Labour and Employment Law:

Cases Materials, and Commentary

SEVENTH EDITION

COMPILED BY A GROUP OF TEACHERS OF LABOUR AND EMPLOYMENT LAW KNOWN AS

The Labour Law Casebook Group

D1247394

Published in 2004 by

Irwin Law
14 Duncan Street
Suite 206
Toronto, Ontario
M5H 3G8

www.irwinlaw.com

ISBN: 1-55221-024-3

Library and Archives Canada Cataloguing in Publication

Labour and employment law : cases, materials and commentary / Labour Law Casebook Group. — 7th ed.

Fourth–5th eds. published under title: Labour law : cases, materials and commentary.
    6th ed. published under title: Labour and employment law : cases, materials and commentary.

Includes bibliographical references and index.

ISBN 1-55221-024-3

    1. Labour laws and legislation—Canada—Cases. 2. Labour laws and legislation—Canada—Textbooks. I. Labour Law Casebook Group. II. Labour and employment law.

KE3108.5.L33 2004   344.7101   C2004-903426-X
KF3320.ZA2L33 2004

The publisher acknowledges the financial support of the Government of Canada through the Book Publishing Industry Development Program (BPIDP) for its publishing activities. The publisher also acknowledges the Government of Ontario through the Ontario Media Development Corporation's Ontario Book Initiative.

Printed and bound in Canada.

2 3 4 5   08 07 06

The Labour Law Casebook Group

Table of Contents

Preface to the Seventh Edition

This is the seventh edition of a book initially brought out in 1970 as the first Canadian law school casebook prepared by a national group of academics — the Labour Law Casebook Group. Labour and employment law have evolved considerably over the decades, and the book has changed accordingly. Beginning with the fourth edition in 1986, we moved away from an almost exclusive focus on collective labour law and added chapters on the individual contract of employment and on statutory regulation, as well as an introductory chapter on the historical and normative foundations of labour and employment law. The growing importance of the *Canadian Charter of Rights and Freedoms*, and of equality issues more generally, led to greater prominence for those subject areas in the fifth edition, which appeared in 1991. In the sixth edition, published in 1998, we added a final chapter on the impact of globalization, the liberalization of trade and the changing role of the state. Over the past few years, for better or worse, the prominence of statutory regulation and *Charter*-based jurisprudence has continued to increase across the spectrum of worker-employer and union-employer relations, and so have the consequences of globalization of the economy. Many of the changes to this seventh edition are designed to help students assess both the current and longer-term importance of those trends.

Preparation of this edition has proceeded in several stages. At a seminar organized by the Labour Law Casebook Group in June 2000 to consider the implications for labour and employment law of recent developments in legal and industrial relations scholarship and practice, presentations by Henry Dinsdale, Joe Rose, David Schneiderman, Elizabeth Shilton and Mark Walters gave us very helpful insights. Each chapter of the previous edition was then revised by a team consisting of a few members of the group. Next, each member of our editorial committee reviewed the draft revisions to a number of chapters. Finally, Bernie Adell, a member of that committee, did a final round of revisions to the entire manuscript, with important support from the Queen's University Faculty of Law in the form of sabbatical leave.

As well as spanning much of the country geographically, the Labour Law Casebook Group includes scholars with a wide range of perspectives on labour and employment law, and more generally on the role of law in society. Making the book read as if was not written by a committee has always been a work in progress, and that remains very true of this edition.

The arrangement of chapters in this edition is the same as in the sixth, and there has been no major reallocation of subject matter between the chapters. However, the material in several of them has been extensively reworked. Where a case or other source that was included in the previous edition also appears in this one, it should not be assumed that the particular excerpt remains the same; many have been shortened or changed in other ways to make them fit better with newer material. The notes and other passages that we have written ourselves to provide transition between excerpts are more clearly identified in this edition by the use of a sans serif typeface.

Every previous edition of the book was published by the Queen's Industrial Relations Centre, to which we are indebted for its support and its efforts on our behalf over so many years. For this edition, we have a new publisher, Irwin Law. The encouragement we have received from Jeff Miller at Irwin Law has been important to us, and so has the painstaking work that Jo Roberts and Erin Metzler have done in the final polishing of the manuscript. We are also grateful for the comments we have received from teachers and students who have used the book in the past. Many parts of this edition build on work done for earlier editions by colleagues who have left the group, and we want to express our continuing appreciation for their contributions.

Finally, we owe much to Harry Arthurs, the group's long-time guiding spirit and taskmaster, for once again getting us down to work on this edition and for steering us through the early stages of its preparation.

The Editorial Committee
April 2004

Chapter 1: **Introduction**

1:100 OUR OBJECTIVES

This casebook has two purposes. One is to provide some familiarity with the legal regimes that purport to regulate workplace relations, and with the normative foundations of those regimes. The other, undoubtedly more important in the long run, is to encourage reflection on whether changes in the organization of work, and changes in the capacity of governments to regulate employment relations in Canada and elsewhere, are outstripping labour and employment law as we know it and endangering its survival.

1:200 THREE LEGAL REGIMES

Labour relations and employment law in Canada are conventionally seen as consisting of three closely interrelated regimes that regulate the employer/employee relationship.

The first regime is the common law of employment, which treats employers and employees as free and equal contracting parties in the buying and selling of labour. It is based on the notion of a contract of employment between employer and employee, formed by negotiation between individuals and enforced by the courts, much like the classic commercial contract. The common law of employment is the subject of Chapter 2 of this book.

Collective bargaining, which is examined in Chapters 3–10, is the second regime. It is based on the realization that the usually inferior economic position of the employee *vis-à-vis* the employer keeps the individual employment contract from being a satisfactory regulatory mechanism. For the negotiation of terms and conditions between individual employers and employees, the collective bargaining regime substitutes collective negotiation between union and employer or between groups of unions and groups of employers. The individual employment contract is replaced by the collective agreement. When adjudication is needed under collective bargaining, it is usually done by specialized administrative tribunals (labour relations boards and arbitration tribunals) rather than by the courts.

Direct statutory regulation is the third regime governing the employer/employee relationship and is the subject of Chapters 11–14. Employment standards legislation on such matters as minimum wages, maximum hours, and health and safety has existed for a long time to protect employees against some of the excesses of the individual contract regime. Until quite recently, such legislation was seen as having a very subordinate role — as being little more than a stop-gap to provide basic protection for employees who remained outside the reach of collective bargaining or whose bargaining power, even when marshalled collectively, was insufficient to provide minimally acceptable employment terms.

In recent decades it has become clear that collective bargaining cannot be relied on to provide as much protection as was once expected of it. Some 40 percent or more of the Canadian workforce remains beyond the reach of collective bargaining. That is so for historical, social, and economic reasons, and because of the length and difficulty of the legal procedures for setting up collective bargaining relationships. Those factors will become apparent in the chapters that follow. All that needs to be said at this point is that the factors limiting the spread of collective bargaining through the workforce have proved to be very persistent and not easily remedied by changes in collective bargaining legislation or in the interpretation and application of that legislation by labour relations boards. Even where collective bargaining has been able to penetrate the hard-to-organize sectors of the workforce, the balance of economic power in those sectors often remains such that unions cannot negotiate terms that are considered minimally acceptable in our society. In addition, even long-standing collective bargaining relationships commonly fail to come to grips with such important but often overlooked issues as health and safety in the workplace and the persistence of unacceptable forms of employment discrimination.

Canadian labour lawyers, and those in many other countries as well, have long understood labour law as constituted in a certain way. They have had a story (a narrative) about the reality of the working world and the manner in which the law applied to that world. The narrative explained and provided a framework for all the details of the various labour laws which applied to work and made them part of a more or less coherent whole. This received wisdom evolved in the twentieth century against the backdrop of economic and social organization which prevailed through much of that century. Most productive activity was organized through continuing employer/employee relationships: employers (firms) entered into long term contracts of employment giving employees security and stability in return for being subordinated to the control of the firm. The law that applied to employees and employers was understood at its most general level as seeking to achieve justice in the contractual relationship known as employment. This is a familiar, if controversial, picture for lawyers — re-regulating contract power in the name of justice.

A problem we now face is that the modern world has conspired to put into question the underpinnings of this way of understanding the world of labour and employment law. Changes in technology and in the social and economic organization of productive activity, as well as the increasingly integrated nature of global systems of consumption and production, have altered the reality that labour law seeks to comprehend and address. As we will see, the resulting problems are quite fundamental. Are the basic categories of employment law (employee and employer) still relevant? Has the old regime in fact produced justice? What new regimes might do so? Is the project of state regulation of labour markets still a viable one? In short, has labour law lost its grip on what it was meant to address? Can it get a grip? These are the questions we wish to set out at the very beginning of our explorations.

In the rest of this chapter, after a look at the changing meaning of work and employment, we will set out a brief overview of the history of our labour and employment law, and we will then explore the controversies, both normative and empirical, which arise out of the received wisdom on this area of law. We will end the chapter with a note on constitutional issues in Canadian labour law. In Chapters 2 to 13, we will review the three regimes in light of the questions and problems referred to in this chapter. In Chapter 14 we will return to an explicit discussion of the fundamental issues raised in this introductory chapter — issues arising from changes in labour market organization and in global affairs.

Although our traditional understanding of this area of law is under pressure, that does not mean that the controversies it organizes will or must disappear. They are likely to remain the core issues. The challenge will be how to understand and address them in their new context.

1:300 WORK AND EMPLOYMENT

The term "work" encompasses a range of activities, which have a variety of social meanings and are subject to various kinds of legal regulation. The forms and meanings of work change through history, as do the legal institutions that regulate it.

Raymond Edward Pahl, "Editor's Introduction: Historical Aspects of Work, Employment, Unemployment and the Sexual Division of Labour" in Raymond Edward Pahl, ed., *On Work: Historical, Comparative and Theoretical Approaches* (Oxford: Basil Blackwell, 1988) 7 at 11–12

Employment is simply one form of work. In the past work was synonymous with toil: an agricultural worker might do some digging or ploughing as part of the collective household labour needed for that household to achieve a modest livelihood; other digging or ploughing could be done as a wage labourer. The distinction between remunerated or non-remunerated labour did not prevent either being equally unpleasant on a cold, wet day. It may be that a given worker might bring different orientations to the task so that there could be more or less resentment and awareness of oppression, depending on whether the work was for the household or for the abbots of the local monastery. Perhaps wage labour was perceived as more constraining in the sixteenth century, as work in the domestic dwelling is perceived as more constraining by some women today. . . .

The notion that one should obtain most, if not all, of one's material wants as a consumer by spending the money gained through employment emerged for the first time in the nineteenth century. Whilst there has, indeed, been a market for labour for at least 800 years in England so that most households probably had some source of income, however erratic and irregular that might be, income generation was not an essential basis for livelihood. Malcolmson remarks that, even as late as the eighteenth century, 'in most households an adequate subsistence depended on a complex of various forms of task work and wage labour: regular, full-time employment at a single job was not the norm.' Indeed, from as early as the seventeenth century, there was substantial resistance to the spread of wage labour. To give all of one's labour power in return for a wage was seen as a grievous

3

loss of independence, security and liberty. 'It takes centuries,' observed Marx, 'ere the "free" labourer, thanks to the development of capitalist production, agrees, i.e. is compelled by social conditions, to sell the whole of his active life, his very capacity for work, for the price of the necessaries of life, his birthright for [a] mess of pottage.'

In pre-industrial times, then, most of an individual's work was done in and for the household. The viability of the household was the crucial priority in life and the work of all members of the household had to be coordinated to achieve that end. Different members had different tasks and these became conventionally established, as we have seen. There was no *a priori* assumption that wage labour was a superior form of work or that men were the natural wage earners. Very often women were the main money earners, either by selling produce at markets or by producing textile goods in their homes in the proto-industrial era of the eighteenth or early nineteenth centuries.

[Reprinted by permission of Blackwell Publishers.]

✳ ✳ ✳

"Employment" is one way of organizing productive activities, or work. In an important sense of the term as we understand it, employment is work organized on the principles of "private ordering," contract, and the market. The employer buys labour from the employee through the device of contract operating in a labour market.

David Beatty, "Labour Is Not a Commodity" in Barry Reiter & John Swan, eds., *Studies in Contract Law* (Toronto: Butterworths, 1980) 313 at 318–24

II   THE MEANING OF EMPLOYMENT

. . . there can be no doubt that immediately prior to the industrial revolution it was land and its attendant customs, rather than employment, which primarily determined how production was to be organized. Both in defining the identity of the members of the society by their relationship to the land, and in regulating the material output of what traditionally had been a subsistence economy, it was the law and custom of land rather than of employment which was the critical device utilized by society in determining how the capacities of its individual members could be co-ordinated with its wants.

. . . the social, political and economic environment in which a society must arrange its affairs will strongly influence how it comes to view the particular purposes served by its most basic social institutions. We understand that it is in their regulation of their most central relationships, like employment, that societies stake out the clearest expression of their social and economic characters. In an obvious respect, the institutions constructed to regulate these relationships mirror the societies' most basic economic and philosophical beliefs. A few examples will suffice to illustrate the point. For instance, in a community where the needs of subsistence can be taken care of by a small proportion of its members, and where the larger part of the population is freed to create surplus produce or, as in our own society, to render services entirely divorced from the imperatives of survival, it would be natural that work, and its institutional superstructure employment, would come to be seen as a means to the more complete forms of personal development than physical survival. . . .

In much the same fashion, the philosophical and religious milieu of a society can strongly influence how its members come to regard their producing activities. Thus, as one would expect, in an increasingly secular society notions of self-determination and realization rather than spiritual salvation come to assume more prominence in the personal meaning of employment. . . . Denied a spiritual justification for their circumstances, employees could be expected to seek more immediate rewards from their work.

Obviously environmental circumstances as well have an effect on how a society comes to regard its basic productive arrangements. In an earlier age when the habitable world appeared to be limitless, when growth could most easily overcome injustice, the choices of exit, of 'going west' could be looked to rationally as a paradigm of problem solving. . . . In those circumstances of available alternatives one could ignore the reckoning that must take place when there becomes, for the vast majority of persons in a particular society, no institution other than employment through which the personal meaning of work can be achieved. By contrast, for many individuals in our own society, there are in fact scarcely any practicable possibilities of exit from this institution. The means by which the personal meaning of work is attained are now effectively controlled by others. Homestead Legislation and Preemption Acts making available opportunities for working with land to the impoverished and unemployed of the eastern cities and of Europe are a relic of our past. Opportunities for establishing the corner grocery or garage are increasingly offered as positions within an employment relationship. In such circumstances, society can be expected to focus more sharply on the opportunities for participation and self-determination that can be accommodated within the institution itself. . . .

Finally of course, one must also be cognizant of the intimate relationship that holds between a society's political circumstances and its understanding of the meaning of work as reflected in the institutions designed to regulate that activity. The coincidence between the way in which society comes to view the social institutions it chooses to regulate its productive relationships and its political processes, reflects and can be explained by its common perception of man. For example, in the society in which our own rules of employment were first developed, the very individuals whose lives would be most directly affected by them were not even represented in the governing processes which established them. They were regarded, quite explicitly, as less than the equal of those who governed them. In that social milieu, of the early and mid-nineteenth century, it would be expected that the attitudes towards work and employment that were currently held, even by the working and employed classes themselves, would be indelibly coloured by their political disabilities. . . . it would only be in future generations, when basic rights of equal citizenship reflected a social acceptance of some intrinsic equality in the condition of all persons, that one would anticipate a similar discounting of our different endowments and abilities to be reflected in all of society's basic social structures. . . .

Accepting the pervasive influence of our social, economic, religious environment, what can one say as to the source and shape of our own understanding of the employment relationship? . . . We are not yet so affluent as a society nor, at least for most of us, so independent as individuals, that we can choose to exercise our capabilities without regard to the social demand for the consequences. Constrained by the imperatives of survival, most individuals are obliged to make their contributions and realize their potential in socially approved ways. In other words, it is the production aspect of the employment relationship that insures some congruity between social expectation and individual aspiration. While separate and distinct from the personal meaning of employment, nevertheless the production function limits the individual quest for participation, contribution and personal meaning within this relationship to ways consistent with and in the contemplation of society's larger needs and wants. In a society in which the identities of its members are materially affected by the exertion of their labour and in which that expression is, for the most part, played out in an employment relationship, it is the production function then, which insures against an institution given over to narcissistic indulgences. And correlatively, it is this root purpose of the relationship which supports, in all systems of employment, the right to terminate for just cause any individual who is unable or unwilling to make his contribution in socially desired ways.

However, . . . [t]he personal meaning of work is seen to go beyond rather than to be completely dependent upon the purposes of production. That, it seems to me, was what the members of the world community, through the International Labour Organization, were affirming at the conclusion of both world wars when they gave expression to the principle that 'labour is not a commodity.' Consistent with the traditional understanding of work relationships generally, this Labour Charter confirmed the existence of a discrete, personal meaning of employment to be defined by other than its social (production) purposes. At its most basic level, this personal end of the relationship is one of subsistence, of physical survival. As we have noted, for most individuals in our own society their physical needs can only be satisfied within this institution. However, at a more sophisticated level, and reflecting the characterization of humans as, for the most part, doers and makers, the identity aspect of employment is increasingly seen to serve deep psychological needs as well.

[Reprinted by permission.]

* * *

For additional reading on the importance of work in the lives of those who do it, see A. Schwartz, "Meaningful Work" (1982) 92 Ethics 634. An unscientific but informative sampling of workers' views on the matter is found in Studs Terkel's *Working* (New York: Avon Books, 1982).

Employment as we understand it is one method of organizing work. It is the predominant context in which human productive activity takes place in Canada. But the employment relationship as we know it is of relatively recent origin. The rise of the contract approach to employment in Canada and the emergence of a labour market are described in H. Pentland, *Labour and Capital in Canada, 1650–1860* (Toronto: Lorimer, 1981).

Labour and employment law regulates only a limited domain of work: that done within the employment relationship in the formal economy. One result is the exclusion of unpaid work from the realm of productive activity. Another result is a lack of attention to its effect on women's labour market participation, both paid and unpaid. The following excerpt notes the importance of unpaid work in the new economy.

Lourdes Beneria, "The enduring debate over unpaid labour" (1999) 138:3 Int'l. Lab. Rev. 287 at 298–302

Emergence of new issues

The attempt to account for unpaid work continues to be important, as current labour market trends raise new questions about the links between paid and unpaid work and about their distribution and boundaries. A transition is currently taking place in the ways in which this distribution is affecting individuals, households and communities across countries.

First, the increasing participation of women in the paid labour force has reinforced the importance of the distribution of paid and unpaid work within the family. This is therefore an important gender equality issue.

Second, in the industrialized world the unemployed and marginalized from mainstream economic life have to negotiate survival strategies that involve an increasing reliance on unpaid work and even some forms of labour exchange not included in conventional statistics. The same can be said for developing countries applying structural adjustment policies, which have resulted in the intensification of unpaid work in the household and in the community.

Third, the high incidence of underemployment and of part-time work in both high-income countries and the developing world results in cyclical or fluid combinations of paid and unpaid work which affect women and men in different ways. As will be argued below, measures of these changes are important to the assessment of variations in living standards and in contributions to social well-being. Similarly the current debate about the 35-hour week taking place particularly in western Europe has many gender implications for the distribution of paid and unpaid work. These discussions are conducted on the assumption that a reduction in working time will help to deal with unemployment. But, as Figart and Mutari have argued, the underlying assumption is that full-time, year-round employment is a social norm constructed around gendered assumptions, for instance that a full-time worker, presumably male, faces limited demands from unpaid work and family life (Figart and Mutari, 1998). A further assumption, they argue, is that the concentration of women in part-time work will continue, regardless of women's preferences. In the same way, households with more than one earner need to address the question of the distribution of working time if they are concerned about gender equality and about ensuring that caring work is fairly shared among household members.

Finally, given that unpaid work represents roughly between a quarter and a half of economic activity, depending on the country, its exclusion from national accounts is difficult to justify. There is some evidence that domestic work is increasing faster than market production. Australian data, for example, indicate that, between 1974 and 1992, household work grew at a rate of 2.4 per cent per year while the corresponding rate for market production was 1.2 per cent (Ironmonger, 1996). This can be attributed to a variety of causes ranging from the rapid increase in the number of small households (resulting in a loss in economies of scale), to the growing proportion of older people in the population, and to growing affluence. Ironmonger (1996) notes that this has happened despite an increase in female labour force participation rates and despite the diffusion of labour-saving household technologies.

All this explains why there has been increasing awareness of the importance of the sex distribution of paid and unpaid work in connection with achieving gender equality. The opening lines of the Human Development Report 1995 underline this point: "One of the defining movements of the 20th century has been the relentless struggle for gender equality ... When this struggle finally succeeds — as it must — it will mark a great milestone in human progress. And along the way it will change most of today's premises for social, economic and political life" (UNDP, 1995, p. 1).

[Reprinted by permission.]

1:400 THE HISTORY OF LABOUR LAW

The concept of employment, which is the fulcrum of labour law, is itself a legal term of relatively recent origin. Moreover, the legal definition is applied to a variety of work situations for a variety of legal purposes.

1:410 The Common Law Contract of Employment

As noted above, working for wages under a negotiated contract is a relatively recent historical phenomenon and took several centuries to emerge. In feudal times production was based on status relations. Servants owed duties of fealty to their masters, who had complete control over them. In the eighteenth century new contract doctrines that facilitated the use of free wage labour emerged. Sir Henry Maine acclaimed the evolution of modern contract as a marvelously progressive development. As the following extract suggests, however, the principles of individual freedom and equal treatment embodied in the common law contract of employment were infused with paternalistic elements, in addition to operating within an overarching system of unequal power.

Alan Fox, *History and Heritage: The Social Origins of the British Industrial Relations System* (London: George Allen and Unwin, 1985) at 7, 14–15, 51

Strains of both paternalist control and individualism were evident in English society from early times, but attempts towards the former strengthened during the sixteenth and early seventeenth centuries. On labour questions both elements of the paternalist equation — authoritarian control and some profession of solicitude — were visible: the first more obviously than the second. Whether or not the superior was punctilious in discharging his own obligations, inferiors were held to theirs. The *Statute of Artificers of 1563* — little more than an attempt to apply, on a national scale, laws, guild rules and municipal regulations going back to the Middle Ages — applied, among other things, the medieval notion of the universal obligation to work by making labour compulsory when employment was offered. . . . It also enabled local justices to punish by imprisonment craftsmen who 'left work unfinished' — a convenient counter to strikes. Vagrancy legislation was particularly revealing of the control element. The essence of the whole paternalist strategy as a mode of social control was that everyone must come under the tutelage, guidance, responsibility and control of some person of superior status. 'No man without a lord' was the phrase which expressed this principle whereby all subjects of the realm were bound within a pyramidal structure of reciprocal obligations of protection and obedience. Given such a conception, 'masterless men' — that is, men lacking any personal and reciprocal bonding of submission to a superior — were a threat to social order and discipline, for they were outside that network of responsible dependencies which was deemed to hold society together. They were accordingly legislated against with extreme ferocity. Successive statutes from the sixteenth century decreed, for 'sturdy beggars,' vagrants and men refusing to work, such punishments as whipping, branding, imprisonment and, during one period, slavery and death. . . . These statutes, which sought both to compel the idle to work and to force them back into the structure of control, remained legally binding until the beginning of the eighteenth century. . . .

. . . [The] emergence of the treatment of labour as a commodity to be bought and sold like any other, though not yet elevated to the status of formally acknowledged proposition in received economic doctrine, became specially apparent in the widespread 'outworking' industries, such as clothmaking, the metal trades, footwear, and others. In these might be found quite sizeable establishments, though large numbers worked in their own homes or in small workshops heavily dependent upon a principal employer or large-scale merchant. This was the outcome of strong economic pressures bursting the bonds of urban monopoly and promoting the growth of so-called 'domestic' industry in the countryside beyond the reach of guild authority. . . .

The growth of individualism had differing impacts upon the dependent lower orders. For those still contained within a traditionally regulated, custom-dominated sector, it might seem only a distant, though potentially disruptive, threat. For those who had come to be directly controlled by it, it could often appear as a disastrous deviation from traditional patterns of personalised control — an abandonment of that diffuse bonding by which, as a reciprocal of their coming under the employer's comprehensive governance, there could be pinned upon him some degree of responsibility for their general welfare. Even though it might be demonstrated that paternalist obligations were more ignored than honoured, there remains significance in the expectation, which bulked large in popular consciousness, that certain social duties of property would be discharged. Men of spirit reacted collectively with outrage when their masters failed them, appealing to principles of 'time immemorial' as leverage against authority and not invariably failing.

What was never abandoned, of course, was the employer's demand for their obedience in the workplace, where the courts invariably supported him. But it was a feature of the growing free labour market, increasingly pervaded by a sharper and more specific conception of contract, that it should be undermining the old notion of each person being contained within a linked pyramid of tutelage, control and diffuse responsibility. Employers were increasingly disposed to throw off such traditional encumbrances in so far as they had survived — for given the English strand of individualism and the lack of a forceful state apparatus to uphold them they had long been more precarious than in some Continental countries. These beginnings of an abdication by those of superior status of their paternalist social control never ceased to disturb some sections of ruling-class opinion and were to excite vocal alarm in the nineteenth century when large-scale consequences began to become apparent. Long before that, they violated the expectations of substantial groups of artisans who appealed to Parliament, town corporations or justices for protection under paternalist statutes and customs only to have quoted at them the tenets of market individualism. But even for them there was not only loss. Instructed by their masters to become independent, many of them took the lesson to heart and became so — not as isolated individual agents, as intended, but as collectives, culturally and socially as well as economically. In these ways the changing English scene was unintentionally weakening, for some groups of workers, such habituated bonds of obedience and deference as there were. Repudiation by their masters of paternalist responsibility left a larger social space within which they could construct a larger independence of spirit and aspiration. . . .

. . . the repudiation of paternalist obligations was revealing ever more clearly . . . that the labour market itself, given the growing disparity of power between employer and individual worker, was an instrument of coercive duress. Of this fact the courts refused to take cognisance. In other spheres of contract the courts had come to accept that 'a contract made by duress or extortion — that is, by actual or threatened violence or imprisonment — could not be upheld.' This was seen as valid morally as well as legally. But ever since 'the devastating analysis by Marx it has been generally realised that this definition of duress as consisting only of threatened violence or imprisonment is impossibly narrow. The formal freedom of the contracting parties can conceal a fundamental inequality of bargaining power which can effectively restrict freedom of choice, even though no physical duress is employed.' The common law courts of the seventeenth century had already made sure, however, that no charge of coercive duress could be read into the dependent position of the individual wage-earner *vis-à-vis* his employer. By concentrating solely on physical coercion the courts made 'no allowance for the various forms of economic coercion which might lead a man "freely" to contract for work for low wages or to pay high prices for food, when loss of life was as much the alternative as it would have been had the agreement been made at the point of a pistol.' . . . In such ways did the old hierarchical structure of power continue to exert itself within what was increasingly proclaimed an open market order of free and equal agents.

[Reprinted by permission.]

✻ ✻ ✻

The notion of using the criminal law to enforce individual contracts of employment persisted in early Canadian legislation. The *Master and Servant Act* provided that an employee who, in violation of his employment contract, refused to go to work or obey lawful commands, was guilty of an offence. Special penalties were also provided for "any tavern keeper, boarding-house keeper or other persons [who] induce or persuade any servants or labourers to confederate for demanding extravagant or high wages." (Repealed by S.C. 1877, c. 35.)

Today, the only vestige of this rigorous enforcement of employment contracts is found in section 422 of the *Criminal Code*, which makes any person "who wilfully breaks a contract" guilty of an offence when he or she knows or reasonably ought to know that the breach will "endanger human life, . . . cause serious bodily injury, . . . expose valuable property . . . to destruction or serious injury," or disrupt public utility or railway service. A saving provision permits a work stoppage by employees engaged in a collective bargaining dispute, provided that all relevant labour legislation is complied with.

1:420 Collective Bargaining

Donald D. Carter, Geoffrey England, Brian Etherington, & Gilles Trudeau, *Labour Law in Canada*, 5th ed. (Deventer: Kluwer; Markham: Butterworths, 2002) at 48–54

The beginnings of the Canadian labour movement antedate the establishment of the Canadian Confederation in 1867. As early as 1794 employees of the North West Fur Trading Company went on strike for higher wages. However, only with the introduction of industry at the beginning of the nineteenth century was a true labour movement begun. Journeymen and craftsmen in the few urban areas, particularly in the building, printing, clothing and shoe trades, began to organize for the purpose of mutual aid and protection and to achieve by united action such objectives as the ten hour day, higher wages and better working conditions. In 1830, for example, the journeymen shoemakers in Toronto went on strike against 'scanty wages . . . beds of straw . . . and tyrannical oppression.' The union movement grew slowly before 1840 owing to depression and labour surpluses but gained momentum in the years prior to Confederation, a period which was further characterized by the affiliation of Canadian unions with their British and American counterparts. This growth brought unionism into collision with the law.

Union organizers were subject to prosecution for the common law crime of conspiracy. The freedom of workers to associate and to alter conditions of work was restricted by legislation modelled upon the English Combinations Act of 1800, such as the Nova Scotia statute of 1816, which prohibited unlawful meetings and combinations for the purpose of regulating wages. Union organizational activities were interdicted as well. In the old Province of Canada, the Master and Servant Act declared the persuasion of labourers 'to confederate for demanding extravagant or high wages' to be unlawful. The common law prohibition against restraint of the course of free trade also affected the civil status of unions. As a result of common law prohibitions, the trade unions were unable to use the courts to enforce any contractual rights they may have achieved, or to protect their property.

In the years following Confederation, labour began to develop a new assertiveness and unity. Local labour councils sprang up in the cities and in 1873, representatives of thirty-five unions formed the first central labour council, the Canadian Labour Union. The C.L.U. resolved to promote union membership, to bring unorganized workers into the C.L.U., and to provide financial assistance to striking unions. Realizing that efforts in these directions would be in vain in view of the existing state of the law, it resolved further to:

> . . . agitate such questions as may be for the benefit of the working classes, in order that we may obtain the enactment of such measures by the Dominion or local legislatures as will be beneficial to us, and win the repeal of all oppressive laws now existing.

This organization petered out in 1877, but it must be credited with arousing in government an awareness of the grievances and aspirations of this segment of the electorate.

In the 1870s the federal government intervened to limit the availability of criminal sanctions to inhibit trade unionism. In part, this reflected the evolution of English law, in part, local political realities. Popular working class support for the nine hour day movement in 1872, and public reaction against the arrest of the strike committee of the Toronto Typographical Union on conspiracy charges, moved Parliament to enact legislative reforms. Trade unions were encouraged to register under a new Trade Unions Act, and thereby to escape the taint of illegality which the common law had assigned them as 'conspiracies in restraint of trade.' The Criminal Law Amendment Act of the same year legalized all strikes except those in which the means employed were calculated to coerce the employer or to prevent him carrying on his business. However, these reforms were not nearly so far reaching in practice as they were held out to be. Whilst the legislation provided that the common law doctrines of criminal conspiracy and restraint of trade did not apply to registered trade unions, the vast majority of trade unions did not register under the federal legislation. Moreover, common law tort doctrines, initially developed in England, were available to restrain trade union activity where the criminal law no longer operated.

However, further amendments in 1875 and 1876 narrowed the definition of criminal conspiracy for the purposes of trade combinations to the performance of acts expressly punishable by law. In 1890, the refusal to work with a workman or for an employer was expressly legalized. By the end of the nineteenth century, the doctrine of criminal conspiracy had ceased to be of practical significance in relation to ordinary labour-management disputes, although it has become, and remains, a central theme in relation to the regulation of business competition.

Another significant development of the 1870s was the definition of the permissible limits of picketing, or 'watching and besetting' as it is called in the Criminal Code. From the outset, violent and coercive conduct was outlawed while the peaceful communication of appeals was permitted. However, when the Criminal Code of 1892 was enacted, the peaceful picketing proviso was omitted. Until it was restored in 1934, the courts tended to deal severely with all forms of picketing, no matter how innocuous.

If the 1870s were a period of legal reform and symbolic advance for the cause of trade unionism the next two decades were to represent a considerable setback. The 'long depression' (mid-1870s to mid-1890s), and the growth of manufacturing on an industrial scale, combined to create abysmal working conditions and nullify the bargaining power of the individual employee. By 1889, as the report of the Royal Commission on the Relations of Capital and Labour disclosed, employers deemed it their prerogative to discipline workers by administering beatings, by imprisonment and by fines; factories were often unsanitary; employees were required to sign agreements to work on religious holidays; the 60 hour week prevailed; and the penalty for joining a union was dismissal and black-listing. These practices stimulated the growth of unionism in the worst years of the depression, and led to the establishment of the Trades and Labour Congress of Canada and the more militant Knights of Labour. By the end of the century, then, it was becoming clear that the repeal of criminal prohibitions against unionism did not automatically place labour organizations on an equal footing with employers.

Unions grew as resource development and national transportation were emphasized as key elements in the emerging national economy. Several provincial governments enacted legislation authorizing third party intervention in order to resolve disputes in industries considered essential for the fragile provincial economies — typically, coal mines, railways and public utilities. These provincial experiments in third party arbitration and conciliation were modelled on legislation enacted in other Commonwealth jurisdictions, and proved to be unsuitable for resolving industrial disputes in Canada prior to the turn of the century. For example, much of this legislation became operative only with the consent of both parties — a condition which usually led the stronger party (typically the employer) to refuse consent.

Industrial disputes in the Western provinces which threatened the federal government's policy of western settlement led to the enactment of three federal statutes — the Conciliation Act [in 1900], the Railway Labour Disputes Act [in 1903], and the Industrial Disputes Investigation Act, 1907. The first authorized voluntary third party conciliation of industrial disputes, the second enabled one of the parties to initiate conciliation and investigation of the dispute by an *ad hoc* tripartite board which was required to issue a normative report, and the third, borrowing the main features of its immediate predecessor, added a prohibition against industrial action by the disputants during the *ad hoc* board's investigation. Like its provincial antecedents, the Industrial Disputes Investigation Act was directed to industries considered to be essential for the Canadian economy. However, unlike the provincial statutes the federal legislation introduced features of Canadian labour relations policy which continue to exist to date — in particular, the requirement that the parties refrain from using economic sanctions until the conciliation board has exhausted its investigation. Furthermore, this statute clearly signalled a conscious policy choice on the part of the federal government to avoid the use of compulsory and binding interest arbitration to settle labour disputes.

Although weakened by constitutional attack, the Industrial Disputes Investigation Act dominated Canadian labour relations policy until the end of the Second World War. In theory the legislation provided for the legitimacy of collective bargaining and the propriety of even-handed government intervention to assist in the establishment of a permanent, bilateral relationship. However, in practice, the Industrial Disputes Investigation Act neither forced employers to bargain with trade unions nor established the terms and conditions of employment. Under this legislation collective bargaining and its outcomes were viewed as essentially private matters between employers and employees.

During the first third of the twentieth century the Canadian economy described a cyclical pattern of growth and recession. The strength and size of the Canadian labour movement tended to ebb and flow with the economy. Moreover, the trade union movement was weakened by internal controversies over international versus national unionism, over the issue of social reform versus higher wages as prime union objectives, over organization of unskilled industrial workers versus organization of skilled craftsmen. Rival labour organizations were formed.

Throughout this period Canada experienced a large increase in industrialization. Foreign investment attracted by extensive natural resources provided the capital required to stimulate economic growth while immigration opened up the West, swelled the unskilled labour force and created larger domestic markets for industry. Between 1901 and 1915 capital investment in Canadian manufacturing quadrupled and, as the capital requirements of industrial enterprises expanded, these enterprises became organized increasingly along corporate lines. In these same years, the number of workers employed in manufacturing rose from 340,000 to 600,000. Labour organization grew even more dramatically, especially during World War I, as union membership swelled from 50,000 in 1901 to 175,000 in 1915 to 250,000 in 1919.

The First World War proved to be extremely important for the Canadian trade union movement. Workers exploited their new-found strength (which was attributable to the brief period of full employment caused by the surge in war production) by engaging in industrial action. The number of workers involved in strikes grew from 43,000 in 1912 to 150,000 in 1919. When the war ended workers were determined to ensure that employers did not take advantage of the changed economic conditions to roll back their collective bargaining gains. This resulted in widespread confrontations between workers, employers and public authorities.

The postwar discontent and conflict is symbolized by the Winnipeg General Strike of 1919. The vast majority of the city's workers demanded union recognition, collective bargaining and the maintenance of working conditions obtained during the war. The entire city was brought to a virtual standstill until the federal government intervened to break the strike. Not only did the federal government use its immigration and criminal powers to deport and imprison strike leaders, it called in armed mounted police reinforced by federal troops. In the end the strike was crushed, as was labour militancy across the country. Throughout the 1920s substantial segments of the industrial work force remained unorganized and little improvement in working conditions was achieved. Working conditions deteriorated during the depression of the 1930s as the massive unemployment caused the power of the unions (together with their membership) to decline dramatically. Unprotected by collective organizations, the lives of individual workers and their families grew increasingly desperate.

Throughout these two decades, the federal legislation — the 1907 Industrial Disputes Investigation Act — had limited impact. The fundamental problem of industrial relations remained the gross disparity of bargaining power as between employers and employed. Given this disparity, employers could ultimately afford to ignore conciliation efforts, to disregard concessions sought, and occasionally secured, by workers in favourable market conditions, and even to make it impossible for workers to bargain collectively. Workers who joined unions were threatened with discharge and then fired; they were easily replaced from the ranks of the unemployed. When unions were formed, employers simply refused to deal with them. And when strikes occurred, either to secure union recognition or for better conditions, employers were almost always able to replace the strikers and to outlast them in any endurance contest.

Increasingly, in the 1930s, industrial strife began to centre on the very basic issue of whether workers would be prevented from associating together for purposes of collective bargaining — not by legislation as in the early days, but by the harsh economic realities. As this issue was being thrashed out on picketlines and street corners throughout North America, unions and employers both began to resort increasingly to coercive and violent tactics. Added to the debilitating effects of the depression, this industrial warfare was doubly damaging.

In 1935 the US Congress passed the National Labour Relations Act (also called the 'Wagner Act' after its sponsor, Sen. Wagner of New York) which exerted a profound, if somewhat delayed, influence on Canadian labour relations policy. This statute explicitly recognized the right of employees to belong to the trade union of their choice and to participate in the process of collective bargaining through that union. To make effective these rights, the statute forbade certain unfair labour practices commonly practised by employers to thwart unionization and imposed upon employers the duty to bargain in good faith with the union selected by their employees.

These elements of the Wagner Act did not come to Canada for almost a decade. In the interim, Canadian unionists continued to struggle against both intransigent governments and employers for the basic right of association and for the fruits which could be won through the practice of collective bargaining. Perhaps the most dramatic episode in this struggle came in 1937 when the Premier of Ontario threatened to use the provincial police to end a strike at the General Motors plant in Oshawa where the company refused to recognize the newly-organized United Automobile Workers. This threat, in turn, precipitated both a cabinet crisis and considerable public protest. In the end, a facesaving compromise emerged in which the union gained some of its demands, but not formal recognition. The incident, however was regarded as a moral victory for industrial unionism and a spur to further organization.

From the mid-1930s onwards there was an attempt by the recently established industrial union movement to organize the semi-skilled workers employed in the new mass production industries on an industrial basis. Between 1935 and 1937 union membership increased from 280,000 to 383,000. Moreover, organized labour began to pressure both the federal and provincial governments for legislative protection of the freedom of association. Between 1937 and 1939 a number of provinces enacted statutes which announced the basic right of association and attempted to protect employees from employer retaliation on the basis of trade union membership. In 1939 the federal government followed suit by amending the Criminal Code to prohibit discrimination or discharge of workers because of their union membership. However, these statutes proved ineffective as they were enforceable only through criminal prosecution. Both the federal and provincial enactments deviated from the Wagner Act in that they failed to provide an administrative tribunal whose function it was to police the provisions of the statute.

The Second World War was a period of rapid industrialization and trade union growth. Trade union membership almost doubled from 362,000 in 1940 to 711,000 in 1945, as the labour shortage and general economic recovery proved conducive to trade union organization. Initially the federal government responded to the increased demand for legislative recognition of trade unions and collective bargaining by issuing exhortary regulations declaring the freedom of association and extolling the benefits of collective bargaining. However, employers refused to bargain with trade unions unless compelled to do so by the union's economic sanctions. As the war continued the failure of the federal government to provide legislative backing for union representation and collective bargaining led to repeated outbursts of industrial unrest. In 1943 the crisis reached its peak as the steel industry was shut down by a nation-wide walkout and one out of every three workers was on strike.

The need to move to an American-style statute became increasingly obvious. In 1943, Ontario became the first jurisdiction to adopt a fully-fledged collective bargaining statute, although its enforcement was entrusted to the Ontario Labour Court (a division of the High Court of Justice), rather than to an administrative board. Experience under the Ontario statute was short-lived, as the federal government preempted the field of collective bargaining in 1944 by enacting P.C. 1003, regulations made under the War Measures Act, which covered virtually all significant industry and economic activity. The federal regulations welded features of the Wagner Act to the long-established Canadian policy of third party conciliation and investigation during a compulsory cooling off period. In particular, P.C. 1003 established a representative tribunal (the National War Labour Relations Board) to administer a regime of collective bargaining which included bargaining unit determination and certification, unfair labour practices and a ban on industrial action during the currency of a collective bargaining agreement. Following the repeal of the federal war-time regulations in 1948, virtually all provinces (and the federal government) adopted Wagner-style labour relations statutes, covering all employees in the private sector.

[© Reprinted with permission from Kluwer Law International.]

✳ ✳ ✳

Much of the above historical survey focuses on the extent to which the state has intervened in the labour market. As the following extract indicates, what sort of intervention is appropriate, and how much of it, has long been at the very heart of debates about labour law.

Harry Arthurs, "Labour Law without the State?" (1996) 46 U.T.L.J. 1 at 1

I   THE LAW OF THE STATE AND THE LAW OF THE WORKPLACE

The notion of law without the state is, if not exactly oxymoronic, at least a challenge to the ingrained assumptions and professional experience of most lawyers. We take law and state to be inextricably linked. A working definition of law is that it is a set of norms authoritatively pronounced by state institutions — the legislature and the higher courts — and enforced by state officials mandated to employ the state's powers of coercion — bureaucrats, policemen, and lower court judges.

Labour law has always represented something of an exception to this definition. The state and its legal system have had an ambivalent, abstracted, even perverse, involvement with the employment relationship. Sometimes the state has followed a conscious policy of absenting itself from the labour market; sometimes it has been highly interventionist. By the beginning of the nineteenth century, *laissez-faire* was displacing older policies of paternalism and mercantilism; almost immediately, however, *laissez-faire* gave way to criminal sanctions against unions, and to administrative regimes designed to protect women and children and promote safety in the workplace. As the administrative regimes began to take hold, they were subverted by hostile judicial interpretations; as the criminal sanctions were gradually relaxed, the new industrial torts took their place. When sporadic conflict gave way to collectively bargained contracts, the courts declined to enforce them; and when as a consequence enforcement was entrusted to arbitrators, the courts insisted on bringing the arbitrators under their tutelage and control. When workers began to take advantage of the relaxation of legal constraints on their ability to organize, legislation was enacted in the 1930s and 1940s to funnel the organizing process through the administrative mechanism of certification; and certification, ostensibly designed to facilitate union organization, soon began to function so as to delay organization and, arguably, to disempower unions. And when workers asserted their new collective power aggressively, their actions were constrained by statutory codes limiting the 'when' and 'why' of strikes, and by judge-written rules concerning the 'where' and 'how' of picketing.

. . . state intervention was sought or resisted, facilitated or impeded, depending on how its presence or absence was seen to affect material interests or ideological belief systems.

Georgian paternalists feared that the state would disrupt traditional master-servant relationships based upon reciprocity and custom; Victorian capitalists feared dilution of their own ability to set wages and working conditions unilaterally under cover of contract; workers feared the use of criminal law and tort law to prevent them from asserting themselves; ideologues of the right feared that state action would distort the 'natural' forces of supply and demand in the labour market; ideologues of the left feared that the state would favour the vested claims of property over those of humanity, social justice, and working-class interests.

Obviously, all of these concerns were justified to some degree, but all were exaggerated: the state had — and has — only a limited capacity to intervene. Notwithstanding all of these perturbations of state policy and action (or non-policy and inaction) it has become increasingly obvious that the largest, and arguably most important, part of labour law is not exclusively or primarily state law. The 'web of rules' governing the complex and dynamic relationship we call employment includes strands of state law, to be sure, but also explicit contracts and implicit understandings, custom and usage, patterned behaviour, cultural assumptions, power relations, and technological imperatives. The state acting alone — even if we wanted it to — could neither replicate nor restrict the variety and volatility, spontaneity and subtlety, power and precision of this web of rules.

Thus, for two hundred years or more, an important task of labour law has been to legitimate, but also to regulate and reform, the indigenous production and enforcement of norms within the workplace. This was true of industries regulated by craft custom, of early manufacturing enterprises, of the first experiments with protective legislation, of initial attempts at 'scientific' management. And — especially because of a desire to ensure to workers the right to participate in the production of norms governing their life at work — it was true of collective bargaining.

This is not to argue that collective bargaining — or any of the other regimes — necessarily operated in total isolation from the state. In various societies, at various times, collective bargaining has been tolerated, encouraged, licensed, regulated, or co-opted by the state. But the most distinctive feature of collective bargaining is not its nexus with the state; rather it is that collective bargaining relies upon employers and workers to generate and enforce the norms which govern workplace behaviour.

True: this is a neutral piece of information. It does not tell us anything about how the state's absence or presence might alter the balance of power in the relationship, or how power in turn might affect the content of collectively bargained norms. True: it has always been possible to argue that the collective bargaining system was able to grow and flourish because it enjoyed formal recognition from the state, and *in extremis* could call upon the state to initiate, facilitate, and enforce its 'private' processes. True: we have become increasingly aware that in the many sectors and dimensions of employment which collective bargaining does not — perhaps cannot — reach, more definitive forms of state intervention are inescapable. True: we have begun to explore the notion (so far rejecting it) that the state should formally guarantee to citizens in the workplace the same rights and freedoms as are guaranteed in other venues by the Charter and other fundamental norms of state law.

But whether we assume that a close affinity exists between the state and labour law, or the opposite, our assumption must be revisited in the light of the rapid and ramifying social, economic, political, and technological developments sometimes referred to collectively as 'the new economy.' These developments are transforming the state, the character of employment, and consequently, labour law.

1:430 HAS QUÉBEC FOLLOWED A SIMILAR PATH?

An understanding of Québec's historical background helps to put into context the distinctive aspects of its approach to labour regulation. By retaining its civilian private law structure, Québec has been able to maintain many continental influences. The philosophical differences separating the civilian and common law traditions are great, and beyond the scope of this brief discussion. However, it is worth pointing out that starting with a civil code means that contractual relations are at their outset regulated by the state, through the codification process. Indeed, the old *Civil Code* of Lower Canada included the relationship between master and servant in separate provisions; the 1994

Civil Code of Québec devotes an entire chapter to a more modern approach to employment relations.

The socio-historical context in Québec adds additional layers of difference to the regulation and implementation of labour and employment law in Québec. For example, the Catholic Church played an important — if not always positive — nineteenth and twentieth century role in shaping the Québec labour movement, and the ensuing legislative framework. The Québec Legislative Decrees system, adopted in 1924 and discussed in Chapter 6:621, was strongly influenced by the Catholic strand of continental approaches to labour. The greater plurality of labour unions in Québec, and the comparatively high rates of unionization are in part attributable to this broader labour militancy and public acceptance of social justice principles. The early links between the movement for sovereignty, including political parties and labour unions, translated into electoral success. What followed initially was a range of progressive labour policies and enactments, including labour standards and occupational health and safety legislation. Moreover Québec has taken proactive legislative measures to ensure that the French language has a predominant place in the workplace. In an increasingly pluralistic society, the 1975 Québec *Charter of Human Rights and Freedoms* has also increasingly been called upon to shape Québec labour and employment law.

Despite its distinct historical background, and only after some struggle between Catholic unions and American-affiliated unions, Québec chose to adopt the Wagner Act framework in 1944 rather than a European model. As a result, it structured its collective bargaining system in a manner similar to the other Canadian jurisdictions. However, through certain distinctive legislative provisions and through judicial and quasi-judicial interpretation, the Québec *Labour Code* (which, despite its title, is simply a standard labour relations statute) and Québec employment law reflect their civilian and historical traditions. Two significant examples in that respect are the relationship between the civilian employment contract, which is widely considered to subsist under collective bargaining, and the interplay between civil law concepts and labour relations concepts, notably on the sale or transfer of an undertaking.

That there are many similarities between labour law in Québec and in common law Canada is illustrated illustrated in the following excerpt:

Marie-France Bich, "Labour Arbitration in Québec" [1993] Lab. Arb. Y.B. 93 at 94–96

[. . .] Québec private law has not been immune to the influence of common law. For instance, commercial law in Québec owes something to a common law tradition that has been adapted to the peculiar demands of a basically codified and legislative law system. The testamentary provisions of our Civil Code draw from both common law and civil law; the institution of the injunction was borrowed from common law. And these are only a few examples; in fact, Québec law is living proof of the interpenetrability of civil law and common law systems, even though both do have and retain their own character and 'génie propre.' This should at least (and at last!) put to rest the myth of their absolute and mutual impermeability.

Employment law is but another example of this convergence. A parallel reading of Christie's *Employment Law in Canada* and Audet, Bonhomme and Gascon's *Le congédiement en droit québécois*, or Aust's *The Employment Contract*, to name but a few, reveals a close resemblance between the legal norms in force in Québec and those in force in other provinces. This, again, is not very surprising: as it is understood in most countries of the western hemisphere, the employee-employer relationship, by its very nature, appears to dictate the development of the law in a certain direction rather than another. The nature of the contract thus transcends the nature of the legal system to which it belongs, at least partly. Take, for instance, the rule which provides that either party to an employment contract of an indefinite duration may terminate it upon reasonable notice: such a rule basically exists everywhere in Canada, subject to the various labour standards statutorily enacted, from time to time, in every jurisdiction. Similarly, the wrongfully dismissed employee has the duty to mitigate his or her loss. The development of these rules may have conformed, whether in Québec or in other provinces, to the particular processes of civil law or common law, but the results, which are largely similar, reflect a common basic understanding of the nature of the employment contract. An additional influence, of course, is that of the geopolitical and economic context, which is factored into the development of the law; this truism also explains the fundamental similarities between the norms and the standards in force in the various Canadian jurisdictions. In a country where both capital and labour have mobility, this convergence is natural, and probably desirable. This is not to say that differences, and sometimes marked ones, do not exist, but the foundations of the various systems are the same.

This may explain why Québec courts have sometimes been unable to resist the lure of common law precedents in matters such as the length of the notice of dismissal or the duty of fidelity and loyalty that the employee owes to his or her employer, and they have regularly quoted judgments from other Canadian courts.

Of course this systemic similarity exists as well in the field of collective labour relations: every Canadian jurisdiction possesses a labour structure based on the recognition of one trade union, certified through a governmentally monitored process on the basis of majority rule, with the union then being entitled to represent all employees within a determined bargaining unit.

[Reprinted by permission of Lancaster House Publishing.]

✳ ✳ ✳

In a nutshell, despite important differences in their legal systems, no fundamental differences can be observed between the employment and labour law in force in Quebec and that in the rest of Canada. This explains why Quebec law is not treated separately in this book. Specific references to Quebec law will be made when needed.

1:500 VALUES AND ASSUMPTIONS

1:510 Introduction

As the historical material set out above suggests, labour law emerges in response to economic and political pressures. Those pressures change over time. So too do the normative discourses used to justify particular responses. It is these normative discourses, values, and assumptions that are the focus of this final section of the chapter.

The common law is rooted in the notion of contract, private ordering, and the values that underlie the market — self-reliance, individualism, liberty for atomistic individuals, and the separation of the private sphere and the public sphere. Some of the values that underlie collective bargaining are the same as those that underlie the common law contract of employment, but some are nor. Collective bargaining departs from the individualistic principles of the market insofar as it allows for concerted action by employees with a view to both a fairer market process and a fairer distribution of the fruits of the market. Nevertheless, collective bargaining is above all a procedural mechanism. Although it introduces a new collective party on the employee side and sometimes on the employer side as well, it ultimately relies on the market to set terms and conditions of employment. In contrast, statutory regulation involves direct governmental intervention in the market/contract process, often in the name of preventing exploitation but also on purely paternalistic grounds. It is obvious that the appropriate scope and interrelationship of the common law, collective bargaining, and statutory regimes cannot be discussed without asking basic questions about such concepts as liberty and equality, fairness and efficiency.

Help in resolving some of the issues in labour and employment law and labour relations can be found by seeking answers to empirical questions, such as the effect of collective bargaining on incomes and the impact of minimum wage legislation. These empirical questions can only be fully answered if we go beyond the language of the legislation or the intricacies of legal doctrine and look to the law in action. However, many of the most important issues cannot be resolved by empirical methods — by collecting more facts — because at bottom they are not empirical questions but questions of ethics or political philosophy. What we may find is that people have different ways of looking at the world and proceed from different premises. The evaluation of premises often cannot be avoided.

What is to be done? Are we left with unprincipled venting of our intuitions? How are choices to be legitimately made? These are the fundamental questions of moral and political choice, in the area of labour and employment law as in so many other areas of legal and social policy. If nothing more is achieved, it is at least possible to advance our understanding of the types of issues involved here.

The materials that follow attempt to do this in several ways. First, by examining some of the normative claims made about the employment relationship, we can become more familiar with the debate and may at least clarify our normative thinking. Second, understanding the normative debates helps us understand many of the most controversial areas of the Canadian law of the employment relationship, where debate on fundamental issues percolates to the surface. Third, considering the materials that follow in relation to the brief historical context provided above helps us realize that concepts such as equality, justice, fairness, and efficiency are essentially contested, and that their meanings depend on one's position in the web of social relations that constitute a particular historical moment.

This is not a book on economics, political philosophy, or ethics, but we cannot avoid the fundamental issues at stake in our labour and employment law. Much has been written, from many philosophical perspectives, about the market model of organizing productive activities. Much attention has been focused on the normative claims made both for and against a market ordering of labour. David Beatty's article "Labour Is Not a Commodity," in section 1:300 above, is a Canadian contribution to that literature. The rest of this chapter tries to give an idea of the various dimensions of the normative debate on the issues before us.

We must begin somewhere and we do so by setting out some relatively recent defences of and attacks on the market mechanism and private ordering, particularly as they relate to employment. In reading the following consider what sorts of arguments are made. Are the arguments consequentialist? That is, are the arguments of the form, "this method of organizing productive activities is desirable because it leads to the following consequences or states of affairs"? (for example, wealth is maximized or efficiency attained). (On consequentialism, see B. Williams, "A Critique of Utilitarianism" in J. Smart & B. Williams, eds., *Utilitarianism: For and Against* [Cambridge: Cambridge University Press, 1973] 77 at 82–93.) Or are the arguments of a different sort, such as, "this method of organizing productive activities is desirable because it respects certain *rights* of people"? (perhaps even if there are adverse consequences, for example with regard to efficiency). Are the arguments of the sort, "society as a whole is better off," or "these rights are protected even if society is worse off"? Or do the proponents argue both grounds, namely that certain consequences are maximized and certain rights protected? What role do the notions of fair process or consent play in the defences and attacks set out below? Finally, do the writings that follow focus on the final distribution (of jobs or money), or on the history and process by which that distribution comes about?

1:520 The Market Model

What does the market model have to say about the employment relationship? A thorough account is given in M. Gunderson, *Labour Market Economics: Theory, Evidence and Policy in Canada* (Toronto: McGraw-Hill Ryerson, 1980). Consider the following.

Armen A. Alchian & William R. Allen, *University Economics*, 3d ed. (Belmont, Calif.: Wadsworth, 1972) at 407–43

'Labor is not a commodity' is a battle cry of some labor groups. Whatever its emotional appeal, the assertion is misleading. Labor service is bought and sold daily. . . .

Economic analysis denies that, in the absence of legal protection for labor, employers would grind wages down to the minimum survival level. An analogy will suggest why. Why are rents on land not ground down by renters to zero? The demands by those who would use the land bid up the rents. Simple supply and demand are in operation. And so it is with labor. The alternative uses and values to which labor could be put are determined by all who compete for it. Potential employers, faced with the available supply, bid wages to whatever level enables them to get an amount of labor that can be put to profitable use. That may be a very high level, if labor is relatively scarce given its productivity function. The price of labor, like that of every other good, depends upon demand and supply forces.

. . . All the considerations in interpreting the demand and supply analysis of price and output effects are applicable to labor services, . . . Suffice it to say, demand-and-supply analysis of *open*-market determination of wages and employment is similar in principle to that for any other good. Underlying is the assumption that people are free agents and can quit or change jobs when they wish, and that at least some will change jobs when knowledge of more attractive openings is available. Employees who entertain offers to look for opportunities elsewhere also permit their current employers to make a counter-bid.

An employer, then, if he is to retain his employees, must detect and match offers of other employers. The employer who does so (through periodic wage and salary reviews and raises), without forcing his employees to seek offers and then ask for a raise, will have to pay no higher wages than if he waited for each employee to initiate negotiations. Job comparison is costly for employees; so the employer who is known to take the initiative in anticipating or matching market offers will find more employees willing to work for him than for one who tries to impose all the costs of job comparison on employees. [Copyright © 1972. By permission of South-Western College Publishing, a division of International Thomson Publishing Inc., Cincinnati, Ohio 45227.]

✻ ✻ ✻

The following is an explanation of the neoclassical economic model in the labour market context.

Steven L. Willborn, "Individual Employment Rights and the Standard Economic Objection: Theory and Empiricism" (1988) 67 Nebraska L. Rev. 101 at 104–33

II. PRICE THEORY, MINIMAL TERMS, AND THE STANDARD OBJECTION

A. The Price Theory Model of the Labor Market

The price theory model of the labor market is a specific instance of the more general neoclassical economic model in which the price of a commodity in a competitive market is determined by its supply and demand. The price theory model describes how the labor market would operate in a perfectly competitive environment. Although by now the basic outline of the model should be familiar to most lawyers, it may be helpful to begin by examining the model in broad relief.

Under the price theory model, the supply of labor and the demand for labor determine the equilibrium wage and the quantity of labor utilized. A basic understanding of labor supply and demand, then, is essential to an understanding of the price theory model.

As indicated in Figure 1, the demand curve for labor generally slopes downward. That is, assuming a fixed supply of capital, the marginal value of each unit of labor to employers declines as the quantity of labor utilized by employers increases. The downward slope

Figure 1

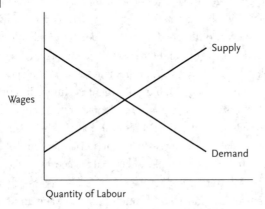

of the demand curve for labor makes sense intuitively. Consider, for example, the demand for manual labor to dig a ditch. One worker using a large shovel may be able to dig 100 feet per day; two workers using medium-sized shovels might be able to complete 150 feet per day; three workers with tiny shovels might be able to complete 180 feet per day; and so on until there are many men with small trowels. The *marginal* product of each unit of labor decreases as more units of labor are added, assuming once again that capital is held constant. The marginal product of the first worker is 100 feet, of the second worker fifty feet, of the third worker thirty feet, and so on. Employer demand for labor depends on the marginal product of labor. An employer might be willing to pay the first worker the equivalent of 100 feet of ditch (the first worker's marginal product), but the second worker is

Figure 2

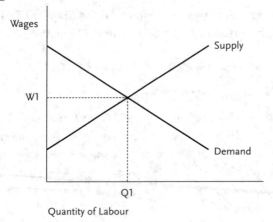

only worth the equivalent of fifty feet of ditch, the third worker only thirty feet, and so on. If we graphed this phenomenon, the marginal product for ditch diggers (which would determine the demand for that type of labor) would slope downward like the demand curve in Figure 1.

The supply curve for labor indicates the quantity of labor that is available at a particular wage rate. The supply curve for labor generally slopes upward, as indicated in Figure 1. Once again, the slope is intuitively sensible because a higher wage would tend to encourage workers to work more hours and to encourage non-workers to enter the labor force.

The intersection of the demand curve and the supply curve determines the equilibrium wage and quantity of labor employed. (See Figure 2). The wage and quantity of labor are in equilibrium in the sense that that level is the only stable position. Employers have no incentive to pay more than the equilibrium wage; as Figure 3 illustrates, they can attract sufficient labor to meet their demand at W1. Indeed, the employer demand for labor at a higher wage, W2, is only Q3. Since there is an excess supply of labor at that wage

Figure 3

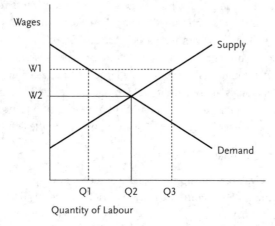

Quantity of Labour

Figure 4

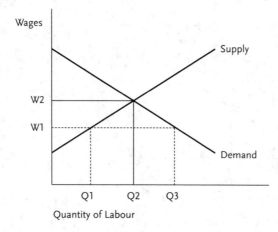

Quantity of Labour

level, (with Q2 willing to work, but employers only willing to hire Q3), workers will be unemployed, which should result in competition between workers for the available jobs, which should drive the wage down toward W1, the equilibrium wage. In much the same way, as indicated in Figure 4, if employers pay a lower-than-equilibrium wage, employers will demand Q2 workers, but only Q3 workers will be available. The resulting competition between employers for the available workers should drive the wage up toward W1. As a result, when wages are higher or lower than equilibrium, there are forces which drive the wages toward equilibrium. In contrast, when wages are at the equilibrium level, these forces are absent. The equilibrium wage is stable because, at that wage, employers can hire the optimal amount of labor given the demand for their products, while workers can optimally balance their demands for work and leisure.

This formal and bloodless picture of the labor market describes only how the market would operate in a perfectly competitive environment. In such an environment, employers and workers would have full, perfect and costless knowledge of the market, including information on wage rates and job openings; employers and workers would be entirely rational, with employers attempting to maximize their profits and workers responding to wage differences and attempting to optimally balance their desires for work and leisure; there would be no externalities; workers would be perfectly mobile and able to change jobs without any costs, and would not act in concert, and employers would be numerous, they would not act in concert, and none would be so large that its decisions would affect the market as a whole. Obviously, these conditions are seldom, if ever, met. Nevertheless, the model is a useful starting point for discussion. When the conditions affect the analysis, as they inevitably do, the discussion can be advanced by easing the conditions.

B. Minimal Terms and the Standard Objection

Minimal terms are nonwaivable, minimum substantive terms of employment which are required by the government. They come in a wide variety of forms. The government might require employers to pay minimum wages, to provide a certain level of maternity rights, to provide a safe workplace, to supply information about plant closings, to pay sev-

Figure 5

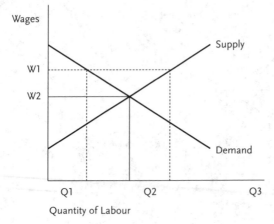

Quantity of Labour

erance pay, to make certain provisions for retirement and possible unemployment, to provide a certain level of health insurance, and so on.

In the abstract, effective minimal terms provide a benefit to workers and impose a cost on employers. All other things being equal, when a minimal term is added to the wage package, both the wage cost to the employer and the effective wages of the workers go up. Minimal terms, at least in the short run, are the equivalent of a wage increase.

The standard objection to minimal terms, then, begins with a consideration of the effects of an exogenous wage increase (i.e., a wage increase that is not the result of changes in labor supply or demand) on the labor market. The effects in the short run should be as indicated in Figure 5. The intersection of the supply and demand curves determines the equilibrium wage, W1. A minimal term imposed by the government would have the effect of a wage increase, raising the wage to W2. The wage increase, in turn, would result in a reduction in the quantity of labor utilized from Q1 to Q3. One part of the standard objection to minimal terms, then, is that minimal terms do not confer any benefits on workers as a class. Any benefits received by one set of workers are paid for (and often more than paid for) by other workers in unemployment. The effects of minimal terms illustrated in Figure 5, however, are not stable. The excess supply of labor creates competition between workers for the available jobs and, as a result, tends to force the wage level back down to equilibrium. Whether the wage actually moves back to (or at least closer to) the equilibrium level depends on whether the employer can avoid the minimal term which effectively raised the wage level by making a compensating change in another part of the wage package. That is, an employer may be able to avoid a minimal term by offsetting the effective wage increase caused by the minimal term with an effective wage decrease in another part of the wage package. For example, a minimal term requiring employers to pay workers for maternity or paternity leave would be avoidable if employers reduced the wages of workers by an amount equivalent to the cost of the required leave program. Some minimal terms may not be avoidable. Minimum wage laws, for example, effectively apply only to low-wage, low-benefit jobs, so offsetting the wage increase by an effective wage decrease in another part of the wage package may not be possible. Most minimal terms, however, should be avoidable, at least in the long run. Even if employers cannot make compensating changes immediately, as in the maternity or paternity leave example, they should be able to do so in the long run, for example, by reducing the rate of increase in wages. When minimal terms are avoidable through compensating changes, wages and quantity of labor should tend to move back to equilibrium.

Another part of the standard objection to minimal terms, then, is that workers and employers will find ways to counteract the desired effects of minimal terms and, indeed, that there are economic forces which drive the parties to do so. Since minimal terms are effective wage increases, they can be counteracted by actual or effective wage decreases in other parts of the wage package. The excess supply of labor encourages the counteraction.

A corollary of this objection is that when wages and quantity of labor move back to equilibrium in reaction to a minimal term, both employers and workers are worse off than they would have been if the minimal term had never been imposed. Using the maternity or paternity leave example again, if the wages and quantity of labor move back to equilibrium, the overall wage package is worth the same as the overall wage package before the minimal term was imposed, but its components are different. Before the minimal term, the package provided no maternity or paternity leave, but a higher wage; after the minimal term was imposed, the package provided maternity or paternity leave, but a lower wage. By hypothesis, the ex post position leaves the parties worse off. In a world with perfect competition, if the parties had wanted that wage package, they would have bargained for it ex ante. Since they did not, imposition of the minimal term frustrates the wage package preferred by the parties.

The standard economic objection to minimal terms, then, is that any perceived benefits to workers are merely illusory. Because imposition of minimal terms is the equivalent of a wage increase and because an exogenous wage increase reduces the demand for labor, any benefits to workers from minimum terms in the short run are paid for by other workers in unemployment. In the long run, minimal terms can usually be avoided by offsetting the effective wage increase from imposition of the minimal terms with wage decreases elsewhere in the wage package. When minimal terms are avoided, employers and workers are worse off than they would have been if minimal terms had not been required in the first place. . . .

III. JUSTIFICATIONS FOR MINIMAL TERMS WITHIN THE PRICE THEORY MODEL

Employers and individual workers face a difficult problem when they wish to enter into a relationship. A number of uncertainties exist which may affect the relationship — uncertainties about the precise work the employer needs done, the ability of the worker to perform it, the employer's long-term need for the work, other work opportunities which may present themselves to the worker, the worker's continued good health, the safety of the workplace, and so on. The proposed relationship is also quite complex — what arrangements should be made for the worker's retirement, for the possibility of a work-related injury, for health insurance, and so on.

Minimal terms can be viewed as a set of ready-made contract terms which deal with many of these difficult issues. The government, for example, requires a certain minimum amount to be set aside for retirement and requires certain safeguards if greater amounts are reserved. To the extent the parties would have included the same or very similar terms in the employment contract even if they had not been required by the government, the minimal terms are efficient. They spare the parties the time and expense of having to negotiate the terms. This effect of minimal terms should be uncontroversial.

Governments generally enact minimal terms, however, not merely to save transaction costs, but to change the substance of the employment arrangement. That is precisely why minimal terms are nonwaivable. It is this goal — to change the employment contract — which runs into the standard objection. When minimal terms are required and they change the arrangements the parties would otherwise have made, the standard objection leads to the conclusion that the parties are necessarily made worse off.

This section considers circumstances in which minimal terms might not be subject to the standard objection but, rather, may enhance efficiency or lead to a more desirable distribution of resources.

A. Efficiency Justifications

1. Collective Terms

Some terms of employment are collective in nature; that is, if they are supplied to one worker, they must also be supplied to other workers. Terms may be collective by their very nature or they may be collective for practical reasons. Health and safety terms, for example, are often collective by their very nature. If an employer supplies clean air or good lighting to one worker, other workers are usually able to share in the benefits. More often, however, terms are collective for practical reasons. When workers work together closely, an eight hour day for one worker may mean an eight hour day for other workers. When one worker demands and receives a new vending machine in the cafeteria, it is likely that other workers will be allowed to use it. When an employer establishes a disciplinary system for a few workers, it may be efficient to use it for all workers.

Collective terms are likely to be underproduced. That is, the terms will often not be offered even though the cost to the employer of providing the terms is less than the value the workers place on the benefits of the terms. To illustrate why this is the case, consider an employer who employs ten workers and who could install Equipment A at a cost of one, which would clean the air in the plant a bit or Equipment B at a cost of twenty, which could clean the air in the plant quite a bit. Assume that each worker would value the cleaner air produced by Equipment A at two and the cleaner air produced by Equipment B at five (i.e., each worker would be willing to accept a reduction in pay of two and five, respectively, in return for the cleaner air). From an efficiency standpoint, the employer should install Equipment B. At a marginal cost of nineteen, the employer can produce cleaner air with a marginal value of thirty (. . .); both the employer and the workers would be better off if the employer installed Equipment B and reduced the workers' aggregate wages by an amount between twenty and twenty-nine.

Because of strategic behavior and information imperfections, however, Equipment B will not always be installed and, indeed, even Equipment A may not be installed in some instances. Consider the calculations of each individual worker who is deciding whether to accept lower wages for cleaner air. Clearly the best outcome for an individual worker would be to refuse to accept lower wages, but to have the equipment installed because other workers accepted lower wages.

In that situation, the worker would be a free rider; she could share in the benefits of the clean air, but would not have to pay for it. If all of the workers engaged in this type of strategic behavior, neither Equipment A nor Equipment B would be installed. Thus, one reason the efficient outcome may not be achieved is that individual workers may engage in strategic behavior designed to position themselves as free riders. . . .

2. Imperfect Information

Imperfect information is a common justification for governmental intervention in markets of various kinds, including labor markets.

Various forms of the argument provide weak and strong justifications for minimal terms.

The conventional argument from imperfect information is that workers cannot enter into optimal employment contracts if they do not have all of the information necessary to evaluate their options. Consider again the worker who is attempting to decide whether to accept a wage reduction in return for a 'for cause' provision which would provide some protection against discharge. If the worker believes that she has some protections against discharge even without a 'for cause' provision when in fact she does not, she is likely to underestimate the value of the provision and, as a result, may fail to buy it even though she should. Other workers may understand the limitations of their protections in the absence of a 'for cause' provision and yet fail to purchase the provision because they underestimate the risk of discharge and, hence, underestimate the provision's potential benefits. Once again, this information failure could lead to an inefficient result — the worker may not buy the 'for cause' provision even though it is worth more to her than the wages.

Imperfect information does not justify intervention, however, merely because individual workers make mistakes. Intervention is justified only if the labor market fails to produce optimal terms because workers make decisions based on imperfect information. Even if many workers make mistakes because of imperfect information, optimal terms may be produced. If some workers seek optimal terms and if employers both wish to attract those workers and cannot distinguish between them and the workers making mistakes, the market should produce optimal terms. In essence, those workers who demand optimal terms protect other workers from the consequences of their limited information. On the other hand, if insufficient numbers of workers seek optimal terms, or if employers do not wish to attract those workers, or if employers can distinguish between those workers and workers with imperfect information, the labor market may fail to produce optimal terms.

Intervention in the labor market is justified, then, if the labor market fails to produce optimal terms because workers make decisions on the basis of imperfect information. This provides only a weak justification for minimal terms, however, because there are other, less intrusive options for remedying this type of information failure. Ensuring that workers receive fuller information on the 'for cause' provision, either by requiring the employer to provide it or by having the government provide it, would remedy the information failure and lead to a more fine-tuned result than simply requiring the 'for cause' provision. It would permit those workers who prefer higher wages even when they have knowledge of the true value of the 'for cause' provision, to continue to receive higher wages.

Another type of information failure provides a stronger justification for minimal terms. If there is information failure not because of limited information, but because workers cannot rationally evaluate the available information, the less intrusive remedial option of providing information may not be effective. Minimal terms may be required to correct the suboptimal choices made by workers.

Information overload and cognitive dissonance are two reasons workers may not be able to effectively evaluate the information necessary to make a choice. Evidence from outside the employment context suggests that there is a point at which additional information becomes dysfunctional; that is, the additional information does not contribute to a better decision because the people to whom it is provided are 'overloaded' and simply cannot process it. To the extent information overload occurs, one would expect it to occur in the employment context. Employment contracts cover a broad range of topics, many of them quite complex; they are often expected to remain in effect for long periods of time; and workers are often poorly equipped to evaluate them. Thus, minimal terms may be justified when there is evidence of information failure and when it is likely that the failure cannot be remedied simply by providing additional information.

Cognitive dissonance may also interfere with the ability of workers to evaluate additional information. Stated generally, cognitive dissonance means that people are uncomfortable when they simultaneously hold two conflicting ideas. People prefer to view themselves as smart and if new information indicates that a prior belief was in error, the new information tends to undermine the preferred self-image. As a consequence, people tend to reject, ignore or accommodate information that conflicts with prior beliefs.

Cognitive dissonance may also justify minimal terms. To illustrate, consider workers who when they first choose a job, choose an industry that is hazardous, but necessarily hazardous because no safety equipment is available to correct the hazards. Over time, cognitive dissonance may lead the workers to believe that the job is really fairly safe. (Smart workers would not work at a hazardous job, therefore the workers must either view themselves as not smart or their jobs as not hazardous. Viewing the jobs as safe is less threatening to the workers' self-image.) If cost-effective safety equipment then becomes available, the workers will not purchase the equipment (by accepting a reduction in their wages). Because of cognitive dissonance, they have come to believe that their jobs are safe even without the equipment. As a result, they are unable to evaluate fairly the value of the newly available equipment. A minimal term which required the equipment to be installed would be necessary to achieve the efficient outcome.

Minimal terms may also correct for information failure from the other side of the ledger — they may increase efficiency by improving the information base of employers. Employers can learn about worker perceptions of the compensation package they offer workers (and, indeed, about worker ideas on ways in which work can be reorganized to enhance productivity) in one of two ways. They can learn when workers quit to take other jobs (exit) or they can learn when workers tell them what they think about the compensation package (voice). Clearly, learning through voice has several advantages for both employers and workers: the costs of job search and transfer are minimized; the investment in job-specific training is not lost; the message is clearer since the communication is direct and the employer need not infer worker perceptions from numerous exits; and so on. Nevertheless, voice is likely to be underutilized:

[W]orkers . . . are unlikely to reveal their true preferences to an employer, for fear the employer may fire them. In a world in which workers could find employment at the same wages immediately, the market would offer adequate protection for the individual, but that is not the world we live in. The danger of job loss makes expression of voice by an individual risky.

Because of this, a minimal term which encourages voice may be efficient. A minimal term requiring cause for discharge, for example, would be likely to cause workers to increase the use of voice to communicate with the employer (because they would be less fearful of discharge when they expressed displeasure), and to decrease correspondingly the use of exit. Thus, the minimal term should result in gains both because the employer has obtained better and quicker feedback from workers which should enable it to make productivity-enhancing changes in the workplace, and because the costs of exit (job search costs, loss of training investment, etc.) can be minimized. If these gains outweigh the costs of administering the 'for cause' system, the minimal term would be efficient.

Minimal terms may lead to a more efficient outcome, then, in several circumstances related to information imperfections. Minimal terms may be efficient when workers do not have the information necessary to evaluate the value of an employment term, when workers are intellectually or psychologically unable to value accurately an employment term, or when employers operate with poor information because workers are reluctant to exercise voice.

3. External Cost

Minimal terms may also be justified when employment terms impose costs on third parties, that is, when there are 'external' costs that are not weighed by employers and workers when they negotiate the employment contract.

Consider an employer that hires a worker who smokes. In a price theory world, the employer would pay the worker less than a worker who does not smoke by an amount equal to the extra costs imposed on the employer by smoking. Thus, if smokers are absent from work more often than non-smokers, the employer should pay a lower wage to a worker who smokes to compensate for the costs to the employer of the extra absences. Considering only the employer and the smoking worker, the price theory world would optimally balance the desire of workers to smoke and the employment costs associated with smoking. A worker would smoke if she valued smoking more than the decrease in pay caused by her smoking. An employer would hire smokers if they would agree to work for an amount sufficiently less than non-smokers to compensate the employer for its increased costs.

Some of the costs of smoking in the workplace, however, may be external, that is, they may be imposed on parties other than the employer and the smoking worker. Fellow workers, health and life insurance companies, social welfare agencies, and others may all bear some of the costs of smoking. To the extent this occurs, the efficient result may not be achieved. The costs of smoking are actually higher than the amount by which the employer reduces the pay of smokers; the employer reduces the pay only enough to recapture its losses, not enough to recapture *all* losses associated with smoking. As a result, some workers will continue to smoke even though they would not if they had to accept a reduction in pay sufficient to cover all of the costs of smoking. There will be 'too much' smoking in the workplace.

Minimal terms can be used to correct for this type of overproduction. The test of efficiency is what the market would have produced if all the costs of workplace smoking were considered. A minimal term which prohibited workplace smoking, or which taxed employers or workers for workplace smoking, would reduce the amount of workplace smoking and may produce an amount of smoking which closer approximates the efficient ideal.

Minimal terms, of course, may overcorrect. A minimal term which prohibited smoking would be likely to produce 'too little' workplace smoking because it would prohibit smoking by workers who would smoke even if they had to absorb all the costs. Even in this situation, however, the minimal term may be justified. If the 'too low' amount of smoking with the minimal term was closer to the efficient ideal than the 'too high' amount of smoking without the minimal term, the minimal term would be justifiable on efficiency grounds. [Reprinted by permission.]

✷ ✷ ✷

How are we to evaluate this view of the market model? By definition it describes a view of the world in which the outcomes (in terms of, say, jobs or incomes) are efficient. Two main questions may be asked here: First, is this an accurate description of how the labour market works? Second, to the extent that it is, what is our view of this state of affairs — is this a good thing?

On the first question, consider the following excerpts from Paul Weiler and Robert Solow.

Paul Weiler, *Governing the Workplace* (Cambridge: Harvard University Press, 1990) at 136–52.

A major premise of this book is that there are fundamental differences between the market for the labor of a human being and markets for other commodities, including the labor of a robot; these differences are (and should be) manifested throughout the entire employment relationship, not only with respect to exceptional concerns such as workplace safety. As good a way as any to appreciate the nature and significance of such differences is to reflect briefly on some peculiar features of contemporary employment, features that are widespread in the real world but anomalous in neoclassical economic theory.

Rigidity of Wages

Perhaps the most widely noted such phenomenon is that when the general demand for labor drops in the economy, the wages and benefits paid to workers usually do not drop; indeed, nominal compensation typically continues to rise. It is true that when severe drops occur in the demand and consequently in the price for particular product lines, special (and usually traumatic) wage concessions may be negotiated in the affected industries (say, in steel or airlines), so that the firms' costs of production can be brought into line with their shrunken revenues. But a general decline in economic activity coupled with a substantial increase in unemployment in the overall labor market is rarely used by employers as a reason to reduce wages to a level which would be sufficient to attract and keep workers who are in surplus supply. Instead, the standard way in which firms adjust to a reduction in consumer demand is to lay off workers and reduce production rather than cut employee wages in order to reduce consumer prices and thereby maintain sales and production. This downward 'stickiness' of wages has emerged as the central problem for contemporary macroeconomic policy, since it is the source of persistent stagflation — a combination of rising prices and substantial unemployment which was especially virulent throughout the seventies. It is this combination which leads policymakers deliberately to induce severe recessions, as they did in the early eighties, to try to wring wage and thence price inflation out of the economy; even such drastic measures have met with only partial success. Whatever may be the source or the cure of such inflexibility in wage levels, what is significant here is the sharp contrast between the labor market and the market for nonhuman commodities. A slump that hits the economy will have a downward impact on the price paid by firms such as General Motors to almost all its suppliers (including vendors of robots), who will themselves have a surplus of product to sell, and to whom GM will feel no obligation to continue paying pre-slump prices or maintain the suppliers' income. Although it is not unique, the labor market is very much a special case in this respect.

Distribution of Wages

Not only are rates of pay not particularly influenced by changes in short-term demand for labor, but they are not strongly correlated with the long-term productivity of the individual worker. Within the firm, the distribution of wages among employees is far more compressed than is the range of differences in their relative productivity, even where such differences can be individually metered. The larger, more sophisticated firms use job evaluation programs that establish rates of pay for the job, not for the individual; and as we saw earlier, progress along that salary scale is based more on length of service than on apparent 'merit.' Though the outside market becomes relevant when the firm must decide where to peg its internal wage structure in the community pay spectrum, surveys conducted of local wage patterns find that there is still a wide disparity in wages paid by different firms for the same type and quality of work. Even more curious, there is a systematic tilt in this pay range under which the larger, more capital-intensive, more profitable firms pay considerably higher wages (and benefits) for the same workers than do their smaller counterparts. The implication, then, is that employees as a group are allowed to share in the overall economic success of their employers even if their individual performance is no better than that of workers in less successful firms; and these wages are distributed in a relatively egalitarian manner within this group of employees, rather than related strongly to individual productive merit. The other side of the coin is that large powerful firms like General Motors and IBM, which can command a discount on almost everything else they buy (money and raw materials as well as robots), pay a premium when they buy labor from human beings.

Internal Labor Market

The allocation of attractive jobs in the more successful firms is done in accordance with what has been called an internal labor market. The selection of workers to be promoted, for example, is made by posting the job vacancy to solicit applications from current employees, then picking one of the internal contenders to fill the position. Only if no suitable candidate can be found inside the firm will the search be broadened to look at outside applicants. To the extent promotion is based on relative ability, it can serve as a substitute for merit pay in that it motivates workers to do better in their present job in order to improve their chances in the competition for better positions. Most firms rely not simply on incumbency, but also to a considerable extent on seniority as a criterion for promotion decisions (seniority counts very heavily for layoffs), thus reducing the level of competition even among workers in the firm. Whatever may be the range and mix of administration and market inside the work force, incumbent employees in these firms are almost entirely insulated from the outside market in the allocation of jobs: they need not worry greatly about an outsider's persuading the company that he will do better in filling a vacancy, and they need worry hardly at all about an outsider's offering to do the work more cheaply in the case of a surplus of employees in a recession. Again, this pattern is almost totally limited to the purchase and sale of human labor, by contrast with the market for almost any other commodity.

Career Employment

These standard features of contemporary employment are closely connected to the phenomenon I described earlier: the long-term career relationship of the worker to the firm. Indeed that kind of relationship is likely to be induced and reinforced by this pattern of administration of job opportunities, wages, and benefits. The implication I drew from the earlier discussion was that an individual's present job becomes more and more valuable to him as he commits more and more of his working life to it while working his way up the internal labor ladder; and that this presents a compelling case for some kind of protection against arbitrary dismissal from the firm and expulsion into the outside market. The crucial point is that the pattern of workers committing themselves to jobs and becoming locked into relationships that can last for decades reduces and inhibits the play of market forces that function most effectively in settings where there is flexibility and mobility in the competition for services.

A number of general comments can be made about these features of the world of work. First, I do not suggest that they are inevitable and universal. Indeed, as we shall see, this employment pattern is of relatively recent vintage. There are many contemporary examples of occupations marked by more casual relationships and more influenced by standard market forces; jobs that range in quality from the migrant farm laborer to the entertainment personality in theater, television, sports, and so on. But the majority of jobs filled by people who are committed to stay in the labor force take the form of this structured career arrangement: in such jobs internal administrative regulation has much more influence than does conventional supply and demand from the external market.

Nor can we bracket these observations from our analysis by assuming these practices to be the hallmark primarily of unionized or union-like public employers — organizations that are supposedly less productive than they might be because they are not required by the market to be efficient in their use of labor. It is fair to say that the origins and impetus of this kind of employment structure are to be found in collective bargaining, and that they continue to remain more pronounced in the union sector. However, administration of employment along the lines I have sketched is also a visible and regular characteristic of nonunion firms; and, even more significantly, of the more successful, more profitable nonunion firms that other employers try to learn from and to emulate. In other words, employers like IBM, General Motors, and the federal government behave very differently in their purchase of labor than in their purchases of other commodities in the marketplace.

WHY TREAT HUMAN LABOR DIFFERENTLY?

The next question is, what is the explanation for the remarkable differences in the market treatment of humans and of robots? In that explanation may be found inspiration and justification for public policies that would alter even more dramatically the market for labor, whether such policies take the form of reconstruction of the labor market through collective bargaining or replacing the market with legal regulation.

It is not difficult to understand why an internal labor market (actually internal labor *administration*) is attractive to the worker who is party to an employment contract. Workers naturally prefer to live in an environment where they have reasonable assurances about what their competition will be, an expectation of advancement in the firm in times of prosperity, and confidence that they will retain their job (or at least be recalled to it) in times of adversity. Employees will find these kinds of assurances and expectations to be far more reliable if judgments about work and pay are insulated from the forces of direct competition with other workers and the sudden shocks to which market competition is prone.

There are two additional reasons most workers prefer such administrative regulation. First, in the modern world a job is the major foundation for the economic welfare of individuals and families; not merely the source of immediate take-home pay, but also of much of the network of insurance protection against illness, disability, aging, and so on. But unlike the owners of almost any other income-producing assets (owners of robots, for example), the worker cannot separate himself from his labor: he cannot diversify his risk by doing business with a variety of customers, some of whom may treat him poorly but most of whom will not. Since at any given time a worker must place all his eggs in one basket, as it were, having a sense of security about what will happen in his current job is far more important than in virtually any other market setting. And for the reasons I gave earlier, it is terribly difficult for workers to spread the risk over time by moving to a comparable new job from one that has proved unstable or unpleasant.

Abstracting from the serious financial costs created by the loss of a job and its perquisites, there are important personal values implicated in the treatment of people at work. Work is not merely an economic function whereby people produce goods and services that are useful to and will be bought by others (although certainly this market exchange dimension is very important). For the employee work is also a major source of personal identity and satisfaction, of his sense of self-esteem and accomplishment, and of many of his closest and most enduring relationships. But at the heart of the employment contract is an undertaking by the worker to subject his person to the authority and direction of the employer (again, in marked contrast to the undertaking made by the owner of the robot). The exercise of such managerial authority is closer, more regular, and often more salient to the worker than is the exercise of government authority. For many of the same reasons we as citizens feel entitled to fair treatment at the hands of government officials, we also feel entitled to comparable consideration from management officials. And as their initial quest for decent compensation and protection on the job is gradually satisfied, workers feel and assert a further claim to meaningful involvement in and influence over the process by which is fashioned the web of workplace rules, with their often fateful human consequences for the employees' lives, both on and off the job.

This is not to imply that even the fairest of treatment by the most responsive of employers guarantees the protection of employees against all adverse happenings at work. Just as governments cannot avert many natural or socioeconomic disasters, so also firms encounter shifts in their external product and capital markets that make them unable to satisfy their workers' expectations of stable employment and rising wages. Few employers guarantee and few employees expect lifetime employment, come what may. But when one considers, instead, the employer's decision to dismiss a particular individual for disciplinary reasons — with the stigma being fired inflicts and the sense of resentment if there was no cause — or, conversely, the decision to favor someone in the award of a raise or a promotion, it is not hard to fathom why workers want their employers to respect, in some fashion or other, the values of personal integrity, equality, and due process that are imposed on government.

This brief sketch of the reasons employees normally prefer administrative regulation to market competition simply repeats what should be evident from our own personal experience. Less obvious, though, is why that facet of the employment relationship should be acceptable to so many employers. Why is self-regulation of management's authority over the work force adopted voluntarily by so many firms, without any significant present-day pressure from either the law or union organization?

Employers did not always perceive that this policy would be to their advantage. Acceptance of the career-type employment relationship dates back no earlier than World War II, and more than half a century of struggle was required to bring it about. The initial organization of factory work in the late nineteenth century was very much in accordance with the market paradigm — the 'drive system' as it was called. In this system, the foreman in charge of a division of the firm's operation recruited the employees he needed from a nomadic population of available workers. The overall wage level went up or down according to conditions in the labor market, and individual workers were paid in accordance with their productivity, measured on a piecework basis or simply assessed by the foreman. If the work load in the factory slackened, the redundant employees were let go with no expectation of a future preference in rehiring based on their previous service; neither was there any regular practice of preferring incumbent workers for promotion into whatever more skilled and attractive jobs happened to open up. In that setting, there was no basis for the employer's devising benefit packages to protect employees against misfortunes that might occur at some time in the future. Indeed, if workers became less productive because of disability or age, they would simply be replaced by younger, more able-bodied workers, who were better able to meet the rigors of factory life. From a socioeconomic perspective, the employment relationship (particularly in manual work, which comprised the majority of jobs at the time) was truly casual and episodic; thus the law's adoption of a strong presumption of an at-will contract was very much in accordance with workplace life.

The interesting question, then, is why has this model almost entirely disappeared from the life, if not the law, of the factory and office, to be replaced by the system of internal administration I just described? One possibility is that employers wanted the benefit of bureaucratic rule, through which senior management could control the exercise of power by people lower down in the hierarchy, and thereby reduce the risk of arbitrariness, favoritism, and simple erratic behavior by their foremen.

While this preference for rules over discretion likely has something to do with the transformation of work, it will not nearly serve as a full explanation. First, supervisory discretion was the price of the firm's having the flexibility to respond to changing market cues: sacrificing it could cost the employer more than regulation would gain. In other words, while one can readily see that the drive system exposed individual employees to considerable risk of arbitrary and discriminatory action, that will not explain why employers would dispense with an arrangement in which they could and did hold the foreman to account for the bottom-line labor productivity and costs produced by whatever style he used in managing his work force.

Second, even a system of bureaucratic rules that proved to have net advantages over market discretion would not explain the *content* of the rules I described, such as the egalitarian tilt to the wage structure or the tendency to reward service more than performance in bestowing jobs and benefits. It is easy to understand why the average employee would be interested in equality and seniority; but what about the employer who, one presumes, is primarily interested in productivity and profitability? What are the special features and challenges of the labor of a human being as far as the employer is concerned? Why might the more rigid administration of a career employment relationship be ultimately more predictive than the more flexible, market-oriented, casual relationship with which modern industrial life began?

Recruitment

One unique feature of human labor is that the worker is a peculiarly free factor of production in the sense that he can leave his job at will. An employer cannot buy and own a worker as it can a robot; indeed, the employer cannot even negotiate a specifically enforceable contract of employment with him. But when workers leave their jobs, others must be recruited to fill their places. The recruiting process itself imposes significant costs on the firm. . . . Since it cannot use the law to force a worker to stay on the job, the employer has to design its employment relationship in a way that gives its workers strong incentives to stay. This is an initial explanation, then, for the variety of features of contemporary employment that mark its transition from the casual to the career form, even though the career form might seem to interfere with the operation of simple, short-term market forces.

Training

Only the smaller share of the financial costs of worker turnover is attributable to the recruiting process. By far the most significant expenditures are those required for training the newly hired worker to perform in the vacant position. Very few jobs have demands which are so rudimentary or necessary skills which are so adequately taught elsewhere that a newcomer can step in and do a satisfactory job immediately. At a minimum, the new employee will have to learn the location and idiosyncrasies of the physical equipment and the routines and expectations of fellow workers. Typically, much of the necessary basic knowledge and skills for the position will have to be learned on the job rather than at school. . . . The employer considers it reasonable to make this investment in the enhanced capacities of its workers because it expects to get a return on the investment in better performance and productivity over the years. But the resulting human capital is in fact embodied in and owned by the worker, who, as I noted above, is legally free to move elsewhere whenever he wants, and in doing so to liquidate instantly the capital investment made in him by the firm. This provides an even stronger incentive for the employer to make another investment in designing attractive employment terms that will reduce turnover in its work force.

Motivation

To secure its side of the employment bargain, the firm must do more than simply retain its employees in their jobs: it must also elicit the optimum level of performance while they are there. This objective confronts another specifically human characteristic. Unlike robots, one cannot program workers to produce a desired response on command, day in and day out. Even with a given level of teaching and training, human beings display a remarkable range in potential performance, the full gamut from perfunctory to consummate. . . . [I]f our goal is not simply profitable businesses, but also a productive economy that supplies its citizens with more and more 'good jobs at good wages,' then it is essential to motivate employees to make a strong, willing commitment to the success of the enterprise rather than simply to do the bare minimum necessary to keep their job. That kind of esprit de corps can be undermined in a number of ways. The work force may get the feeling that individual employees are being treated arbitrarily and unfairly (treatment that is perceived as damaging even if administered to one's fellow workers and friends, not only to oneself). Alternatively, the employees may feel that the business is being run primarily for the short-term goal of raising the rate of return on the shareholders' investment, without a reciprocal management commitment to improve workers' pay and preserve their jobs. Indeed, polls have found that fewer than 10 percent of American workers now believe that if they were to put forth extra effort and thereby enhance the productivity of their operations, it would redound much to their personal benefit rather than just to their employer's. In such an environment, no wonder so many employees feel no particular reason to make sacrifices and try harder in pursuit of a corporate goal, the achievement of which they may not be around to see, let alone to benefit from. Thus the essence of good person-nel practice consists in the communication of a very different message to one's work force in order to enhance its morale and its productivity.

Cooperation

Modern production is much more a social than an individual process. It is hard to imag-ine many goods and services that are produced and supplied by a single worker. The most efficient enterprise then, is not necessarily the one with the most stable, well-trained, and highly motivated individual workers; it is the one with the most cohesive and cooperative team of workers. What a productive team requires are people who complement each other in filling the wide variety of roles in any complex enterprise, with some positions being more attention-getting and rewarding, but with even the journeymen performers being indispensable to the functioning of the whole. Teamwork also requires a willingness on the part of everyone to cooperate with fellow employees in the constantly recurring situa-tions where they interact. A vital example of this is the willingness of veteran employees to transmit the lore of the shop, the equipment, and the position to the newcomer who is being trained on the job.

Again, this sense of cooperation can be threatened by such market-oriented employ-ment practices as attempting to match each worker's pay and benefits precisely to his mar-ginal productivity, where the actual contribution of any individual to the group product is very difficult to measure, at least in a way that will be evident to fellow workers; or setting up a competition for scarce jobs, so that the veteran employee knows that if he trains the newcomer too well, the latter will be able to beat him out for promotions or even bump into the veteran's own job in a layoff. The aim of creating a cooperative, complementary team of employees helps explain, then, not simply the development of rules which limit supervisory arbitrariness to preserve morale, but also the content of such widespread stan-dards as seniority in the allocation of positions, and pay systems that evaluate the job, not the person.

. . . Certainly it was not typically the case that management fashioned these features of the employment relationship to insulate workers from direct exposure to the market because management believed it would be more efficient for the firm. What actually hap-pened was that workers originally developed these practices through their unions and eventually, by means of collective bargaining, forced their adoption throughout modern industry. Once that happened, the management of nonunion firms had a strong incentive to emulate voluntarily the pattern set by collective bargaining relationships in order to avoid being organized themselves.

As the threat of unionization recedes, the psychology of the firm is becoming some-what subtler. A younger, more heterogeneous work force has emerged, one whose collec-tive consciousness has been formed much more by the protest movements of the sixties than by the Great Depression of the thirties. Not only does the new worker find it natural to demand a more satisfying and interesting job, but also it is apparent that many employ-ers treat their employees in a civilized and humane manner and still prosper. Thus any firm that deviates too far from this pattern, that chooses to deny its employees the kind of consideration all its counterparts provide, does so at its own peril. In sum the employer may receive its side of the employment bargain — a stable, trained, motivated, and cooperative team — only if it treats its work force in accordance with norms of behavior that exhibit respect for the employees as human beings. Whatever the explanation, this conclusion is now commonplace in the teaching of human resource management. It is gradually seeping into labor economics, but it has not yet surfaced in the recent efforts by the law and economics school to tackle labor and employment law. To the extent that one wants the future evolution of labor law policy to be informed and influenced by economic analysis, it is critical that labor economics be founded on careful empirical investigation of how labor markets respond to the peculiar needs and concerns of this distinctively *human* commodity, rather than on an effort to force the employment relationship into the procrustean bed of an economic model that accounts quite well for what happens in only certain markets — in markets for money, natural resources, and other inanimate commodities.

Robert Solow, *The Labor Market as a Social Institution* (Oxford: Blackwell, 1990) at 3, 5–10, 28, 31–44, 79

One important tradition within economics, perhaps the dominant tradition right now, especially in macroeconomics, holds that in nearly all respects the labor market is just like other markets. It should be analyzed in much the same way that one would analyze the market for any perishable commodity, using the conventional apparatus of supply and demand. Common sense, on the other hand, seems to take it for granted that there is something special about labor as a commodity, and therefore about the labor market too. (It is not hard to see why one might think that. It is worth pointing out that specialists in labor economics and industrial relations tend to side with common sense in this instance.) . . .

The most elementary reason for thinking that the concept of fairness, and beliefs about what is fair and what is not, play an important part in labor-market behavior is that we talk about them all the time. That is the appeal to common sense. The fact is so obvious that I will not trouble you with examples, except to bet that if you conjure up in your mind a picture of a picket line, the largest word on the placards is likely to be 'UNFAIR.' Let me quote from an essay called 'A Fair Rate of Wages' by no less a person than Alfred Marshall. He says '. . . the phrase is constantly used in the market place; it is frequent in the mouths both of employers and the employed; and almost every phrase in common use has a real meaning, though it may be difficult to get at.' . . . I am going to return to Marshall's essay later. It was called to my attention by Professor R.C.O. Matthews, which seems appropriate because he is the current tenant of the professorship at Cambridge once held by Marshall.

A few days after writing these lines I walked past a group of picketing painters. The word 'UNFAIR' was not to be seen. I was disappointed. When I looked again at the signs, I saw that they said that the X Construction Company 'does not observe COMMUNITY

STANDARDS in wages and working conditions.' It made my day. From the point of view of these lectures, there is no better definition of 'unfair.'

Of course it is conceivable that a phrase or concept that is in everyone's mouth, or even in everyone's brain, should have nothing to do with the reality of outcomes. They may be words, just words, as Kenneth Burke once said of the novel. That seems especially implausible in a context like the labor market where negotiation and bargaining play a fairly conspicuous role. But it is hard to give a conclusive proof of the opposite. Even if the employers and the employed who talk about fairness are not just cynical phonies, their decisions may be entirely controlled by an invisible force, whether they know it or not. All one can do is to offer circumstantial evidence, which is what I try in this lecture, and to show that the view that I am advocating can explain things that the alternative view cannot — I try that in the next lecture. . . .

A second reason for believing that norms of equity and fairness have an effective — and not merely an emotive or symbolic — function in the labor market is that they turn up frequently and prominently in the literature of industrial relations and personnel management. Manuals for the training of people who actually engage in wage setting and wage negotiation teach practitioners that equity and perceived equity, over time and across occupations and firms, are an indispensable characteristic of a good system of industrial relations. Otherwise there will be quits, low morale and accompanying low productivity. Observers of industrial relations confirm this. It seems quite unreasonable to suppose that such statements are just deceptive cover-ups for unrestrained gouging. . . .

The fundamental reason for believing that fairness is a factor in labor markets is what we know about our own society and its culture. Bear in mind that I am speaking now as an ordinary citizen-observer, not as someone with professional knowledge or expertise, though I will in a moment return to report information I have come by more honestly.

We live in a society in which social status and self-esteem are strongly tied both to occupation and income. Of course occupation and income are correlated, but not perfectly correlated. It seems undeniable to me that both occupation and income are significant variables. The way others look at us, and the way we look at ourselves, are both income related, and both are job related at given income. Employment and the income it brings are not simply equivalent to a set of bundles of consumer goods (and savings). But that is exactly the way textbook economics treats them. . . .

Once you admit to yourself that wage rates and employment are profoundly entwined with social status and self-esteem you have already left the textbook treatment of the labor market behind. We all want to be treated as we deserve to be treated, or perhaps better. . .

Persistent unemployment has been a persistent problem for economic theory. It is obviously a problem for the persistently unemployed. They suffer a loss of income, often a deterioration of skills, and sometimes a period of unpleasant uncertainty about the longer future. The problem for the economic theorist is different. What I have been calling textbook economics — the idea that the capitalist economy is a collection of interrelated markets in which supply and demand tend to come into equality — has no good way to explain the fact that fairly high levels of unemployment seem to be able to persist for lengths of time measured in years. A nontrivial part of the history of economics during the past 60 years could be written in terms of the profession's attempts to find a believable story that can account for the facts with minimal damage to the structure of economic theory. . . .

Some economists have already proposed plausible models of the labor market that are capable of accounting in a logical way for the existence and persistence of true unemployment. The more interesting of these, unsurprisingly, seem to be based on a somewhat more sophisticated view of the labor market as a social institution. They allow for a variety of motives and interactions that are conspicuously missing from the standard textbook model.

The leading candidates these days are versions of what are called, in one case, efficiency-wage theory and, in the other, insider-outsider theory. Lectures like these are not the appropriate vehicle for a full exposition; but I have to say something about them to give you an idea of how they work. For one thing, you will have to judge whether the mechanisms they rely on are reasonable interpretations of the reality of labor markets. And secondly I want to add something to them. Both, it seems to me, leave the same gap and are vulnerable to the same criticism; I want to propose a way to complete them.

There are many versions of efficiency-wage theory. They all turn one way or another on the observation that workers employed in modern industry often have some control over their own productivity. They produce more when they are strongly motivated to do so. One way for an employer to provide more motivation is by paying more than other employers do; another is to threaten to fire the excessively unproductive if and when they are detected. It all sounds quite natural, but already we have made a significant break with textbook doctrine: if what I just said is true, actual production depends not only on physical inputs and technology, but also on the wage being paid.

From this point on, alternative versions of efficiency-wage theory proceed to emphasize different facts of life. One of the earliest combines the stick with the carrot: workers also provide effort because being found out and fired for cause is costly. It is more costly the harder it is to find another job, and therefore the higher the current unemployment rate happens to be. Even if each employer finds the carrot initially more efficient than the stick (because detection is costly) and tries to pay more than the others, competition among employers will merely bid up wages with no employer being able to establish a lasting favorable differential. In the end the wage will be driven to levels at which full employment is not viable; all the discipline is, in effect, done by the stick, the threat of unemployment. If there were less unemployment it would pay employers to offer higher wages in the hope of eliciting more productivity from their workers. All would do so; but then with jobs more easily found, and paying more to boot, it would become advantageous for workers to provide less effort and accept the higher risk of being laid off.

There are other styles of efficiency-wage theory. George Akerlof and Janet Yellen have proposed — on the basis of psychological and sociological evidence — what they call the fair-wage-effort hypothesis. In this kinder and gentler version it is not the fear of unemployment and deprivation of wage income that makes individual productivity an increasing function of the wage received, but rather a sort of ethical imperative: if you are paid a fair day's wage you owe your employer a fair day's work. An employer who pays less than a fair day's wage cannot expect to get a fair day's work. It then takes a little analytical machinery to show that a likely outcome is persistent unemployment. (Anyone who wants to go into that can consult the literature.)

I hope all of this strikes you as plausible, even homespun. You could not make it exciting enough for a short story, not even in the New Yorker. But there is a general economic insight hidden in this commonplace description. One important difference between the labor market and the market for fish is that the performance of the worker depends on the price paid for her services. You would not say the same for the performance of a pound of filleted salmon. (By the way, if it should happen that consumers of fish come to judge quality by price — so that salmon tastes better the more you pay for it, just because you pay more for it — then the market for fish will begin to behave unclassically too.) Because the wage rate enters the story in this double role, as a productive factor as well as a simple cost, it is not available simply to balance supply and demand in the usual efficient way. It cannot perform both functions perfectly. It is precisely the character of the labor market as a social institution that makes it generate an inefficiently low level of employment. That is all I want from efficiency-wage theory right now.

The insider-outsider approach starts from a different elementary observation. The group of experienced workers in a firm — the insiders, for short — is likely not to be perfectly interchangeable with other workers — unemployed workers, for instance — who are currently available in the labor market. The economist would say that the insiders generate a rent jointly with the rest of the apparatus of the firm. They are therefore in a position to bargain with the firm over the division of the rent. The rent may arise initially simply because the insiders are more productive in this firm than outsiders would be. It will be enlarged if the insiders can jointly threaten to resist the hiring of outsiders by refusing to train them or to cooperate with them. That may require a certain amount of solidarity. In any case, the insiders can hope to achieve a wage higher than the level that would allow the firm profitably to employ any number of unemployed workers, assuming there are some.

If that is the way the labor market works, then pretty clearly unemployment can persist. Wages are too high for full employment, and the intrinsic advantage and bargaining power enjoyed by insiders is adequate to keep those wages from being eroded by the competition of the unemployed. I will let you make the contrast with the fish market yourself.

These stories connect up with the textbook model in an interesting way. The reason why the textbook model has such a hard time accommodating persistent unemployment is that unemployed workers are supposed to put downward pressure on wage rates by competing for existing jobs. Economists would put that in a more precise and general way. To say that there is true or involuntary unemployment is to say that those without jobs would regard themselves as better off if they were employed in jobs they know how to do at the wages now being paid to those roughly equivalent workers who hold such jobs. In that case (if individuals care only about the goods they consume and the leisure they enjoy) they would feel themselves to be better off if they were employed in jobs they can do even if they were paid ever so slightly less than the going wage in such jobs. If one means by an equilibrium a situation in which no participant can think of anything more advantageous to do than he is now doing, this situation with involuntary unemployment cannot be an equilibrium. Unemployed workers could bid for jobs. In the sort of labor market that underlies the textbook, they should do so.

Both of the novel labor-market stories I have described explain why *employers* would reject competitive offers from the unemployed. The reasons are different in the two models, of course. In the efficiency-wage story, the employer reasons this way. I am offering the wage that I now pay because it is the best wage for me to offer when I take account of its effect on productivity. No doubt the currently unemployed are sincere when they offer to work for a few cents less. But I know that if I were to hire them after a slight wage cut to replace some of my current workers, the newcomers would pretty soon supply less than the optimal amount of effort — less than optimal for *me*, mind you — either because they would have less than the optimal fear of being found out and laid off or because they would feel aggrieved at getting less than a fair wage. Maybe their instant feeling of relief or gratitude at having found a job would deter them for a while. But it would wear off. They are, after all, exactly like their currently employed sisters-in-law, by definition. And that is how I arrived at the going wage in the first place. No, thank you, it is not to my advantage to pay less.

In the insider-outsider case the reason is different but the reality is the same. If I accept any of these wage-cutting offers, I will disturb the balance I have reached with my current insiders. They will very likely make life hard for any small number of outsiders, especially as the insiders will blame the outsiders for the erosion of the wage. The productivity of the enterprise will suffer. If I were to try a wholesale replacement of insiders by outsiders, the loss of firm-specific skills will probably cost me more in profit than a lower wage would bring. Besides, I would merely be replacing my current insiders by a group who would soon become the insiders of the future. And then they would act exactly like their sisters-in-law, by definition. No, thank you, it is not to my advantage to pay less.

This is a powerful result. It resolves an important paradox. When there are a lot of unemployed workers, you might expect employers actively to solicit competitive wage cutting on their part. It rarely happens. The cases when it does happen, usually in deep recession or when there is a serious threat from imported substitutes for the firm's product, are striking enough to call attention to the fact that it does not happen in run-of-the-mill recessions, although the unemployment rate might rise by two or three percentage points and even in average times there appears to be some excess supply of labor. The alternative theories I have sketched at least explain why employers might not try to induce wage cutting and might not accept offers if they came along anyway.

But these stories seem to be incomplete. They do not explain why the unemployed do not at least try to compete for existing jobs by offering to work at less than the going wage. One possible explanation is that they know from hearsay or experience that such offers would be turned down by potential employers. There is undoubtedly something to that.

The collective experience of the labor market (as even relative newcomers must learn) would say that. It would be reinforced by the fact that, in bad times, firms normally let it be known that they are not hiring. Nevertheless, this explanation seems a little lame. It costs very little to try; and the potential gain to any unemployed worker who succeeded would be substantial. There would seem to be some deeper force at work to choke off wage competition from the unemployed. Even in the years of deep recession and import competition, when wage givebacks occurred with some frequency, they were generally initiated by employers, not by competition from the unemployed. The threat was usually to close down a plant, not so often to staff it with unemployed workers. In some European countries, where unemployment rates have been very high by historical standards for an unprecedentedly long time, there has been no tendency for real wages to erode; in fact in some countries they appear to continue rising. One would feel better with a model that explained this apparent unwillingness of unemployed labor to bid actively for scarce jobs. For economists, quite a lot turns on this point. In the absence of any such theory, the temptation is strong to accept the view that measured unemployment is 'voluntary' in the sense that the 'unemployed' are not worse off than their employed sisters-in-law.

One easy way out of this difficulty is the hypothesis that there is some sort of social norm or behavioral injunction that forbids undercutting the going wage as a strategy for unemployed workers. The hypothesis has the advantage that it feels true, precisely because a job is a status as well as a source of income. It does not require any romanticism about solidarity to suggest that competing for an existing job by undercutting the wage might be seen as demeaning, whereas selling off your full load of halibut at the market-clearing price, whatever it may be, would carry no corresponding overtone of betrayal or self-abnegation. The fact that the norm against wage cutting seems to break down in extreme circumstances may only testify to its reality in run-of-the-mill cases. We sense that something has snapped.

I confess that I believe the right answer lies in this direction. But that is hardly an adequate argument. The casual postulation of social norms is altogether too easy a mode of explanation. It will certainly not do for economists, including me, partly because we like to think of ourselves as more hard-boiled than that and partly because we are professionally inclined to think of self-interest as a powerful motive in economic affairs.

An injunction not to engage in wage cutting puts a major strain on unemployed workers. The cost of obeying the norm is undoubtedly diminished by the availability of unemployment insurance and other public assistance benefits. These differ in amount from time to time and place to place. At most times and in most places, the margin of advantage of employment over unemployment remains pretty substantial. Besides, there is plenty of evidence — some of which I described in the first lecture — that a job is a source of self-respect in a way that even moderately cushy unemployment could never be. You have to be pretty obtuse not to realize that very many of the unemployed would much prefer to be working at wage rates currently on offer. Presumably that is why they and their families have been known to celebrate the acquisition of a job. ('Write if you get work.') But then the belief that there is a stable and effective social norm against wage competition for jobs needs some reinforcement of a kind that might come from a showing that obeying such a norm is individually rational, besides performing a social function. That is the sort of argument I now want to make in a non-technical way.

I begin with a general sort of framework and come down to my particular problem later. Probably everyone here knows about the prisoner's dilemma game which, in recent years, has provided a neat vehicle for the study of a whole range of social interactions. We can do without the circumstantial story-line that usually brightens up the description of the situation. The essence of the game is that there are two players, A and B, each of whom must choose one of two possible strategies without any possibility of preliminary communication and certainly without the capacity to make binding commitments about which strategy each will choose. The two strategies available to each player are called Cooperation and Defection, for reasons which emerge from the nature of the game. Each combination of choices, one for each player, leads to a known payoff to each. The particular payoffs have a key property: no matter whether A cooperates or defects, it is to B's advantage to defect; and no matter whether B cooperates or defects, it is to A's advantage to defect. We have to suppose then that both A and B will defect, certainly if they have no particular connection with one another except through a single play of this game. However, if both do defect, the payoff to each of them is perceptibly less than it would have been if both had cooperated. It is individually rational for each player to defect, although each of them knows that it would be jointly and individually better if they were both to cooperate. If they could negotiate a binding agreement beforehand, they would surely agree to cooperate.

There is not much more to say if the players are healthily self-interested and play the game only once. The plot thickens if they have to play the game again and again, for a very long time, even if they remain quite selfish. Then it would be driven home to the players that it would be worth a lot if they could find a way to cooperate effectively. The besetting obstacle to cooperation is the reasonable fear that the other will play you for a sucker and let you cooperate while he or she defects. If the game is played many times, however, there is a possible escape from mutual assured defection. Each player may be able to teach the other, by example and experience if necessary, that each is prepared to punish defection by the other. If A should ever take advantage of B by defecting while B cooperates, B can respond by herself defecting for a whole string of plays. This is costly to B. but the cost may be more than recovered if A is taught a lasting lesson. A may come to realize that the short-run gain from suckering B does not compensate for the long-run loss from a string of mutual defections that might have been mutual cooperations.

(If cooperation is to emerge in this way, it is obviously essential that the game be played more or less forever. There is a well-known problem in the finitely repeated game: the last play is just one-shot; but then the next-to-last play is also effectively one-shot because the last play is bound to result in defection; and thus the whole thing unravels. When we are talking about social phenomena this difficulty is not so acute. Individual players may come and go, but the game — wage bargaining, for example — goes on effectively forever and institutional memory can take over. Alternatively one can make do with a probability that the game will be played at least one more time.)

All this is old stuff and has been much discussed and analyzed by game theorists and others. The political scientist Robert Axelrod has written a well-known book called *The Evolution of Cooperation*, whose subject is well described by its title. Axelrod shows by example that the simplest punishment strategy, which he calls Tit for Tat, does very well in repeated plays of the game against other reasonable strategies. (Tit for Tat starts by cooperating on the first play and then on each succeeding play does whatever its opponent did on the play before. Thus cooperation is rewarded by cooperation and defection is punished by a single defection.) It does not require a vast leap of imagination to see how the habit of cooperation might emerge and be reinforced.

But then the next step could very well be the acceptance and internalization of a social norm: cooperation is the right thing to do in such and such a particular social situation. It is a fair guess that many social norms evolve in just this manner, not merely from prisoner's dilemma contexts. Behavior that has been found to be individually tempting but socially destructive is held to be socially unacceptable. Behavior that has been found to be collectively useful though at least mildly disadvantageous to the individual is held to be the right thing to do. Some conflict between the private and social consequences of actions seems to be a necessary part of the picture, for otherwise there is no need for a specific code of behavior. Too much conflict, on the other hand, could cause a cooperative norm to break down. The last step is the internalization of social norms: we do things because they are the right thing to do, not because we have reckoned all the consequences.

To come back to the labor market, I have something more specific in mind than these rather vague thoughts arising from the prisoner's dilemma. But some of the concepts, like that of a punishment strategy, will play a further role. The problem, remember, is to explain how it can be that unemployed workers do not compete for jobs by offering to work for less than incumbents are getting, although it would appear to be to their advantage to do just that. The solution I want to propose goes as follows. The labor-market outcome is best thought of as a single episode in a repeated game involving firms and workers. In any single episode, some workers are employed and others are unemployed. Being unemployed but sitting tight and accepting the loss that comes with unemployment can be an 'equilibrium strategy' for an unemployed worker. That means that there is an assignment of behavior patterns to each player such that, in the repeated game context, no player can gain from adopting a different strategy if the others stand pat. In such an equilibrium, the behavior pattern assigned to the unemployed worker is the one I have described, and the one we by and large observe. . . .

The last suggestion I want to make is a sort of generalization of the others, and provides a summary note on which I can logically bring these lectures to an end. Earlier I proposed a way of resolving the puzzle of the supply side of the labor market, namely the rarity of active wage competition even under the stimulus of persistent unemployment. The proposal was that the social norm against 'unfair' wage competition could emerge as reinforcement of a particular equilibrium choice of strategies for workers and firms. In that equilibrium, abstention from wage cutting is enforced by the latent threat of reversion to Hobbesian competition. The point I now want to make is that attempts to improve the working of the labor market by making it more nearly perfectly competitive may be misguided. They may be misguided in two ways: first because they might be resisted strongly and thus rendered impractical; and second because they may not be in the best interest of working people, who might be willing to pay a price to avoid having their livelihoods governed by atomistic competition.

[Reprinted by permission.]

* * *

Return now to our second question about the classical economic account of the labour market — not whether it is accurate, the question addressed by Paul Weiler and R. Solow, but, to the extent it is accurate, what are we to make of it?

Two points can be made here. First, it is often said by and about economists that they have or should have little or nothing to say about the "fairness" or "equity" of market outcomes. It is said that efficiency and equity are unconnected concepts. On the other hand, many attempts have been made to defend the system of market ordering on expressly normative grounds. We turn to these overtly normative defences below. But first, consider the proposition that it is possible to separate questions of efficiency from questions of equity.

Lester C. Thurow, *Generating Inequality* (New York: Basic Books, 1975) at 20–26

An outside observer of the economic game can ask two major questions. First, he can ask whether the economic game is an equitable game. What is the distribution of economic prizes across the population? Is the distribution of prizes fair or unfair? Is the mechanism by which prizes are distributed just or unjust? Second, he can ask whether or not the economic game is an efficient game. How large is the average prize? Could the game be reorganized to generate a larger economic prize?

With the death of traditional welfare economics in the 1950s, economic analysis has come to focus almost exclusively on the efficiency questions. Problems of equity are mentioned as important, but they are then treated as too difficult to be discussed or as not the proper area for economists to investigate. Either equity questions are regarded as the province of someone else — philosophers, political scientists, theologians, citizens — or it is assumed that they can only be settled by force. . . .

Not only are equity judgments logically necessary but they are practically unavoidable. Failure to make an overt equity judgment merely leads to the de facto certification of the current market distribution of income and wealth as the equitable distribution of income and wealth. One way or another, each society is forced to reveal its collective preferences with respect to the 'justice' of its distribution of economic prizes. . . . One often hears it said that although there are economic statements to be made about efficiency, there are no economic statements to be made about equity, only personal prejudices. In fact, equity statements stand on the same foundation as efficiency statements. Neither is value free. Both depend upon an underlying set of discussable value judgments. Once these value judgments have been made, there are technical studies to be done on economic equity just as there are technical studies to be done on economic efficiency.

Modern analysis of economic efficiency depends upon the acceptance of Pareto optimality: State A is better than State B if at least one person is better off in A and no one is worse off. A person is better off in A if he prefers to be in A rather than in B. In a weaker version of the same principle, State A is better than State B if those who are better off in State A could adequately compensate those who are worse off in State A. An economy moves toward Pareto optimality in its weaker sense when scarce resources are used in such a way as to maximize potential output. There are more economic prizes to be distributed. With an improvement in efficiency there is a larger bundle of goods and services (including leisure) that individuals can choose among. More is better.

All analysis of economic efficiency depends upon these postulates, which are all thoroughly ethical in nature. Thus, a value judgment is made that each individual is the best judge of his or her own happiness, and that more choice is always better than less. If productivity goes up, society has a wider range of choices among goods and leisure. It is better off. Without such value judgments, 'efficiency' ceases to have any meaning in modern economics.

Paretian efficiency values were easily absorbed into economics because they seemed to be universally held. They are, after all, the values of a liberal-individualistic society. The invocation of universally held value judgments has been the traditional way to avoid discussing values. This occurs partly because we believe what is universally held does not need to be discussed, but also because values that are in fact universally held seem to be intuitively true and are often held to be facts rather than values. To many 'more [choice] is better' is a fact and not a value. But it is easy to see alternative postulates. On a survival hike, less is better. The fewer material aids you start out with the more you have achieved in your survival. Many societies are, and have been, founded on the principle that collective judgments dominate individual judgments. A person is better off in State A if the group decides that he is better off.

We may all share Paretian postulates, but this does not alter the fact that they are value judgments or elevate them beyond the realm of analysis. Take the inviolability of consumer preferences. Given the nineteenth-century belief in the existence of innate wants within the individual, the inviolability of consumers' preferences seemed sensible. Given modern sociology and psychology, the postulate of innate wants is no longer so plausible. We now perceive that every society or culture generates the 'wants' of its population. Moreover, as our knowledge of how 'wants' are generated improves, the activity of generating wants increasingly falls within the domain of deliberate policies. Indeed, a debate on whether our society should try to generate traditional economic 'wants' or other life styles is currently under way.

As this example illustrates, various types of beliefs about matters of fact — especially psychological and sociological matters of fact — can force alterations in values. Similarly, many economic beliefs about matters of fact can affect values. Take such statements as, 'Income equality is bad because it leads to less work,' or, 'Socialism is good because it stops an individual from acquiring economic power over other individuals.' Before going to the barricades over either of these statements, a lot of hard empirical economic research and tough economic analysis must be done. Does income equality lead to less personal effort? Is economic power less concentrated under socialism? When does the adverse work effort effect set in? How should economic power be measured? . . .

✳ ✳ ✳

Is Thurow right?

1:530 Normative Defences and Critiques

Milton Friedman wrote a famous normative defence of the system of market ordering.

Milton Friedman, *Capitalism and Freedom* (Chicago: University of Chicago Press, 1962) at 12–15

The basic problem of social organization is how to co-ordinate the economic activities of large numbers of people. Even in relatively backward societies, extensive division of labor and specialization of function is required to make effective use of available resources. In advanced societies, the scale on which co-ordination is needed, to take full advantage of the opportunities offered by modern science and technology, is enormously greater. Literally millions of people are involved in providing one another with their daily bread, let alone with their yearly automobiles. The challenge to the believer in liberty is to reconcile this widespread interdependence with individual freedom.

Fundamentally, there are only two ways of co-ordinating the economic activities of millions. One is central direction involving the use of coercion — the technique of the army and of the modern totalitarian state. The other is voluntary cooperation of individuals — the technique of the market place.

The possibility of co-ordination through voluntary co-operation rests on the elementary — yet frequently denied — proposition that both parties to an economic transaction benefit from it, *provided the transaction is bi-laterally voluntary and informed.*

Exchange can therefore bring about co-ordination without coercion. A working model of a society organized through voluntary exchange is a *free private enterprise exchange economy* — what we have been calling competitive capitalism.

In its simplest form, such a society consists of a number of independent households — a collection of Robinson Crusoes, as it were. Each household uses the resources it controls to produce goods and services that it exchanges for goods and services produced by other households, on terms mutually acceptable to the two parties to the bargain. It is thereby enabled to satisfy its wants indirectly by producing goods and services for others, rather than directly by producing goods for its own immediate use. The incentive for adopting this indirect route is, of course, the increased product made possible by division of labor and specialization of function. Since the household always has the alternative of producing directly for itself, it need not enter into any exchange unless it benefits from it. Hence, no exchange will take place unless both parties do benefit from it. Co-operation is thereby achieved without coercion.

Specialization of function and division of labor would not go far if the ultimate productive unit were the household. In a modern society, we have gone much farther. We have introduced enterprises which are intermediaries between individuals in their capacities as suppliers of service and as purchasers of goods. And similarly, specialization of function and division of labor could not go very far if we had to continue to rely on the barter of product for product. In consequence, money has been introduced as a means of facilitating exchange, and of enabling the acts of purchase and of sale to be separated into two parts.

Despite the important role of enterprises and of money in our actual economy, and despite the numerous and complex problems they raise, the central characteristic of the market technique of achieving co-ordination is fully displayed in the simple exchange economy that contains neither enterprises nor money. As in that simple model, so in the complex enterprise and money-exchange economy, co-operation is strictly individual and voluntary *provided*: (a) that enterprises are private, so that the ultimate contracting parties are individuals and (b) that individuals are effectively free to enter or not to enter into any particular exchange, so that every transaction is strictly voluntary.

It is far easier to state these provisos in general terms than to spell them out in detail, or to specify precisely the institutional arrangements most conducive to their mainte-nance. Indeed, much of technical economic literature is concerned with precisely these questions. The basic requisite is the maintenance of law and order to prevent physical coercion of one individual by another and to enforce contracts voluntarily entered into, thus giving substance to 'private.' Aside from this, perhaps the most difficult problems arise from monopoly — which inhibits effective freedom by denying individuals alterna-tives to the particular exchange — and from 'neighbourhood effects' — effects on third parties for which it is not feasible to charge or recompense them. . . .

So long as effective freedom of exchange is maintained, the central feature of the mar-ket organization of economic activity is that it prevents one person from interfering with another in respect of most of his activities. The consumer is protected from coercion by the seller because of the presence of other sellers with whom he can deal. The seller is protected from coercion by the consumer because of other consumers to whom he can sell. The employee is protected from coercion by the employer because of other employ-ers for whom he can work, and so on. And the market does this impersonally and with-out centralized authority.

Indeed, a major source of objection to a free economy is precisely that it does this task so well. It gives people what they want instead of what a particular group thinks they ought to want. Underlying most arguments against the free market is a lack of belief in freedom itself.

[© 1962 by The University of Chicago. Reprinted by permission.]

✻ ✻ ✻

What is the normative basis of market ordering, in Friedman's view?

All of the claims made by proponents of market ordering have given rise to compet-ing conceptions and points of view. Some commentators reject the idea that the values involved in defending the market are normatively important. Others claim that although the values involved may be significant the market does not advance or protect them. Still others invoke other values, which are said to be thwarted by market ordering. The extracts that follow illustrate these different points of view.

On the normative importance of merit consider the following.

John Rawls, *A Theory of Justice* (Cambridge: Belknap Press of Harvard University Press, 1971) at 72, 102–4

The existing distribution of income and wealth, say, is the cumulative effect of prior distributions of natural assets — that is, natural talents and abilities — as these have been developed or left unrealized, and their use favored or disfavored over time by social circumstances and such chance contingencies as accident and good fortune. Intuitively, the most obvious injustice of the system of natural liberty is that it permits distributive shares to be improperly influenced by these factors so arbitrary from a moral point of view. . . . No one deserves his greater natural capacity nor merits a more favorable starting place in society. But it does not follow that one should eliminate these distinctions. There is another way to deal with them. The basic structure can be arranged so that these contingencies work for the good of the least fortunate. Thus we are led to the difference principle if we wish to set up the social system so that no one gains or loses from his arbitrary place in the distribution of natural assets or his initial position in society without giving or receiving compensating advantages in return. . . . The assertion that a man deserves the superior character that enables him to make the effort to cultivate his abilities is equally problematic; for his character depends in large part upon fortunate family and social circumstances for which he can claim no credit.

[Reprinted by permission of the publisher, Harvard University Press, Copyright © 1971, 1999 by the Presidents and Fellows of Harvard College.]

Thomas Scanlon, "Liberty, Contract, and Contribution" in Gerald Dworkin, Gordon Berment, & Peter Brown, eds., *Markets and Morals* (Washington: Hemisphere Publishing, 1977) 43 at 43, 61–62

There is a natural prima facie case for the inclusion of market exchange within any distributive system. For, given any distribution of goods taken as just, if two parties would prefer the result of a bilateral exchange to the status quo why not allow them to trade? Institutions that do not allow or do not provide for such exchanges seem to involve objectionable restrictions on the liberty of those to whom they apply. They appear to be inefficient as well, since each such trade, by moving the trading parties to preferred positions and, we may suppose, leaving others unaffected, moves the whole situation closer to Pareto optimality. . . .

. . . Can we say that a system of free contract is clearly preferable to a nonmarket system on the grounds that the restrictions involved intrude less on citizens' control over the development and exercise of their talents? I do not see that this is so. . . . From the fact that institutions of a certain form involve a minimum of nonvoluntary obligations it does not follow that such institutions are to be preferred to others on the grounds that they best promote the relevant forms of liberty. To settle this issue of liberty one must take up the complex empirical question of what the consequences will be, under given social and economic conditions, of the adoption of various institutional arrangements. In particular, it must be shown what the consequences are for the ability of various individuals in the society to maintain control over their own lives and pursuits.

Under a range of possible and, in our experience, not uncommon circumstances, establishment of a system of property rights based on free contract means that some people, in order to gain the means to life, have to devote virtually all their productive energies to whatever tasks and pursuits are desired by those who control the goods necessary for life in their society. The claim of nonmarket institutions is that they can prevent this kind of domination through restrictions on distribution and ownership. Doing this may involve placing limits on how much people can come to own and will also involve decreasing, through taxation, the rate at which people can benefit from the scarcity of their particular talents. It may also involve requiring a certain minimum contribution from every able member of the society as a condition for continued rights to social benefits. . . . Even institutions involving obligations of this sort need not involve direct restrictions on citizens' choice of occupations. Nor is it immediately apparent that such a system would represent a diminution rather than an enlargement of people's ability to choose forms of productive activity that they find rewarding. Certainly, there is much to be learned about the difficult empirical question of how such control can be preserved and enhanced within large scale economic institutions.

[Reprinted by permission.]

C.B. Macpherson, "Elegant Tombstones: A Note on Friedman's Freedom" in *Democratic Theory: Essays in Retrieval* (New York: Oxford University Press, 1973) 143 at 145–47

Professor Friedman's demonstration that the capitalist market economy can co-ordinate economic activities without coercion rests on an elementary conceptual error. His argument runs as follows. He shows first that in a simple market model, where each individual or household controls resources enabling it to produce goods and services either directly for itself or for exchange, there will be production for exchange because of the increased product made possible by specialization. But 'since the household always has the alternative of producing directly for itself, it need not enter into any exchange unless it benefits from it. Hence no exchange will take place unless both parties do benefit from it. Co-operation is thereby achieved without coercion'. . . . So far, so good. It is indeed clear that in this simple exchange model, assuming rational maximizing behaviour by all hands, every exchange will benefit both parties, and hence that no coercion is involved in the decision to produce for exchange or in any act of exchange.

Professor Friedman then moves on to our actual complex economy, or rather to his own curious model of it:

As in [the] simple model, so in the complex enterprise and money-exchange economy, co-operation is strictly individual and voluntary *provided*: (a) that enterprises are private, so that the ultimate contracting parties are individuals and (b) that individuals are effectively free to enter or not to enter into any particular exchange, so that every transaction is strictly voluntary. . . .

One cannot take exception to proviso (a): it is clearly required in the model to produce a co-operation that is 'strictly individual.' One might, of course, suggest that a model containing this stipulation is far from corresponding to our actual complex economy, since in the latter the ultimate contracting parties who have the most effect on the market are not individuals but corporations, and moreover, corporations which in one way or another manage to opt out of the fully competitive market. This criticism, however, would not be accepted by all economists as self-evident: some would say that the question who has most effect on the market is still an open question (or is a wrongly posed question). More investigation and analysis of this aspect of the economy would be valuable. But political scientists need not await its results before passing judgement on Friedman's position, nor should they be tempted to concentrate their attention on proviso (a). If they do so they are apt to miss the fault in proviso (b), which is more fundamental, and of a different kind. It is not a question of the correspondence of the model to the actual: it is a matter of the inadequacy of the proviso to produce the model.

Proviso (b) is 'that individuals are effectively free to enter or not to enter into any particular exchange,' and it is held that with this proviso 'every transaction is strictly voluntary.' A moment's thought will show that this is not so. The proviso that is required to make every transaction strictly voluntary is *not* freedom not to enter into any *particular* exchange, but freedom not to enter into any exchange *at all*. This, and only this, was the proviso that proved the simple model to be voluntary and non-coercive; and nothing less than this would prove the complex model to be voluntary and *non-coercive*. But Professor Friedman is clearly claiming that freedom not to enter into any particular exchange is enough: 'The consumer is protected from coercion by the seller because of the presence of other sellers with whom he can deal . . . The employee is protected from coercion by the employer because of other employers for whom he can work . . . ' . . .

One almost despairs of logic, and of the use of models. It is easy to see what Professor Friedman has done, but it is less easy to excuse it. He has moved from the simple economy of exchange between independent producers, to the capitalist economy, without mentioning the most important thing that distinguishes them. He mentions money instead of barter, and 'enterprises which are intermediaries between individuals in their capacities as suppliers of services and as purchasers of goods' . . . as if money and merchants were what distinguished a capitalist economy from an economy of independent producers. What distinguishes the capitalist economy from the simple exchange economy is the separation of labour and capital, that is, the existence of a labour force without its own sufficient capital and therefore without a choice as to whether to put its labour in the market or not. Professor Friedman would agree that where there is no choice there is coercion. His attempted demonstration that capitalism co-ordinates without coercion therefore fails.

Since all his specific arguments against the welfare and regulatory state depend on his case that the market economy is not coercive, the reader may spare himself the pains (or, if an economist, the pleasure) of attending to the careful and persuasive reasoning by which he seeks to establish the minimum to which coercion could be reduced by reducing or discarding each of the main regulatory and welfare activities of the state. None of this takes into account the coercion involved in the separation of capital from labour, or the possible mitigation of this coercion by the regulatory and welfare state. Yet it is because this coercion can in principle be reduced by the regulatory and welfare state, and thereby the amount of effective individual liberty be increased, that liberals have been justified in pressing, in the name of liberty, for infringements on the pure operation of competitive capitalism.

Max Weber, "Freedom and Coercion" in M. Rheinstein, ed., *Max Weber on Law in Economy and Society*, trans. E. Shils & M. Rheinstein (Cambridge: Harvard University Press, 1954) 188 at 188–91

The formal right of a worker to enter into any contract whatsoever with any employer whatsoever does not in practice represent for the employment seeker even the slightest freedom in the determination of his own conditions of work, and it does not guarantee him any influence on this process. It rather means, at least primarily, that the more powerful party in the market, i.e., normally the employer, has the possibility to set the terms, to offer the job 'take it or leave it,' and, given the normally more pressing economic need of the worker, to impose his terms upon him. The result of contractual freedom, then, is in the first place the opening of the opportunity to use, by the clever utilization of property ownership in the market, these resources without legal restraints as a means for the achievement of power over others. The parties interested in power in the market thus are also interested in such a legal order. Their interest is served particularly by the establishment of 'legal empowerment rules.' This kind of rules does no more than create the framework for valid agreements which, under conditions of formal freedom, are officially available to all. Actually, however, they are accessible only to the owners of property and thus in effect support their very autonomy and power positions. . . . The increasing significance of freedom of contract and, particularly, of enabling laws which leave everything to 'free' agreement, implies a relative reduction of that kind of coercion which results from the threat of mandatory and prohibitory norms. Formally it represents, of course, a decrease of coercion. But it is also obvious how advantageous this state of affairs is to those who are economically in the position to make use of the empowerments. The exact extent to which the total amount of 'freedom' within a given legal community is actually increased depends entirely upon the concrete economic order and especially upon the property distribution. In no case can it be simply deduced from the content of the law. . . .

The private enterprise system transforms into objects of 'labor market transactions' even those personal and authoritarian-hierarchical relations which actually exist in the capitalistic enterprise. While the authoritarian relationships are thus drained of all normal sentimental content, authoritarian constraint not only continues but, at least under certain circumstances, even increases. The larger a structure whose existence depends in some specific way on 'discipline,' for instance a capitalistic industrial plant, the more relentlessly can authoritarian constraint be exercised in it, at least under certain conditions. It finds its counterpart in the shrinkage of the circle of those in whose hands the power to use this type of constraint is concentrated and who also hold the power to have that former power guaranteed to them by the legal order. A legal order which contains ever so few mandatory and prohibitory norms and ever so many 'freedoms' and 'empowerments' can nonetheless in its practical effects facilitate a quantitative and qualitative increase not only of coercion in general but quite specifically of authoritarian coercion. [Reprinted by permission of the publisher, Harvard University Press, Copyright © 1954 by the Presidents and Fellows of Harvard College, Copyright © renewed 1982 by Edward J. Shils]

✻ ✻ ✻

These excerpts from Scanlon, MacPherson, and Weber reveal one of the most long-standing and controversial aspects of the debate on the normative validity of market ordering and contract as the basis for the ordering of labour. The question of whether the relationship between employers and employees is one that maximizes or promotes liberty and is free of coercion is a central element in a marxist critique of capitalist labour arrangements.

This is an issue of great importance. The reality is that the employment relationship in Canada is heavily regulated. There are, as already noted, two major components in the current system of regulation — regulation of the substance of the bargain struck by workers and employers (in the form of minimum wage and other labour standards legislation) and regulation of the process of bargaining (through collective bargaining legislation). The orthodox justification for such regulation of the contract of employment is found in the commonplace slogan 'inequality of bargaining power,' which is a troubling but important notion. What is to be made of it?

A starting point is to note that Adam Smith in *The Wealth of Nations* perceived that it would be the employer who would have an upper hand in bargaining with employees:

> it is not . . . difficult to foresee which of the two parties must, upon all ordinary occasions, have the advantage in the dispute, and force the other into compliance with their terms. . . . In all such disputes the masters can hold out much longer. A landlord, a farmer, a master manufacturer, or merchant, though they did not employ a single workman, could generally live a year or two upon the stocks which they have already acquired. Many workmen could not subsist a week, few could subsist a month, and scarce any a year without employment. In the long run the workmen [sic] may be as necessary to his master as his master is to him; but the necessity is not so immediate. [(1776) vol. 1 at 81.]

But of what normative significance was this insight? The excerpt from Friedman, above, appears to deny that coercion exists in a system of market ordering.

Harry Braverman, *Labor and Monopoly Capital* (New York: Monthly Review Press, 1974) at 52–58

Capitalist production requires exchange relations, commodities, and money, but its *differentia specifica* is the purchase and sale of labor power. For this purpose, three basic conditions become generalized throughout society. First, workers are separated from the means with which production is carried on, and can gain access to them only by selling their labor power to others. Second, workers are freed of legal constraints, such as serfdom or slavery, that prevent them from disposing of their own labor power. Third, the purpose of the employment of the worker becomes the expansion of a unit of capital belonging to the employer, who is thus functioning as a capitalist. The labor process therefore begins with a contract or agreement governing the conditions of the sale of labor power by the worker and its purchase by the employer.

It is important to take note of the historical character of this phenomenon. While the purchase and sale of labor power has existed from antiquity, a substantial class of wage-workers did not begin to form in Europe until the fourteenth century, and did not become numerically significant until the rise of industrial capitalism (that is, the *production* of commodities on a capitalist basis, as against mercantile capitalism, which merely *exchanged* the surplus products of prior forms of production) in the eighteenth century. It has been the numerically dominant form for little more than a century, and this in only a few countries. In the United States, perhaps four-fifths of the population was self-employed in the early part of the nineteenth century. By 1870 this had declined to about one-third and by 1940 to no more than one-fifth; by 1970 only about one-tenth of the pop-ulation was self-employed. We are thus dealing with a social relation of extremely recent date. The rapidity with which it has won supremacy in a number of countries emphasizes the extraordinary power of the tendency of capitalist economies to convert all other forms of labor into hired labor.

The worker enters into the employment agreement because social conditions leave him or her no other way to gain a livelihood. The employer, on the other hand, is the pos-sessor of a unit of capital which he is endeavoring to enlarge, and in order to do so he con-verts part of it into wages. Thus is set in motion the labor process which, while it is in general a process for creating useful values, has now also become specifically a process for the expansion of capital, the creation of a profit.

. . . the technical features of the labor process are now dominated by the social features which the capitalist has introduced: that is to say, the new relations of production. Having been forced to sell their labor power to another, the workers also surrender their interest in the labor process, which has now been 'alienated.' *The labor process has become the responsibility of the capitalist.* In this setting of antagonistic relations of production, the problem of realizing the 'full usefulness' of the labor power he has bought becomes exac-erbated by the opposing interests of those for whose purposes the labor process is carried on, and those who, on the other side, carry it on.

Thus when the capitalist buys buildings, materials, tools, machinery, etc., he can eval-uate with precision their place in the labor process. He knows that a certain portion of his outlay will be transferred to each unit of production, and his accounting practices allocate these in the form of costs or depreciation. But when he buys labor time, the outcome is far from being either so certain or so definite that it can be reckoned in this way, with pre-cision and in advance. This is merely an expression of the fact that the portion of his cap-ital expended on labor power is the 'variable' portion, which undergoes an increase in the process of production; for him the question is how great that increase will be.

It thus becomes essential for the capitalist that control over the labor process pass from the hands of the worker into his own. This transition presents itself in history as the *pro-gressive alienation of the process of production* from the worker; to the capitalist, it presents itself as the problem of *management.*

* * *

Robert Nozick challenged the Marxist view that a worker enters into an employment contract "because social conditions leave him or her no other way to gain a livelihood."

Robert Nozick, *Anarchy, State and Utopia* (New York: Basic Books, 1974) at 253–63

. . . [A]t bottom, Marxist theory explains the phenomenon of exploitation by reference to the workers not having access to the means of production. The workers have to sell their labor (labor power) to the capitalists, for they must use the means of production to produce, and cannot produce alone. A worker, or groups of them, cannot hire means of production and wait to sell the product some months later; they lack the cash reserves to obtain access to machinery or to wait until later when revenue will be received from the future sale of the product now being worked on. For workers must eat in the meantime.* Hence (the story goes) the worker is forced to deal with the capitalist. (And the reserve army of unemployed labor makes unnecessary the capitalists' competing for workers and bidding up the price of labor.)

Note that once the rest of the theory, properly, is dropped, and it is this crucial fact of nonaccess to the means of production that underlies exploitation, it *follows* that in a society in which the workers are not forced to deal with the capitalist, exploitation of laborers will be absent. (We pass over the question of whether workers are forced to deal with some other, less decentralized group.) So, if there is a sector of publicly owned and controlled (what you will) means of production that is expandable so that all who wish to may work in it, then this is sufficient to eliminate the exploitation of laborers. And in particular, if in addition to this public sector there is a sector of privately owned means of production that employs wage laborers who choose to work in this sector, then these workers are not being exploited. (Perhaps they choose to work there, despite attempts to convince them to do otherwise, because they get higher wages or returns in this sector.) For they are not forced to deal with the private owners of means of production. . . .

Whatever may have been the truth of the nonaccess view at one time, *in our society* large sections of the working force now have cash reserves in personal property, and there are also large cash reserves in union pension funds. These workers can wait, and they can invest. This raises the question of why this money isn't used to establish worker-controlled factories. Why haven't radicals and social democrats urged this?

The workers may lack the entrepreneurial ability to identify promising opportunities for profitable activity, and to organize firms to respond to these opportunities. In this case, the workers can try to *hire* entrepreneurs and managers to start a firm for them and then turn the authority functions over to the workers (who are the owners) after one year. (Though, as Kirzner emphasizes, entrepreneurial alertness would also be needed in deciding whom to hire.) Different groups of workers would compete for entrepreneurial talent, bidding up the price of such services, while entrepreneurs with capital attempted to hire workers under traditional ownership arrangements. Let us ignore the question of what the equilibrium in this market would look like to ask why groups of workers aren't doing this now.

It's *risky* starting a new firm. One can't identify easily new entrepreneurial talent, and much depends on estimates of future demand and of availability of resources, on unforeseen obstacles, on chance, and so forth. Specialized investment institutions and sources of venture capital develop to run just these risks. Some persons don't want to run these risks of investing or backing new ventures, or starting ventures themselves. Capitalist society allows the separation of the bearing of these risks from other activities. The workers in the Edsel branch of the Ford Motor Company did not bear the risks of the venture, and when it lost money they did not pay back a portion of their salary. In a socialist society, either one *must* share in the risks of the enterprise one works in, or everybody shares in the risks of the investment decisions of the central investment managers. There is no way to *divest* oneself of these risks or to choose to carry some such risks but not others (acquiring specialized knowledge in some areas), as one can do in a capitalist society.

Often people who do not wish to bear risks feel entitled to rewards from those who do and win; yet these same people do not feel obligated to help out by sharing the losses of those who bear risks and lose. For example, croupiers at gambling casinos expect to be well-tipped by big winners, but they do not expect to be asked to help bear some of the losses of the losers. The case for such asymmetrical sharing is even weaker for businesses where success is not a random matter. Why do some feel they may stand back to see whose ventures turn out well (by *hindsight* determine who has survived the risks and run profitably) and then claim a share of the success; though they do not feel they must bear the losses if things turn out poorly, or feel that if they wish to share in the profits or the control of the enterprise, they should invest and run the risk also? . . .

VOLUNTARY EXCHANGE

Some readers will object to my speaking frequently of voluntary exchanges on the grounds that some actions (for example, workers accepting a wage position) are not really voluntary because one party faces severely limited options, with all the others being much worse than the one he chooses. Whether a person's actions are voluntary depends on what it is that limits his alternatives. If facts of nature do so, the actions are voluntary. (I may voluntarily walk to someplace I would prefer to fly to unaided.) Other people's actions place limits on one's available opportunities. Whether this makes one's resulting action non-voluntary depends upon whether these others had the right to act as they did.

Consider the following example. Suppose there are twenty-six women and twenty-six men each wanting to be married. For each sex, all of that sex agree on the same ranking of the twenty-six members of the opposite sex in terms of desirability as marriage partners: call them A to Z and A' to Z' respectively in decreasing preferential order. A and A' voluntarily choose to get married, each preferring the other to any other partner. B would most prefer to marry A', and B' would most prefer to marry A, but by their choices A and A' have removed these options. When B and B' marry, their choices are not made nonvoluntary merely by the fact that there is something else they each would rather do. . . .

Similar considerations apply to market exchanges between workers and owners of capital. Z is faced with working or starving; the choices and actions of all other persons do not add up to providing Z with some other option. (He may have various options about what job to take.) Does Z choose to work voluntarily? (Does someone on a desert island who must work to survive?) Z does choose voluntarily if the other individuals A through Y each acted voluntarily and within their rights. . . .

* Where did the means of production come from? Who earlier forwent current consumption then in order to gain or produce them? Who now forgoes current consumption in paying wages and factor prices and thus gets returns only after the finished product is sold? Whose entrepreneurial alertness operated throughout?

✻ ✻ ✻

The following excerpt gathers together many of the criticisms of market ordering set out above.

A. Brudner, "Ethical Perspectives on Health Hazards" in *Royal Commission on Matters of Health and Safety Arising from the Use of Asbestos in Ontario, Policy Options* in the *Regulation of Asbestos-Related Health Hazards* (Study No. 3), by C. Tuohy & M. Trebilcock (Toronto: Queen's Printer, 1982) at 5.6–5.9

What, we may ask, constitutes coercion? Alternatively put, what conditions must be satisfied in order that consent may be regarded as free? No one would hesitate to call coercive a situation in which A induces B to sign a contract by a threat of physical violence. This example teaches that mere deliberate choice or voluntariness, while a necessary condition of free consent, is far from being a sufficient one. But the alternative criterion suggested by the example — the absence of personal compulsion — is not satisfactory either. Consider a situation in which A takes advantage of circumstances constraining B's choices in order to secure terms more favourable than he could otherwise obtain. Here one might distinguish between two forms of such advantage-taking: the case of the monopolist who is himself responsible for narrowing the choices available to B, and the case of one who merely exploits a situation of dire need found ready-to-hand. The first type belongs, perhaps, in a category with the example of the threat, since the constraints affecting the will of one party are deliberately imposed by the other. The second type, however, is qualitatively distinct from both, and yet B's consent is no less unfree for its having been forced by impersonal circumstances. If we wish to withhold moral approval from the second type of advantage-taking, then we are driven to the conclusion that the criterion distinguishing non-coercive from coercive agreements is equality. The latter is the only principle sufficiently comprehensive to explain the morally objectionable character of all three types of transaction, and yet sufficiently narrow to save the mutual advantage-taking implicit in bargains generally. On this principle, an agreement is alone morally legitimate if concluded in circumstances purified of all effects of the unequal strength of the parties.

Here, it might be thought, the conditions necessary for a legitimate outcome correspond to those required for an efficient one. Welfare maximization requires, after all, that the individual be capable of giving effect to his preferences. He must have available to him, therefore, a broad range of alternative employments; he must enjoy free movement into and out of these employments; and no one can be permitted to exercise market-wide control of the terms on which employment is offered. The condition of welfare maximization is, in short, freedom of choice, and the condition of freedom of choice is equality of economic power.

Nevertheless, the philosopher's test of a non-coerced choice is probably more stringent than that of an economist. The latter typically regards the classical model of the perfectly competitive market as the ideal standard of a non-coercive framework, as that economic system in which equality and freedom of choice are maximized. He thus takes as given the institution of contract as a means of distributing wealth, as well as the separation of labour and capital implicit in the employment contract. A critique of this model of non-coerced choice might, however, make the following points.

In an advanced market economy there are severe constraints on the extent to which genuine equality is possible in a labour contract. Given the divorce in such an economy between labour and the means of production, and given also the high degree of specialization of skills and functions, a worker cannot sustain himself independently, but must accept wage-employment on terms ultimately imposed by the employer. Furthermore, an exchange economy is characterized by freedom of accumulation and by a system of distribution based on market forces. Such an economy, in that it gives full scope to inequalities of natural endowment and of unearned social advantages, inevitably produces and perpetuates wide disparities of wealth, the cleavage between rich and poor corresponding to that between those who control and those who are excluded from control of the means of production. Neither of these inequalities is remediable by mere regulatory intervention. The first is rooted in the separation between labour and capital, the second in a system of contractual exchange. Both are thus endemic to a capitalist economy. Policies intended to equalize opportunity (e.g., free education, careers open to talent) leave intact the effects of unequal original endowment; policies that redistribute wealth cannot significantly reduce disparities without coming into conflict with the presuppositions of an exchange economy, the engine of which is self-interest and the desire for gain. . . .

✷ ✷ ✷

Given the controversy that surrounds the notions of inequality of bargaining power and coercion in employment contracts, it should come as no surprise that both collective bargaining and statutory regulation have been the subject of extensive debate. These legal regimes have been attacked and defended in normative terms. The debates also have an empirical dimension, which addresses the issue of whether these regimes really benefit those they purport to benefit, and if so, at whose cost (or whether there is a cost).

The most familiar form of direct regulation of the substantive terms of the employment contract is found in minimum wage and maximum hours legislation. The fundamental normative attack on legislative intervention was articulated by Adam Smith in *The Wealth of Nations*:

> The property which every man has is his own labour, as it is the original foundation of all other property, so it is the most sacred and inviolable. The patrimony of a poor man lies in the strength and dexterity of his hands; and to hinder him from employing this strength and dexterity in what manner he thinks proper without injury to his neighbour, is a plain violation of this most sacred property. It is a manifest encroachment upon the just liberty both of the workman, and of those who might be disposed to employ him. As it hinders the one from working at what he thinks proper, so it hinders the others from employing whom they think proper. . . . The affected anxiety of the lawgiver . . . is evidently as impertinent as it is oppressive. [(1776) vol. 1 at 151.]

What are the normative bases of minimum wage laws? Does the fact that such laws apply primarily to certain kinds of employees (women and the young, for example) influence the normative justifications offered?

In addition to the normative attack on substantive regulation in the form of minimum wage legislation, we have already noted that there has been considerable argument about whether minimum wage programs are simply wrongheaded in that they fail to achieve any normative goals and in fact harm the groups they are designed to protect. Many studies argue that minimum wages result in a "significant reduction in employment" (see E. West & M. McKee, *Minimum Wages* [Ottawa: Supply and Services Canada, 1980]). Is this the end of the minimum wage debate? On the basis of what we have read, what arguments can be constructed to demonstrate that this is not the case?

Recall our distinction between two methods of regulating the contract of employment — direct regulation of the substance of the bargain and regulation of the process of bargaining. The thinking behind substantive regulation is straightforward: because of inequality of bargaining power the outcome of the bargain is unfair, and we remedy this by regulating the outcome. Regulation of the process of bargaining by legislation promoting collective instead of individual bargaining is also traditionally justified by talk of inequality of bargaining power. If substantive regulation of the employment contract has been attacked from the market perspective, what of collective bargaining laws? How do market analysts evaluate such laws? Richard Posner summarizes the traditional economic analysis as follows.

Richard Posner, *Economic Analysis of Law*, 2d ed. (Toronto: Little, Brown, 1977) at 239–40

The primary purpose of a union is to control the supply of labor so that the employer cannot use competition among individual labourers to keep down the price of labor. It used to be thought that competition in labor markets would result in depressing wages to the subsistence level — the cost of keeping the worker alive and just healthy enough to work efficiently — but few economists hold this view any longer. The worker has a valuable asset to sell — his productivity (the result of his training, skill, energy) — and there is no a priori reason, and certainly no evidence, to believe that he could not sell it at a price far above his bare subsistence costs without collusion, just as there is no reason to believe that landowners could not rent land for a decent price without colluding. . . .

The *Wagner* and *Norris-LaGuardia Acts*, which insulated most nonviolent union activity, including strikes, from state or federal legal prohibition, was the decisive step in the emergence of a national labor relations policy favorable toward labor monopolizing. The implementation of this policy was in fact followed by a dramatic rise in wage rates in a number of industries. Recall, however, that an increase in price brought about by monopolization is likely to have substitution as well as wealth effects. Employers attempt to substitute cheaper for costlier labor (for instance, by relocating their activities to regions where unions are weak), capital for labor, and white-collar for blue-collar workers. The ultimate effects of unionization on welfare are thus complex. Some workers benefit — those who are paid higher wages in the unionized industries and those who are newly employed by employers seeking substitutes for union labor. So do some shareholders of firms whose competitors formerly paid lower wages than they did but are compelled as a result of unionization to pay the same wage. The losers are the consumers who buy from unionized industries (for those industries will pass along to their consumers a portion, at least, of their higher labor costs), some stockholders and suppliers in those industries, and workers who cannot find employment because of the reduction in the demand for labor brought about by union wage scales.

[Reprinted from *Economic Analysis of Law*, 2d edition, with the permission of Aspen Publishers.]

* * *

In addition to the debate about the market effects of collective bargaining, serious normative attacks have been made on collective bargaining from both the left and the right. It is not hard, in light of what we have read, to construct the argument from the right. But what of the Left's normative criticism? How relevant to collective bargaining are the criticisms of the market model? Which of the normative arguments made against market ordering are applicable here? Consider the following.

David Beatty, "Ideology, Politics and Unionism" in K. Swan & K. Swinton, eds., *Studies in Labour Law* (Toronto: Butterworths, 1983) 299 at 301–14

From hiring halls to university classrooms the received wisdom is passed on that by redressing the imbalance of bargaining power that obviously predominates in the individual employment relationship, collective bargaining will permit employees to participate more meaningfully in the regulation of their working lives and, as a result, secure rules of employment which are more just, equitable and in accord with our sense of fairness and decency.

. . . I argue that collective bargaining does practically nothing to remedy many of the disabilities and inequities generated by the common law system of individual bargaining and actually fosters different injustices of its own. . . . My purpose is to make clear that the system of collective bargaining that has been advocated by unions for the past fifty years systematically discriminates against some of the most disadvantaged and deprived employees in our society. Not only is it a scheme of employment regulation which is neither legally nor practically available to large segments of our employed population but, as critically, it is one which generally rewards those individuals who are already better off with more humane, dignified and fair working conditions. Indeed in many instances, as we shall see, the gains of the winners are paid for directly by those who are made worse off by the system. A system which distributes its goods towards those who already have and away from those who do not, is not one which can easily claim to be in accord with our understanding of industrial justice. . . .

There is no question that some do better. Significantly better. And, given the position of many of these individuals on the lower rungs of the income scale there can be little argument that such results, on their own, are fair and do enhance the dignity of the individuals concerned. But that is hardly determinative of the issue. . . . [T]here are losers in a system of employment regulated by collective bargaining. Who are they, and on what basis are they selected? At whose expense are the winners' gains secured? . . .

In fact, collective bargaining can count three distinct groups of workers for whom its outcomes represent an inequitable and even regressive system of income distribution. . . .

. . . Take the case of the people who are prohibited from bargaining collectively by the exclusions and exemptions that are part of each of the various statutory models in this country. While all of them are not necessary exclusions from collective bargaining legislation, some are. And, while the characters may vary slightly from jurisdiction to jurisdiction, together they are inevitably featured in the introductory statutory pronouncements of the cast of players who are deemed ineligible to perform in the system. In Canada, the traditional exclusions are three-fold. First comes a list of persons to whom the legislation has no application whatsoever, who lie completely outside the scope of legitimate collective bargaining. This group commonly includes domestics employed in private homes and employees in some sectors of the agricultural industry, two of the lowest paid professions in our society. Next comes the usual exclusion of professionals, which in turn is followed by the obligatory managerial prohibition. The latter . . . is thought to be a theoretical imperative of the system.

Surely there is no criterion of industrial justice, substantive or procedural, which can justify the first group of exclusions.

. . . Horizontal inequities exist within the system of collective bargaining as a result of practical, as well as statutory and theoretical, limitations. Even within the group for whom collective bargaining is a legal possibility, for considerably more than half of them it remains as only a possibility. Collective bargaining is just not an available option of employment regulation for large sectors of our employed population. Union organizers know that; they will tell you that the decision not to engage in collective bargaining is not of these people's own choosing. However effective collective bargaining may be for some groups in our workforce it is obviously not a viable nor an available response for the majority of these people. There can be no serious question now, after 50 years during which unions have never been able to reach these employees in the unorganized 'secondary labour markets' of our society, that collectively bargaining over the terms and conditions of their employment is a meaningful possibility for these individuals.

. . . The inequity involves more than just a simple dichotomy of winners and losers. Rather in an 'order of labour' (to borrow Renner's phrase) regulated by a law of collective bargaining, we are looking at a continuum on which each occupational group can, to varying degrees, negotiate a package of material and social advantages different from what they would achieve as individuals in a 'pure' or individualized market solution. How different, of course, depends on the relative strength of their bargaining power. Certain groups, as I have noted, predictably and consistently do well. Indeed some collectives of employees, for example policemen or firemen, are so absolutely certain of completely monopolizing the process because of the importance of the services that they render that we prohibit them from even engaging in collective bargaining. For others, collective bargaining has meant very little; personal service workers in hotels, restaurants, retail trade and clothing are traditionally among our lowest paid workers, notwithstanding the presence of collective bargaining.

The positions of these two groups of workers on a continuum measuring the outcomes generated by the collective bargaining system reveal horizontal and vertical inequities which are endemic to the institution. . . . The gulf that divides these two industrial states tells us that how a group of employees will fare in a system of employment regulated by a law of collective bargaining will depend largely on a set of circumstances over which the individual has little if any control and which are, as a result, highly arbitrary from a moral or social justice point of view. Look at the position of those who are, by the common law system of atomized individual market relationships, dispersed to the least desirable end of the spectrum. Economists have for a long time been telling us that collective bargaining will not likely do very much for individuals employed in industries which pay low wages, either because of the nature of the demand for their labour or because of its inexhaustible supply. Because of these locational and personal circumstances, even if those who presently reject collective bargaining as a viable device by which to regulate the employment relationship changed their views, the experience of their sisters in the low wage communities suggests that they still would not be relatively much better off. That is, even if those groups who have little bargaining power, either because of the endowments at birth or the location of their employment, took up the challenge to participate, they could still claim the system was unjust because of its overall inequitable and perverse distribution of its rights and goods. Their claim would be more than a charge of moral agnosticism. For them the system is inequitable in the sense that it will reward two individuals who are identical in all personal circumstances, in skills, effort, need, etc. and pay them differently because one is located in the auto sector and the other in the laundry industry. More critically, the system is perverse in the sense that to those with relatively rare endowments and skills, who provide services of relatively constant desire, collective bargaining delivers not only the jobs, but the rewards as well. By contrast, to the unskilled, in the secondary labour markets, collective bargaining can scarcely generate an adequate level of income to meet the official poverty standards.

In an obvious way this distributive injustice of collective bargaining is rooted in the same principles which underly [sic] the market system of regulation by individual contracts of employment. Like the individual contract of employment, collective agreements not only distribute wages and other benefits as a price on a commodity, but as well, as we shall consider more fully below, the employee's very rights of citizenship in the workplace vary according to her value to the enterprise. And as the analysis of contract models has shown, valuation in market places is a highly arbitrary exercise. . . .

Neither of these two major determinants of what economists call the marginal product of labour are morally relevant bases on which to ground a system of income distribution, on which to found a schedule of employee rights and rewards. Clearly, locational considerations need not have anything to do with traditional justice values of need, worth or merit. One does not 'deserve' to work in a particular employment setting, such as the auto or garment industry, and it is horizontally inequitable that two individuals of similar endowments, performing the same service, enjoy different rights and benefits in their employment simply because they work in different sectors. . . . Or, to take another example, there is nothing particularly just about a local, single plant employer being constrained by the local labour market to pay her employees a greater wage than that which could be extracted if they were employed by a large multinational, multiplant, multiproduct employer. . . .

But . . . one should harbour no illusions that the other factors, pertaining to the quality of labour, are somehow more deserving of our moral attention. From the point of view of merit, of deserving certain rewards, there is nothing to distinguish skill and endowment qualities — one's native abilities, parental guidance, tangible and intangible inheritances — from the locational factors we have just considered. Both the law of collective bargaining, which permits an occupational group to monopolize the provision of a service, and the law of property which sanctions the monopolization by the professional of the scarcity of her labour, are social constructs which have little to do with moral worth or desert. While there is an obvious incentive justification in recognizing the property a woman possesses in her labour, and even a sense of justice in rewarding her effort, unless severe constraints are imposed to guarantee all employees access to a sufficient property to sustain themselves, even such a property right in one's person is without moral justification. Indeed, unless one denies the assertion that the endowments of people, upon which the skills which stratify the supply of labour are developed, are themselves not deserved, then the argument in favour of merit and meritocracy, of rewarding socially useful effort, leads naturally to the adoption of a much more egalitarian system of rewards than that which is generated by collective bargaining. . . .

In effect, by failing to be sensitive to this argument, and by mimicking the distribution effected by the market, collective bargaining stands condemned of rendering 'morally arbitrary facts [into] ones of great social significance.'

. . . But it is not just on its inverted system of rewards and target inefficiencies that collective bargaining founders. Collective bargaining prejudices the position of many of the worst-off individuals in our society in other ways as well. Specifically, there is strong theoretical support and some empirical evidence to confirm what is for economists the commonplace hypothesis: that the gains secured by those for whom collective bargaining is a powerful instrument for controlling their employment are made at the expense of the lower income groups in our society. There are two logical ways this can be expected to happen. In the first place there will be occasions when the 'supra-competitive' employ-

ment benefits that are secured by a group of employees as a result of their bargaining collectively together will be paid for by those at the lower end of the income scale in the form
of higher prices. If the demand for the ultimate product is sufficiently inelastic, as it commonly is seen to be with various public services, a price (or tax) increase can be used to
offset the increased cost. Either alternative will cause a further depreciation of the already
unjustifiably small share of the national product that is allotted to the low income members of our society.

Alternatively, if the effects of collective bargaining's successes are alleviated by a reduction in the amount of labour that is hired, which will more commonly be the case where
our demand for the product or that labour is not insatiable, the worst-off members in the
nation's distribution of goods will be adversely affected in a different way. In this event, to
the extent that those who are laid off to counteract the increased cost of the collective bargain seek to find employment in alternative markets, as some must inevitably do, there
will be a further depression in the terms and conditions of employment that will be paid
in these secondary, unorganized markets.

[Reprinted by permission.]

✵ ✵ ✵

Paul Weiler has responded to criticisms from both left and right about the impact of collective bargaining.

Paul Weiler, "Promises to Keep: Securing Workers' Rights to Self-Organization under the NLRA" (1983) 96 Harv. L. Rev. 1769 at 1824–27

A complete defense of collective bargaining . . . also requires a response to two traditional objections: first, that organization of employees into cohesive groups seeking a better
deal for themselves imposes a deadweight loss on the economy and thus reduces the size
of the economic pie available to everyone; and second, that increased wages and benefits
for union members are obtained at the expense of unorganized workers.

The first objection is based on the assumption that unionization impairs the allocative
efficiency of the labor market. The union is seen as a cartel, controlling the supply of
labour in order to raise wages above what they would be in a competitive labor market.
Not only does the cartel impose on the system the costs of the strikes and restrictive work
practices that are necessary to establish and maintain these wage gains, but the artificially high price of unionized labor also causes misallocation of capital and labor by both
unionized and nonunionized businesses and thereby reduces the overall productivity of
the economy.

The second objection is concerned with the distributive consequences of unionism.
According to this argument, the ability of a group of employees to achieve wage gains
through collective bargaining depends on their market power, not on their current
income and needs. Such skilled workers as pilots and plumbers regularly win major
increases on top of already-high earnings, while garment workers and clerical workers
find it difficult to sustain any economic gains at all in the face of stiff competition in the
labor market. Worse yet, benefits for the powerful segments of the work force come not

out of capital's share, but rather out of the pockets of other workers, who suffer a decline in the real value of their earnings. On the basis of these perceptions, serious criticisms have been levelled at collective bargaining from the left as well as the right.

Recent empirical research indicates that each of these lines of attack is largely unfounded. Employees who work under a collective agreement may actually be more productive than those employed in an otherwise comparable nonunion environment. To some extent, increased productivity is a result of the much lower turnover that characterizes a unionized work force. Seniority systems, fringe benefits for long-service workers, and the availability of grievance procedures sharply reduce the rate at which workers leave their jobs. The resulting increased stability in the work force leads to fuller development of individual skills and greater cohesion among workers, both of which factors in turn increase productivity. Productivity gains are also spurred by the challenge posed to management to become more sophisticated and efficient when a union capable of winning a sizeable wage premium appears on the scene. There is good reason to believe, then, that collective bargaining can be conducive to a more productive labor market. Thus, unionization may actually generate a substantial part of the additional income it brings to its constituents.

Equally unfounded is the objection that collective bargaining increases income inequality by producing benefits only for elite groups of employees. The total distributional effect of unionization is actually to reduce inequality. The wage-standardizing thrust of collective bargaining tends to narrow the range of income dispersion for jobs within a plant and even among different plants or different employers within the same industry or local labor market. Furthermore, unionization among blue-collar workers reduces the income disparity between blue-collar and white-collar workers. Perhaps most importantly, unionization reduces wage disparities between black and white workers. These egalitarian effects more than compensate for the incremental inequality that stems from the union/nonunion wage differential.

[Copyright © 1983 by the Harvard Law Review Association. Reprinted by permission.]

✳ ✳ ✳

Does this cover all of David Beatty's criticisms?

Debate concerning the normative importance of collective bargaining as an alternative to the individual contracting model has not been confined to the question of economic and distributive impact. Indeed, traditional defences of collective bargaining may rely heavily on other normative assumptions.

Paul Weiler, *Reconcilable Differences: New Directions in Canadian Labour Law* (Toronto: Carswell, 1980) at 30–32

The economic function is the beginning, not the end, of the case for collective bargaining. The role performed by trade unions has never been narrowly pecuniary. Most industrial relations scholars believe that the true function of economic bargaining consists in its civilizing impact upon the working life and environment of employees.

. . . Management is challenged to spell out the principles on which it deals with the employee in her daily life. The employees have a vehicle through which they can forcefully voice their objections when any such standards appear to override their interests with-out compelling reasons. Once the employer has written into a collective agreement the rules by which it will govern the workplace, then any supervisory or departmental edict may be challenged before a neutral arbitrator to test its compliance with these contract standards. An apt way of putting it is to say that good collective bargaining tries to subject the employment relationship and the work environment to the 'rule of law.' Many theo-rists of industrial relations believe that this function of protecting the employee from the abuse of managerial power, thereby enhancing the dignity of the worker as a person, is the primary value of collective bargaining, one which entitles the institution to positive encouragement from the law. . . .

. . . Collective bargaining is not simply an instrument for pursuing external ends, whether these be mundane monetary gains or the erection of a private rule of law to pro-tect the dignity of the worker in the face of managerial authority. Rather, collective bar-gaining is intrinsically valuable as an experience in self-government. It is the mode in which employees participate in setting the terms and conditions of employment, rather than simply accepting what their employer chooses to give them (which, if the employer happens to be benevolent, may be just as generous compensation, just as restrained supervision). If one believes, as I do, that self-determination and self-discipline are inher-ently worthwhile, indeed, that they are the mark of a truly human community, then it is difficult to see how the law can be neutral about whether that type of economic democra-cy is to emerge in the workplace.

[Reprinted by permission.]

✻ ✻ ✻

What sort of argument in favor of collective bargaining is Paul Weiler making? What are the defects of such a defence of collective bargaining? David Beatty outlines his objec-tions to this defence along the following lines.

David Beatty, "Ideology, Politics and Unionism" in K. Swan and K. Swinton, eds., *Studies in Labour Law* (Toronto: Butterworths, 1983) 299 at 319–21

[T]he standard justification of this system of employment regulation is said to rest on the participation it permits to each individual employee in the day to day regulation of her working life. Enter, in the lexicon of John Rawls, the elixir of pure, procedural justice. Argu-ing that the notion of substantive industrial justice is either too general and vague to have any meaning or too defined and specific to have any consensus, proponents of collective bargaining contend that it is the procedures by which the terms and conditions of employ-ment are determined that is important as a matter of industrial justice. And, likening the role of the employee in the fashioning of the rules that govern her behaviour at the work place to that of a citizen in a political democracy, these supporters conclude that collective bargaining does alright by the analogy. As we are fond of chanting, democracy may not be perfect, but it's the best we have.

. . . If this, as the literature would suggest, is the basis on which collective bargaining can satisfy the criterion of industrial justice, it is difficult to conceive of any basis on which the statutory exclusions I described earlier could be allowed to endure. How can the participation of domestics or agricultural workers or indeed management employees in the settlement of the rules by which their productive lives will be regulated be any less important than the participation of any other worker? On what basis can they be exposed to autocratic rulemaking? . . .

But assuming this legislative oversight were recognized as such and the process were extended to all members of society, would that make the case for collective bargaining? Does the analogy hold and if so, does collective bargaining contemplate the kind of pure procedures which would legitimate the distribution of rights and benefits which otherwise appear so perverse?

My answer is that the analogy cannot be maintained, either as a matter of theory or as a matter of fact, and that even if it could, it would not be to a model of democracy that could satisfy the dictates of a procedurally pure system of rule-making. Even if basic rights of due process could be grafted onto the existing system, and collective bargaining could be favourably compared with the operation of democratic processes in liberal societies, there would still remain at least two impenetrable impediments to establishing a connection between it and the conditions of procedural justice. Essentially the argument will be that collective bargaining predicates its rights of participation, just like its system of rewards, on the bargaining power of the individuals involved and that, by doing so, the system not only creates a stratified society, but, as critically, results in the removal of whole areas of control over the industrial society's well-being from the legislative will. As well, by relying on a simple rule of majoritarianism to settle the competing interests of the employees, collective bargaining lacks a theory of and makes no allowance for constitutional rights of participation which the will of the majority cannot override. Consent of the minorities and the worst-off classes in the industrial society, which is so integral to ideals of procedural justice, is foreign to a system of rule-making by collective bargaining. [Reprinted by permission.]

* * *

David Beatty's main point appears to be an allegation of perversity in the distribution of the right of participation and other values collective bargaining is said to confer. Other critics go further by alleging that the fundamental problem of collective bargaining law lies in its legitimation of forms of social organization that are essentially coercive, despite workers' ability to organize collectively. The following excerpt considers what is meant in Canada by free collective bargaining.

Leo Panitch & Donald Swartz, *The Assault on Trade Union Freedoms: From Wage Controls to Social Contract* (Toronto: Garamond Press, updated ed., 1993) at 11–13

The use of the word 'free' does have a crucial double meaning. It suggests that a balance of power prevails between capital and labour, that they face each other as equals, otherwise any bargain struck could scarcely be viewed as one which was 'freely' achieved. It also suggests that the state's role is akin to one of umpire involved in applying, interpreting and adjusting impartial rules. In the first meaning, the structured inequality between capital and labour is obscured; in the second, the use of the state's coercive powers on behalf of capital falls from view. Industrial relations orthodoxy in the post-war era of free collective bargaining premised an acceptance of both meanings of the word 'free.' We will not dwell here on the continued structural inequality between capital and labour. It will suffice to mention the massive inequality in resources available to each party in the relationship. First, in sheer scale, flexibility and durability, capital's material resources continued to overwhelm those of labour. Second, the organizational and ideological resources of labour remained scarcely measurable against the network of associations, organizations, advisory bodies, in-house publications, and mass media, which were owned by, or financially beholden to, capital. Finally, capital's greater access to the state throughout the post-war period has been well documented. The supremacy of capital in this era of free collective bargaining, in both its ideological and coercive dimensions, was captured well by Harold Laski:

> The right to call on the service of the armed forces . . . is normally and naturally regard-ed as a proper prerogative of the ownership of some physical property that is seen to be in danger . . . But we should be overwhelmed if a great trade union in an industrial dis-pute, asked for, much less received, the aid of the police, or the militia or the federal troops to safeguard it in a claim to the right to work which it argued was as real as the physical right to visible and corporal property, like a factory. . . .

Laski, of course, recognized that in 'a political democracy set within the categories of capitalist economies . . . the area within which workers can manoeuvre for concessions is far wider than in a dictatorship.' But he also understood the fact that even within capital-ist democracy, the labour movement is confronted with 'an upper limit to its efforts beyond which it is hardly likely to pass.'

This reference to capital's privileged access to the coercive apparatus of the state brings us directly to the second meaning of 'free' within the term. For the limits beyond which labour was 'hardly likely to pass' were not left to the imagination in Canadian labour pol-icy after World War II. The very same legislation which supported the right to recognition and guaranteed the right to strike, also constrained the nature of bargaining and the exer-cise of union power in a highly detailed manner. The true thrust of the legislation in this respect, has been laid bare unwittingly by labour lawyer Paul Weiler, in defence of the con-ventional interpretation of 'free' collective bargaining:

> There are two parts of a labour code which are central to the balance of power between union and employer. One is the use of the law to facilitate the growth of union represen-tation of organized workers. The other is the use of the law to limit the exercise of union economic weapons (the strike and the picket line) once a collective bargaining relation-ship has become established. . . .

The 'other' part of the labour legislation of the 1940s, to which Weiler referred, was pre-cisely the extensive set of restrictions placed on collective action by unions, establishing one of the most restrictive and highly juridified frameworks for collective bargaining in any capitalist democracy. Modelled after the U.S. Wagner Act, Canadian legislation went 'beyond it,' as Logan noted: '(1) in naming and proscribing unfair practices by unions. . . .

(2) in assuming a responsibility by the state to assist the two negotiating parties. . . . [and] (3) in forbidding strikes and lockouts during negotiations and for the term of the agreement.' . . . Part and parcel of union recognition and the promotion of collective bargaining were a broad set of legal restrictions on eligibility for membership, and the precise circumstances for legal strike action. Apart from restrictions on picketing and secondary boycotts, the most important restriction on the right to strike — and the device ultimately used in 1982 to abrogate the right to strike in the public sector — was the ban on strikes during the term of a collective agreement.

[Reprinted with the permission of Garamond Press.]

✷ ✷ ✷

In light of this attack on "liberal labour law," consider the following discussion of attacks on liberalism.

T. Nagel, "Libertarianism without Foundations," Book Review of *Anarchy, State and Utopia* by Robert Nozick (1975) 85 Yale L.J. 136 at 136–37

Liberalism is the conjunction of two ideals. The first is that of individual liberty: liberty of thought, speech, religion, and political action; freedom from government interference with privacy, personal life, and the exercise of individual inclination. The second ideal is that of a democratic society controlled by its citizens and serving their needs, in which inequalities of political and economic power and social position are not excessive. Means of promoting the second ideal include progressive taxation, public provision of a social minimum, and insulation of political affairs from the excessive influence of private wealth. To approach either of these ideals is very difficult. To pursue both of them inevitably results in serious dilemmas. In such cases liberalism tends to give priority to the respect for certain personal rights, even at substantial cost in the realization of other goods such as efficiency, equality and social stability.

The most formidable challenge to liberalism, both intellectually and politically, is from the left. It is argued that strong safeguards of individual liberty are too great a hindrance to the achievement of economic and social equality, rapid economic progress from underdevelopment, and political stability. A majority of the people in the world are governed on this assumption. Perhaps the most difficult issue is posed by economic power and the political inequality it can create. The criticism from the left is that harmful concentrations of economic power cannot be attacked — or prevented from forming — unless individual actions are more closely restricted than is permitted by the liberal ideal of personal freedom. Radical redistribution is unlikely in a liberal democracy where private wealth controls the political process. A defense against this criticism must either challenge the factual claim or argue that the importance of freedom outweighs these disadvantages.

Liberalism is also under attack from the right. The most conspicuous attacks are not theoretical: the right in its more prominent political manifestations is not particularly attached to individual liberty when that liberty threatens the unequal distribution of wealth and power. But there is also a theoretical challenge from the right, called libertarianism, and while it does not present as serious a moral issue for liberals as does the attack from the left, the two are in some ways symmetrical. Libertarianism, like leftism, fastens on one of the two elements of the liberal ideal and asks why its realization should be inhibited by the demands of the other. Instead of embracing the ideal of equality and the general welfare, libertarianism exalts the claim of individual freedom of action, and asks why state power should be permitted even the interference represented by progressive taxation and public provision of health care, education, and a minimum standard of living.

[Reprinted by permission of the Yale Law Journal Company and William S. Hein & Company from the *Yale Law Journal*, Vol. 85, pp. 136–149.]

✻ ✻ ✻

These debates about the appropriate relationship between the state and the market have become even more important in the modern era of globalization and international economic integration.

1:600 THE EMERGING WORLD

Gordon Betcherman, Kathryn McMullen, and Katie Davidman, *Training for the New Economy: A Synthesis Report* (Ottawa: Canadian Policy Research Network inc., 1998) at 1

First the "new economy." Pundits quibble over the term and exactly what it means, but, fine points aside, there is consensus that a major economic transformation has taken place over the past two decades. This has involved an extension of markets and a retrenchment of government, more open economic borders, a new "technological paradigm" based on microelectronic information and communication technologies, and an ongoing shift to service- and information-based activities. This restructuring, coupled with a range of social, cultural, and demographic changes, has had a significant impact on our working lives. Patterns of labour force participation have changed. Traditional industries, occupations, and communities have declined while new ones have emerged. And the content of work and how it is organized have been evolving rapidly.

Canadians and their governments are uncertain about this new economy and its labour market for two reasons: first, the mediocre performance of the 1990s — the persistently high rates of unemployment, the slow growth in output and productivity, and the stagnant real earnings; and, second, recognition that the "rules of the game" have changed and that no one is quite sure what the new ones should be. What individual strategies make sense for finding a good job and for building financial security? What should firms be doing to enhance competitiveness and business performance? What public policies will support aggregate growth, job creation, and an equitable income distribution?

[Reprinted courtesy of CPRN, all documents are available free at www.cprn.org.]

Patrick Macklem, "Labour Law Beyond Borders" (Public Law and Legal Theory Research Paper No. 02-02, http://papers.ssrn.com/abstract=294313) at 1 and 6

Labour law is an overwhelmingly domestic field of law, characterized by a unique blend of particular rules negotiated by parties to an employment relationship and general legislative imperatives enacted for the protection of workers. Like many domestic legal fields, it has an international counterpart in a set of declarations and conventions that detail rights and obligations with which states, as a matter of international law, must comply. But labour law, traditionally understood, is primarily a constellation of domestic legal initiatives that seek — perhaps not exclusively and no doubt imperfectly — to promote just relationships between employers and employees.

Two dramatic trends are increasingly challenging the traditional capacity of domestic labour law to promote justice in the world of work. The first relates to the introduction of flexible forms of production. What some scholars are calling 'post-fordist' production processes are supplementing and in some cases supplanting traditional forms of mass production dependent on routinized labour hierarchically structured by detailed rules and responsibilities. Facilitated in part by new developments in computer and information technology, these flexible forms of production rely on an increasingly versatile labour force, motivated by a spirit of cooperation and generalism, to produce customized products just in time to meet ever-shifting consumer demand.

The second trend relates to the onset of economic globalization, manifest in the recent spate of bilateral, regional and international agreements, especially those supervised by the World Trade Organization, promoting trade liberalization. By gradually introducing reciprocal tariff reductions and eliminating non-tariff import barriers, these agreements represent the legal superstructure of a new international economic order, where capitalism increasingly operates on a global scale and possesses the capacity to move relatively freely across national boundaries. Economic globalization is both a reflection and result of advanced forms of capitalism and technological innovation overcoming and redefining traditional geographical and political barriers to the production, placement, and sale of goods.

At the same time that these trends are threatening the efficacy of domestic labour law, three new modes of regulation are forming beyond its borders that possess the potential to promote just employment relations at home and abroad. First, the International Labour Organization has assumed the task of articulating labour standards with which all states ought to comply as a matter of international law. The ILO's international presence is not new; it is the primary institutional source of the set of declarations and conventions that for many years has operated as an international mirror of many legal aspirations embedded in domestic labour law. Recently, however, the ILO has begun to advocate state recognition of a core subset of international labour rights in ways that merit attention in light of domestic labour law's aspiration to promote just conditions at work.

Second, a number of international institutions, states, and non-state actors have sought to underscore the significance of international human rights norms in general and labour standards in particular in the context of international, regional and bilateral efforts at trade liberalization. When coupled with a number of recent decisions by the appellate body of the World Trade Organization, proposals to link international human rights with trade liberalization signal that values that domestic labour law historically sought to promote are beginning to influence the nature and direction of international economic law.

Although they involve non-state actors in their promotion, these developments primarily relate to international efforts to hold states accountable to public international labour standards when devising domestic labour market policy. But a third development — one that speaks more directly to firm behaviour — relates to primarily private strategies to subject transnational corporate activity to codes of conduct that impose normative if not legal obligations on firms to treat employees fairly and in a non-discriminatory manner. Corporate codes of conduct potentially enable transnational implementation of international labour standards in ways that do not rely on traditional modes of international legal authority?

Labour law has long sought to promote just conditions of employment through a combination of rules premised on freedom of contract and general legislative imperatives. Rules premised on freedom of contract enable employers and employees, acting either individually or collectively, to negotiate the terms and conditions of employment. General legislative imperatives, such as minimum wage legislation, seek to guarantee a basic set of entitlements to employees regardless of the respective bargaining power of the parties. While their relative influence varies dramatically from country to country, the combination of contractual freedom and a minimum floor of worker entitlements amounts to much of what constitutes domestic labour law in most, if not all, jurisdictions in the world.

Labour law also tends to imagine employers and employees as occupying radically distinct roles in processes of production. Employers are treated as legal actors responsible for the allocation of capital and labour whereas employees are held responsible for supplying the labour necessary for production to occur. In light of this rough division of responsibilities, labour law seeks to enable the parties themselves to determine the terms and conditions of their ongoing relationship against a differentiated background set of general legal entitlements. Employers tend to benefit from a background set of proprietary and managerial entitlements whereas employees typically enjoy a set of legislative entitlements immune from employers' superior bargaining power.

This model of labour law operates relatively successfully in nationally bounded economies primarily dedicated to the mass production of goods and services. Mass production typically requires a centralized, hierarchical, and vertically integrated firm that enables the separation of management and execution of production, the disaggregation of the labour process into specific components and fragmented work tasks, and the establishment and maintenance of a workforce governed by narrowly defined job classifications. To retain workers and minimize training and monitoring costs, employers establish internal labour markets in which seniority provides advancement, and deferred compensation schemes by which workers earn less than their marginal product early in their careers and more later on in their careers. In such an environment, labour law establishes a floor of entitlements by general legislative imperative and authorizes the parties, either individually or collectively, to jointly determine the remaining detailed rules governing their ongoing relationship against a background distribution of property and contractual rights.

But the world in which this model operates is undergoing a dramatic transformation. Through teamwork, participatory production, and atypical forms of employment, flexible forms of production tend to blur boundaries within firms, producing new kinds of workers not easily comprehended by traditional legal categories, including those who benefit from flexibility, those for whom flexibility means disposability, and those who do not possess the requisite skills or opportunities to participate in the opportunities that flexible production provides. Through contracting, subcontracting, outsourcing, and other forms of corporate and institutional collaboration, flexible production also decentralizes decision-making and often blurs boundaries between firms, giving rise to entities designed to be easily redesigned.

As a result, firms are promoting employment relations and transforming into entities that confound the application of legal categories, such as employer and employee, essential to the successful application of domestic labour law regimes. In the words of Manuel Castells, '[w]ho are the owners, who the producers, who the managers, and who the servants, becomes increasingly blurred in a production system of variable geometry, of teamwork, of networking, outsourcing, and subcontracting.' Flexible forms of production simultaneously destabilize labour law's capacity to attach rights and responsibilities to employers and employees while generating distributional consequences that pose dramatic challenges to the capacity of labour law to promote justice at work.

The emergence of flexible forms of production is occurring at the same time that the competitive environment in which production occurs is undergoing a second, related transformation. Economic globalization — the strengthening of international economic interdependence associated with enhanced technological, commercial and financial integration of national economies — is redefining traditional geographical and political barriers to the production, placement and sale of goods and services. With states gradually dismantling tariff barriers and actively seeking new forms of direct foreign investment, corporations enjoy an unparalleled degree of capital mobility. In such an environment, the traditional model of domestic labour law that weds individual or collective contractual freedom with a minimum floor of worker entitlements increasingly appears to create incentives on firms to reduce labour costs by relocating to jurisdictions with less protective labour regulation.

Labour law scholarship has long confronted the allegation that regulatory initiatives harm the very class of persons they are designed to protect. Scholars have noted that there are efficiency gains associated with particular regulatory initiatives that offset losses associated with capital flight; that capital flight engenders efficiency losses associated with training costs, relocation costs, and productivity costs; that the cost of labour is but one of many complex factors, including the economic, social and political stability of the host jurisdiction, that influence relocation decisions; and that justice at work should not always be subservient to efficiency concerns. But these responses appear to increasingly ring hollow in light of heightened competition for foreign direct investment among states and the unparalleled ease with which capital can now move across borders. Capital mobility in an age of economic globalization calls into question a state's ability to attract and retain direct investment and at the same time maintain labour law regimes that manifest a robust commitment to just relations at work.

While each of these trends independently poses formidable challenges to the capacity of labour law to promote just employment relationships, their combination is especially daunting. Flexible production is premised on the assumption that efficiency gains, and thus the ability to obtain comparative advantage over one's competitors, lie less in economies of scale and more in the pace of product innovation, product quality, delivery time, and the maintenance of customer satisfaction. Economic globalization has facilitated the spread of transnational corporations seeking to maximize such efficiency gains by participating in spatially concentrated clusters organized around principles of flexible production, often referred to as territorial production complexes or production chains. Such production processes often 'slice through national boundaries and transcend them in a bewildering array of relationships that operate at different geographical and organizational scales.' Transnational aspects of these production processes possess the potential to elude state efforts at regulation and render difficult the application of traditional forms of domestic labour law. Together, they suggest that those primarily responsible for production — employers and employees — possess identities that are increasingly difficult to for the law to comprehend, while the institutions in which they operate — corporations — appear to exist beyond the reach of sovereign power.

[Reprinted by permission.]

✻ ✻ ✻

As the above excerpt from Betcherman *et al.* notes, a feature of the new economy is that "patterns of labour force participation have changed." As the following chart indicates, not much more than half of the Canadian workforce fits the traditional mould of the employee who has a single, permanent, full-time, long-term job.

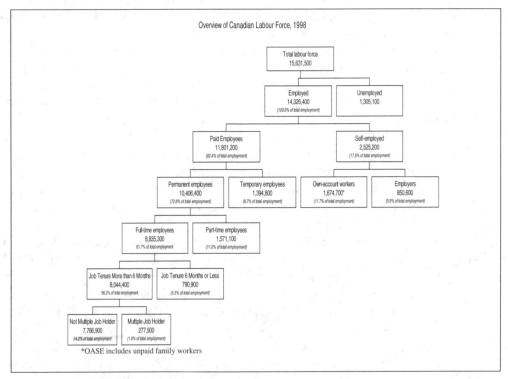

[from G. Lowe, G. Schellenberg, and K. Davidman, *Rethinking Employment Relationships*, (Ottawa: Canadian Policy Research Network inc., 1999) at 5. Reprinted courtesy CPRN, all documents available free at www.cprn.org.]

1:700 OUR NEW PROBLEMS

As the excerpt from Macklem in the preceding section points out, in addition to the other problems adverted to throughout this chapter, Canadian labour and employment law now faces the challenges of globalization. The implications of these challenges, some of which are noted in the following excerpt, will be looked at more closely in Chapter 14.

Brian Langille, "General Reflections on the Relationship of Trade and Labor (Or: Fair Trade Is Free Trade's Destiny)" in Jagdish Bhagwati & Robert Hudec, eds., *Fair Trade and Harmonization: Prerequisites for Free Trade?* **Vol. 2:** *Legal Analysis* **(Cambridge: MIT Press, 1996) 231 at 247–53**

In a world characterized by an internationalized economy and increased mobility of factors of production (other than labor and the nation states which generate regulation), a natural result is the creation of an international market in labor policy. This is problematic given that the nature of labor law is just to question the proper relationship of politics and markets, that is, to establish the proper scope of market regulation. As a result, a political or democratic deficit is created and the increased pressure put upon trade negotiations, such as NAFTA [the North American Free Trade Agreement], to resolve at the level of international political agreement issues such as labor policy, is pressure to take up this political or democratic slack.

Faced with this situation, there are a number of possible policy responses. The Canadian federal election of 1988 was fought dramatically and overtly on precisely which of these responses was most appropriate in the context of the United States/Canada Free Trade Agreement which was then proposed. That debate is not over and remains instructive. The failure of those engaging in that debate to acknowledge what was at stake still resonates down the years of subsequent Canadian politics, and, moreover, exactly the same debate replayed regarding NAFTA.

During the debate which preceded the Canada/U.S. Free Trade Agreement, and which dominated the 1988 Canadian Federal election, two of the most important issues were (1) the direct impact upon Canadian jobs, especially in the manufacturing sector, and (2) the indirect impact of the agreement upon Canadian labor and social policy. On the direct employment effects the Report of the Economic Council of Canada entitled Venturing Forth came to play the role assumed by the Cechinni Report in Europe. In particular, a small positive net impact on job creation over the medium term was predicted, but with significant and predictable adjustment and restructuring effects. The actual direct impact on jobs of the Free Trade Agreement is still extremely controversial and, for the time being, unknowable. Given the complications caused by high interest rates, a high dollar, the recession, and the other elements of internationalization, all that is certain is that Ontario's manufacturing sector has been "hammered," to use a word invoked by Ontario Premier Bob Rae. But by far the most dramatic moments during the 1988 election, and in particular the debate between Prime Minister Mulroney and then Liberal leader John Turner, did not revolve around the direct impact of the proposed Free Trade Agreement, but rather the indirect impact upon Canadian social (including labor) policy. The argument was that putting among other things, Canada's more generous labor policy (on virtually every issue from minimum wages to pay equity to collective bargaining laws resulting in much higher union density) into competition with the 'deregulated' market of America would put inevitable pressure on the Canadian lawmakers to follow suit in order for firms in Canada to remain 'competitive.' For some this was the very reason for the Free Trade Agreement, not an undesirable side effect. But the main defenders of the Free Trade Agreement denied that these policies were 'on the table' or likely to be affected. It cannot escape our attention, however, that since the signing of the agreement we have had, for example, a strident outcry over proposed amendments to Ontario's labor laws on precisely the grounds of competitiveness with U.S. firms operating under the slacker labor regime there.

What is striking about the 1988 debate, however, is that overwhelmingly the perceived public policy choice was all or nothing — either accepting or rejecting the agreement. The two main positions staked out in the debate I have identified as 'status quo/nationalist' and 'classic free trade':

> The big business community in Canada, represented by the Business Council on National Issues, and the Mulroney government, argued for free trade on the neo-classical economic lines. They argued that economies of scale, the theory of comparative advantage, and heightened competition with U.S. firms will create jobs and wealth for Canada. As part of this view little attention was paid to the adjustment costs of the move to the free trade regime. Although lip service was paid to adjustment policy, nothing is said about such policies in the FTA and indeed there may be real problems with certain adjustment policies under U.S. trade law and the subsidies negotiations. And a very clear subtext here concerned the virtues of market ordering and renewed competition on labour market issues which Canadian labour law had taken out of competition or for which it established significant normative baselines.
>
> The status quo/national position was articulated by broad coalition interest groups (the Pro Canada network), the [New Democratic Party], the Liberal Party of Canada and the labour movement . . . [t]hose opposed to the FTA focused upon its indirect effects. They noted that inherent in the pro-FTA agreement, in its celebration of the gains from competition and a much larger marketplace, was the essential idea of putting Canadian labour and social policy into competition with those of America. In this purely competitive exercise, the pressure to lessen the burden of the Canadian regulatory state upon business was said to be straightforward. However, the status quo/nationalist argument, while attending to the direct and indirect costs of trade liberalization, ignored the cost of the status quo protectionist policy. No effort was made to assess whether the costs per job saved from protectionist measures was actually a wise investment.

There was a third, much less well publicized, but better position staked out during the U.S./Canada Free Trade debate. In the main it was made out by academic commentators and is best exemplified in the work of Michael Trebilcock. I have characterized this position as 'adjustment for losers':

> This position is constituted by three elements. First, that the best evidence is that the gains predicted by trade theory will be real. Second, the cost annually per job saved by

protectionist measures are astonishingly high and represent in general, a bad invest-ment. Third that the gains from trade and savings from foregoing protectionism enables us to compensate the losers in the form of adjustment policies and in addition finance the social programmes which are distinctively Canadian. This position does not, howev-er, answer adequately the general argument about the adequacy of (international) market ordering nor the problem of the indirect and downward pressure on Canadian labour and social policy in the absence of baseline norms.

Canadian debate in 1988 was dominated by the first two of these three positions and the idea of a social charter or 'side' agreements played virtually no role. That is, the idea of accepting trade liberalization but with agreement on fundamental social or labor poli-cy, or at least baseline minima, never seriously emerged as a possible option. This idea has now had increased exposure as a result of the NAFTA negotiations to which Canada appended itself. Moreover, the very fact that Canada appended itself to the U.S./Mexico negotiations and the universally accepted explanation for that intervention on our part — that we need to be at the table to ensure the alleged FTA gains are not undermined — point to our commitment, at least sometimes, to the idea that the whipsawing and the bar-gaining down which results from international marketplace negotiations have to give way to multilateral agreements and structures limiting isolated bilateral bargaining outcomes. Put crudely, we perceive in this instance that it is not in our interest to bargain individu-ally and be played one off against the other.

There are clear answers to the positions staked out by the defenders of free trade and their strong opponents in the Canadian debate. The free trade position as argued in Cana-da simply denies what is theoretically obvious and often observed — that there will be increased pressure upon Canadian labor law policy (both legislated and negotiated) to conform to the lower standards set elsewhere. The status quo/nationalist response accu-rately perceives the theoretical and real-life points, but then provides a remedy which is worse than the cure. The problem with that position is not only the effort to make Cana-da an economic island, but a democratic one.

The position staked out by Michael Trebilcock is clearly much more attractive — it is sensitive to the economic gains from trade and the economic costs of protectionism. It is a position endorsed by others. Nonetheless it is insufficiently sensitive to the real crisis in trade theory brought about by the democratic deficit in the establishment of labor and social policy. To excavate this point we must recall the scenario presented by traditional trade theory. In the traditional picture, Bhagwati says, 'Governments played no role.' Now the subsidy idea has captured all governmental activity or inactivity and this is the crisis that trade theory is now confronting. On the other hand, before this crisis governments did have a function which did attract the interests of some trade lawyers: the appropriate dis-tribution of the gains from trade among the members of the nation-state in question. This issue was residual and, although controversial, not conceptually difficult to accommodate. The issue was simply one of distribution of gains between winners and losers and the appropriateness of the policy of 'adjustment for losers.' The issue of what policy stand to take on this distributional issue has been well argued elsewhere. But this debate takes place on familiar terrain: the background of political normalcy within a nation-state. That is, the residual issue of distribution of gains and losses is simply one that will, again, be resolved within the nation-state among the relevant constituencies of capital, labor, and consumers. In this world view governmental action elsewhere is irrelevant because it does not enter the causal chain of trade theory. And governmental action here is completely legitimated by the presence of the relevant constituencies and their equal access to a voice in the political process. Labor and capital were, within the nation-state view of the world, partners in a bilateral monopoly, each with the power of voice, but not, critically, of exit. In this picture then there was a two-way street of democratic legitimacy — the irrelevance of the political processes elsewhere and the legitimacy of resolution of labor policy issues domestically.

There is now a breakdown of this claim to democratic legitimacy — and it too runs in both directions. Governmental activity *elsewhere* is now clearly understood as bearing upon domestic politics. This perception has found expression in the notion of subsidy, level playing fields, and found an outlet at the international trade negotiating table. Furthermore, the mobility of capital and (relative) immobility of labor have broken the traditional mode of understanding of the legitimacy of the resolution of labor law issues in two ways. First, the result is that within any particular state the ground of political legitimacy is shifted. Labor and capital are no longer in a bilateral monopoly within a nation state with equal access to the political processes. Capital has slipped the moorings of the nation-state, labor has not done so. Capital has acquired the option of exit, labor has not done so.

Second, the result is the creation of an international market place in (labor) regulatory policy. Regulatory arbitrage is the expected and observable norm. The primary political task of delimiting the relationship of markets and non-market regulation has been usurped. The fundamental understanding of labor law is directly challenged — it is a dialogue about the appropriateness of market regulation. One view is that the outcome of this debate will be determined by the market. That is, however, to beg the question.

Some observers have commented that this sort of internationalization 'erodes a people's capacity to control its own affairs.' This is correct, but only goes part of the distance required. The problem is that such phenomena erode, to some extent, any people's capacity to control its own affairs, critically so when those affairs are precisely about the scope of market regulation. To claim that this issue should now be settled by the international marketplace is as deep a misunderstanding of the problem involved as we saw with the misunderstanding of the 'inequality-of-bargaining-power' idea.

At this point in the debate proponents of the international market in labor policy may then invoke an argument from 'democracy' or, more likely, 'sovereignty' of their own. Invoking ideas familiar from several contexts, they point out that what pressures Nova Scotia (in the Michelin example) or Ontario (in the reform of The Labour Relations Act) or the United States (in its relationship to Mexican labor law) are simply the choices made by other players in the market for labor policy. Other states make different political decisions (and on the negotiation side, other workers sign different sorts of collective agreements) but that cannot be problematic. . . .

This overlooks the first aspect of our problem — that we are now dealing with an internationalized market in which, from a domestic perspective, only one player has the exit option. Leaving this point aside for the moment, however, there are other very problematic implications here.

As in standard normative defences of market ordering, the choices made elsewhere (in order to legitimately constrain choices here) must be capable of being characterized as free, among other things. The argument is really of the following sort. What is wrong with the people of Mexico, or Malaysia, or Thailand deciding upon a different mix of labor market polices which are attractive to investors? But this rhetorical mode puts extreme pressure upon the validity of the choices made elsewhere by, for example, the Mexican people. On the legislative side it assumes a democratically elected government which is the precondition of a legitimate choice elsewhere. On the negotiation side, it assumes an independent and free labor movement. Both of these assumptions are problematic, not only in many of the states commonly brought to mind in these sorts of debates — Malaysia, Thailand — but in Mexico as well. To the extent that undemocratic regimes maintain standards which undermine ours, they are externalizing their own democratic deficit to our shores. Those arguing for the legitimacy of the constrained choice here (by a legitimate choice elsewhere) have, in many real-life circumstances, a difficult task.

The claim that 'fair traders' insult the 'sovereignty' of other peoples is also a shallow one for a deeper reason. The essence of the claim is that issues which should be decided in Ottawa or Mexico City are now being settled at international trade negotiations in Washington. This insult to the right of self-determination is meant to shame 'fair traders' and to tell them to keep domestic labor law issues on the domestic table, and not risk losing control of them. But this may be a very bad bit of advice. The point that fair traders argue is that Canada (Ottawa) already has, to some extent, lost 'control' of the regulation of labor policy and the reality is that international trade talks provide a forum for regaining some measure of political control over those issues. To put this point another way, our ability to establish our own domestic labor standards has been eroded. These standards will, to some extent, be established internationally. The issue is how, not whether, they will be established internationally. The issue is whether they should be established by the international marketplace in labor policy or via international agreement.

* * *

We now begin our exploration of the three regulatory regimes that make up Canadian labour and employment law: the common law, collective bargaining law, and direct statutory regulation. In planning this casebook, a basic pedagogic decision we had to make was whether to treat the three regimes together, in the sense of considering how all three deal with a particular substantive question (for example, the question of what types of workers are considered to be employees), then moving on to see how all three treat another such question (for example, the principles that govern the termination of employment). This approach would have had the virtue of putting into the same chapter all of the law on a particular substantive question, but at the cost of obscuring the overall structure of each of the three regimes and making it hard to discern the distinctive features of each of them. We judged this cost to be too high. Therefore, we will proceed through each of the three regimes in the roughly chronological order in which they are arranged by the received wisdom: the common law first, then collective bargaining law, and finally, direct statutory regulation. This means that substantive areas which are relevant to all three regimes, such as the principles governing termination of employment, are dealt with in three separate places in this book

As we have tried to make clear in the introduction to this chapter, understanding the three regulatory regimes is a necessary but not a sufficient condition to coming to grips with the broader issues that confront labour and employment law in our times. The question which must be kept in mind throughout the study of the three regimes — a question to which we will return in Chapter 14 — is this: can our traditional understanding of labour and employment law withstand the pressures of contemporary developments in the world around us?

1:800 CONSTITUTIONAL ISSUES

1:810 Three Types of Constitutional Issue

At various points from the 1920s to the present, three major sets of constitutional issues have played an important part in Canadian labour and employment law. Chronologically, the first of the three consisted of those involving the federal/provincial division of powers. These issues still arise fairly often today, and will be discussed in section 1:820 below.

The second set, chronologically, contains what are commonly called "section 96" issues. The *British North America Act, 1867* (1867, c. 3 (UK)) (now the *Constitution Act, 1867*) provides (in sections 96 to 100) that judges of the superior courts in each province must be appointed by the federal government, and also gives those judges considerable security of tenure with a view to protecting their independence. When modern provincial social legislation came onto the scene after the Second World War, it was interpreted and applied by administrative tribunals freshly created for that purpose by the provinces. The members of these tribunals did not enjoy the protections of sections 96 to 100 of the Constitution, and a debate arose over whether they should therefore be prohibited from enforcing rights and granting remedies which resembled the rights and remedies traditionally enforced and granted by the superior courts. The leading case in this area was, and still is, *Labour Relations Board of Saskatchewan v. John East Iron Works Ltd.*, [1949] A.C. 134 (Judicial Committee of the Privy Council).

On its face, this debate was about the independence of adjudicators. On another level, it was about the authority of the legislative branch of government to decide that its social legislation would be administered not by the courts but by specialized tribunals which were expected to be more sympathetic to the redistributive objectives that often characterized such legislation. Because the section 96 debate involved the interface between legislative and judicial authority, it was quite closely related to the long-standing debate over the proper extent of judicial review of administrative decisionmaking — a debate which is at the heart of the field of administrative law.

More than two decades ago, the section 96 debate was considerably damped down by a compromise of sorts. On the one hand, the Supreme Court of Canada allowed the provinces (and the federal government) to give administrative tribunals strong powers to interpret and enforce social legislation. On the other hand, the Supreme Court insisted that no legislature could exempt any tribunal from judicial review, in order to ensure that every tribunal would stay within what the courts saw as the limits of its substantive and procedural jurisdiction. See *Crevier v. Attorney-General of Quebec*, [1981] 2 S.C.R 220 (S.C.C.). At a few points in this book, we will touch upon the very live and constantly evolving administrative law issue of the appropriate standard of judicial review. However, we will make no further mention of the section 96 issue.

The third major set of constitutional law issues — those raised by the *Canadian Charter of Rights and Freedoms* — began to hit labour and employment law just as the section 96 issue was cooling down. *Charter* cases have mostly involved the rubrics of freedom of association under section 2(d), freedom of expression under section 2(b), and the right to equality before and under the law, under section 15(1). Those cases have received a great deal of attention, but there is a considerable division of opinion on the actual impact that they are having and will have in the workplace. Each individual *Charter* case in the labour and employment area can probably best be understood in the context of the specific aspect of that area to which the case relates. Thus, we will not try to summarize the thrust of the *Charter* jurisprudence at this point, but will deal with the most important of its parts in the appropriate chapters below — mainly in Chapter 4 on the coverage of collective bargaining legislation, in Chapter 8 on industrial conflict, and in Chapter 13 on equality rights in the workplace.

1:820 The Federal/Provincial Division of Powers in Labour Relations and Employment Law

The division of powers between the two levels of government in Canada is very complex, and this complexity is reflected in the area of employment and labour relations. The basic rule is easy enough to state: the provinces have jurisdiction over labour and employment matters in industries that are within provincial legislative authority, and the federal government has jurisdiction over labour and employment matters in industries that are within federal legislative authority. However, in borderline cases it can be very difficult to determine what is federal and what is provincial.

Until 1925, it was assumed that the primary responsibility for regulating labour relations and industrial disputes rested with the federal government. After all, the *British North America Act* expressly provided for the federal power to make laws for "the Peace, Order and Good Government of Canada" (section 91), and for "the regulation of trade and commerce" (section 91(2)). Accordingly, Parliament assumed broad control over labour relations by enacting a series of statutes that decriminalized union activity, gave unions legal status, and established mandatory conciliation procedures to make strikes less likely. Most notable among those statutes were the *Trade Unions Act* (S.C. 1872, c. 30), the *Criminal Law Amendment Act* (S.C. 1872, c. 31), the *Conciliation Act* (S.C. 1900, c. 24) and the *Industrial*

Disputes Investigation Act (S.C. 1907, c. 20). However, laws involving individual employment relations — such as master and servant laws, and those on factory conditions and workers' compensation — were generally held to be the responsibility of the provinces.

The course of Canadian labour law changed dramatically with the 1925 decision of the Judicial Committee of the Privy Council in *Toronto Electric Commissioners v. Snider,* [1925] 2 D.L.R. 5. The federal government had decided to appoint a conciliation board under the *Industrial Disputes Investigation Act* to deal with an industrial dispute involving Toronto street railway employees. The employer sought an injunction to block the appointment of that board, arguing that the federal government had no constitutional authority to regulate labour relations in areas of economic activity within provincial legislative jurisdiction. Ultimately, the Judicial Committee, then Canada's final appellate court, held that labour and employment relations between the Toronto Electric Commissioners and their employees were a matter of "property and civil rights" (and perhaps also a matter of "municipal institutions") under section 92 of the *British North America Act,* and therefore fell within provincial competence.

Since *Snider,* the federal government's regulation of employment relations has been confined to the areas of authority given to it by section 91 of the *Constitution Act*: national emergencies, such as occurred during the Second World War; and industries specifically listed in the *Constitution Act* as being federal works or undertakings, as well as operations that are integral to a federal work or undertaking. Today, this means that only about 10 percent of the Canadian work force is regulated by federal legislation, and that 90 percent falls under provincial jurisdiction. In sharp contrast, in the United States the cornerstone constitutional ruling of the American Supreme Court — *Jones v. Laughlin Steel Corp.,* 301 U.S. 1 (1936) — held that the federal government had primary authority to enact labour and employment laws, based on the trade and commerce clause of the *Constitution.* About 90 percent of the American workforce comes under federal jurisdiction.

The principal areas over which the Canadian federal government exercises labour relations jurisdiction include radio and television broadcasting, aviation, postal services, inter-provincial and international transport (such as cross-border trucking, railways, marine ferry services, and shipping), nuclear power and uranium mines, banking, longshoring, and the three northern territories — the Yukon, the North West Territories, and Nunavut. The federal government also has authority over the labour relations of its own employees, including those of federal boards, agencies, and Crown corporations. Virtually every part aspect of the Canadian labour force, including manufacturing, retail trade, and construction, is provincially regulated. The fact that a company in one of those industries does business in more than one province or internationally is generally insufficient to bring its labour relations within federal jurisdiction.

Constitutional issues most often arise in union certification applications, in the form of an argument by the employer that the union which has applied under provincial law to represent its employees should have applied under federal law, or vice-versa: see, for example, *Nordia (Ontario) Inc. v. U.S.W.A.* (2003), 88 C.L.R.B.R. (2d) 295 (C.I.R.B.). However, such issues also arise in a range of other circumstances. Among them are changes in the nature of a business (for example, when a trucking company initiates a new regular shipping route across a provincial or international border), or attempts by one or the other level of government to regulate a company's labour relations: see, for example, *Brewster Transport Co. v. ATU, Loc. 1374 (Re)* (1986), 13 C.L.R.B.R. (N.S.) 339 (C.L.R.B.); *Ottawa-Carleton Regional Transit Commission and ATU, Local 279 (Re)* (1983), 44 O.R. (2d) 560 (C.A.).

Since the enactment of modern labour laws in the 1940s, the Judicial Committee of the Privy Council, and later the Supreme Court of Canada, have decided many division of powers cases involving labour relations. Two of those decisions in particular should be mentioned. In *Canadian Pacific Railway v. A.G. (B.C.)*, [1950] A.C. 122 (P.C.), (the *Empress Hotel* case), the Judicial Committee had to decide whether employees of a Victoria hotel owned and managed by a national railway company came under federal or provincial employment standards legislation. The railway company's transportation operations were clearly in the federal sphere because of their inter-provincial nature. The company argued that its hotel, which was adjacent to its Victoria railway station and received many of its passengers as guests, was an integral part of its railway operations and therefore also came under federal labour and employment legislation.

The Judicial Committee disagreed. It ruled that a company may carry on more than one undertaking, and that those undertakings may fall into different constitutional spheres. If the company's primary undertaking is within federal jurisdiction, and it has other operations that would normally be within provincial jurisdiction, the latter operations will not become federal in character unless they are integral and vital to the company's primary undertaking. Lord Reid could not find that the Empress Hotel was sufficiently integrated with the company's railway operations to bring it under federal jurisdiction.

> It may be that, if the appellant [the employer] chose to conduct a hotel solely or even principally for the benefit of travelers on its system, the hotel would be a part of its railway undertaking. . . But the Empress Hotel differs markedly from such a hotel. Indeed, there is little, if anything in the facts stated to distinguish it from an independently owned hotel in a similar position. No doubt the fact that there is a large and well-managed hotel at Victoria tends to increase the traffic on the appellant's system; it may be that the appellant's railway business and hotel business help each other, but that does not prevent them from being separate businesses and undertakings.

A more recent decision of major importance pointing in the same direction was *Construction Montcalm Inc. v. Minimum Wage Commission*, [1979] 1 S.C.R. 754. Montcalm was a Quebec construction company that had a series of contracts with the federal government to build runways on federal Crown land for the new Mirabel Airport near Montreal. The Quebec Minimum Wage Commission initiated an action against Montcalm, pursuant to the province's minimum wage and construction labour relations statutes, to recover wages, vacation, and holiday pay and other employment benefits on behalf of the company's employees. Montcalm challenged the application of provincial employment law to construction work done on federal Crown land for a federal undertaking.

A sharply divided Supreme Court of Canada ruled against Montcalm. The majority held that doing work on federal Crown lands did not necessarily constitute an extraterritorial enclave where only federal labour law applied. Each case would depend on whether the work was integral to the federal undertaking. While the operation and maintenance of an airport was so closely tied to aeronautics as to fall within federal jurisdiction, the construction of the airport was far enough removed from aviation and aerial navigation to stand on a distinct footing. Mr. Justice Beetz, for the majority, said:

> In submitting that it should have been treated as a federal undertaking for the purposes of its labour relations while it was doing construction work on the runways of Mirabel, Montcalm postulates that the decisive factor to be taken into consideration is the one work that it happened to be constructing at the relevant time rather than the nature of its business as a going concern. . . . This would produce great confusion. For instance, a worker whose job it is to pour cement would from day to day be shifted from federal to provincial jurisdiction for the purposes of union membership, certification, collective agreement and wages, because he pours cement one day on a runway and the other on a provincial highway. I cannot be persuaded that the Constitution was meant to apply in such a disintegrating fashion. . . .
>
> . . . One does not say of them that they are in the business of building runways because for a while they happen to be building a runway and that they enter into a business of building highways because they thereafter begin to do construction work on a section of a provincial turnpike. Their ordinary business is the business of building. What they build is accidental. And there is nothing specifically federal about their ordinary business.

Chief Justice Laskin dissented. He noted that federal public property fell under the exclusive jurisdiction of the federal government under section 91(1)(a) of the *British North America Act*. In his view, there could be no constitutional difference between the construction of a federal undertaking such as an airport, on the one hand, and its maintenance and operation on the other hand. Since only Parliament could authorize a construction project on federal Crown land, Laskin C.J. maintained, it made both constitutional and labour relations sense for the same regulatory regime to govern all aspects of the project.

The majority decision in *Montcalm* emphasized that each employment task at a federal work or undertaking must be examined to determine how essential its relationship is with the core purpose of the undertaking. At an airport, for example, the labour relations of the airline ticket agents, the air traffic controllers, and the baggage handlers would be federal, because their responsibilities are integral to the core operations of the airlines and the airport. However, the work of airport building cleaners, retail employees who sell coffee and magazines, and workers who rent cars and drive limousines would be regulated by provincial legislation, because it is not vital to a core federal undertaking: see *Re Field Aviation Co. Ltd. and I.A.M., Local 1579* (1974), 45 D.L.R. (3d) 751 (Alta. S.C.T.D.), aff'd 49 D.L.R. (3d) 234 (S.C. App. Div.); *Tower Co. (1961) Ltd.*, [1979] 3 Can. L.R.B. R. 255 (O.L.R.B.).

Similarly, a First Nations reserve is not considered an island of exclusive federal jurisdiction, despite the fact that the federal government has exclusive powers over aboriginal affairs under section 91(24) of the *Constitution Act*. A band council office, a health clinic, and a school would normally come under federal labour relations authority, as each of them is an essential aspect of community life. However, a private business operating on the reserve (such as a store or gas station) would likely fall under provincial labour relations jurisdiction: see *Four B Mfg Ltd. v. United Garment Workers of America* (1979), 102 D.L.R. (3d) 385 (S.C.C.); and *P.S.A.C. v. Francis* (1982), 139 D.L.R. (3d) 9 (S.C.C.).

Different but nonetheless instructive tests appear to be used in the transportation industry. At one time, a "pith and substance" test emphasized the proportion of a transportation company's operations that crossed a provincial or international border: *Re Windsor Airline Limousine Services Ltd.* (1980), 20 O.R. (2d) 732 (Div. Ct.)). The test then evolved to focus on whether there were "regular and continuous" border crossings, however miniscule a proportion they were of the company's overall operations: *Ottawa-Carleton Regional Transit Commission and ATU, Local 279 (Re)* (1983), 44 O.R. (2d) 560 (C.A.). More recently, elements of both prior tests have been used, as indicated in the excerpt below from *Windsor Airline Limousine* case. A union had applied to the Ontario Labour Relations Board for certification as bargaining agent for the drivers who worked for a taxi company in Windsor, Ontario, on the American border just across the river from Detroit. The company challenged the constitutional jurisdiction of the OLRB, arguing that its labour relations operations were federally regulated. The company averaged just under 1100 trips per month into the US, which was less than one-half of 1 percent of its total business. Some of the drivers held American immigration permits allowing them to take passengers to and from the US, and the company had both provincial and extra-provincial operating licenses. Its cross-border trips took place at all hours of the day and night, but they were done on demand and not on a regularly scheduled basis.

Re Windsor Airline Limousine Services (c.o.b. Veteran Cab Co.), [1999] O.L.R.B. Rep. Nov/Dec. 1125

CHAPMAN, Vice-Chair

. . .

¶50 . . . the test for determining the constitutional jurisdiction of an undertaking involving extra-provincial carriage is whether or not the work outside the province can be characterized as "regular and continuous" so as to constitute a "connecting" or "extending" undertaking. Just as clearly, though, determining what will meet that test is not capable of simple definition. The conundrum created by the notion of regularity can perhaps be put thus: how regular is regular enough?

¶51 The approaches of labour boards and courts to this area of division of powers litigation . . . have involved the measure of various aspects of an employer's business, and there has been a certain lack of agreement about which measures ought to govern the decision as to jurisdiction. Having reviewed these cases exhaustively, I would suggest, though, that an element of volume is present in all of the tests which have been invoked. As well, adjudicators have tended to look at the nature of the employer's business, and the role of the extra-provincial work in that business, in assessing whether or not the cross-border work is "regular and continuous."

. . .

¶56 There does seem to be a consensus in the case law that any instance of extra-provincial travel will not instantly require federal regulation . . . , as well as the suggestion that some undefined amount of *de minimus* extra-provincial business is permissible for a provincial undertaking. How much is permissible is less clear. . . .

¶57 A review of the actual numbers considered in the various decisions provides no more clear guidance than do these phrases. In the two taxi cases the extra-provincial travel was daily: 60 to 70 trips across the border daily, for a total of less than 2% of the employer's business, in the earlier *Windsor Airline Limousine* decision; and approximately 348 daily dispatches to and from Quebec, constituting a little more than 2% of the total volume of dispatched calls, in the Ottawa Taxi Owners case. . . . [I]n both cases the labour relations of the employer were found to fall within provincial jurisdiction.

¶58 In the trucking cases, many fewer trips per day, representing similar volume as a proportion of an employer's business, have resulted in findings of federal jurisdiction. . .

¶60 . . . Certainly the volume of the work measured only as a percentage of the employer's total business ought not to govern the outcome. The . . . fallacy inherent in such a test . . . can also be seen by considering whether a single but highly remunerative trip ought to result in a finding that the extra-provincial travel was so regular as to require federal regulation. At that same time, though, an analysis of the frequency of the cross-border travel measured only by the absolute volume of that business may be equally misleading, for it fails to take into account what is conceived of as "regular" in a particular business.

¶61 This problem is apparent in the taxi cases, where overall call volume is extremely high, measured for example against the number of runs made daily by a trucking company (or by a charter bus company. . . In this context, even an impressive number of daily trips might fairly be considered *de minimus*. In the case before me, approximately 18 trips across the border are dispatched each day, but this represents less than ½ percent of the employer's daily call volume. Extra-provincial travel is thus regular, if one considers only the interval of the work, which is clearly more than daily (although entirely unscheduled), but at the same time is not frequent, having regard to the number of calls handled daily.

¶62 . . . Having carefully considered . . . all of the decisions reviewed above, I am satisfied that a consideration of the frequency of the extra-provincial travel, compared to the normal pace of the employer's business, is an entirely appropriate way in which to assess whether the extra-provincial undertaking is "regular and continuous." . . .

¶63 The union in its legal submissions emphasized the unique nature of the taxi industry in asserting that the Board ought not to rely upon the case law relating to the trucking and charter bus industries, much less the municipal bus cases, in assessing the appropriate constitutional jurisdiction. Certainly there is ample Board jurisprudence dealing generally with the taxi industry, which does possess various unusual features which have had an impact in applying labour relations principles to the industry. Taxi drivers are generally employees within the meaning of the Act only because they have been found to be dependent contractors who rely upon companies operating dispatch services, the owners of taxi licence plates, and often the owners of vehicles, for their ability to earn a living. Companies like Windsor Airline Limousine are not conventional employers: they generally, but not always, operate dispatch services that advertise the availability of taxi services to the public, and then refer calls for such service to drivers, who pick up the fares and transact directly with the customer; they often own taxi licences, which because of municipal regulation are required for a taxi to be operated, and lease those plates to drivers; and they sometimes also own cars, which are similarly rented to drivers. Drivers pay a variety of fees to brokerages like Windsor Airline Limousine, depending on the nature of their arrangements, which may include dispatch fees, taxi licence rental fees, and/or vehicle rental fees. A driver's income therefore derives directly from the fares paid by customers, less the payments made to the brokerage (and often to other persons, called "associates" in the Board's decisions, who may own plates or vehicles), rather than from any salary paid out by the employer. . . .

¶64 The taxi industry is also regulated by municipal authorities, which issue by-laws controlling important aspects of the business, including the fares charged to customers, the issuance of plates and their transfer and usage, and even the conduct required of drivers. These by-laws are thus central to the ability of brokerages and drivers to earn money in the industry, and have played an important role in the labour relations framework established where drivers have chosen to organize collectively.

¶65 These unique qualities of the taxi industry illuminate the constitutional facts in this matter, and do perhaps distinguish them from the kinds of commercial arrangements which are typical in the other industries considered in the cases reviewed above, including the trucking and charter bus businesses. In the present case approximately half of the drivers have chosen to obtain the clearance necessary to accept from the company referrals for trips across the border, but they are not compelled, as dependent contractors, to be so licensed, nor are they required to accept extra-provincial calls. And the company itself of course carries on no actual operations outside of the province: its dispatch and other services are located in Windsor, and its taxi plates are all issued by the municipal authorities in Windsor. Its only role in terms of extra-provincial business is to refer calls to the various dependent contractors who drive for the company, some of whom will accept those fares and transport them across the border on an unscheduled on-demand basis.

¶66 . . . In all of the circumstances of the present case, I have concluded that, as in the earlier *Windsor Airline Limousine case* and in the decision of the Canada Labour Relations Board in *Ottawa Taxi Owners*, the provision of extra-provincial taxicab services by Windsor Airline Limousine is not carried on a "regular and continuous" basis so as to constitute an "extending or connecting" activity within the meaning of section 92(10)(a) of the *Constitution Act*, 1867.

. . .

¶67 For all of the reasons reviewed above, the Board has determined that the labour relations of the employer fall within provincial jurisdiction, and this Board therefore has jurisdiction to proceed to hear and determine the above-captioned matters.

✻ ✻ ✻

The governing test in non-transportation cases is explained in the excerpt below from the *Murrin Construction Ltd.* case. A union had applied to the British Columbia Labour Relations Board to represent employees of a construction contractor that did track stabilization and maintenance work for the Canadian National Railway (CN), a federally regulated company. The contractor argued that its labour relations fell within federal jurisdiction. The vast majority of its work — at least 80 percent annually over a period of ten years — was done for CN in British Columbia. Nearly all of the work it did on other construction projects fell within provincial jurisdiction, and many of the skills of its employees were readily transferable to those projects. Its work for CN involved the construction of retaining walls to protect trains against rock slides, as well as grade stabilization below track level to prevent the deterioration of the rail tracks. CN's ability to run its trains in British Columbia safely and on schedule depended on the quality of Murrin's track work.

Murrin Construction Ltd. v. Construction & Specialized Workers' Union, Local 1611 (2002), 80 C.L.R.B.R. (2d) 42 (B.C.L.R.B.)

HICKLING, Vice-Chair:

. . .

¶74 . . . the issue is whether the work performed by Murrin and its employees is so vital or essential to the effective operation of the railway as to bring them within the ambit of the *Canada Labour Code.* . . .

¶76 . . . the mere fact that employees have performed in the same kind of work task that can be found in many construction sites, is not determinative. Nor is the fact that the company has performed tasks in areas of the economy that are subject to provincial jurisdiction. If one looks to Murrin's normal or habitual activities, as the case law requires, one finds that its predominant customer since 1992 has been CN. It is not disputed that work for CN has never fallen below 80% of Murrin's total activity. Indeed, in several years the figure hit 100%, and in the last three or four years has ranged from 95% to 100%.

¶77 In the past two or three years there have been a number of significant changes that have strengthened the relationship between Murrin and CN. They include Murrin's increasing specialization, the development of the tie-back wall procedures, its commitment of resources to that activity, and the fact that such work is no longer put out to competitive bidding but is negotiated by Murrin with CN. It is true that those contracts are negotiated on an annual basis, but that is not determinative. . . . Both the duration of the relationship and its exclusivity tend to point to a strengthening of the nexus between Murrin and CN. The work for CN may not be permanent. It may not be guaranteed beyond the expiration of the current contract. . . . However, the present intention of both parties is to continue the relationship for the foreseeable future. The work on tie-back walls is not exceptional, or casual, but is normal, habitual and ongoing.

¶78 . . . Jurisdictional issues are not, of course, decided by reference to a tyranny of percentages. It is not disputed that a significant proportion of Murrin's work is for CN, or that the relationship has been mutually beneficial. Neither of those facts are crucial to the determination of the jurisdictional issue.

¶79 Insofar as corporate relationships are concerned, the evidence is neutral. Murrin is not a subsidiary of CN. There is no relationship between them, other than the commercial one that has developed over the years. The fact that if performed by a department of CN itself, the work would have been regarded as a non-severable part of the core federal undertaking does not lead inevitably to the conclusion that the work is still federal when it is contracted out. Nor, of course, does the fact that it was contracted out to a provincially incorporated company preclude a finding that the work is still within the area of federal competence. . . . More critical is the degree of functional integration of the services with the operations of CN and the latter's dependence upon them.

¶80 The Union suggests that the Employer has failed to establish the necessary degree of functional integration, arguing that compliance with provincial laws relating to wages, hours, and labour relations do not affect the operation of the Railway's business. It asks what the building of retaining walls has to do with the operation of the Railway. Murrin has nothing to do with the laying of track, grinding the rails, or replacing ballast. In short, the Union argues that Murrin has nothing to do with the essential undertaking. Its work is essentially construction work.

¶81 The Employer addresses the issue with quite a different focus. It concentrates on the importance to the Railway of the services Murrin provides and the impact they have upon the ability of the Railway to operate safely and efficiently. Murrin does not undertake work on the track itself. That is true. Nonetheless, it seems to me that it is of vital importance to the Railway to deal with hazards that might prejudice its safe operation, whether the threat comes from unstable rock falling onto the track from above, or erosion undercutting the track bed. Both might lead to derailments, damage to property and injury to life or limb. . . .

¶82 The work is performed on the federal undertaking's property, a factor which has been considered relevant in other cases. . . . In the Employer's submission, the relationship in the present case involves far more than a mere physical connection and a beneficial commercial relationship. As evidence of integration, the Employer points to [its] role in identifying problem areas; in the design of the remedial action; the fact that Murrin's employees are subject to safety regulations established by CN and federal agencies; the safety training provided by CN; the mutual concern and involvement within CN in dealing with environmental issues; regulation by CN of access to the tracks; the coordination of Murrin's activities with CN's operation through the flagperson; the presence of CN technicians on site; as well as the use of specialized equipment to enable Murrin's employees to gain access to remote sites, inaccessible by road. The fact that Murrin's employees may be subject to provincial workers compensation laws (as well as safety rules established by federal agencies and CN) does not dictate a conclusion in favour of provincial jurisdiction. My conclusions are not contingent upon that, but upon an overall assessment of the degree and nature of the integration.

¶83 Insofar as the distinction between construction and maintenance may be helpful in resolving that issue, it seems to me that the work performed by Murrin is closer to the maintenance of CN's operations than to the functions of a general construction company.

. . .

¶85 . . . [I]t is CN's dependence upon Murrin that is important, not vice versa.

. . .

¶87 The work performed by Murrin is vital, essential or integral to CN's operations, and hence falls within federal jurisdiction. As a result, the Union's application under the *Labour Relations Code of British Columbia* is dismissed.

* * *

The perennial difficulty in determining the boundary between federal and provincial jurisdiction is of course not unique to the area of employment and labour relations; it extends across the entire spectrum of division of powers issues. In addition, the existence of eleven different labour law jurisdictions across the country has not altered the fact that every one of those jurisdictions has adopted the principal features of the *Wagner Act* system — labour relations boards, a certification process, binding collective agreements, restrictions on legal strikes, and a mandatory arbitration system — and that their statutory schemes differ largely on matters of emphasis and detail. Many years ago, the argument was made that our decentralized system of labour regulation has resulted in "little laboratories" of experimentation, where reforms can be tested in one jurisdiction, and then more widely adopted if they prove successful: Paul Weiler, "The Virtues of Federalism in Canadian Labour Law," in *The Direction of Labour Policy in Canada* (Montreal: McGill University Industrial Relations Centre), 1977, at p. 58. It can also be argued that the relatively small size of each Canadian jurisdiction makes it easier to administer labour relations law effectively, in contrast to the difficulties faced by the American National Labor Relations Board in regulating almost all of the US workforce: see Peter Bruce, "The Processing of Unfair Labour Practice Complaints in the United States and Ontario," (1990) 45 Relations industrielles 481.

Chapter 2: **The Contract of Employment**

2:100 INTRODUCTION

The contract of employment has been described as the cornerstone of the employment relationship. That undoubtedly remains true in the non-unionized sector, which accounts for a considerable majority of the Canadian workforce. Legally speaking, no one can become the employee of another without making a contract with that person or corporate entity. As we will see in later chapters, the role of the individual contract of employment has been greatly diminished in the unionized sector, but even there, a worker must enter into such a contract in order to be covered by collective bargaining and a collective agreement.

However important the contract of employment may be as a legal phenomenon, the body of law which interprets and applies it has not been very successful at delivering the fruits of industrial citizenship to workers in low to middle-level jobs. In part, this is because of the limited nature of the substantive and procedural rights which the courts have accorded to employees *vis-à-vis* their employers. From a practical standpoint, it is probably even more attributable to the fact that the civil litigation process, which is the main forum for the enforcement of the employment contract, is bedevilled by high costs and long delays and provides a relatively restricted range of remedies. Generally speaking, only higher-level managers and professionals can afford to enforce their common law rights. For realistic protection of their workplace rights and interests, most other workers must look to employment standards legislation (which we deal with in Chapter 12) or to unionization and collective bargaining (which we deal with in Chapters 3 to 10). Indeed, it is largely the failure of the employment contract to deliver industrial justice that has made unionization and employment standards legislation necessary.

With few exceptions, the general principles of contract law govern employment contracts. Those principles assume that a contract — whether it deals with a commercial transaction or with an employment relationship — is a product of relatively free bargaining between parties with relatively equal power. For most workers, however, this assumption is not true; their employer has the power to dictate the terms of employment on a take it or leave it basis. Contract law speaks in the attractive language of freedom of choice and *consensus ad idem*, but the reality is that that the position of employees is usually one of subordination, both before and after the making of the contract.

The principles of contract law assume that the terms of the parties' bargain will reflect their actual intentions, express or implied. The role of the courts is traditionally limited to enforcing the terms of the bargain; that role does not extend to imposing on the parties obligations of the courts' own making. Nonetheless, the courts have fashioned a core of implied obligations which apply to the employee and (perhaps to a lesser extent) to the employer. Those obligations reflect judges' views of what a fair employment relationship involves, having regard to what they see as the requirements of efficient human resource management and the dictates of prevailing social values. Certain implied terms buttress the employer's right to control the day-to-day functioning of the workplace. In this sense, it can be argued that the courts have infused a "status" element into the employment relationship, despite the predominantly contractual basis of that relationship. On the other hand, it can also be argued that in recent years, Canadian courts have been making an effort gradually to move the common law on the contract of employment in a direction that is more mindful of employee rights and interests. As you read through the materials in this chapter, consider whether this has indeed been happening.

Otto Kahn-Freund, "A Note on Status and Contract in British Labour Law" (1967) 30 Mod. L. Rev. 635 at 635, 640–41

The labour law of Great Britain shares with that of the other nations in our orbit of civilisation two essential jurisprudential features: it is based on the contractual foundation of the obligation to work and of the obligation to pay wages, and it is at the same time permeated by a tendency to formulate and to enforce an evergrowing number of imperative norms for the protection of the worker, norms which the parties to the contract cannot validly set aside to the detriment of the economically weaker party. This dual insistence on agreement as the legal basis of at least some of the essential rights and obligations and on mandatory regulation as the source of the content of the relationship has given rise to a jurisprudential dilemma which has so far not been clearly faced in the literature on the subject.

The dilemma arises from the ambiguity of the term 'status' in general jurisprudence. Contemporary writers are fond of reiterating that, under the impact of modern developments, Western society is moving from 'contract' to 'status.' This observation which has been repeated almost mechanically on countless occasions is intended to signify that our society and our law have taken a course in a direction opposite to that traced more than a century ago by Sir Henry Sumner Maine, whose celebrated dictum about the displacement of 'status' by 'contract' is often quoted, but seldom in full. Not infrequently one can sense in the statement that the tendency diagnosed by Maine has been reversed, a conscious or unconscious condemnation of a retrograde evolution. Did not Maine link his famous remark with the analysis of what he called 'progressive societies'? Does not the movement, or rather the alleged movement, from 'contract' to 'status' constitute a 'regression,' a regression from the 'liberal,' 'progressive' environment of the nineteenth century to more primitive forms of social organisation such as those described by Maine in his work? . . .

How can we explain the conceptual confusion between two legal phenomena as different as the imposition of rights and duties irrespective of the volition of the person concerned, and the shaping of a contractual relation into which he has freely entered? Let us admit that in terms of legal policy there may but need not be a common factor. This is the desire to protect persons who, not only, as Maine thought, owing to lack of 'faculty of forming a judgment in their own interests,' but also owing to inferior bargaining power, are liable to be exploited by others. This policy underlies some of the legal provisions or principles which, in Maine's sense, belong to the area of 'status.' They do underlie the law of infants, but certainly not that of aliens. But they also underlie those rules which shape the content of contracts. Yet the legal techniques employed by the two types of legal norms are so fundamentally different that their confusion needs to be explained. Why, then, do English lawyers see a reversion to 'status' in rules which leave the parties free to contract or not to contract, but restrict their freedom to contract except on certain minimum terms?

[Reprinted by permission of Blackwell Publishers.]

Alan Fox, *Beyond Contract: Work, Power and Trust Relations* (London: Faber and Faber, 1974) at 181–84

THE EMPLOYMENT CONTRACT: WAS IT A CONTRACT?

Before we pursue more fully the implications of collective bargaining for our analysis, other questions must be answered if we are to assimilate into that analysis what has been noted so far about the employment relation under industrialization. One of the master symbols of the emergent social order has been seen to be contract. Voluntary agreement forged through bargaining over specific terms, the essence of economic exchange, was seen as the mechanism which articulated atomistic, self-regarding individuals into the collaborative aggregates and linked processes necessary for civil society. How did the employment relation fit into this contractual society and into the ideologies prevalent within it? Can the contract of employment be seen as simply another manifestation of this increasingly pervasive form of exchange?

Certainly one would expect to find a strong ideological drive asserting it to be so. If mediaeval ideology, nourished and sustained by powerful interests, idealized the personalized bonds and commitments of feudal social structure as an equal balance of reciprocal diffuseness, the dominant ideology of newly emergent industrial society might be expected to idealize the employment contract, like all other contracts, in terms of an equal balance of reciprocal specificity. And evidence does indeed suggest a strain in this direction. Laski points to 'a growing sense, both in parliament and in the courts of law, that the nexus between a master and man is purely economic, a relation, not a partnership implying reciprocal social duties.' And did not the evolving law of employment come increasingly during the nineteenth century to emphasize 'the personal and voluntary exchange of freely-bargained promises between two parties equally protected by the civil law alone'? Capitalism indeed 'provides a legitimation of domination which is no longer called down from the lofty heights of cultural tradition but instead summoned up from the base of social labour. The institution of the market, in which private property owners exchange commodities — including the market in which propertyless private individuals exchange their labor power as their only commodity — promises that exchange relations will be and are just owing to equivalence.'

But the impersonal, calculating, low-trust attitudes of economic exchange were never universally accepted by employers, either in practice or in theory. Undoubtedly the general trend throughout the century was towards an 'impersonal management of labor which depended upon the formulation of the conditions of employment and upon elaborate controls which verified the workers' compliance with these conditions.' But persistently in some industries 'management depended upon a personal relationship between an employer and his workers, and hence upon the accidents of personal knowledge as well as upon the well-understood but unformulated relationship of trust which existed traditionally between master and his men.' This persistence might have its roots not only in cultural isolation or inertia but also in a social philosophy which stressed the coincidence of business success with high moral practice and with the principle of the master conducting himself as trustee of his men's 'true best interests.' This philosophy recommending *social* exchange in master-man relations, so far from becoming extinct, was to enjoy a minor revival in circumstances to be examined later.

We must also note the coexistence of ideology celebrating the employment contract as 'the personal and voluntary exchange of freely-bargained promises' with practical attitudes expressing a clear determination that it should be nothing of the kind. Such was the inequality of power between the employer and the individual employee that to describe 'agreements' between them as 'freely-bargained promises' obscured the high probability that for much of the time the latter felt virtually coerced by the former into settling for whatever he could get — a picture hardly consonant with the glories of contract as celebrated by, for example, Spencer. Few of those who lauded the new industrial order were prepared explicitly to emphasize, as did Adam Smith a century before Spencer was writing, that 'it is not . . . difficult to foresee which of the two parties must, upon all ordinary occasions, have the advantage in the dispute, and force the other into a compliance with their terms. . . . In all such disputes the masters can hold out much longer. A landlord, a farmer, a master manufacturer, or merchant, though they did not employ a single workman could generally live a year or two upon the stocks which they have already acquired. Many workmen could not subsist a week, few could subsist a month, and scarce any a year without employment. In the long-run the workman may be as necessary to his master as his master is to him; but the necessity is not so immediate.'

But it was not only that the brute facts of power made the employment contract something a good deal less than contract. Had this been the case we should simply be confronting the commonplace situation of a definition diverging from reality. There was, however, a further ambivalence relating to *definition*. The legal construction which was put upon the contract of employment left it virtually unrecognizable as contract. To appreciate the reason for this the starting point must be that, for employers and their sympathizers, the application of pure contract doctrine to the employment relation, had this ever happened, would have borne a damaging double edge. Certainly there seemed to be a strong legitimizing principle available to hand in the idea, betrayed in practice though it might usually be, of free and equal agents negotiating contractual arrangements on the basis of each seeking to maximize his utilities in competitive markets. The legitimizing strength of this idea could surely be brought to include within its persuasiveness those who con-

tracted to participate as employees in collaborative associations for the production of goods and service, and thereby help to integrate and stabilize the productive system?
[Reprinted by permission.]

2:200 EMPLOYEE STATUS

REFERENCES

Geoffrey England, Innis Christie, & Roderick Wood, *Employment Law in Canada*, 3d ed. (Markham: Butterworths, 1998), c. 2

The law of the employment contract does not regard every exchange of labour for money as constituting an employment relationship. For example, when you have your hair cut, your barber or hairdresser is not your employee, but an independent contractor who runs his or her own business (or perhaps he or she is an employee of the independent contractor who owns the hairdressing shop). The law draws a distinction between employees in the strict sense of the term, to whom the law of the employment contract applies, and independent contractors who are engaged in entrepreneurial activity, to whom the principles of commercial contract law apply. This distinction between employee and independent contractor is absolutely crucial throughout Canadian labour and employment law. Only employees are given rights under the common law of employment, and in normal circumstances only employees are entitled to the protection of employment standards statutes, labour relations statutes, and certain other legislation.

Most people who perform work for others do so as undisputed employees or independent contractors. There is rarely any doubt that an assembly line worker in an automobile manufacturing plant is an employee, or that a plumber who provides services to many different customers is an independent contractor. But there is a significant "gray area" in between. Legislatures have not provided much guidance to the determination of who should be considered an employee, and accordingly courts had to devise their own tests and indicia to assist in this task. The predominant test for the past century has been the *control test*, which identifies employees as those workers who are under the "control" of an employer. Originally, the requirement of control was understood to relate to the manner in which the work was done. This proved to be problematic, as the following excerpt shows. Master and servant are the old-fashioned terms for what we now call employer and employee.

Otto Kahn-Freund, "Servants and Independent Contractors" (1951) 14 Mod. L. Rev. 504 at 505–8

The traditional test was that a person working for another was regarded as a servant if he was 'subject to the command of the master as to the manner in which he shall do his work,' but if the so-called 'master' was only in a position to determine the 'what' and not the 'how' of the services, the substance of the obligation but not the manner of its performance, then the person doing the work was said to be not a servant but an independent contractor, and his contract one for work and labour and not of employment. This distinction was based upon the social conditions of an earlier age: it assumed that the employer of labour was able to direct and instruct the labourer as to the technical meth- ods he should use in performing his work. In a mainly agricultural society and even in the earlier stages of the Industrial Revolution the master could be expected to be superi- or to the servant in the knowledge, skill and experience which had to be brought to bear upon the choice and handling of the tools. The control test was well suited to govern rela- tionships like those between a farmer and an agricultural labourer (prior to agricultural mechanisation), a craftsman and a journeyman, a householder and a domestic servant, and even a factory owner and an unskilled 'hand.' It reflects a state of society in which the ownership of the means of production coincided with the possession of technical knowl- edge and skill and in which that knowledge and skill was largely acquired by being hand- ed down from one generation to the next by oral tradition and not by being systematically imparted in institutions of learning from universities down to technical schools. The con- trol test postulates a combination of managerial and technical functions in the person of the employer, *i.e.*, what to modern eyes appears as an imperfect division of labour. The technical and economic developments of all industrial societies have nullified these assumptions. . . . To say of the captain of a ship, the pilot of an aeroplane, the driver of a railway engine, of a motor vehicle, or of a crane that the employer 'controls' the perform- ance of his work is unrealistic and almost grotesque. But one need not think of situations in which the employee is physically removed from his employer's premises: a skilled engi- neer or toolmaker, draftsman or accountant may as often as not have been engaged just because he possesses that technical knowledge which the employer lacks. . . . No wonder that the Courts found it increasingly difficult to cope with the cases before them by using a legal rule which, as legal rules so often do, had survived the social conditions from which it had been an abstraction. . . .

The control test had to be transformed if it was to remain a working rule and to be more than a mere verbal incantation. . . . the development is in the direction of something like an 'organisation' in preference to a 'control' test. In future the question may perhaps be: 'did the alleged servant form part of the alleged master's organisation?' rather than 'was he subject to his orders in the actual doing of his work?'. . . . in this respect, English law is coming much closer to some of the Continental systems.
[Reprinted by permission of Blackwell Publishers.]

✽ ✽ ✽

Brian A. Langille & Guy Davidov, "Beyond Employees and Independent Contractors: A View from Canada" (1999), 21 Comp. Lab. L. & Pol'y J. 7

III. OUR "TRADITIONAL" PROBLEM

A. The Significance of the Distinction

. . . [T]he concept of "employee" is the "gateway to most (but not all) employment protec- tions at common law and under employment-related legislation." Thus, for example, employment standards acts which regulate the maximum hours of work, overtime, minimum wages, paid vacations, equal pay for equal work, parental leave and more, apply only to "employees." Labor relations acts, which regulate collective bargaining, similarly apply only to "employees." Common-law rights (such as reasonable notice before termination) and obligations (like restriction on competition) generally apply only to employees.

Statutory definitions of "employee" and "employer," if at all existent, are generally not very helpful; they are either vacuous or circular and are often limited to stating exceptions or extensions. Courts were thus intentionally left with the task of inserting content into these concepts and, in effect, determining the boundaries of each regulation's scope of application. Significantly, additional concepts now appear in some pieces of legislation to better define the category of people that should be included within their scope. Terms like "workers" or "dependent contractors" — designed for inclusion of more people within the scope of some protective regulations — can be understood as a response to judges' failure in standing up to their task. Alternatively, they can be seen as providing the courts with better tools for performing this task. It is important to note, however, that even with these statutory additions, the basic distinction between employees and independent contractors — and the courts' task of giving it content — are still fundamental to Canadian labor and employment law and still crucially important.

The employee/independent contractor distinction is becoming significant to more and more workers with the shift from manufacturing to services and with the current changes in the organization of work. If in the past, almost every worker was an indisputable "employee," today the number of cases in doubt is significant and rising. In 1998, out of 14,326,400 employed Canadians, 17.6% were considered self-employed, of which 5.9% were classified as employers and the remaining 11.7% as own-account workers. In addition, at least 28% of the total employment in Canada (approximately four million employees) are in contingent relationships. That includes 9.7% temporary employees, 11% part-time, 5.5% with job tenure of six months or less, and 1.9% multiple job holders. To be clear, in principle, being a temporary, part-time, casual, multiple job holder, or a homeworker does not in itself affect an employee's status; the regular tests as described below apply. But such relationships often put the workers in a position of susceptibility to employers' manipulation and evasion as regards their rights. This includes attempts to exclude the whole relationship from the employment apparatus.

B. Purposive Interpretation

It is a basic rule in statutory interpretation — and as we have noted, a truism about language in general — that the meaning of words be determined with regard to the context and purpose in which and for which they are used. Since the term "employee" appears in different statutes and common-law rules, it may very well have a different meaning in each of these contexts. For example, one can be an employee for purposes of employment standards, but an independent contractor as far as vicarious liability is concerned. . . .

The employee/independent contractor distinction is found in tort law, tax law and other fields, each with very different goals behind it. However, as far as most labor and employment law regulations are concerned, there seems to be one common idea that sheds light on them all — the protection of workers. The accompanying assumption is the existence of an employer that can and should take responsibility for these workers (now "employees"). The basic purpose of the employee/independent contractor distinction in labor and employment law can thus be understood as distinguishing those workers who are in need of a particular sort of protection (and have an identifiable employer) from those who are in a position to protect themselves in the particular regard at issue. There are, of course, specific goals to specific regulations and these should also be taken into account. But the basic purpose of protecting workers that are in need of and are entitled to certain forms of protection *vis-à-vis* their employers unites them all. We will have more to say on that at the concluding part of this essay.

C. The "Fourfold" Test and Other Syntheses

The formulation most frequently used by Canadian courts to determine the existence of employment relationships is that articulated by Lord Wright in a 1947 decision [*Montreal v. Montreal Locomotive Works*]:

> In earlier cases a single test, such as the presence or absence of control, was often relied on to determine whether the case was one of master and servant, mostly in order to decide issues of tortious liability on the part of the master or superior. In the more complex conditions of modern industry, more complicated tests have often been applied. It has been suggested that a fourfold test would in some cases be more appropriate, a complex involving (1) control; (2) ownership of the tools; (3) chance of profit; (4) risk of loss. Control in itself is not always conclusive. . . . In many cases the question can only be settled by examining the whole of the various elements which constitute the relationship between the parties.

These four indicia, in fact, boil down to two questions: (1) whether the worker is controlled by the employer/client; and (2) whether the worker is economically independent, that is, has the characteristics of an independent businessperson (with particular attention given to the chance of profit and risk of loss to this effect). Ownership of expensive tools is simply one indicator of economic independence — creating, to some extent, risk of loss and chance of profit or an ability to take the tools and work elsewhere.

Much attention is still given in the caselaw to the age-old criterion of control. However, the application of this test has changed dramatically over the years. Today, Canadian courts hardly ever settle for the examination of direct control over the worker's activities. It is widely recognized that employment relations often exist without such direction whether because the employee is a specialized professional, because the work requires the use of discretion or simply because it is performed outside of the employer's premises. Instead of direct control, courts have shifted attention to the existence of what may be called "bureaucratic" or "administrative" control. The power to discipline the worker, for example, or to promote her, to give a contrary example, are illustrative of this overall control within the relationship.

Similar developments occurred in Quebec, which follow the civil-law tradition. The main criterion for the existence of [the] employer-employee relationship in Quebec is the existence of "legal subordination" of the employee to the employer. Originally, "legal subordination" encompassed the notion of direction and actual control by a party over the employee's day-to-day work. More recently, however, attention has shifted from control over how the work is done to more general control over the agreed regularity with which it is done and its quality. In practice, this is much like the "bureaucratic" or "administrative" control mentioned above. But the concept of "subordination" — the shift to the worker's point of view — serves to focus attention on why this criterion is relevant to the identification of workers in need of a particular sort of protection. The subordination of some workers means that they are unable to freely and fully pursue their goals and realize themselves to make (or at least take part in) the decisions that directly affect their lives.

The second question mentioned above — whether the worker is economically independent and, in particular, whether he assumes the risk of loss and chance of profit — has gained increased attention alongside control. It is, in fact, designed to examine the degree of dependence of the worker *vis-à-vis* the employer, as a matter of economic reality, on the assumption that dependence puts the worker (now employee) in need of protection. In some cases, the chance of loss or profit has been the decisive criterion; for example, a postmistress in a small community was held to be an independent contractor because she was paid on a commission basis, and "therefore, the more efficient she is, the more money she makes." This can be problematic since the allocation of risks is open to employers' manipulation and the shifting of risks to the worker, by an employer attempting to avoid employment responsibilities, usually leaves the worker with the same need of protection (if not more).

With this problem in mind, it is perhaps better to understand the loss/profit criterion more generally as part of an inquiry into the existence of economic dependency. If this is the ultimate question, courts can more easily bypass employers' manipulation and focus on the economic reality of the relationship. Indeed, in some of the cases, courts have shown willingness to find employment relationships even when the worker assumed most of the risks, but was in fact still in a position of economic dependency.

In short, it seems fair to conclude that the determination of "employee" status in Canada generally rests on two grounds: control and economic dependency. Indeed, it is interesting to note that another test which is sometimes mentioned in the caselaw, the "business integration" or "organization" test, leads in fact to the same two bases. The organization test finds its origins in Lord Denning's statement that,

> under a contract of service, a man is employed as part of the business, and his work is done as an integral part of the business; whereas, under a contract for services, his work, although done for the business, is not integrated into it, but is only accessory to it.

. . . We have seen that both control/subordination and economic dependency are reasonably related to the basic purpose of identifying workers in need of certain forms of protection (with an identifiable employer). Unfortunately, judges sometimes seem to forget this basic goal and in such cases, the application of the tests tends to be rigid and formalistic, with the risk of excluding some workers without real reasoning. . . .

IV. OUR "NEW" PROBLEMS

We have seen that the concept of "employee" has been used to distinguish workers who are in need of certain sorts of protection. The accompanying assumption has always been that there is an identifiable and specific "employer."

This framework indeed fits most of the relationships between workers and their employers/clients. Yet a growing number of workers is left outside of this framework. These are the independent contractors who are in need of similar protection. They are independent, in the sense that they serve different clients and can hardly be seen as dependent on any of them, and yet their position *vis-à-vis* these clients is not one that seems distinguishable from an employee with a single employer. Although independent — and hence considered independent contractors by current definitions — they are in need of protection much like employees. Unlike other independent contractors who are self-dependent entrepreneurs, these workers have such a weak market stance that, like employees, they cannot be said to be self-dependent.

The existence of these non-self-dependent contractors is not entirely new. In the media industry, for example, "freelance" reporters and photographers with very little bargaining power (or any other ability to protect themselves, for that matter) have been quite a common phenomenon for many years, in Canada as elsewhere. But the New Economy has brought a significant rise in such cases, a trend that can be expected to continue and intensify. The plight of the non-self-dependent contractors must now move to the forefront.

A. The New Economy and the Organization of Work

The last two decades of the 20th century have seen dramatic changes in the organization of work. Prominent scholars have already told the story of these changes from a variety of different angles. There is now a proliferation of part-time, casual and temporary (or otherwise short-term) arrangements, more multiple job holders, and more people who work at home. There is much less employment security; in fact, the tacit commitment to long-term relations, which was so central to the industrial order in the post-war era, is said to be an endangered species. Employees who made significant job-specific investments now face a constant risk of losing their job, even in good times. Once they lose their job, they often have no choice but to take a "bad" job based on a contingent relationship and offering less pay, no benefits and no prospects.

More generally, globalization brings with it pressures towards outsourcing and subcontracting. Businesses prefer to focus on core competencies and contract out as much as possible to others. This is beneficial for them for a number of reasons. First, subcontractors sometimes specialize in the specific field and achieve efficiencies that the ordering firm cannot. Second, they can often cut labor costs more easily thanks to their location, a non-unionized labor force and by taking the risks of ignoring labor laws (something which a large, established firm presumably cannot do). And third, due to disparities in bargaining power, subcontractors will often take some of the risks off the ordering firm's back. In most cases, work is subcontracted to firms, and performed by employees of those firms. But sometimes, the subcontractors are merely self-employed workers.

It is in this general context — less security, more contingent relations and [a]tendency towards contracting out work — that some workers find themselves self-employed, many of them involuntarily. To be sure, some of these cases are within the "traditional" problem. When employers misclassify employees as independent contractors to avoid employment responsibilities and achieve better flexibility, the regular distinctions are sufficient (assuming they are applied sensibly and purposively). Such workers should simply be considered employees. When workers are economically dependent upon a specific employer, they should be protected rather than left alone in the "free" market. Indeed, in Canada, such dependent workers enjoy access to collective bargaining and, as we have argued above, should generally enjoy the protection of employment standards legislation as well (at least in part).

Others, however — the non-self-dependent contractors — are not dependent upon any identifiable employer. Our interest here lies with this specific group of workers.

B. Non-Self-Dependent Contractors

It is difficult to come up with data about the number of non-self-dependent contractors. While it is clear that the proportion of own-account self-employed in Canada is rising, we currently lack the critical information that might tell us how many of them are not sufficiently capable of protecting themselves — how many of them are in need of collective bargaining, and perhaps mandatory employment standards, just like employees. A couple of specific examples, while anecdotal, might shed some light on the intensification of this problem.

First, consider the media and entertainment industries. As already noted, the existence of "freelancing" arrangements for photographers and reporters is not new. But it is certainly proliferating; a recent survey of the International Federation of Journalists covering 98 countries found that "the freelance sector was continuing to grow as a proportion of the total journalistic community," with approximately a third now working in freelance capacity. . . .

Similarly, a study of the British book publishing industry revealed that publishing houses increasingly externalize jobs that have low task interdependency, use relatively inexpensive equipment and are cerebral rather than manual in nature. Proofreaders and editors have been externalized — usually involuntarily — and are now likely to work from home as self-employed. The study shows that these workers are typically heavily reliant upon a single client, sometimes their former employer, for over half their work, and upon two clients for over 80% of their work. Their hourly pay is low, and of course they have no holidays, sick leave or pension rights. These proofreaders and editors have lost their constant income-flow and they now find it difficult to deal with uneven "feast or famine" flows of work. The prevalence of such arrangements is expected to continue to grow together with continued restructuring in the industry.

A second example concerns truck owner-operators. While some of them are considered "dependent contractors" in Canada, and hence "employees" for collective bargaining purposes, others have a number of different clients and are accordingly treated as independent contractors. These workers, however, usually lack the bargaining power necessary to reach fair wages and working conditions. Although the demand for truckers is rising — the truck-ing industry in Canada expanded by 5% annually from 1990 to 1998, compared with 1% for airlines and railways and a drop of 1% for marine shipping — owner-operators were not able to translate this demand into better contracts. This problem received public attention in Canada during the early months of February 2000, when protests of independent owner-operators erupted across the country as a result of significant rises in fuel prices. . . . [Reprinted by permission.]

✻ ✻ ✻

For a somewhat different approach to the problem, see Judy Fudge, Eric Tucker, & Leah Vosko, "Employee or Independent Contractor? Charting the Legal Significance of the Distinction in Canada" (2003), 10 C.L.E.L.J 193.

2:300 ESTABLISHING THE EMPLOYMENT RELATIONSHIP

In section 2:100 above, Alan Fox speaks of the common law's assumption that contracts involve "the personal and voluntary exchange of freely-bargained promises." In some contexts, including employment, this assumption was and is at odds with the realities of economic power. As we will see in Chapter 13, because common law judges contin-ued to be reluctant to override freedom of contract, the legislature ultimately intervened in employment and other contexts to suppress discrimination based on religion, race, gender, disability, and various other grounds.

The next case, *Seneca College v. Bhadauria*, considers whether such legislative inter-vention pre-empts subsequent attempts by the courts to change common law doctrine in order to right wrongs which they had earlier condoned. This is a question of particu-lar importance in labour law. In contrast to the courts' historic unwillingness to intrude on freedom of contract, they were very willing to suppress efforts by workers to advance their interests by striking or picketing. Here too the legislature ultimately intervened, and here too questions remain about the relationship between such legislation and the common law — questions that we will return to in Chapter 8.

Thus, *Seneca College v. Bhadauria* is not only about race, or the refusal of an employ-er to hire a prospective employee, or the interpretative interplay between common law and legislation. It is also about the values espoused and the roles played by courts, leg-islatures, and administrative tribunals — values and roles which shift, conflict, and con-verge over time and across various issues. We will return to these issues in Chapters 11, 12, and 13, where we take a closer look at legislated minimum standards and their rela-tionship to the common law (as well as their relationship to collective bargaining).

Seneca College of Applied Arts and Technology v. Bhadauria, [1981] 2 S.C.R. 181 at 182–95

LASKIN C.J.C.: The issue in this appeal is whether this Court should affirm the recogni-tion by the Ontario Court of Appeal of a new intentional tort. The tort was recognized to protect a plaintiff against unjustified invasion of his or her interest not to be discriminated against in respect of a prospect of employment on grounds of race or national origin. The case was argued in the Ontario Court of Appeal on the alternative footing that a civil right of action flowed directly from a breach of *The Ontario Human Rights Code*. . . . Wilson J.A. having found that the tort arose at common law through the invocation of the public policy expressed in the Code as supplying applicable standards, refrained from addressing the alternative argument.

In this Court, considerable emphasis, pro and con, was laid on the question whether a breach of the Code could itself be sufficient to establish civil liability without calling in aid common law principles relating to intentional invasions of legally protected interests. It is common ground that there is no known case in this country, at least in common law jurisdictions, where such a tort is recognized on either of the two grounds on which it was posited by the plaintiff-respondent; nor were counsel able to produce any instance in a comparable foreign jurisdiction.

In my opinion, the attempt of the respondent to hold the judgment in her favour on the ground that a right of action springs directly from a breach of *The Ontario Human Rights Code* cannot succeed. The reason lies in the comprehensiveness of the Code in its administrative and adjudicative features, the latter including a wide right of appeal to the Courts on both fact and law. I will come to the provisions of the Code shortly. For the moment, and for the purposes of this case, it is enough to say that the naked legal question which is raised here came before the Courts below and is before this Court on a motion by way of demurrer under Ontario Rule 126. The facts alleged in the statement of claim are to be taken, therefore, as provable according to their recitation. Of course, no statement of defence has as yet been delivered.

The facts alleged disclose that the plaintiff is a highly educated woman of East Indian origin with an earned Ph.D. degree in mathematics. She holds a valid Ontario teaching certificate and has had seven years' teaching experience in the field of mathematics. In response to newspaper advertisements placed by the defendant College, the plaintiff made some ten separate applications for a teaching position in the period between June 28, 1974 and May 19, 1978. Although letters were sent to her by the College in response to her applications, telling her she would be contacted for an interview, she was never given an interview nor any reason for the rejection of her applications. She alleged that the positions for which she applied were filled by others without her high qualifications but who were not of East Indian origin. She claimed that there was discrimination against her because of her origin and that the College was in breach of a duty not to discriminate against her, and also in breach of s. 4 of *The Ontario Human Rights Code*, as amended. She claimed damages for being deprived of teaching opportunities at the College in which she was still interested and for being deprived of the opportunity to earn a teaching salary. Moreover, she suffered mental distress, frustration, loss of self-esteem and dignity, and lost time in repeatedly applying for advertised positions for which she was denied the opportunity to compete. . . .

What we have here, if the Court of Appeal is correct in its conclusion, is a species of an economic tort, new in its instance and founded, even if indirectly, on a statute enacted in an area outside a fully recognized area of common law duty: see Williams, 'The Effect of

Penal Legislation in the Law of Tort'. . . . It is one thing to apply a common law duty of care to standards of behaviour under a statute; that is simply to apply the law of negligence in the recognition of so-called statutory torts. It is quite a different thing to create by judicial fiat an obligation — one in no sense analogous to a duty of care in the law of negligence — to confer an economic benefit upon certain persons, with whom the alleged obligor has no connection, and solely on the basis of a breach of statute which itself provides comprehensively for remedies for its breach.

It was conceded that the relevant provisions in this case, if applicable, are in s. 4(l)(a) and (b) which read as follows:

4.—(1) No person shall,

(a) refuse to refer or to recruit any person for employment;

(b) dismiss or refuse to employ or to continue to employ any person;

On the facts here, taken as provable, there was a refusal to recruit for employment and, certainly, a refusal to employ. However, a refusal to enter into contract relations or perhaps more accurately, a refusal even to consider the prospect of such relations has not been recognized at common law as giving rise to any liability in tort.

None of the cases considered in the Ontario Court of Appeal, all arising at common law and under the civil law of Quebec, relate to a refusal to recruit or to employ. They exhibit a strict *laisser-faire* policy, even where the business or service whose facilities were denied on the ground of colour or race or ancestry was under government licence. . . . In those cases where a plaintiff succeeded in his claim for damages for denial of services or accommodation on the ground of colour or race, recovery was based on an innkeepers liability.
. . .

The view taken by the Ontario Court of Appeal is a bold one and may be commended as an attempt to advance the common law. In my opinion, however, this is foreclosed by the legislative initiative which overtook the existing common law in Ontario and established a different regime which does not exclude the Courts but rather makes them part of the enforcement machinery under the Code.

For the foregoing reasons, I would hold that not only does the Code foreclose any civil action based directly upon a breach thereof but it also excludes any common law action based on an invocation of that public policy expressed in the Code. The Code itself has laid out the procedures for vindication of that public policy, procedures which the plaintiff-respondent did not see fit to use.

The appeal is, accordingly, allowed, the judgment of the Ontario Court of Appeal is set aside and the judgment of Callaghan J. dismissing the action is restored. . . .

2:310 Where Do the Terms of Employment Come From?

REFERENCES

Geoffrey England, Innis Christie, & Roderick Wood, *Employment Law in Canada*, 3d ed. (Markham: Butterworths, 1998), c. 7

This section, and section 2:320, canvass the problem of what can be called the construction of the contract of employment.

It is unusual for employment contracts to contain comprehensive express provisions on the terms and conditions of employment, except perhaps for top executives, professionals, elite athletes, and entertainers. More commonly, employers put into human resource manuals or other such documents certain terms that they intend to be observed. Then, when a dispute arises, one party or the other may argue that those terms have been incorporated into the employment contract. This can give rise to a minefield of legal difficulties.

Ellison v. Burnaby Hospital Society (1992), 42 C.C.E.L. 239 at 241 (B.C.S.C.)

The plaintiff was initially hired by the defendant as a general duty registered nurse in March 1967. She was gradually promoted within the hospital until she was appointed director of nursing, long term care, in 1989. She remained in that position until she was dismissed on December 10, 1991 following a structural reorganization of nursing administration at the hospital. At the time of her dismissal the plaintiff was 59 years of age and had served the defendant for almost 25 years. . . .

The first question to be resolved in this case is whether the defendant's benefits policy forms part of the contract of employment between the plaintiff and the defendant. The benefits policy was introduced by the defendant in 1988, some 21 years after the plaintiff commenced her employment with the defendant and one year before she was promoted to the position of director of nursing. The plaintiff acknowledges that she received a copy of that document in 1988. She has no recollection of reading it, although she says that she may have glanced at some parts of it. She says that she put it in a folder in a drawer together with other documents related to her employment, such as pay stubs and information on superannuation. She specifically states that she did not know that the benefits policy provided for termination and severance.

The defendant relies on the evidence of Mr. Waldron, vice-president of hospital services for the defendant, who says that the benefits policy forms part of the plaintiff's contract of employment with the defendant. No evidence is given in support of that bald statement. Mr. Waldron also states that he thought he noticed the plaintiff's husband carrying a copy of the benefits policy at a meeting Mr. Waldron attended with the plaintiff on December 2, 1991. Assuming that this is so, and it is not clear that it is, there is no suggestion that either the plaintiff or Mr. Waldron referred to the benefits policy as being part of the contract of employment at that meeting or at any other time prior to the plaintiff's dismissal.

The defendant submits that a person in the plaintiff's position of responsibility must have been aware of the terms of the benefits policy. The defendant points to the fact that the plaintiff was aware that certain of her health benefits were set out in a separate document which she received from the defendant, and that it is reasonable to assume that she was equally aware of the benefits set out in this policy. The defendant says that by claiming some of the benefits which are referred to in the benefits policy the plaintiff must be taken to have accepted the entire policy as part of her contract of employment.

The benefits policy itself does not state that it forms part of the contract of employment between the defendant and any [of] its managerial or non-contract personnel. The policy is divided into 23 parts beginning with an introduction which provides, in part, as follows:

> Welcome to Burnaby Hospital. This booklet, along with the Burnaby Hospital Personnel Information Brochure, has been prepared to describe the complete benefit packages available to all managerial and non-contract personnel along with pertinent information which will make you aware of the current practices of our Hospital.

The policy goes on to describe various benefits provided by the defendant, and it makes several references to other sources of information relating to benefits, including brochures and the employee resources department. The policy is put together as just that — a statement of policy and information. It is not put together with the precision or certainty of terms which one would expect of a document which is intended to create a contractual relationship.

The relevant law with respect to this issue is set out in the case of *Starcevich v. Woodward's Ltd.* . . . . The headnote of that case, which accurately reflects the judgment, provides as follows:

> Before a 'policy' can form part of a contract of employment, there must be evidence that the policy was accepted by both the employer and the employee as a term of the employment contract, and the onus in this respect rests on the party seeking to rely on the policy as a term of the contract. One party cannot unilaterally impose a contractual term on the other. The fact that the plaintiff was aware of the policy, and in fact applied it to others in the course of his employment, did not establish that he accepted the policy as a term of his own employment contract.

Similar statements are found in other cases. . . . [In] *Rahemtulla v. Vanfred Credit Union* . . . , the court stated that the fact that the employee had continued to work after learning of the policy did not lead to the conclusion that the employee had accepted the terms of the policy as part of her contract of employment. The court also stated that there was no evidence that the parties intended the policy to constitute a binding contractual relationship between them.

The defendant submits that the cases referred to by the plaintiff are distinguishable, and it relies on the case of *Greene v. Chrysler Canada Ltd.* . . . which was upheld in the B.C. Court of Appeal for the reasons given by the trial judge. . . . In *Greene* the trial judge found that a notice of lay-off given by the defendant did not amount to a dismissal, apparently because the plaintiff had been provided with two booklets dealing with compensation and benefits which specifically provided for lay-offs, and which the court concluded formed part of the contract of employment. The Court of Appeal concluded that such a finding was justified.

There is no question that a policy or benefits package of an employer can form part of the contract of employment if it is clear that the employer and employee intended it to do so. In this case, however, I am not persuaded that the policy formed part of the contract of employment between the plaintiff and the defendant. The policy was instituted long after the plaintiff was originally hired by the defendant, albeit before she received her last promotion. The policy was simply given to the plaintiff without any request that she read it, or any other indication that the defendant was relying on it as forming part of the contract of employment. The plaintiff glanced at the policy, but did not in any way communicate to the defendant that she accepted the statements set out in the policy as terms of her employment. The language of the policy is not reflective of a contractual document, but rather of an information package.

Since the benefits policy did not form part of the contract of employment between the plaintiff and the defendant, the court must look to the common law to determine the reasonable period of notice which the plaintiff was entitled. . . .

2:320 Implied Terms

REFERENCES

Geoffrey England, Innis Christie, & Roderick Wood, *Employment Law in Canada*, 3d. ed. (Markham: Butterworths, 1998), sections 10.11 to 10.74, 11.49 to 11.178

General contract law principles recognize a difference between implied terms of fact and implied terms of law. Terms of fact are implied on the basis that they reflect the unexpressed factual intentions of both parties. Terms of law are implied on the basis of what the court regards as being reasonable for the parties as a matter of policy. In reality, however, the line between the two categories is frequently blurred; courts sometimes use their view of the parties' unexpressed factual intentions as a basis for imposing on the parties rights and obligations that the judge deems fair and reasonable. A good example is found in the following case.

McNamara v. Alexander Centre Industries Limited (2001), 53 O.R. (3d) 481 (C.A.)

MACPHERSON J.A. (for the court):

A. INTRODUCTION

When an employee is wrongfully dismissed, he or she is entitled to damages as compensation for salary or wages during a reasonable notice period. Depending on the employee's health, the employee may also be entitled to receive disability payments pursuant to the employment contract. The issue on this appeal concerns the relationship between those two potential forms of compensation to the dismissed employee. Specifically, the question is, can the employee retain both payments, or should the disability payments be deducted from the damages awarded for the wrongful dismissal? The resolution of this issue requires a careful consideration and application of the decision of the Supreme Court of Canada in *Sylvester v. British Columbia* . . .

. . .

The appellant Alexander Centre Industries Limited ("ACI") is a company based in Sudbury. It has been engaged in the construction materials supply business for more than 65 years. The owner and Chief Executive Officer of ACI was Cliff Fielding. His son, Jim Fielding, was also involved in the business.

The respondent Kenneth McNamara ("McNamara"), a young chartered accountant and assistant professor at Laurentian University, was hired by ACI in 1971 as its controller. His starting salary was $22,000 and he received the regular benefits, including disability coverage, available to ACI employees. During his career at ACI, McNamara made no direct monetary payments towards those benefits; ACI paid for all the coverage.

McNamara became Vice President of Finance at ACI in 1977 and President in 1986. Between 1990 and 1995 his compensation, by way of salary and bonus, ranged from $175,000 to $267,000.

In the summer of 1995, ACI dismissed McNamara. The circumstances around the dismissal are troubling and disappointing. On July 24, McNamara attended a meeting with the owner, Cliff Fielding. He brought a letter from Dr. Anderson which advised Mr. Fielding that, for medical reasons, McNamara should "be off the job indefinitely." Mr. Fielding took the letter and said something to the effect "your health is important; take care of it."

A week later, on August 1, without further communication and without warning, a letter from Mr. Fielding was delivered by hand to McNamara at his home. It said in part:

> I am distressed to receive the medical information and to learn that your condition will prevent you from ever returning to work at Alexander Centre Industries Limited. It is with regret that I accept that reality and your leaving the company. Obviously, you will be entitled to benefits of the disability insurance coverage with London Life.

McNamara, who had been advised by his family physician, Dr. Bakker, the day before, July 31, that he should stay away from work for two more weeks, contacted ACI's office and tried to arrange a meeting with Mr. Fielding. No meeting took place. McNamara and Dr. Anderson wrote letters to Mr. Fielding explaining that McNamara could return to work in two weeks. ACI did not respond to these letters. McNamara never returned to work. Nor did ACI offer or provide any severance pay to McNamara.

McNamara applied for and received long term disability payments from London Life. He received payments totalling $163,000 from August 1995 to January 15, 1997.

McNamara also filed a complaint for sums owing under the Employment Standards Act, R.S.O. 1990, c. E.14. After a hearing, the Employment Standards Officer ordered ACI to pay McNamara $109,056.73, representing his entitlement to termination notice and severance payments. ACI paid this amount to McNamara in September 1997.

. . .

McNamara brought an action for wrongful dismissal against ACI. At the opening of the trial in April 2000, ACI admitted that its dismissal of McNamara was without cause. Accordingly, the trial proceeded only on the issue of damages. . . .

The trial judge awarded McNamara 24 months compensation in lieu of notice and an additional two months salary because the manner in which ACI dismissed McNamara fell within the category of 'bad faith discharge' as articulated by the Supreme Court of Canada in *Wallace v. United Grain Growers Ltd.* . . . . The trial judge deducted the statutory payments of $109,056.73 from the damages award; this was not a contested matter. However, the trial judge did not deduct the long term disability payments totalling $163,000 from the damages award.

. . .

C. ISSUE

The issue on this appeal is whether the trial judge erred by failing to deduct disability payments McNamara received during the notice period from the damages he received for wrongful dismissal during that period.

D. ANALYSIS

. . . the resolution of this appeal turns almost entirely on the application of the principles enunciated in Sylvester.

In *Sylvester*, an employee of the Government of British Columbia was terminated during a period when he was receiving disability benefits. He received disability payments from the Government's own disability plan. The entire cost of the disability plan was borne by the Government.

The sole issue on the appeal to the Supreme Court of Canada was whether the disability benefits Sylvester received during the notice period should be deducted from the damages he was awarded for wrongful dismissal. The court held that the deduction should take place. Major J., writing for a unanimous court, framed the issue in this fashion, at p. 321:

> Disability benefits . . . are contractual. The question of deductibility therefore turns on the terms of the employment contract and the intention of the parties.

Applying this test, Major J. found that the employment contract did not provide for an employee to receive both disability benefits and damages for wrongful dismissal; moreover, he did not think that such an intention could be inferred.

It is important to note that in *Sylvester* the employer paid both salary and disability benefits. Moreover, the terms of the disability plans established that disability benefits were intended to be a substitute for salary. These are important facts because, near the end of his judgment, Major J. stated a caveat, at pp. 324–25:

> There may be cases where an employee will seek benefits in addition to damages for wrongful dismissal on the basis that the *disability benefits* are *akin to benefits from a private insurance plan for which the employee has provided consideration.* This is not the case here. It is not in dispute that the respondent did not make any contributions to the [short-term and long-term disability plans]. *The issue whether disability benefits should be deducted from damages for wrongful dismissal where the employee has contributed to the disability benefits plan was not before the Court.* [Emphasis added.]

In the present appeal, the entire caveat, and especially the underlined passages, are in play. The trial judge carefully considered *Sylvester*, but thought there were two important distinguishing features between Sylvester's and McNamara's situations.

The first distinction flowed from the "akin to benefits from a private insurance plan" component of Major J.'s caveat. The trial judge said:

Firstly, the plan at Alexander Centre Industries Limited was purchased from a private third party. When the employee was in receipt of benefits, it was not the employer who was paying the employee. The payment came directly from London Life to the employee.

. . .

In my view, this distinction is sound. Although Major J. did not say so explicitly, he must have enunciated the caveat, with its "akin to benefits from a private insurance plan" language, with an eye to the long line of cases culminating in *Cunningham v. Wheeler*, which permits an employee to keep both the damages the employee receives in a tort action and the disability benefits received pursuant to a disability insurance policy, provided the employee contributed in some fashion to the policy.

The trial judge in the present action recognized that in *Sylvester* both salary and disability payments came directly from the employer's pocket whereas in this case ACI was responsible for McNamara's salary but London Life would pay the disability benefits. In my view, she was right to think that this was an important difference. It is one thing to be concerned, as the court was in *Sylvester*, with double recovery when all the money comes from a single source, the employer. The concern should be significantly diminished when the double recovery flows from clear entitlement to two different and legitimate recoveries (damages for wrongful dismissal and disability benefits) *and* neither payor would be responsible for paying even a penny more than it should pay pursuant to its individual obligation).

The second distinction, flowing again from Major J.'s caveat, the trial judge drew between Sylvester's and McNamara's situations was this:

> Secondly, Major J. specifically notes that there was no consideration by the employee for this benefit. Evidence from the Plaintiff, in this case, was directly to the contrary and there was no evidence from the Defendant on the point. McNamara stated that the question of benefits was integral to his discussions on salary at the time of hire, that he would not have accepted the salary but for the benefit package as part of the overall compensation scheme.

As the trial judge pointed out, McNamara's evidence on this crucial point was not contradicted. . . .

In my view, the trial judge was correct to accept that there was in effect a trade-off between McNamara's salary and benefit package, including disability benefits, when he negotiated his employment contract in 1971.

However, accepting the trial judge's finding of fact, . . . do the terms of the employment contract or the intention of the parties suggest deductibility or non-deductibility of disability benefits from damages for wrongful dismissal?

The contract component of this question is easy to answer: there is nothing in the employment contract to suggest an answer either way.

The intention of the parties component is more difficult to answer. It is obvious that the intention of the parties in 1971 would have been that if McNamara worked he would receive a salary and if he could not work due to his illness he would receive disability benefits. But what would McNamara and ACI have intended with respect to this scenario: after 24 years and rising to become President, McNamara becomes ill and within a week is fired? What should he receive by way of damages for wrongful dismissal and disability benefits? Could he keep both? Frankly, I doubt that the parties would have considered any of this in 1971.

Fortunately, in *Sylvester*, Major J. addressed this problem, at p. 324:

> The parties to an employment contract can obviously agree that the employee is to receive both disability benefits and damages for wrongful dismissal. *There may also be cases in which this intention can be inferred*. [Emphasis added.]

What intention can be inferred from the circumstances of the ACI-McNamara employment relationship? It seems to me that there are two possibilities.

If the disability benefits *are* deducted, McNamara will receive his full salary for the entire notice period. However, that salary will be less than it might have been if he had not bargained a trade-off between salary and benefits, and he will forfeit all of the disability payments. ACI, on the other, will derive a huge benefit from the deductibility scenario, solely because it chose an employee's new disability, after 24 years of loyal service, as the moment and reason to fire him. ACI's windfall for acting abominably will be $163,000.

If the disability benefits *are not* deducted, McNamara will be treated generously (salary plus disability payments), but not for a long period of time; the disability payments ended after 17 months, and the damages for wrongful dismissal covered his salary for 26 months (including the *Wallace* two month penalty). ACI, on the other hand, will pay precisely what the law requires it to pay — damages in lieu of reasonable notice for wrongful dismissal.

In my view, in an office in Sudbury in 1971, a *reasonable* employer and a *reasonable* prospective employee, if they turned their minds to the 'what happens if ACI decides to fire McNamara the instant he becomes disabled' scenario, would have agreed on the second result. I so infer. In my view, the reasons of the trial judge are consistent with the same inference. . . .

✻ ✻ ✻

Particular terms may at first be implied into employment contracts on the basis of a judicially inferred intention, but may then be so widely accepted in the relevant labour market that they become part of the 'climate of contracting' which workers and employers do in fact intend to govern their relationship.

It has been suggested that a 'golden thread' in employment contract law has been the courts' desire to facilitate the prevailing system of work organization and human resources management, and to reflect society's moral vision of how work relations ought to be conducted. Nowhere is this more true than in the process of reading terms into the contract. Over the years, the courts have formulated a standardized set of implied rights and duties that reflect the judges' prevailing conception of an ideal employment relationship. The content of those implied terms is not static, but is continually refashioned by the courts to reflect changing conditions in the workplace and society at large.

In theory, the parties are perfectly free to modify such implied terms by negotiating other provisions. The employment contract thus retains a residual free-contract dimension. In practice, however, the parties do not often modify standardized implied terms, especially those favouring the employer. Thus, the code of implied terms gives a strong "status" flavour to employment contract law.

The bedrock obligation on the employee is the implied duty of fidelity. This duty originated in the law of master and servant that predated the Industrial Revolution. At that time, work relations were highly paternalistic. The master, who often shared his home with his workers in the cottage industries, could expect the highest standards of obedience and loyalty. The courts entrenched this expectation in the extensive common law duty of fidelity, which was implied into employment contracts during and after the Industrial Revolution. It gave employers extensive control over workers, especially in the context of the mass production methods that came to dominate the factory system in the late nineteenth and twentieth centuries.

Today, the duty of fidelity remains the cornerstone of employer control over the worker. A leading English authority is *Secretary of State for Employment v. Associated Society of Locomotive Engineers and Firemen and Others (No. 2)*, [1972] 2 All E.R. 949 (C.A.). Railway workers sought to put pressure on their employer by "working to rule" — that is, by applying existing work rules more meticulously than usual, with the result that their work was done more slowly than usual. Under the labour relations legislation in force in England at the time, the legal issue was whether this conduct constituted a breach of the workers' common law contracts of employment. Buckley L.J. said, at p. 972:

> Assuming in the [union's] favour that the direction to work to rule avoided any specific direction to commit a breach of any express term of the contract, the instruction was, nevertheless, directed, and is acknowledged to have been directed, to rendering it impossible, or contributing to the impossibility, to carry on the [employer's] commercial activity upon a sound commercial basis, if at all. The object of the instruction was to frustrate the very commercial object for which the contracts of employment were made. It struck at the foundation of the consensual intentions of the parties to those contracts, and amounted, in my judgment, to an instruction to commit what were clearly breaches or abrogations of those contracts. These are or would be, in my judgment, breaches of an implied term to serve the employer faithfully within the requirements of the contract. It does not mean that the employer could require a man to do anything which lay outside his obligations under the contract, such as to work excess hours of work or to work an unsafe system of work or anything of that kind, but it does mean that within the terms of the contract the employee must serve the employer faithfully with a view to promoting those commercial interests for which he is employed. The contrary view is, in my opinion, one which proceeds upon much too narrow and formalistic an approach to the legal relations of employer and employee and is an approach which, I may perhaps add, seems to me to be unlikely to promote goodwill or confidence between the parties.

The employee's duty of fidelity remains a bulwark of modern Canadian employment law. In *Stein v. British Columbia (Housing Management Commission)* (1992), 65 B.C.L.R. (2d) 181 at 185 (C.A.), Hutcheon J.A. said:

> an employer has a right to determine how his business shall be conducted. He may lay down any procedures he thinks advisable so long as they are neither contrary to law, nor dishonest nor dangerous to the health of the employees and are within the ambit of the job for which any particular employee was hired. It is not for the employee nor for the court to consider the wisdom of the procedures. The employer is the boss and it is an essential implied term of every employment contract that, subject to the limitations I have expressed, the employee must obey the orders given to him.

On the other side of the coin, there are also implied obligations on the employer. Before the Industrial Revolution, the common law of master and servant imposed on employers a relatively extensive duty to secure their servant's well-being, as befitted the paternalistic nature of the employment relationship in that quasi-feudal era. After the Industrial Revolution, the courts continued to apply the servant's duty of fidelity employment with full rigour, but most of the employer's implied obligations went by the board. Nineteenth-century courts did not want the trappings of noblesse oblige from a bygone age to trammel the employer's freedom to pursue profitability in the new economy.

The most notable implied term imposed on employers today is the obligation to give an employee reasonable notice for termination if the employer does not have just cause to terminate the employee. The courts have struggled in recent years with arguments that they should also imply a general obligation on employers to treat employees fairly. This matter is discussed by the Supreme Court of Canada in *Wallace v. United Grain Growers*, found in section 2:520 below.

Under Quebec civil law, as at common law, a court may imply terms into a contract. For instance, the employee's obligation to work under the direction of the employer, and the employer's duty to pay remuneration, are implicit in any contract of employment. See sections 2085 to 2097 of the Quebec *Civil Code*.

2:400 TERMINATING THE CONTRACT OF EMPLOYMENT

2:410 Wrongful Dismissal

Wrongful dismissal is the crucible where the vast majority of employment contract law issues are resolved. Dismissal is 'wrongful' at common law where (a) the employer dismisses the employee without alleging cause and without giving notice or wages in lieu of notice as required by the express or implied terms of the employment contract; or (b) the employee quits in response to repudiatory breach of the employment contract by the employer and sues for damages — the so-called constructive dismissal situation; or (c) the employer summarily dismisses the employee, alleging cause that is not proved; or (d) the employee is dismissed in breach of a statutory rule governing the employment relationship, or in breach of the administrative law duty of procedural fairness if the employment relationship is a statutory one to which the principles of administrative law apply.

2:420 Reasonable Notice of Termination

REFERENCES

Innis Christie, Geoffrey England, & Brent Cotter, *Employment Law in Canada*, 2d ed. (Toronto: Butterworths, 1993) c. 16

Sometimes, though not usually, contracts of employment contain express provisions setting out the amount of notice, or pay in lieu of notice, to which the employee is entitled in the event of termination without cause. As we will see below, in section 2:430, courts sometimes but not always enforce such provisions.

If the contract has no express provision on the amount of notice, courts will look elsewhere for evidence of the parties' factual intentions in that regard. The sources that the courts will examine include the firm's past practice in other dismissals, and policy statements in human resources manuals and other company documents.

Perhaps surprisingly, Canadian courts have seldom determined the notice period in this way. Their usual approach has been to decide what they consider to be a reasonable notice period, without searching for evidence of the parties' unexpressed factual intentions. According to strict contractual principles, this approach should be used only if there is no evidence that the parties intended some other notice period, but in practice most courts follow it wherever there is no explicit notice clause in the contract. Increasing concern in recent years with reducing the costs of firing employees has, however, called this practice into question, as we will see in the *Bartlam* case set out below.

The following case discusses the basic principles used by the courts in determining what is a reasonable period of notice, and considers the controversial issue of the effect of the employee's job status on that determination.

Cronk v. Canadian General Insurance Co. (1994), 19 O.R. (3d) 515 (Gen. Div.), rev'd (1995), 128 D.L.R. (4th) 147 (C.A.)

[In 1993 Edna Cronk was dismissed from her position as a clerk-stenographer as a result of internal restructuring. She was fifty-five years old and had been employed by the company since 1958, save for six years spent raising her children. She sued for damages for wrongful dismissal, and argued that 20 months would have been a reasonable period of notice in the circumstances.]

MACPHERSON J.: Every year in Ontario good and loyal workers lose their jobs through no fault of their own. Companies die or get smaller or make changes. Almost inevitably, the waves that wash over a company and bring these changes are accompanied by a powerful undertow that drags down some of the employees of the company.

In 1993 Edna Cronk got caught in the undertow. She lost her job at a major Canadian insurance company when it made substantial organizational changes. Edna Cronk did nothing to cause the termination of her employment; she was simply dismissed after long years of service. In her world she joined the long ranks of the unemployed. In the legal world she joined the long ranks of plaintiffs in cases bearing the bland rubric 'Wrongful Dismissal.'

In many ways, as will be seen, Edna Cronk's case is similar to the hundreds of other wrongful dismissal claims that arise in Ontario each year. She seeks compensation from her former employer for the loss of her job. The employer acknowledges that some compensation must be paid. But the employer and employee disagree on the question of what amount would constitute fair compensation. The result is a lawsuit which requires this court to set a proper amount.

However, in one important respect this lawsuit is different from many other wrongful dismissal cases. Edna Cronk seeks the equivalent of 20 months' salary as compensation for her dismissal. In a good many cases the Ontario courts have awarded long-serving employees 20 or 21 or 22 months' salary. In all of these cases the dismissed employee was 45 years of age or older, had worked for the company for 20 years or more, and was employed in a reasonably senior management position at the time of dismissal.

Edna Cronk was older than 45 when she was dismissed. She had worked for her company for more than 20 years. But she was not a senior manager, she was essentially a clerical employee with some minor administrative duties.

The pivotal question which this case raises is whether an employee's position in the hierarchy of a company is a major factor in setting the period of compensation to which the employee is entitled when she is dismissed without cause.

This question can be illustrated quite graphically by comparing Edna Cronk's situation to that of the plaintiff in one of the leading Ontario cases in the dismissal domain. Geoffrey Stevens was a renowned journalist and senior manager for the Globe and Mail newspaper for 24 years. When he was fired he was 46 years of age. He was awarded compensation of 21 months' salary by a judge of this court in 1992.

Edna Cronk had been employed by the defendant insurance company for 29 years when she was fired. She was 55 years of age. However, unlike Geoffrey Stevens, she was not a highly visible and renowned employee occupying a senior management position. Viewed from an external perspective, she was in fact an invisible, unknown and junior employee — a small cog in a large corporate enterprise.

The question which this case poses squarely is whether the law of Ontario provides as much protection to Edna Cronk for the loss of her job as it did to Geoffrey Stevens when he lost his job. . . . The plaintiff requests damages in lieu of notice equivalent to 20 months' salary less proper credit for amounts equal to 24 weeks previously paid. The defendant contends that its original offer of nine months' salary was, and still is, reasonable.

The factors to be considered in determining reasonable notice have remained more or less constant for over 30 years. They were enunciated by McRuer C.J.H.C. in *Bardal v. Globe and Mail Ltd.* . . . :

> There could be no catalogue laid down as to what was reasonable notice in particular classes of cases. The reasonableness of the notice must be decided with reference to each particular case, having regard to the character of the employment, the length of service

of the servant, the age of the servant and the availability of similar employment, having regard to the experience, training and qualifications of the servant.

These two sentences constitute the most often cited passage in wrongful dismissal cases, not only in Ontario but throughout Canada. . . .

Several of these factors clearly tell in favour of a generous notice period for Ms Cronk. First, she was 55 years old when she was fired. That is, in my view, a particularly vulnerable age for an employee. She is probably too old to embark upon a lengthy or strenuous retraining programme. Yet she may well be too young to contemplate retirement. The London Life Freedom 55 television commercial paints an attractive picture of the 55-year-old professional woman chucking it all and retreating, with Mustang convertible and surf-board in the rear, to a tropical paradise for a long and deserved retirement. Alas, for most women this commercial is a fantasy. The statistical average Canadian woman struggles to find a job, she receives about 60-70 per cent of the wages received by men doing the same work, she strives to balance family and career, she worries about losing her job, and if she does lose it she desperately seeks to obtain a new job. Edna Cronk was 55 years old when she was fired. But after long years of clerical work at a very modest salary, it is almost certain that she was not able to contemplate the Freedom 55 Mustang convertible and surf-board. She needs another job.

Second, with respect to McRuer C.J.H.C.'s statement regarding the 'availability of similar employment, having regard to the experience, training and qualifications' of the employee, Ms Cronk's position can be described as follows: she has a Grade 12 education; for parts of five decades (1950s to 1990s) her only training has been in the clerical duties domain of an insurance company; she has no qualifications for any other job; she lives in Hamilton and does not have a driver's licence; and her Hamilton employer has fired her because it does not have a job for her. This is not a description that suggests a quick and painless re-entry by Ms Cronk into the work force.

Third, Ms Cronk has worked for a long period of time — 29 years — for the defendant. She has devoted virtually her entire career to the defendant. The case law, throughout Canada, quite properly attaches great significance to what I would call the long and loyal service factor.. . .

Taken together, these three factors would seem to suggest that Ms Cronk should receive a reasonably long notice period. The case law establishes an upper limit of about twenty-four months. It would appear that, applying the *Bardal* factors, Ms Cronk would be entitled to something near this upper limit. And that is in fact what she asks for — 20 months.

Why then does the defendant contend that nine months is the appropriate notice period? There are really two reasons: first, an argument that Ms Cronk's term of employment with the defendant was not, for purposes of compensation in a wrongful dismissal context, 29 years; and second, that the upper limits of reasonable notice periods are reserved for quite senior employees with high salaries and major responsibilities. I will deal with each of these arguments in turn.

(a) Calculation of length of service

Ms Cronk worked for the defendant and its predecessor from 1958–1971 and 1977–1993, a period of 29 years. There is a gap of six years between these two periods of employment. The defendant contends that the gap has legal significance . . .

I disagree with this argument for several reasons. First, it needs to be recorded that the plaintiff is not asserting that the length of her employment should run 'continuously through the interruptions.' In fact Ms Cronk makes no claim for the six-year interruption in her periods of full-time employment with the defendant. . . .

Second, most of the decided cases do not hold that an interruption in employment wipes out the first period for purposes of calculating reasonable notice entitlements. . . .

Third, in the decided cases there are two rationales for not counting an interruption between two periods of employment against the employee: first, if the employee was accorded any seniority or other rights upon rehire in recognition of his or her earlier period of employment; and second, whether the employee actively sought to rehire the employee. There is no evidence either way on the first of these factors in the record in this case. However, there is uncontradicted evidence that the defendant did approach the plaintiff to resume her employment in 1977. . . .

Fourth, Ms Cronk had a very good reason for interrupting her career in 1971. She was about to give birth to a second child and wanted to stay home to raise her children. It would be unconscionable, in my view, for the law to protect employees who interrupt their careers with one employer to take a position with another employer only to return later to the first employer (the situation in cases like *Stevens*, *Roscoe* and *Wilson*) and not to afford similar protection to a woman who interrupts her career with one employer to stay home and raise a family.

Fifth, the interruption in Ms Cronk's employment with the defendant was not a complete one. She worked on a part-time basis for the defendant during the 1971–1978 period. Admittedly, she was not a formal part-time employee of the defendant; she worked through the intermediary of a secretarial services company. But that was not Ms Cronk's decision; it resulted from the defendant's policy at the time of not hiring its own part-time employees.

For all of these reasons, I have no hesitation concluding that Ms Cronk is entitled to be compensated for the full period of her employment with the defendant. That period was 29 years, a very very substantial period indeed.

(b) Relationship between type of employment and reasonable notice periods

The defendant's principal argument against a long notice period was the nature of the plaintiff's work which, the plaintiff and defendant agree, was essentially clerical in nature. The defendant argued that senior management or specialized employees with higher educational training should be awarded longer notice periods than non-managerial employees with little or no higher education or specialized training. The reason offered for this distinction is that the higher an employee's rank or the more specialized the position, the smaller are the number of other similar positions available. Unspecialized workers, such as clerical workers, on the other hand, were said to have a larger range of similar jobs available. There-fore, they would need less time to find reasonable equivalent employment. Furthermore, the defendant contends that there is a greater stigma attached to a senior manager being fired than there is with respect to the dismissal of a clerical worker. The greater stigma pur-portedly makes it more difficult for a senior manager to find equivalent employment.

The stigma component of the defendant's argument can be dealt with quite briefly. I simply do not see how the stigma that a dismissed employee may personally feel, or that may be created in the minds of others, is dependent on the employee's level of employ-ment. A job is a job. It is one of the most important components of the lives of the vast majority of adult Canadians. The loss of a job is almost always a devastating experience, financially and emotionally, for any employee. A secretary or cafeteria worker in a compa-ny who is fired will probably feel just as terrible as would the president of the same com-pany if he or she were fired. And if outsiders attach a stigma to dismissal, it results from the fact of dismissal, not the level of the job from which the employee has been dismissed.

I turn then to the defendant's heavy reliance on the managerial/clerical distinction in the wrongful dismissal domain. The defendant contends that the case law supports the proposition that the higher notice periods are reserved for dismissed senior managers and professionals and are not available to a clerical employee like Ms Cronk.

There is some support for this proposition. Ellen Mole has provided a useful summa-ry of the wrongful dismissal decisions throughout Canada in the 1980–1994 period in her book *Wrongful Dismissal Practice Manual* (1984, with regular loose leaf updates to Febru-ary 1994). Based on her analysis of the cases she has written . . . :

> Generally, a senior, high-level or management employee, or one in a highly skilled, tech-nically demanding position, will be entitled to a longer notice period than a junior, semi-skilled or non-managerial employee. This is sometimes expressed by asking whether or not the employee held a key position with the employer.

I have reviewed the Ontario cases collected and summarized in Ms Mole's book. It will be recalled that Ms Cronk is requesting a notice period of 20 months. I have accordingly concentrated on the decided cases in which the Ontario courts have awarded 19-, 20- and 21-month notice periods. I believe that in the 1980–1994 period there were six cases in this category in which all five of the following factors emerge from the judgments: age when fired, position, length of service, length of period of unemployment following dis-missal, and judicially determined period of notice.

. . .

It is clear that all of these employees held reasonably senior positions. And they all received generous notice periods. The defendant contends that the reason for the 20- and 21-month notice periods — and the factor that separates the six recipients from Ms Cronk — is the greater difficulty these senior, specialized employees will have in securing new employment.

I have great difficulty accepting this argument, for three reasons. First, the defendant has offered no evidence to support its argument. . . .

Second, a close examination of the table above dealing with the six Ontario employees who have been awarded 20- and 21-month notice periods contradicts the defendant's argument at its crucial point. It will be recalled that the defendant asserts that the principal rationale for the long notice periods is the great difficulty these senior employees will have in securing new employment. Yet the average period of post-dismissal unemployment for these six employees was 91/3 months. Ms Cronk was unemployed for almost eight months when this motion was heard, and her unemployment [sic] prospects were very bleak indeed. It is difficult to see how her employment prospects are better than the senior managers in the decided cases.

Third, the reality is — as we are all told by our parents at a young age — that education and training are directly related to employment. The senior manager and the professional person are better, not worse, positioned to obtain employment, both initially and later in a post-dismissal context. Higher education and specialized training correlate directly with *increased* access to employment.

This conclusion is supported by many public documents. One example is the recent study published by the Council of Ontario Universities entitled *The Financial Position of Universities in Ontario: 1994*. The study examined many aspects of the relationship between education and employment. One of those aspects was the unemployment rates in Canada from 1977 to 1992. During that period, the unemployment rate for high school graduates ranged from a low of 7.8 per cent to a high of 14.8 per cent. For people with a university degree, the range was 2.4–5.0 per cent — i.e. three times lower.

Not surprisingly, the picture in Ontario is quite similar to the national picture. In another study published by the Council of Ontario Universities, *Facts and Figures: A Compendium of Statistics on Ontario Universities* (1994), the authors review the same education/ employment relationship, but this time in an Ontario-specific context and in a slightly different time frame, namely 1984–1993. In that ten-year period the unemployment rate for high school graduates in Ontario ranged from 5.7 to 12.5 per cent. For university graduates, the range was 1.6–5.1 per cent. And in Ontario in 1993 — and it was in Ontario in 1993 that Ms Cronk was fired — the unemployment rate for university graduates was 4.2 per cent whereas for high school graduates, like Ms Cronk, it was 12.5 per cent, the highest it had been in the entire decade and almost exactly triple the figure for university graduates. . . .

My conclusion, based on the above data is that it is wrong to contend, as the defendant has, that clerical workers like Ms Cronk or other employees in low level positions should receive a shorter notice period than managers or professionals because the former are likely to obtain new positions more quickly than the latter. Indeed, the data support the opposite conclusion. Statistically speaking, in Ontario in 1993 a fired clerical employee was in a terrible situation with respect to finding employment.

For these three reasons, I do not accept the defendant's argument based on a managerial/clerical distinction. In the six Ontario cases discussed earlier, including the well-known *Stevens* case, the average age of the six dismissed men was 54 years. Edna Cronk was 55 when she was fired. The average length of service of the six men was 22 years. Ms Cronk was employed by the defendant for 29 years. The average post-dismissal period of unemployment of the six men was 91/3 months. Ms Cronk had been unemployed for almost eight months when the hearing of this motion took place and her employment prospects continued to be bleak.

The six men all received notice periods, as determined by the Ontario courts, of 20 or 21 months. There is, in my view, no reason for according Ms Cronk a shorter notice period. The reality is that she is older, has worked for her employer longer, and is less likely to find a new job than most of the six men who have received the 20- and 21-month periods. Accordingly, I award her what she has requested, namely damages in lieu of her notice equivalent to 20 months salary less proper credit for amounts previously paid, plus eight percent for vacation pay. . . .

[The judgment of Macpherson J. was reversed by the Ontario Court of Appeal, in the following judgment.]

LACOURCIERE J.A.: In my opinion, the learned motions court judge's reasons do not justify departing from the widely accepted principle. He erred in doing so on the basis of his own sociological research without providing counsel an opportunity to challenge or respond to the results of the two studies relied upon. . . .

Before taking new matters into account based on statistics which have not been considered in the judgment under appeal, the adversarial process requires that the court ensure that the parties are given an opportunity to deal with the new information by making further submissions, oral or written, and allowing, if requested, fresh material in response.

The result arrived at has the potential of disrupting the practices of the commercial and industrial world, wherein employers have to predict with reasonable certainty the cost of downsizing or increasing their operations, particularly in difficult economic times. As well, legal practitioners specializing in employment law and the legal profession generally have to give advice to employers and employees in respect of termination of employment with reasonable certainty. Adherence to the doctrine of *stare decisis* plays an important role in that respect. . . .

In my opinion, the character of the employment of the respondent does not entitle her to a lengthy period of notice. As pointed out by Saunders J. in *Bohemier v. Storwal International Inc.*, . . . :

> It seems to me that the character of the employment of the plaintiff with Storwal does not entitle him to a lengthy period of notice on the basis of decided cases and the reasons I have stated. If the issue had been addressed at the time he was first employed, it would not have been reasonable for his employer to have agreed to a notice period sufficient to enable him to find work in difficult economic times. In saying this, I hope that it is not thought that I am unsympathetic to the plight of the plaintiff. His claim, however, is based on contract and it is not reasonable to expect that his employer would or could have agreed to assure that his notice of termination would be sufficient to guarantee that he would obtain alternative employment within the notice period.

In calculating the period of notice for this respondent it is necessary to balance the traditional factors enumerated in *Bardal*, *supra*, which the motions court judgment appears to have improperly collapsed into the re-employability factor. While the character of the respondent's employment will restrict her to the level of a clerical, non-managerial employee, the respondent's age and lengthy faithful service for the appellant properly qualify her for the maximum notice in her category.

For these reasons, I would vary the judgment of MacPherson J. so that the plaintiff respondent will recover damages based on a salary calculation covering 12 months from September 9, 1993, including vacation pay for the amount accrued at the date of termination plus the statutory entitlement, less appropriate deductions and after allowing credit for amounts previously paid. . . .

* * *

Weiler J.A. dissented in part, holding that the fundamental objective in determining reasonable notice is to help employees find alternative employment and that occupational character is only relevant as a proxy of employability. She reasoned that if the empirical studies do not support the proposition that high-status workers face greater difficulty than low-status workers in finding alternative employment, the proxy rationale is invalidated and there is no reason why a particular clerical employee such as Cronk should not receive the same notice as a manager under the *Bardal* test if their chances of finding other work are roughly similar. Accordingly, Weiler J.A. would have remitted the case to the lower court for a full inquiry into the empirical validity of the proxy rationale. She did not say that she would overrule the principle that high occupational status automatically attracts a notice premium, but she described it as "troubling" because, in her words, "Our notion of justice is bound up with equality."

Bartlam v. Saskatchewan Crop Insurance Corp. (1993), 49 C.C.E.L. 141 at 148–51, 155–58 (Sask. Q.B.)

[The plaintiff was a senior manager who supervised 650 employees and was sixty-two years old. He had eighteen years' service with the employer, but the first nine were part-time and he was appointed to the senior position only two years before his dismissal. The Court had to decide whether the reasonable notice period should be based on the parties' factual intentions or on broader public policy grounds.]

KLEBUC J.: . . . The principle of reasonable notice was applied in Canada in *Carter v. Bell & Sons (Canada) Ltd.*, . . . where Mr. Justice Middleton . . . concisely stated the principle as follows:

> In the case of master and servant there is implied in the contract of hiring an obligation to give reasonable notice of an intention to terminate the arrangement. . . . This is a peculiar incident of the relationship of master and servant based largely upon custom.

Theoretical Approach to Assessment
While the principle of reasonable notice is well understood, there is a divergence of opinion as to what theoretical approach or test should be followed in determining a reasonable notice period for a specific employment contract. On the one hand is a series of decisions

suggesting that reasonable notice is to be determined by the court as of the date an employment contract was terminated. These decisions do not require the court to consider what the parties would have negotiated at the time they entered into their contract had they directed their minds to such issue or to other matters such as: whether the employee, if he were to leave his or her employment, would be prepared to give the employer the same notice period the court considers reasonable to require the employer to provide the employee. This approach, which for ease of reference I shall refer to as the 'Bardal Approach,' is based on the decision of McRuer C.J.H.C. in *Bardal v. Globe & Mail* . . . where . . . he stated:

> There could be no catalogue laid down as to what was reasonable notice in particular classes of cases. The reasonableness of the notice must be decided with reference to each particular case, having regard to the character of the employment, the length of service of the servant, the age of the servant and the availability of similar employment, having regard to the experience, training and qualifications of the servant.

On the other hand is a series of decisions suggesting that a period of reasonable notice should be determined as of the time the parties entered into their employment contract with the length of the notice to be implied by the court being the same whether the employer or the employee is terminating the employment contract. These decisions direct the court to look at all relevant factors existing at the time the employment contract was entered into and then imply a notice provision of the kind the parties would have agreed to had they considered the same. This approach, which for ease of reference I shall refer to as the 'Lazarowicz Approach,' is based on the decision of Roach J.A. in *Lazarowicz v. Orenda Engines Ltd.* . . . where . . . he said:

> . . . Opinions might differ as to what was reasonable, but in reaching an opinion a reasonable test would be to propound the question, namely, if the employer and the employee at the time of the hiring had addressed themselves to the question as to the notice that the employer would give in the event of him terminating the employment, or the notice that the employee would give on quitting, what would their respective answers have been? . . .

The Manitoba Court of Appeal in *Yosyk v. Westfair Foods Ltd.* . . . approved the approach of Roach J.A. in *Lazarowicz* and refined it. Twaddle J.A. for the court . . . noted:

> The relationship between an employer and an employee is contractual. Save to the extent that statute law imposes a minimum standard, the notice required to terminate employment of indefinite duration is that agreed to by the parties. In many cases, the length of notice will be fixed by express agreement, trade custom or a practice established by the employer. In other cases the implied term is that reasonable notice must be given.
>
> The length of notice which is reasonable is not a matter for subjective judgment. It must be determined having regard to the intention of the parties. The test was stated by Roach J.A., delivering the judgment of the Court of Appeal of Ontario, in *Lazarowicz v. Orenda Engines Ltd.* . . .

. . . In my opinion, it is the proper test in all cases, save for one refinement. The relationship between an employer and an employee is not a static one. During it, the contract is often amended by agreement on such fundamental terms as remuneration and the responsibilities of the employee. In a similar manner, the intention of the parties as to the length of notice required to end their relationship may change. The relevant intent is that which the parties had when the conduct was last changed prior to the events leading to its termination. . . .

In my opinion the Bardal Approach and the Lazarowicz Approach are irreconcilable and when applied to the same facts may lead to substantially different conclusions. . . .

What theoretical approach or test should be applied in Saskatchewan? In considering which of the two noted approaches is the more appropriate for Saskatchewan, attention must be given to the complexity and dynamics of Canada's social and economic environment. Failure to do so could lead to circumstances where the principles of law applied are out of step with the community it is intended to serve. In my opinion, consideration must be given to the dramatic changes that have taken place since the late 1950s and early 1960s. Rapid advances in technology, coupled with enormous gains in scientific knowledge, have increased the speed of change, particularly in the area of commerce and trade. Many established ventures have or will shortly become obsolescent. 'Rust Belts' have become commonplace. Many ventures that did not exist 25 years ago have become a driving force in our economy. Of these new economic activities, many will have a short lifespan.

The community at large generally recognizes that the average employee will have to change jobs or employers, or both four to five times during his or her lifetime. No longer is the concept of a 'job for life,' which was predominantly held in the 1950s and 60s, realistic. While there remain many established corporations with enormous pools of capital, a substantial portion of Canada's economy and new employment opportunities are being created by small corporations, sole proprietorships and partnerships who often have very little capital but many employees. The equity owner is usually personally involved in the day-to-day operation of the venture and may earn little more than his or her employees. These and other factors must be considered in the context of expanded world trade which exposes both employers and employees to the benefits and disadvantages of international competition.

Any approach adopted to imply a period of reasonable notice in an employment contract must be able to effectively and equitably address the economic realities of Saskatchewan's diverse social and economic environment. In my opinion, the Bardal Approach, narrowly applied, is incapable of fulfilling such role. It requires the court to imply a reasonable notice period having regard only to limited criteria. Hence, the court's decision will be a subjective one based on what the judge perceives to be reasonable at the time the employment contract was breached. Such decision may be substantially different than what the parties, and the economic community in which they function, consider appropriate having regard to all relevant factors. . . .

In addition to the degree of capitalization and employee-to-earnings ratio, any theoretical approach adopted must be able to take into account other factors, such as whether the activity involved is gradually becoming redundant or of lesser significance but still capable of providing meaningful employment opportunities in the short run. In these circumstances both the employees, particularly those in management positions, and the employer will be aware of the long term prospects of the activity they are involved in and would have agreed to shorter notice periods had their minds been directed to the subject. In my opinion, a court dealing with such circumstances should be able to imply a shorter notice period even though the employee may have been employed by the employer for a period of 26 years.

There is very little evidence confirming that the Bardal Approach is capable of adequately dealing with complex issues that may arise in diverse circumstances. In fact, the Saskatchewan decisions that I reviewed support my conclusion. In these decisions, there is no indepth discussion of the nature of the activity the employer and employee are involved in, no expert evidence led as to what the 'industry' or 'employment activity' in which the employer and employee are involved in considers to be reasonable notice, or what the parties to the employment contract may have contemplated at the time of entering into the employment contract. In these cases, the evidence appears to have been focused almost exclusively on the nature of the employee's duties, the age of the employee and employment opportunities available, all viewed from the employee's perspective. Counsel in these cases cited authorities, sometime in the form of a matrix, setting out only the duties of the employee, the number of years of employment, the age of the employee and the notice period judicially determined.

The case at bar reflects what commonly occurs when the Bardal Approach is exclusively adopted. Bartlam provided evidence as to his age, level of education, years of employment, and the nature of his duties with his employer, but led no evidence regarding: (a) what he believed the notice period was to be at the time he accepted full-time employment with the Corporation or what he thought the notice period was to be when he accepted his last promotion in 1990; (b) the nature of his employer's business; (c) any policy adopted by the Corporation with respect to notice periods; or (d) what notice periods are generally considered to be reasonable in the industry in which he and the Corporation were involved. Given that Bartlam considered himself to be part of senior management and was responsible for 650 people who reported directly or indirectly to him, he surely had some understanding as to what the Corporation and other employees considered to be reasonable notice for employment contracts similar to his.

The Corporation led no evidence regarding its capitalization, employee-to-earnings ratio or other factors such as organizational changes undertaken due to economic and other events affecting it. Further, its counsel did not vigorously cross-examine the employee on any of the aforementioned points. I am not critical of counsel for either party for they both relied on *Bardal* and were induced by it to limit the scope of their evidence. They put forward very basic evidence and then left it to this court to imply a reasonable notice period based on such evidence.

If the Bardal Approach is to be applied in the future, I am of the opinion from a policy point of view it must be amended to take into account additional criteria. The criteria set out in *Bardal* may have been adequate for the 1950s and early 1960s, but such criteria certainly is inadequate today.

In my opinion, the Lazarowicz Approach, particularly as refined in *Yosyk*, is the better approach for Saskatchewan because it is capable of addressing all relevant criteria when a term of reasonable notice is to be implied, including most of the criteria suggested in *Bardal*, but always in the context of what the employer and the employee would have agreed to having regard to the nature of their employment activity and economic and other factors associated therewith. It facilitates the creation of general understandings and customs in specific industries and activities of the kind which will enable employers and employees to function with a degree of certainty as to what their respective rights and obligations are regarding the giving of notice.

[The Court held that the plaintiff was entitled to twelve months' notice.]

* * *

A controversial technique for reducing the length of reasonable notice periods was introduced in *Bohemier v. Storwal International Inc.* (1982), 142 D.L.R. (3d) 8 (Ont. H.C.J.). Saunders J. held that the notice period could be reduced to help the employer withstand adverse economic conditions, such as then prevailed in Ontario. The Court of Appeal ruled that this factor could be taken into account, but that it must not be given excessive weight. See (1983), 44 O.R. (2d) 361 at 362, per Brooke J.A. The *Bohemier* doctrine fell into disuse during the boom years of the mid to late 1980s, but it re-emerged in the recession of the early 1990s and is still occasionally applied by a minority of courts.

As in the common law provinces, Quebec civil law provides for the possibility of either party terminating an employment contract of indefinite duration without cause by giving notice to the other party. Section 2091 of the Quebec *Civil Code* states that such notice "shall be given in reasonable time, taking into account, in particular, the nature of employment, the special circumstances in which it is carried on and the duration of the period of work." The Code also prohibits the employee from waiving the right to be indemnified if insufficient notice of termination is given (C.C.Q, s. 2092). As in the rest of Canada, there is extensive case law on the meaning of reasonable notice. See particularly *Columbia Builders Supplies Co. v. Bartlett*, [1967] B.R. 111; *Domtar Inc. v. St-Germain*, [1991] R.J.Q. 1271 (Q.C.A.).

2:430 Judicial Supervision of the Contract: Unconscionability and Other Devices to Defeat Written Contractual Terms

In theory, contractual principles strictly govern the interpretation of the contract of employment. For example, if the written contract expressly specifies the length of notice that will be required in the event of termination, that express provision (no matter how unfair it may seem to the court) will theoretically override whatever the common law would consider to be reasonable notice in the circumstances. However, courts are at times willing to circumvent such express contractual provisions where their application might be very unfair to the employee.

The most common devices used to defeat contractual provisions that one party finds harsh or undesirable are these: lack of mutual consent; violation of employment standards legislation (*Machtinger v. HOJ Industries Ltd.*, [1992] 1 S.C.R. 986); pre-contractual fraudulent or negligent misrepresentation by the other party (*Queen v. Cognos*, [1993] 1 S.C.R. 87); invalid variation of an existing employment contract without consideration (*Francis v. Canadian Imperial Bank of Commerce* (1995), 7 C.C.E.L. (2d) 1 (Ont. C.A.); strict *contra proferentum* interpretation of the clauses; and unconscionability.

These devices are most often used by dismissed employees whose written contracts (drafted by the employer) contain harsh termination clauses that purport to preclude reasonable notice. The following case shows the application of the doctrines of unconscionability and lack of mutual consent to such a clause.

Nardocchio v. Canadian Imperial Bank of Commerce (1979), 41 N.S.R. (2d) 26 at 32-36, 38-43 (S.C.T.D.)

[After working for a credit union for several years, the plaintiff was hired by the defendant bank in 1966 to work as a teller at a Nova Scotia branch. In 1975 she became assistant accountant at the branch. She had difficulty getting along with a new co-worker, Holwell. In 1978, when she was 44, the bank dismissed her with three months' pay in lieu of notice and refused to give her any reasons for the dismissal. She sued for wrongful dismissal. In its defence, the bank relied on the terms of the employment contract she had signed when hired in 1966.]

MORRISON J.: . . . Numbered paragraph 4 [of Exhibit 1 — the written contract] indicates that employment may be terminated by the employee upon giving three months prior notice in writing to the bank or terminated by the bank upon giving to the employee three months prior notice in writing or paying to the employee an amount equivalent to three months salary in lieu of such notice.

Numbered paragraph 5 provides that employment may immediately be terminated by the bank without notice or any payment in lieu of notice for good and sufficient cause. The defendant, however, is not relying upon numbered paragraph 5 in its defence and is not suggesting that it was necessary to establish good and sufficient cause in order to dismiss. Rather the defendant relies upon the provisions of numbered paragraph 4 above.

. . .

The plaintiff advanced the following arguments in submitting that paragraph (4) of . . . Exhibit 1 does not disentitle the plaintiff to reasonable notice for the following reasons:

(1) Upon its proper interpretation the provision for termination on three months notice does not apply once a person is appointed to a management position.
(2) The plaintiff should be relieved from the application of paragraph (4) because:
　(a) paragraph (4) is a harsh term, and

(b) determination [sic] provisions are unfair and result from an inequality of bargaining power, and

(3) The dismissal provisions are unenforceable as being contrary to public policy.

The principle of inequality of bargaining power was basically set out by Lord Denning in the case of *Lloyds Bank v. Bundy* . . . :

> Gathering all together, I would suggest that through all these instances there runs a single thread. They rest on 'inequality of bargaining power.' By virtue of it, the English law gives release to one who, without independent advice, enters into a contract upon terms which are very unfair or transfers property for a consideration which is grossly inadequate, when his bargaining power is grievously impaired by reason of his own needs or desires, or by his own ignorance or infirmity, coupled with undue influence or pressures brought to bear on him by or for the benefit of the other. When I use the word 'undue' l do not mean to suggest that the principle depends upon the proof of any wrongdoing. The one who stipulates for an unfair advantage may be moved solely in his own self interest, unconscious of the distress he is bringing to the other. I have also avoided any reference to the will of the one being 'dominated' or 'overcome' by the other. One who is in extreme need may knowingly consent to a most improvident bargain, solely to relieve the straits in which he finds himself. Again, I do not mean to suggest that every transaction is saved by independent advice. But the absence of it may be fatal. With these explanations, I hope this principle will be found to reconcile the cases . . .

Basic to the principle enunciated above is the element that the terms of a contract be very unfair. It seems clear to me that at the time that the plaintiff was hired by the defendant company the terms of the contract insofar as termination is concerned were not very unfair. Indeed, they were not unfair at all but seem quite reasonable. The contract provides for a certain term of notice for the employee who has been employed for six months, for one year and for the employee who has been employed for longer than one year. Consequently the terms of notice with regard to dismissal were not unfair at the time Exhibit 1 was signed. It may be quite true as time went on and as the employee became experienced and more skilled and perhaps highly skilled in certain fields that the termination clauses would then have the effect of being unfair. However insofar as the principle of inequality of bargaining power is concerned it would seem to me that the principle would not be applicable at the time of execution of the agreement, Exhibit 1, because at the particular time the agreement was signed the terms were reasonable.

This brings me to the final point in the plaintiff's argument and that is that the terms of numbered paragraph 4 in Exhibit 1 constitute a harsh term.

In the case of *Allison v. Amoco Production Co.,* . . . MacDonald J. of the Alberta Supreme Court said as follows . . . :

> I find it difficult to believe that it was the intention of the parties after six years of employment when the plaintiff would be entitled to reasonable notice of termination of employment, to continue his employment for an indefinite length of time in more senior positions and after a further 18 years of employment to determine the contract with

only 30 days' notice. If such was to be the intention of the parties, that intention must be expressly and clearly stated. The words used do not clearly state that the contract would terminate on 30 days' notice but only that if the company desires to terminate it it shall give 30 days' notice. These words I do not consider sufficient to abrogate the doctrine of law that reasonable notice must be given. I would consider that the 30 day notice provision if applied would be a harsh term. The case of *W.H. Milsted & Son, Ltd. v. Hamp et al.* . . . is authority for the proposition that harsh terms will not be enforceable.

I have already expressed the opinion that the terms of numbered paragraph 4 of Exhibit 1 were probably reasonable and fair at the time the document was signed for an employee entering into the employment of the defendant company. However, I do not think that the terms of notice are reasonable and fair in the case of an employee who has given faithful service for 12 years to her employer. What was fair in the early part of her employment might certainly not be fair when she has developed new skills and acquired greater experience. . . .

In my opinion Miss Nardocchio received rough treatment at the hands of her employer. The situation which developed could have been solved by a transfer to another branch of either the plaintiff or Mr. Holwell. Faced with this situation the bank management concluded that transferring the plaintiff would only transfer the problem and decided to terminate Miss Nardocchio's employment relying upon the three months notice clause in Exhibit 1. The conclusion reached by the employer in my opinion was not justified in view of Miss Nardocchio's long service, the good ratings she had received over the years, her progress in the bank, and the favourable report of Miss Malone in the spring of 1978. I feel that the bank's treatment of the plaintiff was extremely harsh.

It seems to me that the circumstances surrounding the execution of Exhibit 1 are not as clearly established as they might be. The plaintiff said that she never knew or understood the terms of the agreement and although her signature appears on the document she was never aware of what it contained. There is no evidence from the defendant regarding the specific interview with Miss Nardocchio nor what was said to her. We do have the evidence of Mr. Foote who described his general procedure on hiring but could not recall any specific interview with Miss Nardocchio. It seems to be that it could very probably have happened that Miss Nardocchio was interviewed briefly and handed a paper to sign which she did sign without having its contents clearly explained to her. Certainly the evidence is just as consistent with this conclusion as the conclusion that the document was read over and explained to her and then signed by her. My inference is that the terms of the agreement as to secrecy and faithful performance were emphasized rather than termination provisions.

I am not at all satisfied that Miss Nardocchio knew what she was signing or understood all the terms and conditions of the form. In those circumstances I find it difficult to conclude that there was a meeting of minds on all the terms of the agreement and that there was a mutually agreed upon contract with respect to the termination of employment clauses.

It seems to me that the defendant bank would have been wise to clarify all the terms and conditions of employment to the plaintiff upon her advancement to a management position in 1975. At the very least this would have made it impossible for the plaintiff to plead lack of knowledge of the termination provisions.

I also bear in mind that Miss Nardocchio had never at any stage of her employment been referred to the so-called contract of employment, Exhibit 1, and I accept her evidence that she was not aware of its existence. In these circumstances I consider that the three month notice provision contained in numbered paragraph 4 of Exhibit 1 if applied would be a harsh term and in my opinion that term of the contract is not enforceable. In reaching this conclusion I find that the reasoning of MacDonald J. in *Allison v. Amoco Production Co.* . . . , which I have cited earlier, is applicable. . . .

Having found that the plaintiff's employment was not terminated under the provisions of a binding employment contract and that she was not dismissed for just cause I must then determine what a reasonable amount of notice would have been for the plaintiff in these circumstances. . . .

Having regard for the plaintiff's present age of forty-four years and the difficulty which she has experienced in obtaining new employment and the nature and salary of the position which she held I think that reasonable notice in these circumstances would be one year. . . .

✳ ✳ ✳

In some circumstances, a court may also disregard express language to the effect that the employment relationship is to last only for a defined period of time (a definite term) rather than indefinitely.

Ceccol v. Ontario Gymnastic Federation (2001), 55 O.R. (3d) 614 (C.A.)

MACPHERSON J.A. (for the court):

In the domain of employment law, a fundamental common law principle is that "a contract of employment for an indefinite period is terminable only if reasonable notice is given": see *Machtinger v. HOJ Industries Ltd.*, . . . The principle is not an absolute one; in *Machtinger*, Iacobucci J. described it as a "presumption, rebuttable if the contract of employment clearly specifies some other period of notice, whether expressly or impliedly." (p. 998). Moreover, as Iacobucci J.'s statement of the general principle clearly indicates, it applies only to employees engaged for an indefinite period. The principle does not apply to fixed term contracts. An employee whose contract is not renewed at the conclusion of a fixed term is not dismissed or terminated; rather her employment simply ceases in accordance with the terms of the contract: see *Chambly (City) v. Gagnon*, . . .

The present appeal requires consideration of both the line between fixed and indefinite term employment contracts and the requirements for successfully rebutting the common law presumption of reasonable notice. These issues arise in the context of a 16 year employment relationship between a non-profit athletic association and one of its senior managers which the association terminated, it concedes, without cause. . . .

The respondent, Diana Ceccol . . . , was the salaried Administrative Director of the Federation from September 1, 1981 to May 9, 1997. She was essentially the number two person in a 14-person office. . . .

In July 1981, Ceccol accepted the position of Administrative Director with the Federation, and she commenced employment on September 1, 1981. For the next 15 years and 8 months, Ceccol's employment was governed by a series of one-year contracts. The terms of these contracts were very similar. For convenience, I will refer to the 1996–7 contract which was in force when Ceccol's employment ceased. The crucial provisions of that contract were:

1. TERM

1.1 The Federation hereby hires the Employee and the Employee hereby agrees to serve as the Administrative Director of the Federation for a period of 12 months, commencing July 1, 1996 and terminating on June 30, 1997, unless sooner terminated or extended as hereinafter provided.

1.2 Subject to acceptable performance reviews, this Agreement is subject to renewal, upon the consent of both parties as to terms and conditions.

. . .

5. TERMINATION OF EMPLOYMENT

5.1 The Federation may terminate this Agreement at any time according to the current Employment Standards Act by reason of the Employee's dissipation, violation of reasonable instructions or policies/procedures of the Federation, failure to comply with provisions of this Agreement as herein set out or for other cause. . . .

5.3 The Employee shall have the right to terminate this Agreement at any time by giving reasonable written notice (a minimum of 2 weeks) to the Federation. . . .

5.4 The Federation and the Employee agree to abide by the Ontario Employment Standards Act and regulations concerning notice of termination of employment.

In the late fall of 1996, there were 14 employees at the Federation's head office. On December 3, a staff meeting was called and Harold Sanin, the Vice-President (Administration), presented all of the employees with a written notice: [that their employment would end on June 30, 1997] . . .

In the spring of 1997, most of the senior managers were informed that the Federation would not renew their contracts after June 30. For Ceccol (and for Joe Rabel, the Executive Director), the axe fell on May 9, 1997. . . .

The Federation paid Ceccol her salary and relevant benefits until June 30, 1997. It also offered her *ex gratia* severance payments potentially totalling three months salary if she signed a release. Ceccol declined this offer and commenced a wrongful dismissal action.

The Litigation

. . . the trial judge held that Ceccol was an indefinite term, not a fixed term, employee and that she was entitled to reasonable notice, not the statutory notice in the *Employment Standards Act*, R.S.O. 1990, c. E.14 (*"ESA"*). He fixed the reasonable notice at 16 months but reduced it by four months because of Ceccol's failure to properly mitigate her damages. . . .

The issues on the appeal and cross-appeal are:

1) Did the trial judge err by concluding that Ceccol was an indefinite term employee?
2) Did the trial judge err by concluding that Ceccol was entitled to reasonable notice rather than to the notice provided in the ESA?
3) Did the trial judge err by reducing Ceccol's notice period by four months for failure to mitigate her damages?

. . .

The Federation's Appeal

(a) Duration of Ceccol's employment

The Federation and Ceccol entered into 15 annual contracts. Each contract contained, in article 1.1, a specific final date, June 30 from 1992 onwards. However, the trial judge concluded that Ceccol was not a fixed term employee:

> I find as fact that the plaintiff and all her immediate superiors prior to Sanin, who came on the scene in 1996, believed and acted as if the plaintiff were, what the plaintiff and her witnesses described as a "full-time" permanent employee.

The trial judge gave effect to this shared perception because, in his words, "[i]n the final analysis, in these cases the decision to be made is what are the reasonable expectations of the parties."

I agree with the trial judge's conclusion. His observation about the importance of the parties' reasonable expectations is a faithful application of one of the leading decisions of the Supreme Court of Canada in the contract law domain. In *Consolidated Bathurst Export Ltd. v. Mutual Boiler and Machinery Insurance Co.,* . . . Estey J. said:

> [T]he normal rules of construction lead a court to search for an interpretation which, from the whole of the contract, would appear to promote or advance the true intent of the parties at the time of entry into the contract. Consequently, literal meaning should not be applied where to do so would bring about an unrealistic result or a result which would not be contemplated in the commercial atmosphere in which the insurance was contracted. Where words may bear two constructions, the more reasonable one, that which produces a fair result, must certainly be taken as the interpretation which would promote the intention of the parties.

In this passage, Estey J. linked the factors of the parties' intention and unrealistic or fair results with contractual words that "bear two constructions." Is it fair to conclude that article 1.1 of the Federation-Ceccol contract admits of more than one construction? In my view, it is.

Article 1.1 sets a term of 12 months for the contract. However, article 1.1. also specifically contemplates that the contract may operate either shorter or longer than 12 months: "unless sooner terminated or extended as hereinafter provided." The *longer* life of the relationship is then dealt with in article 1.2 which provides that the contract is "subject to renewal" if the employee has received acceptable performance reviews and if the parties can agree on the terms and conditions of renewal. The *shorter* life of the relationship is dealt with in article 5 of the contract which covers various termination scenarios, including (for sure) termination for cause, termination of probationary employees and termination by the employee, and (possibly) termination without cause.

In my view, this is not a case like [*Gagnon v. Chambly (Ville)*] . . . , where the contract was for a single fixed term and contained no clause dealing with renewal. Rather, there is a renewal provision (article 1.2) and it is explicitly linked to the term provision (article 1.1) by the closing words of article 1.1 ("unless . . . extended as hereinafter provided"). Moreover, it is arguable (I put it no higher) that renewals are not optional. There is a fair amount of language in the contract that contemplates automatic renewal, including the linking of renewals to "acceptable performance reviews" (article 1.2), the requirement that performance reviews "shall be considered in annual salary negotiations" (article 12.1), and the requirement that the employee's salary be negotiated by a specified date before the end of the contract (article 4.2).

. . .

In summary, in my view the relationship between articles 1.1 and 1.2 in the contract is not entirely clear. In particular, the words "subject to renewal" in article 1.2 are not self-defining and cast doubt on the Federation's argument that article 1.1 is effective in creating a clear fixed term contract.

This ambiguity surrounding the extension of the contract (it is worth noting that the contract was in fact renewed 15 times) justified the trial judge's decision to hear, and ultimately to rely on, evidence about the parties' intentions and conduct relating to the contract. That evidence was, as the trial judge found, overwhelming in support of Ceccol's contention that she was hired, and performed for almost 16 years, as an indefinite term employee. . . .

I conclude with this observation. Fixed term contracts of employment are, of course, legal. If their terms are clear, they will be enforced. . . .

However, the consequences for an employee of finding that an employment contract is for a fixed term are serious: the protections of the *ESA* and of the common law principle of reasonable notice do not apply when the fixed term expires. That is why, as Professor Geoffrey England points out . . . , "the courts require unequivocal and explicit language to establish such a contract, and will interpret any ambiguities strictly against the employer's interests."

It seems to me that a court should be particularly vigilant when an employee works for several years under a series of allegedly fixed term contracts. Employers should not be able to evade the traditional protections of the *ESA* and the common law by resorting to the label of 'fixed term contract' when the underlying reality of the employment relationship is something quite different, namely, continuous service by the employee for many years coupled with verbal representations and conduct on the part of the employer that clearly signal an indefinite term relationship.

In the present case, Ceccol served the Federation loyally, professionally and continuously for almost 16 years. The Federation does not say otherwise. I cannot say that the contract which governed their relationship contains the "unequivocal and explicit language" necessary to establish a fixed term contract. I conclude that the employment contract was for an indefinite term, subject to renewal and termination in accordance with other provisions in the contract.

(b) Reasonable notice or not?

The conclusion that a contract is for an indefinite term has as a corollary that, in normal circumstances, the employer can terminate the contract only by providing reasonable notice. This principle is not, however, an absolute one. There is an important exception, set out succinctly by Iacobucci J. in *Machtinger*, at p. 998:

> I would characterize the common law principle of termination only on reasonable notice as a presumption, rebuttable if the contract of employment clearly specifies some other period of notice, whether expressly or impliedly.

The Federation relies on this exception. It submits that article 5.4 expressly specifies some other period of notice. For convenience, I set out article 5.4 again:

> *5.4 The Federation and the Employee agree to abide by the Ontario Employment Standards Act and regulations concerning notice of termination of employment.*

[MacPherson J.A. then set out s. 57(1)(h) of the *Employment Standards Act*, which provides for 8 weeks termination notice for an employee with eight or more years of service with the employer] . . . .

The Federation submits that, reading article 5.4 of the contract and s. 57(1)(h) of the *ESA* together, the result is clear: Ceccol is entitled to eight weeks of statutory/contractual notice, and not reasonable notice under the common law. . . .

I say, candidly, that the Federation's submission on this issue is a plausible one. However, in the end, I am not persuaded by it. . . .

In my view, the absence of "may terminate" wording in article 5.4 which, I underline, is the provision on which the Federation relies, leads to a second plausible interpretation. The interpretation is this: the Federation-Ceccol contract permits only three types of termination — by the employer for cause (article 5.1), by the employer of probationary employees (article 5.2) and by the employee (article 5.3). The contract *does not* deal with terminations without cause. . . .

The question then arises: if article 5.4 is not a provision dealing with terminations without cause, what roles does it play? My answer — and I do not claim it is the only possible answer — is that article 5.4, with its "abide by the [*ESA*] . . . concerning notice of termination" wording, qualifies the three termination scenarios dealt with in articles 5.1–5.3. Article 5.4 says to the parties: if you invoke the right to terminate the employment relationship pursuant to any of articles 5.1–5.3, you must do so in accordance with the *ESA*. . . .

Which of the two plausible interpretations of article 5.4 should govern the Federation-Ceccol employment contract? *Machtinger* instructs that the presumption of reasonable notice can be rebutted only if the employment contract "clearly specifies some other period of notice" (p. 998). I do not think that article 5.4 achieves that high level of clarity.

Moreover, I think it is important to acknowledge what is at stake in the conflicting interpretations put forward by the parties. Ceccol worked loyally and professionally for the

Federation for almost 16 years. Her final salary was $50,000. If she is entitled to only the eight week payment established by the ESA, she will receive approximately $7700. If she is entitled to reasonable notice, which the Federation is content to accept is 16 months, she will receive approximately $66,700.

In an important line of cases in recent years, the Supreme Court of Canada has discussed, often with genuine eloquence, the role work plays in a person's life, the imbalance in many employer-employee relationships and the desirability of interpreting legislation and the common law to provide a measure of protection to vulnerable employees. . . .

These factors have clearly influenced the interpretation of employment contracts. . . .

In the present appeal, there are, as I have tried to demonstrate, two plausible interpretations of article 5.4 of the employment contract. One interpretation would remove the common law entitlement to reasonable notice; the other would preserve it. One interpretation would result in a termination provision which the trial judge described as "especially stringent and onerous"; the other would provide an employee with notice which at common law, both parties accept, is reasonable. One interpretation would provide a loyal and professional 16-year senior employee with $7700 in termination pay; the other would provide her with $66,700. In my view, in each instance the second interpretation is preferable. It is also, in my view, consistent with the leading decisions of the Supreme Court of Canada in the employment law domain. . . .

I would dismiss the appeal . . . with costs.

✻ ✻ ✻

Downsizing and restructuring have taken their toll of rank-and-file workers, middle managers, and senior executives. As the *Cronk* case indicates, the legal response by or on behalf of each group has varied considerably. The dismissal of middle managers and senior executives has attracted the attention of a veritable army of lawyers and personnel experts. However, most ordinary employees simply cannot afford to sue for wrongful dismissal. Litigation is unpredictable and expensive, legal aid is usually not available for wrongful dismissal claims, recovery even for successful litigants is seldom large, and the stakes are high — especially in jurisdictions where the winner is entitled to claim reimbursement of legal costs from the loser. Cronk herself was fortunate; although she lost in the Court of Appeal, her ex-employer did not claim costs against her.

Thus, except for unionized workers, most people tend to seek recourse for dismissal (if at all) under employment standards legislation (discussed in Chapter 12), which guarantees them a minimum period of statutory notice calibrated according to length of service. Typically, this legislation is enforced by officials of the ministry of labour, and the dismissed employee does not have to hire a lawyer or run the risk of further loss in the event of an adverse outcome. In some provinces, mass redundancies, such as the one that resulted in Cronk's dismissal, trigger government efforts to find other jobs for redundant workers or to help them gain further training.

In the late 1990s there were several attempts to use Ontario's *Class Proceedings Act, 1992*, S.O. 1992, c. 6, to bring class actions for wrongful dismissal and damages for reasonable notice on behalf of large numbers of employees affected by downsizing and restructuring measures in the new economy. Having one law firm act for thousands of employees, normally on a contingency fee basis, offered the prospect of a cost-effective way for lower status employees to use civil litigation to enforce their common law rights.

In *Webb v. K-Mart Canada Ltd.* (1999), 45 O.R. (3d) 389, Brockenshire J. of the Ontario Superior Court of Justice certified a class of three to four thousand former K-Mart retail employees across Canada who were dismissed when K-Mart Canada was taken over by the Hudson's Bay Company. The certified class was limited to terminated employees who were unorganized and had been employed on contracts of indefinite duration which did not expressly provide for notice on termination. The class also excluded employees who were terminated for cause. The court noted the access to justice advantages of this type of class action, and its potential for changing corporate termination practices for lower status employees.

However, it is too early to assess the overall effectiveness of this procedure in the wrongful dismissal context. In the K-Mart case, numerous procedural motions have been brought, mostly by the employer, in the years since certification was granted for the class action, and it has been very time consuming and costly to use private adjudicators (mostly retired judges) as referees to assess damages in lieu of notice for individual employees. In one of his procedural rulings, Brockenshire J. held that the process adopted had been counter-productive because the costs were heavy compared to the damages being assessed (*Webb v. 3584747 Canada Inc.*, [2001] O.J. No. 608). Almost two years after the initial certification, Brockenshire J. ordered that the assessment of damages in individual cases be referred to Small Claims Court judges across Ontario rather than to private adjudicators in an attempt to make the procedure cost-effective.

2:440 Constructive Dismissal

REFERENCES

Geoffrey England, Innis Christie, & Roderick Wood, *Employment Law in Canada*, 3d ed. (Markham: Butterworths, 1998), sections 13.24 to 13.80

Strict contractual principles dictate that if the employer commits a repudiatory breach of the express or implied terms of the employment contract, the employee can elect to terminate the contract or sue for damages. Therefore, even though it is the worker who quits, an action can be brought for wrongful dismissal (which is called 'constructive dismissal' in this situation). Were it not for the constructive dismissal doctrine, an employer could make life so miserable for an employee that he or she would be driven from the job without legal recourse.

From the employer's point of view, however, the constructive dismissal doctrine may severely limit flexibility in modifying terms and conditions of employment, because a significant change may constitute a repudiatory breach of the express or implied terms of the employment contract. Today, competitive pressures are forcing Canadian employers to demand a more flexible approach with regard to hours of work, economic benefits, and job duties. Technological advances are constantly challenging old production techniques. The clash between the employer's need for flexibility and the employee's need for security is nowhere more manifest than in the context of constructive dismissal.

Hill v. Peter Gorman Ltd., [1957] 9 D.L.R. (2d) 124 at 125–32 (Ont. C.A.)

LAIDLAW J.A.: The plaintiff was employed by the defendant as a salesman for various periods of time commencing in January 1950 and ending in April 1953. He was re-employed by the defendant by an oral agreement, to commence a new period of employment on November 4, 1953. It was a term of that oral agreement that the plaintiff would receive 2% on the sales made by him of tobacco, 21/2% on confectionery and 3% on sundries. There was no definite term of employment.

Subsequent to the oral agreement made between the parties an agreement in writing was made between them under date December 11, 1953. . . . There is no provision therein and it was not a term or condition of the oral agreement between the parties, that the respondent would assume any responsibility or liability for any account or amount not paid by a customer to the appellant for goods sold to him by the respondent.

During the year 1954, Mr. Peter Gorman, president of the appellant company, was concerned about the state of customers' delinquent accounts. He brought that matter to the attention of the salesmen from time to time at weekly meetings. In the last of such meetings for the month of August 1954, he notified the salesmen, including the respondent, that he was setting up a reserve for bad debts and that 10% would be deducted from their commissions. . . .

The learned trial Judge made basic findings of fact upon which the rights of the parties depend. I quote the all important finding made in these words: 'I am satisfied that the plaintiff Hill did not at anytime accept the procedure adopted by the employer for a deduction of 10% to set up a reserve for bad debts. The parties were never together in this regard.' . . .

There is ample evidence to support the findings of fact made by the learned trial Judge. . . . It follows from the finding of fact made by the learned trial Judge that the plaintiff was entitled to recover from the defendant the amount of money withheld and retained by the defendant from the commissions payable to the plaintiff. Therefore, in my opinion, this appeal should be dismissed with costs.

MACKAY J.A.: I am respectfully of [the] opinion that it cannot be said, as a matter of law, that an employee accepts an attempted variation simply by the fact alone of continuing in his employment. Where an employer attempts to vary the contractual terms, the position of the employee is this: He may accept the variation expressly or impliedly in which case there is a new contract. He may refuse to accept it and if the employer persists in the attempted variation the employee may treat this persistence as a breach of contract and sue the employer for damages, or while refusing to accept it he may continue in his employment and if the employer permits him to discharge his obligations and the employee makes it plain that he is not accepting the variation, then the employee is entitled to insist on the original terms.

I cannot agree than an employer has any unilateral right to change a contract or that by attempting to make such a change he can force an employee to either accept it or quit.

If the plaintiff made it clear to Gorman that he did not agree to the change made in September 1954, the proper course for the defendant to pursue was to terminate the contract by proper notice and to offer employment on the new terms. Until it was so terminated, the plaintiff was entitled to insist on performance of the original contract.

✻ ✻ ✻

Farber v. Royal Trust Co., [1997] 1 S.C.R. 846

GONTHIER J. . . . . This appeal concerns constructive dismissal and the consequent damages. More specifically, the issue is whether the unilateral changes made by the respondent to the appellant's employment contract amounted to constructive dismissal. A collateral issue is whether subsequent events were relevant and admissible in evidence.

I.   FACTS

The appellant began working for the respondent Royal Trust Company in November 1966 as a real estate agent. Because of his excellent work for the respondent, he was promoted a number of times over the years: real estate sales manager at the Chomedey branch (1972); transfer to the branch in Dollard-des-Ormeaux (hereinafter referred to as "Dollard" formerly called the Roxboro branch) (1973); residential sales manager for the Montreal region, then assistant regional sales manager (1976); regional sales manager for Metro-Montreal West (1979); and regional manager for Western Quebec (1982). The appellant was an excellent employee who was respected and appreciated by both his employer and the business community in which he worked.

As regional manager for Western Quebec, the appellant supervised and administered 21 offices employing some 400 real estate agents and 35 secretaries. In 1983, the appellant's region generated a gross income of more than $16,000,000. The appellant's remuneration as regional manager was made up of a guaranteed base salary, commissions and benefits. In 1983, the appellant received $48,802.20 as his base salary and $88,405 in commissions, for a total of $137,207.20. With benefits, the appellant earned $150,000 that year.

On June 4, 1984, the appellant was informed by his immediate supervisor that as part of a major restructuring, the company had decided to eliminate 11 of the 12 regional manager positions across the country, including the appellant's. To replace his eliminated position, the respondent offered the appellant financial compensation and the manager's position at the Dollard branch.

The financial compensation being offered included the following: first, $40,000 as a reorientation allowance payable within two years; and second, an 8.75 percent override commission on the net commissions of the real estate agents at the Dollard branch — by comparison, the respondent's branch managers usually received an override commission of 5.75 percent. However, that rate was to apply only for the remainder of 1984 and 1985. Starting in 1986, the appellant's override commission was to decrease to the usual rate of

5.75 percent. The offer also provided that starting in 1985, the commissions of real estate agents who were below the minimum standard set by the respondent would not be included in the calculation. The appellant was not offered any guaranteed base salary as manager of the Dollard branch; his income was to be made up only of commissions. Finally, the offer provided that the appellant would receive a lump sum of $48,000, which represented the commissions he had earned as regional manager for Western Quebec in the first six months of 1984, the exact value of which was not yet known at the time.

The Dollard branch was one of the most problematic and least profitable in the province. It was not meeting the sales targets set by the respondent and there was even some question of closing it. In 1983, the branch had 22 real estate agents, whose sales amounted to only $616,532. . . .

The appellant considered the respondent's offer unacceptable. To begin with, the position was one he had held eight years earlier and from which he had been promoted. As well, he was insulted by the fact that he was being asked to manage a branch experiencing problems. Finally, he estimated that his income would be cut in half if he accepted the respondent's offer. He therefore initiated discussions with the respondent seeking either to be appointed manager of a more profitable branch or to obtain a guaranteed base salary for the following three years. The respondent refused to change its offer in any way. It told the appellant that he had to assume his new duties on July 6, 1984 or it would consider that he had resigned. The appellant did not go to the Dollard branch on the date in question.

The appellant sued the respondent for damages on the ground that he had been constructively dismissed. On August 11, 1989, the Superior Court dismissed his action. The appellant appealed the decision and, on May 29, 1995, the majority of the Court of Appeal dismissed the appeal . . . Fish J.A., in dissent, would have allowed the appeal. . . .

The issue is whether the appellant was constructively dismissed and, if so, what damages he should be awarded.

A. Constructive Dismissal

I will begin by recalling a few principles. In Quebec, employment contracts are governed by the civil law, including the provisions of the *Civil Code*. . . .

(i) Concept of Constructive Dismissal in the Civil Law

According to art. 1670 C.C.L.C., general contractual principles are applicable to employment contracts. Under art. 1022 C.C.L.C., contracts are binding on the parties thereto: they must fulfil their commitments. The parties cannot unilaterally change the obligations they have incurred under the contract. . . .

In the context of an indeterminate employment contract, one party can resiliate [withdraw from] the contract unilaterally. The resiliation is considered a dismissal if it originates with the employer and a resignation if it originates with the employee. If an employer dismisses an employee without cause, the employer must give the employee reasonable notice that the contract is about to be terminated or compensation in lieu thereof. . . .

Where an employer decides unilaterally to make substantial changes to the essential terms of an employee's contract of employment and the employee does not agree to the changes and leaves his or her job, the employee has not resigned, but has been dismissed. Since the employer has not formally dismissed the employee, this is referred to as "constructive dismissal." By unilaterally seeking to make substantial changes to the essential terms of the employment contract, the employer is ceasing to meet its obligations and is therefore terminating the contract. The employee can then treat the contract as resiliated for breach and can leave. In such circumstances, the employee is entitled to compensation in lieu of notice and, where appropriate, damages.

On the other hand, an employer can make any changes to an employee's position that are allowed by the contract, *inter alia* as part of the employer's managerial authority. Such changes to the employee's position will not be changes to the employment contract, but rather applications thereof. The extent of the employer's discretion to make changes will depend on what the parties agreed when they entered into the contract. R. P. Gagnon made the following comment on this point in *Le droit du travail du Québec: pratiques et théories* (3rd ed. 1996), at p. 66:

> [TRANSLATION] Moreover, to what extent can the employer change the nature of the employee's work or the employee's duties and responsibilities? This issue is increasingly important, *inter alia* because it is often an essential consideration for employees in their employment that they be able to do the job for which they were hired, given both the satisfaction they legitimately wish to derive from it and their concern to maintain and develop their qualifications and skills in their field of work. The answer takes into account the form of and circumstances surrounding the hiring of the employee and thus how much discretion the employer explicitly or implicitly has to exercise managerial authority in this regard. [Citation omitted.]

To reach the conclusion that an employee has been constructively dismissed, the court must therefore determine whether the unilateral changes imposed by the employer substantially altered the essential terms of the employee's contract of employment. For this purpose, the judge must ask whether, at the time the offer was made, a reasonable person in the same situation as the employee would have felt that the essential terms of the employment contract were being substantially changed. The fact that the employee may have been prepared to accept some of the changes is not conclusive, because there might be other reasons for the employee's willingness to accept less than what he or she was entitled to have.

Moreover, for the employment contract to be resiliated, it is not necessary for the employer to have intended to force the employee to leave his or her employment or to have been acting in bad faith when making substantial changes to the contract's essential terms. However, if the employer was acting in bad faith, this would have an impact on the damages awarded to the employee. In the case at bar, there is no question of bad faith by the respondent, which was acting in good faith in reorganizing its hierarchical structure. Thus, the only damages in issue are those that would be awarded in lieu of notice. . . .

Before going on to examine how the courts have applied these principles, I should pause to discuss a point raised by the statement of Fish J.A. of the Court of Appeal, with which Chamberland J.A. concurred, that the doctrine of constructive dismissal, a creature of the common law, has become part of the civil law.

In 1984, in *Lavigne v. Sidbec-Dosco Inc.*, . . . Hannan J. said at p. 28 that the common law rule concerning constructive dismissal has been adopted by Quebec civil law. . . .

As this Court has noted on many occasions, the civil law is a complete system in itself; care must be taken not to adopt principles from other legal systems. Thus, for a legal principle to be applicable in the civil law, it must above all be justified within the system itself. . . .

That being said, it may nevertheless be worthwhile from a comparative point of view to consider how other legal systems have resolved the same issue. . . . In addition, if the rules in the two systems are similar, precedents may be of some relevance. Although they are not binding, the fact that they apply similar or identical principles may be useful for the purpose of explanation and illustration. . . . This is true, *inter alia*, in constructive dismissal cases, in which, as will be seen, the courts have adopted similar solutions based on very similar principles and circumstances. It is therefore worthwhile to consider decisions from both legal systems to find illustrations of how the courts have applied the constructive dismissal concept. . . .

In cases of constructive dismissal, the courts in the common law provinces have applied the general principle that where one party to a contract demonstrates an intention no longer to be bound by it, that party is committing a fundamental breach of the contract that results in its termination.

. . .

Thus, it has been established in a number of Canadian common law decisions that where an employer unilaterally makes a fundamental or substantial change to an employee's contract of employment — a change that violates the contract's terms — the employer is committing a fundamental breach of the contract that results in its termination and entitles the employee to consider himself or herself constructively dismissed. The employee can then claim damages from the employer in lieu of reasonable notice. . . .

The common law rule is therefore similar to that applicable in Quebec civil law when it comes to the concept of constructive dismissal. Thus, although decisions from the common law provinces are not authoritative, it may be helpful to refer to them to see what types of changes the courts have considered fundamental changes to an employment contract resulting in the termination of that contract. However, each constructive dismissal case must be decided on its own facts, since the specific features of each employment contract and each situation must be taken into account to determine whether the essential terms of the contract have been substantially changed.

In a number of decisions in both Quebec and the common law provinces, it has been held that a demotion, which generally means less prestige and status, is a substantial change to the essential terms of an employment contract that warrants a finding that the employee has been constructively dismissed. In some decisions, it has been held that a unilateral change to the method of calculating an employee's remuneration justifies the same finding. Other decisions have found that a significant reduction in an employee's income by an employer amounts to constructive dismissal. . . .

It is clear that the change the respondent unilaterally imposed on the appellant through its June 1984 offer substantially altered the essential terms of the employment contract. At the time the offer was made, any reasonable person in the same situation as the appellant would have come to that conclusion.

To begin with, the change involved a significant, even a serious, demotion for the appellant. He was being offered the manager's position at a single branch in Dollard, which was a position he had held eight years earlier before being promoted four times. As regional manager for Western Quebec, the appellant supervised and administered 21 branches, 17 branch managers, 400 real estate agents and 35 secretaries. The gross income generated by that region was more than $16,000,000. As just the manager of the Dollard branch, the appellant would have been responsible for supervising only 22 real estate agents and 2 secretaries. Moreover, the sales of that branch amounted to less than $700,000. The appellant's responsibilities were therefore being drastically cut, resulting in a considerable loss of status and prestige. . . . Asking the appellant to manage that branch undermined his prestige and status all the more.

In addition, the appellant's salary terms were considerably altered by the change imposed by the respondent. As regional manager for Western Quebec, the appellant's remuneration was made up of a guaranteed base salary, commissions and benefits. As manager of the Dollard branch, he would have received no guaranteed base salary; his income would have been limited to commissions. While the value of a guaranteed base salary is known and can be relied on, the same is not true of an income limited to commissions. That type of remuneration can fluctuate greatly depending on market conditions and, as already noted, those conditions were to say the least inauspicious for the Dollard branch. The unilateral change was extremely detrimental to the appellant's financial security. . . .

When he was asked to manage the Dollard branch, the appellant estimated that his salary would be cut in half if he accepted the offer. At trial, the respondent tried to prove that its offer did not result in such a change to the salary terms of the appellant's employment contract by adducing evidence of what had occurred subsequent to the offer, namely the actual sales figures for the Dollard branch and the Western Quebec region after June 1984. Since the Dollard branch's sales were markedly higher than what the appellant had anticipated, the respondent sought to use the figures to show that if the appellant had agreed to manage the branch, he would in fact have earned more than if he had remained regional manager. The appellant objected to the admission of that *ex post facto* evidence. . . .

Relevance is determined on the basis of what must be proved in an action. In the case at bar, the court had to determine whether the respondent's offer substantially changed the essential terms of the appellant's employment contract. However, since the appellant had to decide whether this was the case at the time he received the offer, the court had to revert to that time to determine whether a reasonable person in the same situation as the appellant would have considered that the offer substantially changed the essential terms of the employment contract. Thus, what is relevant is what was known by the appellant at the time of the offer and what ought to have been foreseen by a reasonable person in the same situation. Evidence of events that occurred *ex post facto* is not relevant unless the sales figures achieved subsequent to the offer could reasonably have been foreseen at the time of the offer.

In the instant case, it is clear that the subsequent sales figures could not reasonably have been foreseen. It was proved that the Dollard branch was in an extremely precarious financial position at the time the offer was made. There was even some question of closing it because its sales were below the minimum set by the respondent. Moreover, when the appellant received the offer, he calculated his projected earnings using documents prepared by the respondent and told the respondent of his projections. The respondent never disputed or even commented on them. Nor is there any evidence in the record that the respondent foresaw that sales at the Dollard branch would increase significantly over the following months. Rather, the evidence shows that the respondent itself anticipated that sales at the Dollard branch would not increase in 1984. . . .

Based on the mere fact that the income of the Dollard branch subsequently improved, the trial judge drew the presumption that such an improvement was reasonably foreseeable by the appellant absent any evidence that exceptional circumstances had arisen in the meantime. In my view, this cannot be the case without other evidence connecting what subsequently happened to the information available at the time of the respondent's offer. The mere fact that an event occurs does not mean that it was foreseeable. The uncertainties of business stand in the way of such a presumption.

The trial judge therefore erred in admitting the *ex post facto* evidence when its relevance to the case had not been established. Moreover, its admission prejudiced the appellant since, in my view and with the utmost respect, it distorted the trial judge's analysis. On the basis of the sales figures of the Dollard branch subsequent to the offer, the judge concluded that the respondent's offer did not substantially change the appellant's employment contract from a salary point of view. However, those figures were not known at the time of the offer and would not have been foreseen by a reasonable person.

With respect, the trial judge erred in concluding that the appellant had not been constructively dismissed in the case at bar. Although he acknowledged that the appellant had been demoted, he found that it was not a factor because the appellant would have been prepared to manage a branch that was . . . "more profitable, more prestigious." However, the issue of whether there has been a demotion must be determined objectively by comparing the positions in question and their attributes. What an employee threatened with job loss is prepared to accept as a replacement position is not the yardstick of the employee's rights, although it may, depending on the circumstances, provide some indication of those rights. In this case, an objective comparison of the positions clearly shows that the appellant was being demoted, and this is simply confirmed by his refusal; even as a compromise, the appellant would have accepted only a manager's position in a more successful branch or a guaranteed salary for three years in compensation for the demotion. The trial judge in fact acknowledged all the differences between the appellant's regional manager position and the respondent's offer. However, he said nothing about or disregarded such significant changes as the loss of a guaranteed base salary and the demotion, which are in themselves sufficient to support a finding of constructive dismissal. In reaching the conclusion that the appellant would have been well advised to accept the offer, he relied primarily on the evidence of what had occurred subsequent to the offer. With respect, he thereby strayed from the real issue, which was whether the offer substantially changed the essential terms of the employment contract. Intervention by this Court is therefore warranted. . . .

The trial judge stated . . . that if he had found that the appellant had been constructively dismissed, he would have awarded the equivalent of one year's remuneration in lieu of notice. Although he did not have to act on his opinion, it is not unreasonable in this case. . . . There is accordingly no reason for this Court to change it. . . .

* * *

Geoffrey England has made the argument that the principles of fundamental or repudiatory breach that underlie constructive dismissal should or would be adapted by common law courts to recognize the need of employers for more flexibility to reorganize the labour process with a view to remaining competitive in the new economy. G. England, "Recent Developments in the Law of the Employment Contract: Continuing Tension Between the Rights Paradigm and the Efficiency Paradigm" (1995), 20 Queen's L.J. 557. The decision of the Ontario Court of Appeal in *Mifsud v. MacMillan Bathurst Inc.* (1989) 70 O.R. (2d) 701, and the lower court decisions in the *Farber* case were seen as early indications of such a trend. However, the Supreme Court of Canada decision in *Farber* seems to indicate an unwillingness to make it harder for employees to claim constructive dismissal.

2:450 Summary Dismissal for Cause

> REFERENCES
>
> **Geoffrey England, Innis Christie, & Roderick Wood, *Employment Law in Canada*, 3d ed. (Markham: Butterworths, 1998), c. 15**

The legal theory of summary dismissal at common law is couched in terms of traditional contract law principles. If an employee commits a breach that is severe enough to constitute a repudiation of the employment contract, the employer has just cause for dismissal. It is entitled to treat the contract as terminated, and to dismiss the employee without notice or pay in lieu of notice. The employer can also sue for damages for losses caused by the employee's dereliction of duty, but this is seldom done.

Courts have given extensive consideration to the question of what sorts of conduct on an employee's part are serious enough to give just cause for dismissal. The Supreme Court of Canada has recently addressed this matter in the following case.

McKinley v. BC Tel, [2001] 2 S.C.R. 161

IACOBUCCI J. —

I. INTRODUCTION

This appeal arises out of a wrongful dismissal action. It calls upon the Court to elaborate the circumstances in which an employer would be justified in summarily dismissing an employee as a result of the latter's dishonest conduct. More specifically, the question is whether any dishonesty, in and of itself, suffices to warrant an employee's termination, or whether the nature and context of such dishonesty must be considered in assessing whether just cause for dismissal exists.

The appeal also raises ancillary questions relating to the propriety of the trial judge's decision to put to the jury questions related to awards for an extended notice period, aggravated damages, and punitive damages. In addition, the parties sought a review of the reasonableness of the jury verdict on various matters decided at trial. A cross-appeal also has been brought, wherein the respondents submitted that, if the Court dismissed the appeal, it ought to dismiss the appellant's wrongful dismissal action outright rather than order a new trial.

For the reasons that follow, I am of the view that this appeal should be allowed and that the jury's verdict should be restored on all questions except that related to aggravated damages. As I would allow the appeal, the cross-appeal must perforce be dismissed.

II. FACTUAL BACKGROUND

The appellant, Martin Richard McKinley, is a chartered accountant who was employed by the respondents, the BC Tel group of companies ("BC Tel"). While working for BC Tel, he held various positions, earned promotions, and received salary increases. In 1991, he became Controller, Treasurer and Assistant Secretary to certain BC Tel companies. But in 1993, the appellant began to experience high blood pressure as a result of hypertension. Initially, this condition was brought under control through medication, and by taking some time away from work. However, by May of 1994, the appellant's health took a turn for the worse. His blood pressure had begun to rise again, and by June of that year, it was rising on a daily basis. Following his physician's advice, the appellant took a leave of absence from work.

By July 1994, the appellant's superior, Ian Mansfield ("Mansfield"), raised the issue of the appellant's termination from his employment. During discussions with his employer, the appellant indicated that he wished to return to work, but in a position that carried less responsibility. He was advised that BC Tel would attempt to find another suitable position for him within its corporate structure. However, alternative employment was never offered to the appellant. Although at least two positions for which the appellant qualified opened during the period in question, these were filled by other employees.

While the appellant was still on leave from work owing to his health condition, Mansfield telephoned him and instructed him to report to the respondents' offices on August 31, 1994. The appellant complied, and on that day, the respondents terminated his employment. By that time, the appellant had worked for BC Tel for almost 17 years and was 48 years of age.

Although the respondents made the appellant a severance offer, this was rejected. According to the appellant, his employment was terminated without just cause and without reasonable notice or pay in lieu of reasonable notice. He thus brought a wrongful dismissal action in the Supreme Court of British Columbia, arguing that his termination was an arbitrary and wilful breach of his employment contract, which was conducted in a high-handed and flagrant manner. The appellant maintained that the respondents' actions amounted to an intentional infliction of mental suffering. He alleged that, as a result of the wrongful dismissal, he lost his employment income and benefits, as well as the short-term disability benefits he was then receiving. He also argued that the dismissal prevented him from qualifying for, or receiving, any long-term disability benefits, and caused him to lose his future pension benefits. As such, the appellant sought an order for general compensatory damages, special damages for the expenses incurred in attempting to find new employment, aggravated damages, and damages for mental distress and the intentional infliction of mental suffering, as well as punitive damages.

Aside from his wrongful dismissal action, the appellant filed an information with the Canadian Human Rights Commission, based on the same allegations of fact. He argued that his dismissal contravened the *Canadian Human Rights Act*, R.S.C., 1985, c. H-6. At the time of trial, he had not yet filed a formal complaint.

The respondents admitted to having terminated the appellant's employment on August 31, 1994. . . .

. . . They . . . argued that just cause for the appellant's summary dismissal existed. Specifically, the respondents alleged that the appellant had been dishonest about his medical condition, and the treatments available for it. This argument was based on the respondents' recent discovery of a letter (dated December 12, 1994) written by the appellant to Dr. Peter Graff, an internal medicine and cardiac specialist, who was one of the appellant's attending physicians. In this letter, the appellant wrote to Dr. Graff acknowledging that, during a previous medical appointment, Dr. Graff had recommended a certain medication — the "beta blocker" — as the next method of treatment for the appellant's hypertension. Although beta blockers were not prescribed at that time, the letter indicated that Dr. Graff had advised the appellant that such treatment should begin upon the latter's return to work, if his blood pressure remained high.

The respondents claimed that the appellant deliberately withheld the truth as to Dr. Graff's recommendations regarding the use of beta blockers and their ability to enable him to return to his job without incurring any health risks. However, the appellant's evidence at trial revealed that, insofar as he was concerned, he had not lied to the respondents.

At trial, the appellant's wrongful dismissal action was heard before a judge and jury. Paris J. held that there was sufficient evidence to put the question of just cause for dismissal to the jury. In instructing the jury on this point, Paris J. stated that, in order for just cause to exist, it must find (a) that the appellant's conduct was dishonest in fact, and (b) that "the dishonesty was of a degree that was incompatible with the employment relationship." Paris J. also held that the jury could consider whether aggravated damages, as well as damages for bad faith in the conduct or manner of the dismissal were warranted. On the other hand, he held that there was no evidence upon which a claim for punitive damages could be based, and thus, this question was not put to the jury.

The jury found in favour of the appellant, awarding him the following amounts: $108,793 in general damages; $1,233 in special damages; $100,000 in aggravated damages; $6,091 in pension contributions; prejudgment interest; and costs. Paris J. refused to make an order for special costs, and for increased costs.

The Court of Appeal for British Columbia set the jury award aside and ordered a new trial. The appellant's cross-appeal on the question of punitive damages was dismissed. According to the Court of Appeal, dishonesty is always cause for dismissal. . . .

III. JUDICIAL HISTORY

A. Supreme Court of British Columbia (Paris J.). . . .

In charging the jury on the issue of dismissal for just cause on the basis of an employee's dishonesty, Paris J.'s instructions were as follows:

> . . . Now what constitutes just cause for dismissal may vary depending upon the circumstances of the case which must be assessed by you the jury. Generally speaking, however, examples of just cause would be an employee's serious misconduct, habitual neglect of duty, incompetence, repeated willful [sic] disobedience, or *dishonesty of a degree incompatible with the employment relationship. The conduct must be such as to undermine or seriously impair the trust and confidence the employer is entitled to place in the employee in the circumstances of their particular relationship. Something less than that is not sufficient cause for dismissal without reasonable notice.* . . . [Emphasis added.]

The question put to the jury on this point asked simply:

> Have the Defendants proven that (unknown to them at the time), cause for dismissal existed when they terminated the Plaintiff on August 31, 1994?

The jury responded to this question in the negative.

B. Court of Appeal for British Columbia. . .

. . . The Court of Appeal held that the dishonesty asserted by the respondents was not as clear as in *McPhillips*, where an employee billed his employer for unauthorized personal expenses. However, it found that Paris J. invited the jury to consider the extent of the dishonesty alleged, and to determine whether this "was of a degree that was incompatible with the employment relationship," and thus "sufficient to warrant dismissal." According to the Court of Appeal, such instructions were incorrect as a matter of law. In this regard, Hollinrake J.A. stated at para. 25:

> Dishonesty within the contract of employment, as is the case alleged here, is cause and that cause is not founded on the basis of the "degree" of the dishonesty.

IV. ISSUES

This appeal raises the following issues:
A. Did the trial judge err by instructing the jury that, to find just cause for dismissal, it would have to find not only that the plaintiff was deceitful, but that the dishonesty was "of a degree that was incompatible with the employment relationship"?
B. Based on the evidence before it, could the jury, acting judicially, have reasonably found that the appellant's conduct was not dishonest and thus, that just cause for summary dismissal did not exist?

. . .

V. ANALYSIS

A. The Standard for Dishonest Conduct in the Employment Relationship

Although this Court has yet to consider the question of whether an employee's dishonesty, in and of itself, necessarily gives rise to just cause for summary dismissal, this issue has been examined by the English courts, as well as appellate and lower courts in Canada. From an analysis of this jurisprudence, no clear principle or standard emerges. Rather, while one line of authority suggests that the nature of the dishonesty and the circumstances surrounding its occurrence must be considered, another seems to indicate that dishonest conduct alone — regardless of its degree — creates just cause for dismissal. A brief review of these two strands of jurisprudence would be useful before determining which should guide this Court's analysis in the present case.

1. Authority Indicating that *Context* Must Be Considered when Assessing Whether Dishonesty Amounts to Just Cause for Dismissal . . .

When examining whether an employee's misconduct — including dishonest misconduct — justifies his or her dismissal, courts have often considered the context of the alleged insubordination. Within this analysis, a finding of misconduct does not, by itself, give rise to just cause. Rather, the question to be addressed is whether, in the circumstances, the behaviour was such that the employment relationship could no longer viably subsist.

The Privy Council's decision in *Clouston & Co. v. Corry* . . . adopted this analytical framework. The question arising in that case was whether an employee's public drunkenness and disobedient conduct warranted his dismissal. The Privy Council's ruling spoke generally to the concept of "misconduct" and held that there was no fixed rule of law to define when termination would be warranted. The question is one of degree. The trial judge must first determine whether there is any evidence to submit to the jury in support of the allegation of justifiable dismissal. He or she also may direct jurors by informing them of the nature of the acts which, as a matter of law, will justify dismissal. However, the ultimate question of whether just cause for such dismissal exists is one of *fact* that the jury must decide. Thus, the Privy Council indicated that it is not sufficient that the jury find misconduct alone, since this will not necessarily provide a basis for dismissal. Rather, the jury must determine that the misconduct is impossible to reconcile with the employee's obligations under the employment contract. . . .

A similar analysis was undertaken in subsequent decisions dealing with this issue. For instance, in *Laws v. London Chronicle, Ltd.*, . . . the English Court of Appeal stated the following. . . .

> [S]ince a contract of service is but an example of contracts in general, so that the general law of contract will be applicable, it follows that, if summary dismissal is claimed to be justifiable, *the question must be whether the conduct complained of is such as to show the servant to have disregarded the essential conditions of the contract of service.* [Emphasis added.]

As such, Lord Evershed, M.R. held that a single act of disobedience justified dismissal only if it demonstrated that the servant had repudiated the contract or one of its essential conditions. In this way, the ruling in *Laws* indicated that an analysis of whether an employee's misconduct warrants dismissal requires an assessment of its degree and surrounding circumstances.

This contextual approach also has been adopted in several decisions by Canadian appellate courts. . . .

. . . [A]ccording to this reasoning, an employee's misconduct does not inherently justify dismissal without notice unless it is "so grievous" that it intimates the employee's abandonment of the intention to remain part of the employment relationship. . . .

The jurisprudence also reveals that an application of a contextual approach — which examines both the circumstances surrounding the conduct as well as its nature or degree — leaves the trier of fact with discretion as to whether a dishonest act gives rise to just cause. For example, in *Jewitt v. Prism Resources Ltd.* . . . Taggart J.A. held that an analysis of the employee's misconduct "in the circumstances" of that case did constitute cause for dismissal. *Jewitt* involved an employee who allowed a co-director's signature to be traced on a balance sheet. In contrast, an examination of the surrounding circumstances in *Hill v. Dow Chemical Canada Inc.* . . . led the Alberta Court of Queen's Bench to conclude that the misconduct in question merely reflected a single incident of "poor judgment." This finding, along with the conclusion that the employee lacked an intention to deceive, caused the court to conclude that the impugned behaviour did not warrant summary dismissal. At issue in *Hill* was an employee's unauthorized donation of bandages and ice packs owned by his employer to a local hockey team, in breach of company procedure. . . .

Cases in which courts have explicitly ruled that the issue of just cause is one of fact to be put to a jury lend further support to an approach that considers the particular circumstances surrounding the alleged employee misconduct. Rather than viewing cause for dismissal as a legal conclusion that *must* be drawn in any case where disobedience (including dishonesty) is proven, these cases indicate that just cause can only be determined through an inquiry by the trier of fact into (a) whether the evidence demonstrated employee misconduct and (b) whether, in the circumstances, such misconduct sufficed to justify the employee's termination without notice. . . .

To summarize, this first line of case law establishes that the question whether dishonesty provides just cause for summary dismissal is a matter to be decided by the trier of fact, and to be addressed through an analysis of the particular circumstances surrounding the employee's behaviour. In this respect, courts have held that factors such as the nature and degree of the misconduct, and whether it violates the "essential conditions" of the employment contract or breaches an employer's faith in an employee, must be considered in drawing factual conclusions as to the existence of just cause. . . .

2. Authority Indicating that Dishonesty *In and Of Itself* Warrants *Dismissal Without Notice*
The broad language used in a second line of decisions indicates that dishonesty, in and of itself, provides just cause, irrespective of the factors and circumstances surrounding the conduct, the nature or degree of such dishonesty, or whether it breached the essential conditions of the employment relationship.

This approach was articulated by the English Court of Appeal in *Boston Deep Sea Fishing and Ice Co. v. Ansell* . . . In that case, an agent had been instructed to arrange for several fishing boats to be built for his employer. The agent then received a secret commission from the boat builder, which the company learned of approximately one year later. The employee's conduct was found to be fraudulent, and this was held to provide ample justification for dismissal without notice. In reaching this conclusion, Bowen L.J. discussed the standard applicable for determining when dishonesty suffices as cause for terminating the employment relationship. At p. 363 he stated:

> [I]n cases where the character of the isolated act is such as of itself to be beyond all dispute a violation of the confidential relation, and a breach of faith towards the master, the rights of the master do not depend on the caprice of the jury, or of the tribunal which tries the question. Once the tribunal has found the fact — has found that there is a fraud and breach of faith — then the rights of the master to determine the contract follow as matter of law.

This passage indicates that once the confidence inherent to the master-servant relationship is breached, just cause for dismissal — *as a matter of law* — is automatically triggered, and must not depend on whether the trier of fact finds that such cause exists. Although Bowen L.J. spoke primarily to fraud, he also indicated that "breach of faith" in general may warrant dismissal. Such broad language suggests that any dishonest conduct which ruptures the trust inherent to the employer-employee relationship provides just cause. . . .

The strict approach . . . resonates in several . . . decisions rendered by Canadian courts, which have held that a finding of dishonesty, in and of itself, creates just cause for summary dismissal. In each of these cases, however, the courts dealt with forms of dishonesty that . . . bordered on theft, misappropriation, forgery or a fraudulent sham. In that connection, the courts drew parallels between dishonesty and fraud, either by noting their common ingredients. . . . In this vein, courts also emphasized that, for dishonesty to amount to cause, the employer must prove intent on the employee's part to engage in deceitful conduct. . . .

This line of jurisprudence seems to indicate that a finding of dishonesty gives rise to just cause as a matter of law. However, I am struck by the fact that, in all of the cases considered here, where cause was found to exist, courts were confronted with very serious forms of employee dishonesty. This point is instructive for determining the proper analytical approach to be adopted in the case at bar.

3. Applicable Standard for Assessing Whether and in What Circumstances Dishonesty Provides Just Cause

In light of the foregoing analysis, I am of the view that whether an employer is justified in dismissing an employee on the grounds of dishonesty is a question that requires an assessment of the context of the alleged misconduct. More specifically, the test is whether the employee's dishonesty gave rise to a breakdown in the employment relationship. This test can be expressed in different ways. One could say, for example, that just cause for dismissal exists where the dishonesty violates an essential condition of the employment contract, breaches the faith inherent to the work relationship, or is fundamentally or directly inconsistent with the employee's obligations to his or her employer.

In accordance with this test, a trial judge must instruct the jury to determine: (1) whether the evidence established the employee's deceitful conduct on a balance of probabilities; and (2) if so, whether the nature and degree of the dishonesty warranted dismissal. In my view, the second branch of this test does not blend questions of fact and law. Rather, assessing the seriousness of the misconduct requires the facts established at trial to be carefully considered and balanced. As such, it is a factual inquiry for the jury to undertake. . . .

. . . I conclude that a contextual approach to assessing whether an employee's dishonesty provides just cause for dismissal emerges from the case law on point. In certain contexts, applying this approach might lead to a strict outcome. Where theft, misappropriation or serious fraud is found, the decisions considered here establish that cause for termination exists. This is consistent with this Court's reasoning in *Lake Ontario Portland Cement Co. v. Groner*, . . . where this Court found that cause for dismissal on the basis of dishonesty exists where an employee acts *fraudulently* with respect to his employer. This principle necessarily rests on an examination of the nature and circumstances of the misconduct. Absent such an analysis, it would be impossible for a court to conclude that the dishonesty was severely fraudulent in nature and thus, that it sufficed to justify dismissal without notice.

This is not to say that there cannot be lesser sanctions for less serious types of misconduct. For example, an employer may be justified in docking an employee's pay for any loss incurred by a minor misuse of company property. This is one of several disciplinary measures an employer may take in these circumstances.

Underlying the approach I propose is the principle of proportionality. An effective balance must be struck between the severity of an employee's misconduct and the sanction imposed. The importance of this balance is better understood by considering the sense of identity and self-worth individuals frequently derive from their employment, a concept that was explored in *Reference Re Public Service Employee Relations Act (Alta.)*, . . . where Dickson C.J. (writing in dissent) stated at p. 368:

> Work is one of the most fundamental aspects in a person's life, providing the individual with a means of financial support and, as importantly, a contributory role in society. A person's employment is an essential component of his or her sense of identity, self-worth and emotional well-being.

This passage was subsequently cited with approval by this Court in *Machtinger v. HOJ Industries Ltd.*, . . . and in *Wallace, supra*, at para. 95. In *Wallace*, the majority added to this notion by stating that not only is work itself fundamental to an individual's identity, but "the manner in which employment can be terminated is equally important."

Given this recognition of the integral nature of work to the lives and identities of individuals in our society, care must be taken in fashioning rules and principles of law which would enable the employment relationship to be terminated without notice. The importance of this is underscored by the power imbalance that this Court has recognized as ingrained in most facets of the employment relationship. . . .

In light of these considerations, I have serious difficulty with the absolute, unqualified rule that the Court of Appeal endorsed in this case. . . .

. . . I favour an analytical framework that examines each case on its own particular facts and circumstances, and considers the nature and seriousness of the dishonesty in order to assess whether it is reconcilable with sustaining the employment relationship. . . .

4. Application to Paris J.'s Jury Instructions

Applying the foregoing analysis to this case, unlike the Court of Appeal, I see no reason to interfere with the trial decision on the basis of Paris J.'s instructions to the jury. . . . Paris J.'s instructions therefore were entirely consistent with the contextual approach discussed above, and thus do not serve as a basis for setting the jury verdict aside.

B. Reasonableness of the Jury Verdict

. . .

In the present case, given the variance in the evidence before the jury, I must conclude that it could have reasonably and judicially found that the appellant did not engage in dishonest conduct of a degree incompatible with his employment relationship. Therefore, the requisite standard for setting aside the verdict was not met, as I now will discuss.

The December 12, 1994 letter from the appellant to Dr. Graff, an internal medicine and cardiac specialist and one of his treating physicians, provides an instructive starting point for the analysis of this issue. In this letter, the appellant requested that Dr. Graff clarify his recollection of the treatment recommended during a medical appointment that had taken place on July 20, 1994. The most relevant passage of this letter for the purposes of the present appeal states the following:

> The only issue that concerns me is that while I agree that you recommended a "beta blocker" as the next method of treatment on July 20, 1994, it is my understanding that you did not want me to start treatment until I returned to work. I remember telling you that BC TEL did not want me back at work until my blood pressure was fully controlled — a concept that bothered you at the time. . . . My recollection is that you said that if I was not returning to the stressfull [sic] job that causing [sic] my elevated blood pressure, then I should remain on Adalat until I was in my new job. If my blood pressure remained elevated in my new job, I was to return to see you to begin a "beta blocker" treatment. You did not issue me a prescription or give me any "beta blocker" samples on July 20.
>
> . . . It does not make sense to me that I would refuse to try "beta blockers" as it also does not make sense that you would prescibe [sic] medication where the apparent cause or trigger was removed!

According to the respondents, this letter revealed the appellant's knowledge of the availability of a medication, namely, the beta blocker, which one of his physicians believed could effectively enable him to return to his former position without any risk to his health. Moreover, the respondents pointed out that, on cross-examination, the appellant testified that Dr. Graff did not discuss any of the adverse side effects of this medication with him. The appellant further testified that Dr. Graff was of the view that, while this medication should not be prescribed at that time, if the appellant returned to work in his former position and his blood pressure continued to rise, there would be a reason to consider administering the beta blockers.

The respondents also argued that this letter indicated that Dr. Graff had implied during the July 20, 1994 appointment that the appellant could return to work, in which case beta blockers might eventually become necessary. However, in voice mail messages left for his immediate superior just after that appointment (on July 20th and 27th, 1994), the appellant stressed that both his family doctor and Dr. Graff were of the view that "a new job, a new change of environment" was what he truly needed. While the appellant alluded to the possibility of trying a "new medication," he indicated that Dr. Graff was of the view that it should not be attempted — given its adverse side effects — if his health could be improved by "a job change in a different kind of environment."

From this evidence, a certain degree of inconsistency can be identified between what the appellant appears to have been told by Dr. Graff, and the information he subsequently conveyed to his employers. The evidence suggests that Dr. Graff believed that the appellant could return to work, even in his former position as Controller, and, if his hypertension became more acute at that point, it could be controlled through the use of beta blockers. However, the voice mail messages of July 20th and July 27th indicate that the appellant did not put this information forward as fully and clearly as he might have. Rather than mention the possibility of returning to his former position if beta blockers were administered, he instead stressed that his physicians were of the view that a change in jobs would in fact be the most beneficial form of "treatment." At trial, however, the appellant admitted on cross-examination that this advice had not in fact been given by his specialist.

This contradiction could raise some suspicion in the minds of jurors as to the trustworthiness of the appellant's character. But, does the evidence lead unquestionably and unequivocally to the conclusion that the appellant's conduct was sufficiently dishonest to provide just cause for summary dismissal? A review of the evidence in its entirety leads me to answer this question in the negative. To my mind, the material in the record provides a sufficient basis for a jury to conclude that the appellant reasonably and truly believed that his physicians, including Dr. Graff, were of the view that beta blockers should be considered only as a "last resort" treatment, and that they were not yet required at that point in time. . . .

The respondents claimed in oral argument that the appellant's falsehood lay in giving Dr. Graff's imprimatur to the notion that beta blockers carried adverse side effects. . . .

. . .

Thus, while there may not have been a full disclosure of all material facts by the appellant, this was not required of him. Rather, the question is whether he engaged in dishonesty in a manner that undermined, or was incompatible with his employment relationship. An analysis of the record as a whole leads me to conclude that the jury, acting judicially, could have reasonably found that this was not the case. For this reason, there is no basis upon which to interfere with the jury's verdict that the respondents had not proven just cause warranting dismissal.

VI. DISPOSITION

For the foregoing reasons, the appeal is allowed, the judgment of the British Columbia Court of Appeal is set aside, and the order of Paris J. is restored, with the exception of the award for aggravated damages, which is struck. . . .

* * *

Quebec civil law is similar to the Canadian common law on this question. Section 2094 of the Quebec *Civil Code* states that "One of the parties may, for a serious reason, unilaterally resiliate the contract of employment without prior notice."

2:460 Procedural Fairness

Canadian courts have not yet held that an employer is under any duty to act with procedural fairness in dismissing an employee, unless the employment is governed by statute. In *Indian Head School Division v. Knight*, [1990] 1 S.C.R. 653 at 668, L'Heureux-Dubé J. said:

> . . . the duty to act fairly does not depend on doctrines of employment law, but stems from the fact that the employer is a public body whose powers are derived from statute, powers that must be exercised according to the rules of administrative law.

If an employer dismisses an employee in breach of a disciplinary or other procedure set down in a statute or in regulations promulgated pursuant to a statute, the dismissal is unlawful: so too if the dismissal violates the administrative law duty of fairness in cases of public or quasi-public sector employees where that duty is applicable. In these circumstances, the dismissal is void *ab initio*. Therefore, the court can grant a discretionary remedy such as a declaration or a mandatory injunction, which will have the effect of reinstating the employee. Of course, such a discretionary remedy cannot be demanded as of right by an employee.

The content of the administrative law duty of fairness toward employees who are employed under statute is discussed by L'Heureux-Dubé J. in the *Indian Head School Division* case, above, at 682–83.

2:500 REMEDIES FOR WRONGFUL DISMISSAL

REFERENCES

Geoffrey England, Innis Christie, & Roderick Wood, *Employment Law in Canada*, 3d ed. (Markham: Butterworths, 1998), c. 16

The remedies available to the wrongfully dismissed worker at common law should be compared with those available under collective agreements for unionized workers; with those available under statutory systems of adjudication provided to non-unionized workers, such as are found in section 240 of the *Canada Labour Code*; and with those available to workers dismissed in breach of human rights and collective bargaining statutes. Only the common law fails to provide for compulsory reinstatement and for make-whole financial awards designed to compensate the employee for his or her real-world losses resulting from the unlawful dismissal.

2:510 Reinstatement

Geoffrey England, "Recent Developments in the Law of the Employment Contract: Continuing Tension Between the Rights Paradigm and the Efficiency Paradigm" (1995) 20 Queen's L.J. 557 at 605–9

The future of the remedy of compulsory reinstatement will be a useful gauge of the shifting balance between the two paradigms [the rights paradigm and the efficiency paradigm]. Courts have traditionally refused equitable or other discretionary remedies that would have the effect of specifically enforcing an employment contract, except where a public officeholder is dismissed in violation of a statutory procedure or the administrative law duty of fairness. This has been justified in part by the principle of mutuality. The courts will not endorse slavery by forcing an unwilling employee to work for an employer, and this has been taken to preclude forcing an unwilling employer to take back a wrongfully dismissed employee. In reality, however, the two situations are not on a par, as it is not tantamount to slavery to reinstate an employee who requests that remedy.

While the practical difficulty of enforcing reinstatement orders has unquestionably contributed to the courts' policy against granting such orders, the main rationale appears to be a reluctance to question the employer's judgment of what is best for the enterprise. The assumption is that mutual trust and confidence have been irretrievably destroyed by the dismissal, or that the production process would otherwise suffer if the employee were reinstated. This is the quintessence of the efficiency paradigm.

In contrast, the rights paradigm envisages some circumstances when reinstatement would be justifiable. One such situation, referred to above, arises where the contract contains an express procedure which the employer has violated in dismissing the employee. In that situation, reinstatement may be ordered pending compliance with the proper procedures, as damages alone cannot fully compensate for the employee's loss of the opportunity to persuade the employer to change its mind before carrying out the dismissal. Mutual trust and confidence would hardly be undermined by requiring the employer to honour obligations of its own making.

Similarly, where the employer fires a worker for an alleged criminal offence, but promises reinstatement if the worker is found not guilty, it seems unfair to allow the employer to renege on the promise. A recent Nova Scotia trial judgment hinted that reinstatement might be appropriate in these circumstances, at least where the worker does not occupy a managerial position.

Second, some workers derive a unique personal benefit from actually doing the job, which money cannot adequately replace. Doctors and university professors develop professional skills and derive vocational satisfaction, as do nurses, pastors, and teachers. Under the rights paradigm, courts have begun to protect this largely psychological benefit by what amounts to a reinstatement order. Thus, an English court has granted an injunction preventing an employer from unilaterally transferring a social worker from a research team on child abuse to less professionally satisfying duties. The Ontario Court of Appeal has granted a declaration that the removal of a clergyman from the rolls of the United Church was void because of failure to comply with the procedures in the Church's constitution. The Court distinguished this situation from the normal employment relationship, but the declaration nonetheless reinstated the plaintiff indirectly. In a Québec case where there was a misunderstanding on whether an orchestra conductor's term contract had been renewed, the court granted an interlocutory injunction reinstating him, pending resolution of the issue at trial. The crucial factor in that case was the unique benefit of remaining in the job, as the conductor did not want to miss a major upcoming performance. However, the Court condemned as outdated the general policy against ordering reinstatement. The principle that an equitable remedy will be granted where damages cannot adequately make up for such vocational losses is plainly applicable to many mainstream employment relationships.

Third, a strong rights argument can be made for reinstatement in order to achieve parity between the common law and other labour law regimes. Reinstatement is the normal remedy for unionized workers under the unjust discharge provisions of collective agreements. It is available, although it is granted more sparingly to non-unionized workers under statutory unjust dismissal provisions in the few Canadian jurisdictions which have such provisions. It is available to all workers, unionized or not, who are dismissed in violation of human rights, health and safety, and labour relations legislation. It is mandated by international labour law conventions which Canada has ratified. Furthermore, increasingly sophisticated personnel management techniques should make it easier, at least for large employers, to reintegrate wrongfully dismissed employees into the workplace. In exceptional circumstances, where the work environment has been irredeemably soured, reinstatement could be denied, as is the practice in arbitration and statutory adjudication.

Recent empirical evidence confirms the limited effectiveness of reinstatement orders in the non-unionized workplace, where there is no employee representation machinery to police how the reinstated employee is treated. One possible solution is to award a sizeable amount of punitive damages in conjunction with the reinstatement order, but the souring effect of such an award could make reinstatement even more precarious. Another possibility is to vest authority for supervising such orders in joint labour-management health and safety committees, or health and safety representatives in smaller firms, but these bodies have not been particularly successful even in their primary function of enforcing health and safety legislation. For the time being, in any event, the chances are that, if reinstatement is adopted at all, it will be limited to situations where the court is enforcing agreed-upon procedural machinery which the employer has chosen to disregard.
[Reprinted by permission.]

2:520 Financial Compensation

The measure of damages for wrongful dismissal is governed by the length of the notice period in the contract of employment, because what makes the dismissal unlawful at common law is the employer's failure to give due notice or wages in lieu. Therefore, the employee can recover only for wages and benefits that he or she would have been legally entitled to during the contractual notice period. We examined the principles for determining the contractual notice period earlier in this chapter. If, for example, the contract of employment expressly provides for four weeks' notice and this satisfies the requirements of the relevant employment standards statute, the employee will receive only four weeks' pay and benefits, even though he or she may remain unemployed for years following the wrongful dismissal.

Furthermore, as outlined in *Ceccol v. Ontario Gymnastic Federation* (2001), 55 O.R. (3d) 614 (C.A.), set out in section 2:430 above, the employee's common law duty to mitigate the financial loss resulting from the dismissal requires that he or she make reasonable efforts to obtain reasonably suitable alternative employment. If the employee fails to meet the duty to mitigate, the damages awarded will be reduced according to his or her degree of inactivity. The leading Canadian case on the nature and extent of the duty to mitigate is the Supreme Court of Canada decision in *Red Deer College v. Michaels*, [1976] 2 S.C.R. 324.

A particularly controversial question in recent years has been whether a wrongfully dismissed employee can claim damages for mental distress.

Wallace v. United Grain Growers Ltd., [1997] 3 S.C.R. 701

IACOBUCCI J. (LAMER C.J.C., SOPINKA, GONTHIER, CORY, and MAJOR JJ. concurring):—

1. FACTS

In 1972, Public Press, a wholly owned subsidiary of the respondent, United Grain Growers Ltd. ("UGG"), decided to update its operations and seek a larger volume of commercial printing work. Don Logan was the marketing manager of the company's publishing and printing divisions at that time. For Logan, the key to achieving this increase in volume was to hire someone with an existing record of sales on a specialized piece of equipment known as a "Web" press.

In April 1972, the appellant, Jack Wallace, met Logan to discuss the possibility of employment. Wallace had the type of experience that Logan sought, having worked approximately 25 years for a competitor that used the "Web" press. Wallace had become concerned over the unfair manner in which he and others were being treated by their employer. However, he expressed some reservation about jeopardizing his secure position at the company. Wallace explained to Logan that as he was 45 years of age, if he were to leave his current employer he would require a guarantee of job security. He also sought several assurances from Logan regarding fair treatment and remuneration. He received such assurances and was told by Logan that if he performed as expected, he could continue to work for Public Press until retirement.

Wallace commenced employment with Public Press in June of 1972. He enjoyed great success at the company and was the top salesperson for each of the years he spent in its employ.

On August 22, 1986, Wallace was summarily discharged by Public Press' sales manager Leonard Domerecki. Domerecki offered no explanation for his actions. In the days before the dismissal both Domerecki and UGG's general manager had complimented Wallace on his work.

By letter of August 29, 1986, Domerecki advised Wallace that the main reason for his termination was his inability to perform his duties satisfactorily. Wallace's statement of claim alleging wrongful dismissal was issued on October 23, 1986. In its statement of defence, the respondent alleged that Wallace had been dismissed for cause. This allegation was maintained for over two years and was only withdrawn when the trial commenced on December 12, 1988.

At the time of his dismissal Wallace was almost 59 years old. He had been employed by Public Press for 14 years. The termination of his employment and the allegations of cause created emotional difficulties for Wallace and he was forced to seek psychiatric help. His attempts to find similar employment were largely unsuccessful.

On September 26, 1985, Wallace made a voluntary assignment into personal bankruptcy. When he commenced his action against the respondent, Wallace remained an undischarged bankrupt. After Wallace had completed his case at trial, UGG moved to amend its statement of defence to assert that as an undischarged bankrupt, Wallace lacked the capacity to commence or continue the proceedings. UGG requested that Wallace's claim for damages for failure to provide reasonable notice of termination be struck out.

The trial judge granted leave to amend the statement of defence and then struck out Wallace's claim for damages for breach of contract. He held that the action in that regard was a nullity from the outset. Wallace's attempt to appeal that ruling was stayed by the Manitoba Court of Appeal pending completion of the trial. The trial resumed and subject to the outcome of the appeal on the bankruptcy issue, Wallace was awarded damages for wrongful dismissal based on a 24-month notice period and aggravated damages.

The Manitoba Court of Appeal reversed the findings of the trial judge with respect to the appellant's capacity to maintain an action for breach of contract. It also allowed the respondent's cross-appeal, substituting a judgment in favour of the appellant based on a 15-month reasonable notice period, and overturned the award of aggravated damages. . . .

[The parts of the judgment dealing with the bankruptcy issue have been omitted.]

The appeal raises five issues:

a. Was there a fixed-term contract?
b. Did the Court of Appeal err in overturning the trial judge's award for aggravated damages resulting from mental distress?
c. Can the appellant sue in either contract or tort for 'bad faith discharge'?
d. Is the appellant entitled to punitive damages?
e. Did the Court of Appeal err in reducing the appellant's reasonable notice damages from 24 to 15 months?

. . .

B. Fixed-Term Contract

The appellant submitted that the courts below erred in rejecting his claim that he had a fixed-term contract for employment until retirement. The learned trial judge exhaustively reviewed all of the circumstances surrounding Wallace's hiring and concluded that there was insufficient evidence to support this claim. The Court of Appeal accepted the facts as they were found by the trial judge and agreed with his conclusion. In light of these concurrent findings of fact, I see no palpable error or other reason to interfere with the conclusion of the courts below.

C. Damages for Mental Distress

Relying upon the principles enunciated in [*Vorvis v. Insurance Corporation of British Columbia*], . . . the Court of Appeal held that any award of damages beyond compensation for breach of contract for failure to give reasonable notice of termination 'must be founded on a separately actionable course of conduct.' Although there has been criticism of *Vorvis*, . . . this is an accurate statement of the law. The Court of Appeal also noted that this requirement necessarily negates the trial judge's reliance on concepts of foreseeability and matters in the contemplation of the parties. An employment contract is not one in which peace of mind is the very matter contracted for . . . and so, absent an independently actionable wrong, the foreseeability of mental distress or the fact that the parties contemplated its occurrence is of no consequence, subject to what I say on employer conduct below.

The Court of Appeal concluded that there was insufficient evidence to support a finding that the actions of UGG constituted a separate actionable wrong either in tort or in contract. I agree with these findings and see no reason to disturb them. I note, however, that in circumstances where the manner of dismissal has caused mental distress but falls short of an independent actionable wrong, the employee is not without recourse. Rather, the trial judge has discretion in these circumstances to extend the period of reasonable notice to which an employee is entitled. Thus, although recovery for mental distress might not be available under a separate head of damages, the possibility of recovery still remains. I will be returning to this point in my discussion of reasonable notice below.

D. Bad Faith Discharge

The appellant urged this Court to find that he could sue UGG either in contract or in tort for 'bad faith discharge.' With respect to the action in contract, he submitted that the Court should imply into the employment contract a term that the employee would not be fired except for cause or legitimate business reasons. I cannot accede to this submission. The law has long recognized the mutual right of both employers and employees to terminate an employment contract at any time provided there are no express provisions to the contrary. In *Farber v. Royal Trust Co.* . . . Gonthier J., speaking for the Court, summarized the general contractual principles applicable to contracts of employment as follows . . . :

> In the context of an indeterminate employment contract, one party can resiliate the contract unilaterally. The resiliation is considered a dismissal if it originates with the employer and a resignation if it originates with the employee. If an employer dismisses

an employee without cause, the employer must give the employee reasonable notice that the contract is about to be terminated or compensation in lieu thereof.

A requirement of 'good faith' reasons for dismissal would, in effect, contravene these principles and deprive employers of the ability to determine the composition of their workforce. In the context of the accepted theories on the employment relationship, such a law would, in my opinion, be overly intrusive and inconsistent with established principles of employment law, and more appropriately, should be left to legislative enactment rather than judicial pronouncement.

I must also reject the appellant's claim that he can sue in tort for breach of a good faith and fair dealing obligation with regard to dismissals. The Court of Appeal noted the absence of persuasive authority on this point and concluded that such a tort has not yet been recognized by Canadian courts. I agree with these findings. To create such a tort in this case would therefore constitute a radical shift in the law, again a step better left to be taken by the legislatures.

For these reasons I conclude that the appellant is unable to sue in either tort or contract for 'bad faith discharge.' However, I will be returning to the subject of good faith and fair dealing in my discussion of reasonable notice below.

E. Punitive Damages

Punitive damages are an exception to the general rule that damages are meant to compensate the plaintiff. The purpose of such an award is the punishment of the defendant. . . . The appellant argued that the trial judge and the Court of Appeal erred in refusing to award punitive damages. I do not agree. Relying on *Vorvis*, . . . Lockwood J. found that UGG did not engage in sufficiently 'harsh, vindictive, reprehensible and malicious' conduct to merit condemnation by such an award. He also noted the absence of an actionable wrong. The Court of Appeal concurred. Again, there is no reason to interfere with these findings. Consequently, I agree with the courts below that there is no foundation for an award of punitive damages.

F. Reasonable Notice

The Court of Appeal upheld the trial judge's findings of fact and agreed that in the circumstances of this case damages for failure to give notice ought to be at the high end of the scale. However, the court found the trial judge's award of 24 months' salary in lieu of notice to be excessive and reflective of an element of aggravated damages having crept into his determination. It overturned his award and substituted the equivalent of 15 months' salary. For the reasons which follow, I would restore the trial judge's award of damages in the amount of 24 months' salary in lieu of notice.

In determining what constitutes reasonable notice of termination, the courts have generally applied the principles articulated by McRuer C.J.H.C. in *Bardal v. Globe & Mail Ltd.* . . . :

> There can be no catalogue laid down as to what is reasonable notice in particular classes of cases. The reasonableness of the notice must be decided with reference to each particular case, having regard to the character of the employment, the length of service of

the servant, the age of the servant and the availability of similar employment, having regard to the experience, training and qualifications of the servant.

. . . Applying these factors in the instant case, I concur with the trial judge's finding that in light of the appellant's advanced age, his 14-year tenure as the company's top salesman and his limited prospects for re-employment, a lengthy period of notice is warranted. I note, however, that *Bardal, supra*, does not state, nor has it been interpreted to imply, that the factors it enumerated were exhaustive. . . . Canadian courts have added several additional factors to the *Bardal* list. The application of these factors to the assessment of a dismissed employee's notice period will depend upon the particular circumstances of the case.

One such factor that has often been considered is whether the dismissed employee had been induced to leave previous secure employment. . . . According to one authority, many courts have sought to compensate the reliance and expectation interests of terminated employees by increasing the period of reasonable notice where the employer has induced the employee to 'quit a secure, well-paying job . . . on the strength of promises of career advancement and greater responsibility, security and compensation with the new organization'. . . .

In my opinion, such inducements are properly included among the considerations which tend to lengthen the amount of notice required. I concur with the comments of Christie et al., supra, and recognize that there is a need to safeguard the employee's reliance and expectation interests in inducement situations. I note, however, that not all inducements will carry equal weight when determining the appropriate period of notice. The significance of the inducement in question will vary with the circumstances of the particular case and its effect, if any, on the notice period is a matter best left to the discretion of the trial judge.

In the instant case, the trial judge found that UGG went to great lengths to relieve Wallace's fears about jeopardizing his existing secure employment and to entice him into joining their company. . . .

In addition to the promise that he could continue to work for the company until retirement, UGG also offered several assurances with respect to fair treatment. . . . Although the trial judge did not make specific reference to the inducement factor in his analysis of reasonable notice, I believe that, in the circumstances of this case, these inducements, in particular the guarantee of job security, are factors which support his decision to award damages at the high end of the scale.

The appellant urged this Court to recognize the ability of a dismissed employee to sue in contract or alternatively in tort for 'bad faith discharge.' Although I have rejected both as avenues for recovery, by no means do I condone the behaviour of employers who subject employees to callous and insensitive treatment in their dismissal, showing no regard for their welfare. Rather, I believe that such bad faith conduct in the manner of dismissal is another factor that is properly compensated for by an addition to the notice period.

In *Lojstrup v. British Columbia Buildings Corp.* . . . the British Columbia Court of Appeal found that *Addis v. Gramophone Co.* . . . *Ansari v. British Columbia Hydro and Power Authority* . . . and *Wadden v. Guaranty Trust Co. of Canada* . . . preclude extending the notice period to account for manner of dismissal. Generally speaking, these cases have found that claims relating to the manner in which the discharge took place are not properly considered in an action for damages for breach of contract. Rather, it is said, damages are limited to injuries that flow from the breach itself, which in the employment context is the failure to give reasonable notice. The manner of dismissal was found not to affect these damages.

Although these decisions are grounded in general principles of contract law, I believe, with respect, that they have all failed to take into account the unique characteristics of the particular type of contract with which they were concerned, namely, a contract of employment. Similarly, there was not an appropriate recognition of the special relationship which these contracts govern. In my view, both are relevant considerations.

The contract of employment has many characteristics that set it apart from the ordinary commercial contract. Some of the views on this subject that have already been approved of in previous decisions of this Court (see e.g. *Machtinger, supra*) bear repeating. As K. Swinton noted in 'Contract Law and the Employment Relationship: The Proper Forum for Reform' in B.J. Reiter and J. Swan, eds., *Studies in Contract Law* . . . :

> . . . the terms of the employment contract rarely result from an exercise of free bargaining power in the way that the paradigm commercial exchange between two traders does. Individual employees on the whole lack both the bargaining power and the information necessary to achieve more favourable contract provisions than those offered by the employer, particularly with regard to tenure.

This power imbalance is not limited to the employment contract itself. Rather, it informs virtually all facets of the employment relationship. In *Slaight Communications Inc. v. Davidson* . . . Dickson C.J., writing for the majority of the Court, had occasion to comment on the nature of this relationship. . . . [H]e quoted with approval from P. Davies and M. Freedland, *Kahn-Freund's Labour and the Law* . . . :

> [T]he relation between an employer and an isolated employee or worker is typically a relation between a bearer of power and one who is not a bearer of power. In its inception it is an act of submission, in its operation it is a condition of subordination. . . .

> . . . The vulnerability of employees is underscored by the level of importance which our society attaches to employment. . . .

> . . . [F]or most people, work is one of the defining features of their lives. Accordingly, any change in a person's employment status is bound to have far-reaching repercussions. In 'Aggravated Damages and the Employment Contract,'. . . Schai noted . . . that, '[w]hen this change is involuntary, the extent of our "personal dislocation" is even greater.'

The point at which the employment relationship ruptures is the time when the employee is most vulnerable and hence, most in need of protection. In recognition of this need, the law ought to encourage conduct that minimizes the damage and dislocation (both economic and personal) that result from dismissal. In *Machtinger* [*v. HOJ Industries Ltd.*], . . . it was noted that the manner in which employment can be terminated is equally important to an individual's identity as the work itself (at p. 1002). By way of expanding upon this statement, I note that the loss of one's job is always a traumatic event. However, when termination is accompanied by acts of bad faith in the manner of discharge, the results can be especially devastating. In my opinion, to ensure that employees receive adequate protection, employers ought to be held to an obligation of good faith and fair dealing in the manner of dismissal, the breach of which will be compensated for by adding to the length of the notice period. . . .

The obligation of good faith and fair dealing is incapable of precise definition. However, at a minimum, I believe that in the course of dismissal employers ought to be candid, reasonable, honest and forthright with their employees and should refrain from engaging in conduct that is unfair or is in bad faith by being, for example, untruthful, misleading or unduly insensitive. In order to illustrate possible breaches of this obligation, I refer now to some examples of the conduct over which the courts expressed their disapproval in the cases cited above.

In *Trask* [*v. Terra Nova Motors Ltd.*] . . . an employer maintained a wrongful accusation of involvement in a theft and communicated this accusation to other potential employers of the dismissed employee. *Jivrag* [*v. City of Calgary*] . . . involved similar unfounded accusations of theft combined with a refusal to provide a letter of reference after the termination. In *Dunning* [*v. Royal Bank*], . . . bad faith conduct was clearly present. Although the plaintiff's position had been eliminated, he was told by several senior executives that another position would probably be found for him and that the new assignment would necessitate a transfer. However, at the same time that the plaintiff was being reassured about his future, a senior representative of the company was contemplating his termination. When a position could not be found, the decision was made to terminate the plaintiff. This decision was not communicated to the plaintiff for over a month despite the fact that his employers knew he was in the process of selling his home in anticipation of the transfer. News of his termination was communicated to the plaintiff abruptly following the sale of his home.

In *Corbin* [*v. Standard Life Assurance Co.*], . . . the New Brunswick Court of Appeal expressed its displeasure over the conduct of an employer who made the decision to fire the employee when he was on disability leave, suffering from a major depression. The employee advised the manager as to when he would be returning to duty and informed him that he was taking a two-week vacation. He was fired immediately upon his return to work. The facts in *MacDonald* [*v. Royal Canadian Legion*] . . . are also illustrative of bad faith conduct. In that case, the defendant employer closed its bar for three months and laid off the plaintiff bartender. While the bar was closed, the executive committee was replaced and the new officers decided to implement a different salary structure for bartenders when the bar reopened. The employer advertised for a bartender at a rate of almost half of the plaintiff's hourly rate. The plaintiff was unaware of any change in his status, and it was only when he saw the advertisement in the newspaper that he learned that he had been dismissed and was not to be offered reinstatement.

These examples by no means exhaust the list of possible types of bad faith or unfair dealing in the manner of dismissal. However, all are indicative of the type of conduct that ought to merit compensation by way of an addition to the notice period. I note that, depending upon the circumstances of the individual case, not all acts of bad faith or unfair dealing will be equally injurious and thus, the amount by which the notice period is extended will vary. Furthermore, I do not intend to advocate anything akin to an automatic claim for damages under this heading in every case of dismissal. In each case, the trial judge must examine the nature of the bad faith conduct and its impact in the circumstances.

The Court of Appeal in the instant case recognized the relevance of manner of dismissal in the determination of the appropriate period of reasonable notice. However, . . . the court found that this factor could only be considered 'where it impacts on the future employment prospects of the dismissed employee' (p. 180). With respect, I believe that this is an overly restrictive view. In my opinion, the law must recognize a more expansive list of injuries which may flow from unfair treatment or bad faith in the manner of dismissal.

It has long been accepted that a dismissed employee is not entitled to compensation for injuries flowing from the fact of the dismissal itself. . . . Thus, although the loss of a job is very often the cause of injured feelings and emotional upset, the law does not recognize these as compensable losses. However, where an employee can establish that an employer engaged in bad faith conduct or unfair dealing in the course of dismissal, injuries such as humiliation, embarrassment and damage to one's sense of self-worth and self-esteem might all be worthy of compensation depending upon the circumstances of the case. In these situations, compensation does not flow from the fact of dismissal itself, but rather from the manner in which the dismissal was effected by the employer.

Often the intangible injuries caused by bad faith conduct or unfair dealing on dismissal will lead to difficulties in finding alternative employment, a tangible loss which the Court of Appeal rightly recognized as warranting an addition to the notice period. It is likely that the more unfair or in bad faith the manner of dismissal is the more this will have an effect on the ability of the dismissed employee to find new employment. However, in my view the intangible injuries are sufficient to merit compensation in and of themselves. I recognize that bad faith conduct which affects employment prospects may be worthy of considerably more compensation than that which does not, but in both cases damage has resulted that should be compensable.

. . . I note that there may be those who would say that this approach imposes an onerous obligation on employers. I would respond simply by saying that I fail to see how it can be onerous to treat people fairly, reasonably, and decently at a time of trauma and despair. In my view, the reasonable person would expect such treatment. So should the law.

In the case before this Court, the trial judge documented several examples of bad faith conduct on the part of UGG. He noted the abrupt manner in which Wallace was dismissed despite having received compliments on his work from his superiors only days before. He found that UGG made a conscious decision to 'play hardball' with Wallace and maintained unfounded allegations of cause until the day the trial began. Further, as a result of UGG's persistence in maintaining these allegations, '[w]ord got around, and it was rumoured in the trade that he had been involved in some wrongdoing' (p. 173). Finally, he found that the dismissal and subsequent events were largely responsible for causing Wallace's depression. . . .

I agree with the trial judge's conclusion that the actions of UGG seriously diminished Wallace's prospects of finding similar employment. In light of this fact, and the other circumstances of this case, I am not persuaded that the trial judge erred in awarding the equivalent of 24 months' salary in lieu of notice. It may be that such an award is at the high end of the scale; however, taking into account all of the relevant factors, this award is not unreasonable and accordingly, I can see no reason to interfere. Therefore, for the reasons above, I would restore the order of the trial judge with respect to the appropriate period of reasonable notice and allow the appeal on this ground. . . .

[McLachlin J., with La Forest and L'Heureux JJ. concurring, dissented in part.]

Chapter 3: Introduction to Collective Bargaining Policy

3:100 INTRODUCTION

We turn now to the second of the three legal regimes governing productive relations in Canada's collective bargaining law. As the material in Chapter 1 makes clear, the shift from the individual contract of employment to the collective bargaining system rested on complex normative and empirical arguments. The accepted or received wisdom is that this second regime represents a procedural mechanism designed to address the perceived limitations of the common law regime. But as the following excerpt shows, it is a peculiar sort of procedural mechanism.

Roy J. Adams, *Industrial Relations under Liberal Democracy: North America in Comparative Perspective* (Columbia, S.C.: University of South Carolina Press, 1995) c. 4

CONTEMPORARY COLLECTIVE BARGAINING

The Modern Employment Relationship

The modern employment relationship is regulated by a complex web of rules. There are rules specifying the amount and nature of remuneration: wages, benefits, pensions, profit sharing, and so on. There are rules that define the nature of the job and the method whereby performance in carrying out job tasks will be evaluated. There are rules denoting appropriate and inappropriate behavior and rules regulating the discipline that may be imposed on those who engage in improper conduct. Within modern employment relations, employers and employees have rights and duties, and there are rules specifying what might be done if rights are not respected and sanctions that may be invoked if duty is not done.

There are many methods for creating this web of rules. The government may establish the rules through the passage of laws and regulations. Under communism, this is the overwhelmingly dominant means for establishing conditions of employment. The rules may be established unilaterally by the employer. In the early nineteenth century, this was the dominant method in all of the countries that are now classified as liberal democracies. The rules may also be unilaterally established by labor organizations. Where they were strong, the early unions developed their own internal rules for minimum wage rates for the trade, for workload levels, and for apprenticeship training. Additionally, they demanded that employers abide by these rules if they wanted to employ any member of the union. More commonly today rules are established through bilateral (union-management negotiations) or multilateral (labor-management-government) processes.

Throughout the contemporary industrialized world, the principle is accepted that employees should be able to influence the conditions under which they work. The dominant institution for putting that principle into action is the bilateral, union-management process of collective bargaining. In many countries, union-management bargaining is supplemented by the use of mechanisms such as workers participation on corporate boards of directors, by the establishment of statutory works councils, by the appointment of labor and business representatives to quasi governmental agencies, and by formal or informal tripartite consideration of socioeconomic policy. It is also supplemented to a degree by individual bargaining. However, most rules in the employment setting apply to everyone in a class (e.g., all production workers, all secretaries, all accountants) and cannot be individually varied. The wage system, pensions, operating hours, and health and safety policy are all critical to individual employees, but cannot be individually negotiated. They may be either imposed unilaterally or negotiated collectively.

North America, and the United States more particularly, is exceptional in its almost exclusive reliance on collective bargaining as the means to make the principle of participation operative. Also exceptional is the requirement that unions must be certified as bargaining agents in discrete bargaining units in order for employers to be expected to recognize and negotiate with them. What we in North America refer to simply as collective bargaining is a very specific variant of bargaining with positive and negative aspects that are not necessarily generalizable. In this chapter, my goal is to place our practice in comparative perspective so that a judgement may be made of its relative merits and problems.

Theoretical Justification of Collective Bargaining

In a democratic nation, the only legitimate justification for any institution is that it is beneficial (or at least not harmful) to the nation as a whole. There is also a widespread consensus that a defining attribute of democracy is that all citizens have a right to participate in the making of decisions that affect their essential interests. To be legitimate, collective bargaining must stand up to these tests. Both in North America and elsewhere, one may find rationales that render collective bargaining consistent with these standards. The theory underpinning public support for collective bargaining in North America, however, is quite different from the one that is embraced in many of the other advanced liberal democratic countries.

Throughout the nineteenth and into the twentieth century, the labor movement and other forces for democracy marched side by side. In European countries, one of the key initial demands of the expanding labor organizations was for the universal adult franchise and for equal rights for all citizens. The demand was for not only political democracy, but also industrial democracy. Theorists argued that adults do not check their citizenship at the door of the factory or office. They do not become subjects or wage slaves. Since the employment web of rules has such an enormous impact on their well being, they have a fundamental right to participate in the making of the rules under which they work. It is recognized that managers in modern corporations and bureaucracies also have responsibilities to shareholders, to the public, and to the local community as well as to the employees. Collective bargaining from this perspective is considered to be one means towards the achievement of industrial democracy.

Many of those in North America who are involved in industrial relations entirely accept this rationale. But there is another more prevalent theory that is accepted by most employers, government officials, and most likely trade union leaders as well. It is particularly prevalent in economic analysis. The theory holds that employees should have a right to bargain collectively if they choose to do so. They should have the right because individual employees have little bargaining power compared to the forces of the huge modern organization. Through unions and collective bargaining, this power may be offset. Implicitly, the employment relationship is regarded as an economic, market transaction rather than a social/political relationship. Even though the American Clayton Act of 1914 specifically declared that "the labor of a human being is not a commodity or an article of commerce," in fact the bargaining power equalization theory, which is commonly cited as the justification for collective bargaining in the United States, seems to affirm the contrary. A corollary of this economic theory of employment relations is that if employees do not want to engage in collective bargaining they should not be compelled to do so. If they are satisfied with their wages, they should have no further interest in the myriad web of rule regulating the employment relationship. If there is no demand for union services then, like purveyors of an outmoded product, unions should wrap up their business and fade into history. Whereas the political theory dictates a universal solution in which everyone is afforded a means to influence the rules under which they work, the economic theory suggests that it is reasonable for those who are receiving a satisfactory price for their labor to forego collective bargaining.

The law regulating the establishment of collective bargaining in North America is based on this proposition of choice, and it has had profound effects on the culture of labor-management relations. No European country bases its regulations on this theory. Instead, most commonly, collective bargaining is accepted as the appropriate means for deciding wages, hours, and other basic conditions of employment. It is expected that all employers will agree voluntarily to enter into negotiations with freely chosen representatives of employees. Recognition, which is a key issue in North America, is of much less import elsewhere. There are indeed some employers who fight to remain beyond collective bargaining, but they are usually small and on the fringes of the system. In most other economically advanced liberal democracies, the large majority of employees have at least some of their conditions of employment established by collective bargaining. Recognition was settled early in the century as a result of the implicit or explicit basic agreements between trade union organizations and employer associations — often with the state as a third party. An implicit understanding supporting these agreements was that collective bargaining (as a form of industrial democracy) should be universally available just as the institutions of political democracy (e.g., the vote and political representation) were universally available. In short, not only did employee-citizens have a right to participate in decisions critical to their welfare, but also employers had a corresponding duty to recognize and negotiate with employee representatives.

No such accord could be reached in North America in the early years of the twentieth century. However, in the 1930s there was a great expansion of the labor movement in both

Canada and the United States, and in both countries legislation was introduced to encourage the practice and procedure of collective bargaining. The implicit tripartite understanding that was reached appeared superficially to be similar to those previously achieved in Europe. Employees who wanted to engage in collective bargaining would have the free and unfettered choice to do so. Most industrial relations experts were fully confident that this stipulation would result in universal collective bargaining. After all, if offered the cost-free and unconstrained opportunity of being able to influence conditions of employment critical to their welfare, who would say no? In fact, the legal procedures that were instituted did not provide the clear choice that they were supposed to provide and, as a result, they did not have the effect they were initially intended to have.

After the cooperative milieu engendered by the war effort subsided, unorganized employers made it known that they had no intention of magnanimously accepting collective bargaining. Instead, they made it clear that they preferred the status quo and that they regarded collective bargaining as unnecessary except as a check on harsh and irresponsible companies. This attitude put employees in a position whereby to choose bargaining was to provoke the wrath of those who had the power to hire and fire. Under such conditions, the choice clearly was not a free one, but was instead constrained by fear of negative consequences. Despite the fettered nature of the process of unionization, many labor experts ingenuously portray the situation as one in which large numbers of North American employees have freely chosen not to become union members.

A favorite explanation for the implicit choice is the purported value of individualism. Thus, according to Bruce Kaufman, "American culture has a strong credo of individualism and a corresponding lack of class identity or consciousness." As a result, he proposes that "before the average American worker will seriously consider joining a union . . . he or she must feel unable to improve the situation at work through individual action." In short, unionization is a reluctant step taken only as a last resort.

It is difficult to test the validity of such statements, but one way of doing so is to look at situations where employees actually have had a cost-free and unfettered choice. Two naturally occurring experiments of that type have happened in Canada. Prior to the 1960s, collective bargaining was not permitted for Canadian federal government employees. However, during that decade the federal government passed a law permitting employees to certify a union as their bargaining agent if they preferred to do so. It was made clear that the employer (the federal government) was entirely neutral with respect to the choice. It would be pleased to bargain with a union if the employees decided that they wanted to negotiate their conditions of work. No stigma of disloyalty would attach to any employees who took that step. On the other hand, if employees were satisfied with the status quo, the government would be pleased to continue unilaterally to establish terms and conditions of employment. Within a few years, essentially all federal government employees, white-collar and blue-collar, technical and administrative, both men and women, had opted for collective bargaining. In the 1970s, essentially the same scenario was repeated for teachers in the province of Ontario. Indeed, I know of no case where employees have refused a bona fide employer offer to negotiate over the full range of conditions of employment without prejudice. If the Wagner Act's promise was kept, every employer would accept the duty to adopt such a policy. However, the reality is that such offers are practically never made.

Certification

The framers of the U.S. National Labor Relations Act, which had as its fundamental purpose the encouragement of collective bargaining, had the following scenario in mind as the way that a bargaining relationship would come into existence. Employees in a factory or office would decide that they would like to discuss their conditions of employment with their employer. They would form or join a union and ask the union to open discussions with the employer. The result would be a mutually acceptable collective agreement. The framers of the act realized that this process might get more complicated. What if some employees wanted one union to represent them and others wanted a different one? What if some employees wanted union A but others were opposed to representation by that organization because of its policies and behavior but preferred union B? If the employer was not convinced that the first union was the choice of the employees, generally he/she could go to the Labor Board and ask it to conduct an investigation. If the board found that the majority of relevant employees wanted union A, then it would issue a certificate to that effect. Once the employer was presented with such a certificate, he/she would be legally required to enter into negotiations with the union with a view towards arriving at a collective agreement.

Voluntary recognition was initially the preferred means of establishing a collective bargaining relationship, but it occurred only infrequently. Employers quickly learned that it was a good idea always to refuse voluntarily to recognize a union no matter how certain they were that it was the choice of the employees. Consequently, the Labor Board had to get involved in nearly every case of recognition and issue orders insisting that a reluctant employer enter into negotiations.

In the early years of its operation, the Labor Board often issued a certificate when the union was able to present evidence that a majority of the relevant employees had become members or had signed cards authorizing the union to negotiate on their behalf. Employers argued that this method was prone to abuse. For example, some employees might be pressured to join a specific union against their wishes. A better method to determine employees' wishes was to hold a vote, even if the great majority of the employees had signed authorization cards.

This proposal seemed to be reasonable. What could be fairer than a vote? In practice, though, it provided employers with time to formulate a campaign designed to dissuade employees from authorizing a union to bargain on their behalf. Claims were made that certain unions were corrupt or undemocratic or prone to strike. These arguments often had a significant effect on employees. In the midst of representation election campaigns, employee support for the union almost always deteriorated once the employer began his/her campaign.

In the early years of the NLRB, this type of campaign was forbidden. It reasoned that the choice of bargaining representative should be between the employee and the union. On that reasoning, employers were ordered to remain silent during organizing campaigns. But employers did not accept that dictum. They challenged it in the courts saying that it was an infringement of their right to free speech. When the Wagner Act was revised in 1947, the employer right to free speech was clearly recognized. From then on the process of establishing collective bargaining was not a matter of free and unfettered employees accepting the opportunity to appoint an agent to represent their interests in the making of the rules of work; instead it became a contest between employers and unions for the hearts and minds of the workers involved, a contest in which employers had a significant advantage because of the authority which they exerted over the employees. An employee who went against the expressed wishes of the employer might very well find his/her prospects for advancement, if not continued employment, jeopardized even though this was supposed to be illegal. Indeed, by the 1960s and 1970s, the practice of illegal victimization of employees for becoming involved in union organizing campaigns had become commonplace. Not only might individual employees be victimized for making use of their right of association, but also the manager against whom an organizing campaign was initiated could have his/her career negatively affected as a result. American companies made union-free status a priority goal and managers who failed to maintain that status would suffer the consequences.

As a result of these developments, the process initially envisioned by the framers of the Wagner Act practically never happens today. The contemporary logic underlying the process of establishing a collective bargaining relationship is entirely different from what it was initially. First of all, non-union employers almost always let their employees know that (contrary to the spirit of universal democratic participation and against the explicit intent of the law to encourage the practice of collective bargaining) they strongly prefer the status quo. As a result, employees who take the initiative to establish collective bargaining are almost certain to arouse the ire of their employer. They are likely to be identified as disloyal. In many cases, despite the injunction against threats and intimidation, they are likely to be dismissed for their involvement in the union. In consequence, the potential costs to any employee of becoming certified are great, and few take the initiative unless the conditions under which they are working are intolerable. Since only dissatisfied workers take the initiative to certify a union as their bargaining agent, the proposition has become established that employers get the union that they deserve. This phrase implies that if any given employer deals fairly with his/her workforce, the employees should have no reason to form or join a union. Instead of a universally desirable means of involving employees in the making of decisions which impact their interests at work, collective bargaining has come to be regarded as an antidote for incompetent or harsh management.

Since no manager wants to be considered incompetent, staying non-union is a high priority personal goal. Moreover, since collective bargaining has, in popular thought, become transmuted from a universally desirable technique to allow employees to participate in employment decisions to a corrective antidote for bad management or a subsidy to a disadvantaged market haggler — morally there is no wrong seen in corporations actively pursuing a policy of remaining non-union. Since corporate managers everywhere cherish control (rather than having to negotiate decisions with any other party), it has become the policy of most to avoid collective bargaining wherever possible. In short, a train of reasoning has been set in place that legitimizes the continuing existence of labor's exclusion from employment decision making and the active defense by employers of their right unilaterally to establish terms and conditions of employment. In this rhetorical context, the establishment of a bargaining relationship is a very adversarial process.

Because employers actively oppose unionization, it is very difficult for collective bargaining to become established. Indeed, in recent years as unionized factories have restructured and downsized, and new service industries have appeared, collective bargaining has shrunk significantly. In the United States today, less than 15 percent of workers in the private sector have their employment interests represented through collective bargaining. Ironically, the legal framework under which this situation has come about is the result of pressure exerted by the labor movement. Employers, by reinterpreting the theory underlying the legislation and by winning court and Labor Board judgements in their favor, have turned the law to their advantage.

From the industrial democracy perspective, the situation in the United States is indeed diabolical. A law intended to encourage collective bargaining is now being used to strangle it. The unions are, for the most part, acquiescing in their own asphyxiation. Many union activists agree with the phrase "the company gets the union it deserves" which suggests that if employees are satisfied with their conditions of work, they have no cause to institute collective bargaining. In addition, few unionists want to see a fundamental change in the law because within the shrinking perimeter where collective bargaining is still practiced, the law continues to be to their advantage. It requires that employers bargain in good faith. The law has permitted the establishment of practices under which the unions have considerable influence on terms and conditions of employment.

The Canadian Variant

Although most American unionists do not support the abolition of the Wagner Act and its replacement by an entirely new approach, many would like to see it reformed. Canada provides the model they would like to see emulated. In the United States, employers as a matter of course contest certification elections and research shows that in the typical campaign, employers are quite successful in weakening support for the union. The Canadian version of the Wagner-Act model which, as in the United States, was first put in place as a result of strong agitation by the labor movement, does not (in most jurisdictions) require a vote. Instead, the union may be certified on the basis of cards — that is evidence that a majority of the relevant people have become union members or expressed their desire to have the union represent them in collective bargaining. Card signing campaigns are typically carried out in secret and majority support is achieved without the employer finding out that a campaign was underway. In order to prevent the materialization of the fears voiced by American employers, commonly if there is any hint that the union has coerced any signature, the entire application is thrown out.

Canadian law is, from a labor perspective, preferable in other ways too. Procedures before the labor boards are more expedited. In the United States, lawyers are often able to delay proceedings while employers take action to make sure that they will win any election. Infringement of the law such as firing people for being involved in a unionization drive is dealt with more severely. Using their make-whole authority, Canadian boards have imposed large financial penalties against employers who have engaged in such activities. Contrary to U.S. practice, Canadian boards will also certify unions even in the absence of a majority. A common tactic in the United States, even after certification, is for employers to engage in surface bargaining — going through the motions, but making no real attempt to achieve agreement. In several Canadian jurisdictions, this problem has been overcome by first contract arbitration. Labor boards have been given the power to have the first contract settled by an arbitrator in those situations where employers do not fulfill their responsibility to bargain in good faith.

These are only some of the ways in which Canadian legislation is more favorable to labor than U.S. law. The major reason for the difference is almost certainly the presence of a viable social democratic political party. In many instances, laws have been changed in labor's favor during periods when the NDP was insurgent. Even where it had little probability of achieving power, it still had an effect by dramatically publicizing and politicizing illicit employer behavior and thereby compelling more conservative governments to take action. In Ontario, for example, a Conservative Party government that was in power for over thirty years passed several apparently pro-labor bills despite a relatively low standing in the polls of the NDP. It was induced to take action because of the ability of the opposition to make political issues of the events giving rise to the change in law.

The problem with the strategy of the U.S. labor movement on this issue is that, despite a much more favorable climate, the extent of bargaining in the Canadian private sector is still much lower than it is in the typical European country. Perhaps 25–30 percent of employees in the private sector are covered by collective agreements compared with a typical European situation of 70–80 percent coverage. In short, adoption of the Canadian model in the United States is not likely to bring about universal participation consistent with the logic of democratic society.

Although there is no comparable system of union recognition in Europe, in France and Belgium there is a considerably different system. In order for unions to sign legally binding collective agreements, and to qualify for participation on various governmental and quasi-governmental bodies, they must be certified. Certification is granted only to "most representative" unions. To be designated as most representative, a union or more often a federation of unions must have strength nationally or in a specific sector. But it need not have a majority. There are several union federations operating in France and most of them have "most representative" status. This system makes it difficult for newly formed unions to get established. Although there is no reason why a new union cannot negotiate on its members' behalf, any agreements that it is able to secure are not legally binding. In Britain, it should be noted, no collective agreements are legally enforceable, but that has not stopped British unions and employers from establishing an extensive system of collective contracts that are usually honored.

Some countries have a system in place which says that employers must negotiate with any union designated by two or more of its employees. Sweden adopted this approach in the 1930s specifically to encourage the recognition of white-collar worker unions. Although employers had extended general recognition to unions representing blue-collar workers in the December Compromise of 1906, they refused to recognize and bargain with their clerical and administrative workers. After the passage of the 1930 Act, however, bargaining for white-collar workers was quickly established with the result that today more than 70 percent of those in the private sector are covered by collective agreements.

Bargaining Structure

The employees to whom any collective agreement applies may be referred to as the bargaining unit. Such units are the basic elements of bargaining structure. A bargaining unit may be composed of a group of employees (e.g., production workers) working in a single plant. This is the most typical bargaining unit in North America. A bargaining unit may also be composed of a class of employees working in all the plants of a single employer. This type of unit is also common in North America. A third type of unit is one in which the collective agreement applies to all of the employees of a certain class who work for any employer who is a member of an employer's association. This is the most common European unit. Such agreements are typically negotiated between one or more unions and the employers' association. Sometimes such agreements are applicable across the whole country (commonly the case in smaller European countries) or only to a region of the country (a common pattern in Germany). In North America, such agreements are the exception, but they are found in industries such as construction, hospitals, shipping, and the railways.

A still different type of unit is one in which the collective agreement applies to all of the employees who are employed by all of the employers who belong to an association which is affiliated to an employer's federation. Such agreements are typically negotiated between national federations of employers and unions. This was the pattern in Sweden from the 1950s until the 1980s and in the other Scandinavian countries. Agreements of this sort on at least some issues have also been negotiated in, for example, Austria, Ireland, France, Belgium, the Netherlands, and Italy. In short, outside of North America these agreements are quite common.

Bargaining units are not mutually exclusive. They may, and commonly do, overlap. In Sweden, for example, for most of the period since World War II negotiations were first held between the national federation of blue-collar workers — LO — and the national confederation of employer associations — SAF. The result would be a frame agreement specifying the general level of wage movement for the next period (commonly a year but sometimes for longer), and some other very general conditions of employment. Additional negotiations would be carried out at industry level to flesh out the national agreement and still additional bargaining would go on at the company level in order to establish local conditions. The system was often referred to as centralized, but a much better term for it would be articulated. Bargaining took place at all levels throughout the system.

In Europe, the center of gravity of bargaining since early in the century has been the industry level, whereas in Canada and the United States the dominant focus is the plant or enterprise. Why is North America different in this regard? It is because of the historical events discussed above. European employers granted recognition at the industry level and expressed a willingness to negotiate at that level in hopes of defending their control of employment and production decisions at the level of the enterprise. Unions agreed to this proposal (and were themselves sometimes the first party to put it forward) because of their object of establishing common rules for workers. Until after World War II, employer strategy was largely successful in minimizing labor influence on the day-to-day affairs of the enterprise. The works councils that had been established in Germany and Austria were largely advisory and had little impact on crucial managerial decisions inside the firm. In other countries, union networks on the shop floor were generally opposed, and for the most part they were not well established. A major exception is Britain where shop steward movements during both world wars created a strong union shop floor presence. Until the last few decades, however, the shop stewards in Britain often operated independently of the national unions.

After World War II, works councils were reestablished in Germany and Austria and were adopted in several other countries. Over the past four decades, both the councils and union networks on the shop floor have been strengthened. In the 1970s, especially, changes in the law in several countries (Germany, Sweden, and the Netherlands) increased the power and authority of shop-floor labor representatives.

The North American employer strategy of contesting union representation on a plant-by-plant basis had an entirely different result. Where unions were strong enough to compel recognition, they were often also able to establish vigorous shop-floor networks. Initially simple, collective agreements over time became increasingly elaborate and placed a burgeoning network of constraints on managerial discretion at the shop floor. As this occurred, the determination of non-union employers to avoid collective bargaining increased. As a result, American employers are often considered to be much more anti-union than European employers. Very likely, their behavior is more a function of the specific characteristics of the system in which they operate, rather than because of their "Americanness." Foreign companies operating in the American environment do not behave notably different from the American-owned companies. Indeed, many large Japanese corporations, which almost without exception recognize and bargain with a union in Japan, follow a policy of union avoidance in the United States. So, too, do German companies.

Decentralized bargaining has some real advantages for the workers involved. Because they are close to the bargaining process, they are more able than workers under broader-based bargaining to see the personal relevance of negotiations. They are able to have more control over it. This process also has advantages for employers. Agreements may be tailor-made to the needs of the particular company or plant whereas under broader-based bargaining, particular companies may be compelled to adhere to standards which they feel are inappropriate to their situation.

On the other hand, decentralized bargaining has some very problematic aspects. Under broadbased bargaining, the negotiators are more in the public spotlight and thus must consider the consequences of their actions on the public and the economy as a whole. In decentralized bargaining, however, the parties are interested only in their own circumstances. Although the cumulative effect of bargaining has significant consequences for the public welfare, no one takes responsibility for that effect. In inflationary times, decentralized bargaining tends to exacerbate wage-price spirals. . . . The most preferable situation is probably one where general issues (such as general wage increases, pensions, and vacation plans) are negotiated at higher levels and specific issues (such as work scheduling, piece rates, and job structure) are negotiated at lower levels. . . .

Collective Bargaining Coverage

Table 4.1 provides estimates of union density and bargaining coverage in Canada, the United States, and several European countries.

It indicates, as mentioned several times above, that the percent of the labor force covered by collective agreements in Europe is much larger than it is in North America. This is due once again to the general agreements that were reached early in the twentieth century. It is also due in part to the existence of a legal instrument called extension of agreements. In countries with these stipulations, the government (usually at the joint request of the union or unions and the relevant employer organization) may extend the agreement to employers outside of the federation. The purpose of extension is to ensure that all relevant employees enjoy conditions of work generally in place in the industry involved and, very importantly, to protect employers in the association from low-wage competition by unassociated employers.

The existence of these requirements is one reason why European employers are very highly associated. In the typical country, a greater percentage of employers belong to their relevant association than do employees to their union. Only by joining are employers able to affect negotiations. Moreover, the unassociated employer is likely to be at a large disadvantage in negotiating with the union. Once the union has an agreement with the association, it can put all of its resources to work in negotiating with the independent employer. It might use the independent as a tool to win concessions that it was unable to win from the association. Faced with such a prospect, many employers have joined the association in order to get the advantage of the standard contract. Several American employers who set up in Europe after World War II went through precisely these steps.

Table 4.1 Union Density and Bargaining Coverage Estimates, Early 1990s

	DENSITY (percent)	COVERAGE (percent)
Austria	44–50	90+
Sweden	80–95	90+
Germany	39–45	90
Netherlands	24–30	75–80
United Kingdom	35–40	55[1]
Switzerland	28–35	65
France	8–12	70–80[2]
Canada	30–40	40–45
United States	15–17	18–22

Notes:

1. In the early 1980s, the British coverage rate was over 70 percent. It has fallen as a result of demographic changes and the policies of the Thatcher government.

2. The French rate was much lower in the 1970s. It has risen dramatically as a result of government legislation requiring employers to initiate wage bargaining on an annual basis.

Table 4.1 also indicates that in the typical country, union density is much lower than bargaining coverage. Many people who are covered by collective agreements are not union members. I will take up this subject in greater depth later on. For now, suffice it to say that the lower density rates are the result of what in North America would be referred to as a free-rider problem. In most European countries, the principle of freedom of association has been interpreted to mean that individuals have the right to join a union free from coercion, threat, or promise of benefit and that right has, unlike the North American situation, been made quite effective. Dismissal of employees for membership or involvement in a union is not a significant problem on continental Europe. On the other hand, freedom of association has also been interpreted in Europe to mean that individuals must have the right not to belong if they so choose. The right of association is like freedom of religion; the right to join is meaningless without the right not to join. As a result, union membership as a condition of employment is illegal in most European countries.

In North America, an entirely different logic is in place. Since North American bargaining agents must fairly represent all of those in a bargaining unit, whether they are union members or not, it is considered reasonable that the union insist that, once the majority has opted for unionization, all of those in the unit should be required to contribute to the resource base which allows the union effectively to represent their interests. In some Canadian provinces, the clash of the two logics has given rise to a middle-of-the-road arrangement. In Ontario, for example, employers may refuse to compel all employees to become union members, but all of those covered by a collective agreement must, at the union's request, pay dues whether they are a union member or not. Although these agency shop agreements (known in Canada as the Rand formula) are sometimes negotiated in the United States, in six Canadian jurisdictions they have been put in place by law. In those cases, the employer may not refuse the request of the union to have such a clause placed in the collective agreement. Canadian unions generally may, in addition, negotiate stronger clauses requiring that all covered employees be union members.

It seems clear that the European situation is much closer to the true meaning of freedom of association than is the North American approach. In North America, some workers are compelled to be union members against their wishes. They have no real freedom of association. This is one additional unfortunate aspect of the North America approach to labor policy. Mandatory membership (or at least dues payment) is a natural concomitant of unit certification. Without the latter, the need for the former would not be so pressing. In short, the Wagner-Act policy framework elicits behavior that is contrary to universally accepted labor standards.

Scope of the Issues

In most countries there is no legal restriction on the issues that may be the subject of collective bargaining. A union may initiate negotiations about everything from wages and hours to the nature of the product to be produced and the organization of the production process. In practice, though, collective bargaining in most countries is essentially concerned with wages, hours, benefits, employment security, and other conditions of work which directly effect employees (such as health and safety). Under industry-wide bargaining, the scope of the issues to be negotiated is typically narrower than under firm-level and plant-level bargaining because any agreement must be applicable to many different situations. Consequently, North American plant-level collective agreements are much longer and contain much more detail than do typical European agreements. Issues such as opening and closing times, lunch breaks, training, piece rates and other incentive pay schemes, vacation schedules, job transfer policies, plant shutdown, or reorganization decisions cannot easily be dealt with in multi-employer bargaining. In Germany and Austria, the works council is provided with a legal mandate to deal with such issues.

Even though European industry-wide bargaining deals with a narrower range of subjects than does decentralized bargaining in North America, it is incorrect to assert, as is sometimes done by North American writers, that European bargaining is over minimums. Annual wage bargaining, for example, typically determines not the minimum wage to be paid, but rather the general rate at which all wages and salaries of the relevant employees will increase.

Ironically, even though decentralized collective bargaining deals with a broader scope of issues than does broader-based bargaining in Europe, the scope of bargaining is more highly regulated in the United States than it is in any other countries. As the result of the Borg-Warner case in 1958, the U.S. Supreme Court divided issues into mandatory and permissive categories. Mandatory issues must be negotiated at the request of one party; permissive issues need not be negotiated at the request of one party; permissive issues need not be negotiated unless both parties agree to discuss them. In the specifics of the Borg-Warner case, the employer demanded that the union negotiate over certain issues that were considered by the union to be its internal affair. For example, the employer insisted that the union submit its last offer to the membership before calling a strike. The court agreed with the union that it should not have to negotiate over such issues. In subsequent cases, employers argued that by the same logic they should not have to negotiate over items that they considered to be internal management issues such as plant shutdowns and relocations, subcontracting, and work reorganization, and the courts agreed with them. The mandatory versus permissive distinction has not been imported into Canada, however, and almost any issue that either party cares to put on the bargaining table is negotiable to impasse.

The limitation of the issues that may be negotiated is a stimulant to labor management conflict. It encourages management to exclude the union from discussions about issues critical to employee welfare and thus it exacerbates distrust and animosity. The European experience (and the Canadian experience as well) suggests that there is little to be gained by the exclusion of issues from the bargaining process.

Bargaining Process

In North America, the collective agreement is typically written, covers all negotiated issues, and lasts for a specific period of time. In Ontario, for example, by law there may be only one collective agreement, it must be written, and it must last for at least one year.

Towards the end of the contract period, the union (and increasingly during the 1980s, the company also) develops a long list of demands. Typically, the list contains many items that it does not legitimately expect to be included in the agreement. Some of these are new issues, and placing them on the agenda is an indication that the party is interested in the issue and that it may be pushed more vigorously in succeeding bargaining rounds. Some issues are on the agenda because some individual or subgroup in the bargaining unit asked that they be included. These issues commonly fall off the table in the course of bargaining.

The parties exchange their list of items, a common agenda is set, and bargaining commences. The bargaining process may take some time. In Canada, it has been estimated that it takes from fifteen to twenty-five meetings in a typical bargaining round for the parties to reach agreement . . .

In Europe, there is more variation on these issues. Bargaining in Northern Europe (Germany, the Low Countries, and Scandinavia) always ends, as it does in North America, in a written agreement which lasts for a specific period of time. But in Southern Europe and Britain, this is not always the case. Much bargaining in Britain (and France and Italy as well) is informal and results in no more than an oral understanding sometimes embodied in notes taken by one of the attendees at a bargaining session. In such cases, the agreement lasts only so long as both parties agree that it will remain in place. When either party wants to alter current understandings it notifies the other. In Britain during the inflationary 1970s, this custom meant that wage negotiations were occurring in some industries every three to six months. In France, the openendedness of the bargaining that took place prior to the reform of the 1980s meant that there would be intense negotiations during some periods and relatively little activity during others. After a period of intense bargaining from the late 1960s to the mid-1970s it slowed down in many industries almost to a halt.

Formal and informal bargaining are not mutually exclusive. Even though there are many oral agreements in Britain, there are also many written collective agreements in effect. That is also true of North America, of course. Many issues come up on a day-to-day basis and they cannot wait for resolution until the contract expires. In North America, however, the typical collective agreement contains a management's rights clause. This clause commonly specifies that any issue not included in the collective agreement may be unilaterally decided by management. During the time that the collective agreement is in effect, management may do whatever it pleases with respect to issues not in the collective agreement.

The typical situation in Europe is quite different. Despite the attempt by employers early in the century to maintain control over internal issues by requiring agreements or understandings like the Swedish December Compromise of 1906, over the years labor's influence over internal issues has increased. Standards generally in effect today require that as new issues not included in the collective agreement arise, the parties will discuss them and attempt to come to an agreement. Indeed in Northern Europe, although unions may not go on strike during the term of the collective agreement over issues included in the agreement, they may raise and strike over issues not included in the agreement. European unions are not compelled or expected by tradition to sign only one collective agreement. In fact, in most countries there are simultaneously several agreements in effect.

Wages are typically negotiated separately from other issues on an annual or biannual basis. Agreements over other issues such as training, technological change, and pensions may be renegotiated periodically, or they may stay in place until one party or the other initiates new negotiations.

The theory behind the single agreement in North America seems to be that employers should not frequently be placed in a strike-threat position because that would be disruptive and inefficient. European practice does not support the theory. Indeed, most strikes are over major issues such as wages and job security. Only rarely do strikes occur between wage rounds. On the other hand, continuous consultation takes considerable pressure off of wage bargaining. In the North American case, the parties must discuss and resolve disputes over as many as 150–200 issues in a bargaining round. Europeans, in any round, focus on only a few, and thus the probability of breakdown is lower.

Note that single-issue bargaining is quite different from multi-issue bargaining. When 150 issues must be resolved in a three or four month period it is almost certain that many of them will fall off the table. On the other hand, if negotiations are over a single issue it is very likely that the parties will find some way to resolve their differences. The North American system practically ensures that many issues, instead of being jointly regulated, will remain in the domain of management's reserved rights.

Another significant difference between European and North American bargaining has to do with initial offers and demands. North American custom requires that the unions ask for much more than they expect to get and that management initially offer much less that it is prepared to settle for. This ritual allows both parties scope for bargaining. They have issues to trade off. Typical European bargaining is much different. When, for example, unions make a wage increase demand, they expect that the final settlement will be very close to the initial proposal. A far-fetched proposal would be ridiculed both by employers and by the press. Indeed, it is generally expected (especially in Northern Europe) that any demand be backed up by serious economic analysis of the likely consequences of the adoption of the proposal. Bargaining in these circumstances often takes on the character of a debate between employer and union representatives over the quality of their economic forecasts and the assumptions on which they are based. It also allows for a good deal of public scrutiny of the process. Many observers have suggested that these characteristics produce results that are economically more sensible and in the overall public interest.

Contract Ratification and Bargaining Authority

In North America, if tentative agreement is reached in any bargaining round that agreement is almost always submitted to the membership of the union for ratification. If the members accept the tentative deal, bargaining comes to a halt, if not bargaining must resume under very difficult conditions. North American employers have complained about this practice for many decades. They argue that since the management bargaining team is expected to be able authoritatively to commit the company to any agreement, the union leadership should have the same power. In Europe, commonly union leaders do have such power. It removes some control from the hands of the membership, but it is felt that it puts pressure on union leaders to negotiate responsible agreements. One major problem with such systems is that in periods of rapid economic change, the leadership may not be able properly to estimate the members' interests. The result may be, as there was in the late 1960s and early 1970s, a rash of wildcat strikes. Ratification is practiced by some British unions and is used in some cases in Belgium, Finland, Germany, Switzerland, Norway, and Denmark.

[Legal Status] of Collective Agreements

Written collective agreements are legally binding in the United States and almost everywhere else except Britain. In the United Kingdom, collective contracts are only gentleperson's agreements. This is one aspect of the so-called voluntaristic policy that was followed by British governments throughout much of the twentieth century. The policy has been that the issues, structure, and process of bargaining should be left up to the parties and that the state should refrain from involvement. That policy has changed significantly in recent decades, however. The Thatcher government, during the 1980s, passed several laws regulating bargaining — for the most part to the disadvantage of the unions.

Typically in Europe, collectively bargained terms become part of the individual contract of each covered employee. That individual contract, though, is much broader in scope than the collective agreement. Theoretically, it contains the entire panoply of rights and duties that regulate the relationship between the employer and the individual employee. If, for example, the employee was hired on the understanding that he/she would be eligible for promotion within six months, then that understanding, whether written or not, is considered to be part of the individual contract of employment. Indeed all explicit or implicit understandings between the individual employee and the employer are deemed to be included in the individual contract, including the terms of any and all collective agreements that establish minimum conditions. Collective agreements almost always contain minimums that cannot be legally negotiated away, but, in many situations and with respect to many issues, individuals may be able to negotiate terms better than those in the collective agreement. This is different from the typical situation in North America where negotiated terms are usually the actual terms. In most countries, individuals may go to court to make effective terms of the contract that employers do not honor. Labor courts in countries such as Germany and France are kept quite busy settling such individual disputes.

Under the Wagner Act model, a different situation exists in Canada and the United States. The Wagner model delegates to the union exclusive bargaining rights. This means that individuals give up their right to enter into individual understandings outside of the collective agreement unless, of course, the collective agreement explicitly provides them with that capacity. The result is that the individual contract of employment, for all practical purposes, ceases to exist in North America where collective agreements prevail. In some cases, this can be to the detriment of the employees. For example, an unorganized employee in Canada may, if dismissed, sue the employer for wrongful dismissal with hopes of winning a settlement of several months pay. Unionized employees lose the right to sue for wrongful dismissal and have only the rights embedded in the union-negotiated collective agreement.

A common misperception of casual North American inquiry into European practice is that European labor courts are, more or less, equivalent to North American grievance procedures. Although there are similarities, there is one difference of such consequence that it renders comparison all but irrelevant. In North America, the grievance procedure is used largely to settle disputes arising in the context of an on-going employment relationship. Employees with problems take them to their shop stewards with the intention that the steward will work out a satisfactory solution with management. In Europe, most disputes that are settled by labor courts are those which occur at the point of separation. Most individuals who file claims with labor courts are no longer employed by the company against which the claim is made. For the most part, claimants are complaining that employers failed to provide them with appropriate compensation (pay in lieu of notice, severance, and vacation pay due) at the point of separation. In North America, similar claims are filed by unorganized employees either with the regular courts or commonly with departments of labor. Grievances in the North American sense of the word are generally settled informally in Europe, although on occasion full-time union officials will intervene on behalf of their members. . . .

Legality of Strikes

During the nineteenth and into the twentieth century, in some cases strikes were illegal. Slowly, the right to strike was granted. Today it is considered to be a fundamental principle of liberal democratic nations. In such countries the right to strike is recognized everywhere in the private sector, but not without qualification. Strikes and other industrial action (slowdowns, work to rule) are regulated in various ways. For example, in Germany a strike is defined as a work stoppage undertaken in pursuit of a collective agreement with respect to terms and conditions of work. By defining it in that manner, political strikes are not classified as strikes and are illegal. This is a common practice in many countries. In Canada, for example, any concerted action to reduce production, such as a slowdown or a work to rule, is defined in most jurisdictions as a strike. It is also usual for governments to require a peace obligation during the period when the agreement is in effect — although commonly the obligation, as noted above, applies only to disputes over issues included in the collective agreement. Usually, if disputes occur over new issues not enshrined in a contract, those issues are negotiable, and if no agreement can be reached strikes may occur over them.

Since the right to strike is a constitutional right in both France and Italy, "no strike" clauses do not exist in statute and cannot be enforced if included in collective agreements.

In the United States, the National Labor Relations Act gives even unorganized employees a strong right to strike. It states that all employees covered by the act have a right to engage in concerted activities (including the right to stop work) for the purpose of mutual aid or protection. Although the courts and the Labor Board have narrowed this right by their interpretation of what it means (e.g., a single employee cannot engage in concerted action), it is still a strong right. In practice, though, it is of little significance. There are few non-union employees who make use of the right. Even though they have the protection of law to do so, it is likely that those who took advantage of the right would be subject to some form of retribution by their employer. The procedures for ensuring adherence to the letter of the law are inadequate and under administrations that are not enthusiastic about applying the law, protection for the worker has been very weak. As a result, the strong right does not have a great deal of practical effect.

In Canada, the situation is quite different. In most jurisdictions unorganized workers do not have the right to strike. If they want to acquire that right they must form a union and take steps to bring themselves under the terms of the appropriate labor relations act. This policy would seem to be very contrary to the international standard that the right to strike should be universal except for clearly defined exceptions — such as forbidding the withdrawal of services that could have serious effects on innocent third parties or the prohibiting of industrial action during periods of national emergency such as wartime.

For the most part, workers who might cause a public emergency by withdrawing their services are employed in the public sector and it is common to have strike restrictions on such employees as police, fire, the military, and the health sector. As noted above, many countries have a blanket prohibition on withdrawal of services by civil servants. Even in France where the right to strike is embedded in the constitution, there are restrictions on the right of certain public sector employees to strike.

As in North America, the state as sovereign may step in and legislate the end of any specific dispute. That step has been taken, not infrequently, in Scandinavia, for example. Although ad hoc legislation to end strikes is very rare in the United States, it is common in Canada, and during the 1970s and 1980s it grew in use. That development led two Canadian observers to argue that the rights of Canadian workers — those in the public sector, at least — were being trampled by the state.

Continuation of Employment

In the United States, when workers go out on strike it is legal for their employers to hire permanent replacement workers in their stead. In short, if workers go on strike in the United States, the result may be the same as quitting their jobs. Only if their union is strong enough to negotiate their return to work will they get their job back from a strikebreaker. This approach is very rare internationally. Indeed, the common situation within the liberal democratic world is for strikers to continue to be considered employees at least for some period of time. Although many countries permit companies to operate during strikes with temporary replacements, once the strike is over the strikers must be given their jobs back. Unlike the United States, Canada follows the international standard on this issue. In the mid-1980s, one province that did not adopt this approach, Alberta, had a major conflict over the issue. When the dust settled it revised its law to fit the Canadian and international standard.

Lockouts

The lockout is the traditional employer counterpart to the strike. If an impasse occurs in negotiations, the employer, or more commonly several employers in an association, tell their employees not to come to work until the dispute is settled. Most commonly, the lockout is used as a counter to a union strategy of striking one or a few plants of a multi-plant employer, or one or a few employers in an employer association. The lockout is used with considerable vigor throughout Northern Europe. In Sweden, the Swedish Employers Federation maintains a large strike insurance fund and has the right to order any member organization to lockout its employees. A few European countries (France, Italy, Portugal) have statutes prohibiting employers from locking out employees.

The lockout is legal in North America. However, because of the prevalence of plant-level bargaining, employers have little need to use it and it occurs only infrequently. Occasionally it is used, however, as an offensive weapon to compel union concessions or to shortcut the union strategy of calling a strike during a favorable time of year.

Grievance Procedures

Disputes occur not only over the terms of new agreements, but also over the interpretation of collective agreements and other understandings which in total compose the contract of employment. To settle interpretation or rights disputes, labor and management in North America have invented the institution of the grievance procedure. Commonly a grievance will begin with an individual employee who believes that some aspect of the collective agreement is not being applied correctly to him/her. The individual will complain to the local union officer — the shop steward who, if the case has merit, will file a formal written grievance. Most probably the issue will first be discussed with the individual's supervisor. If no mutually acceptable solution can be found, the grievance may go to the departmental level and, failing agreement, to the company level. The final step in the procedure in North America is, almost always, binding arbitration by an arbitrator jointly chosen, and jointly paid, by the employer and the union. In this manner, hundreds of thousands of problems are settled every year.

Although arbitration is, in theory, a private institution, a custom has arisen for arbitrators to consult the reasoning of others who have settled similar cases. Because there is a market for them, arbitration cases are published. This custom has led to the establishment of a body of workplace jurisprudence which, although it has little standing in law, has had an enormous effect on the operation of the workplace. For example, a typical North American collective agreement gives management the right to discipline or discharge employees for just cause, but it is left up to arbitrators to decide what the phrase just cause means. Over the years, arbitrators have made it clear that it is permissible for employers to dismiss employees for such behaviors as stealing, drinking or using drugs on the job, excessive absenteeism, and several other offences. If an employee, through the union, challenges a dismissal, arbitrators across North America generally will insist that the penalty reflect the seriousness of the offense, that the employer conducted an equitable investigation and permitted the employee to state his/her case, took the past record and length of service of the employee into account, made sure that the rules were known and applied consistently, and put a system of progressive discipline into effect.

Grievance procedures in Europe are typically much less formal than are those in North America. If an employee has a problem, commonly the procedure is for him/her to take the issue up first with the supervisor. If the result is not satisfactory, several options are then available. In Britain, the employee will go to the shop steward who will then try to work out a solution. Should none be reached, the workers might go out on strike in support of the individual's claim.

In France, there is a statute requiring a special elected official, the *délégué du personnel*, whose job it is to work out grievances. Depending on the issue the *délégué* might call in various government officials and might assist the individual to go to the *prud'hommes* — the bipartite (labor and management) French employment courts. In Germany and Austria, the individual might very well go to one of the works counselors or to the union office in the town. Either a works councillor or a union officer might then try to settle the dispute amicably.

In most European countries, the final step in such informal systems is a labor court — a government institution designed commonly to settle disputes over a range of issues emerging not only from collective agreements, but also from individual agreements and statutes. Individual agreements are very important in Europe, contrary to the situation in the United States and to an extent in Canada. According to common law, whenever anyone accepts employment that person enters into an agreement with the employer which establishes a body of rights and responsibilities for both parties. In fact, all of the understandings entered into by the employer and the employee with respect to each other are considered to be part of the individual contract. Most commonly, collective agreement terms are considered to become part of the individual contract and individuals usually may process their own complaints to court.

Although European labor courts are part of the overall legal system, commonly judges are appointed only after consultation with labor and employer organizations, and they are expected to understand and respect industrial relations customs. In a few countries . . . instead of a labor court, grievances in the last resort are settled by the regular courts. Even in those countries, however, there are special sections overseen by judges sensitive to the concerns of labor and management.

The substantive rules produced by European labor courts and North American arbitration are not that much different. Remarkably, perhaps, the standards of conduct expected of employers and employees in both Europe (under labor courts) and North America (under arbitration) are very similar despite obvious outward differences. The major difference between Europe and North America is the way that the unorganized are treated. As noted above, in the typical European country the great majority of employees are covered by collective agreements and almost all employees have access to labor courts. In the United States, on the other hand, 80–85 percent of employees are not covered by collective agreements, do not have access to grievance procedures ending in binding arbitration, and do not have the benefit of arbitral jurisprudence. As a result, the rights enjoyed by employees under collective bargaining do not extend to the unorganized. The basic principle in the United States is that the unorganized employee may be dismissed at any time for any reason, or for no reason whatsoever. A similar principle holds in Canada except that the employer must provide the employee with reasonable notice. The bottom line is that American workers are liable to much more arbitrary treatment than are workers in most of the liberal democratic world. This is one more result of the exceptional pattern of

American labor relations developments related in the first few chapters. With no class-conscious labor movement to look after their interests, the unorganized in America have acquired fewer rights and privileges than have workers in most other countries. The quality of their industrial citizenship is second-class.

In one respect, North American grievance procedures are much more favorable to workers than are European systems for resolving employment grievances. According to common practice in North America, workers who are unjustly dismissed are reinstated. In Europe, reinstatement is not common. It is available in several countries but, instead of reinstatement, judges commonly have the option of awarding the unjustly dismissed employee financial compensation, and the award of compensation is the usual practice. That is why, as noted above, most claims brought by individual employees to labor courts are claims filed by workers no longer employed by the firm against which the relief is sought. The result is that if an employer is determined to dismiss an employee, he/she may do so contingent upon paying a penalty. As a result, the European employee is perhaps less secure from arbitrary treatment than is the American unionized worker. This is a subject on which future research needs to be done. Do European and North American organized employees enjoy the same or different degrees of freedom from arbitrary treatment? Theoretically, it appears that the North American worker is better protected, but empirical work is needed to test the theory.

The Right of First Interpretation

In North America, if there is a dispute over the terms of a collective agreement the employer has the right of first interpretation. What this means in practice is that if an employer decides that an employee should be fired, that employee is dismissed immediately and removed from the payroll. The arbitrator has the discretion of reinstating the employee with or without back pay depending upon how egregiously mistaken the employer was in carrying out the dismissal in the first place. This principle, which is a sacrosanct aspect of North American practice, is not so universal elsewhere. In Sweden, legislation introduced in the mid-1970s explicitly gave the local union the right of first interpretation in dismissal cases. If the employer wanted to fire someone and the local union did not agree, the individual would continue working and drawing a salary pending the decision of the labor court. In order to prevent the union from making use of this right to disrupt production in pursuit of other objectives (e.g., wage increases) the law called for heavy penalties for unions that made use of its first interpretation rights frivolously. In Germany, also, employees cannot be dismissed individually unless the works council agrees to the dismissal. If the works council disagrees and no mutually acceptable solution can be worked out the issue is settled by reference to a process similar to North American arbitration. Although it is generally accepted in North America that management must have the right of first interpretation in order to prevent chaos, contrary practice in Germany and Sweden has not created intolerable problems. In both countries, the system has worked reasonably well. In short, European experience casts considerable doubt upon North American theory.

Collective Bargaining and the New Industrial Relations

The traditional policy of North American unions has been to bargain hard to win their members the best conditions of employment. Traditionally, the unions have not been interested in becoming involved in the management of the enterprise. Management, on the other hand, generally defined its role as being that of an agent for shareholder inter- ests. As a result, management would seek to acquire labor at the best possible price. Given these perspectives, bargaining was clearly adversarial. Unions always demanded and managers always gave in reluctantly, if at all. Wage bargaining in Europe was similar, although, because it was conducted at higher levels than in North America, the parties were generally more concerned to justify their positions as being in the overall economic interests of the industry and nation.

In recent years, adversarial assumptions have begun to be challenged in North Amer- ica. According to the tenets of the "New Industrial Relations," companies are most pro- ductive if they are able to induce the thorough involvement of employees in their work rather than simply eliciting unenthusiastic acquiescence to orders given. Japanese experi- ence suggests that this is best done if employees are organized in groups and given broad job responsibilities. It also suggests that union-management cooperation over a broad range of issues helps to engender the trust necessary to produce employees highly com- mitted to continuous improvements in quality and productivity. As a result, over the past decade many North American companies have been seeking union cooperation in the establishment of new forms of production and human resource organization. That initia- tive has produced a heated debate in the labor movement. Many labor leaders are com- pletely set against cooperation because they fear that employers will abuse the process by inducing workers to accept more responsibility and to exert more effort without any clear long-term benefit. Others have been convinced, usually after initial reluctance, to give the process a chance. To date, although there have been notable experiments, the spread of labor-management cooperation at the level of the enterprise has been limited and uneven. It is being held back by adversarial traditions and by institutions that elicit distrust rather than a propensity to cooperate. As Kochan and Wever note "no [American] union has so far placed support for alternative forms of participation and representation in the center of its agenda for the future."

In Europe, the situation is quite different. From the early 1970s, Scandinavian unions were leaders in cooperating with management in order to reorganize work to make it simultaneously more satisfying and rewarding to the workers and more productive. In Germany, after some initial reticence, unions have gotten firmly behind work reorganiza- tion schemes.

In North America, adversarial suspicion traditionally has made unions reject the idea of workers' participation on boards of directors, although that reluctance has softened in the 1980s. In Europe, on the other hand, German and Austrian unions have long insist- ed on board participation and, in the 1970s, as a result of labor demands, worker repre- sentation on boards of directors was extended to several other European countries. Because of the broader recognition of labor's critical and constructive role in society, European unions are less reluctant to become involved in participatory schemes. They have less reason to fear that such schemes are plots to wrangle concessions that could not be won through adversarial bargaining.

Conclusions

The objective of this chapter has been to place contemporary North American collective bargaining in comparative perspective. On many dimensions, North American practice is different from the norm elsewhere. Union recognition, the structure of bargaining, the process of bargaining, and dispute resolution techniques such as formal grievance procedures ending in binding arbitration are all unusual in comparative perspective. In some cases, the North American approach is superior to those more common elsewhere. For example, effective reinstatement of unfairly dismissed employees to their jobs is clearly superior to reimbursing employees for the injury sustained. Decentralized bargaining is also advantageous to the extent that it may be tailor-made to the situation of the parties involved, and may be more easily influenced by those regulated by the resultant agreement. On the other hand, the North American industrial relations system has features that are undesirable in comparative perspective.

The concept of union certification has resulted in the establishment of two systems of employment relations. In one, employment decision making is a unilateral employer process. The governance system is authoritarian. The employees have been excluded from the decision-making process altogether. Formally, those employees have the opportunity to opt for collective bargaining, but it is a hobbled and costly choice to be undertaken only in the most dire circumstances. As a result, most North American employees have no representation in the making of rules which critically impact their working lives.

Decentralized bargaining is also problematic in that under such a system no one has any responsibility for the cumulative effect of negotiations. The results of such negotiations are based largely on power rather than principle, and it is very difficult to coordinate fragmentary bargaining with socioeconomic policy.

Power also plays an important part in bargaining in Europe, of course. However, high-level bargaining is inevitably influenced by general policy considerations. Although imperfect, there is in many European countries a general consensus that bargaining should produce outcomes that are consistent with the policy goals of price stability and international competitiveness. There is also broad agreement that wage increases in the aggregate should not exceed what is possible as the result of the advance of productivity.

Because of distrustful attitudes stimulated and perpetuated by the legal framework regulating bargaining in North America, it has been difficult for the parties to embrace the new cooperative systems of production and human resource organization which generally seem to be more efficient and effective than the older Taylorist form of work organization. These systems seem to require labor-management cooperation, but the institutions of bargaining in North America do little to elicit cooperation.

[Reprinted by permission of the University of South Carolina Press.]

✳ ✳ ✳

The following well-known article addresses one of the basic disagreements, at least in North America, about the impact and desirability of collective bargaining.

Richard Freeman & James Medoff, "The Two Faces of Unionism" (1979) 57 The Public Interest 69 at 69–93

Trade unions are the principal institution of workers in modern capitalist societies, as endemic as large firms, oligopolistic organization of industries, and governmental regulation of free enterprise. But for over 200 years, since the days of Adam Smith, there has been widespread disagreement about the effects of unions on the economy. On the one side, such economists as John Stuart Mill, Alfred Marshall, and Richard Ely (one of the founders of the American Economic Association) viewed unions as having major positive effects on the economy. On the other side, such economists as Henry Simons and Fritz Machlup have stressed the adverse effects of unions on productivity. In the 1930s and 1940s, unions were at the center of attention among intellectuals, with most social scientists viewing them as an important positive force in society. In recent years, unionism has become a more peripheral topic and unions have come to be viewed less positively. Less and less space in social-science journals and in magazines and newspapers is devoted to unions. For example, the percentage of articles in major economics journals treating trade unionism dropped from 9.2 percent in the 1940s to 5.1 percent in the 1950s to 0.4 percent in the early 1970s. And what is written is increasingly unfavorable. The press often paints unions as organizations which are socially unresponsive, elitist, non-democratic, or ridden with crime. In the 1950s, 34 percent of the space devoted to unions in *Newsweek* and *Time* was unfavorable; that has risen to 51 percent in the 1970s. Economists today generally treat unions as monopolies whose sole function is to raise wages. Since monopolistic wage increases are socially deleterious — in that they can be expected to induce both inefficiency and inequality — most economic studies implicitly or explicitly judge unions as having a negative impact on the economy.

Our research demonstrates that this view of unions as organizations whose chief function is to raise wages is seriously misleading. For in addition to raising wages, unions have significant non-wage effects which influence diverse aspects of modern industrial life. By providing workers with a voice both at the workplace and in the political arena, unions can and do affect positively the functioning of the economic and social systems. Although our research on the non-wage effects of trade unions is by no means complete and some results will surely change as more evidence becomes available, enough work has been done to yield the broad outlines of a new view of unionism.

UNIONS AS COLLECTIVE VOICE

One key dimension of the new work on trade unionism can best be understood by recognizing that societies have two basic mechanisms for dealing with divergences between desired social conditions and actual conditions. The first is the classic market mechanism of exit and entry, individual mobility: The dissatisfied consumer switches products; the diner whose soup is too salty seeks another restaurant; the unhappy couple divorces. In the labor market, exit is synonymous with quitting, while entry consists of new hires by the firm. By leaving less-desirable jobs for more-desirable jobs, or by refusing bad jobs, individuals penalize the bad employer and reward the good — leading to an overall improvement in the efficiency of the social system. The basic theorem of neoclassical economics is that, under well-specified conditions, the exit and entry of persons (the hallmark of free enterprise) produces a "Pareto-optimum" situation — one in which no individual can be made better off without making someone worse off. Economic analysis can be viewed as a detailed study of the implications of this kind of adjustment and of the extent to which it works out in real economies. As long as the exit-entry market mechanism is viewed as the only efficient adjustment mechanism, institutions such as unions must necessarily be viewed as impediments to the optimal operation of a capitalist economy.

There is, however, a second mode of adjustment. This is the political mechanism, which Albert Hirschman termed "voice" in his important book, *Exit, Voice, and Loyalty*. "Voice" refers to the use of direct communication to bring actual and desired conditions closer together. It means talking about problems: complaining to the store about a poor product rather than taking business elsewhere; telling the chef that the soup had too much salt; discussing marital problems rather than going directly to the divorce court. In a political context, "voice" refers to participation in the democratic process, through voting, discussion, bargaining, and the like.

The distinction between the two mechanisms is best illustrated by a specific situation — for instance, concern about school quality in a given locality. The exit solution to poor schools would be to move to a different community or to enroll one's children in a private school, thereby "taking one's business elsewhere." The voice solution would involve political action to improve the school system, through school-board elections, Parent Teacher Association meetings, and other direct activities.

In the job market, voice consists of discussing with an employer conditions that ought to be changed, rather than quitting the job. In modern industrial economies, and particularly in large enterprises, a trade union is the vehicle for collective voice — that is, for providing workers as a group with a means of communicating with management.

Collective rather than individual bargaining with an employer is necessary for effective voice at the workplace for two reasons. First, many important aspects of an industrial setting are "public goods," which affect the well-being (negatively or positively) of every employee. As a result, the incentive for any single person to express his preferences, and invest time and money to change conditions (for the good of all), is reduced. Safety conditions, lighting, heating, the speed of a production line, the firm's policies on layoffs, work-sharing, cyclical-wage adjustment, and promotion, its formal grievance procedure and pension plan — all obviously affect the entire workforce in the same way that defense, sanitation, and fire protection affect the entire citizenry. "Externalities" (things done by one individual or firm that also affect the well-being of another, but for which the individual or firm is not compensated or penalized) and "public goods" at the workplace require collective decision-making. Without a collective organization, the incentive for the individual to take into account the effects of his or her actions on others, or express his or her preferences, or invest time and money in changing conditions, is likely to be too small to spur action. Why not "let Harry do it" and enjoy the benefits at no cost? This classic "free-rider" problem lies at the heart of the so-called "union-security" versus "right-to-work" debate.

A second reason collective action is necessary is that workers who are not prepared to exit will be unlikely to reveal their true preferences to their bosses, for fear of some sort of punishment. . . . Since the employer can fire a protester, individual protest is dangerous; so a prerequisite for workers' having effective voice in the employment relationship is the protection of activists from being discharged. . . .

The collective nature of trade unionism fundamentally alters the operation of a labor market and, hence, the nature of the labor contract. In a non-union setting, where exit and entry are the predominant forms of adjustment, the signals and incentives to firms depend on the preferences of the "marginal" worker, the one who will leave (or be attracted) by particular conditions or changes in conditions. The firm responds primarily to the needs of this marginal, generally younger and more mobile worker and can within some bounds ignore the preferences of "infra-marginal," typically older workers, who — for reasons of skill, knowledge, rights that cannot be readily transferred to other enterprises, as well as because of other costs associated with changing firms — are effectively immobile. In a unionized setting, by contrast, the union takes account of the preferences of all workers to form an average preference that typically determines its position at the bargaining table. Because unions are political institutions with elected leaders, they are likely to be responsive to a different set of preferences from those that dominate in a competitive labor market.

In a modern economy, where workers tend to be attached to firms for eight or more years, and where younger and older workers are likely to have different preferences (for instance, regarding pension or health-insurance plans versus take-home pay, or layoffs by inverse seniority versus work-sharing or cuts in wage growth), the change from a marginal to an average calculus is likely to lead to a very different labor contract. When issues involve sizeable fixed costs or "public goods," a calculus based on the average preference can lead to a contract which, ignoring distributional effects, is socially more desirable than one based on the marginal preference — that is, it may even be economically more "efficient."

As a voice institution, unions also fundamentally alter the social relations of the workplace. Perhaps most importantly, a union constitutes a source of worker power in a firm, diluting managerial authority and offering members a measure of due process, in particular through the union innovation of a grievance and arbitration system. While 99 percent of major U.S. collective-bargaining contracts provide for the filing of grievances, and 95 percent provide for arbitration of disputes that are not settled between the parties, relatively few non-union firms have comparable procedures for settling disagreements between workers and supervisors. More broadly, the entire industrial jurisprudence system — by which many workplace decisions are based on negotiated rules (such as seniority) instead of supervisory judgment (or whim), and are subject to challenge through the grievance/arbitration procedure — represents a major change in the power relations within firms. As a result, in unionized firms workers are more willing and able to express discontent and to object to managerial decisions.

Thus, as a collective alternative to individualistic actions in the market, unions are much more than simple monopolies that raise wages and restrict the competitive adjustment process. Given imperfect information and the existence of public goods in industri-al settings, and conflicting interests in the workplace and in the political arena, unionism provides an alternative mechanism for bringing about change. This is not to deny that unions have monopolistic power nor that they use this power to raise wages for a select part of the workforce. The point is that unionism has two "faces," each of which leads to a different view of the institution: One, which is at the fore in economic analysis, is that of a monopoly; the other is that of "a voice institution," i.e., a socio-political institution. To understand fully what unions do in modern industrial economies, it is necessary to exam-ine both faces.

THE RESPONSE TO UNIONS

Another crucial point about unions is that their effects will depend upon the response of management. This was stressed by Sumner H. Slichter, James J. Healy, and E. Robert Liv-ernash in their classic volume, *The Impact of Collective Bargaining on Management*. If man-agement uses the collective-bargaining process to learn about and improve the operation of the workplace and the production process, unionism can be a significant plus that improves managerial efficiency. On the other hand, if management reacts negatively to collective bargaining or is prevented by unions from reorganizing the work process, unionism can have a negative effect on the performance of the firm. The important point is that just as there are two sides to the market, demand and supply, there are two forces determining the economic effects of collective bargaining, managements and unions. The economic impact of bargaining and the nature of industrial relations depend on the poli-cies and actions of both. It is for this reason that we use the two terms "collective voice" and "institutional response" to refer to the second view of unionism under consideration.

The monopoly and collective-voice/institutional-response views of the impact of unionism are strikingly different, as [Table I] . . . demonstrates. While no sophisticated adherent of the monopoly model would deny the voice aspects of unionism, and no indus-trial-relations expert would gainsay the monopoly effects, the polar dichotomization use-fully highlights the facets of unionism stressed by the two views. The monopoly and collective-voice/institutional-response views of unionism in many instances give com-pletely opposite pictures of the institution.

According to the former, unions are by nearly all criteria undesirable impediments to the social good; in the latter view, unions have many valuable features that contribute to the functioning of the economy. In the monopoly view, the current dwindling in the per-centage of private-sector wage and salary workers who are unionized (from 37 percent in 1958 to 29 percent in 1974) is a desirable development and should be associated with increased productivity and reduced inequality — and thus ought perhaps to be encour-aged. From the collective-voice/institutional-response point of view, the dwindling of pri-vate-sector unionization has serious negative economic and social consequences and should be an issue of public concern.

Since, in fact, unions have both monopoly and collective-voice/institutional-response compo-nents, the key question for understanding unionism in the United States relates to the relative importance of these two faces. Are unions primarily monopolistic institutions, or are they

Table I.   Two Views of Trade Unionism

UNION EFFECTS ON ECONOMIC EFFICIENCY	UNION EFFECTS ON DISTRIBUTION OF INCOME	SOCIAL NATURE OF UNION ORGANIZATION
Monopoly View		
Unions raise wages above competitive levels, which leads to too little labor relative to capital in unionized firms	Unions increase income inequality by raising the wages of highly skilled workers	Unions discriminate in rationing positions
Union work rules decrease productivity	Unions create horizontal inequities by creating differentials among comparable workers	Unions (individually or collectively) fight for their own interests in the political arena
Unions lower society's output through frequent strikes		Union monopoly power breeds corrupt and non-democratic elements
Collective-Voice/Institutional-Response View		
Unions have some positive effects on productivity — by reducing quit rates, by inducing management to alter methods of production and adopt more efficient policies, and by improving morale and co-operation among workers	Unions' standard-rate polices reduce inequality among organized workers in a given company or a given industry	Unions are political institutions that represent the will of their members
Unions collect information about the preferences of all workers, which leads the firm to choose a "better" mix of employee compensation and a "better" set of personnel policies	Union rules limit the scope for arbitrary actions concerning the promotion, layoff, recall, etc. of individuals	Unions represent the political interests of lower-income and disadvantaged persons
Unions improve the communication between workers and management, leading to better decision-making	Unionism fundamentally alters the distribution of power between marginal (typically junior) and inframarginal (generally senior) employees, causing union firms to select different compensation packages and personnel practices than non-union firms	

primarily voice institutions that induce socially beneficial responses? What emphasis should be given to these two extreme views for one to obtain a realistic picture of the role trade unionism plays in the United States?

To answer these important questions, we have studied a wide variety of data that distinguish between union and non-union establishments and between union and non-union workers, and we have interviewed representatives of management, labor officials, and industrial-relations experts. Although additional work will certainly alter some of the specifics, our research has yielded several important results which suggest that unions do a great deal more than win monopoly wage gains for their members.

EFFECTS ON EFFICIENCY

In the monopoly view, unions reduce society's output in three ways. First, union-won wage increases cause a misallocation of resources by inducing organized firms to hire fewer workers, to use more capital per worker, and to hire higher quality workers than is socially efficient. Second, union contract provisions — such as limits on the loads that can be handled by workers, restrictions on tasks performed, featherbedding, and so forth — reduce the output that should be forthcoming from a given amount of capital and labor. Third, strikes called to force management to accept union demands cause a substantial reduction in gross national product.

By contrast, the collective-voice/institutional-response model directs attention to the important ways in which unionism can raise productivity. First of all, unionism should reduce "quits." As workers' voice increases in an establishment, less reliance need be placed on the exit and entry mechanism to obtain desired working conditions. Since hiring and training costs are lowered and the functioning of work groups is less disrupted when "quit" rates are low, unionism can actually raise efficiency.

The fact that senior workers are likely to be relatively more powerful in enterprises where decisions are based on voice instead of exit and entry points to another way in which unions can raise productivity. Under unionism, promotions and other rewards tend to be less dependent in any precise way on individual performance and more dependent on seniority. As a result, in union plants feelings of rivalry among individuals are likely to be less pronounced than in non-union plants and the amount of informal training and assistance that workers are willing to provide one another is greater. (The importance of seniority in firms in Japan, together with the permanent employment guaranteed many workers there, have often been cited as factors increasing the productivity of Japanese enterprises.) It is, of course, also important to recognize that seniority can reduce productivity by placing individuals in jobs for which they are not qualified.

Unionism can also raise efficiency by pressuring management into tightening job-production standards and accountability, in an effort to respond to union demands while maintaining profits. . . . [m]odern personnel practices are forced on the firm and traditional paternalism is discarded. . . . Most of the econometric analysis of unions has focused on the question of central concern to the monopoly view: How large is the union wage effect? In his important book, Unionism and Relative Wages, H. Gregg Lewis summarized results of this analysis through the early 1960s, concluding that, while differing over time and across settings, the union wage effect averages on the order of 10 to 15 percent. That is, as a result of collective bargaining, a union member makes about 10 to 15 percent more than an otherwise comparable worker who is not a member. Later work, using larger data files which have information permitting more extensive controls and employing more complex statistical techniques, tends to confirm Lewis's generalization. While unions in some environments raise wages by an enormous amount, the average estimated union wage effect is by no means overwhelming.

As predicted by the monopoly wage model, the capital-labor ratio and average "quality" of labor both appear to be somewhat greater than "optimal" in union settings. However, the total loss in output due to this misallocation of resources appears to be minuscule; an analysis done by Albert Rees suggests that the loss is less than 0.3 percent of the gross national product. For 1975, that would have amounted to $21.00 per person in the U.S. Even this estimate may be too high if one considers the other important and relevant distortions in the economy.

THE EVIDENCE ON QUITS AND PRODUCTIVITY

One of the central tenets of the collective-voice/institutional-response model is that among workers receiving the same pay, unions reduce employee turnover and its associated costs by offering "voice" as an alternative to exit. Our own research, using newly available information on the job changes and employment status of thousands of individuals and industry-level turnover rates, shows that, with diverse factors (including wages) held constant, unionized workers do have significantly lower quit rates than non-union workers who are comparable in other respects. . . .

Our analyses of newly available data on unionism and output per worker in many establishments or sectors suggests that the monopoly view of unions as a major deterrent to productivity is erroneous. In some settings, unionism leads to higher productivity, not only because of the greater capital intensity and *higher* labor quality, but also because of what can best be termed institutional-response factors.

Table III summarizes the available estimates of the union productivity effect. The calculations in the table are based on statistical analyses that relate output per worker to unionization, controlling for capital per worker, the skill of workers (in some of the analyses), and other relevant factors. While all of the studies are subject to some statistical problems and thus must be treated cautiously, a general pattern emerges. In manufacturing, productivity in the organized sector appears to be substantially higher than in the unorganized sector, by an amount that could roughly offset the increase in total costs attributable to higher union wages.

Table III. Estimates of the Impact of Unionism on Productivity

SETTING	ESTIMATED INCREASE OR DECREASE IN OUTPUT PER WORKER DUE TO UNIONISM
All 2-digit Standard Industrial Classification (SIC) manufacturing industries[1]	20 to 25%
Wooden household furniture[2]	15
Cement[3]	6 to 8
Underground bituminous coal, 1965[4]	25 to 30
Underground bituminous coal, 1975[4]	-20 to -25

Sources: All calculations are based on the analyses cited below, which control for capital-labor ratios and diverse other factors that may influence productivity.

1 From C. Brown and J. Medoff, "Trade Unions in the Production Process," *Journal of Political Economy*, June 1978, pp. 355–378.

2   From J. Frantz, "The Impact of Trade Unions on Productivity in the Wood Household Furniture Industry," Senior Honors Thesis, Harvard University, March 1976.

3   From K. Clark, "Unions and Productivity in the Cement Industry," Doctoral Thesis, Harvard University, September 1978.

4   From R.B. Freeman, J.L. Medoff, and M. Connerton, "Industrial Relations and Productivity: A Study of the U.S. Bituminous Coal Industry," in progress.

In the typical manufacturing industry, the substantially lower quit rates under collective bargaining can explain about one-fifth of the estimated positive union productivity effect. Kim Clark, in his study of the cement industry, noted that from his discussions with individuals at recently organized plants, it appeared that the entrance of a union was usually followed by major alterations in operations. Interestingly, the enterprise typically changed plant management, suggesting that the union drive was an important signal to top management of ineffective lower-level managerial personnel: The drive thus provided valuable information or shock of a distinctive kind. Perhaps most importantly, the discussions with union and management officials in the cement industry indicated that firms often adopted more efficiency-oriented and less paternalistic personnel policies in response to unionism in order to raise productivity and meet higher wage demands.

On the other side of the picture, our analysis (with Marguerite Connerton) of productivity in organized and unorganized underground bituminous coal mines indicates that as industrial relations in the union sector deteriorated in the late 1960s and 1970s, unionism became associated with negative productivity effects. . . .

To repeat, unionism may increase productivity in some settings and decrease it in others. If the increase in productivity is greater than the increase in average unit costs due to the union wage effect, then the profit rate will increase; if not, the rate of profit will fall. There is limited tentative evidence that, on average, net profits are reduced somewhat by unionism, particularly in oligopolistic industries, though there are notable exceptions. At present, there is no definitive accounting of what proportion of the union wage effect comes at the expense of capital, other labor, or consumers, and what portion is offset by previously unexploited possibilities for productivity improvements.

Finally, it is important to note that despite what some critics of unions might claim, strikes do not seem to cost society a substantial amount of goods and services. For the economy as a whole, the percentage of total working time lost directly to strikes during the past two decades has never been greater than 0.5 percent and has averaged about 0.2 percent. Even "national emergency" disputes — those that would be expected to have the largest repercussions on the economy — do not have major deleterious impacts. Though highly publicized, the days idle because of the direct and indirect effects of strikes represent only a minuscule fraction of the total days worked in the U.S. economy.

PERSONNEL PRACTICES AND EMPLOYEE BENEFITS

Under the monopoly view, the exit and entry of workers permits each individual to find a firm offering the mix of employee benefits and personnel policies that he or she prefers. As noted earlier, however, the efficiency of this mechanism breaks down when there are public goods at the workplace and when workers are not able to change firms easily. In the voice view, a union provides management with information at the bargaining table concerning policies affecting its entire membership (e.g., the mix of the employee-compensation package or the firm's employment practices during a downturn) which can be expected to be different from that derived from the movements of marginal workers. It is likely, then, that the package of employee benefits and employment-adjustment policies will be different in firms covered by collective bargaining than in those that are not. To what extent does the mix of goods at the workplace differ between union and non-union firms?

Data on the remuneration of individual workers and on the expenditures for employees by firms show that the proportion of compensation allotted to fringe benefits is markedly higher for organized blue-collar workers than for similar non-union workers. Within most industries, important fringes such as pensions, and life, accident, and health insurance are much more likely to be found in unionized establishments. . . . [t]he greatest increases in fringes induced by unionism are for deferred compensation, which is generally favoured by older, more stable employees. This is consistent with the view that unions are more responsive to senior, less-mobile workers. . . .

One of the most important personnel decisions made by a firm is how to adjust its employment and wages in response to swings in economic demand: by temporary layoffs, cuts in wage growth, reduced hours, or voluntary attrition. The evidence indicates that the layoff mechanism is used to a much greater extent in unionized than in non-union establishments. It is important to note, however, that the vast majority of these layoffs are temporary, in that the laid-off members await rehire and are recalled after a short spell of unemployment.

By contrast, evidence on the effect on wages of swings in the demand for products shows that the responsiveness of wage rates is smaller in union than in non-union firms. For example, within the typical manufacturing industry during the very severe economic downturn from May 1973 to May 1975 the fraction of hourly blue-collar union members unemployed due to layoffs grew more than twice the comparable fraction for otherwise similar non-members, but the wages of the unionized workers grew by 18.1 percent versus 16.6 percent for non-union workers. More generally, analysis of monthly data covering the 1958-to-1975 period for manufacturing industries indicates that the hourly wages of production workers vary with shipments in such a way as to reduce the need for layoffs to a greater extent in firms that are non-union than in those that are unionized, while there is virtually no such linkage in union settings. These findings reflect the fact that since the late 1950s about two-thirds of the major contract manufacturing workforce has come to be covered by agreements of three years or more, and nearly all have provisions for automatic wage increases.

Why do temporary layoffs dominate alternative adjustment mechanisms to a much greater extent in firms that are unionized than in those that are not? The most reasonable explanation is that under the provisions of most union contracts — which specify that junior workers will be laid off before those with more company service — senior workers, who can be expected to have greater power in organized firms, will generally prefer layoffs over the alternatives.

THE DISTRIBUTION OF INCOME

One of the striking implications of the monopoly view, which runs counter to popular thought, is that union wage gains increase inequality in the labor market. According to the monopoly model, the workers displaced from unionized firms as a result of union wage gains raise the supply of labor to non-union firms, which can therefore be expected to reduce wages. Thus in the monopoly view unionized workers are likely to be made better off at the expense of non-union workers. The fact that organized blue-collar workers would tend to be more skilled and higher paid than other blue-collar workers even in the absence of unionism implies further that unionism benefits "labour's elite" at the expense of those with less skill and earning power. Since many people have supported unions in the belief they reduce economic inequality, evidence that unions have the opposite effect would be a strong argument against the union movement.

In fact, the collective-voice/institutional-response model suggests very different effects on equality than does the monopoly view. Given that union decisions are based on a political process, and given that the majority of union members are likely to have earnings below the mean (including white-collar workers) in any workplace, unions can be expected to seek to reduce wage inequality. Union members are also likely to favor a less-dispersed distribution of earnings for reasons of ideology and organizational solidarity. Finally, by its nature, collective bargaining reduces managerial discretion in the wage-setting process, and this should also reduce differences among similarly situated workers.

Two common union wage policies exemplify unions' efforts to reduce economic inequality. The first is the long-standing policy of pushing for "standard rates" — uniform rates for comparable workers across establishments, and for given occupational classes within establishments. While many large non-union enterprises today also employ formal wage-setting practices, personal differentials based on service, performance, favoritism, or other factors are more common in the non-union than in the union sector. For example, so-called "merit" plans for wage adjustment appear to be less prevalent in the union sector. In the 1970s, while about 43 percent of all companies offered plant employees "wage adjustment based on a merit plan," only 13 percent of major union contracts mentioned these plans. Overall, according to Slichter, Healy, and Livernash, "the influence of unions has clearly been one of minimizing and eliminating judgment-based differences in pay for individuals employed on the same job" and of "removing ability and performance judgments as a factor in individual pay for job performance." One important potential result of these policies is a reduction of inequality, possibly at the expense of efficiency, which may be lessened because the reward for individual effort is reduced. Another important potential result of this policy is that wage discrimination against minorities is likely to be less in unionized than in non-unionized settings.

Union policies favoring seniority in promotion, and job-posting and bidding systems in which workers are informed about new openings and can bid for promotions, can also be expected to have egalitarian consequences. The possibility that arbitrary supervisory judgments will determine the career of a worker is greatly reduced by the development of formal rules which treat each worker identically.

Thus, according to the monopoly model, trade unionism raises inequality, whereas according to the collective-voice/institutional-response model, it reduces inequality. What are the facts?

Our empirical estimates, based on new data, show that standardization policies have substantially reduced wage inequality, and that this effect dominates the monopoly wage effect. When, for instance, the distribution of earnings for male blue-collar workers is graphed, the results for unionized workers in both the manufacturing and non-manufacturing sectors show a much narrower distribution, compressed at the extremes and radically peaked in the middle. For non-union workers, by contrast, the graphs show a much more dispersed pattern of earnings.

In addition to reducing earnings inequality among blue-collar workers, union wage policies contribute to the equalization of wages by decreasing the differential between covered blue-collar workers and uncovered white-collar workers. In manufacturing, though white-collar workers earn an average of 49 percent more than blue-collar workers, our estimates indicate that in unionized enterprises this premium is only 32 percent; in the non-manufacturing sector, where white-collar workers average 31 percent more in earnings than blue-collar workers, the estimated differential is only 19 percent where there are unions.

But to obtain the net effect of unionism on earnings inequality it is necessary to add the *decrease* in inequality due to wage standardization and the *decrease* due to the reduction in the white-collar/blue-collar differential to the *increase* due to the greater wages of blue-collar union workers. Our calculations show clearly that the *dominant* influence affecting earnings inequality is the standardization of rates within the union sector. As a result of the large reduction in inequality attributable to standard-rate policies, the variance in the natural logarithm of earnings (a common measure of inequality) is reduced by 21 percent in manufacturing and by 27 percent in the non-manufacturing sector. Since the distribution of income is, as Christopher Jencks and others have shown, relatively stable in the face of dramatic changes in such important social factors as the distribution of schooling, these effects must be considered large. Unionism thus appears to *reduce* wage dispersion in the United States, which implies that the voice/response effects of the institution dominate the monopoly wage effect on this front. . . .

THE CORRUPTION ISSUE

Under the monopoly view, the potential to use union monopoly power to raise wages and to extort funds from firms — particularly small, weak firms — fosters a significant amount of corruption and undemocratic behavior in the union movement. Many unions are alleged to be run by bosses or racketeers. But while the monopoly view has been highly publicized, the vast majority of evidence appears to support the voice view that unions generally are democratic political organizations and are responsive to the will of their members.

There are, to begin with, internal and external forces that push unions — both locals and internationals — toward being responsive to the wishes of their members. Union constitutions typically mandate democratic procedures and require conventions or referenda to discern the membership's sentiment on important issues, and fair and frequent elections to assess the members' satisfaction with their leadership. While at one time U.S. labor law dealt only peripherally with the internal workings of unions, the Landrum-Griffin Act of 1959 provides strong federal sanctions against corruption and undemocratic practices inside unions. It contains provisions that require local, intermediate, and international unions to hold elections at fixed, reasonably short intervals, that guarantee members a reasonable opportunity to nominate candidates, run for office, and freely criticize union leaders and their policies, that prohibit incumbents from using union funds to support the election of a given candidate for office in the union and from disseminating propaganda for one candidate without doing as much for his or her opponent, and that require officials to file information on the financial affairs of the union and its leaders and on its constitutional provisions. Moreover, the country's labor law provides an election procedure under which a group of workers can decertify its union and become unorganized, replace one union with another, or attempt to change the boundaries of an existing bargaining unit.

The evidence strongly suggests that the vast majority of local and international unions in the U.S. are quite democratic and suffer only rare breaches of internal democracy. From fiscal years 1965 to 1974, only 239 charges of improper conduct affecting the outcome of a union election were judged to have merit, according to information issued by the Department of Labor. Since approximately 200,000 elections were held by local, intermediate, and international unions during this period, the percentage of elections in which there were proven violations is approximately 0.1 percent. Moreover, it is probably true that in a fair number of these cases the violation was due to ignorance of the details of labor law on the part of union officials rather than to an explicit attempt to affect an election's outcome. And while surely there were some improper actions that were either not reported or not proved, the miniscule number of those which were suggests that number must also have been extremely small.

While many national union leaders tend to remain ensconced in office for years, at the local level a fair number of incumbents regularly get unseated, as would be expected in a well-functioning democracy. One pertinent study by Leon Appelbaum analyzed data on the turnover of union leaders in 94 locals in the Milwaukee, Wisconsin area between 1960 and 1962: 40 percent of the officials in office at the beginning of the period were not in office two years later.

The fact that the majority of members in most unions are satisfied with their union's internal operations is shown by the results of union-decertification elections conducted by the National Labor Relations Board. In each year during the past decade, only about 0.1 percent of all union members were in bargaining units that voted to decertify the union representing them.

Finally, recent surveys of members' views of the internal affairs of their unions indicate that the vast majority are satisfied with union operations. About 70 percent said they had "no problems" with their union in 1972–73, while about 80 percent had no problems in 1969–70. Roughly half of those who had problems in 1972–73 regarded them as "slight" or as "not really a problem at all." In both surveys, less than 10 percent of union members were dissatisfied with how democratically their unions were run, the conduct of their union's leadership, or the officials' policies.

The internal operation of unions aside, the collective-voice/institutional-response analysis stresses the role of unionism in increasing democracy at the workplace by providing workers with a channel for expressing their preferences to management and increasing workers' willingness to complain about undesirable conditions. Evidence from surveys of workers' job satisfaction tends to support this view. In these surveys the reported job satisfaction of unionized workers is less than the reported satisfaction of comparable non-union workers. However, the union members are also more likely to state that they are "unwilling to change jobs under any circumstance" or "would never consider moving to a new job," than are their "more satisfied" non-unionized counterparts. The most direct interpretation of the puzzle is that collective organization provides support that encourages the voicing of dissatisfaction. In contrast to most economic benefits, which increase both utility and stated satisfaction, "voice" increases utility while increasing stated dissatisfaction. In addition, because a union will collect more information than an individual and then disseminate it to every member, though union members know that their jobs are significantly better than the alternatives, they will also know that they are far from ideal. And since voice is also a tool of conflict, good strategists, unlike Voltaire's Pangloss, will not proclaim their workplaces as "the best of all possible worlds."

What about the view that unions are corrupt institutions? The evidence from the surveys clearly runs counter to this stereotype. Ninety-nine percent of union members in both 1969–70 and 1972–73 stated that they had "no problems" with graft or corruption among their leaders. Moreover, after a careful analysis of the extent of corruption in the American labor movement, Derek Bok and John Dunlop, writing in 1970, stressed the honesty of most labor leaders:

> Although the record in this country compares unfavorably with that of many other nations, legal safeguards now go far to curb dishonesty and encourage democratic behavior. Probably only a tiny fraction of all union officials in America would stoop to serious abuse. The overwhelming majority of labor leaders are honest men who take seriously their obligation to represent the interest of the members who have elected them to office.

Finally, in what ways has organized labor affected outcomes in the American political arena? Have unions had greater success supporting "special-interest" legislation or "social" legislation that benefits lower-income persons and workers in general? Despite the bad press given some union efforts to obtain "special-interest" benefits from lawmakers, much union political muscle has been devoted to promoting legislation that would be of no obvious material gain to unionized workers — except as members of the overall working population. For instance, organized labor was quite active in pushing for the passage of the Public Accommodation Act of 1964, the Voting Rights Act of 1965, equal-employment-opportunity legislation, anti-poverty legislation, and the Occupational Safety and Health Act of 1971.

On the other hand, most union-favored special-interest legislation has failed to pass Congress, though important legislation opposed by unions as detrimental to their power or even their survival has been passed. The last major piece of legislation regulating collective bargaining and unionism, the Landrum-Griffin bill, was enacted in 1959 over the vociferous opposition of unions, while a mild 1977 labor-law-reform bill strongly favored by unions failed to clear the Congress. Typically, only when unions and management in a particular sector have united in favor of legislation to benefit that sector have unions had much success in gaining support for their "special-interest" legislative proposals.

All in all, though unions fight for self-interest legislation — as do other groups in our pluralist society — they have scored their greatest political victories on more general social legislation. In terms of actual outcomes, unions have been more effective as a voice of the whole working population and the disadvantaged than they have been as a monopoly institution seeking to increase its monopoly power.

EXPLAINING MANAGERIAL OPPOSITION

If, in addition to its negative monopoly effects, trade unionism is associated with substantial positive effects on the operation of the economy and on the performance of firms, why do so many U.S. firms oppose unions so vehemently? There are in fact several reasons.

First, the bulk of the economic gains that spring from unionism accrue to workers and not to owners or managers. Managers are unlikely to see any personal benefits in their subordinates' unionization, but are likely to be quite aware of the costs: a diminution of their power, the need to work harder, the loss of operating flexibility, and the like.

Second, though productivity might typically be higher in union than in otherwise comparable non-union work settings, so too are wages. It would seem, given the objectives and actions of most unions, that the rate of return on capital would be lower under collective bargaining, although there are important exceptions. Thus, there is risk in unionization; the firm may be able to rationalize operations, have good relations with the union, and maintain its profit rate — or it may not. In addition, while the total cost of strikes to society as a whole has been shown to be quite small, the potential cost to a particular firm can be substantial. Since managers — like most other people — dislike taking risks, we would expect opposition to unions even if on average the benefits to firms equal the costs. Moreover, given the wide-ranging differences in the effects of unions on economic performance, at least some managerial opposition surely arises from enterprises in which the expected benefits of collective bargaining are small but the expected costs high. Even the most vocal advocate of the collective-voice/institutional-response view of unionism would admit that, though functional in many industrial settings, unions are not functional in others — and one must expect greater managerial opposition in the latter cases.

Third, management may find unionism expensive, difficult, and very threatening in its initial stages, when modes of operation must be altered if efficiency is to be improved. New and different types of management policies are needed under unionism, and these require either changes in the behavior of current management, or — as appears to be the case in many just-organized firms — a new set of managers.

Finally, U.S. management has generally adopted an ideology of top-down enlightened control, under which unions are seen as both a cause and an effect of managerial failure. In this view, unions interfere with management's efforts to carry out its social function of ensuring that goods and services are produced efficiently. In addition, because unions typically come into existence as a result of management's mistakes in dealing with its workforce, managers frequently resent what unionization implies about their own past performances.

We believe that our analysis of unionism has opened up a host of neglected issues regarding the key worker institution in the American capitalist system. While some of our findings will surely be altered by additional research and some may even be proven wrong, we do believe that our findings present a reasonably valid picture of modern unionism in our country. It stands in sharp contrast to the monopoly view of trade unions and to many popular opinions about them. And if, as we have found, the positive effects of unions are in many settings more important than their negative effects, then the ongoing decline of private-sector unionism — a development unique to the U.S. among Western developed countries — deserves serious public attention.

[Reprinted with permission of the authors and *The Public Interest*, Number 57, Fall 1979, pp. 69–93 © 1979 by National Affairs, Inc.]

* * *

See also Richard Freeman & James Medoff, *What Do Unions Do?* (New York: Basic Books, 1984).

Chapter 4: **Status Under Collective Bargaining Legislation**

4:100 INTRODUCTION

Collective bargaining is an important component of Canadian labour policy. The reach of the collective bargaining regime is therefore both a hotly contested political issue and the subject of extensive litigation, with repercussions for those who are included or excluded and for the rest of the workforce. Not everyone is entitled to bargain collectively under prevailing labour relations legislation. This privilege is reserved for "employees" — a term that is increasingly difficult to define given the growing variety of contractual arrangements in the labour market, such as apply to operators of food franchises, people who work from their homes as consultants or contractors, or casual workers sent by employment agencies. It should be noted that the problem of how to characterize workers in these developing variants of traditional employment is not restricted to collective bargaining; it also arises in assessing whether such workers are covered by legislation on such matters as employment standards, unemployment insurance, workers' compensation, pensions and occupational health and safety.

Moreover, some people who are employees by any definition may be legally ineligible to bargain collectively. If they work for certain kinds of employers — typically those in the public and quasi-public sector — they may be barred from collective action or required to bargain under more restrictive procedures than those set out in general labour relations legislation. If they are employed in certain occupations — predominantly the professions, agriculture, and domestic service — they may be entirely excluded from statutory collective bargaining because, for good or bad, legislatures have concluded that it is inappropriate or unworkable for them. Even employees who work at conventional jobs that come under ordinary labour legislation are denied the right to bargain collectively if they have significant responsibility for representing management in its relations with workers and unions, or if they have other important managerial responsibilities. The rationale for this restriction is that such employees would find themselves in a conflict of interest.

Even if a person is clearly an employee eligible for inclusion in collective bargaining, it is not always clear who his or her legal employer is. Individual entrepreneurs may set up complex and confusing corporate structures for legitimate business reasons, or simply to avoid obligations under labour or tax legislation. The restructuring of companies, and the growth of outsourcing and more flexible methods of production, may mean that workers who were once employed by, say, an automobile manufacturer are now employed by a different entity that is part of the automobile manufacturer's tightly integrated network of suppliers.

As for employee organizations, they are of many kinds, both in the workplace and outside of it — social clubs, groups based on a common ethnic or religious identity, and so on. In order to fall within the statutory definition of a trade union, and therefore be eligible to acquire the privileges and responsibilities of a bargaining agent under labour relations legislation, an organization must have been formed for purposes that include collective representation of its members vis-à-vis their employer. In addition, other questions may arise in determining whether an organization that claims union status is indeed eligible to represent workers. For example, does the organization have sufficient structure and permanence to represent workers effectively? Should it have the right to function as a collective bargaining agent if its internal decion-making processes are not democratic? These are all important public policy questions, though they may often appear to be mere quibbles over the legal interpretation of the key terms "employee," "employer," and "union." The answers to them may affect the balance of power in the particular workplace and across the whole economy.

It should not be assumed that the advent of collective bargaining invariably improves the position of employees, or that denial of access to collective bargaining always disadvantages them. For example, under some labour relations statutes, domestics and agricultural workers are denied collective bargaining rights because of what are often seen as anachronistic or disingenuous arguments about the need to protect the sanctity of the household or the family farm. However, even where those groups have been given bargaining rights, they have seldom been able to use them to much effect. Conversely, medical doctors generally are not employees by any definition and do not formally bargain collectively under conventional labour legislation, but they have been very successful in advancing their economic interests through lobbying, negotiations, public appeals and even work stoppages. These two examples (the former involving the powerless, the latter involving the powerful) suggest that there are very real limits to the effectiveness of our collective bargaining laws in reducing income disparities in society.

In recent decades, fundamental changes in our economy have called into question the logic that underlies the boundaries drawn by labour relations legislation around the right to bargain collectively. That logic is based on the assumption that the legislation will be used by certain kinds of people, namely skilled and semi-skilled blue-collar workers in relatively stable employment relationships with corporate enterprises structured on a traditional hierarchical basis. This assumption may have been reasonably accurate when collective bargaining legislation was introduced during and shortly after the Second World War. It has become less accurate as rapid changes in technology have influenced the shape of employment and corporate organization in the new economy. Will unions be able to organize the growing number of highly skilled knowledge workers employed in organizations where managerial authority is less clearly defined?

At the other end of an increasingly polarized workforce, an even greater challenge for unions is what to do about unorganized workers in the expanding secondary labour market. These employees may often work on a part-time or casual basis, and may need to hold more than one job to make ends meet. The precariousness of their employment raises the question whether, even as a collective, they could muster enough power to bargain effectively under existing labour relations legislation.

As large firms break down into much smaller production units, the attachment of collective bargaining rights to the individual firm — a cornerstone of our present system — may further limit employee bargaining power. It can be argued that our present collective bargaining system only works well in large firms, where unions can collect enough dues revenue to be able to bargain effectively and where the firm itself has the economic and political leverage to pass on the costs of collective bargaining settlements to society at large. Perhaps it is time to re-examine the assumption that access to collective bargaining should depend on a proximate relationship with a particular employer, and to look instead to the worker's attachment to a particular industry.

It may also be time to re-examine who should and should not have access to collective bargaining, and with what consequences. Very affluent "employees" such as elite professional athletes may appear to have no need for collective bargaining, but they enjoy the right to engage in it and they do so very effectively. Distinctly un-affluent "employees" — non-elite musicians and writers, for example — may well need collective bargaining, but cannot have it under ordinary labour relations legislation because they lack a specific employer with whom they can bargain in any conventional sense. Some small businesspeople, such as consultants and the owners of franchised food outlets, may be at the mercy of a single provider of supplies or work opportunities, but they still have no access to collective bargaining. Other people with small businesses — for example, doctors paid on a fee for service basis by government health plans, and lawyers paid by legal aid plans — also have no employer in the conventional sense, but nevertheless manage to bring collective pressure to bear on the source of their income (the government).

Each of these cases presents special problems. If the workers concerned are not covered by labour relations statutes, they may be covered by special legislation. This is the case, for example, with artists and performers who are subject to the federal *Status of the Artist Act*. Doctors and legal aid lawyers may operate under special bargaining and dispute resolution procedures established by statutes, regulations, agreements between the government and professional bodies, or unwritten understandings. In the absence of such arrangements, collective activities are regulated by the general law of the land. The federal *Competition Act* (discussed at the end of section 4:200 below) is very important in this regard. It provides for criminal, administrative, and civil sanctions. Also very important is the common law of tort (discussed in Chapter 8). It gives plaintiffs who are adversely affected by certain kinds of collective economic sanctions the right to sue for damages or injunctions.

The express exclusion from collective bargaining legislation of managerial employees and those employed in a confidential capacity relating to labour relations raises a different concern. This exclusion reflects the classic adversarial paradigm of collective bargaining, which posits a divergence of interest between workers and management and their necessary separation into opposing camps. The appropriateness of that paradigm becomes more questionable as external economic forces generate pressure for greater labour-management co-operation, even within the largest corporations. The emergence of a large group of knowledge workers, and an increasing emphasis on nonhierarchical and participatory management, suggest that the present managerial exclusion may be overly broad.

This same concern arises when considering what types of organizations are granted status as trade unions under collective bargaining legislation. That legislation was originally designed to ensure that company-dominated employee organizations did not preempt the formation of genuine trade unions. Today, however, greater union participation in corporate management, and an increasing employee ownership stake in some unionized companies, raise questions about whether it is still appropriate to require an arm's-length relationship between unions and employers. That requirement must also be looked at in the context of a harsher economy, which has forced many unions and employers to adopt more co-operative approaches in order to maintain the economic viability of enterprises with well-established collective bargaining relationships.

The next sections explore the boundaries of employee status and union status under labour relations law: what types of workers are entitled to make use of collective bargaining statutes, and what types of employee organizations are recognized by these statutes?

REFERENCES

George Adams, *Canadian Labour Law*, 2d ed. (Aurora, Ont.: Canada Law Book, 1993) c. 6; Donald Carter *et al.*, *Labour Law in Canada*, 5th ed. (Markham, Ont.: Butterworths, 2002) pt. 2, c. 3; Harry Arthurs, "The Dependent Contractor: A Study of the Legal Problems of Countervailing Power" (1965) 16 U.T.L.J. 89

4:200 WHO IS AN EMPLOYEE?

National Labor Relations Board v. Hearst Publications Inc. (1944), 322 U.S. 111 at 120–32

[The United States National Labor Relations Board had ordered certain newspapers in the Hearst chain to bargain collectively with the Los Angeles Newsboys Local Industrial Union No. 75. The board's order was quashed by a federal appeals court on the basis that the newsboys were not "employees" within the meaning of the *National Labor Relations Act* (the Wagner Act), and that the employer therefore was not required to bargain with their union. In the following judgment, the United States Supreme Court reversed the appeals court.]

RUTLEDGE J.: The principal question is whether the newsboys are "employees." Because Congress did not explicitly define the term, respondents say its meaning must be determined by reference to common-law standards. In their view "common-law standards" are those the courts have applied in distinguishing between "employees" and "independent contractors" when working out various problems unrelated to the Wagner Act's purposes and provisions.

The argument assumes that there is some simple, uniform and easily applicable test which the courts have used, in dealing with such problems, to determine whether persons doing work for others fall in one class or the other. Unfortunately this is not true. Only by a long and tortuous history was the simple formulation worked out which has been stated most frequently as "the test" for deciding whether one who hires another is responsible in tort for his wrongdoing. . . .

Whether, given the intended national uniformity [in the application of the Wagner Act], the term "employee" includes such workers as these newsboys must be answered primarily from the history, terms and purposes of the legislation. The word "is not treated by Congress as a word of art having a definite meaning . . . ". Rather, "it takes color from its surroundings . . . [in] the statute where it appears . . . , and derives meaning from the context of that statute, which "must be read in the light of the mischief to be corrected and the end to be attained." . . . Congress, on the one hand, was not thinking solely of the immediate technical relation of employer and employee. It had in mind at least some other persons than those standing in the proximate legal relation of employee to the particular employer involved in the labor dispute. It cannot be taken, however, that the purpose was to include all other persons who may perform service for another or was to ignore entirely legal classifications made for other purposes. Congress had in mind a wider field than the narrow technical legal relation of "master and servant," as the common law had worked this out in all its variations, and at the same time a narrower one than the entire area of rendering service to others. The question comes down therefore to how much was included of the intermediate region between what is clearly and unequivocally "employment," by any appropriate test, and what is as clearly entrepreneurial enterprise and not employment. . . . Congress was not seeking to solve the nationally harassing problems with which the statute deals by solutions only partially effective. It rather sought to find a broad solution, one that would bring industrial peace by substituting, so far as its power could reach, the rights of workers to self-organization and collective bargaining for the industrial strife which prevails where these rights are not effectively established. Yet only partial solutions would be provided if large segments of workers about whose technical legal position such local differences exist should be wholly excluded from coverage by reason of such differences. Yet that result could not be avoided, if choice must be made among them and controlled by them in deciding who are "employees" within the Act's meaning. Enmeshed in such distinctions, the administration of the statute soon might become encumbered by the same sort of technical legal refinement as has characterized the long evolution of the employee-independent contractor dichotomy in the courts for other purposes. The consequences would be ultimately to defeat, in part at least, the achievement of the statute's objectives. . . .

The mischief at which the Act is aimed and the remedies it offers are not confined exclusively to "employees" within the traditional legal distinctions separating them from "independent contractors." Myriad forms of service relationship, with infinite and subtle variations in the terms of employment, blanket the nation's economy. Some are within this Act, others beyond its coverage. Large numbers will fall clearly on one side or on the other, by whatever test may be applied. But intermediate there will be many, the incidents of whose employment partake in part of the one group, in part of the other, in varying proportions of weight. And consequently the legal pendulum, for purposes of applying the statute, may swing one way or the other depending upon the weight of this balance and its relation to the special purpose at hand.

Unless the common-law tests are to be imported and made exclusively controlling, without regard to the statute's purposes, it cannot be irrelevant that the particular workers in these cases are subject as a matter of economic fact, to the evils the statute was designed to eradicate and that the remedies it affords are appropriate for preventing them or curing their harmful effects in the special situation. Interruption of commerce through strikes and unrest may stem as well from labor disputes between some who, for other purposes, are technically "independent contractors" and their employers as from disputes between persons who for those purposes, are "employees" and their employers. . . . Inequality of bargaining power in controversies over wages, hours and working conditions may as well characterize the status of the one group as of the other. The former, when acting alone, may be as "helpless in dealing with an employer," as "dependent . . . on his daily wage" and "as unable to leave the employ and to resist arbitrary and unfair treatment" as the latter. For each "union . . . [may be] essential to give . . . opportunity to deal on equality with their employer." And for each, collective bargaining may be appropriate and effective for the "friendly adjustment of industrial disputes arising out of differences as to wages, hours, or other working conditions. In short, when the particular situation of employment combines these characteristics, so that the economic facts of the relation make it more nearly one of employment than of independent business enterprise with respect to the ends sought to be accomplished by the legislation, those characteristics may outweigh technical legal classification for purposes unrelated to the statute's objectives and bring the relation within its protections. . . .

In this case the Board found that the designated newsboys work continuously and regularly, rely upon their earnings for the support of themselves and their families, and have their total wages influenced in large measure by the publishers who dictate their buying and selling prices, fix their market and control their supply of papers. Their hours of work and their efforts on the job are supervised and to some extent prescribed by the publishers or their agents. Much of their sales equipment and advertising materials is furnished by the publishers with the intention that it be used for the publisher's benefit. Stating that "the primary consideration in the determination of the applicability of the statutory definition is whether effectuation of the declared policy and purposes of the Act comprehend securing to the individual the rights guaranteed and protection afforded by the Act," the Board concluded that the newsboys are employees. The record sustains the Board's findings and there is ample basis in the law for its conclusion.

* * *

In defining "employee," it is important to consider whether the scope of collective bargaining should include more than the employment aspects of an economic relationship. If other types of economic arrangements fall within collective bargaining legislation, there may be a conflict with competition policy.

Canadian public policy favours the preservation of business competition, and forbids businesses to enter into conspiracies that would unduly restrict such competition. This policy is embodied in the *Competition Act*, R.S.C. 1985, c. C-34. Section 45(1) of that Act makes it illegal for persons to form combinations that would unduly restrain or injure competition. It should also be noted that section 2(1) of the same Act forbids restraints on or injury to competition respecting "products," which are defined to include not only "articles" but also "services . . . of any description whether industrial, trade, professional or otherwise." Reading these two provisions literally and together, there is a risk that section 45 could prohibit certain union tactics, such as strikes and picketing, as concerted activity designed to restrain or injure competition in the supply of services. However, section 4 of the *Competition Act* provides a general exemption for "combinations or activities of workmen or employees for their own reasonable protection as such workmen or employees" (section 4(1)(a)), and also provides a more specific exemption for arrangements "pertaining to collective bargaining . . . in respect of salaries or wages and terms and conditions of employment" (section 4(1)(c)).

Interestingly, although private parties injured by a violation of the *Competition Act* have had a right to sue for damages since 1975, no such suits have been brought against unions, nor have other proceedings been brought against them under that Act in recent years. This may signal recognition of the fact that competition policy somehow has to be squared with collective bargaining policy. The point is of particular importance in assessing the cases in the following subsection, which deal with the legislative conferral of employee status on individuals who might also be deemed to be entrepreneurs and thus subject to the restrictions of the *Competition Act*.

4:210 Dependent Contractors

Labour boards and courts have constantly struggled with the question of the distinction between an "employee" and an "independent contractor." As we saw in the *Hearst* case in the preceding section, in the absence of legislative guidance decision-makers are sometimes tempted to borrow definitions from the common law. In Canada, one such borrowing produced what is known as the "fourfold test," which is discussed above in Chapter 2 (section 2:200) and below in the *Winnipeg Free Press* case. That test took into account four factors — control of the relationship, ownership of the tools, chance of profit, and risk of loss. The presence of some of these factors and not others, however, sometimes led to confusion and to the exclusion from collective bargaining of groups of workers for whom collective action was both necessary and appropriate. Consequently, some Canadian legislatures adopted "dependent contractor" provisions, which extended the reach of the term "employee" (for collective bargaining purposes) to cover some of the most problematic and marginal parts of the universe of independent contractors. A typical statutory definition of "dependent contractor" is found in the Ontario *Labour Relations Act*, section 1(1):

> "dependent contractor" means a person, whether or not employed under a contract of employment, and whether or not furnishing tools, vehicles, equipment, machinery, mate-

rial, or any other thing, or any other thing owned by the dependent contractor, who performs work or services for another person for compensation or reward on such terms and conditions that the dependent contractor is in a position of economic dependence upon, and under an obligation to perform duties for, that person more closely resembling the relationship of an employee than that of an independent contractor.

The following case applies the concept of the dependent contractor.

Winnipeg Free Press v. Media Union of Manitoba (1999) (Case No. 443/97/LRA) (Manitoba Labour Board)

CHAPMAN, Vice-Chair; WINSTON and MCMEEL, Members

. . .

¶ 17 The initial position stated by counsel for the Free Press was that [newspaper] carriers were not employees within the meaning of the Labour Relations Act. The Media Union, through its counsel, submitted that the Free Press had no status in this matter.

. . .

¶ 23 . . . The Free Press is one of Canada's largest newspapers and has a long and proud tradition in Manitoba, and Winnipeg, in particular. In recent years, there has been a change from afternoon delivery to early morning delivery, and the newspaper now publishes seven days per week. There are several hundred carrier routes and a substantial number of large apartment blocks. These factors, inter alia, have substantially changed how newspapers are delivered. The former image of a young boy or girl, usually in their teens, carrying a bag full of newspapers after school hours and collecting during the evenings, has drastically changed. Today the papers are delivered early in the morning and are at the reader's doorstep in the early hours of dawn. Additionally, the collection of accounts is, for the most part, done by pre-authorized credit card charges or cheques, and there are only a minimal amount of collections done in cash on a bi-weekly basis. The subscriber can now have a paper delivered on a regular basis, and perhaps will never meet the individual who delivers it. The evidence disclosed that there are only a handful of young carriers still employed.

¶ 24 . . . The evidence discloses that carriers are required to attend at a specified depot each morning to pick up their allotment of papers for their particular route. There are six depots, each with a district manager. The Employer's trucks bring the newspapers to the depots. Since attendance is early in the morning, obviously, youths of tender years would not be able to perform that work. In fact, carriers are required to have an automobile.

¶ 25 It is worthwhile to note the evidence of Ms Hyworren, who has been employed as a carrier for some two and one-half years. She has no other occupation at this time, and she and her partner operate three routes. . . . She earns 10.5 cents for each paper delivered, plus she receives a route allowance of 18 cents per kilometer, measured from the depot and through the route. It is anticipated she will deliver approximately sixty papers per hour and would earn approximately $20.00 per day. In addition to the 10.5 cents per paper, she receives certain extras. One extra is 5 cents for the Saturday paper, and there is extra payment for certain coupon books or other handout material one receives with the newspaper. Rates are fixed, and nothing is negotiable except that periodically there may be some discussion about the mileage allowance for a route. It is essential that the person with a route have a car. She recited that at one stage she and her partner tried to operate with one car, but it was not permitted. Periodically route sizes are reduced by virtue of the fact that a number of large apartment blocks have been constructed. . . .

¶ 26 . . . If carriers are ill or for any reason are unable to carry out their work, they are to try and find a replacement, and, if they cannot do so, then the district manager would have a list of extra individuals who would deliver the papers, but the regular carrier's compensation would be reduced. They are required to pick up their papers by 3:45 a.m. . . .

¶ 27 Ms Hyworren confirmed that most subscribers' collections are paid directly to the Employer's office. . . . If a customer were in arrears, a carrier's compensation would be deducted. Carriers were instructed to let a customer go for four weeks without paying the bill, before delivery would stop. However, ultimately, they would get the deducted monies back from the Free Press.

¶ 28 If the truck was not there in time, which occasionally happened because of inclement weather or breakdowns, they had to wait, and there was no extra payment for that time. They were expected to find and get customers, and, if they did receive a new start, they would get some compensation. . . .

¶ 29 . . . Ms Hyworren stated that she had worked for other carriers on occasion, both at their request and at the request of the district manager, and was paid by the Free Press for doing so. Very seldom was she paid by a carrier. . . . Ms Hyworren was adamant that the district manager set the route allowances and determined the route sizes. Although a carrier might discuss it with the district manager, ultimately the carrier had no choice in the matter. Ms Hyworren confirmed that, if there was a breakdown in her vehicle, she was responsible for the cost of repairing it, and, therefore, she was at some financial risk. Additionally, if she got extra customers, she would get a bonus, and, therefore, there was a chance for more profit. Also, if a carrier could negotiate a higher route allowance, there would be more profit.

. . .

¶ 50 On reviewing the duties of district managers, [Rob Covaceuszach, a Free Press executive] stated that they could hire, fire, permit absences, negotiate route allowances, warn employees, and correct their performance. . . . Mr. Covaceuszach acknowledged that the Free Press could instruct a carrier to keep delivering the papers even though an account was in arrears. He stated that carriers could provide substitutes if they are unable to attend and there is no restriction as to who did the work. . . .

¶ 51 There are some nine hundred routes, with some seven hundred carriers, and some carriers have more than one route. . . . Mr. Covaceuszach stated that there were no reference checks and no personnel files were kept with respect to carriers.

¶ 52 In circumstances where a carrier quit and suggested a new carrier, Mr. Covaceuszach stated it would be likely that the recommended carrier would be hired, but the district manager made the decision. In certain circumstances rewards were given to carriers for good service, and, additionally, carriers would receive gratuities from customers. Carriers were not restricted to delivering only for the Free Press, and many hold other full-time positions, and often concurrently delivered other papers, magazines, or advertising material.

. . .

¶ 56 Mr. Covaceuszach was referred to Exhibit 35, which is a notice from the Free Press to customers, and in which it is stated that the Free Press carriers are independent business people and personally responsible for any outstanding monies. Mr. Covaceuszach ultimately agreed that, that statement was somewhat misleading. He also agreed that a carrier could not sell or dispose of his route — any change in carrier was at the discretion of a district manager.

. . .

¶ 90 The question of whether individuals are employees or independent (or dependent) contractors is one that has been before the courts and administrative tribunals for many years. The genesis of the jurisprudence is found in the decision of the Privy Council in *Montreal v. Montreal Locomotive Works.* . . . In that case, and in other subsequent cases, it was stated that the main factors to be considered in such cases were that of control, ownership of tools, chance of profit, and risk of loss. The most significant test, however, and certainly the one to be generally applied, lay in the nature and degree of detailed control over the person alleged to be an employee.

¶ 91 In the *Gelco Express Ltd.* case, . . . this Board . . . said:

> The Board, in reaching its conclusion, had regard to the leading authority, *Montreal v. Montreal Locomotive Works* (1947) 1 D.L.R. 161, where Lord Wright, speaking for the Privy Council, observes:
>
> > In many cases the question can only be settled by examining the whole of the various elements which constitute the relationship between the parties. In this way it is in some cases possible to decide the issue by raising as the crucial question whose business is it, or in other words by asking whether the party is carrying on the business, in the sense of carrying it on for himself or on his own behalf and not merely for a superior.
>
> and, as well, to *McDonald et al v. Associated Trucks Ltd.*, a decision of the Supreme Court of British Columbia, where the following observation is made:
>
> > McCardie J. in *Performing Right Soc. v. Mitchell & Booker (Palais de Danse) Ltd.* . . . , gathers together numerous authorities with regard to the tests to be applied in deciding whether a man is a servant or an independent contractor. He summarizes them thus: "It seems, however, reasonably clear that the final test, if there be a final test, and certainly the test to be generally applied, lies in the nature and degree of

detailed control over the person alleged to be a servant. This circumstance is of course one only of several to be considered, but it is usually of vital importance."

As I have said, so McCardie J. says, the decisions are numerous and he says not always easy to follow. At least they are not always easy to apply to the particular situation. There are many elements to be considered of which some are as follows: the nature of the task undertaken, the freedom of action allowed, the retention of the right to prescribe the exact work and of the power or right to direct the particular work to be done: the fact that the person in question devotes or may be bound to devote either the whole of his time to the work directed or so much thereof as the person directing the work shall require as and when the person receiving directions shall be given such directions. All these are but some of the features to be taken into consideration in deciding whether a person is a servant or an independent contractor.

The statutory definition of "employee" that had prevailed prior to the most recent amendments to the Act made reference to "dependent contractor" to whom the Act made clear the definition of employee extended. The amendments to the definition of employee included deleting the reference to dependent contractor in the definition and deleting the definition of the term.

In Manitoba "dependent contractor" had been defined specifically as meaning:

(i) "dependent contractor" means the owner, purchaser or lessee of a vehicle used for hauling livestock, liquids, goods, merchandise, or other materials other than on rails or tracks who is not employed by an employer but who is a party to a contract, oral or in writing, under the terms of which he is

(i)   required to provide the vehicle by means of which he performs the contract,

(ii) entitled to retain for his own use from time to time any sum of money that remains after the cost of his performance of the contract is deducted from the amount he is paid, in accordance with the contract, for that performance,

(iii) required to operate the vehicle in accordance with the contract.

and [in *Gelco Express*] we note the following:

What is the effect, if any, of the most recent amendment to the definition of employee? The Employer's submission, in effect, is that the amendment returns us to the classic common law tests. The Union submits that the effect of the legislative change is to broaden, not narrow the scope of the relationships captured by the term "employee."

In the Board's view the current definition has the effect of expanding, not restricting, the definitional scope of the "employee" under the Act. The Act now provides that:

k) "employee" means a person employed to do work and includes any person designated by the board as an employee for the purposes of this Act,

The section goes on to say that this designation as an "employee" may be made:

. . . notwithstanding that the person to whom the employee provides services is not vicariously liable for the employee's acts or omissions, . . .

Whether an employee/employer relationship exists has been answered often in common law in the context of issues as to vicarious liability involving circumstances where a third party injured as a result of the negligence of one party attempts to have the negligence of the first party attached to a second party.

The test to be applied by the Board was set out [in *Gelco Express*] as follows:

> To what, if anything, must the Board have regard in exercising its discretion to designate a person as an "employee"? That we must have regard to something cannot be in doubt, but if a specific list of relevant considerations had been contemplated, the Act would have done so. The Board is of the view that what is contemplated now is that we assess the particular circumstances of the relationship in each case against the backdrop of whether or not it presents an appropriate context for the practice and procedure of collective bargaining, in contrast to our prior focus of analyzing facts to determine whether they fell inside or outside a particular classification box. What has been altered by the amendment, in essence, is a matter of form and substance, for we must continue to have regard to the same facts within their labour relations context, but we do so under a mandate that empowers us to designate, not to classify — to exercise a discretion, not to determine a classification.

In the exercise of this discretion, the Board regards our obligation as being along the same lines as expressed by the Ontario Board in *Superior Sand* . . . :

> In the final balance, the Board must be satisfied that the relationship before it, even though it may not bear all of the hallmarks of the typical employment relationship, more closely resembles the relationship of an employee than that of an independent contractor.

In so concluding, the Ontario Board tracked very closely the concluding words in the definition of "dependent contractor" in its Act, i.e. "more closely resembling the relationship of an employee than that of an independent contractor." By contrast to the Ontario legislation, which requires the Board to make a determination as to whether the facts fall within the classification of "dependent contractor," our Act requires the Board to exercise a discretion as to whether a person ought to be considered an "employee" within the meaning of the Act. The mission is the same, but the mandate under which it is conducted is different.

¶ 92 The evolution of the jurisprudence shows that the initial four criterion set out in the Montreal Locomotive Works case, supra, have been vastly expanded. A fairly comprehensive statement of all of those [by the Ontario Labour Relations Board] can be found in *Algonquin Tavern* . . . :

1. The use of, or right to use substitutes.
2. Ownership of instruments, tools, equipment, equipment, (sic) appliances or the supply of materials.
3. Evidence of entrepreneurial activity.
4. The selling of one's services to the market generally.
5. Economic mobility or independence, including the freedom to reject job opportunities, or work when and where one wishes.

6. Evidence of some variation in the fees charged for the services rendered.
7. Whether the individual can be said to be carrying on an "independent business" on his own behalf rather than on behalf of an employer or, to put it another way, whether the individual has become an essential element which has been integrated into the operating organization of the employing unit.
8. The degree of specialization, skill, expertise or creativity involved.
9. Control of the manner and means of performing the work — especially if there is active interference with the activity.
10. The magnitude of the contract amount, terms, and manner of payment.
11. Whether the individual renders services or works under conditions which are similar to persons who are clearly employees.

¶ 93 Before reviewing the criteria with respect to the facts in this particular case, it is perhaps worthwhile to very briefly make one comment on the agreement between the parties (Exhibit 6), supra. There is no question that Exhibit 6 attempts to establish that the carrier is an independent contractor. The test, as stated above, must be based on the particular facts of the case and not simply on the title referred to in the agreement.

¶ 94 Some other criteria were considered, and the list was expanded by the British Columbia Labour Relations Board in the *Semiahmoo Management Ltd.* case. . . .

¶ 96 In view of the *Gelco* decision, *supra,* the definition of independent contractor, as compared to employee, is less significant in Manitoba because of the decision which, as previously quoted, considered the effect of vicarious liability. However, certain questions remain unanswered by the change in the statutory definition. As stated by Vice Chair Parkinson, in the *Semiahmoo* case, *supra:* "The dividing line between them is somewhat fluid and elusive." We have noted that most of the carriers entered into contracts, which identify them as independent contractors. That title is relevant to some extent but it cannot be determinative of the status. This Board has the authority to determine that a relationship is one of employer-employee notwithstanding that the parties have chosen to describe it differently. It is the actual relationship that exists and not the nomenclature chosen by the parties.

¶ 97 The Board is satisfied that, notwithstanding all of the other criteria from time to time established by the jurisprudence, one of the key factors continues to be control over the work and the manner in which it is performed. In this particular case, there is a relatively high degree of control. It may not be to the same extent as found in some employment relationships; nevertheless, the degree of control is substantial. It must be born in mind that the majority of the work is done away from the environment of a factory or printing plant, and, accordingly, to some extent, the degree of control may be lesser than if performed in that structured environment.

¶ 98 It is important to note that the Free Press tells the carriers who the customers are, the manner in which the papers must be delivered, the hours during which the paper must be delivered, the route that is to be taken, and the compensation to be paid. The "tools of the trade" is basically the use of an automobile, which is mandated as a condition precedent to being a carrier, and carriers must have a valid driver's licence. It certainly is not uncommon for employees to be required to use their own automobiles during the course of their employment, and, in our view, that simple fact does not, of itself, determine that the carriers are not employees.

¶ 99 . . . it is clear that the Free Press can unilaterally determine that the carriers are to deliver advertising supplements, coupon books, and other similar items. They are paid for this work but there is no opportunity to refuse to do it.

¶ 100 With respect to the entrepreneurial aspect, i.e. the chance of profit or the risk of loss, we do not consider that particularly significant in this case. Admittedly, if a carrier's car broke down, the carrier would have a loss because of the cost. However, that is not uncommon with anyone who operates a car in the course of his/her employment and who receives an allowance. The only opportunity for an increase in profit is to obtain new customers and/or negotiate a better route allowance. The evidence is clear that, although there can be some negotiation on route allowances, it is only done in a negligible amount of cases, and the prospect of obtaining new customers, when one considers the hours of delivery, is quite remote. Additionally, the range of route allowance compensation is slight. Of considerable significance with respect to the risk of loss is the fact that the Free Press can compel the carriers to continue delivery to non-paying customers, and any loss as a result of that non-payment is absorbed by the Free Press.

¶ 101 It is important to note that carriers are required to attend at designated times, in designated areas, and, if there is any delay in delivery to the carriers, then carriers are required to wait for them, and there is no additional compensation.

¶ 102 The Board has also considered very carefully the fact that carriers can appoint substitutes and that the district manager has very little control over the replacement. However, if a carrier cannot find a substitute, then the district manager, as part of his/her responsibility, must obtain someone to deliver the papers and, accordingly, maintains a roster of individuals for that purpose. The cost of utilizing those replacements is deducted from the carrier's payment. However, the initial appointment as a carrier, the route obtained, the number of newspapers to be delivered, and the route allowance are determined by the Free Press. Although a carrier may, in certain circumstances, have more than one route, routes and the number of the subscribers on a route can be changed in the sole discretion of the Free Press.

¶ 103 Because the carriers have very little realistic opportunity to increase the rate, then they are, in our opinion, economically dependent on the Free Press with respect to the terms and conditions of which they deliver the daily newspaper. . . .

¶ 104 The fact that carriers work only a few hours per day and may work for others is not, in our view, of any particular significance. This is clearly a category of what can be deemed part-time employee. It must be remembered that these individuals work on a seven-day cycle, 365 days per year, except for the limited number of days when the newspaper is not published. There is not any prohibition on carriers delivering other newspapers or doing other work, and the fact that they do not have that restriction is not, in our opinion, of particular significance. There is no fiduciary relationship between the parties, and it is certainly not uncommon for carriers to work more than for one employer and sometimes for employers who are competitors. We have previously noted, with approval, the comments of Vice Chair Parkinson, in the *Semiahmoo* case, supra.

¶ 105 In addition, we have also considered the fact that the Free Press does issue warning letters and reserves the right to terminate an agreement on notice. These are, at the very least, indicators of the normal employment relationship and do not, of themselves, establish that the carriers are independent contractors or non-employees. Perhaps the fact that district managers can impose discipline . . . indicates a criterion which ordinarily applies to employees.

¶ 106 After reviewing all of the above, the Board concluded and ordered that a unit of carriers be certified as follows:

> All newspaper carriers personally employed by the Winnipeg Free Press, in the City of Winnipeg, in the Province of Manitoba, under a written arrangement and who are assigned specific routes, save and except those excluded by the Act.

. . .

* * *

If B hires C to do certain work, and C then hires D and E to do some of that work, can C still be considered an employee of B for the purposes of collective bargaining legislation? According to the British Columbia Labour Relations Board, the answer may be yes. In *Fownes Construction Co.*, [1974] 1 Can. L.R.B.R. 510 at 512, that board said:

What is to be done with owner-operators who own more than one truck and thus employ other drivers to operate them? A person who owns quite a few trucks, whose main concern is renting the trucks with a driver, and who does not regularly drive a truck himself would not come within the scope of the "dependent contractor" provision because he does not "perform work or services" in a manner analogous to an employee. Another person with several trucks may drive one of these trucks regularly, but because of the total character of his business, should not be considered to be "dependent." However, we do not believe that an individual who owns perhaps two trucks, and thus employs a driver to operate one of them, is necessarily removed from the category of "dependent contractor." There is nothing illogical about finding that an individual is, at one and the same time, both an employer and an employee and it can also be true that an individual is both an employer and a dependent contractor. That always turns on a judgment about the facts of the particular case.

The more difficult question is whether an individual, having been found to be a dependent contractor, should appropriately be included in the same bargaining unit as his employee. On the surface, that would seem to produce the kind of conflict of interest which the Code tries to prevent by such provisions as the managerial exclusion from the definition of "employee." However, we are now inclined to the view that this is largely a hypothetical concern in the real world of the construction industry. The opposing problem, which we have already mentioned in the earlier decision, is the owner-operator with two or three trucks becoming a major bone of contention in negotiations between the Teamsters and [the Construction Labour Relations Association] if he must be excluded from the unit. Counsel for Fownes, after arguing that all employers should be excluded, said that "if it is of any comfort, it may be a safe assumption that owner drivers in this category would receive essentially the same treatment as those outside the category." In view of the history of this problem (as reflected in a case such as *Therien v. Teamsters . . .*) we are not so confident in that assumption. For this reason, we are not prepared at this stage to lay down any rule excluding all owner-operators who are also employers from the scope of the bargaining unit. Should there be challenges to the inclusion of any particular individual in the voting constituency . . . , we shall deal with such cases in all of their concrete detail.

Different jurisdictions take different approaches to the appropriate bargaining structure for dependent contractors. Where there is an existing bargaining unit of other employees, the British Columbia *Labour Relations Code*, section 28(1)(b), requires the labour board to "determine whether inclusion of the dependent contractors in the existing unit would be more appropriate for collective bargaining and, if so, require that an application be made to vary the certification." On the other hand, the Ontario *Labour Relations Act*, section 9(5), says:

> A bargaining unit consisting solely of dependent contractors shall be deemed by the Board to be a unit of employees appropriate for collective bargaining but the Board may include dependent contractors in a bargaining unit with other employees if the Board is satisfied that a majority of the dependent contractors wish to be included in the bargaining unit.

The British Columbia provision tends to bring together dependent contractors and other employees in a single bargaining unit, whereas the Ontario provision favours a more fragmented structure. This may help to explain the different approaches to whether a dependent contractor who is also an employer falls within the legislation. Including dependent contractors with other employees for collective bargaining purposes may eliminate any economic advantage to the employer of continuing the dependent contractor arrangement, while separate bargaining units may have the opposite effect. As firms increasingly contract out many of their core functions, this difference in approach becomes more significant.

4:220 Near-Employees

Independent contractor and dependent contractor relationships are by no means the only ones in which services are provided outside the traditional employment relationship. Student nurses, medical residents and interns, articling law students, prison inmates, and participants in training programs and government-funded job creation programs may all supply services in return for some form of remuneration. Do they have access to collective bargaining? The answer appears to depend on how closely the particular relationship resembles traditional employment. In one case, student nurses assigned to a hospital for training were found not to be employees of the hospital. In another case, inmates working for a commercial abattoir on the premises of a correctional centre were considered to be employees of the abattoir.

How about individuals who perform services under "workfare" programs (called "community participation activities" in Ontario) as a condition of receiving welfare benefits? Ontario has specific legislative provisions which state that the *Labour Relations Act, 1995* "does not apply with respect to participation in a community participation activity," and which go on to prohibit anyone engaged in such an activity from being covered by collective bargaining pursuant to the *Labour Relations Act* and even from joining a trade union within the meaning of that Act. Those provisions were originally enacted by the provocatively named *Prevention of Unionization Act (Ontario Works), 1998*, S.O. 1998, c. 17, and are found in the *Ontario Works Act, 1997*, S.O. 1997, c. 25, Schedule A, section 73.1. The International Labour Organization Committee on Freedom of Association has urged the Ontario government to amend them, but to no avail: 330th Report of Committee on Freedom of Assocation, ILO GB.286/11 (Part 1), March 2003, paragraphs 35–37. After you have read the *Dunmore* case, excerpted in the next section of this chapter, consider whether those provisions might be held to violate freedom of association under section 2(d) of the *Canadian Charter of Rights and Freedoms.*

4:300 EXCLUDED EMPLOYEES

As was noted earlier in this chapter, not every type of employee is given access to collective bargaining under general labour relations legislation. The statutory exclusions vary considerably from jurisdiction to jurisdiction. For example, the Ontario *Labour Relations Act, 1995* has a relatively long list of wholly or partially excluded groups: civil servants, firefighters, police officers, domestics, agricultural workers, and members of certain professions. Each of those groups is covered by general collective bargaining statutes in one or more of the other jurisdictions across the country: see Bernard Adell, Michel Grant, and Allen Ponak, *Strikes and Lockouts in Essential Services* (Kingston: Queen's IR Press), 2001, chapter 2.

These divergences call attention to the politics of inclusion, and raise the question whether there are rational grounds for drawing the line at any particular point. They again raise the question whether denial of the right to bargain collectively constitutes interference with freedom of association under the *Canadian Charter of Rights and Freedoms*, and if so, whether such interference can reasonably be justified under section 1 of the *Charter*.

These issues were first addressed by the Supreme Court of Canada in *Delisle v. Canada*, [1999] 2 S.C.R. 989. At issue was whether the complete statutory exclusion of members of the Royal-Canadian Mounted Police (RCMP) from the federal *Public Service Staff Relations Act* was inconsistent with the *Charter* guarantees of freedom of association (section 2(d)) and equal treatment under the law (section 15). The majority judgment held that section 2(d) did not impose upon Parliament a positive obligation of protection or inclusion. In the words of Bastarache J.:

The ability to form an independent association and to carry on the protected activities described below, the only items protected by the statute, exists independently of any statutory regime. Freedom of association does not include the right to establish a particular type of association defined in a particular statute; this kind of recognition would unduly limit the ability of Parliament or a provincial legislature to regulate labour relations in the public service and would subject employers, without their consent, to greater obligations toward the association than towards their employees individually. . . .

A dissenting minority of the Court considered that, on the evidence, the purpose of the complete exclusion of RCMP members from the coverage of the labour relations statute was not merely to withhold collective bargaining rights but to allow management interference in the formation or operation of their labour association. In the dissenters' view, the exclusion was accordingly a breach of freedom of association, in contravention of section 2(d) of the *Charter*. The dissenters went on to hold that securing a stable and reliable police force was a legitimate objective for the federal government to pursue, but that there were a range of less restrictive approaches to police collective bargaining that would allow this objective to be met — approaches that had been taken in various other Canadian jurisdictions. Thus, the dissenters concluded, a complete exclusion from the coverage of the statute was not a reasonable limitation within the meaning of section 1 of the *Charter*.

An alternative argument in *Delisle*, based on the *Charter* guarantee of equality, was also unsuccessful. Section 15(1) of the *Charter* provides that everyone is "equal before and under the law and has the right to the equal protection and equal benefit of the law without discrimination" on the basis of certain enumerated grounds, which do not include one's occupation. The Supreme Court of Canada has extended the protection of section 15(1) to grounds of discrimination which are "analogous" to the enumerated grounds. It has refused to treat occupation as an analogous ground, on the basis that individuals have both the theoretical and practical right to move from one occupation to another.

The RCMP members who were excluded from the protection of the *Public Service Staff Relations Act* could not be described as a particularly disadvantaged group of workers. The holding in *Delisle* with respect to the effect of section 2(d) of the Charter on occupational exclusions from the coverage of labour relations legislation has to be looked at in that light, and in light of the Supreme Court of Canada's subsequent decision in the *Dunmore* case.

Dunmore v. Ontario (Attorney General), [2001] 3 S.C.R. 1016

BASTARACHE J. (McLachlin C.J., Gonthier, Iacobucci, Bastarache, Binnie, Arbour, and LeBel JJ. concurring):

¶ 1 This appeal concerns the exclusion of agricultural workers from Ontario's statutory labour relations regime. The appellants, individual farm workers and union organizers, challenge the exclusion as a violation of their freedom of association and equality rights under the Canadian Charter of Rights and Freedoms. In particular, they argue that the

Labour Relations and Employment Statute Law Amendment Act, 1995, S.O. 1995, c. 1 ("LRESLAA"), combined with s. 3(b) of the Ontario Labour Relations Act, 1995, S.O. 1995, c. 1, Sched. A ("LRA"), prevents them from establishing, joining and participating in the lawful activities of a trade union. In addition, they claim that the LRESLAA and the LRA violate their equality rights under s. 15(1) of the Charter by denying them a statutory protection enjoyed by most occupational groups in Ontario.

. . .

¶ 3 Although agricultural workers have been excluded from Ontario's labour relations regime since 1943, the impetus for this appeal was the passage of the LRESLAA. The LRESLAA was enacted pursuant to an initiative of Ontario's Progressive Conservative government in 1995; it repealed the only statute ever to extend trade union and collective bargaining rights to Ontario's agricultural workers. That short-lived statute, the Agricultural Labour Relations Act, 1994, S.O. 1994, c. 6 ("ALRA"), was enacted pursuant to an initiative of the New Democratic Party government in 1994 following the recommendations in the Report of the Task Force on Agricultural Labour Relations: Report to the Minister of Labour (June 1992). The ALRA lasted from June 23, 1994 to November 10, 1995, during which time the United Food and Commercial Workers Union ("UFCW") was certified as the bargaining agent for approximately 200 workers at the Highline Produce Limited mushroom factory in Leamington, Ontario. The UFCW also filed two other certification applications during the period of the ALRA. . . . These certification activities came to an end when, with the passage of the LRESLAA in 1995, the ALRA was repealed in its entirety. . . .

¶ 4 The most recent embodiment of Ontario's labour relations policy, the LRA, excludes agricultural workers in the following terms:

3. This Act does not apply,

. . .

(b) to a person employed in agriculture, hunting or trapping;

The net effect of the LRESLAA was to re-subject agricultural workers to this exclusion clause. Thus, in addition to challenging the constitutionality of the LRESLAA, the appellants challenge the constitutionality of s. 3(b) of the LRA. . . .

VI. ANALYSIS

A. Freedom of Association

(1) Nature of the Claim

¶ 12 . . . [T]he appellants direct their attack not at legislation restricting collective bargaining per se, but at legislation restricting the "wider ambit of union purposes and activities."

¶ 13 In order to establish a violation of s. 2(d), the appellants must demonstrate, first, that such activities fall within the range of activities protected by s. 2(d) of the Charter, and second, that the impugned legislation has, either in purpose or effect, interfered with these activities. . . .

(2) Scope of Section 2(d)

(a) General Framework

¶ 14 The scope of s. 2(d) was first decided by this Court in a landmark trilogy of labour cases, all of which concerned the right to strike (see *Reference re Public Service Employee Relations Act (Alta.)* . . . ("Alberta Reference"); *PSAC v. Canada* . . . ; *RWDSU v. Saskatchewan.* . . . In the Alberta Reference, McIntyre J. (writing for himself) stressed the double-edged nature of freedom of association, holding that "while [freedom of association] advances many group interests and, of course, cannot be exercised alone, it is nonetheless a freedom belonging to the individual and not to the group formed through its exercise". . . . On the basis of this principle, McIntyre J. confined s. 2(d) to three elements. . . . These three elements of freedom of association are summarized, along with a crucial fourth principle, in the oft-quoted words of Sopinka J. in Professional Institute of the Public Service of Canada v. Northwest Territories (Commissioner), . . . :

> Upon considering the various judgments in the Alberta Reference, I have come to the view that four separate propositions concerning the coverage of the s. 2(d) guarantee of freedom of association emerge from the case: first, that s. 2(d) protects the freedom to establish, belong to and maintain an association; second, that s. 2(d) does not protect an activity solely on the ground that the activity is a foundational or essential purpose of an association; third, that s. 2(d) protects the exercise in association of the constitutional rights and freedoms of individuals; and fourth, that s. 2(d) protects the exercise in association of the lawful rights of individuals. [Emphasis added.]

The third and fourth of these principles have received considerably less judicial support than the others, having only been explicitly affirmed by three of six judges in the Alberta Reference and two of seven judges in PIPSC. . . . Most recently, in Delisle, supra, this Court did not have to rule on the validity of the existing framework because all of the activities involved fell within it. In that case, this Court clarified that s. 2(d) does not guarantee access to a particular labour relations regime where the claimants are able to exercise their s. 2(d) rights independently. . . .

¶ 16 . . . [T]he purpose of s. 2(d) commands a single inquiry: has the state precluded activity because of its associational nature, thereby discouraging the collective pursuit of common goals? In my view, while the four-part test for freedom of association sheds light on this concept, it does not capture the full range of activities protected by s. 2(d). In particular, there will be occasions where a given activity does not fall within the third and fourth rules set forth by Sopinka J. in PIPSC, supra, but where the state has nevertheless prohibited that activity solely because of its associational nature. These occasions will involve activities which (1) are not protected under any other constitutional freedom, and (2) cannot, for one reason or another, be understood as the lawful activities of individuals. As discussed by Dickson C.J. in the Alberta Reference, supra, such activities may be collective in nature, in that they cannot be performed by individuals acting alone. . . . To limit s. 2(d) to activities that are performable by individuals would, in my view, render futile these fundamental initiatives. At best, it would encourage s. 2(d) claimants to contrive individual analogs for inherently associational activities, a process which this Court clearly resisted in the labour trilogy, in Egg Marketing, supra, and in its jurisprudence on union security clauses and the right not to associate (see Syndicat catholique des employés de magasins de Québec Inc. v. Compagnie Paquet Ltée. . . . ("[t]he union is . . . the representative of all the employees in the unit for the purpose of negotiating the labour agreement," hence "[t]here is no room left for private negotiation between employer and employee". . . .); McGavin Toastmaster Ltd. v. Ainscough . . . ("[t]he reality is, and has been for many years now throughout Canada, that individual relationships as between employer and employee have meaning only at the hiring stage". . . . The collective dimension of s. 2(d) is also consistent with developments in international human rights law, as indicated by the jurisprudence of the Committee of Experts on the Application of Conventions and Recommendations and the ILO Committee on Freedom of Association. . . . Not only does this jurisprudence illustrate the range of activities that may be exercised by a collectivity of employees, but the International Labour Organization has repeatedly interpreted the right to organize as a collective right. . . .

¶ 17 As I see it, the very notion of "association" recognizes the qualitative differences between individuals and collectivities. It recognizes that the press differs qualitatively from the journalist, the language community from the language speaker, the union from the worker. . . . [T]he law must recognize that certain union activities — making collective representations to an employer, adopting a majority political platform, federating with other unions — may be central to freedom of association even though they are inconceivable on the individual level. This is not to say that all such activities are protected by s. 2(d), nor that all collectivities are worthy of constitutional protection; indeed, this Court has repeatedly excluded the right to strike and collectively bargain from the protected ambit of s. 2(d). . . . It is to say, simply, that certain collective activities must be recognized if the freedom to form and maintain an association is to have any meaning. . . .

(b) State Responsibility Under Section 2(d). . . .

¶ 20 . . . [H]istory has shown, and Canada's legislatures have uniformly recognized, that a posture of government restraint in the area of labour relations will expose most workers not only to a range of unfair labour practices, but potentially to legal liability under common law inhibitions on combinations and restraints of trade. Knowing this would foreclose the effective exercise of the freedom to organize, Ontario has provided a statutory freedom to organize in its LRA (s. 5), as well as protections against denial of access to property (s. 13), employer interference with trade union activity (s. 70), discrimination against trade unionists (s. 72), intimidation and coercion (s. 76), alteration of working conditions during the certification process (s. 86), coercion of witnesses (s. 87), and removal of Board notices (s. 88). In this context, it must be asked whether, in order to make the freedom to organize meaningful, s. 2(d) of the Charter imposes a positive obligation on the state to extend protective legislation to unprotected groups. More broadly, it may be asked whether the distinction between positive and negative state obligations ought to be nuanced in the context of labour relations, in the sense that excluding agricultural workers from a protective regime substantially contributes to the violation of protected freedoms.

¶ 21 This precise question was raised in Delisle, supra, in which the appellant failed to establish that exclusion from a protective regime violated s. 2(d). . . . [T]he Delisle majority . . . focused instead on the fact that an interference with associational activity had not been made out on the facts of the case. Indeed, in making this finding, I deferred judgment on the appellant's argument that underinclusion could have "an important chill on freedom of association because it clearly indicates to its members that unlike all other employees, they cannot unionize, and what is more, that they must not get together to defend their interests with respect to labour relations". . . . In addition, I left open the possibility that s. 2 of the Charter may impose "a positive obligation of protection or inclusion on Parliament or the government . . . in exceptional circumstances which are not at issue in the instant case." . . .

¶ 22 . . . [I]t seems to me that apart from any consideration of a claimant's dignity interest, exclusion from a protective regime may in some contexts amount to an affirmative interference with the effective exercise of a protected freedom. In such a case, it is not so much the differential treatment that is at issue, but the fact that the government is creating conditions which in effect substantially interfere with the exercise of a constitutional right; it has been held in the s. 2(a) context, for example, that "protection of one religion and the concomitant non-protection of others imports disparate impact destructive of the religious freedom of the collectivity" (see Big M Drug Mart . . .). This does not mean that there is a constitutional right to protective legislation per se; it means legislation that is underinclusive may, in unique contexts, substantially impact the exercise of a constitutional freedom.

¶ 23 This brings me to the central question of this appeal: can excluding agricultural workers from a statutory labour relations regime, without expressly or intentionally prohibiting association, constitute a substantial interference with freedom of association? . . .

¶ 24 . . . [C]laims of underinclusion should be grounded in fundamental Charter freedoms rather than in access to a particular statutory regime. . . . In my view, the appellants in this case do not claim a constitutional right to general inclusion in the LRA, but simply a constitutional freedom to organize a trade association. This freedom to organize exists independently of any statutory enactment, even though the so-called "modern rights to bargain collectively and to strike" have been characterized otherwise in the Alberta Reference, supra, per Le Dain J. . . . . While it may be that the effective exercise of this freedom requires legislative protection in some cases, this ought not change the fundamentally non-statutory character of the freedom itself. . . .

¶ 25 Second, the underinclusion cases demonstrate that a proper evidentiary foundation must be provided before creating a positive obligation under the Charter. . . . [I]t was concluded in Delisle that "it is difficult to argue that the exclusion of RCMP members from the statutory regime of the PSSRA prevents the establishment of an independent employee association because RCMP members have in fact formed such an association in several provinces. . . . In my view, the evidentiary burden in these cases is to demonstrate that exclusion from a statutory regime permits a substantial interference with the exercise of protected s. 2(d) activity. . . .

¶ 26 Assuming an evidentiary foundation can be provided, a third concern is whether the state can truly be held accountable for any inability to exercise a fundamental freedom. . . . [I]t should be noted that this Court's understanding of "state action" has matured since the Dolphin Delivery case and may mature further in light of evolving Charter values. . . . Moreover, this Court has repeatedly held in the s. 15(1) context that the Charter may oblige the state to extend underinclusive statutes to the extent underinclusion licenses private actors to violate basic rights and freedoms. . . . Finally, there has been some suggestion that the Charter should apply to legislation which "permits" private actors to interfere with protected s. 2 activity, as in some contexts mere permission may function to encourage or support the act which is called into question. . . . If we apply these general principles to s. 2(d), it is not a quantum leap to suggest that a failure to include someone in a protective regime may affirmatively permit restraints on the activity the regime is designed to protect. The rationale behind this is that underinclusive state action falls into suspicion not simply to the extent it discriminates against an unprotected class, but to the extent it substantially orchestrates, encourages or sustains the violation of fundamental freedoms.

¶ 27 The notion that underinclusion can infringe freedom of association is not only implied by Canadian Charter jurisprudence, but is also consistent with international human rights law. Article 2 of Convention (No. 87) concerning Freedom of Association and Protection of the Right to Organize, 67 U.N.T.S. 17, provides that "[w]orkers and employers, without distinction whatsoever, shall have the right to establish and . . . to join organisations of their own choosing," and that only members of the armed forces and the police may be excluded (Article 9). In addition, Article 10 of Convention No. 87 defines an "organisation" as "any organisation of workers or of employers for furthering and defending the interests of workers or of employers." Canada ratified Convention No. 87 in 1972. The Convention's broadly worded provisions confirm precisely what I have discussed above, which is that discriminatory treatment implicates not only an excluded group's dignity interest, but also its basic freedom of association. This is further confirmed by the fact that Article 2 operates not only on the basis of sex, race, nationality and other traditional grounds of discrimination, but on the basis of any distinction, including occupational status. . . . Nowhere is this clearer than in Article 1 of Convention (No. 11) concerning the Rights of Association and Combination of Agricultural Workers, 38 U.N.T.S. 153, which obliges ratifying member states to secure to "all those engaged in agriculture" the same rights of association as to industrial workers; the convention makes no distinction as to the type of agricultural work performed. Although provincial jurisdiction has prevented Canada from ratifying Convention No. 11, together these conventions provide a normative foundation for prohibiting any form of discrimination in the protection of trade union freedoms. . . .

¶ 28 In sum, while it is generally desirable to confine claims of underinclusion to s. 15(1), it will not be appropriate to do so where the underinclusion results in the effective denial of a fundamental freedom such as the right of association itself. . . . [T]he burden imposed by s. 2(d) of the Charter differs from that imposed by s. 15(1): while the latter focuses on the effects of underinclusion on human dignity (*Law v. Canada (Minister of Employment and Immigration)) . . .*, the former focuses on the effects of underinclusion on the ability to exercise a fundamental freedom. . . .

(c) Summary of Discussion on Section 2(d)

¶ 30 In my view, the activities for which the appellants seek protection fall squarely within the freedom to organize, that is, the freedom to collectively embody the interests of individual workers. Insofar as the appellants seek to establish and maintain an association of employees, there can be no question that their claim falls within the protected ambit of s. 2(d) of the Charter. Moreover, the effective exercise of these freedoms may require not only the exercise in association of the constitutional rights and freedoms (such as freedom of assembly) and lawful rights of individuals, but the exercise of certain collective activities, such as making majority representations to one's employer. These activities are guaranteed by the purpose of s. 2(d), which is to promote the realization of individual potential through relations with others, and by international labour jurisprudence, which recognizes the inevitably collective nature of the freedom to organize. Finally, while inclusion in legislation designed to protect such freedoms will normally be the province of s. 15(1) of the Charter, claims for inclusion may, in rare cases, be cognizable under the fundamental freedoms. With this in mind, I turn to whether s. 3(b) of the LRA interferes with the appellants' protected freedoms, either in purpose or effect.

(3) Application to the Ontario Legislation

(a) Purpose of the Exclusion

¶ 31 The appellants claim that their exclusion from the LRA was intended to infringe their freedom to organize and, as such, violates the Charter notwithstanding its actual effects. . . . A similar allegation of colourable purpose was assessed in the recent case of Delisle, supra. In that case, s. 2 of the Public Service Staff Relations Act, R.S.C. 1985, c. P-35, was held not to interfere with the unionization of RCMP officers, as the purpose of the provision was simply to withhold from RCMP officers any status or protection created by the Act itself. . . . In the case at bar, a similar analysis yields an ambiguous result. At first blush, it would seem that the purpose of the LRA and the LRESLAA is to withhold from agricultural workers any status or protection created by the former Act, and not to target non-statutory unionization. On the other hand, the appellants point out several comments made by Ontario government officials to the effect that the purpose of the LRESLAA was to prevent "unionization." Upon introducing the LRESLAA to the Ontario Legislature in 1995, for example, the Ontario Minister of Labour stated that "unionization of the family farm has no place in Ontario's key agricultural sector". . . . These troubling comments were made to members of the provincial legislature before they voted on the LRESLAA and, as such, may have reflected the legislature's intention in enacting that statute.

¶ 32 . . . On the other hand, the fact that the LRESLAA pursues a collateral legislative objective, namely the protection of the family farm, makes it difficult to conclude without speculation that this protection was sought through the prevention of unionization per se. While my colleague L'Heureux-Dubé J. marshals compelling evidence to make this point, I remain struck by the fact that s. 3(b) of the LRA does not, on its face, prohibit agricultural workers from forming workers' associations, while it does bar them from all statutory labour relations schemes.

¶ 33 The difficulties of assessing legislative intent cannot be overemphasized. . . . On the facts of this case, . . . I think it is more appropriate to focus on the effects of the impugned provisions, noting that some of the concerns raised by the above comments will inform the s. 1 analysis.

(b) Effects of the Exclusion . . .

¶ 35 The history of labour relations in Canada illustrates the profound connection between legislative protection and the freedom to organize. To illustrate this point, I find it necessary to make three observations about the appellants' exclusion from the LRA. . . .

(i) The LRA is Designed to Safeguard the Exercise of the Fundamental Freedom to Associate
   . . .

¶ 37 The freedom to organize lies at the core of the Charter's protection of freedom of association. . . . As recently as Delisle, supra, L'Heureux-Dubé J. noted that

> "the right to freedom of association must take into account the nature and importance
> of labour associations as institutions that work for the betterment of working conditions
> and the protection of the dignity and collective interests of workers in a fundamental
> aspect of their lives: employment". . . .

Moreover, the importance of trade union freedoms is widely recognized in international covenants, as is the freedom to work generally. In my view, judicial recognition of these freedoms strengthens the case for their positive protection. It suggests that trade union freedoms lie at the core of the Charter, and in turn that legislation instantiating those freedoms ought not be selectively withheld where it is most needed.

¶ 38 By protecting the freedom to organize, s. 2(d) of the Charter recognizes the dynamic and evolving role of the trade union in Canadian society. In addition to permitting the collective expression of employee interests, trade unions contribute to political debate. At the level of national policy, unions advocate on behalf of disadvantaged groups and present views on fair industrial policy. These functions, when viewed globally, affect all levels of society and constitute "an important subsystem in a democratic market-economy system" (see K. Sugeno, "Unions as social institutions in democratic market economies" . . .). For these reasons, the notion that minimum legislative protection cannot be extended to agricultural workers without extending full collective bargaining rights is misguided. Equally misguided is the notion that inherent difficulties in the formation of trade unions, or the fact that unions are in some cases experiencing a decline in membership, diminishes their social and political significance. On the contrary, unions remain core voluntary associations based on the principle of freedom of association.

(ii) Without the Protection of the LRA, Agricultural Workers Are Substantially Incapable of
   Exercising the Freedom to Associate . . .

¶ 41 . . . Not only have agricultural workers proved unable to form employee associations in provinces which deny them protection but, unlike the RCMP officers in Delisle, they

231

argue that their relative status and lack of statutory protection all but guarantee this result. Distinguishing features of agricultural workers are their political impotence, their lack of resources to associate without state protection and their vulnerability to reprisal by their employers. . . . Moreover, unlike RCMP officers, agricultural workers are not employed by the government and therefore cannot access the Charter directly to suppress an unfair labour practice. . . .

¶ 42 . . . [I]t is only the right to associate that is at issue here, not the right to collective bargaining. Nevertheless, to suggest that s. 2(d) of the Charter is respected where an association is reduced to claiming a right to unionize would, in my view, make a mockery of freedom of association. The record shows that, but for the brief period covered by the ALRA, there has never been an agricultural workers' union in Ontario. Agricultural workers have suffered repeated attacks on their efforts to unionize. Conversely, in those provinces where labour relations rights have been extended to agricultural workers, union density is higher than in Ontario. . . . The respondents do not contest this evidence, nor do they deny that legislative protection is absolutely crucial if agricultural workers wish to unionize. . . . For these reasons, I readily conclude that the evidentiary burden has been met in this case: the appellants have brought this litigation because there is no possibility for association as such without minimum statutory protection.

(iii) The Exclusion of Agricultural Workers from the LRA Substantially Reinforces the Inherent Difficulty in Exercising the Freedom to Associate

¶ 43 Their freedom to organize having been substantially impeded by exclusion from protective legislation, it is still incumbent on the appellants to link this impediment to state, not just private action (see Dolphin Delivery . . .).

¶ 45 The most palpable effect of the LRESLAA and the LRA is, in my view, to place a chilling effect on non-statutory union activity. By extending statutory protection to just about every class of worker in Ontario, the legislature has essentially discredited the organizing efforts of agricultural workers. . . . [T]he effect of s. 3(b) of the LRA is not simply to perpetuate an existing inability to organize, but to exert the precise chilling effect I declined to recognize in Delisle.

¶ 46 Conversely, the didactic effects of labour relations legislation on employers must not be underestimated. It is widely accepted that labour relations laws function not only to provide a forum for airing specific grievances, but for fostering dialogue in an otherwise adversarial workplace. . . . [T]he wholesale exclusion of agricultural workers from a labour relations regime can only be viewed as a stimulus to interfere with organizing activity. The exclusion suggests that workplace democracy has no place in the agricultural sector and, moreover, that agricultural workers' efforts to associate are illegitimate. As surely as LRA protection would foster the "rule of law" in a unionized workplace, exclusion from that protection privileges the will of management over that of the worker. Again, a contrast to Delisle, supra, is apposite: a government employer is less likely than a private employer to take exclusion from protective legislation as a green light to commit unfair labour practices, as its employees have direct recourse to the Charter. . . .

¶ 48 In sum, I believe it is reasonable to conclude that the exclusion of agricultural work-ers from the LRA substantially interferes with their fundamental freedom to organize. The inherent difficulties of organizing farm workers, combined with the threats of eco-nomic reprisal from employers, form only part of the reason why association is all but impossible in the agricultural sector in Ontario. Equally important is the message sent by s. 3(b) of the LRA, which delegitimizes associational activity and thereby ensures its ulti-mate failure. Given these known and foreseeable effects of s. 3(b), I conclude that the pro-vision infringes the freedom to organize and thus violates s. 2(d) of the Charter.

B. Section 1

¶ 49 Having established a violation of s. 2(d) of the Charter, the question arises as to whether exclusion from the LRA constitutes a reasonable limit on agricultural workers' freedom to organize. In this regard, s. 1 of the Charter obliges the respondents, as the par-ties seeking to uphold the limitation, to establish both that the objective underlying the limitation is of sufficient importance to warrant overriding a constitutionally protected right or freedom, and that the means chosen to reach this objective are proportionate. . . .

(1) Sufficiently Important Objective

¶ 52 Judging from the parties' evidence, I am satisfied both that many farms in Ontario are family-owned and -operated, and that the protection of the family farm is a pressing enough objective to warrant the infringement of s. 2(d) of the Charter. The fact that Ontario is moving increasingly towards corporate farming and agribusiness does not, in my view, diminish the importance of protecting the unique characteristics of the family farm; on the contrary, it may even augment it. . . .

¶ 53 With respect to the economic rationale, I disagree with the appellants that "[t]he Gov-ernment has provided no evidence that the Ontario agricultural sector is in a fragile com-petitive position or that it is likely to be substantially affected by small changes in the cost and operating structure of Ontario farming." The Attorney General notes that agriculture occupies a volatile and highly competitive part of the private sector economy, that it expe-riences disproportionately thin profit margins and that its seasonal character makes it par-ticularly vulnerable to strikes and lockouts. Moreover, these characteristics were readily accepted by the Task Force leading to the adoption of the ALRA, which recommended a system of compulsory arbitration in order to guard against the economic consequences of strikes and lockouts. . . .

(2) Proportionality
(a) Rational Connection

¶ 54 At this stage, the question is whether a wholesale exclusion of agricultural workers from the LRA is carefully tailored to meet its stated objectives. . . . In my view, the Attor-ney General has demonstrated that unionization involving the right to collective bargain-ing and to strike can, in certain circumstances, function to antagonize the family farm dynamic. The reality of unionization is that it leads to formalized labour-management relationships and gives rise to a relatively formal process of negotiation and dispute resolution; indeed, this may well be its principal advantage over a system of informal industrial relations. In this context, it is reasonable to speculate that unionization will threaten the flexibility and co-operation that are characteristic of the family farm and distance parties who are otherwise, to use the respondent's words, "interwoven into the fabric of private life" on the farm. That said, I hasten to add that this concern ought only be as great as the extent of the family farm structure in Ontario and that it does not necessarily apply to the right to form an agricultural association. In cases where the employment relationship is formalized to begin with, preserving "flexibility and co-operation" in the name of the family farm is not only irrational, it is highly coercive. . . .

¶ 55 Even less convincing than Ontario's family farm policy, in my view, is a policy of denying the right of association to agricultural workers on economic grounds. While this may be a rational policy in isolation, it is nothing short of arbitrary where collective bargaining rights have been extended to almost every other class of worker in Ontario. The reality, as acknowledged by all parties to this appeal, is that many industries experience thin profit margins and unstable production cycles. . . . As Professor Beatty has written, "[i]f indeed collective bargaining increases the costs of labour to the overall detriment of society, then our legislators should repeal the legislation in its entirety rather than selectively exclude those most in need of its protection". . . .

(b) Minimum Impairment

¶ 56 The next issue is whether recognizing the unique characteristics of Ontario agriculture and its resulting incompatibility with the formation of agricultural associations as a reasonable minimum justifies the complete exclusion of agricultural workers from the LRA. The LRA excludes all persons "employed in agriculture, hunting or trapping" from its application, defining agriculture as "farming in all its branches, including dairying, beekeeping, aquaculture, the raising of livestock including non-traditional livestock, furbearing animals and poultry, the production, cultivation, growing and harvesting of agricultural commodities, including eggs, maple products, mushrooms and tobacco, and any practices performed as an integral part of an agricultural operation" (see LRA, s. 1(1)). This provision has been broadly interpreted by Ontario's Labour Relations Board, albeit with some reluctance and interpretive difficulty. In Wellington Mushroom Farm . . . , for example, a majority of the board denied LRA certification to the employees of a mushroom factory, even though the actual growing of the mushrooms took place within a single-storey concrete block building. The majority of the board recognized that the employer's operation did "not differ in any material respect from a typical manufacturing plant," but it concluded that the growing of mushrooms constituted an agricultural activity in the ordinary sense of the term. . . .

¶ 59 . . . The Attorney General makes three arguments in defence of its policy: first, that unionization is not appropriate for the "vast majority" of Ontario agricultural operations; second, that no appropriate dispute resolution mechanism exists for agricultural workers; and third, that extending collective bargaining rights to certain sectors of agriculture would be "arbitrary and impracticable." It is also submitted that legislatures are entitled to a margin of deference when balancing complex matters of economic policy. In my view, these arguments all fail on a single point: they do not justify the categorical exclusion of agricultural workers where no satisfactory effort has been made to protect their basic right to form associations.

¶ 60 This effort need not produce the result most desirable to this Court; however, the legislature must "attempt very seriously to alleviate the effects" of its laws on those whose fundamental freedoms are infringed. . . . [N]either enactment in this case includes a concrete attempt to alleviate the infringing effects on agricultural workers. Not only does the legislation fail to distinguish between different types of agriculture, but there is no evidence that the Ontario Legislature even turned its mind to freedom of association when enacting either statute. Rather, each enactment merely cloned a piece of existing legislation — be it the Wagner Act or the LRA — and, in so doing, relied on studies that had been commissioned by a previous legislature.

¶ 61 In my view, there are at least two ways in which the LRESLAA might impair Charter rights more than is reasonably necessary to achieve its objectives: first, by denying the right of association to every sector of agriculture, and second, by denying every aspect of the right, specially whatever protection is necessary to form and maintain employee associations, to agricultural workers. . . .

¶ 64 . . . [T]he fact that some legislation includes exceptions for smaller or family-run farms, most notably labour codes in New Brunswick and Quebec, as well as the ALRA itself, suggests that such an exercise is eminently possible, should the legislature choose to undertake it. . . .

¶ 65 More importantly, the Attorney General offers no justification for excluding agricultural workers from all aspects of unionization, specially those protections that are necessary for the effective formation and maintenance of employee associations. It might be inferred that in order to protect the family farm and ensure the productivity of the farm economy, the legislature felt it necessary to discourage any form of union and to suffer that agricultural workers be exposed to a raft of unfair labour practices. Yet no policy could, in my view, be more repugnant to the principle of least intrusive means. If what is truly sought by s. 3(b) of the LRA is the protection of the family farm, the legislature should at the very least protect agricultural workers from the legal and economic consequences of forming an association. . . .

C. Remedy

¶ 66 To the extent they substantially impede the effective exercise of the freedom of association, both the LRESLAA and s. 3(b) of the LRA must be declared contrary to the Charter. Given the nature of these enactments, however, determining the appropriate remedy is not without difficulty. First, the respondents point out that the precise effect of striking down the LRESLAA would be to re-enact the statute it repealed, namely, the ALRA. As this Court is not in a position to enact such detailed legislation, nor to confer constitutional status on a particular statutory regime, I prefer to strike down the LRESLAA to the extent that it gives effect to the exclusion clause of the LRA. The precise effect of this remedy is to strike down that exclusion clause, which is the alternate remedy sought by the appellants. This remedy presents its own problems, as it obliges the legislature to extend the full panoply of collective bargaining rights in the LRA to agricultural workers. As such action is not necessarily mandated by the principles of this case, I would suspend the declarations of invalidity for 18 months, allowing amending legislation to be passed if the legislature sees fit to do so. . . .

¶ 67 . . . [T]he Charter only obliges the legislature to provide a statutory framework that is consistent with the principles established in this case. . . . In my view, these principles require at a minimum a regime that provides agricultural workers with the protection necessary for them to exercise their constitutional freedom to form and maintain associations. . . .

¶ 68 In choosing the above remedy, I neither require nor forbid the inclusion of agricultural workers in a full collective bargaining regime, whether it be the LRA or a special regime applicable only to agricultural workers such as the ALRA. For example, the question of whether agricultural workers have the right to strike is one better left to the legislature. . . .

4:310 Professionals

Some Canadian jurisdictions still exclude certain groups of professional employees, such as physicians, lawyers, dentists, and architects, from the scope of collective bargaining legislation. These exclusions are now the exceptions to a general trend that has seen professional employees enthusiastically embrace collective bargaining. Nurses, engineers, teachers, and university professors have led this trend, and have had considerable success in advancing their economic and professional interests through collective action. This success raises the question whether collective bargaining is becoming the preserve of employees who already enjoy a privileged economic position, and whether it increases rather than decreases the income gap between the primary and secondary labour markets, to the further disadvantage of employees at the bottom of the economic ladder.

4:320 Public Employees

Collective bargaining in Canada has its roots in the private sector, and did not spread throughout the public sector until legislative amendments encouraged it to do so from the late 1960s on. Until that time, collective bargaining legislation usually covered employees in the broader public sector, such as hospital and municipal workers, but not those employed directly by government. In many Canadian jurisdictions, civil servants were implicitly excluded from collective bargaining through the application of the canon of statutory interpretation which says that the Crown will be bound by a statute only if the statute so provides by explicit language.

Today, the rate of unionization in the public sector in Canada far exceeds that in the private sector. In a few provinces — Saskatchewan is the paradigmatic case — civil servants are covered by the same collective bargaining legislation as private sector employees. More often, they are covered by special collective bargaining statutes, which may put more restrictions on the subject matter of collective bargaining and on the right to strike. Employees in the broader public sector may be covered by general collective bargaining legislation, but are sometimes placed under special regimes, such as Ontario's *Hospital Labour Disputes Arbitration Act*. For a review of the collective regimes for public sector employees, see Bernard Adell, Michel Grant, and Allen Ponak, *Strikes and Lockouts in Essential Services* (Kingston: Queen's IR Press), 2001, chapter 2.

4:330 Managerial Employees

North American labour relations policy assumes an adversarial relationship between management and union, or at least an arm's length relationship, with a view to avoiding conflicts of interest. Trade unions seek to exclude management personnel from interfering in their internal affairs, and employers seek assurance that the people responsible for creating and executing management policies will not be deflected from their duty to the employer by loyalty to "the other side."

Accordingly, labour relations statutes have traditionally tried to draw a clear line between those who are "employees" and those who exercise "managerial functions": see, for example, the Ontario *Labour Relations Act*, 1995, section 1(3)(b). "Employees" may bargain collectively under the statute, but managers may not. However, this dichotomy is easier to state than it is to apply. The line between manager and employee is not always clear, and it may vary with the approach taken by the particular labour board. Consider the following examples.

Children's Aid Society of Ottawa-Carleton [2001] O.L.R.D. No. 1234 (Ontario Labour Relations Board)

PAMELA A. CHAPMAN, Vice-Chair

[¶1] This is an application for certification. The bargaining unit which is applied for constitutes a group of persons who are employed in various positions with the responding party ("the CAS") but who can all be described generally as "supervisors." The employer has challenged all 43 names on the voters' list at the time the representation vote was ordered, on the basis that all proposed members of the bargaining unit are not employees within the meaning of section 1(3)(b) of the Ontario *Labour Relations Act*, 1995 ("the Act"). A representation vote was taken on May 4, 2000, but the ballot box was sealed pending determination of whether or not there are any employees in the bargaining unit.

[¶ 2] The employees who are supervised by the persons sought to be represented by CUPE in the present application are members of a bargaining unit represented by OPSEU. Those employees generally occupy the positions of Social Worker or Counsellor or are support staff. Throughout the history of that collective bargaining relationship front-line supervisors have been excluded from the OPSEU bargaining unit by way of the following specific exclusion: "Assistant Supervisors . . . (and) persons above the rank of Assistant Supervisor."

[¶ 3] This group of excluded persons has nonetheless for some years dealt collectively (albeit informally) with the employer under the auspices of a staff association. In 1999 the members of the association took a vote and more than 75% expressed their interest in joining a trade union. This decision resulted in the application for certification before me, in which the members of the association seek to obtain formal certification as a bargaining unit represented by CUPE. . . .

[¶ 4] . . . The parties agreed that the employer would call evidence from persons in two of the disputed positions [Gerry Laurin and Katharine Dill], and from the Coordinator of Employment Services [Valerie Flynn]. . . . The Board was asked to provide a ruling on the status of the two persons testifying, in the hope that this interim decision would provide sufficient guidance to the parties such that the entire application might be resolved. . . .

[¶ 6] There are more than 40 people in one of the two classifications in dispute in this application — "supervisors" and "assistant directors" — deployed in the various departments of the CAS, who supervise more than 300 front-line workers who are in a bargaining unit represented by OPSEU. . . .

[¶10] Supervisors are the front-line of management and supervise employees in the bargaining unit directly. They in turn report to either Assistant Directors, who are also alleged by CUPE to be appropriate for inclusion in the proposed bargaining unit, or more often to Directors, who are agreed to be excluded. Directors in turn report either to the Executive Director, who heads the organization, or to the Director of Service who reports to the Executive Director.

[¶11] The job description for supervisors emphasizes their role in supervising the daily work of employees in their area. Flynn testified about the criteria used by the agency when selecting persons for hire into these positions, which emphasizes their ability to manage employees rather than just clinical expertise. Staff who become supervisors take a three day course in "Interactive Management" which trains them in a particular framework for managing performance and discipline issues in the workplace.

[¶ 12] Supervisors are required to do "supervisions" with employees at particular intervals, in order to review their caseload and the progress made. Many of these standards are imposed by the Ministry of Community and Social Services, which sets very particular requirements in terms of record-keeping, contact with clients, etc.

[¶ 13] Flynn described the role the supervisors play in staffing the agency. When a vacancy occurs, the supervisor in the area affected completes a form making a request for staff, which is signed off by the Director and Executive Director. . . . Interview panels are generally made up of three people: two supervisors and a representative from human resources. . . . Both Dill and Laurin have been involved in such interviews, and concurred with the notion that decisions are made on a consensus basis. . . .

[¶ 15] Human resources personnel sometimes "screen" prospective candidates without supervisors present when there is some urgency, . . . but the "receiving" supervisor is consulted before a final decision is made.

[¶ 16] Gerry Laurin, as a supervisor in the Parent Model Homes programme, has had some additional involvement in the hiring of casual employees with only limited involvement by human resources personnel. Most recently, he and another supervisor interviewed a number of potential candidates for casual positions and provided the names and interview questionnaires together with his recommendations to human resources, so that they could complete reference checks and proceed with offers of employment. To avoid delay the supervisors did some of the reference checks as well.

[¶ 17] Laurin also testified that supervisors have in the past had greater independence in the hiring of new staff, with human resources playing only a "supportive" function, but that more recently a different management style has led to greater involvement by professional human resources staff.

[¶ 18] Sometimes permanent positions are filled internally without the use of a formal interview process. Recently 29 contract positions were "converted" to permanent positions, and the candidates were assessed by an evaluation method which did not include an interview, but instead gave significant weight to performance reviews completed by supervisors. . . .

[¶ 19] When an employee earns a permanent position, they are placed on a six-month probationary period. Just prior to the end of that period, human resources forwards to the employee's supervisor a form asking for their recommendation, which is completed and signed by the supervisor and then approved by the Director and by human resources.

[¶ 20] Supervisors carry out the agency's performance review program, completing performance reviews on bargaining unit staff annually. . . . Supervisors review the goals set in the previous round, provide comments as to an employee's success in reaching those goals, and assign a rating. The performance review is then forwarded to the director for signature. Supervisors are permitted to meet with employees to discuss their appraisals before sending them to the Director. Flynn testified that sometimes she is asked by supervisors for advice in framing particular comments, but that there is no requirement that supervisors involve her, and that she does not provide substantive input in that she has no opportunity to assess employees. Dill testified about challenges she faced in managing a particular employee who had had difficulties meeting the reporting requirements. She discussed possible approaches with Val Flynn, and with her Director, at various points during her management of this employee. When it came time to complete the performance review, however, she did not consult with them and simply assigned a poor rating based on the problems she had observed and had discussed with the employee. If she was planning on "failing" someone, though, she would consult with human resources "because of the union."

[¶ 21] Supervisors also carry out the attendance review program, maintaining a calendar which monitors employee attendance.

[¶ 22] Discipline issues usually arise as part of the overall program for the management of employee performance, and are handled by supervisors using the principles of "interactive management" in which they are trained. This involves counselling employees . . . before taking any steps which might appear to constitute conventional discipline. . . .

[¶ 23] Katharine Dill testified that she would never impose formal discipline on an employee without consulting with her Director, and likely human resources as well, although she has issued verbal reprimands and warnings. She did not attribute this approach to any particular prohibition imposed upon her, . . . but rather stated that she felt that with a union in place she would want to ensure that she was "going in the right direction". . . .

[¶ 26] Supervisors schedule employees, assign them cases, and approve overtime and vacation leave within the scope of the agency's policies respecting such leaves.

[¶ 27] Personnel files are maintained by the human resources department but supervisors have access to the files of employees under, or about to be under, their supervision. . . .

[¶ 29] Flynn testified that two supervisors were involved on the management team which bargained with OPSEU for the most recent renewal of the collective agreement. CUPE suggested that supervisors had not previously been involved in collective bargaining, and that the employer had made this assignment only after it learned of the present application. As the two supervisors whose status is being considered in the present decision did not participate in bargaining, this is not a dispute which I need consider at present.

[¶ 30] Flynn also described the involvement of several supervisors in decision-making about a proposed down-sizing on a panel which assessed the skills and abilities of displaced employees and matched them with available jobs. . . . When layoffs did occur in 1995 and 1996 Laurin sat on another committee with another supervisor and a human resources representative charged with the task of implementing the layoffs in accordance with the collective agreement, which required an assessment of the skills, abilities and experience of affected employees in order to reach decisions about layoff and/or redeployment

[¶ 31] Flynn was involved in the grievance procedure as a supervisor when an employee grieved a disciplinary letter which she had issued, attending meetings at the early stages. Dill testified that she had never attended at grievance meetings but assumed she would if a grievance matter arose. . . .

[¶ 32] This application raises again, for the first time in several years, the question of whether or not units made up of persons who supervise employees will be permitted to bargain collectively in Ontario.

[¶ 33] The legal framework for the resolution of this issue is not in dispute. Section 1(3)(b) of the Act provides as follows:

> 1.(3) Subject to section 97, for the purposes of this Act, no person shall be deemed to be an employee,
>
> (b) who, in the opinion of the Board, exercises managerial functions or is employed in a confidential capacity in matters relating to labour relations.

[¶ 34] The question before me is therefore: do the supervisors at the CAS exercise managerial functions within the meaning of section 1(3)(b)?

[¶ 35] The parties placed before me several authorities dealing with the purpose of the managerial exclusion in the Act, which was the starting point for each of their arguments in the present case. The following excerpt from *The Corporation of the City of Thunder Bay* . . . is perhaps the most often-cited discussion of the statutory goals represented by section 1(3)(b):

> 2. Section 1(3)(b) excludes from collective bargaining persons who in the opinion of the Board exercise managerial functions. The purpose of the section is to ensure that persons who are within a bargaining unit do not find themselves faced with a conflict of interest as between their responsibilities and obligations as managerial personnel, and their responsibilities as trade union members or employees in the bargaining unit. Collective bargaining, by its very nature, requires an arm's length relationship between the "two sides" whose interests and objectives are often divergent. Section 1(3)(b) ensures that neither the trade union, nor its members will have "divided loyalties". . . .

[¶ 38] In the present case, the employer has the onus to establish that the supervisors perform managerial functions within the meaning of the Act, given that it is seeking to prevent these persons from obtaining the protections of the Act through collective bargaining. At the same time, though, the status quo, over many years of a collective bargaining relationship between OPSEU and the CAS, has been to treat the supervisors as excluded employees exercising managerial functions, which should be taken into account in considering the demand of the union that collective bargaining now be extended to the first layer of supervisors outside of the existing OPSEU unit.

[¶ 39] Most of the Board decisions interpreting and applying the managerial exclusion have arisen in the context of defining the precise limits of a bargaining unit made up largely of persons who indisputably have the status of employees, where a question arises as to whether a particular person exercising front-line supervision over those employees falls within or without the unit. However, the approach articulated in the *Thunder Bay* case has been applied on a few earlier occasions where, as in the present case, groups of supervisors have sought to bargain collectively in a unit separate and apart from the bargaining unit containing the employees they direct.

[¶ 40] The most well-known of those cases is *Ford Motor Company of Canada Limited.* . . . . In that case the Board reiterated . . . the purposes served by the managerial exclusion "in order to protect the institutional interests of both employers and unions". . . . The Board reviewed many of the examples of "conflicting interests on the shop floor" which have traditionally driven the exclusion of managers from the bargaining units they supervise, but also considered whether the purposes of the managerial exclusion are engaged by a grouping of supervisors into a separate unit:

> 14. In addition to the obvious examples of conflicting interests on the shop floor, there are broader, systemic concerns which require the exclusion of "management" from par-

ticipation in trade union activities. For if management personnel were treated like ordinary employees, and were free to organize or promote particular trade unions, the freedom of these *other workers* could be undermined and the independence of *their trade unions* could be jeopardized. And this problem may not be resolved merely, as here, by segregating the "supervisors" into their own bargaining unit.

15. . . . if "foremen" had the same rights as other employees, what would prevent them, acting in their own interest, from trying to persuade those other workers to join, support or discard a particular union? . . . Section 1(3)(b) not only defines who is *excluded* from the collective bargaining process; it also identifies who is *prevented* from using "managerial" authority to interfere with the collective bargaining rights of others.

16. This is not an academic concern either. What distinguishes "management" from ordinary "employees" is the power that managers exercise over the economic security of their fellow workers — a power which, in the Board's experience, "foremen" have sometimes used to interfere with the right of those workers to engage in collective bargaining through a trade union of *their choice*. . . . That is why section 1(3)(b) is but one of a constellation of statutory provisions designed to segregate "employees" from "management," and ensure that the employees and their unions are entirely independent of managerial influence.

17. . . . Collective bargaining might well be a useful tool for managerial employees, just as it is for ordinary workers. However, the Legislature has determined that the process is better served if those obliged to act on behalf of the employer are completely segregated from the union institutions and the collective bargaining mechanism that employees use to promote their interests. . . .

[¶ 43] The Board has acknowledged in numerous cases that the assessment of whether an individual performs "managerial functions" is an exercise in characterization, with factors pointing in one direction being weighed against those suggesting an opposite result. These decisions are also of course essentially fact-driven, as the particular nuances of authority and discretion vary in each case. To further complicate matters, the scope of a supervisor's ostensible authority is often affected by the unique experience, skills and disposition of a particular incumbent, meaning that two different people apparently occupying the same position may appear to fall on opposite sides of the managerial divide. . . .

[¶ 44] . . . As was said in *The Corporation of the City of Thunder Bay*, "the important question is the extent to which [first line managerial employees] make decisions which affect the economic lives of their fellow employees thereby raising a potential conflict of interest with them". . . . Thus, the parties generally agreed that the Board ought to focus on what have been described as the real indicia of economic power over employees: the power to hire, fire, promote, demote, grant wage increases or discipline employees.

[¶45] The union in the present case took this accepted approach one step further, arguing that the Board ought to further narrow the test for establishing managerial authority by effectively eliminating consideration of other factors which have been discussed in the cases, and looking only at the smaller number of criteria utilized by the British Columbia Labour Relations Board, as confirmed in a decision of the Chair of that Board in 1997, *Cowichan Home Support Society*. . . . The approach taken by that Board is apparent in the following excerpt:

> 150. With respect to managerial status, we have determined that three criteria will now be considered by the Board (the first two being more important, but the latter nonetheless justifying exclusion in appropriate cases). These criteria or factors are:
> (a) discipline and discharge;
> (b) labour relations input; and
> (c) hiring, promotion and demotion.
>
> 151. There is no minimum level of discipline necessary in order to warrant exclusion — particularly in non-industrial settings. In regard to all three criteria, the level of power or authority which must be exercised by the person whose status is in question must be one of "effective determination." Reliance on labour relations or legal advice per se does not detract from the meaningful exercise of managerial authority. We have confirmed under the heading of labour relations input that the underlying issue is one of potential, and not actual, conflict of interest. Such conflict cannot be removed simply through the creation of a separate bargaining unit. The authority to hire, promote and demote employees may be particularly significant in smaller businesses which do no have established labour relations procedures. Lastly, the test for exclusion must be applied with flexibility, taking into account such considerations as the administrative structure of the employer and the size of the operation.

[¶ 46] I am not inclined in this decision to modify the long-standing approach of the Ontario Labour Relations Board, which considers a myriad of factors which may indicate the presence of managerial authority, but which undoubtedly emphasizes the same important criteria identified by the British Columbia Board. It may be that a more focused approach would, as the B.C. Board suggested, "allow more accurate and efficient determination of who constitutes an "employee," but the current test has not been shown to be particularly problematic, nor even to really differ from that which is proposed by the union, in its application to the facts of this case. . . . .

[¶ 48] . . . it is obvious that the size of an employer's operations will change the type of role played by supervisors and must be taken into account in trying to determine whether they exercise real managerial authority. This is particularly the case where the employer has a large unionized workforce. The Board put it this way in *E.B. Eddy* . . . ;

> 34. In a [large] workplace . . . , it is . . . not surprising that the classic managerial duties have been divided up in a hierarchical way, with the lower level managers playing more of a monitoring and reporting role and significant decisions being made at a higher level. In a small workplace, all managerial tasks may be performed by a single individual; but once large numbers of employees are involved, and therefore more supervisors, it makes little sense for each and every supervisor to be engaged in all of those same

tasks. Instead, the pool of managers is likely to be divided in much the way it has been at *E.B. Eddy*, with senior managers, together with human resources professionals who have no direct supervisory responsibilities, setting policies for the management of employees, monitoring the front-line supervisors, and setting working terms and conditions through the bargaining process. The management role would not be complete, however, if these tasks were to be separated from those carried out by the foremen, as the higher level of management is generally not engaged in the direct supervision of employees and would therefore have no effective way to ensure the implementation of its policies, or to obtain information critical to the monitoring of that implementation. The pool of managers must be considered as an organism, which cannot function without all of its parts.

[¶ 49] Also significant is the nature of the managerial or administrative structure adopted in the workplace. The B.C. Board in *Cowichan* contrasted hierarchical structures with many layers of managerial responsibility to the more flattened management structures which are increasingly common. In the present case we see a perfect example of the unique managerial strategies which are often adopted in settings where large numbers of professional employees are employed at both bargaining unit and managerial levels. . . .

[¶ 50] Such professional environments sometimes create forms of supervision which appear at first instance to be managerial but in fact involve the provision of only technical or professional advice to less skilled employees, and the Board must be cautious in examining this form of supervision. On the other hand, that is not to say . . . that professional or technical employees may not also exercise managerial functions. In fact, real managerial authority may be present but difficult to discern in these settings, where collegial modes of decision-making and performance management through counselling may be the norm. . . .

[¶ 51] In the present case we are dealing with just such a large, unionized, and professional environment, and its effect on the nature of the managerial authority exercised by the supervisors is clear. The duties and responsibilities of the persons in dispute are structured in many important respects by the requirements of the collective agreement, and discretion is limited by the requirement for consistency throughout a large organization, and for compliance with the contract, which leads to the adoption of various policies and procedures for the management of staff. As well, the Ministry of Community and Social Services establishes various standards which impact on what supervisors require of employees under their direction. There are professional human resources staff who coordinate the implementation of personnel policies and advise supervisors on particular supervisory challenges. And the style of management consciously adopted by the organization is a consensual and non-confrontational one, described as "interactive management," which means that there are fewer obvious examples of the traditional mechanisms of front-line management.

[¶ 52] Does this context mean that the front-line managers, here the supervisors, do not exercise real managerial authority? In the present case, I have concluded that the supervisors about whom I heard evidence do exercise managerial functions within the meaning of the Act, despite the constraints upon their roles described above.

[¶ 53] First, the supervisors play an important role in both the hiring of casual and contract staff, and the promotion of staff to permanent positions. Supervisors regularly sit on interview panels, and I am satisfied that they have meaningful input into the selection of staff, particularly as to their ability to meet the needs of the area which requires staff, rather than their general suitability for employment with the agency. This contribution is also apparent in the role that some supervisors have played in developing questions or criteria for the interview protocols. . . .

[¶ 54] Is the input of supervisors into hiring and promotion decisions to be discounted given that the final decisions are made by consensus, and therefore no one person has the ultimate authority? In discussing the concept of the "effective power of recommendation" the Board has emphasized that when assessing the role of a front-line manager whose decision making is not entirely independent of senior management "it is necessary to show that his recommendations are really effective, so that, in practice, and to a substantial degree, he becomes the effective decision maker in respect of matters impacting upon his fellow employees". . . . I am satisfied, though, that the supervisors play as important a role in the selection of the people who work under their direction as do any other managers in the organization. It is not the case, for example, that their recommendations are regularly overruled by human resources, Directors or by the Executive Director; the opposite seems true. Surely that level of involvement must meet the test of effective recommendation in a setting like this.

[¶ 55] Supervisors have essentially complete control over the formal performance review program, which has had a critical impact on the ability of contract staff to obtain permanent positions, and on the retention of probationary staff. . . .

[¶ 56] As noted in many earlier cases, involvement in the discipline and discharge of employees is perhaps the most critical indicia of true managerial authority. It is not really in dispute that in the present case the supervisors are the "eyes and ears" of the employer; they are the only members of management who really monitor the work and conduct of employees and they are therefore the ones who are in a position to identify and express management concerns. . . .

[¶ 57] When conduct does not improve, or very serious conduct occurs in the first instance, there is no doubt that the supervisors who testified, and likely any supervisor, would consult with their Director and/or a human resources professional about the appropriate course of action. . . .

[¶ 59] When we consider the disciplinary style encouraged at the CAS, the entirely appropriate reliance upon human resources professionals to provide consistency of approach and professional expertise, and the participatory form of decision-making, it is not surprising that the supervisors have had only limited involvement in imposing formal and/or serious discipline on the employees they direct. . . .

[¶ 60] Having read the decisions in *Ford* and *E.B. Eddy* closely, I am satisfied that the supervisors in the present case, despite the less traditional disciplinary style adopted at the CAS, play at least as significant a role in monitoring employee performance and initiating disciplinary responses where required as did the foremen considered in those decisions. As well, in the present case the supervisors play a significant role in performance appraisal, which has an impact on the promotion and retention of employees, and in hiring; the foremen in *Ford* and in *E.B. Eddy* had no role in hiring, and there was no formal system of performance evaluations. Also important is the fact that, as in the two earlier cases, the supervisors in the present case are engaged full-time in supervisory work and do virtually no bargaining unit work. This, more than anything else, differentiates them from the category of "team leader" as that concept has been developed in the caselaw. . . .

[¶ 67] This leads us to the issue of the ratio of supervisors to bargaining unit employees. . . . The Board has regularly considered the number of front-line managers as compared to the number of employees they supervise, and also the number of higher level managers involved in the direction of the supervisors in issue, in examining the claim that the front-line is indispensable to the management structure as a whole. . . .

[¶ 68] I have concluded that the supervisors about whom evidence was heard play a role in hiring, discipline and performance appraisal such that the mischief to which section 1(3)(b) is directed would likely be engaged should they be found to be employees within the meaning of the Act. Ought that conclusion to be modified by the fact that, by the terms of the present application for certification, they would be in a different bargaining unit than the employees they supervise, represented by a different union?

[¶ 69] The supervisors considered in the *Ford* and *E.B. Eddy* cases were found not to be employees within the meaning of the Act despite the proposal that they be placed in a separate bargaining unit. In British Columbia, the labour relations statute makes specific reference to the possibility of placing supervisors in separate units, and the labour board discusses the significance of that statutory tool in determining employee status in the *Cowichan* case:

> 117. . . . the placement of an individual into a separate bargaining unit does not address the issue of a potential conflict of interest in dealing with the issue of undivided loyalty or commitment. As stated, the issue is one of dual loyalties between the employer and a bargaining unit. . . . [T]he potential conflict of interest . . . is not the one which is internal to the bargaining unit (which will be dealt with under appropriateness); but rather, is directed at maintaining an arm's length relationship between supervisors and any unionized bargaining unit.

[¶ 70] Similarly, this Board in *Ford* emphasized the employer's reasonable expectation that its supervisors will be undivided in their loyalty, concluding that their duties and responsibilities assign to them "a role which inevitably puts them in the employer's camp, pitted against the employees who report to them". . . .

[¶ 72] The presumption that there is an inherent conflict between the interests of employers and any ability to bargain collectively by those to whom it delegates some of its authority, even in a separate bargaining unit, has been challenged by some commentators who bemoan the focus on conflict and adversity of interests which underlies our present system, but it remains a central tenet of the statute under which this application for certification has been brought. As such, I must conclude that the two employees about whom evidence was heard, Katharine Dill and Gerry Laurin, are not employees within the meaning of the Act and as such must be denied access to collective bargaining as structured and facilitated by the Act.

[¶ 73] This ruling of course does not restrict the ability of supervisors at the CAS to deal collectively with their employer as they have done in the past, through a staff association, with or without the assistance of CUPE or some other union. . . .

Re Québec-Téléphone [1996] C.L.R.B.D. No. 36 (Canada Labour Relations Board)

HANDMAN, Vice-Chair; BASTIEN and ARONOVITCH, Members

[¶ 1] . . . Through this application, the union (CUPE) seeks to represent the project officers at Québec-Téléphone . . . together with first and second-level managers. The union's view is that the incumbents of these positions share a community of interest, and accordingly should be included in the same bargaining unit. . . .

[¶ 6] Québec-Téléphone challenges the bargaining unit proposed by the applicant in its amended application. It considers as appropriate only that unit which comprises the project officers. . . . It submits that if the Board decides that first and second-level managers are employees within the meaning of the [*Canada Labour Code*], they must form separate bargaining units due to a lack of a community of interest and the possibility of a conflict of interest with the members of the unit sought. . . . Lastly, the employer argues that the inclusion of these managers would result in Québec-Téléphone being over-unionized given the minimum number of executives required to manage the business properly. . . .

[¶ 9] . . . The issues are two-fold. The first one relates to whether the first and second-level managers, in light of their respective functions, are employees within the meaning of the Code and, if so, whether they share a sufficient community of interest with the project officers to justify being placed in the same unit. . . .

[¶ 12] Section 3(1) of the Canada Labour Code defines "employee" as follows:

> "'employee' means any person employed by an employer and includes a dependent contractor and a private constable, but does not include a person who performs management functions or is employed in a confidential capacity in matters relating to industrial relations."

[¶ 13] There is abundant case law regarding the criteria used by the Board in deciding to exclude certain positions from a bargaining unit by reason of their incumbents not being employees within the meaning of section 3 of the Code, either because they perform management functions or are employed in a confidential capacity in matters relating to industrial relations. . . . [I]n *Canadian Broadcasting Corporation* . . . , the Board summarized succinctly the whole set of factors and criteria which justify the exclusion of certain positions from a bargaining unit because their incumbents are not employees within the meaning of the Code. These are as follows:

a) management exclusion is determined fundamentally on the basis of an individual's effective and regular exercise of decision-making. Or, in other words, what matters is the power to decide, not the power to recommend. . . .

b) the functions over which the power to decide exercises itself are typically those of the management cycle, i.e. planning, organising, staffing, co-ordinating, directing and controlling. . . .

c) the extent, not merely the existence, of authority in financial matters is a key indicator of a position's management content. . . .

d) management is a highly dynamic, not static, concept, and 'its precise ambit is a question of fact or opinion for the Board rather than a question of law'. . . . *Island Telephone Company Limited* . . . spoke of the concept as 'the embodiment of ever-changing corporate structures and processes, work practices, technologies and, ultimately, social values'. . . .

e) determination of management status will rest in the end on the consideration of all factors taken together and on how the specific duties of a position relate to the decision-making framework in place and on the organisational configuration of which it is a part. . . .

[¶ 14] One aspect of the last criterion relates to the need for the Board to take into account the overall bargaining unit structure of the undertaking, and its impact on the company's ability to run its business, when applying these principles to the circumstances of the present case. . . .

[¶ 16] Québec-Téléphone, a telecommunications business, services a very large territory which takes in Québec City and its surroundings within about a 100-km radius, the Gaspé peninsula and the North Shore . . . , and it has some 1,700 employees.

[¶ 17] The company operates in an industry marked by increasing competition and rapid technological innovation. Its activities are not confined to local and long distance telephone service but extend to services such as mobile services, installation, maintenance, and sales and the rental of subscribers' equipment, as well as Internet access.

[¶ 19] The management structure currently includes the chief executive officer, five vice-presidents, 18 division managers (third-level managers), 62 area managers (second-level managers), and 87 section chiefs (first-level managers). The positions of the first two hierarchical levels are those in dispute and the ones which will now be examined. . . .

First-Level Managers and Project Officers
[¶ 22] The first-level managers are section heads. They work in a service outlet in Rimouski or in a remote region within Québec-Téléphone's territory. All but about ten of [the]

first-level managers . . . work in the same geographical location as their immediate superiors. These supervisors are responsible for an operational unit and report to a second-level manager. On occasion, some of them are asked to supervise project officers. . . .

[¶ 23] While first-level managers have significant responsibilities vis-à-vis the planning and day-to-day, or at least regular, performance of the tasks carried out by the staff they supervise, they generally, and on the whole, do so within a rather well-determined framework as regards their actual decision-making authority in matters of financial commitments, hiring and staff evaluation, disciplinary measures and representational functions. For instance, the evidence showed that decisions to create or even abolish positions are made by third-level managers even though managers at lower levels obviously participate in the decision-making process. All the typical activities of first-level managers pertaining to their decision-making authority are subject to very detailed internal policies which strictly limit their range of discretion. . . .

[¶ 24] The supervisors who testified spoke of the large degree of autonomy they enjoyed in running their services and the lack of frequent or significant intervention on the part of their immediate superiors, the second-level managers. However, the evidence reveals that this feeling has more to do with the great familiarity most of them have of the operations or services they direct than with the actual exercise of true discretionary authority which is typical of the management functions recognized by the case law.

[¶ 25] The interaction between analysts and first-level managers was described by the Operations Centre Director, Mr. Julien Godin, who as a second-level manager directs supervisors and, occasionally through them, the analysts. . . . When Mr. Godin spoke of the interaction of the analysts with staff from marketing, planning and engineering on the introduction of a new service such as the digitalization of equipment . . . , he indicated it is incumbent on the analysts to make sure the equipment comes in on schedule, and that this "service is truly operational, that is, from a technical point of view, how things should be done, how the new service should be programmed in the automatic switches". . . .

Second-Level Managers

[¶ 26] The second-level managers have various titles, such as area manager, project leader, change leader, area director and regional director. In short, they are responsible under these various titles for an area of activity on a large part of the company's territory. They exercise direct or indirect supervision over a large portion of the company's employees. Their responsibilities for planning and organizing the company's areas of activity, selecting and evaluating their staff, and financially committing the company are clearly - from the perspective of both content and relations to the company's essential functions - at a higher level than those of their first-level colleagues.

[¶ 27] While second-level managers are subject to the same formal requirements to have their decisions approved by third-level managers when the creation or abolition of positions is involved, their effective authority to make decisions on such matters is obviously greater than that of the first-level managers. . . .

[¶ 28] Mr. Dagnault, Project Leader, New Invoicing System (CBSS), explained that, due to the project's very nature, its long duration and its ever-changing personnel requirements, various teams (for which he himself had to negotiate secondments) were grafted onto a small initial core of employees at various phases of the project. The actual, if not formal, authority vested in him by management in respect of these budgetary and personnel matters came out loud and clear throughout his testimony. . . .

[¶ 30] . . . [T]he invoicing project whose design and implementation had been assigned to Gaston Dagnault is worth examining and analysing. This project, called CBSS, was meant to design and implement a new invoicing software at Québec-Téléphone. It was implemented over a period of more than three years. . . . Management had mandated Mr. Dagnault to lead the entire project through to completion. In this capacity, his essential functions involved the negotiation of a contract to purchase software from a U.S. firm, the numerous alterations of the project's parameters as it was being implemented, the assignments of personnel to the project, the ongoing interaction with the company's senior executives on the one hand, and with outside firms from which services and specific expertise were sought.

[¶ 31] Throughout his testimony, Mr. Dagnault referred to his role as that of "macro-managing" (translation) the project, that is, determining the major phases such as objectives and deadlines, building a team to implement the project and, above all, maintaining relations with senior management to ensure full integration with company operations once the new system was implemented. The scope and level of these functions stand out when we consider that the project's initial total budget was some $7 million which had grown to almost $10 million by the time the project was completed. These circumstances prompted this project leader to deal regularly with the company's senior executives with respect to choices and decisions to be made.

[¶ 32] Of course, not all the second-level positions shared the same functions performed by Mr. Dagnault in his position as project leader. Individual positions are unique in terms of the area concerned, the relative complexity of the project or functions involved as well as the specific organizational context in which they are carried out. That being said, at the time the application was filed, the company had five project leaders, all at the second level, whose functions were similar to those performed by Mr. Dagnault. . . .

[¶ 33] Throughout his testimony, Mr. Godin conveyed a very practical sense of his responsibilities and their level of complexity. They consisted first and foremost in ensuring the "functionality and consistency" (translation) of the sections under his authority. As well, they involved maintaining an ongoing relationship with the other divisions within the company, consistent with his role to determine the orientation of the operations centre in relation to the new services to be offered. That is how he explained the need to continually reorganize the sections in the context of changing products and markets. . . .

[¶ 37] . . . [T]here are co-ordination functions which are shared between the analysts and the supervisors but which entail different requirements and perspectives. The analysts' contribution is based first and foremost on their technical expertise, while that of the supervisors pertains to operational requirements. . . .

Supervisors or First-Level Managers

[¶ 38] What can be concluded from the foregoing examination of the evidence with regard to the questions to be decided by the Board? First, that the supervisors or first-level managers are employees within the meaning of the Code. While their functions . . . are performed in a spirit of openness and with relative operational autonomy, they do not constitute management functions within the meaning of the case law. . . . Whatever decision-making discretion they enjoy — and they do — it is always exercised within a predetermined framework, either through detailed administrative management policies or through essential operational requirements whereby the supervisor must ensure continuity of service. These cases strictly involve an autonomy of means, with these means, for the most part, being clearly defined at the outset.

[¶ 39] Indeed, if first-level managers enjoy a certain margin of autonomy, it is one that stems largely, on the one hand, from the relative ease with which their human resources and financial needs can be predicted and, on the other, from the requirement placed on them to do whatever is necessary to maintain or, in the event of major outages, restore telephone services. The testimony of the supervisors . . . shows that the authorization to exceed normal spending limits on overtime, for example, stems from immediate operational requirements more than from the exercise of any particular financial authority they might enjoy. In short, the supervisors play a major role in Québec-Téléphone's activities but this role is not a managerial one within the meaning of the Code.

[¶ 40] There is, however, one exception to the latter statement: the supervisor of the Havre-Saint-Pierre network, Gérald Smith. The great distance between him and his supervisor, who lives in Sept-Îles, his role of representing the company in this remote region, his authority and his decisions regarding the hiring of staff, as well as the scope of his functions at the regional level, are reasons that justify the exclusion of his position from the proposed unit. . . .

[¶ 41] The question of the community of interest shared by the supervisors and the [second level] project officers remains to be determined. An initial aspect of this question pertains to the very nature of the functions of both positions. It should be noted that the incumbents of these two types of positions, as indicated above, enjoy real operational discretion even though it is not managerial in nature.

[¶ 42] In effect, this autonomy and the range of action associated with it stem primarily, as we saw earlier, from the incumbents' thorough knowledge of the equipment in question, the technical characteristics of a product or process, or the operation or functioning of this equipment or process. There are, of course, significant differences between these two groups in terms of how this knowledge is applied. For example, the project officers' knowledge pertains more to technical concepts and their implementation, whereas the supervisors' knowledge primarily involves the practical and daily operation of the equipment or processes for which they are responsible in conjunction with the employees they supervise. Both positions, however, undeniably involve functions of supervision and co-ordination even though they vary in degree and in method.

[¶ 43] In this regard, it is interesting to note how their respective roles manifest themselves vis-à-vis their interaction with other areas of the business. For example, the first-level managers or supervisors must ensure the continual operation of a service, piece of equipment or set of equipment. For this reason, they, like the analysts, are often called on to deal with other units or areas of the business but these dealings pertain to the practical operation of their service or equipment. Their involvement occurs on a daily basis and focuses on activities associated with the delivery of a service for which they are responsible. . . .

Second-Level Managers

[¶ 47] The first question to be determined in the case of second-level managers is whether or not they are employees within the meaning of the Code. . . .

[¶ 48] The above analysis of the functions of second-level managers showed that the responsibilities assigned to these managers, including the project managers, are significant and involve, unquestionably, management content. As noted earlier, their planning, organizing, directing and evaluating functions are performed at a level and in connection with projects or business processes which involve the company's actual decision-making authority and, by way of consequence, its policy and methods. For this reason, they enjoy a significant measure of discretion. This discretion refers not only to proven technical knowledge, as in the case of the analysts and supervisors, but also to a great extent to their knowledge and use of management processes through regular contacts with the highest levels of the organization.

[¶ 49] The difference between second-level managers and supervisors is more clearly seen in the nature of the relationship each maintains with other areas of the organization. Second-level managers, like the [first-level] analysts or supervisors, maintain contact with these areas but they do so primarily to ensure harmony and co-ordination with the hierarchical functions of management or consistency in the decision-making process for the business as a whole, as Mr. Dagnault's testimony clearly showed. In this way, their involvement differs from that of the analysts or supervisors, which, as we saw earlier, relates primarily to co-ordinating the technical aspects of a project, or to their need to ultimately ensure the functional consistency of the system or the new equipment in question.

[¶ 50] It should be noted, moreover, that the functions of second-level managers have been performed in recent years in an organizational context dominated by many changes in management processes and structures, including a progressive flattening of the hierarchical pyramid. For example, the elimination of two management levels during the 1980s undoubtedly led to a redistribution of management functions relative to the remaining levels, and to a proportional increase in the management content of the second-level managers. This spells a need for them to deal more with the higher echelons of the decision-making hierarchy in order to decide issues pertaining to the company's management process. It will be recalled that, based on our previous analysis, major differences were noted between supervisors and second-level managers on how they interact and relate to senior management. In the first instance, the relationship centres most often on the operation of the company's equipment and daily operations, whereas in the second, it focuses on changes in the company and its management processes.

[¶ 51] . . . In short, the functions of the second-level managers are sufficiently extensive and continuous, in relation to both the nature of the issues to which they pertain and the hierarchical level at which they are performed, to exclude them from the definition of employee within the meaning of the Code. As we saw, these functions involve the exercise of a significant and ongoing discretion with respect to selecting staff, orienting management processes and setting budgets. Consequently, second-level managers, including the project and change leaders at the same level, are excluded from the unit proposed by the applicant. . . .

* * *

As noted above in *Children's Aid Society of Ottawa-Carleton,* there has been considerable criticism of the managerial exclusion. Economists, management theorists and some unionists have advocated more participation by workers in management decisions generally, and especially in those that affect workers directly. A number of European countries have had considerable experience with both works councils of various sorts and employee directors. A few North American companies have also experimented with employee directors. If workers participate in management, the strict dichotomy between management and labour begins to break down, and this creates problems in the application of our current statutory arrangements.

Universities have been a testing ground for the permissible limits of employee participation in management. In Canada, labour boards regard university professors as employees under labour relations statutes, despite their role in the academic governance of the university: see *Mount Allison University,* [1982] 3 Can LRBR 284. The United States Supreme Court took a different view in *National Labor Relations Board v. Yeshiva University* (1980), 100 S. Ct. 856. It held that professors in private universities exercised managerial functions because they sat on university bodies that decided on appointments and promotions, awarded tenure and formulated curricula and teaching methods — matters that would be prerogatives of management in a private business. Not surprisingly, this holding did not meet with universal approval among academics.

Karl Klare, "The Bitter and the Sweet: Reflections on the Supreme Court's 'Yeshiva Decision'" (1983), Socialist Review No. 71 (vol. 13, no. 5) at 122–25

While many of the current workplace participation experiments are unfolding in the context of mature collective-bargaining relationships, the message of *Yeshiva* is that the collective bargaining system as presently organized, at least in contemplation of law, is ill-suited to accommodate reform of the structure of work. The established assumptions about the purposes and meaning of collective bargaining are anti-participatory. Prevailing legal images of the worker are inappropriate for a more complex future in which workers' self-learning and team decision-making emerge as valued productive forces. Indeed, the very rigidity of the law's images of the workplace are what caused an ideal prototype of the worker of the future, the teacher, to be rejected as a candidate for collective bargaining. It would seem, therefore, that unless it is dramatically transformed, labor law will act as a brake upon the capacity of our industrial-relations institutions to adjust and adapt to emergent tendencies in work organization.

Thus, the "traditional crisis of the labor movement" (i.e., diminished political clout, declining percentage of organized workers, assault by law, and brutally adverse economic circumstances) coincides with a "developmental crisis," a question of the future of collective bargaining itself. How will the contending parties respond to the growing datedness of collective bargaining? Will collective bargaining adjust to the needs of the workplace of the future? What is its political meaning in the unfolding story of the post-Taylorist workplace? While we can't yet answer these questions, it is possible to suggest in general terms some of the conceivable lines of direction in the relationship of collective bargaining to job redesign.

A variety of scenarios, arising for several distinct reasons, may occur under which the dominant development will be conflict between collective bargaining and emergent tendencies toward workplace participation. Unions might be fearful that new organizational forms will displace worker loyalty and diminish the shop-floor role and prestige of unions. Indeed, some schemes may be designed to accomplish those ends. The cautious and conservative mentality of most top labor leaders may induce them to discourage or to misperceive rank-and-file interest in workplace participation. Under these circumstances unions may well take their stand against worker-participation schemes that conflict with the practices and institutions of collective bargaining, and they may attempt to use the law as a shield against transformation of workplace organization.

Sources of conflict between collective bargaining and workplace reorganization also exist on the management side. In some cases the vogue of worker participation may be promoted simply to discredit and marginalize unions. Some managers may be genuinely motivated by a desire for reform, e.g., to enhance morale and productivity, but may regard collective bargaining as insufficiently "flexible" to incorporate the changes they envision as desirable. Another possibility is that some managers may attempt to mesh new modes of work with older, hierarchical forms of enterprise governance. To accomplish this goal they will need to discourage any sense of collective solidarity among employees and to make unionization appear as unattractive as possible by persuading employees that it is a barrier to job enrichment and personal responsibility.

Employers seeking to "end run" collective bargaining will of course seek to promote alternative sources of employee identification and self-image that are consistent with management control. Of these perhaps the most important is the ideology of professionalism. The crucial principle that management appropriates and collects the knowledge pertaining to productive processes can only be perpetuated in an era when the employee is increasingly an investigator, learner, and teacher, if cultural, institutional, and legal forces combine to assure the affiliation of employees to management. It is this fact that gives towering significance to the debate about "alignment" in the Yeshiva case and to the effort to portray the faculty's independent professional judgment as inseparable from (and subordinate to) the policies of management.

For the reasons indicated, serious conflict may develop in coming years between the collective bargaining system and developing tendencies toward workplace reorganization. It seems equally plausible, however, that collective bargaining and job redesign might evolve together in a mutually reinforcing fashion. This prospect might also occur in a variety of ways and for a range of reasons. For example, it is conceivable that under the guidance of a new generation of elite supporters and theorists the collective bargaining system could be refashioned so as to accommodate the productivity-enhancing aspects of worker participation while containing and channelling the "destabilizing" aspects. That is, collective bargaining might adapt so as to play the same co-optative and integrating role with respect to workplace reorganization in the future that it has played with respect to industrial unionism in the past.

But, finally, there is the possibility that, in the context of a national debate over paths to social and economic reconstruction, workers and labor supporters could take the initiative in the movement for workplace reorganization. The exciting thing about this prospect is that it will take much more than interstitial adjustment to move forward simultaneously on the collective bargaining and worker control fronts. The labor movement will have to transform totally its conception of collective bargaining in order to regain momentum in linked struggles to organize and to democratize the workplace. To assimilate aspirations for authentic worker participation, collective bargaining will require a new, non-liberal foundation, a guiding conception of industrial democracy that blends the quest for workers' control with the egalitarian principles originally connected to the cause of collective bargaining — collective decision-making, employee self-reliance, solidarity. Perhaps in the end something can be said for the *Yeshiva* decision. It will have performed a service if by the unexampled clarity of its depiction of mainstream collective-bargaining values it prompts us to re-examine those assumptions and to fashion and to fight for alternative, radically democratic foundations for the world of work.

[Reprinted by permission.]

* * *

Canadian labour law has recognized for some time that the managerial exclusion should be tailored to the reality of greater employee participation in the workplace. In *Ontario Public Service Employees Union v. Family Services of Hamilton-Wentworth Inc.*, [1980] 2 Can. L.R.B.R. 76, the Ontario Labour Relations Board considered whether employee-directors of a social service agency exercised the kind of independent decision-making authority which would bring them within that exclusion. The board concluded that because of the nature of the particular employer, the composition of its workforce and its history of employee involvement, the employee-directors should not be considered managers. Quebec's *Labour Code* excludes from the definition of employee "a director or officer of a corporation, unless a person acts as such with regard to his employer after having been designated by the employees or a certified association." This provision clearly contemplates that employee-directors are not to be excluded from collective bargaining.

4:340 Confidential Employees

Except in Quebec, Canadian collective bargaining legislation excludes employees who are employed in a confidential capacity in matters relating to labour relations. This exclusion, like that of managers, is based on the possibility of a conflict of interest, but labour boards are reluctant to apply it as rigorously. The following excerpt considered whether the stenographer at the Simcoe, Ontario branch of a bank should be excluded as a confidential employee.

Canadian Union of Bank Employees v. Bank of Nova Scotia (1977) 77 CLLC 16,090 (Canada Labour Relations Board)

LAPOINTE, Chair:

. . .

[The branch manager's] evidence is that the stenographer has access to personnel records kept in a credenza in his office. These include medical records, performance appraisals, salary increase recommendations, staff ban requests and hiring documents. The stenographer does not have a key to this credenza. She also waits on customers, works at the counter and sells traveler's cheques. The employer submits that this person is not an employee because she is "employed in a confidential capacity in matters relating to industrial relations."

The denial of collective bargaining rights to persons employed in a confidential capacity in matters relating to industrial relations is also based on a conflict of interests rationale. The inclusion of that person in a unit represented by a union might give the union access to matters the employer wishes to hold close in its dealings with the union. These include bargaining, grievance and arbitration strategy. To avoid that conflict and to assure the employer the undivided confidence of certain employees these persons are denied the right to be represented by a union even if they wish to be represented. However, this exclusion is narrowly interpreted to avoid circumstances where the employer designates a disproportionate number of persons as confidential and to ensure that the maximum number of persons enjoy the freedoms and rights conferred by [the *Canada Labour Code*].

To this end this Board and other Boards have developed a three-fold test for the confidential exclusion. The confidential matters must be in relation to industrial relations, not general industrial secrets such as product formulae. . . . This does not include matters the union or its members know, such as salaries, performance assessments discussed with them or which they must sign or initial. . . . It does not include personal history or family information that is available from other sources or persons. The second test is that the disclosure of that information would adversely affect the employer. Finally, the person must be involved with this information as a regular part of his duties. It is not sufficient that he occasionally comes in contact with it or that through employer laxity he can gain access to it. . . .

The stenographer position at Simcoe does not meet these tests. The position involves no access to information with respect to negotiation, grievance or arbitration strategy. It involves no access to, working with or developing of information the employer could withhold from the union if demanded at the bargaining table. . . . Finally, it is unlikely such information will be available to the stenographer when collective bargaining begins and a collective agreement is concluded. The more realistic appraisal is that this information will be developed and maintained at head office or, perhaps, in the regional office. We therefore, find the stenographer is an employee and appropriate for inclusion in the bargaining unit. . . .

☆ ☆ ☆

4:400 QUALIFIED TRADE UNIONS

4:410 The Union as an Organization

Section 3(1) of the *Canada Labour Code* defines a trade union as "any organization of employees, or any branch or local thereof, the purposes of which include the regulation of relations between employers and employees." Similar definitions are found in other statutes across Canada.

Although this definition does not specify that a union must have any particular constitutional structure, labour boards have held that an organization must meet certain requirements of form in order to be recognized as a trade union under labour relations legislation. It has never been entirely clear whether those requirements reflect a simple concern that unions should have a viable organizational framework, or a more ambitious and controversial concern that they should be democratic in their structure and functions.

A related issue, which has arisen frequently, is the extent to which a union's constitutive arrangements must reveal a collective bargaining purpose.

United Steelworkers of America v. Kubota Metal Corporation Fahramet Division and Employees' Association Committee of Kubota, [1995] OLRB Rep April 467 (Ontario Labour Relations Board)

[The United Steelworkers had signed up most of the employees in the company's factory, and had applied for certification as their bargaining agent. However, there was already an "Employees' Association Committee," which had a twenty-year history of negotiating employment agreements with the employer. That Committee intervened to oppose the Steelworkers' application.]

MACDOWELL, Alternate Chair:

. . .

[¶ 15] . . . a "trade union" must originate and operate at arm's length from the employer. A union that receives employer support (etc.) cannot be certified to represent employees nor enter into a collective agreement binding these employees. It is an unfair labour practice for an employer to create or support a "trade union" in order to hinder employees' efforts to seek truly independent representation.

[¶ 16] Under the *Labour Relations Act*, a trade union must be an independent agent of employees. . . . This is important in our scheme of collective bargaining because, once a trade union has established bargaining rights, the employee loses many of the common-law rights that s/he formerly had — including the right to set terms and conditions of employment by individual dealings with the employer, the right to sue on his/her employment contract, and so on. . . .

. . .

[¶19] The [Employees Association] Committee has been a fixture of the Kubota workplace for many years. However, its origins are somewhat obscure. The evidence of its existence begins with an *employee handbook issued by the employer* in 1976. That handbook sets out the employees' terms and conditions of employment. . . . The inference is that the Committee was conceived and created by the employer in order to have a better channel of communication with its employees.

[¶ 20] Later on, the handbook format began to look more like an "agreement" between Kubota and the Committee. . . .

[¶ 21] The "agreement" sets out the employees' terms and conditions of employment. It contains a "grievance procedure," with several steps and a provision for reference to "an independent individual who has been previously mutually agreed upon by both parties" and is empowered to render a decision that is "final and binding upon both parties and the employee or employees concerned . . . .

[¶ 22] However, the "agreement" does not purport to make the Committee the employees' *exclusive* bargaining agent . . . , nor does it contain the mandatory no strike clause. The outside individual designated as the final step in a grievance procedure is not referred to as an "arbitrator." Indeed, the document is not described as a "*collective* agreement" at all. . . . What is striking about the document is the extent to which it does not use the terminology or reflect the processes governed by the *Labour Relations Act.*

[¶ 23] According to [Committee witness] Rick Fagan, the Committee is a largely self-selected group of employees, drawn from the company's various departments, then subdivided into sub-committees. Mr. Fagan testified that the selection of committee members could be by secret ballot. But in practice it does not work that way. He could not recall any election by employees. . . .

[¶ 25] The Committee conducts monthly meetings with members of management to exchange information and address any employee concerns that originate with the Committee or are brought to its attention. Among other things, the Committee meetings provide a platform for the review of production information, productivity issues, profitability, and so on. These meetings occur in the company boardroom during working hours and are attended by members of management. . . .

[¶ 26] It is important to note that . . . there are no general employee meetings to discuss common interests or problems. There is nothing like the kind of "membership" meeting which a union would normally have.

[¶ 27] The Committee has no independent or continuing existence apart from the persons who serve on it from time to time. It has no constitution or by-laws. . . .

[¶ 28] There are no membership dues or fees paid by the employees to the Committee. The Committee has no bank account or other financial wherewithal. Indeed, there is no evidence that the Committee has any assets at all — even so much as a typewriter. The evidence is that any typing or photocopying that may be required for communicating with employees is done by the company's personnel department; and it is interesting to note that when the committee members required information about provincial employment standards, they went to the company to obtain information on whom to contact with the Ministry of Labour.

[¶ 29] . . . Mr. Fagan could only recall two or three "grievances" that were put in writing. He did not know where the grievance forms came from, but presumed that they were developed, printed, and provided by the company.

[¶ 31] Every year or so, the Committee meets with management to discuss the employees' terms and conditions of employment. . . .

[¶ 32] According to Mr. Fagan, the proposals that become part of the agreement are ratified by employees on an individual basis (i.e., there is no meeting for discussion or ratification purposes). . . .

[¶ 33] There is no evidence that the company has ever provided direct financial support to the Committee. On the other hand, having no fees, financial resources, assets, or "membership" (other than the committee members themselves), the Committee is entirely dependent upon the employer for all of the activities in which it is engaged. And while Mr. Fagan testified that he wanted the Committee's activities to be "legal," it was clear that he had no idea what the law might require a "trade union" to be or do, nor was he aware of the collective bargaining framework in which the Committee (it is now said) was purportedly engaged. For example, Mr. Fagan did not know what "conciliation" was, nor was he familiar with the statutory regime regulating collective bargaining.

[¶ 34] This is not to say that the result in this case turns upon the sophistication of the individuals involved, nor whether they put the "right label" on activities which otherwise meet statutory parameters. However, where an entity is asserting that it is a "trade union" with an established collective bargaining relationship under the *Labour Relations Act*, I think that it is reasonable to scrutinize how the organization actually behaves. . . .

[¶ 35] In section 1 of the *Labour Relations Act*, a trade union is defined as an organization of employees formed for purposes that include the regulation of relations between employees and employers. The definition requires that there be an *"organization"* with the specified purposes. The precise nature of that organization is not defined; but certain necessary characteristics can be inferred from the modifying phrase, from the general legal conception of what a trade union is, and from the nature of the rights, obligations, and duties conferred and imposed on trade unions by the Act itself. In *Associated Hebrew Schools of Toronto*, . . . , the Board commented on the formality of structure required in order to constitute a trade union organization under the Act:

10. Once a trade union has come into existence it is a relatively simple matter for others to become members of the organization and thereby enter into a contractual relationship with the existing members. When a new member joins, however, he does so on the basis of a pre-existing constitution. He knows (or at least should know) that it is a trade union which he is joining, that he is entering into a contractual relationship with the other members of the union and that the terms of that relationship are as spelt out in the union's constitution. The more difficult procedure to accomplish is for a group of employees to create a trade union where none has existed before. This process must involve not only the settlement of the terms of a constitution for the union, but also the taking of steps which make it clear that the individuals involved have actually entered into a contractual relationship one with another on the basis of the terms set forth in the constitution.

11. The Board has in a number of cases indicated a series of steps which will generally be sufficient to insure that a trade union has been brought into existence. . . .

These steps may be summarized as follows:
1. A constitution should be drafted setting out, among other things, the purpose of the organization (which must include the regulation of labour relations) and the procedure for electing officers and calling meetings.
2. The constitution should be placed before a meeting of employees for their approval either as originally drafted or as amended at the meeting.
3. The employees attending the meeting should be admitted into membership. In this regard it is well to keep in mind section 1(1) of the Act which defines a union member to include a person who has applied for membership in the union and on his own behalf paid to the union at least $1.00 in respect of initiation fees or monthly dues.
4. The constitution should be ratified by a vote of the members.
5. Officers should be elected pursuant to the constitution.

[¶ 36] The steps outlined in paragraph 11 of the decision in *Associated Hebrew Schools* do not represent the only procedure by which a group of employees can create the structure envisaged by the Act. The Board has recognized that the web of contractual relationships described in those decisions can arise in more than one manner. . . . However, it is of fundamental importance that a contractual relationship be created and maintained. As the Board observed in *Associated Hebrew Schools,* the maintenance of the organization's formal structure requires that new members become party to the contractual relationship by agreeing to its terms, and that can only occur if the terms of that relationship are clear and capable of being ascertained by current proposed members.

[¶ 37] The collection of rules for this contractual relationship is usually called the "constitution" or "by-laws" of the union organization; and it is normally supposed that such rules will be reduced to writing. . . . That is why section 86 of the Act provides:

86. The Board may direct a trade union, council of trade unions or employers' organization to file with the Board within the time prescribed in the direction a copy of its con-

stitution and by-laws and a statutory declaration of its president or secretary setting forth the names and addresses of its officers.

Implicit in this provision is the expectation not only that a trade union will have a constitution or by-laws, or both, but also that the constitution and by-laws, if any, will be reduced to writing.

. . .

[¶ 40] I do not doubt that for many years the Committee has been a useful mechanism by which the employer communicates with employees and explores their concerns. . . .

[¶ 41] However, I am simply unable to conclude on the evidence before me that the Committee — an entity without constitution, assets, or employee members (other than themselves) — possesses a structure sufficiently formal for it to be described as a "trade union" within the meaning of the Act. Indeed, I find that the intervenor is correctly named: it is "a committee" that (on the evidence) was initially fostered by the employer, is intimately engaged with the employer, and is routinely supported by the employer in all of its functions; moreover, without that employer support or "membership" from the employees as a whole, it simply would not be able to function at all. . . .

[¶ 43] A certificate will issue to the applicant, United Steelworkers of America. . . .

* * *

Requiring employees to follow certain traditional procedures in setting up a union can constitute a trap for those who are unwary or inexperienced. For example, in early cases, the Ontario board held that an association could not be considered a trade union if its officers were appointed before its constitution had been adopted. Today, labour boards appear to be insisting on only a minimum of formality, and to be concerned primarily with ensuring the existence of a viable organization that can function as a bargaining agent.

The statutory definitions of a trade union do require that its objects include "the regulation of relations between employers and employees." In *Graham Cable TV/FM, Toronto v. Cable Television Workers Association* (1987), 14 Can. L.R.B.R. (N.S.) 250, the Canada board held that a particular association of employees was not a trade union within the meaning of the *Canada Labour Code* because its true aim was not to regulate employer/employee relations but merely to get the incumbent union out. In the alternative, the board found that there was enough employer influence to impair the fitness of the association to represent the employees.

A more controversial question is whether union status will be reserved for organizations that are democratic in their structure and practices. The meaning of democracy in the context of internal union affairs, and the extent to which labour boards and courts will seek to enforce democratic governance within unions, will be adverted to in Chapter 10, especially in section 10:500. By and large, except for cases of discrimination on grounds prohibited by human rights legislation, labour boards have taken the approach that they do not have the authority to deny trade union status to an otherwise bona fide workers' organization for the reason that it fails to adhere to democratic forms and practices in its internal decisionmaking.

4:420 Employer Influence

Management interference with, or domination of, unions is prohibited by labour relations legislation as an unfair labour practice, as we will see in Chapter 5 below. The policy of protecting union autonomy to ensure that unions act as the authentic voice of employees is also reflected in the denial of employee status to members of management, as we have seen in section 4:330 above, and by statutory provisions preventing employer-dominated organizations from being certified as trade unions.

An example of the latter type of provision is section 15 of the Ontario *Labour Relations Act, 1995*, which forbids certification of a union "if any employer . . . has participated in its formation or administration or has contributed financial or other support to it." This prohibition posed a problem in the sort of situation that frequently occurred with the spread of unionization outside the traditional blue collar context: the effort by an employee association which had included managers among its membership to evolve into a trade union in order to be certified as bargaining agent. For a time, the Ontario Labour Relations Board attempted a sort of compromise resolution to that problem. It held that the association's constitution must exclude from membership anyone who fell within the managerial exclusion, but that the board would not "require an organization seeking recognition as a trade union to correctly guess the [managerial or non-managerial] status . . . of those it is seeking to organize, and to purge [before applying for certification] all those who might be managerial or risk the imposition of the s. [15] bar:" *Children's Aid Society of Metropolitan Toronto*, [1977] 1 Can. L.R.B.R. 129, at 130. In other words, if an association happened to have some people in it who were found by the labour board to be managers but who were not doing management's bidding within the association, that would not disqualify the association from certification if the association's rules made such people ineligible for membership and if they were expelled when their managerial status became known.

Later, the labour board went further, holding that "the fact that the constitution of the Association permits the admission of non-employees and that it in fact does so would not in itself prevent the Association from being considered a trade union within the meaning of the Act:" *Board of Education for the City of Toronto*, [1994] OLRB Rep. August 1098, at paragraph 11. "[T]he structure of the Act," the board said (at paragraph 10), "does not merely tolerate membership by non-employees, it contemplates it." The board concluded (at paragraph 9): "In short, the . . . composition of an organization's membership, although in certain circumstances relevant to the question of whether a trade union is *dominated* by the employer . . . does not enter into the question as to whether that organization is a trade union."

* * *

As is noted earlier in this chapter, developments in technology and the organization of work, and the challenges of globalization, have called into question the appropriateness of the law's continuing allegiance to a model of labour relations that requires an arm's length relationship and an adversarial approach. Employers seeking to capitalize on the desire of their employees for increased responsibility and input into decision-making have instituted a variety of employee participation programs, often giving individual workers or teams responsibility over matters previously dealt with by lower level management. Are employees who have this sort of role in the new economy properly excluded from trade union representation? Along these lines, the Canada Labour Relations Board has held that an employee organization does not have to be committed to an adversarial form of collective bargaining in order to qualify as a trade union: *British Columbia Transit and Transit Management Assn.* (1990), 6 Can.L.R.B.R. (2d) 1 (B.C.L.R.B.). There are few decided cases in this area, perhaps because unions have not often been able to mount successful organizing campaigns in workplaces that use new economy management practices.

Chapter 5: **The Right to Join a Union**

5:100 A HISTORICAL NOTE

This chapter examines the protection afforded by law to the right of employees to choose collective representation by a trade union. The current legal safeguards were developed against a historical backdrop of strenuous and sometimes violent resistance by employers (and at times by government as well) to union organizing efforts — efforts which themselves were not always free of coercive elements. The following excerpt describes a violent episode in a union recognition dispute in Estevan, Saskatchewan, in 1931.

S. Hanson, "Estevan 1931" in I. Abella, ed., *On Strike: Six Key Labour Struggles in Canada, 1919–1949* (Toronto: James Lorimer, 1974) 33 at 43–51

With the formation of a branch of the MWUC [Mine Workers' Union of Canada] in the Souris coal field, a crisis arose that eventually culminated in the September 8 walkout. The operators of the large mines adamantly refused to recognize the new organization as a body with constituted authority to negotiate on behalf of the miners. The miners were equally adamant in their refusal to negotiate independently of their union. When requested by the union to attend a joint meeting of all operators and miners' representatives in the Estevan Town Hall at 8:30 P.M. on September 3 for the purpose of reaching an agreement on hours of work, wages and living conditions, only the operators of six smaller mines complied. The operators of the six deep-seam mines stated:

> We will not meet you [Sloan] or any representative of an organization such as yours which, by your own statement, boasts a direct connection with the 'entire Workers' Unity League and the Red Internationale of Soviet Russia.'

Under these circumstances, the union decided to use its ultimate weapon and voted to cease work at midnight on September 7, 1931. . . .

When mine operators in the Souris coal field awoke on the morning of September 8, only one was in operation. Because Truax-Traer did not employ men underground and its employees were non-union, it was not directly affected by the work stoppage. Sloan intimated that the fifty men engaged in stripping coal and laying track there would be allowed to continue working despite the union's call for a one hundred per cent walkout. He warned, however, that there would be trouble if any attempt were made to have the men load or ship coal. The union further stated that it was prepared to permit coal to be shipped to Dominion Electric Power and the Estevan Hospital, but would vigorously oppose shipments destined for outside markets. Provision was also made for local supply. Soon after the strike began, union officials granted the owners of several hillside mines permission to supply coal for local consumption, and to fill orders from farmers within a twenty-five mile radius of Estevan.

Despite the gestures of goodwill by the union towards those in the vicinity of the coal field who might require fuel, and despite the sympathetic response to the plight of the striking miners by workers and others elsewhere, suspicions quickly arose that the strike might not be altogether peaceful. Hence, to assist the two-man local detachment in quelling any future disturbance, a squad of four RCMP officers arrived in Estevan from Regina at noon on September 8.

As the strike progressed and tension mounted, additional reinforcements were sent to the strike zone. A dozen RCMP under the command of Detective Staff-Sergeant Mortimer arrived and began operating twenty-four-hour-a-day patrols throughout the district for the stated purpose of maintaining law and order. In addition, the Saskatchewan Coal Operators' Association engaged a private force of thirteen special constables to assist police in protecting mine property. . . .

Despite the increasing number of law-enforcement personnel in the district, the coal operators were dissatisfied. Morfit in particular believed that the RCMP were handling the situation poorly. Morfit, 'an American with extreme ideas who has had experience in the Pensylvania [sic] USA strikes,' reportedly stated that 'if this was in the States it would soon be settled . . . the strikers would be mowed down with machine guns if they carried on the way they do up here.'

At the conclusion of a conference held September 18, the coal operators issued a statement charging that the absence of adequate police protection had prevented the reopening of the mines. A few days later, the operators requested that additional police be sent to the strike sector 'to insure protection to life, property and the peaceful operation of our industries.' Their plea fell on deaf ears. The acting attorney-general, the Honourable Howard McConnell, seemingly of the opinion that the Saskatchewan government was not responsible for breaking strikes, stated that the government had been and still was according the mine owners ample police protection in the Estevan district coal field.

At about the same time, M.S. Campbell, chief conciliation officer with the Canada Department of Labour, arrived in Estevan. After a brief conference with the coal operators, he obtained their assurance that if the miners agreed to return to work pending an investigation of their grievances, they would be reinstated in their former positions without discrimination. However, when it became obvious that the operators would not recognize the union, negotiations collapsed and Campbell proceeded to Regina to meet with provincial authorities. Testifying later before a royal commission, Dan Moar, a miner and officer of the MWUC local, stated that upon his arrival Campbell told the miners' committee that the royal commission, headed by Judge E.R. Wylie of Estevan, which had just been appointed to inquire into the labour dispute, could not proceed until the men resumed work. He quoted Campbell as saying that 'the government wasn't going to spend money if we wouldn't go back to work. . . .' When told the men would not do so, Campbell allegedly said: 'If that is your attitude, I am through with you, I leave this morning.' Thus, the stalemate continued and the stage was set for violence.

On September 28, information was conveyed to Estevan Police Chief McCutcheon that the miners intended to hold a 'nuisance parade' in Estevan the following day. The parade was to be held for the purpose of dramatizing the miners' plight in order to gain local support, and to advertise a mass meeting scheduled for the evening of the twenty-ninth in the town hall, at which time Anne Buller, a WUL [Workers' Unity League of Canada] organizer from Winnipeg, would address the assembly. As no application for a permit to hold the parade had been made, Mayor Bannatyne called a special session of the town council for the morning of the twenty-ninth to discuss it, as well as the matter of renting the hall to the strikers. After brief deliberations, council, it has been said, passed a resolution prohibiting the renting of the town hall to the miners, banning the parade and authorizing the Estevan police and the RCMP to prevent any such demonstration. . . .

At 1:30 P.M., on the twenty-ninth, some two hundred miners, all of them evidently unaware that they would soon be confronted by the police, assembled in Bienfait intent on motoring to Estevan, accompanied by their wives and children, to interview Mayor Bannatyne regarding prohibition of the public meeting scheduled that evening in the town hall. At two o'clock the group departed for Crescent Collieries, three miles distant. That mine had been chosen for a rendezvous and soon cars and lorries bearing strikers and their families arrived from various points throughout the district. Here the men boarded lorries, a few of which were draped with Union Jacks, and the women and children entered automobiles for the seventeen-mile journey. The caravan, consisting of thirty or forty vehicles, extending for a distance of a mile along the highway and moving at a speed aptly described as that of a funeral cortège, then threaded its way through the idle mining district, picking up recruits en route. As it approached Estevan, banners proclaiming 'We will not work for starvation wages,' 'We want houses, not piano boxes' and 'Down with the company stores' were unfurled.

Meanwhile, in Estevan the police were reportedly charting strategy to prevent any violation of the town council's edict forbidding any parade or demonstration. They are said to have decided that should any attempt to demonstrate occur, they would concentrate their forces at the limits of the town to prevent the striking miners from entering. Reinforcements had arrived intermittently during the strike, and by the twenty-ninth Inspector Moorhead had forty-seven RCMP under his command. The police were equipped with thirty rifles (one hundred rounds of ammunition per rifle), forty-eight revolvers, forty-eight riding crops and four machine guns capable of firing three hundred shots per minute. Rumours were prevalent that the police also were holding a stock of tear-gas bombs in readiness.

Shortly before 3 P.M., three to four hundred striking miners plus members of their families reached the outskirts of the town. The motorcade approached Estevan from the east on Highway 39 and proceeded west along Fourth Street, the principal thoroughfare, to Souris Avenue, where twenty-two policemen had formed a cordon across the street. Chief McCutcheon approached the lead vehicle and told the strikers: 'Now boys youse had better pull back home for we are not going to allow you to parade through town. . . .' During the ensuing argument, McCutcheon apparently grabbed hold of Martin Day and attempted to pull him down off the lorry. While some of his colleagues were engaged in holding Day back, another struck McCutcheon in the face and knocked him to the ground. It was at this point that McCutcheon ordered Day's arrest and the initial struggle began. The strikers leaped from the lead truck and, led by Martin Day, who shouted: 'Come on boys, come on, give it to them,' rushed the arresting officers.

Almost simultaneously, the fire brigade was called to the scene. Their intervention, however, proved both unavailing and tragic. After a brief encounter, five miners succeeded in driving the firemen from the equipment and prevented the anticipated drenching. One striker climbed up on the engine and declared it 'captured.' He was shot dead on the spot.

Striking miners and their women, wielding clubs and throwing stones and other missiles, then launched the final assault. Hopelessly outnumbered and unable to halt the advancing crowd, the police retreated step by step, firing warning shots above the heads of the demonstrators and at their feet. It was not until the police, 'with blood streaming down their faces,' stood with their backs to the town hall that Inspector Moorhead, accompanied by a squad of about thirty RCMP, arrived on the scene from Truax-Traer. The police then took the offensive and by 4:15 P.M. the mob had been dispersed, leaving in its wake some wounded, dead and dying, and sixty thousand dollars' damage to store fronts, light standards and the fire-fighting equipment.

The grim toll of the battle consisted of three dead and twenty-three injured. Nick Nargan, a twenty-five-year-old miner from Taylorton, died instantly from a bullet in the heart; Julian Gryshko, age twenty-six, died of abdominal bullet wounds. Pete Markunas, a Bienfait miner aged twenty-seven, died in Weyburn General Hospital two days later as a result of bullet wounds to the abdomen. Eight other miners, four bystanders and one RCMP constable also suffered bullet wounds. In addition, eight RCMP personnel and Chief McCutcheon were injured by weapons wielded and thrown by the strikers.

[Reprinted by permission.]

✳ ✳ ✳

Partial accounts of the history of resistance to unionization can be found in J. Fudge and E. Tucker, *Labour Before the Law: The Regulation of Workers' Collective Action in Canada, 1900–1948* (Toronto: Oxford University Press, 2001).

Before the Second World War, a strike or the threat of a strike was the only way for a group of employees to compel a reluctant employer to engage in collective bargaining. Since the 1940s, however, legislation across Canada has required an employer to negotiate with a trade union that has been certified by a labour relations board to represent employees in a defined "bargaining unit." To be certified, the union must usually have the support of a majority of the employees in that unit. How a bargaining unit is defined, and how majority support is determined, will be addressed in Chapter 6. An employer's duty to bargain with a certified union is dealt with in Chapter 7. For the purposes of the present chapter, the important point is that employees no longer need to strike to obtain recognition of their chosen union. Indeed, as is discussed in Chapter 8, recognition strikes are now illegal.

Because an employer is legally obliged to recognize and bargain with a certified trade union, and because many employers prefer not to bargain collectively, management representatives have an incentive to prevent the union from obtaining or retaining the majority support on which its collective bargaining rights are based. Labour relations legislation restricts anti-union activities by an employer during an organizing campaign, and also before and after that campaign — indeed, at any time. Conduct that violates these restrictions is commonly called an unfair labour practice. The legislation also prohibits union unfair labour practices, including improper conduct in attempting to win new members. The focus of most of this chapter is on unfair labour practices during organizing campaigns. Later chapters will deal with such practices at other times.

The regulation of employer unfair labour practices during an organizing campaign rests in large part on the premise that such conduct unduly influences employee choice for or against collective bargaining. That premise was questioned by an American empirical study published in 1976 — *Union Representation Elections: Law and Reality* by Julius G. Getman, Stephen B. Goldberg, and Jeanne B. Herman (New York: Russell Sage Foundation). That study reached the controversial conclusion that illegal employer tactics did not significantly affect the result in a sample of certification votes conducted by the U.S. National Labor Relations Board (NLRB). The following extract comments on that study and on a subsequent one.

Paul Weiler, "Promises to Keep: Securing Workers' Rights to Self-Organization under the NLRA" (1983) 96 Harv. L. Rev. 1769 at 1782–86

[In] *Union Representation Elections: Law and Reality* . . . , Getman and his co-authors concluded that even the most egregious of illegal employer tactics had no discernible impact on the results of NLRB representation elections.

The authors selected a sample of thirty-one hotly contested campaigns from the period 1972–1973. In each unit, shortly after the NLRB had directed a vote, the authors interviewed the employees about whether they had signed a union card and how they intended to vote. The authors then gathered and evaluated information about the ensuing campaign, and finally, after the election, reinterviewed the employees about their impressions of the campaign and how they had actually voted. The authors concluded that the votes of more than 80% of the employees, and hence the results in twenty-nine of the thirty-one elections, could have been predicted from precampaign attitudes and intentions. The other side of the coin was that the campaign was discovered to have very little impact; the employees had scant recall of the issues, and even illegal employer coercion of the most serious kind did not affect a significant proportion of the votes. The importance Getman and his co-authors attributed to their empirical findings can be seen in the policy recommendation they made — a systematic deregulation of the representation election.

On their face, the Getman findings pose a major challenge to my argument that discriminatory discharges and other forms of coercive behavior by American employers have significantly contributed to the steep decline in union success under the NLRA [National Labor Relations Act]. A closer look at the Getman study, however, reveals two critical flaws in its analysis. The first consists in the study's appraisal of the evidence of the impact of coercive campaigning by employers. The authors actually found that, among the surveyed workers who had indicated before the campaign either that they were undecided or that they favored the union, the percentage of votes against unionization was somewhat higher after an illegal employer campaign than after a clean one. The magnitude of this difference, however, was too small to pass a 99% test of statistical significance in such a limited sample. Thus, the authors asserted, one could not conclude with certainty that the observed relation was attributable to anything but chance.

This sort of statistical judgment is hardly sufficient for the making of legal policy. It may be legitimate for Getman and his co-authors to conclude that their own data do not demonstrate with certainty that employer coercion affects employee voting, but it is entirely unjustified to infer from that fact alone that the contrary is true. The failure to find a statistically significant connection between employer intimidation and employee votes in this limited sample neither proves that there is no such relationship nor provides a basis on which to argue that we may safely abandon efforts to protect employee choice. Legal policy must almost invariably be formulated in the absence of absolute certainty about the causes and effects of social phenomena. Given the inherent plausibility of the notion that employees will respond to threats to the jobs that are crucial to their lives, and given that the data in the Getman study indicate that it is more likely than not that such threats do affect employee votes, it is only prudent to take steps that will ensure freedom of choice in the workplace.

In any event, the data gathered by Getman and his co-authors have been used by another scholar, William Dickens, to calculate the actual probabilities that the employer campaigns had varying levels of impact. Dickens' best estimate was that, in the average campaign studied, unfair labor practices reduced the number of pro-union votes by 4%. The reduction was 15% when the unfair labor practices took the form of specific threats or actions against union supporters. Furthermore, when both legal and illegal practices were taken into account, it was more than 99% certain that the typical employer campaign reduced by at least 5% the probability that the average worker would vote for unionization, and it was more than 90% certain that the campaign reduced that probability by at least 10%.

Some might argue that effects of this magnitude do not warrant the kind of concern that the NLRB, the courts, and the Congress have shown for the trends of the last decade. But such a quick dismissal would be unfounded. The importance of the campaign lies in its effect on the ultimate election verdict, and a small shift in the number of workers voting for union representation may have a substantial effect on the number of union victories. This possibility points to the second crucial flaw in the analysis by Getman and his co-authors: their focus on the average voter rather than the election verdict. Their procedure was to interview each employee before and after the campaign, correlate any changes in his decision about union representation with the type of campaign to which he was exposed, and then simply aggregate these results across all the campaigns in order to determine the effect of the campaign on the average voter. The number of election results changed by employer coercion, however, depends not only on how many votes are affected in all campaigns combined, but also on how close the elections are and on how the affected voters are distributed among the different employee units.

The distribution of affected voters is unlikely to be random. Employers' efforts to influence workers' votes will probably be concentrated on swing voters in close elections; and it is in close elections, when workers believe that their votes will really make a difference, that they may pay more attention to the employer's threats about the dire consequences of a union victory. Moreover, employees are affected by peer group support and pressure. Intimidation is more likely to be effective in a unit in which enthusiasm for collective bargaining is marginal than in a unit in which the union enjoys overwhelming support.

The elections studied by Getman and his co-authors show how shifts among small numbers of critically located voters can have large effects on the overall success of union organizing efforts. The unions won just over one-fourth (eight of thirty-one) of the elections studied. To win a majority of those elections, the unions would have had to be successful in eight more campaigns. A shift of only 2% of the total votes cast in the thirty-one elections, if those 2% had been carefully allocated, would have been sufficient to provide the eight additional victories. This simple calculation demonstrates that even a slight impact from employer unfair labor practices may seriously reduce union success in a representation system based on the rule that the majority vote wins and the winner takes all.

Employing a more sophisticated methodology than my back-of-the-envelope calculation, the Dickens study tested for the multiplier effect that marginal changes in employee support had on election results. Dickens used the Getman study's background information about plant settings and employee attitudes to run computer simulations of each of the thirty-one elections. The elections were simulated once on the basis of the campaigns that were actually conducted, a second time on the assumption that illegal practices took place in all campaigns, and a third time on the assumption that all campaigns were clean.

Dickens' results suggest a starkly different conclusion from that reached by Getman and his co-authors. Dickens found that unions would have won 46% to 47% of the elections if the employer had campaigned entirely cleanly (and 53% to 75% of the elections if there had been no campaign at all), but only 3% to 10% if every employer had campaigned with the highest intensity and greatest illegality identified in the sample. Ironically, then, the raw data that Getman and his coauthors so carefully gathered point to precisely the opposite conclusion from the one they drew. A protracted representation campaign, punctuated by discriminatory discharges and other reprisals against union supporters, can have a pronounced effect on the ultimate election verdict.

[Copyright © 1983 by the Harvard Law Review Association.]

* * *

The following is an excerpt from a report which considered whether American labour law met international human rights standards on the protection of freedom of association.

Human Rights Watch, *Unfair Advantage: Workers' Freedom of Association in the United States under International Human Rights Standards*, (2000), Part I: "Summary — Policy and Reality," online at http://www.hrw.org/reports/2000/uslabor

The NLRA declares a national policy of "full freedom of association" and protects workers' "right to self-organization, to form, join, or assist labor organizations, to bargain collectively through representatives of their own choosing, and to engage in other concerted activities for the purpose of collective bargaining or other mutual aid or protection . . .".

The NLRA makes it unlawful for employers to "interfere with, restrain, or coerce" workers in the exercise of these rights. It creates the National Labor Relations Board (NLRB) to enforce the law by investigating and remedying violations. All these measures comport with international human rights norms regarding workers' freedom of association.

The reality of NLRA enforcement falls far short of its goals. Many workers who try to form and join trade unions to bargain with their employers are spied on, harassed, pressured, threatened, suspended, fired, deported or otherwise victimized in reprisal for their exercise of the right to freedom of association.

Private employers are the main agents of abuse. But international human rights law makes governments responsible for protecting vulnerable persons and groups from patterns of abuse by private actors. In the United States, labor law enforcement efforts often fail to deter unlawful conduct. When the law is applied, enervating delays and weak remedies invite continued violations.

Any employer intent on resisting workers' self-organization can drag out legal proceedings for years, fearing little more than an order to post a written notice in the workplace promising not to repeat unlawful conduct and grant back pay to a worker fired for organizing. . . . Many employers have come to view remedies like back pay for workers fired because of union activity as a routine cost of doing business, well worth the price of getting rid of organizing leaders and derailing workers' organizing efforts. As a result, a culture of near-impunity has taken hold in much of U.S. labor law and practice.

[© 2000 Human Rights Watch. Reprinted by permission.]

5:200 PROVING AN ILLICIT MOTIVE

An illicit motive is an essential ingredient of some unfair labour practices in Canada. For example, labour relations legislation commonly prohibits employers from dismissing or discriminating against an employee because he or she is a member of a trade union. See section 94(3) of the *Canada Labour Code* and section 72(a) of the Ontario *Labour Relations Act, 1995*. In many jurisdictions, an employer alleged to have violated such a provision bears the burden of proving the absence of anti-union animus. See section 98(4) of the federal statute and section 96(5) of the Ontario statute.

Duchesneau v. Conseil de la Nation huronne-Wendat [1999] CIRB No. 1 (Canada Industrial Relations Board)

HANDMAN and GUILBEAULT, Vice-Chairs, and GOURDEAU, Member

¶ 1 Mr. Guy Duchesneau filed a complaint pursuant to section 97 of the Code alleging he was suspended and then dismissed from his employment by the Huronne-Wendat Nation because of his union activities.

¶ 2 The reasons provided by the Band Council relate to financial irregularities and other serious violations allegedly committed by Mr. Duchesneau in the exercise of his duties.

¶ 3 Mr. Duchesneau, an employee of the Huronne-Wendat Nation since 1985, had been actively involved in the organization of the workplace. His involvement stemmed from his participation in the Band's human resources file. As one of two elected representatives, he had negotiated on the employees' behalf in 1996 and ultimately an agreement governing Band policy on human resources management was concluded in August of that year. However, the election of a new Band Council in September 1996 resulted in disagreement with many of the negotiated issues and, at an employee meeting held with respect to the position adopted by the new Band Council, the question of unionization arose. Mr. Duchesneau, who had already been in contact with a representative of the Confederation of National Trade Unions (CNTU), was responsible for initiating the union at the Band and was its principal organizer. Two certification applications were presented with respect to the Band's employees, the first being filed on June 13, 1997.

¶ 4 Mr. Duchesneau, who was suspended at the end of May 1997 and subsequently dismissed, considers that the decision to suspend and terminate his employment was motivated by the employer's knowledge of his role as a union organizer and its attempt to interfere in the union's activities. . . .

¶ 5 Mr. Guy Duchesneau began working for the Band in July 1985 as a social service technician and was promoted in 1992 to the position of social service advisor which he held until his dismissal on November 18, 1997. In this capacity, he was responsible for various services in the social sector. One such service was a home assistance program which had an annual budget of $200,000. This program provided residents of the community, needing assistance, with a resource person who would do their household chores for them.

¶ 6 Mr. Duchesneau had "hands on" involvement with this program. He evaluated the beneficiary's needs and determined the services and number of hours to be provided. While the choice of resource person was left to the beneficiary, if unable to do so, Mr. Duchesneau would recommend someone and initiate the service. He had overall responsibility for assuring that the requisite services had been rendered as set out in the monthly reports completed by both the beneficiary and the assistant. Following a verification of these reports, a cheque from the Band was made payable to the beneficiary. It was the beneficiary who then paid his or her assistant.

¶ 7 In May 1997, Mr. Richard Picard, Director of Health and Social Affairs and Mr. Duchesneau's superior, was advised by a delegate chief that Mr. Duchesneau was personally taking care of the financial affairs of Mr. George Edouard Picard, one of the program's beneficiaries. Mr. Richard Picard, concerned that such a practice could constitute a conflict of interest, demanded that Mr. Duchesneau cease providing this service. Following an exchange of correspondence between Mr. Richard Picard and Mr. Duchesneau and in light of Mr. Duchesneau's denial — that he was personally taking care of Mr. George Edouard Picard's financial affairs — which was co-signed by Mr. George Edouard Picard, Mr. Richard Picard closed his file on the matter.

¶ 8 Further information concerning Mr. Duchesneau's involvement in Mr. G.E. Picard's affairs provided by another delegate chief prompted Mr. Richard Picard to review that beneficiary's monthly records. Having noted different signatures for the beneficiary as well as for the same named resource persons, he brought the matter to the attention of the Band's Police Chief who asked the Quebec Provincial Police to carry out an investigation.

¶ 9 Following an investigation by the Quebec Provincial Police, Mr. Duchesneau was arrested on May 28, 1997, for fraud. When questioned by the police investigators, he admitted to having signed the names of resource persons but claimed he had the authority to sign the reports. Mr. Richard Picard suspended Mr. Duchesneau for an indefinite period of time without pay, the same day, and on June 12, 1997, Mr. Duchesneau was charged with forgery. The investigation continued and after finding a number of cheques made to the order of Mr. G.E. Picard had been deposited in the account of Mr. Duchesneau, further charges were laid on August 21, 1997.

¶ 10 Mr. Duchesneau's preliminary inquiry, set for the fall of 1997 was postponed. The Band Council delegated the Grand Chief as well as Mr. Richard Picard, Director of Health and Social Affairs, and Mr. Michel Picard, Controller, to meet with Mr. Duchesneau before making a decision with respect to Mr. Duchesneau's employment. Mr. Duchesneau was asked a number of questions related to the irregularities found and, in the presence of his lawyer, refused to respond. Following this meeting, the Band Council decided to dismiss Mr. Duchesneau and passed a resolution to that effect on November 18, 1997. Mr. Duchesneau was advised of his dismissal that same day on the grounds of having imitated the signatures of G.E. Picard and Raynald Beaupré, having authorized payment for services to Mr. G.E. Picard knowing that the services had not been rendered by the designated person and for having personally cashed cheques made to the order of G.E. Picard.

¶ 11 In response to questions relating to Mr. Duchesneau's role as a union organizer, Mr. Richard Picard testified that he knew that Mr. Duchesneau was an elected employee representative and believed he was involved in the certification application, but maintained that the decision taken had nothing to do with the unionization of the Band's employees.

¶ 12 Mr. Duchesneau stated that he has known Mr. G.E. Picard since his infancy and, over the years, had maintained a close friendship with him. Following surgery in 1994, Mr. G.E. Picard became a beneficiary of the home assistance program.

¶ 13 Mr. Duchesneau explained that he became personally involved when Mr. G.E. Picard told him that the only resource person he would accept was Mr. Duchesneau himself. Mr. Duchesneau initially considered such an arrangement to be problematic since he was responsible for managing the program. However, after discussing the matter with his friend, Mr. Raynald Beaupré, he began to provide the services required by Mr. G.E. Picard, after working hours, and signed Raynald Beaupré's name as the resource person, with Mr. Beaupré's knowledge and consent. He had signed on behalf of Mr. G.E. Picard when Mr. G.E. Picard who was hospitalized and unable to sign on his own had asked Mr. Duchesneau to pay his bills. As for the cheques from the Band addressed to Mr. G.E. Picard which were deposited in Mr. Duchesneau's account, Mr. Duchesneau stated that he was compensated by Mr. G.E. Picard for his work and had accepted payment by cheque rather than cash when he did not need cash. Mr. Duchesneau stated that it was known to the employees of the

Band that he was personally providing services for Mr. G.E. Picard, but he had never advised Mr. Richard Picard, his supervisor, that he was providing these services for remuneration.

¶ 14 Following the Board's hearing, Mr. Duchesneau was acquitted at a preliminary hearing of all criminal charges that had been laid against him.

. . .

¶ 17 The employer, while acknowledging Mr. Duchesneau's role as a union organizer, submits that there was no anti-union animus involved in suspending and terminating his employment. It maintains that the allegations of violations are serious. Mr. Duchesneau, who was responsible for the home assistance program, devised a scheme to pay himself from the community's funds for services, without the employer's knowledge. Given this breach of confidence, the employer claims the dismissal is founded.

¶ 18 Counsel for the complainant claims that Mr. Duchesneau was suspended and dismissed as a result of anti-union animus. He submits that we must consider the particular circumstances in which Mr. Duchesneau provided services for Mr. G.E. Picard as well as Mr. Duchesneau's prominent role in the two certification applications that were filed. He contends that Mr. Duchesneau is identified by everyone as the contact person with the CNTU and even though some elements exist which could bring the Band to question certain of Mr. Duchesneau's activities, the Band used it as a pretext to interfere with the union organizer's activities.

¶ 19 The Code provides employees with the fundamental right to select a bargaining agent and to opt for collective bargaining. In the context of a union organization drive, the Board is particularly careful to ensure that the rights and employment of those involved are protected. Consequently, when a complaint is filed pursuant to section 94(3) of the Code, the Board will examine the employer's behaviour to ensure that anti-union animus was not a consideration in the dismissal of the employee(s) concerned.

¶ 20 In this regard, even if anti-union animus is only a proximate cause, the employer will be found to have committed an unfair labour practice. The applicable test is described in *Yellowknife District Hospital Society et al.* . . . :

> . . . It is a rare experience for labour relations boards to hear an employer who cannot advance a justification for his act — e.g. failure to report to work one day, an act of insubordination to a superior, or merely a re-evaluation of the employee's performance which showed he did not maintain the standard desired. They may be proper motivations for employer actions but experience shows they are often relied upon around the time the employee is seeking to exercise or has exercised his right under section 110(1). To give substance to the policy of the legislation and properly protect the employee's right, an employer must not be permitted to achieve a discriminatory objective because he coupled his discriminatory motive with other non-discriminatory reasons for his act.
>
> For these reasons, if an employer acts out of anti-union animus, even if it is an incidental reason, and his act is one contemplated by section 184(3) (now section 94(3)), he will be found to have committed an unfair labour practice.

. . .

¶ 21   Pursuant to section 98(4) of the Code, where a complaint is presented in respect of an alleged failure by an employer to comply with section 94(3), the complaint is itself evidence that such a failure actually occurred and if the employer alleges that such failure did not occur, the burden of proof is on the employer.

¶ 22   Consequently, the employer bears the burden of proof. To refute this presumption, the employer must satisfy the Board that its actions were not in any way intended to interfere with an employee's legitimate exercise of a right conferred by the Code. . . .

¶ 23   The Board's task is not to determine the appropriateness of the action taken or whether the reasons provided by an employer constitute just cause for dismissal. Rather its role is to determine whether anti-union animus played any part in the decision taken. As the Board stated in *Air Alma Inc.* . . . :

> . . . The reasons for dismissal may very well be justified. Nevertheless, anti-union animus, even if only incidental to the decision to terminate an employee's employment, compromises the objectivity of this decision and makes the employer guilty of unfair labour practice.

. . .

¶ 26   Notwithstanding the employer's argument that Mr. Duchesneau's employment was terminated for just cause, the Board must determine whether or not the decision was also tainted by anti-union animus. Irrespective of the grounds an employer may have to discipline an employee, it is nevertheless guilty of an unfair labour practice if, in addition to cause, there existed any anti-union motivation. . . .

¶ 27   As already indicated, the employer pursuant to section 98(4) of the Code has the burden of proof. In this regard, the Board stated in *Halifax Grain Elevator Limited.* . . . :

> In this case, because section 98(4) places the burden of proof on the employer, it must provide to the Board an explanation for its actions which, on the balance of probabilities, will satisfy the Board that no anti-union animus is present in its decision to take these actions against employees which are covered by section 94(3) of the Code.

¶ 28   In light of the evidence, the Board concludes that the employer has failed to discharge the burden of proof it has pursuant to the Code. On the balance of probabilities, the Board does not find it probable that the complainant's union activities had nothing whatsoever to do with the employer's decision to suspend and terminate his employment.

¶ 29   It was well known that Mr. Duchesneau was involved in organizing a union at the Band. Although he had acted as an employee representative in an informal arrangement with the Band, unionization was a different matter as evidenced by the Chief's negative reactions when ultimately faced with the certification applications that were filed on behalf of the Band's employees.

. . .

¶ 31 . . . Despite the fact that the complainant's assistance to Mr. Picard had been ongoing for a number of years to the knowledge of several Band employees, coincidentally, Mr. Duchesneau's supervisor is alerted to Mr. Duchesneau's activities and irregularities by delegate chiefs during the organizing campaign, shortly before the application for certification is filed and an investigation is begun.

¶ 32 The employer contends that it sought to determine the validity of the allegations raised. However, the evidence does not satisfy the Board that the employer really sought to determine all the relevant facts in connection with the matter.

¶ 33 The employer stated that it was aware that Mr. Duchesneau was involved in the certification applications but that its decision had nothing to do with the unionization of the Band's employees. However, the indefinite suspension without pay or the termination of an employee during an organizing drive who is its leader often has a chilling effect on the organizing campaign. Such action can bring an ongoing drive to an end since it serves as a warning to potential members. . . .

¶ 34 In sum, while Mr. Duchesneau's behaviour was far from exemplary, the Board is not satisfied that Mr. Duchesneau's indefinite suspension without pay and dismissal were not motivated at least in part by the employer's desire to rid itself of a key union organizer and union supporter.

¶ 35 Accordingly, the Board unanimously finds that the employer, in suspending and terminating Mr. Duchesneau, contravened section 94(3)(a)(i) of the Code.

5:300 NON-MOTIVE UNFAIR LABOUR PRACTICES

Although some legislative provisions concerning unfair labour practices refer to motive, others are silent on this point. See, for example, section 94(1)(a) of the *Canada Labour Code* and section 70 of the Ontario *Labour Relations Act, 1995*. The latter section reads as follows:

> No employer or employers' organization and no person acting on behalf of an employer or an employers' organization shall participate in or interfere with the formation, selection or administration of a trade union or the representation of employees by a trade union or contribute financial or other support to a trade union, but nothing in this section shall be deemed to deprive an employer of his freedom to express his views so long as he does not use coercion, intimidation, threats, promises or undue influence.

Is an illicit motive an element of the offence created by this section? If not, does the section outlaw any employer conduct that has the effect of dissuading employees from unionizing or of otherwise dampening the union's activities, no matter why the employer engages in that conduct? The following case raises this question. Consider whether it offers a clear answer. The provisions of sections 64 and 66 of the Ontario statute in effect at the time were identical, respectively, to the current sections 70 and 72.

Canadian Paperworkers Union, Canadian Labour Congress and Its Local 305 v. International Wallcoverings, a Division of International Paints (Canada) Limited, [1983] O.L.R.B. Rep. 1316 at 1328–37

[The company kept its operations going during a legal strike by using agency-supplied strikebreakers who were picked up at secret locations each morning by the agency and driven to the plant in specially adapted vans. The strikers learned that the strikebreakers would be picked up at the Vesta Restaurant one morning, and a number of strikers showed up there at the pickup time. An altercation ensued.

The Board made the following findings of fact with respect to the nine strikers whose dismissal led to this complaint. Strikers D. McCarroll (local union president), Lutes (local union secretary), and Prewal kicked, punched, or otherwise assaulted strikebreakers. Striker M. McCarroll (local union vice-president) attacked and slightly damaged the agency's van, but did not (as the company alleged and perhaps believed) threaten a strikebreaker with a knife. Strikers Brinston, Carrier, and Mez were at the restaurant but did not participate in the attack on the strikebreakers or the van. Strikers Blanchard and Richard were found by the board not to have been at the restaurant at all. All nine of the strikers mentioned above were dismissed by the company's labour relations manager, Clayton, as soon as he was advised of the incident and of the names of the strikers who were thought to have been present.]

ADAMS, Chair: What becomes immediately apparent is the use in sections 66 and 70 of words suggesting a motive requirement whereas section 64 is expressed more in terms of effect. More specifically, section 66 uses the words 'because,' 'seeks' and section 70 the word 'seek.' These words are not to be found in section 64. Instead, section 64 refers to interference. That section is also a very general one cast in terms, inter alia, of interference with the formation, selection or administration of a trade union. On the other hand, sections 66 and 70 are more particular in scope, aimed at particular kinds of improper action which impede or prevent persons from exercising rights under the Act. The result is that any conduct that violates sections 66 and 70 arguably will also offend section 64 but the opposite will not necessarily be so. For this reason, the inter-relationship and scope of these sections (principally sections 64 and 66) are absolutely critical. If section 64 does not require an 'intent' to interfere and sections 66 and 70 do, complainants would be better off filing complaints only pursuant to section 64. The result would be, however, to read sections 66 and 70 out of the Act. This would be a dubious application of legislative intent. On the other hand, interpreting section 64 always to require motive gives little or no effect to the difference in language between the sections.

This tension accounts for the somewhat different treatment accorded to section 64 in [a number of board decisions]. For example in *A.A.S. Telecommunications* . . . , the then Chairman of the Board . . . read into the statute an exception for employer conduct 'that only incidentally affects a trade union.' In this manner the Board proposed, pursuant to section 64, to distinguish between legitimate and illegitimate management initiatives. Presumably an adverse impact on union activity would be characterized as 'incidental' where, relying on its expertise, the Board accepted the employer's action as classic business or collective bargaining activity not inconsistent with the scheme of the Act. In effect, the Board would 'balance' the conflicting interests of labour and management, honouring accepted relationships but being vigilant that intrusions on statutory entitlements have suitable justifications. In fact, labour board analysis of no-solicitation rules has tended to follow non-motive approach after an adverse effect has been established or inferred. This is particularly apparent from the touchstone American cases which have been referred to and relied upon in Canada. . . . However, we wish to stress that 'the balancing' has been more one of examining the record for a legitimate management interest to support the adverse impact on union activity. It has not usually involved a delicate weighing of legitimate but conflicting interests with labour boards being the final arbiters of the right policy mix. We know of no case in Canada or the United States in which a labour board has purported to balance a bona fide exercise of a managerial prerogative, for example, a layoff or subcontracting decision, against its impact on union activity. The no-solicitation cases have looked to identify the managerial interest in a sweeping no-solicitation rule over and above a simple reliance on property rights. Where such an interest is absent, there exists a significant imbalance in favour of the protected activity and this clear imbalance triggers a statutory violation. Indeed, this absence of a managerial interest is the same kind of a condition often justifying an inference of improper motive. The real balancing, in the no-solicitation cases, has been between property rights and statutory rights. Unfortunately, this point was not made in the A.A.S. case which in turn gave rise to a concern within the Board itself over the viability of an unrestrained balancing approach.

In *Skyline Hotels Limited* . . . , the Board indicated its concern about the open-ended nature of section 64 and its potential triggering by any bona fide management action having an adverse impact on trade union activity. In contrast to the *A.A.S.* decision, the *Skyline* decision proposed to avoid this possibility by implying in section 64 a motive requirement while noting that motive need not be established always by direct evidence. In this respect the decision stated . . . :

> The striking aspect of this section is that on its face it makes no mention of anti-union motive or purpose. It simply uses the word 'interfere,' which, in normal parlance, could be taken to connote either intentional or unintentional conduct. . . .
>
> But the Board has always had regard to industrial relations reality, and to the scheme of the Act as a whole, and has never interpreted the section in this manner. To do so would of course render meaningless the other specific provisions of the Act, such as section 58, which clearly require the finding of an anti-union motive. Any discharge of a union organizer, or perhaps of any employee during a campaign, for example, could be litigated successfully by a trade union under section 56, whether or not an anti-union motive could be shown under section 58. It is impossible to contemplate that section 56 creates that kind of unfair labour practice. . . .
>
> *In the absence of an anti-union motive, in other words, it is not a violation of the section if the employer's conduct simply affects the trade union in pursuit of an unrelated business purpose. . . .*

As has often been noted, however, the trade union will not in every case be required to prove by affirmative evidence the existence of an anti-union motive. This is so because the effect of certain types of conduct is so clearly foreseeable that an employer may be presumed to have intended the consequences of his acts . . . *Once such conduct has been established, then as a practical matter (and whether or not section 79(a) of the Act applies to the situation) the onus is upon the employer to come forward with a credible business purpose to justify the conduct. . . .* It is up to the Board then, in all the circumstances, to decide what the motive of the employer really was. [Emphasis added]

In comparing this statement to the *A.A.S.* approach, emphasis must be given to the *Skyline* observation that specific evidence of intent to interfere is not an indispensable element of proof. As the United States Supreme Court explained in *Radio Officers' Union v. NLRB* . . .

Both the Board and the courts have recognized that proof of certain types of discrimination satisfies the intent requirement. This recognition that specific proof of intent is unnecessary where employer conduct inherently encourages or discourages union membership is but an application of the common-law rule that a man is held to intend the foreseeable consequences of his conduct.

Also relevant is the fact that improper motive need not be the dominant purpose underlying disputed conduct for the Act to be breached. It is sufficient that employer conduct only be partially motivated by anti-union considerations. . . . [T]he combined effect of the mixed motive approach and legal inference can result in the striking down of employer conduct where the Board is not prepared to accept tendered evidence of a bona fide business purpose as a complete answer to the adverse impact on trade union activity complained of. However, usually the Board has been reluctant to find by legal inference a partial but improper motive where direct and persuasive evidence of an acceptable business justification has been established by a respondent employer. . . . [W]hen direct evidence of motive is not available, the Board is often required to engage in a form of balancing of conflicting interests in deciding whether to infer an improper (and possibly partial) motive on the evidence before it. Balancing is not eliminated by requiring that motive be established and this, on occasion, has caused motive to be referred to as 'fictive formality.' In this respect, labour law is little different from those other fields of law discussed above. As the United States Supreme Court stated in *NLRB v. Erie Resistor* . . . , the necessary intent may be:

founded upon the inherently discriminatory or destructive nature of the conduct itself. The employer in such cases must be held to intend the very consequences which foreseeably and inescapably flow from his actions and if he fails to explain away, to justify or to characterize his actions as something different than they appear on their face, an unfair labor practice charge is made out. . . . But, as often happens, the employer may counter by claiming that his actions were taken in the pursuit of legitimate business ends and that his dominant purpose was not to discriminate or to invade union rights but to accomplish business objectives acceptable under the Act.

Nevertheless, his conduct does speak for itself — it is discriminatory and does discourage union membership and whatever the claimed overriding justification may be, it carries with it unavoidable consequences which the employer not only foresaw but which he must have intended. As is not uncommon in human experience, such situations present a complex of motives and *preferring one motive to another is in reality the far more delicate task, reflected in part in decisions of this Court, of weighing the interests of employees in concerted activity against the interest of the employer in operating his business in a particular manner and of balancing in the light of the Act and its policy the intended consequences upon employee rights against the business ends to be served by the employer's conduct.* This essentially is the teaching of the court's prior cases dealing with this problem and, in our view, the Board did not depart from it. [Emphasis added.]

Thus the differences between the *A.A.S.* and *Skyline* decisions are not as great as may at first appear. Both approaches involve some balancing; both take into account the scheme of the Act; and, without direct evidence of motive, both approaches in effect require a considerable imbalance of interests in favour of the protected activity before a violation will be established. Unfortunately, however, it cannot be said that the requirement of motive in all claimed applications of section 64 is a superfluous detail and that both approaches always result in the same outcome. A non-motive approach to section 64, by requiring a substantial imbalance of interests, is capable of accommodating the concern that section 66 not be read out of the Act. Usually, the same imbalance will support an inference of improper motive which should negate the superiority of section 64 in the run of the mill section 89 case. On the other hand, the universal requirement of motive for section 64 can deprive the statute of the necessary flexibility to respond to certain troublesome situations which its otherwise general wording would provide.

For example, cases arise where employer conduct has a significant impact on protected activity and, while supported by good faith, does not reflect a persuasive or worthy business purpose. The balance between employer and employee interests may therefore strongly favour the protected activity, but the absence of a motive to interfere precludes a remedy. The no-solicitation cases are one example but not the only illustration of this problem. Indeed, the no-solicitation cases could probably be preserved on a compulsory motive test by employing a legal inference of intended interference notwithstanding the longstanding and consistent application of a no-solicitation rule without discrimination. But the problem transcends the no-solicitation cases. In *NLRB v. Burnup & Sims Inc.* . . . , two employees, who had been active in an attempt to organize the respondent's plant, were discharged as a result of the employer's sincere but mistaken belief that they had threatened to dynamite his plant if the organizational drive was unsuccessful. The situation was therefore somewhat analogous to the submission of the complainant in this case that, as a minimum, Blanchard and Richard were discharged because of a mistaken belief as to their presence at the restaurant. The same argument can also be made with respect to Mark McCarroll's termination to the extent it was based on his alleged threatening with Turnbull's knife. Justice Douglas for the United States Supreme Court in the *Burnup & Sims Inc.* case . . . ruled that a discharge for alleged misconduct arising out of protected activity constituted a violation . . . no matter what the employer's motive when it was shown that the misconduct never in fact occurred. . . .

Such cases can and should be considered pursuant to section 64. The only other course open to us would be to dismiss a complaint where mistake has been established and then carefully scrutinize the employer's subsequent hiring decision when the grievor reapplies for employment. It is our view that such an approach would be too indirect and would not encourage the requisite caution that an employer should exercise when administering discipline in the context of activity protected by this Act. Accordingly, we hold that the respondent violated section 64 of the Act in discharging R. Richard, R. Blanchard and M. McCarroll. They are to be immediately reinstated to their former positions. In the cases of Blanchard and Richard, they are to receive full back pay with interest in accordance with Board policy. McCarroll, however, is to be reinstated without back pay and on terms stated below having regard to the conduct it was established he engaged in. We will not condone such conduct with a back pay order. It is not, however, clear that he would have been terminated for only that misconduct having regard to the company's response to similar actions on the picket line. As for the argument that McCarroll would have been terminated simply for his presence at the restaurant our following findings are applicable.

In this case all of the grievors had been involved in picketing and strike activity which are fundamental rights under the Act. As the Board held in *Dominion Citrus and Drug Ltd.* . . . , lawful strike activity is protected by sections 3 and 66. Picketing, being a normal adjunct of a strike, is also protected. . . .

The respondent, however, contends that the manner in which the grievors attended the restaurant demonstrates that their arrival there was not a simple extension of the picket line, but rather a concerted attempt to interfere unlawfully with the pick-up and the workers involved. In this respect it relies on the numbers of striking employees involved, the way in which they blocked the van with their vehicles, and the physical assault on Mr. Turnbull and Mr. McCarthy. Counsel submits that they were discharged because they were all party to the unprovoked assaults and not for any other reason. We further note that this employer has not committed any earlier unfair labour practices and the collective bargaining relationship is not a recent one involving a first contract.

Subject to our comments on section 64 above, the Board is concerned with the actual motivation of the respondent in acting as it did. The Board must look beneath the stated purposes and focus on the facts established. Like many of the difficult cases brought before this Board, there is no direct evidence that the respondent was improperly motivated. The assault on two innocent persons was unprovoked and constituted serious misconduct. It therefore cannot be said that discharge was a clearly excessive response for those who engaged in the physical assault. The respondent was also under no legal obligation to arbitrate the discharges and trade union officials who engage in misconduct have no immunity from discipline under the Act. Whether Clayton knew that D. McCarroll and L. Lutes, the president and recording secretary, were the individuals along with Prewal who carried out the assault does not and cannot change the matter. These three grievors were the authors of their own misfortune and, on the evidence before us, we are not prepared to draw an inference that discharge was selected, in part, because of their official status and because they were engaged in a strike.

It is important to point out in light of the earlier discussion of principle, that even a non-motive section 64 analysis of these three discharges and refusal to arbitrate would not produce a different result to this point. We have found that, given the circumstances, the decision to discharge was not clearly excessive and by itself a hallmark of anti-union animus. The decision not to arbitrate merited no different characterization. Were we to intervene on the basis of section 64, the Board would be saying that all discipline issued during a strike must be submitted to arbitration because any potential excessiveness could deter participation in protected activity. This extreme sensitivity to protected activity might well be seen as insufficiently sensitive to improper picket-line misconduct and would not obligate trade unions to take all such issues to arbitration instead of placing them on the bargaining table. It would also be difficult to reconcile our sensitivity to any adverse impact on protected activity with the absence of a legal obligation to arbitrate arising under the Act. A clear imbalance in favour of protected activity does not exist. In this type of situation it seems to us that a non-motive approach to section 64 should be reserved for instances of clear mistake or for discipline clearly out of all proportion to the misconduct in issue.

The discharges of Carrier, Brinston and Mez are, however, a different matter. It is clear that these employees were simply present at the restaurant. They did not engage in the assault. We have found above that their presence at the restaurant would be an aspect of protected activity (in effect an adjunct of their strike) unless their sole motivation for attending was to facilitate the assault on Turnbull and McCarthy. M. McCarroll testified that the purpose of the mission to the restaurant was to identify the strike replacements given the strategy of concealment the respondent had adopted. This rationale is a plausible one notwithstanding their manner of arrival. In any event, the respondent decided on termination before it knew of the details of the incident and at no time did it engage in an inquiry which attempted to assess the motives of Carrier, Mez and Brinston in attending. In our view, the speed and severity of the respondent's response indicated a disposition that they had 'no business' being at the restaurant whatever their purpose. On the evidence before us we are prepared to infer that in expanding the circle of discharges beyond those who actually inflicted the assault, the respondent was at least in part objecting to their presence at the restaurant regardless of their motive and seizing upon a response that would make the greatest impression on other employees for the duration of the strike. Accordingly, we find that the respondent breached section 66 in dismissing these three employees. This conclusion would also apply to the Richard and Blanchard discharges. Had the respondent demonstrated to us that it was sensitive to the protected right of striking employees to attend at the restaurant unless their intent was to assault the employees, our conclusion would have been different because these three employees did not testify to permit us to assess their actual intent. There would have been no evidence on which to find a mistaken belief and no basis for inferring an improper motive. Indeed, because these employees did not testify before the Board, we have decided to reinstate them to their former positions with no compensation. We understand that they are facing criminal trials but we are uncomfortable with their decisions not to testify. In the circumstances, our concern for what happened at the restaurant leads us to tailor a remedy for these employees which conveys that concern. No compensation is directed.

Finally, we turn to the dismissal of M. McCarroll which in many respects is the most difficult matter. We have found the respondent to have been mistaken with respect to the alleged knife threat but, on his own admission, McCarroll assaulted the van. Nevertheless, there is no evidence before us that at the time the company decided on the discharges it was directing its attention to anything other than the assaults on the two strike replacements. Moreover, the company had not issued any discipline in relation to earlier mischief on the picket lines at the plant. On the evidence then we are prepared to infer that M. McCarroll was, in part, terminated for just being present at the restaurant in the same manner as Brinston, Mez and Carrier or he was terminated in the mistaken belief that he had physically threatened one of the strike replacements. His termination therefore offends sections 66 and 64 of the Act. However, we are not about to condone the misconduct he did engage in or the incident as a whole by awarding him any back pay. We are, however, prepared to direct his reinstatement to his former position provided that he reimburses or makes arrangements to reimburse the company for the damage inflicted on the van driven by Auger.

✻ ✻ ✻

In *Westinghouse Canada Ltd.*, [1980] 2 Can. L.R.B.R. 469 (O.L.R.B.) (Burkett, Alternate Chair), the employer decided to close a centralized manufacturing operation and open several new plants at different locations. The old plant was unionized, and the new ones were deliberately located in areas where there was little trade union presence. Having determined that the employer was motivated by anti-union considerations, the board concluded that it had committed an unfair labour practice. The board suggested (at page 497) that its conclusion might have been otherwise had the scenario unfolded in a slightly different way:

> Can an employer faced with economic difficulties caused by collective bargaining-related factors (wages, benefits, seniority, work practices etc.) act to remove himself from his collective bargaining relationship? It may well be that it is more profitable to operate without a union than with one but if an employer can react to this reality simply by moving his business the right of employees to engage in collective bargaining would be seriously undermined. What of the employer who is faced with an economic crisis caused by collective bargaining related factors, seeks relief from the union and is met with an unsympathetic or unsatisfactory response? Assuming that these factors could be established, the answer is by no means clear. The question, however, is not raised by the factors of this case. This company was not faced with an economic crisis and notwithstanding the constraints to productivity perceived by it, there is no evidence that the company ever raised its concerns with the trade union prior to making its decision to relocate.

In *Kennedy Lodge Nursing Home* (1980), 81 C.L.L.C. para. 16,078 (O.L.R.B.), the employer had contracted out its entire housekeeping and janitorial functions and had laid off sixteen of sixty-five employees represented by the union. Testimony led by the employer indicated that the decision was made to "save money." In response to the union's argument that the situation was indistinguishable from Westinghouse, the board wrote (at page 473):

> If the cost of doing business is too high in relation to the business revenues generated, the employer, who is motivated solely by correcting that imbalance, is not precluded by the Act from taking that action. Absent restrictions in the relevant collective agreement, business operations are not 'frozen' by the collective relationship so long as the action taken is not in any way motivated by the accomplishment of an unlawful objective.
>
> Business decisions must be made on the basis of the overall viability of an operation — one aspect of which might be the cost of labour. In the *Westinghouse* case it was found that the company's decision to relocate its operations was 'motivated in large part by anti-union considerations.' There was evidence in that case that the company had explicitly set non-union operation as a goal to be achieved. However, in the case before the Board there was no evidence that the fact that the employees had engaged in collective bargaining and were represented by a trade union played any part in the employer's decision to contract out some bargaining unit work. We accept Mr. Duncan's testimony on this point. *Westinghouse* makes it clear that an employer may discontinue operations for cause so long as the decision is not motivated by anti-union *animus*. A desire to save money and thereby increase profits is not equivalent to anti-union *animus* simply because the money saved would otherwise have been paid as wages to employees in the bargaining unit.

In "Equal Partnership in Canadian Labour Law" (1983) 21 Osgoode Hall L.J. 496 at 531, Brian Langille quoted the above passage, and added:

> All one can do is note that this simply collapses the distinction between discriminatory (anti-union) and economic motives, at least in a good number of cases. What is it that the Board wishes to have as evidence of anti-union animus? The rational employer, intent on avoiding the collective bargaining process for rational reasons is protected through this test. Applying this test, it is difficult to see that Westinghouse itself is correctly decided. It seems clear that, absent provisions in the collective agreement empowering the employer to unilaterally make those decisions, employer action violates the act and is a most blatant unfair labour practice. Contracting out to avoid the axiomatic effects of unionization is contracting out with an anti-union animus.

The same employer subsequently entered into an arrangement with an employment agency for the supply of nursing and health aides who would displace about two-thirds of the union's bargaining unit. In the unfair labour practice proceedings that ensued, Kennedy Lodge was found not to have relinquished control over employees performing these "core functions" of the business. Accordingly, the board concluded that it was still the employer or, in the alternative, that it shared control with the subcontractor and was a related employer within the meaning of the legislation. After making these findings the board went on to consider the relationship between contracting out for economic reasons and unfair labour practices. The board stated that where an employer retains control, "an inference can be easily drawn that the employer has acted to replace his bargaining unit employees in order to undermine their collective bargaining rights." Accordingly, Kennedy Lodge was found to have engaged in an unfair labour practice: *Kennedy Lodge Inc.*, [1984] O.L.R.B. Rep. 931.

5:400 ALTERATION OF WORKING CONDITIONS: THE STATUTORY FREEZE

Collective bargaining legislation generally provides for a two-stage "statutory freeze" that prohibits the unilateral alteration of terms and conditions of employment, first during the certification process and then during much of the bargaining process after certification. The pre-certification stage of the freeze begins when an application for certification is filed, and ends when the application is dismissed or soon after the certificate is issued — for example, under the Ontario *Labour Relations Act, 1995*, when notice to bargain is given. At that point, the bargaining stage of the freeze begins, and subsists until the parties are in a legal strike or lockout position. For convenience, both the pre-certification stage and the bargaining stage will be dealt with in this section, although the bargaining freeze will be mentioned again briefly in Chapter 7 (section 7:300).

The freeze aims to restrain employer conduct that may have the effect of undermining the union's organizing or negotiating efforts. Anti-union motive on the employer's part is not required for a breach of the freeze provisions, so even employer action that is taken for a legitimate business purpose may be illegal during the freeze period. It is important to understand that the freeze operates in addition to the other statutory unfair labour practice provisions, and that it supplements rather than displaces those provisions.

The application of the freeze to wages is illustrated by the federal labour board's decision in *Canadian Imperial Bank of Commerce v. Union of Bank Employees* (1979), 80 C.L.L.C. para. 16,002. The great majority of the bank's branches across Canada were not unionized. The union had applied for certification for two branches. The bank's established practice was to give an annual wage increase. During the freeze period after the certification application was filed, the bank gave such an increase to employees outside the two branches covered by the application. The union argued that the employer had violated section 124(4) of the *Canada Labour Code*, which read:

> Where an application by a trade union for certification as a bargaining agent for a unit is made in accordance with this section, no employer of employees in the unit shall, after notification that the application has been made, alter the rates of pay or any other term or condition of employment or any right or privilege of such employees until (a) the application has been withdrawn by the trade union or dismissed by the Board, or (b) thirty days have elapsed after the day on which the Board certifies the trade union as bargaining agent for the unit, except pursuant to a collective agreement or with the consent of the Board.

The denial of the expected wage increase was held to contravene this provision. The board said (at page 367):

Basically, it is 'business as before.' Here, business as before was the granting of the 9% general salary increase. If there are reasons and justifications for altering that situation, the employer can and must obtain the consent of the Board. The need for consent applies, in our view, to the normal day-to-day working conditions, including existing wage rates as well as the wage structure, hours of work, classifications, duties and functions, transfers, layoffs, promotions, etc.

As the following cases suggest, the "business as before" test is often not very helpful.

Simpsons Limited v. Canadian Union of Brewery, Flour, Cereal, Soft Drink and Distillery Workers (1985), 9 Can. L.R.B.R. (N.S.) 343 at 356–60

[The employer was a national department store chain, and was in financial difficulty. The union had recently acquired bargaining rights for one of the employer's warehousing and soft goods manufacturing facilities in Toronto. Just before the union gave notice to bargain, the employer gave layoff notice to more than one-tenth of its nationwide workforce, including a substantial number in the recently certified unit. The functions of most of the laid off employees in that unit were discontinued, but the functions of some of them (those in the drapery workroom) were contracted out. The union alleged a violation of section 79(2) (now section 86(2)) of the Ontario *Labour Relations Act*, which read:

> Where a trade union has applied for certification and notice thereof from the Board has been received by the employer, the employer shall not, except with the consent of the trade union, alter the rates of wages or any other term or condition of employment or any right, privilege or duty of the employer or the employees until,
>
> (a) the trade union has given notice under section 16, in which case subsection (1) applies; or
>
> (b) the application for certification by the trade union is dismissed or terminated by the Board or withdrawn by the trade union.

The board accepted that the layoffs were done without anti-union animus and for legitimate economic reasons. It went on as follows:]

> TACON, Vice-Chair: The Board could have interpreted s. 79 so as to freeze the precise conditions extant at the time the statutory provision was triggered. The Board, though, has consistently rejected that approach as an unreasonable interpretation of the legislation. In the Board's view, such an interpretation would effectively paralyze an employer's operations for the duration of the statutory freeze, a period which could be quite lengthy. In effect, the 'business as before' formulation in *Spar Aerospace* . . . was the Board's response to too expansive a view of employee privileges. To paraphrase *Spar Aerospace*, the employer's right to manage its operation was maintained subject to the condition that the operation conform to the pattern established when the freeze was triggered.
>
> 'Business as before' is a 'slippery' concept to apply to specific fact situations. The focus of the test is the 'pattern of operations,' the employer's 'practice.' Certainly, where the 'practice' is accurately embodied in an employer's policy manual, the application of 'business as before' has been relatively straightforward. . . . There have been other instances

where a practice has been so well entrenched so as to be beyond dispute: *Spar Aerospace*, supra, with respect to annual merit and annual cost of living increases. On the other hand, the 'increased parking fee' cases illustrate the difficulty in looking for a pattern. . . .

The freeze provisions catch two categories of events. There are those changes which can be measured against a pattern (however difficult to define) and the specific history of that employer's operation is relevant to assess the impact of the freeze. There are also 'first time' events and it is with respect to that category that the 'business as before' formulation is not always helpful in measuring the scope of employees' privileges. Some 'first time' events have been readily rejected by the Board, where, for example, the employer has instituted parking fees for the first time during the freeze. . . . On the other hand, the Board has upheld an employer's right to lay-off employees during the freeze (assuming there is no anti-union animus in the decision). . . . This right has been confirmed even where the first instance of layoff occurred during the freeze . . . ; and where the layoffs had occurred elsewhere in the employer's operation but not at the specific location in question. The respondent in the instant case cited *Corporation of the Town of Petrolia* . . . for the proposition that the employer may also contract out work for the first time during the freeze.

Instead of concentrating on 'business as before,' the Board considers it appropriate to assess the privileges of employees which are frozen under the statute, and thereby delimit the otherwise unrestricted rights of the employer, by focussing on the 'reasonable expectations' of employees. The 'reasonable expectations' approach, in the Board's opinion, responds to both categories of events caught by the freeze, integrates the Board's jurisprudence and provides the appropriate balance between employer's rights and employees' privileges in the context of the legislative provisions. . . .

The 'reasonable expectations' approach clearly incorporates the 'practice' of the employer in managing the operation. The standard is an objective one: what would a reasonable employee expect to constitute his or her privileges (or, 'benefits,' to use a term often found in the jurisprudence) in the specific circumstances of that employer. The 'reasonable expectations' test, though, must not be unduly narrow or mechanical given that some types of management decision (e.g., contracting out, workforce reorganization) would not be expected to occur every day. Thus, where a pattern of contracting out is found, it is sensible to infer that an employee would 'reasonably expect' such an occurrence during the freeze. . . .

Finally, the 'lay-off' cases are consonant with the 'reasonable expectations' approach. Very few, if any, work forces are entirely static; fluctuations in the size of the staff complement and its composition are the norm. Employers are generally expected to respond to changing economic conditions through the hiring, termination and attrition of employees. It is in this sense that it is 'reasonable' for employees to expect an employer to respond to a significant downturn in the business with layoffs (or terminations) even where such layoffs are resorted to for the first time during the freeze. The magnitude of the layoffs, of course, must be proportional or relative to the severity of the economic circumstances. Economic justification must be proven where relied on and there must be an absence of anti-union animus. It must also be stressed that, while the expectation of layoffs does not initially depend on the specific history of the employer's operation, there might well be specific evidence with respect to that employer which would negate the otherwise usual 'reasonable expectation' of layoffs in response to an economic downturn.

The 'reasonable expectations' approach also distinguishes between layoffs and contracting out. Where there was a pattern of contracting out, of course, there would be no violation of s. 79 where work was contracted out during the freeze. However, in the Board's opinion, while an employee would reasonably expect a layoff where there was no 'demand,' i.e., where there was an economic downturn, an employee would not reasonably expect that the work would continue to be performed for the benefit of the employer's operation but through contracting out. This is not to say that the employer does not have the right to contract out work during non-freeze periods, except as limited by a collective agreement. During the freeze, however, and unless there is a practice of contracting out, the employer's 'right' to contract out is limited by the employees' 'privilege' of performing the work if the work is to be performed for the benefit of the employer's operation. Contracting out is merely one of the ways an employer might otherwise increase productivity or efficiency which is caught by the freeze; reducing wages, instituting parking fees, ignoring its policy manual are other means of achieving such goals which are proscribed by the statutory provision.

The board concluded (at page 360) that the employees whose functions were discontinued should reasonably have expected to be laid off, given the company's widely known economic problems, and that the company had "demonstrated that the scale of the terminations was related to the economic conditions." However, the contracting out of the drapery workroom functions was held (at page 360) to be a breach of the freeze because it involved "the introduction of a new means to continue to have the work performed (which is outside the employees' reasonable expectations). . . ."

* * *

Does ascertaining the "reasonable expectations" of the employees amount to anything more than a simple determination of where the balance of interests lies? In the following excerpt, the Ontario Labour Relations Board considered this matter, and also considered the relationship of the statutory freeze to the general labour practice provisions and to the duty to bargain, which will be dealt with in Chapter 7. As the board notes, "business as before" is a problematic basis for limiting the scope of employer action once the union has been certified and the common law has been displaced.

Ontario Public Service Employees Union v. Royal Ottawa Health Care Group [1999] OLRB Rep. July/August 711

[The hospital admitted that it had reduced the level of employee benefits during the negotiation of a collective agreement — that is, during the bargaining stage of the statutory freeze. The union brought a complaint that the hospital's actions violated that freeze.]

MACDOWELL, Chair:

. . .

The hospital maintains that it was acting *bona fide*, in response to serious budgetary pressures, and that, in the circumstances, it fairly concluded that reducing benefits was a way of realizing savings, without impairing other employee entitlements and without impinging upon patient care. In the hospital's submission, it was merely carrying on"business as usual" - making modifications to employee benefits as it had done in the past, and in accordance with its own assessment of the situation.

The hospital says that it was entitled to proceed unilaterally. It needed to save money, and reducing benefits was the most appropriate way of doing so. . . .

. . .

[W]hile there may be an "overlap" between the various sections of the Act, in the sense that particular behaviour can engage several provisions at once, each section makes its own contribution to the regulatory scheme, which in turn should be considered as a whole. From that perspective, the freeze captures something that the other provisions do not: bona fide business behaviour that is not motivated by anti-union considerations and may not be a breach of section 17 [the duty to bargain], but is nevertheless prohibited (for a time, at least) because it undermines bargaining. The mischief to which section 86(1) is directed is an unexpected shift in the starting point or basis for bargaining, during the initial stages of that bargaining. . . . [L]acking a requirement for "anti-union motivation," [the freeze provisions] are more accurately viewed as a form of economic regulation, rather than a fault-based prohibition. A "pure freeze case" does not have the pejorative flavour of the traditional unfair labour practice sections. The freeze provisions . . . stipulate that, for a time, even *bona fide* business decisions may be suspended while the bargaining process unfolds. In contrast to the "traditional" unfair labour practice provisions, the freeze is directed more towards facilitating bargaining, than protecting employees from "victimization" at the hands of an anti-union employer. . . .

The problem with the so-called "business as usual" "test" is not simply that it is a "slippery concept" — to use the words of the Board in Simpsons. . . . "Business as usual" has been taken as the "answer" or "end of the enquiry" rather than an "approach" or aid to interpreting difficult language in a particular context. . . . When the words of section 86(1) are read in conjunction with its purpose, and in conjunction with the related provisions of the Act, (especially sections 17 and 73), it is quite evident that an employer cannot carry on "business as before." Once certification is granted, a new legal regime is introduced; and once notice to bargain is given, the employer must not ignore the union or act unilaterally as it might have done in a pre-collective bargaining regime. Indeed, if the employer really does try to carry on "business as before," purportedly exercising managerial "rights" and "prerogatives" derived from the common law of master and servant, it may well collide with the requirements of the statute... Since neither the union nor these statutory requirements were part of the pre-collective bargaining regime, it is quite misleading for an employer to look exclusively to that regime for guidelines on how it should conduct itself in the course of bargaining. . . .

Nor, for the same reason, do the "reasonable expectations of employees" provide an unfailing guideline for what can or cannot be changed during the currency of the statutory phrase. The fact is, that test is just as "slippery" as "business as usual" — not least because it is not at all clear how such "employee expectations" might be ascertained. It is of necessity a Board construct, applied in particular circumstances to give expression to the competing policy considerations underlying the ambiguous language of section 86(1). It is a way of rationalizing competing interests, when the statute itself does not point unambiguously to a particular result. . . .

More to the point: is this focus on "employee expectations" congruent with the language and collective bargaining purpose of section 86(1)? For having just voted in favor of trade union representation, would those same employees not reasonably expect that ... wages and benefits . . . would be bargained about by their trade union? . . . Or are the rights of employees in a collective bargaining regime to be determined by what employees THINK the employer might have done in other pre-collective bargaining circumstances? . . .

✳ ✳ ✳

Chair MacDowell concluded that in the post-certification context, the existing tests had to be augmented by a third approach — one that read the freeze provisions in light of the need to bolster the bargaining process, reinforce the status of the union as bargaining agent and provide a firm (if temporary) starting point for collective bargaining.

The statutory freeze applies only from the date when an application for certification is filed with the labour board. May the employer alter the terms and conditions of employment before that date? Does it matter whether the change is one which benefits the employees? Consider the following passage from a U.S. Supreme Court decision.

National Labor Relations Board v. Exchange Parts Co., (1964) 375 U.S. 405 at 409

HARLAN J.: The broad purpose of ss. 8(a)(1) [of the *National Labor Relations Act*] is to establish 'the right of employees to organize for mutual aid without employer interference.' . . . We have no doubt that it prohibits not only intrusive threats and promises but also conduct immediately favourable to employees which is undertaken with the express purpose of impinging upon their freedom of choice for or against unionization and is reasonably calculated to have that effect. In *Medo Photo Supply Corp. v. Labor Board* . . . , this Court said . . . : 'The action of employees with respect to the choice of their bargaining agents may be induced by favors bestowed by the employer as well as by his threats or domination.' Although in that case there was already a designated bargaining agent and the offer of 'favors' was in response to a suggestion of the employees that they would leave the union if favors were bestowed, the principles which dictated the result there are fully applicable here. The danger inherent in well-timed increases in benefits is the suggestion of a fist inside the velvet glove. Employees are not likely to miss the inference that the source of benefits now conferred is also the source from which future benefits must flow and which may dry up if it is not obliged. The danger may be diminished, if, as in this case, the benefits are conferred permanently and unconditionally. But the absence of conditions or threats pertaining to the particular benefits conferred would be of controlling significance only if it could be presumed that no question of additional benefits or renegotiation of existing benefits would arise in the future; and, of course, no such presumption is tenable. . . .

5:500 EMPLOYER SPEECH

During a union organizing campaign, management representatives often want to communicate with employees, with a view to persuading them not to opt for unionization. What should an employer be allowed to say in those circumstances?

In *National Labor Relations Board v. Federbush Co.*, (1941) 121 F.2d 954 at 957 (U.S. 2nd Circuit Court of Appeals), Learned Hand J. made these often-quoted comments:

> The privilege of "free speech," like other privileges, is not absolute; it has its seasons; a democratic society has an acute interest in its protection and cannot indeed be without it; but it is an interest measured by its purpose. That purpose is to enable others to make an informed judgement as to what concerns them, and ends so far as the utterances do not contribute to the result. Language may serve to enlighten a hearer, though it also betrays the speaker's feelings and desires; but the light it sheds will be in some degree clouded, if the hearer is in his power. Arguments by an employer directed to his employees have such an ambivalent character; they are legitimate enough as such, and pro tanto the privilege of "free speech" protects them; but, so far as they also disclose his wishes, as they generally do, they have a force independent of persuasion. The [National Labor Relations] Board is vested with the power to measure these two factors against each other. . . . Words are not pebbles in alien juxtaposition; they have only a communal existence; and not only does the meaning of each interpenetrate the other, but all in their aggregate take their purport from the setting in which they are used, of which the relation between the speaker and the hearer is perhaps the most important part. What to an outsider will be no more than the vigorous presentation of a conviction, to an employee may be the manifestation of a determination which it is not safe to thwart. The Board must decide how far the second aspect obliterates the first.

Legislation in some Canadian jurisdictions expressly recognizes a right of employer free speech, but adds the qualification that the employer must not use threats, promises or undue influence. The following case shows the importance of this qualification.

United Steelworkers of America v. Wal-Mart Canada Inc., [1997] O.L.R.D. No. 207 (O.L.R.B.) (Upheld on judicial review: *Wal-Mart Canada Inc. v. United Steelworkers of America*, [1997] O.J. No. 3063 (Div. Court), leave to appeal refused [1999] O.J. No. 2995 (Ont. C.A.)).

> JOHNSTON, Vice-Chair: . . . While the union has asserted numerous breaches of the Act by the company, the key allegation in the union's view is that the company raised issues of economic and job security with the employees and then refused to answer questions asked on these matters. In the union's view, the company's failure to answer the question "will the store close if the union is successful" led the employees to conclude that the store would in fact close if the union was successful. Therefore, the union requests that the Board set aside the vote and certify the union pursuant to section 11 of the Act.
> . . .

The company is what was described as a "junior" department store engaged in the selling of merchandise to the public. The store which is the subject of the application for certification is located in Windsor.

Wal-Mart is an American company which in January, 1994 acquired 122 of 144 stores owned and operated by Woolco in Canada, including the Windsor store which is the subject of this application. None of the 122 stores acquired were unionized although 9 of the 22 stores not acquired were unionized. Wal-Mart currently operates 2600 stores worldwide in countries such as China, Brazil, Argentina, Mexico, Puerto Rico and the Philippines. None of these stores are unionized. Wal-Mart is currently planning further expansions and in fact has been expanding.

The company employs full-time and "peak" time or part-time associates. Full-time associates work from 28 to 37 hours per week and peak-time associates work from 6 to 27 hours per week. The store is open from 9:00 a.m. to 9:00 p.m. Monday to Saturday and from 11:00 a.m. to 5:00 p.m. on Sundays. The full-time employees generally work Monday to Friday on a day shift. Peak-time associates fill in hours whenever necessary. The management structure at this store consists of a Store Manager, Mr. Andy Johnston, and 6 assistant managers. There are 40 departments in the store and each one has a person in charge of that department. The department managers are not managerial in the way in which the Board defines that term and the parties have agreed that they are members of the proposed bargaining unit. Above the store manager, is a District Manager, Mr. Tino Borean, who is responsible for a total of 8 stores located in London, Windsor, Sarnia, Chatham and Goderich. The company's head office or "home" office as it was referred to in this case, is located in Toronto. Mr. Jon Sims, the Regional Vice-President of Operations for Region 2 in Canada (Windsor being in Region 2), Mr. Paul Ratzlaff, Director of Associate Relations and Ms. Karen Duff, a Regional Personnel Officer, all work out of the home office.

Mr. Johnston, Mr. Sims and Mr. Ratzlaff all testified before the Board. We heard a great deal of evidence regarding the company's practices and procedures and what was referred to as the Wal-Mart culture.

Wal-Mart seeks to promote an atmosphere or "culture" in its stores which is positive and friendly, customer-oriented and in which associates work together as a family or team.... [I]n support of its goal of regular information sharing with its employees, Wal-Mart holds daily meetings with its staff. The daily morning meeting is held at 8:45 a.m. and is attended by all associates scheduled to commence work up to 9:00 a.m. in the morning. This meeting is held at the front of the store near the courtesy desk. The meeting in this Windsor store is run by either Mr. Johnston or in his absence one of the assistant managers. At this meeting management provides financial information such as sales figures for the previous day as well as information concerning who the top performing department and individuals were on the previous day. New items of stock are discussed as well as issues around safety, shrinkage and loss prevention. An exercise to help associates limber up is also done. The Wal-Mart culture is often discussed by reference to the history of the store and its founder, Sam Walton. Associates are encouraged to participate, become involved and ask questions. The meeting normally ends just before 9:00 a.m. with the Wal-Mart cheer and then the store opens its doors to customers. An additional meeting is held every day after the store closes at 9:00 p.m. It follows the same format as the morning meeting and is an opportunity for the company to provide information to those employees who are not working in the morning and did not attend the morning meeting.

The union commenced its organizing drive on April 14, 1996. The strategy utilized by the in-house organizers in getting employees to sign cards, was to approach employees in the parking lot who were on route or at their cars after having completed their shift, and to ask them to sign a union card. On May 2, 1996, the union filed an application for certification accompanied by 91 membership cards in support of its application. By decision dated May 7, 1996, the Board directed that a representation vote be conducted on May 9, 1996. At the vote, 205 employees voted, 9 ballots were segregated and not counted, 43 ballots were cast in favour of the union and 151 ballots were cast against the union. Between April 14, 1996 and April 27, 1996, the union collected a total of 84 cards or an average of 6 cards per day. Between April 27 and May 2 (a period of 5 days) the union collected a total of 7 cards. The relevance of these numbers will be explained later in this decision.

The company became aware on April 26, 1996 that associates were being approached to sign union cards. An associate advised Mr. Johnston of this fact. As he had previously been instructed to do, Mr. Johnston immediately telephoned Mr. Ratzlaff to tell him of the union's organizing drive. Mr. Ratzlaff is Wal-Mart's labour relations specialist. Prior to being employed by Wal-Mart Mr. Ratzlaff worked for Woolworth. From 1973 to 1989 he held a variety of managerial positions in Woolco stores and eventually was promoted to the position of Director of Personnel for the Woolco division in 1989. In 1992 he was promoted to Director of Labour Relations for Woolworth Canada. Mr. Ratzlaff told the Board that he was quite familiar with the legal and procedural framework concerning union organizing drives.

The first thing Mr. Ratzlaff did was to telephone Mr. Borean to advise him of the situation. Mr. Borean then contacted Mr. Johnston and told him that he would come to the store the next day, Saturday, April 27, 1996 for the morning meeting. Mr. Borean indicated that he was planning a trip to Windsor for that day to attend the funeral of an associate who had worked in the other Windsor store. At the end of this conversation, Mr. Johnston directed one of his assistant managers to telephone all of the associates scheduled to work the next morning to tell them to ensure that they reported for work in time for the morning meeting as Tino Borean was coming to visit the store. Mr. Johnston had the employees contacted because it was the first time Mr. Borean had attended a Saturday morning meeting and he wanted to make sure that all of the scheduled associates attended the meeting and had a chance to hear what Mr. Borean had to say. It was highly unusual for the company to call employees in this fashion and Mr. Johnston was unable to think of another occasion when it had occurred.

Approximately 25 to 30 associates attended the morning meeting on April 27th. After concluding the usual routine, Mr. Johnston introduced Mr. Borean and Mr. Borean spoke. Mr. Borean indicated that he was in Windsor to attend the funeral of an associate who had worked at the other store in Windsor. There is some dispute as to what Mr. Borean said next. Mr. Johnston testified that Mr. Borean then indicated to the associates that he had heard that associates were being approached by other associates in the parking lot to sign union cards. Mr. Borean indicated that if anyone had any questions he would be there for the day to answer them, other than the couple of hours he would spend at the funeral. Ms. Mary McArthur, one of the union's inside organizers was at this meeting. She testified that Mr. Borean said that he had heard that there were people going around trying to sign union cards, that he was at the store to find out why people thought they needed a union and that he would be coming around the sales floor to talk to people about that. Ms. Debbie Kulke, a peak-time associate called by the company to give evidence about this meeting, gave another version of what was said by Mr. Borean at the meeting. She indicated that Mr. Borean stated that he knew that there was some talk about a union going on, that he would be in and out of the store, that he was going to go out and ask people if they had any questions or concerns and that he would be there if anyone had any questions or concerns. If anyone wanted to speak to him they were to feel free to do so. Ms. Norma Passador, another associate called by the company to testify indicated that Mr. Borean said that he had heard there was talk about a union. In her words, "later on he would like to go around and talk to associates and see if there was a problem and if he could handle it himself." There was no dispute that after Mr. Borean finished speaking that Ms. McArthur spoke out saying to the associates gathered that it was illegal for management to interfere or coerce or intimidate them to change their decision, that they had a right to be part of whatever was happening and that they did not have to speak to management. After the meeting concluded Mr. Borean did circulate throughout the store speaking to employees for the majority of the day. We heard no evidence as to the substance of those conversations.

Although it appears he is still employed by the company, Mr. Borean was not called upon to testify. . . . The employer was aware that Mr. Borean's conduct at this meeting and his individual conversations with associates thereafter was asserted by the union to be a violation of the Act. . . . The union urges us to prefer the testimony of Ms. McArthur regarding what Mr. Borean said and did on April 27, 1996. In the circumstances it is appropriate for us to draw an adverse inference from the company's failure to call Mr. Borean. . . .

The line between legitimate employer persuasion and unlawful intimidation or undue influence must be determined on the particular facts of each case. The company contacted the associates scheduled to work an April 27th and told them to ensure that they were at work in time for the morning meeting as Mr. Borean would be attending the store. This was an unprecedented call and sent the message to employees that the meeting was important. The associates who attended this important meeting then heard from Mr. Borean that he is aware of the union and will circulate throughout the store to discuss presumably either in small groups or individually with associates, why they wanted a union or what problems or concerns they had causing them to want a union. Mr. Borean then circulated throughout the store speaking to employees. While the conduct of Mr. Borean is not a violation of the Act, it sets the tone for what is to follow. In addition, not surprisingly, the union's organizing drive began to falter shortly after Mr. Borean's visit.

On Monday, April 29, 1996, Ms. Norma Passador, an associate, approached Mr. Johnston and asked if she could speak at the morning meeting the next day. Mr. Johnston agreed. Ms. Passador did not volunteer and Mr. Johnston did not ask what she wanted to speak about. On Tuesday, April 30th, at the conclusion of the regular morning meeting, Mr. Johnston asked if any associates had any questions and Ms. Passador stated that she had something she wanted to read. She read the following speech:

> I have asked to come here this morning as a concerned associate to voice my opinion against the "alleged" rumor (sic) of a union trying to be put in this store. I have worked in this building for 20 years, 18 with Woolco and the same as many of you with Wal-Mart. When Wal-Mart took over Woolco they let us keep our years of seniority for pension, vacation and rate of pay, this is something they did not have to do, but to me as a senior associate it meant a lot.
>
> The young people in the store that have started this do not realize the consequences involved. For some of them the company is not their future when they finish their schooling they will leave and move on to better jobs in their fields, but for the rest of us this is our only income. I for one would like to know what they think they are going to receive from this action.
>
> I believe we receive what other dept. stores have and then some. I know some of you think when we get our annual raise it should be more this is the retail business and that is how it is run. Eventually even big businesses such as the auto companies will have to accept lower wages. A union will only cause discontentment in our store and I assure you as I am standing here Wal Mart [sic] will not put up with this.
>
> I cannot be called a company person because I complain like everyone else if not more. But I am for for [sic] what's best for me and a union is not it.
>
> Also a word to the associates who have started this. Remember the old ruling used to be 51% and the union is in. WRONG every person MUST have a vote, because now the government steps in and posts a notice in the store when a vote will be taken and we all vote and remember as far as I am concerned the union is not your friend, it is the friend of people who don't like to work. Also please remember that there are people working in union places that do not get all the benefits we have and you all know what they are. Also if anything if anything [sic] comes of this I assure you I will be one of the first associates to cross a picket line because I need my job.
>
> Thank you for listening to me this morning.

When Ms. Passador finished speaking there was considerable commotion. Some of the associates present applauded Ms. Passador's speech, others did not. Either Ms. McArthur or Mr. Dave Cartier (another inside organizer), or both, indicated that they wanted to respond to Ms. Passador's speech. Mr. Borean, who was in attendance at the meeting, did not allow either employee to speak and ended the meeting. He indicated that it was time to open the store as they had customers waiting. It was either 9:00 o'clock or shortly after 9:00 a.m. when the meeting ended.

Later the same day Mr. Johnston approached an associate, Jamie Campbell, while he was working. Mr. Johnston opened the conversation by telling Mr. Campbell about the morning meeting, as Mr. Campbell worked an evening shift, either 4:00 p.m. to 9:30 p.m. or 5:00 p.m. to 9:30 p.m. Mr. Johnston then asked Mr. Campbell if he knew what was going on in the store regarding the union and Mr. Campbell answered that he did. Mr. Johnston asked Mr. Campbell if he had been approached by anyone from the union about signing a union card and Mr. Campbell answered that yes he had been approached. Mr. Johnston next, in Mr. Campbell's words, "went on to say something along the lines of a union would not necessarily benefit the store because all of the benefits and everything would have to be bargained for and he also suggested that neither side would have to agree to any specific details." The benefits or details referred to are what are called stakeholder payments or the profit sharing programme. The last thing mentioned by Mr. Johnston to Mr. Campbell was that some employees had been tricked into signing union cards as they were being told they were signing the card to get more information. Mr. Johnston then advised Mr. Campbell to use his own judgement when he was making decisions.

The union's application for certification was filed with the Board and delivered to the store on May 2, 1996. As Mr. Johnston was on a day off that day, the assistant manager who received the application contacted him at home to tell him of the application. The assistant manager also contacted Mr. Ratzlaff to advise him of what had occurred. Mr. Ratzlaff had the assistant manager fax him the application. Mr. Ratzlaff then contacted Jon Sims and Tino Borean to advise them of the application. In light of the union's application, Mr. Ratzlaff decided to go to the Windsor store the next day. That evening Mr. Ratzlaff, Jonathan Hamovitch, Vice-President of Human Resources Wal-Mart Canada and Robert Wasserman, in-house counsel for Wal-Mart met with counsel who acted on behalf of the company at the hearing. The union's application and the company's response to it was discussed at this meeting. Mr. Ratzlaff was the company official responsible for all matters pertaining to the union's application for certification, the actions taken by the company with regard to it and all of the decisions made on this matter.

. . .

When Mr. Ratzlaff, Mr. Sims and Ms. Duff arrived in Windsor they checked into their hotel and met with Mr. Johnston and Mr. Borean. Mr. Johnston advised them that the tension in the store was incredible so the first item discussed was how the group of managers might defuse the tension, calm the store and continue to serve the customers. Mr. Ratzlaff told the managers how he wanted the morning and evening meetings approached in the days leading up to the vote. He felt due to the Wal-Mart culture that questions regarding the union would come up at these meetings and he wanted to ensure they were handled properly. Therefore he told the management that until the vote was held that he would decide and plan which managers would speak at the meetings and what they would say. Mr. Ratzlaff indicated that he wanted to bring more structure to the meetings before the vote, therefore he would determine the appropriate content for the meetings. Mr. Ratzlaff then had the same conversation with Mr. Borean and Mr. Johnston that he had had with Mr. Sims and Ms. Duff with regard to the questions he anticipated receiving from the associates and how to answer them.

On Saturday, May 4, 1996 Mr. Johnston ran the morning meeting. Mr. Ratzlaff, Mr. Sims, Mr. Borean and Ms. Duff were present at the meeting. Mr. Johnston read from a prepared text and told the employees present at the meeting the following:

The Steelworkers Union applied to the labour board to get in at this store. The labour board will now check to see if the union has enough support for the board to hold a vote on the issue. Does this mean that the union is in? No! It means the union has applied to get in. The union can not [sic] get in until it has a vote. That vote would be by secret ballot and everyone get [sic] to vote no matter if they have signed or not signed a union card.

I want to be sure we get the right answers to your questions. To make that easier, I've put up a question box. You can write down your questions and put them in the box. You don't need to put your name on the question. I'll get answers and give the answers to all of you.

Mr. Johnston indicated that pursuant to Mr. Ratzlaff's instructions he had put the question and answer box up on Friday. Employees were told to put questions in the question box if they wanted to and that management would answer their questions. Mr. Johnston then introduced the three home office managers and Tino Borean to the group of employees present. He told the associates that he had been inundated with questions with regard to the union's application. The additional managers were there to answer questions and to provide information about the union's application and about the vote or anything else. Mr. Ratzlaff also spoke and then the meeting ended. This format with a few additions was followed that evening, at the meeting Sunday and at the two meetings on Monday.

After the meeting concluded, the three home office managers, Mr. Borean and Mr. Johnston began to circulate throughout the store. Mr. Ratzlaff described his approach to employees as follows. He told the Board that sometimes while he was walking around an associate would approach him if they saw him coming. However, more often he would go to an associate who was working and strike up a conversation. If the associate kept working Mr. Ratzlaff would help the person. When they stopped working to talk to him, he would introduce himself and indicate where he was from. Mr. Ratzlaff would then ask the associate if he/she had been present at the morning meeting that day. If the answer was yes then Mr. Ratzlaff would tell the person that "we" (the outside managers) were there to answer questions about the union if they had any or about anything else. Mr. Ratzlaff would indicate that if they wanted to talk about the union issue they would have to raise it with him and it was purely voluntary to do so. If the associate indicated that he/she had not attended the morning meeting then Mr. Ratzlaff would make sure that they knew about the union's application. He would ask if they had seen the notice posted in the employee lounge with regard to the application and if the person had not seen it Mr. Ratzlaff would tell them to feel free to go look at it. If the person had any questions after reviewing the notice he/she was told to approach the managers who were visiting the store or Andy Johnston as any of this group would be happy to answer questions. When he was asked whether the store would close if the union was successful Mr. Ratzlaff indicated that it was not appropriate to answer that question. On one occasion, while being confronted by an inside organizer concerning the effect that the employer's refusal to answer any questions concerning whether or not the store would close was having on employees, Mr. Ratzlaff told a group of employees that he had been given legal advice that it was not appropriate to tell employees what the company might or might not do as a result of the vote.

The approach utilized by Mr. Sims was similar to that of Mr. Ratzlaff. . . . Mr. Sims indicated that his goal was to talk to as many employees as possible and answer their questions on any topic. Mr. Sims recalled being asked whether the store would close if the union got in and the answer he gave was, in his words, "it would be inappropriate to comment on what might or might not happen." . . .

The three home office managers, Mr. Ratzlaff, Mr. Sims and Ms. Duff plus Mr. Borean were in the store circulating amongst the employees from May 4, 1996 until the day of the vote, May 9, 1996. . . .

The union issue came up in one way or another at every morning (and presumably every evening) meeting between May 4th and the day of the vote. After each of the morning meetings concluded, the management group present in the store would move throughout the store for the remainder of the day approaching employees to see if they had any questions. On at least two occasions, both Mr. Sims and Mr. Ratzlaff were advised by one of the union's inside organizers that the refusal of management to answer any questions concerning whether the store would close if the union was successful, was causing employees to fear for their jobs. Management never changed its approach.

On May 5, 1996 between 4 and 5 o'clock Mr. Johnston approached a peak-time associate, Mr. Walter Dinatale. Mr. Johnston asked Mr. Dinatale if he had any questions concerning the union or what was going on in the store. Mr. Dinatale told Mr. Johnston that he did not have any questions. Mr. Johnston then went on to tell Mr. Dinatale that he should not feel pressured into signing anything and that he should feel free to make up his own mind. Mr. Johnston told Mr. Dinatale that a lot of things would change if the union was successful, for example, the stakeholders' benefit would be revoked. Then Mr. Johnston told Mr. Dinatale that if he had any further questions he should speak to a member of management.

In final submissions counsel for the company acknowledged that both Mr. Campbell and Mr. Dinatale were credible witnesses. Given this concession on the part of counsel and the fact that both Mr. Campbell and Mr. Dinatale's recollection of the conversation they had with Mr. Johnston were clearer and more complete than the recollection of Mr. Johnston, we have accepted their version of the conversation. In his conversation with Mr. Dinatale Mr. Johnston made an explicit threat going to Mr. Dinatale's economic security. In threatening to take away benefits if the union was successful, Mr. Johnston breached section 70 of the Act.

At the morning meeting on May 7, 1996, the employees were given the answers to the questions which had been put into the question box. At the end of the meeting Mr. Ratzlaff indicated that all of the employee questions, with answers provided, had been set out in a written document. That written document was available for employees to pick up. The order in which the questions and answers were set out was determined by Mr. Ratzlaff. As it is lengthy we will only set out the first two questions and the answers provided by the company. . . .

Q. "There is an overwhelming concern that if the store unionizes, Wal-Mart will close the store. Is this true?"

A. It would be inappropriate for your Company to comment on what it will or will not do if the store is unionized.

Q."Some people have said that if the store unionized it would be illegal for Wal-Mart to close the store. Is that true?"

A. This statement is not factually correct. What would or would not be legal for your Company to do following the store becoming unionized depends on the factual circumstances and the application of the law against those circumstances. It would be inappropriate for your Company to comment or suggest what those factual circumstances might be.

. . .

As is obvious, the questions pertaining to whether the store would close if the union was successful were answered with the indication that the company could not answer the question. Before leaving the question and answer sheet we would point out that in response to two other questions concerning the store's lease the employer gave the same response. In response to a question concerning profit sharing and a question concerning payment for work on Sundays the company responded by indicating that this was a matter to be decided at the bargaining table. While this answer may have been interpreted as an indication that perhaps the company would not immediately close the store if the union was successful, the kind of mixed message generated by these inconsistent responses is not sufficient to counteract the fear generated by the employer's consistent failure to respond to the direct questions with regard to the store closure.

. . .

We have two concerns with Ms. Passador's speech on April 30, 1996. First of all the company, at the end of Ms. Passador's speech did not distance itself from her comments. Neither Mr. Borean nor Mr. Johnston stated that her comments were not reflective of the company's views on unions and the effect that a union would have in the store. Secondly, even though we accept that there were legitimate reasons for ending the meeting at that point, namely that it was time for the store to open to its customers, by not allowing the union supporters to speak, the associates who were present were left only with the views of Ms. Passador. What is crucial in our view, is the effect that Ms. Passador's comments may have had on employees in the store. What message would the average or reasonable associate hear upon listening to Ms. Passador's speech? . . . Ms. Passador never said that the store would close if the union was successful in its attempt to organize employees. However, because of what she did say an associate listening to her would have likely concluded that she had concerns for her future job security in the event that the union was successful. . . .

It was never suggested that management arranged for Mr. Passador to make the comments she did. We accept that the views expressed were her views. There is nothing wrong with allowing Ms. Passador to speak her mind. However, in light of the fact that the company after inviting questions or comments, did not clarify that the comments were not reflective of the company's views, allowed the spectre of job insecurity to be raised in a situation in which it is reasonable for employees to conclude that it was a legitimate concern. In the circumstances, it would not be unreasonable for some of the associates to conclude that the views of Ms. Passador were reflective of the views of the company and that the company agreed with her assessment of the situation. In allowing this message to be sent at a meeting which management directs and controls, without distancing itself from her remarks or allowing the union supporters the opportunity to balance her remarks, the company has sought to intimidate or unduly influence employees with regard to their decision on union representation contrary to section 70 of the Act. An employer simply cannot allow an employee to make a speech containing the subtle threats to job security such as those contained in Ms. Passador's speech, at a meeting run by management, fail to distance itself from the comments and then silence the union's supporters in the manner in which it did. While the company did not make any threats, it allowed threats to be made in circumstances in which they could be attributed to the company. Ms. Passador's speech had a chilling effect on the union's organizing drive.

The attendance of four outside managers in the store from May 4th to May 9th who spent the vast majority of their time approaching employees while they were working in the store and engaging them repeatedly in conversations regarding the union, was an extremely risky response for the company to have made to the union's organizing drive. . . .

In this case there was no surveillance or pressure being brought upon the union's inside organizers. Nor was there a series of management meetings opposing the union. However, there were daily morning meetings at which the union issue was discussed. At their conclusion the four outside managers would start circulating and continued to do so for the majority of their time until the store closed for the day. They did this for the five days leading up to the vote and on the day of the vote. In the course of these conversations they learned who the union supporters were and who were not union supporters contrary to the protection afforded by the Act. The presence of the four outside managers certainly sent the message that the union issue was a very important one to the company. The Board heard a great deal about the Wal-Mart culture and the open relationship between management, as representatives of the company, and the employees. Given this "culture" it is understandable that Mr. Ratzlaff, as the official co-ordinating the company's response, would want to ensure that resources were available to deal with employee questions. But, there is a big difference between having resources available, which employees can seek out and what occurred in this case. Mr. Ratzlaff's strategy was to have four outside managers, senior managers, constantly approaching employees over a six day period actively soliciting questions from the employees on the union issue. This conduct, four managers (and this is not counting Mr. Johnston who is doing the same thing) repeatedly engaging employees in a conversation about the union, goes beyond mere assistance to employees based on a concern that their questions be answered, and becomes an extremely effective tactic of intimidation or undue influence contrary to section 70 of the Act. As the Board has noted before, an employer cannot hide behind "open door" policies when the effect of the open communications is to put undue influence on employees concerning their selection of a trade union to represent them. This repeated and persistent personal contact initiated by the employer and not requested by the employees was clearly designed to identify the union supporters as well as communicate the message which we will next deal with.

This conduct of the employer, namely the strategy of having four managers constantly engaging employees in conversations about the union, is not the breach of the Act or the conduct in and of itself which led us to conclude that it is appropriate to certify the union pursuant section 11. The conduct of the employer which gave us the most concern, while part of the approach detailed above, was far more harmful to the free will of the employees. . . . We accept that there is a unique culture fostered in this company, one in which employees are encouraged to ask questions and expect to get answers. One of the key concerns of the associates in this store was whether the company would continue to operate the store if the union was successful. . . .

Given the Wal-Mart culture and the expectations of employees that answers to their questions would be given, what would the effect of this refusal to answer such a crucial question be on the average, reasonable associate? In assessing the effect of the refusal to answer it is also important to bear in mind that management over a six day period is continually approaching the associates and asking them if they have any questions about the union's organizing drive. The managers present in the store in the days leading up to the vote entered into dozens of daily one-on-one conversations with associates about the union and when asked, refused to answer any questions with regard to the store closure issue. The company attempted to portray the store closure issue as a union issue and pointed out that it was not raised with a great deal of frequency with the managers. In our view it is irrelevant how many times the associates asked one of the managers this question, as it would not take long for it to "get around" the store that this question was not being answered. Why ask if you knew it would not be answered?

. . . The managers, knowing the effect the refusal to answer the questions of employees with regard to store closure was having, nevertheless continued to refuse to answer any questions on this issue.

In our view you cannot have it both ways. If you adopt the approach of constantly soliciting questions in an environment such as was present in this case, you have to answer them. Either you answer the questions asked or you do not circulate amongst employees in the manner in which management did in this case. . . .

It is always difficult to place oneself in the shoes of the employees in the store to determine what effect the company's campaign would have had on them. However, in the unique circumstances of this case, and we stress that they are unique, we are of the view that the company's failure to answer the questions of associates with regard to the issue of store closure would cause the average reasonable employee to conclude that the store would close if the union got in. Given that the inside organizers told management that this was in fact happening, and management did not change its approach, we are satisfied that the company intended employees to draw this conclusion. There is no legal prohibition against answering questions with regard to store closure by saying that the company would not close and would sit down and negotiate with the union if the union was successful. Obviously, it is only illegal for the company to say that the store would close. Therefore, by not alleviating employees' concerns by answering the question, the company was intentionally fuelling employee concerns. Accordingly, we find that the conduct of the employer in circulating amongst the employees and engaging them in individual and group discussions regarding the union, in the fashion in which it did, and the company's refusal to answer any questions with regard to what the store would do if the union was successful, was a breach of section 70 of the Act. . . .

5:600 SOLICITATION ON EMPLOYER PROPERTY

The workplace is the usual location for union organizing. It is also the employer's property. How should labour legislation balance employees' rights to act collectively with the employer's right to control conduct on its premises?

Canada Post Corporation (1995) 95 CLLC 220-042 (C.I.R.B.)

DOYON, Vice-Chair: On November 24, 1994, the Letter Carriers Union of Canada (LCUC) filed a complaint with the Board alleging that Canada Post Corporation (CPC or the Corporation) had violated sections 94(1)(a) and 94(3)(a)(i) of the Canada Labour Code.

These sections read as follows:

94. (1) No employer or person acting on behalf of an employer shall

(a) participate in or interfere with the formation or administration of a trade union or the representation of employees by a trade union; or

. . .

(3) No employer or person acting on behalf of an employer shall

(a) refuse to employ or to continue to employ or suspend, transfer, lay off or otherwise discriminate against any person with respect to employment, pay or any other term or condition of employment or intimidate, threaten or otherwise discipline any person, because the person

(i) is or proposes to become, or seeks to induce any other person to become, a member, officer or representative of a trade union or participates in the promotion, formation or administration of a trade union, . . .

LCUC alleged that the Corporation contravened the Code by refusing to grant access to employees from other than their own work locations. The employees wanted to canvass co-workers at other CPC premises during non-working hours and within designated lunch areas. The employees were part of LCUC's raiding campaign to replace the Canadian Union of Postal Workers (CUPW) as bargaining agent for the operational bargaining unit [one nationwide unit]. LCUC says the employer had no compelling business reasons or justification to prohibit access at any location to its employees who were not scheduled for work at their own premises. The decision, LCUC says, was aimed at prohibiting the solicitation of employees. In the result, CPC reduced the status of its employees to that of any "stranger" to the Corporation.

The complainant asked the Board to declare that CPC violated the Code by interfering with the organization and formation of a trade union. LCUC also asked the Board to order the Corporation to grant LCUC representatives, who are its employees, access to designated lunch areas, in order to canvass during rest periods and lunch breaks at any of CPC's worksites. LCUC agrees that if membership solicitation takes place on CPC's premises, it should only be carried out in the cafeterias or lunch areas during non-working hours.

The employer's position can be summarized as follows. Firstly, solicitation on the employer's premises would be allowed if it was carried out by employees employed at the worksite, outside of business hours and in non-working areas. Thus, the October 21st, 1994 memorandum signed by Mr. G. Courville, Corporate Manager, Labour Relations, stating that position, which excludes access by employees from other locations or non employees, did not unlawfully restrict organizing activity at the work place. This position reflects the employer's general policy restricting employee access to CPC facilities for any purpose other than to carry out their work, unless prior permission is obtained. Given the nature of CPC's operations, there are valid business and security reasons for this policy. The employer's main concern is security, either at the point of access, as for example in smaller postal stations and depots, or in larger plants, once the person has gone through the security check point.

Secondly, the employer relies on its obligation to act in a strictly neutral manner when two unions are competing to represent a group of its employees, as in the present case.

The employer considered that granting access to its facilities for organizing purposes, when such access is normally prohibited for other purposes, could be seen as favouring LCUC. CPC referred to a letter dated June 9, 1994 on that subject, from Mr. D.W. Tingley, CUPW's National President, requesting that the employer remain neutral vis-à-vis LCUC's efforts to displace CUPW as the certified bargaining agent for the operational unit. One of the contentious issues cited by Mr. Tingley in that letter was allowing LCUC canvassers access to CPC premises.

. . .

The employer's greatest concern is the question of security, given the nature and magnitude of CPC's operations. The Corporation has approximately 52 000 employees who work in 21 mechanized facilities and 400 depots or postal stations. It moves about 30 to 35 million pieces of mail per day, excluding advertisements. Mr. Alan Whitson, Manager, Loss Prevention and Special Projects, stated that not all employees have identification cards. Only certain letter carriers have identification cards, as the Corporation stopped issuing such cards to external workers some time ago. The identification cards that employees do have only give them access to the plant where they normally work, and this has been the practice for several years.

The Corporation's plant security guidelines, in effect since 1989, define non-employees and employees from other plants as "visitors." According to these guidelines, visitors must sign in, visibly display an ID card, and be escorted by an employee, whereas employees carry their CPC identification card at all times. Drivers of any vehicles entering the plants, must stay in certain areas and only use certain entrances and exits.

. . .

At postal stations and depots, security rules are different since occasionally, there are no managers on duty. Visitors to any of these facilities will be questioned as to the purpose of their visit when they enter. Here as well, once visitors are inside, it is unlikely that they would be challenged.

In Mr. Whitson's view, the security of a facility is essential since once CPC has given visitors access to its premises, they are rarely stopped. Despite the fact that visitors should remain where they have business, once they pass the security point, they can virtually circulate as they wish, unless challenged by someone in the plant. Even if this rarely occurs, in Mr. Whitson's experience, there is little control over visitors, and breaches of security can lead to loss of customers and CPC products.

. . .

Mr. Dale Clark, First National Vice-President, testified at CUPW's request. CUPW maintained that granting LCUC supporters access to CPC's premises would amount to assisting the LCUC raid. Access given to LCUC canvassers should be restricted to employees at their own work locations, to neutral areas, outside of business hours; and no access should be granted to any employees on leave or not scheduled to work. He said that if extensive access was given to LCUC canvassers, "there will be major disruption" in the work place.

. . .

The issues the Board must decide, since the parties agree that organizing activities would take place in cafeterias and lunch areas during non-working hours, are:

1. Was CPC's refusal to grant access for organizing purposes, to employees employed at any other CPC worksite, a violation of section 94(1)(a) of the Code?
2. Was CPC's refusal to grant employees access to their own worksite for organizing purposes if the employee was on leave or not scheduled for work, a violation of section 94(1)(a) of the Code?

To answer these questions, the Board must consider whether the employer has demonstrated any valid and compelling business reasons for restricting access.

. . .

Section 94(1))(a) provides union activities with extensive protection. . . . The Board has, however, recognized that not all union activities fall under that provision. In *Brazeau Transport Inc.* . . . , the Board said:

> Union activities — whether those of the union's executive, its officers or its members — must be carried out within the framework recognized by the Code. The only union activities that are protected are those which are recognized by the Code. Section 184 [now 94] cannot serve as an umbrella for all union activities regardless of their merits. A union president who speaks on behalf of his organization's members is clearly taking an action that can always be associated with the performance of union activities. This does not give him free rein to do anything whatsoever at any time because his actions fall within the framework of union activities. To say that it did would force us to recognize anarchy and chaos, which are precisely what the Code seeks to avoid by setting forth rules and a framework within which the said union activities must be carried out.

Section 95(d) of the Code explicitly restricts the exercise of union activities which are protected by section 94(1)(a). It reads as follows:

95. No trade union or person acting on behalf of a trade union shall

. . .

(d) except with the consent of the employer of an employee, attempt, at an employee's place of employment during the working hours of the employee, to persuade the employee to become, to refrain from becoming or to cease to be a member of a trade union; . . ."

This section clearly prohibits union solicitation at the work place during working hours. However, according to the interpretation of this provision by this Board and other relations boards in Canada, section 95(d) does not prohibit organizers from signing up of members in a trade union at the work place, outside working hours. . . .

The Ontario Labour Relations Board, in *Adams Mine, Cliffs of Canada Ltd.* . . . , defined as follows the words "working hours" found in section 71 of the Labour Relations Act, R.S.O. 1980, c. 228, a provision which has the same object as section 95(d) of the Code:

. . . Labour boards have consistently interpreted the phrase 'working hours' to refer only to the period of time during which an employee is required to undertake his duties and responsibilities. Therefore the section does not apply to those periods of time an employee is on company property before shift, during coffee break, during lunch break, or after shift. This is so even if the employee is being paid for such time, otherwise an employer could prevent the exercise of statutory activity by the simple expedient of a money payment. . . .

In the above-mentioned decision, the Ontario Board adopted and applied the interpretation provided by this Board in *Bell Canada*, . . . concerning the right to solicit outside working hours — a right that can only be restricted if the employer can demonstrate the existence of "compelling and justifiable business reasons." The Nova Scotia Labour Relations Board . . . had previously adopted a similar position.

This interpretation of section 95(d), regulating the time frame within which membership solicitation can take place on the employer's premises, is not contested in the present case.

The Board must determine in this case whether employees, who work for an employer operating at several locations, have the right to solicit membership of their co-workers in the same bargaining unit during non-working hours at the company's work locations other than at their own work place. This is the first time that this specific issue is before the Board. Section 95(d) and other sections of the Code do not however define in any way who, acting on behalf of a trade union, has the right to engage or participate in such solicitation.

. . .

An absolute rule of non-admittance concerning union organizing applied to employees not scheduled to work, at any time and at any of the employer's worksites, because of apprehended fears related to security and safety, is not compatible with the provisions of the Code, nor with the jurisprudence of some other labour relations boards. Over the years, labour relations boards have shed light on the meaning and scope of the conditions relating to the exercise of the right of association. We must reiterate that nothing in the Code prohibits an employee from encouraging fellow employees to join a trade union on the employer's premises outside working hours. On the other hand, membership solicitation is an integral part of the expression of the fundamental right of freedom of association provided for in the Code and, in this regard, should be allowed and protected. It should only be restricted for compelling and justifiable reasons, including safety and security concerns.

As the Board stated in *Canada Post Corporation, supra*:

> The purpose of raiding is to displace a certified bargaining agent. The only means to achieve that result is to convince a majority of employees in the bargaining unit to support the raiding union. This activity of persuading employees to become a member of a union during a raid period is essential, and not only incidental to the formation of a trade union. (page 56)

Therefore, the Board concludes that such action is not prohibited by the Code, when it is carried out by those directly affected in collectively choosing a bargaining agent whose task will be to negotiate the terms and conditions of employment of the group of employees included in the bargaining unit. The Board finds that to conclude otherwise would unduly restrict the means of exercising the right of association set out in section 8 of the Code as well as the scope of the protection provided by section 94 of the Code.

Nothing in the Code prohibits an employee who is a member of a bargaining unit from engaging in such solicitation. Therefore, the Board finds that the employer, by prohibiting bargaining unit members from other locations from meeting with fellow employees during non-working hours and in non-working locations within CPC premises, such as cafeterias and lunch areas, is prima facie in violation of section 94(1)(a).

Having said this, there is no doubt that solicitation must nevertheless comply with conditions that ensure a balance between an employer's right to productivity and sound management on the one hand, and on the other hand, the employees' right to freely exercise their right of association.

The balancing test between the parties' interests has been developed over the years by labour boards. It was first established in *Bell Canada, supra*, where it was referred to as the employer's "compelling and justifiable business reasons" to justify that its actions do not amount to interference pursuant to section 94.

In *Ottawa-Carleton Regional Transit Commission, supra*, the Board defined what it considered to be "compelling and justifiable business reasons." In that case, the Board had to determine whether prohibiting employees from wearing union insignia during an organizing campaign constituted interference in union business by the employer.

. . . the Board characterized the reasonableness of an employer's decision to restrict union activities in the following manner:

> "Reasonableness" in the context of restricting a lawful union activity such as the wearing of a union insignia during working hours must surely include the ability to show a detrimental effect on entrepreneurial interests such as, negative customer reaction, security, safety or other business considerations. In other words, "compelling or justifiable business reasons."

In *Canada Post Corporation* . . . , the Board defined "compelling and justifiable business reasons" as follows:

> For an employer to establish compelling and justifiable business reasons, it must show that its operations are being disrupted or that other legitimate business interests are being adversely affected. . . .

In *Adams Mine, supra*, the Ontario Board recognized, as this Board and the Nova Scotia Board did, the right of employees to solicit membership from other employees on the employer's premises outside working hours. The Ontario Board expressed its concerns on the issue of protection of the employer's rights as follows:

> . . . This, of course, does not mean an employer is deprived by the Act of maintaining productivity or discipline or of securing his property from encroachment by strangers with whom he has no relationship.

The meaning and scope of this statement has to be addressed in the present case, since CPC claimed that it had no relationship with employees who intended to solicit membership elsewhere than at their own worksite. For the Board to accept the employer's argument that those employees seeking access to CPC locations for the purpose of promoting LCUC are "strangers" because they do not work at or out of that location would restrict them from attempting to speak to their fellow bargaining unit members on this important issue and unduly limit the employees' right under section 8 in the circumstances. There is one nation-wide bargaining unit in existence in this case. The Board would effectively deprive employees of their right to participate in the formation of the trade union of their choice if it accepted the employer's and intervener's positions and concluded that an employee may only solicit fellow employees at his or her own work location. Consequently, in this case and for the purpose of this decision, it suffices to say that the Board does not consider that employees at one work location are strangers to any other work location such that they can be treated as strangers with whom the employer has no relationship. . . .

> . . . the employer did not point out any specific disruption or adverse effect on its business which could reasonably be anticipated should greater access to its premises be granted as requested by LCUC.

CPC has established a complete set of security guidelines that can be adapted and followed to ensure that LCUC supporters are identified and monitored when they legally canvass on CPC's premises.

> . . . Consequently, the Board orally issued this order at the hearing:

> Canada Post shall grant access to employees in the bargaining unit acting as LCUC representatives for the purposes of canvassing and soliciting union membership during employee rest breaks and lunch periods in the cafeterias and/or lunch areas only. Such access will be subject to CPC security guidelines currently in effect, to the extent they apply in light of this order.

✳ ✳ ✳

In *T. Eaton Co.*, [1985] O.L.R.B. Rep. 491, the Ontario Labour Relations Board held that the employer had unlawfully interfered with the formation of a trade union by applying a blanket rule prohibiting the distribution of union literature on its premises at all times, including when the store was not open to the public and when the employees concerned were not working. The board ruled that the employer could not prohibit the occasional distribution of union literature before the store opened, because this activity would not interfere with the employer's legitimate business interests.

The store in question was located entirely within the Toronto Eaton Centre, an enclosed shopping mall. The mall's managers, Cadillac Fairview, maintained a no-solicitation policy for all areas of the mall, even those rarely used. According to this policy, union organizers were prohibited from soliciting employees to become union members. The board held that Cadillac Fairview also had unlawfully interfered with the formation of a trade union, because the challenged policy lacked a business justification. The Court of Appeal upheld the board's decision in *Cadillac Fairview Corporation v. Retail, Wholesale and Department Store Union* (1989), 71 O.R. (2d) 200. Speaking for the court, Robins J.A. said:

> In my opinion, notions of absolutism have no place in the determination of issues arising under a statute designed to further harmonious labour relations and to foster the freedom of employees to join a trade union of their choice. In this area of the law, as in so many others, a balance must be struck between competing interests which endeavours to recognize the purposes underlying the interests and seeks to reconcile them in a manner consistent with the aims of the legislation . . .
>
> Once Cadillac Fairview was found to have no valid business purpose that would justify its interference with the protected union activity, its property rights were required to yield, at least to the limited extent ordered by the Board, to the employees' s. 3 organizational rights.

Assume that a collective agreement gives a union the right to use bulletin boards on the employer's premises. During a federal election campaign the union posts literature supporting the New Democratic Party. Management then issues a ban on all forms of political campaigning on company premises. Would this ban constitute an unfair labour practice in your jurisdiction? In *Adams Mine* (1983), 83 C.L.L.C. para. 16,011 (O.L.R.B.), such a ban was held not to be an unfair labour practice. The Ontario board concluded (at 14,096):

> . . . the activity is too remotely connected to the dominant purpose of the Labour Relations Act to attract the right asserted by the applicant. In our view, the communications in issue before us are not as connected to concerns of the bargaining unit employees as employees as they are to their concerns as voters. The complainant is therefore not communicating to bargaining unit employees primarily because of its status as their exclusive bargaining representative but rather as an affiliate or supporter of a political party seeking the electoral support of certain employees. In this context, the trade union canvasser is no different than any other political canvasser. A trade union should not be able to use

its certified bargaining agent status to capture an audience for its political canvassing activities.

5:700 UNION UNFAIR LABOUR PRACTICES

The law forbids trade unions from coercing employees to become members, in much the same way as management is forbidden to exert pressure in the opposite direction. Union unfair labour practice cases are much less common than employer unfair labour practice cases. What might explain this difference?

In *Milnet Mines Ltd.* (1953), 53 C.L.L.C. para. 17,063 (O.L.R.B.), threats of violence against organizers and supporters of an intervenor union by supporters of the applicant union led the Ontario Labour Relations Board to dismiss the application, without even holding a vote, because it considered that such intimidation would have a continuing effect. Similarly, in *Canadian Fabricated Products Ltd.* (1954), 54 C.L.L.C. para. 17,090 at 1511–12 (O.L.R.B.), an application by the applicant union to replace the intervenor union as bargaining agent for the respondent company's employees was dismissed on the basis of testimony from several of those employees that the applicant's canvassers had told them that it

> had collective relations with several of the companies upon whom the respondent was dependent for business and that, unless the employees of the respondent became members of the applicant, the members of the applicant employed by other companies would see to it that the respondent's goods were rejected and ultimately the witnesses would find themselves without work and would lose their jobs.

The board concluded (at 1512) that

> [t]hreats of economic reprisals of this nature are forbidden by section 48(1) [now 76] of the [Ontario *Labour Relations Act*] which declares that "no person shall seek by intimidation or coercion to compel any person to become . . . a member of a trade union . . .

5:800 REMEDIES FOR INTERFERENCE WITH THE RIGHT TO ORGANIZE

A test of any legal system is the extent to which its norms are applied in practice. When private actors do not comply voluntarily, effective remedies ensure that the law is implemented. In labour-management relations, remedies play a particularly important role because of the peculiar psychological dimensions of the employment relationship, because time has great tactical importance in a union organizing campaign, and because the parties do not sever their relationship when the litigation is over.

Labour relations legislation typically provides for both quasi-criminal penalties and administrative remedies. Under many of the statutes, certain unfair labour practices are treated as offences subject to prosecution. An aggrieved party may launch a prosecution only with leave from the responsible minister or labour relations board: see, for example, Ontario *Labour Relations Act*, 1995, sections 104–7 and 109.

Administrative penalties are available from a labour relations board. Boards in most jurisdictions have a broad legislative mandate to provide remedial relief. For example, section 96(4) of the Ontario statute authorizes the board to determine what should be done to redress any contravention of the legislation.

When an employer engages in an unfair labour practice by suspending or dismissing an employee, the normal remedy is reinstatement with compensation for lost wages and benefits. Such relief reaches only the harm done to the individual employee, yet the employer's unfair labour practice may have discouraged other employees from supporting the union. Labour relations boards have fashioned a variety of remedies designed to counteract this sort of collective harm.

As is noted above, section 5:300, in *Westinghouse Canada Ltd.*, [1980] 2 Can. L.R.B.R. 469 (O.L.R.B.), the employer closed its old plant and opened new ones in an attempt to escape a union. The Ontario board directed the employer to give employees of the old plant a right of first refusal on the new jobs, with no loss of seniority or fringe benefits, and to pay a relocation allowance to those employees who chose to move. The employer was also ordered to give the union a list of those employed at the new plant, to give the union access to company bulletin boards, and to permit union representatives to address employees during working hours. In addition, the union was awarded compensation for expenses incurred in organizing the new plants. Do you consider these remedial orders to be appropriate and sufficient in the circumstances?

In *United Steelworkers of America v. Radio Shack*, [1980] 1 Can. L.R.B. 99, the Ontario Labour Relations Board, having found that the employer had engaged in several unfair labour practices, awarded a number of remedies, including a direction that the employer post, for a sixty-day period, a notice drafted by the board. This notice informed employees of their rights, stated that the employer had violated those rights, and set out a promise by the employer to comply with both the legislation and the board's orders. Does this type of posting serve a useful purpose? On judicial review, the Ontario Divisional Court refused to interfere with the board's remedy: see *Re Tandy Electronics and United Steelworkers of America* (1980), 115 D.L.R. (3d) 197. Cory J. wrote (at page 215):

> So long as the award of the Board is compensatory and not punitive; so long as it flows from the scope, intent and provision of the act itself, then the award of damages is within the jurisdiction of the Board. The mere fact that the award of damages is novel, that the remedy is innovative, should not be a reason for finding it unreasonable.

Radio Shack may be the high-water mark of the development of labour board remedies. That the courts would continue to set limits on the power of boards to remedy unfair labour practices was made clear by the Supreme Court of Canada's response to the following decision of the federal board.

National Bank of Canada and Retail Clerks' International Union, [1982] 3 Can. L.R.B.R. 1 at 16–18, 24, 32–34 (C.L.R.B.)

[The union was certified to represent employees at the bank's Maguire Street branch in Quebec City. The *Canada Labour Code* imposed a statutory freeze on the terms and conditions of employment from the date of the application for certification until thirty days after the certificate was granted. The giving of notice to bargain led to another statutory freeze, but the union did not give such notice until more than thirty days after being certified. As a result of that delay, neither freeze was in force for about three days. During that interval, senior bank officials met and changed a plan to reduce services at the Maguire Street branch to a plan to close that branch and transfer its accounts to the non-unionized Sheppard Street branch. The union complained that this was an unfair labour practice.]

> FOISY, Vice-Chair: A business decision was taken [in May 1980] by the Bank's officers: the Maguire Street branch would be converted to a limited service branch under the jurisdiction of the Sheppard Street branch. . . . Then came the certification of the Union on June 27, 1980. . . . The thirty-day period began the day following this certification. The thirty days expired. No notice to bargain was sent. What happened? A special emergency meeting of the Bank's officers was held on July 29, 1980. For what reason? By the director of labour relations' own admission, it was because [neither of the statutory freezes] applied. A new decision was then taken by the Bank's officers: the Maguire Street branch would be closed. . . .
>
> After analysing the evidence and weighing the explanations provided by the Bank, the Board considers that it has been established conclusively that the decision to close the Maguire Street branch was motivated by anti-union animus. . . .
>
> [T]he Bank's officers saw a golden opportunity to "get rid of" the Union. The best way of achieving this, according to them, was simply to close the Maguire Street branch. If there were no longer any employees at this branch, the Bank would not have to negotiate with the Union. Moreover, it is for this reason that the Bank hurriedly informed all the employees that the branch would be closed. The Bank wanted to present the employees and the Union with a *fait accompli*: any collective bargaining would be pointless. . . . The building housing this branch was sold shortly after it was closed. In reality, every effort was made to close the books once and for all on the Maguire Street branch; they buried it post-haste.
>
> What is the effect of the Bank's unlawful actions? The Bank wanted to show the employees that they had made a mistake by joining a union. The message was clear and unequivocal: they would have been better off without a union. . . .

[After making the finding of anti-union animus, the board found that there had been a transfer of a business between the unionized and non-unionized branches and an intermingling of employees from the two branches. Without regard to the wishes of the original employees of the Sheppard Street branch, the board held that the union was the bargaining agent for employees at this branch. The board went on to grant remedies for the employer's unfair labour practice.]

> [T]he Union is now bargaining agent for the employees of the Sheppard Street branch. Nevertheless, it has been seriously, perhaps fatally, injured by the unlawful closure of the Maguire Street branch. . . . However, according to the provisions of the Code, it must negotiate a collective agreement with the employer for its group. To do so, it will need the employees' support. It will have to begin by learning who they are and meeting with them.

It will also have to be able to communicate with them. In short, owing to the employer's unlawful action, the Union is in the position where it must recruit members as if it had never been certified. Paradoxically, it must represent all the members of its unit fairly under section 136.1. We must assist it so that, in spite of the employer's unlawful action, it can fulfil the obligations imposed on it by the Code. . . .

From the psychological point of view, the Bank's unlawful action is particularly fraught with consequences in that it gives management employees and those likely to join a union the clear message that the prospect of access to free collective bargaining is not welcomed by the Bank. The public nature of the instant decision and its broad distribution through-out Canada can only give the employer's unlawful action greater publicity. For the objec-tives concerning free access to collective bargaining to be attained, it is important that employees who want to take advantage of this fundamental right perceive it as a mean-ingful one. If employees cannot be sure that the exercise of their right is more than an illusion, it follows that they will not want to exercise it. A right is of value only when effec-tive remedies protect its exercise. . . .

✻ ✻ ✻

The board ordered the employer to give the union lists of employees at the Sheppard Street branch, to allow the union to hold meetings at that branch during working hours, to allow the union to install a bulletin board in the staff area of that branch, and to pay all of the associated costs. These remedies were not challenged in the courts.

In addition, the board directed the employer to send a letter to all employees across Canada saying that it had violated their rights under the *Code* and that it recognized that they had a right to organize and that managers had a responsibility to recognize that right. The board also ordered the bank to deposit $144,000 into a trust fund to be administered jointly by the union and the bank, subject to the board's approval, for the purpose of promoting the *Code's* objectives among all of the bank's employees. The $144,000 figure was estimated to be the amount that had been saved by closing the branch. These remedies were reviewed by the Supreme Court of Canada in the follow-ing decision.

National Bank of Canada v. Retail Clerks' International Union, [1984] 1 S.C.R. 269 at 290–96

CHOUINARD J. (for the Court): . . . In *Canada Labour Relations Board v. Halifax Long-shoremen's Association; Canada Labour Relations Board v. Local 1764 International Longshore-men's Association* . . . , a complaint had been made under s. 161.1 of the Code against two unions who had failed to establish referral rules for hiring halls and who refused to admit certain individuals as members of the union or card men. This considerably reduced their chances of obtaining work, in addition to depriving them of the fringe benefits enjoyed by members and of the right to participate in union affairs. In addition to ordering that rules be adopted for administration of the hiring hall, including rules regarding the admission of members and the issuing of cards, the Canada Labour Relations Board ordered that three of the complainants be admitted as members and that a card be issued to the fourth.

This part of the orders was set aside by the Federal Court of Appeal, but restored by this Court.

In the course of his reasons on behalf of the Court, Laskin C.J. wrote . . . :

> In determining what remedy to prescribe for the breach of s. 161.1 the Board had to be concerned not only to rein in the two unions and to require them to conform to the statutory directions, but also to realize the importance of benefiting the complainants who had courageously acted in the interest of all non-union employees and would-be employees. I agree with the Board that it would not be enough in a case of this kind simply to leave the complainants under the cure of a proper job referral system. The Board thus invoked the very wide powers conferred upon it under s. 189 to require the unions "to do or refrain from doing anything that it is equitable to require [them] to do or refrain from doing in order to remedy or counteract any consequence of such failure to comply that is adverse to the fulfilment of [the] objectives [of s. 161.1]."

. . . the Chief Justice wrote:

> It is rarely a simple matter to draw a line between a lawful and unlawful exercise of power by a statutory tribunal, however ample its authority, when there are conflicting considerations addressed to the exercise of power. This Court has, over quite a number of years, thought it more consonant with the legislative objectives involved in a case such as this to be more rather than less deferential to the discharge of difficult tasks by statutory tribunals like the board.

Earlier, however, he noted . . . :

> At the same time, equitable and consequential considerations are not to be so remote from reparation of an established breach as to exceed any rational parameters.

In *Massicotte v. the Teamsters' Union*, Can L.R.B.R. 427 (Jan. 25, 1980), a complaint was made that a union had failed to represent a part-time employee by refusing to handle his dismissal grievance. After finding that the employee was part of a bargaining unit covered by the collective agreement, the Canada Labour Relations Board authorized him to undertake arbitration proceedings at the Union's expense. Laskin C.J. wrote for the Court . . . :

> However, the Board's wide remedial powers under s. 189, as amended by 1977–78 (Can.), c. 27. s. 68, where it has found a breach of s. 136.1 in the duty of a Union's duty of fair representation, entitled it to permit Massicotte to participate directly in the arbitration through nomination of an arbitrator.

In each of the foregoing cases a relationship can be seen between the act alleged, its consequences and the thing ordered as a means of remedying it. Thus, for example, in *Massicotte* the Board authorized the employee to undertake personally the handling of his grievance, which the Union refused to handle. In *Halifax Longshoremen's Association* the unions' conduct had the effect of depriving the complainants of work. Ordering that they should be admitted as members or issued cards would have the effect of increasing their chances of getting work. . . .

In the case at bar, however, and I say so with respect, this relationship between the alleged unfair practice and its consequences on the one hand and [the trust fund] on the other is in my opinion absent.

The order that there had been a sale within the meaning of s. 144 of the Code guaranteed the continuance of the certificate, which the Board extended to all employees in the new work location, the Sheppard Street branch.

Remedies Nos. 1 to 4, which were not disputed, are designed to ensure that the Union would be firmly established at the new branch.

However, remedy No. 6, regarding the creation of a trust fund to promote the objectives of the Code among other employees of the Bank, which in my view means promoting the unionization of those other employees, is not something intended to remedy or counteract the consequences harmful to realization of those objectives that may result from closure of Maguire Street and its incorporation in the Sheppard Street branch. The fact that a large number of the Bank's other employees are not unionized is not a consequence of closure of the Maguire Street branch, where the Union continued to exist and had its certificate extended. Thus, I consider that this remedy should be set aside.

In accordance with a practice followed by a number of labour relations boards, including the Board, the latter ordered in remedy No. 5 that a letter signed by the president and chief executive officer of the Bank be sent to all employees, including management personnel. . . .

The Bank submitted that this was in actual fact a humiliating letter, that this order is unreasonable and vexatious and that the Board's decision was intended to be not compensatory but punitive, exemplary and humiliating, which constitutes an excess of its powers. The Bank further submitted that the letter repeats the conclusions of remedy No. 6 regarding the creation of the trust fund, which should be set aside.

In my view, this last ground suffices for remedy No. 5 to be likewise set aside. The announcement of the creation of this fund in this letter is at the very least a key feature of the letter. Since remedy No. 6 regarding the fund should be set aside, the Court should also set aside remedy No. 5, regarding the letter which puts emphasis on the fund. . . .

BEETZ J. (Estey, McIntyre, Lamer, and Wilson JJ. concurring): I have had the benefit of reading the opinion of my brother Chouinard, and I concur in his findings and reasons.

Like him, I consider that remedy No. 6 is not a true remedy; but I also think that, like remedy No. 5, it is clearly punitive in nature. It was acknowledged by all counsel at the hearing that the Canada Labour Relations Board has no power to impose punitive measures. . . .

This type of penalty is totalitarian and as such alien to the tradition of free nations like Canada, even for the repression of the most serious crimes.

* * *

The litigation of unfair labour practices is a time-consuming process. A remedy granted after a complaint has been adjudicated on its merits may come weeks or months after the violation was committed. In the meantime, support for the union may have plummeted because of the employer's unlawful conduct. In 1992, the Ontario Labour Relations Board was authorized by statute to grant interim relief pending the final disposition of a complaint. In *Loeb Highland v. United Food and Commercial Workers Union*, [1993] O.L.R.B. Rep. 197, (McCormick, Chair), an employee allegedly fired for participating in an organizing campaign was reinstated pending the adjudication of his complaint on the merits. The board's power to give interim relief was repealed in 1995.

Most of the administrative remedies that seek to protect union organizing activities are process-oriented, in that they attempt to redress the harm caused by illegal employer conduct while leaving employees to choose for or against collective bargaining. Until 1998, the Ontario *Labour Relations Act* provided (in section 11) for the remedy of certifying a union which had been the victim of serious unfair labour practices, even where the union could not prove that it had the support of a majority of the bargaining unit. An illustration of the use of this remedy is found in the *Wal-Mart* case, set out above in section 5:500. In that case, the Ontario Labour Relations Board said:

> The first requirement of section 11(1) is that an employer or someone acting on behalf of the employer must have breached the Act. In this case we are satisfied that in several instances the employer's conduct breached section 70 of the Act.

. . .

> The second and third factors set out in section 11 provide that a certificate is not to be issued pursuant to this section unless the Board is satisfied that no other remedy, including the taking of another representation vote is sufficient to counter the effects of the employer's contravention of the Act. As we have already noted, this is not a typical section 11 case. However, in our view the determinative factor set out in section 11(1)2 is not whether the employer['s] breaches of the Act are flagrant or egregious but whether or not the employer's breaches of the Act result in the Board concluding that a representation vote does not or would not likely reflect the true wishes of the employees in the bargaining unit about being represented by a trade union. The employer in this case is sophisticated and its response to the union's organizing drive reflects this. We have no doubt that the intentionally generated implied threat to job security which occurred in this case had the result of rendering the representation vote taken on May 9, 1996 meaningless. This case is a classic example of a situation in which the conduct of the employer changes the question in the minds of the employees at the vote on May 9th from one of union representation to one of "do you want to retain your employment." . . .

> Section 11(1)3 requires us to consider whether any other remedy short of automatic certification, including the taking of a second representation vote, is sufficient to counter the effect of the employer's contraventions of the Act. We are of the view that a second representation vote in this case would be equally meaningless. We would adopt the comments made by the Board in *Lorraine Products Canada Limited*. . . . that:

>> the threat to job security and/or economic well-being cannot now be erased by either the employer or the Board. It undoubtedly followed the employees into the voting booth on October 5 and would follow the employees into the voting booth in any subsequent vote.

The Board has repeatedly recognized that threats to an employee's job security will undermine the ability of the employees to freely express their views with regard to union representation. Therefore a second vote in this case is not appropriate. . . .

The final question the Board must answer is whether the union has support adequate for the purposes of collective bargaining. On May 2, 1996 when the union filed its application for certification it filed membership evidence on behalf of approximately forty-four percent of the bargaining unit. Although Wal-Mart raised concerns with regard to the membership evidence filed on behalf of one employee and suggested that as a result the Board should generally question the membership evidence in this case, we do not share the employer's concerns. We are of the view that the membership evidence filed in this case is completely reliable. At the time of its application for certification, the union after a very brief campaign, enjoyed the support of forty-four percent of the bargaining unit. One week later as a result of the employer's contravention of the Act that support had plummeted to approximately twenty-one percent. However, as noted we are of the view that this drastic drop in support was not reflective of the true wishes of the employees. Accordingly, we are of the view that the trade union has membership support adequate for the purposes of collective bargaining.

* * *

After the board's decision to issue a certificate in the *Wal-Mart* case, section 11 of the Ontario *Labour Relations Act, 1995* was amended in 1998 to deprive the board of the power to certify a union without a vote where it finds that employer unfair labour practices have undermined the organizing campaign. The amendments restricted the board to ordering another representation vote in such cases.

The board's approach to the use of that limited authority in a case of egregious employer interference with an organizing campaign was shown by *Baron Metal Industries*, [2001] OLRD No. 1210. The employer had used the services of a criminal gang which, among other things, had made death threats against union supporters. The representation vote ended in a tie. The Board ordered that a new vote be held within six months, at a time to be determined by the union. In addition, the Board did the following: directed the employer to provide the union with the names, addresses, and telephone numbers of all employees eligible to participate in the new vote; gave the union the right to distribute leaflets in the workplace prior to the vote; directed the employer to post in the workplace and distribute to each employee a Board notice that the employer had violated the Act; gave the union the right to meet with the employer to discuss the discharge or suspension of any employee before the new vote; directed that all employees in the bargaining unit attend monthly union meetings; allowed the union to designate three representatives to act on its behalf in the workplace; and directed the employer to reimburse the union for its organizing costs. The Board also granted the union additional damages for intimidation and loss of opportunity to bargain.

The criminal law is rarely invoked against employers who engage in anti-union activity. In the following case, the Crown appealed a fine imposed on an employer for the *Criminal Code* offence of conspiring to effect an unlawful purpose, that purpose being to commit unfair labour practices prohibited by provincial labour relations legislation. The Crown argued that the fine was too light in the circumstances.

R. v. K-Mart Canada Ltd. (1982), 82 C.L.L.C. para. 14,185 at 222–23 (Ont. C.A.)

HOWLAND C.J.O.: Prior to 1975, the respondent [K-Mart] maintained a warehouse on Progress Avenue in Scarborough and Local Union No. 419 of the International Brotherhood of Teamsters, Chauffeurs, Warehousemen, and Helpers of America ("the Union") had been certified as the bargaining agent for the respondent's employees at that location.

During 1975, the respondent opened a new distribution centre in Bramalea and some employees were moved from the Scarborough warehouse to the new operation. On April 16, 1975, an application was made to the Ontario Labour Relations Board for certification of the Union as the bargaining agent at the new distribution centre.

The respondent opposed the application and a postponement of the certification vote was granted by the Ontario Labour Relations Board on the representation that the work force of the respondent at Bramalea would be quadrupled to exceed 120 shortly after the centre opened. This representation was made under the signature of Michael Clarke as Vice-President of Personnel and Employee Relations of the respondent. In fact, there was no intention to augment the respondent's work force at Bramalea to this extent.

Centurion Investigation Limited ('Centurion') and Mark-Anada Associates Limited ('Mark-Anada') of which Daniel McGarry was the principal shareholder and officer, had agreements with the respondent to provide security and personnel services. While the application for certification was under consideration, a further agreement was made between Daniel McGarry and senior officials of the respondent whereby a number of employees of Centurion and Mark-Anada would be hired by the respondent to get information about the organizing efforts of the Union, to dissuade other employees from voting for certification, and to vote against certification themselves.

As the number of employees at the new centre did not increase, the Ontario Labour Relations Board ordered a certification vote to take place on September 19, 1975. On September 7 a strategy meeting was held, attended by Daniel McGarry, Jenkins, who was the director of security of the respondent, and Seunik, who was directing the movement of employees to the new centre in Bramalea, together with a number of employees of Centurion. At this meeting discussions took place as to the ways and means of discrediting the Union and its leaders and defeating the certification vote.

The voters' list contained the names of sixteen Centurion employees who were not *bona fide* employees of the respondent. The certification vote took place on September 18 and 19, 1975 and resulted in a tie vote of 30 votes for and 30 votes against certification. Two of the ballots cast were segregated and were further investigated.

At a hearing of the Ontario Labour Relations Board into the circumstances surrounding the certification vote, one Centurion undercover employee gave false evidence detrimental to the Union, in the presence of Michael Clarke. At a later hearing another undercover employee stated in Mr. Clarke's presence that he was a *bona fide* employee of the respondent and that his connection with Centurion was innocuous.

During this period, a productivity flow analysis agreement, back-dated to April 1975, was prepared and signed by Daniel McGarry and Seunik on behalf of the respondent to attempt to explain the influx of undercover employees into the Bramalea distribution centre.

The Ontario Labour Relations Board then directed that a further certification vote be held on January 30, 1976. Before that vote was taken the respondent had obtained new legal advice and had discharged Centurion and Mark-Anada. The second certification vote resulted in 37 votes being cast in favour of certification, and 8 votes against.

After the Union had been certified, it was unable to negotiate a contract with the respondent. A long strike ensued and finally the Union ceased to act as the bargaining agent for the respondent's employees at the Bramalea distribution centre.

The respondent expended over $167,000 to achieve its ends in connection with the certification votes, but this sum may have included, in part, the cost of security services being provided for the respondent.

* * *

The Court of Appeal increased the fine from $25,000 to $100,000. Was this an adequate penalty? Should the courts impose jail sentences on company officers who engage in this sort of conduct? What are the advantages and disadvantages of using the criminal law rather than administrative proceedings?

5:900 THE PROFESSIONAL RESPONSIBILITY OF LAWYERS

Lawyers practicing in the field of labour relations are not uncommonly faced with clients who are contemplating illegal conduct — management representatives who are determined to interfere in an organizing campaign, or union representatives who believe that untimely (and therefore unlawful) strike action will be to their advantage. Parallel situations of course arise in other fields of law practice, but the emotional and ideological overlay of union-employer relations may make the position of labour lawyers particularly difficult — a difficulty which is compounded by the fact that most of them act only for management or labour and never for the other side. This may promote an unusually close identification between lawyer and client — a situation that can have real dangers.

The canons of legal ethics of law societies across Canada prohibit a lawyer from knowingly helping or encouraging a client to break the law, or advising on how to do so in a way that might avoid or limit punishment. Consider what these obligations mean for a lawyer whose management client seems to have weighed the costs of being found guilty an unfair labour practice and to have concluded that it is worth incurring those costs to keep the union out — or for a lawyer whose union client seems to have made a similar cost-benefit analysis with respect to taking illegal strike action.

The following is a decision of the Discipline Committee of the Law Society of Upper Canada.

Law Society of Upper Canada v. Rovet, [1992] L.S.D.D. No. 24

In early January, 1991, A Company learned that certain of its employees were considering joining a union. The company's president, B, spoke to several lawyers who specialize in the representation of employers in labour relations matters, most of whom informed him that there was little the company could do that would be effective in blocking the unionization of the employees.

One of the lawyers with whom B spoke was the Solicitor, who was not as pessimistic about the company's prospects of blocking the unionization attempt as were most of the other lawyers with whom B spoke. B arranged to meet with the Solicitor, and they met for the first time on January 8, 1991. Another executive employed by A Company, C, was also in attendance. The Solicitor outlined the process of union certification under applicable legislation. He told B and C that the number of employees who would be included in the bargaining unit is a critical factor in the success of an organizational drive.

The Solicitor also asked B and C whether A Company had any plans to increase the size of the company's work force, as that would affect the size of the bargaining unit and might have the effect of reducing the proportion of employees who supported the union.

B informed the Solicitor that the company's business had increased significantly in the autumn of 1990 and that an expansion of the work force was justifiable. The Solicitor said that he knew of a company, D Company, which was able to provide employees who were favourably disposed to the employer's interests in an organizational drive, on a contract basis, until the union organizing campaign was over. . . .

Two days later, on January 10, 1991, a representative of D Company met with the Solicitor and B. After preliminary discussions about how many additional employees were justifiable, the Solicitor left the meeting and A and D Company's representative negotiated an agreement in principle that day whereby A Company agreed to utilize the services of D Company and to employ a specified number of workers provided by D Company. The Solicitor was informed of the agreement in principle.

On January 17, 1991, the Solicitor met with representatives of A Company and D Company. At that time, the main terms of an agreement were worked out. The agreement called for a separate, confidential contract to be entered into between D Company and a numbered company owned by the principal shareholders of A Company. This separate contract provided for extra payments to be made to D Company. At the conclusion of the meeting the numbered company made an initial payment to D Company in the amount of $125,000. The numbered company agreed to pay that sum to D Company each week until the certification application was concluded.

Over the next few days the Solicitor drafted the two contracts. The initial drafts of the contract between A Company and D Company, whereby the former agreed to employ certain workers of the latter, were dated December 14, 1990.

On January 23, 1991, the Solicitor met with representatives of A Company and D Company to deal with certain issues which had to be resolved before the contracts could be signed. During or after the meeting, the Solicitor and the others in attendance learned that the union had filed an application for certification the previous week. One effect of

319

the filing of the application was to settle the bargaining unit for the purpose of determining support for the union as of the date of filing. As of the date of filing, there was an agreement in principle between A Company and D Company whereby the former would hire extra workers and the number of workers had been determined and were on standby, but none of them had yet started to work for A Company. A Company nevertheless decided, with the Solicitor's concurrence, to carry into effect the agreed upon strategy of employing workers provided through D Company and to submit that they should be treated as members of the unit and eligible to vote.

On or after January 23, 1991, the Solicitor prepared the two contracts in their final form. The contract between A Company and D Company was backdated to November 23, 1990, and its commencement date was specified as being January 1, 1991.

In addition, at the request of B, correspondence between A Company and D Company was created. This correspondence purported to reflect negotiations between the two companies beginning in early October, 1990, which culminated in the November 23, 1990, contract. This correspondence was generated in draft form by a junior lawyer in the Solicitor's firm in consultation with B, to the Solicitor's knowledge. The junior lawyer gave the draft correspondence to the Solicitor, who then gave them to B and a representative of D Company, E. The letters were then typed on the letterheads of A Company and D Company, and copies were returned to the Solicitor.

In late February, 1991, B and E had a falling out, and B concluded that E would be a liability to A Company if called upon to testify. Another representative of D Company, F, was introduced to A Company. To the Solicitor's knowledge, new backdated contracts and correspondence were prepared and signed. This time F signed on behalf of D Company, as if he had been involved from the beginning.

As the certification process continued, A Company continued to make weekly payments in the amount of $125,000 to D Company.

The Solicitor made his final written submission to the labour relations board in relation to the certification application in a letter dated March 11, 1991. The submission made was voluntary and not required. The statutory reply, which was required, was accurate and was filed. No contractual documents were appended to the voluntary submission. In his letter the Solicitor made the following representations which he knew to be false:

1. That negotiations between A Company and D Company began in October, 1990. (In fact negotiations began on January 10, 1991.); and

2. That the contract was made on November 23, 1990, and that the new workers were employed beginning on January 1, 1991. (In fact there was no agreement in principle until January 10, the terms of the contract were not agreed upon until after the date on which the certification application was filed, and the new workers were not paid for any work they did for A Company until at least January 23, 1991.)

The labour relations board granted the certification application. Shortly thereafter, representatives of A Company consulted with another lawyer, who, after consulting with other senior members of the bar, reported the matter to the Society and to the Solicitor's firm.

The Solicitor's firm thereupon reviewed the Solicitor's file. Because it appeared that several undocumented disbursements (payments to the Solicitor's American Express account) had been charged to A Company, the firm retained an accounting firm, Price Waterhouse, to review the Solicitor's fee billings from April, 1989, to April, 1991.

Price Waterhouse's examination in conjunction with a follow up review by the Society disclosed that the Solicitor charged numerous personal expenses to client files and arranged for the firm to pay these expenses. . . .

The personal expenses which the Solicitor charged to clients as fees included such items as newspaper subscriptions, airplane tickets, automobile expenses, restaurant meals, drycleaning, hardware, baseball and theatre tickets, household items, landscaping, photographs, furniture, ski equipment, clothes, books, and art. It is not possible to determine precisely the amount of personal expenses included by the Solicitor in client fee billings over the period during which the Solicitor was a partner in Fogler, Rubinoff (a period of two years), but the amount is in the range of approximately $35,000. The Solicitor generally reduced the fee billings to accommodate the personal expenses so that he did not overcharge or double bill the client.

The Solicitor has co-operated fully in the Law Society's investigation, and voluntarily undertook not to practise pending the hearing of the complaint. He has not practised, pursuant to his undertaking, since May 11, 1991. . . .

The Committee finds the Solicitor guilty of professional misconduct. . . . The Committee recommends that the Solicitor be suspended from practice for a period of six months from an effective date of June 1, 1991.

The evidence demonstrated that the Solicitor is an intelligent, experienced, wholly competent practitioner of many years experience, who enjoyed an enviable reputation within the legal community and with an apparently sound family relationship.

The character evidence led on his behalf uniformly makes these points:

a) The Solicitor has never been known to have engaged in unethical or improper activities, other than the conduct evident in these complaints.

b) His conduct in respect of the complaints appears to be an aberration, and the Committee is unanimously of the belief that the possibility of the conduct re-occurring is at least remote.

The Solicitor has engaged himself actively in community activities, to the obvious benefit of the public in general.

[This recommendation was considered by Convocation, the governing body of the Law Society of Upper Canada, which made the final decision. Convocation determined that the appropriate penalty was a one-year suspension running from the date of its decision. A dissenting Bencher, whose reasons are excerpted below, was of the view that the solicitor should be disbarred.]

BENCHER LAX (dissenting): Had this been a case of a serious misappropriation of client funds, even in circumstances where a lawyer had never been before the Society previously, the solicitor would have been disbarred. Indeed, Mr. MacKenzie said as much in his submissions to Convocation. However, he also said that Mr. Rovet's conduct had not been regarded in the past as the kind of case which would have attracted a penalty of disbarment. Convocation was referred to several authorities, decided in 1984 and 1985, none of which were on all fours with this case. However, even had they been, that is not to say that they were correctly decided. In any event, as Mr. MacKenzie pointed out, ethical standards imposed on lawyers change over time and if anything, should be higher today than they were in the past. In my view, a solicitor who cheats his partners, lies to an administrative tribunal, and prepares fraudulent documents for submission to the tribunal, engages in conduct which is equally reprehensible as the conduct of a solicitor who misappropriates client funds. In both kinds of cases, there is a serious violation of trust. In both kinds of cases, there is harm suffered. Although it may be easier to point to the direct harm suffered by clients when lawyers steal their money, this does not mean that the harm done in this kind of case is any less damaging. In both, the public is made vulnerable and the ethical standards of the profession and the public's confidence in it are seriously diminished.

* * *

Consider these following questions about the above case.

1. Put aside the issue of improper expense accounts, and focus on the issue of misleading the board. What is a lawyer's duty in this respect? Not to counsel or assist a client to build a record of false facts that would defeat the right of workers to organize? Not to tender those facts in the form of an affidavit? To warn the client not to come forward with false facts? To appear before the board or to complain to the Law Society if he or she gets wind of the possibility that false facts will be or have been tendered to the board?

2. What explanation might Rovet have had for his actions, other than an uncharacteristic lapse of judgment? That he needed the business? That all's fair in love and labour relations? That the practice of gerrymandering the bargaining unit was widespread (witness the availability of the firm that supplied the additional workers and his knowledge of it), and that he was being penalized for what others were doing all the time? That the board was not a court, but a tribunal thought to be unfriendly to employers, and therefore not entitled to the same degree of deference from advocates?

3. What would have happened to a nonlawyer advocate (a union representative or a management consultant, for example) who engaged in similar behaviour? What should have been done with Company D, which supplied the additional workers? What should have been done with Company A, which attempted, with Rovet's help, to mislead the board?

Chapter 6: The Acquisition and Termination of Bargaining Rights

REFERENCES

George Adams, *Canadian Labour Law*, 2d ed. (Aurora, Ont.: Canada Law Book, 1993) c. 7–9; Donald Carter *et al.*, *Labour Law in Canada*, 5th ed. (Markham, Ont.: Butterworths, 2002) 210–44

6:100 THE *WAGNER ACT* MODEL AND THE PRINCIPLE OF EXCLUSIVITY

Before the advent of modern collective bargaining legislation, workers and trade unions had to rely on economic sanctions to induce employers to engage in collective bargaining. Some of the most bitter strikes in North American labour history were fought more over the demand for trade union recognition than on demands for specific improvements in terms and conditions. It was mainly to remedy the problem of union recognition that labour relations legislation was introduced.

As has been noted in earlier chapters, the current North American system of labour law, often known as the *Wagner Act* model, was created in the 1930s in the United States and was adopted across Canada in the aftermath of the Second World War. In every Canadian jurisdiction, there is a statutory procedure (known as certification) which allows a union, upon proving that it has majority support among a unit of employees, to become the exclusive bargaining agent for those employees and to compel their employer to bargain with it on their behalf. An alternative but less common route allows a union to be "voluntarily recognized" by the employer as the exclusive bargaining agent for its employees. In either case, the union is prohibited from exercising economic sanctions in its efforts to acquire bargaining rights. And in either case, it becomes the bargaining agent for all of the employees in the unit, including the minority who did not support certification.

Majority rule and exclusivity of bargaining rights are key principles of our labour law system. They are closely related; exclusivity is justified by the fact that the union has demonstrated that it has the support of a majority of the employees, as well as by the assumption that it is generally to the advantage of all parties to have one clearly identified interlocutor on the employee side.

The *Wagner Act* model was designed to reflect the economic and industrial relations realities of what is sometimes called its golden age — from the 1940s to the 1960s. It was created with large and stable manufacturers in mind, such as Ford and General Motors, and on the assumption that once workers were unionized, they would be able to bargain on a more or less equal footing with their powerful employers. As the following extract explains, some aspects of the *Wagner Act* model are unique to North America.

Roy Adams, "Union Certification as an Instrument of Labor Policy: A Comparative Perspective" in Sheldon Friedman *et al.*, eds., *Restoring the Promise of American Labor Law* (Ithaca: ILR Press, Cornell University, 1994) 260 at 260–65

In comparative perspective, the North American practice of union certification is very unusual. Generally, other countries do not divide the labor force into tiny bargaining units and do not require representatives of employee interests to win the support of the majority of employees in each microunit to acquire government support for recognition. . . .

When the World War I period dawned, a broad consensus had emerged that all employees should be able to participate in the making of the decisions under which they labored. There was, however, no consensus on how that principle should be put into practice. The dominant position among employers was that there should be mechanisms composed entirely of representatives chosen by and from enterprise employees rather than from national unions. The justification was that 'outside unions' had no interest in the welfare of the enterprise and thus were likely to have a disruptive effect on productivity and competitiveness. The solution offered by this group to the participation imperative was the establishment voluntarily by companies of employee representation plans.

The compromise position worked out by the NWLB [National Wartime Labor Board] for the contrary stances of labor and management was acceptable to the American Federation of Labor. The AFL felt confident that under a 'true open shop' system in which employees were free to join or not join but in which employers did not discriminate against those who became active in a union, the free and independent labor organizations would be able to convince the enfranchised employees to vote for union activists and, by demonstrating their ability, attract most employees to their ranks. Employers were not so confident of maintaining control of employment relations under such a system and thus shortly made new demands. At its conference in October 1918, the National Industrial Conference Board (NICB) stated that its members would tolerate what they called 'cooperative representation' (rather than collective bargaining) only if the majority of employees entitled to vote requested such a system by voting in favor of it in an election held on company premises. . . . In the 1930s, when the first National Labor Board was established under the National Industrial Recovery Act, it drew upon this experience to hold elections when the majority status of a bargaining agent was in doubt. . . . Later, the majority principle was embedded in the Wagner Act. . . .

. . . For the unions, certification results in compulsory collective bargaining, backed by a government agency with powers to compel an intransigent employer to enter into negotiations with a view toward signing a written collective agreement. Since achieving recognition for the purposes of collective bargaining is extremely difficult even with the aid of a government agency with substantial enforcement powers, without the aid of such an agency it would no doubt be much more difficult. Since certification leads to legal orders requiring reluctant employers to enter into negotiations, it is generally looked on as a pro-union policy invention. As noted above, however, it was first called for by employer spokespeople and for good reason. From the point of view of the nonunion employer seeking to maintain the status quo, certification has some outstanding positive traits.

First of all, American policy as it has evolved to the present permits the employer to contest employee representation campaigns. . . .

A second major positive aspect of certification from the position of the nonunion employer is that it has entirely dissipated the pressure that existed during the first four decades of the twentieth century for the general enfranchisement of the industrial citizenry. As it has evolved in the United States, certification legitimizes industrial autocracy. Because employees have a means to establish collective bargaining through an electoral process, noncertified employers are considered entirely justified in refusing to recognize and deal with independent unions representing a minority of their employees. . . .

Not only are employers permitted to attempt to maintain unilateral control over the establishment of terms and conditions of employment, they are also forbidden from establishing employee representation plans voluntarily. Their alternative to collective bargaining with independent unions as a means of establishing industrial democracy has been outlawed. The unions successfully argued in the 1930s that such plans generally did not provide for genuine employee representation but instead were used by employers to avoid dealing with organizations freely chosen by the employees themselves. To remove that blockage on the road to real joint regulation of the conditions of work, the Wagner Act outlawed company unions. . . . Because of this development, employers have been effectively relieved of the duty resting upon them earlier in the century to address the democratic void in industry positively.

The result of this evolution is that, in the United States today, only a small and diminishing part of the labor force has in place institutions that allow employees to influence the conditions under which they work. Four out of five American employees have their conditions of employment established within a system of industrial autocracy.

* * *

In recent decades, the feasability of the *Wagner Act* model for acquiring bargaining rights has been called into question by new realities, most notably the increasing globalization of the economy. As you read this chapter's discussion of how that model works and how it might be changed, bear in mind the following excerpts on how globalization has affected the balance of power between corporations, unions, and governments.

Sanford Jacoby, "Social Dimensions of Global Economic Integration" in S. Jacoby, ed., *The Workers of Nations: Industrial Relations in a Global Economy* (New York: Oxford University Press, 1995) 3 at 3–4, 8

We live and work in a global economy; world trade is growing faster than world incomes. . . . Nations feel compelled to change their economic and social policies to conform to global patterns. This pressure is felt particularly by labor market institutions — wage structures, workplace practices, social insurance, and labor relations — all of which have been undergoing major changes in the developed nations. The changes have been accelerated by regional trading pacts such as the European Community (EC) and the North American Free Trade Agreement (NAFTA).

Greater trade has been accompanied by greater mobility of capital. Every day billions of dollars, yen, and other currencies shuttle instantaneously across the planet. To attract and retain fickle investors, nations must rely on their physical infrastructure and their human talents. . . .

World economic growth and productivity rose rapidly during the 1960s but began to slow in the 1970s. The deceleration continued for much of the 1980s and early 1990s; some regions (such as Europe) were affected more severely than others (such as East Asia). Despite the slowing in growth, markets became increasingly internationalized in the 1980s. Trade in goods and services grew rapidly. Meanwhile capital markets transcended national boundaries, a remarkable but not fully intended result of computer technology, 'petrodollar' recycling, and the shift from fixed to floating exchange rates.

Growth of world trade and finance has hastened the spread of multinational corporations (MNCs) that operate in, and depend on, the economies of many world regions. Conversely, MNCs have contributed directly to market globalization via their foreign direct investments. Foreign investment exploded in recent years; between 1983 and 1989 it grew more rapidly than world trade itself. . . .

In the advanced nations, globalization has had mostly a negative effect on organized labor's bargaining power and political influence. Competition from lower-cost producers is exerting downward pressure on wages and employment in many unionized industries, from steel to textiles to apparel. To secure a competitive advantage farther up the value chain, employers are shifting toward the production of more technology-intensive goods and services. This step, however, has harmful consequences for unions, at least in the short term. It reduces the demand for manual workers — who form a large portion of most labor movements — while boosting employment of non-manual employees, a group in which rates of unionization tend to be lower.

Historically, employers were willing to agree to collective bargaining when unions could promise to 'take wages out of competition.' The promise made sense when markets were fixed within national boundaries and employers themselves were immobile. Today, however, markets are international and unions find themselves unable to standardize wages across borders. This situation diminishes their usefulness to employers. Also, modern employers now find it far easier to relocate. Even aircraft can be repaired or paperwork processed almost anywhere in the world. The mere threat of relocation saps labor's bargaining power even further. Government employees are virtually the only group free of this threat. Thus, it is hardly surprising that throughout the advanced countries, unionization rates in the public sector are holding up better than in other industries. . . .

Harry Arthurs, "Reinventing Labor Law for the Global Economy"(2001) 22 Berkeley J.Emp'ment and Lab.L. 271, at 282–83

. . . [G]lobalization has changed the effect of the law by placing groups of workers in different jurisdictions in competition with each other. Employers now have a choice — and are perceived to have a choice — between producing in their own countries using local workers and local suppliers, shifting production off-shore to foreign workers and subsidiaries, or out-sourcing production altogether to foreign suppliers and subcontractors.

Indeed, thanks to technology, service functions such as data entry and call centers are even more easily moved offshore than production functions. Thus workers across the globe are effectively forced to compete for jobs: they must underbid their rivals in other countries by promising not only to be more productive, but to work harder and more cheaply and to be less assertive about their rights.

In a sense, the pressures — or temptations — for employers to shift work to jurisdictions with low labor standards resemble those which prevailed in the United States before the federal commerce power was used to establish a single system of labor law. However, today these competing groups of workers are located in jurisdictions that are sovereign nations, not stated in a federal union, and there appears to be no way to bring them all under one overarching legal regime.

. . . [G]lobalization has helped to attenuate the connections between employers and employees and to dilute the whole notion of community of interest among workers. Whereas employees used to work for an identifiable common employer, today they occupy an often-uncertain location on a global production and distribution chain that links transnational operations, their divisions, subsidiaries and allies to a host of ephemeral local contractors, brokers, and distributors. Whereas employees of a given employer used to share many common interests and characteristics — language, culture, politics, history, legal rights, managerial supervision, and integrated work processes — workers in the global economy may share none of the above. And whereas "employees" used to be pretty much identifiable as such for statutory and social purposes, today more and more workers around the world are self-employed, are reluctant parties to the "new psychological contract" of discontinuous, serial and sometimes contingent jobs, or work under other coercive arrangements that leave their legal status unclear, their economic future uncertain, and their sense of solidarity greatly attenuated. For all of these reasons, it is increasingly difficult for workers in the global economy even to identify their common adversary, let alone to define common expectations, claim common entitlements, or implement common strategies.

. . . [E]ven when workers occasionally transcend these perceptual and conceptual difficulties and organize across national boundaries, they confront systemic difficulties in the form of local labor laws with inconsistent legal rules. Even as between democratic countries where workers have comparable legal protections, and even within industries where operations are integrated across national boundaries, these systemic difficulties are formidable. Just imagine the problem of trying to create a bargaining unit or negotiate a collective agreement that covers all Daimler Chrysler workers in America, Canada, and Germany. Just imagine the complexity of orchestrating a strike of professional athletes that is legal on both sides of the Canada-U.S. border in, say Major League Baseball. [Reprinted by permission.]

* * *

6:200 THE APPROPRIATE BARGAINING UNIT

Describing the North American model as a majority rule system built on a principle of exclusivity is accurate, but is too abstract to explain much about the certification process.

One cannot have a majority in the air; it has to be a majority of some constituency. In Canadian and American labour law, that constituency is called the "bargaining unit."

6:210 Bargaining Unit Determination: General Principles

A bargaining unit is a group of employees defined on the basis of the employer for whom they work and the positions they occupy. In some cases, it consists of all employees of the employer who are engaged in the production of a particular good or service. In other cases, it consists only of a subset of those employees who perform certain tasks. It can include workers employed at only one workplace or at several locations. Certification applications typically involve only one union and one employer — a fact which, as we will see later in this chapter, is often considered to be a serious shortcoming in our labour law system.

A bargaining unit has two distinct functions. First, it serves as an electoral constituency for the purposes of certification and decertification. Second, it serves as the basis for collective bargaining, because a collective agreement drawn up at the bargaining table normally covers all employees in the bargaining unit.

The parameters of the unit will affect the ongoing employer-union relationship in several ways. First, there may be strong pressure toward the compression of wage differentials and toward uniformity in other terms of employment for everyone covered by the agreement. For management, this may facilitate the administration of the enterprise. Employees with special skills or other employment advantages, however, may not wish to be swept into a unit with their fellow workers. The failure of an all-embracing union to meet the needs of special groups may undermine morale or make recruiting more difficult.

Second, if there are a multiplicity of units within a single enterprise, disputes may well occur over which collective agreement governs particular tasks. Inter-union "jurisdictional disputes" may arise over which of two or more unions should have the exclusive right to bargain for a particular group of employees. More often, however, jurisdictional disputes involve a dispute between the members of different unions over who should do certain work — for example, who replaces light bulbs, the janitor or the maintenance electrician? The drawing of bargaining unit boundaries can help to spark or damp down jurisdictional disputes.

Third, the degree of economic pressure that each party can bring to bear on the other will also be affected by the design of the bargaining unit. Economic action in support of negotiation demands is often restricted to the same unit as is covered by the collective agreement. At a certain point, workers within the unit may strike in support of their demands, or the employer may lock them out in support of its demands. In addition, a work stoppage within the unit may interrupt other processes outside it that are functionally integrated. Often these are the only economic pressures that one party can lawfully exert on the other. Strikes or lockouts involving workers outside the unit are unlawful in most jurisdictions unless those workers themselves have the right to strike or their employer has the right to lock them out. Picketing by lawfully striking bargaining unit employees that is directed at other workers may also be outlawed. Issues of this sort are considered in Chapter 8.

The size and shape of the bargaining unit can have a dramatic effect on bargaining power and on the frequency and impact of strikes. If there are many units in a particular enterprise, there is the possibility of a number of legal strikes at different times, which may be quite disruptive and therefore quite effective as a bargaining tactic. If only one unit is on strike, and its members are few in number or not particularly indispensable, the employer may easily be able to continue operating despite the strike. Strategically placed employees can, however, have a tremendous amount of bargaining power, even if their numbers are small. It may make a significant difference whether such employees bargain on their own or as part of a larger group.

The design of bargaining unit structures affects economic power in another way. Each wage settlement is strongly influenced by "coercive comparisons" to earlier settlements for other units. As the number of bargaining units increases, so do the opportunities for such comparisons. The tactic whereby a unit seeks to obtain a settlement better than one previously negotiated by another group is known as leapfrogging. In recent decades, however, this has become more difficult, as many unions have been put on the defensive by recessionary tendencies, labour saving technologies, employer attempts to outsource work to nonunion firms, and growing international competition.

These observations point to the dilemma of defining an appropriate bargaining unit. The optimal unit for effective long-term collective bargaining may be larger than the group within which a union can in the short run obtain the majority support necessary to get collective bargaining started at all. How should these competing considerations be weighed? And should the public interest be considered, as distinguished from the interests of the parties? If so, how should it be identified?

6:220 Delineating the Bargaining Unit

A union seeking certification for a unit that it claims to be appropriate for collective bargaining will apply to the relevant labour relations board. The board must decide whether that unit, or some variation of it, is an appropriate one. Sometimes the legislation is quite specific about what constitutes an appropriate unit — most often where public sector employees are involved. In the private sector, in contrast, boards usually have wide discretion to determine what is an appropriate unit.

The traditional approach to determining an appropriate bargaining unit was set out by Paul Weiler of the British Columbia Labour Relations Board in the leading case of *Insurance Corp. of British Columbia and C.U.P.E.*, [1974] 1 Can. L.R.B.R. 403 at 405–12. The preferred bargaining unit, according to that decision, is a broad one comprising all of the employees of a single employer. The simplest reason is that such a unit is administratively efficient and often facilitates collective bargaining for both parties. It does not impede lateral mobility of employees, and it allows for a common framework of employment conditions. It may also promote industrial peace and stability, by making strikes and lockouts less likely than if there are several separate sets of negotiations.

Another consideration, traditionally described as the most important of all, is whether there is a community of interest among the employees in question. This consideration can often point to the creation of several units in a particular enterprise; employees who differ significantly in such matters as background, skill, type of work, method of payment, and geographical location have frequently been placed in separate units on the basis of the criterion of community of interest. In recent years, however, as the following decision indicates, the use of that criterion has been evolving.

Metroland Printing, Publishing and Distributing Ltd., [2003] O.L.R.D. No. 514 (O.L.R.B.)

McLEAN, Vice-Chair:

. . .

¶2 Metroland Printing, Publishing and Distributing Ltd. ("Metroland") is a large publisher of, among other things, community newspapers. The trade union applied for certification of the following "all employee" bargaining unit of the employees of Metroland in its operation in Midland:

> all employees of Metroland, Printing, Publishing and Distributing Ltd. in the Town of Midland, save and except supervisors, persons above the rank of supervisor, and those employees in bargaining units for which any trade union holds bargaining rights as of the application date (July 31, 2002).

¶3 The employer and the intervenor, Mr. Walker, asserts that the proposed bargaining unit is not appropriate. . . .

FACTS

¶5 Metroland publishes the Midland-Penetanguishene Mirror out of its office in Midland, Ontario. . . . The Mirror is one of 69 community newspapers published by Metroland through various offices. . . .

¶7 The Midland office has two departments. The sales department consists of three advertising representatives and one telemarketing representative. The sales employees are paid on a commission basis. The distribution department, as the name suggests, is engaged in activities to ensure that the paper is distributed to customers. Such activities include warehousing and the recruitment and monitoring of carriers. The employees in the distribution department are hourly paid employees. Two employees, including Mr. Walker, work in the distribution department.

¶8 From time to time the employer hires part time and temporary employees. Part time employees generally work 19 or 20 hours per week and are usually, but not always temporary. In contrast to regular full time employees who receive a full benefit package (life insurance, long term disability, dental, accidental death & dismemberment, extended health care, and access to an employee assistance program), part time and temporary employees do not get a benefit package. Part time employees can be and are sent home if there is no work to be done. Their shift schedule can change on short notice. Full time employees work regular hours on a regular schedule.

¶9 Temporary employees are hired for two purposes: to replace an employee on leave (up to a year) or to assist the company during busy periods (usually 3–4 months). The latter category of temporary employee does not do the same work as regular full time employees. Temporary employees are hired pursuant to a written contract of employment, regular full time employees are not.

¶10 The company also utilizes/trains co-operative students on occasion. They are placed with the company pursuant to a Ministry of Education program. The co-operative students sign a contract supplied by the Ministry and are not paid any salary or benefits. They are assigned a variety of work. The Ministry of Education covers their Workplace Safety & Insurance Board coverage. The employer interviews co-operative students before they start with the company to determine if they are acceptable. . . .

¶12 All of the company's current full time employees began with the company on a one year contract working 19 or 20 hours per week.

ARGUMENT

¶13 The employer asserts that part-time employees, temporary employees and co-operative students should be excluded from the bargaining unit. There should either be one bargaining unit for each of the part time and temporary employee groups or one combined bargaining unit for the temporary and part time employees. Students should be included with the part-time employees.

¶14 The intervenor asserts that the two employees in his department do not want to be represented by the trade union and that therefore the bargaining unit should not include the distribution department.

¶15 The employer urges the Board not to have a "knee jerk" reaction to its proposed bargaining unit(s). Prior to the Bill 40 and Bill 7 amendments to the Act the Board used to make assumptions about the appropriateness of bargaining units (for example with respect to part time and full time employees) but those assumptions have been rejected in favour of bargaining units which are designed to fit the circumstances of each workplace. In this regard community of interest is still a relevant factor when the Board determines bargaining units. In this case the full time employees simply do not have a community of interest with the part-time employees, temporary employees and co-operative students. They are paid differently, they receive different benefits and they work on different schedules.

¶16 The employer relies on the Board's decision in *Hospital for Sick Children*. . . . There the Board stated:

> ¶17. Given that the definition of the bargaining unit can materially affect the ability of employees to organize, and that uncertainties concerning its contours can provoke costly litigation and potentially prejudicial delay, what then is the purpose of the concept of the "appropriate bargaining unit"? Quite simply, it is an effort to inject a public policy component into the initial shaping of the collective bargaining structure, so as to encourage the practice and procedure of collective bargaining and enhance the likelihood of a more viable

and harmonious collective bargaining relationship. . . . [T]he discretion to frame the "appropriate" bargaining unit during the initial organizing phase provides the Board with an opportunity (albeit perhaps a limited one) to avoid subsequent labour relations problems. Now, of course, this is not necessarily the same thing as minimizing administrative problems for the employer or organizing problems for the union. The structures and policies that promote a maximization of the employer's business interests are not those that will necessarily describe a viable bargaining unit, or the only viable bargaining unit — particularly since those interests may include a desire to avoid collective bargaining altogether, or limit its effectiveness. The employer's administrative structures are relevant in determining the bargaining unit, but they are not necessarily to be taken as the conclusive blue print in deciding what is appropriate. Nor is it a matter of simply giving an applicant union what it wants. It is, as we have noted, a matter of balancing competing considerations, including such factors as: whether the employees have a community of interest having regard to the nature of the work performed, the conditions of employment, and their skills; the employee's administrative structures; the geographic circumstances; the employees' functional coherence, or interdependence or interchange with other employees; the centralization of management authority; the economic advantages to the employer of one unit versus another; the source of work; the right of employees to a measure of self-determination; the degree of employee organization and whether a proposed unit would impede such organization; any likely adverse effects to the parties and the public that might flow from a proposed unit, or from fragmentation of employees into several units, and so on.

. . .

¶17 The employer argues that, applying the *Hospital for Sick Children* test, that there are two requirements to a finding that a bargaining unit applied for by a trade union is appropriate: first the employees in the bargaining unit must have sufficient community of interest that they can bargain together and; second, the bargaining unit must not create serious labour relations problems for the employer. In this case, the employer asserts, the groups of employees have almost no community of interest in that they are paid differently, have different hours of work and shift expectations and receive different benefit packages. In addition, the part time, temporary and co-operative students have little real connection to the workplace because they are interested in short term monetary reward rather than a career with the employer.

DECISION

¶18 The starting point for the determination of a bargaining unit is the Board's decision in *Hospital for Sick Children*. I agree with the employer that there are two parts to that test: "*sufficient* community of interest" and no "serious labour relations problems for the employer." I also agree that the Board should not automatically make assumptions about community of interest.

¶19 In my view, the Board's assessment of the level of community of interest required to be sufficient to permit a single bargaining unit has evolved. As the employer rightly asserts, for example, at one time part-time employees were automatically excluded (at the employer's request) from a full time employee bargaining unit. Now the Board frequently places such employees in the same bargaining unit. It is no longer assumed that part time employees have a different community of interest than full time employees. The Board determines an appropriate bargaining unit based on the particular circumstances of each workplace.

¶20 The Board has significant experience in placing disparate groups of employees in one bargaining unit with little apparent negative effect on labour relations. It is now common for employees with quite different terms and conditions of employment and different employment aspirations, including part-time and full-time and temporary employees, to be placed in one bargaining unit. As a result, community of interest has much less influence on the determination of an appropriate bargaining unit than it once may have had.

¶21 This evolution has been recognized in the case law. In *Active Mold Plastic Products Ltd.*, . . . the Board stated:

> . . . Most recently, in *Burns International Security Services* . . . , the Board addressed the utility of the concept of "community of interest." In this decision, it was noted that the term "community of interest" does not usually provide the Board with much assistance in determining whether an applied-for bargaining unit is appropriate. It was observed in this decision that the focus before the Board in bargaining unit determination cases should be upon "concrete problems rather than the sometimes nebulous concept of 'community of interest'." . . .

. . .

¶23 In my view the result of the evolution in the Board's analysis of the determination of an appropriate bargaining unit is that the Board has recognized that employees share a community of interest simply by being employed by the same employer in the same workplace and that employees with quite different terms and conditions of employment can effectively bargain together. In essence, what has happened, is that the "sufficient community of interest" part of the *Hospital for Sick Children* test and the serious labour relations problems part of the test have merged. Employees of the same employer will generally be found to have sufficient community of interest to bargain together unless the placement of them in the same bargaining unit, due to lack of community of interest or otherwise, creates serious labour relations problems for the employer.

¶24 In this case, I am satisfied that the various (groups) of employees at this workplace have sufficient community of interest that they can bargain together. I also see no prospect that the inclusion of all of these categories of employees in a single bargaining unit will create serious labour relations problems for the employer. While the employees in question have different terms and conditions of employment, the differences are not so great so as to cause serious (or likely any) labour relations problems. In addition, given the fact that the majority, or perhaps all, of the current employees began with the company on a part-time contract, the group of employees are all in potentially similar career positions.

¶25 In addition, it is apparent that the employer's proposed bargaining unit would lead to inappropriate bargaining unit fragmentation at the employer's workplace. Fragmentation can itself lead to serious labour relations problems for the workplace parties. Moreover, the Board has frequently said that broader-based bargaining units are better for collective bargaining. As the Board stated in a different context in *Humber/Northwestern/York-Finch Hospital* . . . ,

¶32 This is not to say that "bigger is always better." However, labour relations boards across the country have all recognized the utility of broader-based bargaining structures, because they are more likely to: promote stability, increase administrative efficiency, enhance employee mobility, and generate a common framework for employment conditions for all employees in an enterprise. Bigger bargaining units also have more critical mass, so that they are better able to facilitate and accommodate change. . . .

¶33 In the absence of statutory prescriptions, there is, today, a pronounced preference for broader-based bargaining units, unless that objective collides in a serious way with the employees' ability to organize themselves. Indeed, the Board has often favoured broader-based bargaining units, even in certification situations, where the shape of the unit may well influence whether there will be any collective bargaining at all. The Board has recognized that the *structure* of collective bargaining "*matters*". . . . Fragmented bargaining structures can pose serious labour-relations problems. Conversely, broader based bargaining units make collective bargaining go more smoothly and successfully.

¶34 There is nothing particularly novel about these observations. Nor are they unique to Ontario, or to the Ontario Labour Relations Board. The consolidation of bargaining structures has been ongoing in other jurisdictions for many years (the Post Office, CBC, railways, and airlines come to mind); and policy considerations such as those discussed in the Ontario cases can be found in the reasons of other adjudicators in other jurisdictions. Those boards, too, have been inclined to favour more comprehensive bargaining units unless there are persuasive countervailing considerations. . . .

¶26 In this case there are only a total of approximately 10 employees at the workplace. One of those employees is already in a separate bargaining unit. Therefore, the employer's proposals could lead to a total of three or four bargaining units for a very small workplace. This is unacceptable in such a small bargaining unit even in this industry, which has a history of fragmentation. Finally, to the extent that the students are employees at all, which I doubt, there is no reason why they cannot be included in an all employee bargaining unit.

¶27 As for the position taken by the intervenor, the preceding comments apply equally to Mr. Walker and the other employee in the advertising department. It simply makes no labour relations sense to hive off a small department of two employees into their own separate bargaining unit. Employee wishes are just one of the factors the Board may consider when determining an appropriate bargaining unit. Those wishes are balanced, among other things, against the Board's aversion to fragmentation and the viability of the bargaining unit as a whole. It is not surprising that in this application for certification, there are employees (like Mr. Walker) who do not wish to be represented by a trade union. That is the case in many of the applications for certification which come before the Board. . . .

¶33 The Board finds that:

all employees of Metroland, Printing, Publishing and Distributing Ltd. in the Town of Midland, save and except supervisors, persons above the rank of supervisor, and those employees in bargaining units for which any trade union holds bargaining rights as of the application date . . . constitutes an appropriate bargaining unit.

* * *

Although the *Wagner Act* model was premised on the prevalence of full-time, blue-collar employment in an industrial or manufacturing setting, in more recent years part-time and casual employees in those sectors, and above all in the service sector, have become subjects of prime concern for the union movement and for scholars interested in labour law reform. Part-time and casual employment has been the largest growth segment (and often the only one) in the Canadian labour market since the late 1980s. Part-time employees, defined by Statistics Canada as those who work thirty or fewer hours a week, now make up around 20 percent of the labour force in Canada, and their numbers have been growing steadily throughout the industrial world since the 1950s. With the rise of a globalized economy, industrial economies have been shifting from manufacturing goods to producing services. Part-time employment has grown along with the growth of the service sector; in 1991 that sector accounted for 89 percent of all part-time jobs in Canada. This is especially significant given that service work now makes up 70 percent of total Canadian employment. Most service sector firms are relatively small and face a high degree of competition. As a result, they tend to favour part-time workers, who generally receive lower wages and fewer benefits than full-time workers.

As well as being the fastest-growing segment of the workforce, part-time employment represents the most likely area for female employment. Seventy percent of all part-timers in Canada are women. Working women represent around 40 percent of the total workforce, of which 25 percent is accounted for by women in part-time positions. Some of these women prefer to work part-time, because the flexible hours make it possible for them to attend to childcare responsibilities.

Because part-time workers generally have less job security as well as inferior terms and conditions, they might be expected to be fertile ground for union organizers. A 1984 survey, however, showed that only 19 percent of part-timers were unionized, whereas the figure for full-timers was 41 percent. Many unions traditionally opposed the hiring of part-timers, viewing them as competitors for jobs and as exerting downward pressure on wages. Part-timers often returned this hostility.

As is indicated by the *Metroland* case set out above, boards have been moving toward a more flexible approach to the inclusion of part-timers in bargaining units with full-time employees. Nevertheless, debate continues in the labour law community about how best to handle the growing phenomenon of part-time work.

Casual employees are another group that presents difficult issues of bargaining unit determination. In the following case, the federal board considered whether casual employees ought to be included in a pre-existing bargaining unit comprising the full-time and part-time employees of a particular branch of a bank. The broader question of the appropriateness of single branch certification in the nationwide banks will be discussed in the next section of this chapter.

Canadian Imperial Bank of Commerce (Powell River Branch) v. British Columbia Government Employees' Union (1992), 15 Can. L.R.B.R. (2d) 86 at 87–89

JAMIESON, Vice-Chair:

. . .

What do we mean when we refer to 'casual employees'? Generally speaking, this term has been used to describe employees who are employed on a call-in basis. Usually these employees work very irregular hours as required. When they are called by an employer about their availability for work there is no obligation for them to accept the hours offered. Conversely, there is no obligation upon the employer to call the casuals to work. Normally casuals are paid on an hourly basis plus the minimum percentage of vacation pay. They are not usually entitled to any other benefits.

Much has been written by this Board and other boards about the advisability of including employees who do not work a regular full-time schedule with those who do. . . . What can be drawn from those decisions are several principles which will influence the Board when it is faced with the problem of including or excluding casual employees from bargaining units. Some major concerns for the Board are:

1) The possibility of casual employees preventing full-time employees from having access to collective bargaining. This situation could arise where the full-time employees are outnumbered by casuals who may not be interested in participating in collective bargaining. If the Board were to insist on the inclusion of casuals in these circumstances, the smaller group of full-time employees who may opt for collective bargaining could have their attempts to do so vetoed by the contrary wishes of the casuals.

2) There is a possible negative impact on the free collective bargaining process if casuals are included because in most cases casual employees have a different community of interest from regular full-time or regular part-time employees. Obviously, the bargaining strength of regular employees would be considerably diluted if the bargaining unit was flooded with casuals. These casuals could not be expected to support strike action over issues such as seniority or pensions which have more impact on the employment of regular employees.

3) The Board is also hesitant to confer full collective bargaining rights, including the right to halt operations by strike action, on small groups of casual employees who only have a marginal connection with a given industry.

For these reasons as well as others, the Board has shown a preference for excluding casuals from bargaining units, particularly when dealing with new applications where there are no established collective bargaining relationships.

Notwithstanding the Board's stated preference for bargaining-unit construction excluding casuals, the fact remains that casuals are 'employees' within the meaning of the Code (s. 3) and they do have the rights and protections bestowed upon employees by the statute. The

Board's dilemma has been how to balance the rights of casual employees with those of regular employees and this can only be done depending upon the particular circumstances of any given case. One example of where the Board did include casuals in a bargaining unit with full and part-time employees is *Pacific Western Airlines Ltd.*, (1984), . . . There the Board found it appropriate to include some 21 casuals in a bargaining unit containing 960 or so regular employees. In that instance the Board was also dealing with an application for review where there was an established collective bargaining relationship. There the Board expressed its satisfaction that the usual concerns about including casuals were alleviated in the circumstances before it, i.e., there was no opportunity for the casuals to prevent regular employees from exercising their rights under the Code as they were already organized. Also, there was little possibility of the casuals dominating the bargaining unit because of the large number of regular employees in the unit as opposed to the number of casuals being sought to be added.

In that decision the Board emphasized the importance of identifying a real community of interest between the casuals and the other employees in the bargaining unit. The Board also said that an important consideration is the continuity or the pattern of employment of the casuals notwithstanding the irregularity of the hours worked. . . .

We concur with that view that the continuity of employment should be a telling factor. If an employer has created a regular standby pool of employees upon which it relies to do its extra production work or to fill in for its regular staff on an ongoing basis, this pool of employees should be viewed as an integral part of the employer's workforce. This is not like an employer calling office overload or the likes to fill an occasional vacancy or to deal with an unforeseen increase in the workload.

6:230 Bargaining Unit Determination and the Organizing Drive

Recall again the crucial fact that the bargaining unit performs two main functions: it serves as an electoral district for certification purposes, and it serves as the basis for collective bargaining. These two functions often conflict in cases where an employer has several outlets or branches. Although it may be easier to organize employees branch by branch, single branch bargaining units may not have enough power to engage in effective collective bargaining.

The following readings describe the history of union efforts to organize bank employees in Canada. They illustrate how labour relations boards have grappled with the tension between the bargaining unit's two main functions, and they draw attention to the particular consequences that traditional principles of bargaining unit determination have had for women workers and bank employees.

Elizabeth Lennon, "Organizing the Unorganized: Unionization in the Chartered Banks of Canada" (1980) 18 Osgoode Hall L.J. 177 at 179–84

There are currently ten chartered banks in Canada, functioning through a very widespread network of small branches. While some of these banks are localized, and several are small, the 'Big Five,' which control ninety-one percent of total bank assets, operate throughout Canada. Organization is highly centralized, with most important decisions emanating from the head offices in either Toronto or Montreal. Most have provincial or regional administrative subdivisions as well. . . .

Bank employment patterns are changing slowly in response to changing social and economic conditions, but in general they still reflect the policies of an earlier era. Banks employ a remarkably high percentage of women in comparison with the Canadian labour force as a whole: in 1975 the figure was seventy-two percent. These women are heavily concentrated in low-paying, routine clerical jobs. The Bank of Nova Scotia indicates that while between eighty and ninety percent of its management employees are male, ninety percent of its clerical employees are female. This profile is typical of the industry as a whole. Comparative male/female salary levels reflect this difference in functions.

Working conditions in the banks are fairly typical of 'white-collar' employment. . . . There is a high turnover rate, which the banks estimate variously at between twenty-seven and thirty-six percent. Since turnover is confined largely to clerical (and therefore female) ranks, the figure for this class of employee would be even higher. Compensation levels for clerical employees are somewhat lower than the average for clerical work across all industries in Canada, and this is probably true for management employees as well. . . .

The chartered banks have been notoriously resistant to trade unionism, and there have been only sporadic attempts to organize them over the years. It was not until 1959 that the Canada Labour Relations Board received its first application for certification from a union seeking to represent bank employees. The Kitimat, Terrace and District General Workers' Union, Local 1583 applied for a unit of three workers among a total staff of five in the Kitimat branch of the Bank of Nova Scotia. The bank contested the application on the grounds that the unit was not appropriate for collective bargaining, taking the position that only a national unit would be appropriate. Although the application was dismissed on the basis that the unit was not appropriate, the Board was careful to point out that it was not accepting the argument that only a national unit would be suitable: 'It may well be that units of some of the employees of a Bank, grouped together territorially or on some other basis, will prove to be appropriate, rather than a nation-wide unit.' It was clear, however, that a branch was not an appropriate unit.

This decision understandably daunted the trade union movement. In 1959 the Royal Bank had 503 branches nationally and presented a truly formidable organizing task. The task became even more formidable as branches proliferated with the passage of time. Although the *Kitimat* decision hinted at some more manageable unit, none was readily apparent since the administration of bank personnel was, in fact, largely handled at the national level, as the bank had argued. The response of the trade union movement to the *Kitimat* decision was virtually to suspend organizing for about fifteen years. . . .

Aside from a sprinkling of provincial certifications held by various unions in trust companies and credit unions, the financial sector in 1976 was still virgin territory for the labour movement. . . .

If unions did not appear to be very interested in bank workers, at least some bank workers were interested in unions. This interest crystallized independently in two parts of the country: Ontario and British Columbia. In mid-1976 the first applications for branch certification since *Kitimat* were filed.

The history of the Service, Office and Retail Workers' Union of Canada (SORWUC) and its contact with bank workers is quite different [from the normal union experience]. This union was an outgrowth of the Vancouver women's liberation movement, and was founded in 1972 by the Working Women's Association (WWA), a feminist labour support group. Although WWA members were working women, in general they worked in unorganized workplaces. Their contacts with the trade union movement had been uniformly negative. . . . They felt that there was a pressing need for a union organized and controlled by women and committed to organizing places where women worked. . . .

Although bank workers are mainly women and, thus, are part of SORWUC's natural jurisdiction, the union did not move into the banking field immediately. However, in the spring of 1976 it campaigned with leaflets in Vancouver's downtown area, inviting contact from clerical women interested in organizing. There was a strong response from bank workers and the union decided to follow up on these contacts made in the various branches.

SORWUC and its legal advisors were not at all confident that the CLRB would accept an individual bank branch as a unit appropriate for collective bargaining, although that was always a possibility. . . .

The strategy was, then, to assemble as many applications for certification as possible and to file them in rapid succession. The first was an application for employees at the Victory Square branch of the Canadian Imperial Bank of Commerce in Vancouver, filed on August 16, 1976. Sixteen more branches of various banks applied before the end of 1976. Momentum dropped somewhat after that, but SORWUC had filed a total of twenty-two applications for certification before the first hearings were held in April of 1977.

[Reprinted by permission.]

Service, Office and Retail Workers' Union of Canada [SORWUC] v. Canadian Imperial Bank of Commerce, [1977] 2 Can. L.R.B.R. 99 at 110, 113, 117–25 (C.L.R.B.)

[The applicant asked to be certified for eight bargaining units, each corresponding to a different branch of the bank. The bank claimed that the only appropriate unit was all of its branches across Canada.]

DORSEY, Vice-Chair: The Canadian Imperial Bank of Commerce is one of Canada's 12 chartered banks. It has 34,000 employees and operates a nationwide branch banking system with 1,693 branches in Canada and 114 branches outside Canada. The essence of the branch banking system is that, through the branch, all customers of the bank have access to all the banking facilities of the bank. The bank can concentrate deposits, its lifeblood, and deploy them to work for it wherever there is a profitable market. To make this system effective, each branch is supported by a central pool of resources. . . .

The branch is not a totally autonomous unit and each branch manager cannot organize his branch to suit his personal philosophy or business attitudes. The financial success of the bank depends upon the success of each branch and the ability of the system to service all its customers. Each branch has its own deposit and borrowing customers with their needs, but uniformity of systems promotes efficiency and reduces costs. To this end, several financial and administrative functions are centralized. There are at least 30 financial functions that are centralized to the extent that they require the completion or accounting to be done outside the branch. . . .

What emerges from this picture is an operation that for purposes of efficiency and ease of administration seeks to maintain standardized procedures and uniformity of employment policy. But on the employment side this centralization must not be overemphasized. The picture is well summarized by Mr. Duffield who testified that hiring, assessment, promotion, discipline and termination are usually initiated at the branch level because the bank has to rely upon its managers in its many locations. . . .

The Board is vested with the exclusive authority and responsibility to determine the appropriateness of proposed bargaining units. . . .

Why has Parliament vested this authority and responsibility in the Board? The answer to this question is obvious when the consequences of a certification order are considered.

Once a trade union is certified it is vested with the 'exclusive authority to bargain on behalf of the employees in the bargaining unit' (s.136(1)(a)). The union acquires the right to bargain for all employees in the unit, not just those who are members of the trade union. The issuance of a certification order affects not only union members but other employees as well. They become represented by the certified trade union whether they do not wish any union representation or wish to be represented by another trade union. These employees lose their right to negotiate directly with their employer on terms and conditions of employment. That change in the employment relationship may last indefinitely and is of considerable importance to these employees.

Secondly, the issuance of a certification order has legal consequences for the employer. Once a trade union is certified it may require the employer to bargain collectively with it (s.146). The employer is obliged to bargain in good faith and make every reasonable effort to enter into a collective agreement. It is also precluded, for a time, from unilaterally altering terms and conditions of employment (s. 148).

Thirdly, the public and employer are affected because the issuance of a certification order entitles the union, after having fulfilled the statutory requirements, to undertake a lawful strike (s.180). . . .

In this case the unit proposed by the union is a single location unit — a unit of employees of the employer employed at a branch of the employer's operations. That unit is a unit because it is a 'group of two or more employees' (s.107(1) 'unit'). Is it an appropriate bargaining unit?

It is the experience of this and other labour relations boards that employees consider the single location unit to be a natural unit, because this is where the employees work. In this case, the employees daily or regularly attend to work at the branch location. They work under the supervision of the branch manager and other personnel who, in turn, work in the branch. They have social interchange during the day, develop friendships and acquaintances among fellow employees in the branch, get to know the branch's customers, and perhaps engage in after-hours athletic or social activities.

It is also the common practice of labour relations boards to hold that the single location unit is an appropriate bargaining unit. Provincial boards make this determination when dealing with retail outlets, manufacturing operations, mines and other operations.

This Board makes this determination when dealing with radio or television stations, atomic energy plants and others. It is the consensus among labour relations boards that the community of interest of employees at a single location is sufficient to hold that the single location unit is an appropriate unit.

The Commerce asks the Board to deviate from this natural inclination of employees and practice and consensus of labour relations boards. It asks the Board to find that the only appropriate unit is a unit of all employees of the bank. In this unit would be included most of the Commerce's 34,000 Canadian employees employed in 1,693 branch locations and several data centers, regional offices and head office. It would include tellers, clerks, loan officers and others employed in any one branch with keypunch operators, regional and head office clerical employees, administrators, instructors, security personnel and others.

Why is the bank asking for this unusually large, widespread and diverse unit? It requests this unit in the interest of administrative efficiency and convenience in bargaining, administrative convenience for lateral mobility of employees in a large unit, the desirability of common employment conditions, and a reduction of the potential incidents of industrial unrest. . . .

The second reason it requests this unit is because in its view branch certification would create 'utter chaos' contrary to the public interest. In fact it maintains 'chaos was probably inadequate to describe' the branch unit proposition. The Commerce arrives at this unusual perception of single location unit designation because it perceives the banking industry as the fiscal fibre of the country. The argument is that branch unionization would affect the property rights of all Canadians, i.e., their right to deposit and withdraw money, and would disrupt the mechanism our society relies upon for the money necessary to sustain all elements of society. . . .

Let us examine this position in the larger context of the duty the Board must discharge. The fundamental dilemma the Board confronts in each certification application and bargaining unit dispute is that the bargaining unit serves two basic purposes. It is the initial constituency which will decide whether an applicant union will acquire representational rights to commence collective bargaining. It is also the basis for the bargaining structure that may obtain in the future. This Board and other labour relations boards recognize that in difficult cases, such as this one, any judgment carries its cost. The freedom of choice of employees to group into self-determined units or the most rational, long-term bargaining structure is partially or totally sacrificed. . . .

. . . The express intention of Parliament is the 'encouragement of free collective bargaining' and to support labour and management who recognize and support collective bargaining 'as the bases of effective industrial relations for the determination of good working conditions and sound labour-management relations.' Parliament also 'deems the development of good industrial relations to be in the best interests of Canada in ensuring a just share of the fruits of progress to all.'

This legislative intent can best be achieved by facilitating collective bargaining for employees who choose this procedure for settling their terms and conditions of employment. That can be accomplished by this Board accepting or fashioning bargaining units that give employees a realistic possibility of exercising their rights under the Code. Too large units in unorganized industries will abort any possibility of collective bargaining ever commencing and defeat this express intention of Parliament. At the same time, this does not mean the Board will or should create artificial units based on [the] extent of organizing. This would ignore the purpose of the Board's role.

A real-life example of aborting the possibility of collective bargaining is the Board's decision 18 years ago in *Bank of Nova Scotia, Kitimat* . . . In that case the Board found a single branch unit to be inappropriate. . . .

The experience after the *Bank of Nova Scotia, Kitimat* decision demonstrates that bank employees and trade unions realistically perceived that any form of union organizing was virtually impossible on any basis other than the branch basis. There was some evidence that SORWUC supporters have the zeal to attempt organizing on a broader basis, but zeal is not the basis for interpreting legislative intention.

The practical reality of the employer's proposed bargaining unit is that only an organization or movement with the enormous financial resources to operate nationwide, in a concerted effort, for a long period of time, could make the rights of the Code meaningful for the Commerce employees. This in itself is a restriction of the freedom of employees 'to join the trade union of his choice' (s. 110(1)). Apart from this fact the history of union activity is that unions begin or are based in a particular locale. To organize on a national basis a union of bank employees would have to start to solicit members in one area and then move outward to other areas. By the time it had encompassed the expansive territorial boundaries of Canada the employees in the primary locales would have become disillusioned and perhaps lost interest in any expectation of achieving collective bargaining. Because of the turnover of employees at the Commerce and in the industry, a union seeking to act as a vehicle for bargaining would be on a constant treadmill of soliciting new employees and, at the same time, maintaining the support of members while expanding to new areas. And all of this would occur against the background of no tradition of collective bargaining in the industry.

Do the employer's arguments outweigh these considerations? Administrative convenience, lateral mobility of employees, and the desirability of common terms of employment are interests of the bank and employees. How much will these be compromised by a single branch unit?

The Commerce is an efficient, diversified organization responding to and leading in the complex world of commerce, finance and international business. It is a multi-resourced organization with specialists in banking as well as real estate, taxation, computer systems, government relations, personnel administration, etc. It operates across Canada and adapts to local business practices and labour markets. It structures its work environment, hours of business and wages to local conditions. Its employee benefit program is flexible to account for the differing wishes of its employees. It accepts and adopts changes in government regulation, markets and business practices.

Employees move from one branch to another, most often at their request or agreement. They are seldom required to move. Moves often accompany promotion or promotional opportunities which is a distinct interest of employees, perhaps even more than for the bank. Neither provincial boundaries, climatic conditions nor domestic situations prevent employee acceptance of movement.

These two factors of administrative convenience and lateral mobility of employees are significant to the bank, but we are not convinced that certification and collective bargaining at the branch level cannot result in agreements that accommodate these interests. Commonality of terms and conditions of employment does not entirely exist now. A multitude of employee classifications in a complex structure of delegated responsibility is reflected by varying pay ranges and merit steps in those ranges. Assorted benefit packages accommodate individual preferences. Differing local markets have necessitated different wage scales. We are satisfied that, under branch certification, centralized employer bargaining and the employees' interests in uniformity and equality can result in uniform terms and conditions of employment. This is the proven collective bargaining experience of multi-location employers.

The fourth factor, the reduction of the potential incidents for industrial unrest is linked with the employer's fears of chaos. This fear of hypothetical horribles is the foremost basis for the employer's position. The Commerce fears that an acceptance of SORWUC's position would create a 'monster' that could not be turned around. It points to the disruption resulting from a confusion of bargaining units that is recounted in *British Columbia Railway Company and CAIMAW et al.* . . . as an example, and says the approach of several other British Columbia public sector cases should be applied because the Commerce is akin to a public institution. The basic rationale of these decisions is capsulized in *British Columbia Ferry Corp. and B.C. Gov't Employees Union et al.* . . .

The first distinguishing feature of these cases is that the unions applying for certification define their units in occupational terms. The future results of such a certification would have been that, when these employees withdrew their services, the employer's entire operation could be shut down because the occupations sought were employed in integrated operations employing several occupations. A cessation of work by one occupation could disrupt the entire system. This is not the case here where the unit sought is multi-occupational at a single location. A cessation of work at one location would not prevent the bank at its many other locations from continuing to operate. It would be essentially self-contained within the unit.

The second distinguishing feature of these cases is that they involve a truly public employer or an essential monopolistic enterprise (e.g., the British Columbia Railway Co. or the British Columbia Ferry Corp.). The impact of a work stoppage at these employers has a serious external impact on the public. The Commerce is not a public institution like a provincial monopolistic insurance corporation, a municipality, a workers' compensation board or a provincially run railway. . . .

A collateral position the employer advances is that a branch unit will result in a multiplicity of unions representing a multiplicity of units. This is not the experience in other industries where craft unions have not been historically present. The experience is that unions grow and evolve with jurisdiction over employees in an industry. This is in the interest of employees and unions generally. New unionized sectors or industries often foster the creation of unions to care for their needs. Public sector and white-collar employee unions are recent examples. SORWUC and its Local No. 2 is an obvious example. . . .

In conclusion, the Board has wrestled with the fundamental dilemma of the competing functions of the appropriate bargaining unit concept and its application in this case. We have decided that the single branch location of the Commerce encompasses employees with a community of interest and is an appropriate bargaining unit.

* * *

After the above decision, the union continued to organize bank branches for several months. In 1977 it made twenty-six more applications for branch certification in British Columbia and Saskatchewan, and was successful in sixteen. By the summer of 1978, however, it had withdrawn from bargaining for the vast majority of its units. By 1980 it had withdrawn entirely, and had lost all of its certifications.

What caused this turn of events? The banks — the Royal Bank, the Bank of Nova Scotia, and especially the CIBC — had waged strong campaigns against unionization, to the extent of committing many unfair labour practices. This hostile attitude continued at the bargaining table. The union attempted to bargain with the banks on a multibranch basis. The banks refused, pointing out that the union had been certified only on a branch-by-branch basis and was therefore entitled only to require branch-by-branch bargaining. This tactic stretched the resources of the small feminist union to the breaking point. The banks also announced that their annual across-the-board pay increases would thereafter apply only to nonunion branches. The Canada board initially dismissed the union's complaint that this was an unfair labour practice aimed at further undermining its already declining support (*Bank of Nova Scotia, Vancouver Heights Branch*, [1978] 2 Can. L.R.B.R. 181). The board reversed that decision a year later. However, the union had failed to conclude any collective agreements that would have improved terms and conditions, and it was unwilling to risk calling a strike. This led to its withdrawal from bargaining, and to requests for decertification. Other unions that subsequently attempted to organize in the banking sector were also unable to win better wages or benefits than those at non-unionized branches.

In the above excerpt, Elizabeth Lennon concluded that there were three reasons why the unions largely failed in their attempts to organize the banks. First, the small numbers of staff in each branch-based bargaining unit, and the large number of such potential units, meant that organizational and bargaining costs were huge. Second, the highly centralized nature of the banks and the enormous disparity between their bargaining power and that of a branch-based bargaining unit made it easy for them to resist giving unionized branches any wage increases and benefits not given to non-unionized employees. Finally, frequent transfer of personnel between branches, and high rates of staff turnover, often resulted in the swift disappearance of the initial majority that supported the union, and this led to pressure for decertification.

In the *National Bank of Canada* case excerpted below, the Confederation of National Trade Unions tried to enhance its bargaining power by seeking certification for a unit of all five branches of that bank in Rimouski, Quebec. At that time the National Bank had over 11,000 employees in 577 branches across Canada, the majority in Quebec. After the certification application was filed, the bank closed one of the Rimouski branches, leaving four within the ambit of the application. The bank had no other branches within twenty-five miles.

The bank employed 102 people in Rimouski. There were 86 in the proposed unit, ranging from five at the smallest of the four branches to 46 at the largest. There was relatively little movement of employees into Rimouski from outside branches, but there was more such movement between the Rimouski branches.

Syndicat des Employés des Banques Nationales de Rimouski (CNTU) v. National Bank of Canada (1986), 11 Can. L.R.B.R. (N.S.) 257 at 261–62, 302–05 (C.L.R.B.)

LAPOINTE, Chair: The instant application for certification, encompassing all branches of a chartered bank in Rimouski, Quebec, asks the Board to group all the employees into a single bargaining unit, because it would be appropriate for collective bargaining. It offers the Board the opportunity to review the entire question of certification in the banking industry. . . .

In the Board's original decisions concerning the Canadian Imperial Bank of Commerce in British Columbia and the Bank of Nova Scotia in Ontario, it explained that in its opinion a branch was a natural work place for the people employed there. Given the fact that until 1982 the unions had not proposed any other appropriate unit, and that in Windsor the union involved backed down, the Board has not had the opportunity in dealing with bank branches to rule on any appropriate unit other than the individual branch.

The application under consideration is the first in which a union has taken a clearly different approach. It has concentrated on all the employees of a bank in a city.

At the outset there were five branches. There are now four. The intended scope of the certificate sought does not cover four branches, but an entire city.

The evidence indicated that three of the branches conduct all the business of a branch, while the other is a counter (with no capacity for credit operations). One of the branches is a little larger, and has somewhat more centralized operations (the loans department; one of the employees in the department supervises the other branches, and the employee visits the other branches). . . .

The employer asked the Board not to accept this bargaining unit, which it said would, through the distribution of employees, permit a majority to impose its will on a minority, possibly on all the employees in a small branch. We cannot accept this reasoning, which seems to reject the entire Canadian and North American certification system.

Indeed, if we consider an appropriate industrial bargaining unit, with an employer who operates a single plant, we will find a number of departments in which employees with varying qualifications perform their jobs. Once a labour board determines that there is sufficient community of interest and integration of functions, and similarity of working conditions and system of compensation to conclude that all employees — except, say office employees, members of management and employees in confidential labour relations positions — will be in the unit, does it then ask the applicant union to establish that a majority of employees in each department support the application?

Moreover, with respect to the representativeness in the unit, the Board must say that the applicant has established this. But beyond that, the representativeness of the union is not a result of crushing small branches with an enormous majority in the biggest branch; that is not the evidence.

The bank's labour relations expert, who testified at the public hearing, explained how the bank proceeded when it meets with the union representing a cluster of individually certified branches in a region such as Quebec, for example. Given the logic of not insisting on bargaining separately for each unit, they have decided to bargain as a 'common front.' And so how would current practice be disrupted if the Board certified the unit sought? The common front would be replaced by a committee of the certified union.

What can be said about this new unit? It appeared from the cases decided by the NLRB in the United States that the 'splinter' (the individual branch) is the rule. But in an industry in which an employer has many branches, the retail drugstore industry, it invented the concept of the 'cluster' of establishments.

We prefer this concept to the idea that the branches in a city constitute an appropriate unit. We can only assume that there are several communities in Canada, a country as vast as it is underpopulated, where there are isolated pockets of population with characteristics similar to Rimouski in Quebec: geographical regions where there are concentrations of people which call for the establishment of clusters of branches of chartered banks. Everyone, or almost everyone, knows one another in Rimouski, as opposed to the anonymity of the large towns or cities or metropolises elsewhere.

Thus, we decided that the proposed unit was appropriate for collective bargaining, and we have therefore issued a certification certificate. This is a geographical unit, but the Board would not wish to have it seen as just the same as a unit covering a city.

Furthermore, as the Board has been careful to note, the chartered banks have quite diverse structures and, in fact, each case will have to be studied on its own merits. . . .

In conclusion, the Board intends by this decision to continue its policy of exercising its discretion under s. 125(2) of the Code in such a way as to give the employees 'a realistic possibility of exercising their rights under the *Code*.'

✻ ✻ ✻

In the above decision, the CLRB did not discuss whether the union would have had enough support in each of the four branches to obtain certification for each branch separately, but the board did note that the union's support was not inordinately skewed. Ultimately, the board simply ascertained whether the union had majority support in the four-branch unit as a whole, and the board certified for that unit when it found that the union did have such support.

Regional or cluster units of that sort did not catch on in Ontario. Despite their similarities to banks, trust companies are within provincial jurisdiction, and the CLRB's Rimouski decision can be contrasted with a pair of decisions by the Ontario Labour Relations Board on trust company bargaining units: *National Trust (No. 1)*, [1986]

O.L.R.B. Rep. 250, and *National Trust (No. 2)*, [1988] O.L.R.B. Rep. 168. The union had applied for a unit of seven National Trust branches in Toronto. National Trust had thirty-seven branches in what was then Metropolitan Toronto, which the company divided into into three regions: Central, Metro East, and Metro West. Of the seven branches applied for, six were in Metro East (of fourteen in that region) and one was in Metro West (of seventeen in that region). The union argued that although it had enough support to be certified at each branch separately, and that although seven single-branch units would be an appropriate bargaining structure, a combined unit of all seven branches would be more appropriate. The employer responded that the only appropriate approach would be to have single-branch units side-by-side with three regional units or a unit covering all of Metropolitan Toronto. In the first of the two decisions, the OLRB sided with the union on this question, although it rejected the union's request that full-time and part-time employees should be in the same unit.

In *National Trust (No. 1)*, Vice-Chair Mitchnick's decision that a regional unit would be appropriate was based on what proved to be an erroneous assumption, namely that the union had majority support in each of the seven branches. Because of that assumption, the board thought there was no danger that any of those branches would be swept into collective bargaining against the wishes of most of its employees. In other words, there would have been no tension in the particular case between the bargaining unit's role as an electoral district and its collective bargaining function.

In *National Trust (No. 2)*, Chair MacDowell refused to accept the union's renewed request for a single unit made up of the seven branches because it turned out that the union, contrary to what it had asserted in *National Trust (No. 1)*, had majority support in only four of the seven and was in a position to require a vote in only one of the remaining three. One of the reasons for the refusal was that board would not certify for a multi-branch unit unless the union could show that it had a majority in each branch. In Ontario at the time, a union could be certified without a vote if it provided evidence of support from at least 55 percent of the employees in the unit, and it was entitled to a vote if its support was between 45 and 55 percent.

Even within single-jurisdiction, single-employer enterprises, highly particularistic units may be certified. In a university, for example, there may be separate units for full-time library staff, part-time library staff, electricians, carpenters, machinists, operating engineers, stagehands, security guards, plumbers, sheet metal workers, typesetters, day care workers, faculty, office staff, and teaching assistants. In hospitals, labour boards have segregated service employees, technicians, nurses, security guards, and operating engineers into separate units. In the mining industry, each mining property is generally recognized as a separate bargaining unit.

Whatever the deficiencies of single-branch or single-plant units in terms of employee bargaining power *vis-à-vis* a multi-location employer, unions often seek certification for such units because they may be easier to organize. In *Michelin Tires (Canada) Ltd.*, excerpted below, the company had two plants in Nova Scotia, in Granton and Bridgewater, 150 miles apart. The provincial labour board followed the reasoning in the *SORWUC* case, above, in holding that a unit comprising only the employees at the Granton plant was appropriate. The board rejected Michelin's argument that the only appropriate unit would comprise both plants. The interest in allowing employees to unionize in the first place favoured the conclusion that Granton was an appropriate unit on its own.

United Rubber, Cork, Linoleum & Plastic Workers of America, Local 1028 v. Michelin Tires (Canada) Ltd., [1979] 3 Can. L.R.B.R. 429 at 440–41

> It is undeniable that there is a sacrifice of stability and the likelihood of a strike is increased somewhat by creating a potential for two separate bargaining units. The Board accepts that a strike at one plant would inevitably bring a halt to work at the other. We do not belittle the importance of this consideration, but, simply, have concluded that the other factors favouring Granton as a separate bargaining unit are overriding. While the interdependence of the Granton and Bridgewater plants is physically demonstrable to a somewhat unusual degree, it is not uncommon for separate operations of the same employer to be heavily dependent on one another in an economic sense. Thus a fish plant cannot operate without supplies of fish and a retail outlet cannot operate if there are no shipments from the warehouse. Nobody can fail to be aware of how dependent economic units in today's world are on each other, even where they are not owned by the same employer, but these facts of economic life have never been held to dictate single province-wide bargaining units.
>
> No case was cited to us and we know of none in Nova Scotia where a unit of, essentially, all employees at a single plant has been held not to be appropriate.

* * *

Michelin, which never made a secret of its desire to remain union-free, found a more sympathetic ear in the provincial legislature, which passed section 24A (now section 26) of the *Trade Union Act*, commonly known as the Michelin Amendment, to overturn the board's decision. Under section 26, when an employer operating interdependent manufacturing locations so requests, the board must find that the appropriate unit is one that combines employees from all of the locations.

Brian Langille, "The Michelin Amendment in Context" (1981) 6 Dalhousie L.J. 523 at 546–52

> . . . [D]epending upon one's view of the motives underlying [the Michelin Amendment], it either makes a serious and unnecessary error in reconciling the tension between the two functions of bargaining units, or recognizes that tension and exploits it in order to render organization extremely difficult. The Michelin Amendment, and the Labour Relations Board's order made pursuant to it declare that the appropriate unit consists of both the Granton and Bridgewater plants. If we assume that the purpose of the amendment and the link between it and jobs and development is that industry will be attracted to the province because of the stable (broad base) bargaining structures created by the labour relations board's bargaining unit orders, then it seems clear that the legislation has struck

the balance between the conflicting tensions in bargaining unit theory totally in favour of long-term industrial relations stability at the expense of the other value at stake, the ability to organize at all. . . .

. . . This error may be an unnecessary one. Recent developments in bargaining unit determination in British Columbia demonstrate that it may be possible to reconcile the two functions of a bargaining unit in a most interesting way. It may be possible to both ensure that organization takes place and a broad based and stable bargaining structure results for collective bargaining purposes. It may be possible to have your cake and eat it too. How is this achieved?

In *Amon Investments Limited* (1978) B.C.L.R.B. No. 39/78, the employer had 13 locations within Victoria and Vancouver. The union applied for a unit at one location. The employer, of course, urged that the appropriate unit was one consisting of all thirteen locations, relying on the reasons set out in the *Insurance Corporation of British Columbia* [1974] 1 Can.L.R.B.R. 403, case favouring large units and stable unfragmented bargaining relationships. The union [argued] . . . that a single location was appropriate in order to permit collective bargaining to take place. After reviewing the evidence and the countervailing pressures, the Board concluded that a single location was an appropriate unit but went on to add the following crucial qualification:

> . . . Any union other than the [Applicant] seeking to represent employees of this Employer will be required to gain the support of those employees already represented by the [Applicant]. Further certification applications received from the [Applicant] (and there is one pending at this time) will, if the union has the required support, be disposed of by enlarging the existing unit rather than creating a new additional unit.
>
> Our decision to uphold the present certification, subject to the proviso that future organization of the employees must be accomplished by a variance of the presently certified unit, serves to allow the employees who now desire collective representation to exercise their rights and, at the same time, accommodate the employer's concerns.

What I refer to as the '*Amon* Principle' in my view successfully achieves a reconciliation of the conflicting purposes of the bargaining unit. It enables organization to take place while at the same time ensuring that an unfragmented and thus stable and broad base bargaining structure results in the long run. . . .

If the legislature has determined that long-term stable and broad base bargaining structures are crucial in multi-location manufacturing plants, then it seems to me that the '*Amon* Principle' could profitably be invoked to ensure that that end is achieved without totally ignoring the other function of bargaining unit determination.

But there is one feature of the Michelin case which separates it and makes it a more difficult case than those which we have been discussing. The overwhelming majority of cases involving multi-location employers involve retail chains, fast food outlets, and banks. There is little jurisprudence concerning the manufacturing industry. But more especially there is little jurisprudence on functionally interdependent operations. The chain store, fast food outlet and bank cases are distinguishable because the locations there, although they may be dependent upon other parts of the employer's organization to continue to operate, are not functionally interdependent. The operations of Michelin Tire's two plants in Nova Scotia are unquestionably interdependent as was explained by the Nova Scotia Labour Relations Board. . . .

The thrust of these discussions is that because of the Board's interest in long range industrial stability, functional interdependence is an important element in unit determination. Certifying separately a number of units which are functionally interdependent would lead to instability. Although not well articulated in the House of Assembly Debates, Michelin Tire itself took this argument one step further. It argued that because of functional interdependence a fundamental question of democracy arose in the attempted unionization of Michelin's plants. The focus was not upon the long term but upon the present. The argument was not based upon industrial stability in the future but rather upon a present question of fairness. Because a strike at Granton would put employees at Bridgewater out of work, it would be undemocratic to allow only those employees at Granton to vote upon a decision which would have such an impact on employees at both plants. In abstract form there is certainly merit in this contention. However, there are several problems with this contention as well. First, functional interdependence is pervasive in modern industrial society and crosses employer lines. . . .

Secondly, there is a fundamental problem with this argument from democracy in that it too ignores the basic dilemma faced by labour relations boards in unit determinations. While in some sense it might seem abstractly more democratic to consult all employees at the outset, this ignores the real pragmatic difficulties confronting trade unions in organizing very large bargaining units, especially in the face of an organized employer campaign against unionization. The abstract appeal to the merits of democracy rings very hollow where there is no real equal opportunity to convey information and to consult all sides of the question. This has particular relevance in Michelin's case where the no solicitation rule is still in force. . . . It seems to me that the labour relations boards in striking the balance that they have achieved between the two functions of the bargaining unit are seeking to ensure a fairer degree of political equality.

It also seems to me that the '*Amon* Principle' also removes the potency of the argument from democracy. In the end all are consulted and in a meaningful manner without the sacrifice of long term stability.

[Reprinted by permission.]

6:300 DETERMINING EMPLOYEE SUPPORT

The certification process is built around the concept that the choice of whether or not to have collective bargaining is given to the majority of employees in the bargaining unit. Nonetheless, there are divergences in how the presence or absence of majority support is assessed.

Across North America there are basically four models for determining whether most of employees in a bargaining unit wish to be represented by a trade union. In the United States there is a representation vote in every case, preceded by a fairly long campaign in which the employer is allowed to be a full participant. In Canada, various approaches have been used in effort to limit the opportunity for unfair labour practices by employers or undue influence on employees. The three Canadian models are

1) a quick vote in every case;
2) primary reliance on membership evidence (generally in the form of signed membership application cards), with a brief period after the certification application is filed to allow for change-of-heart petitions; and
3) primary reliance on membership evidence as of the date of application.

Nova Scotia pioneered the quick-vote method. Under section 25 of that province's *Trade Union Act*, a vote is normally held within five days of the filing of an application for certification. The rationale for the quick vote is that it has the perceived reliability of a secret-ballot vote but nevertheless leaves little time for the employer to bring pressure on employees. Ontario followed Nova Scotia's lead, providing for a vote in every case within five days of application unless the board directs otherwise. British Columbia now requires a vote to be held in every case, within ten days of application, unless the vote is to be held by mail, in which case the Board has discretion to set the length of time. Section 32(1)(d) of the Alberta *Labour Relations Code* also requires a vote in every case, with no legislative stipulation on timing, although votes are typically held within two weeks of application.

In other Canadian jurisdictions, votes are possible but are not required. The procedures under the *Canada Labour Code* are premised on the notion that "petitions" reflecting a change of heart on the part of employees are inherently suspect, even if they are not proven to have been inspired by the employer. In general, under the *Canada Labour Code*, such petitions are taken into account only if it is alleged that there was something improper in how the union obtained its membership evidence. Normally, a union is certified if its membership evidence shows that it had majority support on the date of application. The board may also choose a date preceding the date of application if it concludes that employer interference caused the union to lose majority support shortly before the latter date.

The following readings discuss the merits and effects of different ways of determining the level of employee support for unionization.

Paul Weiler, "Promises to Keep: Securing Workers' Rights to Self-Organization under the NLRA" (1983) 96 Harv. L. Rev. 1769 at 1775–78, 1808–16

American labor law has created an elaborate formal procedure for the representation contest. In order to make a sufficient showing of interest for a certification application to the NLRB a trade union must convince at least 30% of the employees in a unit to sign membership or authorization cards. The Board investigates the union's petition, defines the scope of the appropriate bargaining unit, decides whether the conditions for a valid election have been satisfied, and, if they have, conducts a secret ballot vote among the eligible employees. Before the election, both union and employer vigorously campaign in an effort to influence the vote; an extensive battery of legal regulations is aimed at preventing any improper interference with the employees' choice. Assuming that its 'laboratory conditions' for an informed and unrestrained verdict have been satisfied, the Board will either certify the victorious union as the exclusive bargaining representative for the employees (and impose on the employer a corresponding duty to bargain), or, if the union has lost, bar any further elections in the unit for at least twelve months.

In their halcyon days of the early 1940s, American unions fared very well under the formal certification procedure of the NLRA; elections involved more than one million eligible voters annually, and trade unions won approximately 80% of those elections. Union success rates were still high in 1950; but . . . there has been a steady and stark decline ever since, both in the union victory rate in certification elections (from 74% in 1950 to 48% in 1980) and, even more dramatically, in the percentage of voters included in union victories (from 85% to 37%). The result of these trends is that the number of employees successfully organized each year has dropped from 750,000 to fewer than 200,000. In 1950, new certifications raised the level of union representation in the private sector work force by 1.92%; in 1980, the entire organizational effort of American unions under the NLRA increased union density by a near-infinitesimal 0.24%, a rate just one-eighth that of thirty years earlier (and one that was far outstripped by natural attrition from job loss in unionized firms).

. . . To a dispassionate observer, the simplest explanation for the drop in the union victory rate would be that it represents a corresponding drop in interest in collective bargaining among American workers. My thesis, however, is that the decline in union success in representation campaigns is in large part attributable to deficiencies in the law: evidence suggests that the current certification procedure does not effectively insulate employees from the kinds of coercive anti-union employer tactics that the NLRA was supposed to eliminate.

It is the time lag between the filing of a representation petition and the vote, usually about two months, that gives the employer the opportunity to attempt to turn its workers against the union. Typically, the firm will mount a vigorous campaign to fend off the threat of collective bargaining. It will emphasize to its workers how risky and troubled life might be in the uncharted world of collective bargaining: the firm might have to tighten up its supervisory and personnel practices and reconsider existing, expensive special benefits; the union would likely demand hefty dues, fines, and assessments, and might take the employees out on a long and costly strike with no guarantee that there would be jobs at the end if replacements had been hired in the meantime; if labor costs and labor unrest became too great, the employer might have to relocate.

The employees might well dismiss this message as mere bluffing were it not that a determined anti-union employer has at its disposal a potent weapon with which to demonstrate its power over the lives of its employees: the dismissal of selected union activists, in violation of section 8(a)(3) of the NLRA. Dismissal has the immediate effect of rendering these union supporters unable to vote — a consequence that by itself might tip the balance in a close election — and also excludes the discharged employees from the plant, the setting in which they could have campaigned most effectively among their fellow employees. Even more importantly, the dismissal of key union adherents gives a chilling edge to the warning that union representation is likely to be more trouble for the employees than it is worth.

Perhaps the most remarkable phenomenon in the representation process in the past quarter-century has been an astronomical increase in unfair labor practices by employers. . .

The purpose of a representation system, of course, is neither to chalk up a high union victory rate in certification drives nor to channel as many employees as possible into unions. Rather, it is to nurture and protect employee freedom of choice with respect to collective bargaining. Reflection on the differences between the legal techniques used by the United States and Canada to achieve this purpose reveals the crucial assumptions of the American model.

The assumption of the Canadian scheme is that the labor board simply licenses unions to bargain on behalf of employees. Thus, although the system includes a number of safeguards designed to ensure that the union card majority reflects actual employee wishes, its primary objective is a smooth-running administrative procedure that, without much fanfare, will get the parties to the negotiating table as quickly as possible.

By contrast, an ingrained premise of the American model is that certification confers on the trade union a quasi-governmental authority over the employees and therefore requires a procedure comparable to that by which a government is chosen. It is assumed that, even if a union has obtained a solid card majority, the employees need protection against a possibly hasty judgment about unionization that might have resulted from peer group pressure and the bandwagon effect of a whirlwind union organizing drive. Workers should be given the time to listen to the employer's arguments as well as to the union's, time to reflect and perhaps to recant. And what better way to ensure a reasoned decision than by having a campaign followed by a secret ballot election, the same process through which we choose our political leaders?

This view is misleading insofar as it equates the limited role of the union with the role of a legislative body. A trade union does not govern the employees in the unit. Unlike an elected legislature, the union does not have the authority to prescribe conditions in the workplace. All it can do is negotiate with the employer to try to obtain some of the improvements that the union promised the employees in the representation campaign. Only if a contract is achieved will there be any tangible effects on the employees — changes in the distribution of the compensation package, union control over the prosecution of grievances, a union security clause, and so on. But achieving a first contract is a very different challenge for the union from that of simply obtaining certification.

The certification of a union in no way guarantees that the employees will be able to secure a collective bargaining agreement, even if the union has satisfied the most painstaking of representation procedures and won a secret ballot vote. Once the certification stage is passed, the guiding principle of the NLRA is freedom of contract. The employer is under no obligation to offer any tangible benefits to the union. The Act provides the means by which employees who wish to organize into unions in order to deal more effectively with their employers can do so, but it promises them no particular gains as a result. The workers must win these through their own efforts.

Unions force concessions, and ultimately contracts, from employers with the lever of employee pressure — the use or the threat of a strike. Thus, to achieve any degree of real authority in the bargaining unit and to win a decent contract that will give collective action a reasonable prospect of survival, the union must obtain a strike mandate from the employees. In practice this requires not just a bare majority, but a solid one. Only such a mandate will make the employer realize that its employees not only are prepared to vote for unionization in the abstract, but also are willing to put their jobs on the line to secure a collective influence on their employment conditions. The assumption of the Canadian model, in contrast, is that the willingness of the employees to back the union during negotiations is the best measure of the durability of the support for the union shown by the initial card majority. Rather than decide on the basis of easily made promises in a representation campaign that takes place months before serious negotiations begin, the employees can see what their employer actually offers at the bargaining table, compare these offers with what their union demands, and then make up their minds whether to take the risks and make the sacrifices necessary to achieve a favorable collective agreement . . .

After administering a card-based system for five years [in British Columbia], I am satisfied that it not only rests on a more realistic appreciation of the tangible value of legal certification, but also permits a true reading of employees' sentiments about union representation. The system does, however, have one major drawback. Although both the union and the labor board may know that the union has the real support of the employees, the employer — who is prone to genuine self-deception on this score — often remains unconvinced on the basis of cards alone. A secret ballot vote has a symbolic value that a card check alone can never have. It clears the air of any doubts about the union's majority and also confers a measure of legitimacy on the union's bargaining authority, especially among minority pockets of employees who were never contacted in the initial organizational drive.

The Province of Nova Scotia has devised a procedure — the 'instant vote' — that achieves these values while still avoiding the trauma of the bitter representation battle. The Nova Scotia Labour Board must conduct an election no more than five days after it receives a certification petition. In this highly compressed interval, it is nearly impossible for the employer to mount a sustained offensive aimed at turning employee sentiments around through intimidation and discrimination. . . .

. . . [T]he single most important assumption underpinning the NLRA model [is] that the employer is legitimately entitled to play the same role in a representation campaign against the union that the Republican Party plays in a political campaign against the Democrats. Stated this baldly, is the assumption not incongruous? After all, the purpose of the representation process is to permit employees to decide whether collective bargaining or individual bargaining will better advance their own interests. If they choose to deal with their employer collectively, the representation process enables them to license the union, which is itself an organization of employees, to bargain on their behalf. The union is simply a vehicle for collective employee action. The employer, on the other hand, has a primary duty to serve its shareholders. In this respect, its interests are distinct from those of its employees. Of course, the outcome of the election will affect the interests of the employer, but it is precisely because the employer's interests typically diverge from the employees' that it is strange to give the employer a central role in the representation decision.

Let us take a closer look at the political analogy to see whether the campaign between employer and union is really comparable to a contest between Republicans and Democrats for government office. A political campaign produces a verdict about who is to govern the voters. But a newly certified union does not govern even the employees, and it has no authority at all over the employer. The firm remains free to pursue its own interests and priorities, to determine its own personnel or industrial relations policies, and to refuse to make any significant changes in its current compensation package or in the prerogatives of management. The presence of a union sitting at the other side of the table may make it more difficult for the employer to run its business as it chooses, because the employees are now more determined, more cohesive, and better equipped to pursue their own goals. But it is hard to see why the employer should be given a role to play in the process by which employees decide in the first place whether they will deal collectively with the employer.

. . . Because only the employees' interests are supposed to count in the certification decision, the employer can claim no positive right to influence the employees' vote. The law should not restrain the employer's freedom to say what it will about collective bargaining — censorship in the representation campaign has the same offensive flavor that it has in politics or in the arts — but there is no principle of fairness that requires that the representation process be structured to facilitate employer opposition to unionization.

A proponent of the current American model of the extended representation campaign might retreat to one final defense. He might grant that the employer has no inherent right to protect its own interests by campaigning against collective bargaining, yet at the same time he might defend the employer's participation in election campaigns as an aid to informed employee choice. . . .

In my view this is the best case that can be made for the American-style representation campaign. One cannot deal with it simply on a conceptual level; rather, one must examine the empirical assumptions of the argument and appraise the tangible benefits and costs of the system it purports to justify.

My reading of the evidence about the current American experience leaves me unpersuaded of the supposed advantages of the extended campaign. In the first place, the employer has had ample opportunity and incentive to demonstrate the advantages of an individual bargaining regime before the union comes on the scene. Second, American workers are not typically unsophisticated about unionization. They are quite aware of the negative features that their employer may point out to them: dues, strikes, job losses, and so on. . . . Finally, the employer and the union will have sufficient chance for debate during contract negotiations. By the time the employees make up their minds about what they wish to do in negotiations, the issues will be more focused, and the choice will be more informed than it could possibly be at the certification stage. The contribution made by the election campaign to the enlightenment of the employees is marginal at best.

A champion of fully informed employee choice might still ask why we should not pursue even that incremental improvement. In principle I agree that, all other things being equal, a more informed employee choice is a freer one. Unfortunately, we do not have the luxury of choosing between an employer's illumination of the issues for its employees and no employer influence at all. If we design a representation system to elicit the additional enlightenment provided by law-abiding employers, we thereby create both the opportunity and the incentive for illegal coercion of workers by firms that recognize that they can flout the system with relative impunity. Any fair minded review of the trends in this country in the last twenty years makes it clear that our maintaining the present full-blown campaign implies that we have opted for some illumination and a great deal of intimidation.

* * *

Taking Weiler's thesis as a starting point, Jospeh Rose and Gary Chaison looked at the impact on union density rates of the election campaign system used in the United States and the card system used in most of Canada. They concluded that, while density rates in Canada had remained fairly stable, the American system had led to a serious weakening of the union movement.

Joseph Rose & Gary Chaison, "Linking Union Density and Union Effectiveness: The North American Experience" (1996) 35 Industrial Relations 78 at 80–83, 86, 99

The modest [union] membership gains in the United States from 1956 to 1979, an increase of 29 percent, disappeared in the 1980s. Union density has now returned to the levels of the mid-1930s, that is to the levels preceding the great wave in organizing that followed the passage of the Wagner Act. When we consider the period from the early 1960s through 1979, we find that union membership increased but at a slower rate than overall employment, and this caused union density to fall. From 1979 to 1990 union membership fell while employment rose. In 1991 union membership and employment declined proportionately. In 1992 there was a slight increase in employment while union membership fell; and in 1993 union membership increased but at the same rate as employment. Since 1979, [American] unions have lost 4.4 million members.

In contrast to their American counterparts, Canadian unions experienced growth and stability. From 1956 to 1993 union membership increased by almost 200 percent (2.7 million members), and as membership gains exceeded labor force growth, union density rose from 33.3 percent to 37.6 percent. Cross-sectional analyses of employees' characteristics show that Canadian union density is now roughly twice that of the United States even among purportedly harder to organize workers; for example, in 1990, the comparable density rates in Canada and the United States were 29.7 percent and 12.6 percent for female workers, 23.1 percent and 7.0 percent for part-time workers, and 26.9 percent and 13.6 percent for clerical workers. In the years since 1980, a period of tremendous membership losses for American unions, Canadian unions gained nearly 700,000 members.

. . . There can be little doubt . . . that the primary source of union growth in both countries has been the public sector. However, it is noteworthy that Canadian public sector union density is nearly twice that of the United States (61.3 percent versus 36.5 percent in 1990) and that private sector union membership in the United States fell faster than in Canada, widening the gap between the density rates in the two countries. Indeed, recent evidence indicates that structural differences in economies and labor forces account for only 15 percent of the U.S.-Canada unionization gap. Finally, no matter how . . . [one] estimates or interprets density rates, the fact remains that there has been overall growth and recent stability in the Canadian union movement, and that this is in sharp contrast to the significant, continuous decline in the United States. . . .

. . . We believe declining union density [in the United States] also perpetuates itself through its adverse effects on organizing resources and priorities. First, unions with sharply reduced memberships and facing intense employer opposition in negotiations have had to cut back on organizing staff and resources and redirect efforts toward the protection of past bargaining gains. Second, declining density rates mean that unions have less dues income to mount new organizing drives. At the same time, the costs of organizing a given fraction of the non-union workforce rises for each union member. This might not be a major problem if new organizing could readily yield membership gains to cover its costs. But low union density rates increase incentives for employers to remain non-union in order to maintain their competitive positions. As a result, employer opposition increases and organizing campaigns become protracted and more expensive. The high costs and low yields from organizing in low density industries may convince union officers that organizing is not a prudent investment of the members' dues and the staffs' time, particularly if it detracts from the quality of representational services to the present membership. The results are a lower priority for union organizing and self-perpetuating membership losses. The situation has become one in which the costs of organizing the number of new members just to maintain the present rate of union density are prohibitive given the financial resources of labor unions in general. . . .

The greater organizing activity and success in Canada is the result of the interaction of lower employer resistance to unionization and legislation that facilitates organizing. For example, certification is normally based on signed membership cards, some jurisdictions require expedited elections, and labor boards generally have strong remedial powers to discourage employer misconduct during organizing campaigns and the negotiation of first agreements. . . . [R]elative to the union certification elections in the United States, the accelerated certification procedures used in most Canadian jurisdictions reduce the opportunity for, and impact of, illegal employer practices aimed at decreasing employees' support for union representation. . . .

Accordingly, unions confronted by a hostile or unfavorable legal climate, that is, one that does not facilitate unionization, will likely find it more difficult to achieve organizing and bargaining gains, and, as a consequence, density level will fall. Conversely, legal environments supportive of collective bargaining offer greater opportunities for unions to expand membership. As noted previously, differences in public policy, union organizing, and employer resistance have been cited as important determinants of the divergence in unionization in Canada and the United States. One contribution of this study is that it demonstrates that the level and direction of density rates have a circular effect. A labor movement experiencing declines in membership and density rate will be hard pressed to stem the tide of de-unionization and retain its status within the industrial relations system, whereas a labor movement experiencing membership gains and a stable density rate will have greater vibrancy and institutional stability and will be capable of fulfilling its economic, political and social role.

[Reprinted by permission.]

6:400 TIMELINESS OF CERTIFICATION AND DECERTIFICATION APPLICATIONS

The basic principle with respect to the timeliness of a certification application is that a union may apply at any time to be certified as bargaining agent for a unit of employees who are not already covered by collective bargaining. However, there are a number of important exceptions, commonly known as bars, which vary considerably from jurisdiction to jurisdiction and call for close scrutiny of the relevant labour relations statute and the jurisprudence of the particular labour board. The bars are designed to balance the need for stability in a collective bargaining relationship against the employees' right to get rid of a bargaining agent with which they are unhappy and the employer's interest in not having its work force targeted by overly frequent certification campaigns.

Generally speaking, a union that has failed in an earlier attempt to establish majority support in a particular bargaining unit, or that has withdrawn an application either before or after a vote has been held, is barred for a certain period (either by statute or by board practice) from applying again for certification for the same unit. Similarly, because it is unlawful to strike in order to obtain recognition, a board will often dismiss a certification application made with respect to employees who are engaging in an unlawful work stoppage, or will simply adjourn the application until the strike ends.

If the unit of employees in question is already represented by another union, there are tighter bars to a certification application by a rival union. To give newly certified unions a chance to get established, most labour relations statutes allow a union a ten or twelve-month period after certification in which to reach a collective agreement with the employer. During that period, other unions or dissident employees may not apply to displace the new bargaining agent. This bar can be extended by the advent of the statutory conciliation process or by a legal strike or lockout. Unions that are voluntarily recognized generally enjoy less protection than certified unions during the early part of the collective bargaining relationship, to limit the risk of entrenchment of employer-influenced bargaining agents.

If the union concludes a collective agreement, an application to terminate its bargaining rights can still be brought by another union or by employees within the bargaining unit, but only during certain periods (informally called the "open season") — for example, in Ontario, during the last three months of the agreement's term, and in British Columbia during the seventh or eighth month of each year. Additional open season periods arise each year in the case of very long collective agreements, or agreements which provide for automatic renewal.

A bargaining agent will be decertified, and any collective agreement it may have negotiated will be void, if it is established at any time that the certification was obtained by fraud. This type of challenge is more likely to be brought in jurisdictions that allow the assessment of support through a card system than in those where elections by secret ballot are always required.

In some jurisdictions, such as Ontario, statutory amendments in recent years have made it somewhat easier than in the past for employees in the bargaining unit to apply for decertification if they no longer desire union representation. Decertification applications by employees are, however, subject to the same timeliness requirements as decertification applications by rival unions. If a board is given evidence that a certain percentage of employees in the unit no longer support the union, the board will generally order a decertification vote.

A trade union can also have its bargaining rights extinguished if it has abandoned them, for example by failing for a long time to make efforts to negotiate, renew, or administer a collective agreement.

6:500 SUCCESSOR EMPLOYERS, CONTRACTING OUT, AND RELATED EMPLOYERS

6:510 Successor Employers

In the absence of any statutory provision to the contrary, the concept of the "corporate veil" means that a change in the employer's corporate identity puts an end to any statutory bargaining rights by which the "old" employer was bound, and to any collective agreement negotiated pursuant to those bargaining rights. As a result, all Canadian labour relations statutes now have detailed provisions intended to give significant protection to existing bargaining rights where a business has been sold or transferred to a new employer. Typical of this kind of legislation is section 44 of the *Canada Labour Code*, which preserves existing bargaining rights and collective agreements where a business is sold. Such provisions only apply where the labour board finds that the transaction in question does indeed constitute the sale of a business. However, as the following case demonstrates, boards and courts have shown some flexibility in finding a sale of a business even in situations where there has been no apparent exchange between the predecessor and the successor.

Ajax (Town) v. National Automobile, Aerospace and Agricultural Implement Workers Union of Canada (CAW-Canada), Local 222 **(1998), 41 O.R. (3d) 426 (Ont. C.A.) (affirmed by the Supreme Court of Canada , 2000 SCC 23)**

> GOUDGE J.A. (for the court): For many years the Town of Ajax contracted with Charterways Transportation Limited to provide it with the skilled drivers and the limited number of mechanics and cleaners needed to operate the town transit system. These people were employees of Charterways and were represented in their collective bargaining with their employer by the appellant Union, CAW-Canada.
>
> As of January 1, 1993 the Town determined that it would take back the operation of its transit system. It cancelled its contract with Charterways and hired its own drivers, mechanics and cleaners. The vast majority of those hired by the Town came from that

group of Charterways employees who had previously been operating the transit system for the Town.

The Union sought to preserve its bargaining rights by seeking a declaration that these circumstances constituted the sale of a business within the meaning of s. 64, the successor rights provision of the Labour Relations Act, R.S.O. 1990, c. L.2, as amended. The Ontario Labour Relations Board granted the declaration. . . . On the judicial review application brought by the Town, the Divisional Court quashed the Board's decision finding it to be patently unreasonable. . . .

For the reasons that follow I disagree. In my opinion the Board's decision cannot be said to be patently unreasonable. I would therefore allow the appeal and dismiss the application for judicial review.

THE RELEVANT LEGISLATION

Like all provincial labour acts the Ontario Labour Relations Act contains a successorship provision whose purpose is to protect the permanence of bargaining rights when a business or a part of a business is sold or transferred from one employer to another. . . .

That provision is s. 64. For the purposes of this appeal the relevant parts of that section are as follows:

> 64(1) In this section,
>> "business" includes one or more parts of a business;
>> "predecessor employer" means an employer who sells his, her or its business;
>> "sells" includes leases, transfers and any other manner of disposition;
>> "successor employer" means an employer to whom the predecessor employer sells the business.
>> (1.1) This section applies when a predecessor employer sells a business to a successor employer.
>
> (2) If the predecessor employer is bound by a collective agreement, the successor employer is bound by it as if the successor employer were the predecessor employer, until the Board declares otherwise.

The task faced by the Board in this case was to determine whether on the facts as it found them there had been a "sale" of a "business" for the purposes of this section.

THE STANDARD OF REVIEW

The parties to this litigation all agree that in reviewing the decision of the Board the court should apply the standard of patent unreasonableness.

In my opinion, this is clearly the appropriate standard of review. . . .

The Board found that from 1977 to the end of 1992 Charterways contracted to supply the Town with the skilled workforce needed to operate its transit system. Charterways recruited, hired, trained, disciplined, scheduled and deployed the team of drivers and the small number of mechanics and cleaners needed by the transit system. The appellant Union held collective bargaining rights for this group of Charterways employees.

The contract between Charterways and the Town made clear the importance of the continuity and stability of this workforce. Among other things, this helped make the drivers familiar and identifiable to the riding public. In the language of the contract, Charterways undertook that "the same vehicle operators will be regularly assigned to the Transit System to ensure route familiarity, system continuity, and allow passenger recognition."

When Ajax terminated this contract as of December 31, 1992 Charterways had no comparable employment to offer the group of employees who had been working on the Ajax transit contract. However, in taking back this operation the Town conducted its hiring so as to achieve substantial continuity in the workforce operating its transit system. Twenty-three of the thirty drivers hired and three of the four cleaner and maintenance personnel hired had previously performed that work for Charterways on its Ajax contract.

Given these circumstances the Board concluded as follows:

> ... the business [of Charterways] was primarily carried on through the utilization of an identifiable employee complement skilled in the operation of the Ajax Transit System that, through its efforts over the years, it had recruited, trained and coordinated. Particularly bearing in mind the operational requirement that the employee complement remain stable, the work force engaged by Charterways can be considered its most valuable asset. Given its centrality to its operation, then, we conclude it constitutes a distinguishing "part" of its business.
>
> . . .
>
> In summary, we are satisfied that by acquiring the substantial part of the work force previously employed by Charterways to perform its obligations under its contract with the Town, the Town transferred to itself an essential element of that business. Consequently, we conclude that in so doing, Charterways and the Town have transacted a sale of part of a business within the meaning of s. 64 of the Act.

The issue on this appeal is whether the Divisional Court was correct in finding this conclusion to be patently unreasonable. . . .

First, the Divisional Court found that it was patently unreasonable to conclude that in the circumstances of this case there was a sale or transfer. The court put its point this way:

> ... other than terminating their employment because, as the Board found, Charterways had "no comparable employment to offer" to the employees in question, nothing occurred between Ajax and Charterways which can be reasonably said to have caused a "sale, transfer or other disposition" of Charterways' "business or a part thereof." Specifically there was no "nexus," "legal act" or "legal relations". . . .

In my opinion, the Divisional Court erred in this finding. The conclusion that these facts constitute a sale as defined by s. 64 . . . does not give the section a patently unreasonable interpretation. The statutory definition is inclusive: "'sells' includes leases, transfers and any other manner of disposition." Because of the remedial purpose of s. 64, namely the preservation of bargaining rights, this definition is to be given a broad and liberal interpretation. Moreover, it is not required that the transfer take any particular legal form nor take place by way of a legal transaction. In *W. W. Lester . . .*, McLachlin J. put it this way:

Ten of the labour acts have provisions similarly worded to s. 89 of the Newfoundland Act, referring to transactions such as sale, lease, transfer or disposition. (The Quebec Act also contains a successorship provision but the section uses the phrase "alienation or operation.") Although the terms "sale" and "lease" may have restricted meanings, the words "transfer" and "other disposition" have been broadly interpreted to include several types of transactions, including exchange, gift, trust, take overs, mergers, and amalgamation.

In keeping with the purpose of successorship provisions — to protect the permanence of bargaining rights — labour boards have interpreted "disposition" broadly to include almost any mode of transfer and have not relied on technical legal forms of business transactions.

. . .

Notwithstanding the broad discretion in labour boards to determine whether or not the mode of disposition constitutes successorship, the fact remains that in virtually all jurisdictions something must be relinquished by the predecessor business on the one hand and obtained by the successor on the other to bring a case within the section.

Here, as a result of its contractual relationship with Ajax, Charterways had developed a skilled and experienced group of employees which operated the transit system for the Town. This was the business which Charterways carried on for Ajax. When Ajax terminated the contract, Charterways relinquished this work force, most of which was then acquired by Ajax. The nexus between Charterways and the Town is the commercial history without which the Town's acquisition of the work force would not have occurred. This acquisition represents a "transfer" to the Town of that work force. In my opinion, these factors provide a reasonable basis for concluding that what happened here was a sale or transfer within the meaning of s. 64 of the Act. . . .

Second, the Divisional Court found clearly irrational the Board's conclusion that in taking on the employees in question Ajax acquired a "part" of the business of Charterways within the meaning of s. 64 of the Act . . .

This conclusion is also in error in my view. The Board found that the scope of the business engaged in by Charterways for Ajax consisted primarily of the provision of this skilled work force to the Town and that therefore this work force could be considered the most valuable asset of that business. The importance to the Town of the continuity and stability of this work force is reflected in the terms of the contract between the parties and in the results of the hiring done by the Town when it took back the operation of the transit system.

In essence, the Board found that what was transferred was not just the work formerly done by the Charterways employees nor the employees themselves. There was the added value that came with the continuity, experience and stability of this work force. Hence, there was a reasonable basis for the finding that what was transferred to Ajax was a significant part of the business which Charterways conducted for Ajax. . . .

The conclusion of the Board that on the facts before it there was the sale of a part of a business within the meaning of s. 64 of the Act is a finding that is rationally defensible. Its decision cannot be said to be clearly irrational or patently unreasonable.

* * *

6:520 Contracting Out

***Canada Post Corporation v. C.U.P.W. (Nieman's Pharmacy)* (1990), 4 Can. L.R.B.R. (2d) 161 at 174–75, 186–87**

[Nieman's had operated a post office in conjunction with its pharmaceutical and retail business since 1970. In 1987, under a new arrangement with Canada Post Corporation (CPC), Nieman's expanded its postal services to include several additional functions. In 1988 a similar arrangement was made for a second pharmaceutical and retail sales outlet that Nieman's had just opened. The applicant union contended that both of these arrangements constituted a sale of business by Canada Post within the meaning of the *Code*. The employer position was that the arrangement was one of contracting out rather than a sale or transfer of a business.]

JAMIESON, Vice-Chair:

. . .

First we must look to the purpose of these successor rights provisions in the Code. If one studies the jurisprudence, it becomes readily apparent that there is unanimity in previous decisions emanating from this Board and from other jurisdictions that these provisions in labour legislation are designed to preserve existing bargaining rights and to protect rights and privileges acquired by employees under a collective agreement in the event that the employing authority of a business changes hands. Given these objectives, it is generally accepted that s. 44 must be interpreted liberally. A sale of business under the Code can have a much broader meaning than to sell in the commercial sense.

It is also an accepted principle that bargaining rights attach to a business, not to any particular incumbent employees or to chattels or assets, nor to the work. For successor rights to be triggered, there must be more than a transfer of assets or of work. While the transfer of any one or all of the foregoing might be a compelling indicia that a sale within the meaning of the Code has occurred, each on their own is not conclusive. For successor rights to apply, the business as a whole or any part thereof must pass from the seller to the purchaser. For the purposes of a sale under the Code, any part of a business has been defined as meaning a coherent and severable part of a business' economic organization, or a functional economic vehicle or a going concern capable of standing alone. It is not enough that employees of another employer are now doing work previously done by employees of a predecessor employer for a sale of business to have taken place. There must also be some continuity in the employing enterprise for which a union holds bargaining rights, as well as continuity in the nature of the work. The two go hand in hand. . . .

Trade unions obtain their bargaining rights through the certification provisions in the Code. Fundamental to a union becoming a bargaining agent for a group of employees is the expression of a majority wish amongst the affected employees to have the trade union represent them for collective bargaining purposes. Section 44 of the Code was not intended to circumvent the certification process:

> When section 144 was enacted in 1973, it was our understanding that the goal of the legislators was to protect established bargaining rights and benefits accrued through collec-

tive bargaining where new employers assume control of enterprises wherein the employees have already exercised their rights under the Code. In our minds, successor rights were never intended to apply to genuine circumstances of subcontracting, a loss of business to a competitor or where there is a corporate dissolution. It was certainly never anticipated that section 144 would be a vehicle to extend bargaining rights to or impose collective agreements on non-unionized employees or their employers. (*Freight Emergency Service Ltd.* . . .)

. . . What has really happened here is that the implementation of CPC's Corporate Retail Representation Plan has resulted in there being less wicket work for the employees of CPC who are included in CUPW's bargaining unit. Some of that work has been sub-contracted to Niemans where it is now being done by Niemans' employees. What CUPW is saying is, 'That is our work, protect our jobs!' This takes us right back to the 'bargaining rights follow the work' theory which has been rejected by this Board sitting in plenary session. It has also been rejected by the Supreme Court of Canada. The purpose of s. 44 of the Code is not to protect jobs — it is to protect existing bargaining rights and preserve the terms and conditions of collective agreements. The transactions between CPC and Niemans have not resulted in a new employing authority taking over any part of CPC's business that is affected by CUPW's certification order or by its collective agreement. CUPW's bargaining rights have not diminished; the union still represents the same bargaining unit that it represented before postal services were expanded at [the first Nieman's location] and the new postal retail outlet was opened at the [second Nieman's location]. CUPW members still have the same terms and conditions of employment under their collective agreement. The only change is that there has been an increase in the work done outside the bargaining unit. This is a matter for negotiations rather than successor rights, particularly when the work is still being performed within the purview of CPC's business. To find a sale of business in these circumstances would result in the extension of CUPW's bargaining rights to the private sector of CPC's operations where they have never been before. This would be contrary to the intent of s. 44 of the Code.

✻ ✻ ✻

Very commonly, companies subcontract services, such as cleaning or cafeteria services, that are auxiliary to their main business. If a company ends such a contract with one contractor, for whose employees a union has bargaining rights, and gives it to a second contractor, should the second contractor be bound by those bargaining rights? Between 1992 and 1995, the Ontario labour relations statute said yes; it dispensed with the need to demonstrate that a sale of a business had taken place if "substantially similar services are subsequently provided at the premises under the direction of another employer." The Quebec statute has never had a provision of that sort, but in *Ivanhoe Inc. v. UFCW, Local 500*, 2001 SCC 47, the Supreme Court of Canada upheld the Quebec Labour Court's position that a certification could extend to a new subcontractor, at least where the employees of the company contracting out the work had been covered by the certification before the work was originally subcontracted. The Supreme Court emphasized the wide discretion of labour tribunals in determining and weighing the factors to be applied in deciding what is the transfer of an undertaking, and the tribunals' authority to develop specific tests responsive to the situation in a given industry.

In *Sept-Îles (City) v. Quebec (Labour Court)* 2001, SCC 48, the Supreme Court of Canada again accepted the Quebec Labour Court's view that a subcontracting of work alone was in some circumstances enough to ground the transfer of bargaining rights. In that case, it was not an auxiliary function that was contracted out, but a central function — municipal garbage collection.

In 2003, the Quebec government responded to widespread employer objections that such restrictions on subcontracting were impairing the competitveness of Quebec businesses. It amended the successor rights provision of the *Labour Code* (section 45) to provide that bargaining rights do not follow "the transfer of part of the operation of an undertaking" unless what is transferred are not only "functions or the right to operate" but also "most of the elements that characterize the part of the undertaking involved:" SQ 2003, c. 26, s.2.

6:530 Related Employers

Sometimes an employer may carry on business through two or more corporate entities sharing certain facilities and management structures. And sometimes an employer may sell a part of its business to another party within the meaning of the successor rights provisions discussed in the preceding section, but may nevertheless keep considerable control over how that purchaser operates. The form of these arrangements may suggest the existence of more than one employer, and corporate law may indeed treat each of the entities as separate bodies. However, treating them as separate employers for labour law purposes may mean that the union which represents employees in the subordinate entity is unable to bargain with the entity that has real control over the entire operation. To meet this problem, many Canadian jurisdictions provide that the labour board may treat associated or related employers under common control and direction as a single employer for the purpose of bargaining unit determination and for other collective bargaining purposes. Ontario goes so far as to place on the putative employer the onus of disclosing all relevant facts relating to such determination.

The following case illustrates the operation of the "related employer" or "common employer" provisions, and their interface with the successor employer provisions discussed in the preceding section.

White Spot Ltd. v. British Columbia (Labour Relations Board) [1997] B.C.J. No. 1440 (British Columbia Supreme Court)

¶1 MACKENZIE J.: — This is a petition seeking to quash decisions of the Labour Relations Board . . . declaring the petitioner, White Spot Limited [which operated a chain of restaurants in British Columbia] . . . and Gilley Restaurants Ltd. . . . to be a common employer pursuant to s. 38 of the *Labour Relations Code*, R.S.B.C. 1996 c. 244.

¶2 White Spot sold to Gilley the assets and undertaking of a White Spot restaurant in Langley, B.C. The restaurant continues to be a White Spot, operated pursuant to franchise agreements between the petitioner and Gilley. Employees of the Langley restaurant are members of the union, which has a collective agreement with White Spot covering 17 White Spot restaurants in the Lower Mainland. White Spot and Gilley both accept that Gilley is bound by the terms of the collective agreement as a successor pursuant to s. 35 of the Code.

¶3 A panel of the Board made the common employer declaration . . . on the union's application and issued an amended certification.

[The Board had set out the following, at BCLRB No. B191/95, para 51 (Q.L.), as "the most significant [facts] amongst others . . . which lead us to conclude that White Spot and Gilley Restaurants are under common control or direction":

1. White Spot has the substantial control over menu prices and food items despite [the fact] that the WFOA has some input and a few restaurants have different food items.
2. Gilley Restaurants is required to use the White Spot approved suppliers and delivery company. The price of food supplies is in the control of White Spot who negotiates with suppliers. Those prices impact profit by constituting 25% to 30% of total sales. This, coupled with White Spot's control over prices, leads to substantial control over the profit of the franchisee.
3. White Spot requires a marketing fee be paid which it controls for the purposes of promotions and advertising intended to bring business in to all restaurants operating under the White Spot trademark and logo.
4. White Spot requires that a franchisee have a White Spot trained general manager and requires that restaurants operate within its standards. White Spot ensures its standards are met through a comprehensive standards review and frequent quality checks. . . .]

White Spot and Gilley then applied to the Board for reconsideration of the original decision. Another panel of the Board upheld the original panel's decision. . . . White Spot then commenced these proceedings to quash both decisions of the Board. Gilley supported White Spot's petition.

¶4 White Spot contended that the collective bargaining rights of the parties on Gilley's succession to the Langley restaurant are exclusively and automatically determined by the application of s. 35 and the Board has no jurisdiction to "override" the effect of s. 35 by a common employer declaration under s. 38. Mr. Jordan [counsel for White Spot] conceded that s. 38 might have some application if the motive for the succession was an attempt to undermine the union, but there is no such motive here. The Board has concluded that White Spot and Gilley were engaged in a bona fide arm's length transaction for commercial reasons without any ulterior collective bargaining purpose.

¶5 It is agreed on all sides that there has been a succession to the Langley restaurant to which s. 35 applies. Mr. Jordan, on behalf of White Spot, contended that the effect of s. 35

succession is to sever the single bargaining unit for the Langley restaurant and the other unionized restaurants owned and operated by White Spot. Two bargaining units are automatically created by the succession, with the Langley restaurant forming one of them under a collective agreement on the same terms and conditions as the original White Spot collective agreement, except that Gilley is the employer and the bargaining unit is limited to the employees at the Langley site. The union's concern, which apparently led to its application to the Board, was that the Langley employees would lose the benefits of being part of a broader bargaining unit and the ability to deal with White Spot across the bargaining table. . . .

¶6 The issues turn on the interpretation and the interrelationship of the relevant provisions of the Code, namely, s. 38 and s. 35 as follows:

38   If in the board's opinion associated or related activities or businesses are carried on by or through more than one corporation, individual, firm, syndicate or association, or a combination of them under common control or direction, the board may treat them as constituting one employer for the purposes of this Code and grant such relief, by way of declaration or otherwise, as the board considers appropriate.

35 (1) If a business or a part of it is sold, leased, transferred or otherwise disposed of, the purchaser, lessee or transferee is bound by all proceedings under this Code before the date of the disposition and the proceedings must continue as if no change had occurred.

   (2) If a collective agreement is in force, it continues to bind the purchaser, lessee or transferee to the same extent as if it had been signed by the purchaser, lessee or transferee, as the case may be.

   (3) If a question arises under this section, the board, on application by any person, must determine what rights, privileges and duties have been acquired or are retained.

   (4) For the purposes of this section, the board may make inquiries or direct that representation votes be taken as it considers necessary or advisable.

   (5) The board, having made an inquiry or directed a vote under this section, may

      (a) determine whether the employees constitute one or more units appropriate for collective bargaining,

      (b) determine which trade union is to be the bargaining agent for the employees in each unit,

      (c) amend, to the extent it considers necessary or advisable, a certificate issued to a trade union or the description of a unit contained in a collective agreement,

      (d) modify or restrict the operation or effect of a provision of a collective agreement in order to define the seniority rights under it of employees affected by the sale, lease, transfer or other disposition, and

      (e) give directions the board considers necessary or advisable as to the interpretation and application of a collective agreement affecting the employees in a unit determined under this section to be appropriate for collective bargaining.

¶7 The Board relied on two decisions of the Ontario Labour Relations Board in support of its decisions, *Dominion Stores Ltd. and Willett Foods Ltd. and Penmarkay Foods Ltd. . . . ,* and *RPKC Holding Corp.* . . . . In both cases Dominion Stores sold retail grocery stores to the franchisors, RPKC and Penmarkay, triggering a succession invoking the Ontario equivalent of s. 35. The Ontario board granted common employer declarations. Mr. Jordan sought to distinguish those decisions on the ground that the Ontario board found a corporate motivation to weaken the union's collective bargaining position in the franchised operations and perhaps achieve decertification. The Board found no such motivation on the part of White Spot and Gilley for the succession here. . . . While a labour relations advantage may have been one factor motivating the franchise arrangements in the Ontario cases, it was not the dominant factor influencing the Ontario board's decisions. In both cases the board stressed the degree of control exercised by the franchisor under the franchise agreements and the desirability for the union to be able to bargain with the party exercising the dominant influence on the employers' side. The fact that the franchisee was a successor to a collective agreement under the Ontario equivalent of s. 35 was not seen as an obstacle to a common employer declaration.

¶8 The approach taken by the Board here is consistent with the Ontario jurisprudence. The Board was influenced by the single bargaining unit structure which had existed before the Langley restaurant was franchised and the union's desire to "preserve" that structure. As Mr. Jordan stressed, that structure was divided automatically by the s. 35 succession, and the union's application is more accurately characterized as one to restore a pre-existing structure rather than preserve an existing one. . . . Nonetheless, whether it is preservation or restoration, the Board intended a single bargaining unit structure to permit the union to bargain with White Spot as well as Gilley for the Langley employees. The Board has found that White Spot dominates the franchise relationship and that effective bargaining by the union requires that it bargain with White Spot. I do not think that simply because s. 35 created an automatic severance of the bargaining unit on succession, that fact alone precludes the Board from invoking its s. 38 jurisdiction where it considers it to be appropriate.

. . .

¶10 Counsel for White Spot and Gilley both contended that the common employer declaration drags Gilley into bargaining with White Spot for the other restaurants in the bargaining unit still owned and operated by White Spot, in which Gilley has no interest. . . . The form and scope of the existing certification order is a matter of remedy which the Board has the jurisdiction to vary on application by the parties. . . . If White Spot and Gilley wish to pursue complaints about the particulars of the s. 38 remedy granted here they should return to the Board on proper application. The Board's powers under s. 38 are to "grant such relief . . . as the board considers appropriate" which allows the Board latitude to fashion a remedy which meets the exigencies of particular circumstances. . . .

¶11 Gilley advanced an alternative argument that, irrespective of s. 35, the Board was incorrect in concluding that White Spot and Gilley could be under "common control or direction" as required by s. 38, because they are separately owned and managed entities dealing with each other at arm's length. . . .

¶12 The Ontario board's decisions in Penmarkay and RPKC, under very similar statutory provisions, held franchisor and franchisees to be a common employer notwithstanding separate ownership and management, on the basis of the degree of control exercised by the franchisors over the franchisees' activities through the franchise arrangements. Labour relations board jurisprudence, both in British Columbia and Ontario, interprets "common control and direction" as extending to dominant control exercised by a franchisor under franchise agreements with an independently owned franchisee. In my view, the words "common control or direction," in context, are capable of bearing that interpretation. The Board's functional interdependence test is within those parameters. Once that test is met and the interpretation adopted by the Board is one that can reasonably be supported by the wording of the section, the application of the section to any particular circumstances is a matter for the Board. Its exercise of jurisdiction within those limits can only be attacked successfully if its conclusions are patently unreasonable. . . .

¶13 The issue then becomes whether in the particular circumstances the franchisor has sufficient control to justify a declaration. The control exercised by a franchisor in a particular franchise arrangement and whether that degree of control is sufficiently dominant to be common control or direction of the franchised operations are inferences or conclusions of fact flowing from the evidence. The Gilley submission reviewed the facts in detail and argued that Gilley's authority under the franchise arrangements with respect to pricing, labour relations and other aspects of the day to day management, plus the independent financial risk for the operations assumed by Gilley on the purchase, precluded a reasonable conclusion that White Spot dominated the relationship, and the Board's declaration was patently unreasonable. The Board made an extensive inquiry into the franchise arrangements between White Spot and Gilley and reached certain conclusions as to White Spot's degree of control which prompted the declaration. . . . I cannot say here that the Board has so obviously misperceived the evidence before it that its factual conclusions are patently unreasonable.

¶14 The petition is dismissed.

6:600 ALTERNATIVES TO THE *WAGNER ACT* MODEL

In its heyday from the 1940s to the 1960s, collective bargaining was premised on a paradigmatic form of employment — embracing semiskilled factory work, mining, construction and transportation — in which workers generally filled specific, stable jobs. This stability enabled employees to claim a range of very important "job rights" — pay scales, promotion opportunities, layoff protection — based on their seniority and skills. Unions were often able to negotiate elaborate collective agreement language regulating the acquisition and exercise of such rights within each bargaining unit. Workers were prepared to support unions because unions were able to protect job rights.

Today, changes in technology, especially in information technology, have radically altered the means of production, the nature of work and employment, and management strategies. Machines can be more easily retooled to produce new products, so manufacturers are more able to implement "flexible production." Volatile consumer demand, and the increased expectation that demand will drive production, have persuaded manufacturers not to maintain large inventories but to develop networks of suppliers and contractors to provide components as needed — "just in time" production. This in turn allows for rapid expansion or contraction of production without having to invest in plant, or employees who may be standing idle as production fluctuates. The risks resulting from volatility are shifted to the suppliers, whose employees are not in the original bargaining unit and thus cannot benefit from the job rights negotiated by the union.

Changes in technology also permit corporations to control technical specifications and quality when the actual production takes place thousands of kilometres away — in Asia or Latin America, for example. Thus, unionized employers can reduce the amount of work actually done within the bargaining unit in order to cut labour costs. The knowledge that this exit option is available to employers puts great pressure on workers and their unions to lower their demands, and often to surrender job rights and economic benefits won earlier.

Apart from their ability to export jobs to other companies or countries, employers can plausibly argue that workers must become more adaptable if the company is to take full advantage of changes in technology. Flexibility, employers say, is impaired by the old job rights, which are based on the premise that jobs can remain essentially the same for many years. And finally, because new technologies require a greater degree of technical sophistication on the part of workers, employers argue that learning which is derived from and tied to the performance of a given set of operations unique to the bargaining unit is less relevant than general knowledge and skills, which enable employees to perform a wider range of tasks and effectively operate new machinery. This, too, weakens the old system of job rights.

All of these changes have helped to undermine plant-based bargaining units, and traditional job rights that have currency only within such units. If collective bargaining to remain meaningful, it must somehow take place within larger structures that encompass not only a plant's core workforce but all of the workers who contribute to the productive process, including those who work for other companies and perhaps even those who work in other countries. If job rights are to remain worthwhile, they must transcend the old paradigm of static production in traditional bargaining units, and must be based on sophisticated skills and knowledge that can be used both inside and outside of those units. The very point of having a just-in-time network of suppliers is that they not be part of the prime employer's organization.

However, North American collective bargaining — like North American capitalism itself — is atomized and highly decentralized, with a tradition of autonomous and uncoordinated action. Our union, corporate and governmental structures cannot easily accommodate more broadly based collective bargaining that would parallel the emerging paradigms of industrial organization and employment. The essence of traditional North American job rights is that they should be exercised only with reference to the specific operations in which they are grounded, and the notion that collective bargaining should reach across jurisdictional boundaries and encompass operations in another company or another country is something we have not yet come to terms with. In contrast, in some northern European economies for example, labour market policies assume more broadly-based, sectoral collective bargaining, encompassing (say) all automobile and automobile parts manufacturers in a particular region. Training and redeployment of workers on an industry-wide basis are facilitated by tripartite agencies accountable to government and to federations of employers and unions.

6:610 Minority and Occupational Unionism

The readings in this section question the principles of majority rule and exclusivity of bargaining rights that underpin the *Wagner Act* model. Clyde Summers advocates allowing unions to play a role in representing pro-union minorities in particular workplaces. Dorothy Sue Cobble evokes the pre-*Wagner* phenomenon of occupationally organized unions as a possible way to facilitate the organization of service sector workers. Katherine V.W. Stone explores occupational unionism and citizen unionism as potential models for maintaining employee representation in contexts where workers can expect to move frequently from one employer to another.

Clyde Summers, "Unions without Majority: A Black Hole?" (1990) 66 Chi.-Kent L.R. 531 at 532–34, 539–40, 542–43, 545, 547–48

Unions, by their focus on organization campaigns for the purpose of winning elections, have helped foster the assumption that a union without a majority have [*sic*] no significant role to play. The dominant, if not exclusive, emphasis in organizing is not to increase membership, but to obtain majority status. Indeed, during an organizational campaign employees are commonly not asked to join the union, but only to sign cards authorizing the union to represent them. The objective is to obtain the status of exclusive representative through voluntary recognition by the employer or through a Board election. If the union fails in this objective it commonly assumes that it has no continuing role except, perhaps, to try again another year. Unions, thereby, tacitly accept the Board's characterization that if they are not the exclusive representative they have no representation function. In the absence of a majority, the union is not 'present' in the plant. . . .

When the union loses the election, it commonly abandons the field, seldom attempting to maintain a functioning organization in the plant, except where there is hope that the union can mount a winning campaign the next year. The union ceases to exist as an organization representing the interests of those who supported it, and leaves the local leaders in the plant who declared their support of the union to the tender mercies of the employer. . . . All that is left is a black hole.

In the reports and legislative debates, preceding the Wagner Act, the arguments for majority rule were made in the context of competing unions and the necessity that the majority union have exclusive authority to negotiate for all employers. The purpose of an election was to determine which, if any, union was to be given exclusive representation rights, thereby empowering it to represent non-consenting employees. There was no suggestion that a majority, by preferring individual bargaining, could deprive a minority of their right to bargain collectively for themselves through representatives of their own choosing.

Bargaining collectively with a non-majority union for its own members is not impracticable. Indeed, it is practiced, if not legally required, in almost every country which has a system of free collective bargaining. The American notion that an employer has no duty to bargain with a union until it has obtained a majority is unknown and unthinkable in most other countries. In those countries the collective agreement is legally binding only for union members; the employer remains free to provide more, less, or different benefits to non-members and to settle their grievances without the intervention by the non-majority union.

To be sure economic strength of a non-majority may not be great, and the employer might resist agreeing to benefits for members which it was not prepared to extend to other employees. The non-majority union's position, however, would not be significantly different from that of a union which had a majority in a bargaining unit encompassing only a minority of the employer's work force. Negotiation with a non-majority union could serve the purpose of leading each side to understand better the needs and desires of the other side, and help find solutions which might be mutually accepted. More importantly, it could provide a grievance procedure to which individual employees could resort with assurance of an uncompromised advocate. . . .

A more fruitful role for the non-majority union is to help employees know and enforce their individual employment rights. For example, many employees do not know the full scope of their rights under workmen's compensation. . . .

Similarly, in-plant committees could help employees know and enjoy the full measure of their other entitlements such as medical benefits, sick leave, severance pay and pensions provided by employer established plans. The union could help employees claim and collect statutory entitlements such as unemployment compensation, disability pay, social security and various welfare benefits. . . .

The most important potential function of a non-majority union is enforcement of the Occupational Safety and Health Act ('OSHA'). Statutory enforcement procedures provide a series of openings to a union which establishes an active in-plant safety committee. . . .

There is neither time nor need to canvass the functions which non-majority unions could fulfill in making real other individual employment rights under the evolving common law or under statutes, such as plant closure laws, pregnancy leave acts, polygraph and privacy laws, and whistleblowing statutes. There is need, however, to point out that judicially created doctrines establishing employment rights and employment protection statutes are proliferating at a rapid rate, largely because of the recognition that the shrinking sphere of collective bargaining cannot provide protection. The failure of unions to achieve and maintain majorities is increasing the necessity for non-majority unions to play a significant role. When unions cannot represent employees for the purpose of collective bargaining, non-majority unions can represent employees for the protection of individual employment rights. . . .

... Obviously, a non-majority union is no substitute for an economically strong union with complete, recognized bargaining rights. Even at best, a non-majority union can provide less than half a loaf of economic justice and industrial democracy. But a union without a majority can provide workers a measure of protection, either by collective action or legal representation. It can maintain the bonds between those who believe in unions and want to belong, and it can offer a continuing visible presence in the workplace.

Dorothy Sue Cobble, "Making Postindustrial Unionism Possible" in Sheldon Friedman et al. eds., *Restoring the Promise of American Labor Law* (Ithaca: ILR Press, Cornell University, 1994) 285 at 292–94

Much of the current critique of the New Deal system falsely equates all unionism with the form of unionism that became dominant by the 1940s. Thus, the argument goes, if industrial unionism is obsolete, so is unionism per se. This historical amnesia hampers attempts to create new forms of collective representation. Postindustrial unionism does not need to be invented out of whole cloth: it can be reassembled, reshaped, and extended from elements of past and current institutional practice. The institutional practices of what I have termed 'occupational unions' and the nontraditional approaches to representation taken by female-dominated professional and semiprofessional groups such as teachers, nurses, and clericals offer the best guide to the formulation of a postindustrial unionism.

Occupational unionism, the primary model of unionism before the New Deal, was neither Taylorist nor worksite-based. . . . Although not every trade adopted 'occupational unionism' in toto, before the New Deal the majority of organized trades and virtually every single trade that successfully organized mobile workers relied on some elements of occupational unionism. Occupational unions recruited and gained recognition on an occupational or local market basis rather than by industry or individual job site. Their representational systems emphasized occupationally based rights, benefits, and identity rather than worksite-based protections. Longshoremen, janitors, agricultural laborers, food servers, and garment workers, as well as such classic craft unionists as printers, building tradesmen, and performing artists, strove for control over hiring through closed-shop language and through union-run employment exchanges, rosters, and hiring halls; stressed employment security rather than 'job rights' at individual worksites; offered portable benefits and privileges; and took responsibility for monitoring workplace performance.

Occupational unionism flourished because it met the needs of workers and employers outside of mass-production settings. In local labor markets populated with numerous small employers, the unionization of garment workers, restaurant employees, teamsters, and others brought stability and predictability, inhibiting cutthroat competition. Employers gained a steady supply of skilled, responsible labor and an outside agency (the union) that ensured the competence and job performance of its members. In many cases, the union took responsibility for expanding the customer base for unionized enterprises. A floor for minimum wage and working conditions was established. Workers did not gain long-term job tenure but the opportunity to invest in their own 'human capital' through training and experience at a variety of worksites. As long as the unionized sector remained competitive — a goal to which both labor and management were committed — unionized workers also gained real employment security, in that the union helped make them more employable individually and helped ensure there would be a supply of high-wage, 'good' jobs. This unionism, then, in contrast to industrial unionism, never developed rigid seniority rules at individual worksites; it was committed to maintaining employee productivity, high-quality service and production, and to ensuring the viability of unionized firms. In short, it was flexible, cooperative as well as adversarial, and dedicated to skill enhancement and to the creation of a high-performance workplace. . . .

Occupational unionism declined dramatically in the postwar era, in part because of shifts in union institutional practice. . . . Legislative and legal decisions also severely hampered the ability of occupational unions to exert control over their members, to pressure employers for recognition, and to provide services to members and employers. Closed-shop, top-down organizing, secondary boycotts, the removal of members from the job for noncompliance with union bylaws and work rules, and union membership for supervisors all became illegal. Unions lost their ability to organize new shops, to maintain multiemployer bargaining structures, to set entrance requirements for the trade, to oversee job performance, and to punish recalcitrant members. . . .

By the 1960s, occupational unionism was but a mere shadow of its former robust self. Only the building and construction trades (which obtained special legislative language exempting them from some of the new postwar legal restrictions on unions) and certain highly specialized professional groups (such as the performing arts occupations) retained some degree of power and influence. . . . Yet, by the 1960s other alternatives to mass-production unionism were emerging. The professional and semiprofessional employee organizations built primarily by women, for example, initially focused less on extracting economic concessions from individual enterprises and more on the well-being of their industry or sector and on responding to the 'professional' interests of their members. As state bargaining laws and other forces moved them toward more traditional 'bargaining' relations with employers, they shed some of their occupational and associational orientation. Yet, as Charles Taylor Kerchner and Douglas E. Mitchell . . . have argued for teacher unions, many are now moving toward a third stage of labor relations, in which they are as concerned with the welfare of the overall educational system and with meeting the needs of their clients as with protecting their own interests as employees. It is these alternative models of unionism that hold promise for the future.

Katherine V.W. Stone, "The New Psychological Contract: Implications of the Changing Workplace for Labor and Employment Law" (2001) 48 UCLA L. Rev. 519, at 631–633, 640–641, 650–653

[The author notes the radical transformation of employment in recent years, including a change in the implicit understandings that employers and employees bring to their relationship. Dominant 20th century job structures relied extensively on internal markets, with their tacit promise of long-term employment in exchange for employees doing their job and refraining from disruptive oppositional conduct. The emerging paradigm seeks to substitute more flexible forms of work, abandons the implicit promise of job security, and replaces it with a new psychological contract that posits a boundaryless career in which employees will expect to move frequently among employers. The author points out that this new psychological contract and its attendant job structures originated in nonunion environments. She goes on to look at models of unionism that may be able to preserve institutions for employee representation. A few of the specific changes that she recommends for American labour law near the end of the following excerpt are already in place in Canada, but most of them are not.]

One hundred years ago, Beatrice and Sydney Webb identified three different goals of working class collective action and three corresponding roles for labor organizations. They are: (1) to form mutual benefit associations, (2) to create organizations to engage in collective bargaining for job related protection, and (3) to create organizations that can lobby for legislation favorable to employees. The Webbs detailed how English unions, at different times in English history, performed each of these roles.

In the twentieth century, American unions have also played all three roles, but with a heavy emphasis on the second. Both the AFL and the CIO, prior to their merger in 1955, saw their primary function as bargaining for job-related protections. And postmerger, the AFL-CIO continued to emphasize collective bargaining and contract administration as the core function of unionism. Over the past fifty years, international unions and the AFL-CIO have built high-powered research and legal departments to provide support for their bargaining programs, while relegating their legislative departments to secondary roles. The strength of the AFL-CIO unions at their postwar zenith lay in their achievements at the bargaining table, one employer at a time.

In light of the transformation in the workplace, unions now need to develop new methods of operation. While there are many workers still working under the old psychological contract, evidence suggests that new workplace practices are spreading both across the corporate spectrum and through the employment hierarchy. As careers become boundaryless and work becomes detached from a single employer, unions need to become boundaryless as well. They need to develop strategies, skills, and strengths that go beyond single contracts with single employers. They need to move beyond worksite-based collective bargaining and expand into the Webbs' other domains. Unions need to expand upward into the political domain and outward into the community.

In the political domain, unions need to expand their reach so that they represent a wider sector of the workforce in the political process. They need to redefine their mission to include lobbying and political action on behalf of working people generally, to become a working person's version of the American Association of Retired Persons. Unions have long been involved in lobbying on issues of broad concern, such as civil rights and the minimum wage. In recent years, the political and legislative arenas have been ones in which union efforts have been especially effective. But an expanded role for unions in politics and the legislative process would require a major redefinition of both their mission and their membership structure. For example, unions could institute a category of membership that does not involve workplace representation but rather gives individual working people a voice in the political process. The labor law currently discourages union participation in politics through restrictions on the use of dues money for political campaigns and doctrines limiting the scope of protected activity. Rather than discourage unions from participating in politics, the law should be amended to enable unions to expand their role in that domain.

Unions also need to expand their role in the community. In the boundaryless workplace, employees continue to need collective representatives to act as bargaining agents, but not merely on a single-employer basis. Employees need organizations that can bargain with groups of employers for decent wage rates, adequate and portable benefit packages, training, employability, child care, and other features of social welfare. Thus, unions need to find ways to exert influence on a multiemployer basis, across worksites, localities, and regions. In that way, they can help workers acquire skills, provide opportunities for retooling, ensure portability in benefits, create institutions for child care, and in other respects empower individuals to participate in the boundaryless workplace.

In recent years, some unions and labor groups have begun to perform new roles that are responsive to the transforming workplace. Two different models of unionism have emerged as an alternative to traditional employer-centered unionism. The first, new craft unionism, is an occupation-based form of unionism that bargains with industry-wide employer groups to establish minimum standards and provide training, while enabling employees to move freely between employers in the industry. The second, citizen unionism, is a locality-based form of unionism that uses collective pressure to induce corporations to become good corporate citizens of the geographic area in which they are located. While employer-centered unionism will continue to work well for employees within the internal labor market type of employment setting, these two emerging types of unionism can provide representation for employees in the emerging boundaryless workplace.

. . .

1. New Craft Unionism

. . .

Thus, there are emerging examples of new craft unionism that can address some of the problems facing workers in the boundaryless workplace. Members of such occupationally based unions are not guaranteed jobs, but they are able to develop networks with which to find them. Similarly, new craft union members are not guaranteed income, but they work under contracts that contain minimal terms to ensure a living wage. Further, members are not guaranteed protection of their skills from technological change, but the unions provide a mechanism for continual learning.

Overall, then, nonexclusive craft unionism, with embedded contract bargaining and a job-to-job insider contracting employment system, is better suited to the modern workplace than is the industrial union model. However, this form of unionism does not solve all the problems of the boundaryless workplace. While it is inclusive rather than exclusive, the insider contract form of job placement favors insiders and thus reinforces cliques. It poses a serious danger that long-time members will use their own contacts and preroga-tives to monopolize employment opportunities and exclude newcomers, particularly on racial and gendered lines. . . . [A] union hiring hall or a union-maintained referral list would be a preferable method of allocating job assignments than the inside contracting method, because a hiring hall or referral list permits external monitoring for fair employ-ment practices. Another limitation of the new craft unionism in the new workplace is that it may only be suitable for skilled work. If a job requires no skill or training, an employer has no incentive to turn to the union to fill it. And without a closed shop, it is difficult for a union to protect low-skilled workers or workers without occupational mobility paths. But if the laws policing discrimination were strengthened, and if the laws prohibiting the closed shop were eliminated, new craft unionism could prove to be an effective vehicle for boundaryless unionism.

2. Citizen Unionism

Another form of unionism that is emerging to address the boundaryless workplace is geo-graphically-based rather than workplace — or skills-based. Locality-based unions, or citi-zen unions, operate by enlisting all employees in a locality or region to pressure area employers to provide the labor market protections workers need to survive in the bound-aryless workplace. Notwithstanding the growth of the Internet and other pervasive indicia of globalization, most people today still look to their local city, town, or county to provide the basic accouterments of daily life such as schools, libraries, hospital, and parks. Also, while Americans change their residences frequently, most of these moves are within the same county or metropolitan area. Thus, most people would benefit from improvements in their locality's social infrastructure and have a strong incentive to work toward that end. Citizen unionism draws on those impulses.

A geographically-based citizen union is an amalgam of a central city labor council and a worker-based civic association, which includes as its members working people of all types, from all types of workplaces and industries, in a given locality. It exerts pressure on employers in an area to ensure areawide workers the ability to operate in the boundary-less workplace. Citizen unionism is evocative of the "One Big Union" movement in Cana-da in the early years of the twentieth century, in which all workers in a given town or locality organized around the goal of conducting a general strike. In recent years, some contingent worker groups have formed locality-based organizations with the goal, not of calling a general strike, but of creating an effective political and economic pressure group. Citizen unionism is just in its incipiency, however, so this conception of boundaryless unionism can only be described in a sketchy form.

. . .

Citizen unionism is compatible with traditional workplace-based local unions. A citizen union could have area local unions as affiliates and work with them on job-related issues that cut across workplaces. The AFL-CIO's Union-Community program currently engages in locality-based projects of this type. Citizen unionism is also compatible with employer-specific employee caucuses. Such caucuses are emerging with increased frequency in nonunion workplaces, usually around a single issue or comprised of a specific racial or ethnic group. For example, IBM workers recently organized a network when the company converted its pension plan to a cash balance plan in such a way that threatened to defeat many long-term workers' expectations of continually increasing pension benefits. The IBM workers held meetings and utilized email, media, and stockholder resolutions to exert pressure on the company, the Securities and Exchange Commission, and Congress. They were successful in challenging the company policy. The IBM workers' network was comprised of computer specialists, engineers, and technicians — workers who have until now eschewed conventional unionism. The network they formed around the pension issue has affiliated with the CWA. Other single-issue employee caucuses have become a common form of employee protest. Local unions or employee caucuses would benefit from having a local citizen union to give publicity and support to their campaigns, boycotts, and strikes.

. . .

D. REFORMS IN THE LABOR LAW TO FACILITATE BOUNDARYLESS UNIONISM

New forms of unions will require, and create, new types of labor laws. We have already seen some of the ways in which the National Labor Relations Act embodies the old psychological contract's assumption of long-term stable employment. The centrality of the bargaining unit in the labor law creates and reinforces hard boundaries between individual establishments or departments and the rest of the world. Other aspects of the labor law such as the secondary boycott prohibition and the industrial pluralist treatment of arbitration similarly reinforce separatism and discourage boundaryless organizational forms. As the workplace changes and new union practices emerge, there will have to be changes in the labor law to accommodate new forms of employee representation.

To reform the labor law in a way that would facilitate the formation of boundaryless unions would require abandoning those features of the law that treat the unionized workplace as an isolated and separate sphere. For example, to enable new craft unionism to expand, it would be important for the NLRB to abandon the presumption in favor of single establishments and other impediments to multi-employer bargaining. It would also have to abandon the notion that it can identify a "community of interest" in a bargaining unit, and instead permit bargaining units to be determined according to the wishes of the employees involved. This would require a change in the statute. Inclusive craft unionism will also require a change in the secondary boycott laws to permit unions to bargain for terms and conditions that affect workers at establishments within a production network, including an employer's subsidiaries or its joint venture partners. Instead of banning closed shops, the law should permit unions that maintain nondiscriminatory hiring halls or other nondiscriminatory job referral systems to bargain for closed shops. Also, if unions are to develop an insider contracting system, it would be necessary to amend the definition of supervisor in section 2(11) of the NLRA so that lead workers can be union members when they play an inside contractor role.

A further reform that would assist in the formation of new craft unions is the modification of the independent contractor exclusion in section 2(3) by the adoption of an "economic realities" test for determining who is an employee. This change would enable unions to organize workers who have employment relationships with multiple employers.

Other changes in the labor law would be necessary to facilitate the formation of citizen unions and to enable them to bargain with employers in a locality for area standards in compensation, benefits, health and safety, training, and child care. Some of the legal reforms that would facilitate area-wide bargaining for area standards and portable benefits are: (1) to require multi-employer bargaining when a union requests it, (2) to permit unions to engage in coordinated bargaining about the scope of the bargaining unit, (3) to adopt European-style extension laws that extend negotiated standards to all firms of the same type in the same locale, (4) to amend the Employment Retirement Income Security Act to require employer-funded pension and health benefit plans to offer portability and otherwise facilitate movement between employing units, (5) to overturn the Beck decision that restricts union contributions to political and lobbying campaigns, (6) to change the definition of concerted protected activity so that workers are protected in their efforts to act collectively to affect legislation and politics, and (7) to repeal section 8(b)(4) of the NLRA and permit unions to engage in peaceful secondary activity.

Some of the foregoing suggestions have been proposed by others concerned with the growing representation gap and the lack of representation rights for atypical employees. Some are minor revisions in existing rules, some challenge fundamental aspects of the conceptual scheme. None of the proposals will magically produce boundaryless unionism; rather, they are aimed at removing the legal obstacles to this goal. While attempts at labor law reform have not succeeded in the recent past, it is useful to articulate proposals for reform so that legal change can be envisioned. To actually produce a form of representation appropriate to the new workplace will require both a bold vision with broad reach and, at the same time, many small-scale experiments by many local unions, national unions, and other types of workers' groups.

[Reprinted by permission.]

6:620 Broader-Based Bargaining

In addition to calls for minority, occupational and citizen unionism, there has been widespread advocacy (particularly among scholars) of broader-based bargaining as a technique of achieving greater stability in labour relations. Broader-based bargaining implies collective negotiations between a representative employers' association or bargaining agency on one side and a union or association of unions on the other, covering employment relationships in a local, regional, or national labour market.

Proponents of such a system attribute many advantages to it. They argue, for instance, that uniform industry-wide working conditions will remove wages as a competitive factor and focus attention on other factors such as efficiency, design, and quality. They also say that bargaining removed from the individual workplace may produce a more statesmanlike approach on both sides by facilitating the use of dispassionate professionals insulated from the emotional and political pressures of their labour or management constituencies. Another argument is that the potential costs of industry-wide strikes are so great that public opinion will not tolerate them. Moreover, in many industries where small-scale firms predominate, organization on the employer side is needed to offset overwhelming union power. Finally, an employers' organization helps to bring order to an industry by enforcing compliance with industry-wide standards, thereby avoiding the necessity for legal or economic sanctions by the union.

Broader-based bargaining, especially if it is industry-wide, may also mitigate the problem of the contracting out of work by employers to nonunion firms. As we have seen in section 6:520 above, labour relations boards have generally refused to find that firms to which work is contracted out are successor employers bound by any bargaining rights that attached to the work before it was contracted out.

On the other hand, broader-based bargaining has its risks and disadvantages. Taking labour costs out of competition may decrease labour mobility. Industry-wide or regional standards may be unsuitable for particular firms with unique problems. Even more important, perhaps, employers' organizations formed for collective bargaining purposes may (with or without union connivance) become vehicles for the suppression of commercial competition. Finally, the costs of industry-wide strikes, should they occur, are likely to be very great.

Of the multi-employer or industry-wide bargaining relationships that exist in North America, most are private arrangements not required by law. The authority of a bargaining agent to act on behalf of multiple employers or unions rests on ordinary agency principles, and such arrangements may prove to be unsatisfactory for a number of reasons. For one thing, voluntary coalitions are difficult to sustain; individuals have an incentive to refuse to participate in measures designed to further collective goals whenever such measures are detrimental to their particular interests. Those who break ranks may not only protect their own position but also enjoy any enhancement in the general climate produced by the collective action of others. Finally, the public interest will not be weighed when a private choice is made between individual and joint bargaining. Voluntarism does not always work.

Even if management or labour is able to maintain a strong coalition on its side, those on the other side may refuse to engage in joint bargaining. Economic action to enforce demands for multiparty bargaining may not be lawful in some jurisdictions. Certification orders, which usually are limited to one employer and one union, require each party to bargain with the other for the unit defined in the certificate. In jurisdictions where multiparty certification is available, it helps to meet this problem by expanding the scope of the certified unit.

6:621 Broader-Based Bargaining in Quebec

Jean-Guy Bergeron & Diane Veilleux, "The Québec *Collective Agreement Decrees Act*: A Unique Model of Collective Bargaining" (1996) 22 Queen's L.J. 135 at 135–60

Canadian labour relations practitioners and academics are nearly unanimous on the importance of employee participation in the workplace. However, contemporary political and socioeconomic realities, which are leading governments to deregulation and privatization and are inducing companies to restructure their organizations and methods of production, are also leading to fierce questioning of whether the key North American labour law institution of exclusive representation is well-suited to promoting employee participation and protecting working conditions. Other mechanisms which have been proposed for these purposes, such as works councils, plural unionism and sectoral bargaining, are largely untried in North America.

Another model — one with both an existing legal framework and a long history of application — is provided by Québec's distinctive *Collective Agreement Decrees Act* [R.S.Q. c. D-2]. Where unions and employers in a particular sector of economic activity have negotiated a collective agreement, and the agreement has acquired 'preponderant significance' for the regulation of terms and conditions of employment in that sector, the Quebec government (through a process called 'juridical extension') may make a decree rendering certain terms of that agreement applicable to all employers and employees throughout the sector. The basic purpose of the Decrees Act, which has no equivalent in the rest of Canada or the United States, is to ensure decent working conditions in sectors where employees are especially vulnerable, by preventing unfair competition among employers. The act was also intended to further the creation and development of unions and collective bargaining, although it does not directly provide a method to organize workers. It offers a middle road between the direct government imposition of minimum labour standards under the *Labour Standards Act* and the conduct of collective bargaining under the labour relations statute (which is called the *Labour Code* in Quebec).

. . . The *Decrees Act* was enacted on 20 April 1934 during a period of heavy unemployment accompanied by a severe drop in prices and wages. Economic liberalism was prevalent at the time, and there was only limited state regulation of working conditions. The Decrees Act was a product of social corporatism, a doctrine defended by the clergy, the leaders of the [Canadian and Catholic Confederation of Labour], and some members of the French Canadian lower middle class.

Once enacted, the *Decrees Act* was used extensively, as it was the only available legal instrument for ensuring stable labour relations. During the first two decades of the Act's life, the number of decrees increased significantly, rising from 40 in 1935 to 120 in 1959. Since then, however, the number has steadily declined. Today there are only 29 decrees in the manufacturing and services sectors. According to 1992 data, the manufacturing sector accounts for 41 percent of the total aggregate remuneration of employees covered by decrees, while the services sector accounts for 59 percent.

One major factor contributing to the decline in the number of decrees was the enactment in Quebec of labour relations legislation on the model of the American Wagner Act of 1935, which led to loss of interest in the decree system in many sectors. . . .

Government regulation of minimum wage levels has also contributed to the general decline of collective agreement decrees. . . . it was the rapid increase in the minimum wage during the 1970s, and the adoption of the *Labour Standards Act* in 1979, which prompted the significant decline in the use of decrees for establishing working conditions. . . .

The *Decrees Act* allows the government to adopt specific decrees and to 'order that a collective agreement respecting any trade, industry, commerce or occupation shall also bind all the employers in Quebec or in a stated region of Quebec, within the scope determined in such decree. Any party to a collective agreement may request a juridical extension of the agreement. . . . Unions do not have to be certified under the *Labour Code* to be able to make a collective agreement for the purposes of extension; for *bona fide* employee associations without certification, negotiation is conducted on a voluntary basis.

Unlike the *Labour Code*, which provides for enterprise-based collective bargaining, the *Decrees Act* promotes sectoral bargaining. Almost all of the collective agreements which have been extended under the *Decrees Act* have an employer association as a party. These associations group together employers with unionized employees and employers without unionized employees. The agreements they negotiate with a view to extension are binding on both types of employer. For example, in the Woodworking Decree which applies to the Quebec City region, two employer associations are contracting parties. Of the 59 employers in those associations, only 12 have certified unions. They employ 14.7 percent of the unionized workers covered by the decree. The Non-structural Metal Work Decree applicable to the Montreal region has one association as a contracting party. Only three of the 82 employers in that association have certified unions. They employ 16.7 percent of the unionized workers subject to the decree. The Security Guards Decree has two employer associations as contracting parties, and 24 of the 33 employers belonging to these associations have unionized employees, who represent 52.6 percent of the employees covered by this decree.

Agreements may be negotiated on a voluntary basis for the sole purpose of making decrees. . . .

The Minister of Labour may hold an inquiry to determine whether juridical extension is justified. In deciding whether to recommend that the government approve a petition for extension, the Minister takes the following factors into consideration: whether extension would create serious inconvenience because of competition from foreign countries or other provinces; economic conditions in the various regions of Quebec; and whether the provisions of the agreement have acquired a 'preponderant significance and importance' in setting labour conditions.

As the *Decrees Act* does not provide criteria for determining whether a collective agreement has acquired such preponderant significance, the Minister has discretion in this respect. Generally, the following criteria are applied: how many employers have signed the collective agreement, and how many employees work for them; how many employers are not parties to any collective agreement but provide working conditions as good as or better than those in the agreement for which extension is sought; and how many employers are parties to collective agreements that embody better working conditions than those sought to be extended. The extent of membership of the unions which are parties to the collective agreement is not a factor in assessing the preponderant significance of its terms. In fact, the total union presence in industries covered by decrees was only 26.9 percent in 1992 (49.6 percent in the manufacturing sector and 3.1 percent in the services sector). These figures underline the importance to unions of having the option of petitioning for juridical extension.

Although the Minister does consider the wishes of the parties to a collective agreement who are affected by the petition for extension, he or she is not formally bound by those wishes. He or she may approve the extension but modify certain terms of the collective agreement. The Minister also has discretion in matters pertaining to the amendment, prolongation or repeal of the decree. Professor Jean Bernier asserts that the granting of such discretion to the Minister shows that the Act's approach is fundamentally much more regulatory than contractual.

The law does not currently permit the Minister to extend all of the terms of a collective agreement, but only those on matters specified in the *Decrees Act*: wages, hours of work, paid vacations, social security benefits, classification of operations and determination of employee and employer classifications. Social security benefits can include life, health, accident and disability insurance as well as a pension plan. Terms which cannot be extended include those on union dues, union security, seniority rights, promotions, layoffs and arbitration. . . .

Rather than entrusting the enforcement of decrees to the government or one of its administrative bodies, the Act gives that task to a parity committee — that is, a committee consisting of an equal number of employer and employee representatives who are parties to the collective agreement.

Among the various statutory powers of the parity committee is its right to bring proceedings on behalf of employees with respect to any claims (called 'recourses' in the Act) arising under the decree or the Act. . . .

The *Decrees Act* has been called into question many times over the past 20 years. . . . In February 1994, an interdepartmental committee on collective agreement decrees, set up by the Liberal government, submitted a report on the subject, entitled *Rapport du comité interministiériel sur les décrets de convention collective. . . .*

Concerns were expressed that the decree system no longer accorded with social and economic realities; that the system constrained the expansion of sectors faced with international competition and at the same time artificially protected some firms against competition; that it stifled innovation and adversely affected production; and that by providing more favourable working conditions, it hindered the emergence of new enterprises. Non-economic arguments included the following: that the parity committees were not representative, that Quebec was the only province with a decree system, and that the system led to bureaucratic 'disease' and to negative effects on the work environment in particular industries and firms.

The arguments in favour of keeping and, indeed, improving the *Decrees Act* have centred on social factors. From this viewpoint, the law has been a valuable and effective development tool not only for small and medium-size firms but also for entire industries. Parity committees have fostered ongoing communication between employers and unions across an industry and have furthered social and industrial harmony. By preventing unfair competition, decrees have provided decent working conditions in small and medium-sized firms operating in intensely competitive markets. For example, in the security guards sector, of the 150 employers covered by the decree, 57 have unionized employees representing 56.3 percent of the employees covered by the decree. The existence of the decree is particularly important for the 43.7 percent of employees who are not unionized and are working in many small firms. It also prevents those firms from competing unfairly with the unionized firms. Without a decree, a deterioration in working conditions would be very probable. Political authorities cannot ignore the deplorable results which the repeal of the *Decrees Act* would have on such conditions in sectors covered by the Act.

These arguments might explain why, in 1994, the interdepartmental committee echoed the findings of previous working groups in ruling out the idea of repealing the Act and instead proposing to improve the decree system by redefining its role. The committee's recommendations envisioned a closer link between the *Labour Code*, the *Labour Standards Act* and the *Decrees Act*. . . .

On 22 November 1995, the Minister presented a draft bill to amend the *Decrees Act*. While this draft bill has already been amended and will likely be further modified before it is enacted by the Quebec legislature, its main thrust is clearly discernible.

In order to reconcile the collective agreement decree system with other laws in force, the draft bill would limit the possibility of juridical extension to parties to a collective agreement as defined in the *Labour Code*, thereby restricting access to individual certified associations or groups of certified associations. Unlike other Canadian labour relations statutes, the Quebec *Labour Code* does not recognize collective agreements made by non-certified unions, but the *Decrees Act* does so for the purpose of extending such agreements. The proposed amendments to the latter statute would therefore make it impossible to apply the Decrees Act without first going through the certification process in the *Labour Code*, thus preventing some *bona fide* employee associations from obtaining any form of legal recognition. Furthermore, this measure would seem to permanently preclude unions from making any use of the *Decrees Act* to organize small and medium-sized firms in the private sector without first obtaining certification, a process which the union would have to undergo for each and every employer. . . .

[Reprinted by permission.]

* * *

Important changes were made to Quebec's decree system in 1996. The criteria for the extension of collective agreements were redefined to take into account increased international competition. The result has been a decrease in the number of decrees since 1996; by 2000, only four decrees remained in force in the manufacturing sector.

6:622 A Proposal for Broader-Based Bargaining in British Columbia

In 1992 a committee of special advisors to British Columbia's Minister of Labour was charged with reviewing the province's labour laws and proposing reforms that would promote harmonious labour-management relations. In the following excerpt from its report, the committee proposed a novel form of sectoral bargaining as a partial solution to the problems faced by workers in hard to organize sectors. The terms of the proposal sought to avoid a common criticism of sectoral bargaining: that it forces groups of employees into collective bargaining without their consent. The proposal has not been implemented.

John Baigent, Vince Ready, & Tom Roper, *Recommendations for Labour Law Reform: A Report to the Honourable Moe Sihota, Minister of Labour* (Victoria, B.C.: Ministry of Labour and Consumer Services, 1992) at 30–33

Between 1973 and 1984 the [British Columbia] *Labour Code* provided for a form of multi-employer certification whereby employers within a sector could be organized under one certification. We are recommending a return to a modified form of sectoral bargaining for those small enterprises where employees have been historically underrepresented by trade unions.

The current provision in the [British Columbia] *Industrial Relations Act* dealing with multiple employer certification requires the consent of each employer before a multi-employer unit can be certified. Not surprisingly, the provision has never been utilized. The present situation then is one where multiple employer certification is provided for under the statute but virtually impossible to attain.

We consider our recommendations in this area as among the most important and significant we are making. Our recommendations attempt to address the peculiar difficulties that workers in small businesses encounter in seeking union representation.

Statistical information indicates that over 90% of workers in business services, real estate companies, financial institutions, insurance companies and retail trades are unorganized. More than 85% of the workers in restaurants and beverage rooms fall under the same category. These are the fastest growing sectors of the economy and most of the jobs in these areas fall to adult women and part-time youth. And those jobs are often the lowest paying ones in our society.

Existing collective bargaining models, designed for large industrial operations with full-time workforces, have great difficulty operating in these sectors of the economy. Collective bargaining is only viable when there are a sufficient number of employees to justify union organizing and collective bargaining efforts. It is simply impractical and unacceptably expensive for unions to organize and negotiate collective agreements for small groups of workers if their dues cannot begin to cover the costs involved in developing separate collective agreements for each of their work sites. As a result, persons employed as clerical support staff in small business, farm workers or service station attendants do not have any realistic prospect of ever being represented by a trade union under present labour legislation. Yet, these are the very workers who are most in need of trade union representation. Put simply, for these persons certification and collective bargaining rights are illusory. The options are stark: either maintain a status quo in which many workers will seldom achieve collective bargaining rights, or, fashion a model which allows employees in these sectors the option of banding together, for purposes of collective bargaining, with other employees performing the same types of jobs. Only the latter option is consistent with Canada's proposed new *Social Charter* which includes the policy objectives of 'protecting the rights of workers to organize and bargain collectively.' It is also the option consistent with what we have identified as the purpose of new labour legislation — 'to encourage the practice and procedure of collective bargaining . . . .'

Presently, sectoral bargaining exists in Quebec where a 'decree' system imposes uniform wage rates on all employees within a particular sector of the economy. A decree applies whether or not employees at any particular location are unionized. The provisions which were in force in British Columbia for 11 years allowed union to 'sweep' employees of a particular employer into a bargaining unit as long as the overall majority of employees of all employers supported the union. The amendments we have devised eliminate the possibility of employees at one particular location being swept into a bargaining unit against their wishes: instead, our recommendations allow each group of employees within this sector to decide for themselves whether they wish to be represented by a trade union.

The model we recommend would be available only in sectors which are determined, by the Labour Relations Board, to be historically underrepresented by trade unions and where the average number of employees at work locations within the sector is less than 50. A sector has two characteristics: a defined geographical area (e.g. Marpole, Burnaby, the Lower Mainland or the entire Province) and similar enterprises within the area where employees perform similar tasks (e.g. preparing fast food, child care, picking fruit or pumping gas). For example, a sector could consist of 'employees working in fast food outlets in Burnaby.'

We recommend that a union which has the requisite support at more than one work location within a sector could apply for certification of the employees *at those locations*. In addition to demonstrating support at each location, the union would have to prevail in a vote amongst all the employees at the work locations where certification was sought. If successful, the union would be granted certification for a bargaining unit within the sector. Collective bargaining would then take place between the union and the various employers whose employees had become certified. A standard collective agreement would be settled and subsequently, if the union could demonstrate sufficient support at additional locations within the sector, it would be entitled to a variance of its bargaining certificate to encompass the new employees. Any collective agreement in place in the sector would apply to the new employees, but the Labour Relations Board would have the option of tailoring the standard agreement to the exigencies of any particular location.

Once a sector has been declared historically underrepresented any trade union can apply for certification within the sector. Accordingly, in our example, three or four different unions might end up representing employees at fast food outlets in Burnaby, each administering its own collective agreement. This feature has several advantages. It ensures that unions who are certified within a sector are not granted a monopoly on representation rights while offering employees within a sector the option of choosing from more than one union.

The model ensures that employees at each location within the bargaining unit will support the union before a certification is varied to include them. This safeguard meets the most common objection to sectoral bargaining and distinguishes the recommendations from the Quebec system and the earlier British Columbia model.

The model we are recommending has parallels which have been in place for many years in other areas of the economy. Construction workers usually work for several employers each year. Each of their employers is one of several on a construction site where the workforce changes from day to day as different stages of construction are completed. Under normal circumstances it would be impossible to organize construction workers because of the multiplicity of their employers and the changing composition of the workforce. However, collective bargaining has been facilitated for construction workers by the application of a standard collective agreement to all organized worksites and by permitting those workers to avail themselves of union security clauses (basically, the right to invoke non-affiliation clauses which allow them to refuse to work with non-union trades). In a similar way our model would allow special certification processes and the development of standardized collective agreements so that collective bargaining is available in historically underrepresented areas. The point to note is that over the years collective bargaining has worked because it has proven sufficiently flexible to adapt to a variety of new circumstances. Another change is now required.

The system does impose a collective agreement on new employers whose employees elect to join a union during the term of a collective agreement. Too much should not be made of that fact. Under a system of sectoral certification all employers are entitled to participate in the negotiation and renewal of the collective agreement. A collective agreement would be imposed only where an employer became certified during the term of a collective agreement. Even then, our proposal allows the Labour Relations Board a wide discretion to tailor the collective agreement to the peculiar circumstances of any enterprise.

Once certified, an employer would be required to bargain alongside other employers within the sector. That is a common occurrence in many British Columbia industries. Health care, trucking, the woods and pulp and paper — to name only a few — are all industries where a single collective agreement is applied to many different employers. The reality of collective bargaining in British Columbia is that many, if not a majority of, unionized employers operate under collective agreements negotiated on an industry-wide basis. Sectoral bargaining also has advantages for employer organizations and we note that one of the larger employer organizations in the Province (Construction Labour Relations Association) urged us to implement sectoral bargaining in the construction industry.

Opponents of sectoral bargaining assert that it is inconsistent with the trend towards enterprise-based collective bargaining. But that trend is by no means prevalent in all, or even most, sectors of our economy. In those industries where the criteria for sectoral bargaining can be met (historically underrepresented, similar job functions and small work locations), there are usually very standardized terms of employment already in force. One would be hard pressed to discover any major differences in terms and conditions of employment among employees at fast food outlets, medical receptionists, farm workers or domestic workers. Most often, these sectors of the economy are characterized by repetitive tasks, minimum wage levels and part-time employment. In such areas there is every reason to be confident that standardized collective agreements will operate successfully.

. . . Cartels are, of course, undesirable. But it cannot be suggested that there is any real likelihood of cartels occurring in sectors of the economy where the organizational levels presently stand at somewhere less than 10% of the work force. We also note that our proposals allow for a multiplicity of unions within a sector — a feature inconsistent with the notion of a cartel.

The observation that only a few of the submissions directed to us urged sectoral bargaining should be balanced by the observation that those organizations represented the vast majority of workers in the Province and, in one case, a large number of employers. More to the point, the recommendations to enact a form of sectoral bargaining recognizes — as do many labour law theorists — that if collective bargaining is to go forward, it must find ways to make itself more available to those presently beyond its reach.

The issue respecting sectoral bargaining is whether certification procedures should be modified so that collective bargaining is a real option for people working in small workplaces. As a matter of principle, we believe certification should be made available to workers in these areas unless doing so would impose unacceptable restrictions on the rights of others. The model we propose — unlike the earlier British Columbia model — rejects the notion of 'sweeping in' employees at a particular location against their will. There can be no objection on that score. The employer does lose the right to negotiate its own unique collective agreement but that right is more theoretical than real. It is also a small price to pay for the extension of collective bargaining to those workers who otherwise would have no prospect of ever achieving it.

6:630 An Employee Council in Every Workplace?

Some scholars have argued that a major problem with the *Wagner Act* model lies in the fact that it does not provide workplace representation for all employees, but only for units that vote for unionization. Those scholars, including Roy Adams in Canada, often look to the German system as a model which provides for broader-based collective bargaining at regional level and which also — and most importantly — mandates an *employee works council* in every workplace, with employees having the right to choose the members of that council but not the right to vote it out of existence. Adams suggests that the German system comes closer than the *Wagner Act* model to realizing the ideal of democracy in the workplace.

Roy Adams, *Industrial Relations under Liberal Democracy: North America in Comparative Perspective* (Columbia, S.C.: University of South Carolina Press, 1995) at 143–46

From early in their history, a key object of German unions was the achievement of industrial democracy as a natural and essential counterpart of political democracy. German employers were, however, adamantly opposed to dealing with unions on a daily basis in the shop. They argued that they needed discretion to make quick decisions free from constraint in order to operate the production process in an efficient and effective manner. They also argued that the unions had a political agenda that, if manifested in the shop, would result in disruption to the production process. The independent unions, argued the employers, had no commitment to the success of the enterprise.

These opposed positions resulted in a compromise. Employers recognized that employees should have a right to representation at the level of the enterprise, and unions recognized that the right to representation should be universal — that is, it should be available to all employees not just to union members. Legislation putting these principles into effect was passed. It required the establishment of works councils elected by all employees in a company, whether union members/supporters or not. These councils were to have legally specified rights and duties. Unions could nominate candidates in works council elections, but one did not have to be a union member to stand for election. The legislation also required that workers have a minority representation on corporate supervisory boards. . . .

During the Nazi era, the entire system was dismantled. However, codetermination was reestablished after the war. Initially, in the coal and steel industry, employees were granted parity representation on supervisory boards. Chairpersons were to be neutral outsiders who would have the power to break voting ties. The labor side of the directing board, in addition, would be able to designate one of the top corporate executives — the one with responsibility for human resources management. Many of these top management positions were filled by trade union activists who previously had experience as works counselors. The labor movement wanted this parity codetermination system extended to the whole of German industry, but management was opposed and indeed attempted, unsuccessfully, to have the system dismantled once normalcy was reestablished. Outside of coal and steel, as a result, the government reestablished minority labor representation on directing boards. Employees were to elect one-third of the board members and the top executive corps was to be appointed by the board as a whole.

Labor was not satisfied with the situation and, in the mid-1970s, it succeeded in having the law changed to require near parity in large corporations. Both employees and stockholders would elect half the supervisory board members, but there would be no neutral chairperson. Instead, the shareholder side would select the chair who, in the event of a tie, would be able to cast a second tie-breaking vote.

Works councils were also reestablished after World War II with powers similar to [the works councils] of the Weimar Republic. Because the unions were not granted more authority over the councils than they had during the Weimar era, they opposed the Works Constitution Act of 1952. They still were concerned that the councils would become competitors as employee representation agents. However, as a result of diligent organizing efforts, the unions were able to dominate the works councils elections and, by the mid-1960s, the overwhelming majority of councillors were union activists.

The Works Constitution Act simply states that 'works councils shall be elected in all establishments ('Betriebe') that normally have five or more permanent employees with voting rights, including three who are eligible.' Administratively, however, it is left up to the unions or to the individual employees to set up the councils. As a result, the preponderance of large- and middle-sized firms have councils, but commonly in very small firms the necessary steps have not been taken.

In 1972, the powers of the councils were extended considerably. They now have codecision rights over a wide range of firm level issues such as working hours, wage payment procedures, piece rates, individual employment contracts, occupational health and safety, the implementation of vocational training, job classification, and dismissals both individual and mass. On these issues, no decision may be taken unless the works council agrees. Deadlocks are generally settled by reference to binding arbitration, although impasses requiring arbitration occur only very infrequently. The councils are also entitled to economic information about the plans and prospects of the firm, and they must be consulted before technological or work organization changes may be put in place. But, they do not have codetermination rights with respect to such issues. In addition, they oversee the implementation of collective agreements and statutory requirements and negotiate plant agreements necessary to put them in place. The councils are not permitted to organize strikes. Most active works councillors are also trade unionists. The unions have very extensive research and education facilities to provide councillors with the skills they need in order responsibly and effectively to carry out their statutory duties.

Although this system was initially opposed by both labor and management, there is currently a very strong labor-management consensus that it has worked remarkably well. It has allowed change to be introduced without major disruption. Employee representatives (both board members and councillors) have to be informed about tentative plans well in advance of their implementation. The consequences of the change are discussed and means to deal with them are built into implementation plans. Since consensus is sought before implementation, resistance subsequent to the change is kept to a minimum. Moreover, the quality of the decisions taken are considered by many to be better than they otherwise would have been because of the broad base of input. There is general agreement that the requirement to consult and to reach consensus rather than submit disputes to third parties (who might very well hand down inappropriate decisions) has substantially modified managerial style. Traditionally, German culture elicited an authoritarian approach to employment relations. The institutions of codetermination have resulted in a much more collaborative managerial approach. Employee representatives, on the other hand, have been able to become acquainted first hand with the difficult and complex decisions continually facing management. This greater understanding has helped to ensure more cooperation and commitment to decisions taken.

In short, employees have improved their situation because their interests are taken into account when critical enterprise decisions are under discussion, and because there is a genuine effort to reach consensus with respect to those decisions. Employers have also gained because the quality of the decisions has been enhanced and resistance to change has been significantly reduced.

Employers feared that decision making would be slowed down to the point of inefficiency but, in general, that has not happened. For the most part, employee representatives have been willing to defer to managers in areas beyond their expertise. Problems have occurred primarily where managers have failed to produce information necessary to fully evaluate the results of proposed courses of action.

At one time, there were many who believed that codetermination was a fair weather system that would collapse in difficult times. There are no longer many who hold that view because the system has functioned very well even during the turbulent 1980s and early 1990s. . . .

[Reprinted by permission of University of South Carolina Press.]

Chapter 7: **Negotiating a Collective Agreement**

REFERENCES

George Adams, *Canadian Labour Law*, 2d ed. (Aurora, Ont.: Canada Law Book, 1993 — as updated by looseleaf releases) c. 10, subsections 8(ii)(b), 11, and 12; Donald Carter *et al.*, *Labour Law in Canada*, 5th ed. (Markham, Ont.: Butterworths, 2002) pt. 2, c. 4

7:100 INTRODUCTION

The core of collective bargaining legislation is, not surprisingly, *bargaining*. After all, to be able to bargain collectively with an employer is why employees join a union and why unions secure the right to represent employees through certification or voluntary recognition. The status of exclusive bargaining agent both supersedes individual bargaining between employer and employee and carries with it the constraint that an employer cannot bargain with another union.

But the fact that bargaining is at the core of the legislation raises some difficult problems. We tend to think of bargaining as a voluntary exercise between willing participants who seek particular outcomes (a sale or purchase, for example) and who, if things do not go to their liking, are entitled to walk away from the table and seek a better deal elsewhere. Collective bargaining does not quite conform to this model. The employer is often an unwilling party to negotiations; outcomes are open-ended in the sense that collective agreements are almost infinitely variable; the parties cannot simply terminate their relationship and seek other buyers or sellers of labour; and the pressure each can apply to the other — strikes and lockouts — has few counterparts in other bargaining contexts.

All of these peculiarities of collective bargaining law raise a fundamental issue: to what extent can and should the law seek to regulate bargaining behaviour? This issue presents itself in a variety of forms. For example, should the law attempt to prevent a truly recalcitrant employer from merely going through the motions of bargaining? Should it permit the parties to establish whatever terms of employment are mutually agreeable? To what extent should it regulate the use of pressure tactics in the name of the public interest? And assuming the law ought to proscribe some forms of bargaining behaviour, what kind of remedies will effectively keep the bargaining process within appropriate limits?

7:200 THE STATUTORY TIMETABLE

Collective bargaining legislation subjects negotiations to a fairly detailed statutory timetable. This timetable is set in motion, for the first collective agreement, by the certification of a trade union as exclusive bargaining agent; certification entitles the union to serve a notice to bargain on the employer, or the employer to serve a notice to bargain on the union. In relationships that have already seen the negotiation of at least one collective agreement, either party can serve a notice to bargain on the other party when an existing agreement has expired, or within a certain period before its expiry date. The precise period during which notice to bargain for the renewal of an agreement varies from jurisdiction to jurisdiction.

The service of a notice to bargain triggers the start of the statutory "duty to bargain." Under Canadian labour relations statutes, that duty generally has two branches: a duty to bargain "in good faith" and a duty to make "every reasonable effort" to reach a collective agreement. The Supreme Court of Canada in *Royal Oak Mines v. Canada (Labour Relations Board)*, [1996] 1 S.C.R. 369, excerpted in section 7:421 below, described the "good faith" requirement as the subjective element of the duty to bargain, and the "reasonable efforts" requirement as the objective element. Statutes in the three Maritime provinces refer only to "reasonable efforts," and do not mention "good faith," but in those provinces the duty to bargain has been interpreted as having the same subjective and objective elements as in the rest of the country: see *Canadian Union of Public Employees v. Labour Relations Board (Nova Scotia)*, [1983] 2 S.C.R. 311 (the *Digby School Board* case).

Once a notice to bargain has been served, the parties remain under a duty to bargain until they reach a collective agreement. The duty does not require that they succeed in negotiating an agreement, but only that they try. Sometimes, no matter how hard they try, they may reach an impasse. Normally, before they may resort to a strike or lockout, labour relations legislation requires them to go through a conciliation or mediation process, usually under the auspices of the labour ministry. This requirement of conciliation or mediation, which is a long-standing feature of Canadian labour law, is predicated on the idea that the parties acting alone will often be unable to reach an agreement, not because there is no overlap in their respective positions but because bargaining strategies and various obstacles to communication obscure potential points of agreement.

Although the state will intervene to try to help the parties reach an agreement, in general it will not impose one on them. The most important exception to this principle is what is called "first contract arbitration," which allows for state imposition of the terms of the first collective agreement after certification if the parties cannot settle those terms themselves. First contract arbitration is now provided for in most Canadian jurisdictions, and is discussed in section 7:700 below. Other exceptions to the general principle that the state will not impose a bargain on the parties include ad hoc back to work legislation and specific statutes requiring compulsory interest arbitration in certain sectors. The use of these types of legislation varies widely across the country, and will be discussed briefly in Chapter 8 below (section 8:620).

Once a work stoppage (a strike or lockout) becomes legal, the duty to bargain continues, even while a stoppage is actually underway. However, the content of the duty changes significantly in those circumstances. If a party has complied with the duty to bargain but an impasse has nonetheless been reached at the bargaining table, that party is allowed to break off negotiations on the basis that there is no current prospect of progress. In a strike or a lockout, each side hopes that the economic pressure on the other side will prompt concessions. Conversely, a party which thinks it is winning a strike or lockout can take advantage of that situation to toughen its stance. "It would be naive in the extreme," in the Ontario Labour Relations Board's words, "for parties to collective bargaining to expect that conditions which prevailed before a strike or lockout to still prevail afterwards": *Toronto Jewellery Manufacturers Association*, [1979] O.L.R.B. Rep. July 719 at 723.

Normally, a collective agreement will eventually be reached, with or without the assistance of conciliation, and with or without resort to a strike or lockout. Once a collective agreement has been signed, labour relations statutes explicitly provide that (with very few exceptions) conflict in the form of a work stoppage is no longer allowed, and the duty to bargain is suspended until it is time to negotiate a new agreement. It should be noted that American law is different in this respect; in the US, the duty to bargain does continue during the lifetime of the collective agreement, on matters not dealt with in the agreement.

During the life of a collective agreement, the law across Canada entitles the parties to make changes to the agreement if they wish, but only by mutual agreement; neither party can require the other even to discuss any such changes. Every labour relations statute in the country now requires that a process of third-party arbitration, known as grievance arbitration or rights arbitration, must be provided for in every collective agreement in order to resolve differences over the meaning of the agreement; strikes and lockouts are not allowed while a collective agreement is in effect. Chapter 9 and parts of Chapter 10 deal at length with the enforcement of the collective agreement. However, it should be noted here that under the "management rights" doctrine, to be discussed in Chapter 9, grievance arbitration has traditionally been understood as applying only to disputes over matters that are dealt with in the collective agreement, and management generally retains a tight to act unilaterally on matters on which the agreement is silent. As we will see later in this chapter, for some commentators, the fact that the prohibition against strikes during the life of a collective agreement is broader than the reach of grievance arbitration means that a more rigorous duty to bargain should be imposed on management during the negotiation of the agreement.

The only significant exception to the prohibition against strikes or lockouts during the term of a collective agreement is the provision in a few statutes (for example, the *Canada Labour Code*, sections 51–55) that allows for the reopening of the duty to bargain if the employer introduces a technological innovation that is likely to affect the terms and conditions or security of employment of a significant part of the bargaining unit.

7:300 THE BARGAINING FREEZE

Complementary to the statutory duty to bargain are provisions that prohibit changes in terms and conditions of employment after notice to bargain has been given (what can be called the "bargaining freeze"). This is closely related to the "certification freeze," which prohibits changes in terms and conditions during a certification campaign. The basic principles underlying both the certification freeze and the bargaining freeze have been discussed in Chapter 5 above (section 5:400), and will not be dealt with again here.

Jurisdictions across Canada are consistent in tying the start of the bargaining freeze to the serving of notice to bargain, and are also consistent (either expressly or by implication) in bringing the freeze to an end when a new collective agreement is signed or when the union's bargaining rights are terminated. However, where a strike or lockout is looming, there are differences as to the end point of the statutory freeze. In a few jurisdictions, (Alberta *Labour Relations Code*, section 128; British Columbia *Labour Relations Code*, section 45(2)) the freeze runs until there is an actual lawful strike or lockout; if the union is not ready to strike as soon as the law allows strike action to be taken, the employer must institute a lockout if it wants to bring the freeze to an end. In other jurisdictions, the freeze remains in force only until a strike or lockout would be lawful (for example, Ontario *Labour Relations Act*, 1995, section 86(1); Newfoundland *Labour Relations Act*, sections 74(b), 75(b)). In the latter jurisdictions, if the union does not call a strike as soon as the law allows, the employer (though still subject to the duty to bargain with the union) can unilaterally change terms and conditions without actually instituting a lockout. The rationale for allowing such unilateral changes is that the employees are not forced to accept them, as they are free to strike.

7:400 THE DUTY TO BARGAIN IN GOOD FAITH

> REFERENCES
>
> **George Adams, *Canadian Labour Law*, 2d ed. (Aurora, Ont.: Canada Law Book, 1993 — as updated by looseleaf releases) paras. 10.1360–10.1700; Donald Carter *et al.*, *Labour Law in Canada*, 5th ed. (Markham, Ont.: Butterworths, 2002) pp. 299–307**

7:410 Purposes of the Duty to Bargain

Archibald Cox, "The Duty to Bargain in Good Faith" (1958) 71 Harv. L. Rev. 1401 at 1407–9

> Section 8(a)(5) of the *National Labor Relations Act* provides that it shall be an unfair labor practice for an employer "to refuse to bargain collectively with the representatives of his employees". . . . By reading the testimony, the debate, and the history of the times with a large measure of hindsight one can discern four purposes which entered into the enactment of section 8(5).
>
> 1) The simplest and most direct purpose was to reduce the number of strikes for union recognition. Prior to 1935 [when the *National Labor Relations Act* was passed] the outright refusal of employers to deal with a labor union was a prolific cause of industrial strife. . . . The cause could be eliminated by placing an employer under a statutory duty to acknowledge as the legal representative of all his employees any union designated by the majority. In arguing that the act was constitutional the Government placed great stress upon this purpose. . . .

2) The most important purpose of the Wagner Act was to create aggregations of economic power on the side of employees countervailing the existing power of corporations to establish labor standards. When the authors of the act spoke of "inequality of bargaining power" between employee and employer, they had in mind the famous dictum of Mr. Chief Justice Taft:

> [Labour unions] were organized out of the necessities of the situation. A single employee was helpless in dealing with an employer. He was dependent ordinarily on his daily wage for the maintenance of himself and family. If the employer refused to pay him the wages that he thought fair, he was nevertheless unable to leave the employ and to resist arbitrary and unfair treatment. Union was essential to give laborers opportunity to deal on equality with their employer.

> The denial of recognition is an effective means of breaking up a struggling young union too weak for a successful strike. After the enthusiasm of organization and the high hopes of successful negotiations, it is a devastating psychological blow to have the employer shut the office door in the union's face. Imposing a legal duty to recognize the union would prevent such anti-union tactics and thereby contribute to the growth of strong labor organizations.

3) Section 8(5) was also intended to implement the basic philosophy of the act by imposing the duty to engage in collective — as distinguished from individual — bargaining. The courts exemplified the obligation by holding that after a representative has been designated, it is an unfair labor practice for an employer to negotiate wages or other terms of employment with individual employees. It is also possible that Congress meant that the duty to deal with the group — with the collectivity — included a more far-reaching idea usually expressed in metaphors. An employer must look upon labour as an equal partner, and "when we have such a partnership . . . then one partner cannot do anything without consulting the other partner." Or to change the figure, the divine right of the king must yield to a constitutional monarchy, in which a large measure of industrial democracy will prevail. Wages, hours, and conditions of employment should be determined by mutual consent.

4) There were also those who looked upon collective bargaining as a rational process of persuasion. Collective bargaining, it was thought, enables employers and employees to dig behind their prejudices and exchange their views with the result that agreement is reached on many points while on others it is discovered that the area of disagreement is so narrow that compromise is cheaper than battle. As early as 1902 an industrial commission reported:

> The chief advantage which comes from the practice of periodically determining the conditions of labor by collective bargaining directly between employers and employees is, that thereby each side obtains a better understanding of the actual state of the industry, of the conditions which confront the other side, and of the motives which influence it. Most strikes and lockouts would not occur if each party understood exactly the position of the other.

Although there is little doubt that the sponsors of the *Wagner Act* hoped that the statute would accomplish all four purposes, only the first two can be said to have been written into law. There is no real evidence whether the sponsors intended to write the third and fourth directly into the statute or counted upon time and human nature to realize these objectives. Collective bargaining is curiously ambivalent even today. In one aspect collective bargaining is a brute contest of economic power somewhat masked by polite manners and voluminous statistics. As the relation matures, Lilliputian bonds control the opposing concentrations of economic power; they lack legal sanctions but are nonetheless effective to contain the use of power. Initially it may be only fear of the economic consequences of disagreement that turns the parties to facts, reason, a sense of responsibility, a responsiveness to government and public opinion, and moral principle; but in time these forces generate their own compulsions, and negotiating a contract approaches the ideal of informed persuasion.

The purpose of the original *Wagner Act* was to create a necessary balance of economic power. The act also aimed at ideal bargaining. It intruded at least so far as to protect unionization from interference by employers and to compel them to recognize the employees' representatives. Did the statute leave the further consequences to develop without government regulation or did it legislate some of the state of mind and habits of conduct which make up the ideal bargaining relation?

[Copyright © 1958 by the Harvard Law Review Association.]

7:420 Content of the Duty to Bargain

In 1935, Senator Walsh, one of the sponsors of the *Wagner Act* in the American Senate, in defending the inclusion in the statute of a requirement that the employer bargain collectively, described that requirement in minimalist terms:

> When employees have chosen their organization, when they have selected their representatives, all the bill proposes to do is to escort them to the door of the employer and say, "Here they are, the legal representatives of your employees." What happens behind those doors is not enquired into, and the bill does not inquire into it.

As you read the materials that follow, consider to what extent (if at all) that minimalist perception still prevails.

United Electrical, Radio and Machine Workers of America v. DeVilbiss (Canada) Ltd. (1976), 76 C.L.L.C. para. 16,009 at 404–5 (O.L.R.B)

ADAMS, Vice-Chair: . . . a very important function of section 14 [now section 17 of the Ontario *Labour Relations Act*] is that of reinforcing an employer's obligation to recognize a trade union lawfully selected by employees as their bargaining agent. Certainly the freedom to join a trade union of one's choice declared in section 3 of the legislation would be but an edict "writ on water" if an employer could enter into negotiations with no intention of ever signing a collective agreement. But we believe the duty to meet and make every reasonable effort to make a collective agreement has an even more important function in a modern society that for the most part accepts that trade unions have legitimate and important roles to play. That is to say that the duty assumes that when two parties are obligated to meet each other periodically and rationally discuss their mutual problems in a way that satisfies the phrase "make every reasonable effort," they are likely to arrive at a better understanding of each other's concerns thereby enhancing the potential for a resolution of their differences without recourse to economic sanctions — the impact of which is never confined to the immediate parties of an industrial dispute. At the very least rational discussion is likely to minimize the number of problems the parties are unable to resolve without the use of economic weapons thereby focusing the parties' attention in the eleventh hour on the "true" differences between them. . . . Hence it is our belief that the duty described in section 14 has at least two principal functions. The duty reinforces the obligation of an employer to recognize the bargaining agent and, beyond this somewhat primitive though important purpose, it can be said that the duty is intended to foster rational, informed discussion thereby minimizing the potential for "unnecessary" industrial conflict. . . .

Graphic Arts International Union Local 12-L. v. Graphic Centre (Ontario) Inc., [1976] O.L.R.B. Rep. 221 at 229–31

[The employer served notice on the union to renegotiate the collective agreement. The parties met, and the union tabled a list of twelve proposals. The employer responded by indicating its desire to maintain the status quo. The union subsequently applied for conciliation, which did not resolve the dispute. The Minister of Labour decided not to appoint a board of conciliation, thereby setting in motion the statutory "countdown" which would lead to the point at which a strike or lockout could legally be called. The union rejected a compromise proposal made by the employer. A subsequent proposal by the employer was put to the union members, who voted to accept it, and the results of the vote were conveyed to the employer.

In the middle of the negotiations, the union brought a grievance (the MacDonald grievance) under the old collective agreement, alleging that the employer had breached that agreement by hiring a certain person. The union claimed that it had waited until this point to bring the grievance so as not to jeopardize the negotiations. The employer refused to sign a renewal agreement unless the grievance was dropped. Although the parties appeared to have settled all of the outstanding issues between them, the ill feeling generated by the filing of the grievance led the employer to put forward sixteen new demands for changes to the collective agreement. In these proceedings, the union alleged, among other things, that the employer had failed to make every reasonable effort to conclude a collective agreement.]

BURKETT, Vice-Chair: The requirement for rational discussion and full consideration of the issues between the parties is of particular importance in assessing the conduct of the respondent employer in the instant case. The evidence clearly establishes that the respondent took an initial position that it wished to renew the existing collective agreement without change. . . .

The requirements for open and rational discussion of all the issues in dispute stems from the fact that collective bargaining is in essence an exercise in *decision making*. The parties make hard decisions as to the content and timing of their offers and counter offers as they attempt to conclude an agreement. Frequently the most difficult decision facing the parties and often a decision with far-reaching public ramifications, is the resort to economic sanctions. Decisions which determine terms and conditions of employment and which may precipitate strike or lock-out obviously require, as a matter of public policy, open and full discussions. Conduct by one of the parties to the process which inhibits or undermines the decision-making capability of the other is conduct which is contrary to the requirement to bargaining in good faith and make every effort to reach a collective agreement. The failure of the employer to supply the requested wage data in the *DeVilbiss* case supra undermined the decision-making capability of the union in that situation and the Board commented that:

> It is patently silly to have a trade union "in the dark" with respect to the fairness of the employer's offer because it has insufficient information to appreciate fully the offer's significance to those in the bargaining unit.

Lack of full discussion obviously impedes the decision-making capability to the detriment of the collective bargaining process and the relationship of the parties. . . .

The decision-making capability of the parties depends upon not only a full and open discussion of the items which are in dispute but also upon an awareness that the scope of the dispute is limited to those items which have been put into dispute in the early stages of the bargaining process. Decision making does not take place in a vacuum. The parties set the parameters with their early exchange of proposals thereby establishing the framework within which they negotiate. A party which holds back on an item or number of items and then attempts to introduce these matters into the negotiations as the process nears completion, effectually destroys the decision-making framework. A party cannot rationally or properly consider its bargaining position in the absence of absolute certainty that the full extent of the dispute has been revealed. The tabling of additional demands after a dispute has been defined must, in the absence of compelling evidence which would justify such a course, be construed as a violation of the duty to bargain in good faith.

In the instant case the union was not altogether forthright in holding back the MacDonald grievance until it thought the bargaining had concluded. Nevertheless, the action of the employer which gave rise to that grievance occurred during the bargaining process thereby justifying a response by the union within the context of the bargaining process. The evidence establishes that the matter was verbally settled to the satisfaction of all parties and that subsequent to this verbal settlement the company tabled its revised list of demands. The tabling of the grievance did not justify the employer's response especially in light of the fact that the response occurred after a verbal settlement had been achieved. The employer's conduct is in violation of section 14 of the Act in so far as that section requires that the parties act in such a way as to foster rather than undermine the decision-making capability of the parties. . . .

Canadian Association of Industrial, Mechanical and Allied Workers v. Noranda Metal Industries Ltd., [1975] 1 Can. L.R.B.R. 145 at 162

[During negotiations for renewal of a collective agreement, the employer sent a series of letters to each employee in an attempt to bring pressure on the union to alter its position on fringe benefits. One letter emphasized the difference between the company's and the union's positions on that matter. At a subsequent bargaining session, the union asked the employer to disclose the cost to the employer of the benefits in question. The employer refused, taking the position that it was obliged to discuss only the extent of those benefits and not the price at which the employer could purchase them from third party providers. The union alleged, among other things, that this refusal constituted a violation of the duty to bargain in good faith. The board upheld this aspect of the union's complaint, for the following reasons.]

WEILER, Chair: It is a long-established principle of American labour law that a party commits an unfair labour practice if it withholds information relevant to collective bargaining without reasonable grounds. . . . That principle does fit comfortably within the language of [the duty to bargain provision of the British Columbia *Labour Code*]. One would hardly say that an employer who deliberately withheld factual data which a union needed to intelligently appraise a proposal on the bargaining table was making "every reasonable effort to conclude a collective agreement." The policy behind the American rule has been summed up in this comment: "Negotiation nourished by full and informal discussion stands a better chance of bringing forth the fruit of collective bargaining agreement than negotiation based on ignorance and deception."

Having said that, we want to make clear that we are not deciding in this case that this entire body of American doctrine is to be imported into British Columbia. The scope of the obligation which we find in s. 6 of the Labour Code will be developed on a case-by-case basis. But here we do have a particularly arresting situation for the application of that principle. First of all, Noranda's letter of July 5th to the employees raised the issue of the cost of fringe benefits and made this issue a public obstacle to settlement. By that same letter, the Company indicated it did have the data available to make those calculations. Finally, in its letter of July 26th, the Company led the Union reasonably to believe there would be a fruitful discussion of the factual underpinnings of the fringe issues. In our judgment, Noranda could not suddenly reverse gears, as it did in the meeting of August 13th, without significantly prejudicing an opportunity to dissolve this important bar to a settlement. In this respect, we do find that Noranda Metal Industries was in violation of s. 6 of the Labour Code.

* * *

7:421   Substantive and Procedural Obligations Imposed by the Duty to Bargain

At one extreme, it would be a clear breach of the duty to bargain for a party to propose a term that could not legally be included in a collective agreement — for example, a wage rate below the minimum wage required by employment standards legislation, or a union security clause weaker than the minimum required by the labour relations statute. Such substantive statutory requirements are matters of public policy, and a party who proposes that they be violated can hardly be said to be making reasonable efforts to reach a collective agreement.

There is another type of proposal which either the employer or the union can put forward without necessarily violating the duty to bargain, and which the other side can lawfully accept, but which neither side can press to an impasse — that is, to the point of threatening a strike or lockout over it. Generally speaking, these are proposals on matters which affect the parameters of the collective bargaining relationship. Examples are proposals to reduce or expand the size of the bargaining unit as set by the labour board, and proposals to institute or maintain multi-employer bargaining in a situation where bargaining rights exist only on a single-employer basis: see Donald Carter, "The Duty to Bargain in Good Faith: Does it Affect the Content of Bargaining?" in K.P. Swan and K.E. Swinton (eds.), *Studies in Labour Law* (Toronto: Butterworths, 1983), 36 at 42–51.

Apart from these relatively narrow exceptions, the parties to collective bargaining have considerable freedom to exercise their own judgment about what matters to raise at the bargaining table and about which of those matters are worth pressing to (or beyond) the point of impasse, as well as about the tactics they will use in the bargaining process. However, in applying the subjective and objective branches of the duty to bargain, labour boards have developed an extensive body of jurisprudence which places certain restrictions on that freedom. The rest of this section will review and assess those restrictions.

Labour boards have drawn an important distinction between what they characterize as "surface" and "hard" bargaining. Surface bargaining is a breach of the duty to bargain; hard bargaining is not. The meaning of this distinction is explored in the following leading case.

United Steelworkers of America v. Radio Shack, [1980] 1 Can. L.R.B.R. 99 at 123–28, 145 (O.L.R.B.)

[The respondent employer was a branch of Tandy Electronics Limited (Alberta), a subsidiary of Tandy Corporation of Fort Worth, Texas. The complainant union had been certified without a vote under section 7a (now section 11) of the Ontario *Labour Relations Act*, for full-time employees in November 1978 and for part-time employees in March 1979, pursuant to a finding by the Ontario Labour Relations Board that the employer had engaged in extensive unfair labour practices designed to keep the union out. Among those practices were the respondent's failure to comply with a board order to reinstate an employee dismissed for union activity; its involvement in the circulation of an anti-union petition; its warning that it would "move out west" if the union was certified, its statements to employees disparaging the board's procedures; and its distribution of free anti-union T-shirts to employees. There was also evidence from a former Radio Shack security officer, Donald Gallagher, that the respondent's director of personnel and security, Roy Murden, had hired people to infiltrate the union and obtain information on its activities, and had engaged private investigators to photograph everyone who attended union meetings. Murden had told Gallagher that he had been instructed "by Fort Worth to get rid of the union, no matter what the cost." Those activities had apparently all taken place before the union was certified.

On 30 November 1978, the complainant union's staff representative, Frank Berry, served notice to bargain on the respondent. In December Berry asked the respondent for the name, classification, and seniority date of each employee in the unit, and for the details of existing fringe benefits. On 9 January 1979, the respondent sent all employees a memorandum ridiculing the union's request for such information. Two days later, after receiving the union's proposals for a collective agreement, the respondent sent another memorandum to its employees, purporting to assure them that despite the union's demand for a union shop clause, no employee would ever have to pay union dues to work at Radio Shack. On 19 January, right after the first collective bargaining session, management sent employees another memorandum commenting on issues discussed at the bargaining table. On 16 February, after the second bargaining session, a further memorandum of that sort went out.

The respondent's counterproposals, put forward early in 1979, included several highly unusual items. A "relationship" clause would have prohibited the union from publicly mentioning the respondent or any of its employees, orally or in writing, without prior written authorization from the respondent's president, and would have allowed an employer grievance over any such mention to go immediately to arbitration, with the arbitrator being required to order the public withdrawal of the statement and damages of $5,000 to $10,000 a day against the union. A list of "rules and regulations" included eleven heads of prohibited employee conduct, some of them very vague. Any violation would subject the offending employee to immediate discharge.

On 15 December 1978, the parent company sent an American lawyer, Stewart Gordon, to participate in the negotiations. Gordon testified that he did not at first attend the bargaining sessions because of the objections of the respondent's Ontario labour lawyer, Donald McKillop, but that in May 1979 it was decided that he should attend the sessions. This led to McKillop's withdrawal as counsel and to his replacement by Bruce Binning, who became spokesman for the respondent along with Gordon.

Between 7 June 1979, when Binning and Gordon first arrived at the bargaining table, and the end of July, many outstanding issues were settled. Among the few remaining unsettled were the proposed rules and regulations and the union's request for a compulsory dues checkoff (a Rand Formula clause). Gordon and Binning testified that they had by then dropped their demand for the relationship clause, but Berry testified that the union was never told of this. The evidence was unclear on the respondent's willingness to modify its proposed rules and regulations.

Berry testified that Binning and Gordon told him in July 1979 that the respondent was unlikely to give any more ground on the outstanding issues unless the complainant threatened to strike. The parties therefore informally agreed to allow the mediator to time his report so that the employees would be in a legal strike position on 1 August. No settlement was reached, however. A strike began on 8 August and was still on when this matter was heard by the board.

Striking employees testified that during the strike, Jack MacDonald, a security consultant engaged by the respondent, photographed them on the picket line and told them — falsely — that a decertification application was being prepared. MacDonald testified that he said nothing about a decertification application. During the strike, Jerry Colella, vice-president and general manager of the respondent's Canadian operation since February 1979, published in the respondent's in-house publication (entitled *Watts Up*) a letter headed "A Debt of Gratitude." The letter gave profuse thanks to "those Radio Shack employees who have demonstrated their courage and fortitude by exercising their right to work in the face of a strike called by a minority of workers."

The complainant alleged that the respondent had breached sections 14, 56, 58, 59, and 61 (now sections 17, 70, 72, 73, and 76) of the Ontario *Labour Relations Act*, and asked for various remedies.]

ADAMS, Chair: [W]e have no hesitation in concluding that the respondent from November 1978 until June of 1979 utterly failed in its duty to bargain in good faith and make every reasonable effort to make a collective agreement. We are also of the view that its negotiating conduct during this period was a blatant continuation of its earlier anti-union animus and clearly aimed at further dividing its employees and undermining the trade union's statutory role in violation of sections 56, 58, and 61 of the *Labour Relations Act* and their underpinning principles discussed above.

This brings us to the months of June, July and August of 1979 and the Respondent's conduct at that time. There can be no doubt that the parties made "progress" after the insertion of Bruce Binning. A substantial portion of the language that would go into any collective agreement was agreed to between June and August and by the end of July the outstanding central issues had been narrowed to union security, merit wage increases, the transfer clause and the rules and regulations of the Respondent. Gordon testified that he had become dissatisfied with the "direction" of the negotiations by May and in retaining Bruce Binning wished to avoid the commission of any further unfair labour practices. Binning testified that the Respondent's position was not rigid on union security, that it was willing to submit disputed merit increases to arbitration; and that it was willing to review any rule the Complainant thought unreasonable. On the surface all of this evidence appears consistent with the Respondent's claim of a complete "change in heart."

So too, some of Berry's evidence is consistent with this theory. After narrowing the issues to four, Berry agreed to the issuance of a no-board report by the Minister apparently to facilitate the mutual need for a strike deadline. This could be said to be a peculiar approach to take with respect to an employer the Complainant thought was bargaining to destroy it. As the strike deadline approached Berry said that if there could be an agreement on union security and the rules, "everything else would fall into place." The union then waited until it was at least three weeks into its strike before commencing this complaint — a timing which might suggest the Complainant simply miscalculated its capacity to strike the employer, its strength having been dissipated by the Respondent's earlier lawless conduct.

We have, however, a number of serious misgivings which preclude adopting this view. For one thing, neither Gordon nor Binning had the final say in developing the Respondent's negotiating position. Apparently, Jerry Colella had the ultimate responsibility in this respect and Colella was not called to testify. The evidence indicates that Colella was in control of the Respondent from February of 1979 and, thus, would have been party to the earlier bad faith bargaining which we have found occurred up until at least June of 1979. We further note the recent publication of the letter of "thank you" bearing Colella's picture and signature to those employees who have continued to work during the strike and its resemblance to earlier improper tactics aimed at dividing the employees and undermining the Complainant. By itself the letter could be viewed as no more than an emotional response to a heated strike situation, but the overall conduct of the Respondent makes it difficult for the Board to be confident in characterizing the letter this way. Viewed in the totality of the Respondent's conduct, Colella's "thank you" is more suggestive of an unmitigated desire to destroy the Complainant by fostering employee opposition and belies any apparent change of heart. In the context of this case, the publication also constitutes a violation of section 56 as well as casting light on the proper construction to be given the Respondent's other actions.

Apart from Jerry Colella, there has been no significant change in the identity of those people managing the Respondent since the issuance of the certificate for the full-time unit, and yet, no one from the Respondent's management came forward to testify about the underlying basis to the instructions given to Gordon and Binning from June to August in contradistinction to the style of bargaining the Respondent had engaged in before that. Of additional concern is Gallagher's testimony that Murden told him "Fort Worth" wanted to get rid of the union at any cost and that the union would not get a contract within the year following notice to bargain. This testimony was inconsistent with Gordon's evidence that the American parent had been kept in the dark. Indeed, the insertion of Colella by the American parent in February of 1979 is inconsistent with Gordon's view of the Respondent as an independent Canadian subsidiary which was keeping its parent and its advisor in the dark. We are also concerned that neither Murden nor anyone associated with the parent came forward to rebut Gallagher's testimony or to explain to the Board firsthand that such deep-seated attitudes no longer permeated the Respondent's actions. Gordon explained his understanding of the change in attitude, but he is not an officer of either the American parent or the Respondent and his evidence about the change in attitude was, by and large, hearsay. Furthermore, he had no direct knowledge of any communication links between the Respondent and its parent and the role the parent was playing, if any, in the negotiations. Berry dealt exclusively with Gordon and Binning and even in the eleventh hour of the negotiations he doubted the sincerity of the Respondent. With the insertion of a new face in the negotiations, it is not surprising that the union delayed bringing this complaint and instead made a serious effort to test and judge the Respondent's apparent change in heart. That the Complainant called a strike before launching this complaint is not irrelevant to the issues before us but may only reflect its stated uncertainty over the Respondent's true intentions. After hard reflection on this issue, we have come to the conclusion that any ambivalence it may have had over the actual intentions of the Respondent was not unreasonable in the circumstances and ought not to deprive it from asking this Board to make its own judgment about the Respondent's sincerity in light of all the evidence.

In making our assessment, the absence of direct testimony from company officials is of great significance because of the rigid positions taken by the Respondent on the central issues in the negotiations. There can be little doubt that its positions on wages, transfer, union security and rules of conduct cut to the very heart of a collective agreement. That they would be strike issues with the Complainant in the context of this dispute is hardly surprising. That the Complainant would see an anti-union animus connecting the Respondent's position on each of these issues is also not unreasonable given the history to this relationship. Against the background of the Respondent's earlier misconduct, this Board is entitled to a detailed explanation justifying the Respondent's position on each item in order to be satisfied that the positions were not taken for the purpose of provoking the Complainant into an untenable strike.

To be fair to Bruce Binning and Stewart Gordon, they tried to give a rationale for some of the positions taken, but it was clear that they were merely giving their personal interpretations of what they thought the Respondent's intent was. The fact that they told Berry a strike deadline might affect the Respondent's resolve is demonstrative of their limited direct knowledge of the Respondent's motives.

The absence of direct testimony on motivation is of particular importance on the issue of union security because the Respondent's position on this issue fits hand in glove with the entire pattern of earlier unlawful conduct aimed at fostering employee opposition to the Complainant to undermine its status as exclusive bargaining agent for all of the employees in the bargaining unit. Binning testified that the Respondent's position was not rigid on this issue, but saying this does not make it so. The rigidity in a party's position must be gleaned as much from its conduct as from what it says to this Board. While we have no doubt that Bruce Binning thought his client might react differently in the face of a strike, the fact is that it did not. It is also a fact that Colella was the decision maker and he did not come forward to provide the Board with his understanding of the Respondent's current position on this issue and to explain how it differs from the Respondent's intemperate declaration on union security published in its January 11, 1979 newsletter. Nor was he called to explain how his "thank you" note to employees not honouring the picket lines related to the Respondent's earlier improper tactics aimed at discouraging support for the Complainant. From the Respondent's bargaining conduct one can detect no change on the union security issue from the period during which its actions were rife with anti-union animus to the more recent summer period where it claims to have engaged in hard bargaining. Furthermore, we have difficulty with Bruce Binning's explanation that the Respondent's position on union security is simply an unwillingness to agree to a Rand Formula where the union lacks a very large degree of employee support. Where the employer adopting this position has played no significant role in unlawfully contributing to the absence of such support, the position is unobjectionable. Such a difference in principle is not foreign to collective bargaining and cannot, by itself, be considered a product of bad faith bargaining. . . . But where an employer adopts this stance after having engaged in the kind of pervasive unlawful conduct that the Respondent has engaged in, the underlined caveat in the following excerpt from *The Daily Times* leaps out from the rest of the paragraph which the Respondent asked the Board to take note of:

The union claims that the company has coupled its wage offer with an offer of union security which it knows the union cannot accept and which, therefore, is designed to make it impossible to conclude an agreement. Section 36a [now 47] of the *Act* provides that on written request of the trade union there shall be included in the collective agreement a clause providing for voluntary revocable check-off. An offer of the form of union security provided for in Section 36a of the *Act* cannot be in violation of the *Act*. *This is not to say that an intransigent offer of this form of union security coupled with other relevant facts might not cause the Board to conclude in a given case that an employer had failed to bargain in good faith.* Even if the Board were to make such a finding, however, it could not impose a form of union security different than that set out in section 36a of the Act. If the Board was to make an order of the type sought by the trade union in this case, it would be ignoring the policy of voluntarism which is embodied in the Act and, having regard to the provisions of Section 36a, it would be thrusting itself into the role of legislator; a role which it cannot assume. (Emphasis added.)

It is not unusual for the ranks of a union to be swelled by bargaining unit employees after the issuance of a certificate. In fact, Bruce Binning made this point during his testimony. Employees who have been noncommittal may subsequently support the union once it has been certified by the Board. And this is true even for those employees who may have opposed the union prior to certification. But the Respondent did not refrain from the commission of unfair labour practices in November of 1978 after the issuance of the full-time bargaining unit certificate and did not commence to bargain in good faith. For the Respondent to then base its position on union security on an absence of employee support in August of 1979 tends to taint its motivation on this issue with its earlier unlawful conduct. Without persuasive evidence to the contrary, there is no reason for not concluding that the Respondent's rigid position on union security continues to be part and parcel of a longstanding scheme to undermine the statutory role of the Complainant as exclusive bargaining agent.

In coming to this conclusion we are particularly sensitive to the nature of section 36a, the benefit of which a trade union is entitled to as a matter of right and which is all the Respondent has ever been prepared to offer. Section 36a requires an employee to come forward and advise his employer that he wishes union dues to be deducted from his wages. Where an employer has acted as the Respondent has and over so long a period of time, it may require a particularly courageous employee to make such a request. Therefore, when this same employer rigidly ties his position to voluntary revocable checkoff, his conduct is open to the inference that he is motivated by a desire to deter his employees from supporting the union in this manner. The Respondent has, in the circumstances, failed to adduce sufficiently cogent evidence to rebut this inference. It is simply wrong to conclude that offering what the statute requires as a bare minimum in the area of union security cannot be held to constitute bargaining in bad faith. Standing alone this may be the case. But when considered in the light of other employer actions, it can be one of the most coercive elements of a scheme to discourage and undermine trade union support. Surely the Legislature did not intend to preclude the Board from so finding. We therefore find that the

Respondent's position on union security violates sections 14, 56, 58 and 61 of the *Labour Relations Act.* As for counsel's argument that employees have to identify themselves when they go on strike in any event, this submission does not respond to the coercive significance of section 36a to non-member employees and, if the Respondent's own assessment of strike support is accurate, it may be telling that fewer employees than originally supported the Complainant's application for certification are now on strike. In fact, we find it quite remarkable that the Respondent could seriously rely on the "intelligence" about union support gathered by supervisors in developing its position on union security. With the history to this complaint, an employee would have to consider the wisdom of admitting support for the Complainant to the Respondent's supervisors and, as a Board, we are concerned that the Respondent is even monitoring employee sentiment in this respect in these circumstances.

To the extent that absolute rigidness is inconsistent with good faith bargaining and reasonable effort, it should be clear from our reasoning above that we are of the view that an employer can be no more rigid and unbending on union security than he can be on any other issue. Section 36a simply provides the union with a very limited form of union security as a matter of right. Any other form of union security is still clearly negotiable and, thus, an employer's bargaining obligation remains unchanged. Indeed, the very fact that the Legislature thought it necessary to enact section 36a conveys a statutory recognition of how important this issue is to trade unions and the problems associated with employer opposition. It would therefore be strange for this Board to interpret the presence of a provision benefiting trade unions to some limited degree in a manner which would encourage employer resistance and thereby exacerbate collective bargaining conflict in relation to this very sensitive issue. The issue is easily manipulated by an employer intent on undermining the exclusive role of a certified bargaining agent arising as it does in first agreement controversies. The Board must therefore judge bargaining with this fact clearly in mind.

After the long period of bargaining in bad faith that has been established in this case (together with the other unfair labour practices committed by the Respondent), there is an onus to prove the alleged change of heart in the latter stages of negotiations with the most cogent evidence available. This must be so because of the labour relations reality that apparent changes in heart may be little more than an awareness that "hard bargaining" is now sufficient to preclude the execution of any agreement or to cause so unsatisfactory a contract that continued employee support of the Complainant will be impossible. Neither of these approaches to "hard bargaining" is permissible and the Respondent is in the best position to explain its motivation in adopting the bargaining postures that it has.

After carefully analyzing all of the evidence, we have also come, on balance, to the more general conclusion that the Respondent was not bargaining in good faith and making every reasonable effort to enter into a collective agreement from June to August. This is not to deny that "progress" was made in negotiating the language of a possible agreement. But we think it more likely than not that the Respondent's rigid position on union security, as well as other items central to the negotiations, had the purpose of avoiding a collective agreement and was part and parcel of its earlier conduct aimed at undermining the trade union in the eyes of the employees in order to foster its early demise. This conclusion relies heavily on the totality of the evidence, arising as it does in a first agreement context, and draws its conceptual support from the following description of "surface bargaining" found in *The Daily Times*. . . .

> "Surface bargaining" is a term which describes a going through the motions, or a preserving of the surface indications of bargaining without the intent of concluding a collective agreement. It constitutes a subtle but effective refusal to recognize the trade union. It is important, in the context of free collective bargaining, however, to draw the distinction between "surface bargaining" and hard bargaining. The parties to collective bargaining are expected to act in their individual self interest and in so doing are entitled to take firm positions which may be unacceptable to the other side. The Act allows for the use of economic sanctions to resolve these bargaining impasses. Consequently, the mere tendering of a proposal which is unacceptable or even "predictably unacceptable" is not sufficient, standing alone, to allow the Board to draw an inference of "surface bargaining." This inference can only be drawn from the totality of the evidence including, but not restricted to, the adoption of an inflexible position on issues central to the negotiations. It is only when the conduct of the parties on the whole demonstrates that one side has no intention of concluding a collective agreement, notwithstanding its preservation of the outward manifestations of bargaining, that a finding of "surface bargaining" can be made.

We therefore find that the Respondent's more general bargaining posture during the months of June to August was in violation of sections 14, 56, 59, and 61 of the *Labour Relations Act*.

BOURNE, Board Member, dissenting: The history of events at the respondent's location in Barrie, up until May 1979, is unsavoury, to say the least. But it must surely be the events subsequent to that time which are the subject of bad faith bargaining in this instance.

. . . The shadow of negotiations before the entrance of Gordon and Binning has convinced the other members of the Board that the leopard hasn't changed its spots. Yet the evidence persuades me that both parties had entered into "hard bargaining" and had run across intractable positions on both sides by August 8 — the company's stance with regard to the dues check-off being countered by the union's adamant position on rules and regulations as well as the check-off. . .

. . . Events speak louder than words and [the respondent's] new team, which brought a whole grab-bag of unresolved issues down to three between June 7 and August 8, 1979, surely gives an indication of bargaining in good faith.

* * *

Canadian Union of United Brewery, Flour, Cereal, Soft Drink & Distillery Workers, Local No. 304 v. Canada Trustco Mortgage Company, [1984] O.L.R.B. Rep. 1356 at 1363–65

[The union had been certified as bargaining agent at only two of the many Canada Trust branches in Ontario — the St. Catharines and Cambridge branches. It had negotiated a collective agreement for the St. Catharines branch, generally embodying the terms that prevailed in its non-unionized branches, with only marginal improvements. In negotiations for the Cambridge branch, it was willing to offer only very minor improvements over the terms in the St. Catharines agreement.

The union brought a complaint that the employer was bargaining in bad faith in the Cambridge negotiations. The employer's approach, the union argued, was the antithesis of real bargaining, which ought to have given the union the right to participate in or challenge employer decisions that adversely affected employees. After citing its *Radio Shack* decision (above), among others, the board concluded that the employer's behaviour was an example of hard but legitimate bargaining rather than surface bargaining.]

MACDOWELL, Vice-Chair: In recent years the Board has been scrupulous to protect the framework of collective bargaining: the independence of the union, the integrity of its role as the employees' exclusive bargaining agent and the right to information necessary for it to properly perform its statutory role. But the Board has been equally clear that it will not act as interest arbitrator, or prescribe the precise contents of the parties' collective agreement — even in the face of an "egregious" breach of the duty to bargain in good faith (see *Radio Shack* . . .). The content of the agreement is for the parties to determine, in accordance with their own perceived needs and relative bargaining strengths. The legislation enables employees to combine together to bargain collectively and compels the employer to recognize their bargaining agent. It further provides a framework within which there can be an exploration of the parties' differences and a sincere effort to reach some accommodation. Despite the adversarial aspects of collective bargaining, there are substantial areas of mutual interest between employers and employees which informed discussion may reveal. But the statute does not *require* any particular concessions, nor does it stipulate the content of a collective agreement, or even that a collective agreement always must be the necessary outcome of the parties' bargaining.

One cannot quarrel with the proposition that the "duty to bargain in good faith" must encompass an obligation to engage in informed and rational discussion, and in exceptional circumstances an employer's position at the bargaining table may be so patently unreasonable or devoid of apparent business justification as to evidence a desire to avoid any collective agreement altogether. So may an unexplained retreat from a previous agreed position, or the untimely insertion of new issues into the bargaining process. However, the Board must be careful that in adjudicating disputes and giving a reasoned elaboration for its decisions, it does not impose its own model of decision-making as the normative standard for the collective bargaining process. Collective bargaining is not simply a matter of presenting proofs and reasoned arguments in an effort to achieve a favourable outcome, nor is that outcome necessarily arrived at, or explained, by a logical development from given and accepted premises. It is a process in which reason plays a part — but not the only part. There may be a range of potential outcomes or solutions and the ultimate result may have more to do with economic strength than abstract logic. In particular collective bargaining situations there simply may not be any commonly accepted principles or criteria and, in consequence, no objective basis for distinguishing a "claim of right" from a "naked demand." Reason and self-interest are inextricably intertwined. Ultimately the parties may reach agreement only because of a realistic appraisal of the value of their objectives in relation to their ability to obtain them, including the costs they are able to inflict on one another. It may have little to do with what some outsider might consider a "fair" settlement, or a just allocation of rewards to capital and labour.

Rational discussion is an important aspect of the bargaining process. So is power. Persuasion is an effective tactic to gain one's bargaining objectives. So is economic pressure. Whether that system actually results in a "just wage" or "distributive justice," we leave for others to debate. Collective bargaining permits that outcome, but it does not compel it. (For an interesting analysis of the impact of collective bargaining see: *What Unions Do*, by R.B. Freeman & J.L. Medoff. . . .)

The facts of this case provide a graphic illustration of the absence of shared principle, and the predominance of bargaining power as a means of settling the parties' collective bargaining differences. The union seeks to limit the exercise of managerial authority and achieve for its supporters, terms and conditions of employment not only more generous than the employer is willing to pay, but also more generous than the employer is currently paying to hundreds of other employees in identical circumstances. The employer seeks to maintain its managerial prerogatives and provide levels of remuneration consistent with its own assessment of its needs, its own organizational imperatives, and its own perception of the dictates of the market place. There is no obvious way of reconciling these competing interests, nor is there any reservoir of principle to which one can resort to provide the "right answer." No amount of rational discussion or reasoned elaboration will necessarily produce an accommodation. Nor can there always be such accommodation in our system of free collective bargaining which ultimately rests, as it must, on the right of parties to resort to economic sanctions in pursuit of their own self-interest as they define it. Under our statute their only obligation is to endeavour to conclude a collective agreement and if that is the true intent, neither the content nor the consequences of that agreement are of any concern to the Board.

This is not to say that collective bargaining must always be a "zero sum game," or that there cannot be substantial areas of mutual accommodation and joint decision-making. But our statute mandates collective bargaining, not co-determination. Co-determination, or co-partnership may be the result of collective bargaining, but it is not an outcome required by law. Nor was the duty to bargain in good faith designed to redress an imbalance of bargaining power. A party whose bargaining strength allows it to virtually dictate the terms of the agreement does not thereby bargain in bad faith, and that proposition is applicable whether it is the union or the employer which "has the upper hand."

In the circumstances of this case, we are satisfied that the employer's conduct is properly characterized as hard bargaining in pursuit of its own self-interest and legitimate business objectives. It was, and remains, prepared to sign a collective agreement on terms similar to those agreed to in St. Catharines, and, in our view, it was entitled to take into account the relative insignificance of this bargaining unit in its overall organizational scheme. If its rigid insistence on the preservation of management rights has a certain ideological cast, it is one which in our system is recognized as legitimate. There has been no breach of section 15 of the Act. The complaint is therefore dismissed.

* * *

The authors of the following excerpt offer a critique of what they describe as the dominant approach to the duty to bargain — the approach taken by the Ontario board in *Canada Trustco* and in its subsequent decision in *Eaton's* [1985] O.L.R.B. Rep. March 491.

Brian Langille & Patrick Macklem, "Beyond Belief: Labour Law's Duty to Bargain" (1988) 13 Queen's L.J. 62 at 80–87, 91–92

We wish to suggest that this whole structure and way of thinking about the duty to bargain is seriously mistaken. We do not say that this dominant understanding is incapable of processing any complaints in a rational manner. We believe it does so, and this explains, in part, the longevity of this point of view. However, at the heart of the conception lies a serious flaw, a flaw which renders the duty impotent where it is needed the most, in a category of truly hard cases which the current understanding does not even recognize. *Canada Trustco Mortgage* is such a case.

Returning to the opening words of the *Canada Trustco* decision, we find the Board articulating the views of the parties in terms which are perfectly understandable within the prevalent mode of thinking. The union alleges bad faith; the employer replies that it is simply acting in its self-interest. The point to make is that such a conception of the duty to bargain, which assumes or rests upon a supposed distinction between bad faith and self-interest, is bound to fail. It is bound to fail because, by and large, there is no such distinction. Any labour law rule which assumes, draws, or depends upon a distinction between bad faith and self-interest, or between anti-union animus and self-interest, in our view, will not work. In a contractualist bargaining world, self-interest is the only operable notion, the only gauge against which conduct can be measured. By definition, one's self-interest can include an anti-union animus. Acting under an anti-union animus is merely playing the contractualist game.

Now it is true that the current understanding of the duty to bargain in good faith will cover a number of particularly unattractive factual situations — represented, perhaps, by the *Radio Shacks* of this world. The current conception, as has been pointed out, does make one — but only one — change in the pre-existing rules governing contractual bargaining. The duty compels an employer to deal with a trade union. At common law there was no obligation to deal with anyone if one did not want to, regardless of one's reasons for not wanting. By contrast, under a collective bargaining regime, you must be willing to bargain and you must be willing to enter a collective agreement.

Thus it is clear that the duty is not without content. It can capture those employers who view it in their self-interest not to recognize the trade union. If your intent is not to sign a collective agreement because this is your view of how to maximize your self-interest then you are, if the evidentiary problem is overcome, caught by the duty. However, if you are willing to sign a collective agreement, then you can maximize your self-interest. The problem with this neat view of the world is that it captures only: (a) the rational but less powerful, and (b) the irrational but more powerful, employers of this world. It does not capture the rational and powerful employer. That is, a rational and powerful employer will always be willing to sign the collective agreement which maximizes its self-interest. It is simply wrong to think that one can only maximize one's self-interest by not signing a collective agreement. If the content of the agreement is totally "up for grabs" then there is no rational disincentive to signing. If self-interest backed by economic clout can produce any agreement, what disincentive is there to signing? Under our model, once you are willing to sign, all else becomes a matter of "self-interest." Once you cross that hurdle all is relegated to the tautology that whatever is in your self-interest is by definition legitimate; no further reason need be given — none whatsoever. Freedom of contract is absolute.

Our thesis is simply the following: the law has gradually come to grips with the irrational and powerful employers. Our existing conception captures this case. The hole in the heart of the theory is its inability to deal with the rational and powerful employer. And, as we all know, rational employers have appeared on the scene. The bottom line for our labour law must be that there is no distinction, from the point of view of regulating bargaining, between the rational and the irrational employer. Both achieve the same *effect* and both do so for the same motive. One is simply more rational in its pursuit of its objective than the other. It makes no sense to relegate the duty to the role of regulating the irrational powerful anti-union employers of this world, but not the rational ones.

Without substantive content, and with the principle of maximizing one's self-interest, a willingness to enter some collective agreement is merely the requirement of rationality upon the part of the employer. An employer who has superior bargaining power, such that it can dictate the terms of a collective agreement, need not act in an irrational way. There is no difference between refusing to sign any collective agreement and signing a collective agreement the terms of which can be completely dictated and which represent no change from the status quo. In the former situation, the employer refuses to recognize the union; in the latter, the employer refuses to permit the union to be recognized in the collective agreement. One simply achieves through the front door what one could not achieve through the back. Our current conception of the duty simply ignores this point. A powerful, rational, anti-union employer can thus plead self-interest and escape the strictures of the duty. This is what the opening words of *Canada Trustco* tell us, and this is what we all assume. . . .

Thus our current conception of the duty to bargain ignores a whole category of employer behaviour. By relying on a distinction between good faith and self-interest which has the effect of upholding rational anti-union employer tactics, this conception threatens the integrity of legislative schemes designed to "encourag[e] the practice and procedure of collective bargaining" by subjecting their dictates in situations of this sort to an overriding defence of self-interest. In what can be characterized as a series of attempts to mediate the radical potential of this unruly affirmation of freedom of contract, jurisprudence under the duty to bargain contains certain exceptions to the automatic equation of good faith with self-interest — exceptions which, in our view, operate as avoidance techniques and which are only as coherent as the principle which engenders them.

An example of such exception and avoidance can be found in the recent *Eaton's* decision of the Ontario Board. In that case, the Board was faced with an employer who refused to give more at the bargaining table to unionized employees than what it was willing to give its non-unionized employees at other locations. In upholding such a position, the Board relied on the distinction between bad faith and self-interest outlined previously, accepting the argument that an employer is acting according to self-interest when it formulates bargaining proposals designed to minimize the likelihood or unionization at its non-unionized locations and rejecting the view that this constitutes bad faith. The Board stated the following:

> Nothing in the *Labour Relations Act* requires an employer to agree to wages and employee benefits for unionized employees that are superior to those being received by non-unionized employees. See *Canada Trustco*. . . . Neither is there any provision which prohibits an employer when formulating its bargaining position to take into account the likelihood that improvements in the terms of employment for one group of employees will likely impact on other groups. Indeed, logic suggests that this is a consideration frequently taken into account by employers, since an improvement in the employment conditions of one group of employees will logically lead to similar improvements for other employees of the same employer, whether they be unorganized or included in a different bargaining unit.

Stripped to its essentials, the above asserts that employers frequently consider the likely impact of improvements in terms of employment for one group of employees upon another (not yet organized) group of employees. Therefore, the cost of future unionization is part of the calculus of bargaining and affects the content of proposals. The paragraph is telling of the fact that jurisprudence under the duty simultaneously recognizes that minimizing the cost of unionization is self-interested action but represses the idea that such behaviour also amounts to an anti-union animus. The implication of such repression, of course, is that it potentially renders the notion of anti-union animus meaningless. The Board appears to recognize this implication and attempts to mediate it by introducing the following caveat:

> Further, the fact that an employer refuses to give more to unionized employees, does not, by itself, necessarily mean that the employer is seeking to interfere with the formation of trade unions. Such a conclusion might be justified if the terms being offered to organized employees were inferior to those being enjoyed by comparable non-union employees, for this would indicate an intent to punish employees because they had selected trade union representation. Such, however, is not the case here.

Thus the Board quickly distances itself from the idea that, even though an employer can factor in and attempt to minimize the cost of unionization during bargaining in an attempt to reduce the likelihood of future unionization, the employer does not breach the duty by attempting to enshrine terms in a collective agreement *inferior* to those being enjoyed by non-unionized employees. This, in the Board's view, would be acting in bad faith.

The question which presents itself is, of course, why? If one is entitled to take a hard line during bargaining to eliminate incentives on employees at other locations to organize, why is it that an employer cannot demand that unionized employees accept an offer inferior to what non-unionized employees receive? It is presumably in the employer's self-interest to do so, and there is nothing in the logic and rhetoric of our dominant conception of the duty to bargain, so long as the employer was willing to sign the agreement, which would prevent such an action. The notion that the latter move is punitive, while the former is self-interested, avoids the fact that both are punitive, both are self-interested, and both have the same motive and effect. . . .

In sum, the claim made here is that our dominant conception of the duty to bargain is fraught with inconsistency. This is not to say that it is totally useless. But there are serious problems. First, it relies on a distinction between self-interest and bad faith which does not hold up to scrutiny. Acting in one's economic self-interest and acting with an anti-union animus are ultimately indistinguishable: in theory, the former includes the latter and, in practice, it is widely thought that it is in one's economic self-interest to have a non-unionized workplace. The upshot is that our conception of the duty to bargain legitimates bargaining positions designed to eliminate the union from the workplace simply because the employer is amenable to the signing of a contract which ensures that result. Second, our conception of the duty engenders caveats to the equation of good faith and self-interest which, insofar as they rely on the validity of that equation but at the same time attempt to restrain its radical implications through exception and avoidance, are ultimately incoherent.

. . . [T]he purpose of our collective bargaining law is not to promote contractualism, it is to seek justice. Contractualism is a means to the end, not the end itself. Indeed, pure common law contractualism is what we modified and rejected in the name of justice. We say, this method will not get us where we wish to go. Therefore, we create other modes of regulation, including that of the restructured market. Our misunderstanding has been to articulate the means of achieving justice in a way which denies the end in the name of which we utilize those means in the first place. At the same time, and as a result, we achieve the incoherence evident in *Canada Trustco* and *Eaton's*.

Earlier it was argued that there is no distinction between the irrational and rational powerful anti-union employer. Both seek to achieve the same effect and with the same motive. However, under our current conception of the duty, one is excused and the other is not. This cannot be correct. The point is that if the current conception of the duty demands only willingness to sign an agreement (that is, no intent not to sign any agreement) then a rational employer is indifferent to signing a collective agreement which merely embodies the status quo or not signing a collective agreement and thus guaranteeing the status quo. As long as you are willing to sign, any content can be justified in the name of self-interest backed by economic power. The collective agreement need not contain anything but what the statute demands. That is, until recently, almost nothing. There need be no recognition of the role of the union stewards, committees, or other institutions. Not even a bulletin board. Even if these institutions are created they need be given no role, no say, no process, no input, no control. Further, there need be no reduction of arbitrary employer power, no rule of law, no rights of citizenship, no recognition of seniority at all or in any form, no just cause provision, no inroads upon other arbitrary employer actions. What the employer gets is exactly what the employer gets without a collective agreement, and for the same reasons. The statute calls for an arbitration process but that process will

not guarantee substantive rights. Assuming grievances even reach arbitration, the employer will win all the cases. When we witness the use of superior bargaining power to destroy the institutions and processes of collective representation of employees, then we witness the tragedy of the sacrifice of ends of the civilized and democratic workplace to the means of contractualism. We are in effect arguing for minimum substantive content of the duty to bargain — a minimum set of rights to ensure collective voice.
[Reprinted by permission.]

* * *

In *Royal Oak Mines Inc.*, excerpted below, the Supreme Court of Canada considered the extent to which labour boards can scrutinize the contents of bargaining proposals. The majority of the court found that where a party refuses to include in its proposals terms that have been widely accepted in other agreements throughout the particular industry, it may be appropriate for the board to find a breach of that party's duty to make every reasonable effort to reach a collective agreement. Consider how far this judgment goes to address the concerns raised above by Langille and Macklem.

Royal Oak Mines v. Canada (Labour Relations Board), [1996] 1 S.C.R. 369 at 369–89

[The unionized workers of Royal Oak Mines, a company based in Yellowknife, N.W.T., voted overwhelmingly to reject a tentative agreement put forward by the employer. A bitter and violent eighteen-month strike followed, which affected the whole community of Yellowknife and resulted in nine deaths in a bomb explosion. Various attempts to effect a settlement were made during the strike, through mediation and the appointment of an industrial commission under the *Canada Labour Code*. The Canada Labour Relations Board found that the employer had failed to bargain in good faith, by refusing to bargain until a particular certification issue had been resolved and by attempting to impose a probationary period on all returning strikers. However, the board based its decision mainly on what it found to be the employer's most serious violation: the employer's refusal to negotiate until the issue of reinstatement and discipline of several employees accused of serious picket line violence had been resolved.

In light of the long history of intransigence and bitterness between the parties, the board ordered the employer to put back on the table the tentative agreement that it had put forward earlier (and which the union had rejected), with the exception of four items on which the employer had changed its position. The parties were given a thirty-day period to settle those items, after which compulsory arbitration was to be imposed. An application by the employer for judicial review was dismissed by the Federal Court of Appeal. The employer appealed to the Supreme Court of Canada.]

CORY J. (L'Heureux-Dubé and Gonthier JJ. concurring): Section 50(a) of the *Canada Labour Code* has two facets. Not only must the parties bargain in good faith, but they must also make every reasonable effort to enter into a collective agreement. Both components are equally important, and a party will be found in breach of the section if it does not comply with both of them. There may well be exceptions but as a general rule the duty to enter into bargaining in good faith must be measured on a subjective standard, while the making of a reasonable effort to bargain should be measured by an objective standard which can be ascertained by a board looking to comparable standards and practices within the particular industry. It is this latter part of the duty which prevents a party from hiding behind an assertion that it is sincerely trying to reach an agreement when, viewed objectively, it can be seen that its proposals are so far from the accepted norms of the industry that they must be unreasonable.

Section 50(a)(ii) requires the parties to "make every reasonable effort to enter into a collective agreement." It follows that, putting forward a proposal, or taking a rigid stance which it should be known the other party could never accept must necessarily constitute a breach of that requirement. Since the concept of "reasonable effort" must be assessed objectively, the Board must by reference to the industry determine whether other employers have refused to incorporate a standard grievance arbitration clause into a collective agreement. If it is common knowledge that the absence of such a clause would be unacceptable to any union, then a party such as the appellant, in our case, cannot be said to be bargaining in good faith. On this it is significant that the special mediators made the following observation in their second interim report:

> . . . the employer must restrain itself from taking bargaining positions which it surely must know would be unacceptable to virtually any organization of workers. It is one thing to say that circumstances have changed such that the content of the tentative agreement is no longer good enough. It is another to construct unmanageable bargaining gaps. . . .

In some cases a party's behaviour may be so egregious that it can be reasonably inferred that there is an unwillingness to make a real effort to reach an agreement. In those circumstances, while a party may express a desire to reach a collective agreement their actions may clearly indicate that they do not wish to intend to reach an agreement. A refusal to include such basic and standard terms in an agreement as a requirement of a just cause for dismissal clause, or a refusal to negotiate about pensions, or as in this case, a refusal to consider a grievance arbitration clause, leads to the inference that despite any "sincerely and deeply held" beliefs the party claims to have, by taking a rigid stance on such a widely accepted condition, it becomes apparent that the party (here the employer) has no real intention of reaching an agreement. In other words, the employer is breaching the duty to "make every reasonable effort to enter into a collective agreement."

If a party proposes a clause in a collective agreement, or conversely, refuses even to discuss a basic or standard term that is acceptable and included in other collective agreements in comparable industries throughout the country, it is appropriate for a labour board to find that the party is not making a "reasonable effort to enter into a collective agreement." If reasonable parties have agreed to the inclusion of a grievance arbitration clause in their collective agreement, then a refusal to negotiate such a clause cannot be reasonable. The grounds on which an employer may dismiss an employee is of fundamental importance for any association of employees. For an employer to refuse an employee a grievance procedure or some form of due process, by which the employee can challenge his or her dismissal on the ground that it was not for just cause, is to deny that employee a fundamental right. In those circumstances it would be reasonable for a board to infer that no reasonable union would accept a collective agreement which lacked a grievance arbitration clause and that the employer's failure to negotiate the clause indicated a lack of good faith bargaining.

. . . The more appropriate approach would have been for the appellant to agree to the inclusion in the new collective agreement of some form of a grievance arbitration clause for the dismissed employees. It is certainly significant that after the Board decision, once a grievance arbitration process for the dismissed employees had concluded, the process resulted in 44 of the 49 employees being reinstated and/or awarded severance pay.

In summary, on the issue of the Board's finding that the appellant failed to bargain in good faith, I am of the view that this precise issue was by the provisions of the *Canada Labour Code* granted to the Board to decide, and that the courts should not set aside the Board's decision unless it was patently unreasonable. There is overwhelming support for the Board's finding that the appellant breached its duty to bargain in good faith by imposing an unreasonable condition to the collective bargaining process. Accordingly, the decision was clearly not patently unreasonable and the Federal Court of Appeal, recognizing this, properly deferred to the Board's finding.

National Automobile, Aerospace Transportation and General Workers Union of Canada (CAW-Canada) and its Local 2224 v. Buhler Versatile Inc., [2001] M.L.B.D. No. 9 (QL) (Manitoba Labour Board)

KORPESHO, Chair:

. . .

CAW-Canada alleged that B.V.I. had failed to bargain in good faith and failed to make every reasonable effort to conclude a collective agreement with the Applicant Union.

. . .

The original "Versatile" plant began as a family operation in Winnipeg, in 1952, as a manufacturer of tractors and drag-behind equipment. In or around 1987, the plant was purchased by Ford New Holland Canada, Ltd. . . . New Holland was subsequently sold to IHF — Internazionale Holding Fiat S.A. . . .

The plant, throughout its history, experienced the cyclical nature of the agricultural industry, at one time employing up to 1,150 and as few as 70 employees. The current work force in the plant unit numbers approximately 250.

In 1999, New Holland purchased Case International . . . , another major farm tractor and implement manufacturer. The proposed purchase came under the scrutiny of the U.S. Department of Justice, in Washington, D.C., in regard to the potential loss of competitiveness in the industry as a result of this sale. The U.S. Department of Justice subsequently informed New Holland that the Versatile plant had to be sold as a condition of the New Holland-Case merger. At the time of the merger, the Versatile plant produced three tractors: a two-wheel drive model known as the G-70 Genesis; a four-wheel drive model; and a bidirectional model known as the TV140.

. . .

After some nine months of negotiations and meetings with the U.S. Department of Justice, as well as a representative of the Federal Government of Canada . . . B.V.I. purchased the plant in July of 2000. . . .

It is within this backdrop that we get to the allegations before us. There is no question that the CAW-Canada also had serious reservations as to the purchase of New Holland by B.V.I. The CAW-Canada had made it quite clear that B.V.I. was not its purchaser of choice as the Union felt Buhler did not have the corporate presence to enter into a purchase of this size. Having said that, B.V.I. became a party to the Collective Agreement covering the plant employees, which expired September 2000.

The parties' first bargaining session took place on September 29th, 2000, . . . at which time proposals were exchanged. . . .

. . . It was at this meeting that Buhler stated, "My first offer is always my last offer."

. . .

There is no doubt in our minds that the CAW-Canada, from the initial meeting of September 29th, 2000, modified and withdrew certain bargaining proposals, and at the same time asked for written clarification so they could rationally consider certain proposals put forth by Buhler. The Employer, on the other hand, offered less each time they met and failed to provide, as requested, information in relation to its proposals.

. . .

The Alberta Labour Relations Board, in *Alberta Projectionists and Video Technicians Local 302 of the International Alliance of Theatrical Stage Employees and Moving Picture Machine Operators of the United States and Canada v. Famous Players Inc.* . . . , states:

> The duty to bargain in good faith is a cornerstone of the Labour Relations Code. It "gives life and substance to the rights of employers and employees" contained in sections 19. . . .

That board went on to say, at page 12:

> The duty to bargain in good faith has many aspects; breach of one aspect does not imply a breach of all aspects. However, a breach of even one aspect may result in the Board finding a breach of s. 58. Decisions of this Board reveal the variety of obligations inherent in the duty to bargain in good faith. A summary of those obligations include the obligation on:
> - the employer to recognize the trade union as the bargaining agent;
> - the parties to meet;
> - the parties to bargain;
> - the parties to act with the intent of concluding, revising or renewing a collective agreement;
> - the parties to make every reasonable effort to enter into a collective agreement;
> - the parties to engage in full, rational, informed discussion about the issues;
> - the employer to disclose decisions that have been made affecting the bargaining unit;
> - a party, upon request, to provide the other party with information relevant to the issues involved in bargaining;

- the parties to avoid deception in their representations to each other;
- the parties to avoid surface bargaining.

. . .

The parties met and bargained on six occasions prior to the strike. We do not agree with counsel for the Employer that the limited number of meetings should be a significant issue in considering if bad faith bargaining had occurred. On the contrary, the Board is more interested in the quality of negotiations as opposed to the quantity of time expended.

. . .

. . . Buhler, with the exception of the Buhler benefit package, put forth proposals without providing any justification or documentation to support his demands. It is also clear that Buhler was not prepared to discuss, in any rational way, any of the positions put forth by the CAW-Canada. One only has to review the notes of the last bargaining session, held on November 2nd, 2000, where most of Buhler's answers were either: "No; my answer is no; that's a definite no; and you've got to be kidding; no." to almost every query or proposal raised by the CAW-Canada.

It is also our view that Buhler knew, or ought to have known, that certain of his demands that would eliminate a number of longstanding provisions in the existing Collective Agreement, including the current health and welfare benefits and seniority, could not have been accepted by the Union and still have them maintain credibility with its members.

As Adams states [in] . . . his text, *Canadian Labour Law*. . . . :

> The deliberate tabling of inflammatory proposals which would likely provoke a breakdown in negotiations may violate the duty. This must be contracted with the "hard-bargaining" situation where one party insists on onerous terms the other refuses to accept. . . .

In assessing Buhler's demands, we are satisfied that his bargaining tactics went beyond that of "hard bargaining" and contravened the intent of section 63(1) of the Act [the duty to bargain requirement].

Although we are unaware of the negotiating tactics utilized by Buhler with other bargaining agents, we are troubled that his strategy with the CAW-Canada was based on his constant threats of plant closure. Buhler's proposals seemed, at times, to be irrational, to say the least, and at certain times took on a "bait and switch" type of strategy. A number of times through the bargaining sessions Buhler insisted that he would not lock out the employees, yet in those same discussions, threatened to padlock the doors.

The Board understands that parties, from time to time, engage in what has been described as "hard bargaining" to try to persuade the other side to accept a position on a particular issue. This, in our view, is not the case in the matter before us. Buhler consistently displayed an unwillingness to enter into any rational and informed discussions and provide supporting arguments throughout those negotiations. The evidence is clear that each time the CAW-Canada modified its position, Buhler proceeded to offer less. This, in itself, satisfies the Board that he breached the duty to bargain in good faith by purposely avoiding attempts to find some "common ground" to resolving the outstanding issues.

As previously mentioned, Buhler's tactics throughout can only be described as an attempt to bully the CAW-Canada into submission, by threats of selling the operation or padlocking the doors. Buhler and Engel were also quick to place the blame of the failed negotiations on the failure of both the Conciliation Officer and the Mediator for either not transmitting information or not holding face-to-face meetings with the parties. We find these comments unacceptable and consistent with Buhler's attitude that everyone else is responsible for the present situation except Buhler.

There is no doubt, in analyzing this situation, that B.V.I. placed the CAW-Canada in a situation where negotiations were going nowhere and, in fact, in a situation where each time they met, the Employer's offer worsened. Buhler's proposals could best be described as a "moving target."

Counsel for the Employer argued that the CAW-Canada didn't have to go on strike, as other options were available. She argued, for instance, that they could have continued working, and at the same time file an application with the Board alleging the very same bargaining in bad faith allegations. Although that may well have been an option for the CAW-Canada, that is not the question before the Board. The issue is simply, did the actions of the Employer cause the strike to take place. Having heard the evidence of both parties, the answer to that, in the Board's opinion, is an unequivocal yes.

We are satisfied, after considering the totality of the evidence, that the Employer's conduct during the bargaining sessions, up to and including November 2nd, 2000, were such that they contravened the duty to bargain in good faith and to make every reasonable effort to enter into a collective agreement.

. . .

The Board is satisfied that the action of this Employer went beyond hard bargaining. The constant threat of sale and closure; the lack of supporting material to justify Buhler's demands; the switching of positions in the middle of bargaining; the continued deterioration of Buhler's initial offer; Buhler's failure to disclose vital decisions; and his total lack of attempt to seek some common ground can only lead the Board to one conclusion — a breach of section 63(1) of the Labour Relations Act.

* * *

The Manitoba board notes above that the employer's chief executive officer (Buhler) said at the very first bargaining meeting, "My first offer is always my last offer." This approach on the employer's part has echoes of a tactic known as Boulwarism, developed by an American company in the 1940s. That tactic consisted of the employer's placing of a detailed offer on the table at the start of negotiations, and announcing that it would listen to what the union had to say but would not change the offer in any way unless economic conditions changed: *N.L.R.B. v. General Electric Co.*, (1969) 418 F, 2d 736, certiorari denied (1970) 397 U.S. 965.

Should it be a breach of the duty to bargain for an employer to work out carefully in advance exactly how far it is willing to go in order to reach a collective agreement, then state that position at the start of negotiations and stick firmly to it? Conversely, should it be a breach of the duty for a union to insist that the employer accept the same terms that the union has negotiated with other employers in the particular industry?

7:422 Disclosure of Decisions or Plans Substantially Affecting the Bargaining Unit

In the early 1980s, the Ontario board considered the extent to which the duty to bargain in good faith required the employer to disclose to the union information concerning plans for closing or reorganizing plants. In *Westinghouse Canada Ltd.*, [1980] 2 Can. L.R.B.R. 469 at 489 (O.L.R.B.), during negotiations for the renewal of a long-standing agreement, the company had been considering a plan to move one of the manufacturing operations covered by that agreement from its existing location in a highly-unionized area (Hamilton) to several less unionized areas of Ontario. The move, according to the testimony of a company officer, was an "unevaluated likelihood" during the period of the evaluations. At the bargaining table, the union did not ask whether the company had any relocation plans, nor did the company mention that it was considering the matter. Shortly after the renewal agreement was signed, the company announced the move and proceeded to implement it. The union then brought a complaint that the company had breached the duty to bargain in good faith by not informing the union of its plans before the agreement was signed. The union further argued that the decision to move was motivated by an anti-union animus, and therefore constituted an unfair labour practice. The board found that the company had committed an unfair labour practice by moving the plant, but dismissed the complaint of failure to bargain in good faith. The board said that the duty to bargain places an obligation on the employer to respond honestly to union inquiries at the bargaining table about the existence of company plans that may have a significant impact on the bargaining unit, but does not place the employer under a duty to reveal, on its own initiative, plans that have not yet ripened into at least de facto final decisions.

In *Sunnycrest Nursing Homes Limited*, [1982] 2 Can. L.R.B.R. 51, the Ontario board, on the principles enunciated in *Westinghouse*, found a violation of the duty to bargain in circumstances where it was clear that a decision to contract out a substantial portion of the bargaining unit's work had been taken before or during negotiations with the union. In *Plastics CMP Limited*, [1982] O.L.R.B. Rep. 726, a similar result was reached although most of the laid off employees were subsequently hired by the firm that the employer chose to do the work. Consider the following critique of this line of cases, and in particular of the *Westinghouse* decision.

Brian Langille, "Equal Partnership in Canadian Labour Law" (1983) 21 Osgoode Hall L.J. 496 at 517, 519–20

Now the one simple point that needs to be made before turning to *Westinghouse* is this: it is much easier to get away with an agreement which says nothing about issues like plant shutdown or contracting out if the probability of such occurrences is perceived as low. Further, one aspect of perception of low probability is ignorance that future occurrences, contemplated or decided upon, are in the works. In short, the statutory timetable offers the employer not only the *Sunnycrest* incentive not to *implement* changes, but the further incentive (referred to as *Westinghouse* incentives) not to reveal possible or actual decisions upon changes. Rather, the incentive to the employer is to remain silent, lock the union into the agreement, and then reveal the plans or act upon them. It is a system geared to non-disclosure. It is this structuring of incentives, flowing from our statutory timetable and (partially) our arbitration jurisprudence, which generated the *Westinghouse* case. The *Westinghouse* decision and a rash of similar cases reveal that these thoughts about incentives are not idle speculations. Employers have attempted to exploit these incentives to non-disclosure. This, in itself, should lead us to question, for example, Canadian arbitration law on contracting out. Yet non-disclosure is in direct conflict with the duty to bargain in good faith. Westinghouse addresses this conflict. As a starting point, it may be noted that under the general law of contract bargaining, non-disclosure (of latent defects for example) is generally accepted unless there is a duty to disclose. This state of the general law is said to instance the general proposition that there is no duty of good faith in our law of contract. But, of course, under Canadian labour law the parties are under that precise duty of good faith. This can be viewed as the second purpose outlined in *DeVilbiss (Canada) Ltd.* . . . , "to foster rational, informed discussion thereby minimizing the potential for unnecessary industrial conflict." The question left by *Westinghouse* is how well has the Board explicated the content of the duty to bargain over planned changes in the face of the incentives to non-disclosure.

The second objection is much more substantial and it concerns the reasoning invoked by the Board to justify limiting disclosure on the employer's own initiative to cases where the decision has been finalized. This reasoning was determinative of the actual decision in *Westinghouse*. The Board's sole justification for its decision that the silence of the employer about relocation plans under corporate discussion did not violate the bargaining duty is contained in a single extraordinary paragraph.

> The competitive nature of our economy and the ongoing requirement of competent management to be responsive to the forces at play in the marketplace result in ongoing management consideration of a spectrum of initiatives which may impact on the bargaining unit. More often than not, however, these considerations do not manifest themselves in hard decisions. For one reason or another, plans are often discarded in the conceptual state or are later abandoned because of changing environmental factors. The company's initiation of an open-ended discussion of such imprecise matters at the bargaining table could have serious industrial relations consequences. The employer would be required to decide in every bargaining situation at what point in his planning process he must make an announcement to the trade union in order to comply with section 14 [now section 17]. Because the announcement would be employer initiated and because plans are often not transformed into decisions, the possibility of the union viewing the employer's announcement as a threat (with attendant litigation) would be created. If not seen as a threat the possibility of employee overreaction to a company initiated announcement would exist. A company initiated announcement, as distinct from a company response to a union inquiry may carry with it an unjustified perception of certainty. The collective bargaining process thrusts the parties into a delicate and often difficult

interface. Given the requirement upon the company to respond honestly at the bargaining table to union inquiries with respect to company plans which may have a significant impact on the bargaining unit, the effect of requiring the employer to initiate discussion on matters which are not yet decided within his organization would be of marginal benefit to the trade union and could serve to distort the bargaining process and create the potential for additional litigation between the parties. The section 14 duty, therefore, does not require an employer to reveal on his own initiative plans which have not become at least de facto decisions.

Does this sound familiar? Assumptions are made here in the guise of practical industrial relations thinking. The major one is that the Board can and should predict that any effort to bargain collectively (and thus possibly co-determine outcomes) would not have a desirable but rather an adverse effect because the union would act irrationally. . . .

. . . Nondisclosure of plans (not finalized) to shutdown, relocate, or contract out work is simply inconsistent with a duty to bargain in good faith. In *Westinghouse*, the Board avoided this conclusion by wrongly assuming that some issues were not within the scope of the duty. The Board did respond that the union position is adequately protected by the ruling that the employer must respond truthfully to union inquiries about any plans. But the whole point of a duty of disclosure is to put the onus on a party to reveal the information requested. It has always been a deceit to lie in response to a question, even before the Board's holding in *Westinghouse*. As the Board explained in a later decision, "[i]n *Westinghouse* the employer was silent on a substantial issue about which the employer had exclusive knowledge." Well, exactly. Under a system with a duty to bargain in good faith, this provides a complete rationale for disclosure.

From this perspective, the holding in *Westinghouse* that finalized plans must be disclosed looks very peculiar. If we hold that plant relocation is contemplated by our legislation as a fit subject for collective bargaining, then what rational ground can there be for inducing "bargaining" after one party has "finalized its plans?" This remains a mystery. Mac Neil recently and accurately summarized the defects of the *Westinghouse* decision as follows:

> The reason for not requiring the employer to give notice that this type of decision is being considered is said to be that notice would be of marginal benefit to the trade union and would only serve to distort the bargaining process. *The Board seems misguided in its approach.* Firstly, it is acting upon the assumption that the union has and should have no say in the decision-making process. Secondly, it fails to see that rather than distorting the bargaining process, such information rationalizes the process. Both parties should bargain from positions where they each can at least understand the goals and limitations of the other. The bargaining process is distorted if this information is known by only one party. Furthermore, even if the union cannot by reason of inexperience effectively provide useful input into the decision-making process, it will have a greater opportunity to protect the interests of its members by including provisions in the agreement to help through the transition process. By forcing the employer clearly to realize its duty toward the employees that will be affected by a decision to alter operations, the union can help internalize the social costs of the decision.

In summary, if the commitment to the rejection of the limited American approach, and the reasoning underpinning it, regarding the issue of the scope of the duty to bargain is taken seriously, that reasoning should not be let in the back door to limit the *functional content* of that duty.

[Reprinted by permission.]

* * *

Slightly later, in the *Consolidated Bathurst* case below, the Ontario board attempted to respond to some of the criticisms levelled against its *Westinghouse* decision.

International Woodworkers of America, Local 2-69 v. Consolidated Bathurst Packaging Ltd., [1983] O.L.R.B. Rep. 1411 at 1435–45

[From November 1982 until 13 January 1983, the union and the employer negotiated a renewal of the collective agreement covering an all-employee unit in the employer's Hamilton plant. During negotiations, the union sought to persuade the employer to tighten the provisions in the expired agreement dealing with plant closures and severance pay. In the end, the union dropped those demands, and the old provisions were simply renewed. At no point during the negotiations did the company indicate that its Hamilton plant might or would be closed during the term of the collective agreement. On 1 March 1983, a few weeks after the agreement was signed, the employer announced that it was shutting down its Hamilton operation on 26 April 1983.

The union complained that the employer breached its duty to bargain, and advanced three arguments in support of that complaint. First, the union argued that the employer's decision to close the plant had been finalized during bargaining, and therefore had to be communicated to the union under the Westinghouse principle. Alternatively, the union argued that the board ought to reconsider its decision in Westinghouse and require disclosure whenever an employer is "seriously considering an action which if carried out will have a serious impact on employees." Finally, the union urged the board to find a duty to bargain with a union over major and unexpected changes introduced or intended to be introduced during the lifetime of an agreement.

The board refused to extend the duty to bargain into the lifetime of the collective agreement, but after carefully scrutinizing internal and external employer communications on the matter, it held that the employer had in fact made the decision to close the plant before the collective agreement was signed, and that it had therefore violated the duty by failing to disclose that decision during bargaining.]

ADAMS, Chair: Clearly, collective bargaining is an appropriate tool for dealing with the impact of industrial change in a work environment although it is by no means a complete answer to the difficulties thrown up for both labour and management. It enables solutions to be tailored to the needs of the individual participants; trade-offs can be made; and, at the very least, there is the sense of participation in the eventual outcome. Of course, the difficulty with the legal background in Ontario is that the requirement of compulsory no strike clauses together with the absence of a continuing duty to bargain during the term of the agreement, minimizes the likelihood that parties will engage in collective bargaining about these issues. Indeed, it has been pointed out that against the backdrop of the arbitral and collective bargaining framework discussed to this point, there is a real incentive for employers not to make decisions with respect to major change until a union is locked into a collective agreement. . . . Other jurisdictions such as British Columbia, Manitoba, Saskatchewan and the Federal Government have enacted specific provisions to permit bargaining over various types of mid-contract change. . . .

In considering the application of the bargaining duty in this context the Board needs to be sensitive to the limited time span of the duty and the potential for unilateral employer action once the duty ends and a collective agreement is signed. The incentive for non-disclosure or manipulation of decision-making should also be kept in mind when assessing evidence and an employer's stated justification. On the other hand, this Board must be sensitive to the limits of adjudicating policy responses to the general problem of industrial change. The history and complexity of the problem together with the competing values at stake has attracted legislated solutions in other jurisdictions after considerable debate and reflection. An isolated fact situation arising in the context of an unfair labour practice complaint is not a comparable format for fashioning a meaningful policy contribution. The Board must also be sensitive to the statutory purpose of the bargaining duty, the language describing that duty, and the industrial relations implications of one approach over another. A single-minded pursuit of disclosure is inconsistent with the scheme of the Act and sound collective bargaining practices. The same can be said of the opposite direction. The experience before the N.L.R.B. does little to dispel this caution. . . .

We have seen that collective bargaining in Canada has significant temporal as opposed to substantive limitations. These temporal limitations become important in considering and assessing the disclosure requirements Canadian labour boards, such as this one, have begun to fashion through the bargaining duty.

. . . A bargaining agent can claim entitlement to information necessary for it to reach informed decisions and thereby to perform effectively its statutory responsibilities. Disclosure encourages the parties to focus on the real positions of both the employees and the employer. And hopefully with greater sharing of information will come greater understanding and less industrial conflict. Although Canadian experience is limited, the American cases reveal that the employer is under no duty, as a general matter, to provide information until the union makes a specific request for the relevant information. . . . A request identifies a union's interest in specific information and then permits a discussion by the parties on the relevance of the data. The requirement of a request also sharpens a disclosure obligation. Without a request, an employer will be unclear what is needed and why. Indeed, a request is a basic method for receiving information particularly in an adversarial context. A general duty of unsolicited disclosure would be costly, unclear and potentially counter-productive. However, a second and more limited way the bargaining duty requires disclosure arises out of its good faith purpose and does not require a specific request. . . .

One does not have to expand this principle significantly to conclude further that it is "tantamount to a misrepresentation" for an employer not to reveal during bargaining a decision it has already made which will have a significant impact on terms and conditions of employment such as a plant closing and which the union could not have anticipated. Indeed, this is what the Board held in *Westinghouse Canada Limited* in stating:

> Similarly can there be any doubt that an employer is under a section 14 [now section 17] obligation to reveal to the union on his own initiative those decisions already made which may have a major impact on the bargaining unit. Without this information a trade union is effectively put in the dark. The union cannot realistically assess its priorities or formulate a meaningful bargaining response to matters of fundamental importance to the employees it represents. Failure to inform in these circumstances may properly be characterized as an attempt to secure the agreement of the trade union for a fixed term on the basis of a misrepresentation in respect of matters which could fundamentally alter the content of the bargain.

[After reviewing its decision in *Westinghouse*, the board asked itself whether the rulings in that case ought to define the extent of the duty to disclose in the absence of a specific request from the union.]

Against the backdrop of these cases some further reflection is merited. Corporate planning, it is argued, is necessarily complex and dynamic while collective bargaining is an adversarial and tactical process. Typically, unions bargain out provisions on the basis of a work force's experience. For example, as technological change becomes apparent, provisions are sought to cushion the effect. Day to day layoffs are expected and general seniority, recall and severance provisions are negotiated. It is also argued that the parties usually have enough real roadblocks to reaching an agreement without taking to impasse issues which "may" need a collective bargaining response. This may explain why in the *Westinghouse, Sunnycrest . . .* , and *Amoco . . .* cases questions about possible management changes in the future were not asked by *the unions* themselves. Indeed, no request for information was made in the facts at hand. Another disincentive to revealing other than firm decisions without solicitation, it is pointed out, is the uncertainty over when the disclosure obligation arises. At what stage in an employer's thinking about major change is he obligated to reveal "this thinking" to the trade union? Is a recommendation from a corporate planning division sufficient grounds? What if those with the ultimate say have not seen the proposal or have deferred its consideration? What if the planning document contains sensitive information which, on disclosure to the union, might be learned by competitors, customers or suppliers? Premature disclosure may force an adverse decision to be taken that might have been avoided if events had been left to take their course. Corporate thinking about possible closings or relocations may also not be in direct response to labour related costs but rather potential loss of customers, need for expansion or a more advantageous market location. Until a decision is made, is the matter sufficiently ripe for collective bargaining discussions? Another problem relates to the potential severity of labour board remedies. For example the N.L.R.B.'s usual backpay order from the date when disclosure should have been made until an actual impasse is arrived at under a Board bargaining order frequently puts employees in a better position than if the company had met its bargaining obligations, particularly if the plant would have closed anyway. In fact, with this type of order, a trade union might be encouraged not to ask questions about future planning and simply rely on the subsequent assistance of a labour board remedy. It could be reasonably suggested that these types of problems may have contributed to the United States Supreme Court eventually taking plant closure decisions off the bargaining table altogether. What policy justification then supports greater unsolicited disclosure and merits the Board's intervention in the face of these potential difficulties?

Those who argue for unsolicited disclosure beyond firm decisions marshal their arguments along the following lines. They point out that collective bargaining is valuable because of the "say" it gives employees in the decisions which affect them. When an employer fails to disclose changes which are being contemplated, employees are not put on notice of problems which may arise during the term of the agreement. The trade union will, in the usual case, enter into a collective agreement silent on the point which has the effect of providing for unilateral employer initiatives. Secondly, they point out unsolicited disclosure based only on firm decisions is a standard too subject to manipulation. Planning, proposals and decisions can be easily arranged around collective bargaining schedules particularly with the legal onus of proof in an unfair labour practice case involving section 15 residing with the complainant trade union. In response to claimed inherent uncertainty of proposals or plans, they submit that many decisions should not be made without first getting the trade union's response. They argue that in the face of cost-related problems, employees have frequently played a pivotal role in keeping a business functioning or a plant open. They further submit that if such plans are sufficiently concrete to be disclosed when an employer is asked about his intentions by a trade union, as the Westinghouse case suggested, then why is it a factor in the context of disclosure without being asked? In any event, it is submitted that an employee's commitment to a company usually involves years of training, the development of specialized skills and the ordering of his entire life around the employer's business. A decision to shut a plant destroys these human investments in as real a manner as shareholders are affected. It is submitted that some disruption at the bargaining table is a small price to pay for trying to provide workers with a meaningful opportunity to participate in such a fundamental decision. They further point to the fact that from 1966 until just recently the United States labour relations system operated under the *Ozark Trailers Inc.* . . . standard of disclosure which required disclosure once management had "reached the point of thinking seriously about taking such an extraordinary step as relocating or terminating a portion of the business. . . ." It is also pointed out that disclosure of only firm decisions is not likely to set the stage for productive "decision" bargaining. While bargaining does not demand that management ignore its own interests, bargaining is likely to be less productive if management already has its mind made up. It is further emphasized that the bargaining duty only imposes a duty on management to meet and discuss matters with a union. After that, it is free to do as it wishes. Finally, it is submitted that the very unusual and unexpected nature of major business decisions affecting employees explains why trade unions often fail to ask questions about such matters. It is asserted that the failure to ask should be treated, at most, as a technical oversight.

To be accurate, this Board has not said that unsolicited disclosure is only obligated after a board of directors has given its approval. In Westinghouse, the Board used the term *de facto* decision and, we might add, in the context of a decision that was not primarily cost related. In the same decision it also pointed out the supplementary obligation of a company to respond honestly to questions. In this respect we would observe that the bulk of solicited disclosure cases in the United States and the few in Canada that exist have related to factual information or data — wage rates, wage surveys, time studies, insurance costs and other employment related activity. (We point out that this Board has not yet had to set the ground rules to such requests. . . .) Accordingly, it is not at all clear what a company's obligation is, if any, with respect to requests over plans. In *Westinghouse* the Board's reference to requests for such material emphasized the employer's duty to respond "honestly" thereby pointing out that a request could well trigger a misrepresentation which may later be relied upon. Moreover, questions by a trade union on specific plans for significant changes permit the trade union to assess the employer's response and decide whether the issue should be pursued. An equivocal employer response may encourage a bargaining proposal which will not be removed until an acceptable assurance is forthcoming. In short, requests and answers provide a self-regulatory mechanism and permit collective bargaining to resolve these problems, minimizing the need for labour board intervention. A failure to request information of this kind may also, in certain circumstances, suggest the union is satisfied with the appropriateness of a collective agreement (as it will stand) or that it believes it can do little about such significant change — a "What will come, will come" type of attitude. There is also an inherent uncertainty in defining the extent of an unsolicited disclosure duty beyond firm decisions. There is the problem of confidentiality surrounding such plans. And there is the collective bargaining impact of dropping such "incomplete thinking" on a bargaining table. These problems cannot be denied or minimized.

On the other hand, plans and decisions to close a plant can effectively extinguish a bargaining unit and the relevance of the usual terms of a collective agreement. In this context, where a decision to close is announced "on the heels" of the signing of a collective agreement, the timing of such a significant event may raise a rebuttable presumption that the decision-making was sufficiently ripe during bargaining to have required disclosure or that it was intentionally delayed until the completion of bargaining. It can be persuasively argued that the more fundamental the decision on the workplace, the less likely this Board should be willing to accept fine distinctions in timing between "proposals" and "decisions" at face value and particularly when strong confirmatory evidence that the decision-making was not manipulated is lacking. This approach is sensitive to the positive incentive not to disclose now built into our system, and the potential for manipulation. Indeed, a strong argument can be made that the de facto decision doctrine should be expanded to include "highly probable decisions" or "effective recommendations" when so fundamental an issue as a plant closing is at stake. Having regard to the facts in each case, the failure to disclose such matters may also be tantamount to a misrepresentation. We might also point out that there are decisions taken because of costs which really ought not to be made until the underlying problem is discussed with the union to see if adjustments can be made and the decision avoided. However, for the reasons discussed above, we are not willing to adopt the *Ozark*

Trailers test of "thinking seriously" for unsolicited disclosures as urged upon us by the complainant. The failure to reveal such "possibilities" as a general matter is not tantamount to a misrepresentation and therefore lacks the bad faith rationale developed in *Westinghouse* justifying unsolicited disclosure. The purpose of such information would be investigative and to facilitate the rational discussion purpose of the bargaining duty. Accordingly, the purpose of the information and the difficulties detailed above with unsolicited disclosure militate against any substantial expansion of the unsolicited disclosure obligation as elaborated to date. The interests of employees are real but the Board is not ignoring these interests by requiring a questioning approach to disclosure as a general matter. The position urged upon us by the complainant has too much potential for "greater heat than light" at the bargaining table. There is already enough uncertainty over precisely how significant and what nature a decision must be to trigger the unsolicited disclosure duty. Unsolicited disclosure must be understood to be exceptional and centered essentially on a bad faith rationale.

* * *

Applying this reasoning to the facts before it, the board concluded that a *de facto* decision had been made by the employer during negotiations, and that the company's silence amounted to a misrepresentation within the meaning of the Westinghouse doctrine. By way of remedy the board declined, on grounds of practicality, to order the employer to reopen the plant. Instead, it ordered the employer to indemnify the union for the damages it suffered from the loss of opportunity to negotiate on the matter of the plant's closing.

In a world of intensified international competitive pressures, increasingly rapid technological change and growing market uncertainties, restructuring of operations has become increasingly common — and many would argue, often inevitable. But restructuring runs up against the basic assumptions underlying fixed-term collective agreements, which generally have a lifetime of from one to three years. These agreements evolve over time and gradually provide a complex regime of employment rules and entitlements. How should we deal with the consequences of restructuring — by facilitating collective bargaining, or by asking whether it should take place at all? Should we abandon the idea of closed collective agreements, so that the parties can address the fallout of restructuring by resuming collective bargaining before the agreement's term runs out? Or should we look to labour law regimes other than collective bargaining to address the real issues at stake?

7:500 REMEDIES FOR VIOLATING THE DUTY TO BARGAIN

REFERENCES

George Adams, *Canadian Labour Law*, 2d ed. (Aurora, Ont.: Canada Law Book, 1993 — as updated by looseleaf releases) paras. 10.1710–10.2135

In *Radio Shack*, above, section 7:421, in addition to dealing with the content of the duty to bargain, the Ontario board outlined its position on remedies for breach of the duty. The board first stressed that a remedy should not be seen as a penalty. To that end, it held that it would award monetary relief only as compensation to an injured union for pay increases and other benefits it had failed to win as a result of the employer's actions, and not as punitive damages for the employer's breach of the duty to bargain. Second, it held that it could not simply impose a collective agreement on the parties by way of remedy, as this would exceed its statutory mandate and would deviate too far from the principle of free collective bargaining. Instead, the board said, it would resort to other measures such as cease-and-desist orders and orders to bargain in good faith, orders to publish retractions of false or prejudicial statements, and orders to pay the injured party's negotiating costs.

Critics argue that the sorts of relief fashioned by the board in the *Radio Shack* case are not sufficient to secure the objectives of the legislation, and that more far-reaching regulation of bargaining is required. According to those critics, the inability of many groups of employees to negotiate effective rules on matters central to their work relationships, and the poor distributive outcomes they experience under free collective bargaining, point to the need for substantive regulation of bargaining proposals on a standard of reasonableness.

Would it be a good idea for labour boards to move toward such an approach? Does the the Supreme Court of Canada's decision in *Royal Oak Mines*, as reflected in the following excerpt, allow for such an approach?

Royal Oak Mines v. Canada (Labour Relations Board), [1996] 1 S.C.R. 369 at 402–23

[A summary of the facts is given above, in section 7:421. Cory J. set out the test for determining whether a labour board has exceeded its jurisdiction in imposing a particular remedy. The remedy in question in this case was an order that the employer put back on the table an offer it had made earlier in the negotiations, with certain modifications — principally, the addition of a back-to-work protocol specifying that arbitration would be available to adjudicate grievances brought by any employees who were discharged by the employer during the bitter strike which had occurred during bargaining.]

CORY J. (L'Heureux-Dubé and GonthierJJ. concurring): In examining the legislation itself it is apparent that Parliament has clearly given the Canada Labour Relations Board a wide remedial role. The wording of s. 99(2) does not place precise limits on the Board's jurisdiction. In fact, the Board may order anything that is "equitable" for a party to do or refrain from doing in order to fulfil the objectives of the Code. In my view, this was done to give the Board the flexibility necessary to address the ever changing circumstances that present themselves in the wide variety of disputes which come before it in the sensitive field of labour relations. The aims of the *Canada Labour Code* include the constructive resolution of labour disputes for the benefit of the parties and the public. The expert and experienced labour boards were set up to achieve these goals. The problem before the Board was one which Parliament intended it to resolve.

The requirement that the Board's order must remedy or counteract any consequence of a contravention or failure to comply with the Code imposes the condition that the Board's remedy must be rationally connected or related to the breach and its consequences. This requirement is also consistent with the test established in *National Bank of Canada v. Retail Clerks' International Union* . . . , which required that there be a relation between the breach, its consequences and the remedy. Section 99 also provides that the Board may remedy breaches which are adverse to the fulfilment of the objectives of the Code. This empowers the Board to fashion remedies which are consistent with the Code's policy considerations. Therefore, if the Board imposes a remedy which is not rationally connected to the breach and its consequences or is inconsistent with the policy objectives of the statute then it will be exceeding its jurisdiction. Its decision will in those circumstances be patently unreasonable.

. . . In my view the remedy directed by the Board was not patently unreasonable, rather it was eminently sensible and appropriate in the circumstances presented by this case. A judicial review of the order must take into consideration both the complex factual background, and the prior involvement of the Board in this dispute. In this case, the factual background presented to the Board was such that it cried aloud for the imposition of a remedial order.

The unparalleled severity of this labour dispute was well articulated by Dr. Nightingale, a professor at Queen's University who was commissioned by the appellant to study the dispute and advise it as to whether to accept the recommendations of the mediators. He described the course of the dispute in the following terms:

> The complexities of this dispute — including failed conciliation, failed mediation, the rejection of a tentative agreement, a representational dispute within the union, a decertification drive while the strike continues and the continued operation of the mine by the replacement workers — are unusual enough. Add to these, the murder of 9 workers, an ongoing RCMP investigation, intimidation and death threats directed toward miners and their families, violence, including beatings which have spilled over into the community and the Mayor of Yellowknife discussing the possible need for martial law and we have a tragedy without precedent in Canadian labour history. The Black Tuesday clash in the Souris, Saskatchewan coal fields in 1931, the 1969 Inco strike, the 1990 Placer Dome strike and the more recent Brunswick Mining and Smelting strike pale in comparison.

In fashioning an order the Board was obliged to take into account the long violent and bitter history of the dispute. Moreover, the facts in this case are so extraordinary that, if it were necessary, the Board was justified in going to the limits of its powers in imposing a remedy. The appellant's suggestion, that the Board should have rectified the breach by simply ordering the appellant to cease taking such an intractable position on the issue of the dismissed employees and then requiring the parties to recommence bargaining is hopelessly inadequate. In light of the long and turbulent history of the parties' attempted negotiations the typical "cease and desist" order would have been, as the Board described it, "unrealistic and even a cruel waste of time." . . . It was clear that the parties would never come to an agreement on their own with respect to the issue of the dismissed employees. In fact, the Industrial Inquiry Commissioners concluded in their final report that everyone had to be realistic enough to acknowledge that on some of the matters in dispute, "the parties are not likely ever to come to an agreement on their own." Therefore, taking into account this prediction, the unfortunate bargaining history and the effect of the dispute on the community, the Board was correct in recognizing that a more effective remedy was required.

Section 99(2) of the *Canada Labour Code* gives the Board jurisdiction to require an employer "*to do or refrain from doing any thing that it is equitable* to require the employer . . . to do or refrain from doing in order to remedy or counteract any consequence of the contravention or failure to comply that is adverse to the fulfilment of [the] objectives" of the Code. . . .

The breadth of the remedial section gives a clear indication that it was the intention of Parliament that the Board should be given the necessary flexibility to fashion remedies which will best address the entire spectrum of problems and of factual situations which it must confront. It is noteworthy that the section was amended in 1978. Prior to that date, the Code allowed the Board to impose only those remedies which were specifically enumerated. Section 189 (now s. 99(2)) was added in 1978. This provision authorizes the Board to make orders based on the principles of equity. The section now gives the Board both the flexibility and the authority to create the innovative remedies which are needed to counteract breaches of the Code and to fulfil its purposes and objectives. The granting of such a broad discretion to the Board demonstrates that Parliament wished the courts to defer to the Board's experience and expertise in making remedial orders so long as they were not patently unreasonable. . . .

The appellant's prime objection to the Board's remedial order is based on the premise that the Board imposed a collective agreement on the parties, and that in so doing, the Board exceeded its remedial jurisdiction. I cannot accept this contention. The Board did not impose a collective agreement. Instead, the Board made its best effort to identify what the appellant's last offer to the Union had been. The tentative agreement offered by the appellant and thus acceptable to the appellant in April 1992 was the last identifiable proposal put forward by the appellant. While the Union had initially rejected this agreement by an overwhelming majority, the membership had subsequently reconsidered the offer and was prepared to accept it. Therefore, the Board used this tentative agreement, drafted by the appellant, on terms which the appellant was obviously willing to accept as the foundation of its order. The Board ordered the appellant to offer this agreement to the Union, at which time the Union could decide whether or not to ratify it. The Board recognized that the appellant had changed its position regarding some aspects of the tentative agreement. On these, the Board directed the parties to bargain for 30 days and if they failed to reach agreement, they were to be subject to binding arbitration.

It cannot be said that the requirement of the Board that the employer tender the tentative agreement subject to the issues to be negotiated constituted the imposition of a collective agreement. A board is ordinarily acting within its remedial authority in ordering a party to present once again its last offer from which any improper or illegal demands have been deleted. . . . [[T]hat] was accomplished by the Board's reinvoking the tentative agreement. Similarly, a Board generally acts within its remedial jurisdiction when it imposes upon the parties certain terms and conditions of a collective agreement. These two legitimate remedies cannot be added together in order to contend that they constitute an illegal order. There is nothing to suggest that the two remedies are alternatives to each other. In the usual case, one of these remedies would suffice. However, since other efforts to resolve the dispute had been exhausted, the Board concluded that both facets of the order were needed in order to effect a constructive settlement of the dispute.

There are four situations in which a remedial order will be considered patently unreasonable: (1) Where the remedy is punitive in nature; (2) Where the remedy granted infringes the *Canadian Charter of Rights and Freedoms*; (3) where there is no rational connection between the breach, its consequences, and the remedy; and (4) where the remedy contradicts the objects and purposes of the Code. The appellant argued that the Board's order, in this case, failed on both the third and fourth of the above prohibited grounds. Namely, that the order failed both the "rational connection" test and the "policy consistency" test respectively.

(a) Rational Connection

The case of *National Bank* . . . held that there must be a relation between the breach, its consequences and the remedy. However, the necessity for a rational connection is evident from the wording of s. 99(2) which requires that the remedy imposed by the Board be designed to counteract any consequence of the contravention or failure to comply found by the Board. In other words, the Board must be concerned about remedying a specific breach of the Code, and in so doing there must be a relationship between the unfair practice which has occurred, its consequences to the bargaining process, and the remedy imposed.

In the case at bar, there was a clear causal connection between the breach, its consequences and the remedy imposed by the Board. To begin with, the Board identified the breach as being the appellant's intractable position with respect to a form of due process for the dismissed employees. The consequence of this breach was that bargaining was blocked so completely that no collective agreement could ever be reached. As a result of the impasse the serious damage to the community of Yellowknife continued unabated. The nature, extent and effect of the failure to bargain in good faith may in certain circumstances justify, in itself, the imposition of a remedial order. To be valid, such an order must deal with the effect of the breach and comply with the aims and objects of the *Canada Labour Code*. Perhaps more often it will be the failure to bargain in good faith coupled with other factors which will justify a remedial order.

Yet a further consequence of the appellant's intractable position was the frustration of the efforts of the Industrial Inquiry Commission to achieve a settlement. The Commission had recommended that the parties reach an agreement similar to the appellant's April 1992 offer (the tentative agreement), and also suggested that in the four unresolved areas where the appellant had changed its position that the parties should continue to negotiate, with the possibility of binding arbitration if the negotiations failed. The Commission also recommended that the fate of the dismissed employees should be determined in the usual way by third party arbitration. While the Union agreed to the Commission's proposals, the appellant rejected them, primarily because it refused to consider any proposal which would result in the dismissed employees returning to work. Were it not for this the appellant would have, in principle, accepted the recommendations.

Accordingly, the Board ordered the appellant to table an agreement based on its own tentative agreement and the final report of the Commission, including a grievance arbitration clause. This achieved the result that the parties were put back in the position they would have been in were it not for the appellant's violation; namely, with a collective agreement tabled for the Union's consideration. Therefore, there is a clear relation between the appellant's breach of its duty to bargain in good faith, the consequences of that breach and the remedy imposed by the Board.

(b) Policy Consistency
. . .

The appellant contends that the promotion of *free* collective bargaining supersedes all the other objectives of the statute and that the Board's remedial order did not respect the principle of free collective bargaining. This position is untenable. It fails to take into consideration all the other factors which made this dispute in the opinion of two very experienced mediators the worst they had known. . . .

Clearly it can never be forgotten that free collective bargaining is a corner stone of the *Canada Labour Code* and of labour relations. As a general rule it should be permitted to function. Nonetheless, situations will arise when that principle can no longer be permitted to dominate a situation. Where the dispute has been bitter and lengthy; the parties intransigent and their positions intractable; when it has been found that one of the parties has not been bargaining in good faith and that this failure has frustrated the formation of a collective bargaining agreement; and where a community is suffering as a result of the strike then a Board will be justified in exercising its experience and special skill in order to fashion a remedy. This will be true even if the consequence of the remedy is to put an end to free collective bargaining. This follows in part because it is the lack of good faith bargaining by a party which is frustrating the bargaining process and in part because of the other principles and factors the Board is required to consider pursuant to the provision of the *Canada Labour Code*.

In the case at bar, the strike had been bitter and long. The intractable position of the appellant that it would not consider some form of due process for dismissed employees was found to constitute lack of good faith. This position of the appellant certainly put an end to any possibility of true bargaining between the parties. The community of Yellowknife was obviously suffering. In those circumstances it was appropriate for the Board to fashion a remedy. The remedy put forward did not impose a collective agreement on the appellant. Rather the Board used as a basis for the bulk of its remedy the tentative agreement drafted and put forward by the appellant. Obviously this agreement was acceptable to the appellant in April 1992. It is true that it had changed its mind with regard to four matters. On those matters the parties were directed to bargain for 30 days and if they failed to reach agreement they would be subject to binding mediation on those issues. In light of the past history of the intransigence of the parties, no other solution was feasible. . . .

The appeal should be dismissed with costs.

✵ ✵ ✵

In *Buhler Versatile Inc.*, excerpted above in section 7:421, the Manitoba Labour Board found that a legal strike which lasted for more than four months had been precipitated by the employer's serious breaches of the duty to bargain. The major remedy granted by the board was the following: that the employer "immediately compensate each employee who is a member of the bargaining unit represented by the union and who was employed by the Employer/Respondent at the time the strike commenced for all lost wages and employment benefits they would have earned had the strike not occurred." As there were 250 employees in the bargaining unit, this amounted to an award of damages in the amount of several million dollars — by far the largest award for breach of the duty to bargain ever made in Canada.

If a union responds to an employer's illegal bargaining tactics not only by bringing a complaint before the labour board but also by calling a strike, is it appropriate for the board to require the employer to pay employee wages lost as a result of the strike?

7:600 NEW APPROACHES TO COLLECTIVE BARGAINING

Jurisprudence on the duty to bargain strives to protect and reinforce the union's status as exclusive bargaining agent, but it does not tell us much about what actually occurs at the bargaining table. The form of bargaining that traditionally prevails is often called positional or adversarial bargaining, and most of the cases we have looked at in this chapter accept it as the normal approach to union-management negotiations. In Michel Grant's words,

> An important tactical objective in traditional bargaining is keeping the opponent from getting accurate knowledge about one's real position on contentious issues. Only enough information is conveyed to let the other side know what one wants; the negative implications which one's demands may have on the other side's interests are usually hidden and understated. . . .
>
> . . . Once negotiators have taken positions and committed themselves vis-à-vis their principals and their opponents, they will set about to change their opponents' minds while shunning the possibility of changing their own. Arguments based on reason and logic do not necessarily carry a lot of weight in traditional bargaining. Power is more persuasive than reason!
>
> [Michel Grant, *Shifting from Traditional to Mutual Gains Bargaining: Implementing Change in Canada* (Kingston: IRC Press, Queen's University, 1997) at 6]

In recent years, considerable interest has developed in a different approach, often called interest-based or mutual gains bargaining. R. Fisher and W. Ury's *Getting to Yes: Negotiating Agreement Without Giving In* (New York: Penguin, 1991) put forward an alternative to positional bargaining in the form of principled or mutual gains bargaining, and was greeted with enthusiasm by parts of the North American labour relations community.

In the first excerpt below, Richard Chaykowski and Michel Grant outline how mutual gains or interest-based bargaining might work, and how it differs from the traditional model. In the second excerpt, Charles Heckscher gives a concrete example of how mutual gains bargaining has worked in a Canadian oil refinery. In the final excerpt, Ira B. Lobel sounds a note of caution, arguing that many of the assumptions on which mutual gains bargaining rests do not hold in most unionized workplaces, and that labour relations at these workplaces will inevitably continue to be governed by power-based positional bargaining.

Richard Chaykowski & Michel Grant, "From Traditional to Mutual Gains Bargaining: The Canadian Experience" (May 1995) Collective Bargaining Review 79 at 79, 81–82, 86

While many participatory approaches have been introduced in the workplace, the pace of innovation appears to be much slower at the bargaining table, where distributive tactics, expressed as win-lose and we-us approaches by negotiators, still predominate. In the past decade, the topic of mutual gains bargaining (MGB) has increasingly been scrutinized by those preoccupied with the successful adaptation and survival of collective bargaining. Other terms such as principled negotiation, interest-based bargaining, win-win negotiation and reasoned bargaining are used in referring to this new way of reaching a collective agreement. . . .

The 'interest-based' approach emphasizes the importance of negotiations based on information, persuasion and co-operation while coercion is viewed as dysfunctional and counterproductive. First, . . . negotiations [should] be conducted on the basis of the merits of the issues and the problems to be resolved; the more that principles and standards of fairness, efficiency and scientific merit are brought to bear on the issues at stake, the more likely it is that the exchanges will produce a fair and reasonable package. Second, 'merit-based' or 'principled' negotiations allow the parties to achieve mutual benefits when they focus on interests, not on specific, and potentially entrenched, positions. Third, bargainers have to separate the problems to be resolved from the people negotiating the issues; persons in dispute who are committed to their positions 'are more likely to respond to what the other side has said or done than to act in pursuit of their own long-term interests.' Fourth, refraining from positional bargaining means not committing oneself to specific and detailed demands. Thus, each negotiator is able to freely discuss and examine a variety of options before deciding what course of action to pursue.

Finally, principled negotiation requires that the parties use objective criteria in assessing potential solutions; this method shuns ideological and emotional arguments, and calls for the use of data, information sharing, precedents, etc. Resorting to objective criteria should reduce the number of commitments that are made and then unmade, as often occurs during the traditional bargaining process. Negotiations based on persuasion assumes the ability and the will to listen and to put oneself in the other's place, to communicate, and to be reliable and trustworthy. . . .

The impetus for change away from established bargaining practices tends to be pressure resulting from the business environment. Management and unions often look to avoid costly conflicts, achieve superior bargaining outcomes, or modify the fundamental principles that frame their ongoing relationship in order to effect workplace changes that may yield improved productivity and increased competitiveness. Recognizing that many of the desired responses require changes in the bargaining relationship, mutual gains bargaining offers one approach to change. . . .

An interest-based approach is not necessarily confined to the process of collective bargaining. The participants noted that an interest-based approach may reasonably be extended beyond the process of negotiating a collective agreement to develop change in ongoing aspects of the relationship. Labour-management consensus regarding rules governing the workplace may thus go beyond the formal and legal contract to evolve into more flexible forms of 'common understandings'; for example, the parties may prefer to have the opportunity to opt out of, or to renegotiate, a previous deal on some issue rather than entrench it in a formal contract. Mutual gains bargaining encourages continuous discussion and adaptation of workplace rules as both parties gain experience with those rules and adjust to contextual pressures.

. . . there is no systematic line of distinction to be drawn between union-management relations during the process of collective bargaining and the conduct of the relationship during the term of the contract. Improvements in the ongoing relationship may then shape the approach taken in subsequent rounds of collective bargaining. By widening the scope of employment conditions that are subject to co-determination, mutual gains bargaining (as a problem-solving technique) may bring significant changes in the nature and role of the collective agreement itself.

[*Collective Bargaining Review* is a publication of Human Resources Development Canada. Reproduced with the permission of the Minister of Public Works and Government Services Canada, 1997.]

Charles Heckscher, "Searching for Mutual Gains in Labor Relations" in L. Hall, ed., *Negotiation: Strategies for Mutual Gain* (Newbury Park, CA: Sage Publications, 1993) 86 at 95–96

The most extraordinary case of mutual gains relations that I have seen is a Shell chemical refinery in Sarnia, Canada. This plant, which began operations in 1978, is organized in teams: Any one of six teams, with 20 workers each, can run the normal operation on its own. The teams are largely self-governing. Although they began with two management-appointed coordinators, the number and responsibilities of these coordinators have been steadily reduced. Teams manage their own work assignments, scheduling, training, and most issues of discipline. Representatives of the teams, along with management and the union, form a review board that oversees most of the governance issues in the plant.

There is a union here: The Energy and Chemical Workers. They conduct contract negotiations on a 3-year cycle, as in the rest of the industry. What is unusual is the outcome: The contract is less than 10 pages long, compared with 65 pages at a neighboring plant. Only the most basic issues of wages and benefits are put into the contract. The rest — including central concerns such as vacation and overtime scheduling, pay progression, hours of work, and the grievance procedure — is left to a more organic and informal document called the Good Works Practices Handbook. The handbook can be revised by the review board at any time. There have been no strikes in the life of the plant.

This system includes mutual gains bargaining in a highly developed form. The shift schedule, to take just one example among many, was initially unique in the industry: Based on a 12-hour shift, it allows workers to spend a startling two thirds of their time on days, with more free blocks on weekends than at comparable plants. The idea came out of a long process of investigation and brainstorming by workers early in the life of the plant. Both union officials and management were initially opposed to the plan, which ran against long tradition in the industry, but it turned out to be highly successful by every criterion — increasing operating efficiency as well as employee satisfaction. The same process has been successfully applied to other issues, which have often led to strikes in other contexts: Shift schedules, progression systems, technological innovation, and supervisory roles, to name a few, have undergone major changes in policy as a result of discussions within the teams and the review board.

There is no doubt that these employees are highly skilled at negotiating. But what I want to draw attention to is the context that makes it possible:

1. Virtually total sharing of information: The computer records of the company's operations, including productivity and profit figures, are accessible by all employees.
2. Extensive training: Management provides courses in problem solving and team relations as part of the orientation procedure. In addition, the union organizes periodic discussions and reviews of the plant's development, both informally on the job and formally off site.
3. A flexible work force: The workers were deliberately selected with no prior industry experience; they averaged 30 years of age and had a minimum of 12 years of education. They had few preconceptions either about their jobs or about union-management relations, and they had the conceptual skills to deal with complex issues.
4. Support from the parent institutions: The national union is almost unique in the high level of involvement of its rank-and-file members and has consistently backed the innovations at Sarnia. Shell corporate management has been less sure but has been persuaded at crucial points to keep its hands off the system, even when it conflicted with central directives and procedures.

I might add to this context a relatively stable competitive environment. There have been some reductions in the work force over the decade-long life of the plant, but none that required forced layoffs; the pressure has remained within manageable bounds. We do not know yet how far those bounds can be pushed.

[Copyright © 1993 by Sage Publications. Reprinted by permission of Sage Publications, Inc.]

Ira B. Lobel, "Labor-Management Cooperation: A Critical View" (1992) 43 Labor L.J. 281 at 284–88

Collective bargaining . . . involves a multi-issue, multi-person process that makes the categorization of the bargaining process not only impossible but also inappropriate. Union and management, and various groups within each, may have different goals and aspirations in each set of negotiations. Categorization of collective bargaining into interest based disputes simplifies the process to an extent that does not take into account the competing and at times conflicting interests of all of the protagonists in a dispute.

For example, a joint interest in making a company more productive may have conflicting effects on various groups within both labor and management. Increased productivity may help a company make more money to compete and survive in today's economy. Increased productivity may also involve a reduced work force, which may mean laying off employees and thereby posing a practical dilemma for a union and specific employees. Determining who will get laid-off can (and probably should) become a major source of discussion and conflict.

Interest-based bargaining assumes that both benefits and costs, if any, among all the affected parties (from the CEO to the janitor) will be the same. Unfortunately, they rarely are. One group's interests may involve increased profits; another group's interests may be higher wages; another group may simply involve maintaining a job until retirement; and still another group may be interested in increased power. It is simply not realistic to believe that 'betterment of the business,' whatever this means, has the same priority for all employees.

Conflict often revolves around how a finite pie is to be divided. Without even considering the question of stockholders' profits versus employees' interest, one need not look very far in actual bargaining situations to see the complexity of this type of conflict (i.e., Nurses getting more than other groups in a hospital and maintenance men getting an additional adjustment in a manufacturing plant. While all parties in a hospital or plant may understand the need and rationale for this type of adjustment, the reality to many employees is that giving more to a nurse or a maintenance man will in effect mean that he or she gets less).

One of the underlying principles of 'win-win' bargaining is that the 'pie,' or the amount of money available for wages and benefits, can be expanded. While labor management cooperation may often generate increased productivity and thus improve profits, cooperative efforts in many cases simply allow a company to hold its own or stop losing quite as rapidly. In some situations, due to outside forces, business may still decrease. If the pie does not increase, positional or distributive bargaining will remain an important and vital part of the process to help determine how a finite pie gets divided. While interest-based negotiations are appropriate for certain cases or issues, the parties should understand that if there is no resolution of an interest-based dispute, one side will often resort to power and attempt to impose their will on the other.

Certain issues in collective bargaining are more conducive than others to interest-based negotiations. Negotiators and mediators have often attempted to get the parties to work together to resolve these types of issues. For example, orderly systems for promotion, lay-off, and transfer are usually desirable for both a company and a union. Usually based on some form of seniority, these systems are often difficult for any outsider, mediator or otherwise, to fully understand. In many instances, mediators will bring union and management together, and, by asking questions and making suggestions, get the parties to verbalize their various interests. For these types of issues, interest based bargaining works extremely well.

For certain issues, however, the amount of a wage increase, the size of a pension benefit, or the number of holidays, interest-based bargaining simply does not deal with the reality of parties wanting to divide a finite (or shrinking) amount of money in different ways. Cooperation does not necessarily increase the size of the pie.

Collective bargaining, when used as a means for determining wages, hours, and conditions of employment, has always been, and probably always will be, a power-based system. Rights-based bargaining has been used extensively for the resolution of grievances, but rarely do rights get involved in the resolution of the contents of a collective bargaining agreement.

Interest-based negotiations can be a valuable tool available to the parties and the mediators. Interest-based bargaining is particularly appropriate when dealing with specific issues, such as seniority, productivity and possibly health insurance, but not appropriate with the entire collective bargaining agreement (primarily when economic issues are involved).

Interest-based bargaining will have increased utility when management looks more toward long-term solution of business problems. Eliminating concern over layoffs and loss of jobs will do much to allow both sides to concentrate on long term solutions to what may be significant business problems. Workers and management may be much more cooperative if they believe their livelihood is not at stake. Commitments analogous to the Japanese system of lifetime job security helps give employees the security to make suggestions that may eliminate their particular job. Disruptions caused by layoffs, shutdowns takeovers, and buyouts do not promote any type of cooperative attitude among groups of employees.

[Reproduced with permission from the author. © 1992, CCH Incorporated. All rights reserved.]

* * *

Consider whether any aspects of the jurisprudence on the duty to bargain might discourage a move toward mutual gains bargaining.

7:700 FIRST CONTRACT ARBITRATION

REFERENCES

George Adams, *Canadian Labour Law*, 2d ed. (Aurora, Ont.: Canada Law Book, 1993 — as updated by looseleaf releases) c. 10, paras. 10.2140–2237; Donald Carter *et al.*, *Labour Law in Canada*, 5th ed. (Markham, Ont.: Butterworths, 2002) 294–95

Most Canadian jurisdictions make some provision for interest arbitration if the parties do not reach a settlement in negotiations for the first collective agreement after certification. Those provisions differ significantly across the country, on such matters as these:

1) whether the labour ministry screens applications for first contract arbitration, to decide which cases will proceed;

2) whether the labour board ultimately has discretion as to whether to impose a collective agreement;

3) whether the terms of the agreement are to be decided upon by the labour board or by an arbitrator; and

4) whether a finding of breach of the duty to bargain is a pre-requisite to the invocation of the first contract arbitration process.

Manitoba is the only jurisdiction that provides not only for first contract arbitration but also for the imposed arbitration of subsequent collective agreements in cases where there has been bad faith bargaining or where it is unlikely that a settlement will be reached: Manitoba *Labour Relations Act*, sections 87.1–87.3.

Yarrow Lodge Ltd. et al v. Hospital Employees' Union et al. (1993) BCLRB No. B444/93 (British Columbia Labour Relations Board) December 30, 1993

STAN LANYON, Chair:

. . . [T]he principles which we draw from the past experience of the British Columbia Labour Relations Board, our examination of other jurisdictions in Canada, and the policies which now underlie Section 55 [the first contract arbitration provision of the British Columbia *Labour Relations Code*], are as follows:

1. First collective agreement imposition is a remedy which is designed to address the breakdown in negotiations resulting from the conduct of one of the parties. It is not simply an extension of the unfair labour practice remedies for egregious employer conduct.

2. The process of collective bargaining itself, to whatever extent possible, is to be encouraged as the vehicle to achieve a first collective agreement.

3. Mediators should be assigned early into first collective agreement disputes in order to facilitate and encourage the process of collective bargaining and to educate the parties in the practices and procedures of collective bargaining.

4. The timing of the imposition of a first collective agreement (if it is deemed appropriate that one be imposed) should not be at the end of the negotiation process when the relationship has broken down and is irreparable, but rather should take place in a "timely fashion," after the mediator has identified "the stumbling blocks" in the dispute and what is needed in order to "avoid" an irreparable breakdown in the collective bargaining relationship.

In applying these principles, we now set out the following factors which the Board will employ in assessing the conduct of the parties in making its determination under Section 55(6)(b) — whether or not to impose a first collective agreement. The factors are as follows:

a) bad faith or surface bargaining;

b) conduct of the employer which demonstrates a refusal to recognize the union;

c) a party adopting an uncompromising bargaining position without reasonable justification;

d) a party failing to make reasonable or expeditious efforts to conclude a collective agreement;

e) unrealistic demands or expectations arising from either the intentional conduct of a party or from their inexperience;

f) a bitter and protracted dispute in which it is unlikely the parties will be able to reach settlement themselves.

This list is not exhaustive. The Board will monitor first contract applications to possibly refine or amend these factors in the future. . . .

In reviewing the past policy of the Board and the policy of other jurisdictions in Canada, we set out the following criteria to be used by arbitrators in determining the terms and conditions of a first collective agreement. These criteria are in addition to the points made above concerning the term of an imposed collective agreement and the inclusion of certain fundamental collective agreements rights.

Our objective is to provide arbitrators with both guidance and flexibility in determining the actual terms and conditions of employment. These factors are as follows:

1. A first collective agreement should not contain breakthrough or innovative clauses; nor as a general rule shall such agreements be either status quo or an industry standard agreement.

2. Arbitrators should employ objective criteria, such as the comparable terms and conditions paid to similar employees performing similar work.

3. There must be internal consistency and equity amongst employees.

4. The financial state of the employer, if sufficient evidence is placed before the arbitrator, is a critical factor;

5. The economic and market conditions of the sector or industry in which the employer competes must be considered.

* * *

In the following excerpt, Jean Sexton evaluates the operation of the various regimes of first contract arbitration across Canada. He concludes that although only the Quebec experience could be called an unqualified success, first contract arbitration could be an important and effective remedy in other Canadian jurisdictions if their labour relations boards were prepared to use it as extensively as it has been used in Quebec.

Jean Sexton, "First Contract Arbitration: A Canadian Invention" (1991) 1 Lab. Arb. Y.B. 231 at 236–40

The original objectives of first contract provisions were twofold: first, "to put an end to the current dispute" and, second, "to allow the parties to get used to each other and lay the foundations for a more mature and enduring relationship." Evaluation should therefore be on the basis of these objectives. Experiences have been different, as have been the results.

In British Columbia, no single dispute has been referred to the Labour Relations Board since 1979, most likely for political reasons. B.C.'s experience was therefore very limited since only 12 disputes were resolved by the Board, making it dubious that any firm conclusions can be drawn. In examining this limited experience, both Weiler and Cleveland come to the same conclusion, that the main result has been that these first contract provisions have acted as a deterrent to union recognition conflicts. This point finds further support in the experiences of other jurisdictions.

At the federal level, a similar conclusion can be reached. Between 1978 and 1989, the Board intervened in only 10 cases and imposed a first agreement in only 6. No request has been presented to the Board since 1986. Again, so few cases prohibit any firm conclusions. Moreover, one must add that the Canada Labour Relations Board has chosen to apply these first contract provisions in a somewhat restrictive manner so that the parties are reluctant to seek Board intervention.

The Québec experience is totally different. First contract provisions have been regularly applied since they came into force in February 1978. Between that date and March 31, 1987, the Minister of Labour received some 532 requests for first contract arbitration, granted 257 of them (48.3 per cent) and refused 234 demands (43.9 per cent). At the time these data were collected, 41 cases were under review.

I conducted a study of this experience with a special emphasis on what happened after the imposition of a first agreement in all of the 88 cases where an award was rendered before December 31, 1984. Between February 1, 1978 and December 31, 1984, 376 requests for first contract arbitration were addressed to the Minister of Labour. Of these requests, 205 were granted (54.5 per cent), 165 were refused (43.8 per cent), and 6 were still under investigation at the time these data were compiled. Of the requests, 85.6 per cent came from unions, 13.5 per cent from employers, and 1.3 per cent from both. In only 19.5 per cent of these cases was there a strike or lock-out.

The fact that 205 cases were referred to arbitration by the Minister of Labour does not mean that 205 agreements were imposed. Only 88 arbitration awards were rendered since, in 63 cases, the parties signed an agreement before the arbitration board completed its work. In 12 cases, the board decided not to intervene. Union certification was cancelled in 8 cases and the union withdrew its request in 13 other cases. There were also 8 plant closings and, in one case, the arbitration board declared itself without jurisdiction.

I therefore decided to include in my study all 88 cases where there had been an award. A structured questionnaire was administered by telephone. The parties responded in 72 of the 88 cases (81.8 per cent). In 49 of these 72 cases, the imposed agreement had not yet come up for renewal. Sixteen awards were still in force, bargaining was under way in 4 cases, union certifications were revoked or in the process of cancellation in 16 cases, and there were 10 plant shutdowns. These figures suggest that in 22 of the 88 cases, nothing followed the imposition of a first agreement.

The main results of this research are the following:

- only one third of the arbitration boards also acted as mediators during the process;
- in the large majority of cases, the arbitration board did not impose the entire collective agreement, but only some provisions such as wages, hours of work and seniority, to mention the most important;
- in 23 cases, the agreement was renewed at least once;
- of these 23 cases where at least one renewal of agreement was signed, 17 never used the conciliation, mediation or arbitration services of the Ministry of Labour;

- in total, there were 36 renewals of agreement, only 4 strikes occurred and there were no lock-outs;
- bargaining for renewal was relatively expeditious; in only 8 cases were 4 months or more necessary, and in 12 cases it took less than a month;
- nearly half the firms have seen grievances brought to arbitration; for these, between one and five grievances were arbitrated;
- the major disagreement during renewal bargaining was said to be over wages (26 out of 36 cases);
- a comparison of the contents of imposed first agreements and freely bargained agreements in similar industries suggests that arbitrators are more conservative on monetary provisions and as liberal on nonmonetary issues. One exception must be noted: the length of the agreement is greater for freely bargained contracts than for imposed agreements. . . ;
- the labour climate was assessed by respondents in 26 of the renewals. Management described it as from good to excellent in 24 cases while unions shared this view in only 14 cases. Both agree, however, that the climate has improved over time and that they have learned to speak to one another and to come to agreements.

The Québec experience is especially interesting because it has been mostly concentrated in small bargaining units. This tends to contradict Weiler's conclusion that "if the agreement is to have any chance of enduring, the bargaining unit must be large." The examination of the Québec experience supports, at least in part, Weiler's view that "the agreements that the parties will write on their own, under the pressure of a strike, are likely to be much better than those that would be imposed by an outside government agency." However, the data indicated that this was the case for monetary issues only. . . .

First contract arbitration has been shown to be a useful and necessary remedy in those Canadian jurisdictions where it has been given sufficient use. The Québec . . . experience suggest[s] that the more time passes and the greater the number of cases referred, the more successful this remedy will be not only in terms of putting an end to a current dispute but also in terms of getting the parties used to each other and into a more mature and enduring relationship. The deterrent effect is surely noted. But it is still greater when first contract arbitration is known and used. In Québec, no one from either management or unions requested that these provisions be eliminated from the *Labour Code* or that they be made ineffective.

Four further points should be stressed. First, there has been a tendency in Québec and then in Ontario, not to systematically refer cases of arbitration to Labour Boards or their equivalent, but to use arbitrators. I would tend to endorse this approach for reasons of flexibility and efficiency. Moreover, in difficult and very publicized cases, a decision of a Labour Relations Board could affect its credibility and even its perceived neutrality. Finally, most arbitrators are less prone to be as legalistic in approach as the Labour Boards.

Second, the initiator of the idea in B.C. decided that the imposed agreement should be for one year. Weiler agrees that there should be a two year agreement, which would allow time to engage in visible administration of the contract in order to demonstrate the value of collective bargaining in action. Québec and Ontario have followed this path. Bearing in mind this same objective, I suggest going even further. I see no reason why an imposed first agreement could not be as long as the maximum duration of a freely bargained agreement (three years in Québec). Surely, this would be in keeping with the objectives of first contract arbitration.

Third, experience, mostly in Québec, shows that attempts by the arbitrator to engage first in conciliation or mediation are likely to bring successful results. In fact, in most cases arbitrators do not have to arbitrate; they conciliate or mediate, using the threat of arbitration as bargaining power.

Fourth, the success of first contract arbitration largely rests in the hands of its administrators. There is always the danger of a party applying for first contract arbitration in the hope of obtaining more through this process than through regular collective bargaining. The challenge for the administrator is to identify those cases where collective bargaining is not working, while refusing those which do not meet this test.

[Reprinted by permission of Lancaster House Publishing.]

Chapter 8: **Industrial Conflict**

8:100 SOCIAL SIGNIFICANCE AND POLICY PERSPECTIVES

8:110 Industrial Pluralism and Industrial Conflict

As we have seen in the preceding chapter, labour boards have increasingly regulated the bargaining process in recent years. Nevertheless, under general labour relations legislation everywhere in Canada, the ultimate means of dispute resolution is the use of economic sanctions. Thus, the ability to maintain or withstand a work stoppage remains central to collective bargaining. If a union cannot win a strike or lockout, it will probably not get a favourable agreement, and it might not get an agreement at all. In the end, though, only a small minority of bargaining rounds actually lead to strikes or lockouts. For example, in 1988 7 percent of all negotiations for major collective agreements resulted in a work stoppage.

Although the prospect of economic sanctions is generally considered to be a crucial part of the bargaining process, a primary factor driving the evolution of Canadian labour law has been a desire to limit what are seen as the detrimental effects of strikes. The earliest efforts at labour regulation in Canada involved a unitary approach which tended simply to repress strikes, leaving employees unable to withdraw their labour collectively. When this approach proved incapable of containing industrial unrest, Canadian governments (from the late 1800s on) began to move toward a pluralist approach, relying more on dialogue and accommodation as the principal road to industrial peace.

Over the years, this pluralist approach has come to predominate in Canadian public policy. Negotiation and compromise are encouraged, while repression is used more sparingly, in the background. Employers are required to recognize and bargain with certified bargaining agents, and recourse to economic sanctions is hedged about with a set of legal restrictions. On occasion, non-binding third-party intervention by mediators, conciliators, fact finders, and others pushes the parties toward agreement.

A few analysts have argued that legislatures should go further, banning strikes altogether and substituting some form of third-party arbitration of the terms of employment (usually called interest arbitration). They claim that this would not only eliminate disruption but would also lead to outcomes based on justice rather than on sheer economic power. See, for example, David Beatty's criticisms of collective bargaining in "Ideology, Politics and Unionism," above, at 1:530. Canadian policymakers have consistently rejected this option, except in "essential services" and, in some provinces, in other public services. The most common reasons for the reluctance to accept interest arbitration are the absence of agreed standards on which to base awards, the inability of arbitrators to take account of all the economic variables relevant to wage setting in a predominantly market economy, and the danger that the results will be less acceptable to the parties. In recent years, the determination of governments to reduce the public debt has made them more reluctant to leave public sector wage settlements in the hands of arbitrators. We will return to this debate later, in section 8:600.

The rejection by governments of a general system of interest arbitration, combined with a continuing desire to prevent industrial disruption, has led to a persistent tension in Canadian labour regulation. On the one hand, governments try to push the parties to settle their disputes without strikes, by imposing a series of hurdles that must be overcome before economic sanctions can lawfully be invoked. On the other hand, governments generally (though decreasingly) disclaim any influence over the content of settlements.

This distinction between process and outcome is difficult to maintain. In Chapter 7 we saw that labour relations boards, despite misgivings, do to some extent scrutinize substantive bargaining positions in administering the duty to bargain, and in first-contract arbitration they do indeed impose collective agreement terms. Even when boards do not rule on the parties' bargaining positions, the regulation of the process cannot help but influence the outcome. In the materials on strike regulation that follow, you will find echoes of the debate (noted in Chapter 7) on the duty to bargain. In the pluralist literature, the discussion of strike regulation is frequently cast in terms of equality of bargaining power. A certain structure is said to be justified because it promotes equality of bargaining power; another is rejected because it would tip the balance excessively.

The following excerpt states the classic pluralist conception of the role of strikes in collective bargaining.

Paul Weiler, *Reconcilable Differences: New Directions in Canadian Labour Law* (Toronto: Carswell, 1980) at 64–66

It is understandable that there is growing exasperation among the press, the politicians and the general public, about Canada's dismal record of industrial unrest. Nor is it any consolation to explain that much of the recent trend is due to the fact that many of our public sector bargaining relationships were new and immature. Loss of public services due to strike action is not the answer to the problem; to many people that *is* the problem. We hear again the refrain that economic warfare is an outmoded and atavistic method of settling labour disputes. The law must provide a better way to replace such crude, primitive methods of self-help. We have already banned strike action as the means of settling recognition issues or contract grievances. Why should we not complete the circle and ban strikes about negotiating disputes as well, at least in a wide range of important industries? And of course, no one would want to single out just the trade unions for such restrictive action. It is assumed that lockouts by employers would be prohibited as well.

I dare say that there would be near unanimous consensus among the professionals in labour-management relations that that kind of proposal is terribly unwise. They believe that there is, if not a logical necessity, at least a natural affinity between the right to strike and the system of free collective bargaining. Although the elements in that argument are rather commonplace, perhaps it is still worthwhile to spell them out, as a prelude to my discussion of the legal meaning of the right to strike.

The basic assumption of our industrial relations system is the notion of freedom of contract between the union and the employer. There are powerful arguments in favour of that policy of freedom of contract. We are dealing with the terms and conditions under which labour will be purchased by employers and will be provided by employees. The immediate parties know best what are the economic circumstances of their relationship, what are their non-economic priorities and concerns, what trade-offs are likely to be most satisfactory to their respective constituencies. General legal standards formulated by government bureaucrats are likely to fit like a procrustean bed across the variety and nuances of individual employment situations. Just as is true of other decisions in our economy — for example the price of capital investment or of consumer goods and services — so also unions and employers should be free to fix the price of labour at the level which they find mutually acceptable, free of intrusive legal controls.

The freedom to agree logically entails the right to disagree, to fail to reach an acceptable compromise. Most of the time good faith negotiation does produce a settlement at the bargaining table, often without a great deal of trouble. But often enough it does not; and of course it is the failures which generate the visible tumult and shouting. And at that point the collective bargaining system diverges sharply from other components in the market economy.

For instance, if a customer does not like the price for the sale of a car, or a businessman does not like the terms for a bank loan, the assumption is that each will go his own separate way and try to find a better deal elsewhere. The fact that they have reached a deadlock in their individual dealings is not a social problem. That competition among buyers and sellers, lenders and businesses, et al., is the necessary lubricant in the operation of a market economy. But that solution is totally at odds with the system of free collective bargaining. It is precisely because we do not want to allow the employer to quote his price for labour, and to invite his employees to accept those terms or go elsewhere (that is, 'to take it or leave it'), that as a matter of public policy we have fostered the development of collective organization of the employees, to provide a countervailing lever to the bargaining position of their employers (especially of large organizations and aggregations of capital). The whole point of a union is to act as a cartel in the supply of labour, to deny the employer an alternative source, and to force it to reach a mutually acceptable agreement about the terms and conditions of employment. The tacit premise underlying the system is that both employment status and collective bargaining relationship will persist indefinitely through one series of negotiations after another. And it is precisely for that reason that the means of resolving deadlocks in negotiations between union and management becomes a serious social issue.

At the same time we must appreciate the very different perspectives of the employer and the union on that subject. The employer typically has no direct and immediate interest in successfully getting the new contract settlement. That settlement almost invariably will provide for compensation increases, often in sizable amounts. All other things being equal, the employer would just as soon stick with the status quo. (Indeed in an inflating economy unchanged money wage rates mean real gains to the employer and real losses to its employees.) It is the union which ordinarily must take the initiative to move negotiations off dead centre. True, that is not always the case. Sometimes the status quo may be distasteful to the employer. It may have lost an arbitration award interpreting the previous agreement, an award now giving a monetary windfall to its employees. Or it may have had to use unnecessary and costly levels of manpower in its operations (for example manning the presses of a newspaper). Suppose the employer cannot get an agreement from the union to change these requirements in a new contract. In that event, management is entitled to act unilaterally. It can simply post an announcement to its employees that it is reducing the price it will pay for labour and the amount of labour that it is going to use. That is what it means for management to exercise the rights of property and of capital; to be able to propose the terms upon which it will purchase labour for its operations.

What rights and resources do the employees and their union have in response? In essence, they have only the collective right to refuse to work on those terms, to withdraw their labour rather than to accept their employer's offer. That is what a strike consists of. What is its function in the larger collective bargaining system? What contribution does the strike make to resolving the impasse? The employer's operations are shut down without any employees to run them. The employer loses the flow of revenues. In turn the employees are out of work, deprived of their earnings. Thus both sides are being hurt economically. They experience viscerally the pain of disagreement with their opposite numbers at the bargaining table. Soon they realize that it is much less painful to agree, even if they do have to move considerably closer to the terms proposed by the other side. In that way strike action plays an indispensable role in resolving deadlocks in a collective bargaining relationship.

. . . It is a common experience in industrial relations to achieve a midnight settlement on the eve of the strike deadline in difficult negotiations. The ability to compromise simply would not be there unless the parties were both striving mightily to avoid the harmful consequences of a failure to settle. In the larger system it is the credible threat of the strike to both sides, even more than its actual occurrence, which plays the major role in our system of collective bargaining.

Thus a simple legal ban on strike action is totally unacceptable if we are going to have free collective bargaining. I do not mean to suggest that the right to strike is a fundamental, inalienable, personal right, as many trade-unionists assert. The legal right to strike is justified not on account of its intrinsic value, but because of its instrumental role in our larger industrial relations system. We can, and we have, prohibited strikes at many points in the system; for example in the administration of the collective agreement, because we have concluded that there are better techniques for performing that task of dispute resolution: grievance arbitration. But so far we have not been able to agree on an acceptable alternative for contract negotiation disputes, and thus the strike continues to be the indispensable lesser evil in that setting.

[Reprinted by permission.]

✵ ✵ ✵

Professor Weiler begins the above discussion by referring to Canada's "dismal record" of industrial unrest. He was writing at the end of the 1970s, which saw considerable labour upheaval, due in part to inflationary pressures and to the impact of federal anti-inflation legislation. The incidence of strikes has decreased markedly in more recent decades. A comparison of the figures during and after the economic slowdowns of 1982 and 1991 shows us, among other things, that collective bargaining is not insulated from general market forces. The ability to win a strike depends in part on the employer's ability to replace strikers with new workers. This in turn depends on such factors as the rate of unemployment and the skill level of the workforce. The employer's ability to withstand a strike also depends on its position in the product market. At a time of low demand for its goods, the employer may lose little from a temporary shutdown. Striking employees may also find it harder to maintain a strike when other work is scarce. Increasingly, especially in the private sector, unions have had to take account of the fact that international competition may reduce the employer's ability to pay higher wages or to improve other terms and conditions. Because willingness to begin job action often depends on the likelihood of success, strike rates tend to reflect changes in general economic conditions.

What is the true impact of strikes in terms of lost production, profits, and wages? In the mid-1980s the average Canadian worker lost a little less than half a day's work per year because of industrial disputes. But because of the disproportionate effect of strike losses on certain sectors, this small figure represents a considerable social loss, though how much of a loss is difficult to calculate.

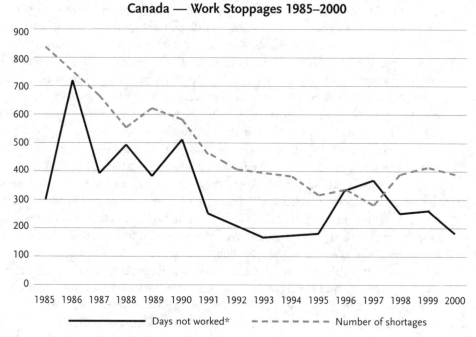

Canada — Work Stoppages 1985–2000

*Days not worked are measured in units of 10,000
Source : Workplace Information Directorate — HRDC

8:120 A Constitutional Right to Strike?

In the years since the adoption of the *Canadian Charter of Rights and Freedoms* in 1982, unions have brought several *Charter*-based challenges to laws which restrict or abrogate the right to strike. That right is not expressly guaranteed in the *Charter*, but unions have argued that it is included in the section 2(d) guarantee of "freedom of association." Other provisions of the *Charter* have also been invoked, such as the guarantee of liberty in section 7 and freedom of expression in section 2(b). However, it is mainly freedom of association that has been relied on, in Canada and elsewhere, as the potential foundation for a constitutional right to strike.

The Supreme Court of Canada addressed the meaning of freedom of association for the first time in the following case, which was one of three decisions (often called the right to strike trilogy) released simultaneously. The brief majority judgment was written by LeDain J. A more detailed analysis was offered in McIntyre J.'s concurring opinion.

Reference Re Public Service Employee Relations Act (Alberta) (1987), 87 C.L.L.C. para. 14,021 at 12,151–63

LE DAIN J.: . . . I agree with McIntyre J. that the constitutional guarantee of freedom of association in s. 2(d) of the *Canadian Charter of Rights and Freedoms* does not include, in the case of a trade union, a guarantee of the right to bargain collectively and the right to strike. . . .

In considering the meaning that must be given to freedom of association in section 2(d) of the *Charter* it is essential to keep in mind that this concept must be applied to a wide range of associations or organizations of a political, religious, social or economic nature, with a wide variety of objects, as well as activity by which the objects may be pursued. It is in this larger perspective, and not simply with regard to the perceived requirements of a trade union, however important they may be, that one must consider the implications of extending a constitutional guarantee, under the concept of freedom of association, to the right to engage in particular activity on the ground that the activity is essential to give an association meaningful existence.

In considering whether it is reasonable to ascribe such a sweeping intention to the *Charter* I reject the premise that without such additional constitutional protection the guarantee of freedom of association would be a meaningless and empty one. Freedom of association is particularly important for the exercise of other fundamental freedoms, such as freedom of expression and freedom of conscience and religion. These afford a wide scope for protected activity in association. Moreover, the freedom to work for the establishment of an association, to belong to an association, to maintain it, and to participate in its lawful activity without penalty or reprisal is not to be taken for granted. That is indicated by its express recognition and protection in labour relations legislation. It is a freedom that has been suppressed in varying degrees from time to time by totalitarian regimes.

What is in issue here is not the importance of freedom of association in this sense, which is the one I ascribe to section 2(d) of the *Charter*, but whether particular activity of an association in pursuit of its objects is to be constitutionally protected or left to be regulated by legislative policy. The rights for which constitutional protection is sought — the modern rights to bargain collectively and to strike, involving correlative duties or obligations resting on an employer — are not fundamental rights or freedoms. They are the creation of legislation, involving a balance of competing interests in a field which has been recognized by the courts as requiring a specialized expertise. It is surprising that in an area in which this Court has affirmed a principle of judicial restraint in the review of administrative action we should be considering the substitution of our judgment for that of the Legislature by constitutionalizing in general and abstract terms rights which the Legislature has found it necessary to define and qualify in various ways according to the particular field of labour relations involved. The resulting necessity of applying section 1 of the *Charter* to a review of particular legislation in this field demonstrates in my respectful opinion the extent to which the Court becomes involved in a review of legislative policy for which it is really not fitted.

MCINTYRE J.: . . . The question raised in this appeal, stated in its simplest terms, is whether the *Canadian Charter of Rights and Freedoms* gives constitutional protection to the right of a trade union to strike as an incident to collective bargaining. . . .

The appellants do not contend that the right to strike is specifically mentioned in the *Charter*. The sole basis of their submission is that this right is a necessary incident to the exercise by a trade union of the freedom of association guaranteed by section 2(*d*) of the *Charter*. The resolution of this appeal turns then on the meaning of freedom of association in the *Charter*.

Freedom of Association and s. 2(d) of the Charter

Freedom of association is one of the most fundamental rights in a free society. The freedom to mingle, live and work with others gives meaning and value to the lives of individuals and makes organized society possible. The value of freedom of association as a unifying and liberating force can be seen in the fact that historically the conqueror, seeking to control foreign peoples, invariably strikes first at freedom of association in order to eliminate effective opposition. Meetings are forbidden, curfews are enforced, trade and commerce is suppressed, and rigid controls are imposed to isolate and thus debilitate the individual. . . .

It is clear that the importance of freedom of association was recognized by Canadian law prior to the *Charter*. It is equally clear that prior to the *Charter* a provincial legislature or Parliament acting within its jurisdiction could regulate and control strikes and collective bargaining. The *Charter* has reaffirmed the historical importance of freedom of association and guaranteed it as an independent right. The courts must now define the range or scope of this right and its relation to other rights, both those grounded in the *Charter* and those existing at law without *Charter* protection. . . .

The Value of Freedom of Association

. . . While freedom of association like most other fundamental rights has no single purpose or value, at its core rests a rather simple proposition: the attainment of individual goals, through the exercise of individual rights, is generally impossible without the aid and cooperation of others. . . .

Our society supports a multiplicity of organized groups, clubs and associations which further many different objectives, religious, political, educational, scientific, recreational, and charitable. This exercise of freedom of association serves more than the individual interest, advances more than the individual cause; it promotes general social goals. Of particular importance is the indispensable role played by freedom of association in the functioning of democracy. . . .

Associations serve to educate their members in the operation of democratic institutions. . . .

Associations also make possible the effective expression of political views and thus influence the formation of governmental and social policy. . . .

Freedom of association then serves the interest of the individual, strengthens the general social order, and supports the healthy functioning of democratic government.

In considering the constitutional position of freedom of association, it must be recognized that while it advances many group interests and, of course, cannot be exercised alone, it is nonetheless a freedom belonging to the individual and not to the group formed through its exercise. While some provisions in the Constitution involve groups, such as s. 93 of the *Constitution Act, 1867* protecting denominational schools, and s. 25 of the *Charter* referring to existing aboriginal rights, the remaining rights and freedoms are individual rights; they are not concerned with the group as distinct from its members. The group or organization is simply a device adopted by individuals to achieve a fuller realization of individual rights and aspirations. People, by merely combining together, cannot create an entity which has greater constitutional rights and freedoms than they, as individuals, possess. Freedom of association cannot therefore vest independent rights in the group. . . .

Collective bargaining is a group concern, a group activity, but the group can exercise only the constitutional rights of its individual members on behalf of those members. If the right asserted is not found in the *Charter* for the individual, it cannot be implied for the group merely by the fact of association. It follows as well that the rights of the individual members of the group cannot be enlarged merely by the fact of association.

The Scope of Freedom of Association in s. 2(d)

Various theories have been advanced to define freedom of association guaranteed by the Constitution. They range from the very restrictive to the virtually unlimited. To begin with, it has been said that freedom of association is limited to a right to associate with others in common pursuits or for certain purposes. Neither the objects nor the actions of the group are protected by freedom of association. This was the approach adopted in *Colly-more v. Attorney-General.* . . .

A second approach provides that freedom of association guarantees the collective exercise of constitutional rights or, in other words, the freedom to engage collectively in those activities which are constitutionally protected for each individual. This theory has been adopted in the United States to define the scope of freedom of association under the American Constitution. Professor L.H. Tribe in his treatise, *American Constitutional Law* (1978), describes the American position, as follows . . . :

[Freedom of association] *is a right to join with others to pursue goals independently protected by the first amendment* — such as political advocacy, litigation (regarded as a form of advocacy), or religious worship.

. . . It will be seen that this approach guarantees not only the right to associate but as well the right to pursue those objects of association which by their nature have constitutional protection.

A third approach postulates that freedom of association stands for the principle that an individual is entitled to do in concert with others that which he may lawfully do alone, and conversely, that individuals and organizations have no right to do in concert what is unlawful when done individually. . . .

A fourth approach would constitutionally protect collective activities which may be said to be fundamental to our culture and traditions and which by common assent are deserving of protection. This approach was proposed by Kerans J.A. in *Black v. Law Society of Alberta*. . . . The court held in that case that legislative restrictions against partnerships for the practice of law between Alberta solicitors and non-resident solicitors violated freedom of association. Speaking for himself, Kerans J.A. stated . . . :

> In my view, the freedom [of association] includes the freedom to associate with others in the exercise of *Charter*-protected rights and *also those other rights which — in Canada — are thought so fundamental as not to need formal expression: to marry, for example, or to establish a home and family, pursue an education or gain a livelihood.* [Emphasis added.]

A fifth approach rests on the proposition that freedom of association, under s. 2(*d*) of the *Charter*, extends constitutional protection to all activities which are essential to the lawful goals of an association. This approach was advanced in *Re Service Employees' International Union, Local 204 and Broadway Manor Nursing Home . . .* by the Ontario Divisional Court. The court held that freedom of association included the freedom to bargain collectively and to strike, since, in its view, these activities were essential to the objects of a trade union and without them the association would be emasculated. . . .

The sixth and final approach so far isolated in the cases, and by far the most sweeping, would extend the protection of s. 2(d) of the *Charter* to all acts done in association, subject only to limitation under s. 1 of the *Charter*. This is the position suggested by Bayda C.J.S. in the *Dairyworkers* case. . . . He said in his reasons for judgment . . . :

> To summarize, a person asserting the freedom of association under para. 2(d) is free (apart from s. 1 of the *Charter*) to perform in association without governmental interference any act that he is free to perform alone. *Where an act by definition is incapable of individual performance, he is free to perform the act in association provided the mental component of the act is not to inflict harm.* . . . [Emphasis added.]

. . . I would conclude that both the fifth approach (which postulates that freedom of association constitutionally protects all activities which are essential to the lawful goals of an association) and the sixth (which postulates that freedom of association constitutionally protects all activities carried out in association, subject only to reasonable limitation under s. 1 of the *Charter*) are unacceptable definitions of freedom of association.

The fifth approach rejects the individual nature of freedom of association. To accept it would be to accord an independent constitutional status to the aims, purposes, and activities of the association, and thereby confer greater constitutional rights upon members of the association than upon non-members. It would extend *Charter* protection to all the activities of an association which are essential to its lawful objects or goals, but, it would not extend an equivalent right to individuals. . . .

The sixth approach, in my opinion, must be rejected as well, for the reasons expressed in respect of the fifth. . . .

I am also of the view that the fourth approach, which postulates that freedom of association embraces those collective activities which have attained a fundamental status in our society because they are deeply rooted in our culture, traditions, and history, is an unacceptable definition. By focusing on the activity or the conduct itself, this fourth approach ignores the fundamental purpose of the right. The purpose of freedom of association is to ensure that various goals may be pursued in common as well as individually. Freedom of association is not concerned with the particular activities or goals themselves; it is concerned with how activities or goals may be pursued. . . .

Of the remaining approaches, it must surely be accepted that the concept of freedom of association includes at least the right to join with others in lawful, common pursuits and to establish and maintain organizations and associations as set out in the first approach. This is essentially the freedom of association enjoyed prior to the adoption of the *Charter*. It is, I believe, equally clear that, in accordance with the second approach, freedom of association should guarantee the collective exercise of constitutional rights. Individual rights protected by the Constitution do not lose that protection when exercised in common with others. People must be free to engage collectively in those activities which are constitutionally protected for each individual. This second definition of freedom of association embraces the purposes and values of the freedoms which were identified earlier. For instance, the indispensable role played by freedom of association in the democratic process is fully protected by guaranteeing the collective exercise of freedom of expression. . . .

One enters upon more controversial ground when considering the third approach which provides that whatever action an individual can *lawfully* pursue as an individual, freedom of association ensures he can pursue with others. Conversely, individuals and organizations have no constitutional right to do in concert what is unlawful when done alone. This approach is broader than the second, since constitutional protection attaches to all group acts which can be lawfully performed by an individual, whether or not the individual has a constitutional right to perform them. It is true, of course, that in this approach the range of *Charter*-protected activity could be reduced by legislation, because the Legislature has the power to declare what is and what is not lawful activity for the individual. The Legislature, however, would not be able to attack directly the associational character of the activity, since it would be constitutionally bound to treat groups and individuals alike. A simple example illustrates this point: golf is a lawful but not constitutionally protected activity. Under the third approach, the Legislature could prohibit golf entire-ly. However, the Legislature could not constitutionally provide that golf could be played in pairs but in no greater number, for this would infringe the *Charter* guarantee of freedom of association. This contrasts with the second approach, which would provide no protec-tion against such legislation, because golf is not a constitutionally protected activity for the individual. Thus, the range of group activity protected by the third approach is greater than that of the second, but the greater range is to some extent illusory because of the power of the Legislature to say what is and what is not lawful activity for the individual. This approach, in my view, is an acceptable interpretation of freedom of association under the *Charter*. It is clear that, unlike the fifth and sixth approaches, this definition of free-dom of association does not provide greater constitutional rights for groups than for indi-viduals; it simply ensures that they are treated alike. . . . It follows from this discussion that I interpret freedom of association in s. 2(*d*) of the *Charter* to mean that *Charter* pro-tection will attach to the exercise in association of such rights as have *Charter* protection when exercised by the individual. Furthermore, freedom of association means the free-dom to associate for the purposes of activities which are lawful when performed alone. But, since the fact of association will not by itself confer additional rights on individuals, the association does not acquire a constitutionally guaranteed freedom to do what is unlawful for the individual.

When this definition of freedom of association is applied, it is clear that it does not guarantee the right to strike. Since the right to strike is not independently protected under the *Charter*, it can receive protection under freedom of association only if it is an activity which is permitted by law to an individual. Accepting this conclusion, the appellants argue that freedom of association must guarantee the right to strike because individuals may lawfully refuse to work. This position, however, is untenable for two reasons. First, it is not correct to say that it is lawful for an individual employee to cease work during the currency of his contract of employment. Belzil J.A., in the Alberta Court of Appeal, in the case at bar, dealt with this point in these words:

> . . . While it is true that the courts will not compel a servant to fulfil his contract of service, the servant is nevertheless bound in law by his contract and may be ordered to pay dam-ages for the unlawful breach of it. It cannot be said that his cessation of work is lawful.

The second reason is simply that there is no analogy whatever between the cessation of work by a single employee and a strike conducted in accordance with modern labour legislation. The individual has, by reason of the cessation of work, either breached or ter-minated his contract of employment. It is true that the law will not compel the specific performance of the contract by ordering him back to work as this would reduce 'the employee to a state tantamount to slavery' (I. Christie, *Employment Law in Canada* (1980), p. 268). But, this is markedly different from a lawful strike. An employee who ceases work does not contemplate a return to work, while employees on strike always contemplate a return to work. In recognition of this fact, the law does not regard a strike as either a breach of contract or a termination of employment. Every province and the federal Parlia-ment has enacted legislation which preserves the employer-employee relationship during a strike. . . . Moreover, many statutes provide employees with reinstatement rights following a strike . . . , and in the province of Quebec the employer is expressly prohibited from replacing employees who are lawfully on strike. . . .

Modern labour relations legislation has so radically altered the legal relationship between employees and employers in unionized industries that no analogy may be drawn between the lawful actions of individual employees in ceasing to work and the lawful actions of union members in engaging in a strike. As Laskin C.J. stated in *McGavin Toastmaster Ltd. v. Ainscough* . . . :

> The reality is, and has been for many years now throughout Canada, that individual relationships as between employer and employee have meaning only at the hiring stage and even then there are qualifications which arise by reason of union security clauses in collective agreements. The common law as it applies to individual employment contracts is no longer relevant to employer-employee relations governed by a collective agreement which, as the one involved here, deals with discharge, termination of employment, severance pay and a host of other matters that have been negotiated between union and company as the principal parties thereto.

It is apparent, in my view, that interpreting freedom of association to mean that every individual is free to do with others that which he is lawfully entitled to do alone would not entail guaranteeing the right to strike. . . . Restrictions on strikes are not aimed at and do not interfere with the collective or associational character of trade unions. It is therefore my conclusion that the concept of freedom of association does not extend to the constitutional guarantee of a right to strike. . . .

Furthermore, it must be recognized that the right to strike accorded by legislation throughout Canada is of relatively recent vintage. It is truly the product of this century and, in its modern form, is in reality the product of the latter half of this century. It cannot be said that it has become so much a part of our social and historical traditions that it has acquired the status of an immutable, fundamental right, firmly embedded in our traditions, our political and social philosophy. There is then no basis, as suggested in the fourth approach to freedom of association, for implying a constitutional right to strike. . . .

While I have reached a conclusion and expressed the view that the *Charter* upon its face cannot support an implication of a right to strike, there is as well, in my view, a sound reason grounded in social policy against any such implication. Labour law, as we have seen, is a fundamentally important as well as an extremely sensitive subject. It is based upon a political and economic compromise between organized labour — a very powerful socio-economic force — on the one hand, and the employers of labour — an equally powerful socio-economic force — on the other. The balance between the two forces is delicate and the public-at-large depends for its security and welfare upon the maintenance of that balance. One group concedes certain interests in exchange for concessions from the other. There is clearly no correct balance which may be struck giving permanent satisfaction to the two groups, as well as securing the public interest. The whole process is inherently dynamic and unstable. Care must be taken then in considering whether constitutional protection should be given to one aspect of this dynamic and evolving process while leaving the others subject to the social pressures of the day. . . . To intervene in that dynamic process at this early stage of *Charter* development by implying constitutional protection for a right to strike would, in my view, give to one of the contending forces an economic weapon removed from and made immune, subject to s. 1, to legislative control which could go far towards freezing the development of labour relations and curtailing that process of evolution necessary to meet the changing circumstances of a modern society in a modern world. . . .

To constitutionalize a particular feature of labour relations by entrenching a right to strike would have other adverse effects. Our experience with labour relations has shown that the courts, as a general rule, are not the best arbiters of disputes which arise from time to time. Labour legislation has recognized this fact and has created other procedures and other tribunals for the more expeditious and efficient settlement of labour problems. Problems arising in labour matters frequently involve more than legal questions. Political, social, and economic questions frequently dominate in labour disputes. The legislative creation of conciliation officers, conciliation boards, labour relations boards, and labour dispute-resolving tribunals, has gone far in meeting needs not attainable in the court system. The nature of labour disputes and grievances and the other problems arising in labour matters dictates that special procedures outside the ordinary court system must be employed in their resolution. Judges do not have the expert knowledge always helpful and sometimes necessary in the resolution of labour problems. The courts will generally not be furnished in labour cases, if past experience is to guide us, with an evidentiary base upon which full resolution of the dispute may be made. In my view, it is scarcely contested that specialized labour tribunals are better suited than courts for resolving labour problems, except for the resolution of purely legal questions. If the right to strike is constitutionalized, then its application, its extent, and any questions of its legality, become matters of law. This would inevitably throw the courts back into the field of labour relations and much of the value of specialized labour tribunals would be lost. . . .

A further problem will arise from constitutionalizing the right to strike. In every case where a strike occurs and relief is sought in the courts, the question of the application of s. 1 of the *Charter* may be raised to determine whether some attempt to control the right may be permitted. This has occurred in the case at bar. The section 1 inquiry involves the reconsideration by a court of the balance struck by the Legislature in the development of labour policy. The court is called upon to determine, as a matter of constitutional law, which government services are essential and whether the alternative of arbitration is adequate compensation for the loss of a right to strike. In the PSAC case, the Court must decide whether mere postponement of collective bargaining is a reasonable limit, given the Government's substantial interest in reducing inflation and the growth in government expenses. In the Dairyworkers' case, the Court is asked to decide whether the harm caused to dairy farmers through a closure of the dairies is of sufficient importance to justify prohibiting strike action and lockouts. None of these issues is amenable to principled resolution. There are no clearly correct answers to these questions. They are of a nature peculiarly apposite to the functions of the Legislature. However, if the right to strike is found in the *Charter*, it will be the courts which time and time again will have to resolve these questions, relying only on the evidence and arguments presented by the parties, despite the social implications of each decision. This is a legislative function into which the courts should not intrude. It has been said that the courts, because of the *Charter*, will have to enter the legislative sphere. Where rights are specifically guaranteed in the *Charter*, this may on occasion be true. But where no specific right is found in the *Charter* and the only support for its constitutional guarantee is an implication, the courts should refrain from intrusion into the field of legislation. That is the function of the freely-elected Legislatures and Parliament.

I would, therefore, dismiss the appeal. . . .

[The reasons of Dickson C.J.C. and Wilson J., dissenting, were delivered by Dickson C.J.C. That dissent included the following discussion of the link between freedom of association and the right to strike in international law, and the relevance of that link to interpretation of the *Charter*.]

[F]reedom of association in the labour relations context has received considerable attention under international law . . .

. . .

International law provides a fertile source of insight into the nature and scope of the freedom of association of workers. Since the close of the Second World War, the protection of the fundamental rights and freedoms of groups and individuals has become a matter of international concern. A body of treaties (or conventions) and customary norms now constitutes an international law of human rights under which the nations of the world have undertaken to adhere to the standards and principles necessary for ensuring freedom, dignity and social justice for their citizens. The *Charter* conforms to the spirit of this contemporary international human rights movement, and it incorporates many of the policies and prescriptions of the various international documents pertaining to human rights. The various sources of international human rights law — declarations, covenants, conventions, judicial and quasi-judicial decisions of international tribunals, customary norms — must, in my opinion, be relevant and persuasive sources for interpretation of the *Charter*'s provisions.

In particular, the similarity between the policies and provisions of the *Charter* and those of international human rights documents attaches considerable relevance to interpretations of those documents by adjudicative bodies, in much the same way that decisions of the United States courts under the Bill of Rights, or decisions of the courts of other jurisdictions are relevant and may be persuasive. The relevance of these documents in *Charter* interpretation extends beyond the standards developed by adjudicative bodies under the documents to the documents themselves. As the Canadian judiciary approaches the often general and open textured language of the *Charter*, "the more detailed textual provisions of the treaties may aid in supplying content to such imprecise concepts as the right to life, freedom of association, and even the right to counsel." J. Claydon, "International Human Rights Law and the Interpretation of the Canadian Charter of Rights and Freedoms" (1982), 4 Supreme Court L.R. 287, at p. 293.

Furthermore, Canada is a party to a number of international human rights Conventions which contain provisions similar or identical to those in the *Charter*. . . . The general principles of constitutional interpretation require that these international obligations be a relevant and persuasive factor in *Charter* interpretation. . . . I believe that the *Charter* should generally be presumed to provide protection at least as great as that afforded by similar provisions in international human rights documents which Canada has ratified.

In short, though I do not believe the judiciary is bound by the norms of international law in interpreting the *Charter*, these norms provide a relevant and persuasive source for interpretation of the provisions of the *Charter*, especially when they arise out of Canada's international obligations under human rights conventions.

(a) The United Nations Covenants On Human Rights

[Dickson C.J.C. discussed the relevant United Nations declarations, principally the *Declaration of Human Rights*, as well as the *International Covenant on Civil and Political Rights and the International Covenant on Economic, Social and Cultural Rights*. Article 8 of the latter Covenant guarantees the right to join a trade union with no restrictions other than those necessary for public order or national security, and guarantees the right of unions to strike "provided that it is exercised in conformity with the laws of the particular country."]

> This qualification that the right must be exercised in conformity with domestic law does not, in my view, allow for legislative abrogation of the right though it would appear to allow for regulation of the right: see *Re Alberta Union of Provincial Employees et al. and the Crown in Right of Alberta* (1980), 120 D.L.R. (3d) 590 (Alta. Q.B.) at p. 597.

[Dickson C.J.C. then discussed article 22 of the *Covenant on Civil and Political Rights*, which guarantees the right to freedom of association, including the right to join a trade union, with the same limitations as article 8 of the *Covenant on Economic, Social and Cultural Rights*.]

(b) International Labour Organization (I.L.O.) *Convention No. 87*

As a specialized agency of the United Nations, with representatives of labour, management, and government, the I.L.O. is concerned with safeguarding fair and humane conditions of employment. In the present appeal, it is important to consider the *Convention (No. 87) Concerning Freedom of Association and Protection of the Right to Organize*, 67 U.N.T.S. 18 (1948), which was ratified by Canada in 1972. . . .

[Dickson C.J.C. listed the various rights protected by I.L.O. *Convention 87*, including the right of workers to organize, draft their own rules, call their own elections, and affiliate with international organizations. The Convention also states that unions cannot be dissolved by national administrative agencies. However, the Convention calls for unions to only exercise their rights pursuant to the "laws of the land" (provided those laws are fair).]

> These provisions have been interpreted by various I.L.O. bodies. . . . The general principle to emerge from interpretations of *Convention No. 87* by these decision-making bodies is that freedom to form and organize unions, even in the public sector, must include freedom to pursue the essential activities of unions, such as collective bargaining and strikes, subject to reasonable limits. . . . The [I.L.O.] Committee of Experts has . . . pointed out

that prohibitions on the right to strike may, unless certain conditions are met, violate *Convention No. 87*:

> In the opinion of the Committee, the principle whereby the right to strike may be limited or prohibited in the public service or in essential services, whether public, semi-public or private, would become meaningless if the legislation defined the public service or essential services too broadly. As the Committee has already mentioned in previous general surveys, the prohibition should be confined to public servants acting in their capacity as agents of the public authority or to services whose interruption would endanger the life, personal safety or health of the whole or part of the population. Moreover, if strikes are restricted or prohibited in the public service or in essential services, appropriate guarantees must be afforded to protect workers who are thus denied one of the essential means of defending their occupational interests. Restrictions should be offset by adequate impartial and speedy conciliation and arbitration procedures, in which the parties concerned can take part at every stage and in which the awards should in all cases be binding on both parties. Such awards, once rendered, should be rapidly and fully implemented. (Freedom of Association and Collective Bargaining: General Survey by the Committee of Experts on the Application of Conventions and Recommendations, Report III (Part 4(B)), International Labour Conference, 69th Session, Geneva, International Labour Office, 1983, at p. 66.)

. . .

These principles were recently applied in relation to a number of complaints originating in Canada, in particular, in Alberta, Ontario and Newfoundland. A number of the provisions impugned as being in violation of Convention No. 87 are the subject of this Reference. It is helpful, in the present context, to look at the Freedom of Association Committee's conclusions and recommendations on the provisions relating to prohibitions on strike activity. These conclusions and recommendations were approved unanimously by the I.L.O.'s Governing Body.

The complaint (Case No. 1247) was launched by the Canadian Labour Congress on behalf of the Alberta Union of Provincial Employees against the Government of Canada (Alberta). In discussing s. 93 of the Public Service Act, which bans strike activity of provincial government employees, the Committee summarized the principles applicable to complaints about infringements of Convention No. 87 as follows:

> 131. The Committee recalls that it has been called to examine the strike ban in a previous case submitted against the Government of Canada/Alberta (Case No. 893, most recently examined in the 204th Report, paras. 121 to 134, approved by the Governing Body at its 214th Session (November 1980). In that case the Committee recalled that the right to strike, recognised as deriving from Article 3 of the Convention, is an essential means by which workers may defend their occupational interests. It also recalled that, if limitations on strike action are to be applied by legislation, a distinction should be made between publicly-owned undertakings which are genuinely essential, i.e. those which supply services whose interruption would endanger the life, personal safety or health of

the whole or part of the population, and those which are not essential in the strict sense of the term. The Governing Body, on the Committee's recommendation, drew the attention of the Government to this principle and suggested to the Government that it consider the possibility of introducing an amendment to the Public Service Employee Relations Act in order to confine the prohibition of strikes to services which are essential in the strict sense of the term. In the present case, the Committee would again draw attention to its previous conclusions on section 93 of the Act.

(I.L.O Official Bulletin, vol. LXVIII, Series B, No. 3, 1985, pp. 34–35). . . .

(c) Summary of International Law

The most salient feature of the human rights documents discussed above in the context of this case is the close relationship in each of them between the concept of freedom of association and the organization and activities of labour unions. As a party to these human rights documents, Canada is cognizant of the importance of freedom of association to trade unionism, and has undertaken as a binding international obligation to protect to some extent the associational freedoms of workers within Canada. Both of the U.N. human rights Covenants contain explicit protection of the formation and activities of trade unions subject to reasonable limits. Moreover, there is a clear consensus amongst the I.L.O. adjudicative bodies that *Convention No. 87* goes beyond merely protecting the formation of labour unions and provides protection of their essential activities — that is of collective bargaining and the freedom to strike. . . .

I am satisfied, in sum, that whether or not freedom of association generally extends to protecting associational activity for the pursuit of exclusively pecuniary ends — a question on which I express no opinion — collective bargaining protects important employee interests which cannot be characterized as merely pecuniary in nature. Under our existing system of industrial relations, effective constitutional protection of the associational interests of employees in the collective bargaining process requires concomitant protection of their freedom to withdraw collectively their services, subject to s. 1 of the *Charter*. . . .

All three enactments prohibit strikes and, as earlier stated, define a strike as a cessation of work or refusal to work by two or more persons acting in combination or in concert or in accordance with a common understanding. What is precluded is a collective refusal to work at the conclusion of a collective agreement. There can be no doubt that the legislation is aimed at foreclosing a particular collective activity because of its associational nature. The very nature of a strike, and its *raison d'etre*, is to influence an employer by joint action which would be ineffective if it were carried out by an individual. . . . It is precisely the individual's interest in joining and acting with others to maximize his or her potential that is protected by s. 2(d) of the *Charter*. . . .

These provisions directly abridge the freedom of employees to strike and thereby infringe the guarantee of freedom of association in s. 2(d) of the *Charter*.

[Dickson C.J.C. then considered whether the legislation could be justified under section 1 of the *Charter*. He concluded that it could not, because the legislation covered workers who did not perform essential services, because it excluded some matters from arbitration without sufficient reason, and because the employees did not have recourse to arbitration as of right.]

* * *

The *Alberta Reference* decision left doubt as to whether aspects of collective bargaining other than the right to strike might still be protected under the constitutional freedom of association. Subsequent decisions of the Supreme Court appear to have resolved that doubt.

Brian Etherington, "An Assessment of Judicial Review of Labour Laws under the *Charter*: Of Realists, Romantics and Pragmatists" (1992) 24 Ottawa L. Rev. 685 at 697–98

In the . . . [*Alberta Reference* decision], three of the six justices made it clear that freedom of association also did not include a right to bargain collectively. McIntyre J., however, was somewhat ambiguous on this question. In his concurring opinion in the PSAC decision he made the obiter comment that his decision on the right to strike did not preclude the 'possibility that other aspects of collective bargaining may receive *Charter* protection under the guarantee of freedom of association.' Nevertheless, that possibility would appear to have been foreclosed by the more recent decision of the Court in *Professional Institute of the Public Service of Canada v. Northwest Territories (Comm'r)* [*PIPS*]. . . .

In *PIPS*, the appellant union had been the bargaining agent for a unit of nurses employed by the federal government in the Northwest Territories until the nurses were made employees of the Territories' government. Under the *Public Service Act* of the Northwest Territories, employees of the government could only be represented in collective bargaining by an association which was incorporated by the Northwest Territories government for the purposes of such bargaining. The decision to recognize an association for bargaining by incorporating it rested in the unfettered discretion of the government, as did the decision of whether to enter into a collective agreement with the incorporated association. The Northwest Territories Public Service Association had been recognized by the government and the nurses could join it. The Northwest Territories government refused to incorporate the PIPSC to represent the group of nurses which had become Northwest Territories employees.

Four of seven Supreme Court justices held that freedom of association in the *Charter* did not protect the right to bargain collectively. Although there were four concurring opinions given by the majority justices, all agreed that the government was under no constitutional obligation to bargain collectively or provide any statutory scheme for collective bargaining by recognition or certification. Hence a legislative choice of how bargaining agents are chosen or mandated was not a matter for judicial scrutiny under the *Charter*. . . .

[Reprinted by permission.]

* * *

The ruling that the freedom of association found in the *Charter* does not include the right to bargain collectively was affirmed by the Supreme Court of Canada in two important cases referred to or excerpted above in Chapter 4 — *Delisle v. Canada (Dep. Att.-*

Gen.), [1999] 2 S.C.R. 989, and *Dunmore v. Ontario (Attorney-General)*, [2001] 3 S.C.R. 1016, 2001 SCC 94. However, the judgment of the majority of the Court in Dunmore moved away from the idea that freedom of association as set out in the *Charter* only pro-tects the collective exercise of activities which can legally be carried out by an individual, and toward the idea that freedom of association can protect some aspects of employee organizing activity which are inherently collective. *Dunmore* also represents a clear move toward the view expressed in Dickson C.J.C.'s dissent in the Alberta Reference case to the effect that the meaning of the freedom of association in the *Charter* should be interpreted with an eye to the somewhat broader meaning that it had acquired in international jurisprudence. In one writer's words, the *Dunmore* decision "seems to have broken the spine of the restricted definition of freedom of association which has governed *Charter* jurisprudence since the *Alberta Reference*": Patricia Hughes, "*Dunmore v. Ontario (Attorney-General)*: Waiting for the Other Shoe" (2003) 10 CLELJ 27 at 55–56. However, Hughes goes on to argue as follows, at 57:

> Whatever 'departures' from previous jurisprudence *Dunmore* may represent, they are only one shoe; the other shoe, waiting to be droppped, is the full realization of the scope of freedom of association to include collective bargaining as a protected activity.

8:200 LEGAL PROHIBITION OF STRIKES AND OTHER ECONOMIC SANCTIONS: THE PEACE OBLIGATION

A strike traditionally takes the form of a complete cessation of work. However, there are a wide variety of employee pressure tactics that fall short of a complete shutdown, and which have become relatively more important in recent years. These include rotating or selective strikes, go-slows, work-to-rule campaigns, "study sessions," overtime bans, co-ordinated sick days, consumer boycotts, picketing, hot declarations, and mass resig-nations. Many of these seek to restrict or disrupt the amount of work done. Others try to induce people not directly involved in the dispute to cease doing business with the target employer.

On the employer's side, the lockout (where the employer closes the enterprise, or a part of it, to try to compel the union to come to terms) is usually cited as the counterpart to the strike. This is somewhat misleading. Employers seldom initiate conflict by shutting down. Usually, the employer simply resists the strike tactics, either by waiting them out or by trying to continue its operations through the use of supervisory personnel, replacement workers, or bargaining unit members who do not heed the strike call. Even when the employer wants to modify an existing collective agreement, a lockout is not usually its first line of attack. It can impose new terms unilaterally, as long as it does so at the proper time and under certain conditions. This is discussed below, in section 8:220.

Thus, the union is usually cast in the role of the aggressor. In inflationary times, it must strike to obtain better terms; in deflationary times, it must strike to prevent the imposition of worse terms. Employers tend to use lockouts only to counter employee tactics: that is, to force a work stoppage at a time of the employer's rather than the union's choosing, or to pre-empt the union's use of rotating strikes or other types of partial stoppage.

8:210 Prohibition of Strikes

Most cases on the definition of the term "strike" address situations where strikes are prohibited by law. For the most part, these prohibitions date from World War II. Before that time, strikes were used by Canadian workers to resolve virtually all types of employment-related disputes — those over the recognition of unions for collective bargaining, the negotiation of new terms of employment, the reinstatement of discharged employees, the enforcement of collective agreements, and the drawing of jurisdictional boundaries between unions. This resort to the strike for many different purposes did not result from any affirmative legal recognition of a right to strike, but from the determination of employees and unions to use the one powerful industrial weapon available to them, often in defiance of legal restrictions. Grudgingly and unsystematically, the legal system began to accommodate the exercise of employees' collective power, leading to a regime of qualified "collective laissez-faire" in prewar Canadian labour relations. Collective bargaining and strikes occurred without express legal authorization, and legal intervention was sporadic.

During World War II, Canadian labour policy took on a dramatically new orientation. In response to demands for continuous war production, Canadian governments instituted a more intensely regulated system of collective bargaining. As explained in earlier chapters, this new system was a modified version of the American *Wagner Act* model. The use of strikes was strictly limited to disputes over the negotiation of collective agreements. In all other circumstances, strikes were banned. Often, the use of economic force was replaced by a new set of mechanisms that were expected to play the role previously played by strikes. These new mechanisms included the certification process for initiating collective bargaining, the duty to bargain, the prohibition of unfair labour practices, and the grievance arbitration process for enforcing collective agreements. Employees can no longer strike to force the employer to recognize a union, or to engage in bargaining, or (perhaps most important of all) to enforce their interpretation of the terms of a collective agreement.

The only significant exception to the ban on strikes and lockouts during the lifetime of a collective agreement is found in the British Columbia, Manitoba, and federal labour relations statutes, which require the employer to give the union advance notice of technological change (as defined in those statutes) during the lifetime of the collective agreement. A duty to bargain then arises over matters arising out of such change, and the bargaining can eventually result in a legal work stoppage. The relevant provisions of the *Canada Labour Code* (sections 51–55) have seldom been used. From 1973 to 1991 there were thirty-three applications to the Canada Labour Relations Board regarding technological change, of which only six went to a hearing.

Another common hurdle to a legal work stoppage is the requirement, dating back to the early years of the twentieth century, that the parties talk to each other before resorting to a strike or lockout. As part of that requirement, labour relations statutes in all jurisdictions except Manitoba and Quebec provide that a dispute must be submitted to conciliation or mediation before a work stoppage may begin, or at least provide that the labour ministry may choose to impose conciliation or mediation. In addition, particularly in recent years, some jurisdictions have added yet other obstacles, including compulsory strike votes (for example, *OLRA* sections 79(3) and (4)) and the right of the employer or the Minister of Labour to demand an employee vote on whether to accept the employer's last offer (for example, *OLRA* sections 41 and 42).

The thrust of all of these limitations is that everywhere in Canada, the legality of a strike or lockout depends above all on whether the various statutory prerequisites just outlined have been met. These requirements are commonly encapsulated by saying that a strike or lockout must be "timely" in order to be legal.

8:211 Definition of "Strike"

The array of legislative restrictions on strikes applies only to conduct that falls within the statutory definition of a strike. As an example, section 3(1) of the *Canada Labour Code* sets out this definition:

> 'strike' includes a cessation of work or a refusal to work or to continue to work by employees, in combination, in concert or in accordance with a common understanding, and a slowdown of work or other concerted activity on the part of employees in relation to their work that is designed to restrict or limit output.

The definitions of a strike in other jurisdictions are similar. All apply (expressly or, as discussed below, by interpretation) to a broad range of tactics that restrict production, including conduct short of a full-scale work stoppage. All require some measure of common action by employees. In three provinces — Alberta, Manitoba, and Nova Scotia — the definition of a strike includes the qualification that the job action must be for the purpose of compelling an employer to agree to terms or conditions of employment. As is indicated below in sections 8:213 and 8:214, the statutes of some other jurisdictions (including British Columbia and the federal jurisdiction) included that qualification at one time but no longer do.

8:212 Actions Constituting a Strike: Common Action or Concerted Activity

What kinds of conduct fall within the definition of a strike? The following case gives an idea of the breadth of the answer to that question. It also describes one situation in which an employer might resort to a lockout in response to protected strike activity.

Communications, Electronic, Electrical, Technical and Salaried Workers of Canada v. Graham Cable TV/FM (1986), 12 Can. L.R.B.R. (N.S.) 1 at 2–4, 9–14 (C.L.R.B.)

> JAMIESON, Vice-Chair: On July 18, 1985, the Communications, Electronic, Electrical, Technical and Salaried Workers of Canada (CWC) . . . filed this complaint alleging that Graham Cable TV/FM . . . had violated s. 184(3)(a)(vi) [now s. 94(3)(a)(vi)] of the *Canada Labour Code* by taking disciplinary action against some of its members because they were participating in lawful strike activities. The employer denied the allegations claiming that

discipline had only been imposed on some employees who had reported for work but who had failed or refused to perform the functions of their job descriptions. . . .

[At the time of the relevant events, the union was in a legal position to strike. Because of the nature of the employer's operations, the union believed that a traditional strike would fail, as management personnel could maintain service for a long time unless there was a major equipment failure. The union therefore decided to work to rule.]

. . . Ms. Cynthia Down, a union steward and a member of the negotiating committee described the programme that was adopted and how it was to be put in place. The job action that was contemplated included slowdowns in some areas and a speed up in others. For example, in the marketing and sales department inside work was to slow down and outside sales were to speed up generating more work for the inside workers. No overtime was to be worked and employees would cease the practice of training others to perform their job functions. In the customer service area only four calls an hour were to be accepted with other incoming calls to be diverted to management persons. Dispatchers would screen orders going to technicians and servicemen were to request audit checks which would slow down the dispatchers. Installers would cease collecting money from customers. The employees also decided that they would no longer whisper amongst themselves about the union, they would speak up. To that end study sessions would be held on each floor to convince management that they were openly standing up for their rights.

The job action programme commenced on the morning of July 4, 1985. Ms. Down was the overall co-ordinator with eight to ten other co-ordinators reporting to her from other areas of the work place. Employees were given strict instructions to act only on the directions of the official co-ordinators. That way there would be some measure of control and there would be absolutely no doubt that the actions were being done in a concerted fashion. . . .

[This kind of job action occurred, with some modifications, from 4 July until 26 July. Beginning on 15 July, the employer warned its employees that they must do the work required by their job descriptions or face discipline. Some employees who continued the job action were suspended. On 26 July 26 the employer required all employees who wished to work to sign the document that follows.]

July 26, 1985
MEMO TO: Graham Cable
FROM:

I am reporting for work and desire to continue to work at Graham Cable TV/FM, commencing 26 July, 1985 as a _____ , in accordance with my job description (see attached), Graham Cable standard procedures, Graham Cable practices and Graham Cable standards.

I agree as a condition to being permitted to enter the premises and report for work that I shall complete my work assignments, as set out above.

_____

Signature

. . .

[Those who did not sign were excluded from the premises.]

The issues before us really come down to what is a strike under the Code? If the work related activities by the employees fall within the definition of a strike they are then protected under s. 184(3)(a)(vi) of the Code and the imposition of discipline by the employer for having participated in those activities would amount to an unfair labour practice.

A strike is defined in s. 107(1) of the Code:

> 'strike' includes (a) a cessation of work or a refusal to work or to continue to work by employees, in combination or in concert or in accordance with a common understanding, and (b) a slowdown of work or other concerted activity on the part of employees in relation to their work that is designed to restrict or limit output;

The protection against discipline or other forms of penalty for having participated in a lawful strike is extremely broad and if one looks at the construction of s. 184(3)(a)(vi) it becomes readily apparent that Parliament intended it to be so:

> 184. (3) No employer and no person acting on behalf of an employer shall (a) refuse to employ or to continue to employ or suspend, transfer, lay off or otherwise discriminate against any person in regard to employment, pay or any other term or condition of employment or intimidate, threaten or otherwise discipline any person, because the person . . . (vi) has participated in a strike that is not prohibited by this Part or exercised any right under this Part;

There are strict limitations in the Code when a strike can legally occur. Section 180 sets out all of the conditions which have to be met before a strike becomes legal. The same restrictions apply equally to a lockout. . . .

Frequently, when job action has been taken in response to mid-contract disputes or during negotiations where trade unions or employees have simply jumped the gun and have initiated job action before they are lawfully entitled to, employers have come to the Board under s. 182 of the Code seeking declarations of unlawful strikes and corresponding cease and desist orders. Through those procedures the definition of a strike in the federal jurisdiction has evolved to the extent that it encompasses a wide range of activities. It can even extend to a refusal to cross a legal picket line which is considered to be a right as a matter of routine in most jurisdictions. . . . In *Canadian Broadcasting Corp.* (No. 236) and *Air Canada*, the Board found that concerted refusals to work overtime were unlawful strikes notwithstanding that the overtime assignments in question were considered to be voluntary under the relevant collective agreements. . . . In the *Air Canada* case the Board also found a concerted refusal to accept acting supervisory assignments to be an unlawful strike regardless of the fact that the assignments being refused were again voluntary under the collective agreement. . . . Other job-related action that has been found to be an illegal strike includes, a concerted work to rule . . . and booking off sick or being otherwise unavailable for assignments. . . . One of the best examples of how wide a net is cast when the Board is assessing the legality of job action is the decision in *Canada Post Corp.* . . . .

There, the Board declared that an unlawful strike had been declared when the Canadian Union of Postal Workers announced that over the Christmas period its members would accept and process mail bearing ten cent stamps which was less than the postage rate required at that time. The key to the Board's apparent strict enforcement of s. 180 lies in the consistent presence of the few factual elements which go to make up a strike under the Code. All of the activities have taken place when the conditions set out in s. 180 have not been met, they were all found to have been done in combination or in concert or in accordance with a common understanding and, they were designed to restrict or limit output. That is all it takes for an unlawful strike to have occurred in the federal jurisdiction.

The broad interpretation of strike that has evolved under the Code really reflects the growing attitude of bargaining agents in today's work environment. As tough economic times continue and jobs are hard to come by, trade unions are looking for ways other than the traditional strike to apply pressures on employers. Particularly in industries where replacement workers are readily obtainable, rotating strikes, overtime bans, work to rule campaigns, slow-downs and many other more imaginative job-related activities are becoming the strike weapon of the day. Besides being less predictable, the strategy of limited or sporadic job action has one main advantage, the union members are not deprived of their income over long periods of time. Having repeatedly told trade unions and other members that those activities are unlawful when they are done at the wrong time, are we now going to tell them that the same activities are not lawful strike activities when they are in a legal strike position? Surely when we are faced with the reverse situation to an unlawful strike as we are now and are being asked to extend the protection of s. 184(3)(a)(vi) to concerted job related activities that have been taken when a strike can lawfully occur, the same standards must apply. It must then naturally follow if the same standards are applied to determine lawful strike activities as the Board has applied to unlawful strikes in the past that almost any concerted activity on the part of employees in relation to their work would fall within the protection contemplated by s. 184(3)(a)(vi) of the Code. We say almost any activity because it goes without saying that however broad the protection under the Code, it cannot be used to shield criminal or other unlawful acts.

Where does that leave employers? Are they left defenceless once a trade union is in a lawful strike position? We think the Ontario Labour Relations Board's comments, when they were faced with similar circumstances to what we have here, are most appropriate (*The Corporation of the City of Brampton* . . .):

> . . . An employer, for its part, is free to take measures designed to limit the disruptive effect of this type of strike activity, such as the increased use of managerial personnel and non-striking employees. An employer is also free to take responsive action through its right to lock out employees. *An employer is not, however, free to discipline or punish employees for engaging in a lawful strike.* (Emphasis added.)

We concur with that assessment of the situation and adopt it as our own. Disruption of an employer's normal operations is what a strike is all about and provided the employees are participating in lawful strike activities their employer is prohibited from taking any of the actions against them that are spelled out in s. 184(3)(a)(vi). . . .

* * *

In 1992 the Canada Board was forced to return to the question of what measures an employer could take in response to rotating or partial strikes. In *C.U.P.W. v. Canada Post Corporation* (1992), 16 Can. L.R.B.R. (2d) 290, the union over the course of one day had engaged in various concerted activities designed to decrease production; at the time, it was in a position to engage in a lawful strike. One such activity was a refusal by employees at a postal station to deliver anything but first class mail. The union handed out summaries of the *Graham Cable* decision, in an effort to persuade its members that the *Canada Labour Code* protected them from being punished for such activities. When the employer responded by refusing to allow employees who had participated in the partial strikes to work the following day, the union filed an unfair labour practice complaint alleging that the employer had discriminated against those employees because they had participated in a lawful strike.

The board held that *Graham Cable* had contemplated that employers could defend their interests by imposing lockouts in response to concerted activity in the workplace. It went on to hold that it must try to distinguish employer conduct that was merely a defensive lockout from conduct that discriminated against or disciplined employees for the exercise of their rights under the Code. The board held that the employer's conduct in this case was merely a rotating defensive lockout, despite the fact that in one instance only those employees who had engaged in strike activity were denied entry to the workplace the next day. The *Canada Post* decision indicates that a lockout might indeed be an effective weapon to counteract partial strike action.

Ontario Secondary School Teachers' Federation v. Grand Erie District School Board, [1999] OLRB Rep. Jan/Feb 44

[The union, while in a legal strike position, had begun a "work to rule" campaign in which its members were instructed, among other things, not to supervise extra-curricular activities or attend staff meetings or parent-teacher interviews. The school board sent a letter to the union threatening legal action on the basis that the work-to-rule campaign was illegal because the duties in question were mandatory for teachers under the *Education Act* and *Regulations*. The union then brought an unfair labour practice proceeding, claiming that the employer's letter constituted interference with protected union strike activity. The employer argued that the work-to-rule activities were not protected "lawful activities" of the union under section 5 of the *OLRA* because the teachers were refusing to perform duties that were required by statute.]

TRACHUK, Vice Chair: ¶ 27 The Board held in its decision of November 10, 1998 that the union's work-to-rule campaign was protected strike activity. The teachers are acting in combination or concert to "limit output" and therefore fall within the definition of strike. The campaign is occurring within the statutorily mandated time frame so it is legal. . . . The fact that the duties the teachers are not performing are part of their statutory employment duties does not remove them from the spectrum of work activities which teachers can refuse to perform during a strike. If they were so removed, a total cessation of work would also not be possible. As the school board concedes however, the Education Act contemplates that teachers have the right to strike and therefore a total cessation of all work is not unlawful. If the right to strike were to be taken away, or limited, it would be part of a clear legislative decision manifest in the statute. Limitations on the right to strike cannot be inferred from the fact that the Education Act includes some duties of teachers, principals and school boards. Although the school board urges the result that the union has to choose between a total strike or no strike at all, that stark choice is not mandated by the statutory scheme. Clearly a concerted refusal to perform some of the occupational duties prescribed by contract or statute cannot be unlawful when a concerted refusal to perform all of those same duties is conceded to be lawful.

. . .

¶ 29   The school board repeatedly referred to the effect the teachers' actions would have on the students and parents. . . . Third parties who are not participants to the negotiations are almost always adversely affected. School board strikes may be some of the most painful because most of those other "parties" are children. As in every strike or lock-out, both sides are attempting to put as much pressure on to the other side as possible. The union achieves this by limiting "output." In a public school board strike the teachers have little ability to inflict economic pressure as there is no economic "output." The pressure asserted by the teachers is political and it is inflicted through the students and their parents because the "output" is education. This reality is not new and if there had been a legislative will that it should not occur the Education Act amendments could have added teachers to the categories of public sector workers who are designated as essential services. But the legislature did not remove the right to strike. . . . The school board can always make wage reductions and change working conditions as this school board has done or it can lock the teachers out.

¶ 31   The school board argued that including the work-to-rule campaign as protected strike activity is analogous to finding that employees in a legal strike position can refuse to participate in a health and safety committee, which is mandated by statute, or to employees of an automobile manufacturer refusing to install safety devices on cars. It is not evident to the Board why those activities would not be legal strike activity if they were undertaken by employees in concert within the statutory time frame. In any case, the Board is prepared to say that these circumstances are not analogous to industrial sabotage which is clearly unlawful and not protected strike activity. The distinction may be understood as refusing to perform assigned work which is clearly contemplated by the definition of strike and is conceptually consistent with that definition versus taking actions which are not part of one's work, are not contemplated by the statute, and which are not conceptually consistent with it. . . .

¶ 32   However, the Board did not find the school board's effort to stop the work-to-rule campaign by sending the October 22, 1998 letter to be a violation of the Act. That letter was conveying the school board's view that the union's actions were illegal and it was contemplating court action. It is often the case that parties accuse each other of engaging in unlawful strikes or lock outs. Such an accusation is not a violation of the Act in itself whether or not the person making it is correct. Parties are entitled to have a view on the legality of each other's actions (even if those theories are somewhat unlikely) and to pursue them in this, or other, forums. It is acting responsibly for one party considering legal action to inform the other that it is considering such action in the hopes of resolving the matter. Such a communication does not manifest the intent to interfere with lawful union activities. Even if section 70 does not require a finding of anti-union animus as claimed by the union, the possible effect of interfering with the union must be balanced against the employer's right to inform the union that it perceives its actions to be unlawful. The employer has not imposed discipline on the employees for engaging in legal strike activity and this situation is therefore distinguishable from those cases.

✵ ✵ ✵

A second element of the definition of "strike" is the concerted nature of the employees' action. What precisely does it mean that the work stoppage must be "in combination, in concert or in accordance with a common understanding"? Is it enough that more than one employee stops work, or must there be an element of co-ordination?

British Columbia Terminal Elevator Operators' Association on Behalf of the Saskatchewan Wheat Pool v. Grain Workers' Union, Local 333 (1994), 94 C.L.L.C. para. 16,060 at 14,500 (C.L.R.B.)

[The employer sought an unlawful-strike declaration and other remedies. The employer argued that there had been a concerted refusal by its employees to work voluntary overtime following the temporary layoff of ten employees in the bargaining unit. The collective agreement explicitly stated that employees could refuse overtime work.]

No direct evidence was presented that the union authorized or orchestrated the employees' refusal to work overtime. However, it is not necessary to prove that point through direct evidence; circumstantial evidence will suffice. . . .

Here the parties were in the midst of collective bargaining. The employees in the bargaining unit had engaged in a concerted refusal to work overtime in circumstances where, in the normal course, a sufficient number would have accepted work. In addition, the employer had been told that the union was clearly opposed to the concept of resorting to overtime when lay-offs were in effect. In light of the above, and in the absence of any evidence to the contrary, the Board must conclude that the union was the architect of the employees' concerted refusal. We found therefore that a strike contrary to section 89 was in effect.

. . . it must be clear that the statutory definition of 'strike' cannot be changed by an agreement of the parties. Nor can the public purpose of 'industrial peace' behind the no-strike provision be avoided by 'contracting out' of the legal obligations of the Code. . . . Of course, the parties can negotiate an employee's individual right to refuse to work and these clauses will be applied in accordance with their given interpretation, subject to arbitration. However, the union or its members cannot use such a clause to circumvent the Code by giving employees the right to refuse collectively to work contrary to section 89. Each separate segment of the Code definition of 'strike' is significant and must be read in conjunction with the other segments. Actions which are acceptable, for individual employees, because of the collective agreement provisions, may constitute an unlawful strike when done 'in combination, in concert or in accordance with a common understanding,' that is aimed, in relation to their work, at restricting or limiting output. . . .

* * *

In *CBC v. Canadian Media Guild*, [1999] CIRB No. 11, memos from officials of the respondent union told members that they had a legal obligation to report for work during a legal strike by another bargaining unit, and also told them that it could not direct them to refuse to cross the other unit's picket line because such a refusal would be an unlawful strike. The memos also stressed that the choice of whether to cross a picket line had to be based on the personal belief or conscience of the individual worker. In addition, they said that the respondent union would back any member who was disciplined for refusing to cross the other unit's picket line, and warned them that they could soon find themselves in the same situation as the other unit (that is, on a legal strike against the employer). Some members of the respondent union did refuse to cross the picket line. The Board held that those refusals were concerted activity and thus amounted to a strike. In support of that conclusion, the Board noted that the union's memos conveyed implicitly conflicting messages. Thus, resort by a union to mixed messages is not likely to succeed in keeping a slowdown or stoppage from being held to be concerted activity.

8:213 The Strike Prohibition and Sympathetic Action

Because the timing of strikes is strictly regulated by statute, the strike ban poses significant obstacles to "sympathetic action" by one group of workers designed to help another group that is involved in a strike or lockout. Any sympathetic action of that sort is likely both to constitute a strike and to be untimely. The following case addresses such a situation, namely the refusal of employees to cross a picket line when they were not themselves in a position to strike legally.

Local 273, International Longshoremen's Association et al. v. Maritime Employers' Association et al., [1979] 1 S.C.R. 120 at 123, 125–26, 137–39

ESTEY J.: The issuance of an injunction against three trade unions certified under the Canada Labour Code . . . is challenged principally on the grounds that . . . refusal by members of the appellant Locals to cross a lawful picket line is not a strike and therefore there is no proper basis for the issuance of an injunction, . . .

Prior to the incidents giving rise to these proceedings, a legal strike was commenced by the members of the National Harbours Board Police employed in the Port of Saint John, and the police, in the course of that strike, established picket lines in the entrance to the port's facilities. The employers of the police were not, of course, the employers of the members of the appellants; the conflict here arose because of the common *situs* of employment around which the police placed a picket line. The members of the three Locals refused to cross the police picket lines and on their failure to do so and to report to work, shipping operations in the Port of Saint John were closed down. . . .

The Locals submitted in this Court that by reason of the universally understood doctrine of 'union solidarity,' it could not have been the intention of Parliament in enacting the Code to have included, in the meaning of 'strike,' the refusal to cross a lawful picket line drawn up around the employees' place of work. Presumably the same argument is extended by the Locals to the terms of their Collective Agreements where the same definitions of 'strike' are employed. This approach to the problem at hand found support in proceedings before the B.C. Labour Relations Board in *MacMillan, Bloedel Packaging Ltd. v. Pulp, Paper & Woodworkers of Canada, Local 5 and Local 8, et al*, where the Board interpreted the statutory definition of strike as including a

> . . . subjective element: a concerted effort by employees undertaken for the specific purpose of compelling an employer to settle a dispute about terms of employment. It is just that motivation which is absent in the normal case of employees honouring a picket line.

The response to this submission is found in the history of the federal labour statute itself. The *Industrial Disputes Investigation Act*, R.S.C. 1927, c. 112, provided in s. 1(k) a definition of strike as follows:

> 'strike' or 'to go on strike,' without limiting the nature of its meaning, means the cessation of work by a body of employees acting in combination, or a concerted refusal or a refusal under a common understanding of any number of employees to continue to work for an employer, in consequence of a dispute, done as a means of compelling their employer, or to aid other employees in compelling their employer, to accept terms of employment;

This statute was replaced in 1948 by the *Industrial Relations and Disputes Investigation Act*, 1948 (Can.), c. 54, which deleted the qualification that the withholding of services be done for the purpose of compelling the employer to accept the proposed terms of employment. The definition, [s. 2(p),] was as follows:

> (p) 'strike' includes a cessation of work, or refusal to work or to continue to work, by employees, in combination or in concert or in accordance with a common understanding;

The Code, in its present form, repeats the 1948 definition. There is no room for doubt now that Parliament has adopted an objective definition of 'strike,' the elements of which are a cessation of work in combination or with a common understanding. Whether the motive be ulterior or expressed is of no import, the only requirement being the cessation pursuant to a common understanding. Here, the concurrent findings foreclose this aspect of this submission.

Refusal to cross a picket line lawfully established by another union cannot be a strike unless it falls within the definition of 'strike' which fortunately for the purposes of this appeal is in substance the same in both statute and contract. This definition requires a cessation of work (a) in 'combination' or (b) in 'concert' or (c) 'in accordance with a common understanding.' In this case the 'concert,' the 'combination' or the 'common under-standing' may be considered to have a common root in the principle of labour organiza-tion which forbids the crossing of picket lines. Section X(b) of the agreement with Local 1039, Article 12:02 of Local 273, and the definition in the Code, when given the ordinary meaning of 'common understanding,' seem to be an attempt by the authors to provide for the very situation where the 'cessation of work' results from a concept jointly held by the employees, such as the principle against the crossing of picket lines. The contract might have been more precise and included in the 'strike' definition, the cessation of work resulting from a refusal to cross a picket line. However, the question is simply: do the words 'in accordance with a common understanding' embrace the more specific provision that a cessation of work resulting from the application of the commonly understood prin-ciple of the labour movement that members of unions should not cross picket lines?' The argument is made more complex here because one of the three Collective Agreements does not define 'strike' and none of the Agreements defines 'stoppage of work.' Given the ordinary meaning of these words, there is no room to import a qualification which would exclude a stoppage of work resulting from one circumstance only, namely the honouring of a picket line by the employees comprising the bargaining unit.

* * *

The extent of the prohibition against concerted sympathetic action in the form of hon-ouring another union's picket line was emphasized in *Progistix-Solutions v. CEP*, [1999] OLRB Rep. March/April 309. The union had instructed its members, when driving in to work, to pause for five minutes per car at the entrance being picketed by members of another bargaining unit who were on a legal strike. This was held to be unlawful strike activity, because it resulted in some employees being late for work.

* * *

What if a collective agreement expressly permits the employees covered by it to refuse to cross a lawful picket line?

Nelson Crushed Stone and United Cement, Lime & Gypsum Workers' International Union, Local Union 494 v. Martin, [1978] 1 Can. L.R.B.R. 115 at 119–20, 125, 128–29 (O.L.R.B)

HALADNER, Vice-Chair: The facts of this case — a refusal by members of one union to cross a picket line maintained by members of another union who are legally on strike against a common employer, where the collective agreement between the employer and the 'non-striking' union contains a provision stating that it shall not be a violation of the agreement (or cause for discharge or discipline) if any employee refuses to cross a legal picket line — raise again the question of the precise scope of the strike definition con-tained in section 1(1)(m) of the Labour Relations Act. . . .

The Board, when applying the statutory definition, has not drawn a distinction between a refusal by employees to cross a picket line and other types of employee activity which result in a disruption of an employer's operation. In all cases, the question is whether the refusal to work on the part of the employees is in combination, in concert, or in accordance with a common understanding within the meaning of section 1(1)(m). In this regard, the Board has held that the definition of 'strike' is not restricted or qualified by the purpose underlying the work stoppage. The Board, moreover, does not allow the parties to qualify the no-strike provision deemed to be contained in every collective agreement. The Board has held that provisions which purport to legalize strike activity during the contract term embody attempts by the parties to contract out of the Labour Relations Act and are, to that extent, invalid. . . .

. . . It is difficult to see any difference in principle between a clause which provides that it will not be a violation of the collective agreement for employees to refuse to cross a legal picket line and a clause which provides that employees will not be so required. Neither clause can make unlawful [sic] that which would otherwise be unlawful — that is, a concerted refusal on the part of employees to work when there is work scheduled. . . .

To conclude that clauses such as Article 4.02 cannot authorize a work stoppage which, in the absence of such a clause, would amount to a 'strike' is not, however, to conclude that such clauses are of no legal effect. . . . such clauses, while invalid to the extent that they purport to contract out of the *Labour Relations Act*, may nevertheless limit the liability of employees and/or the union under the terms of a collective agreement. In addition, such clauses may . . . be sufficiently exculpatory to persuade the Board to decline to grant consent to prosecute where the employees or the union, relying on such a clause, engage in a 'strike.' Whatever the precise extent of the 'collective agreement' protection which such clauses may afford, such clauses can probably be expected to provide a defense to individual employees who may be discharged or disciplined as a result of their refusal, on an individual basis, to cross a legal picket line.

* * *

A "hot cargo" or "hot declaration" clause in a collective agreement typically purports to allow employees to refuse to do any work coming from or destined for another employer who has been declared unfair by the union. Such clauses are inconsistent with the thrust of the O.L.R.B. decision in *Nelson Crushed Stone*. In British Columbia, the approach to sympathetic collective job action is quite different. From 1973 to 1987, and again since 1992, the British Columbia labour relations statute has allowed the labour relations board to give effect to hot cargo clauses, with certain limitations: *Labour Relations Code 1992*, c. 81, s. 164(1). As well, clauses permitting employees to refuse to cross picket lines remain fully effective in British Columbia; the definition of a strike in section 1(1) of the British Columbia statute excludes stoppages or refusals to work that are a direct result of lawful picketing.

Manitoba legislation expressly permits employees to refuse to facilitate the operation or business of a struck employer. The Manitoba *Labour Relations Act* provides as follows, in section 15(1):

An employee who is in a unit of employees of an employer in respect of which there is a collective agreement in force and who refuses to perform work which would directly facilitate the operation or business of another employer whose employees within Canada are locked out or on a legal strike is not by reason of that refusal in breach of the collective agreement or of any term or condition of his employment and is not, by reason of that refusal, subject to any disciplinary action by the employer or the bargaining agent that is a party to the collective agreement.

8:214 Is a Political Protest a Strike?

Whether a purposive restriction should be read into the definition of strike is highly controversial. Labour boards across the country grappled with that issue at the time of the "National Day of Protest," a one-day work stoppage called by the Canadian Labour Congress in 1976 in protest against federal anti-inflation legislation limiting the wage increases obtainable through collective bargaining. Some employers treated employees who stayed away from work as illegal strikers, and considerable litigation ensued. In *British Columbia Hydro and Power Authority and International Brotherhood of Electrical Workers, Local 258 and Local 213*, [1976] 2 Can. L.R.B.R. 410, at 413, the British Columbia Labour Relations Board held that the stoppage did not fall within the definition of a strike set out in the British Columbia Labour Code at that time:

> 'strike' includes
>
> i) a cessation of work, or
> ii) a refusal to work, or
> iii) a refusal to continue to work, or
> iv) an act or omission that is intended to, or does, restrict or limit production or services,
>
> by employees in combination, or in concert, or in accordance with a common understanding, for the purpose of compelling their employer to agree to terms or conditions of employment, or of compelling another employer to agree to terms or conditions of employment of his employees, and 'to strike' has a similar meaning;

The Board reasoned that the latter part of this definition (which was removed in 1984) required a subjective intent on the part of the workers to elicit an employment-related response from an employer, and that no such intent could be found in what was essentially a form of political protest. Chair Weiler held, at 418–19, that such protests were essentially not a matter for collective bargaining law, because they involved disputes between unions and government.

This approach was not adopted in every province that had a purposive element in its statutory definition of a strike. In *Re Robb Engineering and United Steelworkers of America, Local 4122* (1978), 86 D.L.R. (3d) 307 (N.S.C.A.), the Nova Scotia Court of Appeal held that the word "includes" in the definition should be construed broadly, and that a political protest which involved a work stoppage was encompassed by the definition. MacKeigan C.J.N.S. said, at 315–16:

> Workers are free to participate individually in politics and are free, indeed, to cease work individually for any reason or for no reason, subject to job rules as to absenteeism. They are not free to combine by agreement to quit work. Unions' political activities are similar-

ly not restricted, but political freedom does not permit disregard of the law. Unions in exchange for the right of bargaining are pledged to settle, by arbitration or otherwise, 'without stoppage of work' (s. 40(1) of the Act), all differences with employers, and are required not to cause any work stoppage. The Legislature has ordained that a strike may be used only as a collective bargaining sanction when negotiations break down. Four men deciding to go fishing together would not be striking, but if forty men all agreed to quit at the same time, purporting to go fishing, that might well be a strike.

In Ontario and other jurisdictions where the definition of a strike had no purposive component, the National Day of Protest was invariably held to be a strike. See, for example, *Domglas Ltd*. (1976), 76 C.L.L.C. para. 16,050 (O.L.R.B.), upheld (1978), 78 C.L.L.C. para. 14,135 (Ont. Div. Ct.).

In a decision arising from one of several Days of Protest called by the Ontario Federation of Labour to protest labour law reforms enacted in that province in 1995 by a new Conservative government, the Ontario Labour Relations Board reaffirmed its commitment to the *Domglas* approach to political protests that result in work stoppages. In *General Motors of Canada Ltd*., [1996] OLRB Rep. May/June 409, the Canadian Auto Workers argued that the statutory prohibition of collective job action during the term of a collective agreement was invalid insofar as it prohibited political protest strikes, because it contravened the employees' *Charter* freedoms of expression and association. In rejecting this argument, the O.L.R.B. acknowledged that such activity constituted political expression within the meaning of section 2(b) of the *Charter*, but held that the blanket prohibition of strikes during the term of a collective agreement was a reasonable limit under section 1 of the *Charter*. In support of that holding, the board referred to the deference shown by the Supreme Court of Canada to the legislatures in the area of collective bargaining policy. It also noted that the purposive element had been removed from the British Columbia statutory definition of a strike in 1984, after the advent of the *Charter*.

8:220 Economic Sanctions Available to the Employer

8:221 Definition of "Lockout"

As with strikes, labour relations statutes impose restrictions on when employers can declare lockouts. The statutes define "lockout," as in the following example from the *Canada Labour Code*:

> 'lockout' includes the closing of a place of employment, a suspension of work by an employer or a refusal by an employer to continue to employ a number of their employees, done to compel their employees, or to aid another employer to compel their employees, to agree to terms or conditions of employment . . .

Unlike the definition of a strike in most jurisdictions, this definition contains a purposive limitation. Would shutdowns designed as political protests (for example, a refusal to produce oil in protest against a national energy program) be prohibited as lockouts? Why should employer shutdowns be treated differently from similarly motivated employee shutdowns? See *General Motors of Canada Ltd.*, [1996] OLRB Rep. May/June 409, referred to above, for a discussion of this issue.

Note too that the definition of a lockout does not include an unconditional plant closure. If an employer moves to Mexico, that is not a lockout, although a threat to move may be an unfair labour practice. A closure can also be challenged as an untimely lockout if the union can prove that it is merely a bargaining ploy. See *Humpty Dumpty Foods Ltd.*, [1977] 2 Can. L.R.B.R. 248 (O.L.R.B.).

Generally speaking, the same timeliness restrictions which are imposed on the right to strike are also imposed on the right to lock out. In other words, a lockout is timely whenever the employees can legally strike.

Quite similar timelines apply to another employer economic weapon — the unilateral alteration of working conditions. The employer may initiate such alterations at any time following the expiry of the statutory freeze discussed above in Chapter 7 (section 7:300). That freeze usually expires with the acquisition of the right to strike or upon the initiation of a strike or lockout.

The only additional restriction on the employer's use of these weapons flows from the duty to bargain in good faith.

Westroc Industries Ltd. v. United Cement, Lime and Gypsum Workers International Union, [1981] 2 Can. L.R.B.R. 315 at 324–29 (O.L.R.B.)

[The company was engaged in manufacturing operations in several provinces. During negotiations for renewal of the collective agreement at its Mississauga, Ontario, plant, the company concluded that the union was deliberately prolonging discussions in order to conduct simultaneous strikes in other locations, where the collective agreements had later expiry dates. Attempts to bring the Mississauga negotiations to a more rapid conclusion failed, and the company locked out the Mississauga employees. Over a period of several weeks, the company hired some replacements and resumed certain operations. The lockout followed exhaustion of conciliation proceedings. The board found that during negotiations both before and after the lockout, the employer met the standard of good faith required by the legislation. The union complained that the lockout and the hiring of replacements were breaches of the *Ontario Labour Relations Act*.]

> ADAMS, Chair: We have come to the conclusion that both complaints must be dismissed in their entirety. From a review of all of the evidence, we are satisfied that none of the impugned conduct of the respondent company violates sections 14, 56, 58 or 61 of the Act.
>
> . . .
>
> We begin by observing that an employer may properly decide to continue his operations in the face of a strike and, to that end, may hire fresh employees. Section 64 of the Act would appear to contemplate that possibility in that it explicitly provides for the job security of striking employees for a finite period. . . .
>
> Thus, as long as an employer's motive is free of anti-union animus, it seems clear that strike replacement employees can be hired and such action can be a powerful economic weapon in many cases. . . . This being clear, it is of some interest to note that the almost par-

allel treatment of strike and lockout activity by the statute — a treatment that tends to suggest that, for the most part, they are but two sides of the same coin. For example, section 1(2) provides, *inter alia*, that no person shall cease to be an employee by reason only of his ceasing to work for his employer as the result of a lockout or strike. Similar dual references can be found in, *inter alia*, sections 34b, 34d, 34e, 36, 53(3), 63, sections 65 and 66 when read together, 67, 68, sections 82 and 83 when read together, sections 119 and 134a. Indeed, section 64 is the only section of consequence where the dual reference is missing although our later analysis of the lockout replacement capacity of an employer will illustrate why we do not think this discloses a fundamental flaw in the statutory scheme. This parallel treatment, we think, goes some way to suggest that the Legislature saw each party in collective bargaining having a range of economic weapons in its arsenal and that it intended no ground rules with respect to the utilization of such weapons or the initiation of industrial conflict. The legislative scheme, on this latter point, clearly envisages the possibility of an employer locking out his employees before being struck. . . . Moreover, while a lockout singles out those persons employed by an employer who are engaging in collective bargaining, the statute explicitly recognizes this result and makes a distinction between two classes of employer motivation in causing a lockout. Section 1(1)(i) of the Act defines a lockout as including:

> the closing of a place of employment, a suspension of work or a refusal by an employer to continue to employ a number of his employees or to aid another employer to compel or induce his employees, to refrain from exercising any rights or privileges under this Act or to agree to provisions respecting terms or conditions of employment or the rights, privileges or duties of the employer, an employees' organization, the trade union, or the employees;

A timely lockout aimed at inducing employee agreement over terms and conditions of employment is part of the very process of collective bargaining which the Act contemplates. See section 63(2) in the light of sections 14 and 45. On the other hand, a lockout aimed at dissuading employees from exercising rights under the Act is never lawful and the concept of timeliness simply had no application to such activity. . . . A collective bargaining lockout, then, while in some real sense discriminating between those engaged in negotiations and those employees who are not, does not contravene sections 56, 58 or even section 61 because the employer's intent is directed at achieving a collective agreement and not at penalizing his employees for having exercised a right under the statute. Unlawful intent is the hallmark of these sections and a close analysis of the evidence before us in this case discloses no such motivation. As the United States Supreme Court observed in American *Shipbuilding Co. v. NLRB* . . .

> [t]he lockout may well dissuade employees from adhering to the position which they initially adopted in the bargaining, but the 'right' to bargain collectively does not entail any 'right' to insist on one's position free from economic disadvantage. . . .

Employers can lockout to apply economic pressure in order to achieve a collective agreement on the terms they want and, in the instant case, the employer continued to be driven by this purpose. There is also no evidence that the lockout was intended as a 'cheap layoff' or in any way unrelated to the bargaining differences between the parties. We also note that throughout the lockout the respondent has respected the exclusive authority of the complainant as bargaining agent.

Does this analysis change if the employer, after locking out his employees, goes on to replace them in order to operate? Clearly if the employer's motive is directed at avoiding a collective agreement or the punishment of his employees for having exercised rights under the Act, the hiring of replacements should be struck down. In fact, this Board has held that the permanent replacement of an employee does not constitute a lockout because there is nothing conditional in the employer's action. . . . The action is, instead, a dismissal or termination. The permanent replacement of locked out employees would likely amount to a unilateral destruction of the bargaining unit and the withdrawal of recognition of their duly certified bargaining agent. . . . This is the feature of a lockout that makes reference to it in section 64 unnecessary. A permanent lockout of bargaining unit employees would be very difficult to characterize as employer conduct aimed at achieving a collective agreement. But in the instant case, the company clearly hired temporary replacements and paid them at rates found in the expired collective agreement. Full benefit entitlement was not extended to these persons and formal recruitment procedures were not employed. The arrangement was therefore clearly temporary and locked out employees as a group can have their jobs back at any time their bargaining agent is prepared to agree with the respondent. . . .

Counsel for the trade union submits that any form of replacement is unlawful because of the manifest distinction made between unionized employees and other workers, but this ignores the fact that the use of temporary replacements is only marginally more discriminatory than the lockout itself and clearly, in the facts at hand, has the same collective bargaining purpose. Indeed, the temporary replacement of locked out employees may allow an employer to maintain key customers (as was part of the employers' motivation in the case at bar) and, to some degree, ensure that locked out employees will have jobs to return to. But, more fundamentally, the trade union's position is totally at odds with the dynamics of collective bargaining and, if adopted, would permit trade unions to control the timing of economic conflict — the latter being an inestimable strategic advantage and one nowhere explicitly sanctioned in the statute. . . .

For the same reasons that we have found the lockout itself to be lawful, therefore, we find the respondent's use of temporary lockout replacements; its deployments of non-unit personnel; and its subcontracting of bargaining unit work, do not violate any provision of the Labour Relations Act. The initial use of supervisors, clerical employees and subcontractors was aimed at protecting the patronage of key customers against its two major competitors who had substantial excess capacity. The use of temporary replacements was similarly motivated and implemented only after a lengthy lockout and a resulting perception by the employer of the trade union's unresponsiveness. A distinction made by an employer between employees engaged in protected activity and others who are not is, standing alone, sufficient to violate sections 56, 58, or 61. Rather, the basis to an impugned distinction has to be one of hostile purpose aimed at punishing employees or persons for having exercised their rights under the Act. As the definition of lockout reveals, this labour relations concept involves employer conduct that may be based on a proper or improper purpose. Which purpose is in fact the case must be determined on a careful review of all the evidence. In many earlier decisions we have said that first agreement situations are to be subjected to detailed scrutiny by this Board and a lockout with replacements will particularly merit such an approach in a first agreement context. However, in the instant case, the parties have had a longstanding relationship and there is simply no hint of anti-union animus on the evidence before us. . . .

Lastly, regardless of the outcome of these negotiations, we are satisfied that individual employees locked out and replaced by temporary employees continue to have important job security rights under the general unfair labour practice provisions of the statue. After the imposition of a lockout for some considerable duration and without a collective agreement materializing, affected employees may wish to abandon the conflict and return to work despite the apparent continuing resistance of the bargaining agent. The employer's response to such a situation would be closely scrutinized under section 58, *inter alia*, of the Act. However, at present, such rights are not in issue between the parties.

For all of these reasons the matters consolidated herein are dismissed. . . .

* * *

It might be argued that any unilateral alteration of working conditions amounts to a breach of the duty to bargain, for the simple reason that a unilateral change is tantamount to bargaining with the employees individually. This argument seems to have been laid to rest in *Canadian Association of Industrial, Mechanical and Allied Workers, Local 14 v. Paccar of Canada Ltd.*, [1989] 2 S.C.R. 983 at 1007–15 (per La Forest J.). In the case of unilateral employer-instituted changes to working conditions after the end of the statutory freeze, the duty to bargain appears to require only that the employer must first give the union an opportunity to accept the proposed terms before acting on its own, and that the employer's conduct must otherwise show a willingness to conclude a collective agreement: see *Canadian National Railways Co. and Council of Railway Unions* (1993) 23 CLRBR (2d) 122 (CLRB).

8:300 LEGAL FORUMS REGULATING INDUSTRIAL CONFLICT

In section 8:200, above, we focused mainly on the role of labour relations boards in deciding what is a strike or lockout for the purpose of labour relations legislation. Most of the court decisions that we looked at involved judicial review of board decisions, on administrative law grounds.

The primacy of labour relations boards in the regulation of industrial conflict is quite recent, however, and is neither completely nor firmly established. Before the advent of labour relations statutes and other modern employment legislation, the courts were, by and large, the only adjudicative forum governing strikes and other forms of industrial action. In those days, the study of labour law consisted mainly of the study of criminal law and common law tort doctrines restricting industrial action, and of such related matters as whether trade unions had the legal status to sue and be sued in the courts.

Today, most aspects of the collective bargaining process are governed by a unified regulatory regime administered by labour relations boards. That is not true, however, of strikes and lockouts and of related activities such as picketing. In this area, courts, labour relations boards, and grievance arbitrators all have a thumb in the regulatory pie.

Common law tort doctrines have been used for well over a century by the ordinary civil courts to regulate strikes and picketing. They have also been used to ground the awarding of damages to compensate victims, and the awarding of injunctions. But tort law applies to the full range of human conduct, and its doctrines are not designed to respond to the specific realities of labour relations.

Canadian collective bargaining legislation determines whether and when strikes are legal, and sometimes also proscribes conduct that encourages or supports illegal strikes or is carried on in furtherance of illegal strikes. In most jurisdictions across the country, primary responsibility for the enforcement of such legislation is given to labour relations boards. The remedial authority of those boards generally includes the power to make cease and desist orders against certain types of industrial action and to award compensation for losses resulting from such action. Board procedures usually require an attempt to resolve disputes through negotiation or mediation prior to adjudication.

Violation of collective bargaining legislation may also lead to prosecutions in the criminal courts and to penal sanctions. This rarely occurs today.

Through convention and because of the requirements of labour relations statutes, such as section 48(1) of the Ontario *Labour Relations Act, 1995*, collective agreements contain no-strike clauses which are enforced through the grievance procedure in the agreement and ultimately through arbitration. Arbitrators can award damages for violation of a no-strike clause, and may also have the authority to issue orders prohibiting the recurrence of industrial action. Almost all collective agreements also prohibit employers from disciplining employees except where there is just cause.

Accordingly, a strike or lockout, or an episode of picketing or other conduct that occurs during a strike or lockout, can give rise to proceedings in several forums — an action in the civil courts, a labour relations board proceeding, a prosecution in the criminal courts, and an arbitration proceeding involving an employer claim for damages or an employee grievance against discipline imposed by the employer. Because each of these forums applies a different subset of the broad array of legal rules that govern industrial conflict, whether a remedy will lie against a particular labour relations tactic may well depend on where relief is sought. Finally, the constitutionality of the legal rules in question may be challenged under the *Canadian Charter of Rights and Freedoms*, and such a challenge may be made in any of the proceedings just mentioned.

8:310 The Courts

8:311 Criminal Jurisdiction
Courts play a significant role in some labour disputes through their administration of the general criminal law. Basic *Criminal Code* prohibitions against assault, mischief, and other forms of trespass to persons and property, which we will not examine here, may

be violated by conduct engaged in during a labour dispute. See Jonathan Eaton, "Is Picketing a Crime?" (1992) 47 Relations industrielles 100.

There is, however, a less familiar criminal offence, called "watching and besetting," that is particularly relevant to industrial conflict. Section 423 of the *Criminal Code* states:

> 423(1) Every one who, wrongfully and without lawful authority, for the purpose of compelling another person to abstain from doing anything that he has a lawful right to do, or to do anything that he has a lawful right to abstain from doing, . . . (f) besets or watches the dwelling-house or place where that person resides, works, carries on business or happens to be, . . . is guilty of an offence punishable on summary conviction.
>
> (2) A person who attends at or near or approaches a dwelling-house or place, for the purpose only of obtaining or communicating information, does not watch or beset within the meaning of this section.

The application of the offence of watching and besetting in situations of industrial conflict, and the applicability of the saving clause in section 423(2) when the picketing goes beyond communicating information, are discussed by Jonathan Eaton, above, at 102–10.

An important practical effect of the use of criminal law in labour disputes is that it leads to the involvement of the police in the regulation of picket line behaviour. The police have at times allowed themselves to become closely identified with the interests of employers. In recent years, however, sophisticated police forces have come to see themselves as neutrals, attempting on-the-spot mediation between picketers and others who encounter a picket line.

Penal prosecutions under labour relations legislation provide another potential avenue for court involvement in strikes. This avenue has remained significant in Quebec, where any interested party can bring a prosecution for contravention of the *Labour Code*, including the ban on strikes. These prosecutions are heard by the Labour Court (a division of the Court of Quebec), with an appeal to the Superior Court by way of trial de novo. Only penal sanctions, principally fines, are available as remedies. The significance of such prosecutions is likely to decrease because the *Labour Code* has recently been amended to create a labour board with broad remedial powers.

In all other jurisdictions, access to penal prosecutions has been reduced or eliminated. Sections 104–09 of the Ontario *Labour Relations Act 1995* are typical. Before a prosecution can be launched, consent must be obtained from the labour relations board (or in some jurisdictions, the Minister). This consent is seldom sought, and rarely granted save in egregious cases. Even when consent is obtained, prosecution is almost never proceeded with. Even a successful prosecution, coming to trial long after the events at issue and leading to fines payable to the Crown and not the victim, is very rarely thought to be worth the trouble.

8:312 Civil Jurisdiction

In practice, the courts' civil jurisdiction has been much more important than their criminal jurisdiction. Civil actions can bring immediate relief through injunctions forcing illegal strikers back to work, restricting picketing, or limiting the use of other economic sanctions, except in jurisdictions where (as will be discussed later) injunctions have been displaced to some degree by labour relations board remedies. Damages may also be available in certain circumstances.

More will be said later in this chapter about injunctions and damages as remedies. Before looking at remedies, however, we must look at some of the principal causes of action that have been used (and sometimes are still used) against industrial action.

8:313 Tort Illegalities

Civil suits with respect to industrial action have sometimes been based on breach of contract, especially where no collective bargaining relationship exists, but in practice such suits are usually based on tort. Nominate torts such as assault, trespass, and defamation, which protect basic interests in physical security of the person and property and in reputation, can ground such suits and sometimes do. More important in the area of industrial action, however, are a group of generally newer and more complex torts commonly known as the "economic torts." They were designed to provide redress against losses resulting from hostile use of the collective strength of economic adversaries, especially collective employee strength exerted through strikes and boycotts. The best-established and most frequently used of these torts are conspiracy and inducing breach of contract.

The development of the economic torts by the English courts is a fascinating story, which we do not have the space to recount. An excellent account is given by K.W. Wedderburn, "Strike Law and the Labour Injunction: The British Experience, 1850–1966" in *Report of a Study on the Labour Injunction in Ontario*, by A.W.R. Carrothers, vol. 2 (Toronto: Ontario Department of Labour, 1966) at 603. Wedderburn describes how the English courts invented new economic torts, or relaxed the requirements of existing ones, in order to deal with outbursts of trade union militancy.

The doctrinal requirements of the economic torts will be summarized in the following paragraphs, in roughly the form in which they were developed by English courts up to about 1975, prior to major statutory changes in English labour law which are not relevant to Canada. As should become apparent by the end of this chapter, Canadian courts have not applied the requirements of the English court decisions rigorously or consistently, but have often bent or disregarded them in order to facilitate the granting of remedies against industrial action, especially in cases of secondary picketing in support of legal strikes. Some feel for the technical requirements of the economic torts is necessary, however, in order to understand the approach of Canadian courts to industrial conflict.

The Tort of Conspiracy to Injure by Lawful Means
This requires

1) a combination of two or more persons;
2) an intention to cause economic injury to the plaintiff and the causing of such injury; and
3) a predominant purpose or motive that the courts do not recognize as being a legitimate interest.

The courts have recognized the traditional collective bargaining activities of unions, including the demand for a closed shop, as legitimate interests. See *Crofter Hand Woven*

Harris Tweed Co. v. Veitch, [1942] A.C. 435 (H.L.). In Ontario, section 3(1) of the *Rights of Labour Act*, R.S.O. 1990, c. R33, provides as follows:

> An act done by two or more members of a trade union, if done in contemplation or furtherance of a trade dispute, is not actionable unless the act would be actionable if done without agreement or combination.

This would appear to eliminate conspiracy to injure as a cause of action in labour cases, subject, however, to the fact that the courts have interpreted secondary picketing as going beyond the scope of a "trade dispute." This matter will be examined further in the discussion on secondary picketing, below, section 8:420.

The Tort of Conspiracy to Injure by Use of Unlawful Means
This requires

1) a combination of two or more persons;
2) an intention to cause economic injury to the plaintiff; and
3) the use of unlawful means to cause the injury.

In *Rookes v. Barnard*, [1964] A.C. 1129, the House of Lords held that any illegality (in that case, a breach of the defendants' contracts of employment) would suffice as unlawful means.

The Tort of Directly Inducing Breach of Contract
This requires

1) an intention by the defendant to cause economic injury to the plaintiff;
2) knowledge by the defendant that there is a contract between the plaintiff and a third party;
3) the use of lawful means by the defendant to persuade the third party to breach the contract;
4) a breach of the contract; and
5) economic injury to the plaintiff as a reasonable consequence of the breach.

The requirements of knowledge and persuasion have been whittled away significantly in recent decades. The requisite knowledge will exist if the defendant ought reasonably to believe that a contractual relationship exists, even if he or she may not know of its terms, or if the defendant acts "recklessly," without caring whether a contract exists. As for the element of persuasion, it is enough that the defendant conveys information to a third party whom the defendant would like to see act in a certain way (for example, to honour a picket line) and the third party does in fact act in that way. There is a defence of "justification" to this tort, but the pursuit of union objectives has traditionally not been considered as justification. See Lord Pearce's judgment in *Stratford v. Lindley*, [1965] A.C. 269 (H.L.), and compare it with *Thomson v. Deakin*, [1952] Ch. 646 (C.A.).

The Tort of Indirectly Procuring Breach of Contract by Unlawful Means
This requires

1) an intention by the defendant to cause economic injury to the plaintiff;

2) knowledge by the defendant that there is a contract between the plaintiff and a third party;
3) a threat by the defendant to use unlawful means against the third party unless the latter breaches his or her contract with the plaintiff, or the actual use of unlawful means for that purpose by the defendant;
4) a breach of the contract between the plaintiff and the third party; and
5) economic injury to the plaintiff as a necessary consequence of the breach.

The key to this tort is unlawful means. Under *Rookes v. Barnard*, above, any technically illegal conduct can suffice for the purposes of the tort, whether that conduct be a crime, another tort, or a breach of contract. The defence of justification has traditionally not been available where unlawful means are present, but Lord Denning intimated otherwise in *Morgan v. Fry*, [1968] 2 Q.B. 710 (C.A.).

Direct Interference with Contractual Relations Falling Short of Breach
This tort was "discovered" by Lord Denning in *Torquay Hotel Co. v. Cousins*, [1969] 2 Ch. 106 (C.A.). It requires

1) an intention by the defendant to injure the plaintiff economically;
2) an action by the defendant that has the effect of hindering or preventing performance of a contract between the plaintiff and a third party; and
3) that the defendant's action was a direct cause of that result.

In *Acrow (Automation) Ltd. v. Rex Chainbelt*, [1971] 3 A11 E.R. 1175 (C.A.), Lord Denning added the qualification that the action causing the interference must be unlawful. Nonetheless, Canadian courts appear to be applying the tort according to Lord Denning's original, less rigorous formulation.

The Tort of Intimidation
This requires

1) an intention by the defendant to injure the plaintiff economically;
2) a threat by the defendant to use unlawful means against a third party unless the latter takes action that will injure the plaintiff economically; and
3) action by the third party against the plaintiff which is lawful in itself but which causes the plaintiff economic injury.

The key element is again unlawful means. *Rookes v. Barnard*, above, held that if the threatened act is illegal in any way, be it a crime, a tort, or a breach of contract, that is sufficient to constitute unlawful means.

The Tort of Intentional Injury by Use of Unlawful Means
This residual tort requires

1) an intention by the defendant to injure the plaintiff economically, and
2) use by the defendant of unlawful means, in the *Rookes v. Barnard* sense, to cause the injury.

No combination is needed.

The potency of the foregoing torts in strikes and picketing becomes apparent if we imagine a fairly typical scenario of a union picketing a large construction site at which several other unionized trades are working. What sorts of tort illegalities might be present?

Some provinces have enacted legislative provisions restricting or abolishing certain of these torts, particularly those that do not require illegal means. See, for example, the British Columbia *Labour Relations Code*, sections 66 and 69, and the Ontario *Rights of Labour Act*, section 3(1). Nevertheless, the economic torts remain of some importance, especially where the collective employee action in question does not constitute a breach of labour relations legislation or of any other statute (for example, where there is a legal strike supported by peaceful picketing). In such cases, the economic torts are still often called on as a basis for restricting secondary action. We will refer to them again in the discussion on secondary picketing, below, section 8:420.

When an industrial action constitutes a breach of a labour relations statute, the economic torts are less important. Courts have taken the position that a violation of labour legislation is itself enough to ground liability in tort, either because such a violation constitutes a tort in itself or because noncompliance with the statute constitutes the element of illegality necessary to make out one of the economic torts. A crucial step in this direction was taken by the Supreme Court of Canada in *Gagnon v. Foundation Maritime Ltd.* (1961), 28 D.L.R. (2d) 174, where the violation of a statutory strike ban was held to constitute unlawful means for the purpose of the tort of conspiracy to injure by unlawful means.

In other areas of law, it is not normally assumed that violation of a statute which is silent on the question of civil suit automatically gives rise to a cause of action. Indeed, the contrary is true; if a statute prohibits certain conduct and provides its own form of recourse for those affected by such conduct, they must pursue the remedies provided by the statute and cannot sue civilly: *Seneca College of Applied Arts and Technology v. Bhadauria* (1981), 124 D.L.R. (3d) 193 (S.C.C.). In the context of industrial conflict, however, the courts have departed from this approach and have been willing to base civil actions on breach of the labour relations statute alone, without even trying to make the breach into a component of an identifiable tort. In *International Brotherhood of Electrical Workers v. Winnipeg Builders Exchange*, [1967] S.C.R. 628, the Supreme Court of Canada upheld an injunction against a strike that was untimely and therefore illegal under the labour relations statute and the no-strike clause of the collective agreement. Cartwright J., for the Court, did not rely on any economic tort, but simply held, at 640, that

> the purposes of the *Labour Relations Act* would be in large measure defeated if the Court were to say that it is powerless to restrain the continuation of a strike in direct violation of the terms of a collective agreement binding on the striking employees and in breach of the express provisions of the Act.

In ordering the strikers back to work, Cartwright J. also departed from the common law's long-standing refusal to order the specific performance of employment contracts, discussed below, Chapter 2. At 640 he wrote:

There is a real difference between saying to one individual that he must go on working for another individual and saying to a group bound by a collective agreement that they must not take concerted action to break this contract and to disobey the statute law of the province.

In *Maritime Employers' Association*, above, section 8:213, the basis of liability again seems to have been violation of the labour relations legislation and the applicable collective agreements, no other cause of action being mentioned.

✻ ✻ ✻

Some courts have begun in recent years, when asked to grant an injunction based on one of the above-mentioned economic torts, to indicate a willingness to give weight to striking workers' interests in peaceful picketing in support of a lawful strike, even where that picketing has secondary effects. Most notable in this regard is *Pepsi-Cola Beverages (West) v. R.W.D.S.U., Local 558* (1998), 167 D.L.R. (4th) 220 (Sask. C.A.) [leave to appeal to SCC granted, [1998] S.C.C.A. No. 624; appeal heard 31 October 2000]. The Saskatchewan Court of Appeal noted the constitutional value of freedom of speech raised by such picketing and indicated that the courts should limit their function to maintaining the peace and should not move to restrain such picketing unless the plaintiff has made out all of the constituent elements of the tort in question with sufficient certainty to warrant court intervention. See excerpts from *Pepsi-Cola Beverages (West) v. R.W.D.S.U., Local 558*, below at 8:420.

8:314 The Legal Capacity of Trade Unions to Sue and Be Sued

The foregoing brief outline of the civil jurisdiction of courts over industrial action raises the threshold issue of whether a trade union has the legal capacity to sue or be sued in a civil action. This question is significant in several areas of labour law — industrial conflict, the enforcement of collective agreements, the law of internal union affairs — in short, wherever a court action is contemplated by or against a union. This is the first point where the question arises in this book, so it will be dealt with here.

At common law, a trade union is traditionally considered to be a voluntary unincorporated association, and therefore not a legal entity. It is deemed to be held together merely by a web of implied bipartite contracts between each member and every other member, and these contracts are deemed to incorporate the terms set out in the union's constitution. To avoid making unions and other unincorporated associations legally liable for the actions of members over whom they might have little or no control, the common law has long taken the position that such associations cannot be sued (or sue) in their own names unless a statute says they can. Courts have often sought to circumvent this obstacle where a union is being sued for taking illegal industrial action.

The following is the leading case holding that the traditional common law position has been overridden by Canadian labour relations legislation.

International Brotherhood of Teamsters v. Therien, [1960] S.C.R. 265 at 268–69, 271–78

[Therien was an independent trucking contractor who contracted with City Construction Co. to provide his own services and those of several drivers whom he employed. The collective agreement between City Construction and the Teamsters provided that City Construction would hire only union members. The union demanded that Therien become a member. He refused, arguing that as an employer himself he was not an "employee" for the purposes of the statute and the collective agreement. The union responded by threatening to picket City Construction's work sites if Therien remained on the job. As a result, City Construction terminated its contract with Therien, who sued the union for damages and an injunction.]

LOCKE J.: This is an appeal from a judgment of the Court of Appeal of British Columbia which dismissed the appeal of the present appellant, the defendant in the action, from a judgment of Clyne J. By that judgment the respondent recovered general damages in the sum of $2,500, special damages for loss of profit for a named period, and was granted an injunction restraining the appellant from interfering with the plaintiff, his agents or servants or any of them, in the operation of his business by endeavouring to induce or coerce the plaintiff to join the defendant union or from negotiating or dealing with any person, firm or corporation in any way to induce or coerce the plaintiff to join the said union. . . .

The appellant is a trade union, as that expression is defined in the *Labour Relations Act*, 1954 (B.C.), c. 17, s. 1. Local No. 213, the appellant in these proceedings, is an organization forming part of an international union which has its headquarters in the United States.

. . . While no evidence was given upon the point, it appears to have been assumed throughout that the union had been certified as the bargaining agent of these employees under the provisions of the *Labour Relations Act* and was, accordingly, empowered to contract in writing on their behalf in regard to their working conditions, rates of pay and other matters commonly forming part of a collective agreement. . . .

That damage to the respondent resulted from these actions cannot be disputed. By way of defence to the action the appellant says, firstly, that it is not a legal entity which may be found liable in tort, and secondly, that the evidence does not disclose a cause of action, either at common law or under the *Industrial Conciliation and Arbitration Act*. . . .

The question as to whether a trade union certified as a bargaining agent by a statute in the terms of the *Labour Relations Act* of British Columbia may be made liable in an action, either in tort or contract, has not heretofore been considered by this Court.

In *Taff Vale Railway v. Amalgamated Society of Railway Servants* [[1901] A.C. 426] the action was brought against a trade union registered under the *Trade Union Acts* of 1871 and 1876 for an injunction restraining the union, its servants and agents and others acting by their authority from watching or besetting the Great Western Railway Station at Cardiff. A motion made on behalf of the union before Farwell J. to strike out the name of that defendant on the ground that it was neither a corporation nor an individual and could not be sued in a quasi-corporate or any other capacity was dismissed.

It appears to me to be clear that, had it not been that the trade union was registered under the *Trade Union Act*, the action against it by name would not have been maintained. Provision was made by the Act of 1871 for the registration of trade unions and they were given power, *inter alia*, to purchase property in the names of trustees designated by them and to sell or let such property. The trustees of any registered union were empowered to bring or defend actions touching or concerning the property of the union and might be sued in any court of law or equity in respect of any real or personal property of the union. The union was also required to have a registered office and to make annual returns to the Registrar appointed under the Act yearly, and any trade union failing to comply with the provisions of the Act and every officer of the union so failing was made liable to a penalty.

Farwell J. [whose judgment was affirmed by the House of Lords] said that the fact that a trade union is neither a corporation nor an individual or a partnership between a number of individuals did not conclude the matter. After pointing out that the Acts legalized the usual trade union contracts, established a registry of trade unions giving to each an exclusive right to the name in which it was registered and authorized it through the medium of trustees to own a limited amount of real estate and unlimited personal estate, said in part . . . :

> Now, although a corporation and an individual or individuals may be the only entity known to the common law who can sue or be sued, it is competent to the Legislature to give to an association of individuals which is neither a corporation nor a partnership nor an individual a capacity for owning property and acting by agents, and such capacity in the absence of express enactment to the contrary involves the necessary correlative of liability to the extent of such property for the acts and defaults of such agents. . . .
>
> Now, the Legislature in giving a trade union the capacity to own property and the capacity to act by agents has, without incorporating it, given it two of the essential qualities of a corporation — essential, I mean, in respect of liability for tort, for a corporation can only act by its agents, and can only be made to pay by means of its property. . . . The proper rule of construction of statutes such as these is that in the absence of express contrary intention the Legislature intends that the creature of the statute shall have the same duties, and that its funds shall be subject to the same liabilities as the general law would impose on a private individual doing the same thing. It would require very clear and express words of enactment to induce me to hold that the Legislature had in fact legalised the existence of such irresponsible bodies with such wide capacity for evil. . . .

It was, undoubtedly, as a result of the judgment in the *Taff Vale* case that the *Trade Disputes Act* of 1906 (c. 47) which amended the *Trade Union Acts* of 1871 and 1876 was passed. That Act did not alter the law as declared by the House of Lords as to registered trade unions being entities which might be held liable in tort, but declared the rights of persons on behalf of trade unions to carry on what has now become to be known as peaceful picketing, and further declared that an action against a trade union or any members or officials thereof on behalf of themselves and all other members of such union in respect of any tortious act alleged to have been committed by or on behalf of the union should not be entertained by any Court.

It was clearly, I think, in consequence of the *Taff Vale* decision that the Legislature of British Columbia enacted the *Trade Union Act* of 1902 (c. 66). This Act declared that no trade union or the trustees of any such union shall be liable for damages for any wrongful act or omission or commission in connection with any strike, lock-out or trade or labour dispute, unless the members of such union or its council or other governing body shall have authorized, or shall have been a concurring party in such wrongful act: that no such trade union nor any of its servants or agents shall be enjoined, nor its funds or any of such officers be made liable for communicating to any person facts respecting employment or hiring or in persuading or endeavouring to persuade by fair or reasonable argument any workman or person to refuse to continue or become the employee or customer of any employer of labour. Section 3 of that Act further declared that no trade union or its agents or servants shall be liable in damages for publishing information with regard to a strike or lock-out or for warning workmen or other persons against seeking employment in the locality affected by any strike, lock-out or labour trouble or from purchasing, buying or consuming products produced by the employer of labour party to such strike.

It will be seen that the British Columbia Act, by its reference to trade unions as such, as well as to the servants and agents of such unions restricting their liability in tort to the extent defined, recognized the fact that a trade union was an entity which might be enjoined or become liable in damages for tort. . . .

By the *Labour Relations Act*, s. 2, a trade union as defined includes a local branch of an international organization such as the appellant in the present matter. Extensive rights are given to such trade unions and certain prohibitions declared which affect them. The Act treats a trade union as an entity and as such it is prohibited, *inter alia*, from attempting at the employer's place of employment during working hours to persuade an employee to join or not to join a trade union, from encouraging or engaging in any activity designed to restrict or limit production or services, from using coercion or intimidation of any kind that could reasonably have the effect of compelling any person to become or refrain to become a member of a trade union and from declaring or authorizing a strike until certain defined steps have been taken. By s. 7 if there is a complaint to the Labour Relations Board that a union is doing or has done any act prohibited by ss. 4, 5 or 6, the Board may order that the default be remedied and, if it continues, the union may be prosecuted for a breach of the Act. By s. 9 all employers are required to honour a written assignment of wages by their employees to a trade union. A union claiming to have as members in good standing a majority of employees in a unit appropriate for collective bargaining is entitled to apply to the Labour Relations Board for certification as the bargaining agent of such employees and, when certified, to require the employer to bargain with it and, if agreement is reached, to enter into a written agreement with it which is signed by the union in its own name as such bargaining agent. Throughout the Act such organizations are referred to as trade unions and thus treated as legal entities. . . .

Were it not for the provisions of the *Trade-unions Act* and the *Industrial Relations Act* if the union was simply an unincorporated association of workmen, it would not, in my opinion, be an entity which might be sued by name. . . . Such an unincorporated body not being an entity known to the law would be incapable of entering into a contract: . . . . That, however, is not the present case. . . .

The granting of these rights, powers and immunities to these unincorporated associations or bodies is quite inconsistent with the idea that it was not intended that they should be constituted legal entities exercising these powers and enjoying these immunities as such. What was said by Farwell J. in the passage from the judgment in the Taff Vale case which is above quoted appears to me to be directly applicable. It is necessary for the exercise of the powers given that such unions should have officers or other agents to act in their names and on their behalf. The legislature, by giving the right to act as agent for others and to contract on their behalf, has given them two of the essential qualities of a corporation in respect of liability for tort since a corporation can only act by its agents. . . .

. . . In the absence of anything to show a contrary intention — and there is nothing here — the Legislature must be taken to have intended that the creature of the statute shall have the same duties and that its funds shall be subject to the same liabilities as the general law would impose on a private individual doing the same thing. *Qui sentit commodum sentire debet et onus.*

In my opinion, the appellant is a legal entity which may be made liable in name for damages either for breach of a provision of the *Labour Relations Act* or under the common law.

* * *

Locke J. went on to hold that the union had committed the tort of intentionally causing economic injury by unlawful means — that is, by breaching the labour legislation which required that disputes over the application of a collective agreement were to be settled by arbitration and not by industrial action or the threat of it.

Canadian legislatures have taken various approaches to the question of the legal capacity of unions for litigation purposes. Some make no mention of the matter in any statute, with the result that the holding in *Therien* governs. Others have enacted provisions similar to section 23(1) of the Alberta *Labour Relations Code*, which provides that unions can sue or be sued "for the purposes of this Act." Proceedings arising from industrial action have been held to fall within the purposes of the Act. At the other extreme is Ontario, which since 1944 has had the following provisions in its *Rights of Labour Act*:

> Section 3(2) A trade union shall not be made a party to any action in any court unless it may be so made a party irrespective of this Act or of the *Labour Relations Act*.
>
> Section 3(3) A collective bargaining agreement shall not be the subject of any action in any court unless it may be the subject of such action irrespective of this Act or of the *Labour Relations Act*.

Section 3(2) has often been held to render the holding in *Therien* inapplicable in Ontario, and to preclude suits by or against unions in their own names. Where neither *Therien* nor a specific statutory provision allows a union to be sued, it may be possible to bring a "representative action" against named officers of the union, on the basis that they "represent" the interest of the entire membership in the particular matter. Courts, however, have often held "that it is not proper or convenient to allow a plaintiff to obtain what would in effect be a personal judgment against every member of an unincorporated body for the tortious act of one or some of its officers or members": *Body v. Murdoch*, [1954] O.W.N. 658 at 658–61, Marriott Senior Master. To avoid putting the personal assets of individual members in jeopardy, the courts have usually restricted representative actions to situations where the union has a trust fund, the terms of which would allow it to be used to satisfy a judgment — and very few unions have such funds. See Douglas J. Sherbaniuk, "Actions By and Against Trade Unions in Contract and Tort" (1958) 12 U.T.L.J. 151.

In *Professional Institute of the Public Service of Canada v. Canada (Attorney General)* (2002), 222 D.L.R. (4th) 438 (Ont. C.A.)., Goudge J.A. (for the court) held that the *Rights of Labour Act*, being a provincial statute, did not preclude a suit in the Ontario courts by a union operating within the federal jurisdiction. Although the case before him did not involve unions operating within the provincial jurisdiction in Ontario, Goudge J.A. in an *obiter dictum*, expressed the view that it was time to do away totally with the restriction in section 3(2) on the capacity of unions to sue and be sued. After referring to *Berry v. Pulley* [2002] 2 S.C.R. 493, excerpted below in Chapter 10 (section 10:500), Goudge J.A. said, at paragraph 45:

> Although it is not necessary to decide in this case, the answer I have given to the application [to unions within federal jurisdiction] of s. 3(2) of the [*Rights of Labour Act*] might well be different for unions governed by the [*Ontario Labour Relations Act*], something which could force them to attempt to access the courts using the antiquated and uncertain vehicle of the representative action. . . . Such a result would seem inconsistent with the broad, principled approach to the legal status of unions found in [*Berry v. Pulley*]. That approach reflects the reality that, across the country, unions share a common history and, speaking generically, perform common functions, and are governed by common legislative provisions. Viewed against this commonality, if s. 3(2) creates an anomalous result for some unions in a single province, it may be time, after more than 50 years, that it be revisited for possible revision.

In *United Nurses of Alberta v. Alberta (A.G.)* (1992), 89 D.L.R. (4th) 609, the Supreme Court of Canada held that a union had sufficient legal status to be prosecuted for criminal contempt of court.

8:315 Civil Remedies: Damages and Injunctions

Damages
Outside the labour context, the conventional remedy for a civil wrong is damages. Damages have on occasion been awarded in cases arising out of labour disputes. In *United Steelworkers of America v. Gaspé Copper Mines Ltd.* (1970), 10 D.L.R. (3d) 443 (S.C.C.), damages of $1.75 million (and thirteen years' interest) were assessed against a union for admittedly criminal and tortious conduct committed during an illegal strike.

The deliberate commission of a tort — whether it is a nominate tort such as assault or trespass, or an economic tort such as conspiracy — gives rise not merely to a claim for compensatory damages to make the injured plaintiff whole, but also to punitive damages. Punitive damages are intended to discourage the defendant and others from repeating the tort, and may be assessed in whatever amount the court believes is necessary to accomplish that result. The potential of this kind of award in a labour dispute is easily imagined.

Nevertheless, employers have rarely pursued such claims to judgment, and even more rarely have they collected on them in full. More commonly, the existence of the suit, or the damage award if there is one, is used by the employer as a bargaining counter to obtain a settlement, either for a lesser amount of damages or for favourable collective agreement terms. Damages can be awarded by a civil court only after pleadings, discovery, and trial — a time-consuming process that can take years, during which time the union may continue to pursue the impugned conduct, inflicting harm on the employer and accumulating bargaining counters to trade off against an ultimate unfavourable tort judgment.

These substantial practical impediments have made actions in damages very rare indeed. They have become rarer still as a result of the decision of the Supreme Court of Canada in *St. Anne Nackawic*, set out below.

Injunctions

Injunctions have always played a much more significant role than damages in labour disputes, because of the speed and relative ease with which they can be obtained and because they immediately prohibit the industrial action in question rather than merely granting a monetary remedy long after the fact. Throughout Canada, injunctions used to be the principal means of enforcing limitations on industrial action. More recently, labour legislation in several provinces has sought to replace injunctions with cease-and-desist orders issued by labour relations boards. But as we will see, in most of those jurisdictions injunctions retain a crucial role in the regulation of picketing.

The labour injunction was, and to an extent still is, a focal point for union hostility. It generated violent political controversy and searching academic criticism in the United States, where its use was largely suppressed by the *Norris-LaGuardia Act* of 1932, and in Canada: see A. Carrothers, *The Labour Injunction in British Columbia* (Toronto: CCH Canadian, 1956), and *Report of a Study on the Labour Injunction in Ontario* by A. Carrothers, vol. 1 (Toronto: Ontario Department of Labour, 1966).

The technique generally developed by the courts to make speedy relief available was the interlocutory injunction. This type of injunction, granted on motion, was designed to preserve the status quo pending a full trial, in circumstances where the applicant was in danger of suffering irreparable harm that could not be adequately compensated for by money damages awarded after the event. In theory, it was contemplated that the merits of the plaintiff's claim would ultimately be tested in a full trial, but in fact, in labour matters, the interlocutory proceeding has almost always disposed of the case. By the time a full trial can be arranged, months can pass and the controversy can become moot.

The courts have developed a three-stage test for deciding whether to grant an interlocutory injunction. This test is quite simple to state but difficult to apply. It was summarized by Sopinka and Cory JJ. of the Supreme Court of Canada in *RJR-MacDonald Inc. v. Canada (A.G.)*, [1994] 1 S.C.R. 311 at 334:

> . . . First, a preliminary assessment must be made of the merits of the case to ensure that there is a serious question to be tried. Secondly, it must be determined whether the appli-

cant would suffer irreparable harm if the application were refused. Finally, an assessment must be made as to which of the parties would suffer greater harm from the granting or refusal of the remedy pending a decision on the merits.

An example of the application of this test in a case of aggressive picketing in support of a legal strike is provided by *Urban Parcel Services Ltd. v. Canadian Union of Postal Workers and Mapp* (1992), 107 N.S.R. (2d) 63 (S.C.T.D.). Kelly J., at 72, quoted the following from an unreported judgment of Glube C.J. of the same court in 1990:

> I must express my deep concern that the court continues to be used to deal with labour-management disputes. . . . In my opinion the use of the courts to deal with labour-management disputes is a practice which is not appropriate as the courts are thrust into an almost untenable position and our procedure, which is rigid, tends to entrench the parties' opposing positions. Often, whether it is actually so or not, the court begins to feel that it is being used as a bargaining tool.

These comments are in line with a number of serious concerns expressed over the years about the use of interlocutory injunctions in cases of industrial conflict. One concern focused on undue haste in the proceedings. In urgent cases, the courts had the power to grant an interlocutory injunction *ex parte*, without notice, and often did so on the mere allegation by the plaintiff that there was no time to give the defendant notice. Even when normal notice requirements were observed, the notice period (two days in Ontario) was often insufficient for the defendant to gather evidence in reply.

A related concern involved laxness with respect to proof. Normally, evidence is given in interlocutory proceedings by means of affidavits, with the courts seldom exercising their power to hear *viva voce* evidence. Although the defendant technically had the right to cross-examine the deponent who made the affidavit, in fact the time required to do so could only be purchased by obtaining the union's agreement that the injunction should issue in the meantime. Given this virtual immunity both from cross-examination and reply evidence, affidavits were often drafted in vague and general terms and often contained half-truths or untruths.

A third concern was that interlocutory orders are not normally appealable except with the consent of the court. Such consent has rarely been given in labour matters. Accordingly, the great bulk of decisions in labour injunction cases were by courts of first instance, and there was relatively little opportunity for appeal courts to rationalize conflicting lines of trial decisions or even to correct errors below.

A fourth concern related to the broad scope of labour injunctions, which were typically directed against the named defendants, "their servants or agents, and anyone having knowledge of this order." This had the effect of binding persons who might have interests quite different from those of the named defendants, but who, in any event, had no opportunity of coming to argue that they ought not to be bound by the order.

In response to these concerns and others, some legislatures have reformed injunction procedures. For example, the Ontario *Courts of Justice Act*, section 102, provides that no injunction may be given on an *ex parte* basis. Where an injunction is given on an *inter partes* basis, a number of safeguards are imposed: affidavit evidence is limited to facts "within the knowledge of the deponent," who may be required by the other side to appear for cross-examination; at least two days' notice of motion must be given to the union and any other persons affected by the injunction; and the maximum duration of the injunction is four days. An exception is made with respect to service of notice where the delay would result in "irreparable damage or injury, a breach of the peace or an inter-ruption in an essential public service," and the judge believes that it is "otherwise . . . proper" to dispense with notice. In that event, reasonable steps must be taken to put the other side on notice of the application, and material facts must be established by oral evidence. In addition, no injunction of any kind can be given unless the court is sat-isfied that 'reasonable efforts to obtain police assistance, protection and action to pre-vent or remove any alleged danger of damage to property, injury to persons, obstruction of or interference with lawful entry or exit from the premises in question or breach of the peace have been unsuccessful.' (see below, 8:410).

Finally, all of the above protections apply only to actions "in connection with a labour dispute," which is defined as "a dispute or difference concerning terms . . . of employ-ment . . . regardless of whether the disputants stand in the proximate relation of employ-er and employee" (section 102(1)). These provisions have given rise to considerable litigation over whether certain actions are taken "in connection with a labour dispute." This is a point of particular significance in cases of so-called secondary action (see below, section 8:420).

Even in provinces where the power to grant injunctions has not been restricted by leg-islation, courts have themselves adopted certain safeguards. It is now very rare, for example, for labour injunctions to be granted *ex parte*.

Controversy over the labour injunction also extends to certain aspects of its enforce-ment. As long as an injunction stands, it must be obeyed even though its validity is chal-lenged. Disobedience constitutes contempt of court, which is punishable in summary proceedings by fine or imprisonment, the severity of which is at the judge's discretion. What constitutes disobedience of an injunction is also a matter for judicial discretion, but because contempt is a common law crime, it must, in principle, be strictly proven.

In *United Nurses of Alberta v. Alberta (A.G.)*, [1992] 1 S.C.R. 901, the wide divergence of views in this area was reflected in a sharp division in the Supreme Court of Canada over the propriety of using a criminal contempt proceeding to enforce an order prohibit-ing an illegal strike by nurses, who had no right to strike in Alberta. The order in this case was not a court injunction but a labour board's cease-and-desist order, which had been registered as an order of the court. In the majority judgment, which held that the particular circumstances were appropriate for use of a criminal contempt proceeding, McLachlin J. wrote, at page 933:

> While publicity is required for the offence, a civil contempt is not converted to a criminal
> contempt merely because it attracts publicity, as the union contends, but rather because
> it constitutes a public act of defiance of the court in circumstances where the accused

knew, intended or was reckless as to the fact that the act would publicly bring the court into contempt.

In this case there was ample evidence to support the conclusion that the union chose to defy court orders openly and continuously, with full knowledge that its defiance would be widely publicized and, even putting the union's case at its best, it did not care whether this would bring the court into disrepute.

Criminal contempt, thus defined, does not violate the *Charter*. It is neither vague nor arbitrary. A person can predict in advance whether his or her conduct will constitute a crime. . . .

Cory J., dissenting, wrote at page 919:

The imposition of huge fines in labour disputes such as the $400,000 fine in the case at bar is contrary to the intent of the *Labour Relations Act*. The use of criminal contempt proceedings and the imposition of such crushing penalties are inappropriate except in circumstances of violence or threats of serious violence. The concerns voiced by the respondent [Attorney General] that, without the criminal contempt power, the courts and labour boards will have difficulty enforcing their orders and that respect for the rule of law will be threatened are, in my view, groundless in light of the effective alternate remedies that were available.

* * *

British Columbia, alone among Canadian provinces, decided as long ago as 1973 to adopt a more far-reaching solution than Ontario to the many problems posed by the labour injunction. The British Columbia *Labour Relations Code*, in sections 136–37, purports to abolish the courts' authority to grant injunctions in labour matters, providing instead for regulation by the labour board. The courts, however, may still grant an injunction when the conduct complained of "causes immediate danger of serious injury to an individual or causes actual obstruction or physical damage to property," and they have in fact claimed a jurisdiction broader than that expressly reserved to them: see *Better Value Furniture v. Vancouver Distribution Centre Ltd.* (1981), 122 D.L.R. (3d) 12 (B.C.C.A.).

In theory, before a civil court can take jurisdiction over any matter and grant any remedy, including an injunction, the plaintiff must assert a recognized cause of action. This basic principle, which has not always been scrupulously respected in labour injunction cases, has been restricted to some extent by *Brotherhood of Maintenance of Way Employees v. Canadian Pacific Ltd.* (1996), 21 B.C.L.R. (2d) 201 (S.C.C.), which held that the required right of action can lie in another forum. In the *Canadian Pacific* case, that other forum was grievance arbitration, because the underlying dispute involved the interpretation of a collective agreement. Arbitrators generally do not have the authority to make interim orders except in procedural matters, and the Supreme Court of Canada pointed to that fact as justification for the granting of an injunction by the courts in order to avoid allegedly irreparable harm while the matter was going through arbitration.

The *St. Anne Nackawic* case is the leading decision of the Supreme Court of Canada on two aspects of the law on the remedies available for illegal industrial action. One aspect is the very narrow scope that remains for civil actions for damages in respect of industrial action which contravenes a collective agreement. This matter will be looked at below in Chapter 9 (section 9:631), with respect to the enforcement of collective agreements. The other aspect, more central to the concerns of the present chapter, relates to the continued availability of court injunctions against unlawful industrial action, even when a collective agreement is in force and the arbitral forum is therefore available to the injured party. *St. Anne Nackawic* thus bears witness to the entrenched status of the injunction in Canadian industrial dispute law, notwithstanding the thrust of modern labour relations legislation.

St. Anne Nackawic Pulp & Paper Co. Ltd. v. Canadian Paper Workers Union, Local 219, [1986] 1 S.C.R. 704 at 708–14, 717–27, 731

[The respondent union represented two bargaining units — mill workers and office workers — at the appellant company's pulp and paper mill in New Brunswick. The office workers went out on a legal strike and picketed the mill. The mill workers, who could not legally strike because their collective agreement was in force, stayed out in sympathy with the office workers. The company began a court action three days after the strike began, and obtained an interlocutory injunction two days later. The mill workers did not return to work until after a finding of contempt of court was made against the union and three of its officers. Two weeks later the mill workers went out again. Despite another contempt order, they did not return to work until the office workers' strike was settled a few days later. The company then claimed damages against the union for the losses caused by the mill workers' strike.

The New Brunswick court held that it had the authority to award damages against the union because of the illegal strike, and it fined the union for the two instances of contempt. On appeal, the union challenged the court's jurisdiction to award damages to enforce the collective agreement. The union did not challenge the court's jurisdiction to issue the interlocutory injunction, nor did it challenge the findings of contempt. However, the Supreme Court of Canada considered whether the lower court could grant an injunction to enforce the no-strike clause of a collective agreement, as well as whether it could award damages for that purpose.]

> ESTEY J.: This case raises for the first time in this Court the question whether a court of otherwise competent jurisdiction is authorized to receive a claim by an employer for damages against a trade union, the bargaining agent for its employees, by reason of a strike which was allegedly, and on the record before this Court, apparently, illegal under the applicable labour relations statute, and which was at the same time a breach of a collective agreement to which the employer and the trade union are parties. . . .
>
> . . . There are numerous instances where the courts have issued injunctions in such circumstances, and the jurisdiction to do so was settled in *International Brotherhood of Electrical Engineers, Local Union 2085 v. Winnipeg Builders' Exchange.* . . . The courts have

also awarded damages in similar circumstances . . . but in those cases the issue of the jurisdiction of the court to do so was not challenged by the parties. . . .

In its pleadings, the appellant based its claim on the following ground:

> The said unlawful strike referred to in paragraph 6, was in breach of the Collective Agreement between the Plaintiff and the Defendant and in violation of the Industrial Relations Act.

The collective agreement referred to was the one between the mill unit and the appellant. It . . . provided that, 'There shall be no strike, lockout, stoppage, slow-down or restriction of output during the life of this Agreement.' The relevant sections of the Industrial Relations Act, R.S.N.B. 1973, c. 1-4, as amended, are as follows:

> 53(1) Every collective agreement shall provide that there shall be no strikes or lock-outs so long as the agreement continues to operate.

> 91(1) Where a collective agreement is in operation, no employee bound by the agreement shall strike . . . .

The Act further provides, however, and this is what led to the trial judge's reservation of the question of the court's jurisdiction as a preliminary matter, that:

> 55(1) Every collective agreement shall provide for the final and binding settlement by arbitration or otherwise, without stoppage of work, of all differences between the parties to, or persons bound by, the agreement or on whose behalf it was entered into, concerning its interpretation, application, administration or an alleged violation of the agreement, including any question as to whether a matter is arbitrable.

Where a collective agreement does not so provide, a very comprehensive arbitration clause is, by s. 5(2), deemed to be a provision of the agreement. The collective agreement between the appellant and respondent in this case did provide for arbitration. Clause 8 provided a procedure to be followed in the 'Adjustment of Complaints' which culminated in the appointment of a three member arbitration board whose decision would be 'final and binding upon both parties to the Agreement.' . . .

The preliminary question raised by the trial judge prior to trial, put simply, is whether, given the comprehensive provision for the submission to arbitration of all differences between the parties to a collective agreement, the court has any jurisdiction to hear a claim arising out of that agreement. . . .

An early consideration of the relative jurisdictions of court and arbitration board to entertain claims for breach of a collective agreement is found in *McGavin Toastmaster Ltd. v. Ainscough* . . . , where the employees claimed severance pay under their collective agreement after their employer had closed the plant during an illegal strike. Laskin C.J., writing for the majority, raised the issue of the Court's jurisdiction to hear a claim based on interpretation of a collective agreement which provided for grievance procedures and binding arbitration of such issues. He wrote . . . :

> There was no contention in defence that the appropriate proceedings should have been by way of arbitration under the collective agreement, and it does not appear that any

such position was taken either before the trial judge or in the British Columbia Court of Appeal. This Court refrained therefore in this case from taking any position on this question and is content to deal with the legal issue or issues as having been properly submitted to the Courts for adjudication.

The same approach was taken in the *Winnipeg Teachers' Association* case, . . . , *per* Martland J. . . . . The majority of the Court in that case acknowledged as well founded an employer's claim for damages arising out of the employees' 'work to rule' under the collective agreement. Laskin C.J., however, writing in dissent, took the position that if the parties had raised the issue, he would have allowed the appeal solely on the basis that . . . :

> . . . the machinery for determining contract disputes as prescribed by the collective agreement is not only better suited than resort to the Court, but ought to have been resorted to here for resolving what emerged as a difference about the nature or scope of the contractual obligation of the appellant's members and of the appellant itself. . . .

There are a significant number of decisions doubting the jurisdiction of the courts to hear claims based on the interpretation or application of collective agreements containing provision for binding arbitration. The earlier cases seemed to establish two exceptions to this principle. First, the courts have been held in a number of cases to have jurisdiction in a case where, although the claim depends entirely upon a right created by the terms of a collective agreement, the court is not required, in enforcing the right, to interpret the agreement. An example is *Hamilton Street Railway Co. v. Northcott*, . . . in which a prior arbitration had established the right of a group of employees to unpaid wages, but had not settled the amounts owing to each member of the group. The latter issue was held to be within the Court's jurisdiction.

The second exception consists of cases where the claim can be characterized as arising solely under the common law, and not under the collective agreement. An example is *Woods v. Miramichi Hospital* . . . a case involving a claim by an employee, a member of a bargaining unit, for damages for wrongful dismissal. . . .

In cases where the claim concerned an entitlement originating in the collective agreement, and the proper interpretation of the agreement was disputed, the courts uniformly have denied that they have jurisdiction: . . .

If there were nothing more than the collective agreement between bargaining agent and employer, the courts might still have applied the common law to its enforcement at the suit of the bargaining agent or the employer. The collective agreement embodies a holding out, a reliance, a consent and undertaking to perform, mutual consideration passing between the parties, and other elements of contract which would expose the parties to enforcement in the traditional courts. There would be, of course, a basic difficulty as to the status of the absent third party, the employee, and perhaps the absence of an identifiable benefit in the bargaining agent. All this is overcome by the statute, and the question whether worthwhile enforcement could be realized at common law is, therefore, of theoretical interest only. The missing elements are the status of the members of the bargaining unit and the appropriate forum. The legislature created the status of the parties in a process founded upon a solution to labour relations in a wholly new and statutory framework at the centre of which stands a new forum, the contract arbitration tribunal. Furthermore, the structure embodies a new form of triangular contract with but two signatories, a statutory solution to the disability of the common law in the field of third party rights. These are but some of the components in the all-embracing legislative program for the establishment and furtherance of labour relations in the interest of the community at large as well as in the interests of the parties to those labour relations. . . .

The collective agreement establishes the broad parameters of the relationship between the employer and his employees. This relationship is properly regulated through arbitration and it would, in general, subvert both the relationship and the statutory scheme under which it arises to hold that matters addressed and governed by the collective agreement may nevertheless be the subject of actions in the courts at common law. These considerations necessarily lead one to wonder whether the *Miramichi* case, *supra*, and cases like it, would survive an objection to the court's jurisdiction if decided today. The more modern approach is to consider that labour relations legislation provides a code governing all aspects of labour relations, and that it would offend the legislative scheme to permit the parties to a collective agreement, or the employees on whose behalf it was negotiated, to have recourse to the ordinary courts which are in the circumstances a duplicative forum to which the legislature has not assigned these tasks. . . .

. . . The courts have no jurisdiction to consider claims arising out of rights created by a collective agreement. Nor can the courts properly decide questions which might have arisen under the common law of master and servant in the absence of a collective bargaining regime if the collective agreement by which the parties to the action are bound makes provision for the matters in issue, whether or not it explicitly provides a procedure and forum for enforcement. There is, therefore, little practical scope left to the second general exception identified above. As to the first exception, that is, that the court may enforce the terms of a collective agreement where its meaning is not disputed, this Court decided in *Brunet* . . . and *Shell Canada Ltd. v. United Oil Workers of Canada* [1980] . . . that there is no difference in principle between a dispute over the 'application' of a collective agreement and one relating to its 'violation.' The jurisdiction of the courts ought not, therefore, to depend on whether the parties dispute the meaning or application of the terms of a collective agreement. . . .

What is left is an attitude of judicial deference to the arbitration process. . . . It is based on the idea that if the courts are available to the parties as an alternative forum, violence is done to a comprehensive statutory scheme designed to govern all aspects of the relationship of the parties in a labour relations setting. Arbitration, when adopted by the parties as was done here in the collective agreement, is an integral part of that scheme, and is clearly the forum preferred by the legislature for resolution of disputes arising under collective agreements. From the foregoing authorities, it might be said, therefore, that the law has so evolved that it is appropriate to hold that the grievance and arbitration procedures provided for by the Act and embodied by legislative prescription in the terms of a collective agreement provide the exclusive recourse open to parties to the collective agreement for its enforcement.

This, however, appears to conflict with the long-settled jurisdiction of the courts to issue injunctions restraining illegal strike activity during the currency of a collective agreement: *International Brotherhood of Electrical Engineers, Local Union 2085 v. Winnipeg Builder's Exchange, supra, International Longshoremen's Association, Locals 273, 1039, 1764 v. Maritime Employers' Association*. . . . It can be surmised that many, if not all, of the cases in which injunctions have issued, started life as claims for an injunction together with other relief, including damages to compensate an employer for losses suffered during an illegal strike. . . . The history of labour law in our country since World War II reflects a rather straightforward pattern whereby the parties would take recourse to the superior courts by an action for injunction, declaration and damages in which an interlocutory or interim injunction was sought with a view to driving the other party back to the labour relations process prescribed by statute. Rarely would the action proceed beyond the interlocutory injunction stage.

An injunction is as much an action to enforce the no-strike clause in a collective agreement as is an action for damages. If the former is available, so in principle should be the latter. Thus, if it is confirmed that the courts have no business interpreting, applying or enforcing collective agreements in any way, the jurisdiction to enjoin strikes illegal by virtue of their occurrence during the term of a collective agreement, unquestioned since *Winnipeg Builder's Exchange, supra*, is called into doubt. This would have the unfortunate result of putting an employer whose assent to a collective agreement indicates his willingness to bargain in good faith with the union and to fulfill the expectations of the collective bargaining regime, in a more restricted position than an uncooperative employer who may never have signed an agreement, and who is not therefore subject to binding arbitration. This prejudice may be more apparent than real, however, as in fact it entails only a shift of forum and procedure, but not necessarily a real deprivation of ultimate remedy.

The statutory context may be viewed as ambiguous on this issue. Though setting out a scheme in which arbitration plays a central role, the legislation does not enact any privative clause explicitly ousting the jurisdiction of the courts to deal with breaches of collective agreements which clearly, under the legislation, regulate the legal rights of the parties and are binding and enforceable in the proper forum. This is in contrast to the practice in all provincial and federal labour relations statutes of expressly excluding the courts from any power of review by any procedure of the determinations by the statutory labour relations board. The absence of such legislative action in the case of the boards of arbitration established by contract, even in the provinces where such boards have been held to be statutory and not private, is perhaps revealing of the presence of a legislative intent to continue some role for the traditional courts in the labour relations pattern. What the statute does is to establish a preference for arbitration of a particular sort over other means of dispute settlement, by establishing a procedure to be followed where the parties do not expressly provide for any other method of resolving their differences. Where the parties so choose, however, the New Brunswick Act, in common with most of the other Canadian labour relations statutes, does not actually require the parties to resort to arbitration (the Ontario *Labour Relations Act*, R.S.O. 1980, c. 228 is an exception in this respect . . .). It requires a provision in the collective agreement for 'final and binding settlement by arbitration *or otherwise*, without stoppage of work.' The emphasized words indicate that, if they so choose, the parties may validly provide for a variety of other sorts of settlement mechanisms, including recourse to the courts . . . Thus, even where the parties, as here, have chosen arbitration, it may be argued that s. 55(1) of the New Brunswick Act is insufficient to oust the inherent jurisdiction of the superior courts. . . .

There is the further consideration that the Act appears to recognize concurrent jurisdiction to deal with aspects of illegal strikes in the statutory board, the courts, and arbitrators acting under the provisions of collective agreements. Section 102(3) provides:

102(3) A declaration made under this section does not affect any proceeding in any court or any proceeding under the provision of a collective agreement, where the question of a lawful or unlawful strike . . . is in issue.

This may be seen to accord with the reason for enactment of the arbitration provisions. As suggested by Lord Russell in *Young v. Canadian Northern Ry. Co.* . . . , the appropriate course of action for workers who had a grievance under a collective agreement at common law was to engage in concerted action, usually a strike, in order to force the employer's compliance. Labour legislation was enacted largely to regulate industrial relations with an eye to preserving industrial peace: per Cartwright J., as he then was, in Winnipeg Builders' Exchange, supra, at p. 640. A cornerstone in this legislative edifice was to make strike action or lock-out illegal during the currency of a collective agreement. In exchange for restricting the right to strike and lock-out, the legislation made collective agreements binding and enforceable. . . .

This . . . may be taken as indicated by the fact that grievances are directed to be settled by arbitration 'without stoppage of work.' It would, accordingly, be illogical to permit a union to plead in defence to court proceedings brought to restrain an illegal strike that the employer should have resorted to arbitration, when the conduct in issue is the very conduct which the provision for arbitration and the statutory prohibition were designed to prevent. . . .

The avoidance of the disruptive effect of cessation of production of goods and services except in well defined circumstances is one of the basic design features of labour relations legislation. Another feature of labour legislation is the provision for rapid restoration of normal bargaining relations. Long or repeated abstentions of the parties from participation in the remedial processes of collective bargaining and grievance processing defeats the program. Slow and expensive processes of dispute resolution likewise render the statutory scheme less beneficial and perhaps unavailable to the community. The labour arbitration board came into being because of this reality.

In a limited role, the ready access by the parties to the court system provided by the community for the disposition of differences however arising in the community, can itself be another bulwark against the deterioration of employer-employee understanding. The interlocutory injunction by summary process but of limited life, for example as governed by the *Judicature Act* of Ontario, now the *Courts of Justice Act*, 1984 (Ont.), c. 11, s. 115, finds its origin in this reality. It is, of course, open to the legislature to close this access, as it has done in the case of the privative clauses relating to the labour relations boards themselves. . . .

. . . it is apparent that the cases affirming the courts' injunctive power do not purport to create a power in the courts to enforce the terms of collective agreements. Rather, they enforce the general law as embodied in the statute, which includes both an express prohibition on strikes during the currency of a collective agreement and provision for binding and enforceable arbitration which, in many cases, would resolve the dispute underlying illegal strike activity. An injunction restraining a strike also upholds incidentally the rights of an employer under a collective agreement, and specifically enforces the individual obligations of the employees on whose behalf the collective agreement was negotiated pursuant to the *Industrial Relations Act* of New Brunswick, *supra*. Such incidental effects, as the *Winnipeg Builders' Exchange* case, *supra*, demonstrates, are not sufficient reason to deny an injunction to prevent immediate harm arising out of a clearly illegal act, where no adequate alternative remedy exists. . . .

Therefore, I conclude that the courts below were correct in law in recognizing that the claim for damages must be advanced in the contractual forum of an arbitration board. This is so where legislation requires the parties to establish a mechanism for dispute resolution, and whether the arbitration board so established is 'statutory' or is private in nature. This appeal does not require comment upon the question of the range or remedies the board may apply in disposing of differences arising under the collective agreement, as we are here concerned only with a claim for damages. On the other hand, it should be said for clarity and completeness, because the issue of the availability of a court injunction and other judicial remedies was ever present in the arguments presented by the parties to this Court, that the initial process in injunction undertaken by the court in these proceedings was within the jurisdiction of the court, and that this jurisdiction has not been reduced by the labour relations statute or indeed by the presence of the collective agreement and its provision for arbitration.

✳ ✳ ✳

The New Brunswick legislation on which *St. Anne Nackawic* was based did not empower the labour board to issue cease-and-desist orders in the case of illegal strikes. The only remedy available from the board was a declaration that a strike was illegal. It is unclear whether Estey J.'s comments regarding injunctions would have been different had the cease-and-desist power existed. In *Attorney General for Ontario v. O.T.F.* (1997), 36 O.R. (3d) 367 (Ont. S.C.), the court refused the government's request for an interlocutory injunction to bring an end to a province-wide teachers' strike, in part because the government had made no attempt to use the Ontario Labour Relations Board procedures for that purpose before seeking a court injunction.

8:320 The Role of Labour Relations Boards

As we have seen above, in 8:200, labour relations boards are clearly the principal forum for enforcing the limitations on strikes and lockouts set out in labour relations legislation. It is the boards that have the statutory duty to determine whether there has been a strike or lockout, and if there has, whether it is legal under the legislation. As we have also seen, however, courts have retained for themselves some role in assessing the statutory legality of strikes in civil actions for injunctions or damages, and the existence of an illegal strike or some other breach of statute may be held to provide the element of illegality required for a cause of action in tort. And as will be discussed below, in 8:400, a rather confusing interplay between the roles of courts and boards still characterizes the regulation of picketing, especially peaceful picketing that occurs during a legal strike or lockout. Only in British Columbia has an explicit legislative attempt been made to delineate the roles of the board and the courts in regulating industrial conflict, and to restrict the role of the courts. Other jurisdictions, including Ontario, have in recent decades amended their labour relations statutes to expand the board's remedial powers with respect to industrial conflict, but they have not expressly limited the authority of the courts. Sometimes, however, the courts will refuse to act when a comparable remedy is available from a specialized tribunal. See, for example, *Attorney General for Ontario v. O.T.F.*, above, and *McKinlay Transport v. Goodman* (1978), 78 C.L.L.C. paragraph 14,161 (F.C.), referred to in the *National Harbours Board* judgment set out below.

For a very long time, labour relations boards had little or no specific remedial authority over illegal strikes. In Ontario, for example, the board's only power was to declare the strike illegal. Oddly, this declaratory remedy proved reasonably effective. When the parties were in doubt about whether their actions were lawful, the declaration enlightened them, and they usually complied. When there was no such doubt, as in the case of a wildcat strike during the term of a collective agreement, the declaration alerted them to potential consequences such as a claim for damages, a criminal prosecution, or the discharge of illegally striking employees. This often altered the dynamics within the bargaining unit, encouraging some members to urge a return to work and giving those who were more militant a reason to back down.

Other advantages of declaratory relief over directive orders, especially in the context of politically motivated strikes of the sort that characterized the 1995 and 1996 Days of Protest in Ontario, were spelled out by Chair MacDowell of the Ontario board in *General Motors of Canada Limited*, [1996] O.L.R.B. Rep. May/June 409 at 452–54. Among them were the avoidance of the spectre of criminal contempt proceedings and the affirmation of the basic assumption of collective bargaining legislation that "self-regulation and private ordering are an appropriate (and perhaps the best) method of workplace governance."

The declaratory authority of some labour relations boards has in recent decades been supplemented by a very broad and flexible remedial jurisdiction. For example, section 100 of the Ontario *Labour Relations Act, 1995*, reads as follows (the italicized passage was added in 1984):

> 100. Where, on the complaint of a trade union, council of trade unions, employer or employers' organization, the Board is satisfied that a trade union or council of trade unions called or authorized or threatened to call or authorize an unlawful strike or that an officer, official or agent of a trade union or council of trade unions counselled or procured or supported or encouraged an unlawful strike or threatened an unlawful strike or that employees engaged in or threatened to engage in an unlawful strike *or any person has done or is threatening to do an act that the person knows or ought to know that, as a probable and*

reasonable consequence of the act, another person or persons will engage in an unlawful strike, the Board may so declare and it may direct what action, if any, a person, employee, employers' organization, trade union or council of trade unions and their officers, officials or agents shall do or refrain from doing with respect to the unlawful strike or threat of an unlawful strike.

Our main concern in this part of the chapter is not with the relationship between the powers of boards and courts, but with the approach that the boards take toward the regulation of illegal industrial action. The following decision illustrates that approach.

National Harbours Board v. Syndicat national des employés du Port de Montréal, [1979] 3 Can. L.R.B.R. 502 at 503–18 (C.L.R.B.)

[The union had called two one-day work stoppages while a conciliation commissioner was attempting to bring about a new collective agreement, and had also instituted an overtime ban. This affected the transhipment of grain through the Port of Montreal, disrupting export shipments. The employer complained that the union's actions were untimely and unlawful, and sought relief under the *Canada Labour Code*, section 182 (now section 91). The union argued that its members had become impatient with the slowness of the conciliation commissioner, that its use of limited sanctions was an attempt to "channel" employee discontent, and that it had to prove to the employer that it enjoyed support among the employees. The union acknowledged that the board's officer had managed to speed up the conciliation commissioner, and that it was now satisfied with his diligence. Finally, the union argued that the employer had violated the overtime provisions of the collective agreement, and that the protest tactics had no serious consequences.]

LAPOINTE, Chair: It should be explained here that the Board's jurisdiction as created by the provisions of . . . section 182 has existed only since Parliament's adoption of Bill C-8 and its implementation on June 1, 1978.

Being aware of the positive role that Parliament intended the Board to play in cases involving work stoppages, the latter therefore immediately developed a policy for applying this new jurisdiction. This policy bears the mark of the desire not only to remedy the symptoms of problems arising in labour relations but also to do so in particular by determining the source of the malady causing the problems.

The Board has now an experienced, dedicated support team composed of labour relations officers, and in the case of every application filed under section 182 or 183 (which, as the counterpart of section 182, deals with lockouts), it can rapidly establish a date for a public hearing. However, at the same time, it immediately sends one of its officers to the scene of the dispute. The latter will then do his utmost, by meeting with the parties and using the method of his choice, to discover where the shoe pinches in the case of an unlawful work stoppage (strike or lockout). He has complete authority with the full support of the Board to resolve the problem in order to avoid a public hearing.

If he fails, he merely reports this fact to the Board panel assigned to hear the case and then the Board sits and hears the parties.

The judiciousness of this approach seems clear in that to date, the Board has heard only three of over twenty applications of this nature. . . .

. . . This practice and the policy underlying it are based on the Board's conviction that Parliament did not intend, by giving this new jurisdiction [to issue cease-and-desist orders] to the Board, to create a remedy that was identical and parallel to that still offered by the courts of the land.

It should be remembered, moreover, that Parliament's action in part reflected a reiterated request by central labour bodies in Canada . . . that the legislator transfer to labour tribunals the jurisdiction of regular courts as regards injunctions. These labour bodies alleged that only specialized tribunals could really unravel problems in the case of bitter labour disputes characterized by work stoppages. . . .

. . . After giving the party in question the opportunity to be heard, the Board may decide not to issue an order even when faced with facts showing that an unlawful work stoppage exists. Everything depends on the higher interests to be satisfied in given circumstances: these higher interests may be summarized very simply. They involve creating or helping to create the factual situation most likely to promote healthy and orderly labour relations. In order to accomplish this, the Board believes that in cases of unlawful work stoppages which are the result of disturbances in the relations between the parties, it is important to identify the cause in order to determine the remedy. This is what it has instructed its officers to do in their meetings with the parties before the public hearing. . . . However, even in the event that the Board's officer fails, it may happen that the board will conclude after a public hearing that it may take the same action either by issuing an order containing specific directives conducive to remedying the cause of the disturbance or by refusing to issue an order.

It seems that this view of the Board corresponds to that of the regular Courts. In fact, in *McKinlay Transport Limited v. Goodman* . . . , a case in which a party wanted the Federal Court to issue an injunction and for which the judgment is dated July 27, 1978, shortly after implementation of Bill C-8, Thurlow J. stated the following: . . .

> . . . [E]ven though the legislation does not specifically purport to withdraw from the Superior Courts' jurisdiction to issue injunctions in respect of conduct arising out of labour disputes, it seems to me that the Court can and ought to take into account in exercising its discretion that Parliament has shown its disposition that such matters be dealt with by the Board of the principles which it applies of the legislation rather than by the Courts. It is perhaps unnecessary to add that Court injunctions have not been notoriously successful as a device for achieving harmonious labour relations or for resolving labour disputes.
>
> A further aspect of the matter with respect to the exercise of discretion is that there is nothing before me to show that prompt and effective relief is not obtainable by the plaintiff in appropriate proceedings therefor before the Canada Labour Relations Board. . . .

In effect, as the late shipping season delayed delivery of grain in the ports on the St. Lawrence, one of which was Montreal, there was a rapid increase in activities involving the unloading of vessels from the Great Lakes and the loading of ocean-going vessels. The employer has been very vulnerable for the last few weeks and will continue to be for a while yet. A large number of vessels are waiting to be loaded or unloaded.

The union's interests would be best served by collective bargaining in a situation of extreme pressure, namely the strike situation, if said bargaining and the strike occurred during this very peak of activities at the Port of Montreal. There is nothing inherently wrong with this union viewpoint.

Consequently, when the Board discovered between April 12 and 18, 1979, through the services of its labour relations officer, that what was bothering the union was the slowness of the conciliation commissioner's procedure, it anchored the re-establishment of the status quo by its interventions in obtaining a speed up of this procedure prior to the parties acquiring the right to stage a lawful work stoppage. The Board was successful in its attempts and even the union stated through its chief negotiator that it was satisfied in this regard on May 8, 1979, the date of the hearing regarding the employer's amended application. However, the employer complained that this status quo was again upset on May 4, 1979 and that it was in danger of remaining upset, depending on certain of the respondents' activities. On May 8, 1979, everyone was waiting from one moment to the next for the conciliation commissioner to file his report.

It is thus clear that in spite of the agreement concluded, which allowed the Board to help accelerate the process without intervening, the respondents or some of them again lost their patience on May 4, 1979 and a restive atmosphere prevailed subsequently from this date until May 8, 1979 inclusive. . . .

In short, the respondent employees and their union began before the time stipulated in the Code to partially exercise the ultimate form of pressure in collective bargaining. This is prohibited by the legislator.

The respondent union sought through its main spokesman to transform these transgressions into virtues when it endeavoured to justify them by saying that it had attempted in this way to channel the discontent, prove to the employer that the 'troops' were following it and thus avoid the worst, presumably, a complete unlawful strike.

We can neither close our eyes to these violations nor excuse them in the current circumstances because over and above the plain fact of the violations per se, we must take into account the fact that by imposing time periods and interposing third parties, the legislator was seeking to achieve a well-defined goal, namely, to increase the opportunities for the parties to settle their differences without resorting to the ultimate sanction. But, he wanted still more. He also wanted the two parties to be on an equal footing at all times with respect to the means of exerting pressure that each of them had at its disposal. . . .

Some people try to justify these transgressions by claiming that the insertion of the stages calling for the intervention of third parties constitutes poor labour legislation. It is not for us to form an opinion on this matter. However, it must be understood that if people are not happy with the legislation, the solution is to get it amended. In the meantime, parties must act honestly and legally.

* * *

The board issued an order requiring that the workers "perform the duties of their employ-ment and . . . refrain from any concerted illegal activity," and that the union refrain from authorizing or declaring such activity and distribute the order to its members.

Following the board's order, employees still refused to report for overtime work. The employer sought the board's consent to prosecute the strikers and the union. The board authorized prosecution [1979] 3 Can. L.R.B.R. 514, but only against the union. The board also directed that any prosecution must be brought before the collective agreement was signed, to avoid allowing the prospect of a prosecution "to become a sword of Damo-cles during the term of the next collective agreement. . . ."

The remedial discretion of the Canada board is not absolute, however. In *Syndicat des employés de production . . . de l'Acadie v. Canada (Labour Relations Board)* (1984), 84 C.L.L.C. para. 14,069, the Supreme Court of Canada held that the board did not have the power to order the submission of an issue to expedited arbitration as part of its reme-dy for an illegal strike.

8:330 The Arbitrator's Role in Industrial Conflict

Grievance arbitration is treated mainly in Chapter 9, which looks at the administration of collective agreements. But because grievance arbitrators play a central role in award-ing damages for illegal strikes and in determining the justness of disciplinary measures imposed by employers for employee conduct in connection with both legal and illegal strikes, these matters will be treated here.

8:331 Awards of Damages by Arbitrators

Most collective agreements contain a no-strike clause, sometimes by legislative decree. Violation of a no-strike clause is a breach of the agreement and may be the subject of arbitration proceedings at the instance of the employer. As we saw in *St. Anne Nackaw-ic*, grievance arbitrators have the authority — indeed, the exclusive authority — to award damages against the union for such a breach. But they will do so only if the union itself is responsible for the breach.

Re Oil, Chemical & Atomic Workers & Polymer Corporation (1958), 10 L.A.C. 31 at 33–35, 37–39

[A strike occurred during the lifetime of a collective agreement. The company brought a grievance under the agreement, alleging that the union had violated the no-strike clause (article 8.01) and claiming damages against the union for the losses that it suffered as a result of the strike.]

> LASKIN, Chair: Counsel for the company urged, with some vigour, that art. 8.01 involved an automatic liability of the union under each agreement upon mere proof of the occur-rence of a strike. . . . this Board cannot accept the argument of automatic liability. On the other hand, it must equally reject the contention of the respondents herein that liability arises only if there is an official strike, that is one called or sanctioned under the prescrip-tions of the union constitution and by-laws. . . .

. . . A union may contract (and for arbitration purposes a collective agreement is a contract) to accept liability for the conduct of a member but if it does so its ensuing responsibility does not arise under any principle of vicarious liability but by virtue of a contractual
obligation. A union normally has officers and employees who, under varying circumstances, may implicate it in vicarious liability for tort and in so-called personal liability in
contract. But members of a union are not, as members only, either employees or servants
of a union, or its agents, and their actions are not the actions of the union for which the
latter must respond either in tort or in contract. A union member cannot, as such, bind the
union in contract or make it liable vicariously for his tortious conduct merely by representing that he is acting for the union. Apart from principles of estoppel and kindred doctrines,
upon which it is unnecessary to dilate here, his acts are no more the acts of his union than
the acts of a mere shareholder in a corporation are the acts of the corporation. . . .

. . . art. 8.01 'must mean that the union undertakes that there will be no stoppages by
persons in the bargaining unit whom it purports to control, that is the members. Or, that
there will be no stoppages by any of the workers in the bargaining unit, whether members or not. Or that it will not through its proper officers sanction or direct or condone or
encourage stoppages by any persons in the bargaining unit.' . . .

This board agrees that the third alternative . . . is the proper one to apply to the interpretation of art. 8.01. . . . The board understands well enough how difficult it can be to
pinpoint responsibility for the initiation of a work stoppage or, as here, a refusal to report
for work, but the difficulty does not warrant accepting mere surmise as a substitute for
evidence. In short, the real basis, and the only basis, for the company's grievances must
be the alleged failure of the respondents to take prompt and necessary steps to bring the
strike to an end. . . .

Stewards or committeemen who are put forward by a union as its representatives for
departmental or area grievance adjustment must be expected to know that their very status and function underlines the impropriety as well as the illegality of a strike while the
collective agreement is in force. Thus it follows that a strike called or instigated by a steward or committeeman in his area is a strike for which the union must accept liability under
art. 8.01. Steward action is union action in this respect. It does not follow, however, that
given a situation where a strike arises by spontaneous employee action, or otherwise but
without union complicity, that the stewards or committeemen implicate the union if they
severally fail to take affirmative action to bring the strike to an end. Direction of 'back to
work' efforts may be in the hands of officers on a higher level and the stewards would
understandably be subordinate to them. If those officers did nothing towards the termination of the strike, union liability would be established by that fact and not by any inaction
or passivity of the stewards as such. Two points are, however, important in connection with
the position of stewards or committeemen in a situation, such as the one before this
board, that calls for affirmative union action to bring a strike to an end. If the stewards or
committeemen join the strikers in any demonstration, such as a picket line march, this
would be evidence which might show, unless explained away, that the union was encouraging a continuation of the strike. Much would depend on the duration and other circumstances of the participation of the stewards or committeemen in the demonstration.

Secondly, the presence of stewards or committeemen among the strikers at any mass demonstration would invite immediate action by union executive officers to procure their withdrawal as a tangible sign that the union is not supporting the unlawful strike. . . .

* * *

In *Attorney General for Newfoundland v. Newfoundland Association of Public Employees* (1977), 74 D.L.R. (3d) 195 at 209 (Nfld. S.C.), Goodridge J. suggested a long list of measures that, in the circumstances before him, the union hierarchy might have taken to avoid liability when an illegal strike occurred:

1. Where a strike could have been foreseen, meetings of each unit involved should have been convened by the association executive who should have ordered the members not to strike;
2. After the strikes began the association should have convened unit meetings to order the members back to work;
3. Persuasive leaflets should have been placed in the hand of each employee outlining the legal and practical situation;
4. The special nature of their work–the care of those who could not care for themselves — should have been emphasized; . . .
5. Association executive and staff members should have visited the picket lines to persuade the strikers to return to work;
6. Unit executive members should have been called on the carpet and told in no uncertain terms to return to work themselves, and to order the others to return;
7. Press, radio and TV coverage to the extent that it was available should have been used to persuade the employees to return;
8. The association should have forthwith suspended the shop stewards;
9. The association should have forthwith suspended the unit executives;
10. The association should have fined, suspended or otherwise disciplined any member who participated in the strikes; and
11. Finally, the association should have clearly indicated to all that in this dispute it was on the side of management and generally acted resolutely to determine the strike.

If damages are awarded against the union, what is the proper measure of damages? The normal contractual measure of compensation for breach? Some variant of compensatory damages permitting adjustment downward when the employer has provoked the strike by its own misconduct, or upward when the union's conduct was egregious? A non-compensatory measure calculated to discourage future misbehaviour and encourage good relations between the parties?

8:332 Employer Disciplinary Action against Strikers

Involvement by an employee in an illegal strike does not in itself rupture the employment relationship. However, it does expose the employee to discipline for cause, and leading an illegal strike will clearly be held by an arbitrator to justify heavier discipline than mere passive participation.

Involvement in a *legal* strike is quite different. The *Graham Cable* decision, above, 8:212, makes clear that it is an unfair labour practice for an employer to discipline employees because of their participation in a legal strike. More difficult is the question of employer discipline imposed not for the act of striking but for the employee's conduct during the strike.

Rogers Cable T.V. (British Columbia) Ltd., Vancouver Division et al. v. International Brotherhood of Electrical Workers, Local 213 (1987), 16 Can. L.R.B.R. (N.S.) 71 at 77, 84–85, 90–93 (C.L.R.B.)

[The company had attempted to maintain operations during a very bitter legal strike. The union had picketed vigorously, blocking access to company premises and using flying picket squads to follow company vehicles and harass employees doing bargaining unit work. The company hired security guards, and the police were often called in to respond to picketing incidents. The company obtained three injunctions against picket line conduct, and a union business agent and twenty-two members were found guilty of contempt of court for disobeying the injunctions. The union then complained to the labour board that the company had committed an unfair labour practice by imposing disciplinary suspensions on eight employees for alleged misconduct on the picket line. Some of the eight were awaiting sentence for contempt, and three faced criminal charges for the acts for which the company disciplined them.]

> JAMIESON, Vice-Chair: The specific allegations against the eight union members ranged from yelling, cursing and swearing, puncturing tires on company vehicles, pounding vehicles with pieces of wood, breaking mirrors on company vehicles, opening propane valves on vehicles, cutting cables to disrupt service to customers, to threatening persons with knives. . . .

[Section 184(3)(a)(vi) of the *Canada Labour Code* provided that it was an unfair labour practice for an employer to take any reprisals against an employee for having "participated in a strike that is not prohibited by this Part or exercised any right under this Part. . . ."]

> The union . . . took the position that an employer has no authority at law to discipline for any act committed during a lawful work stoppage. The logic for this argument is that an employer's right to discipline is a derivative of the employment contract whether it be collective or individual. Once a legal work stoppage is in progress by way of a strike or a lockout, there is no employment contract in effect. The employees no longer hold themselves out to be subject to employer discipline, thus the employer has no powers of discipline left to exert. The union says that picket line activities, legal or illegal, are a matter of public order and the employer's only recourse is to the courts through criminal or civil actions. . . .
>
> In the over-all scheme of the Code, strikes and lockouts are expected to be temporary suspensions in the employment relationship during which collective bargaining differences are ironed out. While these periods of economic sanctions last, employees have no obligation to report to work or to perform services on the employer's behalf. The employ-

er on the other hand need not provide work to the employees, in fact, he has a legal right to call on others to perform the services necessary to keep the business operating. . . .

Once a strike or lockout is over and when the full employer-employee relationship is restored, we can see nothing in the Code to prevent an employer from using its restored disciplinary powers to deal with acts of employees that occurred during the work stoppage, provided of course the discipline is not for reasons prohibited by s. 184(3)(a)(vi). Once employees do return to work they may find themselves accountable under employment law if they have participated in acts of violence or wilful damage against the property or persons of the employer.

This situation is not altogether dissimilar to where employees conduct themselves in a manner that is detrimental to their employment relationship while they are away from work on any other authorized leave of absence such as vacations, sick leave or just off duty for the week-end. In those instances, arbitration cases in general treat employers' powers of discipline as diminished in scope. The analysis seems to be directed at protecting the personal freedoms of employees and takes the form of imposing a higher standard of reasonableness on an employer's claim that discipline was justified. Arbitral jurisprudence on the scope of an employer's authority to discipline for off duty conduct appears to limit the exercise of disciplinary powers to circumstances where the conduct of the employee undermines the viability of the employment relationship. . . .

In this complaint, the IBEW speaks about there being no duties or obligations remaining from the expired contract of employment, regardless if the contract is collective or individual. We would point out that in this case, like so many others where there is a lawful work stoppage, the new collective agreement was made retroactive to [a date] which was many months before the work stoppage occurred. The employer did not actually use its disciplinary powers until after the new collective agreement was entered into therefore we see no basis for the union's argument. . . .

The facts before us show no indication of anti-union animus on the part of the employer. Certainly, the employer took a hard position at the bargaining table to achieve its collective bargaining goals, but there was never any suggestion that it was trying to rid itself of the union. This was further supported by the return-to-work arrangements entered into by the company and the union whereby all of the union members returned to work. . . .

The evidence also clearly shows that the employer did not, or does not intend to discipline the eight union members because they participated in a lawful strike. The discipline has nothing to do with the withdrawal of their labour or their participation in normal picket line activities. Without in any way adjudicating upon the merits of the allegations against the union members affected by this complaint, we would like to make it clear that acts of violence or of wilful damage or any other such unlawful acts are not lawful activities of a trade union that are guaranteed as fundamental rights under s. 110 of the Code. Nor do they fall within the protection offered by s. 184(3)(a)(vi) of the Code.

Taking everything into consideration, we find that the employer has not contravened s. 184(3)(a)(vi) of the Code as alleged. The complaint is dismissed.

8:400 THE REGULATION OF PICKETING

In many strikes and lockouts, picket lines become the focus of the conflict. Strikers seek to disrupt the employer's operations by dissuading customers, suppliers, and other employees from doing business with their adversary. Employers, for their part, commonly attempt to maintain access to the premises, so supervisors and other non-striking employees can come to work and materials can be moved in and out. In hotly contested disputes, employers may bring in replacement workers.

A considerable body of common law and statute law has developed to regulate picketing. The diversity of sources, of means of enforcement, and of lawmakers' attitudes toward labour/management relations confounds any attempt to make definitive statements about what is permitted and what is not. The various forms of regulation do, however, draw a distinction between two types of picketing: primary and secondary. Picketing is generally held to be primary if it is done at the struck employer's place of business, and secondary if it is done anywhere else (for instance, at the premises of a customer who continues to sell the struck employer's goods). As we will see, courts and labour boards tend to be much more permissive toward primary picketing than toward secondary picketing.

As was indicated in the *St. Anne Nackawic* case (above, section 8:315), most Canadian labour relations statutes do not explicitly deal with picketing. This legislative silence has been interpreted as leaving the courts with the major role in the regulation of picketing, and labour boards with only a secondary role. British Columbia is the major exception. The following provisions of the British Columbia *Labour Relations Code* give the board considerable power over picketing, to the substantial exclusion of the courts.

1(1) "picket" or "picketing" means attending at or near a person's place of business, operations or employment for the purpose of persuading or attempting to persuade anyone not to

(a) enter that place of business, operations or employment,

(b) deal in or handle that person's products, or

(c) do business with that person,

and a similar act at such a place that has an equivalent purpose.

65 (3) A trade union, a member or members of which are lawfully on strike or locked out, or a person authorized by the trade union, may picket at or near a site or place where a member of the trade union performs work under the control or direction of the employer if the work is an integral and substantial part of the employer's operation and the site or place is a site or place of the lawful strike or lockout.

(4) The board may, on application and after making the inquiries it requires, permit picketing

(a) at or near another site or place that the employer causing a lockout or whose employees are lawfully on strike is using to perform work, supply goods or furnish services for the employer's own benefit that, except for the lockout or strike, would be performed, supplied or furnished at the site or place where picketing is permitted by subsection (3), or

(b) at or near the place where an ally performs work, supplies goods or furnishes services for the benefit of a struck employer, or for the benefit of an employer who has locked out,

but the board must not permit common site picketing unless it also makes an order under subsection (6) defining the site or place and restricting the picketing in the manner referred to in that subsection.

136(2) . . . the board has and must exercise exclusive jurisdiction in respect of

. . .

(b) an application for the regulation, restraint or prohibition of a person or group of persons from

. . .

(ii) picketing, striking or locking out, or

(iii) communicating information or opinion in a labour dispute by speech, writing or other means.

The following case raises many of the policy issues involved in this statutory substitution of administrative for judicial regulation. The thrust of the decision is that if acts which are illegal independently of the labour relations statute are committed in the course of picketing, the courts retain jurisdiction to deal with them. This remains true everywhere in Canada.

Canex Placer Limited (Endako Mines Division) v. Canadian Association of Industrial, Mechanical and Allied Workers, Local 10, [1975] 1 Can. L.R.B.R. 269 at 272–75 (B.C.L.R.B.)

[During a legal strike at the company's mine, large numbers of picketers totally blocked access to the mine by standing in the road and by uttering what the Board described as "some isolated threats of violence." The company applied to the Board for an order prohibiting such conduct.]

WEILER, Chair: The legal issue before us is whether the Board has the power to prohibit that behaviour. . . .

Here the subject of the complaint . . . was activity occurring on a picket line. [The Board referred to the presence in the Labour Code of an earlier version of the provisions set out above.]

. . . [T]he conduct [of the picketers] . . . is illegal, at least at first blush, because it violates the requirements of quite different areas of the law of this province. These may include the Criminal Code's prohibition of assault or threats of violence, the Highway Act offence of obstruction of traffic, the common law torts of assault and battery, and so on. How may the Labour board, on a . . . complaint under the Labour Code, exercise the power to enforce this entire body of the general law? . . .

The . . . Code . . . creates a division of labour in the administration of the law that may affect picketing activity. Under the previous Trade-unions Act, the courts enforced both the labour law and the criminal or tort law facets of picketing. Now the Labour Relations Board is given exclusive jurisdiction over the industrial relations regulation of picketing while the courts remain charged with jurisdiction over its criminal or civil law features. The source of this change in the Code is found in the recommendations of the Woods Report, *Canadian Industrial Relations*, (1968):

621. The laws of industrial torts have particular relevance to conduct relating to the 'why,' 'where' and 'when' of picketing. The general law of torts and delicts (civil wrongs), of general application to society at large and generally designed to protect persons and property, relates to the 'how' of picketing. This distinction leads us into disparate recommendations for the 'why,' 'where' and 'when,' and for the 'how.' Briefly, because conduct relating to the first three facets of picketing is peculiar to the industrial relations system of collective bargaining, we recommend a form of codification of the law respecting 'why,' 'where' and 'when,' and a repeal of the common law of industrial torts in respect of cases where the code applies. We recommend also that adjudication under the Code be assigned to a reconstituted Canada Labour Relations Board . . . with a remedy, among other things, of restraining and mandatory orders to replace the equity injunction now available in the courts . . .

630. We would not change the substantive law relating to the form — that is, the 'how' — of picketing. Generally, we do not think there is a case for giving to persons who choose to engage in acts of picketing any relief from general laws for the protection of the person and property, such as assault, battery, defamation, trespass, nuisance, and so on. Nor do we think protection should be extended against civil liability for conduct that is a violation of the criminal law. . . .

This is not to ignore what appeared to be the major support for the contrary conclusion, the policy argument that the Code should be interpreted as eliminating judicial injunctions entirely from labour disputes. The contention was that the distinctive process and atmosphere of a labour relations board should deal even with the problems of violence on the picket line. . . . Dean Arthurs put it this way:

The practical difficulty is that in the course of deciding, for example, that messages disseminated by the pickets are defamatory, or that their behaviour constitutes an assault, the court is really determining the efficacy of the picketing. 'Defamation' may consist merely in a failure adequately to disclose that the primary focus of the dispute is at another of the employer's business premises. 'Assault' may consist merely in 'pointing, grimacing and staring.' And in determining that the tort of coercion has been committed, the court may well be defining the legitimate ambit of pressure available to a union seeking to enforce its collective agreement. By the astute selection of a cause of action . . . the employer may bypass the whole integrated body of statutory rules administered by the labour relations board. . . .

But . . . there may be a serious constitutional issue in granting the Board jurisdiction over this kind of conduct. Apparently, the legislature can grant the Board power to enforce the strikes and picketing sections of the Code. . . . The reason is that the Board is simply directed to enforce an additional segment of the comprehensive Labour Code, rather than applying the traditional common law torts to the economic conflict. . . . Very different legal problems would be raised if a provincial administrative agency were empowered to enforce the general criminal or civil law, even if only in the labour relations context. Before the Code is interpreted as taking that constitutional risk, there should be a clear statement of the legislature that this is its intention. . . .

[In the preceding paragraph, Chair Weiler was referring to the effect of sections 96 to 100 of the *Constitution Act*, as interpreted by the Privy Council and the Supreme Court of Canada.]

* * *

In some other jurisdictions (including Alberta and Ontario), labour relations statutes have been amended in recent decades to give labour boards broad remedial authority with respect to illegal strikes and to conduct which causes such strikes. The Ontario *Labour Relations Act, 1995*, for example, gives the Ontario board the power to issue cease-and-desist orders when, among other things, "any person has done or is threatening to do any act [and] the person knows or ought to know that, as a probable and reasonable consequence of the act, another person or persons will engage in an unlawful strike" (section 100). The Alberta *Labour Relations Code*, sections 82 and 152, restricts picketing to the striking employees' place of employment, authorizes the board to regulate picketing at that location, and empowers the board to control a wide range of "dispute-related misconduct." Since the enactment of such provisions, labour boards and courts have shared the regulation of picketing, in an implicit and uneasy partnership.

On the eve of the 1996 Days of Protest called by the labour movement in Toronto against the policies of the Ontario government, senior officers of certain unions and labour federations publicly urged people to picket Toronto Transit Commission (TTC) sites so that the TTC would be unable to operate. In *Toronto Transit Commission*, [1996] O.L.R.B. Rep. Sept./Oct. 889, the Ontario Labour Relations Board declared that those officers had breached the statutory prohibition against doing anything that would likely lead to an illegal strike (section 83(1)). The Board also granted a limited cease and desist order against picketing at certain places that were critical to the movement of TTC employees and vehicles. Alternate Chair Herman wrote, at 892–93:

> . . . the Board does not have a general jurisdiction over picketing; rather, it deals, in circumstances such as those at hand, with questions of unlawful strikes or unlawful picketing, where the individuals on strike or likely to strike are not legally entitled to do so. If the strike itself is lawful, then the Board does not deal with particular picket line activity, and whether it might be unlawful. That jurisdiction is the courts'. . . .
>
> It is important to understand what the Board is not dealing with in this application, and that is the question of whether the TTC can conduct its operations without interference from the protests. . . . The TTC asks only that no picketing occur prior to 6:30 a.m. on each day, because by that time its collectors will have been able to enter the stations.

After 6:30 a.m., the TTC does not request that we issue any order. The remedy sought by the TTC in this respect reflects the jurisdiction and concern of this Board, that no unlawful strike occur. Except as is necessary or incidental to this issue, this Board does not deal with ensuring that the TTC can fully operate. Indeed, had the TTC sought a prohibition against picketing outside subway stations at any time during the day or night, the Board would not grant it, because there is nothing before us to indicate that such a remedy is necessary to ensure that employees do not have to cross picket lines.

The second point worth making is to re-emphasize that significant Charter rights are at issue in the circumstances. Even though the Board is satisfied that there must be some limits placed upon the rights of people to express themselves and to assemble, in order to ensure that no unlawful strike occurs, any limitation should be as narrow as possible, reflecting the significant and critical rights at issue. We are not dealing here with a typical employer-employee dispute, nor indeed, with a typical labour relations dispute. The provisions of section 83 have of course been breached, but any remedial response should restrict freedom of expression or freedom of assembly as little as possible in the circumstances. Just as the Board did in *Sarnia Construction Association*, . . . where as a remedial response the Board established two gates around a construction site, one for striking employees and one for all other employees, similarly the Board should look here to establishing a remedial response that goes no further than is necessary to ensure that no unlawful strike occurs.

In *Progistix-Solutions Inc.* [1999] O.L.R.B. Rep. March/April 309, the O.L.R.B. reiterates and explains the view that its statutory power to regulate picketing or other conduct in support of a strike is not as broad as that of the British Columbia Board, and is essentially limited to situations where the conduct in question is causing an illegal strike.

8:410 Primary Picketing

Both labour boards and courts tend to allow a wide scope for primary picketing in support of a legal strike, if the picketing is focused directly on the business of the struck employer and affects third parties only in their dealings with that employer. When these conditions are met, the only limitations tend to be those based in general tort law and criminal law, such as the prohibitions against physical obstruction, assault, property damage, and trespass. Sometimes these issues are framed in terms of the watching and besetting provision of the *Criminal Code*, cited above, section 8:311. The question thus is whether the picketing is "peaceful" and "informational" or violent and obstructive. Because these restrictions on picket line conduct come from the general law, they are enforced by the ordinary courts.

It is clear in principle that assault, trespass, obstruction, and the like are outside the limits of peaceful picketing and are not tolerated by the courts. However, the reality is somewhat more nuanced, as is reflected in these words of Sedgwick J. of the Ontario Court (General Division) in *National Gallery of Canada v. Public Service Alliance of Canada* (2001) (unreported, at para. 12):

The courts recognize that implicit in picketing activities is some degree of interference with the civil and legal rights of others. Some give and take on the picket line, that goes beyond the bounds of normal polite conversation, is to be expected.

The next two cases explore the limits of this "give and take."

Harrison v. Carswell, [1976] 2 S.C.R. 200 at 202–05, 209, 212–13, 216–20

DICKSON J.: The respondent, Sophie Carswell, was charged under *The Petty Trespasses Act*, of Manitoba, R.S.M. 1970, c. P-50, with four offences (one on each of four days) of unlawfully trespassing upon the premises of the Fairview Corporation Limited, trading under the firm name and style of Polo Park Shopping Centre, located in the City of Winnipeg, after having been requested by the owner not to enter on or come upon the premises. The appellant, Peter Harrison, manager of Polo Park Shopping Centre, swore the informations. The charges were dismissed by the Provincial Judge but on a trial de novo in the County Court Mrs. Carswell was convicted and fined $10 on each of the charges. The convictions were set aside by the Manitoba Court of Appeal. . . .

With great respect, I am unable to agree with the majority reasons, delivered in the Court of Appeal by Chief Justice Freedman for I find it difficult, indeed impossible, to make any well-founded distinction between this case and *Peters v. The Queen*. . . , decided by this Court four years ago in a unanimous decision of the full Bench. . . .

It is urged on behalf of Mrs. Carswell that the right of a person to picket peacefully in support of a lawful strike is of greater social significance than the proprietary rights of an owner of a shopping centre and that the rights of the owner must yield to those of the picketer. . . .

The submission that this Court should weigh and determine the respective values to society of the right to property and the right to picket raises important and difficult political and socio-economic issues, the resolution of which must, by their very nature, be arbitrary and embody personal economic and social beliefs. It raises also fundamental questions as to the role of this Court under the Canadian constitution. The duty of the Court, as I envisage it, is to proceed in the discharge of its adjudicative function in a reasoned way from principled decision and established concepts. I do not for a moment doubt the power of the Court to act creatively — it has done so on countless occasions; but manifestly one must ask — what are the limits of the judicial function? There are many and varied answers to this question. Holmes J. said in *Southern Pacific Co. v. Jensen* . . . : 'I recognize without hesitation that judges do and must legislate, but they can do it only interstitially; they are confined from molar to molecular actions.' Cardozo, *The Nature of the Judicial Process* . . . , recognized that the freedom of the Judge is not absolute in this expression of his review:

> This judge, even when he is free, is still not wholly free. He is not to innovate at pleasure. He is not a knight-errant, roaming at will in pursuit of his own ideal of beauty or of goodness. He is to draw his inspiration from consecrated principles. . . .

Anglo-Canadian jurisprudence has traditionally recognized, as a fundamental freedom, the right of the individual to the enjoyment of property and the right not to be deprived thereof, or any interest therein, save by due process of law. The Legislature of Manitoba has declared in *The Petty Trespasses Act* that any person who trespasses upon land, the property of another, upon or through which he has been requested by the owner not to enter, is guilty of an offence. If there is to be any change in this statute law, if A is to be given the right to enter and remain on the land of B against the will of B, it would seem to me that such a change must be made by the enacting institution, the Legislature, which is representative of the people and designed to manifest the political will, and not by the Court.

I would allow the appeal, set aside the judgment of the Court of Appeal for Manitoba and restore the judgment of the County Court Judge.

LASKIN C.J.C. (dissenting): . . .The locale is a shopping centre, in which a large number of tenants carry on a wide variety of businesses. The shopping centre has the usual public amenities, such as access roads, parking lots and sidewalks which are open for use by members of the public who may or may not be buyers at the time they come to the shopping centre. There can be no doubt that at least where a shopping centre is freely accessible to the public, as is the one involved in the present case, the private owner has invested members of the public with a right of entry during the business hours of his tenants and with a right to remain there subject to lawful behaviour. . . .

An employee of a tenant in the shopping centre participated in a lawful strike and then proceeded to picket peacefully on the sidewalk in front of the tenant's premises. The struck employer took no action to prohibit the picketing and, on the record, an action by the employer would probably have been unsuccessful. The owner of the shopping centre introduced himself into the situation and told the picketer, the respondent in this appeal, that picketing was not permitted in any area of the shopping centre and if she did not leave she would be charged with trespass. He advised her to move to a public sidewalk which was some distance away. She continued to picket on the shopping centre sidewalk and charges against her under *The Petty Trespasses Act*, R.S.M. 1970, c. P-50, followed.

[*R. v. Peters*] also involved picketing in a shopping centre. However, the picketing there arose not out of a labour dispute with an employer tenant of premises in the shopping centre, but was by way of a boycott appeal against the selling of California grapes. . . .

The first question put to this Court in the *Peters* case was framed as follows:

> Did the learned Judges in appeal err in law determining that the owner of the property had sufficient possession of the shopping plaza sidewalk to be capable of availing itself of the remedy for trespass under the *Petty Trespass Act* R.S.O. 1960 Chapter 294, Section 1(1) [now *Trespass to Property Act*, R.S.O. 1980, c. 511]?

This question, a strictly legal one without any context of fact, was answered unanimously in the negative by the full Court of which I was a member. The Court gave the briefest of oral reasons . . . , and I regarded the answer as a response to a narrow question of whether a shopping centre owner can have sufficient possession of a sidewalk therein to support a charge of trespass under the provincial Act. The question, to me, was whether the owner had divested itself of possession so as to make the shopping centre sidewalk a public way upon which there could be no trespass as against such owner in any circumstances.

It is, of course, open to others to read this Court's disposition of the *Peters* case differently but I can say for myself that the brief reasons would not have sufficed had the question that was asked been put in a factual frame as is often done when questions are formulated for the consideration of this Court. For me, it follows that the Peters case is neither in law nor in fact a controlling authority for the present case which came to this Court not upon specific questions of fact but at large so as to enable this Court to consider both law and fact as they bear on the position inter se of the shopping centre owner and of the lawful picketer in a legal strike. . . .

This Court, above all others in this country, cannot be simply mechanistic about previous decisions, whatever be the respect it would pay to such decisions. What we would be doing here, if we were to say that the Peters case, because it was so recently decided, has concluded the present case for us, would be to take merely one side of a debatable issue and say that it concludes the debate without the need to hear the other side. . . .

The respondent picketer in the present case is entitled to the privilege of entry and to remain in the public areas to carry on as she did (without obstruction of the sidewalk or incommoding of others) as being not only a member of the public but being as well, in relation to her peaceful picketing, an employee involved in a labour dispute with a tenant of the shopping centre, and hence having an interest, sanctioned by the law, in pursuing legitimate claims against her employer through the peaceful picketing in furtherance of a lawful strike. . . .

* * *

The Manitoba Legislature responded by amending the *Petty Trespasses Act* to overrule *Harrison v. Carswell*: S.M. 1976, c. 71, s. 2 (R.S.M. 1987, c. P-50). Section 66 of the British Columbia *Labour Relations Code* provides that "No action or proceeding may be brought for (a) petty trespass to land to which a member of the public ordinarily has access . . . arising out of strikes, lockouts or picketing permitted under this Code. . . ."

From 1993 to 1995, section 11.1 of the Ontario *Labour Relations Act* expressly allowed picketing during a lockout or a legal strike on "premises to which the public normally has access and from which a person occupying the premises would have a right to remove individuals." In a case involving food service concessions in university buildings, this provision was held not to give the Ontario Labour Relations Board the sole jurisdiction to decide whether the public normally had access to particular premises: *Queen's University v. C.U.P.E., Local 229* (1994), 120 D.L.R. (4th) 717 Ont. C.A.).

As explained in the *Canex Placer* decision (above, 8:400), courts still have the authority, everywhere in Canada, to restrain picketing activity that involves violence or other breaches of what the Woods Report called "general laws for the protection of the person or property." However, even where such a breach is alleged, some legislatures (for reasons discussed above, at 8:315) have required that police intervention be sought before an injunction may be granted.

Industrial Hardwood Products (1996) Ltd. v. International Wood and Allied Workers of Canada, Local 2693 (2001), 52 O.R. (3d) 694 (Ont. C.A.)

[During a lawful strike, the plaintiff employer hired replacement workers and used vans to take them in and out of the plant. For about three months, picketers consistently obstructed entry and exit of the vans, except when the police were there. The Ontario *Courts of Justice Act*, section 102(3), provided as follows:

> 102(3) In a motion or proceeding for an injunction to restrain a person from an act in con-nection with a labour dispute, the court must be satisfied that reasonable efforts to obtain police assistance, protection and action to prevent or remove any alleged danger of dam-age to property, injury to persons, obstruction of or interference with lawful entry or exit from the premises in question or breach of the peace have been unsuccessful.

The employer had made a blanket request that the police be at the plant entrance every day at 8 a.m. and 5 p.m. The police had turned down this request for lack of resources, but they had responded to any specific calls made when the picketers were actually blocking access.

The employer was granted an interlocutory injunction limiting the number of pickets to four at each entrance and allowing them only to communicate information to people who wanted to receive it, and only for up to five minutes per vehicle. The union appealed, arguing that because the police responded whenever they were called, and did ensure access to the plant while they were there, the employer had not met the condi-tion in section 102(3).]

GOUDGE J.A.:

. . .

[14] Two considerations provide the backdrop for the proper interpretation of s. 102(3). First, there can be no doubt about the vital role that picketing plays in labour disputes. It provides striking workers with the collective opportunity to seek to persuade others of the rightness of their cause. It allows them to express through collective action their solidari-ty in pursuit of that cause. And it provides an important outlet for collective energy in what is often a charged atmosphere. . . .

[15] Second, s. 102 of the Courts of Justice Act reflects the understanding of the Legisla-ture that regulation of picketing in a labour dispute requires unique attention. It must be done with care, balance and sophistication. This section provides the code for granting injunctions in labour disputes. It was first enacted in response to the Royal Commission Inquiry into Labour Disputes by the Honourable Ivan Rand and has remained essential-ly unchanged. It set up significant new requirements that had to be met before the court could be called on to regulate a labour dispute with injunctive relief. One of these require-ments, the predecessor to s. 102(3), reflected the view of Commissioner Rand that in all cases adequate police assistance must be shown to have been unavailable.

[16] The policy foundation for this requirement is clear. Strikes and the picket lines that go with them are evolving human dramas where risks of property damage, personal injury or obstruction of lawful entry are best controlled by flexible and even-handed polic-ing. Only where this fails should the court, with its blunt instrument of the injunction, be resorted to. . . .

[18] How then should the court determine whether the pre-condition set up by s. 102(3) has been met, particularly in a case like this where there is little or no evidence of prop-

erty damage or personal injury, but where each day the picketers obstruct lawful entry until the police arrive?

[19] The appellants argue that where, as in this case, the police respond on each occasion and on arrival are able to provide proper entry to or exit from the plant, the pre-condition is not met. They argue that police assistance has not failed to prevent obstruction of lawful entry or exit.

[20] I do not agree. The section does not purport to assess the success of police assistance in preventing obstruction of lawful entry only once the police arrive. This would require the insertion into the subsection of the words "once the police arrive" after the word "prevent." Moreover, the Legislature surely did not contemplate that day after day a company could have access to its premises blocked until whenever the police arrive without being able at some point to resort to the court. The interpretation urged by the appellants would implicitly sanction an indefinite breach of the law. I do not think the Legislature intended this.

[21] On the other hand, s. 102(3) must be interpreted with a realistic understanding of the role of picketing in a labour dispute. The number of picketers is an important expression of solidarity in the taking of collective job action. Pending police assistance, there may well be some inconveniencing or impeding of those seeking to pass through the picket line. The police response to requests for assistance will not always be immediate given their other policing responsibilities. The first failure of the police to respond instantaneously to a request for help does not necessitate the conclusion that police assistance has failed and that therefore the court can be resorted to. Absent questions of property damage or personal injury, a robust society can accommodate some inconvenience as a corollary of the right to picket in a labour dispute before the court will conclude that police assistance has failed, and that it has jurisdiction to intervene with injunctive relief.

[22] In my view, the essence of the pre-condition set up by s. 102(3) was captured by Osborne J. (as he then was) in Mack (Canada) Inc. v. I.A.M.A.W. Lodge No. 2281. . . . As he said there, the section places an onus on the applicant to satisfy the court that the applicant has made reasonable efforts to obtain police assistance and that those efforts have not resulted in an acceptable degree of control in light of the factors set out in the section: the risks of property damage, personal injury or obstruction of lawful access to the premises.

[23] In a case like this one, involving not property damage or personal injury, but obstruction of lawful entry or exit, the relevant considerations will include the degree of the obstruction, its duration on each occasion and how many days it has gone on. The question posed by s. 102(3) is whether in all the circumstances reasonable efforts to obtain police assistance have failed to result in an acceptable degree of control of the situation. . . .

[26] After almost three months, this pattern of daily picketing was clearly established. So too was the police response that could be expected, despite the company's reasonable efforts to obtain their assistance. The result was complete obstruction of lawful access for significant periods of time over a significant number of days. Hence, I conclude that in

the light of the factors set out in s. 102(3) the company has demonstrated that its reasonable efforts to obtain police assistance have failed to result in an acceptable degree of control of the situation.

[27] This ground of appeal therefore cannot succeed.

[Goudge J.A. then discussed several other claims made by the appellant union, including the claim that the injunction was unnecessarily broad. He held that the prohibition against delaying vehicles for more than five minutes each was reasonable, but that it was unreasonable to limit to four the number of picketers at each entrance.]

[39] . . . once the police arrived, the picketers, regardless of their numbers, complied with the requests of the police to provide access. The problem here was not the number of picketers but the delay in the arrival of the police. In these circumstances, limiting the number of picketers goes further than necessary to prevent a recurrence of the demonstrated obstruction of access. It unreasonably restricts an important aspect of the employees' right of expression.

8:420 Secondary Picketing

Hersees of Woodstock Ltd. v. Goldstein (1963), 38 D.L.R. (2d) 449 at 450–56 (Ont. C.A.)

AYLESWORTH J.A.: The matter arises out of a labour dispute between Deacon Brothers Sportswear Ltd. of the City of Belleville, which may conveniently be referred to as the Deacon Company, and the Union mentioned in the style of cause, [Amalgamated Clothing Workers of America (CLC)] referred to as the Union. The appellant [Hersees] is in no way interested in the dispute and has no difficulties with its own employees but in the ordinary course of its business as a retail merchant sells as part of its stock-in-trade from time to time, goods manufactured by the Deacon Company. Neither the respondents nor the Union of which they are members, have any business relationships whatsoever with the appellant and no quarrel with it unless it be appellant's refusal to accede to the request made of it by the respondents to which I shall later refer. On August 12, 1960, the Union was certified by the Ontario Labour Relations Board as the collective bargaining agent for the employees of the Deacon Company but following the report of a conciliation board that company refused and has continued to refuse to conclude a collective agreement with the Union.

The material before the Court consists of two affidavits — one by William Hersee of the appellant and the other by the respondent, Stanley Clair. Hersee deposes that on August 22, 1962, he was approached by Clair who represented himself to be the President of the Union Label Department of the Canadian Labour Congress; that upon Clair ascertaining that appellant did business with the Deacon Company, Clair requested appellant to cancel any orders it had with the Deacon Company; that Clair said if this were not done appellant's store would be picketed; that Clair's request was refused; that appellant then 'had no orders' with the Deacon Company; that on August 28th and following days, one or two pickets bearing placards stationed themselves in front of appellant's place of business. Hersee also deposes to his belief that the picketing thus carried on will have a detrimental effect on appellant's business.

. . . While I am not prepared to disturb [the lower court's] findings negativing conspiracy and nuisance, I think with respect . . . that there was a contract extant between appellant and the Deacon Company and that respondents, acting individually at least, tried to induce appellant to break it. I think further that the chief, if not only purpose of the subsequent picketing, was to force appellant's hand in this respect and thus indirectly to bring pressure to bear upon the Deacon Company.

In this day and age the power and influence of organized labour is very far indeed from negligible. 'Loyalty to the picket line' is a credo influencing a large portion of any community such as the City of Woodstock with its own District Labour Council and numerous member unions; nor does the matter rest there, for doubtless to many private citizens not directly interested in the labour movement the presence of pickets before business premises is a powerful deterrent to doing business at those premises. . . .

. . . To me, and I should think to anyone seeking to do business at the appellant's premises, the inference [to be drawn from the picketing] is unmistakable — Hersees is in a dispute of some kind with organized labour; don't become involved! I think any other conclusion is simply unrealistic and I would hold on the facts of the case that appellant's apprehension of damage to its business as a result of the picketing is completely justified.

Upon this branch of the case, therefore, I summarize my conclusions as follows: appellant had a contract with the Deacon Company; respondents knew of the contract and attempted to induce appellant to break it by picketing his premises; such picketing is a 'besetting' of appellant's place of business causing or likely to cause damage to appellant; not being 'for the purpose only of obtaining or communicating information' the picketing is unlawful — *Criminal Code*, 193-54 (Can.) c. 51, s. 366 [now s. 423] — and it ought to be restrained.

But even assuming that the picketing carried on by the respondents was lawful in the sense that it was merely peaceful picketing for the purpose only of communicating information, I think it should be restrained. Appellant has a right lawfully to engage in its business of retailing merchandise to the public. In the City of Woodstock where that business is being carried on, the picketing for the reasons already stated, has caused or is likely to cause damage to the appellant. Therefore, the right, if there be such a right, of the respondents to engage in secondary picketing of appellant's premises must give way to appellant's right to trade; the former, assuming it to be a legal right, is exercised for the benefit of a particular class only while the latter is a right far more fundamental and of far greater importance, in my view, as one which in its exercise affects and is for the benefit of the community at large. If the law is to serve its purpose then in civil matters just as in matters within the realm of the criminal law, the interests of the community at large must be held to transcend those of the individual or a particular group of individuals. I have been unable to find clear and unequivocal precedent for this principle in any of the numerous decisions at all relevant to the question, to be found anywhere in Canada. . . . certain judicial observations would tend to support this conclusion but in each of such cases the secondary picketing which was the subject-matter under consideration, embraced one or more admittedly unlawful elements such as trespass, intimidation, nuisance or induce-ment of breach of contract. . . . Despite, however, the inclusion in these cases of second-ary picketing of the unlawful elements I have mentioned, I deduce therefrom a trend toward if not a positive statement of the principle I have enunciated. . . .

. . . condemnations of the secondary picketing [by the Supreme Court of Canada in *A.L. Patchett & Sons Ltd. v. Pacific Great Eastern R. Co.*] as being illegal do not appear in a con-text which suggests that they are based upon the inclusion in the picketing of the extrin-sic unlawful elements mentioned elsewhere in the judgments and I view them as declaring secondary picketing to be illegal per se. Upon this ground also I would restrain the respondents.

I would allow the appeal with costs, set aside the judgment and direct judgment against respondents with costs restraining respondents, their servants, agents and any persons acting under their instructions from watching, besetting or picketing or attempt-ing to watch, beset or picket at or adjacent to appellant's place of business.

Consolidated Bathurst Packaging Ltd. v. Canadian Paperworkers Union, Local 595, [1982] 3 Can. L.R.B.R. 324 at 337–39, 342–43 (O.L.R.B.)

[The union lawfully struck four of Ontario's five major manufacturers of cardboard car-tons. Some of their customers increased their orders from the fifth manufacturer (the applicant) whose employees were not on strike. The union then picketed the applicant's plants. Some of its employees refused to cross the picket line. The applicant sought an order from the labour board under section 92 to stop the union from picketing and to stop it from procuring an unlawful strike contrary to section 74. The union argued:

1) that the applicant was an "ally" of the struck firms and would benefit if they obtained a lower settlement;
2) that the picketing was protected under section 76(2), which excluded liability for an act that might reasonably be expected to cause other people to engage in an unlaw-ful strike if that act was "done in connection with a lawful strike"; and
3) that the courts had exclusive jurisdiction to regulate picketing.]

ADAMS, Chair: Sections 74 and 92 must be interpreted in the context of the other provi-sions of the statute and of industrial relations practices. Similarly, the Board's discretion under section 92 must be exercised in the light of these same considerations. It is from this perspective that the Board has said that section 74 must be read and applied with due regard to the legislation policy expressed in section 76. See *Canteen of Canada Limited* . . . Picketing is a traditional method employed by workers to publicize their employment dis-putes and to attract support. If section 74 was applied literally by this Board, picketing at their workplace by employees lawfully on strike would be restrained if honoured by other employees of the struck employer or by the employees of suppliers providing goods and services to the struck location. Section 76(1) is aimed more broadly and directly at picket-ing in that it applies to 'persons' as opposed to trade union officials and requires only the finding that persons will engage in an unlawful strike as the probable and reasonable consequence of the picketing and not that an unlawful strike has occurred. However, by section 76(2) the Legislature has made it clear that it does not intend to restrain picketing done 'in connection with a lawful strike.' In other words, accommodation is made for the traditional exercise of picketing conduct. This Board has therefore read section 74 in light of section 76(2) and declined to restrain, under either section 92 or 135, the involvement of union officials in picketing properly associated with a lawful strike. This case, like *Sarnia Construction Association* . . . , raises the issue of the scope of picketing envisaged and permitted under the Act. Is this picketing in connection with a lawful strike within the meaning of the Act?

Ontario has not chosen to provide a detailed code for picketing such as exists in the Province of British Columbia. Rather, more like the [American] National Labor Relations Act, the Act begins with the premise that all actions causing unlawful strikes are themselves unlawful and then a very general exemption is provided for 'any act done in connection with a lawful strike' to accommodate labour's traditional exercise of picketing activity. Prior to the enactment of section 20 of the Judicature Act [now section 102 of the Courts of Justice Act] and the Board's cease and desist remedial jurisdiction, section 76(2) was largely irrelevant. *Ex parte*, interim and final injunctive relief was available in the courts in actions brought against picketers and framed in common law terms. Section 76(2) simply was a defense to a prosecution under the Act but was not seen as founding a positive statutory right. However, the courts did try to rationalize common law tort and contract laws with lawful strike action and important accommodations were made for picketing arising out of an otherwise lawful strike and confined to the primary work location. . . . Secondary picketing — the picketing of an innocent third party to a labour dispute — was clearly unlawful both at common law and under the Labour Relations Act. See *Hersees of Woodstock Ltd. v. Goldstein* . . .

However, the situation in the courts with respect to labour relations conflict was significantly affected by the passage of section 20 of the Judicature Act. This enactment sets down stringent rules for the availability of injunctive relief in a labour dispute. 'Labour dispute' is defined very broadly and, in such a dispute, an injunction is only available if the court is satisfied 'that reasonable efforts to obtain police assistance, protection and action to prevent or remove any alleged danger of damage to property, injury to persons, obstruction of or interference with lawful entry upon or exit from the premises in question or breach of the peace have been unsuccessful'. . . . However, Ontario courts have had to interpret the meaning of 'labour dispute' to determine the application of section 20 and have held that picketing directed at neutral third parties or at employers not connected with a labour dispute falls outside the section and is amenable to injunctive relief. But in so holding, the courts have tried to ensure that an applicant has not involved himself in a labour dispute. . . .

At the very time the courts were being restrained in their involvement in labour disputes, this Board was being given more extensive remedial powers to control and regulate all forms of industrial relations conflict. Indeed, this jurisdiction was recognized by the court with respect to picketing. . . . In the case of picketing, general substantive guidelines were already in place and this new remedial jurisdiction therefore provided the labour relations community with an alternative forum to the courts. The Board's substantive mandate clearly differs from that of the courts and it cannot be said the two jurisdictions are congruent. . . . However, cases decided under section 20 of the Judicature Act involve a somewhat similar balance of competing factors and can provide useful guides in particular cases. This Board is obligated to determine whether "the act done" (i.e. picketing) is 'in connection with a lawful strike.' One interpretation might be that as long as the picketers are on lawful strike somewhere in Ontario they can picket anyone and anywhere else without restriction by this Board. We do not, however, believe that the Legislature intended to insulate picketing to this extreme extent. Rather, the emphasis of section 76(1) is on affording positive protection against picketing. Reading subsections (1) and (2) together, we believe the Legislature intended to protect innocent third parties from the effects of labour disputes while, at the same time, accommodating the traditional actions of employees involved in lawful strike action, i.e. picketing. To use the classic jargon of this area of labour relations, the Legislature has attempted to maintain a balance between the rights of unions to engage in primary activity and the rights of secondary employers to remain free from the direct involvement in the disputes of others. . . . This Board is required to determine whether particular actions complained of are done in connection with a lawful strike understanding that section 76(2) does not sanction action directed at a person or employer wholly unconcerned in a disagreement between another employer and his employees. Picketing directed at a neutral third party is not in connection with a lawful strike occurring between other parties within the meaning of the subsection. Such actions may, depending on the circumstances, violate both sections 76(1) and 74 and can be remedied under sections 86 and 92. . . .

[The board then considered whether the applicant had become an "ally" of the struck companies by selling its products to their customers during the strike.]

. . . [A] customer or secondary employer may attempt to reduce the impact of the strike on his business as long as it does not reduce the impact of the strike on the primary employer by enabling him to continue his business. No alliance will usually exist where the impetus for substitutions comes solely from the customers of the struck primary employer and the services are not undertaken for the primary employer's account or his name. . . . But abstract pronouncements are not appropriate and the Board should be reluctant to develop per se rules in this area. Each case must be analyzed in light of the established facts, the industrial relations realities, and competing policy considerations.

Against this analysis we cannot find that the facts established before us justify the finding that the applicant is an ally or has allied itself to the struck employers. . . . The applicant is a natural manufacturer for the customers to have recourse to in that the applicant was already performing work for such customers. There is no evidence that the customers are being directed to the applicant by the struck employers or that there is any kind of arrangement by which the struck employers will compensate the customer for any increased cost in having their work performed elsewhere. The applicant has also spurned completely new business. While there is some evidence to indicate that the customers may well return a portion of their patronage to the struck employers at the conclusion of the strike there is no clear understanding that this will be the case and we are satisfied that the applicant is interested in retaining this work if this is at all possible. The applicant also has bona fide concerns over customer reaction if it were to turn its large clients away in their time of need. We have been troubled by the joint meetings of the employers, including the applicant, in January and subsequently in August of this year. Employee suspicions of an arrangement are somewhat understandable in the context of these meetings. The applicant also has a real interest in the outcome of the negotiations involving the struck employers in that this settlement has been a pattern settlement in previous rounds. But a thorough review of the 'minutes' produced does not disclose an understanding that the applicant perform struck work and that the meetings were anything more than informational in purpose. It must be remembered that the unions take an industry approach to their bargaining and it is natural for employers who are affected by their industry-wide efforts to exchange information, concerns and views. On the evidence before us we cannot find that the applicant has gone beyond this purpose or that it is acting in a manner other than as a true competitor to the struck employers in performing work that is clearly arising from the unavailability of the struck employers to perform work for their customers. . . . Accordingly, we find that the applicant is a neutral and that the picketing directed at it is not in connection with a lawful strike within the meaning of section 76(2). . . .

* * *

Despite the fact that the Ontario Labour Relations Board has accepted jurisdiction over picketing in support of a legal strike in cases such as *Consolidated Bathurst*, and uses criteria similar to those used by the courts in deciding when picketing is secondary and therefore not protected by the statutory provisions sheltering activity carried on "in connection with a lawful strike," the Ontario courts continue to entertain applications for injunctions against secondary picketing without adverting to any idea of deference to the board: see, for example, *A.B. McLean Ltd. v. United Steelworkers of America, Local 2251*, [1991] 91 C.L.L.C. 14,018 (Ont. Ct. (Gen. Div.)).

In *Domtar Construction Materials Ltd. v. International Brotherhood of Teamsters, Local Union No. 213*, [1976] 1 Can. L.R.B.R. 81 (B.C.L.R.B.), the seven striking employees of a Domtar warehouse picketed a Domtar gypsum plant employing seventy production workers and located some distance away, shutting down that plant. Sales from both the warehouse and the gypsum plant were handled by Domtar's marketing division, located at the site of the warehouse but not on strike. Apart from this, the warehouse and gypsum plant functioned with substantial independence. The board prohibited the picketing, describing it as enabling the small warehouse unit to bring "an excessive and disproportionate degree of economic pressure" to bear on the employer.

Similarly, in *Irving Oil Ltd. v. Canadian Paperworkers Union, Local 601* (1990), 108 N.B.R. (2d) 91 (Q.B.), employees on strike against a paper company owned by the Irving family were enjoined from picketing retail outlets of an oil company owned by the same family. There was no evidence, Higgins J. wrote, that the oil company "has involved itself in any active meddling or transfer of human or physical resources to strip it of its neutrality and to give rise to [the] so-called "ally" doctrine" (at page 104). The applicable statutory provision, section 104 of the New Brunswick *Industrial Relations Act*, R.S.N.B. 1973, c. I-4, prohibited picketing anywhere but "at the employer's place of business, operations or employment," and the court held that the oil company was not the employer of the strikers.

British Columbia is the only Canadian jurisdiction with detailed legislative provisions on picketing. Such provisions, some of which are referred to above, have been in force since 1973 and have been amended from time to time in accordance with the changing political complexion of the provincial government. The *Labour Relations Code*, S.B.C. 1992, c. 82, states in section 67 that "Except as provided in this Code, a person shall not picket in respect of a matter or dispute to which this Code applies." What sorts of picketing are and are not allowed is set out in section 65:

(1) In this section

'ally' means a person who, in the board's opinion, in combination, in concert or in accordance with a common understanding with an employer assists the employer in a lockout or in resisting a lawful strike;

'common site picketing' means picketing at or near a site or place where

(a) 2 or more employers carry on operations, employment or business, and

(b) there is a lockout or lawful strike by or against one of the employers referred to in paragraph (a), or one of them is an ally of an employer by or against whom there is a lockout or lawful strike.

(2) A person who, for the benefit of a struck employer, or for the benefit of an employer who has locked out, performs work, supplies goods or furnishes services of a nature or kind that, except for a lockout or lawful strike, would be performed, supplied or furnished by the employer, shall be presumed by the board to be the employer's ally unless he or she proves the contrary.

(3) A trade union, a member or members of which are lawfully on strike or locked out, or a person authorized by the trade union, may picket at or near a site or place where a member of the trade union performs work under the control or direction of the employer if the work is an integral and substantial part of the employer's operation and the site or place is a site or place of the lawful strike or lockout.

(4) The board may, on application and after making the inquiries it requires, permit picketing

(a) at or near another site or place that the employer causing a lockout or whose employees are lawfully on strike is using to perform work, supply goods or furnish services for the employer's own benefit that, except for the lockout or strike, would be performed, supplied or furnished at the site or place where picketing is permitted by subsection (3), or

(b) at or near the place where an ally performs work, supplies goods or furnishes services for the benefit of a struck employer, or for the benefit of an employer who has locked out, but the board shall not permit common site picketing unless it also makes an order under subsection (6) defining the site or place and restricting the picketing in the manner referred to in that subsection.

(5) In subsection (4) 'employer' means the person whose operation may be lawfully picketed under subsection (3).

(6) The board may, on application or on its own motion, make an order defining the site or place at which picketing that is permitted by subsection (3), or that is permitted under subsection (4), may take place and where the picketing is common site picketing, the board shall restrict the picketing in such a manner that it affects only the operation of the employer causing the lockout or whose employees are lawfully on strike, or an operation of an ally of that employer, unless it is not possible to do so without prohibiting picketing that is permitted by subsection (3) or (4), in which case the board may regulate the picketing as it considers appropriate.

(7) For the purpose of this section, divisions or other parts of a corporation or firm shall, if they are separate and distinct operations, be treated as separate employers.

Thus, section 65(3) allows primary picketing in support of a lawful strike at the site of the strike, and sections 65(2) and (4) permit (or authorize the board to permit) picketing at other sites of the struck employer or at the site of an ally as defined in section 65(1). Section 65(7) makes clear that the picketing of separate divisions of a struck corporation or firm is to be treated as secondary rather than primary.

It is interesting that all three members of a committee appointed in 1992 to advise on reform of the statute agreed that these provisions should remain intact. In the words of John Baigent, the union representative on the committee, they all agreed "that neutral employers should be insulated, as much as possible, from the effects of legal picketing." Ted Roper, the management representative, stated that they also agreed that employees should not be allowed to picket "non-struck 'secondary' locations of their own employer": J. Baigent, V. Ready, & T. Roper, *Recommendations for Labour Law Reform: A Report to the Honourable Moe Sihota, Minister of Labour* (Victoria, B.C.: Ministry of Labour and Consumer Services, 1992), app. 4 at 1, 9.

The rest of section 65 deals largely with common site picketing, and it is here that the members of the advisory committee disagreed to some extent. The union representative argued (app. 4 at 1) that employees should have an unfettered right to picket at their own worksite, even if that site is shared by a separate division of the struck employer. The employer representative argued (app. 4 at 8) that "[i]nvestors want to be assured that a labour dispute in one of their operations will not spill over to others," and that "it is not consistent with that reality to permit a labour dispute at a particular operating division of a company to affect non-struck operations." The neutral member, Vince Ready, proposed the compromise solution of adding the "unless" clause that now appears at the end of section 65(6). He stated (app. 4 at 5):

I do not draw a distinction between uninvolved employers and separate divisions of the same corporate entity which are not involved in the labour dispute. In both cases, picketing should be confined to the location where employees involved in the labour dispute work. Where separate divisions share a common site, picketing should be confined, to the extent possible, to the division engaged in the strike or lockout: i.e. where the employees work. . . .

Currently, the Act would require the Board to eliminate picketing in a common site picketing situation where there was no way to confine the pickets to the operation of the struck employer without affecting the uninvolved party. I believe that the Board should have discretion in such circumstances.

A leading discussion of the "ally" doctrine is found in *Liquor Distribution Branch v. Hiram Walker & Sons Limited*, [1978] 2 Can. L.R.B.R. 334 (B.C.L.R.B.), Weiler Chair.

Pepsi-Cola Canada Beverages (West) Ltd. v. Retail, Wholesale and Department Store Union, Local 558 (2002) 208 D.L.R. (4th) 385 (SCC)

[During a legal strike and legal lockout between the Pepsi-Cola distributor in Saskatoon and its employees, strikers engaged in various types of picketing and other acts in support of their bargaining position. Some of those acts were clearly illegal because they involved violence or the picketing of private homes. However, the case dealt mainly with the peaceful picketing of a number of retail stores which sold Pepsi products but had no corporate connection to the Pepsi-Cola company, and only that part of the judgment is excerpted below.

In the court of first instance, Pepsi-Cola applied for and was granted an interlocutory injunction prohibiting picketing "at any location other than [Pepsi's own] premises"— that is, prohibiting all secondary picketing. The Saskatchewan Court of Appeal struck down that prohibition. In a unanimous judgment written by McLachlin C.J.C. and LeBel J., the Supreme Court of Canada upheld the Court of Appeal decision.]

MCLACHLIN C.J.C. and LEBEL J.: — This case raises the issue of when if ever secondary picketing — typically defined as picketing in support of a union which occurs at a location other than the premises of that union's employer — may be legally conducted. . . .

The law on this issue has been clarified by legislation in a number of Canadian provinces. Saskatchewan has legislated to abolish the tort of restraint of trade in the union context: The Trade Union Act, R.S.S. 1978, c. T-17, s. 27. However, apart from this it has left the common law in place. The Union, supported by the Canadian Labour Congress and the Canadian Civil Liberties Association, argues that the common law as presently articulated is difficult to apply and unnecessarily curtails the right to free expression. Pepsi-Cola, on the other hand, defends the present rule as workable and appropriate to protect business interests and prevent labour disputes from spreading to non-parties to the dispute.

For the reasons that follow, we conclude that secondary picketing is generally lawful unless it involves tortious or criminal conduct, and that the Saskatchewan Court of Appeal correctly disposed of the issues on this basis. . . .

IV. ISSUES

The main issue in this appeal is the legality of secondary picketing at common law. A secondary issue is whether the employer, Pepsi-Cola, can apply for relief against secondary picketing, or whether only the third parties affected by secondary picketing may apply.

V. ANALYSIS

1. Preliminary Questions

Two preliminary issues arise: (1) whether the courts have the power to make the sort of change advocated by the Union; (2) if so, how the Charter may affect the development of the common law.

On the first issue, we conclude that the change in the common law here at issue lies within the proper power of the courts. The status of secondary picketing at common law remains unsettled and inconsistent across jurisdictions. The Court in this case is not required to overturn a well-established rule at common law, but rather to clarify the common law given two strands of conflicting authority, each with some claim to precedent. Resolution of the conflicting lines of authority lies well within the powers of a court of common law. . . .

The second preliminary issue is how the Charter may affect the development of the common law. Here again the answer seems clear. The Charter constitutionally enshrines essential values and principles widely recognized in Canada, and more generally, within Western democracies. Charter rights, based on a long process of historical and political development, constitute a fundamental element of the Canadian legal order upon the patriation of the Constitution. The Charter must thus be viewed as one of the guiding instruments in the development of Canadian law.

This Court first considered the relationship between the common law and the Charter in R.W.D.S.U. v. Dolphin Delivery Ltd., [1986] 2 S.C.R. 573, 33 D.L.R. (4th) 174, where McIntyre J. concluded, at p. 603:

> Where, however, private party "A" sues private party "B" relying on the common law and where no act of government is relied upon to support the action, the Charter will not apply. I should make it clear, however, that this is a distinct issue from the question whether the judiciary ought to apply and develop the principles of the common law in a manner consistent with the fundamental values enshrined in the Constitution. The answer to this question must be in the affirmative. In this sense, then, the Charter is far from irrelevant to private litigants whose disputes fall to be decided at common law.

The reasons of McIntyre J. emphasize that the common law does not exist in a vacuum. The common law reflects the experience of the past, the reality of modern social concerns and a sensitivity to the future. As such, it does not grow in isolation from the Charter, but rather with it.

Although s. 2(b) of the Charter is not directly implicated in the present appeal, the right to free expression that it enshrines is a fundamental Canadian value. The development of the common law must therefore reflect this value. Indeed, quite apart from the Charter, the value of free expression informs the common law. As McIntyre J. observed in Dolphin Delivery. . . :

> Freedom of expression is not, however, a creature of the Charter. It is one of the fundamental concepts that has formed the basis for the historical development of the political, social and educational institutions of western society.

At the same time, it must be recognized that the common law addresses a myriad of very diverse relationships and seeks to protect a host of legitimate interests not engaged by the Charter. Salient among these are the life of the economy and individual economic interests. Common law rules ensure the protection of property interests and contractual relationships. Nevertheless, where these laws implicate Charter values, these values may be considered.

In Hill v. Church of Scientology of Toronto, . . . the Court adopted a flexible balancing approach to addressing alleged inconsistencies between the common law and Charter values:

> Charter values, framed in general terms, should be weighed against the principles which underlie the common law. The Charter values will then provide the guidelines for any modification to the common law which the court feels is necessary.

The Court also cautioned that: "Far-reaching changes to the common law must be left to the legislature". . . Finally, the Court determined that the party alleging an inconsistency between the common law and the Charter bears the onus of proving "that the common law fails to comply with Charter values and that, when these values are balanced, the common law should be modified". . . . It is upon this basis that we proceed to balance the values at stake in the present appeal.

2. The Competing Values and Interests

(a) Historical Perspective of the Function of Picketing in a Labour Dispute

. . . it has come to be accepted that, within limits, unions and employers may legitimately exert economic pressure on each other to the end of resolving their dispute. Thus, employees are entitled to withdraw their services, inflicting economic harm directly on their employer and indirectly on third parties which do business with their employer. Employers are similarly entitled to exert economic pressure on their employees through the use of lockouts and, in most jurisdictions in Canada, through the hiring of replacement workers.

. . . The legally limited use of economic pressure and the infliction of economic harm in a labour dispute has come to be accepted as a legitimate price to pay to encourage the parties to resolve their differences in a way that both can live with. . . .

(b) Picketing and Free Expression

. . .

In labour law, picketing is commonly understood as an organized effort of people carrying placards in a public place at or near a business premises. The act of picketing involves an element of physical presence, which in turn incorporates an expressive component. Its purposes are usually twofold: first, to convey information about a labour dispute in order to gain support for its cause from other workers, clients of the struck employer, or the general public, and second, to put social and economic pressure on the employer, and often by extension, on its suppliers and clients. . . .

. . . Picketing represents a continuum of expressive activity. In the labour context it runs the gamut from workers walking peacefully back and forth on a sidewalk carrying placards and handing out leaflets to passersby, to rowdy crowds shaking fists, shouting slogans, and blocking the entrances of buildings. Beyond the traditional labour context, picketing extends to consumer boycotts and political demonstrations. . . . A picket line may signal labour strife. But it may equally serve as a physical demonstration of individual or group dissatisfaction on an issue.

For the purposes of this appeal, we find it unnecessary to define picketing in a detailed and exhaustive manner. We proceed rather on the basis that picketing may involve a broad range of activities, from the "traditional" picket line where people walk back and forth carrying placards, to the dissemination of information through other means.

Picketing, however defined, always involves expressive action. As such, it engages one of the highest constitutional values: freedom of expression, enshrined in s. 2(b) of the Charter. This Court's jurisprudence establishes that both primary and secondary picketing are forms of expression, even when associated with tortious acts: Dolphin Delivery, supra. The Court, moreover, has repeatedly reaffirmed the importance of freedom of expression. It is the foundation of a democratic society. . . .

Free expression is particularly critical in the labour context. As Cory J. observed for the Court in U.F.C.W., Local 1518 v. KMart Canada Ltd., . . . "For employees, freedom of expression becomes not only an important but an essential component of labour relations". . . . The values associated with free expression relate directly to one's work. A person's employment, and the conditions of their workplace, inform one's identity, emotional health, and sense of self-worth. . . .

. . . It is through free expression that employees are able to define and articulate their common interests and, in the event of a labour dispute, elicit the support of the general public in the furtherance of their cause. . . . As Cory J. noted in KMart, . . . "it is often the weight of public opinion which will determine the outcome of the dispute."

Free expression in the labour context benefits not only individual workers and unions, but also society as a whole. . . .

This said, freedom of expression is not absolute. When the harm of expression outweighs its benefit, the expression may legitimately be curtailed. Thus, s. 2(b) of the Charter is subject to justificative limits under s. 1.

The same applies in interpreting the common law to reflect the Charter. The starting point must be freedom of expression. Limitations are permitted, but only to the extent that this is shown to be reasonable and demonstrably necessary in a free and democratic society.

(c) Protection of Innocent Third Parties to Labour Disputes

On the other side of the balance lie the interests of the employer and third parties in protection from excessive economic and other harm as a result of picketing and other labour action. As previously discussed, one important objective of labour picketing is the infliction of economic harm on the employer with an eye to compelling a favourable resolution of the dispute. Thus, expressive action in the labour context, as in other situations, may cause economic harm. However, the appellant argues that economic harm arising from labour disputes should be confined to the actual parties to the dispute — it should not be permitted to harm innocent third parties, who have neither influence over the outcome of the dispute, nor the ability to bring it to a close.

The appellant emphasizes that secondary picketing expands the labour dispute beyond its core, increasing both the incidence of picketing and the number of businesses and persons affected by it. The targets of secondary activity, such as retailers of a struck product, may suffer considerable economic damage, which may in turn affect customers and employees, as well as a host of other business relations. The appellant contends that the interests of these third parties, as well as public order generally, compel restraints on the scope of picketing activity.

On this point, the appellant relies on Dolphin Delivery, supra. In that case, the union represented the locked-out employees of Purolator, an Ontario-based courier service. Dolphin undertook to supply delivery service to Purolator customers in the Vancouver area during this lockout. The union planned to picket Dolphin's premises, and Dolphin succeeded in getting an injunction to prohibit the intended picketing. The union challenged the injunction all the way to this Court, where it was ultimately upheld.

The challenge to this restriction on secondary picketing was framed as a violation of the union's right to freedom of expression under s. 2(b) of the Charter. As no picket line ever went up, the Court chose to assume that the picketing would have been peaceful and that Dolphin's unionized workers would have respected the picket line. In the end, McIntyre J. found that the Charter did not apply, and the injunction was upheld on the basis of the common law tort of inducing breach of contract.

McIntyre J. was of the view that if the Charter did apply, the injunction could have been justified under s. 1. While acknowledging that all picketing (even where accompanied by tortious conduct) involves some element of expression, McIntyre J. recognized the legitimacy of some curtailment of secondary picketing in order to prevent the economic harm of labour disputes from spreading too broadly into the community. McIntyre J. stated . . . :

> When the parties do exercise the right to disagree, picketing and other forms of industrial conflict are likely to follow. The social cost is great, man-hours and wages are lost, production and services will be disrupted, and general tensions within the community may be heightened. Such industrial conflict may be tolerated by society but only as an inevitable corollary to the collective bargaining process. It is therefore necessary in the general social interest that picketing be regulated and sometimes limited. It is reasonable to restrain picketing so that the conflict will not escalate beyond the actual parties. While picketing is, no doubt, a legislative weapon to be employed in a labour dispute by

the employees against their employer, it should not be permitted to harm others. [Emphasis added.]

To the extent that the appellant relies on the obiter comments in Dolphin Delivery to support the notion that secondary picketing in itself is a tort, the appellant's argument must fail. First, as Cory J. cautioned in KMart, . . . these comments from Dolphin Delivery must be read in the specific context of that case. . . . McIntyre J. held that the picketing in question would have been tortious, amounting to inducing breach of contract. McIntyre J. stated . . . that "[o]n the basis of the findings of fact that I have referred to above, it is evident that the purpose of the picketing in this case was to induce a breach of contract between the respondent and Supercourier," and again . . . , "[i]n the case at bar . . . [w]e have a rule of the common law which renders secondary picketing tortious and subject to injunctive restraint, on the basis that it induces a breach of contract." It was therefore on the assumption that the anticipated picketing would have been tortious that McIntyre J. proceeded with the s. 1 analysis — not on the basis of secondary picketing being illegal per se. As such, Dolphin Delivery did not make any final pronouncement on the legality of secondary picketing as such, and up until now, the issue has never been addressed directly by this Court.

Secondly, although McIntyre J.'s comments reflect a concern with the interests of third parties to labour disputes who may incur collateral damage, they should not be read as suggesting that third parties should be completely insulated from economic harm arising from labour conflict. As Cory J. noted in KMart, . . . the objective of the restraint on picketing in Dolphin Delivery was to ensure that third parties did not "suffer unduly from the labour dispute over which it has no control". . . . Therefore, third parties are to be protected from undue suffering, not insulated entirely from the repercussions of labour conflict. Indeed, the latter objective would be unattainable. Even primary picketing frequently imposes costs, often substantial, on third parties to the dispute, through stoppages in supplies or the loss of the primary employer as a customer. . . . Indeed, labour disputes in important sectors of the economy may seriously affect a whole town or region, even the nation itself. As McIntyre J. recognized in the above quote, the social cost of a labour dispute is often great. Yet this impact on third parties and the public has never rendered primary picketing illegal per se at common law to protect the interests of third parties.

So we are left with this: innocent third parties should be shielded from "undue" harm. This brings us to the question that lies at the heart of this appeal. How do we judge when the detriment suffered by a third party to a labour dispute is "undue," warranting the intervention of the common law? . . .

3. Potential Solutions — Surveying the Landscape

Picketing engages distinct and frequently clashing interests among the parties affected by a labour dispute. The present appeal casts the right of unions to freely express their views on the conditions of their employment and the facts of a labour dispute against the resulting potential for economic damage to third parties. . . .

Three possible options emerge from the parties' submissions:

1) an absolute bar on secondary picketing (the "illegal per se" doctrine);
2) a bar on secondary picketing except for "allied" enterprises (the modified "Hersees" rule); and
3) permitting secondary picketing unless the picketing amounts to a tort or other wrongful conduct.

We will consider each option in turn.

(a) The Illegal Per Se Doctrine

This view holds that secondary picketing is illegal per se, in the manner of an independent tort, even in the absence of any other wrongful or illegal act.

The doctrine turns on location. It rests on a distinction between picketing the premises of the employer against whom the union is striking (primary picketing) and picketing other premises (secondary picketing). Primary picketing is legal unless it involves tortious or criminal conduct, while secondary picketing is always illegal.

The "illegal per se" doctrine for secondary picketing originates from the obiter comments of the Ontario Court of Appeal in Hersees. . . .

The decision in Hersees . . . reflects a deep distrust of unions and collective action in labour disputes. An expressive act that is legal and legitimate if done by an individual suddenly becomes illegal when done in concert with others. Aylesworth J.A.'s reasons reflect the common sentiments of early 19th century legislation and subsequent judgments which held that the combination of workers in pursuit of their economic interest was unlawful and against public policy. . . . The effect of these judgments was to discount the importance of freedom of expression in the labour law context, a point which will later be discussed in greater detail. . . .

(b) Exceptions to Hersees — The Primary Employer and Ally Doctrines

Over time, necessary refinements to the bold "illegal per se" doctrine have riddled it with difficult exceptions. As a threshold matter, courts would refuse to enjoin picketing where the employees were found to be engaged in "primary" rather than "secondary" picketing. In some of these cases, the courts found that the location of the picketing, although not necessarily the primary workplace of the employees, was nonetheless owned by the same employer. The courts would also "lift the corporate veil" and refuse to enjoin picketing at the parent company, or at a company which shared corporate ownership with the primary employer. . . . The picketing would therefore not be characterized as "secondary"; hence the definition of secondary picketing referred to in these reasons.

However, forbidding picketing at any place other than the primary employer's workplace continued to create difficulty. For example, strict application of the Hersees doctrine would effectively deny a union the ability to picket its own employer if, by virtue of a shared driveway, for example, an otherwise unrelated employer would also be affected. Courts have nevertheless allowed picketing in these circumstances, provided it is primarily directed at the struck employer. However, the search for primary purpose may, at times, prove a rather subtle intellectual exercise, as some courts have found. . . .

Another exception to the strict Hersees approach is the ally doctrine (although there is a significant degree of overlap between this doctrine and the other exceptions discussed in this section). Some courts, while suggesting secondary picketing may be illegal per se, have refused to enjoin picketing where the struck operation was effectively assisting the employer in carrying on business during a labour dispute. . . .

Similarly, courts have refused injunctions where third parties allowed struck employers to conduct a business from their warehouse, on the basis that the secondary location was effectively a place of business for the employer. . . . Concerns such as these have required courts to make delicate distinctions regarding the amount of warehousing, for example, as evidence of the degree of co-operation between the primary and secondary employer. . . .

These modifications to the Hersees doctrine have softened its harshest effects on unions and picketing, but have made the common law difficult to implement in a consistent, clear manner. . . .

Despite these difficulties, the Ontario Court of Appeal and courts in some other provinces continue to apply the obiter of Hersees that secondary picketing is illegal per se. . . . On balance, few judgments reflect the Hersees doctrine in its strictest form, but some courts continue to apply a modified version.

(c) Permitting Secondary Picketing Unless it Involves a Tort or Crime

A third approach starts with the proposition that all picketing is permitted unless it can be shown to be wrongful or unjustified (the "wrongful action" model). It defines wrongful or unjustified picketing as picketing that involves a tort (a civil wrong) or a crime (a criminal wrong).

Prior to the decision of the Ontario Court of Appeal in Hersees, there was no clear pronouncement on the issue of whether picketing activity should be enjoined by the common law in absence of an independently actionable tort, such as nuisance, inducing breach of contract, intimidation or trespass. However, authority for the wrongful action model can be found in the decision of this Court in Williams v. Aristocratic Restaurants (1947) Ltd. . . . In that case, the issue was whether the picketing activity by a striking union at the location of non-unionized restaurants belonging to the same employer was unlawful. The picketing in question involved two workers walking back and forth on a sidewalk in front of the targeted restaurant carrying placards which stated that the proprietor did not have a labour agreement with the union. The majority found that the picketing activity in question did not amount to trespass, unlawful assembly, nuisance, or any other criminal or tortious activity. As such, the activity remained lawful (although, as discussed, this form of picketing would probably fall within the "primary employer" or "ally" exceptions to the Hersees doctrine).

Even after Hersees, a number of Canadian courts have expressly declined to adopt its classification of secondary picketing as illegal per se; instead, they have refused injunctions to enjoin secondary picketing unless it involves tortious or criminal conduct. . . . This approach stems from the proposition, as articulated by Cameron J.A. for the majority in the court below, that "[g]enerally speaking, picketing constitutes an exercise of the fundamental freedom of expression which can only be circumscribed by laws, whether statutory, regulatory, or common, that accord with the constitutional norms of the Canadian Charter of Rights and Freedoms". . . .

4. Resolving the Conflict: The Wrongful Action Model

Having canvassed the interests at stake and the conflicting approaches the law has adopted to reconcile them in the context of secondary picketing, we now confront the issue before us — which approach best balances the interests at stake in a way that conforms to the fundamental values reflected in the Charter?

We conclude that the third approach — the wrongful action model that makes illegal secondary picketing which amounts to tortious or criminal conduct — best achieves this goal. The following considerations, some of which involve overlapping themes, lead us to this conclusion.

(a) Conformity to Charter Methodology

While freedom of expression is not absolute, and while care must be taken in the labour context to guard against extending the more severe effects of picket lines beyond the employer, if we are to be true to the values expressed in the Charter our statement of the common law must start with the proposition that free expression is protected unless its curtailment is justified. This militates against a rule that absolutely precludes secondary picketing, whether harmful or benign, disruptive or peaceful. The preferred methodology is to begin with the proposition that secondary picketing is prima facie legal, and then impose such limitations as may be justified in the interests of protecting third parties. . . .

(b) Protection of the Value of Free Expression

The wrongful action approach best protects the values of contemporary Canadian society as they find expression in the Charter. . . . The Hersees rule, even in its modified form, denies free expression any value outside primary picketing. . . .

(c) Avoidance of Excessive Emphasis on Protection from Economic Harm

In Hersees, the Ontario Court of Appeal appears to have viewed the issue as a conflict between a public right to trade and the rights of a smaller group, the union, to advance its purely private interests. The public interest in free expression and societal debate on working conditions and labour conflict receives no mention. The Hersees doctrine casts the economic protection of third parties from the effects of labour disputes as the pre-eminent concern of the law, regardless of the resulting incursion on free expression.

If the legal foundation of the hierarchy of rights proposed in Hersees was doubtful at the time, it is even more problematic in light of the enactment of the Charter and contemporary labour relations.

(d) Adequate Flexibility

Not only do the Hersees and modified Hersees rules deny adequate protection for free expression and place excessive emphasis on economic harm, they do this in a rigid, inflexible way. These rules are more about shutting off the message than regulating the activity. By contrast, a wrongful action approach is sufficiently flexible to accommodate both interests. Courts may intervene and preserve the interests of third parties or the struck employer where picketing activity crosses the line and becomes tortious or criminal in nature. It is in this sense that third parties will be protected from "undue" harm in a labour dispute. Torts such as trespass, intimidation, nuisance and inducing breach of contract, will protect property interests and ensure free access to private premises. Rights arising out of contracts or business relationships will also receive basic protection. Torts, themselves the creatures of common law, may grow and be adapted to current needs.

In summary, a wrongful action approach to picketing allows for a proper balance between traditional common law rights and Charter values, and falls in line with the core principles of the collective bargaining system put in place in this country in the years following the Second World War.

(e) Rationality

A wrongful action approach to picketing is clearer and more rational than the absolute or modified prohibition approach represented by Hersees. The Hersees or modified Hersees approach uses location as the primary criterion for determining when picketing is legal. Yet the reason for prohibiting picketing is not its location, but its character and impact — the wrong it represents and damage it does. Location is merely a legal marker, and not a very satisfactory one at that; as we have seen, the Hersees jurisprudence is dominated by formalistic debates centring on location.

The wrongful action approach, by contrast, focuses on the character and effects of the activity, as opposed to its location. It gets at the heart of why picketing may be limited. . . . Picketing which breaches the criminal law or one of the specific torts like trespass, nuisance, intimidation, defamation or misrepresentation, will be impermissible, regardless of where it occurs.

(f) Avoidance of the Primary-Secondary Picketing Distinction

It follows from this analysis that the difficult and potentially arbitrary distinction between primary and secondary picketing is effectively abandoned on a wrongful action approach to picketing. Secondary picketing has been, as we have seen, location defined. Indeed, many of the difficulties the courts have encountered over the years in defining secondary picketing flow from how to determine the relevant location. A conduct approach based on tortious and criminal acts does not depend on location. All picketing is allowed, whether "primary" or "secondary," unless it involves tortious or criminal conduct.

We should not lament the loss of the primary-secondary picketing distinction. It is a difficult and arbitrary distinction that deserves to be abandoned. . . .

(g) Avoidance of Labour/Non-labour Distinctions

The wrongful action approach treats labour and non-labour expression in a consistent manner. The Hersees rule, by contrast, effectively creates an independent tort of secondary picketing that applies only in the labour context. This distinction is difficult to justify. . . . We can find no persuasive reason to deprive union members of an expressive right at common law that is available to all members of the public. . . .

(h) Balance of Power

Pepsi-Cola argues that the potential harm to the employer from secondary picketing may be much greater than the harm that would result from primary picketing alone, and that allowing secondary picketing may tilt the balance of power too much in the unions' favour. . . .

Judging the appropriate balance between employers and unions is a delicate and essentially political matter. Where the balance is struck may vary with the labour climates from region to region. This is the sort of question better dealt with by legislatures than courts. Labour relations is a complex and changing field, and courts should be reluctant to put forward simplistic dictums. Where specialized bodies have been created by legislation, be it labour boards or arbitrators, they are generally entrusted to reach appropriate decisions based on the relevant statute and the specific facts of a given situation. Mediation and arbitration are also assuming increasingly important roles in the resolution of labour disputes. If the Saskatchewan Legislature had enacted a comprehensive scheme to govern labour disputes, then it might be argued that allowing secondary picketing would disturb a carefully crafted balance of power. In the absence of a legislative scheme, however, we find it difficult to say that determining illegal picketing on the basis of tortious or criminal conduct — an approach that prevailed at common law prior to Hersees — will unduly undermine the power of employers vis-à-vis employees.

We emphasize that the validity of legislation is not at stake in this appeal. It is the absence of such legislation that requires us to look to the common law to resolve the issue of the legality of secondary picketing. Nothing in these reasons forestalls legislative action in this area of the law. Within the broad parameters of the Charter, legislatures remain free to craft their own statutory provisions for the governance of labour disputes, and the appropriate limits of secondary picketing.

(i) Undue Harm to Neutral Third Parties

It is argued that although secondary picketing may yield a benefit for a limited class of people, the neutral retailers' right to trade is "far more fundamental and of far greater importance . . . for the benefit of the community at large" (Hersees. . . .)

The first difficulty with this argument is that it gives no weight to free expression. As discussed above, this runs counter to Charter methodology and values.

A second difficulty is that the argument overstates the interests of third parties by positing a "fundamental" right to trade in the struck good. Again as discussed above, the basis for this purported fundamental right is unclear.

A third difficulty is that the argument glosses over the fact that third parties — producers and consumers — are harmed even as a result of primary picketing. . . . To the extent that harm to neutrals is a rationale for restricting secondary picketing, it is also a rationale for restricting primary picketing.

Fourth, the argument contravenes at least the spirit of the Charter by sacrificing an individual right to the perceived collective good rather than seeking to balance and reconcile them. . . .

It is important that neutral third parties be protected from wrongful conduct and that labour disputes be prevented from unduly spreading: . . . We are not persuaded, however, that it is necessary to ban all secondary picketing in order to accomplish these goals. Prohibiting strike conduct which is tortious or criminal offers protection against a wide variety of misconduct associated with strike action. Insofar as conduct is non-tortious, it is not clear that more is required to protect third parties.

(j) The "Signalling" Effect

An extension of the previous argument is that secondary picketing is per se unjustified because it has the effect of "signalling" that people must not do business with neutral third parties. Expression through a picket line may "signal" that the line is a barrier and hence acquire coercive impact. . . .

This signalling effect, it is argued, goes beyond expression and becomes coercion. Many people, as a matter of principle or habit, will not cross a picket line. . . .

The first point to note is that the signalling effect should be carefully assessed. . . . Doubtless there is a kernel of truth in this concept. Some people will see a picket line and automatically refuse to cross it, out of respect, sympathy, or the fear of an implied confrontation. It should be remembered, however, that this concept arose originally to describe the response to picketing among other unionized employees. . . . Moreover, the so-called signalling effect . . . may vary sharply, depending on whether the dispute happens in a small tightly knit, and highly unionized community, or at a strongly organized construction site used by several employers. . . . In a large urban centre, where the population is diverse, and where the per capita unionization rate is low, the signalling effect may be exaggerated. We should be mindful to remember the words of caution written by Rand J. several years ago in Aristocratic Restaurants . . . about peaceful picketing and its effect and the fact that it could be taken pretty well in stride by the common person:

> Through long familiarity, these words and actions in labour controversy have ceased to have an intimidating impact on the average individual and are now taken in the stride of ordinary experience . . .

A second observation is that the signalling argument implicitly suggests that to the extent that picketing has a coercive signal effect, it is not expressive and hence not worthy of protection. We find such a suggestion problematic. It is difficult to see how a signal can be other than expressive; by definition, a signal is meant to convey information to others. . . . It seems better to us to admit that signalling is expression, the limitations of which must be justified. At this point, however, signalling ceases to suggest a special rule; rather, the question is when expressive signalling can be justifiably limited.

This brings us to a third difficulty with the signalling argument. Used to buttress the proposition that secondary picketing is per se illegal, it amounts to a special rule for union speech. As discussed under (g) above, it is difficult to explain why expression in the labour context should be treated as fundamentally less important than expression in other contexts. It is far from clear that union speech is more likely to elicit an irrational or reflexive response than, for example, speech by a political organization. If we say that the signalling effect justifies a special prohibition in the labour context, does it not follow that signalling in other contexts may also justify blanket prohibitions? Moreover, it seems clear that freedom of expression is not confined to "rational" speech. Irrationality may support according less protection to particular kinds of speech. But it does not justify denying all protection as a matter of principle.

A fourth problem with the signalling argument is that not all secondary picketing relies on the coercive potential of the picket line. A distinction is sometimes drawn between secondary picketing whose aim is to disrupt the production of the secondary employer (either by dissuading the secondary employer's employees from working or by persuading consumers not to deal at all with the secondary employer until it discontinues its commercial relationship with the primary employer), and secondary picketing whose aim is merely to persuade consumers not to purchase from the secondary employer the products of the primary employer. (As an example of the latter form of labour activity, workers striking against a tobacco manufacturer might picket convenience stores in an effort to persuade customers to substitute another manufacturer's brand of cigarettes for the brand manufactured by the primary employer.) The danger of a coercive picket line that depends on a signalling effect is clearly much greater in the case of union activity whose aim is to harm the secondary employer. The danger of coercion and signalling is much less in the case of secondary picketing aimed merely at persuading consumers not to purchase the product of the primary employer.

The United States Supreme Court recognized this distinction in National Labor Relations Board v. Fruit and Vegetable Packers and Warehousemen, Local 760. . . :

> Peaceful consumer picketing to shut off all trade with the secondary employer unless he aids the union in its dispute with the primary employer, is poles apart from such picketing which only persuades his customers not to buy the struck product.

We should therefore be mindful not to extend the application of the signal effect to all forms of union expression. As Cory J. noted in KMart . . . : "It is the 'signal' component of conventional picketing which attracts the need for regulation and restriction in some circumstances" (emphasis added). Given the diverse range of activities captured by the term "picketing," it is apparent that the signal effect operates to a greater degree in some situations than in others. We conclude that signalling concerns may provide a justification for proscribing secondary picketing in particular cases, but certainly not as a general rule.

(k) Does a Wrongful Action Rule Offer Adequate Protection?

Having concluded that there is no principled ground on which to ban secondary picketing per se and that an approach requiring tortious or criminal conduct is preferable, the practical question remains: does a wrongful action rule offer sufficient protection for neutral third parties when weighed against the value of free expression? . . . In other words, . . . is it too permissive in that it does not provide a mechanism to permit neutral third parties to raise valid justifications — justifications that might prevail under s. 1 of the Charter had the matter arisen as a Charter case?

At this point we may usefully review what is caught by the rule that all picketing is legal absent tortious or criminal conduct. The answer is, a great deal. Picketing which breaches the criminal law or one of the specific torts like trespass, nuisance, intimidation, defamation or misrepresentation, will be impermissible, regardless of where it occurs. Specific torts known to the law will catch most of the situations which are liable to take place in a labour dispute. In particular, the breadth of the torts of nuisance and defamation should permit control of most coercive picketing. Known torts will also protect property interests. They will not allow for intimidation, they will protect free access to private premises and thereby protect the right to use one's property. Finally, rights arising out of contracts or business relationships also receive basic protection through the tort of inducing breach of contract. . . .

. . . while the wrongful action approach is grounded on conduct and hence less arbitrary than the per se illegal rule of Hersees . . . , the way torts or crimes are defined may introduce its own measure of arbitrariness. Some of the relevant torts require an unlawful act or the threat of an unlawful act. This makes the relevant inquiry circular: secondary picketing is unlawful if it is tortious but it is tortious only if it is unlawful. Other torts may end up drawing arbitrary lines. Inducing breach of contract, for example, requires (obviously) a contract. The result might be that a neutral employer who has a long-term contract with the primary employer may be protected from secondary picketing, whereas a neutral employer who sells the same products without a long-term supply contract would not be protected.

Despite some anomalies, it is safe to assert that a wrongful action-based approach will catch most problematic picketing — i.e. picketing whose value is clearly outweighed by the harm done to the neutral third party. Moreover, the law of tort may itself be expected to develop in accordance with Charter values, thus assuring a reasonable balance between free expression and protection of third parties.

Moreover, to the extent that it may prove necessary to supplement the wrongful action approach, the courts and legislatures may do so. Doubtless issues will arise around the elaboration of the relevant torts and the tailoring of remedies to focus narrowly on the illegal activity at issue. Doubtless too, circumstances will present themselves where it will become difficult to separate the expressive from the tortious activity. In dealing with these issues, the courts may be expected to develop the common law sensitively, with a view to maintaining an appropriate balance between the need to preserve third party interests and prevent labour strife from spreading unduly, and the need to respect the Charter rights of picketers. The legislatures too may play a role. Clarification of the status of picketing at common law should not be viewed as a restriction on legislative intervention. Rather it should be seen merely as a tool to assist the courts where federal and provincial laws remain silent. As mentioned earlier, different circumstances in different parts of the country may call for specially tailored legislative regimes. Legislatures must respect the Charter value of free expression and be prepared to justify limiting it. But subject to this broad constraint, they remain free to develop their own policies governing secondary picketing and to substitute a different balance than the one struck in this case.

5. Status to Seek an Injunction

In this case, Pepsi-Cola, the primary employer, sought an injunction to restrain picketing and demonstrations at the premises of independent third parties.

Cameron J.A. for the majority of the Court of Appeal, held that picketing is not subject to injunctive relief unless accompanied by the commission of a tort actionable at the instance of the primary company (i.e. Pepsi-Cola). Wakeling J.A., in dissent, concluded that Pepsi-Cola had suffered adequate injury and loss by the secondary picketing and thus would have allowed it to maintain an action for injunctive relief.

We would favour Cameron J.A.'s approach for the following reasons.

First, this approach is consistent with the wrongful action approach to secondary picketing. Since the wrongful action approach recognizes that secondary picketing is lawful where there is no tortious or criminal conduct, it follows that Pepsi-Cola should only be allowed to initiate injunction proceedings where it has been subjected to a tort or a crime — not where it has merely been the target of peaceful secondary picketing.

The contrary view, espoused by Wakeling J.A., is based on accepting secondary picketing as an independent tort against the primary company. The approach we adopt is inconsistent with such a tort. It follows that allowing Pepsi-Cola to maintain an action for injunctive relief on the basis of secondary picketing alone should also be rejected.

This does not mean that Pepsi-Cola has no ability to maintain an action for injunctive relief in a secondary picketing situation. It simply means that Pepsi-Cola would have to base its claim on a specific tort. Not all torts limit the cause of action to the person primarily affected by the actions of another. Intimidation serves as a good example. The elements of intimidation include both intimidating the plaintiff and intimidating others, to the injury of the plaintiff. Thus, as Cameron J.A. points out, in the context of labour-management disputes, intimidation would be actionable at the instance of the employer whether the person intimidated be the employer or an employee. Hence, the tort-based approach only limits Pepsi-Cola's cause of action to the extent that it is limited by the tort itself.

VI. APPLICATION AND CONCLUSION

The Chambers judge enjoined [the picketing of the retail stores] on the basis that such picketing involved the tort of "conspiracy to injure" the third parties. However, s. 28 of the Saskatchewan Trade Union Act expressly abolishes this tort. In effect, such a tort would render secondary picketing per se illegal. Therefore, we agree with the majority of the Court of Appeal that this injunction cannot be supported on the basis relied on by the Chambers judge. We also agree with the majority of the Court of Appeal that the conduct of the Union provided no basis for inferring any other tort, much less crime. It was peaceful informational picketing. It was aimed at supporting the strike and harming the business of Pepsi-Cola by discouraging people from trading or buying Pepsi-Cola's products. It did not amount to the tort of intimidation, which has to do with the intentional infliction of loss by unlawful means. Nor did the pickets support the tort of interference with contractual relations. First, Pepsi-Cola did not establish the required contractual basis under which the outlets allegedly acquired its product for resale. Second, the evidence as to picketing was, in the view of the Court of Appeal, "so ambiguous as to have made it impossible to conclude that the picketers . . . induced the breach of any contract or hindered its performance". . . .

We would therefore dismiss the appeal. . . .

✿ ✿ ✿

The Supreme Court of Canada's treatment of the economic torts in the Pepsi-Cola judgment is discussed by Chris Rootham *et al*, "The Expanded Scope of Union Protection under the *Charter*," (2003) 10 CLELJ 161 at 170–185.

Labour relations statutes in three provinces (Alberta, New Brunswick, and Newfoundland) prohibit all secondary picketing, even if the picketed party is an economic ally of the struck employer. For example, the Alberta Labour Relations Code states, in section 82(1), that picketing may take place at the "striking or locked out employees' place of work and not elsewhere." After the *Pepsi-Cola* decision, in *Alberta (Attorney General) v. Retail Wholesale Canada, Local 285 (Brewers Distributors)*, [2001] 6 W.W.R. 643 (Alta. Q.B.), where the primary employer had in effect moved its business to the secondary employer's premises during a strike, the court upheld the opinion of the Alberta Labour Relations Board that the complete statutory ban on secondary picketing was in breach of the *Charter* protection of freedom of expression because it went farther than was necessary to meet "the pressing and substantial objective of preventing economic damage to neutrals in a labour dispute."

For a discussion of the potential effect of the Pepsi-Cola judgment on less restrictive forms of legislative regulation of picketing, and on labour board jurisprudence in this area, see Bernard Adell, "Secondary Picketing after *Pepsi-Cola*: What's Clear and What Isn't?" (2003) 10 CLELJ 135, at 149–59.

In *British Columbia Government Employees' Union v. British Columbia (A.G.)* [1988], 2 S.C.R. 214 at 243–44, Chief Justice McEachern of the British Columbia Supreme Court granted an injunction, ex parte and on his own motion, prohibiting legally striking government employees from picketing courthouses. McEachern C.J.S.C. held that such picketing constituted a criminal contempt of court. The Supreme Court of Canada held that unlike the action of the court in *Dolphin Delivery* (referred to in the *Pepsi-Cola* judgment above) in granting an injunction based on the common law in a proceeding between two private parties, McEachern C.J.S.C.'s granting of this injunction was subject to scrutiny under the *Charter*. Dickson C.J.C. said:

> At issue here is the validity of a common law breach of criminal law and ultimately the authority of the court to punish for breaches of that law. The court is acting on its own motion and not at the instance of any private party. The motivation for the court's action is entirely 'public' in nature, rather than 'private.' The criminal law is being applied to vindicate the rule of law and the fundamental freedoms protected by the Charter. At the same time, however, this branch of the criminal law, like any other, must comply with the fundamental standards established by the Charter.

The Supreme Court of Canada nevertheless upheld the injunction on the ground that free access to the courts was essential to the vindication of fundamental rights, especially *Charter* rights. The Court adopted the following passage from the British Columbia Court of Appeal judgment:

> We have no doubt that the right to access to the courts is under the rule of law one of the foundational pillars protecting the rights and freedoms of our citizens. It is the

preservation of that right with which we are concerned in this case. Any action that interferes with such access by any person or groups of persons will rally the court's powers to ensure the citizen of his or her day in court. Here, the action causing interference happens to be picketing. As we have already indicated, interference from whatever source falls into the same category.

In *Ontario Public Service Employees' Union v. Ontario (Attorney-General)*, (1996) 47 C.P.C. (3d) 189 (Ont. Gen. Div.), the above judgment was relied on to uphold an injunction against the peaceful picketing of a courthouse by legally striking provincial public servants. Evidence was adduced that the picketing did not dissuade anyone from entering the courthouse. However, the court was of the view that the picketing itself constituted an interference with the administration of justice, even if no one respected the picket line.

8:500 JOB RIGHTS OF STRIKERS

8:510 Employee Status during a Strike

The "right to strike" is not expressly granted by labour legislation. Nor, according to the Supreme Court of Canada, is it granted by the Constitution (above, section 8:120). Rather, it is implied from the statutory recital of the right of employees to take part in the "lawful activities" of unions, from the prohibition on strikes until such prerequisites as conciliation and strike votes are met, and from the prohibition of employer retaliatory action designed to eradicate the union or punish strikers.

The extent of the protection afforded striking workers depends on whether the strike is legal. This section will examine employee status during a legal strike - that is, whether and to what extent employees retain a right to their jobs during such a strike. It will not discuss the effect of strikes on employment benefits such as pension entitlements, seniority rights, vacations, sick pay, and severance pay, although this can be of great concern to striking employees. (For one discussion, see Geoffrey England, "The Legal Response to Striking at the Individual Level in the Common Law Jurisdictions of Canada" (1976) 3 Dal. L.J. 440.) On employee status during illegal strikes, see *McGavin Toastmaster Ltd. v. Ainscough*, below, section 10:220.

The following case provides the foundation for an analysis of employee status during a legal strike.

R. v. Canadian Pacific Railway Co. [*The Royal York Case*] (1962), 31 D.L.R.(2d) 209 at 211, 216, 218–20 (Ont. H.C.)

[This was an appeal by way of stated case from a provincial criminal court's dismissal of an unfair labour practice charge against the Royal York Hotel. During the course of a legal strike, the hotel's management sent the following letter to strikers:

1. On June 26th I wrote you enclosing Form A — Resignation, and Form B — Return to Work, and asked you to sign either form and return it by July 15th. I again wrote you

on July 10th in this same connection, and also outlined the new wage rates and working conditions now in effect.

2. As you did not indicate your availability for duty or otherwise, in accordance with paragraph 4 of letter dated 26th June, we are closing your employment record at the Royal York Hotel effective 16th July, 1961. . . .

McRuer C.J.H.C. held that this letter amounted to an unfair labour practice. With respect to section 1(2) of the Ontario *Labour Relations Act*, which provided that no one "shall be deemed to have ceased to be an employee by reason only of his ceasing to work for his employer as the result of a lock-out or strike," he said:]

MCRUER C.J.H.C.: This subsection preserves the relationship of employer and employee for the purposes of the statute notwithstanding a strike and even though the true relationship of employer and employee may have been terminated at common law on account of the strike. . . .

I think the Act throughout recognizes that there may be employees who are reporting for work and employees who are on strike and it forbids the employer to dismiss or threaten to dismiss members of either class because they engage in lawful union activities. . . .

. . . One of the purposes of s. 1(2) is to preserve for employees their rights as such while they are on strike. The Act creates a statutory class of employees, *viz.*, employees on strike. In the United States of America it has been consistently held before and since the *Wagner Act*, which contains a provision somewhat similar to s. 1(2) of the Ontario Act, that the relationship of employer and employee continues notwithstanding a strike unless that relationship has been abandoned . . . If I were to come to any other conclusion on the construction of section 1(2) the result would be that when a collective agreement comes to an end and conciliation proceedings have been exhausted an employer will be at liberty to lay down terms that employees could not be expected to accept with the consequence that if they went on strike they would lose all their pension rights, their insurance rights and seniority rights. To so interpret the law would destroy the security built up by old and experienced employees and leave it subject to the will of the employer. This would appear to be contrary to the whole course of the development of labour legislation for half a century. . . .

. . . Counsel asks the question, 'If the law is as I have stated it to be, what is the legal position where a strike is never concluded by a settlement?' This is a question that it may not be necessary for me to answer. However, I think the answer is quite simple. In such a case the employees have either gone back to work, taken employment with other employers, died or become unemployable. Such employees could not any longer, adapting the language of s. 1(2), be deemed to have ceased to be employees by reason only of their ceasing to work for their employer as the result of a strike.

* * *

The decision of McRuer C.J.H.C. was affirmed by the Ontario Court of Appeal, and by the Supreme Court of Canada, *sub nom. C.P.R. Co. v. Zambri* (1962), 34 D.L.R. (2d) 654. Cartwright J. wrote, at 664:

> It is said that the Act does not in terms declare the right to strike, but I find myself in agreement with [union counsel's] argument that the right is conferred by s. 3 which reads:
>
>> 3. Every person is free to join a trade union of his own choice and to participate in its lawful activities.
>
> It is clear on the findings of fact made by the learned Magistrate that the strike with which we are concerned was an activity of the union; I have already expressed my opinion that it was lawful; it follows that s. 3 confers upon the six employees, all of whom are members of the union, the right to participate in that lawful activity. I conclude therefore that the participation in the strike by the employees was the exercise of a right under the Act.
>
> . . .

Locke J. added this important *dictum*, at 657, with respect to the permanent replacement of lawful strikers.

> While unnecessary for the disposition of this appeal, I wish to express my dissent from the opinion that has been stated that if a strike is never concluded by settlement the relationship declared by ss. (2) of s. 1 continues until the employee has either gone back to work, taken employment with other employers, died or become unemployable. When employers have endeavoured to come to an agreement with their employees and followed the procedure specified by the *Labour Relations Act*, they are at complete liberty if a strike then takes place to engage others to fill the places of the strikers. At the termination of the strike, employers are not obliged to continue to employ their former employees if they have no work for them to do, due to their positions being filled. I can find no support anywhere for the view that the effect of the subsection is to continue the relationship of employer and employee indefinitely, unless it is terminated in one of the manners suggested.

In several provinces, the use of "professional strikebreakers" has been expressly forbidden: see, for example, the Ontario *Labour Relations Act*, section 78. This prohibition is particularly significant for relatively small bargaining units of unskilled or semiskilled workers, where security firms and labour contractors manage to undercut vulnerable unions by supplying temporary personnel to enable employers to maintain operations. In several well-publicized cases, these tactics were accompanied by the use of agents provocateurs or other illicit devices to further undermine the union.

Quebec and British Columbia have much broader provisions that forbid employers from hiring even temporary replacement workers or using certain classes of ongoing employees to perform bargaining unit work. Ontario enacted similar legislation in 1992, but it was repealed in 1995. See below, section 8:520, for a discussion of such legislative restrictions.

In other jurisdictions, where the hiring of replacements continues to be part of the employer's tactical arsenal, a controversial issue remains: can the employer maintain operations by using permanent replacements to fill the strikers' jobs without commit-ting the unfair labour practice of refusing to employ someone because of his or her par-ticipation in the lawful activities of a trade union? Legislators in Ontario and Manitoba, influenced by the above *dictum* of Locke J. in *Royal York*, thought this would not be an unfair labour practice, and moved to protect employees by giving former strikers an explicit statutory right to return to their jobs even if replacement workers are in those jobs. The Manitoba provisions are the widest. They state that work being done by replacements at the end of a strike or lockout is work which "becomes available" for the purpose of allowing returning strikers to reclaim it, and that returning strikers must be recalled on the basis of their seniority at the beginning of the stoppage, unless the par-ties agree otherwise. The Manitoba provisions also make it an unfair labour practice for the employer to hire or threaten to hire anyone to perform struck work "for any period of time longer than the duration of the lockout or legal strike" (Manitoba *Labour Rela-tions Act*, sections 11–13.) In Ontario, the protection is more limited in that the striker must make an "unconditional" application for reinstatement within six months of the commencement of the strike (*Labour Relations Act, 1995*, section 80). Following a bitter strike in which the entitlement of strikers to return to work was very much at issue, Alber-ta also enacted a general right to reclaim one's job (*Labour Relations Code*, section 88).

As the following extracts reveal, the *dictum* of Locke J. in *Royal York* may no longer reflect the effect of general unfair labour practice provisions in this area.

Canadian Air Line Pilots' Association [C.A.L.P.A.] v. Eastern Provincial Airways Ltd. (1983), 5 Can. L.R.B.R. (N.S.) 368 at 409, 407 (C.L.R.B.)

[During a lawful strike the company maintained operations by, among other things, hir-ing eighteen new pilots to fill the strikers' positions and promising those new employ-ees that they would retain their jobs after the strike. Some nine weeks into the strike, the employer offered to conclude a return to work agreement with the striking union, clause 12 of which read as follows (at 409):

> . . . It is agreed that when the strike ends, all pilots presently involved in the strike will be considered on layoff due to a sudden cessation of work caused by a work stoppage of employees. . . . Pilots will be recalled to openings in accordance with their seniority. For these purposes, an opening is an available vacant position in a status according to opera-tional requirements. However, it is understood that the problems of returning to normal operations and the requirements of retraining make it impractical to recall pilots in accor-dance with the provisions of the collective agreement for a temporary period. It is agreed, therefore, that pilots may be recalled out of seniority in accordance with operational requirements for a period of 60 days following the date of signing of this Return to Work Agreement. Following that, and unless the parties mutually agree to extend the period, the provisions of Article 7 of the Collective Agreement [regarding seniority] will apply for all further recalls.
>
> It is agreed that no grievance shall be filed by CALPA or any pilot, as a result of the non-application of the Collective Agreement regarding recalls during the above men-

tioned period. Furthermore, it is agreed and understood that the reactivation of the provisions of the Collective Agreement regarding seniority shall not affect the status and base location of any pilot, who was already on active flying duty, or who had commenced, or been scheduled to commence training on the date of the signing of this Return to Work Agreement.

One of the union's claims was that this offer violated section 184(3)(a)(vi) of the *Canada Labour Code*, which made it an unfair labour practice for an employer to "refuse to employ or to continue to employ . . . or otherwise discriminate against any person in regard to employment . . . because the person . . . has participated in a strike that is not prohibited by this Part . . ." The board found in favour of the union.]

JAMIESON, Chair: EPA [Eastern Provincial Airways] takes the position that in the absence of statutory provisions providing for the reinstatement of employees at the end of a strike, and, where there is nothing to restrain an employer from operating during a strike or restricting the hiring of new employees, its insistence that the new pilots not be replaced by returning strikers, is not unlawful.

EPA relied on extensive North American industrial relations jurisprudence which would overawe any tribunal by the mere mention of the impressive list of prominent and respected authors and adjudicators in this field. Particular emphasis was placed on two Ontario Labour Relations Board decisions: *Mini-Skool Ltd.* . . . and *The Becker Milk Company Limited.* . . . It is our view that there is nothing particularly relevant in those cases to the facts before us in this case. They deal primarily with the rights of employees under s. 73 of the Ontario legislation. . . .

We shall not go through the other cases to distinguish them, they are all so clearly dependent upon the interpretation given the particular statutory provisions in the relevant jurisdictions. . . .

If the Code only contained s. 107(2), which is a standard provision in most jurisdictions [preserving the 'employee status' of strikers], it would be open to argument that to retain 'employee status' does not necessarily mean a guarantee of a job. But, Parliament went much further than s. 107(2) to protect the continued employment of those who exercised their rights under the Code. The construction of s. 184(3)(a)(vi) could leave absolutely no room for doubt that employees cannot be deprived of any term or condition of employment whatsoever because of participation in a lawful strike. If an employee is so deprived, a reason, other than the exercise of the right to strike, must be present.

What reasons does EPA have for laying off some 18 pilots at the end of a lawful strike? The jobs are still there, the aircraft are the same and there has been no change in the equipment as far as we know. Other than the changes to the content of the collective agreement, the only difference there would be at the end of the strike from when it began . . . is that there are 18 additional pilots. Pilots who have been lawfully hired in the same manner as any other pilot hired by EPA. They have the same working conditions, in fact, they are still on probation. . . . How does EPA propose to avoid laying off the new pilots rather than the strikers, keeping in mind that such lay-offs are normally governed by art. 7 of the collective agreement? . . .

While we do not wish it said that we are interpreting the collective agreement, the effect of [the proposed] clause 12 is rather obvious. The seniority provisions which normally govern the employment relationship at EPA would be suspended long enough for EPA to accomplish what it could not lawfully do otherwise. That is, to keep the new pilots and those who crossed the picket lines to work during the strike on the active workforce out of seniority. Clause 12 also provides EPA with a 60 day opportunity to selectively recall whom it wishes, out of seniority or alternately, not to recall those that it does not wish to recall. And, to add insult to injury, CALPA and the pilots would be required to forego their right under the collective agreement to grieve their displacement by junior pilots. What could be more blatantly discriminatory? And, what is the reason for all of this? EPA cannot escape the answer!

Such conduct by EPA is contrary to s. 184(3)(a)(vi) of the Code, and we so find.

✻ ✻ ✻

Pursuant to the recommendations of a task force in 1996 (in its report entitled *Seeking a Balance*, below, section 8:520), the *Canada Labour Code* was amended (by S.C. 1998, c. 26, s. 37) to provide, in section 87.6, that legal strikers or locked out employees must be reinstated in preference to any replacement worker "who was not an employee in the bargaining unit on the date on which notice to bargain collectively was given. . . ."

The question of the applicability in Ontario of the reasoning in the *Eastern Provincial Airways* decision is complicated by section 80 of the Ontario *Labour Relations Act, 1995*, which allows strikers individually to return to their jobs during the first six months of a legal strike. If a strike is still on after six months, can the *Eastern Provincial Airways* rationale apply? In *Mini-Skool Ltd.* (1983), 5 Can. L.R.B.R. (N.S.) 211, the Ontario Labour Relations Board held that it was not an unfair labour practice for an employer to retain junior employees who had returned to work before the six-month limit in preference to more senior employees who wished to return after that point. In *Shaw-Almex Industries Ltd.* (1986), 15 Can. L.R.B.R. (N.S.) 23, on the other hand, the board held that the *Mini-Skool* decision depended on a finding that the employer had no improper motive for extending a preference to the junior employees. In *Shaw-Almex*, the employer's expression of feelings of loyalty to the replacement workers, and its failure to make out the claim that their skills had surpassed those of the returning strikers, led to a finding of improper motive in retaining the replacement workers in preference to the strikers, even though the strike had lasted longer than six months. Another possible distinction between the *Shaw-Almex* and *Mini-Skool* cases was that the replacement workers in *Shaw-Almex* had been hired for the first time during the strike, whereas in *Mini-Skool* the junior employees had been hired before the strike, had gone on strike, and had returned to work under section 80.

In *Ottawa Citizen* [1999] O.L.R.D. No. 1445 (Q.L.), vacancies arose after a legal strike, and the employer filled them with people who had been replacement workers during the strike rather than with those who had been on strike. Although the employer had clearly been anxious to hire back the particular replacement workers, the O.L.R.B. found that it had met the burden of proving that it did so because of the competence they had shown during the strike rather than because of anti-union animus.

In *Canadian Association of Smelter and Allied Workers, Local No. 4 v. Royal Oak Mines Inc.* (1993), 93 C.L.L.C. para. 16,063 at 14,510–14, a long and bitter strike was dragging on, and a rival employee association applied to decertify the striking union, as was allowed by the *Canada Labour Code*. The Canada Labour Relations Board held that replacement workers should not be considered to be in the bargaining unit or to be eligible to take part in the decertification vote, because they had only "a temporary, precarious status" and their interests were "not only divergent from but squarely opposed to those of the permanent workforce." In 1998, section 29(1.1) was added to the *Canada Labour Code* to make explicit the exclusion from the unit of anyone "hired or assigned after [the beginning of collective bargaining} to perform all or part of the duties" of a striker or a locked out employee: S.C. 1998, c. 26 s. 13.

8:520 Replacement Worker Laws

Since 1977, Quebec's *Labour Code* has contained what are often called anti-strikebreaker provisions — provisions which have sharply restricted the use of replacement workers (R.S.Q. 1977, ss. 109.1–109.4). During a strike or lockout employers are forbidden to use most classes of employees to perform the work of the struck bargaining unit. All employees within the bargaining unit must cease work. The only employees who may fill their places are those who both fall within the managerial exclusion and were working in the struck operation before the beginning of the current negotiations. There is a limited exception for work designed to prevent the destruction or serious deterioration of property, and it may be permissible for an employer to have the work done by a subcontractor at another location. Thus, although these provisions do not explicitly require the employer to cease operations, they greatly curtail its ability to maintain production. They reinforce Pierre Verge's argument that under Canadian labour relations statutes, the right to strike is vested in the union and not in workers individually: see P. Verge, "Syndicalisation de la grève" (1983) 38 Relations industrielles 475.

Perhaps because the anti-strikebreaker provisions met with very strong opposition from employers when they were introduced in 1977, only very limited redress was made available in the event of a breach of those provisions. The *Labour Code* expressly contemplates two kinds of redress: investigation leading to a non-binding report, and prosecution leading to a fine. An employer may well ignore the investigation and wait for the prosecution to come to trial, which only happens long after the dispute has ended. In the meantime, the employer's bargaining power will have been enhanced by the use of replacements. In practice, the only effective remedy has been injunctive relief from the ordinary courts, and this has not always served unions well.

Despite the controversy which surrounded the anti-strikebreaker provisions in their early years, it is fair to say, a quarter-century later, that they have become well integrated into Quebec labour law. This is indicated by the fact that they were not called into question during the debate which led to amendments to the *Labour Code* in 2001 (S.Q.

2001, c. 27). Those amendments could, however, have a significant impact on the way the anti-strikebreaker provisions are administered. A labour board similar to those in other jurisdictions has been created, and it has very broad remedial powers, with respect to the anti-strikebreaker provisions as in other areas. Those powers include the authority to issue cease and desist orders. How they will be used remains to be seen.

Since its enactment in 1992, the British Columbia *Labour Relations Code* (S.B.C. 1992, c. 82, s. 68) has prohibited employers from using the services of paid or unpaid replacement workers. A replacement worker is defined as a worker who

1) is retained after the date on which notice to bargain is given or the date on which bargaining commences;
2) ordinarily works at another of the employer's places of work;
3) is transferred to a strike or lockout location after the date mentioned in (1); or
4) is employed by or engaged by the employer, or supplied to the employer by another person, to perform the work of an employee in the strike or lockout unit or the work ordinarily done by a person who is performing the work of an employee in the strike or lockout unit.

The British Columbia provisions, unlike the Quebec provisions, do not prohibit employees in the struck unit from returning to work while the strike continues.

In Ontario, provisions to prohibit the use of replacement workers were enacted in 1992 but repealed in 1995.

Policy issues with respect to replacement worker legislation are explored in the following excerpts from an article on American labour law. The excerpts refer to the *MacKay Radio* doctrine, which is based on *dicta* of the United States Supreme Court in *NLRB v. MacKay Radio & Telegraph Co.* (1938), 304 U.S. 333, at 345–46, that an employer "is not bound to discharge those hired to fill the places of strikers, upon the election of the latter to resume their employment, in order to create places for them."

Paul Weiler, "Striking a New Balance: Freedom of Contract and the Prospects for Union Representation" (1984) 98 Harv. L. Rev. 351 at 389–94, 412–14

... [F]ew rules of American labor law have been as heavily criticized as the legality of hiring permanent strike replacements. But contrary to the tacit assumption of its critics, overturning that doctrine would merely scratch the surface of the problem of inequality of bargaining power — especially as experienced by the newly certified unit struggling to win a first collective agreement — because the employer would still be entitled to operate its plant during the strike.

We must therefore grapple with the tougher question whether the law should completely bar employers from continuing operations during a legal strike. A plausible case can be made that it should. Enabling the employer to keep its business going blunts the normal 'double-edged sword' of the strike and tilts the balance of power at the bargaining table sharply in its favor. Still worse, this employer 'right' is exercised most effectively against small units of relatively unskilled employees and in periods and regions of considerable unemployment; female workers in largely nonunion, 'secondary' labour markets, not auto and steelworkers, are those who must face the threat of *Mackay Radio*. There is thus a close correspondence between the types of workers whose attempts to better their lot through free collective bargaining are most contained by outside economic forces and the types of workers who actually experience the adverse effect of this additional legal resource conferred by the Supreme Court on their employers.

This argument that employers should be altogether barred from operating their business during a strike no doubt has some force. Nevertheless . . . there are substantial and ultimately persuasive objections to using the law in this way in order to maintain a fair equilibrium in bargaining power. . . .

Under current law, the employer can insulate itself from the mutual economic pressure on which a regime of free collective bargaining depends by hiring replacements in order to continue operating during the strike. I argued earlier that we should overturn the feature of the *Mackay Radio* doctrine that authorized the hiring of 'permanent' replacements. Employers who exercise this right put at grave risk both the strikers' jobs and the future of collective bargaining within the unit. Such a power is not justified by the 'legitimate and substantial' interests of employers, most of whom will be able to recruit replacements even without offering them a rather ephemeral 'permanent' status.

More important, *Mackay Radio* authorizes employers to continue operating during a legal strike by their employees. Although even the most critical American commentators rarely confront this aspect of the opinion, overturning it should no longer be considered unthinkable. A social democratic government in Quebec, sympathetic to the labor movement, has recently taken this step. The Quebec Labor [*sic*] Code does not actually prohibit employers from operating during a strike, yet it bans the use of almost all strike replacements for this purpose. Not only workers hired off the street, but also the firm's non-unit employees, outside contractors, and even bargaining unit workers who prefer not to go on strike are barred from working during the strike. Only management personnel, at most a skeleton staff able to provide minimum services, may be used by the struck establishment.

Reflection on this recent, highly controversial development in Quebec law forces us to grapple with some profound issues of principle in American labor law. Under American law, it is usually assumed that a deadlock at the bargaining table should be broken by the mutual economic pressure generated by a work stoppage — the employees' loss of wages and the employer's loss of production and sales revenues. If, however, the employees go on strike and the employer continues to operate, the contest becomes quite one-sided: the employees feel most of the financial pressure, and their employer can bide its time until the union concedes. Should the law ensure a fairer contest by prohibiting the use of any strike replacements, temporary as well as permanent?

I do not believe so, for two reasons. First, the employer's right to hire replacements to reduce the impact of a strike is, to a large extent, reciprocal to the employees' right to take other jobs in order to protect themselves against their loss of income. True, most workers are unable actually to exercise this legal right; on the other hand, most struck firms find little consolation in the *Mackay Radio* doctrine. Moreover, unions are often able to find work for many of their striking members — especially if the workers are skilled, the labour market is tight, and the union supplies workers through a hiring hall. The availability of this option to some workers, such as electricians in the construction industry, may accentuate the disparity in power between the union and small firms with which it deals and may thus allow the union to extract an unfairly large wage premium. If the labor laws forced employers to experience the losses of a strike as a real incentive to compromise at the bargaining table, fairness would require that the same legal constraints be placed on union members. But there are major problems, in both principle and practice, in trying to enforce such an intrusive restraint on workers' freedom to support themselves and their families during collective work stoppages.

This consideration gives rise to my second objection to outlawing employers' use of strike replacements. Were we to bar the recruitment of replacements or the strikers' taking on other jobs, the law would insulate the parties from outside competition. Such insulation runs very much against the grain of a market-based system of collective bargaining, as the following example illustrates. An employer has been paying average wages of $6 per hour. The employees, believing that they are underpaid, join a union. Eventually, good-faith bargaining gets under way. The employer is now willing to offer an increase to $7 per hour, but the employees strike, insisting on $9 per hour — the wage in the standard union contract. Assume that the law prohibits the employer's hiring even temporary replacements who would gladly work for the $7 per hour already offered to the union. Such a rule in effect empowers the unionized employees unilaterally to fix a wage floor — $9 per hour — that their employer must pay if it wishes to have the bargaining unit's work performed. Correspondingly, if the law barred the employees who go out on strike from taking work elsewhere, the employer could unilaterally set a ceiling — here, $7 per hour — on the wage that these employees could earn for their services.

In a system of free collective bargaining, neither result is acceptable. I do not mean to suggest, of course, that the law should place no limits on the parties' abilities to expose each other to the coldblooded test of the labor market. As I have argued, the legal right to strike should be defined in a way that will foster the long-term employment relationship, by protecting striking employees not only against outright discharge, but also against forfeiture of their jobs to permanent replacements. But I feel quite uncomfortable with the kind of one-sided intervention provided for in the recent Quebec legislation.

✻ ✻ ✻

In 1995 the federal Minister of Labour appointed a task force to review part 1 of the *Canada Labour Code*, the law governing collective bargaining for private-sector employers and unions in the federal jurisdiction. As part of its mandate the task force considered proposals for the adoption of replacement worker legislation.

Seeking a Balance: Canada Labour Code Part 1 Review (Ottawa: Supply and Services Canada, 1996) (Chair: A. Sims; Members: P. Knopf & R. Blouin) at 124–28, 131

DIFFERENT PERSPECTIVES ON WORK AND WORK STOPPAGES

Part of the question involves the balance of power between labour and management. However, underlying the issue is a more fundamental difference between the parties about what bargaining rights entail. From an employer's perspective, the obligation to bargain is an obligation to bargain over the terms of work for their employees. They retain, in their view, the residual right to get the work done in other ways, restrained only by any commitments that they make through collective bargaining (for example, a prohibition on contracting out). Such commitments end, in any event, once a work stoppage takes place.

From the union's perspective, employees retain a permanent connection to their job until terminated. The Code maintains employees' status during a work stoppage, and protects them against retaliation for exercising their right to strike. Employees often perceive themselves as having almost a proprietary right not just to employment, but to the performance of the work. They therefore see it as an invasion of this proprietary right when someone else takes over their job.

There are also differences of view over what a strike is all about. Some see collective bargaining as an important market instrument. The strike or lockout tests competing views of the market value of work. The union maintains that the work is worth a specified price; the employer, in turn, believes it can get the work done for less. The availability of willing replacement workers and the efficiency with which they perform the work tests these assumptions. If replacement workers are unavailable or unsatisfactory, the employer is persuaded to raise its offer. If they work well, this pressures the employees, through their union, to reduce their demands to the market level.

Others see the strike as being fought on the more limited field of the financial ability of the employer to survive a shutdown versus the ability of the employees to survive without wages. Under this perception, the employer is seen as garnering an unfair advantage by maintaining a revenue stream during a shutdown. Employers argue that employees are not precluded from seeking alternative employment during a work stoppage and that to achieve balance, employers should not be prohibited from using alternate sources of labour.

THE POTENTIAL FOR VIOLENT CONFRONTATION

One argument advanced in favour of anti-replacement worker legislation is the need to avoid violent incidents that can arise when replacement workers attempt to cross picket lines set up by striking or locked out workers.

No one favours violence, however caused. But violence is not, and need not be, an inevitable consequence of the use of replacement workers. Unions advance this argument somewhat gingerly, and employers resent it being advanced at all. In the employer's view, to restrain its options because those on strike may become violent is seen as punishing the victim, not the perpetrator.

Neither side of this argument is fully justified. Experience shows that violence most often occurs when replacement workers and strikers come into contact with each other in a heated labour dispute. Sensible measures to reduce that potential should be considered seriously. Sometimes it is the strikers that instigate violence and sometimes, but by no means at all times, this is due to encouragement from their leadership. We recognize the important efforts taken by many union leaders to discourage violence in such situations. But it is not always the fault of the strikers or their union. Replacement workers and front line supervisors have also, on occasion, engaged in their fair share of provocative conduct.

In our experience, it is the threat of permanent job loss, and taunting about that between replacement workers and strikers, that raises picket line pressures towards the potential for violence. Creating a clear statutory right to return to work, eliminating the threat of permanent replacement, should moderate some of the deepest tensions.

In other areas of workplace regulation, employers and employees work hard to protect the personal integrity of the worker. We see this in our strict attitude towards safety hazards and the fact that we treat personal and particularly sexual harassment as intolerable actions. We recognize that it is simply unacceptable, no matter what the circumstance or alleged justification, to expose workers to physical harm or undue abuse. This same fundamental assumption must be accepted for the picket line. Labour and management must both take responsibility for the conduct of those they represent, or those who represent them, in such situations.

IMPACT ON INVESTMENT

Employers argue that any introduction of anti-replacement workers legislation will create an environment hostile to investment and scare away sources of capital, costing jobs and security.

A related, but more subtle argument, is that such legislation will gradually affect the way employers structure their business affairs, reducing their dependence upon their permanent workforce in favour of subcontracting and similar practices.

The investment argument arises partly because some provinces have anti-replacement workers legislation while others do not. Despite the vigour of the argument, we found disappointingly little research available on the impact that different provincial laws (particularly in Quebec) had on investment decisions.

Many investors are said to compare our laws to U.S. laws. U.S. laws currently permit the use not only of temporary but permanent replacement workers. However, these laws are also subject to an exception. U.S. law includes the concept of the unfair labour practice strike or lockout. If a dispute is engendered by illegal activities, such as ridding the workplace of the union, then an employer may not make permanent replacements and striking workers have a right to return to work.

IMPACT ON THE DURATION AND RESULTS OF STRIKES

How do anti-replacement workers laws affect the incidence, duration or results of labour disputes? We wish we could point to a conclusive answer but we cannot. Often labour and management supported their positions by referring to 'studies' which were neither named or filed with us for review. Closer analysis revealed that there are few definitive studies. Those that do exist arrive at somewhat different conclusions.

One 1993 study of Canadian manufacturing agreements, by John W. Budd of the University of Minnesota, entitled 'Canadian Strike Replacement Legislation and Collective Bargaining: Lessons for the United States,' concludes 'there is no evidence to support the contention that the presence of legislation affecting the use of strike replacements significantly alters relative bargaining power and the wage determination process or significantly impacts strike activity.'

A second study, however, by Peter Cramton, Morley Gunderson and Joseph Tracy, respectively of the University of Maryland, University of Toronto and Columbia University, entitled 'The Effect of Collective Bargaining Legislation on Strikes and Wages,' and published in 1994, finds that prohibiting the use of replacement workers during strikes is associated with significantly higher wages and more frequent and longer strikes. The Gunderson study compared private sector contract negotiations involving 500 or more workers from 1967 to March 1993. Particularly significant is their conclusion that 'As predicted by theory, the ban on replacement workers is associated with longer strike durations (a 37% increase).' The authors acknowledge however, that their conclusions are based only on a comparison with Quebec.

VARYING VULNERABILITY OF EMPLOYERS

Employers are unequally vulnerable to a prohibition on replacement workers. Some employers are vastly more susceptible to competition from non-union competitors. Other employers have a capital plant that requires regular maintenance even during a shutdown. Some can stockpile or reorganize during a shutdown, while others cannot. This alters the power balance and can thus skew wage settlements in different ways for different workplaces. The impact of a prohibition on employing replacement workers would therefore be quite uneven.

FREQUENCY OF USE

Some argue that the laws should prohibit replacement workers because so few employers use them anyway. For some employers, particularly with specialized work, there is no alternative workforce to call upon. In other industries, stockpiling (by suppliers or customers) gives sufficient protection against the full force of a strike. Many other employers choose not to risk the adverse labour management relationships that can result from using replacement workers. In the federal jurisdiction, external replacement workers were hired in about 25% of the 48 work stoppages under the *Canada Labour Code* which occurred during the period 1991 to 1994.

While it is true that most employers neither plan for nor use replacement workers, the law can nonetheless be an important consideration for collective bargaining strategies. Unions and employers may both modify their behaviour depending on their ability or lack of ability to operate with replacement workers. In this sense, it is not the actual use, but the threat of use and the perceived ability to use replacements that is important to the balance of bargaining power.

THREAT TO COLLECTIVE BARGAINING RIGHTS

Some argue that it is not the ability to use replacement workers itself that is objectionable so much as its frequent abuse. They point out the correlation between the use of replacement workers and efforts to undermine the trade union and destroy its bargaining agency.

This argument mirrors experience with the duty to bargain in good faith. Labour boards have moved to restrain bargaining proposals that indicate an intention to dislodge the union rather than to achieve a particular bargaining result. The distinction between this form of bad faith bargaining and hard bargaining is never easy to discern. However, such conduct is often accompanied by other conduct indicative of the same intention. While labour boards are reluctant to interfere with genuine bargaining positions, they are not, nor should they be, reluctant to intervene when bargaining positions become thinly disguised unfair labour practices aimed at undermining the union's right to represent employees. . . .

RECOMMENDATIONS:
There should be no general prohibition on the use of replacement workers.
Where the use of replacement workers in a dispute is demonstrated to be for the purpose of undermining the union's representative capacity rather than the pursuit of legitimate bargaining objectives, this should be declared an unfair labour practice.
In the event of a finding of such an unfair labour practice, the Board should be given the specific remedial power to prohibit the further use of replacement workers in the dispute.
[*Seeking a Balance* is a publication of Human Resources Development Canada. Reproduced with the permission of the Minister of Public Works and Government Services Canada, 1997.]

✽ ✽ ✽

In 1998, the following provision was added to the *Canada Labour Code*, by S.C. 1998, c. 26, s. 42, pursuant to the above recommendations:

Section 94(2.1): No employer or person acting on behalf of an employer shall use, for the demonstrated purpose of undermining a trade union's representational capacity rather than the pursuit of legitimate bargaining objectives, the services of a person who was not an employee in the bargaining unit on the date on which notice to bargain collectively was given and was hired or assigned after that date to perform all or part of the duties of an employee in the bargaining unit on strike or locked out.

That provision was complemented by this one, enacted by S.C. 1998, c. 26, s. 37:

Section 87.6: At the end of a strike or lockout not prohibited by this Part, the employer must reinstate employees in the bargaining unit who were on strike or locked out, in preference to any person who was not an employee in the bargaining unit on the date on which notice to bargain collectively was given and was hired or assigned after that date to perform all or part of the duties of an employee in the unit on strike or locked out.

For an empirical study of the effect of anti-replacement-worker legislation in Canada, see P. Crampton, M. Gunderson, and J. Tracy, "Impacts of Strike Replacement Bans" (1999) 50 Lab. L.J. 173.

8:600 ALTERNATIVES TO STRIKES?

Strikes and lockouts are traditionally seen as the engine that drives collective bargaining. But they have consequences, real or imagined, that make many observers uneasy — economic costs, exacerbation of the confrontational character of employment relations, and impact on essential services. Other observers argue that working conditions should be based on some idea of justice, not on economic power: "From a political perspective, the strike threat system is an anomaly. It is analogous to the medieval method of dispute resolution known as trial by combat": Roy J. Adams, "Two Policy Approaches to Labour-Management Decision Making at the Level of the Enterprise: A Comparison of the Wagner Act Model and Statutory Works Councils" in W. Craig Riddell, ed., *Canadian Labour Relations* (Toronto: University of Toronto Press, 1986) 87 at 103.

We have already looked at many legal manifestations of the ambivalence of Canadian public policy toward strikes, such as extensive statutory restrictions on the timeliness of job action and court decisions denying *Charter* protection to the right to strike. Especially in the public and parapublic sectors, which we have not dealt with specifically in this book, Canadian legislatures have often gone much further and imposed a wide variety of standing and ad hoc statutory restrictions on strikes, sometimes with a view to balancing government budgets or limiting inflation and sometimes to maintain essential services. From the 1960s through the 1980s, such statutory restrictions were quite frequently used, leading to a climate of what one study called "permanent exceptionalism": Leo Panitch & David Swartz, *The Assault on Trade Union Freedoms: From Wage Controls to Social Contract* (Toronto: Garamond Press, 1993). They were used less often during the 1990s, when economic circumstances tended to discourage resort to strikes and to cast some doubt on the conventional view that the right to strike increases employee bargaining power. As noted below in section 8:620, the apparently declining efficacy of the strike led some governments, including that of Ontario, to bring an end to standing compulsory arbitration schemes for Crown employees and to give those employees the right to strike. However, at the end of the 1990s and the turn of the new century, a revival of employee militancy in health care and other parts of the public and parapublic sectors has led to a revival of ad hoc legislation to end or prohibit specific strikes.

8:610 Essential Services Legislation

The rapid growth of collective bargaining in the public and parapublic sectors since the mid-1960s has led to more frequent conflict between the right to strike and lock out and the public right to the maintenance of essential services. In the private sector, too, the essential services issue has had to be confronted in jurisdictions that have banned the use of replacement workers during legal strikes. As noted above, section 8:520, such bans exist in Quebec and British Columbia.

Widespread concern exists that the public will suffer undue hardship from stoppages by certain strategically placed groups of workers — most commonly, perhaps, health care workers, but also those who provide other services such as policing, public transit, electricity and water supply, garbage collection, snow clearing, and teaching. There is a countervailing view among other observers, however, including many who have been involved in such stoppages on both sides, that too wide a range of services are thought to be essential, and that even those which are truly essential can safely be reduced to a much lower level than usual for considerable periods. What about industries of substantial economic importance, where safety is not in issue? Back-to-work legislation has been used frequently on the railways, in the post office, and in other industries (such as the Saskatchewan dairy industry and the Quebec construction industry). Differing conceptions of what is an essential service are discussed by Bernard Adell, Michel Grant, and Allen Ponak, *Strikes in Essential Services* (Kingston: Queen's IRC Press, 2001), at 9–13 and 29–30.

Employer representatives tend to favour removing the question of essential services from the bargaining table and addressing it elsewhere — that is, through direct legislative specification of the types and levels of services that must be maintained in the event of a work stoppage, or through a legislatively mandated adjudicative process administered by a tribunal of some sort. Unions, on the other hand, tend to be suspicious of any mechanism that limits the right of their most strategically placed members to withdraw services, because of the impact such limitations have on bargaining power.

These conflicting views have led to a wide variety of legislative approaches in different jurisdictions across Canada, and sometimes even in different sectors in the same jurisdiction, with respect to the determination of essentiality and the manner of regulating strikes and lockouts once a particular service is deemed essential. Some jurisdictions, including Alberta, simply deny the right to strike to large parts of the public and parapublic sectors. Others, including Saskatchewan, allow a much broader right to strike, but quite readily use ad hoc legislation to prohibit or end work stoppages in what are considered to be essential services. Still others, including Quebec, British Columbia, and the federal public service, give an adjudicative tribunal the responsibility for regulating such stoppages in accordance with legislatively specified criteria. Adell, Grant, and Ponak, above, outline the different approaches at 13–14, and evaluate them at 195–205.

Since the early 1980s, Quebec has relied on a specialized essential services tribunal called the Conseil des services essentiels, which has a detailed statutory mandate under the provincial Labour Code and has developed an extensive body of jurisprudence. The Conseil is generally thought to have been quite successful in ensuring the provision of essential services in what the Code (section 111.0.16) calls "public services" — municipal services, transit, electricity, garbage collection, and some others. British Columbia gives the task of designating essential services and overseeing their maintenance to its Labour Relations Board, after having experimented with other adjudicative mechanisms.

A hallmark of the current procedures in Quebec and British Columbia is that they put the employer and the union themselves at the forefront of the process, by requiring them to try to agree on what services are essential. As well, both provinces place much emphasis on mediation.

Michel Grant & France Racine, *Services essentiels et stratégies de négociation dans les services publics* (Québec: Ministry of Labour, 1992) at 11–14, 41 (translation)

The mandate of the [Québec Conseil des services essentiels] . . . looks only to the protection of public health and safety in the context of an anticipated or actual strike in a public service, with respect to which a government order has been made (s. 111.0.17 of the *Labour Code*). . . . in principle, the Conseil . . . does not try to help the parties reach a collective agreement. The responsibility for identifying and providing essential services is given to the parties. They are supposed to negotiate an agreement on those matters. If they cannot do so, the union must put forth a list of the essential services which it proposes to perform during the strike (s. 111.0.18). The same section empowers the Conseil, on its own initiative or at the request of one of the parties, to provide mediation services to help the parties reach an essential services agreement.

In practice, the Conseil only intervenes after the union has given strike notice [at least seven days before the strike] (s. 111.0.23). The Conseil then assesses the adequacy of the proposed essential services as set out in the agreement or list (s. 111.0.19). It has very broad discretion in that regard in the area of public services [as distinct from health and social services]. The Conseil's case law affirms that its assessments of adequacy are based solely on the criterion of protection of public health and safety. In applying that criterion, it takes account of the time of year when the strike occurs, the type of services involved, the qualifications of the employees designated to provide the essential services, and the type and length of the stoppage in question.

The Conseil can hold a hearing and, if it decides that the services which have been proposed or which are actually being performed are not adequate, it makes recommendations to the parties and a report to the Minister (ss. 111.0.19 and 20). The government can then suspend the right to strike if it decides (usually on the basis of the Conseil's report) that there is a danger to public health or safety (s. 111.0.24). The Conseil can also conduct an inquiry in the event that the requirements of the statute or the terms of the list or agreement are not complied with (s. 111.16). It can then make an order 'if it considers that the conflict is or is likely to be prejudicial to a service to which the public is entitled' or that the essential services in question have not been performed, and it can grant whatever remedy it deems appropriate in light of the harm suffered (s. 111.17).

. . . In referring to 'a service to which the public is entitled,' s. 111.17 goes beyond the concept of truly essential services. . . .

When these essential service provisions were enacted in 1982, it was widely thought that they would spell the end of union pressure tactics in the public services. . . . However, the respondents we interviewed generally agreed that the legislation has not affected the parties' bargaining power. The statistics on wage increases tend to confirm that view.

The data we gathered from employers and unions show clearly that in the public services we studied, unions have been able to adapt their bargaining strategies, especially with respect to the nature and frequency of pressure tactics. In the municipal sector, short rotating strikes appear to have replaced the unlimited total strike. The great majority of the people we interviewed did emphasize, however, that this change in union strategy has lengthened the bargaining process. The wage losses of union members from strikes are less abrupt, but extend over a longer period. . . .

The success of unions in adapting to the requirements of the legislation perhaps reflects . . . growing realism on their part as to the limits of the public's willingness to tolerate the right to strike in public services. . . . We believe that the legislation has met its objectives, and that the experience shows that the right to collective bargaining can be reconciled with the public's overriding right to the protection of its health and safety. [Reprinted with permission.]

* * *

An interesting contrast to the success of the Conseil des services essentiels in the area of public services is provided by its relative failure in the area of health and social services. In the latter area, the Conseil does not have much discretion to decide what proportion of normal services should be treated as essential; it is bound by a scale of rigid statutory minima that range from 55 percent of normal services for child protection and social service agencies to 80 percent for acute care hospitals and 90 percent for long-term care and psychiatric institutions. For a discussion of the operation of the Conseil des services essentiels, see Adell, Grant, and Ponak, referred to above, at 36–40 and 67–106.

The structure and application of the British Columbia essential services provisions (sections 72 and 73 of the *Labour Relations Code*, S.B.C. 1992, c. 82) are outlined in *School District No. 54 v. Bulkley Valley Teachers' Ass'n* (1993), 19 Can. L.R.B.R. 269 (B.C.L.R.B.). In that case, the risk that students in their last year of high school would lose their year led the Labour Relations Board to hold that a strike by their teachers would pose "a threat to the health, safety or welfare of the residents of British Columbia" within the meaning of section 72 of the *Code*. After a change of government in 2001, section 72 was amended to allow the government to order the Labour Relations Board to designate as essential any services necessary "to prevent immediate and serious disruption of the provision of educational programs": see section 72(2.1), enacted by S.B.C. 2001, c. 33, section 11(b).

In recent years, a multitude of difficult issues have arisen in applying the British Columbia essential services provisions. For example, how many hours a week should management personnel be expected to work during a strike? Must the employer give the union an on-site strike headquarters? Should the daily scheduling of essential services be done by management or the union? See T. Knight & C. Sand, eds., *Essential Services Designation Conference: Proceedings* (Vancouver: University of British Columbia Centre for Labour and Management Studies, 1995); Adell, Grant, and Ponak, above, Chapter 5.

8:620 Interest Arbitration

This section looks at "interest" arbitration, as opposed to "grievance" arbitration. Interest arbitration, sometimes called compulsory arbitration, is designed to replace the strike as the mechanism for resolving bargaining disputes. If the parties cannot agree, work continues and an arbitrator sets the terms that will govern their future relations, in effect writing their collective agreement for them. In contrast, grievance arbitration, which will be examined in Chapter 9, involves the application of an existing agreement, where one party alleges that the other has violated that agreement.

Mediation is often used prior to arbitration, in order to clear away as many issues as possible. In a variant known as "med-arb," the arbitrator first tries to mediate the dispute, then adjudicates those issues that remain unresolved.

Allen Ponak & Loren Falkenberg, "Resolution of Interest Disputes" in A. Sethi, ed., *Collective Bargaining in Canada* (Scarborough, Ont.: Nelson, 1989) 260 at 272–86 (references omitted)

> The rapid growth of public sector collective bargaining in the late 1960s and throughout the 1970s presented policy makers with a new dilemma. While the right to strike was well entrenched in the private sector, substantial reservations existed about permitting public employees to withdraw their services. The basis for these reservations was essentially twofold: (1) a belief that public sector work stoppages, involving irreplaceable and in some cases essential services, would place an intolerable burden on the public; and (2) a perception that the combination of political and economic pressure generated by public sector strikes would place too much power in the hands of public employee unions.
>
> The dilemma arose in finding substitutes for the right to strike. A number of American states had prohibited public sector work stoppages but had failed to provide mechanisms for the final resolution of impasses. This approach simply resulted in illegal strikes. Most Canadian jurisdictions, on the other hand, opted for some form of compulsory arbitration when the right to strike was removed by statute. By and large, arbitration accomplished the objective of eliminating work stoppages. Illegal strikes have occasionally taken place in the face of arbitration (a well-publicized example is the Montreal police strike in 1969), but such occurrences have constituted rare exceptions. Canadian public employees, albeit with great reluctance in some cases, have accepted the prohibition on strikes where arbitration is available as a substitute.
>
> Unfortunately, compulsory interest arbitration, while alleviating concern about public sector work stoppages, presents a number of problems of its own. Industrial relations systems in virtually all democratic countries place a high premium on permitting labour and management to negotiate their own collective agreements through the give-and-take of the bargaining process. Almost all available evidence suggests that compulsory arbitration systems reduce the likelihood that the parties will in fact be able to reach an agreement at the bargaining table. . . .
>
> Three major reasons have been advanced to explain why compulsory arbitration reduces the likelihood of negotiated settlements. First, interest arbitration generally pro-

duces a lower cost of disagreement than does a strike. Put another way, the fear of going to arbitration is usually less than the fear of a work stoppage. Part of the reason parties settle in negotiations under right-to-strike systems relates to the substantial consequences of not settling. Strikes are usually expensive and painful propositions for the worker, the employer, or both. The same is less likely to be true in an arbitration system where the consequences of actually using an arbitrator may not be particularly onerous. In short, the threat of a strike is a powerful inducement to settle; arbitration systems lack such an inducement.

A second factor that is thought to inhibit negotiated settlements under arbitration systems is the fear that concessions made during bargaining may prove harmful if an arbitrated settlement is eventually required. Whether well-founded or not, a widespread perception exists that arbitrators 'split the difference' between the two parties' positions in arriving at their decisions. Accordingly, negotiators are reluctant to make bargaining concessions that might narrow the differences to their side's detriment; thus, there is a tendency to adopt extreme positions and maintain them. The inhibiting impact of arbitration on compromise activity is frequently referred to as the chilling effect.

The third major reason advanced for the reduced incidence of settlement under arbitration systems is that arbitration is habit forming. It is suggested that negotiators become accustomed to rely on arbitration as an easy way out of making difficult decisions and eventually lose the ability to settle in negotiations. This tendency has been referred to as the narcotic effect, with negotiators becoming 'addicted' to the arbitration process. As time passes, fewer and fewer settlements are achieved at the bargaining table as the temptation to rely on the 'quick fix' of an arbitrated agreement becomes irresistible.

USE OF ARBITRATION IN THE CANADIAN PUBLIC SECTOR

. . . Arbitration is most likely to be obligatory for fire fighters, police, and civil servants. At the other end of the spectrum, it is not mandated in any jurisdiction for general municipal employees (i.e., inside and outside workers, local transit).

The most commonly used form of interest arbitration in Canada is the traditional or conventional form of arbitration. Under conventional arbitration procedures, the arbitration board is free, after receiving submissions from the union and the employer, to fashion its solution to the issues in dispute. The board is permitted to accept the union or the employer position, it can split the difference down the middle, or it can derive its own compromise position on the issues. Subject to very broad constraints of reasonableness, the arbitration board can issue the award it feels is most appropriate under the circumstances and that award becomes the new collective agreement.

Although rarely used in Canada, many jurisdictions in the United States use a form of arbitration called final offer selection (FOS). Final offer selection differs from conventional arbitration in that the arbitrator is required to choose the position submitted by management or by the union, without alteration. In other words, the arbitration board is not free to fashion its own solution by adopting a middle position; it is forced to choose one side's proposal or the other's. Depending on the jurisdiction, a total package format or more flexible issue-by-issue format is used. . . .

A third type of arbitration system, choice of procedures (COP) was pioneered in the 1967 Public Service Staff Relations Act, which granted collective bargaining rights to federal civil servants. It continues to be used in the federal sector as well as British Columbia, Saskatchewan, and some American states. Under a choice-of-procedures system, one of the parties (in Canada, the union) can specify at some point prior to or during negotiations whether an impasse will be resolved through a work stoppage or arbitration. . . . Experience has shown that arbitration is chosen much more frequently than the strike. . . .

SETTLEMENT RATE

There is little disagreement that arbitration systems reduce the incidence of negotiated settlements compared to strike-based systems. The most meaningful comparisons in this regard are among public sector jurisdictions. . . .

The major variable of interest . . . is settlement rate, defined as the proportion of negotiations that are settled by the parties without resort to the final mechanism of dispute resolution. Under arbitration systems, this would be the proportion of negotiations in which no arbitration award was issued; under right-to-strike systems, settlement rate means the percentage of negotiations where settlement was achieved without a work stoppage.

. . . The broadest data set [for public sector systems with the right to strike] is for the province of Ontario and covers over 600 negotiations during a four-year period [1979–82] for teachers, hydro-electric utility workers, and municipal employees (including mass transit). The Ontario data show a settlement rate of 93 percent, a figure that appears to be a reasonable median rate for public sector strike-based systems.

. . . Under conventional arbitration, the ability of labour and management to settle without the help of an arbitrator ranges between 65 and 82 percent. The average settlement rate would appear to be approximately 75 percent. The settlement rate goes up to the 85-percent range under final-offer selection, but still falls short of settlement rates achieved under strike-based systems.

The data, therefore, unequivocally supports the proposition that arbitration systems reduce the likelihood of negotiated settlements compared to strike-based dispute procedures. The gap between the two systems is approximately 18 percent under conventional arbitration and eight percent under final-offer selection procedures.

The data cannot answer the policy question, however, of whether the settlement rate difference between strike and arbitration systems is acceptable or not. . . . After all, even under the least productive arbitration systems, negotiators still manage to settle without arbitration two-thirds of the time. The fact that one out of three negotiations requires an arbitrator's intervention may well be a price that has to be paid for the overall public good. Such tradeoffs might be less palatable, however, in situations where settlement rates are much lower or where the groups involved are arguably less essential.

THE CHILLING AND NARCOTIC EFFECTS

The theoretical underpinnings of the perceived inadequacies of interest arbitration rest on two related concepts, the chilling and narcotic effects. . . . Chilling is assumed to occur when one or both parties are unwilling to compromise during negotiations in anticipation of an arbitrated settlement; the narcotic effect is an increasing dependence of the parties on arbitration, resulting in a loss of ability to negotiate. . . .

[The authors then discuss several empirical studies on the chilling effect and narcotic effect, and observe that the findings of those studies are generally inconclusive.]

The most common method of assessing the narcotic effect is the proportion of units going to arbitration over time. It is assumed that if arbitration is addictive, more and more units will resort to it with each round of negotiations. . . .

In summary, the empirical research suggests that: (1) a chilling effect may occur with conventional arbitration but is less likely with final offer selection; and (2) while some parties may become dependent on arbitration (narcotic effect), the majority does not repeatedly use the process. These conclusions notwithstanding, there remains considerable confusion among studies in terms of inferences drawn with much of the confusion relating to a lack of clarity over appropriate measures. . . .

[From *Collective Bargaining in Canada*, 1st ed. by Sethi, A.S. © 1989. Reprinted with permission of Thomson Learning: www.thomsonrights.com. Fax 800-730-2215.]

James O'Grady, *Arbitration and Its Ills* (Kingston, Ont.: School of Policy Studies, Queen's University, 1994) at 5–35 (bibliography at end of excerpt)

2 WHAT WE BELIEVE WE KNOW ABOUT ARBITRATION IN THE PUBLIC SECTOR

Experience with mandatory arbitration in both Canada and the United States has produced a considerable body of research literature. This literature evaluates the impact of arbitration and examines the criteria that shape arbitrators' awards. This section of the paper endeavours to summarize the principal conclusions and observations that have emerged from the research literature.

1. *Although research findings are not unanimous, the weight of evidence supports the view that arbitration has an upward bias on relative wages in the public sector.* . . .

Surveying the literature in 1983 for the Ontario Economic Council, Gunderson concluded that 'the evidence on the effect of arbitration on settlements is mixed . . . but most [find] a slight positive effect'. . . .

A more recent study supports the Gunderson view. This study, carried out by Currie and McConnell, is the most extensive, empirical review of Canadian experience with compulsory arbitration. Currie and McConnell reviewed the results of collective bargaining in 426 large public sector units, i.e., bargaining units with more than 500 employees. They further confined their survey by the requirement that bargaining units must have negotiated at least four agreements over the period 1964 to 1987. Currie and McConnell conclude that 'on average, wage settlements are highest under compulsory arbitration.' They estimate that 'a switch from right-to-strike to compulsory-arbitration legislation increases wages by between 1 and 2 percent of the wage or by between 6 and 12 cents [per] year of settlement.' The 'arbitration premium' estimated by Currie and McConnell is higher than that suggested by other studies. . . .

2. *There are significant variances among arbitrators in the weight that they attach to different criteria. . . .*

3. *Productivity, ability-to-pay and labour market disequilibria factors play little role in shaping arbitral decisions.*

This finding is consistent across studies. D.A.L. Auld et al. concluded that arbitrators' awards were determined by factors that were different from those shaping negotiated wage increases. In his review of public sector wage determination for the Anti-Inflation Board, Gunderson found that ability-to-pay, productivity and minimum living standards ranked among the least important factors in determining arbitrated wage increases. Ontario arbitrator Martin Teplitsky stated his position unequivocally in a 1981 award determining the wages for Windsor police officers. In that award, he wrote that 'the ability of the employer to pay in the public sector is irrelevant'. . . .

Arbitrators have not, in general, attached weight in their awards to such disequilibria indicators as 'job queues' or 'quit rates'. . . .

4. *Comparability factors carry, by far, the greatest weight in arbitrators' decisions. Indeed, so great is the weight attached to comparability that it tends to marginalize other criteria.*

The classic statement of the importance of comparability was set out by Harry Arthurs in an award handed down shortly after the Ontario legislature enacted the *Hospital Labour Disputes Arbitration Act* in 1965. In that decision Arthurs wrote:

> instead of permitting the parties to discover labour market realities by a withdrawal of labour, they are instructed to submit to arbitration. But arbitration is made to substitute for the strike and should therefore likewise be considered an exercise in discovering labour market realities. This being so, it is to relevant wage comparisons that we must look.

Empirical studies confirm the importance of comparability factors. . . . Currie and McConnell . . . conclude that comparability factors are twice as significant in determining wage increases where the right to strike is superseded by arbitration. This finding applies both when wage increases are arbitrated and when they are bargained. In other words, it is the availability of arbitration, not the fact of arbitration, that causes comparability factors to be so important. Swimmer notes that comparability leads most arbitrators to give more weight to wage increases among unionized employers than to economy-wide trends. This biasing of comparability towards unionized employers arises from the predominant view among arbitrators that arbitration's purpose is to replicate a bargained outcome, not an outcome that proceeded from unilateral determination by an employer.

The weight attached to comparability can, however, lead to serious tensions. Harry Arthurs warned of these tensions in his *Welland County Hospital* decision. Arthurs suggested that basing arbitration awards on settlements negotiated at other hospitals would become 'increasingly artificial after all hospital wages have been determined one or more times by compulsory arbitration.' Paul Weiler echoed this concern in a 1969 decision. He wrote:

> after a time the arbitration decisions themselves become a major factor determining the kinds of settlements which will be agreed to. . . . The level of private agreement [i.e., non-arbitrated settlements] will tend to reflect the trends in the awards. If this is the case, one completes the vicious circle if the awards are themselves justified by patterns of wages arrived at by settlement. . . .

5. *Arbitrators do not appear to attach significant weight to deferred compensation, viz., the costs of providing pension benefits and termination benefits. Nor do arbitrators assign any special importance to implied commitments to annual merit increments or to greater degrees of job security. The costs of pay equity adjustments do not appear to have affected arbitration awards. Directing arbitrators to consider 'total compensation' appears to have comparatively little impact on arbitral practice. . . .*

6. *Arbitration is rarely chosen freely by the parties to a collective agreement. It is especially rare in the private sector.*

The parties to a collective agreement are always free to choose arbitration to resolve an impasse in bargaining. The evidence, however, is that they rarely do so. . . . The federal *Public Service Staff Relations Act* is unique in providing the union with a choice of routes to resolve a bargaining impasse. The evidence from the *PSSRA* is that in the initial years, unions were more inclined to choose arbitration. However, union attraction to arbitration declined over time.

Except when back-to-work legislation is enacted, arbitration in the private sector is exceptionally rare. The important exception is the provision in some labour codes for arbitration of first agreements. These provisions are typically triggered by a union in a weak bargaining position. . . .

To say that both employers and unions in the private sector do not voluntarily choose arbitration is to understate their antipathy to third parties determining the provisions of their collective agreements. Morley Gunderson captured the views of both unions and employers in the private sector:

> The fact that voluntary arbitration is rare in the private sector . . . indicates that labour and management, when not compelled to do otherwise, almost invariably prefer the costs and consequences of a possible strike to the uncertainties of an arbitrated settlement. . . .

. . .

9. *Mandatory arbitration appears to diminish the proportion of settlements achieved through negotiation.*

The evidence for this was discussed in the first part of this paper. It was noted that under compulsory arbitration, voluntary settlement rates fall from approximately 93 percent to 70 percent.

10. Arbitrators tend to award conservatively on non-compensation issues.

While the impact of arbitration on wages has been studied extensively, there has been no systematic examination of arbitral treatment of non-compensation issues. Generally, seniority rules tend to be much weaker in the public sector than in the private sector. As well, classification systems are more likely to be managerially determined. Public sector collective bargaining, therefore, may be judged 'conservative' to the extent that it has not significantly disrupted the pre-collective bargaining *status quo* on these issues.

Arbitrators may be reluctant to alter managerial practice lest their awards lead to unintended effects. Indeed, some adjudicators have criticized both unions and management for putting issues before arbitration boards which a third party is presumptively less capable of understanding than the parties themselves. Arbitration is clearly not a process that exhibits a propensity to be innovative. Indeed, being risk averse, the parties probably do not wish arbitration to be innovative. It seems likely that the disinclination of arbitrators to be innovative, along with the diminished incentive that arbitration gives to the parties to reach voluntary settlement, imparts a degree of conservatism overall to human resource management. . . .

3   COMPULSORY ARBITRATION IN ONTARIO

. . . Paul Weiler commented that 'advocacy of binding arbitration is now de rigueur across a wide spectrum of opinion among politicians and pundits. They consider arbitration not a painful necessity, but a positive virtue.' Ten years later, the pendulum appears to have swung. The desire to escape from the perceived upward bias of wage arbitration may now rank alongside with, or even take precedence over, the concern for stability that led to the legislated imposition of interest arbitration in the first place.

Legitimacy

A system of wage determination that is viewed as 'rigged' against workers will suffer a loss of legitimacy in the eyes both of those workers and others who sympathize with them. The benchmark by which wage determination systems are viewed is free collective bargaining, viz., collective bargaining that is not subject to third-party review or adjudication. Any system of wage determination that departs from the free collective bargaining model is potentially subject to an erosion of legitimacy. This is particularly true of compulsory arbitration and post-settlement reviews of wage agreements. Presumptively such systems risk a loss of legitimacy if they lead to wage increases that are generally below the averages being achieved in the private sector.

When employees view a system of wage determination as 'rigged' against them, a potentially significant instability is introduced. The possibility of defiance becomes real. Ontario had five such episodes between 1974 and 1981.

Legitimacy is an intangible and immeasurable characteristic of a wage determination process. It is not readily susceptible to social science investigation. Legitimacy is nonetheless an important goal of public policy. Proposals that would address a perceived upward bias in wage arbitration at the expense of legitimacy are unlikely to prove durable.

Efficiency

Agreements negotiated by the parties are presumptively more likely to be workable than arrangements imposed by a third party who is often inadequately informed and has only a limited stake in the terms being awarded. Most of the economic analysis of collective bargaining and arbitration dwells on measurable compensation. Collective bargaining, however, addresses significantly more than wages and benefits. In addition to matters involving job security and seniority rights, a collective agreement may also address job duties, occupational health and safety and staffing levels. Paul Weiler has noted a tendency for contentious public sector issues such as classroom size and two-person police cars to wind up in front of an arbitrator. In other situations, arbitrators have been called upon to address such issues as staffing levels in hospital wards or in correctional institutions. Setting aside accountability questions, these are topics that may be ill-suited to determination by a third party. . . .

BIBLIOGRAPHY

Auld, D.A.L. *et al.* (1981). 'The Effect of Settlement Stage on Negotiated Wage Settlements in Canada,' *Industrial and Labor Relations Review*, 34 (January).

Currie, Janet and Sheena McConnell (1991), 'Collective Bargaining in the Public Sector: The Effect of Legal Structures on Dispute Costs and Wages,' American Economic Review 81, 4 (September):693–718.

Gunderson, Morley (1977), 'Criteria for Public Sector Wage Determination,' Anti-Inflation Board Discussion Paper.

Gunderson, Morley, John Kervin and Frank Reid (1986), 'Logit Estimates of Strike Incidence from Canadian Contract Data,' *Journal of Labor Economics* 4 (April):257–276.

Weiler, Paul (1980), *Reconcilable Differences: New Directions in Canadian Labour Law* (Toronto: Carswell).

[Reprinted by permission.]

* * *

An important example of the declining use of interest arbitration in recent years is provided by the Ontario public service. Until 1993, provincial Crown employees in Ontario had no right to strike, and were covered by arbitration. Faced with a very large and growing budget deficit, and believing that arbitration meant higher wages and decreased managerial flexibility, the New Democratic Party government, against the wishes of the Ontario Public Service Employees' Union, passed the *Crown Employees Collective Bargaining Act, 1993*, S.O. 1993, c. 38. That Act ended the system of interest arbitration for most of the public service, replacing it (in section 28) with a right to strike substantially more restricted than the equivalent right under the *Labour Relations Act*. Among the most important of the restrictions on the right to strike is an extensive procedure (sections 30–42) with respect to essential services. That procedure includes a requirement (which in some respects parallels the provisions in the Quebec and British Columbia statutes discussed above, section 8:610,) that the parties attempt to negotiate agreements for the provision of essential services in the event of a strike. This requirement led to many months of arduous bargaining after the Act was passed.

A Conservative government came into office in Ontario in 1995, in time for the first round of strike-route negotiations. It promptly amended the *Crown Employees Collective Bargaining Act, 1993* to impose further restrictions on the right to strike. In 1996 a bitter five-week strike ensued, and the negotiated settlement left the government with considerably more flexibility to downsize and otherwise restructure the public service.

For an analysis of current problems facing public sector labour relations, including some discussion of the future of interest arbitration, written by an architect of the *Crown Employees Collective Bargaining Act, 1993*, see P. Warrian, *Hard Bargain: Transforming Public Sector Labour-Management Relations* (Toronto: McGilligan Books, 1996). On the Ontario Conservative Government's effort to change some aspects of the dynamic of interest arbitration referred to above by O'Grady, by requiring that the arbitrators be chosen from a group of retired judges rather than from among the usual candidates, see *Canadian Union of Public Employees v. Ontario (Minister of Labour)* 2003 S.C.C. 29.

Chapter 9: The Collective Agreement and Arbitration

9:100 INTRODUCTION

If the collective bargaining process discussed in Chapters 7 and 8 brings a settlement, the terms will be embodied in a collective agreement (sometimes informally called a "contract") between the union and the employer. This chapter deals with the enforcement of such agreements, first at common law and then under modern labour relations legislation.

Disputes over the interpretation and application of collective agreements are commonplace. An employee may claim that the agreement was violated when he or she was disciplined, rejected for promotion, laid off, denied benefits, or subjected to some other unwelcome treatment. A union may challenge a management practice affecting the workforce at large, or affecting the union in its role as bargaining agent. Or, less commonly, an employer may claim that the union has not met its obligations under the collective agreement.

Modern Canadian labour relations legislation does not permit a power contest over disputes of this sort. Strikes and lockouts are banned during the term of a collective agreement, and every agreement must provide a dispute settlement process to resolve disputes over whether the agreement has been complied with. Some statutes specify that this process must take the form of grievance arbitration. However, even where arbitration is not specifically mandated, it is used almost universally because no practical alternative has been found.

Collective agreements almost always provide for an informal grievance procedure through which the parties attempt to resolve their disputes without resorting to arbitration. If a grievance is not resolved in this way, either party may invoke arbitration, as a form of third-party adjudication. Arbitrators make legally binding rulings based upon evidence and argument presented by the parties in an adversarial hearing. The parties to a dispute normally choose the person who will act as arbitrator. Tripartite boards of arbitration (consisting of a nominee of each party and an impartial chairperson) were widely used at one time, but single arbitrators are now more common in most jurisdictions.

Mandatory grievance arbitration is often said to be the *quid pro quo* for the ban on mid-contract work stoppages, in the sense that a union is required to give up the strike as a means of enforcing the collective agreement but gains access to arbitration in exchange. This notional bargain has no parallel in the commercial world, where contracting parties are free to use both economic warfare and legal proceedings. As we will see, the idea of a notional bargain also overlooks issues not addressed by the collective agreement, over which strikes are not permitted and over which arbitrators have no jurisdiction.

Lawyers tend to see arbitration as serving only an adjudicative function. Yet arbitration, like the grievance procedure which precedes it, performs other functions as well. Some of the purposes served by the grievance process were described by Neil Chamberlain, *The Labor Sector* (New York: McGraw Hill, 1965), at page 247:

> The grievance procedure is . . . a many splendored thing. It is in part the judicial process of applying terms of the agreement to particular situations, as it is most frequently pictured. It is also the mechanism through which the first-line representatives of union and management engage in a continuing contest over the exercise of authority in the shop . . . The grievance process is also a device which strategic groups within the union can use to engage in factional bargaining on their own behalf, sometimes challenging the authority of the union in the doing but more often able to clothe their purpose in "grievances" which have at least the air of legitimacy about them. And finally, the grievance process, in the hands of sophisticated practitioners, can be made an instrument for more effective administration within the shop.

The arbitration process may also play an important role in the retention of employees. Allowing employees to air their complaints before an arbitrator might deter them from leaving. In *What Do Unions Do?* (New York: Basic Books, 1984) R. Freeman and J. Medoff demonstrated that turnover is lower in American workplaces with a union than in those without. They attributed the difference to the "collective voice" offered by unions which serves as a substitute for "exit."

REFERENCES

Donald Brown & David Beatty, *Canadian Labour Arbitration*, 3d ed. (Aurora, Ont.: Canada Law Book, 1988) c. 1; George Adams, Canadian Labour Law, 2d ed. (Aurora, Ont.: Canada Law Book, 1993) c. 12; Donald Carter *et al.*, *Labour Law and Industrial Relations in Canada*, 5th ed. (Markham, Ont.: Butterworths, 2001), pp. 363–398

9:110 The Common Law View of Collective Agreements

Before the advent of modern labour relations legislation in the 1940s, collective agreements were generally unenforceable at law. A system of binding arbitration had not yet developed, and Canadian courts were unwilling to entertain civil actions based on collective agreements.

Three major common law obstacles stood in the way of the enforcement of collective agreements by civil action. First, as we have seen above in section 8:314, trade unions were not considered to have the legal capacity to make binding contracts or to sue or be sued in their own name. Because they sought to affect the operation of the labour market, they were thought to operate in illegal restraint of trade. Because they were unincorporated associations of individuals, they were treated as being without legal status. Second, the courts doubted that employers and unions intended their collective agreements to be legally binding, rather than mere informal understandings. Third, traditional rules of privity of contract were held to prevent individual employees from enforcing collective agreements to which they were not themselves parties.

Young v. Canadian Northern Railway, [1931] 1 D.L.R. 645 at 649–50 (P.C.)

[A collective agreement, called Wage Agreement 4, was in force between the Railway Association of Canada, representing employers, and Division 4 of the Railway Employees' Department of the American Federation of Labor, which negotiated on behalf of railway employees. The plaintiff was not a member of Division 4. In 1920 the defendant railway hired him as a machinist, telling him that he would receive the going rate for machinists but not giving him a written employment contract. In addition to rules on hours and wages, Wage Agreement 4 provided that in the event of a workforce reduction, junior employees would be laid off first, in accordance with a seniority rule.

Young was laid off out of order of seniority. He sued for damages for wrongful dismissal, lost in the Manitoba courts, and appealed to the Judicial Committee of the Privy Council. At the time, no Canadian jurisdiction had labour relations legislation of the sort now in force across the country.]

LORD RUSSELL: . . .The fact that the railway company applied [Wage Agreement 4] to the appellant, is equally consistent with the view that it did so, not because it was bound contractually to apply it to him, but because as a matter of policy it deemed it expedient to apply it to all. If the conduct of the railway company in applying the provisions of the agreement to the appellant could only be explained by the existence of a contractual obligation to the appellant so to do, it would be not only permissible, but necessary to hold that the existence of the contractual obligation had been established. In the circumstances, however, of the present case, their Lordships find themselves unable so to decide. But the matter does not quite rest there. When Wage Agreement 4 is examined, it does not appear to their Lordships to be a document adapted for conversion into or incorporation with a service agreement, so as to entitle master and servant to enforce inter se the terms thereof. It consists of some 188 "rules," which the railway companies contract with Division 4 to observe. It appears to their Lordships to be intended merely to operate as an agreement between a body of employers and a labour organization by which the employers undertake that as regards their workmen, certain rules beneficial to the workmen shall be observed. By itself it constitutes no contract between any individual employee and the company which employs him. If an employer refused to observe the rules, the effective sequel would be, not an action by any employee, not even an action by Division 4 against the employer for specific performance or damages, but the calling of a strike until the grievance was remedied. If, in the present case, the appellant has suffered any injustice at the hands of the railway company, it was in the power of Division 4 to obtain justice for him had they chosen so to do. It is suggested that Division 4 chose not so to do, because the appellant was a member of a rival organization. Assuming the suggestion to be well founded, the moral thereby pointed would appear to be that in the case of an "open" shop, the protection which an agreement such as Wage Agreement 4 affords to a workman who is not a member of the contracting labour organization, is to be measured by the willingness of that body to enforce it on his behalf. . . . In the result their Lordships are of the opinion that this appeal should fail and be dismissed with costs, as they have already humbly advised His Majesty.

* * *

The courts' refusal to enforce collective agreements prompted legislative reform. In 1943, Ontario enacted the *Collective Bargaining Act*, S.O. 1943, c. 4, creating a new branch of the Supreme Court of Ontario, called the Ontario Labour Court, with the power to render binding interpretations of collective agreements. However, resort to the Ontario Labour Court was not compulsory.

In 1944, the federal government, using its wartime emergency powers to override provincial legislative jurisdiction in labour relations, promulgated the *Wartime Labour Relations Regulations*, P.C. 1003. This was the first time that a Canadian labour relations code required every collective agreement to provide a procedure for settling disputes over the interpretation of the agreement without resort to a strike or lockout. As noted above, this is now a standard feature of collective bargaining legislation across Canada.

9:120 Grievance Arbitration as a Distinctive Form of Adjudication

Proponents of grievance arbitration contend that it offers a very different form of adjudication than the courts do. Arbitrators are labour law or indutrial relations specialists usually selected by the parties, whereas judges are appointed by the state and are usually legal generalists. The parties to a collective agreement are free not only to choose their arbitrator but also to design an arbitration process to meet their particular needs. This form of self-government is one of the hallmarks of Canadian collective bargaining law.

As well as being labour law specialists, most arbitrators are lawyers trained in the common law. Arbitration awards are subject to review by judges who are steeped in the common law. As you work through this chapter, consider whether arbitral jurisprudence is shaped mainly by the labour relations environment or by the common law heritage of individual employment law.

9:200 MANAGEMENT RIGHTS

Re United Steelworkers of America and Russelsteel Ltd. (1966), 17 L.A.C. 253 at 253–60

ARTHURS, Chair: On October 25, 1965, three employees filed a grievance in the following terms:

The grievors contend that the company has violated our collective agreement by removing the regular truck drivers from their jobs and replacing them with persons who are not regularly employed in the bargaining unit.

> The Union requests that the truck drivers be immediately returned to their job as truck drivers and paid retroactively for all loss of earnings as a result of this violation and also all other bargaining unit employees suffering loss of earnings as a result of this action be returned to their jobs and paid retroactively for all loss of earnings.

The facts underlying this controversy are hardly in dispute. Prior to the date of the grievance, the company leased trucks from another firm, but employed four truck drivers to drive them. Sometime during the week prior to the grievance, these leasing arrangements were terminated, and the company entered into a contract with another firm for the supply of both trucks and drivers. With this arrangement, the grievors' services as drivers became superfluous, and they were offered a choice of either going to work for the contractor, or remaining in the employ of the company as warehouse labourers. Each of these alternatives offered the grievors a lower wage rate than they were receiving in their capacity as truck drivers.

We are thus confronted with a classic case of contracting out, complicated only by the fact that prior to the action here complained of, the company leased trucks rather than owned them. From the union's point of view, this latter fact is at best neutral and at worst presents additional support for the company's action as an extension of its earlier practice. Therefore, unless we hold the grievance otherwise valid, there will be no need for us to comment upon the effect of the prior leasing arrangement.

There can hardly have been a more contentious issue in the field of labour arbitration in the past 10 years than that of contracting out. While in part, the controversy is prompted by the extremely serious repercussions of contracting out for both the employee and the union, it has, as well, assumed a symbolic significance which pervades the entire area of collective agreement administration. This significance stems from the fact that the divergent views of arbitrators as to the propriety of contracting out, represent polar positions in the approach to the construction of collective agreements. On the one side, there is the 'reserved rights' school which permits contracting out in the absence of some express prohibition in the collective agreement. Arbitrators who have embraced this school take the position that the typical management rights clause reserves to the employer all of his precollective bargaining rights, save those which were expressly bargained away in collective negotiations. On the other hand, there is the school of which (formerly Professor) Laskin J. is perhaps the leading spokesman. As expressed in what has now become classic language in *Re United Electrical, Radio & Machine Workers of America, Local 527, and Peterboro Lock Mfg. Co. Ltd.* . . . , this view holds that . . . :

> The introduction of a Collective Bargaining regime involves the acceptance by the parties of assumptions which are entirely alien to an era of individual bargaining. Hence, any attempt to measure rights and duties in employer/employee relations by reference to the pre-collective bargaining standards is an attempt to reenter a world which has ceased to exist.

Inevitably, in a case of this kind, there are strong pressures upon a board of arbitration to declare its philosophical allegiances, to adopt a series of broad principles, and to derive a solution of the particular case on the basis of a general approach. However, we believe that so far as possible such pressures are to be resisted. Reliance on overbroad philosophical considerations may preclude the pragmatic and realistic solutions to particular problems which would be of most assistance to labour and management in a given bargaining relationship. By such an approach, there is a risk that the lessons of experience, the ever-changing industrial environment, the nuances of the particular situation, might disappear from view. This is not to say that a gradual and economical adumbration of principle ought not to occur. As principle emerges from particular situations, it assists the parties in resolving subsequent disputes without recourse to arbitration. As similar cases are decided over a period of years by a large number of arbitrators, the parties may be able to realistically evaluate the odds upon particular language being construed in a particular way. And as opposing statements of principle confront each other, there being no ultimate appellate tribunal, pressures are generated for compromise between the two positions.

Little purpose would be served by verbal analysis of the several dozen reported cases which constitute the Canadian jurisprudence on the subject. A statistical summary of these cases in a valuable paper presented in 1964 to the Labour Relations Section of the Canadian Bar Association showed that at that time 26 of the 32 reported cases favoured the company's position in the result, while only six favoured the union's. Extending this analysis down to the present day, an even more pronounced trend in favour of the company position is discernible, as 11 cases have since favoured the company's position while only two have favoured the union. The 'box score' since the issue first arose in the mid-1950s is 37 reported cases favouring the company's position, and only eight favouring the union's.

The fact that arbitrators have accepted management's right to contract out almost five times as frequently as they have denied it, does not in and of itself compel this board to a conclusion. As already noted, there is no appellate tribunal whose decisions can reconcile the conflicting awards of the many arbitrators who have considered this matter. Moreover, as is well known, no doctrine of stare decisis operates in labour arbitration. Thus, we are technically free to interpret the agreement as we think right. Looked at as an original question, there may have been much to recommend the 'Laskin' position; indeed it is a position which is widely accepted in labour arbitration in the United States. But to whatever extent the collective bargaining climate may pervade contract interpretation in other areas, in the matter of contracting out, it can no longer be said to do so. Our reason for so holding is in fact rooted in the 'Laskin' approach, for Professor Laskin himself refers to the 'climate of employer/employee relations under a collective agreement.' In our view this 'climate' is of decided relevance, but it is not a climate solely generated by or confined to the relationships between the particular company and the particular group of employees. As well, the 'climate' reflects and in turn contributes to a broader climate prevailing throughout a particular industry, often extending generally to all collective bargaining relationships, and sometimes even borrowing general legal and social concepts from beyond the world of industrial relations. A few examples will suffice to demonstrate the relevance of this broader 'climate.' The traditional craft jurisdictions peculiar to the construction industry may, in a given case, be of extreme importance in interpreting the recognition and job assignment provisions of collective agreements in that industry. The need to vindicate a foreman's authority in order to ensure the orderly progress of work, is a concept well known and widely applied by arbitrators in all organized industries in determining the existence of 'just cause' for discipline or discharge under collective agreements. And broad notions of procedural fairness developed beyond the context of labour arbitration are frequently a guide to arbitrators called upon to decide similar questions in their special context.

In pursuing our task of industrial meteorology, then, we cannot ignore the fact that part of the 'climate' within which labour and management operate in Ontario is the controversy over contracting out. See in this regard Young, *The Contracting Out of Work*. . . . The wide notoriety given to labour's protests against this practice, the almost equally wide notoriety, especially amongst experienced labour and management representatives, of the overwhelming trend of decisions, must mean that there was known to these parties at the time they negotiated the collective agreement the strong probability that an arbitrator would not find any implicit limitation on management's right to contract out. It was one thing to imply such a limitation in the early years of this controversy when one could not speak with any clear certainty about the expectations of the parties; then, one might impose upon them the objective implications of the language of the agreement. It is quite another thing to attribute intentions and undertakings to them today, when they are aware, as a practical matter, of the need to specifically prohibit contracting out if they are to persuade an arbitrator of their intention to do so. . . .

This brings us to the next, and crucial, question: did the parties by express language in the agreement restrict management's rights to contract out? The union drew the board's attention to art. 2 of the collective agreement:

> 2.01. The Company recognizes the Union as the sole collective bargaining agent for all its employees at its Plant in Vaughan Township, including employees formerly covered under separate agreements in Leaside and Rexdale, save and except foreman, persons above the rank of foreman, and office staff.

> 2.02. Persons whose regular jobs are not in the bargaining unit shall not work on any jobs which are included in the bargaining unit except for purposes of instruction, experimenting, or in emergencies when regular employees are not available.

The union contends that the employees of the independent contractor are 'persons whose regular jobs are not in the bargaining unit,' that in driving trucks for the company they are doing 'work on . . . jobs which are included in the bargaining unit,' and that none of the exculpatory conditions which might relieve the company from complying with art. 2.02 are present. Accordingly, the union contends that art. 2.02 has been violated by the company's action in contracting out. . . .

Over and against this interpretation, however, the company introduced evidence to demonstrate that in several contracts executed by locals of the United Steelworkers of America, and in contract proposals submitted to another company, Hugh Russel & Sons Ltd., Montreal, a clear distinction was drawn between a so-called 'working foreman' clause (such as art. 2.02) and a clause prohibiting contracting out. We must note, as persons familiar with collective agreements, that this distinction is frequently drawn. On the company's thesis, the union's knowledge of distinction between a contracting out clause and a 'working foreman' clause must lead this board to the conclusion that the union did not realistically expect the company to bargain away its right to contract out when it procured acceptance of the 'working foreman' clause. . . .

On balance, we are persuaded by these arguments of the company and feel obliged to hold that art. 2.02 was not designed to bear the weighty load the union seeks to heap upon it. Rather, it was designed to preserve the integrity of the bargaining unit from any encroachment by foreman or non-bargaining unit employees. We must, therefore, hold that the agreement does not forbid the company to contract out work.

Finally, we think it important to note that our decision is based upon the interpretation of the agreement before us. We take no general position on the 'reserved rights' controversy. On the other hand, we do not foreclose the possibility that different problems may be presented by contracting out shown to flow from a desire to destroy the bargaining relationship, or from anti-union sentiments, or primarily prompted by a desire to subvert the wage structure of the agreement. Whether such situations give rise to arbitrable controversies, or whether relief must be sought under the *Labour Relations Act*, we do not consider. No evidence was presented to us as to any of these matters. Moreover, no argument was advanced to us that the violation might consist in failing to bargain with the union beforehand, rather than in the very act of contracting out. . . . The grievance is dismissed.

✳ ✳ ✳

Harry Glasbeek, "Voluntarism, Liberalism, and Grievance Arbitration: Holy Grail, Romance, and Real Life" in Geoffrey England, ed., ***Essays in Labour Relations Law*** **(Don Mills, Ont.: CCH Canadian, 1986) 57 at 84–86**

COLLECTIVE BARGAINING AND THE INSIDIOUSNESS OF CONTRACT OF EMPLOYMENT IDEOLOGY

There is really very little mystery as to why grievance arbitrators have felt compelled to accept some of the same premises as the much decried common law courts did. What is so neatly hidden from view by the emphasis on the argument that the collective agreement is a dynamic, noncontractual document, is that each employer still enters into a discrete, individual contract of employment with every single employee in the bargaining unit. Indeed, it is not unfair to say that some liberal pluralists go to great lengths to obscure this fact. They do so by belittling its significance.

I note here Laskin C.J.'s apparent triumph in *McGavin Toastmaster*, when he declared, in line with his own views consistently expressed since the time of *Peterborough Lock*, that, but for the contract of hiring, the legal incidents of individual contracts of employment are immaterial. This pronouncement has been repeated with general approval in Canadian labour relations jurisprudence. Yet, while it may be true to say that there are few, if any, significant *legal* consequences to the fact of individual contract formation in collective bargaining situations, it is not true to say that it has no *substantive* effects.

There is a curious imbalance to the process which we call collective bargaining. After an agreement has been reached the employees are asked to give up the best means of expressing their free will, namely their power to use their bargaining power. In what I can only describe as the epitome of the liberal style, the return promise exacted from the employer is that he is not to use his equivalent economic bargaining power during the life of the collective agreement, that is, he may not lockout the bargaining unit employees. Why is it then, that he can curtail the amount of work that they shall do during the life of the collective agreement? The answer lies in the fact that he, the employer, is seen as a single free will, exercising his individual contractual sovereignty. He can always remove himself from the contractual relationship he has with each and every one of his employees, provided that he gives the appropriate notice, pays the appropriate benefits, etc., which the contractual obligations taken on by him require. The quid pro quo (the reciprocity so dear to private contract law doctrine) is that each employee can, as a sovereign contracting party, also refuse to continue to perform her contractual obligations. But, when a single employee removes herself, the disruption to the enterprise is seldom of any real importance. When the employer removes himself, there also would be little impact if he merely removed his physical person, his personal intellectual ability, his personal emotional input. But, of course, that is not what he removes: he removes his property, his investment; in this context, he shortens hours, diminishes the bargaining unit size, etc. Provided he can show that he does not do this to force workers to accept different terms and conditions than were agreed upon during the collective bargaining process, he will be permitted to do so because it is of the essence of 'personhood,' as envisaged by liberals, that his property is part of his very nature. This, of course, was the very approach which led to the difficulties for liberals after they had embraced the contract of employment as the mechanism for furthering voluntarism. They did not immediately recognize that a contract would always be one of duress if there was marked inequality of this order. Yet, it was the fact that the owner of property had the right to invest or deinvest at will which made the individual contract of employment so oppressive and which made liberals, looking for a way out, welcome the collective bargaining mechanism so warmly. Now, it turns out that it is these unaltered tenets of that precollective bargaining period which counter, effectively, the liberal pluralists' attempt to overcome its pitfalls. To put it bluntly, while, according to collective bargaining theory, the now more equivalent power of the workers enables them to detract from the naked power that the right to private property had given employers, to be effective they must, concretely and specifically, get him to yield up control over that property.

The idea that a person and his property are one remains then, inviolate, subject to special agreements to the contrary. This means that his right to do with it as he wills must be respected. Here note that the property owner still sets the agenda as he always did. Before there can be any collective bargaining, that is, before there can be an attempt to detract from the free use of property power which employers might use to coerce employees, an employer must decide whether or not to invest. He remains because of his right to own property, the initiator. He can, therefore, still determine where, when, into what, and how much to invest; what processes to use, what quantity and quality of goods and services to produce, etc. In this context, the notion that equality of bargaining power can be created is nonsense; all that can be hoped for is more equivalence. As any scheme which permits one party to choose whether or not to invest while the other must invest is theoretically oppressive, we can see that the essential nature of a collective agreement is not as different from that of the individual contract of employment as liberal pluralists would have us believe. It is also apparent now why grievance arbitrators assume that managerial prerogative is to be respected as much as it has been: the employer is ceded the right to manage *his* property. It is clear why the refined employee duties to obey, to exercise skill, to act in good faith and with fidelity have been carved out by grievance arbitrators. In short, it is manifest that increased control to the joint-manager, the trade union, is an increase in 'control to,' whereas the employer's 'control over' remains largely intact. If this is so, and true voluntarism cannot be achieved through the contract of employment regime because the employer always retains 'control over' the enterprise, this is also true of the institution which we now call collective bargaining.

[Reprinted by permission.]

✻ ✻ ✻

For a similar critique of the failure of industrial pluralists to reconcile the promise of industrial democracy and joint sovereignty under collective bargaining with continued adherence to basic premises of capitalism, see K. Van Wezel Stone, "The Post-War Paradigm in American Labor Law" (1981) 90 Yale L.J. 1509.

Paul Weiler, "The Role of the Labour Arbitrator: Alternative Versions" (1969) 19 U.T.L.J. 16

Two themes run through most discussions of the nature of the arbitrator's role. On the one hand, he is expected to act as a lawyer-judge, bringing 'legalist' tools to bear on the interpretation of the collective agreement, his only charter for action. On the other hand, he is alleged to have certain distinctive qualities, of expertise and experience, which legitimate actions that are based on peculiar 'nonlegal' criteria, in particular the maintenance of a peaceful, uninterrupted, and fair industrial enterprise.

The first theory of the arbitrator as judge, contains within itself an essential ambiguity concerning the appropriate mode of judicial action. Some arbitrators feel that they must confine themselves to decisions which are based only on an explicit and specific provision in the collective agreement. In attributing a meaning to such a provision they restrict their assessment of the parties' will to the bare surface of the arrangement, the 'literal' or dictionary meaning of the words. Other arbitrators may feel that it is even more appropriate to delve beneath the surface of the text of a contract clause and assign a meaning which is most compatible with the purpose of the parties in selecting this text. When such a mutually agreed-to purpose is divined, these arbitrators may also feel it appropriate to develop and elaborate the principles it implies and then apply these principles to the instant case before them.

The second theory of the arbitrator's role, the arbitrator as 'labour relations physician,' holds that it is sometimes legitimate for an arbitrator to extend or limit what can fairly be said to be the meaning of an agreement (whether derived purposively or literally), in the light of certain overriding labour relations goals. This theory also contains within itself an essential ambiguity. Some advocate the arbitrator acting as a 'mediator,' attempting to get specific, individualized, consensual accords between the parties and thus enhancing the process of free, collective bargaining even during the administration of the agreement. Others argue that arbitrators must become aware of their necessary position as an 'industrial policy maker' and attempt intelligently to lay down authoritative, general policies, in the interests of the public as well as the immediate parties.

Each of these different theories, when worked out in detail in the literature, is sufficiently complex and sophisticated that it takes account of, and tends to shade into, each of the others. However, I am going to formulate abstract models in order to illustrate the institutional logic of each of the distinctive value judgments which lie at the roots of the different theories. . . . Each assumes that there is an intrinsic, reciprocal relationship between the job we ask arbitration to perform, the design of the institution within which arbitrators operate, and the manner in which we expect them to reach their decisions.

LABOUR ARBITRATION AND INDUSTRIAL CHANGE

Before going on to explicate each of these models in greater detail, I will briefly describe the substantive problem in connection with which I first worked them out. This problem concerns the legal consequences of management responses to changing economic, technological, and social conditions during the term of a collective agreement. Because of the substantial gains in security and stability in a collective bargaining relationship, there is a noticeable impetus in the direction of longterm agreements. On the other hand, it is increasingly recognized that it is impossible to foresee in advance all the labour relations problems inherent in changing industrial conditions. Moreover it is believed undesirable to delay agreement in order to pin down, by specific language, the contractual consequences of changes foreseen from afar, and only in the abstract. For these reasons, the precise impact of the agreement in regard to industrial change must be ambiguous.

Management is required to take the initiative in ordering relations within the plant to best take account of the new demands posed by altered circumstances. This initiative can take various forms. Work may be subcontracted either within or without the plant or it may be transferred outside the bargaining unit or to a plant not covered by the agreement. Management may assign work previously performed by one employee to a new or different job classification or it may vary, or add to, the work assigned to the individual employee. It may close down unprofitable parts of the company's operation (or even the whole of its operations), or it may relocate the plant from an unprofitable site. Finally it may change work rules, or working conditions (e.g., by instituting a compulsory retirement age) which may not affect existing jobs as much as it does the overall amenities incident to the previous plant operation.

It is obvious that such unilateral initiative will affect adversely the interests of employees and unions who have built up certain expectations and attitudes concerning the status quo. In Ontario, by reason of the statutory policy requiring a no-strike clause in every agreement, the union is denied the remedy of self-help. As a consequence, grievances concerning these harmful effects of management-instituted changes are processed through to the arbitrator. The latter is faced with a problem which he must resolve without the aid of any concrete intention or specific language of the parties directed to its solution. This particular issue has formed the battleground over which the dispute about the appropriate role of the arbitrator has been largely conducted.

THE ARBITRATOR AS MEDIATOR

One of the models we can entitle 'the arbitrator as mediator.' This model conceives of arbitration as being at the end of a continuous spectrum, which extends backward through the mutual adjustment of grievances to the original negotiation of the terms of a collective agreement. The paradigm case for this model involved a complex industrial establishment, with many divergent, conflicting centres of interest, and requiring continual, intelligent adjustment of problems in the light of previously settled policies. Collective bargaining is the logical application of a free market economy to the problem of the terms and conditions of employment, when the latter is informed by a concern for industrial democracy. In other words, it allows the employees to wield sufficient power to participate in the determination of their conditions of employment, and makes the touchstone for the latter their mutual acceptability to the various interests inherent in the enterprise, and not their conformity to some governmental policy about the 'public interest.' Hence arbitration must first be perceived as an essential part of industrial (or economic) self-government.

The next important facet of the model is the recognition that collective bargaining is sharply distinguished from other forms of contract negotiation (and administration), because the parties at interest are inextricably wedded together in a permanent relationship. . . . any attempt to subject the ongoing enterprise to detailed prescriptions is not only impossible (because of the human incapacity to anticipate all problems for as far in the future as the normal collective agreement extends), but also undesirable (first, because of the unlikelihood of intelligent solutions to these problems in the abstract, and, second, because the necessity of arriving at final agreement requires statement in general and rather ambiguous principle, as opposed to specific detail). . .

Into this situation is inserted the arbitrator, who is expected to settle those disputes, and solve those problems, left unresolved by mutual grievance adjustment. . . . the legalistic, adjudicative resolution of the dispute is unsuited for parties who must live together with each other following the decision, who will be affected in later negotiating situations by positions taken early in an adversary posture, and who will have to take the consequences of 'victories' which are not wisely addressed to the substantive problems.

Hence this model envisages the arbitrator as, ideally, performing the function of mediation. He can utilize private sources of information to get at the 'real' facts which define the labour relations substance of the grievance (rather than the 'artificial' case which filters through in the adversary context where the 'cards are not on the table'), and thus ensure that his decision does not impinge in a harmful way on the industrial relationship within which it becomes a precedent. The basic criterion for all decisions should be their 'mutual acceptability,' including especially the willing acquiescence by any 'losing party.' Of course the best evidence of such acceptability will be the actual agreement by the parties to the decision. The arbitrator should utilize all available resources to achieve this agreement, or at least to tailor the eventual decision in a way which preserves the essential interests of the losing party.

THE ARBITRATOR AS INDUSTRIAL POLICY-MAKER

. . .

For functional reasons an ever-growing gap has developed between ownership in the company or membership in the union and effective control of the decisions which are made on behalf of the institution. It is becoming more and more evident that it is fictional to speak of these decisions being 'private' only, with their effects confined only to those who participate immediately.

Since control by the market or by the affected constituencies is no longer possible, it becomes the function of legal and governmental policy to exert some control. One available representative of the public is the arbitrator. This is particularly true in jurisdictions where the parties have no untrammelled veto on the choice of an arbitrator (for instance, where they apply to a minister of labour who makes the appointment, rather than supplying panels of names). In Canada and in the United States the legal and social conditions no longer permit the arbitrator to believe he can fulfil his responsibilities by ensuring that his decisions are 'mutually acceptable' to each of the immediate parties. He has larger responsibilities to the 'public interest' of the society of which collective bargaining is an integral part. Out of this changing environment has emerged another model of the arbitration process, that of the 'arbitrator as industrial policymaker.'

This theory makes much the same assumptions about the necessarily ambiguous and 'open' quality of many of the provisions of the collective agreement, insofar as they apply to the types of problems raised in arbitration, if, as the arbitrator attempts to solve these problems, he cannot meaningfully base his decisions on principles that can be distilled from any actual, mutual agreement of the parties. Because of the legal and social developments described above, arbitrators have been delegated the power to make authoritative judgments, allocating values among the many different participants within the industrial community. . . .

. . . the mode of decisionmaking which the arbitrator adopts must reflect the position he occupies. He is no longer justified in using 'conceptual' reasoning, deriving his conclusion from legal principles found within the agreement, the statutory or common law of the jurisdiction, or from a body of accepted, reported, arbitration precedents. The arbitrator should base his decisions on their functional relationship to what he believes to be the appropriate goals of the industrial society in whose government he is participating. Such goals include not only the maintenance of the productivity of the industrial enterprise, and the viability of collective bargaining as the technique for establishing working conditions, but also the commitments of the wider political community to the values of due process.

Although the need for general rules applicable to more than the instant case is also a concern for the arbitrator in some cases, it must often take second place to the latter's function as a flexible resolver of disputes. . . . The role of the arbitrator is peculiarly 'nonlegal,' and, as in early equity, his 'lay'judgment is sought 'to focus on a specific dispute and to reflect the contemporary conscience of the community in its resolution, with both utility and integrity.'

The distinctive value in this model is its perception of the fact that the arbitrator himself really decides those issues which are not reached by any meaning that can be honestly attributed to the agreement. . . . The 'policymaker' model lays bare the legal and social power attached to the office of the arbitrator, and the responsibilities to the wider public interest that this necessarily involves. . . .

Yet I do not believe that those who have advocated this legal theory have fully appreciated the institutional significance of the fact that the imposition of implied restrictions on subcontracting, for instance, represents an authoritative value judgment by the arbitrator, and that his choice of the appropriate term in the agreement be adequately responsive not only to the private interests of the parties represented before him, but also the private interests of the subcontractor and his employees, and the public interest in a productive economy with fair conditions of employment. . . .

THE ARBITRATOR AS ADJUDICATOR

Unlike the first two theories of the arbitrator's role, the adjudicative model rests its case largely on the design of the institution within which labour arbitration is carried on. It holds that the nature of the substantive policies which arbitrators should strive to achieve are and should be limited by the structural means within which they operate. Moreover, the maintenance of enduring institutions such as labour arbitration, and the continuance of wide acceptability for its decisions, is itself a sufficient reason for self-restraint, by participants in the institution in the pursuit of substantive goals such as job security. In other words, the fact that an institution such as arbitration is presented with an opportunity to relieve against more or less apparent industrial ills, even when there is no likelihood of short-run relief elsewhere, may not justify action that is inconsistent with established expectations about the proper limits of arbitral reasoning and decisionmaking. In the long run, the most important social value in industrial relations is the continued existence of procedures and institutions which shape and control the struggle carried on within them.

The distinctive role of adjudication is based on the assumption that arbitration is similar to the judicial process.

. . .

What are the reasons that purportedly justify the use of labour arbitration in its adjudicative form? Four are usually suggested: (1) inexpensiveness; (2) speed; (3) informality; and (4) arbitral expertise.

. . .

To summarize the model very briefly, it conceives of the arbitrator as an adjudicator of specific, concrete disputes, who disposes of the problem by elaborating and applying a legal regime, established by the collective agreement, to facts which he finds on the basis of evidence and argument presented to him in an adversary process. Hence, the arbitration process mirrors the division of functions conventionally adhered to in political life. There, a legislative body establishes the rules or principles which are to govern the private conduct of those subject to its enactments. Then, an adjudicative body settles disputes arising out of this private conduct, by evaluating the latter in the light of these established rules and principles. The key elements defining the adjudicative model are (1) settlement of disputes, (2) adversary process, and (3) an established system of standards which are utilized in the process to dispose of the disputes. . . .

This model, then, envisages the collective agreement as a more or less successful attempt to institute a governing legal system in the plant. The parties to the agreement are required to orient their own activity and relationships in the light of the standards established by the agreement. This does not mean that the parties are not entitled to change the rules as they go along, motivated by a sense of the need for accommodation of immediate goals in the light of long-range interests. However, the collective agreement furnishes the standards for evaluating their conduct as 'right' or 'wrong,' 'legal' or 'illegal.' . . .

An adversary process of adjudication (by contrast with an umpire or inquisitorial system) entails a relatively passive role by the arbitrator who is expected to decide the case on the basis of evidence adduced, and reasoned arguments made, by the parties themselves. It is precisely because this is how the institutional structure is designed that it is illegitimate (within the confines of this model) to distinguish between the 'artificial' facts of the case, as prepared and presented by the parties, and the 'real' facts learned by the arbitrator through his resources outside the record (perhaps when his nominees 'put their cards on the table'). . . .

Most important of all, it should be obvious why 'arbitration as adjudication' requires the existence of standards for decision, standards which are the objects of a consensus of all the participants in the process. This is due to the fact that the preparation and presentation of the case for decision is achieved by parties working separately from each other and from the person or group which is to decide the case. In order to single out and abstract from an undifferentiated concrete situation those facets which appear to be relevant to this resolution of the dispute, and argue for or against their use as reasons for a particular decision, there must be standards available which categorize certain types [of] situation as requiring certain legal results. For instance, suppose there is a promotion in a plant available, and two people want it, and the union supports one, and the company another. There must be some standards telling everybody which facets of the whole life history and present status of each are relevant for selection between them (i.e., training, or time with the company are usually relevant; union status or marital relationship to the supervisors are usually not relevant). Furthermore, the parties, at the time they prepare the case and while they present it, must have some awareness of the standards defining the arbiter's criteria for decision, in order that this enhance the quality of the results, and their sense of meaningfully participating in the process. The whole institution becomes a charade, absent such a consensus concerning standards for decision. Since the purpose of adjudication is to maintain the legal system set up by the agreement, by settling the disputes which occur in its administration, the standards to be used are those established by the agreement.

We can summarize the thesis of the . . . [arbitrator as adjudicator] model as follows: the whole institutional structure of arbitration, its incidence, access to it, mode of participation in it, the bases for decision, the nature of the relief available in it, are all defined by and flow naturally from its function, which is to dispose of private disputes arising out of primary conduct by granting relief to parties on the basis of an evaluation of this conduct in the light of the 'legal' standards established by this agreement.

THE ARBITRATOR'S ROLE IN THE 'OPEN' OR 'UNWRITTEN' AREA OF THE AGREEMENT

. . . An arbitral decision is unacceptable as a mere 'fiat' of the arbitrator and finds its authoritative force or legitimacy in the reasoned opinion which justifies it. This tendency is based on real considerations of the function and makeup of arbitration which, as we have seen, presuppose 'objective' premises and standards as the starting point for arbitral argument. However, the premises relied on in the subcontracting and other analogous areas just do not have the mutually intended and established content necessary for those conclusions (limitation on unilateral change) to be derived from them. Nor is the arbitrator warranted in reasoning in accordance with what he believes to be most consistent with legislative policies and standards, to remake the parties' contract for them. The legislative presumption is that freedom of contract, not compulsory "interest dispute" arbitration, is the rule. Hence, the conclusion of the . . . [arbitrator as adjudicator] model of the arbitral process, which I accept, is that these decisions are inconsistent with a proper conception of the arbitrator's role, and that any short-run substantive gains (which themselves are quite debatable) do not justify such misuse of grievance arbitration (with possible harmful consequences for the "acceptability" of the latter).

AN INSTITUTIONAL ANALYSIS OF ARBITRAL POLICY-MAKING

. . . In deciding whether a limited 'policymaking' role is suitable for arbitration, there are several dimensions along which the existing institution may be assessed: (1) accountability and legitimacy; (2) rationality and adequacy, and (3) effectiveness. At present, it seems safe to say that the institution is designed with the primary role of adjudication in mind. The issue is whether the existing structure is compatible, at certain key points, with the adoption of an overt policymaking role in this field of industrial change.

. . . In the case of the ad hoc arbitration system, the arbitrator holds office completely at the pleasure of each of the parties. . . .

Hence, subject to the limitation of the residual power of the minister of labour, the need for accountability in labour policymaking is substantially satisfied. What is not so apparent is the capacity of the arbitrator, acting within the framework of labour arbitration, to engage in intelligent development of a common law of the administration of the agreement. The vast majority of arbitration cases in Ontario are decided by men whose backgrounds are either in the judiciary, in law teaching, or on the labour relations board. All these men have either legal training or essentially legal experience. They are in a position to specialize in the labour relations field, and to become knowledgeable and surefooted in dealing with the typical problems posed in labour arbitration. However, as far as industrial relations as a whole is concerned, their interest is necessarily secondary, and their experience is essentially as an outsider. No one can seriously contend that, unaided, they are equipped to establish new, general policies adequately resolving the competing interests in job security and industrial change.

Is the institution of labour arbitration designed to furnish this aid? The typical hearing is conducted by lawyers on either side, or by labour relations consultants and/or international union representatives, or by personnel managers and/or union local business agents. Although the industrial background to a specific dispute may be thrashed out by cooperative discussion at the beginning of the meeting, the record for the decision is prepared through the examination of witnesses. Again I believe it a fair statement that the personnel who are presently available and involved in Ontario labour arbitration are unequipped to establish with any degree of probability the disputed policy facts which must underlie a new common law of labour arbitration.

Since, as we have already seen, the arbitrator does not have the expertise necessary to justify his taking 'official notice' of such controverted facts, he must rely on other resources. Yet he does not have the facilities or staff which are available to legislatures or administrative agencies, enabling him to make factual studies, evaluate proposals with the aid of experts, suggest legislative hypotheses in order to get the reaction of all interested parties, and then formulate a final compromise which takes adequate account of what has been learned. Because labour arbitration has been designed as adjudication, the arbitrator is essentially passive and dependent on the efforts of the parties to prepare a record and argument for him. Because they invited him in only when a dispute arises, his policymaking activity can only be sporadic and at random. Thus he does not have the opportunity to test and amend his policies and to avail himself of information feedback for this purpose. . . .

Hence I conclude that, even on pragmatic grounds, there is no justification for the arbitrator stepping outside his appropriate adjudicative role and donning the cloak of industrial policymaker. . . .

AN ALTERNATIVE VEHICLE: COLLECTIVE BARGAINING

I have argued that the type of limitations imposed by arbitrators on management initiatives are often a misconceived resolution of the conflicting interests involved. . . . Arbitration, because of its institutional and functional character, is suited for problems whose resolution can be achieved by the elaboration and application of established standards. Mutually accepted standards which could afford a sufficient basis for a reasoned solution to this problem simply do not exist in the conventional case of unilateral changes in working conditions. Here there is a framework of agreed-to principles and purposes from which we can reason to a more or less probable and plausible conclusion. However, in the job security situation, we leave this penumbral area of the agreement and embark on what are, essentially, the uncharted waters of the unwritten area of the relationship. Not only is there no consensus between union and management as a basis for a rational decision, but the arbitrator necessarily has a distorted perspective from whence it is difficult to perceive the claims of third parties and the general public.

I hope that my attempted justification of these conclusions has not been misinterpreted as a brief for the present legal regime. The existing institutional arrangements are radically deficient because they do not allow the interests of union and employees a fair access to the decisionmaking process. They constitute a disincentive to the use of the technique of free collective bargaining, which, after all, is the statutory policy for establishing working conditions. Moreover, because collective bargaining has given way almost completely to the unilateral prerogative of management, the substantive policies that have become established over a large portion of the economy are totally inadequate.

What is needed is a set of arrangements which allows the law in arbitration to be neutral as between the claims of union or management in this area. At present, the existence of the statutory, absolute, no-strike clause imposes a limitation on the employees' power to respond to employer initiatives and this furnishes a powerful attraction to arbitrators to imply a similar limitation on management's power to take these initiatives. We want a device which will allow arbitrators to declare, in a meaningful fashion, that, although employer conduct is not legally prohibited, neither is it legally permitted. . . .

The logical solution to these problems is relatively simple, in principle, although there are many difficult questions of detail which must be settled. The duty to bargain must be held to continue during the terms of a collective agreement in a meaningful fashion. In this way, it will be made clear to both parties that the union has no right under the agreement to block employer initiatives but, at the same time, that the employer has no legal permission under the agreement to change working conditions. The terms under which changes are to be made are yet to be settled by negotiation. In order to facilitate collective bargaining the employer should be required to give notice of his intention to make changes affecting collective bargaining and then to make a good-faith attempt to reach an agreement about when and how the changes are to be made. Such a duty to bargain in good faith to an agreement or impasse can be enforced through the labour board with appropriate remedies. Of course, such a duty would be defeasible by agreement between the parties about such matters as subcontracting, etc.

However, because of the traditional inefficacy of such a legal duty to bargain, and because negotiations by themselves can be a charade on the employee's part, the union must be free to enforce their own claims through the traditional and legitimate weapon of the strike. Hence, the compulsory no-strike clause must be deleted from the collective agreement, at least to the extent that the strike is over a matter not 'covered' by the collective agreement. Such a legislative change would give the union a fair opportunity to make their interests felt in the process of decision-making leading up to technological or organizational changes. Moreover, it would give employers the incentive to deal with the problem of job security, and the minimization of the effects on employees of industrial change, in the original collective agreement. The union would be able to offer in exchange a more or less extensive promise not to strike. We could expect the same development that has occurred in the USA, where unions and employers have tailored the extent of the arbitration and no-strike clauses, and their provisions dealing with industrial change and job security, to their own individual needs.

The legal regime I have proposed is another alternative to the present options of unilateral management discretion or governmental imposition of the terms of the agreement (via a disguised form of compulsory, 'interest-dispute' arbitration). I believe it is the solution which is most compatible with the existing, legislatively-established policy of free, collective bargaining about employment conditions. This logical development of the statutory scheme will also serve to remove the arbitrator from the dilemma with which he is presently faced, a situation which often tempts him to go beyond his proper institutional role. [Copyright © University of Toronto Press. Reprinted by permission of the University of Toronto Press Incorporated (www.utpjournals.com).]

Brian Langille, "Equal Partnership in Canadian Labour Law" (1983) 21 Osgoode Hall L.J. 496 at 532–36

E. THE ARBITRATION JURISPRUDENCE ON CONTRACTING OUT

It has already been indicated that it is trite to state that in Canada a unilateral employer decision to contract out work with resulting terminations is unimpeachable in arbitration unless the collective agreement contains express provisions controlling or forbidding such actions. This point of arbitration law has been established and well known for some years. Most labour lawyers are familiar with the struggle within our law for this point and the eventual victory of the point of view permitting contracting out. The turning point is now widely held to be the decision in *Russelsteel Ltd.*, wherein Professor Arthurs compiled his 'box score' on the issue and declared the winner. This point is so familiar now that it is sufficient merely to drop a reference to the Russelsteel decision in order to end a discussion of this matter. *Russelsteel* seems a fixed star in the arbitral firmament. It is said that this now forms part of the 'climate' of collective bargaining in Canada, thus turning Professor Laskin's (as he then was) own words on himself, Laskin being the chief proponent of the losing view. . . .

A key to understanding the contracting out controversy lies in noting that beneath the surface discussion about that specific issue there was a much more profound debate, that being, it is submitted, the debate about equal partnership. Professor Weiler has outlined the deeper debate as follows:

> Looking back at the cases from the Fifties, one can see two competing versions of the role of the arbitrator. These two conceptions diverged sharply in their handling of a crucial, practical problem: the response of the arbitrator to industrial change, initiated by management decisions to subcontract work, introduce new technology, and shuffle work assignments.
>
> The majority persuasion was articulated by many lower court judges who, ironically enough, doubled as the bulk of the arbitrators in Ontario for the first fifteen years. Their thesis may be summarized as follows. The collective agreement is essentially a written contract. There is nothing that extraordinary about it. It will be interpreted in the standard, literal fashion. The arbitrator should not stray beyond the four corners of the document unless he is absolutely compelled to. But when the surface language used by the parties does not readily supply the answer to a particular grievance, then the arbitrator should have recourse to the background presuppositions supplied from established areas of contract law, in particular the individual contract of employment between the 'master and servant.' One central assumption in that legal tradition was management's freedom to run the business, to exercise the rights of property and capital, to take the initiative in changing the methods of operation if that appeared profitable. Only if the par-

ties positively agreed to clear and specific written restrictions on that 'reserved right' could an arbitrator restrain such a management decision, to subcontract part of the operation for instance.

An alternative, more promising conception of the arbitral rule is being worked out by a few arbitrators, especially by Bora Laskin, then professor of labour law at the University of Toronto (now Chief Justice of the Supreme Court of Canada). Laskin was quick to recognize the inevitable gaps in collective agreements, and to utilize extrinsic aids (such as the history of negotiations or the previous administration of the collective agreement) to decipher the actual expectations of these parties. More important, when there was no persuasive evidence that these parties had mutually agreed to the precise disposition of the problem presented by a grievance, Laskin believes that the labour arbitrator must recognize fundamental differences between the old world of 'master and servant' and the new 'climate of the collective agreement.' The arbitrator must actively develop the common law of the labour contract based on the needs and expectations of Canadian unions and employers in the second half of the twentieth century, not on English judicial precedents drawn from the second half of the nineteenth century.

The lesson of history is, of course, that the 'reserved rights' theorists won the day on the issue of contracting out. . . . From this perspective, the contracting out controversy can be viewed as merely another manifestation of our recurring phenomenon. This is merely another part of the overall structure in which participants in the labour relations system have sought to inject a viewpoint which is fundamentally at odds with our legislation's basic starting point. This point is clearly made in Professor Weiler's account of the reserved rights theory set out above, where he stated:

> One central assumption in that legal tradition was management's freedom to run the business, to exercise the rights of property and capital, to take the initiative in changing the methods of operation if that appeared profitable.

Of course in the arbitration context those arbitrators advocating the reserved rights theory did not (and did not have to) promote this point of view in the extreme form . . . that these reserved management rights were (under the legislation) inalienable rights. Rather, the thesis was that the rights inhered in management until expressly alienated in the collective agreement. But the key to the reserved rights theory is . . . [that] it embraces a vision of pre-collective bargaining de facto employer control which casts a long shadow into the collective bargaining era. An analogy to libertarian rights theorists, who insist that the inherent 'rights' of man in a state of nature cast a long shadow over social organization, is apt.

At the level of implication of the terms in a contract, those who opposed the reserved rights theorists argued that terms reflecting a lack of negotiating power ought not be implied in a contract negotiated in a context of more equal bargaining power. This is the basic flaw with Canadian contracting out jurisprudence. Approval for one possible outcome of the contracting process led reserved rights theorists to weigh the scales in favour of employers, to grant the employers a head start in negotiations by guaranteeing that employers were given certain rights for free. The role of the union was to try to make inroads into these employer or management rights. Professor Weiler has written at length on the role of the arbitrator when faced with a change in the enterprise, such as contracting out. He is still of the view that the arbitrator should not imply restrictions upon 'management' powers to contract out, arguing that:

> If the trade union is to secure these kinds of rights for its members, then it should have to pay them at the bargaining table, not receive them as a gift from the arbitrator.

The great difficulty with this is that it ignores the result that the employer gets its rights 'as a gift from the arbitrator.' The following general points can be made. First, that it is not open to arbitrators in Canada to assume that there are any management rights either inherent or reserved. That, which has been repeatedly pointed out, is simply not the law in Canada. The view in *Russelsteel* is at odds with basic principles in our legislative system. What employers and unions get under our legislation is a comprehensive duty to bargain collectively. If the rights do not flow expressly or impliedly *from the agreement*, it is impossible to see where they would come from. Second, that if arbitrators rejected the approach of *Russelsteel* and brought a neutral approach to the issue of interpreting collective agreements, it may well be that there would still be agreements which do not address the issues under consideration. If powers are granted to management or the union, fine. If, however, the agreement is truly silent, then Professor Weiler is right in saying that an arbitrator cannot create provisions out of whole cloth. But what this amounts to is that the agreement is silent, not that it supports an 'inherent' management power to act unilaterally. It can be argued, in a large number of cases, and for reasons set out above, such action would constitute an unfair labour practice.

The *Russelsteel* view is a thorn in the side of a coherent theory of Canadian labour relations legislation's view of equal partnership and a roadblock to the effecting of the purposes of Canadian labour law. Under *Russelsteel* there is an incentive offered to employers not to engage in collective bargaining of vital issues within the scope of the duty to bargain. This surely cannot be right. Furthermore, *Russelsteel* drives us to an irrational law of unfair labour practices. This too cannot be right. Thirdly, *Russelsteel* negates collective bargaining during the term of the collective agreement by placing all of the losses for a (real) failure to bargain on the employees and the union. All of these effects are generated by a view of 'management' rights which is at odds with the assumptions of the legislation. Perhaps more fundamentally, and in sum, *Russelsteel* undermines and thwarts collective bargaining and equal partnership in Canadian labour law. A reversal of the thinking in *Russelsteel* would offer incentives to the parties to engage in collective bargaining over these issues during the open season. This would promote the purposes of the legislation. Furthermore, a reversal of *Russelsteel* would mean that under an agreement which was (truly) silent on the issue of contracting out, the employer will have to negotiate with the union during the term of the agreement. The long run effect will be, however, to reject the idea that all the losses are borne by the union and the employees, and to structure a set of incentives so as to make these issues subject to collective bargaining. Much of what has been said about *Westinghouse* [[1980] O.L.R.B. Rep. 577] would become irrelevant. To put it simply, rejecting *Russelsteel* would enable us to have a coherent theory of our legislation's view of equal partnership.

[Reprinted by permission.]

✳ ✳ ✳

Russelsteel, above, involved a consideration of the authority of the arbitrator where the collective agreement was silent on a particular matter.

A related issue in more recent Canadian arbitral jurisprudence is whether management rights expressly recognized in the collective agreement are qualified by an implied duty of fairness.

Re Metropolitan Toronto Board of Commissioners of Police v. Metropolitan Toronto Police Association (1981), 33 O.R. (2d) 476, 124 D.L.R. (3d) 684 at 687-88 (Ont. C.A.)

[Overtime work was needed for the purpose of taking inventory. The employer refused to assign that work to certain employees to whom it had been assigned in the past. Those employees brought a grievance to the effect that the employer's allocation of the work was unreasonable. Arbitrator Maureen K. Saltman, in an award partially reported at (1980), 26 L.A.C. (2d) 117, upheld the grievance. She said:

> In fact, the collective agreement makes no mention of either inventory work or of the distribution of overtime. Moreover, the agreement as a whole does not give rise to any inference that the grievors were entitled to the work.
>
> In addition, I am of the view that merely because the grievors performed the work in past, this does not give them a right to claim the work in future . . . Since the collective agreement does not confer on the grievors a right to the work, the matter comes within the management rights clause. . . . . This clause gives the board the right and power to manage the operation, which would include selecting personnel to take inventory. . . .
>
> Were the grievors in this case excluded from the inventory for irrelevant reasons, i.e., reasons which were not related to the performance of the inventory or because of personal animosity?
>
> . . .
>
> The thrust of the board's complaint against the grievors was their attitude toward their work, rather than their actual work performance. . . . [T]he grievors' attitudes would only be a relevant consideration in the selection of personnel for the inventory if there was reason to believe that their attitudes would adversely affect the inventory. Since there was no evidence that their attitudes interfered with their regular work, in my opinion, it is not reasonable to assume that their attitudes would interfere with the inventory work. Also, the grievors always performed adequately at past inventories. . . . In the absence of a reasonable basis for excluding the grievors, I must conclude that the board made an improper discrimination.
>
> It should be noted that, since the collective agreement puts no limits on the distribution of overtime, the board was entitled to select personnel for inventory on any basis which was reasonably connected to the management of the operations. I find, however,

that the board excluded the grievors because the supervisor . . . did not like their attitude, which in this case was irrelevant to the performance of the inventory work. I find further that the denial of the inventory work as a response to their perceived attitudes was an unfair discrimination for which they should be compensated.]

On an application for judicial review, the Ontario Court of Appeal set aside the arbitrator's award. Houlden J.A. said:

. . .

Ms. Kenny submitted that we should imply a term in the collective agreement that the management rights clause would be applied fairly and without discrimination. With respect, we do not agree. Article 17.06 of the collective agreement provides:

17:06 The Arbitrator shall not have any power to add to, subtract from, alter, modify or amend in any way, any part of this Agreement nor otherwise make any decision inconsistent with this Agreement, which expresses the full and complete understanding of the parties on remuneration, benefits and working conditions.

Moreover, as can be seen, art. 3.01(b) specifically refers to discrimination in promotion, demotion or transfer, and to disciplining a member without reasonable cause and permits these matters to be the subject of a grievance. The collective agreement is a detailed document covering some 40 pages. Having regard to the nature of the agreement, and to its provisions, we see no necessity in this case to imply a term that the management rights clause will be applied fairly and without discrimination. If such a term were to be implied, it would mean that every decision of management made under the exclusive authority of the management rights clause would be liable to challenge on the grounds that it was exercised unfairly or discriminatively. In our opinion, this would be contrary to the spirit and intent of the collective agreement.

The arbitrator erred, therefore, in finding that the grievance could be founded on a failure by the Board to exercise fairly and without discrimination the rights conferred on it by the management rights clause. When the arbitrator determined that there was no provision in the collective agreement that governed the taking of inventory and the distribution of overtime, she should have ruled that she had no jurisdiction to deal with the dispute because of an alleged improper exercise of management rights. . . .

* * *

Re Council of Printing Industries of Canada and Toronto Printing Pressmen and Assistants' Union No. 10 et al. (1983), 42 O.R. (2d) 404 (C.A.) (leave to appeal to the Supreme Court of Canada refused (1983), 52 N.R. 308n)

[The employer had selected five temporary employees for classification as permanent employees. The union grieved that five more senior temporary employees should have been selected, on the basis of their seniority. The employer's position was that the selection should generally be done on the basis of scores on supervisors' evaluations, but in one case this was trumped by a "no family" rule.

The collective agreement included the following provisions:

4 Except as specifically limited by this Agreement, the entire management of the business in the pressroom of the Company is vested in the executives of the Company and without limiting the generality of the foregoing, shall include the employment, discharging, direction and promotion of employees.

6.03 All other things being reasonably equal, seniority shall govern as between individual employees in all cases of rehiring, laying off of staff, or promotion to higher rated positions within jurisdiction of this Agreement.

22 The Employer shall permanently classify thirty-four (34) employees under this Agreement.

. . .

22(f) The Employer agrees that during periods of press shutdown for preventative maintenance and cleanup, no permanently classified employee shall be laid off.

The arbitration board rejected the union's argument that the collective agreement expressly required that the choice of employees for permanent classification be done by seniority. However, the board held that the employer was obliged to act in a *bona fide* manner, and had not done so. The board found that the supervisors' evaluation scores had been arrived at arbitrarily in some respects, and that the blanket "no family" rule was far too broad to be a reasonable response to concerns about conflict of interest.

The Ontario Court of Appeal upheld the arbitration board's decision, in the following terms:]

MACKINNON A.C.J.O.: . . .

The board held . . . :

> We have reviewed all of the provisions of the agreement and must conclude that the parties did not intend art. 6.03 to govern the permanent classification of employees under art. 22. The only way in which the article could apply is if the permanent classification of an employee under art. 22 could be said to constitute a 'promotion to a higher rated position' within the meaning of art. 6.03.
>
> . . .
>
> Accordingly, because the permanent classification does not result in a higher rate of pay, it cannot be said, on the wording of this agreement, that the permanent classification amounts to a promotion.

The Board then stated the issue in these words:

> However, is the company given a free hand to make such decisions in any way it pleases? For example, could it permanently classify employees according to hair colour or sunny disposition? What if its decision was made in bad faith or based on criteria suggesting invidious discrimination?

The Board then goes on to discuss the effect of classification on seniority and says . . . :

> Once permanently classified, an employee is more or less immune from layoff and this means that the impact of contractions in the Company's workforce must be borne by the

so-called temporary employees. In other words, the job security rights of employees classified by the company under art. 22 are said to be an exception to the seniority rights provided by art. 6, in effect abridging the latter rights of all employees not so classified. If this is a proper construction of the agreement as we think it is, the well-known arbitral concern over the abridgment of seniority rights reflected in the following quotation would support the implication of a contractual intent that the company must exercise its discretion under art. 22 in a reasonable manner, without discrimination, bad faith or arbitrariness.

The majority award of the board clearly dealt with the issue before the board as being an interpretation of the effect and intent of art. 22 in light of the whole collective agreement. From our reading of the award the majority were not purporting to deal with the management rights clause per se . . .

It can be seen that in determining their approach to the interpretation of art. 22, the majority of the board was of the view that the company's interpretation of its rights or obligations under that article, seriously affected the seniority rights given by art. 6. This is supported by the company's position, taken in the other two grievances, which position was referred to at the beginning of these reasons, that permanently classified employees are protected from all layoffs. The majority concluded, although many words were used, that the mandatory obligation to permanently classify must be done in a bona fide fashion. They then proceeded to consider whether the carrying out of the permanent classification obligation had indeed been discharged in a bona fide fashion and concluded, on their interpretation of the facts, that it had not. We are, of course, not called on to review that conclusion, if we conclude that on a reasonable interpretation of the governing article the board was entitled to enter upon such an assessment.

. . .

In our view, the interpretation placed on art. 22 by the board in light of the whole collective agreement was one it could reasonably bear, or to use the words of some of the authorities in this field, the interpretation is not "patently unreasonable." Being of this view the court's jurisdiction is exhausted and the appeal [against the decision of the Divisional Court setting aside the award] must succeed.

✳ ✳ ✳

David Beatty, "The Role of the Arbitrator: A Liberal Version" (1984) 34 U.T.L.J. 136

. . .

The issue of the nature and scope of management's rights in a collective bargaining relationship . . . raising as it does questions about the legitimate and appropriate role of the arbitral process, is too important to leave unanswered. . . .

Reduced to its essentials the legal or interpretative issue which is posed by a general recognition of authority in the internal bureaucratic procedures of management is whether decisions which are effected within them are absolute and beyond any form of impartial third-party review. The central question (to which the Court of Appeal in the two judgments [*Metropolitan Toronto Board of Commissioners of Police* and *Council of Printing*

Industries of Canada, above] has given two opposing answers) is whether management's 'right' to decide how to run its business is immune from any involvement by the persons most affected by such decisions, except in so far as the express language of the agreement provides otherwise or whether, alternatively, management's decision-making authority is impressed with implied obligations of fairness and reason. More pragmatically, the question is: when a collective agreement grants an employer a power of decision either in a broad delegation of managerial authority (as in *Re Metropolitan Toronto Board of Commissioners of Police*) or in a particular grant of discretion (as in *Re Council of Printing Industries of Canada*) and whether it does so explicitly or implicitly, is the employer thereby empowered to act in an arbitrary or even capricious way? For example, in the absence of any provision in the agreement explicitly prohibiting it from so doing, might an employer unilaterally introduce a surveillance system in its plant simply to satisfy a perverse curiosity to snoop on others unobserved, or might it require an employee to present herself in a costume it found pleasing to its eye? Alternatively, might management carry out a decision to reduce its labour costs by contracting out all or part of the work traditionally performed by its employees in the bargaining unit to a contractor who employed others at non-union rates or by integrating those duties in the functions performed by its own unorganized (supervisory) staff? Or, to take a final example, could employers choose to retire, layoff, or deny a leave of absence or an overtime opportunity to one employee rather than another simply in virtue of their preference for the colour of hair or political affiliation of the latter, unless it was explicitly constrained in the agreement not to do so?

At least in a system of industrial relations which grounds itself in the liberal-democratic tradition of law, it would seem inconsistent with and contrary to the most basic conceptions of justice and fairness if individuals could be treated in the ways just described. A commitment to liberal precepts of equality of liberty, to the basic entitlement of all individuals to be the authors of their own (occupational) plans in life seems to rule out decisions so central to one's existence being predicated on such idiosyncratic and subjective whims of others. . . . Liberal theory postulates an equality between individuals in their right to self-definition and self-government which renders intolerable rules and results in which, as with the examples I have used, some are given an authority to control others in an entirely arbitrary and discriminatory way.

. . . The idea [of the contrary argument] is simply that if, as the conventional collective agreements invariably stipulate, the parties have jointly willed that some decisions are to be effected exclusively by management within its own bureaucratic procedures, then the primacy we attribute to our democratic lawmaking processes requires us to respect the resolutions that the parties themselves have achieved rather than paternalistically impose solutions of our own. In the phrase of the court's judgment in *Re Metropolitan Toronto Board of Commissioners of Police*, it would be contrary to the 'spirit and intent' of the collective agreement, with its status as a legitimate product of the legislative process, to imply a criterion of fairness and reasonableness when the parties have failed or refused to do so themselves.

. . . In this essay I want to argue against that view and claim that we have always had available to us a method of analysis capable of resolving disputes about the exercise of managerial discretion — and of doing so in a way which satisfies our ambition to ensure that individuals are treated fairly, that is, with equal concern and respect, while simultaneously preserving the integrity of the democratic lawmaking processes we have created to govern their working lives. I want to argue that we have the legal tools to avoid the confusion and conflict which has so far clouded this issue and which, as we have seen, continues to characterize the existing jurisprudence . . . a rigorous theory of the nature and role of a labour arbitrator in a liberal regime of collective bargaining holds the key which allows us to break the deadlock and finally (and actually quite effortlessly) fashion solutions to what, in the final analysis, is an issue about the extent to which the decisionmaking processes in the places where we work must conform to the rule of law, to the most basic precepts of the legal theory on which our model of collective bargaining is founded. . . .

My objective, then, is to propose a theory of arbitration which builds upon the idea of law as a creative, evolving act of interpretation going beyond a search for subjective intention, and to show how and why it is more appropriate than negotiation or bargaining as a way of achieving a synthesis of our competing allegiances to procedural justice and substantive fairness. . . .

The first part of the essay examines the claim that an arbitrator simply has no legal authority or institutional mandate to enter upon the question of how management effects those decisions which the parties have, either in the standard management's rights clause or by their silence, delegated to it to make as it sees fit. The idea, which follows directly from a rigidly positivistic perception of law, is simply to deny the legitimacy of any role for an arbitrator whenever the parties have decreed that management has the authority to do as it pleases. While the claim carries with it the appearance of a certain straightforward logic, on closer analysis it can be shown seriously to distort the role which the courts themselves have sanctioned for arbitrators. . . .

As we shall see, it is based on or at least illustrative of a theory of politics and social organization which gives unquestioned priority to property rights and denies individuals any meaningful opportunity to participate on a whole set of questions and decisions which, in the examples I have used, can be seen to affect the most detailed and the most significant aspects of their working lives. In labour law terms, a version of the arbitral function that is limited to the written text of a collective agreement carries with it the diminution rather than the enhancement of the liberal commitment to lawmaking procedures which respect the autonomy of each individual because it denies individuals access to arbitration on issues on which they have already been forbidden to exercise their right to strike.

Even if one were satisfied as to the legitimacy of arbitrators developing a 'common law of the shop' to flesh out the rights and responsibilities of the parties and to give meaning to the written text of a collective agreement, doubts might still (and for many do) remain as to the effectiveness of the arbitration process in generating viable solutions. Here the concern is not so much that arbitration is not a proper process of social ordering as that for these sets of issues it is not an appropriate one. . . .

In the second part of the essay I will take up these ideas and consider whether it can be said that to the extent that arbitrators become involved they must necessarily act as policymakers, as managers of the enterprise, in a process which, in its forms and procedures of participation (presentation of proofs, reasoned argument), is not well suited to such a task. I shall be concerned primarily to show how and why, both in theory and in practice, the characterization of arbitration as an exercise of unfettered policymaking cannot be made to stick. . . .

In the final section of the essay I suggest that, in a society which structures its system of labour relations within a liberal framework of law, there are strong reasons for preferring adjudication to negotiation as a technique for resolving such disputes; I suggest not simply that arbitrators and courts have it within their authority to develop and apply doctrines of fairness and reasonableness in constraining how management exercises its discretion, but that legislatures should expressly incorporate this version of arbitration into their legislation. . . . Like an employment standard of procedural justice, arbitration should be made accessible to all individuals as a means to ensure that their interests have received equal concern and respect, and that their autonomy has not been unnecessarily abused or sacrificed in or by any of the decision-making processes of the workplace.

ARBITRATION AS INTERPRETATION

. . .

The reserved rights thesis, with its particular assumptions as to the nature and scope of the collective agreement, has not, unsurprisingly, gone unchallenged. Indeed there has always been a competing thesis, sometimes characterized as the joint sovereignty theory of collective agreements, which rejected the historical, temporal analysis implicit in the reserved rights approach and which, envisaging the enactment of collective bargaining as making a complete break with the past, came to perceive the written terms of the collective agreement as representing a more limited grant of rule-making authority. . . . Advocates of this theory make the assumption that in addition to the express provisions of the collective agreement there will be, . . . 'a common law worked out empirically over [the] years . . . to give meaning and consistency to the Collective Agreement on which it is based.' Rather than signalling a limit to the scope of their jurisdiction, silence on the face of agreements, alerts arbitrators to the task of discovering and 'working pure' this industrial, common law of the shop, from 'the customs and unwritten understandings, established practices and sound industrial relations standards' which are part of the ongoing enterprise. Parallelling precisely the role of the courts in the interpretation of commercial contracts or in constitutional adjudication, the role of the arbitrator in the interpretation, application, and administration of the collective agreement is not limited simply to the reading of documentary language. On this view, the context in which the collective agreement is negotiated is as essential to the task of discovering the most reasonable meaning of the agreement as are its written terms.

. . . As a positivist description of the law which governs the role of the arbitrator, the reserved rights thesis and the cases which build on its assumptions can quite easily be shown to be wrong. Our courts' own pronouncements, however erratic they may have been, demonstrate a clear recognition that context (including a common law of the shop) must influence text; that no words stand by themselves admitting of a single unambiguous and absolute meaning.

The most obvious source of implied rights and obligations lying outside the written terms of an agreement which may constrain the exercise of management's, or indeed the union's, authority has always been the totality of established ('past') practices which have permeated the details of industrial life and which the express provisions of the agreement have, for the reasons touched on earlier, consciously avoided. It has always been understood that, simply because there are pragmatic reasons and external constraints which may cause the parties not to reduce all the rules and practices which regulate daily life in the workplace to writing, it does not follow as a matter of logical necessity (to say nothing of sound industrial relations standards) that in those areas and on those subjects the rule of law has been suspended. Indeed, quite the contrary. From the outset for many commentators, as a matter of interpretation and as a deduction from the theory of collective bargaining of which it was a part, a collective agreement was understood, "unless a contrary intention [was] manifest, to carry forward for its term the major terms and conditions of employment, not covered by the [written terms of] the agreement, which prevailed when the agreement was executed." . . .

ARBITRATION AS AN EMPLOYMENT STANDARD

It would seem, then that once it is established that the disputes which have traditionally arisen with respect to how management exercises a discretion delegated to it by the agreement are, both in theory and in practice, amenable to resolution by arbitration, the claim in favour of negotiation as the preferred process of social ordering collapses. Once the institutional integrity and practical viability of arbitration to resolve such matters is established, it makes no sense to argue for its displacement by negotiation. Quite the contrary. There is no reason to believe that the bargaining process which regulates labour relationships is so intrinsically superior to all other rulemaking or legislative procedures that it can dispense with an independent criterion to assess the justice of its outcomes. . . .

Indeed, once the institutional legitimacy and capacity of the arbitral process has been established, the more coherent response is surely to recognize how, in acting more in the capacity of labour directors than that of managing directors, arbitrators can contribute towards, if not guarantee, the procedural fairness of the entire collective bargaining system of which they are a part. Whatever benefits the negotiation process might provide, the availability of arbitration would ensure that some minimum condition of procedural justice, like an employment standard of due process, was enjoyed by everyone contributing to the productive wealth of the society. As a minimum standard, an arbitral principle of fairness would enhance rather than derogate from the negotiation process. It would provide a limited but nonetheless effective means of individual involvement in decisions which affect a person's working life on which the negotiation process could build. Like a minimum wage, it would preclude those who are most vulnerable from trading what the rest of society regard as essential conditions of their autonomy. It would ensure that a basic feature of the rule of law, a minimum condition of justice, governed the working lives of everyone in society, and not just those who have the bargaining power to negoti-ate for it.

. . . Realistically, however, the recent decisions of the courts in Ontario and the division of opinion in the arbitral community do not provide cause to be optimistic that these adju-dicative processes have the will to work the law pure. The history of confusion and con-tradiction which distinguishes their collective treatment of the issue suggests that a legislative amendment will be necessary for the liberal theory of arbitration to be fully realized. . . .

✳ ✳ ✳

The ongoing debate on the management rights doctrine, and on whether arbitrators could review management decisions for fairness or reasonableness, prompted the Man-itoba legislature to amend its *Labour Relations Act* to require (in section 80) that collec-tive agreements expressly require the employer to act reasonably, fairly, and in good faith in administering the agreement. In *Metropolitan Stores (MTS) Ltd. v. Manitoba Food and Commercial Workers, Local 832*, [1988] 5 W.W.R. 544, a trial court held that section 80 does not infringe the *Canadian Charter of Rights of Freedoms*, as section 7 of the *Char-ter* does not protect economic or commercial interests.

9:300 DISCIPLINE AND DISCHARGE

Almost all collective agreements provide that an employee is not to be disciplined or discharged except for just cause. Such provisions mark a radical departure from the common law approach to discipline and discharge. The difference is discussed in the *William Scott* case set out below. A "just cause" clause is required by statute in that province, but such a provision typically is included in agreements in jurisdictions where it is not mandated by legislation. Note that the role of the British Columbia Labour Rela-tions Board differs from that of other boards in Canada, insofar as it has statutory authority to review the decisions of arbitrators.

William Scott & Company Ltd. v. Canadian Food and Allied Workers Union, Local P-162, [1977] Can. L.R.B.R. 1 at 1–6 (B.C.L.R.B.)

WEILER, Chair: This is an application under s. 108 of the Labour Code. Section 108(1)(b) entitles the Board to set aside an award on the ground that it is 'inconsistent with the prin-ciples expressed or implied in the Code.' The Labour Code addresses itself directly to the issue of discharge of an employee. First, s. 93(1) requires that:

> Every collective agreement shall contain a provision governing the dismissal or disci-pline of an employee bound by the agreement and that provision, or another provision, shall require that the employer have a just and reasonable cause for the dismissal or dis-cipline of an employee;

Then, in any grievances brought to challenge discharge under that clause of the agreement, the Code confers this statutory authority on the arbitrator:

> 98. For the purposes set out in s. 92, an arbitration board has all the authority necessary to provide a final and conclusive settlement of a dispute arising under the provisions of a collective agreement, and, without limiting the generality of the foregoing, has authority . . .
>
> (d) to determine that a dismissal or discipline is excessive in all the circumstances of the case and substitute such other measure as appears just and equitable.

The wording of each of these provisions of the Code embodies the significant 1975 amendments contained in Bill 84. This explicit legislative attention to the problem of discharge and discipline testifies not only to the serious impact these measures may have on the individual employee, but also to the need to provide adequate, peaceful machinery for reviewing such cases as an antidote to possible industrial unrest in the bargaining unit.

In this, the first s. 108 application in which the Board has analyzed this legislative language, we wish to emphasize the significance of the legal change from discharge as a pure matter of contract law, under the individual contract of employment, to discharge as the subject of legislative policy governing the collective agreement between employer and trade union. Without reviewing the common law of master and servant in any detail, suffice it to say that the contract of employment allowed the employer to dismiss an employee without notice for cause (some relatively serious forms of misconduct which, in the eyes of the law, made the continuance of the employment relationship undesirable). But that particular doctrine of the common law can be appreciated only in light of two other features of the master-servant relationship. First of all, even in the absence of cause on the part of the employee, the employer could unilaterally dismiss an employee with reasonable notice, or with pay in lieu of notice. This meant that employees had no legal expectation of continuity of employment even if their performance was satisfactory and work was available. Secondly, if an employee was guilty of some misconduct at work, the employer had no other form of discipline available. The contract of employment did not entitle the employer to suspend the employee, for example. The presence of these two subsidiary doctrines naturally coloured the common law analysis of what constituted 'cause' for discharge, in two respects: first, the law concentrated on the immediate incident which triggered the discharge, rather than the situation of the individual employee; secondly, gradually the law took the view that certain serious forms of misconduct automatically justified discharge (e.g. insubordination, dishonesty, or disloyalty) on the grounds that these amounted to a fundamental breach of the contract of employment.

The nature of the legal right to discharge an employee has taken on a very different hue in the world of collective bargaining. A classic depiction of that new reality is contained in the award of the arbitrator in the crucial case of *Port Arthur Shipbuilding*:

> . . . the collective agreement does create an entirely new dimension in the employment relationship: it is the immunity of an employee from discharge except for just cause, rather than the former common law rule of virtually unlimited exposure to termination. Whatever may have been the early views of labour arbitrators, it is common knowledge

that over the years a distinctive body of arbitral jurisprudence has developed to give meaning to the concept of 'just cause for discharge' in the context of modern industrial employment. Although the common law may provide guidance, useful analogies, even general principles, the umbilical cord has been severed and the new doctrines of labour arbitrators have begun to lead a life of their own. . . .

No doubt this legal shift is ultimately attributable to such socio-economic factors as the transformation of the personal relationship of 'master and servant' in a small firm into the impersonal administration of a large industrial establishment by a personnel department. But within the collective agreement itself, there were specific, contractual features which required from arbitrators a different conception of discharge.

First of all, under the standard seniority clause an employer no longer retains the unilateral right to terminate a person's employment simply with notice or pay in lieu of notice. Employment under a collective agreement is severed only if the employee quits voluntarily, is discharged for cause, or under certain other defined conditions (e.g. absence without leave for five days; lay-off without recall for one year, and so on). As a result, an employee who has served the probation period secures a form of tenure, a legal expectation of continued employment as long as he gives no specific reason for dismissal. On that foundation, the collective agreement erects a number of significant benefits: seniority claim to jobs in case of lay-off or promotion; service-based entitlement to extended vacation or sick leave; accumulated credits in a pension plan funded by the employer. The point is that the right to continued employment is normally a much firmer and more valuable legal claim under a collective agreement than under the common law individual contract of employment. As a result, discharge of an employee under collective bargaining law, especially of one who has worked under it for some time under the agreement, is a qualitatively more serious and more detrimental event than it would be under the common law. At the same time, the standard collective agreement also provides the employer with a broad management right to discipline its employees. If an individual employee has caused problems in the work place, the employer is not legally limited to the one, irreversible response of discharge. Instead, a broad spectrum of lesser sanctions are available: verbal or written warnings, brief or lengthy suspensions, even demotion on occasion. . . . Because the employer is now entitled to escalate progressively its response to employee misconduct, there is a natural inclination to require that these lesser measures be tried out before the employer takes the ultimate step of dismissing the employee, and thus cutting him off from all of the benefits associated with the job and stemming from the collective agreement.

Recognizing the cumulative impact of these contractual developments flowing from the modern industrial environment, Canadian labour arbitrators did gradually evolve quite a different analysis of discharge grievances. . . .

. . .

Unfortunately, this indigenous arbitral solution was abruptly aborted by the Supreme Court of Canada, when it reversed the Ontario Court of Appeal and the arbitrator in *Port Arthur Shipbuilding Co. v. Arthurs et al*:

The task of the board of arbitration in this case was to determine whether there was proper cause. The findings of fact actually made and the only findings of fact that the board could possibly make establish that there was proper cause. Then there was only one proper legal conclusion, namely, that the employees had given the management proper cause for dismissal. The board, however, did not limit its task in this way. It assumed the function of management. In this case it determined, not whether there had been proper cause, but whether the company, having proper cause, should have exercised the power of dismissal. The board substituted its judgment for the judgment of management and found in favour of suspension.

The sole issue in this case was whether the three employees left their jobs to work for someone else and whether this fact was a proper cause for discipline. *Once the board had found that there were facts justifying discipline, the particular form chosen was not subject to review on arbitration.* [Emphasis added.]

On its face, that passage seemed to suggest that if an arbitrator found some employee misconduct, no matter how trivial, then management had a totally unreviewable discretion to select any form of discipline, no matter how heavy, up to and including the dismissal of a long service employee. Although some arbitrators attempted to mitigate the impact of such a draconian doctrine. . . . Canadian legislatures uniformly considered it necessary to overturn Port Arthur Shipbuilding by statutory reform. Section 98(d) of the Labour Code, the provision under analysis in this case, is the vehicle through which the B.C. Legislature has sought to place on a contemporary, industrial relations footing the law of discharge under a collective agreement.

We have reviewed this historical background to s. 98(d) to emphasize strongly its central thrust. The B.C. Legislature, in common with all other Canadian legislatures, wished to eradicate once and for all the residual traces of the common law of master and servant which had surfaced in *Port Arthur Shipbuilding* and which would prevent an arbitrator coming to grips with the 'real substance' and 'respective merits' of a discharge grievance (s. 92(3)) and thus impair the ability of arbitration to provide a satisfactory resolution of such disputes 'without resort to stoppages of work' (s. 92(2)). For that reason, it is not legally correct for an arbitrator in a discharge case to assume that the common law definition of 'cause' remains unchanged under the Code, subject only to the possibility that an arbitrator might exercise an ill-defined discretion to rescue an employee from the 'normal' legal consequences of discharge and substitute a lesser penalty on 'equitable' grounds. An arbitrator who approaches a discharge grievance with that reluctant state of mind simply is not proceeding in accordance with the principles of the Labour Code.

Instead, arbitrators should pose three distinct questions in the typical discharge grievance. First, has the employee given just and reasonable cause for some form of discipline by the employer? If so, was the employer's decision to dismiss the employee an excessive response in all of the circumstances of the case? Finally, if the arbitrator does consider discharge excessive, what alternative measure should be substituted as just and equitable?

Normally, the first question involves a factual dispute, requiring a judgment from the evidence about whether the employee actually engaged in the conduct which triggered the discharge. But even at this stage of the inquiry there are often serious issues raised about the scope of the employer's authority over an employee, and the kinds of employee conduct which may legitimately be considered grounds for discipline. . . . However, usually it is in connection with the second question — is the misconduct of the employee serious enough to justify the heavy penalty of discharge? — that the arbitrator's evaluation of management's decision must be especially searching:

i) How serious is the immediate offence of the employee which precipitated the discharge (for example, the contrast between theft and absenteeism)?

ii) Was the employee's conduct premeditated, or repetitive; or instead, was it a momentary and emotional aberration, perhaps provoked by someone else (for example, in a fight between two employees)?

iii) Does the employee have a record of long service with the employer in which he proved an able worker and enjoyed a relatively free disciplinary history?

iv) Has the employer attempted earlier and more moderate forms of corrective discipline of this employee which did not prove successful in solving the problem (for example, of persistent lateness or absenteeism)?

v) Is the discharge of this individual employee in accord with the consistent policies of the employer or does it appear to single out this person for arbitrary and harsh treatment (an issue which seems to arise particularly in cases of discipline for wildcat strikes)?

The point of that over-all inquiry is that arbitrators no longer assume that certain conduct taken in the abstract, even quite serious employee offences, are automatically legal cause for discharge. [The author then referred to recent awards holding discharge to be too severe a penalty, in the particular circumstances, for instances of theft, falsification of records and assault on a supervisor.] Instead, it is the statutory responsibility of the arbitrator, having found just cause for some employer action, to probe beneath the surface of the immediate events and reach a broad judgment about whether this employee, especially one with a significant investment of service with that employer, should actually lose his job for the offence in question. Within that framework, the point of the third question is quite different than it might otherwise appear. Suppose that an arbitrator finds that discharge and the penalty imposed by the employer is excessive and must be quashed. It would be both unfair to the employer and harmful to the morale of other employees in the operation to allow the grievor off 'scot-free' simply because the employer over-reacted in the first instance. It is for that reason that arbitrators may exercise the remedial authority to substitute a new penalty, properly tailored to the circumstances of the case, perhaps even utilizing some measures which would not be open to the employer at the first instance under the agreement (e.g. see *Phillips Cables*, . . . in which the arbitration board decided to remove the accumulated seniority of the employee).

REFERENCES

Donald Brown & David Beatty, *Canadian Labour Arbitration*, 3d ed. (Aurora, Ont.: Canada Law Book, 1988) c. 7

9:310 Rules Regulating Employee Conduct

C.U.P.E., Metropolitan Toronto Civic Employees' Union, Local 43 v. Metropolitan Toronto (Municipality of) (1990), 74 O.R. (2d) 239 (C.A.)

TARNOPOLSKY J.A.:

1. THE APPEAL AND THE ISSUES

In its decision, the [arbitration] Board ruled that it was not precluded from considering six grievances challenging a unilaterally imposed employer rule requiring ambulance drivers/attendants to utilize certain emergency warning lights and sirens while responding to all calls designated "emergency." On the evidence before it, the Board found that there was no valid reason or employer interest in implementing the rule, and held further that any discipline imposed upon drivers/attendants for breach of such rule would be unjust.

Upon application for judicial review of the Board's decision by the Municipality of Metropolitan Toronto (hereinafter referred to as the employer), the Divisional Court quashed the Board's decision, holding that the Board's interpretation of the collective agreement was patently unreasonable.

The issues in this appeal are whether the Divisional Court erred in holding that the Board's decision should be quashed on the ground that the Board fell into reviewable error, in holding that:

1) the grievances in the instant case were arbitrable in the absence of actual discipline; and

2) the employer was required to act reasonably in promulgating rules with disciplinary consequences.

2. THE FACTS

The grievances in this case were filed as a result of a change of policy with respect to the use of warning lights and sirens on ambulances owned by the employer. The six grievors are all ambulance drivers or attendants.

Prior to June 10, 1982, ambulance crews followed a four-fold priority system in responding to calls: Codes 1 and 2 for nonemergency transfer calls; Codes 3 and 4 for emergencies. When the call was designated Code 3 by the dispatcher, the driver had discretion over the use of lights and sirens. When the call came as a Code 4, the use of such devices was mandatory.

By memorandum dated June 10, 1982, the employer replaced these designations with a simple "emergency/non-emergency" scheme. When the call was designated "emergency," lights and sirens were to be used on the way to the patient in all circumstances. The grievors believed the change in procedures to be counterproductive, unreasonable and unsafe both for themselves and for the public. Without waiting for disciplinary procedures to be imposed if they violated the new rules, the grievors filed their grievances on June 18, June 19 and August 16, 1982 . . . .

Essentially, the effect of the change, from the point of view of the drivers/attendants was to deprive them of the discretion they had previously enjoyed as to the use of lights and sirens in some, but not all, emergency cases. According to the employer's witnesses at the arbitration hearing, the basic impetus for the change was the employer's growing concern about the dispatchers' ability to categorize an emergency call as Code 3 (discretionary use of lights or sirens) or Code 4 (no discretion permitted). The employer conceded that the removal of discretion was part of a concerted effort to standardize the "system," to ensure that individual actors could not be blamed if the "system" failed. There was no real evidence of any significant problem with response time prior to June 10, 1982, although management's witnesses stated that there had been some public dissatisfaction expressed at the sight of emergency vehicles responding to calls "as if they had all day."

For its part, the Union maintained that the change was both unnecessary and unsafe — ambulance drivers are conscious of the need to respond to all calls as promptly as possible *in the circumstances.* The Union maintained that the driver was the best judge of the circumstances, given his or her training, experience, and familiarity with the responses of other drivers to the presence of emergency vehicles. According to the Union's witnesses, the response to the use of lights and/or sirens was generally one of panic, often resulting in unpredictable behaviour on the part of some motorists. This, in turn, created a situation for the driver which one witness described as being "like driving through a mine field." Only when the call truly merited it did the drivers feel they should take what they considered to be substantial risks with their own safety and the safety of other drivers on the road. The general preference of the drivers called as witnesses was for a "tailored" response system. . . .

. . .

5. THE SCOPE OF JUDICIAL REVIEW

It is conceded by both sides that the Board's decision may be overturned by this court only if (a) the Board wrongly found it had jurisdiction under the collective agreement to consider the grievance or (b) the Board acted within jurisdiction, but in a manner which was "patently unreasonable". . . .

In applying the test to the present case, the following conclusions emerge. First, the Board's decision is subject to review if the Board erroneously construed the collective agreement as confirming power on it to hear a disciplinary grievance in the circumstances of the case, i.e., prior to any discipline being imposed. Second, the application for judicial review should succeed if the Board, in holding that the rule was unreasonable, interpreted the collective agreement in a patently unreasonable manner.

6. JURISDICTION TO HEAR THE GRIEVANCE AND THE "OBEY NOW, GRIEVE LATER" RULE

. . .

While Steele J. found no legal basis for the adoption of the "obey now, grieve later" rule as it was applied by the Board in the present appeal, in *Wardair Canada Inc. v. C.A.F.A.A.* . . .

a different panel of the Divisional Court seems to have found the argument based on the rule to be quite plausible. *Wardair* was released two months after the judgment under appeal. At issue was whether the arbitrator had exceeded his jurisdiction by hearing a grievance filed subsequent to the grievor's compliance with a directive forbidding males to wear earrings. The arbitrator based his ruling that he had jurisdiction on three arguments. The first of these was that by placing a letter in the grievor's file, instructing him to comply with the directive, the employer had implicitly disciplined him. The second was the "obey now, grieve later" rule. The third basis for jurisdiction was the principle of reasonable contract administration, about which I will say more later. With respect to the "obey now, grieve later" argument, Craig J. stated . . . :

> The rule "obey now and grieve later" is one that makes for or encourages peace in the work place and harmonious relations between employers and employees. In my opinion the arbitrator did not err in applying this rule in the same way as though discipline had been administered to the grievor for insubordination. Upon compliance with its order Wardair cannot be heard to say that there is no right to grieve. . . .

Although Craig J. cites no particular authority for his statement in *Wardair, supra*, the "obey now, grieve later" rule has long been a part of our labour law regime. The nature of and rationale behind the rule is summarized by Donald J.M. Brown and David M. Beatty, in *Canadian Labour Arbitration* . . . :

> One of the most basic and widely accepted rules of arbitral jurisprudence holds that employees who dispute the propriety of their employer's orders must . . . comply with those orders and only subsequently, through the grievance procedure, challenge their validity.
>
> The rationale for this general principle is said to lie in the employer's need to be able to direct and control the productive process of his operations, to ensure that they continue uninterrupted and unimpeded even when controversy may arise, and in its concomitant authority to maintain such discipline as may be required to ensure the efficient operation of the plant. . . .

The majority of the Board justified its use of the "obey now, grieve later" rule, by saying that it would be "hypocritical, and transparently so, to deny employees the promise of the rule having exposed them to its command." In other words, if the purpose of the rule is to avoid insubordination and anarchy in the workplace, the obvious trade-off is that employees in a unionized environment will have the right to grieve rules, the breach of which would likely have led to discipline, even as they continue to obey them.

Would avoiding this directive give rise to discipline? Counsel for the employer did not strongly argue that it would not, although he did argue strenuously that the directive was within the exclusive contractual competence of the employer until and unless a driver/attendant was actually disciplined for not using lights or sirens in responding to an emergency call. The fact is that, subsequent to the filing of the original grievances, some employees were disciplined for failure to obey the directive. Even had this not occurred, the likelihood is that management would have taken a dim view of the breach of a policy going to the heart of its "system-oriented" approach. It is not idle speculation to presume that discipline, up to and including dismissal for repeated infractions, would have been imposed.

Furthermore, if discipline were imposed, it likely would have been grieved. Once the grievance reached the stage of arbitration, the arbitrator would have been compelled by Article 3.01(ii) of the collective agreement to determine if the "employee has been discharged or disciplined without reasonable cause." The Board stated that this task would require it, *inter alia*, to examine the directive for reasonableness. This point will be examined later. Suffice it to say that *this* Board, at least, would have embarked on virtually the same inquiry if the grievance had arisen from actual discipline as it embarked on to deal with "discipline in the abstract." The only major difference, of course, is that, if the grievors had been insubordinate, the mere fact of their insubordination might have been held against them. . . .

The Divisional Court found that the Board had been patently unreasonable in hearing a grievance based on "discipline in the abstract." However, on the strength of the foregoing, it seems clear that under an "obey now, grieve later" rule, an arbitrator is practically *required* to take jurisdiction to hear a grievance against a directive, at least in a case where a breach is likely to constitute insubordination and subject the employee to disciplinary action. In my respectful opinion the Board, in taking jurisdiction, acted in accordance with both the letter and spirit of the collective agreement; its actions were neither patently unreasonable nor (using the more interventionist test) wrong in law. To decide otherwise would be to invite anarchy in the workplace. . . .

Counsel for the employer strongly disputed the Board's preliminary ruling that it could infer from the collective agreement that management had a duty to act "reasonably," even when exercising "its uncontrolled discretion" under Article 3.01(iii) "generally to manage . . . and without restricting the generality of the foregoing, to select, install and require the operation of any equipment, plant and machinery". . . .

Article 3.02 of the collective agreement in the present appeal *specifically obliges* the employer to exercise its discretion in Article 3.01 in a manner not "inconsistent with the provisions of this agreement." Accordingly, the Board held as follows:

> Management cannot use its powers under the management rights clause to issue directives, rules, or orders which undermine the reasonable cause provision. Even in the absence of Article 3.02 it is a fundamental principle of interpretation that the collective agreement ought to be read as a whole, and that one provision ought not to be read in a way which negates another. The presence of Article 3.02 . . . puts the point beyond doubt. The Employer cannot, by exercising its management functions, issue unreasonable rules and then discipline employees for failure to follow them. Such discipline would simply be without reasonable cause. To permit such action would be to invite subversion of the reasonable cause clause.

The major opposing argument is, of course, based on *Re Metropolitan Police, supra.* There, the collective agreement was substantially the same as that in the present appeal. Addressing the question of whether the collective agreement imposed a duty to act reasonably in awarding overtime, Houlden J.A. stated . . . :

Having regard to the nature of the agreement, and to its provisions, we see no necessity in this case to imply a term that the management rights clause will be applied fairly and without discrimination. If such a term were to be implied, it would mean that every decision of management made under the exclusive authority of the management rights clause would be liable to challenge on the grounds that it was exercised unfairly or discriminatively. In our opinion, this would be contrary to the spirit and intent of the collective agreement.

It is worth noting, however, that just before arriving at this conclusion, Houlden J.A. made allowance for the case in which powers conferred on management by a management rights clause "are . . . circumscribed by express provisions of the collective agreement." It would seem that this was exactly the loophole used by this court in *Re Council of Printing Industries, supra*, to find a duty to act reasonably. The arbitrator's use of Article 3.02 and of the "reasonable cause for discipline" provision in Article 3.01(ii) is of a similar character. In neither of these cases was the provision relied on *entirely* explicit. However, it does not seem patently unreasonable to view the collective agreement in a holistic manner, where even management rights may be circumscribed in order to avoid negating or unduly limiting the scope of other provisions.

As well, neither *Re Metropolitan Police, supra*, nor *Re Council of Printing Industries, supra*, was a case involving a rule with disciplinary consequences. Several arbitrators have stated that all company rules with disciplinary consequence must be reasonable. Indeed, Brown and Beatty, *Canadian Labour Arbitration*, . . . assert that the principle limiting the power to make rules, even where there is a management rights clause, is "universally accepted among arbitrators". . . .

The final Union argument that should be noted is based on a notion of reasonable contract administration. The Union relies on the decision of this court in *Greenberg v. Meffert*. . . . This was a case involving a contract of employment between a real estate agent and her employer. The contract provided the employer with the "sole discretion" to disburse commissions to the agent in the event her employment was terminated. Speaking on behalf of the court, Robins J.A. held that the employer's discretion had to be exercised reasonably, honestly, and in good faith. He stated . . . that:

> . . . the nature of this contract and the subject-matter of the discretion are such that the company's decision should be construed as being controlled by objective standards. . . .
>
> In contracts in which the matter to be decided or approved is not readily susceptible of objective measurement? — matters involving taste, sensibility, personal compatibility or judgment of the party for whose benefit the authority was given — such provisions are more likely construed as imposing only a subjective standard. On the other hand, in contracts relating to such matters as operative fitness, structural completion, mechanical utility or marketability, these provisions are generally construed as imposing an objective standard of reasonableness. . . .
>
> In the absence of explicit language or a clear indication from the tenor of the contract or the nature of the subject-matter, the tendency of the cases is to require the discretion or the dissatisfaction to be reasonable. . . .

Like the analogy with respect to standing, it is difficult to apply this case in the context of collective bargaining. Nonetheless, it is true that a collective agreement is an intricate contract, which attempts to reflect the outcome of bargaining on a myriad of issues. It is also true that parties intent on reaching a settlement do not always have the time, the incentive, or the resources to consider the full implications of each and every phrase. There is, therefore, a place for some creativity, some recourse to arbitral principles, and some overall notion of reasonableness. See, for example, David M. Beatty, "The Role of the Arbitrator: A Liberal Version". . . . The presence of an implied principle or term of reasonable contract administration was also acknowledged by Craig J. in *Wardair, supra*. . . .

There is nothing in the Board's findings of fact which could be depicted as patently unreasonable; they were scarcely challenged by the dissenting Board member. Moreover, in imposing a duty on the employer to exercise its discretion to make rules with disciplinary consequences in a reasonable fashion, the Board gave the collective agreement an interpretation that it reasonably and logically could bear. . . .

9:320 Disciplinary Penalties

Re Cook and Ontario (Ministry of Labour) (1979), 22 L.A.C. (2d) 1 at 3–6 (Crown Employees' Grievance Settlement Board)

[Cook, a construction safety worker employed by the Ministry of Labour, had been discharged for submitting fifty-five fraudulent inspection reports and for claiming travelling expenses for fictitious visits to construction sites. Nevertheless, he asked that the penalty be reduced because his misconduct was attributable to alcoholism and he had since made efforts to control his problem.]

SWINTON, Vice Chair: . . . This Board has the power to reduce a disciplinary penalty pursuant to s. 18(3) of the Crown Employees Collective Bargaining Act, 1972 (Ont.), c. 67. That section reads:

> 18(3) Where the Grievance Settlement Board determines that a disciplinary penalty or dismissal is excessive, it may substitute such other penalty for the discipline or dismissal as it considers just and reasonable in all the circumstances.

In this particular case, the fraudulent conduct in which Mr. Cook engaged cannot be condoned. The construction safety officer plays an important monitoring and enforcement role under the Construction Safety Act, 1973 and the fraudulent actions of the grievor must be regarded as just cause for dismissal. Nevertheless, in the particular circumstances of this case, it is the opinion of the Board that the penalty of discharge is excessive and a lesser penalty should be substituted pursuant to s. 18(3).

In coming to this conclusion, the Board is not saying that alcoholism provides an excuse for any misconduct which can be related to an employee's alcoholism. In this case, the Board is not in any way condoning what Mr. Cook did and a lengthy period of suspension through reinstatement without back pay reflects that conclusion. However, we are not dealing here with an offence against the criminal law, in which drunkenness short of automatism provides no excuse for an offence, although counsel for the employer drew an analogy to the criminal law. In the employment setting, we must balance both employer and employee interests in discipline cases in an effort to determine whether the employee can benefit from corrective discipline and continue to provide the employer with good service. Discharge can have serious repercussions for any employee for the blemish on his record will seriously jeopardize future job prospects. In the case of an employee with alcohol problems it can have added personal significance in the added anxiety caused which can undermine chances at rehabilitation. Therefore, if the employee can solve his alcohol problem, it is advantageous to keep him in the workplace. Of course, there are limits to the employer's responsibility to maintain alcoholic employees and at some point the employer must take steps to protect himself, other employees and those whom they serve (here, the public), from the costs and effects of retaining this type of employee.

In his study, *Grievance Arbitration of Discharge Cases*, George Adams has noted that there is a high rate of reinstatement by arbitrators in alcohol-related offences, yet these offences have the least successful reinstatement experience, with subsequent discharge in 50 percent of the cases and recurring discipline in 20 percent. . . . This is in part attributable to the failure of arbitrators to concern themselves with the rehabilitation of the alcoholic employee and to impose conditions on reinstatement that both recognize alcoholism as an illness and provide for its treatment. . . . See also B.J. Hill, 'Alcoholism and the World of Work' in National Academy of Arbitrators, Arbitration – 1975. . . .

In this particular case, the question is whether Mr. Cook's alcohol problem can be resolved and whether he can fulfil his job duties satisfactorily. After hearing the evidence, the Board feels that both results are possible in Mr. Cook's case. He has made a sincere effort at rehabilitation over the last few months, and the prognosis for success from experts such as Father Charbonneau and Dr. Yaworsky is encouraging. Father Charbonneau testified that the Brentwood Clinic had had an 80 to 85% success rate with clients in the grievor's circumstances, that is, married men with children. He feels that the grievor is ready to return to work. Mr. Cook has admitted his problem, which is a first step toward rehabilitation of alcoholics. He appeared to the Board to be sincere in his desire to try to end his dependency. His wife is very supportive and she testified as to the positive effects of the treatment at Brentwood.

Mr. Cook had a good record while with the Ministry of Labour. The two men who had supervised him in his years in the Windsor office, Mr. Smith and Mr. Greenlaw, both expressed their satisfaction with his work performance, and his disciplinary record was clear. According to Dr. Yaworsky and the grievor, his misconduct in falsifying the inspection records was directly attributable to his alcoholism for he needed to carve out time for his drinking. It would seem that, given a second chance, and with his present rehabilitation efforts, Mr. Cook will be able to resume working at the previous satisfactory level of performance now that his alcohol problem is under control.

Clearly, it is important to take steps to ensure that the present progress towards rehabilitation continues. The grievor has shown that he needs the support of a programme such as Brentwood to structure his efforts at rehabilitation, for his earlier attempts to end his dependency on his own have failed. Therefore, while the Board will order that the grievor be reinstated, it is on the condition that he continue the Brentwood programme for at least one year or notify his supervisors of any change in his programme. In addition, he must enter the Ontario Government's Program on Alcoholism.

These formal conditions will only provide partial solutions to rehabilitation. The grievor will also need the support and understanding of his supervisor and co-workers. It would be beneficial for Mr. Cook if his supervisor could be involved in his continuing rehabilitation. This might take the form of his supervisor attending educational orientation sessions so that he could better understand and assist Mr. Cook in his adjustments to recovery. We note that supervisor training is part of the policy contained in the Government programme on alcoholism. Perhaps as well, the employer could give Mr. Cook access to an internal resource professional counsellor whom he could contact as necessary. Of course, the final responsibility for resolving the alcohol dependency problem must rest with Mr. Cook himself.

Therefore, the Board will allow the grievance pursuant to s. 18(3) of the Crown Employees Collective Bargaining Act, 1972, and order that Mr. Cook be reinstated to his position as construction safety officer, without back pay and accrual of service credits, and subject to the conditions that he enter the Government programme on alcoholism and continue the Brentwood programme for at least one year or advise his employer of any change in that programme. His performance should be monitored during this year and if deterioration is evidenced as a result of alcoholism then his continued employment should be reviewed.

* * *

By reinstating the grievor without backpay, the above award effectively substituted for discharge the lesser penalty of an unpaid suspension as long as the interval between dismissal and reinstatement. Is this an appropriate outcome, given the nature of the grievor's misconduct and the other relevant circumstances?

One of the factors that led the arbitrator in the above case to order reinstatement was the grievor's success in overcoming his alcohol problems after the termination. The Supreme Court of Canada has more recently considered whether arbitrators should consider evidence of what happens after an employee had been fired. In *Compagnie Minière Quebec Cartier v. Quebec (Grievances Arbitrator)*, [1995] 2 S.C.R. 1095, the company had dismissed the grievor because he had repeatedly missed work, in part because of serious problems with alcohol. On earlier occasions, the employer had reduced disciplinary penalties in exchange for his promises to undergo alcohol rehabilitation treatment. He had not kept those promises. After the dismissal giving rise to the grievance, the grievor underwent a successful course of treatment for alcoholism. The arbitrator held that the company had been justified in dismissing him on the facts that existed at the time of dismissal, but that reinstatement should be oredered in light of his subsequent successful treatment. The Supreme Court of Canada held that the arbitrator had exceeded his jurisdiction by relying on "subsequent-event" evidence as grounds for reinstatement. L'Heureux-Dubé J. wrote, at pp. 1101–2:

> This brings me to the question I raised earlier regarding whether an arbitrator can consider subsequent-event evidence in ruling on a grievance concerning the dismissal by the

Company of an employee. *In my view, an arbitrator can rely on such evidence, but only where it is relevant to the issue before him. In other words, such evidence will only be admissible if it helps to shed light on the reasonableness and appropriateness of the dismissal under review at the time that it was implemented.* Accordingly, once an arbitrator concludes that a decision by the Company to dismiss an employee was justified at the time that it was made, he cannot then annul the dismissal on the sole ground that subsequent events render such an annulment, in the opinion of the arbitrator, fair and equitable. In these circumstances, an arbitrator would be exceeding his jurisdiction if he relied on subsequent-event evidence as grounds for annulling the dismissal. To hold otherwise would be to accept that the result of a grievance concerning the dismissal of an employee could vary depending on when it is filed and the time lag between the initial filing and the final hearing by the arbitrator. Furthermore, it would lead to the absurd conclusion that a decision by the Company to dismiss an alcoholic employee could be overturned whenever that employee, as a result of the shock of being dismissed, decides to rehabilitate himself, even if such rehabilitation would never have occurred absent the decision to dismiss the employee. (Emphasis added.)

The Supreme Court of Canada made no mention of section 100.12(f) of the *Quebec Labour Code*, which was enacted in response to the Court's earlier decision in *Port Arthur Shipbuilding*. That provision empowers an arbitrator in a discipline case to "confirm, amend or set aside the decision of the employer and . . . substitute therefor the decision he deems fair and reasonable, *taking into account all of the circumstances concerning the matter*" (emphasis added). Is the Supreme Court's ruling consistent with this legislation?

According to the Court, "subsequent-event evidence" may be considered by an arbitrator when it "helps to shed light on the reasonableness and appropriateness of the dismissal under review at the time that it was implemented." Applying this test in *Toronto (City) Board of Education v. O.S.S.T.F., District 15*, [1997] 1 S.C.R. 487, the Court quashed the decision of an arbitrator who excluded post-discharge evidence. The case revolved around three letters written by the grievor (a teacher) to his employer (a school board). The first letter contained what could be perceived as veiled threats to the lives of the employer's Director of Education and others. It was written during the hearing of a complaint the grievor had filed with the Ontario Human Rights Commission alleging that the employer systemically discriminated against persons of South-Asian origin. The second letter was more explicitly threatening. The grievor was dismissed as a result of those two letters. After the grievance was filed, he wrote the third letter. It was less abusive and threatening than the first two but, according to the Court (at pp. 519 and 520), it exhibited "the same extreme views, hyperbolic comparisons and total lack of judgment." Empowered by the collective agreement to "modify the penalty" imposed by the employer, a majority of the arbitration board determined that the grievor should be reinstated subject to stringent monitoring and summary dismissal if the previous conduct was repeated. The arbitration award did not take into account the third letter written after the dismissal. In quashing the award, Cory J. (for the Supreme Court of Canada) wrote, at p. 519:

It is true that the third letter is, to some extent, "subsequent-event evidence" since it was written after the dismissal of [the grievor]. However it has been decided that such evidence can properly be considered "if it helps to shed light on the reasonableness and appropriateness of the dismissal": *Compagnie Miniere Quebec Cartier v. Quebec (Grievances Arbitrator).* . . . In this case, it would not only have been reasonable for the arbitrators to consider the third letter, it was a serious error for them not to do so.

Was the Court consistent in requiring the use of post-discharge evidence in *Toronto (City) Board of Education*, after having rejected its use in the *Quebec Cartier* case?

Fourteen empirical studies of discharge cases, five using Canadian data, are summarized by Allen Ponak, "Discharge Arbitration and Reinstatement: An Industrial Relations Perspective," [1992] 2 *Labour Arbitration Yearbook* 31. Ponak noted that research findings on arbitral use of reinstatement have been remarkably consistent across time and space. He said, at p. 33:

> Discharge is upheld slightly less than one-half of the time, meaning that more than half of all grievors are reinstated. Approximately one out of five grievors receives a complete reinstatement [without any lesser penalty]. More often, however, if discharge is not upheld some grounds for discipline are found and approximately one of three grievors is reinstated with suspension substituted for termination.

As to the work experience of reinstated grievors, Ponak provided a capsule summary of the research results, at p. 38:

> [T]hose employees who return to work usually prove to be productive workers. As rated by their employers, well over half of reinstated grievors are deemed to perform satisfactorily or better. Only a very small proproportion of returning employees are subsequently terminated for cause.

A more detailed discussion of the aftermath of reinstatement is found in this earlier study of Ontario discharge cases.

George W. Adams, *Grievance Arbitration of Discharge Cases: A Study of the Concepts of Industrial Discipline and Their Results* (Kingston: Industrial Relations Centre, Queen's University, 1978) at 66, 86

> A summary of results pertaining to employee rehabilitation can be reported thusly. Of the 128 employees who returned to work with lesser discipline, 37.5 percent experienced some form of subsequent discipline including discharge, and 24.2 percent of the 128 employees were involved in a recurrence [of the same offence]. If a successful reinstatement is to be measured by the absence of any subsequent discipline, the collective success rate of the arbitration tribunals involved in this study is in the order of 63 percent. This 'rate of success' is comparable to earlier studies and, predictably, much at odds with the poor results of rehabilitation in the criminal law field. . . . Therefore, while the correction and rehabilitation justifications for punishment in the criminal law field may be wan-

ing this is not so in industrial relations. Indeed, as a general matter, these results appear to vindicate the corrective approach to discipline forged by arbitration tribunals. . . .

Forty-eight percent of all employers thought that lesser penalty reinstatements were successful from the viewpoint of their relationship with the reinstated employee. Fifty-one percent were satisfied with the employee's performance in terms of productivity, attendance and willingness to cooperate and 65 percent thought that the employee had progressed normally in terms of promotion, merit increases and added responsibility. . . . Looking at the impact of reinstatement on the grievor's fellow employees, 55 percent of the responding employers believed that reinstatement had not adversely affected their relationship with other employees. Sixty-eight percent of the employers advised that workplace morale had not been harmed and 78 percent said that there had been no increase in the conduct for which the grievor was discharged. Eighty-six percent of the employers also said that the grievor's relationship with his supervisor was not adversely affected and 75 percent reported that the supervisor's authority over other employees was not undermined.

This statistical information goes to establish that the reinstatement decisions of arbitrators have not had an adverse impact on the discipline of the workplace. Workplace morale has gone largely unaffected and a qualitative assessment of employee performance reveals that both the grievors and their fellow employees have responded well to disciplinary action. All of these findings are consistent with those of earlier studies and provide justification for extending the corrective discipline approach.

[Reprinted by permission.]

9:400 CONTRACT INTERPRETATION

Disputes about the precise meaning of a collective agreement are commonplace. The wording of a typical agreement does not provide an unambiguous answer to many questions that arise in the workplace. Consider why most agreements are incomplete in this sense.

Paul Weiler, *Reconcilable Differences: New Directions in Canadian Labour Law* (Toronto, Ont: Carswell, 1980) at 92–93, 98

The collective agreement is, if not a unique, certainly an unusual kind of contract. It is vastly different from the individual sales transaction or employment engagement upon which the common law judiciary had cut its teeth in the contract arena. Modern collective agreements cover hundreds, even thousands of employees, not just in single locations or enterprises, but often across an entire industry. The parties deal searchingly with the entire relationship of employer and employee: not just with wages, but also with premium pay, holidays, vacations, leaves of absence, health and welfare plans, pension benefits, seniority rights and layoffs, promotions or transfers, protection from discharge, union security, occupational health and safety, technological change, and much more. And the parties must try to project into the future their views about what should be done about each one of these issues for contract periods which can last three years or even longer. To say the least, the task of interpreting that kind of agreement is a difficult and delicate one.

Rarely is the answer to a hotly contested dispute found clearly expressed within the four corners of the written document . . . .

There are inevitable limits in the detail which the negotiators can draft and agree to. They are often under heavy pressure to reach a settlement at the eleventh hour to avoid a strike. The focus of their attention is on the amount of the wage increase, the economic impact of improvements and fringe benefits, the provision of greater job security for the workers, and so on. Each of the items could present any number of background issues about who is eligible, and for exactly what. For example, the memorandum of settlement may provide for an across-the-board percentage wage increase which is "retroactive to the expiry date of the last agreement." Does that increase apply to employees in the unit who may have worked a couple of months after the end of the previous contract, but whose employment was terminated shortly before this settlement was actually reached? The parties may have agreed to vacation pay of 6% of an employee's yearly "earnings." Does one include in earnings not just the regular hourly wages received, but also overtime and shift premiums, statutory holiday pay, sickness or accident indemnity, or the previous year's vacation pay itself? These are examples of the monetary provisions in the agreement which normally are phrased with some precision. The fundamental job security clauses are usually expressed as broad standards: "no employee shall be discharged or disciplined except for "just cause"; "preference in promotion (or layoff) will be given to the senior employee with the qualifications and ability to perform the job." Arbitration cases are replete with issues of principle which have arisen in the application of these standard discharge or seniority provisions. As to the literally tens of thousands of such penumbral issues which might arise in the operation of typical clauses in a sophisticated collective agreement, the negotiators for the parties have neither the foresight, nor the time, nor the inclination to canvass more than a handful of them and to try to reach mutual agreement about what they want done.

[Reprinted by permission.[

* * **

When a dispute over one of these "penumbral issues" arises, how should it be resolved? Should the arbitrator seek to find a mutual understanding between the employer and union who are parties to the collective agreement being interpreted, perhaps in what transpired between them when negotiating the agreement — "negotiation history" — or in the way the now contested issue was previously handled in the administration of the agreement — "past practice"?

9:410 Negotiation History

Re Noranda Metal Industries Ltd., Fergus Division v. International Brotherhood of Electrical Workers (1983), 44 O.R. (2d) 529 at 530–38 (Ont. C.A.)

DUBIN J.A.: Pursuant to the terms of a collective agreement, dated September 1, 1981, effective to August 31, 1983, an arbitrator was appointed to resolve a grievance brought by the union. The arbitrator was called upon to interpret art. 3.02 of the agreement which provided as follows:

3.02. *During negotiations it was agreed* that the company has the right to subcontract, but in no case shall each subcontracting result in bargaining unit employees being laid off or losing their employment *or being likewise affected.* (Emphasis added.)

The union claimed that the company had violated that clause by subcontracting work to complete the replacement of an acid-waste line at its Fergus plant without offering those employees within the bargaining unit, qualified to do the work, an opportunity of performing that work on a voluntary basis and at overtime rates. Initially the work was performed by skilled tradesmen within the bargaining unit during normal working hours as part of the regularly scheduled non-overtime work of such tradesmen.

In determining whether the company had violated the clause, the arbitrator admitted and considered evidence as to what had transpired during negotiations and evidence of past practices as an aid in interpreting the meaning to be given to the article.

Briefly, the evidence relied upon was to the effect that the 'or being likewise affected' language of the article was expressly represented by the company to meet the concern expressed by the union, during negotiations, that union members could be denied overtime as a result of contracting out. As a result, the union withdrew a request to rephrase the article. The arbitrator relied upon the extrinsic evidence in holding that the company had violated the article. In arriving at his award, the learned arbitrator stated as follows:

. . .

> *Upon due consideration of the evidence and argument of the parties, it is my conclusion that the 'or being likewise affected' language of art. 3.02 was intended to protect bargaining unit employees from losing overtime hours as a result of contracting out by the company. . . .*

The main evidence for the union regarding what was included within the scope of the 'or being likewise affected' language of art. 3.02, was given by Mr. A.W. Schaefer, the business manager of the local union. Mr. Schaefer testified that he was present at the negotiation of art. 3.02 into the collective agreement and that the article has remained the same since that time. In this regard, Mr. Schaefer testified that the first time that art. 3.02 appeared in the collective agreement was in the 1978 agreement. It was suggested by the company during 1977 negotiations leading to that agreement. He stated that it was submitted by the company to accommodate concerns expressed by the union regarding the possibility of maintenance people being denied opportunities to work as a result of contracting out by the company. The language of art. 3.02, he testified, was suggested by the company to cover this situation.

Mr. Schaefer further testified that the 'or being likewise affected' language of the article was expressly represented by the company to cover off an express concern of the union during those negotiations that union members could be denied overtime as a result of contracting out. He was firm in his testimony that the company made that specific representation to him. This testimony was unshaken on cross-examination.

Further, Mr. Schaefer testified that this interpretation of the 'or likewise affected' language was confirmed to him by the company during a union-management meeting sometime in 1978. According to his testimony, this meeting was called because the plant administration had changed, and there were indications to the union that line supervision on the floor did not understand the import of art. 3.02 in this regard. He recalled that in addition to himself at this meeting, there were Frank Wood, the then chairman of the union committee, and the chief steward of the union. He testified that he could not recall the names of management personnel at that meeting because 'the management changes so often' that it is difficult for him to recall the precise persons to whom he spoke after the passage of so much time. . . .

The sole witness for the company was Mr. Ken Faulconbridge, the personnel manager at the Fergus plant for the past 13 years. Mr. Faulconbridge testified that it was never apparent to him that in negotiations the company gave up the right to contract out as suggested by the union. He further testified that in the early stages of the current round of negotiations, the union proposed an amendment to art. 3.02 which specifically required the company to give work to bargaining unit employees on an overtime basis rather than to contract it out. He testified that the company rejected this more specific language because it would affect the efficiency with which the company could run its operation. . . .

Both Mr. Schaefer and Mr. Faulconbridge agreed in their testimony that in response to these objections the union withdrew their proposed amendment at an early stage in negotiations. Mr. Schaefer testified that the union did so because the more specific language did not appear to be necessary in the light of assurances from management representation that they already had the coverage they desired. He further explained that the only reason that the union had proposed the more specific language in the first place was that, again, new line supervision on the plant floor did not appear to be conversant with the prior understanding of the parties regarding the overall effect of the article. . . .

Upon due consideration of the foregoing arguments, I conclude that the 'or being likewise affected' language of art. 3.02 was intended, within reasonable bounds, to require the company to offer overtime to a member of the bargaining unit in the relevant skill group prior to engaging in contracting out. I accept the evidence of Mr. Schaefer regarding the existence of the understandings that, he testified, occurred during the negotiations and were confirmed on an informal basis in the meeting with management during the term of the 1978 collective agreement. Mr. Schaefer gave his testimony in a forthright and non-evasive manner. His evidence was unshaken on cross-examination. His inability to recall the identities of management personnel seemed to be understandable in light of the fact, which appeared to be acknowledged by all at the hearing, that there had been considerable turnover among management personnel at the Fergus plant. I do not attach considerable significance to Mr. Schaefer's inability to produce notes taken during the relevant negotiations, particularly in the light of the fact that the uncontradicted testimony of Mr. Johnson regarding the offering of overtime prior to contracting out confirmed in substantial respect Mr. Schaefer's testimony. . . .

(Emphasis added.)

. . .

With respect, I think the majority of the Divisional Court erred in quashing the award of the arbitrator in this case. The arbitrator was called upon to interpret the article in issue in light of two competing submissions as to its meaning. The company contended that the clause related only to job security and, therefore, the phrase 'or being likewise affected' had to be construed in that light. The union contended that the article was to preserve income-producing opportunities for members of the bargaining unit and thus the term 'or being likewise affected' was designed to protect the employees from any loss of their income-producing opportunities by contracting out work. In determining the true intention of the parties as expressed by the language of the article, the arbitrator favoured the latter interpretation.

The majority of the Divisional Court concluded that the clause was unambiguous and thus extrinsic evidence could not be resorted to aid in its interpretation. Mr. Justice White was of the contrary view. It is apparent from the reasons of the arbitrator that he felt that both the contention of the company and of the union were plausible interpretations and thus the clause was ambiguous. It is difficult to conclude that he made a jurisdictional error in so concluding in light of the division of opinion of the Divisional Court on this very issue. I agree with Mr. Justice White that the clause was patently ambiguous and the arbitrator was entitled to resort to extrinsic evidence to assist him in ascertaining the true intentions of the parties, but, in any event, he was entitled to resort to extrinsic evidence to determine whether there was any latent ambiguity, or in applying it to the facts. . . .

If the arbitrator in this case had refused to admit the extrinsic evidence and the article in question had been interpreted in the manner contended for by the company, there would have been a gross injustice. It is apparent that during negotiations the union was concerned that new management personnel were unfamiliar with the intent of the section and were dissuaded from seeking clarification on the express representation of the clause, as worded, met their concern and did protect their income-producing opportunities.

* * *

Did the arbitrator's use of negotiation history in this case produce a more acceptable outcome than would otherwise have resulted?

9:420 Past Practice

In *Noranda Metal Industries*, excerpted immediately above, the arbitrator made passing mention of the employer's practice of contracting out work only if bargaining employees declined to do it on overtime. The following award considers when "past practice" should be used to resolve an ambiguity in a collective agreement.

International Association of Machinists v. John Bertram & Sons Co. (1967), 18 L.A.C. 362 at 367–68

WEILER: If a provision in an agreement, as applied to a labour relations problem, is ambiguous in its requirements, the arbitrator may utilize the conduct of the parties as an aid to clarifying the ambiguity. The theory requires that there be conduct of either one of the parties, which explicitly involves the interpretation of the agreement according to one meaning, and that this conduct (and, inferentially, this interpretation) be acquiesced in by the other party. If these facts obtain, the arbitrator is justified in attributing this particular meaning to the ambiguous provision. The principal reason for this is that the best evidence of the meaning most consistent with the agreement is that mutually accepted by the parties. Such a doctrine, while useful, should be quite carefully employed. Indiscriminate recourse to past practice has been said to rigidify industrial relations at the plant level, or in the lower reaches of the grievance process. It does so by forcing higher management or union officials to prohibit (without their clearance) the settling of grievances in a sensible fashion, and a spirit of mutual accommodation, for fear of setting precedents which may plague either side in unforeseen ways in future arbitration decisions. A party should not be forced unnecessarily to run the risk of losing by its conduct its opportunity to have a neutral interpretation of the terms of the agreement which it bargained for.

Hence it would seem preferable to place strict limitations on the use of past practice. . . . I would suggest that there should be (1) no clear preponderance in favour of one meaning, stemming from the words and structure of the agreement as seen in their labour relations context; (2) conduct by one party which unambiguously is based on one meaning attributed to the relevant provision; (3) acquiescence in the conduct which is either quite clearly expressed or which can be inferred from the continuance of the practice for a long period without objection; (4) evidence that members of the union or management hierarchy who have some real responsibility for the meaning of the agreement have acquiesced in the practice.

9:500 EQUITABLE AND REMEDIAL AUTHORITY OF THE ARBITRATOR

9:510 Promissory Estoppel in Arbitration

Canadian National Railway Co. v. Beatty (1981), 34 O.R. (2d) 385 at 386–94 (H.C.)

OSLER J.: This was an application for judicial review of the award of David M. Beatty, dated February 12, 1981, concerning the extent of the designated waiting period of the weekly indemnity benefits plan established pursuant to art. 30 of a collective agreement between the applicants and the respondent union.

Canadian Pacific Limited (Communications Department) made an agreement with Canadian Telecommunications Union, having effect from January 1, 1979 to December 31, 1981. It is common ground that a partnership agreement was reached between that company and Canadian National Railway Company providing that business should be carried on by those companies jointly as CNCP Telecommunications. The employees of Canadian Pacific, referred to throughout as CPT, became employees of the partnership referred to throughout as CNCP. CPT has, at all relevant times, been party to broadly based railway-industry-wide collective bargaining involving, among others, Canadian Pacific Limited (formerly Canadian Pacific Railway Company), Canadian National Railways and approximately 20 unions, including the respondent union. The end result of the bargaining process was a settlement referred to as a master agreement which is the basis for revisions, as required, to the various collective agreements between the signatories.

The master agreement dated May 16, 1956, introduced provisions for the establishment of a supplemental agreement respecting health and welfare, and a master agreement dated March 14, 1967, fundamentally revised that agreement so as to provide that:

> . . . payment of weekly indemnity benefits on account of sickness to provide for such weekly indemnity benefit payments to commence on the fourth day of absence account sickness instead of the eighth day as at present . . .

A further amendment to the master agreement was made December 11, 1974, providing that sick benefit payments to eligible employees would be made:

> . . . from the first day in case of accidental injury; from the first day of sickness if hospitalized, and from the fourth day in other cases of sickness.

As a result of such master agreements, the supplemental agreement between the parties, to which the applicant became a party by virtue of the successor provisions of the *Canada Labour Code*, R.S.C. 1970, c. L-1, as set out in s. 144(2)(c) [now see ss. 40-46], was amended successively so that at the time of the arbitration it provided as follows:

> 3(b) Weekly Indemnity Payments . . . will commence from the first day in case of a non-occupational accidental injury, from the first day of sickness if hospitalized and from the fourth day in other cases of sickness.

The partnership agreement under which the present applicant became a party to the collective agreement as a successor employer was made on March 18, 1980. Shortly thereafter, namely on December 23, 1980, CNCP gave notice to the union that it intended to consistently apply the provisions of the collective agreement and the employee benefit plan supplemental agreement and enclosed with the notice a copy of one which was to be posted on all notice boards throughout the CNCP system, as was done during the week of January 5, 1981. That notice draws attention to the employee benefit plan supplemental agreement and to the waiting periods set out above. The fourth paragraph of the notice reads as follows:

> Your attention is drawn to the fact that no provision is made for payment during the first three days of an illness where hospitalization is not required. In the past certain groups of employees received, subject to certain conditions, payment of wages during this three-day waiting period. It is not the intent of CNCP to continue this discriminatory practice and in future all CNCP employees will be treated equally in accordance with the provisions of the Employee Benefit Plan.

The grievance and arbitration provisions of the agreement provide for an attempt to agree on a statement of fact and issue and, in the present case, such was prepared and submitted to the arbitrator. Paragraph 10 of that statement of fact sets out that:

> For many years CPT paid certain members of the bargaining unit wages respecting absence due to sickness during the period of time before indemnities under the plan became due.

Paragraph 11 of the statement set out in part that:

> Such payments were not consistently accorded to all members of the bargaining unit.
> They were accorded to only the following employee groups: . . .

There then follows a list of groups of employees to whom such payments were accorded and a similar list of groups of employees to whom such advance payments were not accorded. According to the statement, some 664 employees are found in the first group and 415 in the second.

By reason of the urgency and importance of the matter, the parties agreed to omit the preliminary proceedings and to proceed directly to arbitration, agreeing upon Mr. D.M. Beatty as the sole arbitrator. The union grieved at the company's unilateral termination of a benefit provided for under the collective agreement and claimed that the company was in violation of arts. 1 and 30 of that agreement, the latter being the article establishing the employee benefit plan, part of which has been set out above.

As set out in the statement of fact, the union contention was that the company was in violation of those articles by unilaterally terminating a benefit provided for under the agreement and the union sought that the company be required to withdraw the directive dated December 29th and 'to revert to its previous policy in respect of the affected employees.'

The company contended that the grievance was inarbitrable for the reason that the alleged 'previous policy' is not subject to the grievance procedure nor would an order requiring CNCP to implement such a policy be within the jurisdiction of the arbitrator. It submitted 'that there was no such previous policy, that the company was entitled and indeed required to consistently apply the collective agreement and that in any event as a successor employer it was not bound by any alleged "previous policy" of the predecessor employer.' The company submitted that the grievance should be dismissed.

In acknowledging the union's grievance and confirming the acceptability of Mr. Beatty as sole arbitrator, the company, by letter dated January 23, 1981, advised the union that it was its intention 'to file a preliminary objection with respect to the arbitrator's jurisdiction, as the matter of a previous past practice is not, in our opinion, subject to the grievance procedure established in our collective agreement.'

Section 155(1) of the *Canada Labour Code* provides that every collective agreement is to contain a provision for final settlement by arbitration or otherwise of all differences concerning 'its interpretation, application, administration or alleged violation.' Article 27 of the agreement complies with that requirement by providing for the ultimate submission to an arbitrator of 'any dispute or grievance arising between the parties relating to the interpretation, application or administration of this agreement, including any question as to whether a matter is arbitrable, or when an allegation is made that this agreement has been violated.'

Counsel for the applicants agreed that in order to succeed he had the burden of persuading the Court that the arbitrator lacked jurisdiction to make the order sought and which he granted by requiring the employer to continue the practice as it had been found to exist. Counsel for the applicant at first took the position that by his award the arbitrator had made a change in the agreement and that he was prohibited from doing so, notably by the decision of the Supreme Court of Canada in *Port Arthur Ship Building Co. v. Arthurs et al.* . . . :

> It [a board of arbitration] has no inherent powers to amend, modify or ignore the collective agreement.

We are all of the view that the arbitrator here did none of these things.

The other principal submission advanced by counsel for the applicant was that the arbitrator had no authority to make use of the equitable doctrine of estoppel by conduct to expand an agreement and that he had done so in the present instance.

We agree that the arbitrator did apply the doctrine of estoppel by conduct and ordered that the company continue the practice of payment without the waiting period to those employees who were members of the group to whom this privilege had been accorded for many years. As the issue was put by the arbitrator . . . :

> The issue then, as joined, represents a textbook illustration of the well rehearsed tune of estoppel by conduct. Although it appears in its written submission that the employer may think otherwise, I do not believe it is any longer a debatable issue that an arbitrator has the jurisdiction to entertain such a submission. Indeed at the hearing, Mr. Flicker [for the company] conceded that it was too late in the day to deny the arbitral practice of applying the doctrine of the terms of the parties' relationship. Arbitrators do it (see Brown and Beatty, *Canadian Labour Arbitration*) . . . and courts have condoned it.

The arbitrator later sets out the principle as enunciated by Denning L.J. in *Combe v. Combe.* . . . That exposition of the doctrine was as follows:

> The principle, as I understand it, is that where one party has, by his words or conduct, made to the other a promise or assurance which was intended to affect the legal relations between them and to be acted on accordingly, then, once the other party has taken him at his word and acted on it, the one who gave the promise or assurance cannot afterwards be allowed to revert to the previous legal relations as if no such promise or assurance had been made by him, but he must accept their legal relations subject to the qualification which he himself has so introduced, even though it is not supported in point of law by any consideration, but only by his word.

Elsewhere, Denning L.J. is said to have explained that the doctrine is only applicable where the parties have already entered into a definite and legal contractual or analogous relationship, when there exists some conduct or promise which induces the other party to believe that the strict legal rights under the contract will not be enforced or will be kept in suspense and that 'having regard to the dealings which have taken place between the parties' it will be inequitable to allow that party to enforce their strict legal rights.

The arbitrator found as a fact, as he was bound to do in view of the agreed statement, that the employer adhered to a course of conduct which reasonably induced the union to believe that the entitlement of the employees in question to sickness benefits would not be governed by the strict legal rights set out in art. 30 but rather would conform to the long-standing practice of paying wages during a waiting period. He found also that it would be inequitable to allow the employer to insist on the terms of art. 30 as the limit of its obligation to the employees. As submitted to the arbitrator by the union, if there had been any indication given by the employer that it had intended to commence applying the terms of art. 30 strictly despite the opposite practice of so many years, the union would have had the opportunity of seeking to negotiate a clause in the agreement to preclude the employer from so doing. . . . the arbitrator finds:

> The detrimental reliance then of assuming the practice would continue, lies in the union's inability to require the employer to negotiate its change in its practice during the life of this agreement. After a practice of this duration, if the employer anticipated changing it, it had an 'affirmative duty' to alert the union of its intention in order to give it an opportunity to negotiate a note of the kind the parties fashioned for their vacation package.

The employer argued also that even if the doctrine of estoppel could be applied, its position as a successor employer relieved it of any obligations other than those found in the strict wording of the agreement.

To this the arbitrator replied that s. 144 [now ss. 44–46] of the *Canada Labour Code* providing that a successor employer 'is bound by any collective agreement that is . . . applicable to the employees employed in the business' does not mean bound only by the written terms of such agreement. In the view of the arbitrator, that provision should be read as 'embracing any obligations that arise out of and are related to those terms of the agreement even if they are not expressly set out in writing.' In other words, the employer must accept the agreement to which it succeeds subject to all the equities, if any, that attach to such agreement.

The arbitrator has exclusive jurisdiction to decide all questions arising out of the application of the collective agreement. He has found that in its application the agreement is subject to the restriction which the employer has itself created by its long-standing practice of payment, notwithstanding the waiting period provided for in the written terms of the agreement. We can find nothing in his findings of fact or his conclusion that would permit us to interfere with his award unless, as submitted by the applicants, the arbitrator was wrong in his statement that it is too late in the day to exclude the doctrine of estoppel by conduct from application to collective labour agreements.

While it may be abundantly clear that arbitrators in recent years have assumed the right to apply the doctrine, it may not be quite so free from doubt, as the arbitrator appears to assume, that the practice has been condoned or approved by the courts.

Counsel for the applicant relies heavily upon the judgment written by me for the Divisional Court, in which Wells C.J.H.C. and Parker J. joined, in *Re Hospital Com'n, Sarnia General Hospital and London District Building Service Workers' Union Local 220, S.E.I.U.,* . . . in which is found the following:

> As to estoppel by conduct, it is rarely, if ever, that such principles can arise in proceedings such as those being reviewed. . . .

At this point I stress first that there is a fundamental difference between the role of a court granting rectification and that of a tribunal applying the doctrine of estoppel by conduct.

In the case of rectification the court is asked to find that the document purporting to contain the agreement between the parties does not in fact do so, and was executed by both parties under a common mistake. The court must determine what in fact was the actual agreement between the parties, and rectify the documents accordingly. Such a process goes far beyond the interpretation, application or administration of the agreement, which is the usual jurisdiction of an arbitrator in a labour case, and was the jurisdiction of the arbitrator in the case at bar.

In estoppel by conduct, on the other hand, there is no question before the court or tribunal as to what in fact was the agreement between the parties. The question is whether the agreement, or part thereof, should be applied, having regard to the conduct of the parties. Questions of the application of collective agreements are squarely within the jurisdiction of arbitrators in labour disputes. . . .

Reflection and a perusal of many arbitration cases, including those to which the present arbitrator made reference, has persuaded me that the judgment in the *Sarnia Hospital Com'n* case, *supra*, to the extent that it doubted whether the principle of estoppel by conduct could arise in labour arbitration proceedings, was too sweeping, as well as going beyond what the decision of the case required. True, a collective agreement, like a contract, should be construed without reference to extrinsic evidence if it is clear upon its face. What the arbitrator did here, however, was not to interpret the agreement but to make a finding as to its proper application and to give consequential relief.

That finding surely fits within the principles enunciated by Denning L.J. in *Combe v. Combe, supra*. By its conduct in persistently paying many classifications of employees from the first day of illness in the face of a clause providing for a waiting period, the company gave the union an assurance which was intended to affect the legal relations between them. The union took the company at its word and refrained from requesting a formal change in the agreement. The company should not now be allowed to revert to the previous relations as if no such assurance had been given. . . .

* * *

On the use of estoppel in arbitration in Quebec, see R. Blouin and F. Morin, *Droit de l'arbitrage de grief*, 4th ed. (Cowansville: Éditions Yvon Blais, 1994) at 259; C. D'Aoust and L. Dubé, *L'estoppel et les laches en jurisprudence arbitrale* (Montréal: École de relations industrielles, Université de Montréal, 1990).

9:520 Damages

Re Polymer Corp. and Oil, Chemical & Atomic Workers (1959), 10 L.A.C. 51 at 54–65

Although arbitrator Bora Laskin's views on joint sovereignty have not prevailed, his perspective on arbitral authority to award damages for a breach of the collective agreement was upheld in *Re Polymer Corporation & Oil, Chemical & Atomic Workers International Union, Local 16-14*, [1961] O.R. 176 (H.C.J.), affirmed by [1961] O.R. 438 (C.A.), and further affirmed *sub nom Imbleau v. Laskin*, [1962] S.C.R. 338.

In the *Polymer* case, the union had called a strike in breach of the collective agreement. In an earlier award, the arbitration board had held that it had the authority to grant damages to the employer for losses caused by the strike. When the board recon-vened to assess the quantum of damages, the union reopened the issue of whether it had the power to award damages. The collective agreement said nothing about the awarding of damages, and it contained this standard limitation on arbitral authority:

Article 7.03. The Board of Arbitration shall not have power to alter or change any of the pro-visions of this Agreement or to substitute any new provisions for any existing provisions nor to give any decision inconsistent with the terms and provisions of this Agreement.

The award was as follows.

LASKIN: . . . The burden of union counsel's argument against the board's authority to assess damages is that no such relief is stipulated in the governing collective agreement either generally or in particular relation to breach of a no-strike clause such as art. 8.01. Further, for the board to assess damages would be to add to the collective agreement in the teeth of art. 7.03 which forbids the board to alter, or change, or substitute new for any existing terms or to give a decision inconsistent with such terms. The collective agree-ment itself limits the issues which may be referred to a board, not only by art. 7.03 but also by art. 7.01. On the basis of this exposition, union counsel takes the stand that dam-ages as a remedy for a collective agreement violation which results in loss to the innocent party cannot be awarded in the absence of clear agreement by the parties in that behalf, either generally in a collective agreement or specifically under a particular submission. Counsel emphasized that the collective agreement is a product of voluntary action, and the parties cannot be deemed to have committed themselves beyond that which they expressed in their contractual undertakings.

For what it is worth this board must reject union counsel's contention that the award of this board is made final and binding only through the election of the parties and not through compulsion of legislation or regulation. Section 19 of the Industrial Relations and Disputes Investigation Act, RSC 1952, c. 152, indicates a legislative policy of final settle-ment by arbitration of what may be termed contract interpretation disputes; and while it is true that such a requirement depends on whether a party invokes s. 19 to have such a provision included in a collective agreement (where they have not mutually incorporated it), the fact is that its inclusion is not a matter of agreement only; it may be forced upon one party by the other. . . . It could not escape counsel's appreciation that if a union need not answer in damages for breach of a collective agreement obligation involving a compa-ny in pecuniary loss, neither need a company answer in damages for breach of a collective agreement obligation involving the union or an employee in pecuniary loss; unless, of course, in either or in both cases there is explicit provision for an award of compensation.

It seems to this board that fundamental to any approach to the issue is some under-standing of the history and purpose of resort to 'final' or 'binding' arbitration, to use the terms which appear respectively in s. 19 of the Industrial Relations and Disputes Investi-gation Act and art. 7.04 of the governing collective agreement. As a matter of history, col-lective agreements in Canada had no legal force in their own right until the advent of compulsory collective bargaining legislation. Our Courts refused to assume original jurisdiction for their enforcement and placed them outside of the legal framework within which contractual obligations of individuals were administered. The legislation, which in the context of encouragement to collective bargaining sought stability in employer-employee relations, envisaged arbitration through a mutually accepted tribunal as a built-in device for ensuring the realization of the rights and enforcement of the obligations which were the products of successful negotiation. Original jurisdiction without right of appeal was vested in boards of arbitration under legislative and consensual prescriptions for finality and for binding determinations. In short, boards of arbitration were entrusted with a duty of effective adjudication differing in no way, save perhaps in the greater responsibility conferred upon them, from the adjudicative authority exercised by the ordinary Courts in civil cases of breach of contract. That the adjudication was intended to be remedial as well as declaratory could hardly be doubted. Expeditious settlement of grievances, without undue formality and without excessive cost, was no less a key to successful collective bargaining in day-to-day administration of collective agreements than the successful negotiation of the agreements in the first place. Favourable settlement where an employee was aggrieved meant not a formal abstract declaration of his rights but affirmable relief to give him his due according to the rights and obligations of the collective agreement. In some jurisdictions, as for example, Ontario, this view was emphasized by the fact of statutory withdrawal of the application of Arbitration Acts from labour arbitrations, thus excluding the kind of curial review which was open to the parties to commercial arbitration. To have proposed to union negotiators that collective agreements, so long ignored in law and left to 'lawless' enforcement by strikes and picketing, should continue to be merely empty vehicles for propounding declarations of right when the right to strike during their currency was taken away, would be to mock the policy of compulsory collective bargaining legislation which envisaged the collective agreement as the touchstone of the successful operation of that policy.

What was true in the case of aggrieved employees or aggrieved union could be no less true in the case of aggrieved employers. They too were sensitive to the need for stability which collective agreements could produce, and no less alive to the need for effective machinery to resolve disputes arising in the day-to-day administration of such agreements. In admitting their own responsibility for due observance of collective agreement obligations they could not be expected to agree to any lesser standard of performance by unions and employees. These considerations are aptly summed up in that part of art. 1 of the agreement between the parties herein which recites 'their desire to provide orderly procedure for collective bargaining, and for the prompt and equitable disposition of grievances.'

It is desirable at this point to point up a distinction between the imposition of penalties and the award of damages. It is a distinction taken, and in this Board's view, properly taken, in the award in *Re U.A.W. and C.C.M.* . . . . This board, sitting as a civil tribunal to resolve contract interpretation disputes, has no punitive function but is charged only with redressing private wrongs arising from breach of obligations assumed as a result of negotiation. The board's remedial authority, if it has any, must be addressed to the vindication of violated rights by putting the innocent party, so far as can reasonably be done, in the position in which he or it would be if the particular rights had not been violated. The redress, if any can be given, must be suited to or measured by the wrong done. A board of arbitration is not, however, a criminal court. True enough, it may play a role in passing upon or modifying a penalty imposed by an employer as a matter of discipline, but in so doing it is merely assessing the permissible limits of employer action taken under the collective agreement and not fashioning a penalty to reward an innocent party.

. . .

. . . The pivotal issue is simply whether the exercise of arbitral authority encompasses the effectuation of the right and the enforcement of the obligation which are submitted for both original and final adjudication. One would ordinarily think, especially if seized of any knowledge of the history of collective bargaining and its legislative implementation, that if there is any area of adjudication where abstract pronouncements, devoid of direction for redress of violations, would be unwelcome it would be in labour arbitration. Such attenuation of arbitration authority must surely be found in explicit restriction rather than in implicit limitation.

It may be useful to pursue the point under discussion in relation to the 'intention of the parties' argument that is from time to time advanced in labour arbitration cases no less than in commercial contract adjudication. Thus, it is said that if the parties intended to make themselves answerable before a board of arbitration in damages they would have said so; and since many collective agreements contain specific reference to an arbitration board's remedial powers where discharge or lesser discipline is involved, the 'intention of the parties' argument is buttressed by reliance on the maxim *expressio unius exlusio alterius*. Whatever may be the intention of the parties as to the binding effect of their reciprocal rights and obligations, the statutory prescription of s. 18 of the Industrial Relations and Disputes Investigation Act makes the collective agreement terms binding on the union as well as on employer and employees covered thereby. Moreover, s. 19 carries the statutory policy further by reinforcing the binding character of a collective agreement with binding adjudication of disputes concerning its interpretation or violation. It seems to this board that whether one appraises the situation in terms of the statutory effects alone, or in terms of the intention of the parties (which must be viewed in the light of the statute), the result is the same; and there is nothing in the language of the agreement in this case to suggest that the parties have in any way tried to qualify this result. Indeed, they could not if they tried; and we are remitted again to consideration of the scope or meaning to be given to their (compelled) intention that the collective agreement shall be binding and that any alleged violation shall be submitted to binding arbitration.

As good an analogy as can be found on this issue lies in the field of international law and, particularly, in the effect given by international law to the voluntary submission of nations to adjudication of disputes arising under treaties to which they are parties. Thus, in the *Chorzow Factory* case of 1927 between Germany and Poland, the Permanent Court of International Justice said . . . :

It is a principle of international law that the breach of an engagement involves an obligation to make reparation in an adequate form. Reparation therefore is the indispensable complement of a failure to apply a convention and there is no necessity for this to be stated in the convention itself.

. . . One of the submissions of union counsel appears to be that there is a difference in an arbitration board's remedial authority where an employee claims redress under the collective agreement and where a company claims redress. The only differences, so far as this board can see any, are in the nature of the obligation which is allegedly violated and in the readier measure of loss, if loss is shown. The fact that a collective agreement stipulates the worth of an employee's labour in a wage schedule merely simplifies a tribunal's assessment of damages. It adds nothing to its powers. There is no need to emphasize that the difficulty of assessing damages has never been a reason for denying a claim thereto based on an established breach of contractual or other obligation owed to the claiming party. . . .

It follows from what has been said that the union's challenge to this board's power to award damages for breach by the union of art. 8.01 is rejected and the board will proceed to assess the company's damages at a hearing to be convened by the board upon advice from the company that particulars as mentioned at the outset of this award have been furnished to the union and upon receipt of copies by members of the board.

* * *

It is now well accepted that an arbitrator may award damages in accordance with general contract principles, even if there are no specific provisions to that effect in the collective agreement: *St. Anne Nackawic Pulp & Paper Company Ltd. v. Canadian Paperworkers Union, Local 219*, [1986] 1 S.C.R. 704.

9:530 Rectification

As with damages, it was arbitrator Bora Laskin who led the way in asserting the authority of arbitrators to apply the general contract principle of rectification (correcting a mutual error made by the parties when reducing the terms of the collective agreement to writing): *W. Harris & Company* (1953), 4 L.A.C. 1531.

However, arbitrators' authority in respect of rectification has had a more checkered history than in respect of damages. In *Re Metropolitan Toronto Board of Commissioners of Police and Metropolitan Toronto Police Ass'n* (1972), 26 D.L.R. (3d) 672 (C.A.) (aff'd on other grounds by S.C.C), the Ontario Court of Appeal said:

In 'applying the doctrine of rectification' the arbitrator made two separate and distinct errors:

i) As a consensual arbitrator he had no power whatever to rectify the collective agreement. If the collective agreement did not represent the true bargain between the parties, the party asserting this to be so could bring an action [in court] for rectification, but as Judson J., said in Port Arthur Shipbuilding Co. v. Arthurs et al., [1969] S.C.R. 85 . . . the arbitrator '[had] no inherent powers to amend, modify or ignore the collective agreement.'

ii) He ignored an express term of the agreement itself, cl. 17 of which reads:

'An Arbitrator . . . shall not have power to add to, subtract from, alter, modify or amend any part of this Agreement . . .'

In later years, many arbitrators declined to follow this ruling. They saw it as anomalous that arbitrators were allowed to invoke promissory estoppel, and thus not to follow the strict letter of the agreement (see section 9:510), but were not allowed to use rectification to correct simple mistakes in the wording of the agreement. It also seemed to be inconsistent with the Polymer approach to arbitral authority to award damages.

More recently, in *P.S.A.C. v. NAV Canada* (2002), 212 D.L.R. (4th) 68, the Ontario Court of Appeal held that an arbitrator does have the authority to rectify a collective agreement where its written terms do not correspond to the parties' intentions. According to the Court, contract clauses which prohibit an arbitrator from amending or modifying the collective agreement do not preclude the granting of a remedy by way of rectification, as that remedy does not operate to alter the agreement but simply to correct terms which have been mistakenly drawn. The Court saw the arbitral authority to apply the equitable doctrine of rectification as flowing from the exclusive jurisdiction of arbitration to resolve disputes arising under a collective agreement.

9:600 EXTERNAL LAW AND MULTIPLE FORUMS

9:610 Arbitration and Employment-Related Statutes

The "employment bargain" is affected not only by the collective agreement, but also by many statutory regimes, including those in relation to human rights, employment standards, occupational health and safety, workers' compensation, and, in some jurisdictions, pay equity and employment equity. The extent of the authority of arbitrators to apply those statutory regimes has been a major issue over the past three decades.

Parry Sound (District) Social Services Administration Board v. Ontario Public Service Employees Union, Local 324 2003 SCC 42

IACOBUCCI J. (McLachlin C.J., Gonthier, Bastarache, Binnie, Arbour, and Deschamps JJ. concurring):

¶1 This appeal raises questions about the application of human rights and other employment-related statutes in the context of a collective agreement. More specifically, does a grievance arbitrator have the power to enforce the substantive rights and obligations of human rights and other employment-related statutes and, if so, under what circumstances? As I discuss in these reasons, I conclude that a grievance arbitrator has the power and responsibility to enforce the substantive rights and obligations of human rights and other employment-related statutes as if they were part of the collective agreement. Consequently, I would dismiss the appeal.

I. BACKGROUND

¶2 Joanne O'Brien was a probationary employee of the appellant District of Parry Sound Social Services Administration Board and a member of the respondent Ontario Public Service Employees Union (the "Union"). Her terms of employment were governed by a collective agreement negotiated between the parties. For the purposes of this appeal, the most important provision of the collective agreement is Article 5.01:

ARTICLE 5 — MANAGEMENT RIGHTS

5.01.

The Union recognizes that the management of the operations and the direction of the employees are fixed exclusively in the Employer and shall remain solely with the Employer except as expressly limited by the clear and explicit language of some other provision of this Agreement and, without restricting the generality of the foregoing, the Union acknowledges that it is the exclusive function of the Employer to:

. . .

(b) hire, assign, retire, promote, demote, classify, transfer, direct, lay off, recall and to suspend, discipline or discharge employees who have successfully completed their probationary period for just cause provided that a claim by an employee who has successfully completed his/her probationary period that she/he has been disciplined, suspended or discharged without just cause may be the subject of a grievance and dealt with as hereinafter provided;

¶3 . . . On its face, Article 5.01 is sufficiently broad to include the right of the employer to discharge an employee. . . . Article 8.06(a), under the heading "Grievance Procedures," states that "a probationary employee may be discharged at the sole discretion of and for any reason satisfactory to the Employer and such action by the Employer is not subject to the grievance and arbitration procedures and does not constitute a difference between the parties."

¶4 Prior to the expiry of her probationary term, Ms. O'Brien went on maternity leave. Within a few days of returning to work, the appellant discharged her. On June 26, 1998, Ms. O'Brien filed a grievance with the Union. The grievance alleged as follows:

I grieve that I have been discharged from my position without justification and that this decision was arbitrary, discriminatory, in bad faith and unfair.

At the arbitration hearing, the appellant objected on the basis that the Board of Arbitration (the "Board") did not have jurisdiction over the subject matter of the grievance. It was the appellant's submission that the collective agreement clearly expressed that it was the parties' intention that the discharge of a probationary employee was not arbitrable. The appellant submitted that the parties have the right to make such a bargain and that it would be a jurisdictional error for the Board to resolve the dispute.

II. RELEVANT LEGISLATIVE PROVISIONS

¶5 *Employment Standards Act*, R.S.O. 1990, c. E.14

44. An employer shall not intimidate, discipline, suspend, lay off, dismiss or impose a penalty on an employee because the employee is or will become eligible to take, intends to take or takes pregnancy leave or parental leave.

64.5 (1) If an employer enters into a collective agreement, the Act is enforceable against the employer with respect to the following matters as if it were part of the collective agreement:

1. A contravention of or failure to comply with the Act that occurs when the collective agreement is in force.

. . .

(2) An employee to whom a collective agreement applies (including an employee who is not a member of the trade union) is not entitled to file or maintain a complaint under the Act.

(3) Despite subsection (2), the Director may permit an employee to file or maintain a complaint under the Act if the Director considers it appropriate in the circumstances.

(4) An employee to whom a collective agreement applies (including an employee who is not a member of the trade union) is bound by a decision of the trade union with respect to the enforcement of the Act under the collective agreement, including a decision not to seek the enforcement of the Act.

Labour Relations Act, 1995, S.O. 1995, c. 1, Sch. A

48.(1) Every collective agreement shall provide for the final and binding settlement by arbitration, without stoppage of work, of all differences between the parties arising from the interpretation, application, administration or alleged violation of the agreement, including any question as to whether a matter is arbitrable.

48.(12) An arbitrator or . . . an arbitration board, as the case may be, has power,

(j) to interpret and apply human rights and other employment-related statutes, despite any conflict between those statutes and the terms of the collective agreement.

. . .

Human Rights Code, R.S.O. 1990, c. H.19

5.(1) Every person has a right to equal treatment with respect to employment without discrimination because of race, ancestry, place of origin, colour, ethnic origin, citizenship, creed, sex, sexual orientation, age, record of offences, marital status, same-sex partnership status, family status or handicap.

. . .

IV. ISSUES

¶14 The principal question in this appeal concerns the Board's finding that Ms. O'Brien's grievance is arbitrable. In reviewing this finding, the primary substantive question to be answered is whether the substantive rights and obligations of the Human Rights Code are incorporated into a collective agreement over which the Board has jurisdiction. A second question that arises is whether it was appropriate for the Court of Appeal to determine that the subject matter of the grievance is arbitrable on the basis that the substantive rights and obligations of the ESA are incorporated into the collective agreement.

¶15 I also note that the Ontario Human Rights Commission has intervened in this appeal for the purpose of ensuring that its jurisdiction is not ousted because the aggrieved employee is a party to a collective agreement over which the Board has jurisdiction. The Commission submits that if the Court finds that the grievance is arbitrable, the Board and the Commission have concurrent jurisdiction. In my view, it is unnecessary to determine this matter at the present time. Consequently, in concluding that a grievance arbitrator has the power and responsibility to enforce the substantive rights and obligations of the Human Rights Code in this case, I make no holding on whether the jurisdiction of the Human Rights Commission is ousted by that of the Board.

V. ANALYSIS

A. What is the Appropriate Standard of Review?

¶16 Where an arbitration board is called upon to determine whether a matter is arbitrable, it is well-established that a reviewing court can only intervene in the case of a patently unreasonable error. . . .

¶17 This high degree of curial deference to the decisions of arbitration boards is necessary to maintain the integrity of the grievance arbitration process. . . . The protective clause found in s. 48(1) of the LRA is the legislative recognition that the basic nature of labour disputes requires their prompt and final resolution by expert tribunals.

¶18 The patent unreasonableness standard is a very high standard that will not easily be met. In Canada (Director of Investigation and Research) v. Southam Inc., . . . the Court described the difference between an unreasonable and patently unreasonable decision in the following terms:

> The difference . . . lies in the immediacy or obviousness of the defect. If the defect is apparent on the face of the tribunal's reasons, then the tribunal's decision is patently unreasonable. But if it takes some significant searching or testing to find the defect, then the decision is unreasonable but not patently unreasonable. . . . If the decision under review is sufficiently difficult, then perhaps a great deal of reading and thinking will be required before the judge will be able to grasp the dimensions of the problem. . . . But once the lines of the problem have come into focus, if the decision is patently unreasonable, then the unreasonableness will be evident. . . .

. . .

B. Was the Arbitration Award Patently Unreasonable?

¶19 . . . the collective agreement is the "foundation" of a grievance arbitrator's jurisdiction. Absent a violation of the collective agreement, a grievance arbitrator has no jurisdiction over a dispute; if the alleged misconduct does not constitute a violation of the collective agreement, there is no basis on which to conclude that a dispute is arbitrable.

¶20 In the present case, the parties are in agreement that the express provisions of the collective agreement in question impose no fetters on the employer's right to discharge a probationary employee. The Union, however, submits that s. 5(1) of the Human Rights Code is implicit in the collective agreement between the parties. If this is the case, there is no doubt but that the discriminatory discharge of a probationary employee is arbitrable. Under s. 5(1), every person has a right to equal treatment with respect to employment without discrimination. Ms. O'Brien's grievance — that she was discharged for discriminatory reasons — falls squarely within s. 5(1) of the Human Rights Code. . . .

¶21 Consequently, the critical issue to be determined at the arbitration hearing was whether or not the substantive rights and obligations of the Human Rights Code are incorporated into each collective agreement over which the Board has jurisdiction. . . . If the critical question that the tribunal must answer is a question of law that is outside its area of expertise and that the legislature did not intend to leave to the tribunal, the tribunal must answer that question correctly.

¶22 The question of whether the substantive rights and obligations of the Human Rights Code are incorporated into each collective agreement over which the Board has jurisdiction is not, in my view, a question that the legislature intended to leave to the Board. The Board's expertise does not lie in answering legal questions of general applicability, but, rather, in the interpretation of collective agreements and the resolution of factual disputes related to those agreements. . . .

¶23 For the reasons that follow, it is my conclusion that the Board was correct to conclude that the substantive rights and obligations of the Human Rights Code are incorporated into each collective agreement over which the Board has jurisdiction. Under a collective agreement, the broad rights of an employer to manage the enterprise and direct the work force are subject not only to the express provisions of the collective agreement, but also to statutory provisions of the Human Rights Code and other employment-related statutes.

(1) The Case Law

¶24 The leading case regarding the effect of employment-related statutes on the content of collective agreements is McLeod v. Egan. . . . Prior to McLeod, the prevailing view was that an arbitrator was not authorized to apply statutes in the course of grievance arbitration other than as an aid to interpreting a collective agreement. . . . On this view, an arbitrator had no alternative but to construe and apply a collective agreement in accordance with its express terms and conditions. If the alleged misconduct did not constitute a violation of an express provision of the collective agreement, the subject matter of the dispute was not arbitrable. In McLeod, however, the Court established that it is necessary to look outside the collective agreement in order to ascertain the substantive rights and obligations of the parties to that agreement.

¶25 In McLeod, the appellant employee alleged that he had been disciplined for refusing to work beyond 48 hours in a week. The collective agreement between the parties contained a broad management rights clause that expressly stated that the control of all operations and working forces, including the right to discipline employees and to schedule operations, is vested solely in the employer, subject only to the express provisions of the collective agreement. There were no provisions of the collective agreement that limited the right of an employer to require an employee to work overtime beyond 48 hours a week. In the absence of language limiting the broad power vested in the employer, the arbitrator concluded that insofar as the collective agreement was concerned the employer was entitled to discipline an employee who refused to work in excess of 48 hours a week.

¶26 The Court, however, concluded that an arbitrator must look beyond the four corners of the collective agreement in order to determine the limits on an employer's right to manage operations. Under a collective agreement, this right is subject not only to the express provisions of the agreement, but also to statutory provisions such as s. 11(2) of the Employment Standards Act, 1968, S.O. 1968, c. 35 (the "ESA, 1968"). Martland J. held as follows, at p. 523:

> The basic provision of the Act is that which places a maximum limit upon the working hours of an employee of eight in the day and forty-eight in the week. Any provision of an agreement which purported to give to an employer an unqualified right to require working hours in excess of those limits would be illegal, and the provisions of art. 2.01 of the collective agreement, which provided that certain management rights should remain vested in the Company, could not, in so far as they preserved the Company's right to require overtime work by its employees, enable the Company to require overtime work in excess of those limits.

Put another way, the absence of a provision that expressly prohibits an employer from requiring an employee to work in excess of 48 hours a week does not mean that the right to manage operations includes the right to violate s. 11(2) of the ESA, 1968. Management rights must be exercised not only in accordance with the express provisions of the collective agreement, but also in accordance with the employee's statutory rights. . . .

¶27 . . . I believe it important to consider carefully what it was that made the collective agreement in McLeod objectionable. In McLeod, the collective agreement did not expressly state that the employer was authorized to require overtime beyond 48 hours a week. It did, however, contain a broad management rights clause that recognized the employer's right to control all operations and working forces, including the right to discipline employees and to schedule operations. The collective agreement was objectionable because the powers it extended to the employer were sufficiently broad to include the power to violate its employees' rights under s. 11(2) of the ESA, 1968.

¶28 As a practical matter, this means that the substantive rights and obligations of employment-related statutes are implicit in each collective agreement over which an arbitrator has jurisdiction. A collective agreement might extend to an employer a broad right to manage the enterprise as it sees fit, but this right is circumscribed by the employee's statutory rights. The absence of an express provision that prohibits the violation of a particular statutory right is insufficient to conclude that a violation of that right does not constitute a violation of the collective agreement. Rather, human rights and other employment-related statutes establish a floor beneath which an employer and union cannot contract.

¶29 As a result, the substantive rights and obligations of the parties to a collective agreement cannot be determined solely by reference to the mutual intentions of the contracting parties as expressed in that agreement. . . .

¶30 In some sense, McLeod is inconsistent with the traditional view that a collective agreement is a private contract between equal parties, and that the parties to the agreement are free to determine what does or does not constitute an arbitrable difference. But this willingness to consider factors other than the parties' expressed intention is consistent with the fact that collective bargaining and grievance arbitration has both a private and public function. . . . This dual purpose is reflected in the fact that the content of a collective agreement is, in part, fixed by external statutes. Section 48(1) of the LRA, for example, dictates that every collective agreement must provide for final and binding settlement by arbitration of all differences arising under a collective agreement. Section 64.5(1) of the ESA provides that the Act is enforceable against an employer as if it was part of the collective agreement. In each collective agreement, certain procedural requirements and substantive rights and obligations are mandatory. In McLeod, the Court determined that these include the obligation of an employer to exercise its management rights in accordance with the statutory rights of its employees.

(2) Application of the Case Law

¶31 As in McLeod, the collective agreement at issue in this appeal expressly recognizes the employer's broad right to manage the enterprise and direct the work force as it sees fit, subject only to express terms providing otherwise. . . . Under the traditional view, the management rights recognized therein are unlimited, except to the extent that the express provisions of the collective agreement provide otherwise. In the absence of a provision in the collective agreement that limits the right of the employer to discharge a probationary employee for discriminatory reasons, Ms. O'Brien's grievance is non-arbitrable.

¶32 . . . Just as the collective agreement in McLeod could not extend to the employer the right to require overtime in excess of 48 hours, the collective agreement in the current appeal cannot extend to the appellant the right to discharge an employee for discriminatory reasons. . . .

¶33 The one factor that distinguishes this case from McLeod is the fact that there is more evidence that the parties to the agreement specifically turned their minds to the subject matter of the grievance and agreed that it was not arbitrable . . . Article 8.06(a) might be understood as an explicit expression of the parties' mutual intention that the discriminatory discharge of a probationary employee is not arbitrable.

¶34 In response to this line of argument, I should state that I am not entirely comfortable attributing this intention to the parties. Although the language of Article 8.06(a) is broad, it cannot be established, as a matter of fact, that the parties reached a common understanding that the discriminatory discharge of a probationary employee is non-arbitrable. It is more likely, in my view, that the mutual intention was to affirm the right of the employer to discharge a probationary employee who did not perform his or her tasks to the employer's satisfaction. . . . I find it unlikely, however, that it was the parties' mutual intention to affirm the right of the employer to discharge a probationary employee on the basis of human rights grounds, namely, race, ancestry, place of origin, colour, ethnic origin, citizenship, creed, sex, sexual orientation, age, record of offences, marital status, same-sex partnership status, family status or handicap.

¶35 But even if Article 8.06(a) does, in fact, reflect a common intention that the discriminatory discharge of a probationary employee is not an arbitrable dispute, I remain of the view that Ms. O'Brien's grievance is arbitrable. One reason I say this is that s. 48(1) of the LRA states that every collective agreement shall provide for the final and binding settlement by arbitration of all differences between the parties arising under the collective agreement. Section 48(1) prohibits the parties from enacting provisions stating that a violation of the collective agreement is non-arbitrable. By the operation of s. 5(1) of the Human Rights Code, the right of probationary employees to equal treatment without discrimination is implicit in the collective agreement, and thus the discriminatory discharge of a probationary employee constitutes a violation of that agreement. To the extent that Article 8.06(a) establishes that an allegation that the discriminatory discharge of a probationary employer is non-arbitrable, it is void as contrary to s. 48(1) of the LRA.

¶36 More fundamentally, the interpretation of Article 8.06(a) that it reflects a common intention is inconsistent with the principle that under a collective agreement an employer's right to manage operations and direct the work force is subject not only to the express provisions of the collective agreement but also to the employees' statutory rights, irrespective of the parties' subjective intentions. . . . Even if the parties to the agreement had enacted a substantive provision that clearly expressed that, insofar as the collective agreement is concerned, the employer possessed the right to discharge a probationary employee for discriminatory reasons, that provision would be void. Put simply, there are certain rights and obligation that arise irrespective of the parties' subjective intentions. These include the right of an employee to equal treatment without discrimination and the corresponding obligation of an employer not to discharge an employee for discriminatory reasons. To hold otherwise would lessen human rights protection in the unionized workplace by allowing employers and unions to treat such protections as optional, thereby leaving recourse only to the human rights procedure.

¶37 The effect of my analysis is to modify Article 8.06(a). Under this analysis, it is only a probationary employee being discharged "at the sole lawful discretion of and for any lawful reason satisfactory to the Employer" that does not constitute a difference between the parties. Any exercise of this discretion otherwise than in accordance with a probationary employee's rights under the Human Rights Code and other employment-related statutes is an arbitrable difference under the collective agreement.

(3) Section 48(12)(j) of the LRA.

¶38 Having determined that McLeod established that an employer's right to manage the operations and direct the work force is subject not only to the express provisions of the collective agreement but also to the right of each employee to equal treatment without discrimination, the question that arises is whether this principle applies under s. 48(12)(j) of the LRA. Put directly, did the enactment of s. 48(12)(j) displace or otherwise restrict the principles established in McLeod? . . .

¶40 . . . I believe that the amendments to the legislation affirm that grievance arbitrators have not only the power but also the responsibility to implement and enforce the substantive rights and obligations of human rights and other employment-related statutes as if they were part of the collective agreement. If the right of an employer to manage operations and direct the work force is subject to both the express provisions of the collective agreement and the employee's statutory rights, then it follows that a grievance arbitrator must have the power to implement and enforce those rights.

¶41 This conclusion is consistent with the modern approach to statutory interpretation. As this Court has repeatedly stated, the proper approach to statutory interpretation is that endorsed by the noted author E. A. Driedger, in Construction of Statutes (2nd ed. 1983), at p. 87: "the words of an Act are to be read in their entire context and in their grammatical and ordinary sense harmoniously with the scheme of the Act, the object of the Act, and the intention of Parliament". . . .

(i) The Plain and Ordinary Meaning of Section 48(12)(j) of the LRA

¶42 The primary factor that supports this conclusion is the very language of s. 48(12)(j), which provides that an arbitrator has the power "to interpret and apply human rights and other employment-related statutes, despite any conflict between those statutes and the terms of the collective agreement."

¶43 The power to interpret and apply a particular statute would, in my view, ordinarily be understood to include the power to implement and enforce the substantive rights and obligations contained therein. . . .

¶44 The appellant submits that the power to interpret and apply human rights and other employment-related statutes arises only when there is a direct conflict between the collective agreement and the statute. . . .

¶45 . . . In any event, I am of the view that the inclusion of a management rights clause that is sufficiently broad to include the right of management to discharge a probationary employee for discriminatory reasons gives rise to a conflict between the statute and the collective agreement.

(ii) The Scheme of the Act

¶46 The appellant's primary submission is that an arbitrator has the power to interpret and apply human rights and other employment-related statutes if, and only if, it already has been determined that the arbitrator has jurisdiction over the subject matter of the grievance. According to the appellant, an arbitrator's primary source of jurisdiction is s. 48(1), which states that each collective agreement shall provide for final and binding settlement by arbitration of a difference arising out of that agreement. Section 48(12)(j), on the other hand, sets out the powers that an arbitrator possesses once it already has been determined that a grievance is arbitrable. On this view, the power to interpret and apply other statutes is merely one among nine other incidental powers that an arbitrator may exercise for the purpose of resolving a difference over which she or he already has jurisdiction.

¶47 To a certain extent, I would agree. Indeed, the structure of s. 48 does seem to suggest that an arbitrator is intended to interpret and apply human rights and other employment-related statutes for the purpose of resolving a dispute that is arbitrable. . . .

¶48 But even if it is true that a dispute must be arbitrable before an arbitrator obtains the power to interpret and apply the Human Rights Code, it does not thereby follow that an alleged contravention of an express provision of a collective agreement is a condition precedent of an arbitrator's authority to enforce the substantive rights and obligations of employment-related statutes. Under McLeod, the broad right of an employer to manage operations and direct the work force is subject not only to the express provisions of the collective agreement but also to the statutory rights of its employees. This means that the right of a probationary employee to equal treatment without discrimination is implicit in each collective agreement. This, in turn, means that the dismissal of an employee for discriminatory reasons is, in fact, an arbitrable difference, and that the arbitrator has the power to interpret and apply the substantive rights and obligations of the Human Rights Code for the purpose of resolving that difference.

¶49 Consequently, it cannot be inferred from the scheme of the LRA that it was the legislature's intention to displace or otherwise restrict the legal principles enunciated in McLeod. The appellant's submissions in respect of the structure of s. 48 are consistent with the conclusion that the substantive rights and obligations of the Human Rights Code are implicit in each collective agreement over which an arbitrator has jurisdiction. If an arbitrator is to enforce an employer's obligation to exercise its management rights in accordance with the statutory provisions that are implicit in each collective agreement, the arbitrator must have the power to interpret and apply human rights and other employment-related statutes. Section 48(12)(j) confirms that an arbitrator does, in fact, have this right.

(iii) Policy Considerations

¶50 In respect of policy considerations, I first note that granting arbitrators the authority to enforce the substantive rights and obligations of human rights and other employment-related statutes advances the stated purposes of the LRA, which include promoting the expeditious resolution of workplace disputes. As this Court has repeatedly recognized, the prompt, final and binding resolution of workplace disputes is of fundamental importance, both to the parties and to society as a whole. . . . It is essential that there exist a means of providing speedy decisions by experts in the field who are sensitive to the workplace environment, and which can be considered by both sides to be final and binding.

¶51 The grievance arbitration process is the means by which provincial governments have chosen to achieve this objective. . . . Recognizing the authority of arbitrators to enforce an employee's statutory rights substantially advances the dual objectives of: (i) ensuring peace in industrial relations; and (ii) protecting employees from the misuse of managerial power.

¶52 Granting arbitrators the authority to enforce the substantive rights and obligations of human rights and other employment-related statutes has the additional advantage of bolstering human rights protection. Major J. [dissenting in this case] correctly observes that if the dispute is non-arbitrable, aggrieved employees have available the same mechanism for enforcing fundamental human rights as any other member of society: they may file a complaint before the Human Right Commission. But the fact that there already exists a forum for the resolution of human rights disputes does not mean that granting arbitrators the authority to enforce the substantive rights and obligations of the Human Rights Code does not further bolster human rights protection. As discussed above, grievance arbitration has the advantage of both accessibility and expertise. It is a reasonable assumption that the availability of an accessible and inexpensive forum for the resolution of human rights disputes will increase the ability of aggrieved employees to assert their right to equal treatment without discrimination, and that this, in turn, will encourage compliance with the Human Rights Code.

¶53 A countervailing consideration is the fact that the Human Rights Commission has greater expertise than grievance arbitrators in the resolution of human rights violations. In my view, any concerns in respect of this matter are outweighed by the significant benefits associated with the availability of an accessible and informal forum for the prompt resolution of allegations of human rights violations in the workplace. It is of great importance that such disputes are resolved quickly and in a manner that allows for a continuing relationship between the parties. Moreover, expertise is not static, but, rather, is something that develops as a tribunal grapples with issues on a repeated basis. The fact that the Human Rights Commission currently has greater expertise than the Board in respect of human rights violations is an insufficient basis on which to conclude that a grievance arbitrator ought not to have the power to enforce the rights and obligations of the Human Rights Code.

¶54 ... in its submissions before this Court the intervener, Human Rights Commission, stated that it believes that the grievance arbitration process has an important role to play in the resolution of human rights issues. It did not intervene on the basis that arbitrators should not have the power to resolve human rights issues, but on the basis that arbitrators and the Board should have concurrent jurisdiction. This suggests that the Commission also is of the view that grievance arbitrators have sufficient expertise to hear alleged violations of the Human Rights Code.

(4) Conclusion
¶55 For the foregoing reasons, the Board was correct to conclude that the substantive rights and obligations of the Human Rights Code are incorporated into each collective agreement over which an arbitrator has jurisdiction. Because of this interpretation, an alleged violation of the Human Rights Code constitutes an alleged violation of the collec-

tive agreement, and falls squarely within the Board's jurisdiction. Accordingly, there is no reason to interfere with the Board's finding that the subject matter of Ms. O'Brien's grievance is arbitrable. The Board's finding that the discriminatory discharge of a probationary employee is arbitrable is not patently unreasonable.

C. The Court of Appeal's Application of the ESA

¶56 The foregoing analysis is sufficient to dispose of the appeal. The Board's finding that the subject matter of Ms. O'Brien's grievance is arbitrable was not patently unreasonable and should be upheld. However, even if there was no basis on which to conclude that the alleged violation of the Human Rights Code is arbitrable, I would still be of the opinion that the analysis furnished by the Court of Appeal would provide sufficient grounds to conclude that Ms. O'Brien's grievance is a proper subject of the arbitration process.

¶57 In substantive terms, there is no doubt but that the application of ss. 44 and 64.5(1) of the ESA leads to the conclusion that the subject matter of Ms. O'Brien's grievance is arbitrable. Under s. 64.5(1), the terms and conditions of the ESA are enforceable against an employer as if they were part of the collective agreement. Under s. 44, an employer is prohibited from dismissing an employee because the employee intends to take or takes pregnancy leave. The joint effect of ss. 44 and 64.5(1) is that each collective agreement is deemed to contain a provision that prohibits the discharge of a probationary employee because she took or intends to take pregnancy leave. Thus, the subject matter of Ms. O'Brien's grievance clearly constitutes a dispute that arises under a collective agreement over which the Board has jurisdiction.

. . .

(2) Procedural Considerations

¶63 The appellant's primary submission in respect of this argument is that the Union is statute-barred from relying on the ESA. Section 64.5(4) of the ESA states that:

> An employee to whom a collective agreement applies (including an employee who is not a member of the trade union) is bound by a decision of the trade union with respect to the enforcement of the Act under the collective agreement, including a decision not to seek the enforcement of the Act.

According to the appellant, s. 64.5(4) binds a union to a prior decision not to seek enforcement of the ESA. Under this view, the respondent Union is bound by its prior decision not to seek enforcement of s. 44 of the ESA at the initial hearing. However, this interpretation of s. 64.5(4) is inconsistent with both its words and its fundamental purpose.

¶64 First, s. 64.5(4) clearly states that an employee is bound by a decision of the trade union with respect to the enforcement of the Act under the collective agreement. It does not, however, provide that the union is bound by a decision not to seek enforcement of the ESA. If the purpose of s. 64.5(4) was to bind a trade union to its prior decision not to seek enforcement of the ESA, one would have expected the legislature to have used language indicating as much. . . .

¶65 This interpretation of s. 64.5(4) is consistent not only with its words but also with its basic purpose, namely, to ensure that the union has sole carriage over employment standards issues that arise during the currency of a collective agreement. This accords with established principles governing labour-management relations. Section 64.5(2), for example, provides that an employee to whom a collective agreement applies is not entitled to file or maintain a complaint under the ESA. Section 64.5(3), in turn, provides that notwithstanding subs. (2) the Director of Employment Standards may permit an employee to file or maintain a complaint under the Act if the Director considers it appropriate in the circumstances. Each subsection suggests that the default presumption is that the union must decide whether or not to pursue a particular grievance. Section 64.5(4) reinforces this principle by binding an employee to the decision of a union not to seek enforcement of the ESA. The purpose of the provision is not to bind a union to a prior decision not to pursue an ESA complaint, but, rather, to affirm the principle that an employee to whom a collective agreement applies is not entitled to file or maintain a complaint under the Act.

¶66 Consequently, s. 64.5(4) has no effect in this appeal. This case does not involve an individual employee who seeks to file or to maintain a complaint under the ESA despite the fact that the Union has decided not to seek enforcement of her rights under the Act. . . .

. . .

¶73 MAJOR J. (for himself and LeBel J., dissenting):

I respectfully disagree with the reasons of Iacobucci J.

¶74 Are all employment and human rights statutes incorporated into every collective bargaining agreement? Collective agreements occupy an important role in Canadian management-union relations. As both parties are experienced in various components of labour law including grievance procedures, the courts should reluctantly interfere and only when necessary. In this case, there were alternatives available to the parties . . . Because I believe that courts should assume that parties may set out the limits of their agreements absent express or implied legislative override, and because the parties should be bound by the form and substance of the grievance they chose, I would allow the appeal.

. . .

¶93 . . . Under McLeod, the parties attempted to explicitly "contract around" the protections conferred by statute, which is clearly impermissible. Here, the parties simply chose not to come to agreement on certain kinds of disagreements, explicitly choosing to remove the arbitrator's jurisdiction. The common law rule that parties may not contract in contravention of public policy does not require parties to agree to arbitrate violations of statutory rights.

¶94 Under this more restrained reading of McLeod, . . . explicit statutory directions override conflicting provisions of collective agreements, but they do not affect the parties' ability to define the limits of their agreement. Parties remain free to exclude certain classes of employees, such as probationary, part-time, or temporary employees, from some of the provisions of the agreement, just as they remain free to exclude certain kinds of disputes from the jurisdiction of the arbitrator. They do this by limiting the scope of the grievance procedure on some matters or acknowledging that a party retains the right to make a unilateral final decision on certain questions.

¶95 Although these labour agreements are entered into under the collective bargaining framework established by the Labour Relations Act, 1995, they are essentially private contracts of significant public importance. The decision to inject legislative protections into these private contracts is a serious one, though clearly one within the powers of a legislature. A court should not lightly infer such intent. When the Ontario legislature wishes to insert such protections directly into collective bargaining agreements, it knows how to do so explicitly and clearly. For example, s. 64.5(1) of the Employment Standards Act reads:

> If an employer enters into a collective agreement, the Act is enforceable against the employer with respect to the following matters as if it were part of the collective agreement:
>
> 1. A contravention of or failure to comply with the Act that occurs when the collective agreement is in force.

There is no equivalent provision in the Human Rights Code.

. . .

¶100 Collective agreements reflect the outcome of a sometimes difficult process of negotiation. The content of the agreement may reflect the acknowledgment of the union that it should not be called upon to deal with matters it is not equipped to deal with or that might cause conflicts within its membership. Where remedies are available elsewhere, the silence of the agreement may reflect the wishes of the union that those remedies be used in preference to the remedies available under the agreement. Silence in the agreement does not indicate a denial of a right or its remedies. On the other hand, overloading the grievance and arbitration procedure with issues the parties neither intended nor contemplated channelling there, may make labour arbitration anything but expeditious and cost-effective. The present case speaks for itself in this respect.

¶101 O'Brien's dismissal is not arbitrable because her Union and her employer agreed not to cover the dismissal of probationary employees in their collective agreement, and the legislature did not intend to require that they do so. She must seek the vindication of her rights before the Human Rights Commission, as would any employee not covered by a collective agreement. . . .

✥ ✥ ✥

The difficult question of the interface between the human rights forum and grievance arbitration will be discussed from the vantage point of the human rights process in section 13:350 below.

9:620 Arbitration and the *Canadian Charter of Rights and Freedoms*

At least where the arbitrator's power derives from statute, arbitrators' orders are subject to the *Charter*, since the adjudicator is a creature of statute who "does not have the power to make an order that would result in an infringement of the *Charter*". *Slaight Communications Inc. v. Davidson*, [1989] 1 S.C.R. 1038, 59 D.L.R. (4th) 416, 93 N.R. 183.

Whether the *Charter* applies to the arbitral dispute itself depends on whether there is a nexus with government: *Douglas/Kwantlen Faculty Assn. v. Douglas College*, [1990] 3 S.C.R. 570. The *Charter* applied to the dispute in *Douglas College* because community colleges were sufficiently subject to government control to be considered part of the apparatus of government. Similarly, in *Lavigne v. Ontario Public Service Employees' Union*, [1991] 2 S.C.R. 211, the Supreme Court of Canada held that the application of the Charter to union security provisions in the collective agreement turned on a finding that the employer was a governmental actor and its acquiescence to a union request for a Rand Formula clause in the collective agreement was sufficient to constitute governmental conduct.

9:621 Arbitral Jurisdiction to Give *Charter* Remedies

Although the Supreme Court of Canada had held in *Douglas College* that a labour arbitrator had the jurisdiction to hear Charter challenges by virtue of section 52 of the *Constitution Act, 1982*, the Court had left open the status of the arbitrator under section 24(1) of the *Charter*; that is, could an arbitrator be "a court of competent jurisdiction?" That issue was addressed in the following case.

Weber v. Ontario Hydro, [1995] 2 S.C.R. 929

[Weber, an employee of Ontario Hydro, took an extended leave of absence because of back problems. Hydro paid him the sick benefits stipulated by the collective agreement. As a result of the information it obtained through private investigators who used false identities, Hydro suspended Weber for abusing his sick leave benefits. Grievances against Hydro were settled. Weber also commenced a court action based on the torts of trespass, nuisance, deceit, and invasion of privacy, as well as breach of sections 7 and 8 of the *Canadian Charter of Rights and Freedoms*, claiming damages for the surveillance. Under section 45(1) (now section 48(1)) of the Ontario *Labour Relations Act*, every collective agreement "shall provide for the final and binding settlement by arbitration . . . of all differences between the parties arising from the interpretation, application, administration or alleged violation of the agreement."]

> McLACHLIN J. (for the majority): . . . *Douglas College* . . . involved a grievance before a labour arbitrator. In that case, as in this, *Charter* issues were raised. It was argued, *inter alia*, that a labour arbitration was not the appropriate place to argue *Charter* issues. After a thorough review of the advantages and disadvantages of having such issues decided before labour tribunals, La Forest J. concluded that while the informal processes of such tribunals might not be entirely suited to dealing with constitutional issues, clear advantages to the practice exist. Citizens are permitted to assert their *Charter* rights in a prompt,

inexpensive, informal way. The parties are not required to duplicate submissions on the case in two different fora, for determination of two different legal issues. A specialized tribunal can quickly sift the facts and compile a record for the reviewing court. And the specialized competence of the tribunal may provide assistance to the reviewing court . . . *Douglas/Kwantlen Faculty Assn. v. Douglas College* also answers the concern of the Court of Appeal below that the *Charter* takes the issue out of the labour context and puts it in the state context. While the *Charter* issue may raise broad policy concerns, it is nonetheless a component of the labour dispute, and hence within the jurisdiction of the labour arbitrator. The existence of broad policy concerns with respect to a given issue cannot preclude the labour arbitrator from deciding all facets of the labour dispute.

This brings us to the question of whether a labour arbitrator in this case has the power to grant *Charter* remedies. The remedies claimed are damages and a declaration. The power and duty of arbitrators to apply the law extends to the *Charter*, an essential part of the law of Canada: *Douglas/Kwantlen Faculty Assn. v. Douglas College* . . .; *Cuddy Chicks Ltd. v. Ontario (Labour Relations Board)* . . . ; *Re Ontario Council of Regents for Colleges of Applied Arts & Technology and Ontario Public Service Employees Union.* . . . In applying the law of the land to the disputes before them, be it the common law, statute law or the *Charter*, arbitrators may grant such remedies as the Legislature or Parliament has empowered them to grant in the circumstances. For example, a labour arbitrator can consider the *Charter*, find laws inoperative for conflict with it, and go on to grant remedies in the exercise of his powers under the *Labour Code*: *Douglas/Kwantlen Faculty Assn. v. Douglas College* . . . . If an arbitrator can find a law violative of the *Charter*, it would seem he or she can determine whether conduct in the administration of the collective agreement violates the *Charter* and likewise grant remedies. . . .

It is thus Parliament or the Legislature that determines if a court is a court of competent jurisdiction; as McIntyre J. puts it [in *Mills v. The Queen*, . . .] the jurisdiction of the various courts of Canada is fixed by Parliament and the Legislatures, not by judges. Nor is there magic in labels; it is not the name of the tribunal that determines the matter, but its powers. (It may be noted that the French version of s. 24(1) uses '*tribunal*' rather than '*cour*.') The practical import of fitting *Charter* remedies into the existing system of tribunals, as McIntyre J. notes, is that litigants have 'direct' access to *Charter* remedies in the tribunal charged with deciding their case.

It follows from *Mills* that statutory tribunals created by Parliament or the Legislatures may be courts of competent jurisdiction to grant *Charter* remedies, provided they have jurisdiction over the parties and the subject matter of the dispute and are empowered to make the orders sought.

[In this case, because the grievances had been settled, the courts had no jurisdiction to determine the *Charter* claims raised in those grievances. Thus, McLachlin J. said, it was not necessary to decide whether Ontario Hydro was subject to the *Charter*.]

✻ ✻ ✻

In *Nova Scotia (Workers' Compensation Board) v. Martin*, 2003 SCC 54, the Supreme Court of Canada affirmed the authority of administrative tribunals to apply the *Charter* in cases involving governmental action. Gonthier J. said, for the entire Court, at paragraph 3:

> I am of the view that the rules concerning the jurisdiction of administrative tribunals to apply the *Charter* established by this Court in *Douglas/Kwantlen Faculty Assn. v. Douglas College* . . . , *Cuddy Chicks Ltd. v. Ontario (Labour Relations Board).* . . , and *Tétreault-Gadoury v. Canada (Employment and Immigration Commission)* . . . , ought to be reappraised and restated as a clear set of guidelines. Administrative tribunals which have jurisdiction — whether explicit or implied — to decide questions of law arising under a legislative provision are presumed to have concomitant jurisdiction to decide the constitutional validity of that provision. This presumption may only be rebutted by showing that the legislature clearly intended to exclude Charter issues from the tribunal's authority over questions of law.

"Canadians," Gonthier said at paragraph 29, "should be entitled to assert the rights and freedoms that the Constitution guarantees them in the most accessible forum available, without the need for parallel proceedings before the courts. . ."

9:630 Multiple Forums

An employee whose union files a grievance and subsequently invokes arbitration under a collective agreement may also have claims under other statutes, or at common law. The employee may therefore want to bring a civil action or file a complaint under human rights legislation, and the same set of facts may lend themselves to complaints under other employment-related statutes.

9:631 Arbitration and Civil Actions

St. Anne Nackawic Pulp & Paper Co. Ltd. v. Canadian Paperworkers Union, Local 219, [1986] 1 S.C.R. 704, is set out above in section 8:315, in connection with the availability of injunctions against strikes in breach of collective agreements. In *St. Anne Nackawic*, the employer had obtained an interim injunction against an illegal strike by the union, and then sued in tort for damages resulting from the strike. The case established that, with some exceptions, the grievance and arbitration procedure under the collective agreement has exclusive jurisdiction to deal with disputes arising between the parties to the agreement, and that the jurisdiction of the courts was therefore ousted. Estey J., for the Supreme Court of Canada, held that permitting concurrent actions would undermine the statutory mandatory arbitration scheme, but that there remained a residual discretionary power in courts of inherent jurisdiction over matters such as injunctions.

The later case of *Weber v. Ontario Hydro* is excerpted above, in section 9:621, on the question of arbitral jurisdiction to hear *Charter* issues and grant *Charter* remedies. However, the main issue in Weber was the extent to which the arbitral regime ousts the jurisdiction of the courts in civil matters. The following excerpts are from the majority judgment on that issue.

Weber v. Ontario Hydro, [1995] 2 SCR 929

McLACHLIN J.:

. . .

The crucial question we face is when employees and employers are precluded from suing each other in the courts by labour legislation providing for binding arbitration. It is common ground that s. 45(1) of the Ontario *Labour Relations Act* prevents the bringing of civil actions which are based solely on the collective agreement.

. . .

The cases reveal three different views on the effect of final and binding arbitration clauses in labour legislation. I shall deal with each in turn.

[McLachlin J. explained why, in her view, neither the concurrent model nor the model of overlapping jurisdiction was satisfactory. Under the concurrent model, the courts have jurisdiction over common law or statutory claims even where they arise in the employment context. *Ste. Anne Nackawic* stood for the principle that mandatory arbitration clauses in labour statutes deprive the courts of concurrent jurisdiction. However, in determining whether the arbitral regime has exclusive jurisdiction, '[t]he issue is not whether the action, defined legally, is independent of the collective agreement, but rather whether the *dispute* is one "arising under [the] collective agreement."' In this case, the Ontario statute made arbitration the only available remedy for differences arising out of the collective agreement. The word 'differences' referred to the dispute between the parties, not to the legal actions which one may be entitled to bring against the other.

> The object of the provision — and what is thus excluded from the courts — is all proceedings arising from the difference between the parties, however those proceedings may be framed. Where the dispute falls within the terms of the Act, there is no room for concurrent proceedings.

Furthermore, permitting concurrent actions would undermine the goal of the collective bargaining regime, which was to resolve disputes quickly and economically with a minimum of disruption.]

. . .

> On [the model of overlapping jurisdiction,] notwithstanding that the facts of the dispute arise out of the collective agreement, a court action may be brought if it raises issues which go beyond the traditional subject matter of labour law.
>
> . . . In so far as it is based on characterizing a cause of action which lies outside the arbitrator's power or expertise, [the overlapping spheres model] violates the injunction of the Act and *St. Anne Nackawic* that one must look not to the legal characterization of the wrong, but to the facts giving rise to the dispute. It would also leave it open to innovative pleaders to evade the legislative prohibition on parallel court actions by raising new and imaginative causes of action. . . . This would undermine the legislative purposes underlying such provisions and the intention of the parties to the agreement. This approach, like the concurrency model, fails to meet the test of the statute, the jurisprudence and policy.
>
> . . .

The final alternative is to accept that if the difference between the parties arises from the collective agreement, the claimant must proceed by arbitration and the courts have no power to entertain an action in respect of that dispute. There is no overlapping jurisdiction.

On this approach, the task of the judge or arbitrator determining the appropriate forum for the proceedings centres on whether the dispute or difference between the parties arises out of the collective agreement. Two elements must be considered: the dispute and the ambit of the collective agreement.

In considering the dispute, the decision-maker must attempt to define its 'essential character,' to use the phrase of La Forest J.A. in *Energy & Chemical Workers Union, Local 691 v. Irving Oil Ltd.* . . . . In the majority of cases the nature of the dispute will be clear; either it had to do with the collective agreement or it did not. Some cases, however, may be less than obvious. The question in each case is whether the dispute, in its essential character, arises from the interpretation, application, administration or violation of the collective agreement.

Because the nature of the dispute and the ambit of the collective agreement will vary from case to case, it is impossible to categorize the classes of case that will fall within the exclusive jurisdiction of the arbitrator. However, a review of decisions over the past few years reveals the following claims among those over which the courts have been found to lack jurisdiction: wrongful dismissal; bad faith on the part of the union; conspiracy and constructive dismissal; and damage to reputation . . . .

This approach does not preclude all actions in the courts between employer and employee. Only disputes which expressly or inferentially arise out of the collective agreement are foreclosed to the courts: *Elliott v. De Havilland Aircraft Co. of Canada Ltd.* . . .; *Butt v. United Steelworkers of America* . . .; *Bourne v. Otis Elevator Co.* . . . . Additionally, the courts possess residual jurisdiction based on their special powers, as discussed by Estey J. in *St. Anne Nackawic* . . . .

Against this approach, the appellant Weber argues that jurisdiction over torts and Charter claims should not be conferred on arbitrators because they lack expertise on the legal questions such claims raise. The answer to this concern is that arbitrators are subject to judicial review. Within the parameters of that review, their errors may be corrected by the courts. The procedural inconvenience of an occasional application for judicial review is outweighed by the advantages of having a single tribunal deciding all issues arising from the dispute in the first instance. This does not mean that the arbitrator will consider separate 'cases' of tort, contract or *Charter*. Rather, in dealing with the dispute under the collective agreement and fashioning an appropriate remedy, the arbitrator will have regard to whether the breach of the collective agreement also constitutes a breach of a common law duty, or of the *Charter*.

The appellant Weber also argues that arbitrators may lack the legal power to consider the issues before them. This concern is answered by the power and duty of arbitrators to apply the law of the land to the disputes before them. To this end, arbitrators may refer to both the common law and statutes: *St. Anne Nackawic*; *McLeod v. Egan*. . . . As Denning L.J. put it, '[t]here is not one law for arbitrators and another for the court, but one law for all': *David*

Taylor & Son, Ltd. v. Barnett. . . . This also applies to the *Charter: Douglas/Kwantlen Faculty Assn. v. Douglas College.* . . .

It might occur that a remedy is required which the arbitrator is not empowered to grant. In such a case, the courts of inherent jurisdiction in each province may take jurisdiction. This Court in *St. Anne Nackawic* confirmed that the New Brunswick Act did not oust the residual inherent jurisdiction of the superior courts to grant injunctions in labour matters. . . . Similarly, the Court of Appeal of British Columbia in *Moore v. British Columbia* . . . accepted that the court's residual jurisdiction to grant a declaration was not ousted by the British Columbia labour legislation, although it declined to exercise that jurisdiction on the ground that the powers of the arbitrator were sufficient to remedy the wrong and that deference was owed to the labour tribunal. What must be avoided, to use the language of Estey J. in *St. Anne Nackawic* . . . is a 'real deprivation of ultimate remedy.'

. . .

APPLICATION OF THE LAW TO THE DISPUTE IN THIS CASE

On the interpretation outlined above, the question is whether the conduct giving rise to the dispute between the parties arises either expressly or inferentially out of the collective agreement between them.

The appellant contends that the dispute in this case falls outside the collective agreement. The act of hiring private investigators who used deception to enter his family home and report on him does not, he contends, relate to the interpretation, application or administration of the collective agreement. It is not in its essential character a labour matter; it is rather a matter of the common law and the constitutional rights of himself and his family. It follows, he submits, that the arbitrator does not have jurisdiction over the claims and that the courts may entertain them. . . .

Article 2.2 of the collective agreement extends the grievance procedure to '[a]ny allegation that an employee has been subjected to unfair treatment or any dispute arising out of the content of this Agreement. . . .' The dispute in this case arose out of the content of the Agreement. Item 13.0 of Part A of the Agreement provides that the 'benefits of the Ontario Hydro Sick Leave Plan . . . shall be considered as part of this Agreement.' It further provides that the provisions of the plan 'are not an automatic right of an employee and the administration of this plan and all decisions regarding the appropriateness or degree of its application shall be vested solely in Ontario Hydro.' This language brings the medical plan and Hydro's decisions concerning it expressly within the purview of the collective agreement. Under the plan, Hydro had the right to decide what benefits the employee would receive, subject to the employee's right to grieve the decision. In the course of making such a decision, Hydro is alleged to have acted improperly. That allegation would appear to fall within the phrase 'unfair treatment or any dispute arising out of the content of [the] Agreement' within Article 2.2.

I conclude that the wide language of Article 2.2 of the Agreement, combined with item 13.0, covers the conduct alleged against Hydro. Hydro's alleged actions were directly related to a process which is expressly subject to the grievance procedure. While aspects of the alleged conduct may arguably have extended beyond what the parties contemplated, this does not alter the essential character of the conduct. In short, the difference between the parties relates to the 'administration . . . of the agreement' within s. 45(1) of the *Labour Relations Act.* . . .

* * *

The test in *Weber* — whether the dispute in its "essential character" arises out of the collective agreement — may at times indicate that the existence of another statutory regime will oust the jurisdiction of the arbitrator. In *Regina Police Assn. Inc. v. Regina (City) Board of Police Commissioners*, [2000] 1 S.C.R. 360, a police officer tried to withdraw his resignation, which he had submitted in an attempt to avoid disciplinary action. The Chief of Police did not permit him to withdraw the resignation, and the union grieved. Did the arbitrator have jurisdiction to hear the matter, or did it have to be heard under the *Saskatchewan Police Act*, which governed discipline and dismissal in police forces? The collective agreement stated that its provisions were not to be used where the *Police Act* and Regulations applied.

Bastarache J., for the Supreme Court of Canada, said that "the rationale for adopting the exclusive jurisdiction model [in *Weber*] was to ensure that the legislative scheme in issue was not frustrated by the conferral of jurisdiction upon an adjudicative body that was not intended by the legislature." Although the collective agreement addressed termination, it did not govern dismissal for cause, whereas the *Police Act* and Regulations provided a complete code for disciplinary matters. The "essential character of the dispute was disciplinary," the Court held, so the procedures under the *Police Act* applied and the matter was not arbitrable.

* * *

In *Weber*, the union had settled the grievances brought on Weber's behalf, but, the Supreme Court of Canada held, he was now precluded from bringing a civil action himself. Thus, in a situation where a unionized employee might previously have had access to the courts, he or she is now more heavily dependent on whether the union will take a grievance on his or her behalf. This problem will be discussed in the next chapter, in section 10:230, in connection with the Supreme Court of Canada decision in *Allen v. Alberta*, 2003 SCC 13.

The passages from the Supreme Court of Canada judgment in *Weber* set out in section 9:621 and earlier in this section indicate that the Court saw the exclusive jurisdiction model as applying to Charter claims as well as common law claims. The Ontario Court of Appeal in *Weber* had held that the exclusive jurisdiction model should be applied to common law claims, but that it could not be applicable to *Charter* claims because it would make a person's access to courts for enforcement of his or her most fundamental individual rights contingent upon support from the union as a collectivity. The majority of the Supreme Court of Canada did not address this very significant issue in Weber. For this and other reasons, the decision has been controversial, as the following excerpt indicates.

Michel Picher, "Defining the Scope of Arbitration: The Impact of Weber: An Arbitrator's Perspective" (1999–2000), Lab. Arb. Y.B. 99, at 108–10, 114–17, 144–47

. . .

The decision of the Supreme Court of Canada in *Weber v. Ontario Hydro* in 1995, and its aftermath in a number of court decisions and arbitration awards, gives cause to wonder whether the success of arbitration may ultimately be its undoing. In Canada, in contrast to the United States, labour arbitration is a statutorily mandated procedure for the resolution of disputes concerning the application, interpretation or administration of the provisions of a collective agreement. Notwithstanding its statutory underpinnings, however, labour arbitration has evolved as an essentially private and consensual process whose procedures and scope have traditionally been controlled by the parties themselves. Before examining the reasoning and result in *Weber*, it is critical to appreciate the evolution of the limitations of arbitrability as fashioned by unions and employers, and long affirmed by arbitrators in Canada. The parties to collective agreements have always recognized that to make all workplace disputes arbitrable is unrealistic. While the enlightened participants in a collective bargaining relationship may wish to see justice and fairness in all things, they do not want to encourage all manner of grievances or surrender the day-to-day life of the workplace to micro-management by arbitrators.

A myriad of aspects of the employment relationship may not be appropriate for regulation under the terms of a collective agreement. Understandably, therefore, not all complaints or conflicts arising in the workplace setting have been made amenable to final and binding resolution through arbitration. In their own mutual interest employers and unions have long agreed to keep certain matters out of the arbitration arena. While arbitration is a simplified and informal quasi-judicial process, it nevertheless occasions substantial expenditures of time and money for employers and unions. The decision to arbitrate is therefore not taken lightly, a reality of collective bargaining which has its own value in the settlement of disputes.

Considerable mischief would operate if trade unions found themselves able, and therefore politically compelled, to grieve and arbitrate virtually all perceived workplace injustices, whether or not they arise under the precise terms of the collective agreement. The loss of an employees' parking lot or the discontinuation of the annual gift of a Christmas turkey to employees may cause employees affected to feel 'aggrieved' or unfairly treated. However, if the collective agreement makes no provision for employee parking or Christmas turkeys, and contains no omnibus provision for the general preservation of all existing privileges, a trade union has traditionally been without any contractual leverage to bring a related grievance which can progress to arbitration. That state of affairs is not the result of any shortage of bargaining power on the part of trade unions, nor is it reflective of some social injustice within the collective bargaining regime. It is a reflection of the conscious decision, wisely made, by trade unions and employers alike, that access to arbitration is a precious commodity which should be limited to contractual rights and obligations of substance and value to employees collectively, as well as to the employer.

. . .

A most disturbing dimension of the decision of the Supreme Court of Canada in *Weber v. Ontario Hydro* is the apparent failure of the Court to recognize and understand these delicate and critical limitations of the labour arbitration system, and the central role of all-important principles of arbitrability. In light of court and arbitration decisions following *Weber*, there is also cause for concern, that the good intentions and 'pro-arbitration' bent of that decision may prove to be a Pandora's box of unforeseen negative consequences for individual rights, as well as for labour arbitration and collective bargaining itself.

For good reason, parties to collective agreements have carefully fashioned ways of discussing general allegations of unjust treatment. Recognizing that there is a value to allowing employees to vent their complaints, including complaints which do not relate to the substantive provisions of the collective agreement, many have fashioned collective agreement provisions which allow employees, through their trade unions, to raise non-arbitrable issues in the pre-arbitration steps of the grievance procedure. Typically, the language of such collective agreements will provide that an employee who feels that he or she has been 'unjustly dealt with' may file a grievance, and the complaint may be advanced through the pre-arbitration steps of the grievance procedure. The collective agreements are generally categorical, however, that such complaints are not to proceed beyond the discussions which form part of the grievance procedure, and are not arbitrable.

. . .

Central to [McLachlin J.'s] reasoning [in *Weber*] is the perception that the grievance and arbitration provisions of the collective agreement 'are broad, and expressly purport to regulate the conduct at the heart of this dispute.' Specifically, she notes that article 2.2 of the collective agreement allows a grievance to be filed in respect of '[a]ny allegation that an employee has been subjected to unfair treatment or any dispute arising out of the content of this Agreement'. . . .

Unfortunately, the Court failed to understand that broad allegations of unjust treatment were never intended to be arbitrated and that the grievance procedure, established under article 2 of the collective agreement, is distinct from the arbitration procedure, separately provided for under article 3. Of that there can be no doubt. Article 3.1 of the collective agreement then before the Court, titled 'Arbitration,' a provision not discussed by the majority or in dissent, expressly provides as follows:

This procedure shall not apply to Union allegations of unfair treatment.

. . .

Although Ontario Hydro and the Power Workers' Union expressly agreed that allegations of 'unfair treatment' arising under the 'wide language of article 2.2 of the Agreement' were not arbitrable, the Court rested much of its decision requiring arbitration on this provision. In the result, the central reasoning of the Supreme Court of Canada in a decision of enormous importance to the labour relations community is reducible to a logical *non-sequitur*: because his collective agreement allows him to grieve unjust treatment, a board of arbitration has exclusive jurisdiction to arbitrate Weber's *Charter* and tort claims. However, claims of unjust treatment were, by the clear terms of the collective agreement, inarbitrable.

The Court based its reasoning on the fact that the sick benefits, whose alleged abuse by Weber triggered the surveillance, were part of the collective agreement. McLachlin J.'s comment that the dispute fell within the grievance procedure because 'the wide language of art. 2.2 of the agreement [unjust treatment], combined with item 13.0 [sick benefits], covers the conduct alleged against Hydro,' and her further observation that the employer's actions were 'directly related to a process which is expressly subject to the *grievance procedure*,' are beyond reproach (emphasis added). The Court's reasoning breaks down, however, when grievability is confused with arbitrability.

Further, as the subsequent court and arbitral jurisprudence . . . demonstrates, the line of jurisdictional fence-plotting has been made extremely wobbly and unpredictable for judges and arbitrators attempting to apply Weber because of the ambiguity of the Court's two-fold test for vesting exclusive arbitral jurisdiction: the nature of the dispute and the ambit of the collective agreement. As is becoming painfully evident, courts and arbitrators are frequently at a loss to define those disputes which arise inferentially from the collective agreement. Bearing in mind that legislators in their wisdom have long required that collective agreements be in writing, and that arbitrators have generally been sensitive not to imply unduly rights and obligations not reduced to writing, absent some clear indication in the language or scheme of the collective agreement itself, the new concept of matters arising 'inferentially' from the collective agreement creates an unprecedented standard upon whose application honest adjudicators will inevitably differ, and in relation to which employers and unions may exercise less contractual control and predictability.

. . . While a compelling case can be made that the resolution of *Charter*, statutory and common law issues by boards of arbitration, subject to judicial review for standards of absolute correctness, in keeping with *McLeod v. Egan* is a positive step for the administration of justice, providing single-forum efficiencies and the benefit of expert tribunal insights in the initial analysis of *Charter* issues for the benefit of reviewing courts it is unfortunate that so monumental a decision as *Weber* should rest, in substantial part, on what appears to be mistaken reasoning.

There is also a substantial argument to be made, which is in fact espoused in some quarters of the union movement, that far from being a victory for trade unions and collective bargaining, *Weber* will, in the end, prove to be an anti-union decision, at least in its consequences. As generally democratic institutions with relatively limited resources, unions have reason, after *Weber*, to fear the pressures that will now mount to pursue wide-ranging claims far beyond the scope of grievances traditionally brought to arbitration. They may be forced, under the threat of accusations of breach of their duty of fair representation, to bring or defend claims of defamation and negligence, as well as a multitude of statutory and *Charter* claims at arbitration. Labour arbitration itself, originally conceived as an informal and less costly alternative to the courts to resolve relatively simple contractual disputes, may increasingly become the forum for a much broader range of claims that are not contractual in their essence, involving more extensive and complex forms of evidence, resulting in awards and remedies of a kind which would have been unimaginable and would have been seen as undesirable by legislators and practitioners involved in the establishment and evolution of what, until now, has been the relatively efficient and expeditious labour arbitration process.

At the first and most obvious level, those parties to collective agreements in Canada whose grievance and arbitration provisions are comparable to those considered by the Supreme Court of Canada in *Weber* should be concerned that the decision of the Court can be construed as obliterating the fences which they have erected to protect the privileged ground of arbitrability. . . . Presumably arbitrators themselves will be able to protect the fences of arbitrability in cases where the collective agreement, like the Hydro/PWU agreement, expressly contemplates that general complaints of unfairness are not arbitrable. However, while it may be expected that the Supreme Court will have occasion to clarify, and indeed rectify, this aspect of the Weber decision, it remains open for some to argue that the result in Weber demonstrates the Court's intention that grievable 'unfairness' complaints, including *Charter*, statutory and common law claims, are arbitrable, notwithstanding contrary language expressly negotiated within the terms of a collective agreement. It is to be hoped that, in the end, common sense will prevail, and that neither arbitrators nor courts will conclude that the parties to a collective agreement intended arbitration to be the exclusive forum for such open-ended claims, absent clear and unequivocal contractual language to support such a conclusion.

Few would question the value of single-forum efficiencies for the resolution of collective agreement-based claims having several facets, which might otherwise involve litigation before two or more tribunals or courts. . . . It is, however, an entirely different order of things for trade unions to take on the burden of enforcing statutory and Charter rights which have only a marginal employment connection, or for them to be compelled to vindicate common law rights traditionally protected by the courts, such as actions in defamation never before arbitrable. The wisdom of forcing employers to defend such claims in labour arbitrations is equally questionable. Those familiar with collective bargaining and labour arbitration know well that union and employee grievances can involve a high degree of interpersonal conflict, with a substantial emotional charge. That reality, coupled with the jurisdictional green light of *Weber*, provides a heady mix. Until *Weber* is clarified and reasonably restricted in a manner consistent with the long-term interests of collective bargaining, it may prove to be a Trojan horse for unions, employers and organized employees alike.

. . .

. . . In Canada, post-*Weber*, the concern is that arbitrators will assume jurisdiction beyond the intended scope of the collective agreement, based on an overly broad characterization of the 'nature of the dispute' and the 'ambit of the collective agreement,' to use the two-fold terminology of McLachlin J. At first blush many, including this author, welcomed the single forum rationale of Weber. However, as demonstrated in the cases to date, the concept of disputes 'which expressly or *inferentially* arise out of the collective agreement' as a basis for exclusive arbitral jurisdiction has proven dangerously ambiguous, undermining the common law rights of individuals and threatening a long-established and rational understanding of the limits of arbitrability, so essential to sound labour relations and a viable labour arbitration process controlled by the parties themselves.

. . . If Weber is broadly interpreted, the focus of arbitrators could shift from their traditional role of facilitating the smooth functioning of collective agreements to vindicating individual rights at the expense of long-term collective bargaining relationships. When the main subject-matter of labour arbitration expands from disputes about overtime provisions, call-in pay and statutory holidays to include bitter personal conflicts about negligence, defamation and other emotion-charged individual rights, arbitration itself may come to be perceived as an instrument that promotes conflict and human discord, in ways that do not ultimately serve the best long-term interests of employers, unions or employees.

. . . Likewise, *Weber* can be a positive step forward if it is understood as a logical extension of *McLeod v. Egan*, facilitating the single-forum resolution of genuine collective agreement disputes which the parties themselves intended to be arbitrable, notwithstanding that those disputes have a related *Charter*, statutory or common law dimension. In Canada, it will be incumbent on the courts, arbitrators and practitioners of labour relations to appreciate the consequences for the arbitration process and the danger for collective bargaining itself in giving Weber too broad an interpretation. Subject to well-established precepts of public policy, the critical concept of arbitrability must never be allowed to go beyond the contractual control of the parties themselves.

In a healthy and responsive legal system, 'law' is not a moral imperative handed down from on high. Rather, it is the product of human interaction and mutual expectations developed at the grassroots, carefully nurtured over time. Recognizing that truth, labour arbitration will be better served if arbitrators, in the face of *Weber*, return to the first of first principles and ask, 'What did the parties intend?'

For their part, employers and unions would do well to be explicit in their collective agreements. They must appreciate the potential cost to their relationship, and to their respective resources, if the vindication of personal claims consumes the arbitration agenda. They should be clear if they do not intend tort claims such as defamation and negligence to be arbitrable. They should also specify that *Charter* and statutory issues are arbitrable only for the purposes of dealing with an alleged violation of their collective agreement, or as otherwise required by statute. With these adjustments, and a degree of understanding by the courts and arbitrators, labour arbitration will retain its proper focus of interpreting and applying collective agreements and facilitating the collective bargaining process. In the end employers, unions and employees will be better served.

[Reprinted with permission of Lancaster House Publishing.]

For a more recent discussion of the problems arising from Weber, and how courts and arbitrators have been dealing with those problems, see John-Paul Alexandrowicz, "Restoring the Role of Grievance Arbitration: A New Approach to *Weber*," (2003) 10 C.L.E.L.J. 269, forthcoming. For a treatment of those problems that puts more emphasis on the relationship between arbitration and other tribunals, see Richard MacDowell, "Labour Arbitration: The New Labour Court?" (2000) 8 C.L.E.L.J. 121.

9:700 JUDICIAL REVIEW OF ARBITRATION

The scope of the arbitrator's role is delimited by the parameters established by judicial review of arbitration awards. It was not until the 1960s that the Supreme Court of Canada began taking an active role in the interpretation of collective agreements, on judicial review of arbitration awards. Since that time a substantial body of case law on the reviewability of arbitration awards has developed.

The watershed decision of the Supreme Court of Canada was *C.U.P.E., Local 963 v. New Brunswick Liquor Corporation*, [1979] 2 S.C.R. 227, which directed the courts to take a strongly deferential approach to the decisions of labour boards, largely because of the high degree of specialized expertise of those boards. The Court has generally taken a similar approach to the review of grievance arbitration decisions. The following case shows, however, that even the application of the "patent unreasonableness" test may involve close scrutiny of the language of the collective agreement and the arbitrator's reasoning.

Canada Safeway Ltd. v. Retail, Wholesale and Department Store Union, Local 454, [1998] 1 S.C.R. 1079

[The nature of the grievance and the relevant provisions of the applicable collective agreement were set out as follows in the dissenting judgment of L'Heureux-Dubé J., at paragraph 3:

> The employee Ms. Hardy grieved the drastic reduction in her scheduled hours and the dramatic change to her employment relationship. In assessing this matter, the Board reviewed the collective agreement's scheduling provisions to find that the employer's conduct constituted a breach of Article A-1.01(2), which provides:
>
> > A-1.01 . . .
> > 2. A weekly schedule of daily hours for part-time employees shall be posted by Thursday at 6:00 P.M. for the following week. . . .
>
> It is complemented by Article A-1.04, the "most available hours" clause, which reads:
>
> > A-1.04 . . .
> > 2. Effective March 23, 1986, in the scheduling of part-time employees in a store, the most available part-time hours of work on a weekly basis shall be assigned to such employees within the store within the classification and department on the basis of seniority provided the employee has the qualifications and ability to handle the work to be performed in a competent manner. . . .
> >
> > . . .
> >
> > 4. Regular part-time employees will have their schedule for the following work week posted along with other employees in the store. . . .
>
> This obligation on the employer to schedule part-time employees for the most available hours within a department on the basis of seniority is limited to department and job classification. But in the case of a "reduction" to part-time or layoff under Article 12.03, seniority governs an employee's right to access available hours across departments. This Article reads:
>
> > 12.03 Full-time or part-time seniority as defined in 12.01 above shall govern in case of reduction to part-time, layoff and recall, providing the employee involved has the qualifications and ability to handle the work to be performed in a competent manner.]

¶40 CORY and McLACHLIN JJ. (for the majority): — Is it patently unreasonable to conclude that an employee whose actual hours of work remain constant, but whose scheduled hours are reduced, was constructively laid off? That is the issue which must be addressed in this case.

FACTUAL BACKGROUND

¶41 Kelly Hardy began working at Safeway as a part-time deli clerk in 1986. As well, she received training which enabled her to work in the meat department under a different job classification. She was scheduled to work in both departments for a total average of 37 hours per week. Ms. Hardy worked a certain but not specific number of hours pursuant to a schedule and the balance of her hours was on a call-in basis. A schedule of employee hours was posted every Thursday for the following work week and if call-in hours became available, part-time employees would receive a telephone call indicating their services were required.

¶42 In 1989, Ms. Hardy's scheduled hours dropped to between 30 and 37 hours. She was advised that her dual role as deli clerk and meat clerk was no longer acceptable. She chose to continue in the meat department because she expected that more work hours would be available. However, after the transfer, her scheduled hours fell even further to between 24 and 26 hours. They were then further reduced to one four-hour shift per week. As a result of the "call-ins," however, her actual hours of work did not change significantly.

¶43 At this time, junior employees in the deli department, in which Ms. Hardy had originally been trained, were being assigned more scheduled hours than she was receiving in the meat department.

¶44 Ms. Hardy grieved the reduction in her scheduled hours, alleging it violated the "most available hours clause" of the collective agreement, and requested scheduled hours in the deli department. The "most available hours clause" of the collective agreement required the assignment of part-time hours on the basis of seniority "within the classification and department" provided the employee's qualifications and ability met the requirements.

. . .

ARBITRATION BOARD (1994), 44 L.A.C. (4TH) 325

¶45 Ms. Hardy's grievance was upheld by the majority of the Arbitration Board. It found that the substantial reduction in her hours, combined with the scheduling of more junior employees to perform work which she was qualified to perform, constituted a "constructive layoff" which gave her the right to 'bump' less senior employees and to be scheduled across department classifications.

¶46 Although the layoff question was not specifically raised in Ms. Hardy's grievance, the Board found it was linked to her complaint about the reduction in her hours.

¶47 The Board noted that the collective agreement required that the employer post a schedule of hours to be worked by part-time employees by 6:00 p.m. each Thursday for the following week and that seniority governed the assignment of part-time hours.

¶48 The Board concluded that Ms. Hardy's loss of scheduled hours did not result from her hours being assigned to more senior employees or from there being no available hours. Instead, it resulted from the employer's desire for flexibility in scheduling which would reduce costs. The Board found that the fact that Ms. Hardy's scheduled hours had been reduced to one four-hour shift per week while she continued to be needed for significantly more hours indicated that Safeway was underutilising the scheduling provision of the collective agreement. Although the collective agreement did not prohibit Safeway from calling employees in as their services were required, the Board concluded that the employer could not schedule hours at such a minimal level as to deprive the obligation to schedule work of any meaning.

¶49 The Board held, at p. 336, that the employer "breached the scheduling provisions of the collective agreement in a manner that has resulted in . . . the grievor receiving substantially fewer scheduled hours . . . and . . . a constructive lay-off has occurred." It concluded that Ms. Hardy should enjoy the benefits of a laid-off employee and that the seniority provisions should be applied, giving her preference over junior employees to do work for which she was qualified.

¶50 One of the three Board members dissented. He found it illogical that a part-time employee who worked the same number of hours, in the same store, in the same department and in the same classification could be said to have been laid off. Further, he disagreed with awarding the grievor layoff remedies for a breach of the scheduling provision. Rather, the proper remedy should have been an order to correct the scheduling deficiencies.

. . .

RELEVANT LEGISLATION

¶57 The *Trade Union Act*, R.S.S. 1978, c. T-17, s. 25:

25. — (1) Where a collective bargaining agreement contains a provision for final settlement by arbitration, without stoppage of work, of all differences between the parties to or persons bound by the agreement or on whose behalf the agreement was entered into concerning its meaning, application or violation, the finding of the arbitrator or the board of arbitration shall:

(a) be final and conclusive;

(b) in regard to all matters within the legislative jurisdiction of the Legislature of Saskatchewan be binding upon the parties; and

(c) be enforceable in the same manner as an order of the board made under this Act.

WHAT IS THE APPROPRIATE STANDARD OF JUDICIAL REVIEW?

¶58 Where labour relations tribunals are called upon to interpret or apply a collective agreement under the umbrella of a privative clause, a reviewing court can only intervene in the case of a patently unreasonable error. . . . This high degree of curial deference is essential to maintain the integrity of the system which has grown to be so efficient and effective in the resolution of disputes arising in the sensitive field of labour relations. The nature of labour disputes requires their speedy resolution by expert tribunals. The protective clause found in the Trade Union Act is the legislative recognition of the fundamental need for deference to the boards' decisions.

¶59 Section 25(1) of the Act states that the finding of the arbitrator or board of arbitration is "final and conclusive" and "binding upon the parties." Although this is not a true privative clause, it is very close to it. In United Brotherhood of Carpenters and Joiners of America, Local 579 v. Bradco Construction Ltd., . . . Sopinka J. considered a statute pertaining to a board of arbitration which contained a similar statutory provision. It was to the effect that issues arising from the interpretation of a collective bargaining agreement were to be submitted to arbitration "for final settlement." It was held that judicial deference to the decision of the arbitration board was warranted. The sage observation was made that an unlimited scope of judicial review would thwart the goal of mandatory arbitration to provide an efficient and cost effective manner of resolving disputes in this field. Those comments are appropriate to this case.

¶60 Further, in the case at bar, the Board was acting within its exclusive jurisdiction to interpret and apply the collective agreement when it considered whether the layoff provisions were applicable to Ms. Hardy's situation. It follows that there can be no doubt that the appropriate standard of review in this case is one of patent unreasonableness.

¶61 This standard of review has now been well established and accepted. It imposes a deferential approach to judicial review. This is a very high standard which will not easily be met. . . .

¶62 In order to justify judicial intervention, the arbitrator's decision must be more than simply unreasonable. In Canada (Director of Investigation and Research) v. Southam Inc., [1997] 1 S.C.R. 748, at para. 57, Iacobucci J. described the difference between an unreasonable and a patently unreasonable decision as follows:

> The difference . . . lies in the immediacy or obviousness of the defect. If the defect is apparent on the face of the tribunal's reasons, then the tribunal's decision is patently unreasonable. But if it takes some significant searching or testing to find the defect, then the decision is unreasonable but not patently unreasonable.

¶63 A reviewing court cannot intervene simply because it disagrees with the reasoning of the arbitration board or because it would have reached a different conclusion. To do so would be to usurp the power of the administrative tribunal and to remove from it the ability to arrive at erroneous conclusions within its area of specialized expertise.

¶64 If a Board purports to act in a manner that clearly exceeds its jurisdiction as set out in its empowering legislation, its decision is incorrect and thus invalid but it would also be patently unreasonable. There are, as well, certain specific egregious errors which are so patently unreasonable that a Board decision should be set aside. It may be helpful to review briefly the cases in which this Court has indicated that a board's decision could be found to be patently unreasonable.

. . .

¶68 We must now turn to a consideration of whether the arbitration board's award in this case was patently unreasonable.

WAS THE ARBITRATION BOARD'S AWARD PATENTLY UNREASONABLE?

¶69 There is no suggestion of unfair procedure or bias. The inquiry therefore focuses on whether the Board applied the wrong principles or applied the correct principles in the wrong way, for example, by making an award which is not supported by the evidence or by reason.

¶70 We have concluded that the Board made a patently unreasonable error of law in defining the change in Ms. Hardy's working conditions as a constructive layoff. Ms. Hardy's scheduled hours dropped from 37 or more hours per week to one four-hour shift per week. Her total hours worked, however, remained relatively constant because she was regularly called in to work by the employer. In our view, the term "layoff" as used in labour law refers to the denial of work to the employee. As a matter of law, a layoff cannot be found where the employee continued to work the usual number of hours, as here. We also conclude that the Board erred in failing to characterize Ms. Hardy's grievance in terms of the labour agreement and in imposing a remedy not rationally connected to the breach alleged. It follows that the Board's decision that a constructive layoff occurred is patently unreasonable.

¶71 The labour agreement in the case at bar does not define "layoff." We must therefore look at the cases to see how courts and labour arbitrators have defined it. They suggest that "layoff" is used in the law of labour relations to describe an interruption of the employee's work short of termination. A "layoff," as the term is used in the cases, does not terminate the employer-employee relationship. Rather, it temporarily discharges the employee. The hope or expectation of future work remains. But for the time being, there is no work for the employee. Such an employee, it is said, is laid off.

¶72 Reference to a few of the cases illustrate this use of the term. In Air-Care Ltd. v. United Steel Workers of America, [1976] 1 S.C.R. 2, at p. 6, Dickson J. (as he then was) adopted the following definition of layoff:

> "Lay-Off" is not defined in the Quebec Labour Code, R.S.Q. 1964, c. 141. However, the Shorter Oxford English Dictionary defines "lay-off" as follows: "Lay-off, a period during which a workman is temporarily discharged" and Nouveau Larousse Universel, Tome 2 "Mise à pied"; "retrait temporaire d'emploi."

The controlling idea of a layoff as a disruption (as opposed to termination) of the employment relationship is echoed by Vancise J.A. in University Hospital v. Service Employees International Union, Local 333 U.H. (1986), 46 Sask. R. 19. Stating that a layoff occurs when the employee-employer relationship is "seriously disrupted," Vancise J.A. noted at p. 28 that Black's Law Dictionary, 5th ed., defines layoff as "A termination of employment at the will of the employer. Such may be temporary (e.g. caused by seasonal or adverse economic conditions) or permanent."

¶73 While in common parlance the term "layoff" is sometimes used synonymously with termination of the employment relationship, its function in the lexicon of the law is to define a cessation of employment where there is the possibility or expectation of a return to work. The expectation may or may not materialize. But because of this expectation, the employer-employee relationship is said to be suspended rather than terminated.

¶74 The suspension of the employer-employee relationship contemplated by the term "layoff" arises as a result of the employer's removing work from the employee. As stated in Re Benson & Hedges (Canada) Ltd. and Bakery, Confectionery and Tobacco Workers International Union, Local 325 (1979), 22 L.A.C. (2d) 361, at p. 366:

> Arbitrators have generally understood the term "lay-off" as describing the situation where the services of an employee have been temporarily or indefinitely suspended owing to a lack of available work in the plant. . . .

¶75 It follows that for there to be a layoff, there must be a cessation of work. If the employee continues to work substantially the same number of hours, his or her grievance is not, whatever else it may be, a layoff. . . .

¶77 In light of the conclusion that the Board made a patently unreasonable error in finding Ms. Hardy was laid off when she had suffered no reduction of hours, it may be useful to enquire as to what lay behind the Board's reasoning. In our view, the Board made three errors. First, it defined layoff too broadly. Second, it wrongly analogized the situation before it to the legal concept of constructive dismissal. Finally, it failed to place sufficient emphasis on the terms of the collective agreement which governed the remedies for the workplace changes that Ms. Hardy experienced. We will deal with each of these errors in turn.

¶78 The Board defined layoff generally as a disruption of the employer-employee relationship. Having found that the reduction of Ms. Hardy's scheduled hours and their replacement by unscheduled hours breached an obligation to schedule in Article A-1.01(2) of the collective agreement and disrupted the employer-employee relationship, it seems to have assumed that there must also have been a layoff. The error in this reasoning stems from defining layoff as synonymous with a work disruption. Many things may constitute a disruption of the employer-employee relationship. A layoff is merely one of them. It cannot be inferred from the fact that there was a disruption in the employer-employee relationship that there was a layoff. A layoff, as the foregoing authorities demonstrate, is the specific type of disruption that occurs as a result of a cessation of work.

¶79 The second error in the Board's reasoning was to treat constructive layoff as analogous to constructive dismissal. . . .

¶80 In fact, the analogy between constructive dismissal and constructive layoff is false. Constructive dismissal recognizes the fact that a drastic change in conditions of employment may be tantamount to terminating the employment relationship, entitling the employee to notice or damages in lieu of notice. Layoff simply refers to the temporary cessation of employment, for which damages are not available. The two concepts are quite different, as are the legal consequences that flow from them. It is conceivable that an employer's denial of scheduled hours to an employee in favour of other, more junior employees, could, in appropriate circumstances, support an argument of constructive dismissal outside the collective bargaining context. But unless the hours were reduced to the point that there has been a cessation of the employee's employment, there has been no layoff.

¶81 The Board's final error lay in failing to apply the collective agreement properly to Ms. Hardy's grievance. The relations between the parties were governed by the collective agreement. If the dispute fell under the terms of that agreement, no recourse to common law concepts like constructive dismissal or its alleged cousin, constructive layoff, was proper. Ms. Hardy alleged a violation of the collective agreement, in particular the "most available hours clause" and Letter of Understanding No. 5. In fact, the "most available hours clause" provided for assignments on the basis of seniority only within the employee's classification and department. It did not provide for cross-classification transfer of part-time employees on the basis of seniority and the Board concluded that it had not been violated. Instead, the Board, through the purported common law doctrine of constructive layoff, converted Ms. Hardy's scheduling complaint into a layoff complaint and gave her a remedy available under the layoff provision — the right to be scheduled to work across classifications (Article 12.03 says that seniority governs in the case of lay-off of part-time employees). It found that the employer had breached Article A-1.01(2) by ceasing to pre-schedule Ms. Hardy for the hours she worked and relying on the call in procedure. In the Board's view, this breach of the scheduling provisions, which resulted in Ms. Hardy receiving substantially fewer scheduled hours while junior staff in other classifications were being scheduled to work, constituted a constructive layoff.

¶82 The Board did not find that, apart from the purported layoff, Ms. Hardy had the right to be scheduled across classifications. Rather, it found that she had that right because she had been laid off. Yet it based its conclusion that Ms. Hardy had been laid off on the fact that junior staff in other classifications were being scheduled to work. In effect, by importing a concept of constructive layoff not found in the collective agreement, the Board gave a remedy for the scheduling grievance not specified in the agreement. To put it another way, the remedy the Board granted is not rationally connected to the breach alleged and runs counter to the provisions of the collective agreement. It creates an internal contradiction within the collective agreement that is patently unreasonable.

¶83 We conclude that the decision of the Board was patently unreasonable. . . .

✻ ✻ ✻

Although the "patent unreasonableness" standard governs when arbitrators apply the provisions of the collective agreement, when they apply external statutes their decisions must meet the higher standard of "correctness." This remains true despite the recent enhancement of arbitral jurisdiction to interpret and apply such statutes: see *Interna-*

tional Union of Operating Engineers, Local 772 v. Philip Utilities Management Corp., [2001] O.J. No. 1815 (Ont. C.A.) (Q.L.).

9:800 THE FUTURE OF THE GRIEVANCE RESOLUTION PROCESS

Arbitration of mid-contract disputes has been required by statute since the 1940s. In the early years, arbitration was hailed by many as a fast, inexpensive, and informal method of grievance resolution controlled by the disputing parties. Since the 1970s, however, criticisms of the conventional arbitration process have been voiced more and more often.

9:810 The Critique of Conventional Arbitration

9:811 Cost and Delay

The self-governing nature of arbitration has implications for who bears the cost of adjudicating grievances. Unlike judges who are paid by the state, arbitrators are paid by the parties who appoint them. The employer and union each pay one-half of the arbitrator's account for services and disbursements including those related to travel and hearing-room rental. Legal fees are another expense often incurred at arbitration. A survey of labour and management representatives, conducted by Wagar in the mid-1990s, found employers were represented by lawyers at 79 percent of hearings and unions had legal representation 57 percent of the time. Employers reported the average cost of an arbitration to be $8,020 and unions reported an average cost of $7685. See T. Wagar, "The Arbitration Process: Employer and Union Views" [1996–97] Labour Arbitration Yearbook 3.

Several empirical studies on delay in arbitration are summarized in A. Ponak, W. Zerbe, S. Rose, & C. Olson, "Using Event History Analysis to Model Delay in Grievance Arbitration" (1996), 50 Industrial and Labor Relations Review 105–6:

> Research in Ontario showed that the elapsed time from grievance filing to arbitration award increased from 250 days in 1973 . . . to 301 days in 1980 and 345 days (expedited awards excluded) by 1983. . . . Investigations in Alberta indicated that elapsed time for grievance resolution grew from approximately seven months in the early 1970s . . . to 345 days by the mid-1980s. . . . A review of the experience in Newfoundland from 1980 to 1992 found that elapsed time increased an average of eight days per year over the twelve year period. . . . Cases reported in [*Labour Arbitration Cases*] in 1975 took an average of 283 days from filing of the grievance to issuance of the arbitration award; by 1987/88 the average elapsed time had increased to 428 days.

9:812 Legalism

Harry Arthurs, "The New Economy and the New Legality: Industrial Citizenship and the Future of Labour Arbitration" (1999), 7 Canadian Labour and Employment Law J. 45 at 50–51 and 54–57

> In all democratic societies, there has been a movement to legally empower citizens. Canada, for example, over the past 20 years or so, has adopted the Charter, class actions, con-

tingency fees and many other legal innovations: a radical expansion of rights and remedies which ordinary citizens can supposedly use to right bureaucracy, resist corporate overreaching and vindicate their personal dignity and freedom. . . . That, at least, is one tendency of the New Legality, a tendency that is entirely consistent with the anti-state, individualistic philosophy of the New Economy. But paradoxically, the New Economy has also helped to create something of a juridical no-man's land, a serious gap between law's promise and law's performance, a gap that is another feature of the New Legality. How did this come about? . . .

And then there is the "low tech" crowd, ordinary unionized workers, who have fairly simple problems requiring speedy, cheap, informal, practical and context-specific solutions. For these individuals, arbitration once served as an appropriately modest form of technology. Some of you may have heard stories of that golden age; some of you may even remember it. Hearings were short; lawyers tended to be house-broken and operated within the tacit assumptions of the system; arbitrators — lower court judges and law professors — generally had a day job and sat down after the hearing to write an award, not a Victorian novel. What happened? What happened was that the technology of arbitration went up-market when the first edition of *Brown and Beatty*, a comprehensive arbitration text, was published 20 years ago, only shortly before the adoption of the *Charter*. This book — like many forms of digital technology — stores a huge amount of data, permitting rapid, total, cheap and convenient recall of every arbitration precedent since, as we used to say, "the memory of man runneth not."

Moreover, this new high technology not only made total recall of arbitration awards possible: it made total recall virtually inevitable. Like most technologies, this one has produced a number of consequential effects that have fundamentally altered social relations and institutional structures. It has shifted the discourse of arbitration — the way people talk about issues — from a labour relations vernacular to a legalistic vernacular. It has shifted responsibility for advocacy decisively away from lay representatives and in favour of lawyers who are at home in the new vernacular. It has shifted the way arbitrators decide cases in a similar direction. By doing all of those things, it has increased the formalism, length, delays and costs of arbitration. And, of greatest importance, it has shifted the nature of the process from one in which results were measured by their positive industrial relations consequences to one in which they are measured by their conformity to the established jurisprudence.

This increasing legalization or juridification of labour arbitration, I would argue, leaches its way back into the grievance procedure, where much effort is now devoted to building a record for adjudication rather than to seeking sensible settlements. Ultimately, it reaches bedrock: the style and content of collective agreements, which have become longer, more convoluted and technical. Finally, just as technology comes to be governed by standards which facilitate interchange between and convergence of systems, the development of an organized corpus of arbitration doctrine will ultimately require that we modify arbitrators' law — the indigenous, idiosyncratic and distinctive "law of the shop" — so that it conforms more closely to "real" law, judges' law — the law one would use to validate commercial contracts, exclude evidence in a criminal trial or interpret the *Constitution*.

Of course, *Brown and Beatty* is not the only evidence of the New Legality at work in labour arbitration. . . .

Judges are another example. Labour arbitration had been practised on a voluntary basis since the nineteenth century, and was first mandated by Canadian law in 1944, by PC 1003. But until the Polymer case in the early 1960s — no one had imagined that awards might be judicially reviewed. However, once the judges got hold of the notion that they could micro-manage the arbitration process, could force arbitrators to adhere to the courts' version of law, there was no holding them back. Only at the end of the 1970s — in the *CUPE* case — did the Supreme Court finally draw breath to suggest that perhaps labour tribunals might be allowed a little latitude, that a little judicial self-restraint might not come amiss. But *CUPE* was too little and came too late. The habit of judicial review was too deeply entrenched by then; and it was shortly to be reinforced by the adoption of the *Charter*. It is not so much that the *Charter* applied directly to arbitration: technically, it affected only proceedings involving crown agencies or statutory adjudicators appointed under the *Canada Labour Code*. Rather, the *Charter* was important because it gave legs to the New Legality: arbitrators, counsel and academic commentators came to see themselves as immersed not in the grubby little enterprise of solving problems in the workplace, but in the great work of transforming society by bringing Law, Justice and Due Process to one of its most arbitrary, power-ridden and peremptory relationships.

Legislatures assisted this great work, from time to time. In Manitoba, for example, arbitrators acquired the statutory power to apply a principle of substantive fairness. In Ontario, arbitrators were mandated to apply the *Human Rights Code* and other employment-related statutes; in fact, recent Ontario legislation requires employees to seek their remedies under employment standards and other legislation through arbitration where possible, rather than through administrative procedures. . . .

As a result of all of this to-ing and fro-ing, Ontario arbitrators have been implicated more and more deeply in the general administration of labour and employment law, *Charter* law, administrative law and human rights law, and they preside and pontificate more and more like common law judges — which I do not mean as a compliment. Whether they are acting out of fear of being judicially reviewed, in response to the pressures of their clientele, out of a belief that the judges have got it right, or because they lack the imagination and insight to do otherwise, I frankly do not know. What I do know is that the New Legality has drawn them farther and farther away from their original mandate of administering the unique law of the parties as expressed in their agreement and in their shop floor practices.

Finally, the arrival of the New Legality in the field of arbitration did not just happen; it was not simply imposed on labour and management by absent-minded academics or high-minded judges. The New Legality was invoked to transform arbitration because someone thought it served a purpose. What purpose? The purpose of transforming the original, historic pre- and post-war character of arbitration as a cheap, informal and effective way of keeping peace under the collective agreement. And whose purpose? The purpose of those who no longer believed in the regime of workplace governance which arbitration helped to maintain.

Here is where the New Economy and the New Legality again come together. Arbitration makes a lot of sense, for an employer, if you are fighting a rearguard action against new contract language won by the union or are trying to discipline an insurgent workforce; it makes much less sense for an employer if technology and restructuring have broken the union's power, if Mexico beckons, or if decertification has suddenly become a realistic possibility. Arbitration is, to say the least, extraneous to any of these scenarios, and if it must be endured in the meantime, then there is every reason to make it work as badly as possible. [Reprinted with permission of Lancaster House Publishing.]

9:820   Alternatives to Conventional Arbitration

Growing concerns about cost, delay, and legalism have produced a number of reforms to the grievance resolution process in recent years. Statutory reforms have been enacted in some provinces. Across the country, parties to some collective bargaining relationships have tailored alterations to their own systems for resolving disputes.

9:821   Grievance Mediation

In British Columbia, Manitoba, New Brunswick, and Saskatchewan, the province provides settlement officers who endeavour to assist employers and unions to resolve grievances without resort to arbitration. Unlike an arbitrator who focuses exclusively upon rights, a settlement officer acting as a mediator can also take account of the competing interests which underlie a dispute.

The Ontario government supplied settlement officers from the late 1970s until the early 1990s, but it no longer does. The Ontario experience with grievance mediation is reviewed in Joseph Rose, "The Emergence of Expedited Arbitration" (1991) 1 Lab. Arb. Y.B. 13. Rose found that 67.7 percent of the grievances referred to mediation were resolved by the parties with the assistance of settlement officers. He estimated that the average cost of a mediated settlement to each party was $245, which was $1,550 less than conventional arbitration. He reported that mediated settlements typically were achieved within three weeks of the request for arbitration: about six months faster than the average time required to deal with a grievance in conventional arbitration.

Mediation is not the sole province of settlement officers appointed by the government. In more and more cases, independent "neutrals," most of whom previously functioned largely as arbitrators, are being appointed by employers and unions to mediate grievances. In addition, arbitrators themselves are now more frequently venturing into mediation during arbitration hearings, sometimes at the suggestion of the parties but perhaps more often on their own initiative.

9:822   Statutory Expedited Arbitration

Legislation in several provinces provides for a process of expedited arbitration, with the arbitrator being chosen by a public agency rather than by the parties to the dispute. The hearing must commence within a specified number of days — for example, in Ontario, twenty-one days — after the process is invoked. The widespread use of expedited arbitration in Ontario is described in Rose, above, section 9:821:

The evidence indicates that expedited arbitration has been accepted as an alternative to conventional arbitration. As shown in Table 2, there were 8,174 awards reported between 1980–1981 and 1985–1986, of which 2,178 or 26.6 percent were expedited cases. . . . As a percentage of total arbitration activity, expedited arbitrations have grown from 4.2 percent of all awards in 1980–1981 to 39.4 percent of the total in 1985–1986. . . . The increased demand for expedited arbitration largely reflects a substitution for conventional arbitration rather than an increase in arbitration activity [pages 18 and 19].

Statutory expedited arbitration ensures hearings begin promptly but does not prevent a hearing from lasting multiple days spread over a number of months. Rose estimated the elapsed time between an incident giving rise to a grievance and an expedited arbitration award to be four months, seven and one-half months shorter than the corresponding period in conventional arbitration.

As this type of expedited arbitration does nothing to curtail the length of hearings or the use of lawyers, it has no impact on legalism and no direct impact on costs. The expense of arbitration may be indirectly effected in the long-term as a result of an increase in the supply of arbitrators who are acceptable to both labour and management. The agency which names expedited arbitrators maintains a roster of those eligible to receive such appointments. Candidates typically are added to the roster based upon the recommendation of a labour/management advisory committee. Once on the roster, fledgling arbitrators have an opportunity to demonstrate their ability (or lack thereof) to employers and unions in expedited cases. Competent new entrants soon find themselves being chosen by employers and unions to arbitrate disputes that have not been referred to statutory expedited arbitration, as Rose reports (at pages 19–20):

[E]xpedited arbitration has reduced the parties' reliance on a small corps of arbitrators. Again, in 1970 five arbitrators were responsible for 76 percent of the arbitration caseload in Ontario. Since the introduction of expedited arbitration, 20 arbitrators completed a training program and were added to the province's list of approved arbitrators. After entering the profession, these newly trained arbitrators have issued over 1,000 awards, including 20.3 percent of the awards issued in Ontario in 1985–1986. Initially, newly trained arbitrators relied almost exclusively on ministerial appointment involving expedited cases. This dependence has declined in recent years, suggesting that they are gaining acceptability. For example, in 1985–1986 over one-quarter of the newly trained arbitrators' caseloads involved non-expedited arbitrations.

9:823 Tailor-Made Expedited Arbitration
The parties to some collective bargaining relationships have designed their own expedited arbitration procedures. Unlike statutory expedited arbitration, such procedures typically limit the length and formality of hearings. Private systems of this sort have become more common in recent years but are still the exception and not the rule. Michel Picher describes one long-standing system of expedited arbitration.

Michel Picher "The Canadian Railway Office of Arbitration: Keeping Grievance Hearings on the Rails" [1991] 1 Labour Arbitration Yearbook 37, at 38, 44, 46–53

At a time when the cost and delay of the ad hoc system of grievance arbitration in industrial relations have become a subject of growing concern to unions and employers alike, the simplified and accelerated system of arbitration that has served Canada's railway industry for close to 25 years has much to commend it. The shortened procedures and efficiencies of scale realized by the operation of a single permanent office of arbitration, governing a substantial number of employers and unions, under a uniform set of rules, have provided stable and efficient service in this important area of labour relations at a fraction of the cost incurred under the system of ad hoc arbitration commonly utilized in other industries. If the opinions of the consumers of the system are to be believed, their savings in hearing time and cost have not been at the expense of quality, either in the process, in the "bottom line" of adjudicated results, or in the satisfaction of the managers and employees affected.

A visitor to the Canadian Railway Office of Arbitration (CROA) in Montreal on a hearing day will see a process that has little resemblance to the "long form" of arbitration hearing that generally follows the procedures of a civil trial. The CROA system also differs dramatically from "shop floor" arbitration or expedited arbitration resulting in oral, non-precedential rulings . . . Normally hearings last between one and two hours, although they are sometimes shorter. Five to seven cases are generally heard in a day, with a written decision, usually from one to four pages in length, normally issuing within the same week. The management and union representatives who present the bulk of the cases are capable and seasoned advocates, well schooled in the procedures and precedents of the CROA. Their participation is central to its success.

The grievances heard are not simply small claims. They range from minor discipline and wage disputes to discharge grievances and cases involving critical contract interpretation, including issues such as work jurisdiction and contracting out, which may have substantial monetary ramifications. . . .

The procedures of the CROA are governed by the terms of the memorandum of agreement establishing the Office. Central to the expeditious hearing of the cases is the requirement . . . that at the hearing each party file and read a written brief outlining the facts, arguments and jurisprudence relied on in support of its position. The briefs are filed, however, only after the parties have provided the Office with a written Joint Statement of Issue one month in advance of the hearing, or if they cannot agree, *ex parte* statements. . . .

The requirement of written briefs and supporting documentation is critical for the successful operation of the CROA system. In this author's experience, in the ad hoc stream of arbitration, parties will too often come to a hearing inadequately prepared, tending to shape their case as the hearing proceeds, depending on what the other party puts forward. The result can be unproductive delays for objections and adjournments as lawyers confer with their clients, often to be briefed on an unanticipated fact or development in the adversary's case. . . .

Time saving is also promoted by the rule that the parties must put their full case between two covers of a brief before they come to the hearing. As the highest appellate courts have long realized, nothing begets clarity and precision in the presentation of facts and arguments so much as the requirement that they be reduced to writing in a relatively brief form. A brief is typically 10 to 20 pages long and contains the history of the dispute, the facts pertinent to the grievance, the provisions of the collective agreement that are in issue and the position of the party, in the form of its argument, including reference to arbitral or court precedents, statutes and railway operating rules, often in the form of federal regulations, that may be pertinent. Exhibits are filed as appendices to the brief, thereby allowing ready access to all necessary documentation.

At the hearing witnesses may be called, but this is done exceptionally. In many cases, particularly those that do not involve discipline, the grievor and local management do not attend the hearing. As a general rule, the decision to hear evidence under oath is reserved until after both parties have presented their briefs. At that point the material points of fact which are not agreed upon are more clearly identified, and the testimony of witnesses can be limited to those facts that bear on the merits of the grievance and which are clearly in dispute.

The fact-finding efficiency of the CROA system is impressive. Too often the award in an ad hoc arbitration will, in a case that has consumed one or more days of oral testimony, begin with the paradoxical observation: "The material facts are not in dispute." The CROA system forces the parties to make that discovery on their own, before the hearing, and not at its conclusion. The resulting difference in time and cost expended is significant. . . .

What does an analysis of the time taken for the hearing and disposition of an arbitration under the CROA reveal as compared to arbitrations in the traditional ad hoc stream? The largest part of my arbitral practice involves ad hoc arbitrations. A review of all types of cases which I read during a recent calendar year discloses that the average ad hoc arbitration case heard to completion in that period required two days of hearings. . . . As noted above, CROA cases are heard, almost without exception, in one to two hours, at a rate of five to seven cases in a day. . . .

Generally speaking, the time for processing a grievance from the precipitating incident to the date of the award is roughly the same under the CROA as in ad hoc cases. For the reasons related above, however, the time utilized by the parties under the CROA in the pre-arbitration stage is generally more productive. . . .

Precise cost comparisons are difficult to make. . . . As consumers of the ad hoc system are well aware, the time spent by managers, union staff and employee witnesses in hearings which, on average, take two days, and in some cases can take much more, also represents a significant cost factor.

A further expense item of major importance which it is impossible for me to quantify and compare is the cost to the parties of legal counsel. In my own ad hoc practice lawyers present the parties' case in the great majority of arbitrations. By comparison, as noted above, the substantial majority of cases heard in the CROA are not pleaded by lawyers.

Certain dollar comparisons can, however, be made as regards the cost of arbitration itself, disregarding the expense of lawyers and staff time or employee time expended both in preparation and at the hearing. . . . [T]he average cost of hearing a single case under the CROA system is roughly 29.4 per cent of the cost of the typical ad hoc arbitration. In other words, consumers of the CROA service spend less than one-third of what is spent by parties who purchase arbitration services on an ad hoc basis. . . .

The lower cost per arbitration of the CROA system has a significant impact on the issue of access to justice. While the CROA docket attempts to give priority to discharge cases, it must ultimately accommodate all grievances filed. Because of the low unit cost of CROA arbitrations, unions are able to process to arbitration substantial numbers of wage claims . . . as well as the most minor of disputed discipline cases. Claims of $200 or less are not unknown. In my experience, cases of that kind, which do involve a felt wrong of some importance to the grieving employee, rarely find their way to final arbitration in the ad hoc stream, because it is simply too costly to have them heard.

[Reprinted with permission of Lancaster House Publishing.]

✳ ✳ ✳

In "Cost and Delay in Labour Arbitration: Is There a Silver Lining?" [1999–2000] 1 Lab. Arb. Ybk. 317, arbitrator Kevin Burkett describes the expedited arbitration processes adopted by Canada Post, Ontario Hydro, and Air Canada, as well as the C.R.O.A. process discussed by Picher above. He notes that all of these systems share the following characteristics which differentiate them from the usual arbitration framework: exchange of information or submission of briefs in advance; recognition that a full-blown hearing is not necessary in most if not all cases; restrictions on the involvement of legal counsel; time limits on argument; and the speedy issuance of brief written or oral awards, often without precedential value.

9:824 Adjudication by a Public Agency

Bernard Adell, *Adjudication of Workplace Disputes in Ontario: A Report to the Ontario Law Reform Commission* (unpublished, 1991) at 120–22

The private aspects of the present grievance arbitration system seem to work well enough for unions and employers who are able and willing to pay, in money and often in terms of delay as well, to have exactly the adjudicator they want and the procedure they want. . . .

However, there is one major and, I think, answerable objection to requiring the parties to collective agreements to use a private adjudicative process — the cost, and the differential impact of that cost on rich and poor parties. Arbitrators' fees and expenses may not be much of a problem for large employers and large bargaining units, but many small locals and small employers can rarely afford to incur those costs. I was told by a senior officer of one of the largest and most respected unions in Canada that even in his union, some locals can never afford to incur them, even where they have a grievance that would probably be upheld at arbitration. This is unsatisfactory. . . .

It is simply unacceptable, in my view, that the only process available for the enforcement of collective agreements is one in which the parties have to pay the adjudicator, and one to which access is therefore conditional on being able to do so. That situation is made even more unacceptable by the fact that many newly organized bargaining units consist of low paid employees in small and often remote workplaces.

I see no reason not to let the parties to a collective agreement continue to use a private grievance arbitration process — to choose and pay for their arbitrator themselves — if they both agree to it. But the key is agreement. If one of the parties would prefer that disputes over the meaning of the agreement go to a wholly public adjudicative process, that is where they ought to go. I suggest that the *Labour Relations Act* be amended to provide that unless a collective agreement says otherwise, unresolved issues of interpretation or application of that agreement are to be decided by a public tribunal.

[Reprinted by permission.]

Chapter 10: The Individual Employee Under Collective Bargaining

10:100 INTRODUCTION

Canadian labour relations law is wholly predicated on the twin concepts of majoritarianism and exclusivity. Once a trade union proves that it enjoys majority support in a bargaining unit, it becomes the exclusive bargaining agent for that unit, and no one else is allowed to bargain on behalf of any of the employees in the unit. As we will see below, the same principle of exclusivity governs the carrying of grievances to arbitration. As we will also see, the law explicitly allows the negotiation and enforcement of union security provisions, including those that require union membership as a condition of employment. All of these features are based on the premise that trade unions need effective bargaining authority and a substantial degree of internal solidarity.

In principle, the individual employee's freedom of choice is given legal expression only through his or her vote for or against an applicant union. Once that vote and those of the other members of the bargaining unit have determined that there will be a bargaining agent, individual freedom is suspended for a substantial period. Majoritarianism, in other words, leads to exclusivity. In incurring the obligation to bargain collectively, the employer acquires the corresponding right to be confronted by only one adversary — one that can speak for every employee in the unit.

Ever since they were first established under the American *Wagner Act* of 1935, the twin pillars of majoritarianism and exclusivity have been attacked by employers and by others who are opposed in principle to collective bargaining or who are concerned about what they perceive to be excessive union power. Many of these attacks have been framed as defences of individual workers' rights — the "right to work," for example. In reality, however, their main object has often been to weaken the representation rights of unions and to dilute their strength.

Even some supporters of collective bargaining and trade unions, however, have increasingly been calling into question the principles of majoritarianism and exclusivity. See, for example, Roy J. Adams, "A Pernicious Euphoria: 50 Years of Wagnerism in Canada" (1995) 3 C.L.E.L.J. 321. First, it is said, these principles unduly inhibit the growth of new arrangements, such as works councils, which could provide workers with a collective voice even when they were not represented by a certified bargaining agent. Second, it is claimed, they prevent the emergence of minority unions that could express a broader array of worker aspirations. Third, they are said to unnecessarily constrain the freedom of association of individual workers who would prefer to belong to minority unions or to no union at all. This last criticism has also been couched in constitutional terms, as a violation of section 2(d) of the *Canadian Charter of Rights and Freedoms*. See David Beatty, *Putting the Charter to Work* (Montreal and Kingston: McGill-Queen's University Press, 1987) at 135–55. The *Charter* argument, however, was rejected by the Supreme Court of Canada in the *Lavigne* case, below, section 10:600.

If majoritarianism and exclusivity are too firmly entrenched in our industrial relations system to be struck down by the courts or dismantled by legislatures, the issue then becomes the extent to which legitimate concern for individual and minority rights can be addressed within the existing structures. There may be no real evidence of wide-spread abuse of such rights, but abuses clearly do occur at times. There is increasing acceptance of the view that more effective protection of minority and individual rights is implicit in the ideals of a democratic society, and also of the view that such protec-tion is necessary to the effective functioning of the collective bargaining system and to its attractiveness to unorganized workers. It is very much open to debate whether pro-tection of minority rights can best be achieved by reinvigorating grassroots democracy within unions, by facilitating judicial intervention at the suit of aggrieved individuals, by introducing closer administrative scrutiny of internal union affairs, or by encouraging unions themselves to adopt new constitutional and institutional arrangements.

Before turning to that debate, we will consider some of the most common areas in which individual and collective interests collide under a regime of collective bargaining: the displacement of the regime of individual contracts when a union acquires bargain-ing rights, the union's authority in negotiating a collective agreement, and the union's authority in processing grievances under that agreement.

REFERENCES

George Adams, *Canadian Labour Law*, 2d ed. (Aurora, Ont.: Canada Law Book, 1993) pt. 5; Donald Carter *et al.*, *Labour Law and Industrial Relations in Canada*, 5th ed. (Markham, Ont.: Butterworths, 2001) 211–234, 363–369; Michael Mac Neil, Michael Lynk, & Peter Englemann, *Trade Union Law in Canada* (Aurora, Ont.: Canada Law Book, 1994) cc. 2, 4, 6–10

10:200 THE PRIMACY OF THE COLLECTIVE AGREEMENT

10:210 Bargaining with other Unions or with Individual Employees

Once a union has acquired majority support and has been certified or recognized as a bargaining agent, the employer is precluded from bargaining with any other union or any other person or organization on behalf of any employees in the bargaining unit, unless and until the union's bargaining rights are terminated pursuant to statute. This was confirmed many years ago in *International Brotherhood of Boilermakers v. Sheafer-Townsend Ltd.* (1953), 53 C.L.L.C. para. 17,058 (O.L.R.B.).

Another long-established but perhaps less obvious rule is that an employer may not bargain directly with individual employees where there is a statutory bargaining agent. The North American *locus classicus* on this point is the United States Supreme Court decision in *J.I. Case Co. v. National Labor Relations Board* (1944), 321 U.S. 332. In that judgment, however, the court left open the possibility that an employer and an employee might make a binding contractual arrangement related to the employment relationship if the arrangement "is not inconsistent with a collective agreement or does not amount to or result from or is not part of an unfair labor practice." The leading Canadian case on this question is *Syndicat catholique des employés de magasins de Québec Inc. v. Compagnie Paquet Ltée*, [1959] S.C.R. 206, where Judson J. said:

> There is no room left for private negotiation between employer and employee. Certainly to the extent of the matters covered by the collective agreement, freedom of contract between master and individual servant is abrogated. The collective agreement tells the employer on what terms he must in future conduct his master and servant relations. . . . The terms of employment are defined for all employees, and whether or not they are members of the union, they are identical for all.

This blanket prohibition of bargaining between employers and individual employees on any matter dealt with in the collective agreement is virtually unknown outside of the United States and Canada. It has been increasingly called into question in recent years, as unionization has gradually spread to sectors where employees tend to be highly individualistic. Athletes are an example, and so are artists. For discussion of a federal statute that tries to create a new collective bargaining framework for performing artists, see Elizabeth MacPherson, "Collective Bargaining for Independent Contractors: Is the Status of the Artist Act a Model for Other Industrial Sectors?" (1999), 7 C.L.E.L.J. 355.

The *Canada Labour Code* (section 54), and the statutes of the Atlantic provinces and Manitoba, provide that an employee may "present his personal grievance to his employer at any time." This provision has been held not to "raise a duty on the employer to deal with the grievance in disregard of the collective agreement," or to preclude the parties from imposing prerequisites (procedural or other) on taking grievances to arbitration: *Lunenberg Police Association v. Lunenberg (Town of)* (1980), 118 D.L.R. (3d) 590 at 604 (N.S.S.C. A.D.), leave to appeal to the Supreme Court of Canada refused.

10:220 The Eclipsing of the Individual Contract of Employment

The collective agreement binds unions, the employees they represent, and employers. In the following case, it was the employer that was trying to avoid the provisions of a collective agreement, but the decision has clear implications for similar attempts by individual employees.

McGavin Toastmaster Ltd. v. Ainscough, [1976] 1 S.C.R. 718 at 721–33

[The respondent employees worked at the appellant company's Vancouver plant. The collective agreement provided that any employees who lost their jobs because of a plant closure would be entitled to severance pay. The company decided that it would close the plant. In protest, and while the plant was still open, the employees went on strike. The strike was illegal because it occurred during the lifetime of the collective agreement. A few days later, while the strike was in progress, the company carried out its plan to close the plant. The closure was for legitimate economic reasons. The company refused to pay the repondent employees severance pay as required by the collective agreement, because it claimed that the act of striking illegally had disentitled them to it, pursuant to the contract law doctrine of repudation. The employees sued the company for the severance pay, and won in the British Columbia courts. The company appealed.]

LASKIN C.J.C.: This Court raised, *suo motu*, the question whether the matter in issue here ought properly to have been submitted to arbitration under the grievance and arbitration provisions of the collective agreement between the appellant and the plaintiffs' trade union. In correspondence exchanged between solicitors the question of arbitration was raised and then dropped, and Court proceedings were instituted on May 12, 1971. There was no contention in defence that the appropriate proceedings should have been by way of arbitration under the collective agreement, and it does not appear that any such position was taken either before the trial Judge or in the British Columbia Court of Appeal. This Court refrained therefore in this case from taking any position on this question and is content to deal with the legal issue or issues as having been properly submitted to the Courts for adjudication.

... the issues taken both at trial and on appeal were (1) whether there was a repudiation by each employee of his contract of employment, by reason of the unlawful strike, entitling the company to terminate it and whether the company did so; (2) whether the concerted refusal to work terminated the employer-employee relationship; and (3) whether the unlawful strike constituted a breach of a fundamental term of the contracts of employment of the respective striking employees so as to disentitle them to call upon the company to perform its obligations, in this case the obligation to give severance pay.

... I do not think that in the face of labour relations legislation such as existed at the material time in British Columbia, in the face of the certification of the union, of which the plaintiffs were members, as bargaining agent of a specified unit of employees of the company and in the face of the collective agreement in force between the union and the appellant company, it is possible to speak of individual contracts of employment and to treat the collective agreement as a mere appendage of individual relationships. The majority of this Court, speaking through Judson J. in *Syndicat Catholique des Employés de Magasins de Québec, Inc. v. Compagnie Paquet Ltée* ... said this in a situation where a union was certified for collective bargaining under Quebec labour relations legislation:

> There is no room left for private negotiation between employer and employee. Certainly to the extent of the matters covered by the collective agreement, freedom of contract between master and individual servant is abrogated. The collective agreement tells the employer on what terms he must in the future conduct his master and servant relations. . . .

The situation is the same in British Columbia where the legislation in force at the material time stated explicitly that a collective agreement entered into between a union and an employer is binding on the union, the employer and the employees covered thereby: see *Mediation Services Act*. . . .

The reality is, and has been for many years now throughout Canada, that individual relationships as between employer and employee have meaning only at the hiring stage and even then there are qualifications which arise by reason of union security clauses in collective agreements. The common law as it applies to individual employment contracts is no longer relevant to employer-employee relations governed by a collective agreement which, as the one involved here, deals with discharge, termination of employment, severance pay and a host of other matters that have been negotiated between union and company as the principal parties thereto. To quote again from the reasons of Judson J. in the *Paquet* case:

> If the relation between employee and union were that of mandator and mandatary, the result would be that a collective agreement would be the equivalent of a bundle of individual contracts between employer and employee negotiated by the union as agent for the employees. This seems to me to be a complete misapprehension of the nature of the juridical relation involved in the collective agreement. The union contracts not as agent or mandatary but as an independent contracting party and the contract it makes with the employer binds the employer to regulate his master and servant relations according to the agreed terms.

The collective agreement in the present case makes the foregoing abundantly clear. Wages and hours of work are, of course, dealt with, and persons who come into the employ do so on the terms of the collective agreement as to wages and hours. They also come under the terms of the collective agreement as to promotion, layoffs, rehiring and preference of transfers to shifts, all of which are regulated in this case by art. XVI of the collective agreement, headed 'Seniority.' Article V deals with hiring procedure, and gives the union the prior right to supply staff subject to certain exceptions. Discharge is dealt with both in art. IV and in art. VII. Central to all the benefits and obligations that rest upon the union, the employees and the company under the collective agreement are the grievance and arbitration provisions, about which nothing more need be said here. Standing at the forefront of the substantive terms of the collective agreement is art. I under which the union is recognized by the company as 'the sole collective bargaining agency for all employees coming under the jurisdiction of this agreement.' There is in this collective agreement ample support for the observations of Judson J. in the *Paquet* case.

In my view, therefore, questions such as repudiation and fundamental breach must be addressed to the collective agreement if they are to have any subject-matter at all. When so addressed, I find them inapplicable in the face of the legislation which, in British Columbia and elsewhere in Canada, governs labour-management relations, provides for certification of unions, for compulsory collective bargaining, for the negotiation, duration and renewal of collective agreements. The *Mediation Services Act*, which was in force at the material time in this case, provided in s. 8 for a minimum one year term for collective agreements unless the responsible Minister gave consent to earlier termination, and provided also for the making of collective agreements for longer terms, subject to certain termination options before the full term had run. Neither this Act nor the companion *Labour Relations Act*, R.S.B.C. 1960, c. 205, could operate according to their terms if common law concepts like repudiation and fundamental breach could be invoked in relation to collective agreements which have not expired and where the duty to bargain collectively subsists.

In *Re Polymer Corp. and Oil, Chemical & Atomic Workers Int'l Union, Local 16-14* . . . McRuer C.J.H.C. observed . . . that a collective agreement 'is not that sort of contract that can be terminated by repudiation by one party merely because the other party has broken one of its terms.' In *CPR Co. v. Zambri,* . . . this Court recognized that the common law relations of employer and employee had been altered by the labour relations legislation of Ontario that was involved in that case, legislation that was comparable to that in British Columbia to which I have referred. Judson J., speaking for four members of this Court said . . . of the *Zambri* case that:

> When a collective agreement has expired, it is difficult to see how there can be anything left to govern the employer-employee relationship. Conversely, when there is a collective agreement in effect, it is difficult to see how there can be anything left outside except possibly the act of hiring.

The references I have made to the collective agreement in this case, which was in force during the events that gave rise to this litigation, lends substance to the words of Judson J. What is, in truth, left for consideration on the appellant's submissions is whether, notwithstanding the existence and binding effect of the collective agreement, the plaintiffs had ceased to be employees by reason only of their unlawful strike and hence had by their own act excluded themselves from the benefits provided by art. XX of the collective agreement.

The applicable legislation, the *Mediation Services Act*, s. 23, prohibits an employee who is bound by a collective agreement from striking during the term of the agreement. It was open to the company in this case to take disciplinary action against the plaintiffs for participating in an unlawful strike, and it is arguable (although this is not before this Court) that discharge would have been held to be for sufficient cause in the light of all the circumstances, if this issue had gone to arbitration. The company did not, however, take any action against the striking employees and, indeed, insisted in this statement of defence that the employees were not discharged but had, in effect, quit their jobs. No doubt they had quit work, but, far from quitting their jobs, the record shows that they had resorted to strike action as a means of emphasizing their concern for retention of jobs in the plant and as a means of persuading the company to reconsider its decision to curtail available jobs, a decision which was part of an overall plan to phase out the Vancouver operation. Even on the basis of common law concepts, the opinion was unanimous below that the unlawful strike did not per se terminate the employer-employee relationship, and I think this is plainly right, and *a fortiori* in the light of governing labour-management relations legislation. It was open to the company to act in relation to the unlawful strike by positive action against the strikers; and, whether or not it saw in the strike an opportunity to accelerate its longer term plan to close out its Vancouver operations, its failure to act against the employees save by closure of the plant brought it within the severance pay obligations at art. XX of the collective agreement.

I would dismiss the appeal with costs.

10:230 The Pre-eminence of Grievance Arbitration

In *McGavin Toastmaster*, above, section 10:220, the Supreme Court of Canada raised the issue of whether the parties should have followed the grievance arbitration process instead of resorting to court. Because the parties did not object to court jurisdiction during the proceedings, the issue was not pursued in that decision. Had the point been dealt with, the Court might simply have ruled that the courts lacked the jurisdiction to consider the case brought by the employer. Such a conclusion has been reached in a long line of cases where court jurisdiction has been challenged.

The issue involves both a question of forum (court versus grievance arbitration) and a consideration of whether the collective agreement can be bypassed. Can the collective agreement and the grievance arbitration processes under its umbrella be circumvented by characterizing the dispute as one outside the collective agreement? The party seeking to do this may be the employer, the union, or an individual employee — either an employee who is acting in concert with the union or one who is trying to bypass the collective agreement as a means of challenging the union. Regardless of who is trying to avoid the grievance process or why, the courts have increasingly tended to foreclose that possibility, through reliance on provisions in labour relations statutes requiring final settlement of disputes between the employer and the union. Recall *Weber v. Ontario Hydro*, *supra*, section 9:631, in which a tort and Charter action for invasion of privacy, beyond the settled grievance, was dismissed for want of jurisdiction. Court jurisdiction was similarly held to be lacking in *New Brunswick v. O'Leary*, [1995] 2 S.C.R. 967, in which the employer was told its only recourse (for alleged damage to a vehicle resulting from its being driven with a flat tire by O'Leary in the course of his work) was to grievance arbitration.

The Supreme Court of Canada has recently addressed the issue, in the following case.

Allen v. Alberta [2003] 1 S.C.R. 128

[The respondents were boiler inspectors who had been employed by the Alberta government and represented by the Alberta Union of Provincial Employees under the provincial *Public Service Employee Relations Act*. The applicable collective agreement provided for severance pay if an employee was terminated. The government decided to privatize most of its boiler inspection services, so it gave the respondents notice of termination. Under the collective agreement, they would have been entitled to severance pay. However, the government and the union negotiated a written settlement, in the form of a letter of intent, to the effect that the respondents would be offered jobs with the private organization that was taking over boiler inspection, and that if they accepted those jobs they would lose their status as public servants and their entitlement to severance pay under the collective agreement. The letter of intent said that it was not part of the collective agreement and was not grievable under that agreement.

The respondents accepted jobs with the private organization and resigned from their government jobs. Years later, they sued in the courts, claiming that they had not resigned voluntarily and asking for a declaration that they were entitled to severance pay under the government collective agreement. The time limit for bringing a grievance under the collective agreement had passed long before. The government applied to strike out the suit as showing no reasonable cause of action. A trial judgment granting that application was reversed by the Alberta Court of Appeal but was restored by the Supreme Court of Canada.]

LEBEL J. (for the Court):

. . .

The problem facing our Court is well defined and narrow. Its solution depends on the proper application of principles set out by our Court in *St. Anne Nackawic Pulp & Paper Co. v. Canadian Paper Workers Union, Local 219.* . . . Those principles were refined in the later cases of *Weber v. Ontario Hydro* . . . and *Regina Police Assn. Inc. v. Regina (City) Board of Police Commissioners.* . . . In a nutshell, these cases stand for the principle that, in accordance with the legislative intent evidenced by the labour relations schemes implemented since the Second World War in Canada, such as the Alberta statutes which apply in this appeal, disputes arising out of the interpretation, application or violation of a collective agreement should be dealt with exclusively under the grievance procedure established in accordance with the agreement or the relevant labour legislation. As a general rule, provided though that they fall within the ambit of the collective agreement, such disputes should be disposed of by labour arbitrators and regular civil courts do not retain concurrent jurisdiction over them.

The judgment of our Court in *St. Anne Nackawic* brought to an end a long period of jurisprudential development and uncertainty as to the respective roles of labour arbitrators and courts in the enforcement of collective agreements. It adopted a model of exclusive jurisdiction of arbitrators over disputes arising from collective agreements, rather than upholding the overlapping jurisdiction of common law courts over such conflicts. This model reflects the nature of the labour relations regime which has existed in Canada for a number of years. A certified bargaining agent holds exclusive bargaining rights in respect of a group of employees. It represents all the members of the unit and negotiates with the employer to arrive at a collective agreement that defines their employment conditions. This agreement binds the union, the employees and the employer. The union is held to a duty of fair representation of the employees it represents.

The *Weber* and *City of Regina* cases have addressed the problem of identifying those disputes which are within the scope of the arbitrator's jurisdiction. In these judgments, our Court has adopted a flexible and contextual method which seeks to avoid formalistic classifications. The analysis should focus on an inquiry into the essential nature of the dispute:

> The question in each case is whether the dispute, in its essential character, arises from the interpretation, application, administration or violation of the collective agreement. *Weber, supra,* per McLachlin J. . . .

Our Court re-affirmed the validity of this analytical approach in *City of Regina.* It acknowledged that labour arbitrators have been granted broad jurisdiction over labour disputes. Nevertheless, only disputes which explicitly or inferentially arise out of a collective agreement are foreclosed to the courts (*City of Regina,* at para. 22, per Bastarache J.). In order to ascertain whether the dispute arises out of the collective agreement, the essential nature of the dispute must be identified. At the same time, it is necessary to consider the ambit of the agreement and whether it covers the facts of the dispute:

> Simply, the decision-maker must determine whether, having examined the factual context of the dispute, its essential character concerns a subject matter that is covered by the collective agreement. Upon determining the essential character of the dispute, the decision-maker must examine the provisions of the collective agreement to determine whether it contemplates such factual situations. It is clear that the collective agreement need not provide for the subject matter of the dispute explicitly. If the essential character of the dispute arises either explicitly or implicitly, from the interpretation, application, administration or violation of the collective agreement, the dispute is within the sole jurisdiction of an arbitrator to decide. [*City of Regina*, at para. 25.]

The application of this analytical method can lead to but one conclusion in the present case: the claim of the respondents was a dispute arising out of the application or violation of a collective agreement. Severance pay had been provided under s. 15.03 of the collective agreement. Any entitlement to severance was based on the collective agreement. Absent this provision, the respondents' right to the severance pay they claim does not exist. The letter of intent did not change the legal situation of the parties. Any claim that severance pay had been lost through resignations procured under duress would have fallen in all its aspects within the jurisdiction of the arbitrator. In the course of the arbitration, the question as to whether the letter of intent was a bar to the claim would have been raised and dealt with by the arbitrator. Even if it was not formally a part of the collective agreement, the letter was at least an agreement which addressed potential grievances and the status of employees who were being transferred to a new employer. In a context where no claim of unfair or inadequate union representation had been advanced, such issues remained a matter for the arbitrator and for the process of collective negotiation between the employer and the union.

Much was made in the course of this appeal of the argument that such a result appeared inherently unfair, as it would leave respondents without a proper forum for their claims. First, as noted above, they failed even to at least explore before the proper arbitral forum whether they had rights under the collective agreements. Secondly, inasmuch as any rights they might have asserted, on the facts of this case, would flow from collective contracts, the shifting of the disputes from an arbitration board to the regular civil courts would neither change the substantive nature of their rights nor add to them. . . .

* * *

The major exception to the principle in the above case is where the employee and employer have made an individual contractual arrangement before entering into the employment relationship (for example, an arrangement to the effect that the employee will continue to be paid at the level at which he or she was paid at in a previous job, or that the employee will be in the job for a certain number of years). Several decisions have held that the employee may bring a civil action in the courts to enforce such a "preemployment contract," whether or not its provisions are consistent with the collective agreement that applies to the employee once the employment relationship begins. The Supreme Court of Canada affirmed that exception in *Goudie v. Ottawa (City)*, 2003 SCC 14. Is the exception consistent with what Laskin C.J.C. said in the *McGavin Toastmaster* case, above, about the pre-eminence of the collective agreement under a regime of collective bargaining?

The requirement of recourse to grievance arbitration ties the fate of the individual employee to that of the union. In *McGavin Toastmaster*, *Weber*, and *O'Leary* the employees were not at odds with their unions. There is nothing in those cases, however, that suggests that the outcomes would have been different had there been conflicts between the unions and the individual employees. The possibility of conflict between an employee and a union is dealt with under the rubric of the union's duty of fair representation.

10:300 THE DUTY OF FAIR REPRESENTATION

A workforce is a matrix of differing interests and abilities. Skilled and unskilled, young and old, male and female, racial minorities and dominant groups, "social reformers," the exponents of "business unionism," anti-union activists — all perceive the terms and conditions of employment from quite different perspectives. The union must reconcile these varying interests. It is assisted in this task by its power to bind all members of the bargaining unit, to exclude individual bargaining, and to administer the grievance arbitration machinery. The union's exclusive bargaining rights, and its corresponding obligations, put it in a position where it can (and indeed must) seek to compromise or otherwise adjust the important differences within its ranks. In the long run, a union's survival depends as much on its ability to resolve these differences as on its capacity to deal with the employer.

Beyond these inevitable tensions, minority and individual rights and interests are sometimes violated by oppressive or arbitrary union action — action that is qualitatively different from, for example, striking a compromise between employees who want more take-home pay and those who prefer higher pensions. In particular situations, moreover, the values underlying collective bargaining may point one way in support of a collective right or interest, while other fundamental values in our society may point to the vindication of the right or interest of a competing individual or minority. Finding legal standards to resolve such conflicts has been a slow and difficult process.

Within our statutory regimes of labour relations, the primary mechanism for addressing these issues has been through the concept of the union's duty of fair representation (DFR), which is the concomitant of the union's exclusive authority to bargain. Like the duty to bargain, the DFR applies not only with respect to the union's own members but also with respect to any non-members who may be in the bargaining unit. The DFR was first formulated in the United States, in the following case of blatant racism.

Steele v. Louisville & Nashville Railroad Co., 323 U.S. 192 at 199–208 (1944)

[The Brotherhood of Locomotive Firemen and Engineers was certified under the American *Railway Labor Act* as bargaining agent for all firemen employed by the defendant railway. Under the union's constitution, black employees were explictly denied the right to be members. In accordance with a demand by the union, new collective agreement provisions were negotiated limiting the percentage of black firemen, and also limiting their seniority rights and employment opportunities. The purpose was to benefit the union's white members and ultimately to exclude all black employees, who were not given the opportunity to express their views on the matter.

The plaintiff, a black fireman, sued for an injunction against the implementation of the collective agreement, and for damages. His action failed in the Alabama courts, and he appealed to the United States Supreme Court.]

STONE C.J.: . . . we think that Congress, in enacting the *Railway Labor Act* and authorizing a labor union, chosen by a majority of a craft, to represent the craft, did not intend to confer plenary power upon the union to sacrifice, for the benefit of its members, rights of the minority of the craft, without imposing on it any duty to protect the minority.

. . .

Unless the labor union representing a craft owes some duty to represent non-union members of the craft, at least to the extent of not discriminating against them as such in the contracts which it makes as their representative, the minority would be left with no means of protecting their interests or, indeed, their right to earn a livelihood by pursuing the occupation in which they are employed. While the majority of the craft chooses the bargaining representative, when chosen it represents, as the Act by its terms makes plain, the craft or class, and not the majority. The fair interpretation of the statutory language is that the organization chosen to represent a craft is to represent all its members, the majority as well as the minority, and it is to act for and not against those whom it represents. It is a principle of general application that the exercise of a granted power to act in behalf of others involves the assumption toward them of a duty to exercise the power in their interest and behalf, and that such a grant of power will not be deemed to dispense with all duty toward those for whom it is exercised unless so expressed.

. . . We hold that the language of the Act to which we have referred, read in the light of the purposes of the Act, expresses the aim of Congress to impose on the bargaining representative of a craft or class of employees the duty to exercise fairly the power conferred upon it in behalf of all those for whom it acts, without hostile discrimination against them.

This does not mean that the statutory representative of a craft is barred from making contracts which may have unfavourable effects on some of the members of the craft represented. Variations in the terms of the contract based on differences relevant to the authorized purposes of the contract in conditions to which they are to be applied, such as differences in seniority, the type of work performed, the competence and skill with which it is performed, are within the scope of the bargaining representation of a craft, all of whose members are not identical in their interest or merit. . . . Without attempting to mark the allowable limits of differences in the terms of contracts based on differences of conditions to which they apply, it is enough for present purposes to say that the statutory power to represent a craft and to make contracts as to wages, hours and working conditions does not include the authority to make among members of the craft discriminations not based on such relevant differences. Here the discriminations based on race alone are obviously irrelevant and invidious. Congress plainly did not undertake to authorize the bargaining representative to make such discriminations. . . .

The representative which thus discriminates may be enjoined from so doing, and its members may be enjoined from taking the benefit of such discriminatory action. No more is the Railroad bound by or entitled to take the benefit of a contract which the bargaining representative is prohibited by the statute from making.

. . . While the statute does not deny to such a bargaining labor organization the right to determine eligibility to its membership, it does require the union, in collective bargaining and in making contracts with the carrier, to represent non-union or minority union members of the craft without hostile discrimination, fairly, impartially, and in good faith. Wherever necessary to that end, the union is required to consider requests of non-union members of the craft and expressions of their views with respect to collective bargaining with the employer and to give to them notice of and opportunity for hearing upon its proposed action.

. . .

We conclude that the duty which the statute imposes on a union representative of a craft to represent the interests of all its members stands on no different footing and that the statute contemplates resort to the usual judicial remedies of injunction and award of damages when appropriate for breach of that duty.

The judgment is accordingly reversed and remanded for further proceedings not inconsistent with this opinion.

10:310 The Development of the Duty of Fair Representation in Canada

Tim Christian, "The Developing Duty of Fair Representation" (1991) 2 Lab. Arb. Y.B. 3 at 3–6, 17, 20

The duty of fair representation is the crossroads for the conflict between individual and collective rights in labour relations. The collective bargaining system is built on two assumptions — that an exclusive bargaining mandate should be conferred on a union enjoying majority support and that individual claims should be subordinated to the majority will. The regulatory scheme thus imposes a utilitarian model: the greatest good will be achieved by satisfying the greatest number. The duty of fair representation has developed as a procedural check on majority rule and has become a friction point between unions and individual employees.

There are two competing views of the role which trade unions ought to play in resolving individual grievances in the North American regulatory system — that primacy should be given to collective interests as represented by the union or that primacy ought to be given to individual interests.

The view that union interests ought to prevail was most ably expressed by Archibald Cox in his well-known article 'Individual Enforcement of Collective Bargaining Agreements,' . . . in which he argued that permitting individuals to advance claims to arbitration would impede the development of good labour relations in four ways. First, it would undermine the union's role in developing the 'law of the plant.' Rather than permitting the union to implement a coherent strategy of monitoring and selectively enforcing important provisions in the collective agreement, the pursuit of ad hoc individual claims would lead to divergent rulings. Second, permitting individuals to pursue claims would undermine the prestige and authority of the union. If some individuals were to secure better settlements or awards through their own efforts than the union was able to secure, the union would look relatively ineffective. This could lead to the development of dissenting groups and a competition with the exclusive bargaining agent, thus undercutting labour relations stability. Third, the possibility of dissension and competition could make union officials reluctant to settle claims early in the grievance process, leading to more arbitrations and uncertainty. Fourth, it would be difficult to distinguish between those claims which could legitimately be brought by an individual and those which could only be brought by a trade union.

While agreeing that permitting individuals access to the arbitration process would provide the best protection against incompetent or arbitrary union officials, Professor Cox argued that the cost of such an arrangement would be too high. There would be too many claims in which the interests of one employee would be contrary to the interests of his fellows, resulting in serious impairment of the grievance process. In a later article, 'Law and the National Labor Policy,' . . . and adopted by the B.C.L.R.B. in *Rayonier Canada (B.C.) Ltd.,* . . . Professor Cox summed up his position in a paragraph which has since been handed down from board to board and adopted as an axiom in the geometry of labour relations. He said:

> . . . the union's function is to resolve the competition by reaching an accommodation or striking a balance. The process is political. It involves a melange of power, numerical strength, mutual aid, reason, prejudice, and emotion. Limits must be placed on the authority of the group, but within the zone of fairness and rationality this method of self-government probably works better than the edicts of any outside tribunal.

Ultimately, Professor Cox called for the development of a duty of fair representation rather than giving individuals unlimited access to the arbitration process.

The opposite view, that individual rights ought to take precedence over collective rights, was expressed by Professor Clyde Summers in his classic article, 'Individual Rights in Collective Agreements and Arbitration'. . . . He argued that it was important to bear in mind that the object of collective bargaining legislation was not just to stabilize relations between labour and management but to provide benefits to individual employees. After canvassing the variety of ways in which a union might fail (sometimes for legitimate and sometimes for improper reasons) to advance a claim to arbitration, Professor Summers concluded that the arbitration process should be altered to accommodate individual claims. He examined the problems with such a system but concluded it was preferable to development of the duty of fair representation proposed by Professor Cox. He suggested that new statutory rules should be developed which would permit individuals to pursue their claims to arbitration. He said . . .

The most important point here is that a framework of basic rules can be constructed which will express the statutory policies and reflect the needs both of the collective parties and of individual workers. As the details are filled in these needs can be further accommodated. As the structure takes shape it becomes increasingly evident that even with modest judicial inventiveness most of the needs can be met. Many of the problems which at first loom large shrink to manageable size or disappear when placed in the context of the total structure of rules. To be sure, these legal rules will require some changes by the collective parties in their habits of thinking and in their practices of administering agreements, for the rules proceed from the premise that collective bargaining is not merely a private device to serve their collective needs but also has the public purpose of improving the dignity and worth of the individual. There is no reason to fear that the institution of collective bargaining is so fragile or that the grievance procedure is so brittle as not to be able to adjust to a recognition of individual rights.

Lying between the views that there should or should not be an individual right to pursue claims to arbitration is a third position — that only those interests which are critical to an individual's employment status and which do not engage collective interests should be pursuable to arbitration by the individual. This position was expressed by Professor Paul Weiler in *Reconcilable Differences: New Directions in Canadian Labour Law* . . . who argued that sacrificing individual interests to the collective security was not justified in those cases where an employee claimed to have been unjustly dismissed. The devastating impact on the employee was disproportionate to the inconvenience which might be suffered by the union if such a claim were pursued to arbitration. Further, the potential adverse impact on the union could be minimized if the individual were required to bear the cost of arbitration.

In my view, having argued successfully that discharge is a kind of 'industrial capital punishment,' such that arbitrators must closely scrutinize the employer's justification for it, trade unions can hardly argue that there is such a pressing need for their power to deny the individual employee the right to get his case before that arbitrator. . . .

As the following review of legislative provisions and judicial decisions will indicate, it is the view of Archibald Cox that has prevailed. Individuals have no right to pursue claims to arbitration regardless of whether critical job interests are involved. However, while individual rights have not been increased by legislation, the practices of labour boards have been affected by the debate and it appears that the level of scrutiny is higher where critical job interests are engaged. . . .

FAIR REPRESENTATION IN COLLECTIVE BARGAINING

In Alberta, Manitoba, Newfoundland, Saskatchewan and, since a 1984 amendment to the Canada Labour Code, under federal jurisdiction, the duty is restricted in its application to the union's administration of the collective agreement. Legislation in British Columbia, Ontario and Quebec goes further and requires that unions observe the duty in the conduct of collective bargaining. A review of the cases indicates that unions in these jurisdictions are subject to a minimal level of scrutiny in their conduct of negotiations. They have a broad discretion to fashion bargaining demands which may disregard the wishes of individuals or minority groups; trade off items thought appropriate, including individual grievances; and agree to terms that adversely affect individuals or groups of employees. What the duty demands is a modicum of procedural not substantive fairness, and while the views of employees in the unit should be canvassed, they need not be followed. . . .

FAIR REPRESENTATION IN THE ADMINISTRATION OF THE COLLECTIVE AGREEMENT

While the scope of the duty will continue to evolve as new fact patterns are considered by labour relations boards, a settled core of understandings exist. As a review of the recent cases indicates, the duty consists of several elements. The union is obliged to investigate the facts of a grievance, to hear the grievor's side of the story, to make an unbiased assessment of the merits, to inform the grievor of steps being taken on his or her behalf, to seek the grievor's agreement to any settlement, to avoid acting with gross negligence in representing the grievor, and to obtain such assistance as is reasonable given the seriousness of the loss to the grievor and the resources of the union. Ultimately, though, the union is not obliged to pursue any particular grievance to arbitration. Even where critical job interests are affected, the union is well within its rights to refuse to pursue a matter provided the decision not to proceed is reached after due deliberation. Labour boards across the country seem to agree on several basic points. . . .

[Reprinted by permission of Lancaster House Publishing.]

✽ ✽ ✽

As is clear from the above excerpt, most Canadian jurisdictions now expressly recognize the DFR in some way in their labour relations statutes. The three Maritime provinces do not. There, a complainant must rely on what is known as the "common law duty of fair representation." Although that terminology has been used by the Supreme Court of Canada, it is something of a misnomer in that the duty arises solely by implication from the labour relations statute.

The common law DFR is very similar in substance to the express statutory DFR, but the common law duty is enforced by the courts rather than by the labour relations board, and there are significant differences in the remedies available. Courts are restricted to awarding monetary relief whereas the statutory jurisdiction of labour boards is usually broader. These differences seem to be of substantial practical significance. In jurisdictions where an explicit statutory duty allows recourse to a labour relations board, DFR complaints are quite numerous. In jurisdictions where the employee must rely on the courts, complaints are few.

10:320 The Duty of Fair Representation in the Negotiation of a Collective Agreement

The genesis of the duty of fair representation, set out in *Steele*, above, section 10:300, involved a challenge to what the union had negotiated in the collective agreement, not merely a challenge to how the collective agreement was being administered. Most DFR claims since then have been about contract administration, but some have related to the negotiation of the collective agreement.

Bukvich v. Canadian Union of United Brewery, Flour, Cereal, Soft Drink and Distillery Workers, Local 304 and Dufferin Aggregates (1982), 82 C.L.L.C. para. 16,156 at 593–601 (O.L.R.B.)

PICHER, Vice-Chair: . . . This is a complaint under section 68 of the *Labour Relations Act*. The five grievors were laid off from their jobs as dependent contractor owner-operators of tandem trucks working out of a quarry at Milton operated by Dufferin Aggregates. The unusual twist is that their layoffs were, in effect, initiated by the union. The grievor[s] claim that the actions of the union which resulted in their layoffs were in violation of its duty of fair representation described in section 68 of the Act.

The facts are not in dispute. In July of 1978 the respondent was certified by this Board as bargaining agent of all drivers working at or out of the Milton quarry. . . . The current agreement, the product of a strike in the summer of 1980, is in effect from June 15, 1980 until December 31, 1982.

When the current collective agreement was executed, the unit numbered thirty-four drivers. Because of the nature of the services rendered, with drivers being paid by the load, the company is indifferent as to the number of drivers in the quarry as long as there are enough to handle the work available. The drivers on the other hand, who own their own trucks and have considerable financing costs and operating expenses to meet, are concerned with keeping a limit on the number of trucks in the quarry, to maximize their own revenues. To that end the following provisions were negotiated into the collective agreement:

Article IV

4.01 The company will establish a drivers' list based on seniority. The number of drivers on such list shall not exceed thirty-four (34). . . .

4.02 There shall be no layoff during the life of this Agreement, it being understood that the drivers will share available work in accordance with present practice.

4.03 Drivers will receive available loads in accordance with the practice presently in effect.

4.04 The Company is entitled to call in truckers not on seniority list as it sees fit provided that, so far as practicable and the requirements of the Company's customers can be met satisfactorily, drivers on the seniority list shall have first call on loads at all times.

The evidence establishes that conditions in the industry have caused a continuing attrition in the number of drivers in the bargaining unit. At one time there were fifty-six drivers at work. There were forty-five at the time of certification. Shortly before the layoff that is the basis of this complaint, there were thirty-three drivers, three of whom quit. After the layoff, at the time of the hearing, there were twenty-one owner-operators at work.

The dependency of the drivers in the bargaining unit on the work available at Dufferin is a matter of record. They do not obtain any meaningful income from alternative sources. . . .

The hardship experienced by the drivers is due in part to a general decline in the construction industry and to an increased use of independent trucking contractors who operate larger tractor trailer units. . . . There was then little reason to doubt that the company would respond to an initiative of the union to amend the collective agreement to allow it to lay off junior drivers and distribute the available work among a smaller pool of senior drivers.

A group of senior drivers began to act on that prospect through the early months of 1981. A petition favouring the insertion of a layoff provision in the collective agreement was circulated among the senior drivers. As a result a meeting of the bargaining unit was held on June 3, 1981 to entertain a motion which would have authorized the union executive to re-open negotiations with the company to amend the no-layoff provision of the agreement. The motion passed by a margin of 14 to 10. The union executive, however, under the direction of Mr. Cameron Nelson, the full-time union officer who chaired the meeting, ruled that the vote was not sufficient to authorize re-opening the contract because it was passed by only a minority of the employees eligible to vote. It appears that under the union's rules a change of that magnitude requires a majority of all employees in the bargaining unit. . . .

Undaunted, the senior drivers, led by shop steward, A. Levin, petitioned again. A further meeting was held on July 13, 1981. . . .

After some two hours of heated discussion a secret ballot vote was taken: the motion to re-open the contract carried 18 to 12, a majority of the employees in the bargaining unit.

The inevitable followed. The union executive, bound to carry out the wishes of the majority, approached the company and negotiated an amendment of the collective agreement. The amendment, tentatively agreed to on August 14, 1981, provided: . . .

4.02 Should the Company find it necessary to lay-off members of the bargaining unit due to lack of work, it shall do so in reverse order of seniority. During periods of lay-off, the Company shall maintain a lay-off list of drivers and shall recall them in order of seniority when work becomes available.

On August 19, 1981, a final meeting of the bargaining unit was held to ratify the amendment. That meeting, again chaired by Mr. Nelson, is not irregular in respect of its procedures. The evidence establishes that adequate notice and a full opportunity to participate and vote was afforded all drivers in the bargaining unit. As expected, after a predictably stormy meeting, the amendment was ratified.

Two weeks later, by letter dated September 3, 1981, the company notified the union that nine drivers were laid off effective 5:00 p.m., September 4, 1981. There can be little doubt that the layoff had a harsh impact on the drivers affected. One of the grievors, Mike D'Alonzo, was unable to find other haulage work and was forced to sell his truck because of an inability to meet his finance payments. Mr. Bukvich testified that because of his financing obligations he may have to choose between losing his truck and losing his home. He is angry that the union could have permitted such a result through a process which he described as 'the rich getting together . . . voting member against member'. . . .

In this case the complainants ask the Board to conclude that the decision to effectively eliminate the jobs of a minority is in itself a violation of the duty to fairly represent the members of the minority. Counsel for the complainants argues that the grievors had a contractual right and expectation to work out of the quarry over the life of the collective agreement, and that to re-open the contract to undo that right is a violation of their vested rights inconsistent with the duty of fair representation.

As compelling as that argument may seem, in my view it does not assist the understanding of the issue to simply assert that the members of a minority have an absolute right to be protected against negative consequences to their job security. The collective agreement is a contract made between the employer and the union. They are the parties to it, and any benefits which it confers on individual employees are necessarily subject to the possibility of amendment between the parties. In this regard it should be recalled that a collective agreement is not 'a bundle of individual contracts between employer and employee negotiated by the union as agent for the employees'. . . .

That is not to say that a trade union can with impunity disregard the interests of the employees it represents or take either a hostile or an indifferent attitude where employees' critical interests are at stake. In discharging its duty to fairly represent all of the employees in a bargaining unit a union must address its mind to the circumstances of those who may be adversely affected by its decision. It has a duty to weigh the competing interests of the employees it represents and make a considered judgment the procedure and result of which must be neither arbitrary, discriminatory nor in bad faith.

Counsel for the complainants submits that in this case the union has not properly balanced the interests of the two groups of employees involved. He argues that if the union cannot show that the marginal advantage which the union's decision gives the majority outweighs the disadvantage to the minority, it has violated the duty of fair representation. In other words, he maintains that the union must justify its decision, and absent such justification the Board should conclude that the union's action is in violation of the duty of fair representation.

That submission must be considered with great caution. To adopt that standard in an unqualified way risks placing the Board in the position of being the arbiter of the political correctness of a union decision. The weighing of competing interests and the ultimate choice as to which outcome is preferable is a highly subjective decision, inevitably influenced by the inherent values, viewpoints and preferences of the decision maker. In the collective bargaining context such choices are highly political, and to that extent unions are required to act as responsive political bodies.

In bargaining changes that affect the competing interests of employees a union has a two stage involvement: firstly it must be the forum for resolving the conflict between sometimes irreconcilable employee interests; secondly it must act as the spokesman for the interests that carry the day. Once the internal choice is made the union must approach the employer with the force and conviction of a body with a single voice. To view the union in this later stage as the antagonist of the minority is to misconceive the process. Professor Cox, in discussing the processing of grievances, usefully summarized this dimension of union activity as follows:

> When the interests of several groups conflict, or future needs run contrary to present desires, or when the individual's claim endangers group interests, the union's function is to resolve the competition by reaching an accommodation or striking a balance. The

process is political. It involves a melange of power, numerical strength, mutual aid, reason, prejudice, and emotion. Limits must be placed on the authority of the group, but within the zone of fairness and rationality this method of self-government probably works better than the edicts of any outside arbiter. A large part of the daily grist of union business is resolving differences among employees poorly camouflaged as disputes with the employer.

The weight of authority supports the view put forward by counsel for the complainants that special considerations attach to any decision by a union that alters or abrogates the job security of employees. That is especially true in relation to seniority rights. Seniority rights, built up over time, usually over a number of successive collective agreements, represent an employee's stake in critical interests such as promotion, pension rights and his rights of layoff and recall. The concept of seniority comes as close as any to approximating a form of industrial relations property right for the individual employee. . . .

This case involves the elimination of a work sharing guarantee in favour of a provision of layoffs by seniority. A work sharing provision is one of a number of means, like seniority, like provisions prohibiting the contracting out of bargaining unit work, or like classification schemes, whereby job security can be directly affected. It is obviously a fundamental provision in any collective agreement, expressing as it does the choice and expectation of the employees respecting the allocation of work in times of scarcity. . . .

Work sharing has deep and abiding importance for the employees who are under it. Because it impacts on job security it represents an employee interest just as critical as a seniority provision. Action by a union to change or eradicate a work sharing or no-layoff provision must, therefore, be viewed as seriously and be judged by the same standards as a change in seniority provisions. That is particularly so where, as here, employees have had the security and benefit of such a provision through successive collective agreements. The impact in this case is more dramatic still: as dependent contractors, the complainants do not contribute to the Unemployment Insurance scheme. For them the consequences of a layoff are particularly hard, and the analogy to a change in seniority ranking provisions is extremely close. . . . The appropriate standard to be adopted by this Board is not unlike that expressed by the Court in the judicial review of the decisions of arbitrators: the Board should ask not whether the decision is right or wrong or whether it agrees with it — rather it should ask whether it is a decision that could reasonably be made in all the circumstances, even if the Board might itself be inclined to disagree with it. Used in this sense 'reasonable' must mean the rational application of relevant factors, after considering and balancing all legitimate interests and without regard to extraneous factors.

In this case the evidence leaves little doubt that the union was faced with a deteriorating economic situation in early 1981. The number of trucks in the quarry had been continuously reduced by attrition over the previous three years. Following the strike in the summer of 1980 conditions had continued to decline with some ten or eleven owner-operators leaving the quarry. In January of 1981 to remain competitive the drivers agreed to postpone the implementation of a negotiated rate increase from January 1, 1981 to April 1, 1981. In May the union agreed to drop the haulage rate by a further 25 cents in hopes of remaining competitive with independent truckers and retaining a larger volume of work. Because of the downturn in construction generally, and the increased use of larger independent trailer trucks, the drivers in the bargaining unit were only barely surviving.

In this regard the evidence of Milovan Stanisic is particularly instructive. Called as a witness by the complainants, Mr. Stanisic has worked as a driver in the quarry for nine years. He believed he stood approximately 17th or 18th in seniority at the time the issue of re-opening the contract arose. Mr. Stanisic favoured the layoff provision. By his own unchallenged account, he did not know what number of employees would be laid off if the contract were re-opened and was given no assurance that he would not. He decided however, that he would be better off either out of the quarry entirely working elsewhere, or in the quarry sharing a viable volume of work among a smaller number of trucks. In his own words 'I had to protect myself, sitting there doing little work with high costs — I had to protect myself from going out of business.' For Stanisic marking time in the quarry was intolerable; he preferred the risk of layoff with the alternative chance of better work in the quarry, to the seemingly hopeless stagnation of the previous months.

That is not to say that Stanisic's view was shared by everyone. . . . It would be unrealistic to think that most if not all drivers voted without giving some thought to their chances of survival. The fact, however, that some drivers in the position of Mr. Stanisic were willing to risk the unknown on the simple basis that the economic status quo was intolerable to them is in my view a compelling factor in understanding the decision which was made and assessing the objective justification for it.

This was a crisis decision — like a decision about how to determine who will survive in an overcrowded lifeboat. If the union had decided to transfer work from the minority to the majority in a time of relative prosperity, where its obvious motive was to increase the already profitable position of some drivers at the expense of others, it would be difficult to avoid the conclusion that its decision was in violation of the duty to provide representation free of invidious favouritism. That is clearly not the situation. . . . The only difference under work sharing as compared to under layoffs by seniority is that as the volume of work diminished attrition would be by order of poverty. Drivers with greater financial obligations would be less able to survive lean periods than those who owned their trucks outright. Under that system, given continual shrinkage, the poor would go first and the rich would go last.

The drivers were in a 'no win' situation. Absent an upturn in the volume of business (in which case layoffs would not be a problem) someone was going to be hurt by the economic pressure. In these circumstances can the union be faulted for choosing an alternative by which those with the longest investment of service in the quarry should go last? The union was not content with a system which, in effect, gave the shrinking work in the quarry to those with the financial strength to bid for it. It chose instead to let seniority prevail. In asking whether the ultimate decision is one that could be reasonably made I do not see how the union can be faulted for preferring what a particularly helpful study has called a political mode of allocation over a market mode of allocation in a time of scarcity. . . .

This Board cannot conclude that in the difficult circumstances facing it, the union's decision to alter its system of work allocation was without objective justification. Without ignoring the hardship on the junior employees who were eventually affected by the union's decision, I must conclude that the decision to renegotiate the work sharing provision was one which the union was entitled to make in the circumstances, and that neither the motive nor the consequences of its decision violated its duty of fair representation. For reasons elaborated above, I am also satisfied that the procedure followed by the union was free o[f] arbitrariness, discrimination or bad faith.

For the foregoing reasons the complaint is dismissed.

* * *

Despite the outcome in the above case, the Board clearly refused to treat as conclusive the fact that a majority of the employees in the unit supported the union's action in renegotiating the worksharing provisions. Other decisions give more weight to the existence of such majority support, even where there is a sharp conflict of interest between majority and minority. An example is provided by *Ouellet v. Syndicat des travailleurs et travailleuses de Deauville* (1983), 83 C.L.L.C. para. 14,054 (Que. Lab. Ct.). Before union certification in 1982 for the employees of a restaurant, the employer's practice was to take back an employee who had been on maternity leave as soon as an opening arose, even if the leave had been longer than the eighteen weeks envisaged in the labour standards statute. The complainant, who started to work at the restaurant in 1976, took an eleven-month maternity leave in 1979–80. When the first collective agreement was being negotiated in 1982, the union bargaining committee decided that any employee who had taken more than an eighteen-week maternity leave would be given a seniority date which coincided with her return from leave rather than her initial date of hire. The complainant asked the union to reconsider that rule in her case. Rather than putting that question to the entire bargaining unit, the union put it only to those employees who were junior enough to be directly affected by the outcome. Those employees voted to give the complainant a 1980 seniority date, which gave her much less job security than a 1976 date. In rejecting the complainant's duty of fair representation complaint, the Labour Court said (at 12,285):

> Having the matter voted on only by those members who were directly affected by it was a debatable course of action. On the other hand, when a union decides whether to make an exception in a particular case, it is perhaps normal to put the question only to those who are directly concerned. In any event, that was the choice which the union made, and intervention under the duty of fair representation is not appropriate. [Translation.]

As is noted in the excerpt from Tim Christian's article in section 10:310 above, the negotiation stage has been omitted from the ambit of the DFR in Alberta, Manitoba, Newfoundland and Labrador, and Saskatchewan — that is, in most of the jurisdictions with an express statutory duty. For example, the Saskatchewan *Trade Union Act*, section 25.1, says that the duty applies "in grievance or rights arbitration proceedings." Similarly, section 37 of the *Canada Labour Code* was amended in 1984 to limit the duty to "the representation of any of the employees in the unit *with respect to their rights under the collective agreement* that is applicable to them" (emphasis added).

However, it is doubtful that section 37 of the federal *Code* has achieved its purpose. In *Via Rail Canada Inc. v. Cairns* (2001), 200 D.L.R. (4th) 35, leave to appeal to the Supreme Court of Canada refused, (2001) S.C.C.A. No. 338, the federal board had held that the statutory freeze provisions of the *Code* preserved rights under an expired collective agreement for the duration of the freeze, so a union's bargaining about those rights was subject to the DFR. In dismissing an application for judicial review, the Federal Court of Appeal said (at paras. 54 and 55):

> [The employer and the union] argue that extending the duty of fair representation to collective bargaining offends the principle of free collective bargaining. They argue that such an extension would destroy the necessary give-and-take of contract negotiations by restraining the union from bargaining away any existing rights. I disagree. The existence of a duty of fair representation does not preclude a union from making concessions with respect to existing rights or privileges of its members as part of the bargaining process. What it does do, is to require that the union, in making those concessions not act in a manner that is arbitrary, discriminatory or in bad faith during the collective bargaining process.
>
> To hold otherwise would be to allow a union to simply put off dealing with controversial matters. . . , so as to address them with the employer during collective bargaining instead of during the term of the collective agreement. While dealing with the matters during the term of the collective agreement would give rise to a duty under s. 37, delaying negotiations would shelter the union from scrutiny under s. 37. In my opinion, an interpretation that allowed such a result would be irrational and absurd.

✻ ✻ ✻

The following decision of the Supreme Court of Canada also shows that it is not always easy to separate the negotiation and the adminstration of a collective agreement. The case is the leading authority on the effect of the DFR on a union's authority to settle or trade off grievances.

Centre hospitalier Régina Ltée v. Quebec (Labour Court), [1990] 1 S.C.R. 1330 at 1334–64

[The plaintiff employee had been dismissed for absences due to illness. Her union filed a grievance, which was scheduled to be heard by an arbitrator. Prior to the hearing, the union and the employer renegotiated the collective agreement, with the union agreeing to settle all pending grievances in exchange for certain concessions in the new agreement. The plaintiff was not a party to this settlement. She brought a complaint alleging violation of the union's duty of fair representation. The Labour Court found the duty to have been breached and ordered the initial grievance to be arbitrated. The employer unsuccessfully sought judicial review in the Quebec courts, and appealed to the Supreme Court of Canada.]

L'HEUREUX-DUBÉ J. (for the Court):

> . . . this case puts in question the finality of the settlement of grievances between an employer and a union in light of an employee's right to arbitrate a grievance filed against his dismissal. In the present case the settlement in question was concluded without the

employee's participation and was part of a general agreement to settle grievances on the occasion of the renewal of a collective agreement. . . .

This appeal essentially turns on the interpretation of the mechanisms established by ss. 47.3 to 47.6 [of the Quebec *Labour Code*, referred to as L.C.], regarding a union's duty of representation covered by s. 47.2 L.C. At the time this dispute arose, these provisions . . . read as follows:

47.2 . . . A certified association shall not act in bad faith or in an arbitrary or discriminatory manner or show serious negligence in respect of employees comprised in a bargaining unit represented by it, whether or not they are members.

47.3 . . . If an employee who has been the subject of dismissal or of a disciplinary sanction believes that the certified association is, in that respect, violating section 47.2, he shall, if he wishes to invoke this section, submit a written complaint to the Minister within six months. The Minister shall appoint an investigator who shall endeavour to settle the dispute to the satisfaction of the interested parties and of the certified association.

47.4 . . . If no settlement has been reached within fifteen days of the appointment of the investigator or if the association does not carry out the agreement, the employee shall, if he wishes to invoke section 47.2, apply to the Court within the fifteen ensuing days to request that his claim be referred to arbitration.

47.5 . . . If the Court considers that the association has violated section 47.2, it may authorize the employee to submit his claim to an arbitrator appointed by the Minister for decision in the manner provided for in the collective agreement, as in the case of a grievance. Sections 100 to 101.10 apply *mutatis mutandis*. The association shall pay the employee's costs. . . . The Court may, in addition, make any other order it considers necessary in the circumstances.

47.6 . . . If a claim is referred to an arbitrator pursuant to section 47.5, the employer shall not allege the association's non-observance of the procedure and delays provided for in the collective agreement for the settlement of grievances.

. . .

The duty of fair representation raises thorny problems when, as here, by its very function the union has an obligation to defend the interests of members of the bargaining unit as a whole, as well as those of an individual employee. These interests can be and often are indeed divergent. . . .

. . . even when the union is acting as a defender of an employee's rights (which in its estimation are valid), it must take into account the interests of the bargaining unit as a whole in exercising its discretion whether or not to proceed with a grievance. The union has a discretion to weigh these divergent interests and adopt the solution which it feels is fairest. However, this discretion is not unlimited. Simply saying that the union has the right or power to 'sacrifice' any grievance, which it feels is valid at that stage, during negotiations with the employer, in order to obtain a concession of better working conditions or other benefits for the bargaining unit as a whole, would be contrary to the union's duty of diligent representation of the employee in question. On the other hand, completely rejecting the possibility that the union and the employer may settle a great many grievances in negotiations for a new collective agreement, or on other occasions, would be to ignore the reality of labour relations. . . . [There is a] necessity for a union to have some discretion in collective bargaining to 'swap' grievances, even when they appear to be valid. . . .

. . . There will be situations where the abandonment of an apparently valid grievance by the union will have such consequences for the employee in question that it will substantially restrain the union's discretion. When, for example, the purpose of the grievance is to challenge a dismissal, the employee will not accept any half measures: only reinstatement will be a suitable remedy. Some have suggested that in such a case the union has no discretion and the employee's right to have his grievance arbitrated is absolute. Professor P. Weiler, for example, commenting on the duty of fair representation, writes (*Reconcilable Differences: New Directions in Canadian Labour Law* . . .):

> I just think that there are limits to the sacrifice which can be made to individual rights in the pursuit of decent collective bargaining relationships, and that that limit is reached here. What is distinctive about this situation is that the dismissed employee who is denied access to his day in arbitration will not share any of the future benefits of that spirit of union-management cooperation. He should not have to pay the price of sacrificing his chance to keep his job.

This proposition was considered by this Court in *Gagnon* [*v. Canadian Merchant Service Guild*], where Chouinard J. noted that the Canada Labour Relations Board had rejected such an approach. . . . *Gagnon* itself appears to sanction a more flexible rule. In 'The Duty of Fair Representation: A Theoretical Structure' . . . Julia Clarke proposes a compromise position recognizing the union's discretion to evaluate the merits of a dismissal grievance as well as the extreme repercussions dismissal poses for the employee. However, given the harsh consequences of dismissal, 'swapping' apparently valid grievances of this nature for a collective benefit is prohibited altogether:

> In addition, there is some support for giving the unions less leeway in dealing with discharge grievances than in other matters. The consequences of discharge — loss of the employee's job as well as the pension and seniority benefits he may have built up over years of employment — are drastic enough to impose stricter restraints on union discretion. *The concern for job security might warrant a rule that would prohibit swapping discharge grievances altogether.* [Emphasis added.]

Accordingly, without necessarily accepting this statement in absolute terms, a union must recognize the importance of an employee's individual interest when exercising its discretion whether or not to proceed with a grievance against a dismissal or disciplinary sanctions. Of course, it goes without saying that if the employee consents to the agreement reached between the union and the employer, the validity of such a 'swap' would be viewed differently.

It is against this background that the provisions of the Quebec *Labour Code* in this regard must be considered. It should be noted at the outset that none of the provisions at issue are at variance with the general principles enunciated by the courts and doctrinal authorities. On the contrary, I consider that the wording of ss. 47.2 et seq. L.C. is admirably consistent with the view that the union's discretion is limited when confronted with a choice between its duty of care toward an employee and that of representing the members of the bargaining unit. Professor Jean-Denis Gagnon observes in this connection ('Le devoir de représentation des associations de salariés en droit canadien et québécois') . . . :

> [Translation:] *The precarious position in which an employee may find himself after being laid off or dismissed, or when severe disciplinary action has been taken against him, was expressly recognized by the Quebec legislator in ss. 47.2 et seq., which deal with the duty of representation imposed on associations.* While recognizing that this duty is imposed on unions in all cases where they are acting as spokesmen or representatives of an employee group, the legislator has nevertheless created a specific remedy to ensure that this duty is observed, only in cases of 'dismissals' or 'disciplinary action.' In all other cases an employee who wishes to complain of his association's attitude and force it to act or change its attitude must use various general remedies contained in the *Labour Code* and other legislation. [Emphasis added.]

I agree. The legislator has clearly indicated his preference here by specifying in s. 47.3 L.C. those extreme cases in which arbitration of a grievance may survive its abandonment by the union: namely, cases of dismissal and disciplinary sanctions. . . .

This choice is consistent with the general recognition that it is important for an employee to retain his employment, in view of the potentially devastating effects on him. . . .

The Quebec legislator's choice to distinguish the rights of an employee facing dismissal from other less serious situations is . . . in accordance with a consistent line of scholarly and judicial authority. . . .

This having been said, the question here is whether, applying these principles, the union has infringed its duty of fair representation, as defined in s. 47.2 L.C, with respect to Cécile Montigny. It seems clear that the union disposed of her grievance without her consent, indeed without even telling her. It is equally clear that the grievance was one regarding dismissal, and thus covered by s. 47.3 L.C. . . .

. . . the appellant argues that allowing recourse to the procedure in ss. 47.3 et seq. L.C. in such cases would have the unacceptable consequence of casting doubt on, and even overturning, both any agreement that might be concluded between a union and an employer at the expense of the employer's rights, and the stability of collective labour relations in Quebec generally. An employer could no longer assume that agreements made with a union were final.

I myself regard such apprehension as greatly exaggerated, in view, inter alia, of the limited number of cases covered by the legislation, cases of dismissal or disciplinary sanctions in which the union has failed in its duty of fair representation. However, such concerns cannot be ignored as they reflect a fear that the delicate balance existing in collective labour relations will be upset. . . .

The union's credibility as a valid and exclusive spokesman for the employees included in the bargaining unit continues to be one of the essential elements of this process. However, it must be recognized that the legislator is fully competent to adjust the balance between employee rights and union monopoly on representation as against the rights of the employer within the framework of collective labour relations, so as to make them as harmonious as possible. . . .

The legislator's decision that the right of employees to retain their employment should be given preference is a conclusion which fits in with the general framework of *Labour Code* provisions, in which the legislator is constantly seeking to provide protection for employee rights. This does not mean serious hardship for the employer. First, as regards the referral to arbitration of a grievance settled with the union, it will be in a position comparable to that following a unilateral discontinuance by the union . . . or a preliminary dismissal of the grievance. . . . Second, as regards the *quid pro quo* for the agreement to settle the grievance, if any, the latter may be the subject either of an eventual action by the employer against the union, or of an order by the Labour Court under the second paragraph of s. 47.5 L.C., but we do not have to decide that point here. Section 47.6 L.C. also creates an exception in favour of the employee by preventing the employer from relying on non-compliance with time limits. . . .

It follows from this analysis that the Labour Court's power to refer to arbitration a grievance already settled between the employer and the union in contravention of s. 47.2 L.C. is firmly based not only on the wording of ss. 47.2 to 47.6 L.C., but also on the provisions of the *Labour Code* as a whole, and is consistent with current judicial and scholarly opinion in labour relations in North America. . . .

In conclusion, I am of the view that the Labour Court did not in this case [Translation] 'make an error going to jurisdiction,' according to the criteria laid down by the courts, and that both the Superior Court and the Court of Appeal properly refused to exercise their superintending and reforming power.

Accordingly, for all these reasons I would dismiss the appeal with costs throughout.

10:330 The Duty of Fair Representation in the Administration of a Collective Agreement

In jurisdictions where the duty of fair representation clearly covers both negotiation and administration of the collective agreement, the bulk of the cases involve contract administration and grievance processing. Nonetheless, as the following often-cited decision on the nature of the duty in collective agreement administration indicates, an element of negotiation may be present in the form of a practice by the employer and the union of not enforcing the apparent meaning of the agreement in certain circumstances.

Rayonier Canada (B.C.) Ltd. v. International Woodworkers of America, Local 1-217, [1975] 2 Can. L.R.B.R. 196 at 198–207 (B.C.L.R.B.)

[Employee Anderson complained that Rayonier had violated the collective agreement by denying him certain seniority rights due to him under that agreement, and that the union had breached its duty of fair representation by not carrying his resulting grievance to arbitration.]

WEILER, Chair: Marpole Sawmill is a division of Rayonier. Its employees are represented by the IWA in a certification which also covers the employees of Rayflo Silvichemical plant, another division of Rayonier which is located on the same property as the sawmill. Both groups of employees are covered by the master collective agreement between the IWA and Forest Industrial Relations. However, they are treated as separate entities by the parties, each with its own elected Plant Chairman, Shop Committee, contract ratification votes, and separate seniority lists.

Last July 26, 1974, as a result of the serious economic condition of the lumber industry, there had to be a massive work reduction in the sawmill. This produced a layoff of more than 200 men, including almost all of the maintenance tradesmen. In particular, it affected the two main subjects of these proceedings, Ross Anderson and Angelo Nasato, both of whom were journeymen welders in the sawmills. Nasato's seniority date was listed as April 19, 1957, while Anderson, the next welder on the list, is dated November 17, 1964. In accordance with its previous practice, Rayonier had arranged to offer some work at Rayflo to the employees at Marpole who were being laid off. On this occasion it had a job for Nasato, but not for Anderson.

A few days later, Rayonier decided that it could conveniently proceed with a new scrubber-barker installation at Marpole during the Mill shutdown. This meant there would be work for some tradesmen, including two welders, and the work would be paid for at new construction rates. However, when Tribe, the foreman, phoned Nasato and offered him this work, Nasato was reluctant to return to Marpole for a short-term project and give up his steady job at Rayflo which would likely last throughout the layoff at the sawmill. Tribe did not insist that Nasato return; instead, he contacted Anderson and the next junior welder on the seniority list, and the latter two were recalled to Marpole for work during August.

Eventually, the sawmill returned to production in mid-fall. However, Nasato remained at Rayflo until November 15, when he was laid off there. He returned to Marpole Sawmill on the date. A week later, on November 22nd, there was another layoff in the sawmill, again affecting the welders. This time, though, there was no work available at Rayflo because of the reduction in effect there. As a result, Nasato was retained at Marpole and Anderson was laid off until his recall on December 5th (losing a total of six working days in that period).

It was this last occurrence and its aftermath which produced these complaints. Accordingly, it is important to be aware of its background. For years, Rayonier and the IWA have operated under an informal arrangement for layoffs and recalls at Marpole. The senior employee is entitled under the agreement to be recalled before the junior employee. However, it is not unusual, especially for tradesmen, for there to be intermittent recalls for short-term jobs during a protracted slowdown. A senior employee may have secured a steady alternate job, perhaps outside of the Lower Mainland, which will probably continue during the entire foreseeable layoff at Marpole. Naturally, he will be reluctant to give up this job to respond to a recall for work at Marpole which may last for just a few days.

Recognizing this, Marpole has adopted the practice of allowing the senior employee to decline to return to work in these circumstances and going on to the next man on the seniority list. There may be an exceptional case where the senior man has special qualifications required by Rayonier for its work, in which case Rayonier will insist that he accept the recall, but this is a rare occurrence. We were given a list of 17 employees who had used this arrangement dating back to 1958. The Union knows of and approves the practice, and it had been reaffirmed in August 1974 in discussions between Murray, the Plant Chairman, and Fleming, the Personnel Supervisor, about the Nasato case itself.

Anderson was aware of the long-standing practice and knew that this was the reason why Nasato had not reappeared at Marpole in August. However, for his own reasons, he decided to challenge the contractual basis of the practice on the occasion of the second layoff in November. In his view, when Nasato did not return to Marpole in August, he lost his place on the seniority list. When he did return on November 15th, he should be placed on that list far below Anderson. Hence, when the next work reduction occurred on November 22nd, it was Nasato who should have been laid off and Anderson who should have been retained.

Naturally enough, Anderson did not find a very sympathetic ear in the Union to listen to this claim. . . .

[Anderson filed a grievance, which the union, after normal internal discussions, decided to drop. He then brought this complaint to the board.]

What is the content of the duty of fair representation imposed on a union? Section 7(1) requires that a trade union not 'act in a manner that is arbitrary, discriminatory or in bad faith in the representation of any of the employees' in the unit. . . .

. . . The union must not be actuated by bad faith in the sense of personal hostility, political revenge, or dishonesty. There can be no discrimination, treatment of particular employees unequally whether on account of such factors as race and sex (which are illegal under the Human Rights Code) or simple, personal favouritism. Finally, a union cannot act arbitrarily, disregarding the interests of one of the employees in a perfunctory matter. Instead, it must take a reasonable view of the problem before it and arrive at a thoughtful judgment about what to do after considering the various relevant and conflicting considerations.

These phrases express the duty imposed on the union in general and abstract terms. The case before us . . . typifies the most intractable and the most litigated specific issue raised in the fair representation area. Does the union have the authority to settle, or to refuse to press, a grievance which the affected individual employee wants to have proceeded with? It is argued that a collective agreement is a contract establishing the law of the plant. As such, it entitles the individual employee to certain rights and engenders the expectation that these will be secured. If the employee feels that his rights have not been respected by the employer, then he should have access to some neutral forum to obtain a binding adjudication of his claim. The preferred mode of adjudication under a collective agreement is arbitration, and customarily the union controls access to that forum through its authority over the grievance procedure. But it has been vigorously argued that if an employee wants to have his claim to some contract benefit established in arbitration, the union acts arbitrarily, and thus in violation of its duty of fair representation, in denying him that right. The leading exponent of this view expressed its rationale in these terms.

> . . . the collective parties can change the general rules governing the terms and conditions of employment, either by negotiating a new agreement or by formally amending the old. The individual has no right to have the contract remain unchanged; his right is only to have it followed until it is changed by proper procedures. Although contract making (or amending) and contract administration are not neatly severable, they are procedurally distinct processes. Most union constitutions prescribe the method of contract ratification, and it is distinct from grievance settlement; the power to make and amend contracts is not placed in the same hands as the power to adjust grievances. Indeed, many union constitutions expressly bar any officer from ratifying any action which constitutes a breach of any contract. Through the ability to change the agreement, the collective parties retain a measure of flexibility. They are not free, however, to set aside general rules for particular cases, nor are they free by informal processes to replace one general rule with a contrary one. Summers, C.W. *'Individual Rights in Collective Agreements and Arbitration'*. . . .

Most courts, labour boards, and commentators have rejected this individual rights position. The contrary view — that the union retains control over grievances subject to a duty of fair representation — derived originally from a law review article by Cox, *'Rights under a Labour Agreement'* . . . and his analysis was accepted by the [United States] Supreme Court majority in *Vaca v. Sipes*:

> In providing for a grievance and arbitration procedure which gives the union discretion to supervise the grievance machinery and to invoke arbitration, the employer and the union contemplate that each will endeavour in good faith to settle grievances short of arbitration. Through this settlement process, frivolous grievances are ended prior to the most costly and time-consuming step in the grievance procedures. Moreover, both sides are assured that similar complaints will be treated consistently, and major problem areas in the interpretation of the collective bargaining contract can be isolated and perhaps resolved. And finally, the settlement process furthers the interest of the union as statutory agent and as co-author of the bargaining agreement in representing the employees in the enforcement of that agreement. See Cox, *'Rights Under a Labor Agreement'*. . . .

In turn, that conclusion was followed by the Ontario Labour Relations Board in the *Gebbie* decision . . . interpreting an Ontario provision with language almost identical to our own:

> One of the most difficult areas in applying the duty is in the settlement of grievances. We think it clear that the union's obligation to administer the collective agreement gives it the right to settle grievances. An employee does not have an absolute right to have his grievances arbitrated. . . .

In our judgment, that same view should be taken of the authority permitted to the union under s. 7 of the Labour Code in handling individual grievances.

... the administration of a collective agreement is not simply the enforcement of individual contract claims: it is also an extension of the collective bargaining process. As such, it involves significant group interests which the union may represent even against the wishes of particular employees. ...

[Grievance procedures and arbitration] can function successfully only if the union has the power to settle or drop those cases which it believes have little merit, even if the individual claimant disagrees. This permits the union to ration its own limited resources by arbitrating only those cases which have a reasonable prospect of success. But even if the employee were willing to finance the union's share of arbitration himself, this would not protect management from the cost of having to defend against frivolous grievances. Such a protection for the employer is a necessary quid pro quo from the union if the latter expects management to be reasonable in conceding those other claims which are well-founded, rather than attempt to wear down the union by making it take every case to arbitration to get relief. It is important as a matter of industrial relations policy that a union must be able to assume the responsibility of saying to an employee that his grievance has no merit and will be dropped.

There is a second group interest in the settlement of grievances which applies even to cases which might succeed in arbitration. While a grievance may originally be brought by one individual, it is not unusual for it to involve a conflict with other employees as well as with the employer.

... Rather than relying on the arbitrator's interpretation of the vague language of the agreement drafted a long time ago, it is normally more sensible for the parties to settle that type of current problem by face-to-face discussions in the grievance procedure, with the participation of those individuals who are familiar with the objectives of the agreement and the needs of the operation and are thus best able to improvise a satisfactory solution. Again, if the employees are to have the benefit of this process and of the willing participation of the employer in it, the law must allow the parties to make the settlement binding, rather than allowing a dissenting employee to finesse it by pressing his grievance to arbitration.

... There is an ample body of experience, both in the American cases and also under the Ontario Labour Relations Act, defining the kinds of situations in which it is proper and those in which it is wrong for the union to deny a grievor access to the arbitration process. The judgment in particular cases depends on the cumulative effect of several relevant features: how critical is the subject matter of the grievance to the interest of the employee concerned? How much validity does his claim appear to have, either under the language of the agreement or the available evidence of what has occurred, and how carefully has the union investigated these? What has been the previous practice respecting this type of case and what expectations does the employee reasonably have from the treatment of earlier grievances? What contrary interests of other employees or of the bargaining unit as a whole have led the union to take a position against the grievor and how much weight should be attached to them?

... This is almost a textbook example of a situation in which it was perfectly proper for the union to drop an individual grievance.

Recall first that Anderson was objecting to the workings of the practice adopted by the Union and the Employer for short-term intermittent recalls during a lengthy layoff.

. . . It is a significant benefit to the bargaining unit, one which is wholly compatible with the principle of seniority, to allow the employee the option of returning to work for [a short] period or asking his supervisor to try someone else. . . .

Nasato had an even more dramatic interest in conflict with Anderson's position. Anderson claimed that he should have been retained at work on November 22nd and until December 5th in preference to Nasato. This was not on the basis that Anderson was entitled to longer seniority himself. Rather, it was because Nasato had allegedly lost all his seniority on the theory that his employment should have been treated as terminated in August. Instead of seniority dating back to 1957, Nasato's current seniority standing would begin running on November 15, 1974. Accordingly, while by the time his grievance was underway, Anderson was back at work and seeking only compensation for lost wages, his case was based on an interpretation of the agreement which would permit — indeed, would require — Marpole to treat Nasato as a brand new employee, on probation, and the junior person on the tradesmen's seniority list. Again unquestionably, the impact of an unfavourable decision about the case would fall much more heavily on Nasato than on Anderson. Because of its implications for the position of both Nasato as an individual and the employees in the unit as a whole, we can understand why the IWA would be reluctant to have Anderson succeed on his grievance.

But was the IWA deliberately sacrificing Anderson's firmly-established rights under the collective agreement? [The board examined the seniority provisions of the collective agreement and held that they were not wholly clear on whether an employee had to return to work immediately when recalled or could postpone his or her return if the employer so allowed.]

. . . We have sketched the opposing arguments in this case but we do not believe we should go further and adopt one of them as the correct reading of the agreement. Under Article XXX, there is a special procedure for interpretation of this agreement, one which should not be pre-empted by this Board unless this is necessary for the performance of our statutory obligations.

. . . One must not lightly assume that there is a 'right' interpretation to be divined in the collective agreement of this issue. Rather, the parties to this agreement have been faced with the industrial relations problem of minimizing the impact of a layoff on the employees and they dealt with it in a spirit of co-operation, using the clauses of the contract as guideposts. While the balance struck by the parties in this case over-rode the immediate claim of Anderson, it did so for the quite legitimate reason of advancing the more pressing needs of the other employees. Under the language of this agreement, read in the history of its application, one could not argue that Anderson had any contrary rights clearly conferred by the collective agreement nor that he had any firm expectation that he would be treated as more senior than Nasato. The 'method of self-government' of these parties operated in this case 'within the zone of fairness and rationality' and should not be reversed by 'the edicts of any outside tribunal'. . . .

✻ ✻ ✻

Labour Boards have been on guard against collusion between the complaining employ-ee and the respondent union. In *Crewdson and Stebeleski v. International Brotherhood of Electrical Workers, Local 1541* (1992), 18 Can. L.R.B.R. (2d) 107 at 109 (C.L.R.B.), Vice-Chair Jamieson commented as follows:

> Let us say immediately that it is not the practice of this Board to accept 'guilty pleas' in duty of fair representation complaints. If this were so, it would be an easy matter for trade unions to counsel members to file complaints when access to arbitration has lapsed for one reason or another. The union could then plead guilty and have the Board order the matter to arbitration. For example, many complaints to the Board rest on allegations that the bargaining agent has missed a crucial time limit in a collective agreement. If the Board were to accept guilty pleas in these situations, it would be a convenient way for trade unions to circumvent these time limits in the collective agreement. In fact, there have been instances in the past where trade unions have literally pled guilty in these sit-uations and the Board has found that there was no violation of the Code.

* * *

It is clear from the decision of the Supreme Court of Canada in *Parry Sound (District) Social Services Administration Board v. Ontario Public Service Employees Union, Local 324* 2003 SCC 42, set out above in Chapter 9 (section 9:610), that grievance arbitrators have the jurisdiction to hear and decide employee grievances that allege violation of statutes dealing with the employment relationship, including human rights statutes. When a union processes a grievance that involves a fundamental statutory right, such as the protection against discrimination on the ground of disability, does the DFR impose a higher standard of conduct on the union than when it processes other types of griev-ance? The answer, so far, is probably yes. See Bernard Adell, "The Union's Duty of Fair Representation in Discrimination Cases: The New Obligation to Be Proactive," [2001–2002] I Lab. Arb. Y.B. 263.

The following decision, by the Saskatchewan Labour Relations Board, is the first one that dealt explicitly with this question. The requirement on the part of the employer and the union to accommodate employees with disabilities is considered in more detail in Chapter 13 (section 13:300).

K.H. v. CEP, Local 1-S (Re), (1997), 98 C.L.L.C. ¶220-020 (Sask. L.R.B.) at paras. 79–116

[K.H. was dismissed from his job after he refused to submit to an independent medical examination demanded by the employer as a result of interpersonal problems he had been having with co-workers. His own physician and the employer's physician agreed that he suffered from depression, but they disagreed on how best to treat that illness. The union investigated a series of grievances filed by K.H., including the dismissal griev-ance, but decided in each case not to take the grievance to arbitration, partly because of its assessment that K.H. should have agreed to an independent medical examination. Section 25.1 of the Saskatchewan Trade Union Act prohibited the union from acting in a way that was "arbitrary, discriminatory or in bad faith" in representing a member of the bargaining unit. K.H. complained that the union had treated him in a discriminatory way, in breach of that provision.]

BILSON, Chair; CAUDLE and BELL, Members: . . . The significant question in relation to this application is whether the Union behaved towards K.H. in a way which was discriminatory, and it is necessary to consider the implications of this term.

. . .

A significant amount of the discussion of discrimination in the workplace has been devoted to a consideration of whether particular workplace rules or policies have a disadvantageous impact on persons or groups who can be identified in terms of one of the categories protected from discrimination under human rights legislation. The scrutiny of workplace practices or policies to identify instances of discrimination has, inevitably, implicated collective agreements, which are one of the sources of guidelines or rules which govern the expectations and requirements for employees.

. . .

In *Central Okanagan School District v. Renaud* . . . , the Supreme Court of Canada made it clear that, in a unionized workplace, the trade union representing employees is bound by the duty to accommodate. In that case, which dealt with the relationship between provisions in a collective agreement concerning scheduling of work, and the situation of an employee whose religious convictions prevented her from working on Friday nights, the Court held that a trade union could become a party to discrimination, either by collaborating in the institution of a rule or policy having an adverse impact of a discriminatory nature, or by taking a position which would constitute a barrier to efforts by the employer to ameliorate a discriminatory practice.

. . .

In many of the cases such as *Renaud, supra,* which have dealt with the duty to accommodate, the focus has been on particular rules or policies followed by an employer, whether in accordance with a collective agreement or otherwise, and on the question of whether, to the extent these rules or policies constitute a term of employment, they represent a "bona fide occupational requirement or qualification" (BFORQ). . . .

Under the Saskatchewan *Human Rights Code,* R.S.S. 1978, c. S-24.1, an employer is entitled to impose legitimate occupational requirements. Section 16(7) of the Code reads as follows:

> The provisions of this section relating to any discrimination, limitation, specification or preference for a position or employment based on sex, disability or age do not apply where sex, ability or age is a reasonable occupational qualification and requirement for the position or employment.

In Saskatchewan, then, an employer is clearly entitled to characterize a rule or policy as a BFORQ as a defence to an allegation of discrimination, and cases such as *Renaud, supra,* make it clear that a trade union may be considered a party to such discrimination in appropriate cases.

Section 18 of the *Code,* however, imposes on trade unions a separate obligation not to discriminate against members:

No trade union shall exclude any person from full membership or expel, suspend or otherwise discriminate against any of its members, or discriminate against any person in regard to employment by any employer, because of the race, creed, religion, colour, sex, sexual orientation, family status, marital status, disability, age, nationality, ancestry or place of origin of that person or member or the receipt of public assistance by that person or member.

Though this provision is part of a statutory scheme which contemplates the adjudication of complaints by boards of inquiry under the auspices of the Saskatchewan Human Rights Commission, it is our view that the notion of discrimination connected with the duty of fair representation must comprehend discrimination in the sense intended in the *Code*.

If this is the case, then the duty to accommodate may be relevant in determining whether there is an expectation that a trade union will make adjustments in procedures or policies normally followed in order to prevent the discriminatory impact which their typical operation would have on members of classes enumerated in the Code. The question in this connection is not whether there is something the Union could or should have done to prevent discriminatory action on the part of the Employer — though this might be a relevant question in a different context — but whether the Union is required to adopt a differential approach to some employees in order to avoid discriminating against them.

It has been pointed out that implicating trade unions in the duty to accommodate as it may apply in the workplace may place an unfair burden on them.

. . .

Certainly, we accept that one must be cautious about attributing to a trade union more authority than they possess to alter the terms and conditions which have a discriminatory impact of the kind prohibited in human rights legislation.

In any case, . . . the question of whether a trade union has been a participant in the creation of a discriminatory rule, or has failed to get out of the way of efforts to remove the discriminatory circumstances — which was the subject of discussion in *Renaud, supra* — is not the essential issue in this case.

In this case the issue is a less contingent one, and arises from the direct obligation of a trade union to deal with members in a non-discriminatory way. This issue is whether the policies and practices followed by the Union in dealing with the circumstances of K.H. were discriminatory, and whether their discriminatory effect could have been lessened by taking reasonable measures.

There were differences of opinion about many things in this case, but there was never a disagreement over the basic fact that K.H. was suffering from a mental disorder at the time he requested time off from work. . . .

As we have seen, the Union responded to the difficulties in which K.H. found himself by filing a series of grievances on his behalf. The process followed by the Union in handling these grievances was characterized by a high degree of structure, extensive discussion by Union officers and representatives at different levels, careful record-keeping, and the opportunity for appeal of unfavourable decisions to a meeting of Union members. [The union officers involved] were experienced and well-trained representatives of their members, who approached their tasks in a conscientious manner, and in accordance with well-established Union policies. In their discussions of the grievances, these officers and other members of the local executive took into account a range of factors, and investigated the facts before coming to a decision.

Among the factors which they considered, and which they raised when the grievances were being discussed with representatives of the Employer, were the medical problems which were faced by K.H. In our view, however, they failed to make allowance for the fact that K.H. was a disabled person. In this respect, though the process they followed might have been more than sufficient to satisfy their duty to represent employees fairly, it was inadequate to address the particular situation of K.H., and had a differential impact on him which must be considered to constitute discrimination.

. . .

In this case, . . . the Union seems to have bought into the notion of the third party medical examination required by the Employer without adequate attention to the possible legitimacy of the reservations expressed by K.H. and by Dr. Katz [K.H.'s physician], and without articulating the rationale for acceding to this requirement.

The Union also seems to have accepted that the paradigm of "progressive discipline" which provided the framework for the actions taken against K.H. constituted an acceptable way of addressing his conduct. They did not raise the question of whether this whole framework was irrelevant to someone with a mental disability of the kind suffered by K.H.

. . .

In formulating and defining the nature of the obligations imposed by the duty of fair representation, labour relations boards have acknowledged that trade unions have limited resources, that they are largely dependent on the services of volunteers, and that they are entitled to place the rights or claims of individual employees in the balance with the overall good of the bargaining unit. We do not think it is unreasonable, however, to expect trade unions, like other organizations and institutions, to come to terms with the concepts of discrimination which have come to the fore in Canadian society as a result of the passage of human rights legislation, as they carry out their responsibilities to the employees who rely on them.

. . .

The Union may have handled the grievances diligently from the point of view of the normal operation of the grievance procedure. An ordinary employee might have little to complain of. Nonetheless, by limiting the scope of the grievance process to the normal sequence of investigation and discussion, by accepting the framework of progressive discipline, by, in effect, allowing the medical opinion of Dr. Barootes [the employer's physician] to govern what happened to K.H., the Union used the grievance procedure in a way which had a discriminatory effect on K.H. because of his mental disability.

As a number of witnesses called on behalf of the Union observed, a trade union is not required to pursue all grievances to arbitration. They may take into account the best use of their resources, and the results of their investigation of the facts. Neither are they required, however, to withdraw all grievances at the earliest opportunity, and it would not, in our view, impose an unreasonable burden on the Union to have expected them to keep the grievances in existence, and to insist on a consideration of the case of K.H. as a whole.

We would not claim that it is an easy task for trade unions to find ways of ensuring that policies and practices they have devised — which may serve fairly and adequately the legitimate expectations of ordinary employees — are applied with sufficient flexibility that these policies will not have a discriminatory effect on individuals or groups within a bargaining unit. It is likely that none of these challenges are more difficult than those related to mental disabilities. K.H. himself acknowledged that his disability made it difficult for him to respond rationally, consistently, or co-operatively in all of his dealings with the Union or other employees. His mental condition made it difficult for him to assess his own situation, to articulate his concerns, or to deal effectively with the representatives of the Union who were responsible for overseeing his grievances. It was, in our view, particularly difficult for him to gain any benefit from the appeal mechanism available to him.

One must have some sympathy for the representatives of the Union who were responsible for dealing with the grievances filed on behalf of K.H. They approached their tasks in good faith, and reasonably conscientiously, and were no doubt frustrated by the difficulties and delays which occurred. Nonetheless, it is our view that overall the Union failed to take sufficient account of the disability experienced by K.H., and that they therefore discriminated against him in handling his grievances.

. . .

Bernard Adell, "Collective Agreements and Individual Rights: A Note on the Duty of Fair Representation" (1986) 11 Queen's L.J. 251 at 254–58

. . . it will be impossible to make the duty of fair representation into a basket strong enough to hold all of the individual rights eggs. The low standards which the duty imposes upon unions are only one problem. Long, cumbersome proceedings are another. The Ontario Labour Relations Board has developed a two-stage procedure for fair representation complaints involving grievance processing. In the first stage, the board decides whether the union breached its duty of fair representation in the way it handled the grievance. At that stage, the merits of the grievance are supposed to be gone into only as far as is necessary to enable the board to assess the legality of the union's conduct — but that is often quite far. If the board finds that the union was in breach of its duty, the board remits the grievance to the second stage: adjudication on the merits by an arbitration tribunal. Although this procedure shows impeccable respect for the jurisdictional boundary between the board and the arbitral process, it can require a great deal of repetition and it does nothing to speed the employee's way to a remedy.

The less sophisticated the employee, and the less well-connected he is with such guardian angels as rival unions, the more intimidating the substantive and procedural barriers will be to him. Most important of all, duty of fair representation proceedings have the inherent flaw of pitting employee against union, in what is too often a bitter internecine fight, before even getting to the main event: the employee's claim against the employer. Is it necessary to make a prolonged, three-sided donnybrook out of a controversy which might well yield quickly to a one-step, bipartite hearing on the merits between employee and employer?

That leads straight into the third possible channel of recourse — a right in the individual employee to carry his own grievance to arbitration if the union refuses or neglects to do so. Alfred Blumrosen argued in 1959 that employees should have control over what he called 'critical job interest' grievances, which he defined as those involving discharge or 'major disciplinary action which will substantially destroy the employment relationship,' those involving a claim for payment for work already done, and those involving job seniority. Paul Weiler has suggested a modified version of that approach, confined to discharge cases. He would not extend it to seniority cases, not even job seniority cases, because, as he puts it, seniority grievances often involve 'a legitimate conflict of interest between two members of the bargaining unit.' Such conflicts of interest, Professor Weiler clearly feels, are better suited to resolution by the union than by an arbitrator.

There are good reasons, which seem to me to get better as time passes, for going farther and giving any grievor covered by a collective agreement the right to carry any grievance to arbitration himself if the bargaining agent will not. The fairly brief history of the duty of fair representation has shown how awkward it is for an outside tribunal — even as sophisticated a tribunal as a labour relations board — to police a union's internal deliberations. Although I have seen no empirical evidence on this point, it seems probable that requiring unions to build up files of the sort which will protect them from unfair representation complaints imposes a drain on their resources out of all proportion to any gains which may accrue to individual employees.

Additionally, I would argue that whenever the law gives a substantive right to someone, as it does to an individual employee to enjoy the fruits of collective bargaining as contained in a collective agreement, it ought (in the absence of compelling reasons to the contrary) to provide a procedural means of enforcing that substantive right. That argument gains strength, in the context of grievance handling, from the central role which collective agreement rights play in the lives of individual employees. It is not only job *retention* grievances that may be of critical importance to particular employees, but also what can be called job *tolerability* grievances — those over such matters as shift work, overtime scheduling and major working conditions, especially where health or safety is involved. Grievances affecting job *level* — for example, job posting and employee selection grievances — can also be critical to ambitious employees. If a good case can be made for allowing individuals to carry their job retention grievances to arbitration, is the case really much weaker for these other kinds of grievances?

Giving employees the right to take their own grievances to arbitration would undoubtedly pose some dangers. Whether the arbitrating was done in the usual way or by a special panel of arbitrators or a special tribunal, there would be a risk that the entire arbitration system might be overburdened by a large influx of new cases. However, I do not think that is likely to happen. Aggrieved individuals who cannot persuade their unions to act for them may at times be persistent and cantankerous, but they are not very numerous, nor do they tend to be very rich or powerful. They usually lack substantial resources unless they are supported by a rival union, whose primary objective may well be to discredit the incumbent bargaining agent. To grievors who are out to get the bargaining agent, a straightforward arbitration proceeding against the employer is likely to be less appealing than the three-party, two-stage circus provided by a duty of fair representation proceeding, where the union is cast as the principal defendant right from the outset. As for the other type of individual grievor — the type who is truly acting on his own — it should not take long to become widely known that grievances rejected by one's own union had little chance of succeeding at arbitration.

A high likelihood of losing might not in itself deter many grievors with strongly felt but wholly ill-founded grievances. However, a requirement that a losing grievor had to pay his own costs, perhaps on a scale appropriate to his means, should be quite an effective deterrent against frivolous use of the arbitration procedure. It would probably not be necessary to take the further step of requiring an unsuccessful grievor to pay the employer's costs as well as his own, and that step might place such a heavy financial disincentive on grievors of modest means as to make illusory the new right which I am arguing for. However, it could be kept in reserve in case a further disincentive turned out to be needed.

As for the employer, it is true that he is now largely free, in the short run at least, from any need to go behind the union's assurance that it will not pursue a grievance. In contrast, under the reform I am proposing, he would have to treat any grievance settlement worked out with the union as tentative until the individual grievor had exhausted or abandoned his right to proceed on his own. That would be an inconvenience to the employer. However, because I believe individuals would make only limited use of such a right, I do not expect it would be a very severe inconvenience.

It might be argued that the availability of arbitration over the objections of the bargaining agent would undermine the latter's authority and would make employees unappreciative of union representation. This strikes me as an argument of sound and fury, without much substance. No union which does a reasonably conscientious and competent job of screening grievances should have much fear that its rejects would be warmly received by arbitrators.

Citing the important 1978 *Canada Labour Code* amendments allowing unorganized employees with twelve months' service to have discharge grievances arbitrated, Paul Weiler suggests that it would be incongruous to continue to allow unions to deny that right to organized employees. This is a valid point, and one which is likely to become relevant to more than discharge grievances as the statutory rights of unorganized employees are increased. It is yet another reason for giving organized employees a broad right to invoke grievance arbitration themselves when their unions fail or refuse to do it for them.

Finally, I would like to make some mention of experience outside our borders. Most Western European countries have a standing tribunal, often called a labour court, the jurisdiction of which varies from country to country but which generally includes the adjudication of individual employee complaints against employers about the violation of employment rights. Access to those tribunals is not limited to unions or to individuals whose cases are supported by unions. In Sweden, for example, as Clyde Summers wrote some years ago, 'the individual has rights under the collective agreement which his organization can neither bar nor barter away.' A Swedish employee may take his claim to the courts if the union refuses to do so, even if the union has purported to settle the matter against his wishes. According to Professor Summers, the fears of those who opposed giving such a right to the individual have not materialized. Only a very small percentage of the Labour Court's cases have been brought by individuals acting on their own. In addition, 'the fears that the parties would be deprived of needed flexibility in administering the collective agreement have not been realized,' because the Swedish Labour Court, in interpreting collective agreements, has been sensitive to the interests of the collective parties. It is hard to imagine that Canadian arbitrators, who depend on the collective parties for most of their business, would be any more inclined to neglect such interests.

It is true that the concept of exclusivity of bargaining rights in Canadian collective labour law, together with the strong focus of Canadian union activity at the workplace level and the virtually complete withdrawal from individual employees of the right to negotiate terms of employment superior to those in the collective agreement, may give exclusive union control over grievance processing an appearance of rationality in our country which it could not have in Europe. Furthermore, the legitimacy of unions is more widely accepted by employers in most Western European countries than in Canada, with the result that European unions may have less reason to fear that an individual right to press grievances will be misused as a stick with which to beat the union. Still, despite such important differences as these, I think Western European experience supports the view that we exaggerate the risks of giving individual employees the right to take their own grievance to arbitration.
[Reprinted by permission.]

☆ ☆ ☆

The high numbers and low success rate of duty of fair representation complaints have prompted concerns about frivolous complaints wasting the time and resources of labour boards and unions alike. In response to such concerns, some jurisdictions have adopted filter mechanisms to enable boards to dispose of such complaints without an oral hearing. See the British Columbia *Labour Code*, section 13; the Canada *Labour Code*, section 98; and the Ontario *Labour Relations Act*, 1995, section 99(3).

Thomas Knight, "Recent Developments in the Duty of Fair Representation: Curtailing Abuse in British Columbia" [1996–97] Lab. Arb. Y.B. 151 at 152–58

Unquestionably, the duty of fair representation is a necessary safeguard of individual rights within the framework of the collective agreement, given the union's right of exclusive representation. Nonetheless, empirical research in the 1980s on the actual experience in British Columbia revealed that the overwhelming majority of fair representation complaints are ultimately rejected and that individuals and factions within unions make 'tactical' use of the duty to advance their personal or political agendas at the expense of the union and its elected officers. Given the political sensitivity of individual rights, tactical leverage can be derived from threatening to file a fair representation complaint or actually proceeding with one, regardless of the substantive merits of the complaint.

Though this perspective on the duty of fair representation aroused controversy, subsequent survey research involving a large sample of union officers further confirmed the tactical use of the duty of fair representation in the grievance process itself in the form of threats to file complaints against union officers should the union compromise or drop a grievance. The net effect of these unintended consequences of the duty of fair representation, it was found, was that significant amounts of time, energy and money were being spent prosecuting grievances, sometimes all the way to arbitration, that the union would otherwise settle or drop. This article reports on a response to these problems in the 1993 B.C. *Labour Relations Code* and preliminary experience under the new *Code* over the first 2 years it has been in effect.

THE DUTY OF FAIR REPRESENTATION UNDER B.C. LABOUR LAW

Table 1 summarizes fair representation complaint traffic under the original *Labour Code* (1975–1987), the *Industrial Relations Act* (1988–1992) and the present *Labour Relations Code*. The table documents the spectacular growth in the annual number of fair representation complaints filed, along with a relatively steady (until 1993) proportion of complaints settled prior to a formal hearing and the large proportion of complaints dismissed by the Labour Relations Board, frequently after a formal proceeding. The table also reveals the consistently small proportion of complaints that result in formal Board orders granting the complaint and providing a remedy. Not reported in the table are the number of complaints not proceeded with by complainants, which increased more than tenfold, from 9 in 1993 to 120 in 1994.

Table 1   Duty of Fair Representation Complaints in B.C., 1975–94*

Year	Total Handled		Settled		Dismissed		Granted	
------	% change	#	#	%	#	%	#	%
1975	—	17	3	18	14	82	—	0
1976	+53	26	15	58	11	42	—	0
1977	+112	55	24	44	30	54	1	2
1978	−7	51	25	49	23	45	3	6
1979	+61	82	47	57	33	40	2	3
1980	+5	86	45	52	39	45	2	3
1981	−2	84	53	63	28	33	3	4
1982	+7	90	46	51	43	48	1	1
1983	+38	124	57	46	61	49	6	5
1984	+1	125	70	56	52	42	3	2
1985	+13	141	78	56	52	42	3	2
1986	−39	86	34	40	50	58	2	2
1987	−6	81	32	40	43	53	6	7
1988	+30	105	34	32	64	61	7	7
1989	−25	9	33	42	43	54	3	4
1990	+19	94	26	28	67	71	1	1
1991	+9	102	37	36	59	58	6	6
1992	+27	130	43	33	81	62	6	5
1993	−12	114	32	28	69	61	4	4
1994	+64	187	17	9	49	26	1	1

*Source: *Annual Reports*, Labour Relations Board and Industrial Relations Council of B.C.

In February 1992, the new B.C. Minister of Labour appointed a Committee of Special Advisors with a broad mandate to recommend an overall industrial relations strategy for the Province. A Sub-Committee of Special Advisors, consisting of John Baigent, Vince Ready and Tom Roper, was appointed to 'review the *Industrial Relations Act* and bring forward recommendations for change having regard for the need to create fair laws which will promote harmony and a climate conducive to the encouragement of investment in British Columbia.' The Sub-Committee of Special Advisors commented as follows on the duty of fair representation and the statutory provisions they recommended:

> . . . Our concern is that unions, employers and the complainant are often forced to expend considerable amounts of time and financial resources in circumstances where the complaint may not be justified. The ability to avoid unnecessary costs is a desirable objective in itself. Unless the tribunal can quickly adjudicate duty of fair representation complaints, the potential of protracted fair representation proceedings can adversely affect the resolution of disputes between a trade union and an employer. It is not uncommon for a trade union today to proceed with a grievance arbitration, where it might otherwise not have done so, to avoid the cost of defending a fair representation challenge, even though that challenge may be unmeritorious. Simply stated, it may be less expensive and more expeditious for a trade union to simply run a case through arbitration rather than defend an unmeritorious fair representation complaint. Accordingly, the process by which duty of fair representation complaints are adjudicated can have a very real negative impact on the labour relations between an employer and a trade union and on the settlement of grievances. Our recommendation would be to provide a process by which the Board could effectively adjudicate fair representation complaints without requiring submissions or holding hearings, in every case.

Accordingly . . . section 13 of the *Labour Relations Code* provides a screening procedure for fair representation complaints in the form of an explicit *prima facie* test that would-be complainants must satisfy before the Labour Relations Board will proceed with a fair representation complaint. Section 13(1) provides, in full:

> If a written complaint is made to the board that a trade union, council of trade unions or employers' organization has contravened section 12, the following procedure must be followed:
> (a) a panel of the board shall determine whether or not it considers that the complaint discloses a *prima facie* case that the contravention has occurred;
> (b) if the panel considers that the complaint discloses a prima facie case, it shall
>   (i) serve a notice of the complaint on the trade union, council of trade unions or employers' organization against which the complaint is made and invite a reply to the complaint from the trade union, council of trade unions or employers' organization, and
>   (ii) dismiss the complaint or refer it to the board for a hearing.

The Sub-Committee of Special Advisors recommended increasing the onus on individual complainants to show that the facts warrant proceeding with a complaint and requiring formal submissions from the union and, as necessary, the employer. In effect, the Sub-Committee acknowledged that many fair representation complaints against unions are either frivolous or mischievous and that this fact adds unnecessarily to the cost and delay associated with the grievance and arbitration processes, as well as with actual fair representation complaints brought to the Labour Relations Board. In essence, the new fair representation provisions in section 13 were intended to create a 'filter' against unmeritorious complaints that would help promote a faster and cheaper resolution of such disputes, in turn establishing a more appropriate balance between individual and collective rights and interests.

CASE LAW ON THE FAIR REPRESENTATION *PRIMA FACIE* TEST

. . . Though the case law is not extensive, the Labour Relations Board has clearly sought to reinforce a *prima facie* standard that demands concrete evidence from complainants before the door will be opened to their complaints and formal submissions required. Board panels have sent clear signals to complainants that they must bring forward more than their own opinions and insinuations of union misconduct, on the one hand, and an assurance to elected union officers that the exercise of conscientious judgment will satisfy the duty of fair representation, on the other. It remains to be seen how these signals will affect the actual incidence of complaints and the grievance and arbitration process.

THE IMPACT OF *LABOUR RELATIONS CODE* SECTION 13

Referring again to Table 1, several preliminary observations as to the potential effect of section 13 may be made. The proportion of complaints dismissed has actually decreased over the 2 years since the *Labour Relations Code* has been in force for which complete statistics are available. Not reported in the table is the fact that roughly half of the complaints dismissed in 1993 and 1994 were found to lack a *prima facie* basis. In 1994 the proportion dismissed fell by almost half despite a dramatically increased volume of fair representation complaints — a trend which appears to be holding in 1995. However, as noted previously, a dramatic increase in the number of complaints abandoned by complainants occurred, from 9 in 1993 to 120 in 1994.

Hence, while the Board may be proceeding cautiously in applying the section 13 'filter' to fair representation complaints, the Board's message to would-be complainants may be reflected in the jump in complaints not proceeded with. Many may simply have had their bluffs called. At the same time, the substantial increase in complaints filed may reflect a stiffening of unions' resolve not to arbitrate grievances they judge to be unmeritorious, based partly on the assurance that the Board will scrutinize fair representation complaints more stringently than in the past and that it is no longer cheaper (financially or politically) to arbitrate than to defend against a fair representation complaint at the Labour Relations Board. . . .

[Reprinted by permission of Lancaster House Publishing.]

Knight's observations on the impact of section 13 are borne out by the following more recent figures provided by the British Columbia Labour Relations Board. The figures show a significant increase in the number of duty of fair representation complaints in 1998 and 1999, but they also demonstrate that many are being filtered by the *prima facie* test and that the number of complaints not proceeded with remains very high.

Duty of Fair Representation Complaints in B.C. 1998–99

Year	Filed	Disposed Of	Not Proceeded With	Settled	Dismissed*	Granted
1998	243	263	140	16	103 (46)	4
1999	230	228	96	21	106 (46)	5

* Number in brackets denotes number of cases in which no *prima facie* case was found

10:340 The Duty of Fair Referral

The right to exclude applicants from membership in a union is of much greater importance in industries — principally construction and longshoring — where union hiring halls exist. In those industries, employers are highly fragmented, and a job with a particular employer usually does not last long enough for an employee to acquire substantial seniority rights. Rather than hiring their own employees, employers in the construction and longshoring industries commonly look to a union to provide the workers needed on a job-by-job or even a day-by-day basis. The union thus becomes, to a degree, employer as well as bargaining agent — a dual role that can provide an important element of job security to workers who would otherwise lack any such security. But this concentration of powers — inherently conflicting powers, perhaps — in the hands of the union exposes workers to abuses as serious as those perpetrated by the most autocratic employers in other industries. Unions that run hiring halls obviously have a strong interest in limiting admission to the union, in order to keep up the demand for the services of their existing members.

Nauss and Roberts v. Halifax Longshoremen's Association, Local 269 of the International Longshoremen's Association and Maritime Employers' Association, [1981] 1 Can. L.R.B.R. 188 at 204–11 (C.L.R.B.)

[Under a hiring hall provision in the collective agreement between the union and the employers' association, the union agreed to take responsibility for supplying enough workers each day to do the longshoring work available that day in the Port of Halifax. The employers' association agreed to employ only longshoremen assigned by the union.

Longshoremen Nauss and Roberts were not union members and were therefore treated unfavourably by the union with respect to work assignment through the hiring hall. Nauss had unsuccessfully applied for union membership. Roberts had unsuccessfully applied for the lesser status of cardholder. In this proceeding, Nauss and Roberts alleged that the union had discriminated against them in the application of its membership rules, contrary to section 185(f) of the *Canada Labour Code*, and that it had not made or posted rules for the operation of the hiring hall as required by section 161.1 of the *Code*. The Canada Labour Relations Board held that in addition to the union's failure to make and publicize such rules, the operation of the hiring hall had several other undesirable features. Among them were the preference given to relatives of union officers with respect to union membership and the arbitrary way in which memberships and work assignments were handed out. The board also commented on hiring halls in general.]

DORSEY, Vice-Chair: By the 1970s legislators were becoming concerned about the fair operation of hiring halls and their impact upon the rights of individuals although their undoubted worth has been constantly recognized. The concerns are amply captured in a recent American study.

> The union hiring hall has been one of the major developments in twentieth century labour relations. It has provided many industries with a means for efficiently matching unemployed workers with job vacancies and has replaced a system of haphazard, unjust, and corrupt employment practices. Yet it has also developed substantial problems of its own.
>
> A hiring hall is fraught with potential for abuse, and, indeed, that potential is all too frequently realized. The largely unreviewable discretion of union business agents and inadequate protection for workers can combine to make hiring halls a mixture of whim, nepotism, prejudice, and irrationality. Hiring halls satisfy important and legitimate needs in the 'casual' employment industries, where jobs are usually short term and employers and employees have little opportunity to sustain a meaningful working relationship. The union halls routinely provide qualified workers and save the employers from conducting endless numbers of personnel searches. Simultaneously, the halls offer workers a convenient source for jobs; unemployed workers need only report to the appropriate hiring hall officials and then wait for referrals. The lengths of the waits would ideally be determined by methods that are rational and fair for all employees.
>
> Unfortunately, the referral systems are not always rational and fair. Too often, there is no 'system' at all and unions typically vest undue discretion in the hiring hall officials. Even in good economic times, such men can have undue power over individuals' opportunities to earn a living. The potential for abuse grows particularly acute, however, when jobs are scarce, as they are now in many sectors of the construction and maritime industries. (Robert M. Bastress, 'Application of A Constitutionally-Based Duty Of Fair Representation To Union Hiring Halls' . . .).

When union security clauses or other arrangements make a union operated employment referral system the only access to employment, then the union effectively hires employees for the employer. When union hiring or dispatch to work is dependent in part or entirely on union membership then it is an integral part of the system intended to be regulated by section 161.1. In that circumstance rules required under section 161.1 must necessarily include rules for access to union membership. The two cannot be separated. Nor can it be said the union may view itself and conduct its affairs as the voluntary association the law once viewed it as. It is a legal entity . . . and it has become a quasi-public or public institution. The dimensions of its responsibilities and the scrutiny of its affairs is no longer confined to employees in a fixed bargaining unit who are hired and acquire employee status by employer decision. It has a responsibility to the person who is a potential employee and looks to the union's system of referral and membership rules as a source of employment. In keeping with this context the Board has stated:

> Matters affecting employees, which under the usual collective bargaining regime are contained in collective agreements and subject to the grievance and arbitral procedures, are found in the union's referral rules, the application of which, in the absence of section 161.1, would be totally within the union's unsupervised control. The Board views its role under section 161.1 as being to provide a means by which a person subject to the union's referral rules can have a third party adjudication of the application of the rules in the same fashion as the unilateral decisions of an employer can be subject to the scrutiny of arbitrators under a collective agreement. . . .

> . . . This union has been run and has behaved more as a privileged exclusive club than as a modern trade union. . . .

> We find the union has contravened section 161.1 in that it has not established rules [on the operation of the hiring hall] and posted them as required. . . .

> [The union is ordered to] prepare a set of rules for employment referral, including rules for admission to union membership and issuance of cards. . . .

> [The board directed the union to admit Nauss and Roberts to membership and cardholder status, respectively, in order to] bring home to the union and those using its employment referral system the seriousness of its task and the shoddy manner in which it has been conducting its affairs. . . .

* * *

Review proceedings challenging the board's jurisdiction to order the union to admit the complainants to membership went all the way to the Supreme Court of Canada, *sub. nom. Canada Labour Relations Board and Nauss et al. v. Halifax Longshoremen's Association, Local 269*, [1983] 1 S.C.R. 245. Laskin C.J.C., for the Court, held that in the extraordinary circumstances of this case, the Court should not interfere with a remedy 'bottomed squarely on the involvement of the complainants in an allegation of breach which was firmly established and which required redress and protection to them as individuals in addition to the redress provided by the board to other non-union employees.'

In *Lockhart and Wilson v. Local 1764, International Longshoremen's Association*, [1981] 1 Can. L.R.B.R. 213 at 225–26, the Canada Labour Relations Board reached the important conclusion that the duty of fair referral under section 161.1 of the *Code* applied not only to hiring halls but "to all forms of referral, including the simple closed-shop situation." The Board said:

> If a union may in any manner effect a referral of a person to employment, pursuant to a collective agreement, the section is applicable. If union membership is part of the assignment, designation, dispatching, scheduling, selection, etc. of a person then there must be rules including rules with respect to acquisition, retention and loss of union membership.

10:400 UNION SECURITY CLAUSES

Under the principles of majoritarianism and exclusivity, representation of an employee by a union does not necessarily require that the employee be a member of the union. The precise relationship between representation and membership generally depends on what sort of union security provision is included in the collective agreement, and that is normally a matter for negotiation between union and employer. Although the possible varieties of union security provisions are almost endless, they fall into five broad types:

i) The closed shop

A closed shop provision requires that one must be a union member before being hired. All Canadian jurisdictions permit closed shop provisions in collective agreements but limit their effects in certain ways. Whether a collective agreement contains such a provision is a function of the union's bargaining strategy and bargaining strength. In some industries, such as construction, closed shop provisions are quite common.

In appearance, a closed shop provision gives the union a great deal of control over who is eligible to be an employee. In practice, union discretion is substantially fettered by statutory regulation, to be discussed below, section 10:500.

ii) The union shop

A union shop provision requires that employees must become union members in order to keep their jobs. The union shop differs from the closed shop in not using union membership as a screening device for determining who is eligible to be hired. Union shop provisions may be included in collective agreements if the parties so decide. As in the closed shop situations, the ultimate result of a union shop provision is a convergence between union membership and bargaining unit membership.

iii) Maintenance of membership

A "maintenance of membership" provision does not require an employee to join the union. However, it does specify that once the employee does join, he or she must remain a member or lose their job. The Saskatchewan *Trade Union Act* provides (in section 36) for a model union security provision which must be included in a collective agreement at the union's request. It embodies a maintenance of membership requirement for existing employees and a union shop requirement for new employees.

iv) The agency shop, or Rand Formula

What is known as the Rand Formula was first proposed by Justice Ivan Rand of the Supreme Court of Canada in his successful mediation of a major automobile strike in 1946. See *Ford Motor Co. of Canada v. U.A.W. - C.I.O.*, reprinted in 1 C.L.L.R. para. 1245, at 1356–63. A Rand Formula clause does not require employees to be members of the union, but does require that they pay to the union an amount equivalent to union dues. The idea is that because each employee in the bargaining unit gets the benefit of the collective agreement, he or she should have to pay a share of the union's costs, but should be allowed to register opposition to the union and its goals by declining to join. The

Rand Formula may in fact give some dissenters an incentive to join, so that they will have a voice in union decisions in return for their money. Subject to religious objector provisions, discussed below, several jurisdictions have made the Rand Formula a statutory minimum for private sector collective agreements, either automatically (Manitoba and Quebec) or at the union's request (Canada, Newfoundland, and Ontario).

The logic of the Rand Formula has been challenged, especially in respect of union expenditures directed toward purposes other than collective bargaining. A *Charter* challenge based on both freedom of expression and freedom of association failed in the Supreme Court of Canada in *Lavigne v. Ontario Public Service Employees Union*, below, section 10:600.

v) Voluntary checkoff

A voluntary checkoff provision is the weakest form of union security clause. It requires the employer to deduct union dues from an employee's wages, if the employee so authorizes, and remit those dues to the union. The voluntary checkoff is the statutory minimum in Alberta, British Columbia, New Brunswick, Nova Scotia, and Prince Edward Island.

10:410 The Religious Objector

The following excerpt has been adapted from Michael Lynk, "Union Democracy and the Law in Canada" (2000), 21 Journal of Labor Research 37, at 49–50.

> In a majoritarian system of industrial relations, the issue invariably arises about balancing the requirement for unions to be funded by the employees they represent and who enjoy the fruits of collective bargaining with, on the other hand, the freedom of an employee not to associate.
>
> One facet of the union security issue in Canada is the accommodation of employees who object to joining a trade union or paying union dues because of a genuine religious belief or conviction. Six jurisdictions — Alberta, British Columbia, Canada, Manitoba, Ontario, and Saskatchewan — have religious objector provisions in their labour legislation. While the statutory provisions vary in their detail from jurisdiction to jurisdiction, they generally allow employees with religious-based objections to unions to apply to the governing labour relations board for an order exempting them from union membership and the payment of union dues.
>
> If an employee making a religious exemption application is successful, the labour relations board will usually exempt that employee from any compulsory union membership, and order that her or his union dues be paid instead to a designated registered charity. In applying the religious exemption provision, many labour boards have developed a stringent test for applicants to meet. In *Barker and Teamsters, Local 938*, (1986), 86 C.L.L.C. 16,031, the Canada Labour Relations Board laid out a four-part test that requires an employee applying for the exemption to satisfy both subjective and objective criteria:
>
> i) the employee must object to all trade unions;
> ii) while the belief need not be based on a specific tenet of a religious faith, the employee's case is stronger if it is;

iii) the belief must be objectively related to a belief in the Divine; and

iv) the employee's religious belief must be sincere, and not be a rationalization of a personal antipathy to unions.

The following year, in *Wiebe and C.P.A.A.* (1987), 87 C.L.L.C. 16,032, the Canada Board raised the threshold even higher by adding a fifth component — whether the grant of an exemption is a "compelling necessity" for the employee — which the Board said was necessary to protect the integrity of the Rand Formula system.

Labour boards in Canada have strictly limited access by employees to the religious belief exemption. Personal beliefs by conscientious objectors to unions, even if deeply held, are insufficient to meet the criteria of *religious* conviction. Objections to unions that are based on mixed motivations, where political, social, or other non-religious reasons mingle with and predominate over religious ones, have also been regularly refused. Employees whose religious beliefs are opposed only to a specific union policy — such as support for abortion rights or the cause of the Palestinians — have been generally unsuccessful because their opposition was not to unions *per se*. As well, Roman Catholic employees who have asserted a religious objection to unions have frequently failed to acquire an exemption, primarily because their own church has endorsed unions and supported the right of workers to organize.

On the other hand, employees have been generally granted a religious exemption where they have shown that their personal history of conscientious objection to unions was closely tied to their religious faith, or where a religious faith specifically prohibited financial support of, or membership in, a union. In *Staub and CUPE, Local 411*, [1976] 1 Can. L.R.B.R. 261, the British Columbia Labour Relations Board granted an exemption to a member of the Seventh Day Adventist Church because he objected to all unions, he lacked any predominately political motive, and his church had an explicit position that opposed its members from belonging to, or participating in, unions.

[Reprinted by permission]

10:500 THE LEGAL PROTECTION OF UNION MEMBERSHIP RIGHTS

The duty of fair representation, discussed above, section 10:300, allows any employee in the bargaining unit (even one who is not a union member) to bring a complaint against the union if the employee feels that it has not fairly represented her or his interests *vis-à-vis* the employer.

A different set of legal issues arise when a union member has a complaint about an internal union matter — for example, about the conduct of a union election, about a fine levied for crossing a legal picket line, about expulsion from the union for a breach of the constitution, or about a decision to merge with another union. The governing legal instrument in such matters is generally the union constitution, and the initial forum for vindicating membership rights is the union's internal trial and appeal procedure. If the member is dissatisfied with the fairness of that procedure, she or he can launch a challenge in the courts, subject perhaps to the prerequisite of exhausting the union's internal procedures or showing that they are fundamentally biased. With several specific exceptions (discussed below), labour legislation across the country does not generally attempt to regulate internal union affairs.

Contract doctrine provides the legal basis for the courts to intervene in internal union matters. Unions are usually unincorporated associations, and have no distinct legal personality. Thus, the courts have had to develop a legal fiction in order to take jurisdiction over union-member disputes. When the following passage was written, this legal fiction held that the union constitution was not a contract between the member and the union (since an unincorporated union has no common law legal status), but that it provided the content for a network of individual contracts between the member and every other member. This is often called the "web of contracts" theory.

Michael Mac Neil, Michael Lynk, & Peter Engelmann, *Trade Union Law in Canada* (Aurora, Ont.: Canada Law Book, 2001 update), at 1-1 to 1-3; 9-6

The status of trade unions raises political, theoretical and practical legal questions going to the very heart of our system of organizing workplace relations. Our society attempts to solve many of its disputes by framing issues in terms of legal rights, and the ascription of legal status is a means of translating political, social and cultural values into a form by which we can measure the worth of social actors. With our social and political order largely committed to liberal values, it is not surprising that the dominant legal person is the individual human being. With our economic order committed to capitalism and market arrangements, it is not surprising that corporations are treated as if they were human beings, and are considered to be legal persons. However, the liberal capitalist premises on which much of our legal system is based, has had a much more difficult time in developing a coherent vision of how trade unions should be treated. The collectivist principles which are central to trade union action . . . have caused the judiciary and legislatures to struggle to fit trade unions into the conceptual framework which guides our understanding of legal personality. . . .

The legal status of trade unions arises in two contexts. One is the relation between the union and external actors such as employers, the state, or persons who claim to be affected by the actions of the trade union. The second is the relation between the union and its members. . . .

. . . [T]he fiction/concession theory . . . best explains judicial and legislative approaches to the legal status of trade unions in Canada. . . . The . . . theory describes the personality of the group as artificial, the product of authority given to the group either by its members or by the state. The group is seen as having only those powers which are conceded to it by the state. In the absence of state concession, the group is nothing more than a collection of individuals, and cannot effectively claim rights or be subject to obligations other than the rights and obligations of individual members. Those rights and obligations, in the absence of statutory provisions, arise from the contractual nexus among the members, and any claims they may have to property of the group. This theory helps to explain the view that dominated the common law, holding that unincorporated associations were not legal persons, but that legislative rules could grant legal personality within statutorily defined bounds. It also explains how the courts nevertheless allowed actions against union members as a group, through the device of representative or class actions, purporting to hold individuals collectively liable for the action of the group. . . .

Contract theory [upon which the fiction/concession theory is based in labour law] undoubtedly has an air of unreality about it. The theory assumes that each member of the trade union is making a contract with each of the other members, so that in even in a trade union of 1,500 persons, there would be over a million contracts. A member does not in fact think of himself or herself as forming such a vast number of contracts, but rather as entering into a relation with the union as an entity. It is contractual in the sense of being a consensual arrangement, but it is not one based on promises between members. The danger of thinking of the relationship as contractual is that it invites the courts to act as appellate bodies, interpreting the contracts and providing relief to a member for any violation, no matter how trivial, of the constitution and by-laws. The threat to union autonomy is obvious. . . .

[Reproduced with the permission of Canada Law Book Inc., 1-800-263-3269, www.canada-lawbook.ca.]

The fiction of a web of individual contracts of membership based on the terms of the union constitution was recently put to rest by the Supreme Court of Canada in *Berry v. Pulley*, excerpted below. As background to this case, look again at *International Brotherhood of Teamsters v. Therien*, [1960] S.C.R. 265, excerpted above in Chapter 8 (section 8:314).

Berry v. Pulley, [2002] 2 S.C.R. 493, 2002 SCC 40

[This case involved a dispute between the pilots of Air Ontario and those of Air Canada. The two groups belonged to the same union — the Canadian Air Line Pilots Association (CALPA) — which, like most unions, was an unincorporated association. Their respective employers were engaged in merger talks. The union constitution provided that in the event of such a merger, the two groups of pilots were to negotiate an integrated seniority list. In those internal union negotiations, the Air Canada pilots insisted that the Air Ontario pilots should be "endtailed" on the new seniority list, meaning that even the most senior Air Ontario pilots would have less seniority than the most junior Air Canada pilots. In contrast, the Air Ontario pilots insisted that the two seniority lists be fully "dovetailed," so that the service they had accumulated with Air Ontario would be fully recognized after the merger.

Michel Picher, the arbitrator appointed by the union to settle the dispute, released a ruling in 1995 that fell between the positions of the two unions. He directed that 15 per cent of the Air Canada pilots should be dovetailed with the most senior Air Ontario pilots, but that the Air Canada pilots should generally be higher on the seniority list than their years of service would indicate. The CALPA president accepted the Picher award, but the Air Canada pilots voted to reject it, insisting on no dovetailing at all. They subsequently left CALPA to form their own union, the Air Canada Pilots Association (ACPA).

Because the Air Canada pilots never presented the revised seniority list to their employer, the Picher award was never put into effect.

The Air Ontario pilots brought a class action against the Air Canada pilots, suing them personally for damages in contract and tort because of their refusal to accept the Picher award. The Air Ontario pilots argued that each CALPA member had been a party to a contract with every other member, that those contracts incorporated the terms of the CALPA constitution, and that the refusal of the Air Canada pilots to abide by the Picher award breached those contracts, resulting in damages to the Air Ontario pilots.

A motion by the Air Canada pilots to dismiss the action was granted by the motions judge, whose decision was upheld by the Ontario Court of Appeal. The Air Ontario pilots appealed to the Supreme Court of Canada.]

IACOBUCCI J.:

A. A Brief Overview of the Historical Development of the Union Contract and Union Status

[34] The use of a contractual model to characterize union membership arose in the early part of the 20th century as a consequence of the rising prominence of trade unions in England. The general rule at common law was that unions, as unincorporated associations, had no legal status. As a result, members could not bring suit against the union itself and courts would normally only engage in union affairs in order to protect the property interests of the members, refusing to interfere to enforce the rules of the association. . . . As the role of trade unions became more significant, and unions were able to exercise significant control over employers and employees alike, common law courts sought to establish a basis for a legally enforceable obligation on unions to follow their internal rules, thereby protecting the rights of individual union members.

. . .

[37] In the seminal Canadian case of [*Orchard v. Tunney*] a union member sued members of the union's executive board in tort for infringing his rights under the union constitution. In addressing the character of the rights and obligations relating to union membership, Rand J. (for the majority) looked to the Taff Vale and Bonsor decisions [of the House of Lords] for the basis of his judgment; however he noted that those decisions were grounded in the fact that the English Trade Union Acts had granted significant rights to trade unions, and that there was no comparable legislation in Manitoba. Thus, with no basis upon which to follow these English decisions, Rand J. was unable to find that trade unions in Manitoba had legal status or personality.

B. The Union Contract and Union Status in the Modern Context

[46] . . . the world of labour relations in Canada has evolved considerably since the decision of this Court in *Orchard, supra*. We now have a sophisticated statutory regime under which trade unions are recognized as entities with significant rights and obligations. As part of this gradual evolution the view has emerged that, by conferring these rights and obligations on trade unions, legislatures have intended, absent express legislative provisions to the contrary, to bestow on these entities the legal status to sue and be sued in their

own name. As such, unions are legal entities at least for the purpose of discharging their function and performing their role in the field of labour relations. It follows from this that, in such a proceeding, a union may be held liable to the extent of its own assets.

[47] Viewed in this modern context, the proposition that a trade union does not have the legal status to enter into contracts with its members is implausible. The impediments that prevented Rand J. in *Orchard, supra,* from holding that by joining a union, the member contracts directly with the union as a legal entity, have been overcome. In order for trade unions to fulfill their labour relations functions, it is essential for unions to control and regulate their internal affairs. Since the regulation of union membership is a fundamental part of the role of trade unions, it is only logical that it should fall within the sphere of activities for which unions have legal status. It follows that unions must have sufficient legal personality to enter into contracts of membership, and that this is an aspect of union affairs for which legislatures have impliedly conferred legal status on unions. In addition, I agree with Lord Morton's statement in *Bonsor, supra,* that there are no "vital differences" between an action in tort and an action in breach of contract brought by a member against the union, and to draw a line between the legal status to be sued in tort and the legal status to enter into contracts with its members is arbitrary and illogical.

[48] In light of the above, the time has come to recognize formally that when a member joins a union, a relationship in the nature of a contract arises between the member and the trade union as a legal entity. By the act of membership, both the union and the member agree to be bound by the terms of the union constitution, and an action may be brought by a member against the union for its breach; however, since the union itself is the contracting party, the liability of the union is limited to the assets of the union and cannot extend to its members personally. I say that this relationship is in the nature of a contract because it is unlike a typical commercial contract. Although the relationship includes at least some of the indicia of a common law contract (for example offer and acceptance), the terms of the contractual relationship between the union and the member will be greatly determined by the statutory regime affecting unions generally as well as the labour law principles that courts have fashioned over the years. With this in mind, for ease of reference I will refer to the membership agreement between the individual member and the union as a contract.

[49] Having said that there exists an enforceable contract between union members and the union, I believe it is worth elaborating on several factors which make this contract unique. First, it is essentially an adhesion contract as, practically speaking, the applicant has no bargaining power with the union. Moreover, in many situations, union membership is a prerequisite to employment, leaving the individual with little choice but to accept the contract and its terms. Finally, it must be borne in mind that a statutory labour relations scheme is superimposed over the contract between the member and the union, and can create legal obligations. Consequently, the contract must be viewed in this overall statutory context. For example, the statutory right of members to be represented by the union of their choice implies that the contract only exists as long as the members maintain that

union as their bargaining agent, and no penalty could be imposed by the contract against members for exercising this statutory right. As it is not necessary to interpret the terms of the membership contract or determine its scope on the facts of this case, I decline from elaborating further on these matters. I simply note that the unique character and context of this contract, as well as the nature of the questions in issue, will necessarily inform its construction in any given situation.

[50] In my view, the above characterization not only fulfills the practical purpose of providing a basis from which the terms of the union constitution may be enforced, but it also serves as an accurate and realistic description of the nature of union membership. The individual applies for membership with the union. It is the union, represented by its agents, that accepts the individual as a member, and this individual agrees to follow the rules of the union. Aside from the fact that the relationship between the union and its members fits naturally into the contractual model, in today's labour relations context, the public has come to view unions as associations with the responsibility to discharge their obligations to members; it would be inconsistent with this view to deny unions the right to enter into legally enforceable contracts with these members.

[51] I emphasize that the above recognition of the legal status of trade unions does not automatically extend to other unincorporated associations. The unique status of trade unions is a consequence of the complex labour relations regime governing their existence and operations. By statute, labour unions have been endowed with significant powers and corresponding duties. They are granted the monopoly power to act as the exclusive bargaining agent for a group of employees, and they have a corresponding duty to bargain fairly on their behalf. As well, union membership is often a prerequisite to employment, forcing members to join the union based on its prescribed terms. By acceding to union membership, the individual agrees to be bound by the union constitution, the terms of which will almost inevitably include internal disciplinary provisions in the event of a breach by the member. In light of the significant powers and duties of the union vis-à-vis its members, and in particular its ability to enforce the terms of the membership agreement internally, it is only logical to hold that the legislature has intended unions to have the status at common law to sue and be sued in matters relating to their labour relations functions and operations.

C. Existence of a Contract *Inter Se* Between Union Members

[52] Given the recognition of the special form of contractual relationship which exists between a trade union and each of its members, the question remains whether there is any basis for maintaining the proposition that there exists a web of contracts between each of the union members *inter se*, and, if so, whether this relationship can form the basis for a breach of contract claim against union members.

[53] As discussed above, the idea that union members were joined to each other through a web of contracts arose as a legal fiction designed by courts as a way to exert jurisdiction over the internal affairs of a trade union. It allowed courts to circumvent the lack of legal

status of unions and hold unions liable through the medium of its membership. By characterizing the liability as that of the group, the execution of the judgment was limited to the assets of the union.

[54] With the acknowledgment of the legal status of unions relating to the fulfilment of their labour relations role, I agree with the view that the legal fiction of a web of contracts between members is no longer necessary. A member wishing to sue his or her union for breach of the constitution is not impeded by a lack of legal status. Since the underlying problem which led to the establishment of the fiction has been resolved, in the absence of some compelling reason to maintain it, the idea that union members are contractually connected to each other should likewise be abandoned.

[55] As an initial matter, I would find it difficult, if not impossible, to conclude that the traditional indicia of a contract exist between the members of a union. For example, it stretches the imagination to suppose that each and every member of a union makes an offer of membership to an individual who then accepts these various offers, or vice versa, or that there takes place some mutual exchange of consideration between and among perhaps thousands of members. This is in contrast with the ease with which the relationship between the member and the union fits into the contractual model. In my view, it is simply unrealistic to posit that such a web of contracts exists between union members. Moreover, I agree with the courts below that it is not within the reasonable expectations of union members that they could be held personally liable to other members for breaching the union constitution. As well, the union constitution does not generally set out obligations which exist between individuals. It is mainly concerned with the obligations of the individual to the union (e.g. to pay dues, to participate in job action, etc.) as well as laying out how the union will be governed and conduct its affairs.

[56] The respondents argue that the concept of a contractual relationship between the members should be maintained and enforced in this case in order to fill a gap that would otherwise exist in the labour relations scheme. In my view, there is no gap in this case that needs to be filled; if the appellants were in fact wronged, there are remedies that were and are available to them that appear to be fair and reasonable.

[57] First, although the Air Canada pilots subsequently left CALPA, at the time the alleged wrongs were committed, they were still members of CALPA and internal remedies were available to the Air Ontario pilots. . . .

[58] In addition to these internal procedures, if the appellants were of the opinion that CALPA was not adequately addressing the alleged misdemeanours by the Air Canada MEC [master executive council], the appellants may have been able to bring a complaint before the CIRB against CALPA for failing in its duty under s. 37 of the Canada Labour Code, to fairly represent the appellants in the bargaining of seniority rights. Although the appellants and respondents disagreed on whether the duty of fair representation was broad enough to encompass this situation, the essential point here is that the appellants failed to pursue any of these internal or CIRB procedures. In this connection, the appel-

lants conceded at trial that there were internal remedies available to them which they elected not to pursue. . . . In addition, aside from the availability of internal procedures and CIRB proceedings, it is well established that tort claims may lie between union members, and in this case, the tort actions have been allowed to proceed.

[59] However, apart from the fact that there were and are remedies available to the appellants in these particular circumstances, on a more general level, it seems problematic for a court to fill legislative gaps in the labour relations scheme by contorting what is essentially a contractual metaphor into a basis for a breach of contract action. Absent an independent basis for recognizing a breach of contract action between members, the mere argument that there exists a legislative gap is insufficient justification for transforming this contractual metaphor, initially created to provide a foundation for finding group liability, into a concrete basis which allows for personal liability to exist between union members.

[60] On a policy level, if courts were to allow disagreements between union members to result in claims against their personal assets absent the existence of an identifiable wrongdoer in breach of some duty, like the required elements of a tort action, this would have a chilling effect on union democracy. The importance of the democratic rights of union members, including the right to dissent, was pointed out in *Tippett v. International Typographical Union, Local 226* (1975), 63 D.L.R. (3d) 522 (B.C.S.C.), at p. 546:

> All members of trade unions have the unqualified right to speak out against the manner in which union affairs are conducted. There is a right of dissent. There is a right to seek decertification, subject to the condition that no member of a union shall conspire with his employer to injure his union. I point out, moreover, that dual unionism is a fact of life in this Province. No person can be expelled or penalized by a trade union for insisting on his rights.

Exposing the personal assets of dissenting union members to liability would be antithetical to this "unqualified right" of union members to speak out against the agenda of their bargaining agent. The result would be to discourage member participation in union affairs and to erode union democracy.

[61] As well, I agree with [the motions judge] that trade unions would find it difficult to recruit members or obtain certificates to bargain collectively if the act of joining a trade union exposed individuals to personal liability in damages to other members for alleged breaches of provisions of the constitution. Further, if union members were permitted to bring suit against other members instead of resorting to internal dispute resolution mechanisms where breaches of the constitution were alleged, the ability of unions to resolve internal conflicts would be hindered. This loss of control over internal affairs would undermine the ability of unions to present a united front to employers and pursue the collective interests of their members.

[62] To summarize, on grounds of both law and policy, I conclude that there is no contract between union members based on the terms of the union constitution. In light of the finding that the union itself can be held liable in breach of contract, there is no need

to maintain the "complex of contracts" model. In addition, to interpret this model so as to allow for personal liability between union members would be contrary to its purpose and intent and would have negative consequences on the operation of the labour relations scheme in this country.

[63] However, this is not to say that union members do not have some obligations inter se. By joining a union, the member agrees to follow the rules of the union, and, through the common bond of membership, union members have legal obligations to one another to comply with these rules. If there is a breach of a member's constitutional rights, this is a breach by the union, and the union may be liable to the individual. Similarly, the disciplinary measures in the constitution can be imposed by the union on a member who contravenes the union's rules. A failure by the union to follow these disciplinary procedures may cause it to breach its contractual obligations to the other members, giving rise to corresponding contractual remedies.

[64] In addition to potential internal procedures, a failure by the union to insist on compliance with the constitution or impose disciplinary measures for its breach may allow members to initiate proceedings either at the CIRB, or the courts, depending on the nature of the complaint. Aside from actions against the union, a member who is harmed by the breach of the union's rules by another member may, if the requisite elements are present, have an action in tort against that member.

VI. CONCLUSION

[65] For these reasons, I would dismiss the appeal with costs.

*** *** ***

Although the courts maintain final supervisory authority over internal union affairs through the law of contract, and although labour relations boards have been given limited statutory jurisdiction to hear complaints by members against their unions, not many cases have been decided in this area by the judiciary or by labour boards. Canadian legislatures, unlike those in the United States and Britain, have refrained from enacting legislation that intrudes deeply into internal union affairs. One reason, according to many observers (including the authors of the following excerpt), is that Canadian unions are generally democratic and not corrupt, and therefore do not require close public regulation to ensure that their affairs are kept in order.

Michael Mac Neil, Michael Lynk, & Peter Engelmann, *Trade Union Law in Canada* (Aurora, Ont.: Canada Law Book, 2001 update), at 6-3 to 6-7

> The Canadian approach of statutory abstinence from the regulation of internal union elections and union officers is the product of four factors. First, Canadian unions have historically encouraged a culture of democratic practices, and they have been able to give voice to both the employment and the social aspirations of their membership. Most industrial relations observers in Canada would concur with the conclusions reached by the 1996 federally appointed Task Force which reviewed the *Canada Labour Code* that: "Canadian trade

unions exhibit a high level of internal democracy and genuinely represent the interests and wishes of their membership." Other recent independent reviews of labour legislation — most notably in British Columbia in 1993, Ontario in 1992 and, earlier, federally in 1968 — have echoed the same views. Union leadership in Canada has changed office on a regular basis both on the national and local level, it has in recent years avoided most hard-left and hard-right splits, and its membership and leadership has of late become more racially and gender diverse. As well, many unions in Canada have strived to achieve not only collective bargaining gains, but also to encourage forms of social unionism that would build durable relations with other community and national organizations on a range of political and social causes.

Second, unions in Canada have generally avoided both the stain of corruption that has tainted some parts of the American labour movement, as well as the spectra of unbridled militancy that had, fairly or unfairly, characterized a number of British unions. Certainly, there have been alarming, if sporadic, incidents of corruption in Canadian union leadership, and occasional episodes of intimidation in union elections. The most serious episode involved the Seafarers' International Union in the 1950s and early 1960s, which, after having been actively encouraged by the federal government of the day to oust the left-leaning union that represented seafarers on the Great Lakes, initiated a reign of thuggery and corruption until its leadership was removed following a federal commission of inquiry. However, the unions that encouraged or tolerated patterns of corruption or violence in Canada were generally outside the mainstream labour congresses, or were expelled once the mainstream leadership was satisfied that the patterns were endemic. As a result, the record of corrupted labour authority in Canada has been infrequent.

Third, as a consequence of these first two reasons, there has never been a sustained political or popular demand in Canada for a significant legislative intrusion into internal union affairs. The cry for "union democracy" has never acquired the hot-button persona in Canada that it achieved in the United States and Britain. Nor has the use of the term "union bosses" ever strongly resonated in the contemporary media or in popular speech. Canadian employers have generally, if reluctantly, accepted the fundamental premises of collective bargaining, and they have not either built up a significant antiunion consulting industry nor have they sought as a common strategy to undermine the legitimacy of unions as representatives of employees. Although conservative federal and provincial governments have been elected with some regularity since the *Wagner Act* model was introduced, they have respected the prevailing consensus among the industrial relations parties that the present level of statutory oversight of union affairs has been appropriate. Even when conservative provincial governments have significantly re-written labour legislation in order to restrict the organizing abilities and other powers of unions — such as in British Columbia in 1982 and 1987, in Alberta in 1988, and in Ontario in 1995 — they have rarely touched the existing degree of regulation of the internal affairs of unions. Part of this forbearance emanates from the active presence of social democratic parties in Parliament and in most provincial legislatures — the New Democratic Party in English Canada, and the Bloc Québecois and the Parti Québecois in Québec — that have articulated the labour movement's positions on industrial relations. In turn, the political presence of these social democratic parties has depended, in part, on the relative strength of the labour movement — the 2000 unionization rate was 32 percent — among the Canadian work force, and its assertive attention to social and political concerns beyond the workplace.

And fourth, the traditional British common law concept of unions as voluntary organizations — and therefore entitled to self-government — has long influenced Canadian legislators and courts. This approach, articulated through a long line of English judicial case law and subsequently adopted by the courts into Canadian law, likened trade unions to voluntary associations such as social clubs and political parties. The English and Canadian courts viewed the membership relationships of these organizations as purely personal and contractual, and they therefore would not review an internal decision of a union except on narrow procedural grounds. Although the law in England changed directions judicially in the 1950s, and legislatively in the 1980s, to become more interventionist, this legal theory has had a longer life in Canada. Even as the Canadian courts themselves have recently shed some of their traditional legal inhibitions about reviewing internal union decisions, while retaining a highly legalistic approach towards reading union constitutions, their supervisory role in practice is still only infrequently called upon.

However, whether there is a role for the statutory regulation of internal union elections and the conduct of union officers has been actively debated in legal academic literature. In Canada, Geoff England and Bill Rees have advocated a measure of statutory intervention to plug what they see as current gaps in the common law. Specifically, they suggest legislative safeguards to protect a member's right to oppose an incumbent leadership, and to ensure fair election procedures that would be regulated by a specialist tribunal. Their remarks echo earlier arguments made by James Dorsey and by the 1968 Woods Task Force on Industrial Relations, who each recommended some statutory form of a union member's bill of rights. This argument for greater legislative intervention is premised not so much upon any historic or current pattern of abuse of democratic rights, as it is upon the increasing political and social role of unions in society. The rationale is that, with this growing political and social role, the public now has a particular interest in the internal operations of unions.

Opposed to this view are several of the leading British scholars on labour law. The late Otto Kahn-Freund argued that a union, as a fighting body of working people susceptible to outside hostile forces working from within, cannot have an overdose of elective democracy imposed upon it. Trade unions are primarily organizations designed to defend and advance their members' working conditions, and not to provide an exercise in civic government. Between democracy and autonomy, he wrote, 'the law must come down on the side of autonomy.' More recently, Lord Wedderburn has written that the issue of trade union democracy must be placed within the power system of labour-management relations. The statutorily imposed forms of elective union democracy in the United States and Britain, he argues, have resulted in weakening the role of the labour movement as an engine of collective bargaining and as a force for social change, a result likely intended by the conservative governments that enacted the legislation.

Any legislative judgment in the future as to whether statutory intervention of any degree is warranted to regulate the conduct of trade union elections and officers in Canada should be determined with at least the following three aspects in mind: the efficacy of judicial oversight, the ability of trade unions to provide democratic self-regulation, and the necessity for the internal democracy of trade unions to be statutorily regulated in comparison to other socially influential organizations, such as corporations, political parties and religious institutions. Those few industrial relations studies that have examined the character of political life in Canadian unions have found that unions are as democratic as other organizations in Canadian society, and far more democratic than the companies that they face across the bargaining table. The most serious obstacle to greater democracy within Canadian unions appears to lie not in the character of their leaders, nor in any particular strictures in their constitutions and rules, but in the generally low participation of the membership in the political life of unions, except in moments of conflict or crisis. Democratic life in British and American unions, with much more extensive legislative intervention, appears to be no greater than in Canadian unions. This may well be an area that is not amenable to legal reform.

[Reproduced with the permission of Canada Law Book Inc., 1-800-263-3269, www.canada-lawbook.ca.]

✻ ✻ ✻

Only a few Canadian jurisdictions provide for any significant degree of legislative oversight of internal union affairs. Three provinces — Alberta, British Columbia, and Saskatchewan — require that internal union disciplinary hearings must comply with the requirements of natural justice. The British Columbia Labour Relations Board, in *Coleman and Office and Technical Employees' Union, Local 378* (1995), 28 C.L.R.B.R. (2d) 1, at pages 27–8, said that in the particular context of an internal trade union hearing, the requirements of natural justice include the following:

- Individual members have the right to know the accusations or charges against them and to have particulars of those charges.
- Individual members must be given reasonable notice of the charges prior to any hearing.
- The charges must be specified in the constitution, and there must be constitutional authority for the ability to discipline.
- The entire trial procedure must be conducted in accordance with the requirements of the constitution; this does not involve a strict reading of the constitution, but there must be substantial compliance with the intent and purpose of the constitutional provisions.
- There is a right to a hearing; the ability to call evidence and introduce documents, and the right to cross-examine and to make submissions.
- The trial procedures must be conducted in good faith and without actual bias; no person can be both witness and judge.
- The union is not bound by the strict rules of evidence; however, any verdict reached must be based on the actual evidence adduced and not influenced by any matters outside the scope of the evidence.
- In regard to serious matters, such as a suspension, expulsion, or removal from office, there is a right to counsel.

In *Coleman*, several former members of a local union executive had been disciplined by their union for opposing the decision to raid the membership of another union. In finding that their internal disciplinary hearing had largely complied with the dictates of natural justice as required by section 10(1) of the British Columbia *Labour Relations Code*, the Board, at page 26, acknowledged the tension between individual and collective rights that frequently arises in such conflicts.

> Individual members of a trade union must be permitted to pursue their own trade or profession, earn a living, participate in the internal affairs of their union, and not be interfered with in any manner other than a lawful one. Conversely, trade unions find their greatest strength in their collective nature, and this may involve compromises between the interests of individual members and the collective interests. It is the enforcement of these trade-offs, and the requirement of a strong and united front that may involve a degree of control or discipline over those who may be seen to threaten that collective good.
>
> It is clear that the democratic tradition, which trade unions uphold, is strengthened, not weakened, by the fair balance which they strike in the administration of these trade-offs. It is this view of the nature and role of trade unions in our society that will inform the framework for our interpretation and administration of s. 10 of the Code.

For an elaboration of the view that the courts (under the influence of Lord Denning) have been too intrusive in their application of procedural fairness rules to internal trade union proceedings, see: Michael Lynk, "Denning's Revenge: Judicial Formalism and the Application of Procedural Fairness to Internal Union Hearings" (1997), 23 Queen's L.J. 115.

A number of Canadian labour relations statutes stipulate that trade unions cannot impose disciplinary penalties against members in a discriminatory manner. For example, the British Columbia *Labour Relations Code* states, in section 10(2):

> No trade union shall expel, suspend or impose a penalty on a member or refuse membership in the trade union to a person, or impose any penalty or make any special levy on a person as a condition of admission to membership in the trade union or council of trade unions
>
> (a) if in doing so the trade union acts in a discriminatory manner, or
>
> (b) because that member or person has refused or failed to participate in activity prohibited by this Code.

Other jurisdictions have comparable provisions, but with added stipulations related to a person's job status. For example, the *Canada Labour Code* provides as follows:

> 95. No trade union or person acting on behalf of a trade union shall . . .
>
> (e) require an employer to terminate the employment of an employee because the employee has been expelled or suspended from membership inthe trade union for a reason other than a failure to pay the periodic dues, assessments and initiation fees uniformly required to be paid by all members of the trade union as a condition of acquiring or retaining membership in the trade union. . . .

The distinction between the two types of provision can be demonstrated by the example of an employee who works during a lawful strike. It is generally assumed that a union is within its rights in refusing membership, expelling from membership, or disciplining an employee for strikebreaking activity. Such union action does not breach provisions comparable to section 10(2) of the British Columbia *Labour Relations Code*. The implication of section 95 of the *Canada Labour Code* and parallel provisions elsewhere, however, is that an employee expelled from union membership for strikebreaking cannot be dismissed from his or her job even if the collective agreement requires union membership as a condition of employment.

To understand the position of an individual employee, it is thus necessary to examine the interaction among the union's constitution and membership rules, the union security provisions in the collective agreement, and the applicable statutory provisions on internal union affairs.

Solly v. Communications Workers of Canada, [1981] 2 Can. L.R.B.R. 245 at 252–58 (C.L.R.B.)

[Solly was a long-service Bell Canada employee who was opposed to militant trade unionism but not to all forms of unionism. He had been very active in the nonmilitant union that was supplanted as bargaining agent for Bell employees in 1976 by the Communications Workers of Canada. In 1977, during the CWC's first bargaining round, Solly circulated an open letter reaffirming his opposition to the CWC and to the use of the strike weapon, and stating his intention to continue working in the event of a strike. He worked during a rotating strike from June to August of 1979 and for the first part of a full strike in August, but he began to have a change of heart and stopped working when the full strike was two weeks old. He obtained a CWC membership application in September, but did not submit it because a local union bylaw was passed imposing a fine of $50 a day on nonstrikers.

In March 1980, when that bylaw was revoked, Solly finally applied for membership. Although he testified before the Canada Labour Relations Board that his attitude had changed and that he had become willing to participate in lawful strikes, he did not communicate those facts to the union at any relevant time. His membership application was considered by the union and rejected because, in the Board's words, the union "did not want a member who would not honour a picket line." The CWC constitution provided that members could be disciplined for working during an authorized strike. Solly did not lose his job as a result of his failure to acquire union membership, because the applicable collective agreement contained only a Rand Formula clause and thus did not require membership. Solly complained to the Board that the CWC's denial of membership was in breach of section 136.1 and sections 185(f) and (g) of the *Canada Labour Code*, which are set out in the following excerpt from the Board's decision.]

> DORSEY, Vice-Chair: This complaint presents the Board with a problem about which voluminous social, political, economical and legal writings have been published. The intensity of the conviction with which competing perspectives and opinions have been expressed on this question is only second to the passion that motivates their statement. We do not propose to review all this literature or explore its history and merits. In a brief fashion, reflec-

tive of argument of the parties, we will place the issue in its statutory setting of Part V of the *Canada Labour Code* and state our conclusion on the legal merits of the complaint.

In the absence of legislation individuals had no enforceable right to membership in a trade union. The courts viewed trade unions as unincorporated voluntary associations analogous to a private club upon whose members an additional member could not be forced (see M.A. Hickling, 'The Right To Membership Of A Trade Union'. . .). This view of unions does not correspond to a realistic appraisal of the role, authority and responsibility of a trade union acting as exclusive bargaining agent in a collective bargaining regime. . . . Today some legislation expressly ensures security of employment if union membership is denied (see *The [Newfoundland] Labour Relations Act*, 1977, Stats. Nfld. 1977, c. 64, s. 30ff).

The *Canada Labour Code* expressly requires unions, as a condition of certification, not to restrict membership eligibility. . . .

Legislators have recognized for many years that the permission of union security clauses in collective agreements and their enforcement ought to be balanced by restrictions on the loss of employment as the result of loss of union membership (see Earl E. Palmer, *Responsible Decision-Making in Democratic Trade Unions* . . .). The federal legislation was once selective and addressed only the question of dual unionism (see Industrial Relations Disputes Investigation Act, R.S.C. 1952, c. 152, s. 6(2)). Today union security provisions are permitted in collective agreements, . . . but loss of union membership for any reason other than failure to pay periodic dues assessments, and initiation fees to the union may not result in loss of employment (sections 185(e) and 184(3)(a)(ii)).

Internal union disciplinary authority may be exercised for reasons other than failure to pay dues, assessments and initiation fees and it may take forms other than expulsion. To prevent and remedy abuse of this authority unions may not act against members because they have participated in proceedings under the Code . . . or because a person refused to perform an act contrary to Part V of the Code . . . or by discriminatorily applying rules of membership or discipline. . . . In the United States the substantive and procedural protection accorded union members is more extensive. There is a useful general discussion in Thomas J. Keeline, *NLRB and Judicial Control of Union Discipline*, 1976 and Janice R. Bellace and Alan D. Berkowitz, The *Landrum-Griffin Act: Twenty Years of Federal Protection of Union Members' Rights*, 1979.

One action of a member that evokes a harsh and immediate response from a union is working during a lawful union-sponsored strike. . . .

> . . . There is little doubt that if employees were free to return to work during the strike, without fear of being subjected to reasonable discipline for violating the rules and regulations governing their union membership, the union would experience severe difficulty both in maintaining the effectiveness of that particular strike and in mounting similar activity in the future. The power to fine or expel strikebreakers is essential if the union is to continue as an effective bargaining agent. Thus, while the union's interest is best vindicated by disciplining its members for strikebreaking, the public interest is in seeing that such discipline does not exceed what is reasonable in the circumstances.

(Goldblatt [*Union Membership and Individual Rights in Labour Law*, 1975]. . . . See also Clyde W. Summers, 'Legal Limitations on Union Discipline' . . . .)

Most of the literature and cases deal with expulsion or discipline of members because there has been far less development in the law on the rights of non-members to be admitted to membership. There has been some consideration of the situation of former members who seek readmission . . . . Some judicial passion for the right to membership if it is a condition of work received little support or legislative endorsement . . . .

Some major restrictions on the union's discretion in granting or denying membership were made in 1978 in the federal jurisdiction when Parliament enacted a duty of fair referral on unions engaged in the referral to employment under a collective agreement. The most commonly thought of method of union referral is the hiring hall. But Parliament did not restrict its obligations to this method of referral. . . . The Board has interpreted Parliament's intention and this section to encompass non-hiring hall situations where acquisition of union membership is a condition of employment and requires unions to include membership rules in the rules required to be established. . . . In this case, the union is not engaged in the referral of persons for employment to Bell Canada. The Union security provision in the collective agreement is a Rand formula.

. . . The Board has expressly stated the duty of fair representation does not apply to internal union affairs . . . . Solly alleges the union contravened its duty under section 136.1. If the union acted improperly it was not in the representation of Solly *vis-à-vis* the employer. Solly makes no complaint in this regard. The duty of fair representation is not the appropriate vehicle for any redress in this case. The complaint alleging a breach of this section is therefore dismissed.

We must now consider the alleged contravention of sections 185(f) and (g), which state:

185. No trade union and no person acting on behalf of a trade union shall . . .

(f) expel or suspend an employee from membership in the trade union or deny membership in the trade union to an employee by applying to him in a discriminatory manner the membership rules of the trade union;

(g) take disciplinary action against or impose any form of penalty on an employee by applying to him in a discriminatory manner the standards of discipline of the trade union; . . .

In administering and interpreting sections 185(f) and (g) the Board must start from some basic premises. First, the sections are intended to protect and advance individual rights against the previously unfettered authority of the union organization. Second, they do not abolish the right of the union to expel, suspend or discipline members or deny membership to non-members. This must be kept in mind when interpreting section 134(2) and leads to the conclusion that unions may be certified when membership is denied to individuals because of certain actions they have undertaken but not if the union has discriminatory policies in respect of qualifications for membership. . . . Section 134(2) does not intend to guarantee membership to all employees in a bargaining unit.

The legislation recognizes unions must have institutional interests that may be advanced if they are to function as effective collective bargaining agents and democratic organizations. Clearly their financial interests are of major importance. Parliament recognizes this when it permits loss of employment when union membership is lost through failure to contribute financially. But Parliament does not and cannot ensure union members participate meaningfully in their union and its affairs. (See the discussion in Seymour Martin Lipset, 'The Law and Trade Union Democracy.' . . .). All it can do is foster a climate where participation is available to those who wish it. The final decision on the acceptability of candidates for membership is left to be fashioned by the union which is only restricted from certain prohibited discriminatory conduct. One of the restraints on the union is that of sections 185 (f) and (g).

The task left to the Board is not to set standards for what unions may consider vital institutional interests or to dictate when those interests must yield to the interests of an individual. Our task is to ensure the union does not act discriminatorily and one measure is the reasonableness of the union's action. . . . The Board does not determine the scope of offences for which a union may discipline or deny membership. . . . This does not mean the Board is not concerned about union membership rules. The application of rules, whether written or not, that are discriminatory in themselves will be a breach of sections 185(f) and (g) (see *Gérard Cassista* . . .).

The problem faced by the legislators and the Board in assessing the limits of Parliament's control of internal union affairs is difficult. The essential difficulty is to balance the competing interests that flow from the reality that individuals find real security and protection of their rights through association, but the associated organization best ensures its efficiency by limiting the freedom of those who have entered into it.

Strike breaking is a long established offence in unions. The Saskatchewan Labour Relations Board recently said this about strike breaking: 'It is difficult to imagine any other act by a member which a union would consider to be more treasonous conduct to it.' The legislation it administers permits a union to enforce a union security clause and compel dismissal from employment where a member is expelled for having 'engaged in activity against the trade union.' Activity against a union was . . . described by the Saskatchewan Board as including any crossing of a union-authorized picket line. Strike breaking 'defies the will of the majority of the members of the bargaining unit' and 'threatens the effectiveness of the strike, and, in many cases, the very life and existence of the union local'. . . .

Here the clear policy of the union was against strike breaking. Solly engaged in this activity when he broke ranks with the employee decision to strike. He gave the union no indication that he would not act similarly in the future. It was reasonable for the membership committee and general meeting to believe he would act again as he had in the past. It was equally reasonable for his actions to be considered when he sought membership. He was not singled out for individualized or any special treatment and the union's reason for denial of membership is clearly reasonable. We therefore find the union did not contravene sections 185(f) or (g). . . .

10:600 UNION SECURITY PROVISIONS AND THE ROLE OF UNIONS IN SOCIETY

Unions obviously play a key role in our statutory regime of labour relations, and the involvement of individual employees in unions allows them to participate in determining conditions at work. But unions have a broader significance as institutions in civil society. In his essay, 'Bowling Alone: America's Declining Social Capital' (1995) 6 Journal of Democracy 65, Robert Putnam used union membership as one of several indicators of social engagement in the United States. He suggested that such engagement was declining in virtually all spheres — politics, unionism, churches and bowling leagues, the largest single collective activity in which Americans were engaged. Putnam located American unions within the larger, rather sorry, picture of declining civic participation throughout society. Ironically, during the 1996 American presidential election, unions became more active than they had been for years — yet for the first time, less than half of all eligible voters exercised their right to vote for a presidential candidate.

Canadian unions have traditionally been much more active in politics, and remain so. They tend to support what they deem to be worthy causes locally, nationally and abroad. They lobby for the adoption of legislation that directly favours union interests, such as amendments to labour relations statutes, and for the adoption of social and economic policies that favour workers, minorities, and the nonworking poor. Many unions, both federally and provincially, have chosen to align themselves with the New Democratic Party, either formally or informally, and unions in Quebec have generally supported the Parti Québécois.

The relationship of unions to the NDP has, however, become rather contingent and contentious. That party has come under fire for its dependence on union support, all the more so because unions have been losing public sympathy in recent years. Nor has union support necessarily delivered many votes to the NDP; in recent years, more and more workers have been voting for other parties. Nor, finally, are unions always pleased with policies adopted by NDP governments; for example, in the case of the 1990–1995 Ontario NDP government, they became very displeased, and many stopped supporting the party altogether.

All of these developments form part of the backdrop to the next case, in which Lavigne, an anti-union dissident, tried to limit the capacity of unions to participate in politics by seeking a court order prohibiting the use for political purposes of dues collected under union security arrangements. A right-wing lobby group, the National Citizens' Coalition, provided support for Lavigne throughout the course of the litigation.

Lavigne v. Ontario Public Service Employees Union, [1991] 2 S.C.R. 211

[Lavigne was a teacher in a community college that had a collective agreement with the Ontario Public Service Employees Union. The agreement had a Rand Formula provision, which required teachers to pay the equivalent of union dues as a condition of employment but did not require them to join the union. Lavigne did not challenge the requirement to pay union dues. However, he claimed that his constitutional rights of freedom of expression and freedom of association under ss. 2(b) and 2(d) of the *Canadian Charter of Rights and Freedoms* were violated by the union's use of some of its funds, of which his dues were a part, for purposes other than collective bargaining — for example, support of the NDP; aid to various causes, including nuclear disarmament and abortion rights; opposition to construction of the Toronto Skydome; and support for Oxfam, striking British mine workers and Nicaraguan health care workers.

Because Ontario community colleges were under substantial government control, the Supreme Court of Canada held that they were governmental actors within the meaning of s 32 of the *Charter*, and that the provisions of the applicable collective agreement therefore had to respect employees' *Charter* rights. However, the Court unanimously dismissed Lavigne's claim that the union's use of a portion of his dues for political purposes violated his *Charter* rights.]

WILSON J.: . . . The fact that the appellant is obliged to pay dues pursuant to the agency shop clause in the collective agreement does not inhibit him in any meaningful way from expressing a contrary view as to the merits of the causes supported by the union. He is free to speak his mind as and when he wishes. Nor does his being governed by the Rand formula have such an effect. It is a built-in feature of the Rand formula that union activities represent only the expression of the union as the representative of the majority of employees. It is not the voice of one and all in the bargaining unit. I find therefore that the appellant's s. 2(*b*) right has not been infringed. . . .

Although it is not necessary for me to consider s. 1 of the Charter in light of my conclusion that neither s. 2(*d*) nor s. 2(*b*) has been infringed, I am considering its application in case my conclusion is in error and for the sake of completeness.

. . . Mr. Lavigne maintains that, while compelling non-members to pay the equivalent of union dues is rationally connected to the objective of promoting industrial peace, this is so only in so far as those dues are put to pure 'collective bargaining' purposes. It is the appellant's position that to confer a complete discretion upon the union to spend the dues as it sees fit, and in particular to spend dues on political parties and issues unrelated to the particular workplace in which dues payers are employed, does not further the goal of industrial harmony. In other words, Mr. Lavigne contends that the provision is overbroad.

. . . Some commentators have suggested that, even if the interests of unions are considered to be primarily economic, there is none the less plenty of justification for permitting them to contribute to causes removed from the particular workplace. For example, Professor Etherington . . . states. . . :

> The attempt to distinguish the economic and political concerns rests on themisguided premise that unions can represent the economic interests of workers effectively without engaging in political activity. If this was ever more than a myth, it is certainly not the case in a post laissez-faire society in which government intervention and regulation in most spheres of economic and social life is a daily event. In such a society, it is necessary for unions to engage in political activity to ensure that governmental regulation takes a form that is favourable, or at least not adverse, to the economic interests of its constituents. If they do not, they may find that their bargaining position vis-à-vis employers has been

substantially weakened or undermined by government legislation or policy. [Emphasis in original.]

Similarly, Benjamin Aaron, in his article 'Some Aspects of the Union's Duty of Fair Representation' stated . . . :

> The welfare of organized labour is affected not only by so-called 'labour legislation,' but also by executive, legislative, and judicial decisions with respect to monetary and fiscal policy, defence, education, health, and many other issues. Finally, policies are made by men, and it is sheer sophistry to argue that although a union may legitimately support certain legislative objectives, it may not spend its funds to secure the election of candidates whom it hopes or has reason to believe will work to achieve labor's goals.

I agree with Professors Etherington and Aaron that union involvement outside the realm of strict contract negotiation and administration does advance the interests of the union at the bargaining table and in arbitration. However, I do not believe that the role of the union needs to be confined to these narrow economic functions. In the past, this court has not approached labour matters from an exclusively economic perspective. For example, in Slaight Communications . . ., Dickson C.J.C. adopted the expression of Professor David Beatty that 'labour is not a commodity'. . . The idea that is meant to be captured by this expression is, I think, that the interests of workers reach far beyond the adequacy of the financial deal they may be able to strike with their employers. . . . the Chief Justice made it clear that the interests of labour do not end at some artificial boundary between the economic and the political. He expressed the view that "'[a] person's employment is an essential component of his or her sense of identity, self-worth and emotional well-being'" (quoting from the *Alberta Reference* . . .) and that viewing labour as a commodity is incompatible with that perspective. Unions' decisions to involve themselves in politics by supporting particular causes, candidates or parties, stems from a recognition of the expansive character of the interests of labour and a perception of collective bargaining as a process which is meant to foster more than mere economic gain for workers. From involvement in union locals through to participation in the larger activities of the union movement the current collective bargaining regime enhances not only the economic interests of labour but also the interest of working people in preserving some dignity in their working lives. . . .

. . . if Mr. Lavigne's *Charter* rights have indeed been infringed, that infringement has been occasioned through measures that significantly modify its impact. Some of the key features of the scheme are worth repeating: the union may only compel the payment of dues from each member of the bargaining unit after a majority of those employees have exercised their choice to be represented by the union; all employees are free to join the union or not, and the bargaining agent may not discriminate against any member of the bargaining unit on the basis of union membership; and if the members of the bargaining unit find that they are unhappy with their bargaining representative, they may take a vote to decertify the union.

Taking these factors into account it seems to me that the legislature has opted for a very reasonable and fair compromise. The union, once certified, has been permitted to exercise authority over the members of the bargaining unit in many respects. However, with that authority comes a great deal of responsibility. As well, the entire process of union representation carries the hallmark of democracy. This is not a case of the heavy hand of government coming down and enforcing its will with little or no regard for the rights and freedoms of those affected. The features of the scheme suggest to me that, while other means might have been available to the legislature to achieve its objective, none is clearly superior in terms of both accomplishing the goal of promoting collective bargaining and respecting as far as possible the rights of individual employees. . . .

The *Charter* does not require the elimination of 'minuscule' constitutional burdens. . . .

LA FOREST J.:

. . .

To take the first step in the *Oakes* test . . . , what can be said to be the state objective in compelling someone like the appellant to pay dues to the Union knowing that those dues could be used to fund activities not immediately relevant, or at all relevant to the representation of his interest at the bargaining table? There appear to be two closely interrelated objectives

The first is to ensure that unions have both the resources and the mandate necessary to enable them to play a role in shaping the political, economic and social context within which particular collective agreements and labour relations disputes will be negotiated or resolved. The balance of power between management and labour at any given time or in any particular industry or workplace is a product of many factors. It is, in part, clearly a product of factors specific to the industry or workplace in question, such as productivity, and the existence or non-existence of a history of bitter strikes and sharp practice. But it is also in part a product of more general factors, such as the prevailing public sentiment as to the importance of unions or the state of the economy. It is also a product of the state of government legislation and policy, most obviously in the area of labour relations itself, but also in regard to social and economic policy generally. Government policy on day-care, for example, will affect what a union can achieve for its members at the bargaining table. If universal day-care is paid for by taxpayers as a whole, union negotiators in a particular workplace will not have to pay for it by making wage concessions as a way of convincing the employer to provide it. Even if the government introduces certain taxes, the balance of power between workers and management may be affected. Concerned to cushion their membership against a tax's inflationary effect, unions may have to make concessions in areas they would otherwise have fought for, such as vacation time or worker safety. This, then, is one of the principal objectives that lies behind the government's willingness to force contribution to union coffers knowing that it will be spent on things not immediately related to collective bargaining on behalf of the workers making the contributions.

The second government objective I have alluded to explains why government puts no limits on the uses to which contributed funds can be put. This objective is that of contributing to democracy in the workplace. The integrity and status of unions as democracies would be jeopardized if the government's policy was, in effect, that unions can spend their funds as they choose according to majority vote provided the majority chooses to make expenditures the government thinks are in the interest of the union's membership. It is, therefore, for the union itself to decide, by majority vote, which causes or organizations it will support in the interests of favourably influencing the political, social and economic environment in which particular instances of collective bargaining and labour-management dispute resolution will take place. The old slogan that self-government entails the right to be wrong may be a good way of summing up the government's objective of fostering genuine and meaningful democracy in the workplace.

✳ ✳ ✳

In the following case, the Supreme Court of Canada confronted the even more controversial question of whether the *Charter* right to freedom of association was violated by a statute that compelled workers to join a union in order to be employed in a particular industry.

R. v. Advance Cutting and Coring Ltd., [2001] 3 S.C.R.209, 2001 SCC 70

[A Québec statute known as the *Construction Act*, R.S.Q., c. R-20, set up a scheme of province-wide bargaining in the construction industry similar in some respects to statutory schemes applicable to that industry in other provinces. In certain ways, however, the Québec statute went further than those in other provinces. It named five union federations as recognized bargaining agents, and it required every construction worker to join one of the five (he or she could choose which one) in order to obtain the "certificate of competence" that was a prerequisite to employment in the industry. Only a limited number of certificates of competence were available in each region of the province.

Several construction firms were convicted and fined under the *Construction Act* for employing workers who did not have the requisite certificates. A number of contractors, real estate developers, and construction workers brought a claim under the *Canadian Charter of Rights and Freedoms* that the convictions should be set aside on the ground that the Act violated employees' freedom of association — and more precisely, that freedom of association under the Charter included the right not to associate. The Québec government and the unions defended the statutory scheme as the only practical response to a long history of strife, violence, and dysfunctional labour relations in the construction industry. The matter eventually reached the Supreme Court of Canada.

A fragmented Supreme Court upheld the legislation by the narrowest of margins. Four separate judgments were written. L'Heureux-Dubé J., speaking only for herself, was the only judge who held that the freedom of association did not include the right of non-association. In her view, such a right would be antithetical to the purpose and scope of freedom of association, which was to protect the collective pursuit of common goals. Alternatively, she said, if there was a right of non-association, it was not violated by this statutory scheme, but even if there was a violation, it was justified under section 1 of the *Charter*.

The other eight judges were all of the view that the freedom of association did indeed include the right of non-association. However, they split three ways on whether that right had been violated, and on the issue of justification under section 1.

What turned out to be the dissenting judgment, written by Bastarache J. and concurred in by McLachlin C.J. and by Major and Binnie JJ., held that the right not to associate had been violated, and that the violation was not justified under section 1. In Bastarache J.'s opinion, the compulsory unionization scheme established by the Construction Act in and of itself represented a form of ideological coercion not justified under section 1. No specific evidence of the ideological views of the unions in question was required, the dissenters said; the mere fact that workers were required to participate in and indirectly support a system of state-sponsored and forced association was enough. Bastarache J. was also of the view that the historical problems of labour relations in the provincial construction industry could not justify such an incursion on freedom of association. He was very unimpressed with the device of competency certificates; in his view (with which the majority did not really take issue), the statute envisaged that those certificates were to be given out not on the basis of competence but on the basis of residence in the particular region and past employment in the industry.

What was in effect the majority judgment was written by LeBel J. and concurred in by Gonthier and Arbour JJ. Like the four dissenters, LeBel J. held that freedom of association included the right not to associate. However, like L'Heureux-Dubé J., he held that the right not to associate had not been violated in this case, and that even if it had been violated, the violation was justified in light of the problems which had led to the enactment of the *Construction Act*. Excerpts from the judgment of LeBel J. are set out below.

The swing vote was cast by Iacobucci J. Writing only for himself, he agreed with Bastarache J. that the *Construction Act* violated the right of non-association, making a total of five judges who found such a violation. However, Iacobucci J. agreed with LeBel J. and L'Heureux-Dubé J. that the violation was justified under section 1, making a total of five judges who reached that conclusion.]

LEBEL J.:

. . .

The *Construction Act* imposes an obligation to join a union group. The obligation remains, nevertheless, a very limited one. It boils down to the obligation to designate a collective bargaining representative, to belong to it for a given period of time, and to pay union dues. The Act does not require more. At the same time, the Act provides protection against past, present and potential abuses of union power. Unions are deprived of any direct control over employment in the industry. They may not set up or operate an office or union hall (ss. 104 and 119 of the Act). No discrimination is allowed against the members of different unions. Provided they hold the required competency certificates, all workers are entitled to work in the construction industry without regard to their particular union affiliation. Specific guarantees against discrimination are found in ss. 94 and 102. Section 96 grants members clear rights of information and participation in union life. The law allows any construction worker to change his or her union affiliation, at the appropriate time. As it stands, the law does not impose on construction workers much more than the bare obligation to belong to a union. It does not create any mechanism to enforce ideological conformity.

[Turning to the political role of unions and union members in contemporary Canadian society, LeBel J. said:]

The fact that unions intervene in political social debate is well known and well documented and might be the object of judicial notice. Indeed, our Court acknowledged the importance of this role in the *Lavigne* case. Several ideological currents have criss-crossed the history of the Quebec labour movement. It was never unanimous about its direction, even about the need to enter the political arena or involve itself in broader societal issues beyond the horizon of the bargaining unit. (See P. Verge and G. Murray, *Le droit et les syndicats*. . . .) These authors underscore the weakness of the formal links between the Quebec unions and political parties. . . . They add that it is impossible to determine whether union political positions had any real influence on their members. . . . More recent studies of voting attitudes seem to indicate that, in fact, Canadian unions exert very little influence on the voting behaviour of their members, as at least one Canadian political party, the NDP, has found repeatedly to its sorrow (see A. Blais et al. "Making Sense of the Vote in the 2000 Canadian Election". . . .)

Taking judicial notice of the fact that Quebec unions have a constant ideology, act in constant support of a particular cause or policy, and seek to impose that ideology on their members seems far more controversial. . . . In this case, it cannot be said that some form of politicalization and ideological conformity which allegedly flows from the political and social orientation of the labour movement is self-evident. Instead, such views evidence stereotypes about the union movement as authoritarian and undemocratic, and conjures images of workers marching in lock step without any free choice or free will, under the watchful eye of union bosses and their goon squads.

In fact, democracy undergirds the particular form of union security provided for by the Construction Act. Throughout the conflicts and difficulties that marred the history of the construction industry, a critical flaw of the regime appeared to be the lack of participation in the life of unions and the need to re-establish and maintain member control over their affairs. While it also facilitated the evaluation of the representativeness of the unions, the obligation to choose and join a union answered this critical need in a way that a different union security arrangement, like the Rand Formula, would not have addressed. The dues check-off scheme, like the Rand formula, disposes of the free rider problem, but the employee remains outside the life of the union. In other security arrangements, a member may choose to remain aloof and refrain from attending meetings, voting for union officers and taking part in discussions. Affiliation means that he or she has, at least, gained the ability to influence the life of the association whether or not he or she decides to exercise this right. . . .

Union members seem to act very independently from their union when it comes to the expression of their political choices and, even more so, to their voting preferences, come election time. Existence of attempted ideological conformity, let alone its realization, seems highly doubtful. . . .

In this context, there is simply no evidence to support judicial notice of Quebec unions ideologically coercing their members. Such an inference presumes that unions hold a single ideology and impose it on their rank and file, including the complainants in this case. Such an inference would amount to little more than an unsubstantiated stereotype.

BASTARACHE J. (dissenting):

. . .

In this case, the fundamental values that must be protected in the workplace include freedom of conscience, mobility, liberty, freedom of expression and the right to work. The necessity of considering the totality of the rights and values that are interrelated when dealing with forced association in the workplace, in my opinion, points to the need to take a broad view of the *Charter* right not to associate.

This approach is supported by consideration of this freedom in light of international conventions and the jurisprudence of this Court.

The United Nations *Universal Declaration of Human Rights* states:

> Article 20
>
> . . .
>
> 2. No one may be compelled to belong to an association.

In addition, the United Nations *International Covenant on Economic, Social and Cultural Rights*, 993 U.N.T.S. 3, provides that:

> Article 8. 1. The States Parties to the present Covenant undertake to ensure:
>
> (a) the right of everyone to form trade unions and join the trade union *of his choice*, subject only to the rules of the organization concerned, for the promotion and protection of his economic and social interests. No restrictions may be placed on the exercise of this right other than those prescribed by law and which are necessary in a democratic society in the interests of national security or public order or for the protection of the rights and freedoms of others; [Emphasis added.]

This Court has regularly made reference to and relied upon the aforementioned international documents in interpreting fundamental freedoms in the *Charter*.

. . .

To suggest that the unions in the present case are not associated with any ideological cause is to ignore the history of the union movement itself. . . .

The legislation in question here is complex; it creates an entire labour relations scheme which governs, amongst other matters, union membership, employers associations, collective bargaining and the creation of the Commission de la construction du Québec and committees on construction and vocational training.

The mis en cause argues that the action against the appellants was directed solely at their failure to obtain competency certificates. According to the mis en cause, there is a distinction between this requirement and the requirement to become a member of one of the five recognized employee associations. I disagree with this assertion. The scheme of the Act provides that both requirements must be met as conditions precedent to working in the construction industry in Quebec; these conditions are certified together on one document, referred to as the competency certificate, and the only way to receive such a certificate pursuant to s. 39 of the Act is if both conditions have been met. . . .

. . . It is because of the collective force produced by membership that unions can be a potent force in public debate, that they can influence Parliament and the legislatures in their functions, that they can bargain effectively. This force must be constituted democratically to conform to s. 2(d).

. . .

. . . Ideological constraint exists in particular where membership numbers are used to promote ideological agendas and, as noted in *Lavigne* . . . , this is so even where there is no evidence that the union is coercing its members to believe in what it promotes. . . .

The vast majority of Canadians must work for a living and, as such, working is a compelled fact of life; however, in the present situation, the appellants are not arguing that being forced to work with a particular group or to participate in employment-related activities violates s. 2(d). This is not a case where workers dispute the payment of mandated union dues; the restrictions in this case are much more severe than that in *Lavigne*. The Rand formula mandates payment of union dues for the betterment of all workers; in this case, the workers are being forced to join a union. . . .

. . . pursuant to s. 30, construction workers can only be placed on the employer's list and join a union pursuant to s. 32 if they were a resident of Quebec in the previous year, worked 300 hours in that year and were under 50 years of age. The Commission de la construction du Québec forwards a card to the workers on this list (s. 36). No employer may use the services of a person in the construction industry unless that person holds one of these cards (s. 39). Therefore, if the s. 30 requirements are not met, a person may not join one of the five unions and, as a result, cannot work in Quebec. In addition, as acknowledged by the Commission de la construction du Québec . . . , at the material time, there were regional quotas in place which also limited the number of workers in each predetermined region within the province. For persons living in and outside the province of Quebec, their ability to join one of the unions and thereby work in the construction industry is severely restricted by these arbitrary requirements. . . . The same may be said for a person who has never left the province but simply did not work in the industry in the previous year or a person who wishes to train and start working in the industry for the first time.

. . .

In summary, there are severe restrictions on the right of a person to join one of the five chosen unions in order to work in the construction industry in Quebec. Even if the conditions imposed by s. 30 of the Act were permissible limitations on freedom of association, the regional quotas would still need to be justified under s. 1. They unduly infringe the ability of workers to join a union, which is a prerequisite for working in the construction industry in Quebec. As such, they are an infringement of the s. 2(d) freedom of association.

. . .

I accept that it is in the public interest to have structured collective bargaining and to provide for competency requirements; these are no doubt pressing and substantial objectives. But I have difficulty accepting that these are the true objectives of the impugned provisions. The legislation brings into play restrictions on the admission to the industry, cancellation of the ability to have a non-unionized business, restrictions on bargaining rights, imposition of regional quotas and impingement of regional mobility.

Regarding the relationship between forced association and the objective stated, the mis en cause submits that it is essential to collective bargaining in this area to limit the number of actors in this industry. This is an argument based on the history of labour relations in Quebec. However, as stated above, the mis en cause has failed to show that permitting structured collective bargaining is the true purpose of these provisions as drafted. Further, any justification based on competency is untenable. The actual requirements of s. 30 and the regional quotas have little if anything to do with the professional competence of workers in the construction industry. This was noted by Judge Bonin who stated that "[t]he certificate's main purpose was to maintain hiring priority." Being a resident of Quebec in the previous year, having worked a set number of hours in that year, and being less than 50 years old, do not verify competence. The same may be said for the regional quotas and control over regional mobility within the province. As such, I find there is no rational connection between the objective and the measures taken.

. . .

Further, when considering the public interest nature of collective bargaining, I fail to see how s. 30 and the regional quotas minimally impair the positive and negative components of the freedom of association. While recognizing the importance of collective bargaining in the public interest, if this was in fact the objective of these provisions, there is no evidence that it need result in government control over admission to the work force based on the factors discussed above or result in a denial of the democratic principle. As was shown by the factual situation in Lavigne, there are other choices that a government can make which support collective bargaining. The imposition of a Rand formula, for instance, would allow for collective bargaining to continue without the requirement that workers actually join a union. Furthermore, with respect to a means to protect the negative right, had there been no problem with the positive right in this case, the government could possibly have instituted a clause allowing those who did not wish to join a union to simply abstain while continuing to pay union dues to the representative union in the majority or to a collective "pot" to be divided equally among all five representative unions.

Chapter 11: **Statutory Regulation of Employment**

11:100 INTRODUCTION

In this chapter and the two that follow, the focus shifts to statutory regulation of the employment relationship. Chapter 12 looks at employment standards legislation, which deals (among other things) with minimum wages, hours of work, maternity leave, and termination of employment. The subject of Chapter 13 is human rights, pay equity, and employment equity legislation. Other employment law statutes, not considered in this book, include those on unemployment insurance, occupational health and safety, workers' compensation, and pensions. All of these statutes generally apply both to employees engaged under individual contracts of employment and to employees covered by collective bargaining. Although statutory regulation of the employment relationship has a very long history, much of the legislation discussed in Chapters 12 and 13 is of relatively recent origin.

Statutory regulation and its institutions are probably the least well-known part of our law of employment. Until fairly recently, law school courses in this area tended to focus exclusively on collective bargaining law, and the practice of labour and employment law mainly involved collective bargaining and the common law action for wrongful dismissal. As we have seen, the common law approach to employment consisted of regulation through the device of the contract of employment, although it was a very special type of contract. A principal objective of employment law is to secure justice in the employment relationship, and a prevalent view is that for most employees justice is not achieved through the negotiation of individual contracts of employment, because of inequality of bargaining power (see above, section 2:100). Collective bargaining is a procedural technique designed to redress this inequality.

Direct statutory intervention attacks the perceived problem of unfairness not through the procedural device of regulating the negotiating process, but by directly enacting standards to govern the employer-employee relationship. The normative justification for such intervention overlaps to some extent, but not entirely, with the justification offered for collective bargaining law. The following excerpt offers a historical overview of the battle between advocates of statutory regulation and proponents of a free labour market.

Barry Reiter, "The Control of Contract Power" (1981) 1 Oxford J. Legal Stud. 347 at 348–53

It is important to appreciate at the outset the implausibility of a claim that society should be organized on the basis of private contracting behaviour. The claim advocates apparent anarchy and amoralism. Never before the birth of faith in markets had gain been advanced as an inherently worthy motive. Nor had economic structures ever been sharply differentiated from social structures and relations. But in an effort to throw off feudal and religious shackles, to release energy and to give vent to new theories of social justice, a broad coalition was forged over the sixteenth through the nineteenth century. The coalition, including economic liberals, utilitarians, and classes rising in power politically and intellectually, adduced powerful arguments in support of the market. The central benefits they attributed to organization in this form included the following. First, the market would provide powerful incentives motivating individuals to work and to produce wealth in society. The resultant gain would improve the lot of all (or of most, depending on the economist) individuals in society. The notion of incentives could be, and indeed was, pushed to the point of urging the necessity of a substantial level of poverty in society and of starvation as a sharp stick to keep the incentive structure keen.

Second, market organization offered promises of efficiency. The consumer would determine what society produced: the cheapest mode of production of the right quantities of goods and an efficient distribution network were explicit outcomes of the model. Third, market organization would allow for innovation. This was a particularly critical attribute given the substantial barriers to innovation that had been erected by the guilds and other local protective arrangements. Fourth, the market meant freedom from imposition by governmental or religious authorities. This freedom offered a consent basis to society, a basis seen both as good in itself and as a legitimating force. Finally, the market promised justice. The entire notion of market rewards and failures could be and was linked to a personal merit principle.

The case was powerful, but it was never wholly accepted. Instead, strange and shifting alliances of intellectual and political power combined to prevent the excesses of the market through the assertion of political power. Society reacted in a 'spontaneous outburst' to assert its primacy over economics. The details of the social reaction and the proof of what I assert about its success are provided in Polanyi's classic study, *The Great Transformation* and in Atiyah's interesting and extensive recent work, *The Rise and Fall of Freedom of Contract*. It may suffice to describe the nature of the rejection of market principles in one critical sector only, that of 'the supply of labour.' The commodification of labour was a critical step necessary to establish a market-based economy. Older feudal notions of the relationship between workers and those responsible for them had to give way if mobile labour was to be available to be bought and sold as supply and demand dictated. The commodification of labour was not really achieved even in theory until the repeal of the Poor Laws in 1834. However, as the momentum to turn labour into a commodity grew, the social reaction was already taking shape. It appeared in the form of the reassertion and the continued assertion of values limiting market values in respect of human labour. The force of the social reaction demonstrates that the nineteenth century was anything but an era of *laissez-faire*. The best known reactions involve those associated with the various Factory

Acts, dating from 1833. The Acts dealt with employment of children, hours of work, and safety matters. Similar legislation regulated other important industrial sectors. A bureaucracy was created, industrial inspection Commissions were established, Reports were issued and legislation followed frequently. Combination laws were enacted early in the nineteenth century and Truck Acts were passed frequently thereafter. All of this social reaction occurred early in the 'era of market economy.'

Today, the dimensions of the reaction are even more apparent. Industrial codes and related legislation govern virtually every aspect of employment: hiring, union rights and responsibilities, hours of work, health and safety standards, compensation for injury, redundancy arrangements (in some cases), minimum or prescribed wage rates (in many cases), terms of payment, pension and unemployment benefits. In modern society, it is a fact that all but the most subsidiary features of the 'labour contract'are determined by institutions other than contract. The labour relationship is governed by political rather than market power. Similarly, the permitted uses of lands and of capital were never and are not now determined by other than a most tightly controlled market. The same may be said of all other significant features of modern life. Contract may be a medium, but as a social directing and organizing principle, it is left well to the margins.

In the face of the powerful case adduced by the 'market coalition' how could this be so? The answer has been provided by students of the social sciences. First, it is important to realize the historical fallacy on which the market economists built their theory. When Adam Smith said that the division of labour in society was dependent on the existence of markets, on 'man's propensity to barter, truck and exchange one thing for another' he was quite clearly historically wrong. This fact is not adduced so much to cast doubt on Smith's historical facility as to point out the striking nature of the theory he advanced. Nowhere before had society been subservient to economics, and a sharp break with the past would have been necessary in order to implement the dramatic change in the relationship between social and economic principles that the classical economists and the utilitarians were, therefore, advocating. Second, it became apparent early on that the classical economic-utilitarian theory did not work even in its own terms: the problem of ignorance among members of the public was a pervasive one and the liberals' hopes for education as the cure proved futile; the problem of monopolies (natural and otherwise) appeared quickly, and posed a major challenge. Third, the problem of inequalities threatened the moral basis of the theory. To the extent that individuals began with different endowments of money, opportunities, or even human abilities, the merit basis of the market system faltered. Fourth, it became apparent that contract was not simply a two-party affair. The market produced externalities of significant proportion: society must be and was concerned about injured workers, ruined social fabric, and ecological chaos. Fifth, the preservation of the institution of the market itself required vigorous suppression of market principles: total freedom had to be limited in order that there could be any freedom. Thus legislation was clearly necessary to prevent the exercise of monopoly power and some action was essential to prevent the enforcement of restrictive covenants that would serve to limit the participation the contract model was designed to foster. Intervention in the market was also necessary to slow the pace of change that might occur too rapidly thereby threatening to bring down the entire structure.

Finally, and most importantly, market theory simply did not take enough account of social values other than those concerned with efficiency and (measurable) net gains. On one hand, *a priori* values could be asserted against the anarchy of contract. Thus it could be argued that individuals and land were not commodities, or that they were not mere means but were, rather, ends. Or different visions of equality could be asserted. While contract may be said to foster certain forms of equality, it is apparent that other more levelling forms can be advocated in its place. On the other hand, less fundamental but nevertheless conflicting values could be asserted against 'market values.' Paternalistic notions could be advanced in support of the view that the consumer cannot choose best, and that choice by others might be preferable. Health, safety and moral values might claim priority on an other-than-market calculus. From the time of John Stuart Mill onward, it was apparent that classical economics had little to contribute on important issues of distribution though it could say much about efficiency.

Many of these difficulties were appreciated very early in the nineteenth century, and it was clear by the last quarter of that century (if not well before) that arguments founded on 'freedom of contract' would not carry much independent weight. In the end, and in respect of contract as a social organizing principle, we have witnessed a 'death of contract' quite different from that which has been the subject of intense debate of late. We have observed the replacement of the idea that contract alone might be the balance wheel of society by one suggesting that political institutions ought to perform this role instead. 'Contract' has become recognized as in need of extensive political manipulation. Ultimately, 'the market' turns out to have been a short term bridge philosophy carrying society from a period of organization in religious and feudal terms to the modern era of democratic political direction. A contemporary theory of contract must recognize these facts by rejecting 'the market' in favour of an institutionally mixed and discretionary measure of social progress.

[By permission of Oxford University Press.]

As you read the materials in the next two chapters, consider which of the three legal regimes examined in this book — common law, collective bargaining, and statutory regulation — offers the best approach to regulating the employment relationship. Some commentators argue that the enactment of legislation on such matters as minimum wages, pay equity, and health and safety indicates that both the common law and collective bargaining have failed to protect employees adequately. This argument implies that the terms and conditions of employment established by statute are substantially different from those resulting from individual or collective bargaining. Other commentators have disputed the accuracy of this assumption, at least with respect to some types of legislation. Who is right? Does the answer vary for different types of legislation or different types of employees? Have some groups of employees fared particularly poorly under individual contracts of employment or collective agreements? Which of the three regimes offers employees and employers the greatest opportunity to participate in establishing the terms of their relationship? Also stop to consider to what extent legislated terms and conditions of employment are actually applied in Canadian workplaces, especially non-union workplaces.

Chapter 12: **Employment Standards Legislation**

12:100 INTRODUCTION

Statutes in every Canadian jurisdiction set out a range of minimum terms and conditions of employment. Those statutes provide what often called a "floor of rights" which cannot legally be undercut by contracts of employment in the non-unionized sector or by collective bargaining in the unionized sector.

As songwriter Paul Simon once put it, "One man's ceiling is another man's floor." The parties to a common law employment relationship or to a collective bargaining relationship are legally free to negotiate terms more beneficial to employees than the statutory minima. However, individual employees, or for that matter their union, may not have enough bargaining power to do so. For many employees, the floor of rights represents the full extent of their rights *vis-à-vis* the employer.

This floor of rights is set out in a wide variety of statutes, whose titles and contents differ considerably across Canada. The employment standards statute (or its equivalent) is the broadest and most basic, covering a range of subjects mentioned below. Other statutes typically address such subjects as occupational health and safety, workers' compensation, employment agencies, pension benefits, human rights, equal pay, apprenticeship, fair wages, industrial standards, and smoking in the workplace. Also relevant is the federal *Employment Insurance Act*. A few of those statutes are touched upon in other parts of this book.

In terms which are also pertinent to Canada, an American writer has said:

> Minimal terms are certainly not a new phenomenon. They can be found in English law as early as 1464 in the late Middle Ages, and have a long history in this country as well. In recent years, however, the importance of minimal terms in this country has increased as the significance of collective bargaining has diminished. The government has increasingly stepped in to require minimal terms which, it was once hoped, would be provided through the collective bargaining process.
>
> Minimal terms present a basic challenge to the student of labour law. Unlike collective labor relations, the subject does not have a natural organizing principle. Minimal terms are found in dozens, if not hundreds, of separate laws; they pursue different and sometimes conflicting policy objectives; they have separate and diverse enforcement schemes.
>
> Steven L. Willborn, "Individual Employment Rights and the Standard Economic Objection: Theory and Empiricism," (1988) 67 Nebraska L. Rev. 101, at 102–3.

In this chapter, we focus on provincial employment standards statutes, which in themselves cover many different subject areas. Obligations imposed on employers by employment standards legislation vary from jurisdiction to jurisdiction, but commonly include matters such as: paying wages when due; respecting the statutory minimum wage; keeping employment records; sending certain types of data to government agencies; providing employees with breaks and rest periods; respecting maximum hours of work; paying overtime premiums; providing a certain level of fringe benefits to part-time workers; granting vacations, statutory holidays, and various types of leave, such as maternity/paternity and child-rearing leave; laying off or dismissing employees, either individually or in large numbers; and participating in labour adjustment programs in the event of mass termination. A practicing lawyer must closely scrutinize the details of the employment standards statute and the accompanying regulations in the particular jurisdiction, because they may vary significantly from those in other jurisdictions and are likely to change often.

It is impossible within the space constraints of this book to do justice to all of the matters dealt with in employment standards legislation. To illustrate the broader issues involved in legislating employment standards, this chapter will focus on the following subject areas:

1) hours of work and overtime;
2) minimum wages; and
3) dismissal for economic reasons and for misconduct on the employee's part.

The crucial issue of who is covered by the legislation is also considered, as are some aspects of the interface between statutory and common law enforcement processes. First, however, we will address a few important background issues.

The historical evolution and future development of the statutory floor can only be understood in the light of the widely-perceived deficiencies in the capacity of the common law employment contract and the free labour market to deliver socially acceptable terms and conditions of employment to a significant proportion of the population — a matter considered at some length in Chapters 1 and 2 of this book. The employment contract is based on the rhetoric of freedom and equality, but in practice, superior bargaining power often allows the employer to dictate the terms. Moreover, when an employee's common law contractual rights are violated, the cost and delay of civil litigation are potent disincentives to starting a lawsuit. Thus, as noted in Chapter 2 above, the great majority of common law wrongful dismissal cases involve relatively high-level managers and professionals. Employment standards legislation and other such statutes with their own enforcement procedures provide the only realistic way for lower-level employees to vindicate their rights. Nevertheless, as we will see in various parts of this chapter, enforcing employment standards legislation can be extremely difficult.

Employment standards legislation was developed in part to advance the personal dignity and autonomy of the individual, a goal that became increasingly prominent on the Canadian political agenda in the decades after World War II. Sustained economic growth during the post-war period gave Canadian employers and governments the financial ability to create today's relatively extensive statutory floor.

Tighter economic conditions in the past two or three decades have forced many employers to become more efficient, and have pressured all levels of government to reduce their debts and deficits. Some commentators argue that the increasing need to compete globally has made the statutory floor too burdensome for Canadian employers, and that it should be cut back or at least not extended further. Some provincial governments have adopted this view, and have amended their statutes to (for example) limit the classes of workers protected by the legislation or make it easier for employers to acquire exemptions from certain provisions. Other commentators argue that the current statutory floor is not an unwarranted drain on efficiency. For one thing, they say, employees who are treated well will be more productive. For another, legislated minimum wages and benefits ease competitive pressures on employers by reducing the scope for labour-market bidding wars.

The international dimensions of contemporary competitive pressures are explored in Chapter 14 below. A useful introductory review is S. Deakin & F. Wilkinson, "Rights v. Efficiency? The Economic Case for Transnational Labour Standards" (1994) 23 Industrial L.J. 289.

It is important not to fall into the trap of seeing employment standards legislation as the exclusive preserve of non-unionized workers. As is indicated in various parts of this book, including Chapters 9, 10, and 13, the statutory floor is of ever-growing importance to collective bargaining. Unions with little bargaining power may find that they cannot obtain better terms and conditions than those required by statute. Even strong unions may content themselves with what the legislation provides in certain areas, such as pensions, in order to seek better terms in areas of more immediate concern to their members, such as wages and job security.

Furthermore, unions may prefer to use statutory procedures to enforce legislated rights because they are quicker or cheaper or offer broader remedies than the grievance and arbitration machinery of the collective agreement. A good example is provided by health and safety legislation, under which the vast majority of complaints are brought by unionized workers. Of course, it is also possible that non-unionized workers may be ignorant of their statutory rights or too afraid of employer reprisals to try to enforce them. To save public funds, some governments in recent years have taken steps to preclude the use of statutory employment standards enforcement processes by unionized employees, and to require such employees to pursue even their statutory rights through the grievance and arbitration procedure in their collective agreement.

The level of the substantive statutory floor can be influenced by collective bargaining, since the benefits that unions secure in collective agreements may eventually find their way into the legislation. In addition, union political leverage may influence governments to raise the floor. In this regard, however, unions claim to find themselves on the horns of a dilemma. On the one hand, their quest for social justice is a crucial part of their *raison d'être*, and an important part of their overall message. On the other hand, there may be less incentive for workers to unionize if the legislation protects them at no cost to themselves. Some empirical studies have found that the appeal of trade unionism to the unorganized diminishes as statutory employment standards coverage expands. See Jean-Guy Bergeron, *Unionization in the Private Service Sector*, Ph.D. thesis, University of Toronto, 1993.

Even the most impressive statutory rights are illusory if they remain unenforced. The reader needs to be aware of the procedures for enforcing the employment standards legislation in his or her province, for there are important differences in this regard. Typically, the process begins with an aggrieved worker filing a complaint with an employment standards officer in the provincial ministry of labour, although such officers may themselves detect violations during periodic spot checks of workplaces. When a complaint is filed, the officer will normally attempt to mediate a settlement, failing which he or she will issue an decision. If there has been a breach of the statute, the officer will, where appropriate, order the employer to indemnify the employee for his or her losses.

An employment standards officer's order can usually be appealed to a higher level of departmental authority, or to an independent tribunal (either a specialized adjudicator or the labour relations board). The decisions of such tribunals are binding, subject only to judicial review by the courts. A quasi-criminal prosecution can be brought against the employer with the consent (depending on the jurisdiction) of the attorney general or the labour minister. Such consent will generally not be granted unless the employer has flagrantly or continually violated the Act. Maximum fines are specified, and are usually relatively low. The employer is typically prohibited from taking any reprisals against an employee for filing a complaint, and reinstatement with full compensation is provided as a remedy. If an employer is ordered to pay money owing to an employee, there is an impressive panoply of legal devices for collecting those payments.

REFERENCES

Geoffrey England, Innis Christie, & Roderick Wood, *Employment Law in Canada*, 3d ed. (Markham: Butterworths, 1998) c. 19

The procedures just described may seem impressive on paper, but enforcing employment standards legislation has been extremely difficult. If you were a non-unionized worker who needed to keep your current job, and you knew that your employer was improperly withholding part of your statutory vacation pay, would you file a complaint with an employment standards officer? Not surprisingly, the 1994 report of the federal Advisory Group on Working Time and the Distribution of Work (below, section 12:400) described noncompliance with the Ontario *Employment Standards Act* as "prominent." The report attributed this state of affairs to the low probability of violators being caught, the low likelihood of their being prosecuted even if caught, and the relatively small fines levied on those who were successfully prosecuted. To this list can be added the fear of employer reprisals. Finally, the efficacy of enforcement mechanisms is obviously dependent on the resources that the government allocates to them.

Roy Adams, "Employment Standards in Ontario: An Industrial Relations System Analysis" (1987) 42 Relations industrielles 46 at 50–57

Should a disagreement occur between an employer and an employee over the application of an employment standard, the *Employment Standards Act* envisions the following procedure (in simplified form) being implemented. First it is expected that the employee will discuss the issue with his/her employer. The Ministry provides advice to employees and employers unsure about their rights and obligations. In 1984–85 the [Employment Standards] Branch received about 725,000 telephone inquiries of which approximately 40% were from employers. The Branch also conducted about 29,000 in-person interviews.

If the employee is unable to arrive at a satisfactory resolution of the issue through direct discussion with the employer then he/she may file a claim in writing with the Employment Standards Branch. When written claims are filed an officer of the Ministry is appointed to investigate. Officers first attempt to work out a satisfactory solution to the problem between the parties. In short, the officer first behaves similarly to that of a conciliator or mediator. If no satisfactory solution can be worked out, then the officer assumes a role like that of the grievance arbitrator under collective bargaining and decides the issue in favour of either the employer or employee. If the decision is in favour of the employee then an order is issued to that effect. An order carries with it a financial penalty equivalent to 10% of the value of the officer's monetary award or $25 whichever is more. Most, but not all, awards have monetary consequences. Employers may appeal judgements against them to neutral referees appointed on an ad hoc basis by the Director of Employment Standards. Employees are not entitled to such an appeal but may have a second investigation by another Employment Standards officer.

How well does this procedure work when compared to the grievance procedure under collective bargaining? In fact, it does not come off very well in the comparison.

First of all, very few regular employees ever file employment standards grievances. . . . Instead, the great majority of complaints are filed by people who have left the employer against whom the complaint is filed. Most are, in effect suing for remuneration due to them. The preponderance of formal employment standards disputes occur at the point of severance rather than in the context of an on-going employment relationship as is common under collective bargaining. The primary function of the disputes procedure under employment standards is not to resolve disputes arising out of day-to-day employer-employee relations. Instead, the Employment Standards Branch is primarily a collection agency. The internal jargon of the Branch recognizes this fact. In annual reports of the Ministry data is provided not on the number of disputes resolved but rather on the number of "collections by issue" which the Branch made during the year. No mention at all is made of disputes settled in the course of an ongoing employment relationship.

Despite this experience, it is clear that the Ontario legislature intended the disputes procedure to be used by regular employees because it included strong language against victimization of grievors in the Act.

Article 57 states that:

No employer shall,
a) dismiss or threaten to dismiss an employee
b) discipline or suspend an employee
c) impose any penalty upon an employee or
d) intimidate or coerce an employee, because the employee,
e) has sought the enforcement of this Act or the regulations

f) has given information to an employment standards officer

g) has participated in or is about to participate in a proceeding or hearing under this Act or

h) testifies or is required to testify in a proceeding or hearing under this Act. (*Employment Standards Act*, 1982).

For engaging in victimization an employer may be fined up to $10,000 and be put in jail for six months. The employee may be reinstated with compensation. An employer who fails to comply with an order to reinstate may be fined $100 for each day of noncompliance.

Article 57 cases are very rare. They are so rare that the Branch does not keep records of them. In response to my request for data the Branch did an informal survey of long service officers. Between them three cases were identified. One was decided in favour of the employer and two were decided in favour of the employee. . . . This experience is very different from that under collective bargaining where effective reinstatement after a dismissal found to be unwarranted is a frequent enough occurrence. . . .

The probable ineffectiveness of the strong sounding sanctions against victimization is indicated by the Ministry procedure for dealing with the odd complaint received from an employee in an on-going relationship. Instead of initiating an investigation on behalf of the employee the Branch conducts (or pretends to conduct) a "routine" or "preventive" investigation. The employer is informed that the Branch has decided to inspect his records as part of its regular oversight activities. According to interviews with ESB officials the identity of the complainer is kept secret precisely because it fears that the employer will illegally victimize employees who file complaints. This procedure is probably not very effective because true random investigations are rare. The number of "preventive" investigations reported to have been carried out annually declined from 1,183 in 1981/82 to 321 in 1984/85. . . . In short, when the Ministry tells an employer it intends to carry out a routine investigation it is likely that the employer will reason that someone "blew the whistle." In small enterprises it should not be difficult for employers to determine likely "whistle blower" candidates. Less than 30 employees work in the average enterprise against which a complaint is filed in Ontario. . . .

The conclusion that I draw from these observations is that there is no effective disputes procedure available to unorganized employees who have a disagreement with their employer about the application of employment standards. No doubt such disputes often are settled amicably by discussion between employer and employee just as most grievances are settled at the first step of the grievance procedure under collective bargaining. . . . However, if the employee is unable to persuade the employer about the correctness of his/her position then he/she cannot place much confidence in the available procedure to provide a just outcome. As it now stands, the final practical resolution to unresolved disputes occurring in the context of an on-going relationship is unilateral decision by the employer. One cannot be confident that such a system is capable of providing justice. . . .

. . . If the Employment Standards Branch is really a collection agency one may ask how good of a collection agency is it? If an employee quits the job or is dismissed and the employer refuses to give to him/her vacation pay or wages due will the Branch ensure that payment is made? In an average year during the 1980s one employee in seven (ca. 15%) who validly complains to the ESB does not receive what is due to him/her.

Delinquent employers (those against whom valid complaints are filed) may be divided into three primary groups: the Sulkers, the Shysters and the Bankrupted.

THE SULKERS

This group is composed of employers who are sedentary (not mobile) and solvent. In a typical case the employee leaves (quits or is fired) subsequent to an angry exchange. Feeling a sense of righteous indignation the employer refuses any payment to the "ungrateful" or "disloyal" employee. In most of these cases the ESB does not eventually collect on behalf of the employee. To do so it may have to enlist the assistance of the courts or the local sheriff. Procedures are available under which the Branch may seize the employer's bank accounts as well as redirect payments due from a third party. One section of the ESB specializes in the application of such legal techniques.

THE SHYSTERS

This group of employers deliberately set out to defraud employees. One common pattern is for an "entrepreneur" to set up a summer business. Towards the end of the summer wage payments to employees are stopped and when the last job is done the employer disappears. This type of white collar criminal often maintains multiple bank accounts and several shell corporations. The procedures of the Branch are very ineffective against them. The primary weapon is court prosecution but because that process is costly there has been a conscious decision to decrease its use. In 1978–79 some 60 active prosecutions were resolved but since 1982/83 there have been no more than four cases a year.

THE BANKRUPTED

When companies became insolvent employees often find it difficult to collect remuneration due to them. . . . Bankruptcy is within the federal jurisdiction. Under the federal law secured creditors (e.g. financial institutions) have priority over employees. Should there be any money left over when it comes the turn of the employees to collect they are only entitled to remuneration earned in the three months prior to bankruptcy up to a maximum of $500. Termination pay is generally not considered to be remuneration within the meaning of the federal act. Vacation pay, the most common collection issue does have some protection from the priority list in the *Bankruptcy Act*. According to the Ontario *Employment Standards Act* employers are "deemed to hold vacation pay accruing due to an employee in trust . . .". Property held in trust is not considered to be part of the bankrupt's estate and therefore the ESB may be able to collect such payments over the claims of the creditors. Pensions and construction industry wages are protected by similar "trust" devices. In cases involving insolvency short of bankruptcy employee claims may have somewhat more security than they do under the *Bankruptcy Act*. Although the priority list is essentially the same, the maximum remuneration collectable is higher (i.e. $2000 vs. $500) and there are no restrictions with regard to when the wages were earned. Finally, officers and directors of corporations may be held personally liable for unpaid wages. However, the recent Ontario Commission into Wage Protection in Insolvency Situations noted that such provisions "have been enforced only sporadically". . . . The Commission also found that in 1982–83 some 36,00 workers in insolvency cases initially were owed vacation pay and 72% collected; some 16,000 employees were owed wages but only one fourth collected; approximately 15,000 workers were owed pay in lieu of notice and another 3,700 were owed severance pay but few "if any" collected. . . .

One may conclude from this review that employees who leave reputable, stable employers in Ontario may be reasonably certain that the available procedures will protect their interests. The probabilities are high that they will eventually receive the remuneration to which they are entitled. However, for people who unfortunately become involved with unscrupulous employers or happen to find themselves working for a company going bankrupt the prospects are not good. Current procedures do not adequately protect their interests.

What could be done? Employers who deliberately defraud employees could be more vigorously and regularly prosecuted. Prosecution is, however, expensive and there is no guarantee that a more extensive effort would have a significant deterrent effect. On the other hand the present system is one in which the potential criminal has little reason not to commit the crime.

In order to protect workers in bankruptcy situations, most developed countries have established wage protection schemes. The European Economic Community in 1980 "adopted a directive requiring Member States to guarantee employees' claims through assets independent of the employer's operating capital". . . . Three Canadian provinces (Manitoba, Quebec and New Brunswick) have established such schemes although the one in New Brunswick is not yet operative and the Quebec scheme functions at present only for the construction industry. A wider Quebec plan has not yet been declared in force. [Editor's note: the Manitoba legislation has been repealed, as has similar legislation later introduced in Ontario.]

Basically wage protection plans provide that employees of a bankrupt firm may collect remuneration due to them from a government agency. The agency then acquires the right to collect from the administrators of the bankruptcy. The Manitoba plan provides even broader protection. All employees on whose behalf the government is unable to collect within 30 days may be paid out of the fund. There is no requirement that the delinquent firm be insolvent. . . . The Brown Commission into wage protection in Ontario made a similar recommendation but severance pay (required in plant shutdown situations in Ontario) would be excluded from the definition of "unpaid wages." Pay in lieu of notice (required under common law and the employment standards statute) would also be excluded as it is in Manitoba.

Commissioner Brown gave three reasons for the exclusions. First, severance pay and termination pay are not earned in the same sense as are wages and vacation pay. For example, neither would be payable if the employee resigned voluntarily or was terminated for cause. Secondly, both severance pay and termination pay would defer eligibility for unemployment insurance benefits. Finally, severance pay and pay in lieu of notice, if paid, would be very expensive. For example, the Brown Commission estimated that during the one year period from April 1, 1982 to March 31, 1983, unpaid wages and vacation pay amounted to about six million dollars. On the other hand, "claims for pay in lieu of notice and for severance pay together totalled nearly $31 million of which little, if any, was collected". . . . Making an amount of such size annually payable, Brown concluded, would "likely result in a reduction in credit to labour intensive business". . . . It might also "increase the risk of an employer deliberately not giving employees notice, knowing than an insurance fund would provide them with wages in lieu". . . .

From a broad economic perspective Brown's recommendation would appear to be reasonable and prudent. Individual employees, unable to collect what otherwise would be due to them, might see the matter differently.

[Reprinted by permission.]

* * *

In 1996 and again in 2000 the Ontario *Employment Standards Act* was amended to change the rules regarding enforcement of the act by unionized employees. The new provision reads:

99. (1) If an employer is or has been bound by a collective agreement, this Act is enforceable against the employer as if it were part of the collective agreement. . . .

(2) An employee who is represented by a trade union that is or was party to a collective agreement may not file a complaint alleging a contravention of this Act that is enforceable under subsection (1) or have such a complaint investigated.

(3) An employee who is represented by a trade union that is or was party to a collective agreement is bound by any decision of the trade union with respect to the enforcement of this Act under the collective agreement, including a decision not to seek that enforcement.

(4) Subsections (2) and (3) apply even if the employee is not a member of the trade union.

(5) Nothing in subsection (3) or (4) prevents an employee from filing a complaint with the Board alleging that the decision of the trade union with respect to the enforcement of this Act contravenes section 74 of the Labour Relations Act, 1995.

Section 74 of the *Labour Relations Act* establishes a union's duty of fair representation (DFR) toward its members. As we saw in Chapter 10, unions generally have a veto over the enforcement of collective agreement provisions on behalf of employees in the bargaining unit, subject only to the requirements of the DFR. Because of the above provision, the same now appears to be true with respect to the enforcement of the provisions of the *Employment Standards Act*.

The Ontario Act was also amended to provide new rules on the relationship between statutory entitlements and common law rights. The Act prohibits employees from filing a complaint under the Act for unpaid wages or benefits, or for severance or termination pay, while pursuing a parallel civil claim for wrongful dismissal. These provisions apply even where the employee claims that the employer owes more than the maximum amount that can be awarded under the Act and the employee's civil claim seeks only the difference between the two amounts.

12:200 COVERAGE OF THE LEGISLATION

REFERENCES

Geoffrey England, Innis Christie, & Roderick Wood, *Employment Law in Canada*, 3d ed. (Markham: Butterworths, 1998) paras. 2:1–2:39

Employment standards statutes normally apply only to "employees," but they define "employee" in very general terms. Courts and tribunals have interpreted "employee" purposively, to bring within the legislation those workers who are in a position of economic subordination to their employer and are part and parcel of their employer's business and to exclude those who are independent entrepreneurs running their own businesses. Employment standards legislation is not designed to shield true entrepreneurs against the risks of the marketplace. This is why economic subordination cannot be the sole determinant of employee status; many entrepreneurs can be dependent on another business for much or even all of their revenue but retain a degree of independence from that other business that is incompatible with an employment relationship.

When negotiating their individual employment contracts, few employees attempt to bargain for changes in the substance of how work is organized. Therefore, the potential exists for employers to attempt to design working relationships that prevent workers from qualifying as employees under employment standards legislation. Difficult economic conditions in recent decades have led many employers to do exactly this. The proliferation of self-employment and other forms of so-called atypical work such as home-based work, telecommuting, casual work, and part-time work is in large part a response to the high cost of employing regular employees. Relatively few of these atypical workers are true entrepreneurs; often they are as powerless as regular employees, but their status under employment standards legislation is often uncertain.

12:300 STATUS UNDER THE LEGISLATION

The scope of employment standards legislation depends on the statutory definition of employee and employer. As we have seen, above, chapters 2:300 and 4:200, both the common law and the various collective bargaining statutes provide definitions or tests for determining what are employment relationships. To what extent should the common law definition of employee influence the definition of employee under employment standards legislation?

The following decision under the Ontario *Employment Standards Act* by designee Donald Carter offers an illuminating example of the approach adjudicators often take to interpreting the language of their enabling statute.

Re Becker Milk Co. (1973), 1 L.A.C. (2d) 337 at 337–48

CARTER: On 27 September, 1972, the Honourable Fern Guindon, Minister of Labour, directed me in the following terms:

This will serve to designate you as the person to enquire into whether the following named individuals [known as store managers] or any of them were, during the periods opposite their names, employees of the Becker Milk Co. Ltd. within the meaning of the Employment Standards Act, and if so, whether the only work of them or any of them was supervisory or managerial in character during the said periods:

The named individuals, along with the relevant period of time, are as follows:

Abe Hajjar — November 4, 1971 to March 27, 1972;

Millum Arsenijevich — February 7, 1972 to May 21, 1972;

Dimitrios Dristsas — January 3, 1972 to May 8, 1972;

Marson Najem — February 1, 1972 to May 4, 1972.

There are two questions that the Minister has directed me to answer: first, whether the named persons were employees of the Becker Milk Co. Ltd. (the company) within the meaning of the Employment Standards Act. Secondly, if they were employees, whether the only work performed by them was supervisory or managerial in character.

The starting point for this inquiry must be s. 1 of the *Employment Standards Act*, the interpretation section of the Act. This section includes the following definitions:

1(c) "employee" includes a person who,

(i) performs any work for or supplies any services to an employer,

(ii) does homework for an employer, or

(iii) received any instruction, or training in the activity, business, work, trade, occupation or profession of the employer;

(d) "employer" includes any person who as the owner, proprietor, manager, superintendent, or overseer of any activity, business, work, trade, occupation or profession, has control or direction of, or is directly or indirectly responsible for, the employment of a person therein;

These definitions provide some guidance as to the extent of the statute, indicating that the statute does not apply to all situations where a person supplies work or services. The Act expressly states that these services must be supplied to an "employer" in order for a person to be considered as an employee. The definition of "employer" appears to contemplate a relationship in which some control is directed or asserted over the person rendering services. This control test is the traditional test used to distinguish between the employment situation and the situation where work or services are supplied by an independent contractor. Consequently, it appears that the *Employment Standards Act* does exclude from its ambit those persons in the business of supplying services.

This interpretation appears consistent with the purposes of the legislation. The *Employment Standards Act* is legislation establishing minimum standards of employment for the Province of Ontario. The statute governs such matters as hours of work, overtime pay, minimum wages, equal pay for equal work, vacations with pay, and termination of employment. The subject-matter of the legislation indicates that the Legislature did not contemplate the regulation of the supply of services by independent businessmen but, rather, was concerned with those situations where the supplier of services was tied to another by an employment relationship.

The next step is to determine the factors indicating whether a person supplying work or services is doing so as an independent businessman, not as an employee. Since the Act provides no guidance on this matter, it is necessary to examine how this question has been answered in other contexts, and then to determine whether these answers are appropriate to the present situation. The case of *Montreal v. Montreal Locomotive Works Ltd. et. al.*, . . . a case concerning liability for municipal taxation, appears to represent the landmark decision on the question of when a person can be said to be carrying on business independently. In delivering the judgment of the board, Lord Wright states that this question can be answered by the application of a fourfold test . . . :

> . . . In earlier cases a single test, such as the presence or absence of control, was often relied on to determine whether the case was one of master and servant, mostly in order to decide issues of tortious liability on the part of the master or superior. In the more complex conditions of modern industry, more complicated tests have often to be applied. It has been suggested that a fourfold test would in some cases be more appropriate, a complex involving (1) control; (2) ownership of the tools; (3) chance of profit; (4) risk of loss. Control in itself is not always conclusive. Thus the master of a chartered vessel is generally the employer (sic) of the shipowner though the charterer can direct the employment of the vessel. Again the law often limits the employer's rights to interfere with the employee's conduct, as also do trade union regulations. In many cases the question can only be settled by examining the whole of the various elements which constitute the relationship between the parties. In this way it is in some cases possible to decide the issue by raising as the crucial question . . . whether the party is carrying on the business, in the sense of carrying it on for himself or on his own behalf and not merely for a superior. . . .

The detailed examination of the control component clearly indicates that control must be a relevant consideration when determining the applicability of the Employment Standards Act. It appears reasonable that minimum employment standards should only be imposed where a person does in fact control the work situation of another. . . .

The work situation of the four named persons during the specified periods must now be examined to determine whether these persons were independent businessmen, or merely employees of the company. All four persons were subject to the terms of an employment agreement made between them and the company, in which they agreed to perform services as store managers. In addition, certain aspects of their work situation were governed by operating procedures of the company not specified in the employment agreement.

Looking first at the factors of chance of profit and risk of loss, one is led to the conclusion that the work situations of the four store managers do not contain these factors. The evidence indicates that these persons were not in the business of buying and re-selling goods. All stock handled by these four persons remained the property of the company, with any surplus in inventory accruing to the benefit of the company. On the other hand, the store managers were allowed an allowance of $2 a day for shrinkage due to pilferage or breakage, with any shrinkage exceeding this amount becoming the financial responsibility of the manager. However, the store manager was not responsible for a loss of inventory resulting from theft due to break-ins. This limited accountability for loss of inventory does not appear to provide the element of risk of loss that was contemplated by Lord Wright, since it cannot be said that the store managers were engaged in any real entrepreneurial exercise. On the contrary, the accountability for loss of stock points to a significant degree of control being exercised by the company over the store manager.

Another risk faced by the company managers is the possibility that they may forfeit a $1,000 performance bond delivered to the company upon the execution of the employment agreement. Under the agreement, the company has the right to set off against the bond any liability to the company resulting from a default under the agreement. Furthermore, if the manager fails to give the company seven days' notice of his intention to quit, the company is entitled to recover the full amount of the bond as liquidated damage for loss of profits and good will. The risk of losing the performance bond, however, does not necessarily mean that the element of risk of loss contemplated by Lord Wright is present in this situation. It would appear that the performance bond is one method by which the company asserts control over the store manager. Consequently, the performance bond can hardly be said to point to the fact that the store managers are independent entrepreneurs.

Ownership of the tools is the next factor to be considered. Under the arrangement between the company and the store manager, the company retains ownership of the place of business, the fixtures contained in that place of business and all merchandise sold at that place of business. Furthermore, the retail sales tax licence for each location is taken out in the name of the company, not in the name of the store manager. Not surprisingly, the company also holds the insurance policy on all the assets. Finally, even the shirts and aprons worn by the store manager and his assistants are owned by the company, with the company supplying laundering at its expense. These facts clearly indicate that the store managers do not supply any of the tools of the trade, but merely provide their own labour.

Although three branches of Lord Wright's fourfold test indicate that the store managers are not independent businessmen, this is not conclusive of the matter. The company submits that, due to the absence of control, the store manager is still a person in the business of contracting his own labour rather than acting as an employee. It was argued by the company that the store manager had a discretion to determine his hours of work, that the store manager was free to hire others to assist him, and that he had a discretion in the ordering of goods.

Although hours of work are not specified in the employment agreement, Mr. Harold Keene, manager of store operations for the company testified that it was company policy that the stores be open from 9 a.m. to 11 p.m., seven days a week. Article 6 of the employment agreement requires the store manager to devote his whole time to his duties as store manager and prohibits him from engaging in any other business without the written consent of the company. Mr. Keene testified that in his experience there had never been a case where a manager had engaged in any other business. Since the arrangement between the manager and the company requires that the manager devote 100% of his working time to the interests of the company, it must be concluded that the store manager is in over-all responsibility for his store during the hours that it is open. The evidence also indicates that the duties required of the store manager would necessitate his presence at the store for most of the time in which the store was open. Thus, the store manager's actual discretion to control his hours of work is very slight.

Under the employment agreement, however, the manager is given a discretion to hire assistants. Article 7 of the agreement states:

> The manager will, at all times, employ sufficient help to be approved by and subject to the continued approval of Becker's to conduct the business in a manner satisfactory to Becker's and the manager shall at all times be responsible for the actions and conduct of such employees while in the manager's store. The total wages for said help are to be paid from the earnings of the manager. The above mentioned wages, if not paid in full, together with any and all invoices for merchandise received by and not charged to the manager, all unsaleable merchandise in said store, all damages or missing equipment, or any obligation upon Becker's arising because of the action or non-action of the manager, shall become a liability of the manager due and owing to Becker's at time of termination of this contract.

The company argued that this discretion to hire, fire, and supervise store help made the store manager an employer himself, leading to the conclusion that he was an independent businessman. The evidence indicated that store managers did in fact have a fairly wide discretion in hiring, at times hiring friends or family informally without obtaining the formal approval of the company. On the other hand, the company's supervisors would often provide advice to store managers on the suitability of certain persons as store help. Furthermore, under company operating procedures, the manager was required to fill out a store help registration form for each person employed as store help, although at times this procedure does not seem to have been enforced. The company then assumed responsibility for the administration of payment to the store help, even though the payment was ultimately deducted from the remuneration of the manager. Moreover, the company interest in the store help extended beyond the provision of these administrative services. In the regular inspections carried out by the company supervisors and shoppers, the appearance and manner of store help was one factor taken into account. Furthermore, the company did provide the uniform to be worn by the store help and also provided for the laundering of these uniforms.

In view of the control asserted over store help by the company, it must be concluded that the store help are in fact employees of the company, not of the store managers. The mere fact that payment of store help is deducted from the remuneration of the managers cannot be conclusive. The reality of the situation contradicts any appearance that might be created by this form of payment. On the facts, it appears clear that the company had a direct hand in both the selection and retention of store help. Consequently, it cannot be said that the store managers are in the business of providing man-power services for the company. The fact that at times the company assumed responsibility for the administration of payments to the store help, and the fact that at all times the company also asserted some degree of supervisory control over the store help can only lead to the conclusion that the company is the real employer of such persons.

The company also argued that the discretion of the store manager in ordering inventory pointed to the fact that he was an independent businessman. The evidence indicated that the store manager did possess some discretion in this area, as he was responsible for keeping the store fully stocked. This discretion, however, was a limited one, since the store manager could only order from certain suppliers designated by the company. In addition, with respect to the ordering of cigarettes, the store manager had little discretion since the company asserted very close control over store inventories of such a high value item. Consequently, it appears clear that the discretion possessed by store managers was no greater than that possessed by employees who exercised a purchasing function.

There are a number of other factors weighing against the company argument that the store managers are merely in the business of supplying their labour to the company. In most cases, persons employed by the company as store managers were trained initially by the company, indicating that this is not the situation of a skilled labourer in the business of contracting out his labour. Moreover, the fact that the store manager cannot work for anyone else without the permission of the company reinforces the conclusion that the store managers were not contractors of labour.

Secondly, close control is asserted by the company over the store manager by a very efficient accounting system. Store managers are made accountable for both cash and inventory. By an arrangement with the banks, the company insures that a cash deposit is made daily. Inventory checks are carried out on a monthly basis, sometimes more frequently. Frequent visits are paid to the various outlets by both supervisors and shoppers. All of these facts indicate that the company is not only concerned with achieving a particular result, but also with the manner in which that result is achieved.

Thirdly, the company, under the employment agreement, has a broad power to terminate the relationship with the store manager. Article 14 of the agreement provides that the agreement with the manager can be terminated at any time, whether for cause or not. As a result, the company could terminate the relationship for such matters as insubordination, dishonesty, absenteeism as well as for the reason that the job was not being properly performed. The evidence indicates that the company did use this legal leverage to assert close control over the store managers.

Weighing all the elements of the work situation, it must be concluded that the four store managers were not acting as independent businessmen. . . .

The second question required to be answered is whether the only work performed by these employees is supervisory or managerial in character. Unfortunately, the *Employment Standards Act* provides no guidance in answering this question. Section 14(2) of the Act merely states that:

> 14(2) Subsection 1 [the maximum hours section] does not apply to an employee whose only work is supervisory or managerial in character, or of a character exempted by the regulations.

Some guidance to what constitutes a managerial or supervisory employee is found in the jurisprudence of the Ontario Labour Relations Board.

The *Falconbridge* decision indicates that supervision of other employees is a primary *indicia* of the managerial employee. This factor, however, is not the only one that must be considered. Some employees can clearly be considered managerial, even though they do not exercise any direct authority over other employees. Such persons may be given a wide discretion to conduct business on behalf of their employer, so that it must be said that they are engaged in actually managing the employer's operation. For example, an employee with a wide responsibility for making purchases on behalf of his employer could be said to be exercising a managerial function.

Examining the facts in this case, it can be said that the four named persons did exercise certain managerial functions. As was stated earlier, these persons did have some discretion in the hiring, firing and supervision of store help. Although this discretion does not lead to the conclusion that they are independent businessmen, it does lead us to conclude that these persons are given the responsibility to supervise other employees. Furthermore, on the facts, these persons did have considerable discretion in ordering inventory for the company, pointing to the exercise of another type of managerial function.

On the other hand, the four store managers also performed a wide range of tasks that were not managerial or supervisory in nature. The evidence indicated that the store manager performed such duties as waiting on customers, stacking the shelves, and maintaining the cleanliness of the premises. This type of work is clearly not managerial or supervisory in nature. Thus, the employment situation was one containing managerial and non-managerial elements in almost equal proportions.

The question is whether all of the work performed by the store managers must be managerial in order to fall within the s. 14(2) exception [now repealed]. The use of the adjective "only" to modify "work" indicates that the exception is a narrow one. The plain meaning of the words used indicate that work must be exclusively managerial or supervisory in order to fall within the exception. Thus, in answer to the second question, it cannot be said that the only work of the four named persons during the specified periods was supervisory or managerial in character.

＊ ＊ ＊

On judicial review, designee Carter's decision was upheld by the majority of the Divisional Court of Ontario, sub nom *Re Becker Milk Co.* (1973), 41 D.L.R. (3d) 503 (Ont. Div. Ct.), on the basis that he made no error of law. In a dissenting judgment, Fraser J. said, at pages 506–7:

Instead of directing his mind to the question remitted to him, i.e., whether the respondents were employees within the statutory definition contained in the Act, the designee directed it to the question of whether they were independent contractors within the criteria laid down for such a determination by cases decided under common law, under civil law, or under statutes containing definitions of "employee" and "employer" entirely different from those in the Act. In my opinion, he asked himself the wrong question and there is error in law on the face of the record.

＊ ＊ ＊

Even if a worker is an employee within the meaning of an employment standards statute, he or she may belong to one of the many occupational groups that are excluded from the statute's coverage or are treated less advantageously than other employees with respect to particular benefits. For example, in Ontario the Act does not apply, either in whole or in part, to: inmates in correctional institutions; persons enrolled in "workfare" programs; judges; members of the clergy; agricultural workers; domestic workers; and members of self-regulating professions such as lawyers, doctors, and architects. The reasons for these exclusions vary. Lawyers and doctors are regulated by their own legislation and self-governing institutions and are seen as capable of setting their own terms and conditions of employment for their members. At the other end of the economic scale, domestic and agricultural workers are excluded from minimum wage and overtime provisions because lawmakers have decided that these employment relationships are not amenable to the restrictions imposed by the Act. Such exclusions have been criticized for denying basic statutory protections to groups that need them most.

In addition, an individual employer may be able to apply for a temporary or ongoing permit to vary some of the provisions of the Act with respect to its work force.

It is necessary to check very carefully the statute and associated regulations of each jurisdiction, for the exclusions and exemptions can be difficult to identify and are often of more than peripheral importance. The Donner Report (section 12:400 below) found that in 1985, 20 to 25 percent of the paid workforce in Ontario was covered by a provincial permit granting an employer an exclusion or an exemption.

The following decision shows the importance of such exclusions and exemptions.

Renaud (Re), [1999] B.C.E.S.T.D. No. 462 (B.C. Employment Standards Tribunal)

JAMIESON, Adjudicator

OVERVIEW

This decision deals with an appeal brought against a Determination issued on June 3, 1999, wherein the Director found that Mike Renaud owed $27,566.07 being overtime wages, statutory holiday pay and compensation for length of service to Ms. Candice Spivey whom he had hired as a personal care attendant. The grounds for the appeal . . . is basically that the Director erred in finding that Ms. Spivey was not a "live-in home support worker" or a "sitter" as defined in the Employment Standards Act Regulation (the Regulation) and thereby excluded from Employment Standards Act (the Act), or at least from the entitlement to overtime pay.

. . .

FACTS

Mike Renaud is a ventilator-dependent complete quadriplegic who requires personal care attendance on a 24 hour basis. His condition came about as a result of a motor vehicle accident.

Ms. Spivey was hired and paid directly by Mr. Renaud as a personal care attendant and she worked from September 30, 1998 to February 28, 1999. Ms. Spivey held no qualifications for this type of work and was trained on the job during the first two or three weeks she was there by Mrs. Nancy Renaud, Mike Renaud's mother.

Ms. Spivey worked at Mr. Renaud's residence three days per week, Sunday, Wednesday and Friday. The daily hours were 24 hours from 8.00 a.m. on the reporting day until 8:00 a.m. the following morning. Ms. Spivey was paid on the basis of a 13 hour day at the hourly rate of $16.00 per hour. The other 11 hours were considered to be her rest period. However, she was on call during the night to attend Mr. Renaud's needs. To facilitate this, Ms. Spivey slept on a couch in the living room at night and, in the event this becomes a consideration later, she was not charged for board and room.

The duties performed by Ms. Spivey included typical care giver functions such as bathing, dressing, feeding, lifting from bed to chair, chair to bed, tidying up and generally being there to help if an emergency arose. Other daily duties involved trachea care, suctioning, bowel care and changing the condom catheter. Ms. Spivey also accompanied Mr. Renaud on outings, doing the driving in his specially equipped vehicle to places like movies, shopping and to restaurants and bars.

In the Determination under review, the Director's Delegate concluded that on the basis of the foregoing facts, Ms. Spivey was not a "live-in home support worker" a "night attendant" or, a "residential care worker," which are all excluded by the Regulation from the hours of work and overtime provisions of the Act.

The Delegate then went to address the definition of work:

One other definition under the Act needs to be examined in making a determination in this matter and that is the definition of "work." The complainant has alleged that she was required to be at the employer's place of residence for a 24 hour basis for which she received only 13 hours of pay. The employer states that although she was required to be there for 24 hours per day she wasn't required to perform work during the entire 24 hour period, in other words there was lots of down time that the complainant was not providing services for the employer. The Act defines "work" as follows:

[1 (1)] "work" means the labour or services an employee performs for an employer whether in the employee's residence or elsewhere.

(2) An employee is deemed to be at work while on call at a location designated by the employer unless the designated location is the employee's residence.

The complainant is required to remain at a specific location, that is, the employer's residence. She is required to be at the employer's residence to attend to his needs should they be required. As the complainant is still under the employer's direction and control and not free to pursue her own interests and is at a place designated by the employer she is entitled to be paid for the full 24 hours that she is at the employer's residence.

I find that the complainant is entitled to be paid wages for 24 hours per day while on shift and that she is entitled to overtime wages pursuant to section 40 for all hours in excess of 8 in a day. As the complainant has been paid straight time for 13 hours each day the adjustment will be a half time adjustment for the hours of work between 8 and

11 hours per day and straight time for the hours between 11 and 13 hours. All hours in excess of 13 hours are owing at double time.

THE APPEAL

. . .

. . . Mr. Renaud submits that Ms. Spivey was a sitter as defined in the Regulation, and thus excluded from the Act:

> "sitter" means a person employed in a private residence solely to provide the service of attending to a child, or to a disabled, infirm or other person, but does not include a nurse, domestic, therapist, live-in home support worker or an employee of
> a) a business that is engaged in providing that service, or
> b) a day care facility;"

In support of this position Mr. Renaud points out that Ms. Spivey does not fit into any of the exclusions in the definition, not being a nurse, therapist etc., and that she was employed in a private residence solely for the purpose of attending to the needs of a disabled or infirm person.

In response dated July 9, 1999, Candice Spivey, through Counsel, . . . denies she was a sitter within the meaning of the Regulation. In this respect, Ms. Spivey emphasizes that she was a full-time employee who was required to stay at the Renaud home 24 hours per day during which she provided much more than sitting services.

. . .

A major theme of the argument on Mr. Renaud's behalf goes to the amount Candice Spivey would earn if the Determination is upheld. This works out to about $600.00 per day, which is absurd according to Mr. Renaud, considering that the minimum daily wage for live-in home support workers under the Act is $70.00 per day. He submits that the money he has been allowed for this type of care would last only a few years instead of a lifetime if he is forced to pay these kinds of wages. This would result in him having to rely on government assistance programs which in his opinion could mean a loss of dignity and independence.

In response to this, Counsel for Ms. Spivey suggests that it is an option for Mr. Renaud to employ three care attendants for eight hour shifts and thus avoid paying overtime rates.

. . .

ANALYSIS

Despite the differences in the evidence regarding the duties and functions Ms. Spivey actually performed and the number of hours worked, the summary of duties set out earlier in this decision will suffice for my purposes. While she may or may not have performed some of these duties on a regular basis, it fairly represents what the job generally required. Moreover, the fact that Ms. Spivey was required to be there for a full twenty-four hour shift, three times per week, for which she was paid thirteen hours at a straight-time rate of $16.00 per hour is undisputed.

While the central issues here are clearly whether Candice Spivey was a . . . sitter, I believe that it would be helpful in this case to take a brief look at where all of these differently defined classes of employees in the care attendant field fit into the overall statutory scheme of the Act and the Regulation.

"night attendant" means a person who,

(a) is provided with sleeping accommodation in a private residence owned or leased or otherwise occupied by a disabled person or by a member of the disabled person's family, and

(b) is employed in the private residence, for periods of 12 hours or less in any 24 hour period, primarily to provide the disabled person with care and attention during the night,

but does not include a person employed in a hospital or nursing home or in a facility designated as a community care facility under the Community Care Facility Act or as a Provincial mental health facility under the Mental Health Act or in a facility operated under the Continuing Care Act;

"residential care worker" means a person who,

(a) is employed to supervise or care for anyone in a group home or family type residential dwelling, and

(b) is required by the employer to reside on the premises during periods of employment, but does not include a foster parent, live-in home support worker, domestic or night attendant; . . .

Under Section 34 of the Regulation, live-in home support workers, night attendants and residential care workers are excluded from the hours of work and overtime requirements of Part 4 of the Act.

The basis for these exclusions would appear to be the common requirement for some degree of residency at the place of employment in these jobs, coupled with the long hours that employees in this field are considered to be on duty, while they may only be required to perform specific duties periodically. This makes it extremely difficult to distinguish actual working hours from down time.

Accordingly, Section 16(1) of the Regulation sets a daily minimum wage of $70.00 for live-in home support workers and Section 22 of the Regulation requires that residential care workers be allowed eight (8) consecutive hours as a rest period. For each interruption of this rest period, residential care workers must receive the greater of two (2) hours at the regular rate of pay or pay for the actual hours of work caused by the interruption.

Sitters are of course, excluded from the Act itself, by virtue of Section 32 (1) (c) of the Regulation.

. . .

Looking at the Determination under review against that background, I must agree with the Delegate's conclusion that Ms. Spivey does not fall within the definitions of a live-in home support worker [defined as a person who is paid through a government program], a night attendant or, a residential care worker.

. . .

Dealing now with whether Ms. Spivey was a sitter and thereby excluded from the Act, I note that nowhere in the Determination does the Delegate entertain the possibility that the arrangements between Mr. Renaud and Ms. Spivey could fall within the definition of a "sitter." I will not speculate as to why not.

In any event, in light of the argument here about Ms. Spivey providing services beyond those contemplated by the definition of a sitter, and what was said in [*R. v. Mills*] . . . , regarding the meaning of "attend," this aspect of the definition has to be revisited to determine if there really is a meaningful distinction between providing "care and attention" and "attending."

Using Webster's Revised Unabridged Dictionary, (1998, Micra Inc.) and Webster's New World Thesaurus, it is readily apparent that the full meaning of attend goes well beyond waiting on, escorting or accompanying, especially when used in the context of health care attendants.

Attending, which is the actual term used in the definition of sitter, includes, "the work of caring for or attending to someone or something." Conversely, care also includes "the work of caring for or attending to someone or something." Clearly, for the purposes of giving the words in the definition their plain and ordinary meaning, these terms must be taken to be synonymous.

Consequently, Ms. Spivey cannot be eliminated from being a sitter on the basis of the argument that she did more than simply attend to Mr. Renaud's needs as interpreted in the Mills case. In fact, taking the evidence as a whole, sketched against the plain language of the text in the definition of a sitter in the Regulation, it is difficult to avoid the reality that Ms. Spivey falls squarely within this definition, i.e., she was hired to work in a private residence, solely to provide the service of attending to Mr. Renaud, who is a disabled or infirm person.

Granted, Ms. Spivey worked on more than a casual basis, which the Director says should be a persuasive factor against her being found to be a sitter. However, if we look back to [the Thompson Report] at pages 73 & 74, where sitters are discussed, it can be seen that this concern was specifically addressed:

> A sitter is defined as a person employed in a private residence solely to provide the service of attending to a child, or to a disabled, infirm or other person, but does not include a nurse, therapist, domestic, homemaker or an employee of a business providing that service or a day care facility. The Commission heard that the intent of this section was to exclude the occupation traditionally known as "babysitter" provided by school age children and adults.
>
> The Commission also learned that some live out domestics think that they are not covered by the Act because they or their employers believe that they are sitters as defined in the Act. Recommendations in this Report concerning domestics raised the matter of the relationship of their work with sitters. The intent of these recommendations is to ensure that they cannot be converted to the status of "sitters" at the end of the regular working day. The Report does not intend to extend coverage to persons providing services for children, parents or immediate family members on a casual basis. Minimum

standards of employment should be available for employees who provide personal care services on more than casual basis. The same distinction used for newspaper carriers and part-time employees, i.e., 15 hours per week, is appropriate to separate casual and regular work.

. . .

The Commission then went on to recommend that a person who provides personal care services for 15 hours or less per week should be excluded from the Act.

Obviously, had this recommendation been adopted, the distinction that the Director asks me to imply between casual care givers and people who work more than on a casual basis, would appear in the Regulation. However, for whatever reasons, the recommendation was not adopted and I cannot read into the Regulation what is not there.

Consequently, I find myself in the same position as the Adjudicator in Dolfi. Being every bit as bound by the plain language of the definition of sitter, I must find albeit reluctantly, in the given circumstances that Ms. Spivey was indeed a sitter as defined in the Regulation and thus excluded from the minimum standards of employment prescribed by the Act.

Accordingly, the appeal must succeed. . . . the Determination in question is hereby cancelled in its entirety.

12:400 HOURS OF WORK AND OVERTIME

There are three current issues of pressing public concern in relation to the regulation of hours of work under employment standards legislation. First, there is the paradox that full-time employees in some occupations are working extremely long hours while other people are either unemployed or working fewer hours per week than they would like. Second, there is a growing demand among many employees for more flexible hours of work than the traditional forty-hour week allows, and for access to more flexible leaves of absence for educational, family, and other purposes. Third, employees who work part-time (usually defined as twenty-four or fewer hours per week) are generally treated less favourably under their employment contracts than full-timers. They usually receive less pay, they often are not entitled to fringe benefits such as medical and dental insurance and pensions, and have encountered even greater difficulties than full-timers in enforcing their statutory rights.

These issues were addressed in the following report.

Report of the Advisory Group on Working Time and the Distribution of Work (Ottawa: Supply and Services Canada, 1994) (Chair: Arthur Donner) at 15–21, 24–25

The paradox of our times is that many Canadians today work long hours while many others have no work at all. Increasingly, people who want full-time, permanent employment have to settle for part-time, temporary or seasonal work. This form of "underemployment" is as troubling as unemployment, since more and more people are relying on these nonstandard or contingent jobs.

Counting both full-time and part-time employment, the typical work week of Canadians has been declining gradually to the current average of 37 hours. This is slightly lower than the standard work week; i.e., the legislated "norm" in each province, which for most Canadians is 40 hours a week or more. But statistics can be deceiving. The prime reason for the decline in average hours of work has been that so many more people are working part-time. Full-time workers have retained virtually the same average usual work week (just over 42 hours a week) since 1975. Those working part-time average about 15 hours per week.

Two patterns have recently emerged. First, actual hours worked by some full-time workers are now on the increase. Second, most of the new jobs created in Canada have been part-time employment, while most of the loss during the last two recessions has been in full-time work. As a result, today 23 percent of all jobs in the Canadian labour market are part-time, compared with only 14 percent in 1975. . . .

In the middle of a protracted period of high unemployment, it is ironic that large numbers of people in convenience stores, on assembly lines, behind retail counters, in secretarial pools, in management and professional offices are working considerably longer than 40 hours per week. If finding a more equitable distribution of work is the goal, those working long hours and short hours become the principal focal points for change.

One significant element ties those who have too little or no work to those who have too much: increasingly, their situations are involuntary. In turn, this takes its toll not just on people's personal lives but on society as a whole. More Canadians are experiencing increased stress whether due to a time crunch or a money crunch. . . .

With more adults in the family working than worked 20 years ago (especially parents of young children) finding the appropriate balance between work and everything else is becoming more of a daily challenge. Could a better allocation of working time relieve current tensions, with more family time, more time for learning, and more leisure time for those now working and more working time and income for those now unemployed or underemployed?

The Changing Patterns of Working Time

The relationship between employer and employee has undergone very considerable changes in the last generation. New work arrangements are eclipsing yesterday's model of a stable working life. Among the contributing factors and developments are the growth of irregular work shifts, the importance of high fixed costs for some employers, and the impact of technological change on working time. . . .

Polarization

We have seen that, while Canadians work an average of 37 hours a week, this is a result of two distinct trends. More jobs offer only short hours, more jobs seem to require longer hours. Together these trends are squeezing out jobs with traditionally normal weekly hours.

The situation reflects the current state of the labour market: more jobs are part-time; more women are balancing paid work with work in the home; more people are self-employed; more workplaces are getting by with lower staffing levels; and both paid and unpaid overtime work are on the increase. It also reflects economic realities. The service sector predominates in the economy and it has the highest concentrations of part-time work. Hours of work are also increasing in some sectors because of competitive pressures and opportunities. Business cycles also have an impact, with longer hours when the economy is expanding and shorter hours when it is in recession. Finally, more people hold more than one job, and this is one reflection of the polarization problems.

In 1976, 71 percent of the work force worked between 35 and 40 hours a week. By 1993, with the increase in part-time workers and those putting in unusually long hours, the proportion of regular-hour workers had dropped substantially. What is striking is the rapid increase in people, particularly men, working very long hours. By July 1994, 22 percent of all employed males were putting in 50 hours or more per week, up from 17 percent in 1976. The "50+ hour club" of workers is at the heart of the discussions that follow. Clearly, the trend toward polarization has a gender bias. Of the 2.1 million Canadians working fewer than 30 hours a week in 1993, more than two-thirds (69 percent) were women. When the job involves long hours, however, the proportions are completely reversed: 70 percent of those working 50 or more hours are adult males.

Polarized hours of work mean polarization of opportunity and income. This is one of the chief explanations for the growing economic inequality in Canadian society. People who work long hours are more likely to have high incomes.

This group often works in sectors where employers — driven by cost considerations, skill availability, and concern for flexibility — want to use their skilled work force to the maximum. Paid overtime among hourly workers tends to be concentrated in resource industries, heavy manufacturing, communications, and transportation: industries that are largely male dominated. These occupational groups are most likely to be paid above average wages to begin with, many as unionized workers earning good hourly wages and significant overtime pay. Professionals and managers, who may or may not be paid overtime, also tend to work long hours.

But in addition to those relatively well-paid, there are others who are scrambling to make enough to get by who are working long hours. This second cluster of workers includes those who are so poorly paid on an hourly basis that they are forced to work extremely long hours to make ends meet. A high concentration of women work in these activities. With hours becoming more variable, as is increasingly the case in the retail and service sectors, workers are often forced to take on more than one job to ensure survival from week to week. About 6 percent of the labour force now hold more than one part-time job.

Finally, some people work long hours on a temporary or seasonal basis, alternating with long periods of unemployment, for example in food processing, construction, fisheries, and forestry. These sectors have distinctive production-oriented demands on labour time which, in many cases, are difficult to alter.

The greatest concern lies in the long hours worked throughout the year on a regular basis in non-seasonal sectors. For example, industries such as auto, steel, mining, and managerial and professional occupations traditionally rely heavily on regular long hours. This raises questions about the culture of long hours and the degree to which Canadians should re-examine the hours they work annually.

We turn now to the seemingly ironic phenomenon of increasing paid and unpaid overtime in an economy currently hobbled by double-digit rates of unemployment.

Paid Overtime

Those working long hours consist of two groups: those paid for overtime and those unpaid. In general, the two groups break down into hourly workers, who get paid overtime, and salaried workers, who often work unpaid overtime (assuming that their "normal" work week is in the 40-hour range).

The situation is more ambiguous for salaried workers, however. Some have defined hours of work and are entitled to overtime pay, although some in this group have difficulty in accessing that pay. There also exists a layer of senior managerial or professional workers whose hours of work are basically undefined.

Under statutory requirements, the employer is commonly obligated to pay overtime at 1.5 times the regular rate of pay once the legislated number of 11 standard-hours has been worked. However, this varies considerably across Canada. Collective agreements may also specify a higher premium and/or an earlier daily or weekly trigger for such pay.

Even in the depth of the last recession, in November 1991, 800,000 Canadians (6.5 percent of the labour force) worked overtime for pay. On average these people worked nearly eight extra hours a week. To provide a sense of the scale of this phenomenon, that is 6.4 million hours of overtime worked in Canada every week. Evidence in North America and Europe shows that, where working-time reductions are sustained and meaningful, about half the reduced time translates ultimately into new jobs. Thus if only one-half of those 6.4 million hours were converted directly into new full-time jobs, it could mean up to 80,000 additional persons employed full-time, full-year in Canada, with considerable savings to employers. But is that likely?

Overtime trends and layoffs have traditionally been closely connected to peaks and troughs in the demand for goods and services, including the different phases of the business cycle. While Canada's economic recovery from the last recession is certainly well under way, it is not unusual for employers in the early stages of a recovery to rely on overtime rather than additional hirings while they assess how secure the increased demand for their products or services will be. A sustained increase usually will lead to personnel recalls or additional hirings, but the decision will vary from one enterprise to the next.

Over the course of the last recession, some 400,000 manufacturing workers (20 percent of the total) lost their jobs. Manufacturing output has since recovered to pre-recession levels. However, only about 100,000 workers (or one-quarter of those laid off in the recession) had been hired back by manufacturers as of July 1994. Part of the reason is higher productivity, but increased overtime is also part of the story. Hourly paid workers in manufacturing averaged 2.2 hours of paid overtime every week throughout 1993, *matching the peak pre-recession overtime level of 1988.*

Particularly high levels of overtime were regularly worked in transportation equipment (auto, auto parts, aerospace, an average of 3.3 hours per worker in the industry); refining (3 hours); primary metals and machinery industries (2.9 hours); and paper (2.8 hours).

These averages conceal the fact that most overtime is worked by a subgroup who often work very long hours or an extra shift per week. Because the use of overtime in these sectors is quite regular and sustained, it should be possible to convert a proportion of these overtime hours into relatively well-paid new jobs or the rehiring of laid-off workers.

Apart from manufacturing, the highest incidence of paid overtime is in mining. High levels of paid overtime, averaging 11 hours per week for those working the extra time, also occur in utilities and communications, transportation, and construction. These tend to be male-dominated and unionized industries with above-average base rates and arrangements for overtime pay.

On average, men are twice as likely to work overtime as women, and when they do they average longer overtime hours.

In any given week, at least one in 10 male workers in Canada will work paid overtime, compared with only 6 percent of women. Among both men and women, overtime hours peaked for those aged 25 to 34, at a time when many of these workers are starting families.

People in clerical, sales and service occupations where most women work have considerably less opportunity for overtime, whether paid or unpaid. Those women who do work paid overtime are most commonly employed in the health and social services, retail trade, and business services fields. But these occupations tend to have low base rates of pay.

Paid overtime occurs more often among highly paid workers, and most overtime is paid in cash rather than time off. In the private sector, where paid overtime is most prevalent, only one in six collective agreements has provision for compensatory time off. . . .

It is not known what proportion of those working paid overtime do so completely voluntarily. Even in the unionized setting, almost two-thirds of collective agreements do not include even the limited right to refuse overtime work. Very few jurisdictions provide it as a legislated right for workers. . . .

Unpaid Overtime

Paid overtime gives only half the picture. Statistics Canada's best estimate is that, in 1991, as many as half a million Canadians worked overtime without pay.

The same survey suggests that a higher proportion of women than men work unpaid overtime. Of women reporting that their actual hours exceeded their usual hours of work, only 43 percent said they had been paid for their overtime. For men, using the same definition of overtime, over half (54 percent) were paid.

These findings are consistent with our earlier observations with respect to fiscal pressures in both the private and public sectors where budgetary cutbacks are making unpaid overtime a regular feature of work practices. This is especially the case in such parapublic sectors as health care, education, and community social services where, despite fiscal restrictions on paid overtime, the urgency of and necessity to provide service prompts workers to put in longer hours just to get the job done.

While long hours are in part driven by economic circumstance, a destructive "long-hours" culture has developed among some workers, largely generated by employment insecurity. Clearly these pressures are prompting employers and employees to work longer hours. But the question arises, is this trend necessary? Or is it a result of an out-dated and inefficient managerial culture?

Many informed human resources practitioners today recognize that a long-hours culture is ultimately counterproductive. In a promising development, some of Canada's leading businesses are stressing the need for senior managers and others to lead by example. . . .

Time and Money: Reactions to the Idea of Fewer Hours of Work

Throughout this chapter the theme of reduced work time has been connected to long-term improvements in standards of living, measured in both income and leisure. Can the redistribution of working time benefit more Canadians in today's climate? This question can be answered only if working time is, again, connected to income.

It has been repeatedly pointed out that the configuration of working hours and the availability of work in general are largely determined by employers and their assessment of the demand for their products or services. The thing that drives business is customers' orders not what working hours might be preferable. That said, working time has changed over the last century and there is clearly still some latitude in how work is organized, even in the highly competitive world of the 1990s.

If there are to be reductions to and a redistribution of working time, working people must feel that such new arrangements would benefit them indirectly. If a more just dis-tribution of work is to occur in society, some people will have to give up the extra hours they now work and often the extra pay as well.

In the only survey of its kind, the Conference Board of Canada asked Canadians in 1985 if they would trade money for time. The ensuing 1987 report, *Hours of Work: Trends and Attitudes in Canada*, is highly suggestive . . . .

At the time of the survey, about a third of Canadians said they preferred to work less time, and a third preferred to work more time. One-third said they would make no change. Of those seeking increased hours worked the vast majority were persons who worked part-time or persons who had low incomes. The preference for reduced working hours was strongest among those with relatively high incomes. For example, among women between the ages of 25 and 34, only about one in five of those with household incomes less than $20,000 would consider reducing work time. But among those in the same group with household incomes of more than $60,000, almost two-thirds said they would forgo income for more time off.

Among those sampled who were interested in reduced hours of work, the most popu-lar option was a four-day week. Taking off more time each year was the second choice, and early retirement the third. The group showed little interest in simply working fewer hours each day. The preference was to "pay for" the reduced work time from future earnings. While some would take the additional leisure time with a commensurate pay reduction, most were not prepared to take an immediate cut in income, even though the relative after-tax cost of reducing work time is considerably less for the well-off than for the poor.

The survey strikingly captures Canadians' "indeterminate" mood regarding working time, at least in the mid-1980s. If it has validity today it strongly suggests that any movement to significantly shorten hours has to be the end result of largely voluntary and prag-matic agreement between the parties themselves in individual workplaces. Whether or not those workplaces are subject to collective bargaining, the voluntary principle remains central to this report. At a time of quickening global competition and increased job polar-ization and insecurity, it ensures that any redistribution or reductions in work time are compatible with the respective responsibilities of employers and employees.

Thus the Advisory Group is not recommending a legislated move to a four or four-and-one-half-day work week. But we anticipate that as Canada moves into the 21st century, and as productivity improvements give rise to annual growth dividends that Canadian employ-ers and employees may share, the momentum towards shorter and more flexible working hours will mount in both the public and private sectors.

[The *Report* is a publication of Human Resources Development Canada. Reproduced with the permission of the Minister of Public Works and Government Services Canada, 1997.]

✻ ✻ ✻

Canadian employment standards statutes follow two approaches to limiting working hours and overtime. The first is the "market" approach, which establishes a definition of "standard working hours" per day, week, or month and requires the employer to pay an overtime premium (usually 50 percent higher than the regular rate of pay) for excess hours worked. Under this approach it is for the employer to decide whether overtime assignments are cost-effective. The second approach also specifies a threshold above which an overtime premium is payable, but goes further by setting a maximum number of hours that can be worked in a defined period, which the parties cannot exceed even if they want to. Some provinces combine features of both approaches in their legislation.

Some employers face irregular production cycles (as in the trucking industry) or unusual labour and product marketing conditions that regularly call for working hours above the statutory ceiling or overtime threshold. To protect such employers from incur-ring undue labour costs, most provinces have a system for granting permits to exempt them from the usual statutory restrictions. However, the employee's need for adequate time off work must also be taken into account.

Generally, a permit is granted at the discretion of the provincial ministry of labour. As was noted above, section 12:300, in 1985, 20 to 25 percent of the paid workforce in Ontario was covered by some kind of permit. British Columbia's Thompson Report, below, section 12:500, recommended that a vote of the affected employees be held before a permit was issued, with 65 percent having to be in favour. Such a requirement, which already exists in some provinces, would help to meet the concern that permits are sometimes granted as a result of political lobbying rather than for reasons of economic necessity.

The *Report of the Advisory Group on Working Time and the Distribution of Work* makes the following recommendations, at page 65:

6) The Advisory Group notes that marked disparities exist in the legislated standard work week across Canada. We recommend that the legislated standard work week be no longer than 40 hours per week in any jurisdiction.

7) The Advisory Group recommends that federal and provincial governments periodically review the legislated standard work week to ensure that the standard moves with the normal full-time work week in their jurisdiction.

8) The Advisory Group recommends that employees be given the right to refuse overtime work after the legislated standard work week of 40 hours and that this right be incorporated into employment standards legislation.

9) The Advisory Group recommends that employers and employees utilize time off in lieu of overtime pay after the standard work week.

Before it was amended in 2000, the Ontario *Employment Standards Act* set the maximum number of hours an employee could work at forty-eight per week. The new Act raises this maximum to sixty, but only where the employee agrees to work those hours. The Act now requires overtime pay for hours worked in excess of forty-four per week or, if the employee agrees, by compensation in the form of one and one-half hours of paid time off for each hour of overtime worked. It is notable that the Act now makes the extent of its protections concerning hours of work and overtime heavily contingent upon written or oral agreements between individual employees and the employer. Some have questioned whether that is consistent with the most commonly accepted purpose of employment standards legislation — to create minimum statutory standards to protect society's most vulnerable workers from some of the consequences of the inequality of bargaining power that often results from unrestrained market forces.

Reforms to legislation on hours of work must also consider flexible working arrangements and leaves of absence. Canadian employment standards acts provide for three major types of leaves of absence: annual paid vacations; designated paid holidays; and maternity, parental, and adoption leaves. Employers do not have to pay wages to employees on maternity, parental, or adoption leave. Instead, for employees who qualify for federal payments, the federal employment insurance fund provides a percentage of insurable earnings during the leave; it is for the employer to decide whether to top up the difference. (See the *Employment Insurance Act*, S.C. 1996, c. 23, sections 22, 23.) Leaves of absence for other reasons, such as a death in the family or voting in an election, are also commonly provided for by statute.

There is increasing recognition that the traditional system for providing leaves of absence fails to address the need of many Canadian workers for more flexible working hours. The federal government has recently increased the combined period of maternity and parental benefits to fifty weeks; some provinces have legislatively increased periods of leave to correspond with these entitlements. The Ontario statute now provides for ten days of annual emergency leave without pay for employees who need to take care of a spouse, child, same-sex partner, or other family member, but only where the employer has at least fifty employees.

Legislation on hours of work must also take into account the unique problems associated with part-time and other atypical work. It has long been known that part-time work is proliferating in the modern economy, that part-timers generally have inferior wages, fringe benefits, and career development opportunities, and that women are heavily concentrated in part-time occupations. Other forms of atypical work such as home-based work, temporary work, and self-employment contracting are also increasing. In 1994 the Advisory Group Report had this to say about atypical forms of work (at page 65):

12) The Advisory Group recommends that employment standards be vigorously enforced, especially for part-time workers and those outside the normal workplace environment. Special attention should be paid to non-standard workers to ensure that they are fully covered and protected under employment standards, have access to collective bargaining rights, and receive at least the minimum hourly wage and other workplace-related social benefits.

13) The Advisory Group recommends that a registry be created in all jurisdictions to cover employees who work at home. Employers would be obliged to provide information on hours of work and pay for their home-based employees. It should include a mechanism to enable employees to register and to verify the accuracy of the information about their hours of work and their pay.

14) The Advisory Group recommends that employers be required to provide prorated benefits to regularly employed part-time employees.

* * *

In British Columbia, the 1994 Thompson Report (*Rights and Responsibilities in a Changing Workplace: A Review of Employment Standards in British Columbia* [Victoria, B.C.: Ministry of Skills, Training and Labour]), at page 101, recommended the following reforms to the law relating to part-timers:

The Commission recommends that employees who work 15 hours or more for an employer continuously for 6 months or more should be eligible for proportional coverage by all nonstatutory fringe benefits available to full-time employees, except for pensions. Eligibility for pensions will be regulated by the *Pension Benefits Standards Act*. Part-time employees will be responsible for paying the costs of fringe benefit coverage not borne by employers. Employers should have no liability to pay wages in lieu of fringe benefit coverage for employees who are not eligible or who choose not to accept coverage. The Ministry should have the authority to grant variances to this requirement under appropriate circumstances.

* * *

Currently, only Saskatchewan has legislated mandatory prorated benefits for part-time workers, under the complex provisions in sections 23–26 of the *Labour Standards Regulations 1995*, R.R.S. c.L.-1, Reg. 5, Sask. Gaz. enacted pursuant to section 45.1 of the *Labour Standards Act*.

Ontario has a registration system for "homeworkers." These are individuals who perform paid work in their own homes, not cleaners or caregivers who work in the homes of others. Before the enactment of the Ontario *Employment Standards Act*, 2000, it was unlawful for employers to hire a person to do defined homework without obtaining a permit from the Director of Employment Standards. The current Act has eliminated the permit requirement, but in sections 15(2) and 15(6) it does require employers to maintain a register with information about homeworkers for three years after the employment relationship ends.

Implementing legislation on hours of work has also presented special difficulties in the organized workplace. The following demonstrates the difficulty of cross-regime thinking on the part of decision makers.

Re Falconbridge Nickel Mines Ltd. (1983), 42 O.R. (2d) 179 at 180–87, 195-201 (C.A.)

GOODMAN J.A. (dissenting): Sudbury Mine, Mill & Smelter Workers' Union, Local 598 ("the union") appeals from the order of the Divisional Court dated January 18, 1982, pursuant to leave granted by order of this court dated March 1, 1982. The Divisional Court order quashed the decision, dated July 13, 1981, of Rory F. Egan, a referee appointed pursuant to the provisions of the *Employment Standards Act, 1974* (Ont.), c. 112, wherein he found that Falconbridge Nickel Mines Limited ("the employer") had failed to comply with s. 25(1) of the Act by failing to pay overtime rates to employees who worked in the employer's smelter for all hours worked in excess of 44 hours in any period of seven consecutive days.

The facts which gave rise to these proceedings are as follows. The director of employment standards, having received a report from an employment standards officer to the effect that the employer may have failed to comply with s. 25(1) of the Act by failing to pay overtime pay to employees employed at its Sudbury smelter, appointed the referee on May 26, 1981, to conduct a hearing, pursuant to the provisions of s. 51 of the Act. The hearing was held on June 26, 1981.

The provisions of s. 25 of the *Employment Standards Act, 1974* (now RSO 1980, c. 137, s. 25) are as follows:

25 (1) Except as otherwise provided in the regulations, where an employee works for an employer in excess of forty-four hours in any week, he shall be paid for each hour worked in excess of forty-four hours overtime pay at an amount not less than one and one-half times the regular rate of the employee.

(2) In complying with subsection (1), no employer shall reduce the regular rate of wages payable to an employee.

(3) Where an employer has not made and kept complete and accurate records in respect of an employee pursuant to clause II(1)(a), an employment standards officer may determine the regular rate of and the number of hours worked by the employee in each day and week.

The circumstances which gave rise to the issues before the referee had their origin in the introduction by the employer in the spring of 1978 of a four-crew schedule operating in a four-week cycle. At this time there was in existence a collective agreement between the parties which terminated on August 21, 1978. This agreement by art. 11, under the heading "Hours of Work" and subheading "Overtime" provided as follows:

11.01 Time worked will be calculated in units of one-half hour.

11.02 Employees shall be paid at the rate of one and one-half time the applicable hourly rate for time worked:

(a) in any 24-hour period in excess of 8 hours except where such excess time worked due to regular change of shift.

(b) in any scheduled work week in excess of 40 hours less amounts paid pursuant to (a) above.

11.03 Overtime work shall be distributed as equally as practicable among those employees who would normally perform such work within their respective first-line supervisor's group or in their particular workplace or area. An employee excused from working overtime shall be regarded as having been given an opportunity to work overtime for the purpose of this provision. Records of such amounts of overtime worked and of declined opportunities shall be made available for inspection by an employee concerned on request.

11.04 Should the Company call out any employee to work he shall be paid at a rate of one and one-half times the applicable hourly rate for time worked by him with a minimum of 4 hours at his applicable hourly rate.

By art. 11.20 the collective agreement established the work week as follows:

11.20 The work week shall commence at 8 a.m. Sundays. This section shall not be construed to mean that all men on the day shift will start exactly at 8 a.m.

Similar provisions were contained in succeeding collective agreements between the parties dated November 25, 1978, and August 21, 1979, respectively, the latter of which terminated on August 21, 1982.

There is no dispute that the employer was entitled to operate a four-crew schedule in a four-week cycle. This operation can best be illustrated by reproducing the relevant part of ex. 1 filed at the hearing and reproduced by the referee in his reasons for decision:

PRESENT 4-CREW SCHEDULE

	1 S MT WT F S	2 S MT WT F S	3 S MT WT F S	4 S MT WT F S
'A'	D D D D D X X	X X N N N N N	N N X X A A A	A A A A X ⒹD
'B'	A A A A X ⒹD	D D D D D X X	X X N N N N N	N N X X A A A
'C'	X X N N N N N	N N X X A A A	A A A A X ⒹD	D D D D D X X
'D'	N N X X A A A	A A A A X ⒹD	D D D D D X X	X X N N N N N

As explained by the referee, the letters 'A', 'B', 'C' and 'D' in the left-hand column are used for the purpose of identifying the four crews who man the schedule. The numbers 1, 2, 3 and 4 at the top of the columns indicate the sequence of work weeks as established by the collective agreement. These are delineated by the vertical lines. The letters 'D', 'N' and 'A' in the schedule represent the day shift, night shift and afternoon shift. The letter 'X' indicates days off for the crew involved. The circled 'D's are days upon which one-sixth of the crew of that shift are not scheduled. They are replaced by other employees. The parties agree that this circumstance is not relevant to the issues in the proceedings.

An examination of the schedule shows that it provides for seven consecutive working days for each of the crews at some time within the four-week schedule. The shifts comprised eight hours so that in some periods of seven consecutive days an employee worked 56 hours. The schedule in use at no time provided for the first of such seven consecutive shifts to be worked on a Sunday or Monday so that the seven consecutive shifts were worked partly in one "work week," as defined in the collective agreement, and partly in another. Accordingly, none of those shifts qualified for overtime pay under art. 11.02(b) of the collective agreement as the schedule did not require any employee to work more than 40 hours in a scheduled work week. It was, however, the position of the union before the referee, the Divisional Court and this court that the employees were entitled to overtime pay pursuant to the provisions of s. 25(1) for all hours worked in excess of 44 hours in any period of seven consecutive days.

That submission was based upon the provisions of the Act. The interpretation provisions of the Act provide by s. 1(q):

(q) "week" means a period of seven consecutive days;

and by s. 1(r):

(r) "work week" means a week of work established by the practice of the employer or determined by an employment standards officer.

The definition of "week" is clear and unambiguous. The wording of s. 25(1) is clear and unambiguous. By inserting the definition of "week" for the word "week" in s. 25(1) it would read:

Except as otherwise provided in the regulations, where an employee works for an employer in excess of forty-four hours in any period of seven consecutive days, he shall be paid for each hour worked in excess of forty-four hours overtime pay at an amount not less than one and one-half times the regular rate of the employee. . . .

In interpreting the provisions of the Act, one must keep in mind its general purpose. The statute sets forth a set of minimum terms and conditions of employment relating to hours of work (Part IV, ss. 17 to 22); wages (Part V, s. 23); overtime pay (Part VI, s. 25); public holidays with pay (Part VII); vacations with pay (Part VIII, ss. 29 to 32); pregnancy leave (Part IX, ss. 35 to 39) et al.

The statutory rights are conferred on all employees: see s. 2(2). They cannot be taken away by contract nor can they be waived by the employee or a union on his behalf: see s. 3. Section 1(e) of the Act defines "employment standard" as follows:

1. In this Act. . . .
(e) "employment standard" means a requirement imposed upon an employer in favour of an employee by this Act or the regulations;

Section 4(1) of the Act provides:

4(1) An employment standard shall be deemed a minimum requirement only.

There can be no doubt that the *Employment Standards Act*, 1974 is a statute remedial in nature. As such it must receive such fair, large and liberal construction and interpretation as will best ensure the attainment of the object of the Act according to its true intent, meaning and spirit: *Interpretation Act*, s. 10.

In my opinion, the provisions of s. 25 relating to overtime pay impose a requirement on employers in favour of employees and set up an employment standard within the meaning of the definition of those words in the Act. Although the Act does not purport to restrict the number of consecutive days in which an employee can be required to work, it does restrict the total number of hours that an employee can be required to work in a day and in a week subject to increase with the approval of the director: see ss. 17 to 20. It is to be noted that in setting the limit of the number of hours to be worked the Act refers in s. 17 to "forty-eight in the week" and in s. 18 to "shall not exceed forty-eight hours in a week." The word "work" is absent in describing "week" in each instance. Section 25 provides for a premium by way of overtime pay where an employee is required to work in excess of 44 hours in a period of seven consecutive days. The purpose of setting up such a standard can only be to discourage employers from requiring employees to work in excess of 44 hours and/or to recognize that work in excess of such hours during such a limited period, is sufficiently burdensome by reason of the concentration of work hours to warrant pay at a rate higher than the regular rate of pay. If the interpretation given by the Divisional Court and sought to be maintained by the employer prevails, namely, that while the word "week" in s. 25 means seven consecutive days, the seven consecutive days are those that coincide with the "work week" established by the employer, then it is possible for the employer to set up a work schedule as it has done in this case which would require the employees to work as much as 56 hours in seven consecutive days without entitlement to any overtime pay. Indeed, if the employer's submission and the Divisional Court's decision are correct, then it would be possible for the employer to schedule an employee to work four hours on Monday and eight hours each day from Tuesday through to the following Thursday and four hours more on Friday for a total of 88 hours without a full day's rest and without overtime pay because the hours of work would not have exceeded 44 hours in a work week. It must be acknowledged, however, that in such a case, under the provisions of the collective agreement under consideration the employee would be entitled to four hours overtime pay. In the absence of a provision similar to art. 11.02(b) no overtime pay would be payable. . . .

HOULDEN J.A. (Robins J.A. concurring): Goodman J.A., in his reasons for judgment, has accurately stated the facts, and it is unnecessary to repeat them. I would only make this comment on them. It is clear that, under the terms of the collective agreement, the employees have no claim for overtime pay, Falconbridge having complied fully with its provisions. If the referee is correct in his interpretation of s. 25(1) of the *Employment Standards Act, 1974* (Ont.), c. 112, then Falconbridge will be obligated to pay overtime to its employees, even though no such obligation exists under the collective agreement. The issue is: Do the provisions of s. 25(1) dictate this result? The referee found that they do.

The Divisional Court disagreed. I agree with the Divisional Court, and I will endeavour to state briefly my reasons for reaching this conclusion.

I agree with the Divisional Court that the referee had to be correct in his interpretation of s. 25(1); it was not sufficient for his interpretation of the statute to be "not patently unreasonable." The referee was not interpreting a constituent statute, nor was his decision protected by a true privative clause. The case is governed, therefore, by *McLeod et al. v. Egan et al. . . .* , and not by *Canadian Union of Public Employees Local 963 v. New Brunswick Liquor Corp. . . .*

Section 1(q) of the Act defines "week" as meaning a period of seven consecutive days. Section 25(1) applies "where an employee works for an employer in excess of forty-four hours in any week." If the section is interpreted strictly, then, as Goodman J.A. has pointed out, Falconbridge employees are entitled to be paid overtime for hours worked by them in excess of 44 hours during any period of seven consecutive days.

In a lecture in the Special Lectures of the Law Society of Upper Canada, 1976, on "Employment Standards in Ontario," . . . Paul Hess, Q.C., made the following comments on ss. 1(q) and 25(1):

> The word "week" is defined by clause 1(q) as a period of seven consecutive days. The definition may appear to be unnecessary but administrative experience with some employers established its practical necessity to avoid argument that a week meant seven working days as selected by the employer from time to time. The seven consecutive days comprising the week for subsection 25(1) are not the same as the calendar week. It may be any seven consecutive days and is taken to be those days which are established by practice or custom by the employer or in the industry.

This accords with the Divisional Court's interpretation of the Act, and with respect, I agree with it.

In interpreting a section of the Act, the Act must be read as a whole. . . . A word, expression or provision of an Act is not to be given an interpretation inconsistent with the context: the *Interpretation Act*, RSO 1980, c. 219 s. 1(1)(b). When s. 25(1) of the *Employment Standards Act* is read in the context of the entire Act, I think it is clear that "week," where a "work week" has been established, means a period of seven consecutive days coinciding with the "work week." I rely on the following provisions of the Act for this conclusion:

1. The word "week" is defined in s. 1(q) as follows:

   (q) "week" means a period of seven consecutive days;

The clause does not, however, say when the period of seven consecutive days begins or ends. To get those dates, it is necessary to go to the definition of "work week" in s. 1(r) which provides:

   (r) "work week" means a week of work established by the practice of the employer or determined by an employment standards officer.

In this case, the collective agreement provides that the work week shall commence "8 a.m. Sundays." Hence, a "work week" has been established that satisfies the requirements of s. 1(r).

I agree that "week" in s. 25(1) means a period of seven consecutive days, and if no "work week" has been established in either of the two ways provided in s. 1(r), the week would be calculated by reference to that period. If, however, a "work week" has been established in one of the two ways provided in s. 1(r), as in this case, the seven consecutive days are, in my opinion, to be calculated by reference to that period.

2. The amount to be paid to an employee for overtime pay by s. 25(1) is "not less than one and one-half times the regular rate of the employee."

Section 1(m) defines "regular rate" as follows:

(m) "regular rate" means,
    (i) the wage rate of an employee for an hour of work in a regular non-overtime work week.
    (ii) where subclause (i) does not apply, the average hourly rate calculated by dividing the wages of an employee earned in a week by the number of hours the employee worked in that week where the employer has made and kept in accordance with this Act complete and accurate records thereof, or
    (iii) where subclauses (i) and (ii) do not apply, the hourly rate determined by an employment standards officer;

If "week" in s. 25(1) was intended to be restricted to "a period of seven consecutive days," then there would be no need to refer to "the wage rate of an employee for an hour of work in a regular non-overtime work week." The method of calculating overtime pay would be that set out in s. 1(m)(ii), i.e., you would divide the wages of the employee earned in a period of seven consecutive days by the number of hours that the employee worked in that week. If, however, "week" in s. 25(1) is interpreted in the manner that I have indicated, then there is good reason for calculating "regular rate" in the manner set out in s. 1(m)(i). By defining "week" in this manner, s. 25(1) becomes consistent with s. 1(m)(i).

. . .

. . . To conclude, reading s. 25 in the light of the statute as whole and not in isolation, I am satisfied that the term "week" as used in the section was intended to mean a period of seven days coinciding with the "work week." The contrary interpretation advanced by the union, in my opinion, is inconsistent with other relevant provisions of the Act and its regulations and produces a result inconsonant with the general scheme of the legislation. I may add that I feel reinforced in my conclusion by the fact that the union, a very experienced bargaining agent, concluded two collective agreements after the four-crew schedule in question first came into operation in which overtime and premium pay provisions were agreed to, and made no suggestion for almost three years that the scheduling entitled employees to overtime pay under the *Employment Standards Act* or that the company was in violation of any of its obligations under the Act. I think it clear that, as between the parties, the result urged by the union is manifestly unfair. In my opinion, a proper interpretation of the legislation does not compel that result. . . .

✻ ✻ ✻

12:500 LOW PAY AND THE STATUTORY MINIMUM WAGE

REFERENCES

Geoffrey England, Innis Christie, & Roderick Wood, *Employment Law in Canada*, 3d ed. (Markham: Butterworths, 1998) paras, 8.79–8.96

Increasing the minimum wage is unfortunately ineffective as the sole means of eradicating low pay. For example, the traditional view among economists is that if labour costs increase too much, employers may hire fewer workers or cut back on training and educational programs for existing employees, thereby harming those whom the minimum wage laws are designed to benefit. This effect is enhanced in industries where employers must compete against those in other jurisdictions with much lower wages. A minority of economists, however, have recently argued that the disemployment effect of increasing the minimum wage is exaggerated, if it exists at all. The theory behind this view is examined in J. Harold McClure Jr., "Minimum Wages and the Wessels Effect in a Monopsony Model" (1994), 15 Journal of Labor Research 271.

Whatever the merits of the economic arguments, it seems clear that the minimum wage is an important component of the statutory "floor" for many workers.

Rights and Responsibilities in a Changing Workplace: A Review of Employment Standards in British Columbia (Victoria: Ministry of Skills, Training and Labour, 1994) (Chair: Mark Thompson) at 81–84

Given the interest in the minimum wage, it is surprising how little information exists on who receives these wages, the impact of the minimum wage on compensation and the effects of raising the minimum wage on employment. The last topic is a complex one requiring sophisticated research techniques, but the first two call for rather simple data collection.

One controversial aspect of the minimum wage is who actually receives it. Statistics Canada conducted a Labour Market Activity Survey from 1986 to 1990. Data from the 1989 survey, when the minimum wage in B.C. was $4.50 for adults and $4.00 for persons under 18 years, revealed that 3.2 percent of employed workers, about 45,000 persons were earning the minimum wage. Half of those workers were between 15 and 19 years old, two thirds of whom were females. The survey found that about 30 percent of low wage earners reported just one family member was working. By contrast 46 percent reported two family earners and 22 percent, three or more family members holding a job. There was no information on the level of compensation of the other family members who were employed. About 60 percent of low wage workers were employed in the service sector in the 1986 survey. Agriculture also employed a relatively large proportion.

The Commission heard many employers argue against raising the minimum wage and that differentials be retained or established. Yet when asked, very few of these employers actually paid the minimum wage. A few started workers there and then gave a raise a few weeks later. Most who discussed this point paid between $6.00 and $7.00 per hour. Their concern about the higher minimum wage was the impact an increase would have on those rates slightly above the minimum, as workers would expect to receive an increase approximately the same as any rise in the legal minimum. One exception to this generalization is the restaurant industry, where some of the more expensive restaurants pay their servers the minimum wage with the expectation that they will earn much more in gratuities. The major gap in knowledge is the link between the minimum wage and other rates of pay. National data from 1991, when the minimum wage was $5.00 in British Columbia, indicated that 5.6 per cent of full-time male workers, and 8.2 percent of full-time female workers earned less than $10,000 per year, and 5.7 percent of males and 11.5 percent of females earned between $10,000 and $15,000 for working between 49 and 52 weeks.

Thus, after looking at hourly wage rates and family income data, it is safe to assume that between 5 and 10 percent of full-time British Columbia workers earn more than the minimum wage, but less than $8.00 per hour, and that about 60 percent of these are female. A *relatively small* number of persons earn the minimum wage, and most of them are under 19 years of age. If only full-time workers are considered, there should be few persons under 19 years of age included in this group. However, some part-time workers receiving hourly wages in this range would prefer full-time employment. There is evidence that low wage earners frequently rely on welfare during the course of a year. . . .

[T]he purchasing power of the adult minimum wage has varied considerably in the last 24 years. The high period was in 1972–1977, when the value of the minimum wage was approximately $8.00 in 1992 dollars. After that, the value of the minimum wage sank steadily through 1986, as the minimum did not rise between 1981 and 1986. By 1992, the minimum wage in constant dollars was lower than it was in 1981. Comparing the minimum wage with other compensation levels in the economy yields much the same result. Between 1970 and 1979, the 40 hours' work at the minimum wage was equal to about half of average weekly earnings. By 1990–1992, the same number of hours was about 40 percent of average weekly earnings. . . . much the same trend occurred in other provinces during the 1980s. Minimum wages rose slowly or not at all during and after the 1982–1983 recession, so that by the beginning of the 1990s, the minimum wage was equal to approximately 40 percent of average weekly earnings in all regions of the country.

There is evidence that increasing the minimum wage reduces employment, although the magnitude of the relationship is uncertain. In a review of the evidence on the relationship between minimum wages and employment prepared for the Canadian Association of Administrators of Labour Legislation, a policy specialist in the British Columbia government found that Canadian and American studies indicated that a 10 percent increase in the minimum wage causes a short-term decline in employment of 1 and 2 percent. Recent research in Ontario concluded that raising the minimum wage to 60 percent of the average weekly earnings (an increase of 13 percentage points) would raise the unemployment rate for women and young workers between 1.8 and 2 percent. The latest research done in the United States found that increases in the minimum wage of 10 percent may cause no declines in employment. . . .

Academic research currently available typically addresses the impact on employment of increases in the minimum wage in the order of 10 percent. There are no estimates of the effects on employment levels of increases in the minimum wage of 25 or 30 percent, but the Commission has concluded that such changes would cause significant reductions in employment, especially in small businesses and the hospitality sector. The Commission heard from restaurant owners who explained how they had reduced employment by eliminating hostesses or bus persons after the minimum wage rose in this province. An Ontario study concluded that labour accounts for about 30 percent of the restaurant industry costs. The emphasis on declines in employment must be balanced by the increases in the incomes of low wage workers when the minimum wage rises. Over a longer term, the immediate employment effects of raising minimum wages are dissipated, since some persons' income rises and others' falls.

It is also necessary to point out that the purchasing power of the current minimum wage is now substantially below the levels of the 1970s and approximately 10 percent less than 1980. Low-paid workers in British Columbia felt the effects of the 1980s recession long after other workers had benefitted from the recovery.

✻ ✻ ✻

The minimum wage does not apply to all workers. Most provinces exclude certain categories of workers, such as agricultural labourers and articling students. As well, there is often more than one "minimum." In Ontario, the hourly minimum wage for most workers in 2001 was $6.85. For students under eighteen who worked less than twenty-eight hours per week, it was $6.40, and for employees who regularly served liquor as part of their job, it was $5.95: *Ontario Employment Standards Act Regulations*, O.Reg. 285/01, sections 2, 5(1). These differentials and exclusions are supposed to give employers an incentive to hire certain types of workers. They may be open to challenge under section 15(1) of the *Canadian Charter of Rights and Freedoms*, for discriminating on the basis of age and other prohibited grounds.

12:600 DISMISSAL AND EMPLOYMENT STANDARDS LEGISLATION

This section examines the issue of dismissal and the interplay between common law standards and employment standards legislation. It begins by reviewing the relationship between the notice provisions in the statutes and at common law. It then looks at two kinds of dismissal: for economic reasons, and for unsatisfactory performance due to misconduct or incompetence.

Machtinger v. HOJ Industries Ltd., [1992] 1 S.C.R. 986

IACOBUCCI J. (La Forest, L'Heureux-Dubé, Sopinka, Gonthier, and Cory JJ. concurring):

This appeal concerns the contractual rights of employees who are dismissed without cause by their employers. Specifically where a contract of employment provides for notice periods less than the minimum prescribed by the applicable employment standards legislation, which in this case is the *Employment Standards Act*, R.S.O. 1980, c. 137 (the "Act"), and absent any claims of unconscionability or oppression, is an employee entitled to reasonable notice of dismissal, or to the minimum statutory notice period? The answer to this question is of considerable importance to employees.

Indeed, it has been pointed out that the law governing the termination of employment significantly affects the economic and psychological welfare of employees. . . .

FACTS

The two appellants were employed by the respondent HOJ Industries Ltd., which was a new and used car dealer. The appellant Marek Machtinger ("Machtinger") began working as a car salesperson for the respondent in 1978. Machtinger was continuously employed by the respondent except for a three-month period in 1980. On June 24, 1985, Machtinger was dismissed by the respondent, which has not alleged that it had cause for dismissal. At the time Machtinger was dismissed, he was credit manager and rust-proofing sales manager for the respondent. His earnings in his last full year of employment were $85,342.36. The appellant Gilles Lefebvre ("Lefebvre") also began working for the respondent in 1978. He also discharged on June 24, 1985, and again the respondent has not alleged that it had cause to dismiss him. Lefebvre was sales manager for the respondent at the time of his dismissal. In his last full year of employment his earnings were $74,220.79.

At issue in this case are the contracts of employment entered into between the appellants and the respondent. Machtinger entered into two contracts with the respondent. The second contract, dated January 11, 1985, was for employment for an indefinite period. The relevant portion of the contract is the termination provision, which reads as follows:

> Termination — Employer may terminate employment at any time without notice for cause. Otherwise, Employer may terminate employment on giving Employee 0 weeks notice or salary (which does not include bonus) in lieu of notice. Bonus, if any, will be calculated and payable only to the date of the giving of notice of termination.

The contract is on a preprinted form, with a blank space left for the notice period. The digit zero has been handwritten in the blank space.

The relevant contract between the respondent and Lefebvre was dated January 10, 1985, and was also for an indefinite period. The termination clause is in every respect identical to that in the document signed by Machtinger, except that the period of notice for termination without cause is two weeks, that is, the word "two" has been handwritten into the space left blank for the notice period.

The appellants acknowledged at trial that, save for the effect of the provisions of the Act, the termination provisions were valid. The appellants make no allegations of unconscionability or oppressive acts on behalf of the respondent. After Lefebvre and Machtinger were dismissed, the respondent paid each of them the equivalent of four weeks' salary. . .

STATUTORY PROVISIONS

Employment Standards Act, R.S.O. 1980, c. 137

1. In this Act, . . .
    (e) "employment standard" means a requirement imposed upon an employer in favour of an employee by this Act or the regulations;

2. . . .

(2) This Act applies to every contract of employment, oral or written, express or implied,

    (*a*) where the employment is for work or services to be performed in Ontario; or

    (*b*) where the employment is for work or services to be performed both in and out of Ontario and the work or services out of Ontario are a continuation of the work or services in Ontario.

3. Subject to section 4, no employer, employee, employers' organization or employees' organization shall contract out of or waive an employment standard, and any such contracting out or waiver is null and void.

4. (1) An employment standard shall be deemed a minimum requirement only.

(2) A right, benefit, term or condition of employment under a contract, oral or written, express or implied, or under any other Act or any schedule, order or regulation made thereunder that provides in favour of an employee a higher remuneration in money, a greater right or benefit or lesser hours of work than the requirement imposed by an employment standard shall prevail over an employment standard.

6. No civil remedy of an employee against his employer is suspended or affected by this Act.

40. (1) No employer shall terminate the employment of an employee who has been employed for three months or more unless he gives, . . .

    (*c*) four weeks notice in writing to the employee if his period of employment is five years or more but less than ten years; . . . and such notice has expired.

(7) Where the employment of an employee is terminated contrary to this section,

    (*a*) the employer shall pay termination pay in an amount equal to the wages that the employee would have been entitled to receive at his regular rate for a regular non-overtime work week for the period of notice prescribed by subsection (1) . . . and any wages to which he is entitled;

ISSUE ON APPEAL

This appeal raises one issue, namely: if an employment contract stipulates a period of notice less than that required by the *Employment Standards Act*, R.S.O. 1980, c. 137, is an employee who is dismissed without cause entitled to reasonable notice of termination, or to the minimum period of notice required by the Act?

ANALYSIS

A. Introduction

At least on their face, the two contracts at issue in this case represent attempts to contract out of the minimum notice periods required by the Act. Under these circumstances, the question posed by this appeal is deceptively simple: of what significance is an attempt to contract out of the minimum notice requirements of the Act?

Howland C.J.O. held that, although the contractual terms were in breach of the Act, they were nonetheless relevant to determining the intention of the parties as to what the notice period should be. Specifically, Howland C.J.O. held that the terms of the contracts entered into by the parties were such as to make it unnecessary and improper for the court to imply a term of reasonable notice. Instead, Howland C.J.O. gave effect to the intention of the parties, as evidenced by the terms of the contracts they entered into, and held that the appellants were entitled only to the minimum notice period set out in the Act.

With respect, I cannot agree with the reasoning of the Chief Justice of Ontario, and I have come to the conclusion that the appeal must be allowed. I divide my analysis into three parts. In the first part, I discuss the common law presumption that reasonable notice is required to terminate contracts of employment for an indefinite term. In the second part, I review the impact of the provisions of the Act on the two contracts at issue in this appeal. Finally, I turn to a consideration of the policy dimensions of the issue before us.

B. Reasonable Notice at Common Law

The history of the common law principle that a contract for employment for an indefinite period is terminable only if reasonable notice is given is a long and interesting one, going back at least to 1562 and the *Statute of Artificers*, 5 Eliz. 1, c. 4. The *Statute of Artificers* prohibited employers from dismissing their servants unless sufficient cause had been shown before two justices of the peace: see S.M. Jacoby, "The Duration of Indefinite Employment Contracts in the United States and England: An Historical Analysis". . . . By the middle of the nineteenth century, however, English courts were beginning to imply a term into contracts of employment that the contract could be terminated without cause provided that reasonable notice was given. Although it was initially necessary to prove the incorporation of a custom of termination on reasonable notice into the contract in each particular case, the English courts gradually came to accept reasonable notice as a contractual term to be implied in the absence of evidence to the contrary: M.R. Freedland, *The Contract of Employment*. . . . In Canada, it has been established since at least 1936 that employment contracts for an indefinite period require the employer, absent express contractual language to the contrary, to give reasonable notice of an intention to terminate the contract if the dismissal is without cause: *Carter v. Bell & Sons (Canada) Ltd.* . . .

The parties devoted considerable attention in argument before us to the law governing the implication of contractual terms, and specifically to the relevance of the intention of the parties to the implication of a term of reasonable notice of termination in employment contracts. The relationship between intention and the implication of contractual terms is complex, and I am of the opinion that this appeal can and should be resolved on narrower grounds. For the purposes of this appeal, I would characterize the common law principle of termination only on reasonable notice as a presumption, rebuttable if the contract of employment clearly specifies some other period of notice, whether expressly or impliedly.

This is the approach taken by Freedland, *supra*, who states that, "the pattern of contract now generally accepted and applied by the courts in the absence of evidence to the contrary is one of employment for an indefinite period terminable by either party upon reasonable notice, but only upon reasonable notice." . . . The same approach was adopted by the Ontario Court of Appeal in *Prozak v. Bell Telephone Co. of Canada.* . . . Writing for the court, Goodman J.A. noted . . . that, "if a contract of employment makes no express or specifically implied provision for its duration or termination, there is likely to be implied at common law a presumption that the contract is for an indefinite period and terminable by a reasonable notice given by either party. . .". Basically, this is also the approach taken by I. Christie, in *Employment Law in Canada*. . . .

What constitutes reasonable notice will vary with the circumstances of any particular case. The most frequently cited enumeration of factors relevant to the assessment of reasonable notice is from the judgment of McRuer C.J.H.C. in *Bardal* . . . :

> There can be no catalogue laid down as to what is reasonable notice in particular classes of cases. The reasonableness of the notice must be decided with reference to each particular case, having regard to the character of the employment, the length of service of the servant, the age of the servant and the availability of similar employment, having regard to the experience, training and qualifications of the servant.

Hollingworth J. referred to the factors set out in *Bardal* in determining what would constitute reasonable notice for the two appellants. His determination in this respect was not challenged in this appeal.

C. *The Employment Standards Act*

It was acknowledged by the appellants and the respondent that, but for the possible effects of the Act, no issue as to the validity of the employment contracts would have arisen. The presumption at common law that a contract of employment for an indefinite term is terminable only on reasonable notice would have been rebutted by the clear language of the contract specifying shorter notice periods. But what is the effect of the Act?

The Act provides for mandatory minimum notice periods. The provision relevant to the appellants is set out in s. 40(1)(c) of the Act, which provides that an employer must give any employee who has been employed for five years or more but less than ten years four weeks' notice of termination. Section 40(7)(a) provides that, if the required notice is not given, the employer shall pay the employee an amount equivalent to his or her regular wages for the period of notice.

It is also clear from ss. 4 and 6 of the Act that the minimum notice periods set out in the Act do not operate to displace the presumption at common law of reasonable notice. Section 6 of the Act states that the Act does not affect the right of an employee to seek a civil remedy from his or her employer. Section 4(2) states that a "right, benefit, term or condition of employment under a contract" that provides a greater benefit to an employee than the standards set out in the Act shall prevail over the standards in the Act. I have no difficulty in concluding that the common law presumption of reasonable notice is a "benefit," which, if the period of notice required by the common law is greater than that required by the Act, will, if otherwise applicable, prevail over the notice period set out in the Act. Any possible doubt on this question is dispelled by s. 4(1) of the Act, which expressly deems the employment standards set out in the Act to be minimum requirements only.

What is at issue in this appeal is the effect, if any, to be given to a term of an employment contract which does not comply with the minimum notice requirements of the Act.

Is such a term capable of displacing the common law presumption of reasonable notice? The effect of ss. 3 and 4 of the Act is to make any attempt to contract out of the minimum employment standards of the Act by providing for lesser benefits than those minimum employment standards, "null and void." The two contracts at issue on this appeal do attempt to contract out of the minimum notice period set out in s. 40(1)(c) of the Act by specifying notice periods shorter than the statutory minimum. Accordingly, the two contracts are not in compliance with the mandatory language of s. 3 of the Act, and those portions of the two contracts specifying the notice periods are "null and void."

In argument, the respondent accepted that the attempt to contract out of the provisions of the Act was "null and void," but argued that the documents should be considered as evidence "that contracts were entered into which expressed clearly the intention of the parties with respect to notice of termination." I cannot accept this argument. In *Rover International Ltd. v. Cannon Film Sales Ltd.* . . . , the Court of Appeal was faced with a contract which was entirely void. Kerr L.J. refused to look to the terms of the contract to limit the recovery of the appellant in *quantum meruit* . . . :

> . . . if the imposition of a "ceiling" in the present case were accepted, then the consequences could be far-reaching and undesirable in other situations which it would be impossible to distinguish in principle. It would then follow that an evaluation of the position of the parties to a void contract, or to one which becomes ineffective subsequently, could always be called for. We know that this is not the position in the case of frustrated contracts, which are governed by the Law Reform (Frustrated Contracts) Act 1943. It would cause many difficulties if the position were different in relation to contracts which are void ab initio. By analogy to [the respondent's] submission in the present case, in deciding on the equities of restitution the court could then always be called upon to analyse or attempt to forecast the relative position of the parties under a contract which is ex hypothesi non-existent. This is not an attractive proposition, and I can see no justification for it in principle or upon any authority.

In this case we are not faced with an entirely void contract, but a contract of which one clause is null and void by operation of statute. I would nonetheless apply the reasoning of Kerr L.J.: if a term is null and void, then it is null and void for all purposes, and cannot be used as evidence of the parties' intention. If the intention of the parties is to make an unlawful contract, no lawful contractual term can be derived from their intention. In *Erlund v. Quality Communication Products Ltd.* . . . , Wilson J. was faced with a contract of employment which was void by reason of the *Statute of Frauds*. Relying on *James v. Thomas H. Kent & Co.* . . . , Wilson J. held that in the absence of a valid contract, he had no choice but to imply a term that the employee was entitled to reasonable notice.

Moreover, because the Act declares the notice provisions of the contracts in dispute to be null and void, it seems to me that the proper question to ask in determining the parties' intention is: what did the parties intend should the notice provisions be found to be null and void? There is simply no evidence with which to answer this question. In *Suleman v. British Columbia Research Council* . . . , Lysyk J., on facts analogous to those in the case at bar, found that there was no evidence of the parties' intention in the face of minimum employment standards with which the employer was required to comply. Lysyk J. was considering the effect of s. 2(1) of the *Employment Standards Act*, S.B.C. 1980, c. 10, which is very similar in wording to s. 3 of the Act. Lysyk J. concluded as follows . . . :

> I find nothing in the evidence in the present case to warrant the conclusion that the parties, had they turned their minds to the subject, would have agreed to substitute for the void contractual term the minimum period of notice required by statute instead of looking to the common law standard of reasonable notice.

POLICY CONSIDERATIONS

I turn finally to the policy considerations which impact on the issue in this appeal. Although the issue may appear to be a narrow one, it is nonetheless important because employment is of central importance to our society. As Dickson C.J. noted in *Reference Re Public Service Employee Relations Act (Alta.)* . . . :

> Work is one of the most fundamental aspects in a person's life, providing the individual with a means of financial support and, as importantly, a contributory role in society. A person's employment is an essential component of his or her sense of identity, self-worth and emotional well-being.

I would add that not only is work fundamental to an individual's identity, but also that the manner in which employment can be terminated is equally important.

Section 10 of the *Interpretation Act*, R.S.O. 1980, c. 219, provides that every Act "shall be deemed to be remedial" and directs that every Act shall "receive such fair, large and liberal construction and interpretation as will best ensure the attainment of the object of the Act according to its true intent, meaning and spirit." The objective of the Act is to protect the interests of employees by requiring employers to comply with certain minimum standards, including minimum periods of notice of termination. To quote Conant Co. Ct. J. in *Pickup* [*v. Litton Business Equipment Ltd.*]. . . , "the general intention of this legislation [i.e. the Act] is the protection of employees, and to that end it institutes reasonable, fair and uniform minimum standards." The harm which the Act seeks to remedy is that individual employees, and in particular non-unionized employees, are often in an unequal bargaining position in relation to their employers. As stated by Swinton . . . :

> . . . the terms of the employment contract rarely result from an exercise of free bargaining power in the way that the paradigm commercial exchange between two traders does. Individual employees on the whole lack both the bargaining power and the information necessary to achieve more favourable contract provisions than those offered by the employer, particularly with regard to tenure.

Accordingly, an interpretation of the Act which encourages employers to comply with the minimum requirements of the Act, and so extends its protections to as many employees as possible, is to be favoured over one that does not. In this regard, the fact that many individual employees may be unaware of their statutory and common law rights in the employment context is of fundamental importance. As B. Etherington suggests in "The

Enforcement of Harsh Termination Provisions in Personal Employment Contracts: The Rebirth of Freedom of Contract in Ontario" . . . , "the majority of unorganized employees would not even expect reasonable notice prior to dismissal and many would be surprised to learn they are not employed at the employer's discretion."

If the only sanction which employers potentially face for failure to comply with the minimum notice periods prescribed by the Act is an order that they minimally comply with the Act, employers will have little incentive to make contracts with their employees that comply with the Act. As Swinton and Etherington suggest, most individual employees are unaware of their legal rights, or unwilling or unable to go to the trouble and expense of having them vindicated. Employers can rely on the fact that many employees will not challenge contractual notice provisions which are in fact contrary to employment standards legislation. Employers such as the present respondent can contract with their employees for notice periods below the statutory minimum, knowing that only those individual employees who take legal action after they are dismissed will in fact receive the protection of the minimum statutory notice provisions.

In my view, an approach more consistent with the objects of the Act is that, if an employment contract fails to comply with the minimum statutory notice provisions of the Act, then the presumption of reasonable notice will not have been rebutted. Employers will have an incentive to comply with the Act to avoid the potentially longer notice periods required by the common law, and in consequence more employees are likely to receive the benefit of the minimum notice requirements. Such an approach is also more consistent with the legislative intention expressed by s. 6 of the Act, which expressly preserves the civil remedies otherwise available to an employee against his or her employer.

Moreover, this approach provides protection for employees in a manner that does not disproportionately burden employers. Absent considerations of unconscionability, an employer can readily make contracts with his or her employees which referentially incorporate the minimum notice periods set out in the Act or otherwise take into account later changes to the Act or to the employees' notice entitlement under the Act. Such contractual notice provisions would be sufficient to displace the presumption that the contract is terminable without cause only on reasonable notice. . . .

Finally, I would note that the Act sets out what the provincial legislature deems to be fair minimum notice periods. One of the purposes of the Act is to ensure that employees who are discharged are discharged fairly. In the present case, the employer attempted to contract with its employees for notice periods which were less than what the legislature had deemed to be fair minimum notice periods. Given that the employer has attempted, whether deliberately or not, to frustrate the intention of the legislature, it would indeed be perverse to allow the employer to avail itself of legislative provisions intended to protect employees, so as to deny the employees their common law right to reasonable notice.

CONCLUSION AND DISPOSITION

I would conclude that both the plain meaning of ss. 3, 4 and 6 and a consideration of the objects of the Act lead to the same result: where an employment contract fails to comply with the minimum notice periods set out in the Act, the employee can only be dismissed without cause if he or she is given reasonable notice of termination.

Accordingly, the appeal should be allowed. . . .

* * *

Following *Machtinger*, the courts have required unequivocal and explicit language to establish that a terminated employee had intended to surrender his or her common law or statutory rights. Any ambiguities in the employment contract will be interpreted strictly against the employer's interest. The courts have applied these principles because they have accepted that employers usually have much more bargaining power when an employment contract is being negotiated. A good example of this new direction taken by the Canadian courts after *Machtinger* is *Ceccol v. Ontario Gymnastic* (2001), 55 O.R. (3d) 614 (C.A.), set out in Chapter 2, at 2:430. For more on the evolution of employment rights in the courts through the 1990s, see Brian Etherington, "Supreme Court of Canada Decisions and the Common Law of Employment: Shifting the Balance Between Rights and Efficiency Concerns?" (1999), 78 Can. Bar Rev. 200.

12:610 Economic Dismissals and Employment Standards Legislation

> REFERENCES
>
> **Geoffrey England, Innis Christie, & Roderick Wood, *Employment Law in Canada*, 3d ed. (Markham: Butterworths, 1998), paras. 14.1–14.65**

There has been a massive increase in terminations for economic reasons (usually called layoffs) during the various economic slumps since the early 1980s. In theory, the non-unionized employee in such a situation has some protection under his or her employment contract. Because redundancy does not provide just cause for summary dismissal at common law, the employer must provide "reasonable notice," or wages in lieu of notice, before terminating the employee. As explained in Chapter 2, this right may be of little practical value to most employees because it is enforceable only through a civil action, which is likely to be unrealistically slow and costly.

Unionized employees may enjoy a certain degree of protection against layoffs under the seniority provisions of collective agreements. However, as the following excerpt from the Carrothers Report suggests, collective bargaining has its drawbacks when it comes to handling redundancy.

Report of the Commission of Inquiry into Redundancies and Lay-offs (Ottawa: Labour Canada, 1979) (Chair: A. Carrothers) at 92–93, 250–51

> . . . [First,] Canada operates in a market economy consisting of a mixture of private enterprise, government regulation and state enterprise. Second, Canada is characterized by a relatively open economic system, in that international trade is an important element of our total production and consumption. Third, the industrial relations system which has been adopted as being the most compatible with the foregoing phenomena is collective bargaining; but the collective bargaining system as it operates within the country today is

far from comprehensive either in its coverage of the labour force or its coverage of subject matter. Fourth, external forces, principally in the area of world trade, have an impact on the Canadian world of work, producing problems of job dislocation. Fifth, job dislocation can occur because of corporate decisions taken in the private sector outside Canada. These external decisions have a particular impact in situations of monopoly where market forces cannot otherwise react.

The task of this Commission is to recommend ways in which human resources can better be managed in "change" situations, that is, how lay-offs can be avoided or limited, or hardship alleviated when lay-offs occur. While both the current industrial relations system and public labour market policy are essential to the development of a socially satisfactory and rational system of human resource management at the level of the enterprise, neither is currently sufficient in itself. . . .

The collective bargaining process is adversary in nature and many representatives of the parties of interest would not have it otherwise, for they know the rules of the game, they know how to make them work and they resist government interference in the process. It, however, carries with it its own attitudes. Some collective agreements do deal with facets of the issue of redundancy. Nevertheless, redundancy is an economic and social issue in which there is a general public interest, involving as it does unemployment and public costs relating thereto, costs to the community, especially the dependent community, and claims on social welfare programs. It is argued in this report that the adversary process does not lend itself well to the management of redundancy problems because the search for solutions requires something more from the employer than the maximization of profits and the attitude that the union is to be tolerated only as an adversary. It requires a non-legalistic, egalitarian search for viable solutions that minimize hardship to the individual and charges, direct and indirect, to the public purse.

It is recognized that the initial decision to effect a change is a matter of management responsibility. However, the consideration of the avoidance of lay-offs flowing from the decision, and the consideration of the lessening of hardship flowing from unavoidable terminations of employment, together with the provision of sufficient time to consider these matters, call for consultation between the parties of interest, with appropriate involvement of government services, to produce effective results. . . .

[The *Report* is a publication of Human Resources Development Canada. Reproduced with the permission of the Minister of Public Works and Government Services Canada, 1997.]

* * *

The Carrothers Report recommended the introduction of an adjustment policy that would require employers to notify and consult with employees or their union with respect to large-scale (or mass) terminations. In response to the Carrothers Report, several provinces have required the use of joint employer/employee consultative committees in certain mass termination situations. Other measures have included statutory minimum notice and severance pay requirements.

The notice and severance pay provisions in employment standards statutes are only one of the strategies used in Canada to facilitate labour adjustment. For an overview, see

Pradeep Kumar, *Labour Market Adjustment Issues in Canada: An Industrial Relations Perspective* (Kingston, Ont.: Industrial Relations Centre, Queen's University, 1991).

The basic level of protection is found in the provisions of the employment standards legislation regarding notice of termination or wages in lieu. Generally, the length of required notice increases with the employee's service with the particular employer, up to a specified limit. The emphasis on seniority reflects a limited form of property interest in the job, but it also supports the view that the statutory notice period represents earnings that are deferred as a form of insurance against termination.

The next level of protection consists of the mass termination provisions found in the employment standards statutes in all jurisdictions. These provisions typically require the employer to give additional notice to affected employees where large numbers are to be laid off within a defined period. The rationale is that it will be more difficult for employees to find other work if large numbers of them enter the labour market simultaneously. The empirical evidence shows that receiving early notice of layoffs makes it easier for employees to find alternative work and helps relieve some of the psychological stress of losing a job. See A. Zippay, "Advance Notice and Post Displacement Job Losses" (1992) 10 Journal of Labour Economics 1. The mass-termination provisions commonly contain exemptions that roughly parallel the statutory exemptions in single-employee termination provisions.

As well, employers are usually required to notify the labour ministry of plans for a mass termination, so that the ministry can help the parties alleviate the impact of the layoffs. In many jurisdictions, including Ontario, Manitoba, New Brunswick, Quebec, British Columbia and the federal jurisdiction, the ministry may appoint a joint committee consisting of representatives of the employer, the employees (or their union), and government to formulate plans for coping with the mass termination. In all but one of these jurisdictions, it is the employer who finally decides what the plan will be when the committee has concluded its deliberations. The exception is the federal jurisdiction, where the ministry can appoint an adjudicator to impose an adjustment plan if the committee cannot agree on one. Nevertheless, the adjudicator has no authority to veto or delay an employer's decision to implement layoffs, but only to set the conditions under which the layoffs will proceed.

Roy Adams heralds the federal scheme as a "revolutionary" development in Canadian employment law because it gives even non-unionized workers a right to participate in collective decision making with their employer. The fact that compulsory adjudication is available to impose an adjustment plan if the employer and the employees cannot agree gives teeth to what would otherwise be just another form of joint consultation, and shows that the right to participate is to be taken seriously.

In Ontario and the federal jurisdiction, permanently displaced employees in defined mass-termination situations are entitled to a severance payment based on their length of service with the employer, in addition to their other statutory entitlements. The justification for this is of more than mere academic interest. In *Stevens v. The Globe and Mail* (1996), 28 O.R. (3d) 481, the Ontario Court of Appeal held that severance pay must be deducted from damages for wrongful dismissal. On the other hand, some courts have held that severance pay vests in the worker as a form of deferred wages and is therefore not deductible from damages for wrongful dismissal. Can you see any weaknesses in the deferred wages rationale?

As yet, no province has given laid off employees a statutory right to be recalled if work becomes available. Such a right is endorsed in para. 24(l) of the International Labour Organization's 1982 *Termination of Employment Regulations*. What difficulties might arise in implementing it? Consider how collective agreements handle recall rights, as discussed in D. Brown and D. Beatty, *Canadian Labour Arbitration*, 3d ed. (Aurora: Canada Law Book) at 6:2354.

12:620 Dismissal for Cause and Employment Standards Legislation

> REFERENCES
>
> **Geoffrey England, Innis Christie, & Roderick Wood, *Employment Law in Canada*, 3d ed. (Markham: Butterworths, 1998) c. 15**

There is a continuing tension in our labour and employment law between protecting the employee's personal dignity and autonomy and establishing a legal framework for employers that will enable them to make profits. Nowhere is this tension more apparent than in the determination of what constitutes just cause for dismissal. As noted above, the costs and delay of civil litigation often mean that non-unionized employees may in reality have little protection against unjust dismissal under the contract of employment. Unionized employees, on the other hand, usually enjoy relatively comprehensive, cheap, and fast safeguards against unjust dismissal under the collective agreement, and have access to the remedy of reinstatement. One might expect that employment standards statutes would have incorporated equivalent protection against unjust dismissal for non-unionized workers, given the growing sensitivity of Canadian public policy to equality issues in recent decades.

Indeed, the International Labour Organization's *Termination of Employment Recommendation 1963* (Recommendation no. 119), which the federal government has ratified, requires the enactment of just cause protections enforceable through independent adjudication and bolstered by the remedy of reinstatement. Yet this has not happened, except in the three jurisdictions mentioned below (Nova Scotia, Quebec, and the federal jurisdiction). The lack of trade union political pressure for such initiatives may be one explanation; a major reason why employees join unions is to secure protection against unjust dismissal. Others argue that from the employers' perspective, it would be too expensive to fire workers under such legislation. This contention has been challenged by some British studies, such as Bob Hepple, "The Fall and Rise of Unfair Dismissal" in W.E.J. McCarthy, ed., *Legal Intervention in Industrial Relations: Gains and Losses* (Oxford: Blackwell, 1992) 94. Can you think of any ways in which such legislation might benefit employers? The Thompson Report on employment standards legislation in British

Columbia, referred to in section 12:500 above, recommended (at page 145) against incorporating protection against unjust dismissal.

The most comprehensive statutory protection against unjust dismissal of unorganized workers is found in sections 240 to 246 of the *Canada Labour Code*. Parallel provisions in Quebec (*Labour Standards Act*, section 124) and Nova Scotia (*Labour Standards Code*, section 71) are somewhat more limited than the federal scheme, because they require, respectively, qualifying periods of three years and ten years of continuous service with the employer. The qualifying period in the federal jurisdiction is only twelve months.

The just cause standards developed by adjudicators under the statutory provisions just mentioned are very similar to those applied by collective agreement arbitrators and discussed above in Chapter 9. Unlike arbitrators, however, adjudicators under the *Canada Labour Code* order reinstatement relatively infrequently, partly because of the practical difficulties of supervising such orders without the presence of a union in the workplace. In 1997–98, reinstatement was ordered in only sixteen out of fifty-three adjudications where dismissal was ruled unjust.

In "Section 240 of the *Canada Labour Code*: Some Current Pitfalls" (2000), 27 Manitoba Law Journal 17–43, Geoffrey England made the following observations, at pages 29–30, on the weakness of the reinstatement remedy in a non-unionized workplace:

> The practical difficulties of making reinstatement succeed in the face of employer opposition are almost insurmountable. Although flagrantly disobeying a reinstatement order may ultimately result in the employer being found in contempt of court, the employer may take the worker back, but make life so miserable that the employee is eventually driven to resign. Indeed, a worker who resigns shortly after being reinstated may be worse off financially than if he or she had been initially awarded compensation on a "make whole" basis. The employer, therefore, may ultimately succeed in being rid of the employee. An important empirical study of the post-reinstatement experience of non-unionized federal workers in Quebec conducted by Professor Trudeau reported that approximately two-thirds of reinstated workers perceived that they had been "unjustly" treated by their employer. Approximately 38 percent of those employees had resigned by the time the study was carried out. In comparison, reinstatement is very successful in the unionized sector due to the presence of the union to police the order.

Although adjudicators under sections 240 to 246 of the *Canada Labour Code* have been reluctant to reinstate unjustly dismissed employees, some have fashioned broad "make whole" remedial orders in an effort to provide appropriate compensation to the employee. The purpose of such remedies is to put the employee in the financial position that she or he would have been in had the unjust dismissal not occurred.

In the article referred to above, England lists the following among the considerations that adjudicators have used:

i) What was the employee's likely career path at the workplace, given such factors as the employee's age and occupational position and the size of the employer?

ii) What are the chances of the employee finding another suitable job, given the condition of the labour market?

iii) What were the employee's other incidental monetary losses, such as use of a company vehicle or the opportunity to earn overtime pay?

iv) Did the employee suffer any non-financial harm from the unjust dismissal, such as mental suffering or damage to his or her professional reputation)? and

v) Are there other appropriate non-monetary remedies, such as a fair reference letter, a re-writing of the employee's personnel record, or access to employment counseling and retraining?

In the following case, the Supreme Court of Canada has endorsed the broad grant of remedies to adjudicators appointed under sections 240 to 246 of the *Canada Labour Code*.

Slaight Communications Inc. v. Davidson (1989), 59 D.L.R. (4th) 416 (S.C.C.)

LAMER J. (dissenting in part): An adjudicator appointed by the Minister of Labour pursuant to s. 61.5(6) [now s. 240] of the *Canada Labour Code*, R.S.C. 1970, c. L-1, made an order in favour of an employee based on s. 61.5(9) of the Code. The employer challenged the said order but its appeal was dismissed by the Federal Court of Appeal. With leave of this court, the employer is now appealing here from this judgment of the Federal Court of Appeal. The outcome of this appeal involves determining whether, under s. 61.5(9) of the *Canada Labour Code*, as it read at the time of his decision, the adjudicator had the power to make the order at issue.

FACTS

Respondent had been employed by appellant as a "radio time salesman" for three and a half years when he was dismissed on the ground that his performance was inadequate. It is not in dispute that when he was dismissed respondent received all moneys to which he was entitled under his employment contract.

However, respondent filed a complaint with an inspector alleging that he had been unjustly dismissed. As the parties were unable to settle this complaint and respondent asked that it be referred to an adjudicator, the Minister of Labour appointed an adjudicator to hear and decide the matter in accordance with the Code.

After hearing the evidence and the submissions of the parties, the adjudicator made an order directing the employer to pay respondent as compensation the sum of $46,628.96 with interest at the rate of 12% and to pay his counsel the sum of $42,500 to reimburse him for the legal costs incurred. The said order further imposed on the employer an obligation to give respondent a letter of recommendation certifying that he had been employed by Station Q107 from June, 1980 to January 20, 1984, and that an adjudicator had found he was unjustly dismissed and indicating the sales quotas he had been set and the amount of sales he actually made during this period. It should be noted that the order made specifically indicates the amounts to be shown as sales quotas and as sales actually made. Finally, the order directed appellant to answer requests for information about respondent only by sending this letter of recommendation.

[Lamer J. then set out the adjudicator's order as summarized in the preceding paragraph. The first four clauses of that order, relating to the payment of commissions, interest, and costs, were not challenged in the Supreme Court of Canada. The rest of the order read as follows:]

Under the power given me by paragraph (c) in subsection (9) of Section 61.5, I further order:

That the employer give the complainant a letter of recommendation, with a copy to this adjudicator, certifying that:

(1) Mr. Ron Davidson was employed by Station Q107 from June, 1980 to January 20, 1984, as a radio time salesman;

(2) That his sales "budget" or quota for 1981 was $248,000, of which he achieved 97.3 percent;

(3) That his sales "budget" or quota for 1982 was $343,500, of which he achieved 100.3 percent;

(4) That his sales "budget" or quota for 1983 was $402,200, of which he achieved 114.2 percent;

(5) That following termination in January, 1984, an adjudicator (appointed by the Minister of Labour) after hearing the evidence and representations of both parties, held that the termination had been an unjust dismissal.

I further order that any communication to Q107, its management or staff, whether received by letter, telephone or otherwise, from any person or company inquiring about Mr. Ron Davidson's employment at Q107, shall be answered exclusively by sending or delivering a copy of the said letter of recommendation.

Appellant is challenging in this court only the parts of the order relating to (1) the sending of a letter of recommendation and (2) the prohibition on answering a request for information in any other way than by sending this letter. . . .

LEGISLATION

The following legislation is relevant to this appeal:

Canada Labour Code

61.5(9) Where an adjudicator decides pursuant to subsection (8) that a person has been unjustly dismissed, he may, by order, require the employer who dismissed him to

(a) pay the person compensation not exceeding the amount of money that is equivalent to the remuneration that would, but for the dismissal, have been paid by the employer to the person;

(b) reinstate the person in his employ; and

(c) do any other like thing that it is equitable to require the employer to do in order to remedy or counteract any consequence of the dismissal.

Canadian Charter of Rights and Freedoms

1. The *Canadian Charter of Rights and Freedoms* guarantees the rights and freedoms set out in it subject only to such reasonable limits prescribed by law as can be demonstrably justified in a free and democratic society.

2. Everyone has the following fundamental freedoms:

(a) freedom of conscience and religion;

(b) freedom of thought, belief, opinion and expression, including freedom of the press and other media of communication;

(c) freedom of peaceful assembly; and

(d) freedom of association. . . .

32(1) This Charter applies

(a) to the Parliament and government of Canada in respect of all matters within the authority of Parliament including all matters relating to the Yukon Territory and Northwest Territories; and

(b) to the legislature and government of each province in respect of all matters within the authority of the legislature of each province.

ANALYSIS

To begin with, appellant argued that the adjudicator had no power to make these parts of the order since the orders he is authorized to make under s. 61.5(9)(c) must be of the same kind as the orders expressly mentioned in s. 61.5(9)(a) and (b), in view of the word "like" that appears in the English version.

As can readily be seen, the English and French versions of s. 61.5(9)(c) are different. Section 61.5(9)(c) of the English version confers a general power on the adjudicator as follows:

61.5(9) Where an adjudicator decides pursuant to subsection (8) that a person has been unjustly dismissed, he may, by order, require the employer who dismissed him to . . .

(c) do any other like thing that it is equitable to require the employer to do in order to remedy or counteract any consequence of the dismissal. (My emphasis.)

The French version, for its part, does not contain any word or expression equivalent to the word "like" used in the English version. The general power conferred on the adjudicator is conferred in the following language:

61.5(9) Lorsque l'arbitre décide conformément au paragraphe (8) que le congédiement d'une personne a été injuste, il peut, par ordonnance, requérir l'employeur . . .

(c) de faire toute autre chose qu'il juge équitable d'ordonner afin de contrebalancer les effets du congédiement ou d'y remédier.

First of all, therefore, these two versions have to be reconciled if possible. To do this, an attempt must be made to get from the two versions of the provision the meaning common to them both and ascertain whether this appears to be consistent with the purpose and general scheme of the Code.

In the case at bar I consider, like the Federal Court of Appeal judges, that the presence of the word "like" in para. (*c*) of the English version was not intended to limit the powers conferred on the adjudicator by allowing him to make only orders similar to the orders expressly mentioned in paras. (*a*) and (*b*) of that subsection, and does not have that effect. Interpreting this provision in this way would mean applying the *ejusdem generis* rule. I think it is impossible to apply this rule in the case at bar since one of the conditions essen-

807

tial for its application has not been met. The specific terms (here the orders referred to in paras. (*a*) and (*b*)) which precede the general term (the power conferred on the adjudicator in para. (*c*) to make any order that is equitable) must have a common characteristic, a common genus. As Maxwell writes in *Maxwell on the Interpretation of Statutes*, 12th ed. . . . :

> Unless there is a genus or class or category, there is no room for any application of the *ejusdem generis* doctrine. . . .

In the case at bar I do not see what characteristic could be described as common to a compensation order and a reinstatement order. The only "denominator" which seems to me common to these two orders in the context of s. 61.5(9) is the fact that these orders are both intended to remedy or counteract the consequences of the dismissal found by the adjudicator to be unjust. However, para. (*c*) expressly provides that an order made under that paragraph must be designed to remedy or counteract any consequence of the dismissal. This "common denominator" cannot therefore assist in the application of the *ejusdem generis* rule, since the legislator has already expressly provided that the orders the adjudicator is empowered to make must have this characteristic. Even if I were to admit that the English version should prevail over the French version, which I do not admit, I would still consider that this provision is ambiguous and that the most rational way of interpreting it is to say that the presence of the word "like" in this version does not have the effect of limiting the general power conferred on the adjudicator. This interpretation is in any case much more consistent with the general scheme of the Code, and in particular with the purpose of Division V.7, which is to give non-unionized employees a means of challenging a dismissal they feel to be unjust and at the same time to equip the adjudicator with the powers necessary to remedy the consequences of such a dismissal. Section 61.5 is clearly a remedial provision and must accordingly be given a broad interpretation. . . .

Appellant further argued that the adjudicator exceeded his jurisdiction since there is no connection between the order made in the case at bar, the dismissal and the consequences of that dismissal. I cannot entirely agree with him in this regard. The part of the order dealing with the sending of a letter of recommendation is, in my view, clearly meant to counteract the consequences of the dismissal found to be unjust by the adjudicator. This part of the order is designed to prevent the employer's decision to dismiss respondent from having negative consequences for the latter's chances of finding new employment. The letter of recommendation is intended to correct the impression given by the fact of the dismissal, by clearly indicating that the dismissal was found by an adjudicator to be unjust and by clearly setting out certain "objective" facts relating to respondent's performance. The situation is therefore very different from that which existed in Re *National Bank of Canada and Retail Clerks' Int'l Union*. . . .

In that case the Canada Labour Relations Board had found that the National Bank of Canada, which had closed a unionized branch and incorporated it in a non-unionized branch, had taken its decision for anti-union reasons and had therefore infringed s. 184(1)(*a*) and (3)(*a*) of the *Canada Labour Code*. These provisions prohibit an employer, *inter alia*, from interfering with the formation or administration of a trade union and from suspending, transferring or laying off an employee on the ground that he is a member of a trade union. The Canada Labour Relations Board had therefore ordered the bank to do a number of things. Among these were that it create a trust fund to further the objectives of the Code among all its employees and send the employees a letter telling them this fund had been created. The order specifically indicated what the wording of this letter should be and prohibited the employer from adding or deleting anything in its wording.

Chouinard J., with whose reasons the other members of this court concurred, said that in his opinion the part of the order prescribing the creation of a trust fund should be set aside since there was no relationship between this remedy and the alleged act and its consequences. He thought that the announcement of the creation of the fund was the key feature of the letter the employer was required to send, and concluded that this part of the order should suffer the same fate as that reserved for the part of the order dealing with the creation of the fund. Beetz J., for his part, added that in his opinion both the creation of the fund and the letter were open to the interpretation that they resulted from an initiative taken by the National Bank of Canada, reflecting the views of the bank and in particular its approval of the *Canada Labour Code* and its objectives. He stated that in his opinion this part of the order was contrary to the democratic traditions of this country and so could not have been authorized by the Parliament of Canada.

In the case at bar the letter the employer is required to give respondent is of a different nature from the letter the National Bank of Canada was required to send in that case. It expresses no opinions and simply sets out facts which, as counsel for the appellant admitted at the hearing, and it is important to note this, are not in dispute. Ordering an employer to give a former employee a letter of recommendation containing only objective facts that are not in dispute does not seem to me to be as such unreasonable. Such an order may be completely justified in certain circumstances, and in the case at bar there is nothing to indicate that the adjudicator was pursuing an improper objective or acting in bad faith or in a discriminatory manner. As this order was not unreasonable, it is not the function of this court to examine its appropriateness or to substitute its own opinion for that of the person making the order, unless of course the decision impinges on a right protected by the *Canadian Charter of Rights and Freedoms*.

Accordingly, I am not prepared to say at this stage that the nature of this part of the order is such that the adjudicator necessarily exceeded his jurisdiction in making it. Quite apart from the constitutional argument that this order infringes the freedom of expression guaranteed by the *Canadian Charter of Rights and Freedoms*, therefore, I consider that the adjudicator had the power to make this part of the order at issue here. The only limitation placed by s. 61.5(9) on the type of order the adjudicator can make is that any order must be designed to "remedy or counteract any consequence of the dismissal." In my view, this part of the order is clearly intended for that purpose.

However, I take a different view of the part of the order that prohibits the employer from answering a request for information about respondent other than by sending this letter of recommendation. Although this part of the order is probably meant to remedy or counteract the consequences of the dismissal, I believe that the issuing of this letter in such a context could be interpreted as meaning that appellant has no comments to make regarding the work done by respondent other than those mentioned in the letter. In such circumstances, it could thus be construed as expressing, at least by implication, appellant's opinion in this regard. Although requiring someone to write a letter is not unreasonable as such, the requirement becomes wholly unreasonable when the circumstances are such that the letter may be seen as reflecting their opinions when that is not necessarily the case. This part of the order does not prohibit the employer from stating facts found to be incorrect at the hearing, which might have been reasonable and justified: it prohibits the employer from making comments of any kind. In my view the effect of this part of the order, by thus prohibiting the employer from adding any comments whatsoever, is to create circumstances in which the letter of recommendation could be seen as the expression of appellant's opinions. As my brother Beetz J. so admirably phrased it in *National Bank of Canada* . . . :

> This type of penalty is totalitarian and as such alien to the tradition of free nations like Canada, even for the repression of the most serious crimes.

Parliament cannot have intended to authorize such an unreasonable use of the discretion conferred by it. A discretion is never absolute, regardless of the terms in which it is conferred. This is a long-established principle. H.W.R. Wade, in his text titled *Administrative Law*, . . . says the following . . . :

> For more than three centuries it has been accepted that discretionary power conferred upon public authorities is not absolute, even within its apparent boundaries, but is subject to general legal limitations. These limitations are expressed in a variety of different ways, as by saying that discretion must be exercised reasonably and in good faith, that relevant considerations only must be taken into account, that there must be no malversation of any kind, or that the decision must not be arbitrary or capricious.

This limitation on the exercise of administrative discretion has been clearly recognized in our law, by *C.U.P.E., Local 963 v. New Brunswick Liquor Corp.* . . . and *Blanchard v. Control Data Canada Ltd.* . . . inter alia. Whether it is the interpretation of legislation that is unreasonable or the order made in my view matters no more than the question of whether the error is one of law or of fact. An administrative tribunal exercising discretion can never do so unreasonably. . . .

In the case at bar I consider that the adjudicator was not authorized by s. 61.5(9)(c) to order the employer not to answer a request for information about respondent except by sending the letter of recommendation containing the aforementioned wording, since such an order is patently unreasonable. Though the adjudicator clearly had jurisdiction to make an order he felt to be equitable and proper, he lost this jurisdiction when he made a patently unreasonable decision. . . .

It now remains to assess in light of the *Canadian Charter of Rights and Freedoms* the part of the order we have found to be not unreasonable in terms of the rules of administrative law. The fact that the part of the order relating to sending the letter of recommendation is not unreasonable from an administrative law standpoint does not mean that it is necessarily consistent with the *Charter*.

The fact that the *Charter* applies to the order made by the adjudicator in the case at bar is not, in my opinion, open to question. The adjudicator is a statutory creature: he is appointed pursuant to a legislative provision and derives *all* his powers from the statute. As the Constitution is the supreme law of Canada and any law that is inconsistent with its provisions is, to the extent of the inconsistency, of no force or effect, it is impossible to interpret legislation conferring discretion as conferring a power to infringe the *Charter*, unless, of course, that power is expressly conferred or necessarily implied. Such an interpretation would require us to declare the legislation to be of no force or effect, unless it could be justified under s. 1. . . .

There is no doubt in the case at bar that the part of the order dealing with the issuing of a letter of recommendation places, in my opinion, a limitation on freedom of expression. There is no denying that freedom of expression necessarily entails the right to say nothing or the right not to say certain things. Silence is in itself a form of expression which in some circumstances can express something more clearly than words could do. The order directing appellant to give respondent a letter containing certain objective facts in my opinion unquestionably limits appellant's freedom of expression.

However, this limitation is prescribed by law and can therefore be justified under s. 1. . . .

To determine whether this limitation is reasonable and can be demonstrably justified in a free and democratic society, . . . one must examine whether the use made of the discretion has the effect of keeping the limitation within reasonable limits that can be demonstrably justified in a free and democratic society. . . .

The test that must be applied in such an assessment has been largely defined by my brother Dickson C.J.C. in *R. v. Oakes*. . . . According to that test, the objective to be served by the disputed measures must first be sufficiently important to warrant limiting a right or freedom protected by the Charter. Second, the party seeking to maintain the limitation must show that the means selected to attain this objective are reasonable and justifiable. To do this, it will be necessary to apply a form of proportionality test involving three separate components: the disputed measures must be fair and not arbitrary, carefully designed to achieve the objective in question and rationally connected to that objective. The means chosen must also be such as to impair the right or freedom as little as possible, and finally, its effects must be proportional to the objective sought.

I consider that the objective sought by the order made in the case at bar is sufficiently important to justify some limitation on freedom of expression. The purpose of the order is clearly, as required by the Code and as I indicated above, to counteract, or at least to remedy, the consequences of the dismissal found by the adjudicator to be unjust. . . . I think it is important for the legislator to provide certain mechanisms to restore equilibrium in the relations between an employer and his employee, so that the latter will not be subject to arbitrary action by the former. These observations should not be taken as meaning that in my view all employers necessarily try to abuse their position. However, it cannot be denied that some employees are in an especially vulnerable position in relation to their employers and that the forces involved are usually not equal. Accordingly, I think that mechanisms designed to remedy or counteract the consequences of an unlawful action taken by an employer are justified in such a context. It should also be noted that in these circumstances the limitation on rights or freedoms is not in fact made until after the act committed by the employer has been found by an adjudicator to be unlawful, and only in order to remedy the consequences of that act found to be unlawful.

An order directing the employer to give respondent a letter of recommendation containing objective facts also seems to me to be reasonable and justifiable in these circumstances. It has the three characteristics necessary to meet the proportionality test. As I mentioned earlier, the purpose of the letter of recommendation is to correct the impression given by the fact of the dismissal, by clearly indicating that the dismissal was found by an adjudicator to be unjust, and by clearly indicating certain "objective" facts that are not in dispute regarding the respondent's performance. A reinstatement order is not always desirable and a compensation order is not always adequate to remedy the consequences of an unjust dismissal. It is possible in some cases for a dismissal to have very negative consequences on the former employee's chances of finding new employment. It seems to me, therefore, that there will be times when such an order is the only means of attaining the objective sought, that of counteracting or remedying the consequences of the dismissal. It is certainly very rationally connected to the latter, since in certain cases it is the only way of effectively remedying the consequences of the dismissal. It is also limited to requiring that the employer state "objective" facts which, in the case at bar, are not in dispute and do not require the employer to express any opinion, since the part of the order regarding the prohibition on answering a request for information about respondent other than by issuing this letter has been found to be unreasonable, and accordingly outside the jurisdiction conferred on the adjudicator. The employer may thus, if this part found to be unreasonable is removed, indicate for example that he was directed to write the letter and that it therefore does not necessarily contain all his views about the work done by respondent. Taking these circumstances into account, I do not see any way of attaining this objective in the case at bar without impairing the employer's freedom of expression. Finally, I consider that the consequences of the order are proportional to the objective sought. As I have already said, the latter is important in our society. The limitation on freedom of expression is not what could be described as very serious. It does not abolish that freedom, but simply limits its exercise by requiring the employer to write something determined in advance. This limitation on freedom of expression mentioned in the *Charter* is thus in my opinion kept within reasonable limits that can be demonstrably justified in a free and democratic society. In making this part of the order, therefore, the adjudicator did not infringe the *Charter* and acted within his jurisdiction. . . .

Accordingly, I would allow the appeal at bar, reverse the judgment of the Federal Court of Appeal, invalidate the order made by the adjudicator and refer the matter back to him so he may make a new order consistent with the instant judgment; the whole with costs.

DICKSON C.J.C. (WILSON, LA FOREST, and L'HEUREUX-DUBE JJ. concurring): . . . I have had the benefit of reading the opinion of Justice Lamer and I am in complete agreement with his discussion of the applicability of the *Charter* to administrative decision-making. I also agree with his conclusion that the positive order made by Adjudicator Joliffe (to draw up and to give the respondent a specified letter of reference) infringes s. 2(b) of the *Charter* but is saved by s. 1. However, with regard to the negative order (that any inquiry about the respondent's employment at Q107 be answered exclusively by the letter of reference which is the subject of the positive order), I must respectfully disagree with the conclusion of Lamer J. that it is patently unreasonable, thereby obviating the need to consider the *Charter*. Furthermore, not only am I of the view that the negative order is reasonable in the administrative law sense but I also believe that it is reasonable and demonstrably justified in the sense of s. 1 of the *Charter*. . . .

It cannot be over-emphasized that the adjudicator's remedy in this case was a legislatively-sanctioned attempt to remedy the unequal balance of power that normally exists between an employer and employee. Thus, in a general sense, this case falls within a class of cases in which the governmental objective is that of protection of a particularly vulnerable group, or members thereof. In *R. v. Edwards Books & Art Ltd.* . . . I stated for the majority . . . :

> In interpreting and applying the *Charter* I believe that the courts must be cautious to ensure that it does not simply become an instrument of better situated individuals to roll back legislation which has as its object the improvement of the condition of less advantaged persons. When the interests of more than seven vulnerable employees in securing a Sunday holiday are weighed against the interests of their employer in transacting business on a Sunday, I cannot fault the Legislature for determining that the protection of the employees ought to prevail.

Consistent with the above view of the place of the *Charter*, I can think of no better way to describe the employment relationship than as expressed in P. Davies and M. Freedland, *Kahn-Freund's Labour and the Law* . . . :

> [T]he relation between an employer and an isolated employee or worker is typically a relation between a bearer of power and one who is not a bearer of power. In its inception it is an act of submission, in its operation it is a condition of subordination . . . The main object of labour law has always been, and we venture to say will always be, to be a countervailing force to counteract the inequality of bargaining power which is inherent and must be inherent in the employment relationship. Most of what we call protective legislation — legislation on the employment of women, children and young persons, on safety in mines, factories, and offices, on payment of wages in cash, on guarantee payments, on race or sex discrimination, on unfair dismissal, and indeed most labour legislation altogether — must be seen in this context. It is an attempt to infuse law into a relation of command and subordination.

The objective of both the positive and negative orders made by Adjudicator Joliffe is sensitive to the reality identified by Kahn-Freund, Davies and Freedland. The courts must be just as concerned to avoid constitutionalizing inequalities of power in the workplace and between societal actors in general. It must be recalled that *Oakes* . . . stated that

> The underlying values and principles of a free and democratic society are the genesis of the rights and freedoms guaranteed by the Charter and the ultimate standard against which a limit on a right or freedom must be shown, despite its effect, to be reasonable and demonstrably justified.

As long as the proportionality test is met, it would not, on the facts of this case, be in accordance with those underlying principles and values for the *Charter* to be successfully invoked by an employer. The inequality in one employment relationship would be continued even after its termination with the result that the worker looking for a new job would be placed in an even more unequal bargaining position vis-à-vis prospective employers than is normally the case. On the facts of this case, constitutionally protecting freedom of expression would be tantamount to condoning the continuation of an abuse of an already unequal relationship.

PROPORTIONALITY

(a) Rational connection

The negative order is very much rationally linked to the objective, no less than the positive order. The adjudicator was plainly of the view that the respondent had been the subject of some kind of personal vendetta or "set-up," as Mahoney J. termed it, *supra* . . . which had been initiated by the employer's general manager and executed by its sales manager, the latter of whom was Mr. Davidson's immediate superior.

As I have indicated, the representative of the employer was found to have engaged in bad faith and duplicitous conduct, giving misleading evidence about Mr. Davidson's work performance both at the time of his dismissal and during the unjust dismissal hearing. Further, in deciding that reinstatement was not a viable remedy, the adjudicator gave as his reason that "[t]here is no sign that he would receive fair treatment by and employer which has made such vigorous efforts to justify the indefensible." With this proven history of promoting a fabricated version of the quality of Mr. Davidson's service and the concern that the employer would continue to treat him unfairly if he went back to work for the employer, it was rational for the adjudicator to attach a rider to the order for a reference letter so as to ensure that representatives of the employer did not subvert the effect of the letter by unjustifiably maligning its previous employee in the guise of giving a reference.

(b) Minimal impairment

In my view, there was no less intrusive measure that the adjudicator could have taken and still have achieved the objective with any likelihood. To the extent there was a likelihood that representatives of Q107 would not be content to pass on the letter of reference absent the kind of untrue comments that had resulted in the finding of unjust dismissal, the letter of reference would have been rendered illusory to the same degree of likelihood.

While an order of additional monetary compensation would clearly be less intrusive upon the appellant's freedom of expression, it would not be an acceptable substitute. Even if the adjudicator had ordered that Mr. Davidson could come back once he had secured a job and be granted compensation, above and beyond unemployment insurance, for the actual period out of work, this would only be compensation for the *economic* effects of lack of employment not the *personal* effects. This is directly contrary to the objective sought to be achieved by the order, which is securing new employment in the shortest order possible: the corollary of this objective is, of course, a concern to alleviate the personal problems associated with being out of work . . . .

Monetary compensation can only be an alternative measure if labour is treated as a commodity and every day without work seen as being exhaustively reducible to some pecuniary value. As I had occasion to say in *Reference re Public Service Employee Relations Act (Alta.)* . . . , "[a] person's employment is an essential component of his or her sense of identity, self-worth and emotional well-being." Viewing labour as a commodity is incompatible with such a perspective, which is reflected in the remedial objective chosen by the adjudicator. To posit compensation as a less intrusive measure is, in effect, to challenge the legitimacy of the objective.

Consider the facts of this particular case. The letter was tightly and carefully designed to reflect only a very narrow range of facts which, we saw, were not really contested. As already discussed, unlike in *National Bank* . . . the employer has not been forced to state opinions ("views and sentiments," per Beetz J. . . .) which are not its own. Rather, the negative order seeks to prevent the employer from passing on an opinion, such prohibition being closely tied to the history of abuse of power which had been found to exist. Furthermore, that prohibition is very circumscribed. Firstly, it is triggered only in cases when the appellant is contacted for a reference and, secondly, there is no requirement to send the letter to anyone other then prospective employers. In sum, this is a much less intrusive and carefully designed order than that in *National Bank* in which the bank was required to send to a very large audience (all the employees and management staff of the bank) what amounted to a letter of contrition which conveyed the impression that certain opinions expressed therein were those of the employer.

Finally, it cannot be ignored that a letter such as this may not have a great beneficial impact on an employee's job hunt. The letter is very neutral in tone, totally unembellished as it is by any opinion customary in letter of reference, and it refers to the fact of the finding of unjust dismissal. It seems to me that the adjudicator went no further than was necessary to achieve the objective and, even then, the measures adopted by the adjudicator cannot be said to have done more than to have enhanced, as opposed to having ensured, the chances of the respondent finding a job. The adjudicator did not in any sense pursue the objective without regard to the appellant's right to free expression.

(c) Deleterious effects

It is clear to me that the effects of the measures are not so deleterious as to outweigh the objective of the measures. . . . As was said in *Oakes, supra* . . . , among the underlying values essential to our free and democratic society are "the inherent dignity of the human person" and "commitment to social justice and equality." Especially in light of Canada's ratification of the *International Covenant on Economic, Social and Cultural Rights*, . . . and commitment therein to protect, *inter alia*, the right to work in its various dimensions found in art. 6 of that treaty, it cannot be doubted that the objective in this case is a very important one. In *Reference re Public Service Employee Relations Act (Alta)*, . . . I had occasion to say . . . :

> The content of Canada's international human rights obligations is, in my view, an important indicia of the meaning of the "full benefit of the *Charter*'s protection." I believe that the *Charter* should generally be presumed to provide protection at least as

great as that afforded by similar provisions in international human rights documents which Canada has ratified.

Given the dual function of s. 1 identified in *Oakes*, Canada's international human rights obligations should inform not only the interpretation of the content of the rights guaranteed by the *Charter* but also the interpretation of what can constitute pressing and substantial s. 1 objectives which may justify restrictions upon those rights. Furthermore, for purposes of this stage of the proportionality inquiry, the fact that a value has the status of an international human right, either in customary international law or under a treaty to which Canada is a state party, should generally be indicative of a high degree of importance attached to that objective. This is consistent with the importance that this court has placed on the protection of employees as a vulnerable group in society.

In normal course, the suppression of one's right to express an opinion about a subject or person will be a serious infringement of s. 2(b) and only outweighed by very important objectives. In the foregoing analysis, I have sought to show that the negative order was minimally intrusive in a relative sense and also that the careful tailoring of both parts of the order has made this a much less serious infringement of s. 2(b) than, for instance, occurred in the *National Bank* case.

CONCLUSION

In conclusion, I am of the opinion that both of the adjudicator's orders at issue (the positive order and the negative order) infringe s. 2(*b*) but are saved by s. 1. I would answer both constitutional questions in the affirmative and dismiss the appeal with costs.

12.630 The Interface between Statutory and Common Law Forums

> REFERENCES
>
> **Geoffrey England, Innis Christie, & Roderick Wood, *Employment Law in Canada*, 3d ed. (Markham: Butterworths, 1998), paras. 8.59–8.74 and c. 20**

A contemporary issue in employment law and statutory employment standards, that has received much judicial attention but has yet to be settled, is the question of finality in litigation. This is sometimes expressed in the related concepts of issue estoppel and *res judicata*. The law places a premium on permitting a litigant to advance a dispute only in one legal forum. Once the litigated dispute has been decided by the initial forum, the litigant should not be able to re-try essentially the same issue in another. The public policy reasons for restricting the multiple litigation of the same issue include the drain on public resources, the potential for inconsistent results, the burden of costs on the respondent, and the delay in resolving the issue. Yet the courts have been reluctant to restrict a litigant from pursuing a claim in a second forum if a strict application of issue estoppel or *res judicata* would result in unfairness.

With a variety of potential forums to litigate employment issues, legislatures and the courts have regularly faced the vexing issue of how broad to cast the rule on litigation finality. For example, the Ontario Legislature enacted amendments to the *Employment*

Standards Act in 1996 which prohibited an employee who had already filed a complaint under the Act for termination pay or severance pay from initiating a civil action for wrongful dismissal: section 64.3. Yet the courts, while endorsing the general principle against the re-litigation of a legal dispute, have regularly sought to refine the rules on issue estoppel and *res judicata* to allow for exceptions. Indeed, whenever one court has articulated a strict rule that would significantly reduce the possibility of pursuing a dispute in a second legal forum (as in *Rasanen v. Rosemount Instruments Ltd.* (1994), 17 O.R. (3d) 267 (C.A.)), a subsequent ruling seems to undo some of the strictness. The following decision of the Supreme Court of Canada is an example of the latter type of ruling. It discusses the competing policy concerns involved in developing a workable doctrine of issue estoppel.

Danyluk v. Ainsworth Technologies Inc., [2001], 2 S.C.R. 460

[In October 1993, while still an employee, Danyluk filed a complaint under the Ontario *Employment Standards Act* claiming that her employer owed her $300,000 in unpaid commissions. Shortly afterwards, the employer escorted her off the worksite, and maintained that she had resigned.

Danyluk met with an employment standards officer in January 1994. The officer wrote to the employer, seeking some documentation. In March 1994, Danyluk's lawyer, having heard nothing from the officer, initiated a court action for wrongful dismissal, and included a claim for the unpaid wages and commissions that were already the subject matter of the ESA complaint. The employer eventually sent the requested documentation to the officer in June 1994, but did not send copies to Danyluk. Nor did the ESA officer send her any of the documents, or give her any opportunity to respond to the employer's position. Eventually, in September 1994, the ESA officer advised the employer, but not Danyluk, that the officer had rejected her claim for the unpaid commissions. However, the officer ordered the employer to pay Danyluk $2,300, which represented the two weeks' pay in lieu of notice owing under the Act. In October, Danyluk finally received a letter from the ESA officer outlining the decision and explained that Ms. Danyluk could appeal the matter to the Director of Employment Standards. Danyluk decided instead to proceed with her civil action.

The employer subsequently brought a motion to strike from Danyluk's civil action her claim for the unpaid wages and commissions, arguing that they were barred by issue estoppel because of the ESA proceedings. The Ontario Court (General Division) granted the motion, and allowed only the claim for damages for wrongful dismissal to proceed. The Ontario Court of Appeal upheld that decision, and Danyluk appealed to the Supreme Court of Canada.]

BINNIE J. for the Court:

The law rightly seeks a finality to litigation. To advance that objective, it requires litigants to put their best foot forward to establish the truth of their allegations when first called upon to do so. A litigant, to use the vernacular, is only entitled to one bite at the cherry.

The appellant chose the ESA as her forum. She lost. An issue, once decided, should not generally be re-litigated to the benefit of the losing party and the harassment of the winner. A person should only be vexed once in the same cause. Duplicative litigation, potential inconsistent results, undue costs, and inconclusive proceedings are to be avoided.

Finality is thus a compelling consideration and judicial decisions should generally be conclusive of the issues decided unless and until reversed on appeal. However, estoppel is a doctrine of public policy that is designed to advance the interests of justice. Where as here, its application bars the courthouse door against the appellant's $300,000 claim because of an administrative decision taken in a manner which was manifestly improper and unfair (as found by the Court of Appeal itself), a re-examination of some basic principles is warranted.

The law has developed a number of techniques to prevent abuse of the decision-making process. One of the oldest is the doctrine estoppel *per rem judicatem* with its roots in Roman law, the idea that a dispute once judged with finality is not subject to relitigation. . . . The bar extends both to the cause of action thus adjudicated (variously referred to as claim or cause of action or action estoppel), as well as precluding relitigation of the constituent issues or material facts necessarily embraced therein (usually called issue estoppel): G.S. Holmested and G.D. Watson, *Ontario Civil Procedure* (loose-leaf), vol. 3 supp., at 21'17 *et seq.* Another aspect of the judicial policy favouring finality is the rule against collateral attack, i.e., that a judicial order pronounced by a court of competent jurisdiction should not be brought into question in subsequent proceedings except those provided by law for the express purpose of attacking it. . . .

The preconditions to the operation of issue estoppel were set out by Dickson J. in *Angle* [*v. Minister of National Revenue*]. . . :

(1) that the same question has been decided;

(2) that the judicial decision which is said to create the estoppel was final; and,

(3) that the parties to the judicial decision or their privies were the same persons as the parties to the proceedings in which the estoppel is raised or their privies.

. . .

The appellant's argument is that even though the ESA officer was required to make a decision in a judicial manner, she failed to do so. Although she had jurisdiction under the ESA to deal with the claim, the ESA officer lost jurisdiction when she failed to disclose to the appellant the case the appellant had to meet and to give the appellant the opportunity to be heard in answer to the case put against her. The ESA officer therefore never made a "judicial decision" as required. The appellant also says that her own failure to exercise her right to seek internal administrative review of the decision should not be given the conclusive effect adopted by the Ontario Court of Appeal. Even if the conditions precedent to issue estoppel were present, she says, the court had a discretion to relieve against the harsh effects of estoppel per rem judicatem in the circumstances of this case, and erred in failing to do so.

A. The Statutory Scheme

1. The Employment Standards Officer

The ESA applies to "every contract of employment, oral or written, express or implied" in Ontario (s. 2(2)) subject to certain exceptions under the regulations, and establishes a number of minimum employment standards for the protection of employees. These include hours of work, minimum wages, overtime pay, benefit plans, public holidays and vacation with pay. More specifically, the Act provides a summary procedure under which aggrieved employees can seek redress with respect to an employer's alleged failure to comply with these standards. The objective is to make redress available, where it is appropriate at all, expeditiously and cheaply. In the first instance, the dispute is referred to an employment standards officer. ESA officers are public servants in the Ministry of Labour. They are generally not legally trained, but have some experience in labour relations. The statute does not set out any particular procedure that must be followed in disposing of claims. ESA officers are given wide powers to enter premises, inspect and remove documents and make other relevant inquiries. If liability is found, ESA officers have broad powers of enforcement (s. 65).

On receipt of an employee demand, generally speaking, the ESA officer contacts the employer to ascertain whether in fact wages are unpaid and if so for what reason. Although in this case there was a one-hour meeting between the ESA officer and the appellant, there is no requirement for such a face-to-face meeting, and clearly there is no contemplation of any sort of oral hearing in which both parties are present. It is a rough-and-ready procedure that is wholly inappropriate, one might think, to the definitive resolution of a contractual claim of some legal and factual complexity.

There are many advantages to the employee in such a forum. The services of the ESA officer are supplied free of charge. Legal representation is unnecessary. The process moves more rapidly than could realistically be expected in the courts. There are corresponding disadvantages. The ESA officer is likely not to have legal training and has neither the time nor the resources to deal with a contract claim in a manner comparable to the courtroom setting. At the time of these proceedings a double standard was applied to an appeal (or, as it is called, a "review"). The employer was entitled as of right to a review (s. 68) but, as discussed below, the employee could ask for one but the request could be refused by the Director (s. 67(3)). At the time, as well, there was no monetary limit on the ESA officer's jurisdiction. The Act has since been amended to provide an upper limit on claims of $10,000 (S.O. 1996, c. 23, s. 19(1)). Had the ESA officer's determination gone the other way, the employer could have been saddled with a $300,000 liability arising out of a deeply flawed decision unless reversed on an administrative review or quashed by a supervising court.

2. The Review Process

The employee, as stated, has no appeal as of right. Section 67(2) of the Act provides that an employee dissatisfied with the decision at first instance may apply to the Director for an administrative review in writing within 15 days of the date of the mailing of the employment standards officer's decision. Under s. 67(3), "the Director may appoint an adjudicator who shall hold a hearing" (emphasis added). The word "may" grants the Director a discretion to hold or not to hold a hearing. The Ontario Court of Appeal noted this point, but said the parties had attached little importance to it.

It seems clear the legislature did not intend to confer an appeal as of right. Where the Director does appoint an adjudicator a hearing is mandated by the Act. Further delay and expense to the Ministry and the parties would follow as a matter of course. The juxtaposition in s. 67(3) of "may" and "shall" (and in the French text, the instruction that the Director "*peut nommer un arbitre de griefs pour tenir une audience*" (emphasis added)) puts the matter beyond doubt. The Ontario legislature intended the Director to have a discretion to decline to refer a matter to an adjudicator which, in his or her opinion, is simply not justified. Even the adjudicators hearing a review under s. 67(3) of the Act are not by statute required to be legally trained. It was likely considered undesirable by the Ontario legislature to give each and every dissatisfied employee a review as of right, particularly where the amounts in issue are often relatively modest. The discretion must be exercised according to proper principles, of course, but a discretion it remains.

If an internal review were ordered, an adjudicator would then have looked at the appellant's claim de novo and would undoubtedly have shared the employer documents with the appellant and given her every opportunity to respond and comment. I agree that under the scheme of the Act procedural defects at the ESA officer level, including a failure to provide proper notice and an opportunity to be heard in response to the opposing case, can be rectified on review. The respondent says the appellant, having elected to proceed under the Act, was required to seek an internal review if she was dissatisfied with the initial outcome. Not having done so, she is estopped from pursuing her $300,000 claim. The appellant says that the ESA procedure was so deeply flawed that she was entitled to walk away from it.

B. The Applicability of Issue Estoppel

1. Issue Estoppel: A Two-Step Analysis

The rules governing issue estoppel should not be mechanically applied. The underlying purpose is to balance the public interest in the finality of litigation with the public interest in ensuring that justice is done on the facts of a particular case. (There are corresponding private interests.) The first step is to determine whether the moving party (in this case the respondent) has established the preconditions to the operation of issue estoppel set out by Dickson J. in *Angle, supra*. If successful, the court must still determine whether, as a matter of discretion, issue estoppel *ought* to be applied. . . .

The appellant was quite entitled, in the first instance, to invoke the jurisdiction of the Ontario superior court to deal with her various monetary claims. The respondent was not entitled as of right to the imposition of an estoppel. It was up to the court to decide whether, in the exercise of its discretion, it would decline to hear aspects of the claims that were previously the subject of ESA administrative proceedings.

2. The Judicial Nature of the Decision

A common element of the preconditions to issue estoppel set out by Dickson J. in *Angle, supra*, is the fundamental requirement that the decision in the prior proceeding be a *judi-*

cial decision. According to the authorities . . . , there are three elements that may be taken into account. First is to examine the nature of the administrative authority issuing the decision. Is it an institution that is capable of receiving and exercising adjudicative authority? Secondly, as a matter of law, is the particular decision one that was required to be made in a judicial manner? Thirdly, as a mixed question of law and fact, *was* the decision made in a judicial manner? . . .

The main controversy in this case is directed to this third aspect, i.e., is a decision taken without regard to requirements of notice and an opportunity to be heard capable of supporting an issue estoppel? In my opinion, the answer to this question is yes. . . .

In my view, with respect, the theory that a denial of natural justice deprives the ESA decision of its character as a "judicial" decision rests on a misconception. Flawed the decision may be, but "judicial" (as distinguished from administrative or legislative) it remains. Once it is determined that the decision-maker was capable of receiving and exercising adjudicative authority and that the particular decision was one that was required to be made in a judicial manner, the decision does not cease to have that character ("judicial") because the decision-maker erred in carrying out his or her functions. . . . The decision remains a "judicial decision," although seriously flawed by the want of proper notice and the denial of the opportunity to be heard.

. . .

In summary it is clear that an administrative decision which is made without jurisdiction from the outset cannot form the basis of an estoppel. The conditions precedent to the adjudicative jurisdiction must be satisfied. Where arguments can be made that an administrative officer or tribunal initially possessed the jurisdiction to make a decision in a judicial manner but erred in the exercise of that jurisdiction, the resulting decision is nevertheless capable of forming the basis of an estoppel. Alleged errors in carrying out the mandate are matters to be considered by the court in the exercise of its discretion. This result makes the principle governing estoppel consistent with the law governing judicial review . . . and collateral attack. . . .

Where I differ from the Ontario Court of Appeal in this case is in its conclusion that the failure of the appellant to seek such an administrative review of the ESA officer's flawed decision was fatal to her position. In my view, with respect, the refusal of the ESA officer to afford the appellant proper notice and the opportunity to be heard are matters of great importance in the exercise of the court's discretion, as will be seen.

I turn now to the three preconditions to issue estoppel set out by Dickson J. in *Angle, supra.* . . .

3. Issue Estoppel: Applying the Tests

(a) That the Same Question Has Been Decided

A cause of action has traditionally been defined as comprising every fact which it would be necessary for the plaintiff to prove, if disputed, in order to support his or her right to the judgment of the court. . . . Establishing each such fact (sometimes referred to as material facts) constitutes a precondition to success. It is apparent that different causes of action may have one or more material facts in common. In this case, for example, the existence of an employment contract is a material fact common to both the ESA proceeding and to the appellant's wrongful dismissal claim in court. Issue estoppel simply means that once a material fact such as a valid employment contract is found to exist (or not to exist) by a court or tribunal of competent jurisdiction, whether on the basis of evidence or admissions, the same issue cannot be relitigated in subsequent proceedings between the same parties. The estoppel, in other words, extends to the issues of fact, law, and mixed fact and law that are necessarily bound up with the determination of that "issue" in the prior proceeding.

The parties are agreed here that the "same issue" requirement is satisfied. In the appellant's wrongful dismissal action, she is claiming $300,000 in unpaid commissions. This puts in issue the same entitlement as was refused her in the ESA proceeding. One or more of the factual or legal issues essential to this entitlement were necessarily determined against her in the earlier ESA proceeding. If issue estoppel applies, it prevents her from asserting that these adverse findings ought now to be found in her favour.

(b) That the Judicial Decision Which Is Said to Create the Estoppel Was Final

As already discussed, the requirement that the prior decision be "judicial" (as opposed to administrative or legislative) is satisfied in this case.

Further, I agree with the Ontario Court of Appeal that the employee not having taken advantage of the internal review procedure, the decision of the ESA officer was final for the purposes of the Act and therefore capable in the normal course of events of giving rise to an estoppel.

I have already noted that in this case, unlike *Harelkin, supra*, the appellant had no right of appeal. She could merely make a request to the ESA Director for a review by an ESA adjudicator. While this may be a factor in the exercise of the discretion to deny issue estoppel, it does not affect the finality of the ESA decision. The appellant could fairly argue on a judicial review application that unlike Harelkin she had no "adequate alternative remedy" available to her as of right. The ESA decision must nevertheless be treated as final for present purposes.

(c) That the Parties to the Judicial Decision or Their Privies Were the Same Persons as the Parties to the Proceedings in Which the Estoppel Is Raised or Their Privies

This requirement assures mutuality. If the limitation did not exist, a stranger to the earlier proceeding could insist that a party thereto be bound in subsequent litigation by the findings in the earlier litigation even though the stranger, who became a party only to the subsequent litigation, would not be. . . . The mutuality requirement was subject to some critical comment by McEachern C.J.B.C. when sitting as a trial judge in *Saskatoon Credit Union Ltd. v. Central Park Ent. Ltd..* . . . , and has been substantially modified in many jurisdictions in the United States. . . .

The concept of "privity" of course is somewhat elastic. The learned editors of J. Sopinka, S. N. Lederman and A. W. Bryant in *The Law of Evidence in Canada* (2nd ed. 1999), at p. 1088 say, somewhat pessimistically, that "[i]t is impossible to be categorical about the degree of interest which will create privity" and that determinations must be made on a case-by-case basis. In this case, the parties are identical and the outer limits of "mutuality" and of the "same parties" requirement need not be further addressed.

I conclude that the preconditions to issue estoppel are met in this case.

4. The Exercise of the Discretion

The appellant submitted that the Court should nevertheless refuse to apply estoppel as a matter of discretion. There is no doubt that such a discretion exists. In *General Motors of Canada Ltd. v. Naken*, . . . Estey J. noted, at p. 101, that in the context of court proceedings "such a discretion must be very limited in application." In my view the discretion is necessarily broader in relation to the prior decisions of administrative tribunals because of the enormous range and diversity of the structures, mandates and procedures of administrative decision makers.

In [*British Columbia (Minister of Forests) v. Bugbusters Pest Management Inc.* . . .,] Finch J.A. (now C.J.B.C.) observed, at para. 32:

> It must always be remembered that although the three requirements for issue estoppel must be satisfied before it can apply, the fact that they may be satisfied does not automatically give rise to its application. Issue estoppel is an equitable doctrine, and as can be seen from the cases, is closely related to abuse of process. The doctrine of issue estoppel is designed as an implement of justice, and a protection against injustice. It inevitably calls upon the exercise of a judicial discretion to achieve fairness according to the circumstances of each case.

Apart from noting parenthetically that estoppel *per rem judicatem* is generally considered a common law doctrine (unlike promissory estoppel which is clearly equitable in origin), I think this is a correct statement of the law. Finch J.A.'s *dictum* was adopted and applied by the Ontario Court of Appeal in [*Schweneke v. Ontario*], at paras. 38 and 43:

> The discretion to refuse to give effect to issue estoppel becomes relevant only where the three prerequisites to the operation of the doctrine exist. . . . The exercise of the discretion is necessarily case specific and depends on the entirety of the circumstances. In exercising the discretion the court must ask — is there something in the circumstances of this case such that the usual operation of the doctrine of issue estoppel would work an injustice?
>
> . . .
>
> . . . The discretion must respond to the realities of each case and not to abstract concerns that arise in virtually every case where the finding relied on to support the doctrine was made by a tribunal and not a court.

. . .

In the present case Rosenberg J.A. noted in passing at pp. 248–49 the possible existence of a potential discretion but, with respect, he gave it short shrift. There was no discussion or analysis of the merits of its exercise. He simply concluded, at p. 256:

> In summary, Ms. Burke [the employment standards officer] did not accord this appellant natural justice. The appellant's recourse was to seek review of Ms. Burke's decision. She failed to do so. That decision is binding upon her and her employer.

In my view it was an error of principle not to address the factors for and against the exercise of the discretion which the court clearly possessed. This is not a situation where this Court is being asked by an appellant to substitute its opinion for that of the motions judge or the Court of Appeal. The appellant is entitled at some stage to appropriate consideration of the discretionary factors and to date this has not happened.

The list of factors is open. They include many of the same factors listed in [*R. v. Consolidated Maybrun Mines Ltd.*] in connection with the rule against collateral attack. . . . The objective is to ensure that the operation of issue estoppel promotes the orderly administration of justice but not at the cost of real injustice in the particular case. Seven factors, discussed below, are relevant in this case.

(a) The Wording of the Statute from which the Power to Issue the Administrative Order Derives
In this case the ESA includes s. 6(1) which provides that:

> No civil remedy of an employee against his or her employer is suspended *or affected* by this Act. [Emphasis added.]

This provision suggests that at the time the Ontario legislature did not intend ESA proceedings to become an exclusive forum. (Recent amendments to the Act now require an employee to elect either the ESA procedure or the court. Even prior to the new amendments, however, a court could properly conclude that relitigation of an issue would be an abuse: *Rasanen, supra, per* Morden A.C.J.O., at p. 293, Carthy J.A., at p. 288.)

While it is generally reasonable for defendants to expect to be able to move on with their lives once one set of proceedings — including any available appeals — has ended in a rejection of liability, here, the appellant commenced her civil action against the respondents before the ESA officer reached a decision (as was clearly authorized by the statute at that time). Thus, the respondents were well aware, in law and in fact, that they were expected to respond to parallel and to some extent overlapping proceedings.

(b) The Purpose of the Legislation
The focus of an earlier administrative proceeding might be entirely different from that of the subsequent litigation, even though one or more of the same issues might be implicated. In *Bugbusters, supra*, a forestry company was compulsorily recruited to help fight a forest fire in British Columbia. It subsequently sought reimbursement for its expenses under the B.C. *Forest Act*. . . . The expense claim was allowed despite an allegation that the fire had been started by a Bugbusters employee who carelessly discarded his cigarette. (This, if proved, would have disentitled Bugbusters to reimbursement.) The Crown later started a $5 million negligence claim against Bugbusters, for losses occasioned by the forest fire. Bugbusters invoked issue estoppel. The court, in the exercise of its discretion, denied relief. One reason, *per* Finch J.A., at para. 30, was that

> a final decision on the Crown's right to recover its losses was not within the reasonable expectation of either party at the time of those [reimbursement] proceedings [under the *Forest Act*].

A similar point was made in *Rasanen, supra*, by Carthy J.A., at p. 290:

It would be unfair to an employee who sought out immediate and limited relief of $4,000, forsaking discovery and representation in doing so, to then say that he is bound to the result as it affects a claim for ten times that amount.

A similar qualification is made in the American *Restatement of the Law, Second: Judgments,* 2d (1982), vol. 2 ' 83(2)(e), which refers to

> procedural elements as may be necessary to constitute the proceeding a sufficient means of conclusively determining the matter in question, having regard for the magnitude and complexity of the matter in question, the urgency with which the matter must be resolved, and the opportunity of the parties to obtain evidence and formulate legal contentions.

I am mindful, of course, that here the appellant chose the ESA forum. Counsel for the respondent justly observed, with some exasperation:

> As the record makes clear, Danyluk was represented by legal counsel prior to, at the time of, and subsequent to the cessation of her employment. Danyluk and her counsel were well aware of the fact that Danyluk had an initial choice of forums with respect to her claim for unpaid commissions and wages. . . .

Nevertheless, the purpose of the ESA is to provide a relatively quick and cheap means of resolving employment disputes. Putting excessive weight on the ESA decision in terms of issue estoppel would likely compel the parties in such cases to mount a full-scale trial-type offence and defence, thus tending to defeat the expeditious operation of the ESA scheme as a whole. This would undermine fulfillment of the purpose of the legislation.

(c) The Availability of an Appeal

This factor corresponds to the "adequate alternative remedy" issue in judicial review. . . . Here the employee had no right of appeal, but the existence of a potential administrative review and her failure to take advantage of it must be counted against her. . . .

(d) The Safeguards Available to the Parties in the Administrative Procedure

As already mentioned, quick and expeditious procedures suitable to accomplish the objectives of the ESA scheme may simply be inadequate to deal with complex issues of fact or law. Administrative bodies, being masters of their own procedures, may exclude evidence the court thinks probative, or act on evidence the court considers less than reliable. If it has done so, this may be a factor in the exercise of the court's discretion. Here the breach of natural justice is a key factor in the appellant's favour.

Morden A.C.J.O. pointed out in his concurring judgment in *Rasanen, supra,* at p. 295: "I do not exclude the possibility that deficiencies in the procedure relating to the first decision could properly be a factor in deciding whether or not to apply issue estoppel." . . .

(e) The Expertise of the Administrative Decision Maker

In this case the ESA officer was a non-legally trained individual asked to decide a potentially complex issue of contract law. The rough-and-ready approach suitable to getting things done in the vast majority of ESA claims is not the expertise required here. A similar factor operates with respect to the rule against collateral attack (*Maybrun, supra,* at para. 50):

> . . . where an attack on an order is based on considerations which are foreign to an administrative appeal tribunal's expertise or *raison d'être*, this suggests, although it is not conclusive in itself, that the legislature did not intend to reserve the exclusive authority to rule on the validity of the order to that tribunal.

(f) The Circumstances Giving Rise to the Prior Administrative Proceedings

In the appellant's favour, it may be said that she invoked the ESA procedure at a time of personal vulnerability with her dismissal looming. It is unlikely the legislature intended a summary procedure for smallish claims to become a barrier to closer consideration of more substantial claims. (The legislature's subsequent reduction of the monetary limit of an ESA claim to $10,000 is consistent with this view.) As Laskin J.A. pointed out in [*Minott v. O'Shanter Development Co.*] . . . :

> . . . employees apply for benefits when they are most vulnerable, immediately after losing their job. The urgency with which they must invariably seek relief compromises their ability to adequately put forward their case for benefits or to respond to the case against them . . . .

On the other hand, in this particular case it must be said that the appellant with or without legal advice, included in her ESA claim the $300,000 commissions, and she must shoulder at least part of the responsibility for her resulting difficulties.

(g) The Potential Injustice

As a final and most important factor, the Court should stand back and, taking into account the entirety of the circumstances, consider whether application of issue estoppel in the particular case would work an injustice. Rosenberg J.A. concluded that the appellant had received neither notice of the respondent's allegation nor an opportunity to respond. . . .

Whatever the appellant's various procedural mistakes in this case, the stubborn fact remains that her claim to commissions worth $300,000 has simply never been properly considered and adjudicated.

On considering the cumulative effect of the foregoing factors it is my view that the Court in its discretion should refuse to apply issue estoppel in this case.

V. DISPOSITION

I would therefore allow the appeal with costs throughout.

✻ ✻ ✻

For further reading, see Sean Doyle, "The Discretionary Aspect of Issue Estoppel: What Does Danyluk Add?" (2002) 9 Canadian Labour and Employment Law Journal 291; and Craig Flood, "Efficiency v. Fairness: Multiple Litigation and Adjudication in Labour and Employment Law" (2001), 8 Canadian Labour and Employment Law Journal 383.

Chapter 13: **Equality in Employment**

13:100 INTRODUCTION

Labour law has long been grounded in equality considerations; diminishing the inequality of bargaining power between employers and employees requires that employees be allowed to act in concert through trade unions. Today, when we speak of equality rights in the workplace, we are more likely referring to protections against discrimination — to diminishing sexism, racism, and homophobia or to enhancing the ability of persons with disabilities to participate fully in the workforce. In this regard, labour relations are subject to the constraints of equality law, just as other areas of life are. The equality provisions of the *Canadian Charter of Rights and Freedoms* apply to labour and employment legislation and to its application by administrative tribunals, as well as to any employment relationship that has a nexus with government. Human rights legislation applies to employers, unions, and employees in the public and private sectors, and it may take primacy over other legislation. Grievance arbitrators have jurisdiction, to an increasing degree, to apply human rights legislation and the equality provisions of the *Charter*. Other statutes also explicitly promote particular aspects of equality. Pay equity legislation, for example, reflects important policy decisions about equality relationships in the workplace and about the social status of employees.

In this chapter, we address some of the most pressing equality issues involved in labour relations, a few of which were mentioned in earlier chapters. We begin with an overview of the meanings given to equality and the identification of equality-seeking groups. We then discuss specific areas of equality law, such as sexual harassment law, pay equity law, and the employer's duty to accommodate, as they apply in the labour and employment context. Some traditional labour relations principles, such as respect for seniority, must be reconciled with equality requirements. We also discuss the interface between different forums that enforce equality rights in the workplace.

13:200 THE CONCEPT OF EQUALITY

13:210 Theoretical Development of the Concept

Equality is a complex concept. It has evolved in many different arenas, it reflects the contribution of many different disciplines, and it is highly contextual. "Equality and inequality," one writer has said, "are political constructions; both their conditions and their definitions vary across space, time, and philosophical families:" Jane Jenson, "Rethinking Equality and Equity: Canadian Children and the Social Union," in Edward Broadbent, ed., *Democratic Equality: What Went Wrong?* at 111.

Our contemporary understanding of social equality has its roots in a commitment to political and legal equality, which is embodied in principles such as "one person, one vote" and the right to equal treatment before the law. These are examples of formal equality; the capacity to enjoy them and use them effectively is often dependent on social or economic status.

Proponents of formal equality may go no farther than to accept that arbitrary barriers should not be placed in the way of anyone's *opportunity* to improve his or her condition. Underlying the notion of formal equality is the objective of treating people more or less the same — that is, emphasizing the qualities they have in common and reducing the extent to which they are treated on the basis of irrelevant characteristics. However, if one begins with the assumption that, for example, only males are capable of being lawyers, high school principals, or skilled tradespeople, excluding women (explicitly or in practice) from those lines of work will not be seen as a denial of equality rights. Under this status-based approach to equality rights, anyone who was treated in a manner appropriate to his or her status was seen to be treated equally.

Taking the commitment to equality one step further leads to the idea that people should be judged on their individual merit and not be excluded from pursuing opportunities or receiving benefits because of particular characteristics, such as class, race, sex, religion, or disability. This idea of equality of opportunity represented a step forward from the earlier status-based concept to a liberal concept of equality based on the right of each individual to achieve whatever can be achieved through his or her own efforts. Yet when we look below the surface of this liberal ideal, it becomes obvious that because of their economic status, some people are better placed than others to develop their aptitudes.

The beginnings of anti-discrimination theory are based on the moral equality of human beings, and are found in the idea that no one should be denied opportunities on the basis of characteristics which are unrelated to his or her objectives. Such characteristics tend to be those that are with us from birth, such as race or sex, or those to which our society otherwise gives a high value, such as religion. The domestic development of anti-discrimination theory reflected developments at the international level during the post-World War II period, which saw the enactment of international human rights conventions in response to the egregious treatment of Jews, homosexuals, and other minorities, who had been castigated simply because they were Jews, homosexuals, or members of another minority. It was hoped that strong statements about common humanity would prevent a recurrence of similar events, but that hope has not materialized. As well, both international and domestic human rights theory and practice have been criticized as reflecting a eurocentric bias: because human rights law places so much emphasis on the individual, the argument runs, it fails to reflect communal values that are fundamental to certain cultures.

As noted above, anti-discrimination law initially stressed "sameness," emphasizing the fact that all human beings share common characteristics simply because they are human beings. Whatever its strengths, that approach overlooked the ways in which people can be treated unequally under a veil of equal treatment. The gradual realization of this shortcoming in recent decades led to the development of the distinction between direct and indirect discrimination and the duty to accommodate.

The distinction between direct and indirect discrimination was based on the recognition that there can be discrimination without an intention to discriminate. Ostensibly neutral job requirements are often developed without consideration of their impact on members of particular groups. A job requirement that an employee be able to lift heavy weights might have a disparate impact on women or on people with particular disabilities, even if the employer does not actually intend to exclude them from the job. A requirement that employees work on Saturdays may not be intended to discriminate against those whose religion makes Saturday a day of rest, but it nevertheless has a disproportionate impact on them. In such cases, the issue becomes whether it is truly necessary that every employee be able to meet the particular requirement, or whether an accommodation can be reached to allow the job to be filled by someone who cannot meet the requirement because of a protected attribute such as sex or religion. However, the interplay between direct and indirect discrimination on the one hand, and the duty to accommodate on the other, led to the development of complex doctrines that made the law very difficult to apply. In 1999, in the *Meiorin* case, set out below in section 13:222, the Supreme Court of Canada sought to simplify the law. *Meiorin* also reflected the now widely-accepted view that difference should not be measured from a majority-oriented baseline, and that what is sometimes required is not merely the accommodation of individuals but the changing of existing standards to bring them into line with non-majority needs. This is in accord with the perception that individual cases of discrimination do not exist in isolation from broader social conditions.

The evolution in the concept of equality has been accompanied by an evolution in the identification of the groups protected by anti-discrimination law. Initially, a few categories were identified on the basis of seemingly immutable attributes such as race and sex. Today, human rights legislation recognizes a much wider variety of grounds, which may include family status, marital status, and criminal record. Not only changing social mores, but technological advances as well, are having an impact in this regard. For example, genetic testing may indicate that a person has an above-average chance of contracting a particular disease, and someone may now be HIV-positive for many years without developing AIDS. The Report of the Canadian Human Rights Act Review Panel (*Promoting Equality: a New Vision* (2000)) recommended that people in such situations should not be subject to discrimination because of their "predisposition to being disabled." The situation of transgendered people provides another example: protection from discrimination on the basis of sex and disability does not meet all of the distinctive problems they face, so the Review Panel recommended that gender identity be added as a protected ground.

13:220 Application of the Concept of Equality by the Courts

Although understanding different approaches to the concept of equality requires us to look at a variety of sources — philosophical and political, among others — we also need to understand how the law sees that concept. The main sources of equality law in the labour relations context are found in section 15 of the *Canadian Charter of Rights and Freedoms* and in human rights statutes, and in the interpretation of those instruments by appellate courts. We may look elsewhere for criticisms of those legally derived meanings, but they are the meanings that will apply when equality issues are raised in the labour context.

Until the enactment of human rights legislation, there was no way to challenge inequality directly where issues such as race or sex were involved. Provincial legislation prohibiting Chinese from working in mines was successfully challenged more than a century ago on division of powers grounds; it was held to trespass on federal authority over "naturalization and aliens" under section 91(25) of the *Constitution Act, 1867*. Not much later, however, a provincial statute prohibiting Chinese employers from hiring white women was held to be within provincial authority becasuse its primary purpose was found to be protective. See *Union Colliery Co. v. Bryden*, [1899] A.C. 580 (P.C.) and *Quong Wing v. The King* (1914), 49 S.C.R. 440, respectively. The first detailed statute codifying equality in employment as a basic human right was the Saskatchewan *Bill of Rights Act*, S.S. 1947, c. 35. It was a quasi-criminal legislation that required proof of an invidious intent: its sanctions were penal, focusing on fines and imprisonment. Attacking discrimination by punishing the perpetrators of discrimination proved ineffective, however, and other provincial legislatures passed statutes designed to give victims compensation and relief. In 1951 Ontario passed the first human rights statute — the *Fair Employment Practices Act*, S.O. 1951, c. 24. Slowly, during the next two decades, the other provinces and the federal government enacted similar legislation. Over the years the prohibited grounds of discrimination under those statutes were expanded, as were the areas of activity to which they applied, the administrative machinery for their enforcement, and the range of remedies available. In *Seneca College of Applied Arts and Technology v. Bhadauria*, [1981] 2 S.C.R. 181, excerpted above in Chapter 2 (section 2:300), Laskin C.J. held that a civil action could not be brought to vindicate equality rights set out in human rights statutes, because those statutes themselves provided a comprehensive administrative and adjudicative regime for the protection of such rights.

Human rights legislation constituted the major source of equality law until section 15 of the *Canadian Charter of Rights and Freedoms* came into force in 1985. When the Supreme Court of Canada decided its first case under section 15 of the *Charter* — *Andrews v. Law Society of British Columbia*, [1989] 1 S.C.R. 143 — it sought guidance from contemporary jurisprudence under human rights legislation. The idea that intention is not required for a finding of discrimination, the idea that discrimination need not be overt or direct but may result from a disparate impact on a particular group, and the idea that attaining equality may require treating people differently — these were all imported into the interpretation of section 15 of the *Charter* from the Supreme Court of Canada's human rights jurisprudence.

A number of the leading early human rights cases involved the workplace. For example, in *Ontario (Human Rights Commission) v. Simpsons Sears Ltd.*, [1985] 2 S.C.R. 536 (*O'Malley*), a department store employee objected to working on Friday nights and Saturdays on religious grounds. Although the employer had legitimate reasons for requiring employees to work on Friday night and Saturday and did not intend to discriminate against O'Malley, the Supreme Court of Canada held the requirement to be discriminatory because it had a disparate impact on anyone of her religion. The Court ordered the employer to accommodate O'Malley by scheduling her time differently, as long as the rescheduling did not impose an undue hardship on the employer. Thus, *O'Malley* established that intention was not required for a finding of discrimination, and it also introduced the idea of the duty to accommodate.

Human rights legislation requires accommodation, and (for some prohibited grounds, such as disability) it permits the defence that in the particular circumstances, an otherwise discriminatory requirement is a "bona fide occupational requirement" (BFOR). Accommodation is mandatory if it can be effected without causing what the legislation refers to as "undue hardship" to the employer or to other employees. However, if the employer establishes that no accommodation is possible without undue hardship, then the employer has made out the BFOR defence. Human rights commissions in some jurisdictions (including Ontario) have developed detailed but non-binding guidelines for assessing what constitutes undue hardship.

In 1989, in the *Andrews* case referred to above, the Supreme Court of Canada rejected the formal equality approach that it had developed under the *Canadian Bill of Rights*, which was the non-constitutional predecessor to the Charter. In particular, the Court rejected the "similarly situated" test, under which "things that are alike should be treated alike, while things that are unalike should be treated unalike in proportion to their unalikeness." In holding that section 15 of the *Charter* guaranteed substantive and not merely formal equality, the Court said: "Consideration must be given to the content of the law, to its purpose, and its impact upon those to whom it applies, and also upon those whom it excludes from its application."

Andrews established a three-stage test for determining whether there had been a breach of subsection 15(1). To prove a breach, a plaintiff had to show that the impugned legislation or other governmental action did all of the following: that it (1) made a distinction (2) which resulted in a disadvantage (3) on the basis of an enumerated ground set out in section 15(1) or an "analogous" ground — that is, a personal attribute which is immutable (in that it is impossible or very difficult to change) and which is characteristic of a disadvantaged group. In Andrews, citizenship, which was a qualification for being called to the Bar of British Columbia, was held to be an analogous ground.

The test for determining whether there has been a breach of section 15 of the Charter has evolved since Andrews, although it is still treated as the leading case. The most significant departure came with a 1995 group of cases known as the equality trilogy: *Egan v. Canada*, [1995] 2 S.C.R. 513; *Miron v. Trudel* [1995] 2 S.C.R. 418; and *Thibaudeau v. Canada*, [1995] 2 S.C.R. 627. In those cases, none of which involved employment, a minority of the Court added the requirement that a complainant must show that the distinction being challenged is not relevant to the purpose of the legislation. However, in subsequent decisions (including *Vriend v. Alberta*, set out below), the Court avoided this dispute by saying that it did not matter which approach was used in the particular case.

13:221 Relationship between Legislatures and Courts

Recent developments in equality law, particularly under the *Charter*, have led to debate about the appropriate role of the courts and legislatures in this area. Legislatures must, of course, comply with the *Charter* as interpreted by the courts, unless they are willing to invoke section 33 of the *Charter* (the "notwithstanding" clause). The following excerpt from the *Vriend* case confronts the "division of labour" debate, and provides a further illustration of how the Supreme Court of Canada addresses equality issues under the *Charter* in the employment context.

Vriend v. Alberta, [1998] 1 S.C.R. 493

[Throughout Delwin Vriend's employment as a laboratory co-ordinator by King's College in Alberta, his work had been evaluated positively. In 1990, in response to an inquiry by the president of the college, Mr. Vriend disclosed that he was gay. In 1991, after the college's board of governors adopted a policy disapproving of homosexuality, the college dismissed him. The sole reason given was his non-compliance with the college's policy. Mr. Vriend tried to file a complaint with the Alberta Human Rights Commission, under the *Individual's Rights Protection Act* (IRPA) (later renamed the *Human Rights, Citizenship and Multiculturalsim Act*), to the effect that his employer had discriminated against him because of his sexual orientation. The Commission advised him that he could not bring such a complaint, because the IRPA did not include sexual orientation as a protected ground. (When Mr. Vriend filed his complaint, the IRPA listed the following prohibited grounds of discrimination: race, religious beliefs, colour, gender, physical disability, mental disability, age, ancestry, and place of origin. Later, but before the matter was decided by the Supreme Court of Canada, marital status, source of income, and family status had been added.)

Mr. Vriend sued for a declaration that the omission of sexual orientation from the IRPA contravened section 15 of the *Canadian Charter of Rights and Freedoms*. He won at trial, lost in the Alberta Court of Appeal, and appealed to the Supreme Court of Canada. Cory and Iacobucci JJ. wrote a joint judgment for the majority of the Court, Cory J. dealing with the section 15 issue and Iacobucci J. with the section 1 issue and the remedy.]

CORY and IACOBUCCI JJ. (for the majority of the Court):

. . .

Despite repeated calls for its inclusion sexual orientation has never been included in the list of those groups protected from discrimination. In 1984 and again in 1992, the Alberta Human Rights Commission recommended amending the *IRPA* to include sexual orientation as a prohibited ground of discrimination. In an attempt to effect such an amendment, the opposition introduced several bills; however, none went beyond first reading. Although at least one Minister responsible for the administration of the *IRPA* supported the amendment, the correspondence with a number of Cabinet members and members of the Legislature makes it clear that the omission of sexual orientation from the *IRPA* was deliberate and not the result of an oversight. The reasons given for declining to take this action include the assertions that sexual orientation is a 'marginal' ground;

that human rights legislation is powerless to change public attitudes; and that there have only been a few cases of sexual orientation discrimination in employment brought to the attention of the Minister.

In 1992, the Human Rights Commission decided to investigate complaints of discrimination on the basis of sexual orientation. This decision was immediately vetoed by the Government and the Minister directed the Commission not to investigate the complaints.

In 1993, the Government appointed the Alberta Human Rights Review Panel to conduct a public review of the *IRPA* and the Human Rights Commission. When it had completed an extensive review, the Panel issued its report. . . . The report contained a number of recommendations, one of which was that sexual orientation should be included as a prohibited ground of discrimination in the Act. In its response . . . , the Government stated that the recommendation regarding sexual orientation would be dealt with through this case. . . .

. . .

V. ANALYSIS . . .

B. Application of the *Charter*

I. Application of the *Charter* to a Legislative Omission

Does s. 32 of the *Charter* prohibit consideration of a s. 15 violation when that issue arises from a legislative omission?

. . .

McClung J.A. in the Alberta Court of Appeal criticized the application of the *Charter* to a legislative omission as an encroachment by the courts on legislative autonomy. He objected to what he saw as judges dictating provincial legislation under the pretext of constitutional scrutiny. In his view, a choice by the legislature not to legislate with respect to a particular matter within its jurisdiction, especially a controversial one, should not be open to review by the judiciary:

> When they choose silence provincial legislatures need not march to the *Charter* drum. In a constitutional sense they need not march at all . . . The *Canadian Charter of Rights and Freedoms* was not adopted by the provinces to promote the federal extraction of subsidiary legislation from them but only to police it once it is proclaimed — if it is proclaimed. . . .

There are several answers to this position. The first is that in this case, the constitutional challenge concerns the *IRPA*, legislation that has been proclaimed. The fact that it is the underinclusiveness of the Act which is at issue does not alter the fact that it is the legislative act which is the subject of *Charter* scrutiny in this case. Furthermore, the language of s. 32 does not limit the application of the *Charter* merely to positive actions encroaching on rights or the excessive exercise of authority, as McClung J.A. seems to suggest. . . .

It is suggested that this appeal represents a contest between the power of the democratically elected legislatures to pass the laws they see fit, and the power of the courts to disallow those laws, or to dictate that certain matters be included in those laws. To put the issue in this way is misleading and erroneous. Quite simply, it is not the courts which limit the legislatures. Rather, it is the Constitution, which must be interpreted by the courts, that limits the legislatures. This is necessarily true of all constitutional democracies. Citizens must have the right to challenge laws which they consider to be beyond the powers of the legislatures. When such a challenge is properly made, the courts must, pursuant to their constitutional duty, rule on the challenge. It is said, however, that this case is different because the challenge centres on the legislature's failure to extend the protection of a law to a particular group of people. This position assumes that it is only a positive act rather than an omission which may be scrutinized under the *Charter*. In my view, for the reasons that will follow, there is no legal basis for drawing such a distinction. In this as in other cases, the courts have a duty to determine whether the challenge is justified. It is not a question, as McClung J.A. suggested, of the courts imposing their view of 'ideal' legislation, but rather of determining whether the challenged legislative act or omission is constitutional or not.

. . .

The respondents contend that a deliberate choice not to legislate should not be considered government action and thus does not attract *Charter* scrutiny. This submission should not be accepted. They assert that there must be some 'exercise' of 's. 32 authority' to bring the decision of the legislature within the purview of the *Charter*. Yet there is nothing either in the text of s. 32 or in the jurisprudence concerned with the application of the *Charter* which requires such a narrow view of the *Charter*'s application.

The relevant subsection, s. 32(1)(b), states that the *Charter* applies to 'the legislature and government of each province in respect of all matters within the authority of the legislature of each province.' There is nothing in that wording to suggest that a positive act encroaching on rights is required; rather the subsection speaks only of *matters within the authority of the legislature*. Dianne Pothier has correctly observed that s. 32 is 'worded broadly enough to cover positive obligations on a legislature such that the *Charter* will be engaged even if the legislature refuses to exercise its authority'. . . .

C. Section 15(1)

1. Approach to Section 15(1)

The rights enshrined in s. 15(1) of the *Charter* are fundamental to Canada. They reflect the fondest dreams, the highest hopes and finest aspirations of Canadian society. When universal suffrage was granted it recognized to some extent the importance of the individual. Canada by the broad scope and fundamental fairness of the provisions of s. 15(1) has taken a further step in the recognition of the fundamental importance and the innate dignity of the individual. . . . In order to achieve equality the intrinsic worthiness and importance of every individual must be recognized regardless of the age, sex, colour, origins, or other characteristics of the person. . . .

It is easy to say that everyone who is just like 'us' is entitled to equality. Everyone finds it more difficult to say that those who are 'different' from us in some way should have the same equality rights that we enjoy. Yet so soon as we say any enumerated or analogous group is less deserving and unworthy of equal protection and benefit of the law all minorities and all of Canadian society are demeaned. It is so deceptively simple and so devastatingly injurious to say that those who are handicapped or of a different race, or religion, or colour or sexual orientation are less worthy. Yet, if any enumerated or analogous group is denied the equality provided by s. 15 then the equality of every other minority group is threatened. That equality is guaranteed by our Constitution. If equality rights for minorities had been recognized, the all too frequent tragedies of history might have been avoided. It can never be forgotten that discrimination is the antithesis of equality and that it is the recognition of equality which will foster the dignity of every individual.

[Cory J. then reviewed what several Supreme Court of Canada decisions had said about how section 15 should be interpreted. He concluded that "any differences that may exist in the approach to s. 15(1) would not affect the result."]

The essential requirements of all these cases will be satisfied by enquiring first, whether there is a distinction which results in the denial of equality before or under the law, or of equal protection or benefit of the law; and second, whether this denial constitutes discrimination on the basis of an enumerated or analogous ground.

2. The *IRPA* creates a Distinction Between the Claimant and Others Based on a Personal Characteristic, and Because of That Distinction, It Denies the Claimant Equal Protection or Equal Benefit of the Law

(a) Does the IRPA Create a Distinction?

The respondents have argued that because the *IRPA* merely omits any reference to sexual orientation, this 'neutral silence' cannot be understood as creating a distinction. They contend that the *IRPA* extends full protection on the grounds contained within it to heterosexuals and homosexuals alike, and therefore there is no distinction and hence no discrimination. It is the respondents' position that if any distinction is made on the basis of sexual orientation that distinction exists because it is present in society and not because of the *IRPA*.

These arguments cannot be accepted. They are based on that 'thin and impoverished' notion of equality referred to in [*Eldridge v. British Columbia (Attorney-General)*]. It has been repeatedly held that identical treatment will not always constitute equal treatment. . . . It is also clear that the way in which an exclusion is worded should not disguise the nature of the exclusion so as to allow differently drafted exclusions to be treated differently. . .

It is clear that the *IRPA*, by reason of its underinclusiveness, does create a distinction. The distinction is simultaneously drawn along two different lines. The first is the distinction between homosexuals, on one hand, and other disadvantaged groups which are protected under the Act, on the other. Gays and lesbians do not even have formal equality with reference to other protected groups, since those other groups are explicitly included and they are not.

The second distinction, and I think, the more fundamental one, is between homosexuals and heterosexuals. This distinction may be more difficult to see because there is, on the surface, a measure of formal equality: gay or lesbian individuals have the same access as heterosexual individuals to the protection of the *IRPA* in the sense that they could complain to the Commission about an incident of discrimination on the basis of any of the grounds currently included. However, the exclusion of the ground of sexual orientation, considered in the context of the social reality of discrimination against gays and lesbians, clearly has a disproportionate impact on them as opposed to heterosexuals. Therefore the *IRPA* in its underinclusive state denies substantive equality to the former group. . . .

[Cory J. rejected the argument that the distinction is not created by law, but by society, and therefore should not be subject to review under the *Charter*.]

Although the respondents try to distinguish this case from *Bliss v. Attorney General of Canada* . . . , the reasoning they put forward is very much reminiscent of the approach taken in that case. . . . There it was held that a longer qualifying period for unemployment benefits relating to pregnancy was not discriminatory because it applied to all pregnant individuals, and that if this category happened only to include women, that was a distinction created by nature, not by law. This reasoning has since been emphatically rejected. . . .

(b) Denial of Equal Benefit and Protection of the Law

It is apparent that the omission from the *IRPA* creates a distinction. That distinction results in a denial of the equal benefit and equal protection of the law. It is the exclusion of sexual orientation from the list of grounds in the *IRPA* which denies lesbians and gay men the protection and benefit of the Act in two important ways. They are excluded from the government's statement of policy against discrimination, and they are also denied access to the remedial procedures established by the Act.

Therefore, the *IRPA*, by its omission or underinclusiveness, denies gays and lesbians the equal benefit and protection of the law on the basis of a personal characteristic, namely sexual orientation.

3. The Denial of Equal Benefit and Equal Protection Constitutes Discrimination Contrary to Section 15(1)

In [*Egan v. Canada*], it was said that there are two aspects which are relevant in determining whether the distinction created by the law constitutes discrimination. First, 'whether the equality right was denied on the basis of a personal characteristic which is either enumerated in s. 15(1) or which is analogous to those enumerated.' Second, 'whether that distinction has the effect on the claimant of imposing a burden, obligation or disadvantage not imposed upon others or of withholding or limiting access to benefits or advantages which are available to others'. . . . A discriminatory distinction was also described as one which is 'capable of either promoting or perpetuating the view that the individual adversely affected by this distinction is less capable, or less worthy of recognition or value as a human being or as a member of Canadian society, equally deserving of concern, respect, and consideration'. . . . It may as well be appropriate to consider whether the unequal treatment is based on 'the stereotypical application of presumed group or personal characteristics'. . . .

(a) The Equality Right is Denied on the Basis of a Personal Characteristic Which Is Analogous to Those Enumerated in Section 15(1)

In *Egan*, it was held, on the basis of 'historical social, political and economic disadvantage suffered by homosexuals' and the emerging consensus among legislatures . . . , as well as previous judicial decisions . . . , that sexual orientation is a ground analogous to those listed in s. 15(1). Sexual orientation is 'a deeply personal characteristic that is either unchangeable or changeable only at unacceptable personal costs'. . . . It is analogous to the other personal characteristics enumerated in s. 15(1); and therefore this step of the test is satisfied. . . .

(b) The Distinction Has the Effect of Imposing a Burden or Disadvantage Not Imposed on Others and Withholds Benefits or Advantages Which Are Available to Others

(i) Discriminatory Purpose

[In response to arguments that the reason the Alberta Government excluded sexual orientation from the legislation was itself discriminatory, Cory J. held that it was not necessary to decide the point since a finding of discrimination does not rely on intention and the discriminatory effects of the omission were sufficient to find discrimination.]

(ii) Discriminatory Effects of the Exclusion

The effects of the exclusion of sexual orientation from the protected grounds listed in the *IRPA* must be understood in the context of the nature and purpose of the legislation. The *IRPA* is a broad, comprehensive scheme for the protection of individuals from discrimination in the private sector. . . .

The commendable goal of the legislation . . . is to affirm and give effect to the principle that all persons are equal in dignity and rights. It prohibits discrimination in a number of areas and with respect to an increasingly expansive list of grounds.

The comprehensive nature of the Act must be taken into account in considering the effect of excluding one ground from its protection. It is not as if the Legislature had merely chosen to deal with one type of discrimination. In such a case it might be permissible to target only that specific type of discrimination and not another. . . . The case at bar presents a very different situation. It is concerned with legislation that purports to provide comprehensive protection from discrimination for all individuals in Alberta. The selective exclusion of one group from that comprehensive protection therefore has a very different effect.

The first and most obvious effect of the exclusion of sexual orientation is that lesbians or gay men who experience discrimination on the basis of their sexual orientation are denied recourse to the mechanisms set up by the *IRPA* to make a formal complaint of discrimination and seek a legal remedy. Thus, the Alberta Human Rights Commission could not hear Vriend's complaint and cannot consider a complaint or take any action on behalf of any person who has suffered discrimination on the ground of sexual orientation. The denial of access to remedial procedures for discrimination on the ground of sexual orientation must have dire and demeaning consequences for those affected. This result is exacerbated both because the option of a civil remedy for discrimination is precluded and by the lack of success that lesbian women and gay men have had in attempting to obtain a remedy for discrimination on the ground of sexual orientation by complaining on other grounds such as sex or marital status. Persons who are discriminated against on the ground of sexual orientation, unlike others protected by the Act, are left without effective legal recourse for the discrimination they have suffered.

. . .

Apart from the immediate effect of the denial of recourse in cases of discrimination, there are other effects which, while perhaps less obvious, are at least as harmful. In *Haig*, the Ontario Court of Appeal based its finding of discrimination on both the 'failure to provide an avenue for redress for prejudicial treatment of homosexual members of society' and 'the possible inference from the omission that such treatment is acceptable' (p. 503). It can be reasonably inferred that the absence of any legal recourse for discrimination on the ground of sexual orientation perpetuates and even encourages that kind of discrimination. The respondents contend that it cannot be assumed that the 'silence' of the *IRPA* reinforces or perpetuates discrimination, since governments 'cannot legislate attitudes.' However, this argument seems disingenuous in light of the stated purpose of the *IRPA*, to prevent discrimination. It cannot be claimed that human rights legislation will help to protect individuals from discrimination, and at the same time contend that an exclusion from the legislation will have no effect.

However, let us assume, contrary to all reasonable inferences, that exclusion from the *IRPA*'s protection does not actually contribute to a greater incidence of discrimination on the excluded ground. Nonetheless that exclusion, deliberately chosen in the face of clear findings that discrimination on the ground of sexual orientation does exist in society, sends a strong and sinister message. The very fact that sexual orientation is excluded from the *IRPA*, which is the Government's primary statement of policy against discrimination, certainly suggests that discrimination on the ground of sexual orientation is not as serious or as deserving of condemnation as other forms of discrimination. It could well be said that it is tantamount to condoning or even encouraging discrimination against lesbians and gay men. Thus this exclusion clearly gives rise to an effect which constitutes discrimination.

The exclusion sends a message to all Albertans that it is permissible, and perhaps even acceptable, to discriminate against individuals on the basis of their sexual orientation. The effect of that message on gays and lesbians is one whose significance cannot be underestimated. As a practical matter, it tells them that they have no protection from discrimination on the basis of their sexual orientation. Deprived of any legal redress they must accept and live in constant fear of discrimination. These are burdens which are not imposed on heterosexuals.

Perhaps most important is the psychological harm which may ensue from this state of affairs. Fear of discrimination will logically lead to concealment of true identity and this must be harmful to personal confidence and self-esteem. Compounding that effect is the implicit message conveyed by the exclusion, that gays and lesbians, unlike other individuals, are not worthy of protection. . . . The potential harm to the dignity and perceived worth of gay and lesbian individuals constitutes a particularly cruel form of discrimination.

Even if the discrimination is experienced at the hands of private individuals, it is the state that denies protection from that discrimination.

. . .

In excluding sexual orientation from the *IRPA*'s protection, the Government has, in effect, stated that 'all persons are equal in dignity and rights,' except gay men and lesbians. Such a message, even if it is only implicit, must offend s. 15(1), the 'section of the *Charter*, more than any other, which recognizes and cherishes the innate human dignity of every individual'. . . . This effect, together with the denial to individuals of any effective legal recourse in the event they are discriminated against on the ground of sexual orientation, amount to a sufficient basis on which to conclude that the distinction created by the exclusion from the *IRPA* constitutes discrimination.

3. 'Mirror' Argument

[The Government argued that if the complaint succeeded in this case, human rights legislation would always have to include the same protected grounds as the *Charter*, thus restricting legislative choice. Cory J. concluded that it was not necessary to decide the point. Although omissions may be vulnerable to challenge under the *Charter*, he said, "it is simply not true that human rights legislation will be forced to 'mirror' the *Charter* in all cases."]

Whether an omission is unconstitutional must be assessed in each case, taking into account the nature of the exclusion, the type of legislation, and the context in which it was enacted. The determination of whether a particular exclusion complies with s. 15 of the *Charter* would not be made through the mechanical application of any 'mirroring' principle, but rather, as in all other cases, by determining whether the exclusion was proven to be discriminatory in its specific context and whether the discrimination could be justified under s. 1. If a provincial legislature chooses to take legislative measures which do not include all of the enumerated and analogous grounds of the *Charter*, deference may be shown to this choice, so long as the tests for justification under s. 1, including rational connection, are satisfied.

. . .

[Having concluded that the omission violated section 15, the Court moved to consideration of whether it was justified under section 1. Iacobucci J. held that the Alberta Government had not shown that the omission of sexual orientation as a protected ground under the *IRPA* satisfied the "pressing and substantial objective" part of the *Oakes* test. This was enough to defeat the Government's section 1 argument, but Iacobucci J. went on to apply the other branches of the Oakes test. With respect to the requirement that there be a rational connection between the objective and the impugned omission, the Government argued that "a rational connection to the purpose of a statute can be achieved through the use of incremental means which, over time, expand the scope of the legislation to all those whom the legislature determines to be in need of statutory protection." In response to that argument, Iacobucci J. said:

The incrementalism approach was advocated in *Egan* by Sopinka J. in a context very different from that in the case at bar. Firstly, in *Egan*, where the concern was the exclusion

839

of same-sex couples from the *Old Age Security Act*'s definition of the term 'spouse,' the Attorney General took the position that more acceptable arrangements could be worked out over time. In contrast, in the present case, the inclusion of sexual orientation in the *IRPA* has been repeatedly rejected by the Alberta Legislature. Thus, it is difficult to see how any form of 'incrementalism' is being applied with regard to the protection of the rights of gay men and lesbians. Secondly, in *Egan* there was considerable concern regarding the financial impact of extending a benefits scheme to a previously excluded group. Including sexual orientation in the *IRPA* does not give rise to the same concerns. . . .

In addition, in *Egan*, writing on behalf of myself and Cory J., I took the position that the need for governmental incrementalism was an inappropriate justification for *Charter* violations. I remain convinced that this approach is generally not suitable for that purpose, especially where, as here, the statute in issue is a comprehensive code of human rights provisions. In my opinion, groups that have historically been the target of discrimination cannot be expected to wait patiently for the protection of their human dignity and equal rights while governments move toward reform one step at a time. . . .

In the last part of his judgment, Iacobucci J. addressed the question of how the Court should remedy the constitutional defect in the legislation. He concluded that this was an appropriate occasion for the Court to read the words 'sexual orientation' into the relevant sections of the Act.]

✻ ✻ ✻

Subsequently, in *Law v. Canada (Minister of Employment and Immigration)*, [1999] 1 S.C.R. 497, the Supreme Court of Canada sought to reconcile the divergent approaches it had taken to section 15 of the Charter. Subsection 15(1), Iacobucci J. said in *Law*, is designed to

> prevent the violation of essential human dignity and freedom through the imposition of disadvantage, stereotyping, or political or social prejudice, and to promote a society in which all persons enjoy equal recognition at law as human beings or as members of Canadian society, equally capable and deserving of concern, respect and consideration.

"Human dignity," Iacobucci J. went on, "is harmed when individuals and groups are marginalized, ignored, or devalued, and is enhanced when laws recognize the full place of all individuals and groups within Canadian society."

The issue was whether the denial to the plaintiff of survivor benefits under the Canada Pension Plan was discriminatory. She was thirty years old, and the governing statute specified a minimum age of thirty-five for the receipt of survivor benefits by anyone who, like her, had no dependent children and no disability. The Court decided that this minimum age requirement did not contravene section 15, as it did not affect the plaintiff's human dignity. The legislation was designed to assist older surviving spouses, who were less likely than she was to obtain employment. Although the denial of benefits was a disadvantage to her, the Court said, it was not likely to be a substantial disadvantage.

An important element of the section 15 analysis — the meaning of equality in the context of the need for differential treatment — was articulated most fully in *Eaton v.*

Brant County Board of Education, [1997] 1 S.C.R 241. Although it was not an employment case, Eaton is relevant to the situation of employees with disabilities. It concerned a child with cerebral palsy who could not any means of communication, had a visual impairment, and used a wheelchair. As it was permitted to do by the governing statute, the Ontario Special Education Tribunal had decided to place the child in a special classroom rather than accede to her parents' wishes that she receive her education in a regular classroom. In deciding that neither the statute nor the tribunal decision violated the child's equality rights under section 15(1) of the *Charter*, Sopinka J., for the majority of the Court, said:

> The principles that not every distinction on a prohibited ground will constitute discrimination and that, in general, distinctions based on presumed rather than actual characteristics are the hallmarks of discrimination have particular significance when applied to physical and mental disability. Avoidance of discrimination on this ground will frequently require distinctions to be made taking into account the actual personal characteristics of disabled persons. . . .
>
> The principal object of certain of the prohibited grounds is the elimination of discrimination by the attribution of untrue characteristics based on stereotypical attitudes relating to immutable conditions such as race or sex. In the case of disability, this is one of the objectives. The other equally important objective seeks to take into account the true characteristics of this group which act as headwinds to the enjoyment of society's benefits and to accommodate them. Exclusion from the mainstream of society results from the construction of a society based solely on "mainstream" attributes to which disabled persons will never be able to gain access. Whether it is the impossibility of success at a written test for a blind person, or the need for ramp access to a library, the discrimination does not lie in the attribution of untrue characteristics to the disabled individual. The blind person cannot see and the person in a wheelchair needs a ramp. Rather, it is the failure to make reasonable accommodation, to fine-tune society so that its structures and assumptions do not result in the relegation and banishment of disabled persons from participation which results in discrimination against them. The discrimination inquiry which uses the attribution of "stereotypical characteristics" reasoning as commonly understood is simply inappropriate here. It may be seen rather as a case of reverse stereotyping which, by not allowing for the condition of a disabled individual, ignores his or her disability and forces the individual to sink or swim within the mainstream environment. It is recognition of the actual characteristics, and reasonable accommodation of these characteristics which is the central purpose of s. 15(1) in relation to disability.

13:222 The "Unified Approach"

In 1999, in the *Meiorin* case, which involved the interpretation of human rights legislation rather than the *Charter*, the Supreme Court of Canada tried to simplify the relationship between direct and indirect discrimination, BFORs, and the duty to accommodate. In doing so, it articulated a new three-stage test for deciding whether a standard which appears to be discriminatory is in fact a BFOR.

British Columbia (Public Service Employee Relations Commission) v. BCGSEU, [1999] 3 S.C.R. 3 (the *Meiorin* case)

McLACHLIN J., for the Court:

. . .

II. FACTS

Ms. Meiorin was employed for three years by the British Columbia Ministry of Forests as a member of a three-person Initial Attack Forest Firefighting Crew in the Golden Forest District. The crew's job was to attack and suppress forest fires while they were small and could be contained. Ms. Meiorin's supervisors found her work to be satisfactory.

Ms. Meiorin was not asked to take a physical fitness test until 1994, when she was required to pass the Government's "Bona Fide Occupational Fitness Tests and Standards for B.C. Forest Service Wildland Firefighters" (the "Tests"). The Tests required that the forest firefighters weigh less than 200 lbs. (with their equipment) and complete a shuttle run, an upright rowing exercise, and a pump carrying/hose dragging exercise within stipulated times. The running test was designed to test the forest firefighters' aerobic fitness and was based on the view that forest firefighters must have a minimum "VO2 max" of 50 ml.kg-1.min-1 (the "aerobic standard"). "VO2 max" measures "maximal oxygen uptake," or the rate at which the body can take in oxygen, transport it to the muscles, and use it to produce energy.

The Tests were developed in response to a 1991 Coroner's Inquest Report that recommended that only physically fit employees be assigned as front-line forest firefighters for safety reasons. The Government commissioned a team of researchers from the University of Victoria to undertake a review of its existing fitness standards with a view to protecting the safety of firefighters while meeting human rights norms. The researchers developed the Tests by identifying the essential components of forest firefighting, measuring the physiological demands of those components, selecting fitness tests to measure those demands and, finally, assessing the validity of those tests.

The researchers studied various sample groups. The specific tasks performed by forest firefighters were identified by reviewing amalgamated data collected by the British Columbia Forest Service. The physiological demands of those tasks were then measured by observing test subjects as they performed them in the field. One simulation involved 18 firefighters, another involved 10 firefighters, but it is unclear from the researchers' report whether the subjects at this stage were male or female. The researchers asked a pilot group of 10 university student volunteers (6 females and 4 males) to perform a series of proposed fitness tests and field exercises. After refining the preferred tests, the researchers observed them being performed by a larger sample group composed of 31 forest firefighter trainees and 15 university student volunteers (31 males and 15 females), and correlated their results with the group's performance in the field. Having concluded that the preferred tests were accurate predictors of actual forest firefighting performance — including the running test designed to gauge whether the subject met the aerobic standard — the researchers presented their report to the Government in 1992.

A follow-up study in 1994 of 77 male forest firefighters and 2 female forest firefighters used the same methodology. However, the researchers this time recommended that the Government initiate another study to examine the impact of the Tests on women. There is no evidence before us that the Government has yet responded to this recommendation.

Two aspects of the researchers' methodology are critical to this case. First, it was primarily descriptive, based on measuring the average performance levels of the test subjects and converting this data into minimum performance standards. Second, it did not seem to distinguish between the male and female test subjects.

After four attempts, Ms. Meiorin failed to meet the aerobic standard, running the distance in 11 minutes and 49.4 seconds instead of the required 11 minutes. As a result, she was laid off. Her union subsequently brought a grievance on her behalf. The arbitrator designated to hear the grievance was required to determine whether she had been improperly dismissed.

Evidence accepted by the arbitrator demonstrated that, owing to physiological differences, most women have lower aerobic capacity than most men. Even with training, most women cannot increase their aerobic capacity to the level required by the aerobic standard, although training can allow most men to meet it. The arbitrator also heard evidence that 65 percent to 70 percent of male applicants pass the Tests on their initial attempts, while only 35 percent of female applicants have similar success. Of the 800 to 900 Initial Attack Crew members employed by the Government in 1995, only 100 to 150 were female.

There was no credible evidence showing that the prescribed aerobic capacity was necessary for either men or women to perform the work of a forest firefighter satisfactorily. On the contrary, Ms. Meiorin had in the past performed her work well, without apparent risk to herself, her colleagues or the public.

III. THE RULINGS

The arbitrator found that Ms. Meiorin had established a *prima facie* case of adverse effect discrimination by showing that the aerobic standard has a disproportionately negative effect on women as a group. He further found that the Government had presented no credible evidence that Ms. Meiorin's inability to meet the aerobic standard meant that she constituted a safety risk to herself, her colleagues, or the public, and hence had not discharged its burden of showing that it had accommodated Ms. Meiorin to the point of undue hardship. He ordered that she be reinstated to her former position and compensated for her lost wages and benefits. . . .

The Court of Appeal . . . did not distinguish between direct and adverse effect discrimination. It held that so long as the standard is *necessary* to the safe and efficient performance of the work and is applied through individualized testing, there is no discrimination. The Court of Appeal (mistakenly) read the arbitrator's reasons as finding that the aerobic standard was necessary to the safe and efficient performance of the work. Since Ms. Meiorin had been individually tested against this standard, it allowed the appeal and dismissed her claim. The Court of Appeal commented that to permit Ms. Meiorin to succeed would create "reverse discrimination," i.e., to set a lower standard for women than for men would discriminate against those men who failed to meet the men's standard but were nevertheless capable of meeting the women's standard.

IV. STATUTORY PROVISIONS

The following provisions of the British Columbia Human Rights Code, R.S.B.C. 1996, c. 210, are at issue on this appeal:

Discrimination in employment

13(1) A person must not,

(a) refuse to employ or refuse to continue to employ a person, or

(b) discriminate against a person regarding employment or any term or condition of employment

because of the race, colour, ancestry, place of origin, political belief, religion, marital status, family status, physical or mental disability, sex, sexual orientation or age of that person or because that person has been convicted of a criminal or summary conviction offence that is unrelated to the employment or to the intended employment of that person.

. . .

(4) Subsections (1) and (2) do not apply with respect to a refusal, limitation, specification or preference based on a bona fide occupational requirement.

V. THE ISSUES

The first issue on this appeal is the test applicable to s. 13(1) and (4) of the British Columbia Human Rights Code. The second issue is whether, on this test, Ms. Meiorin has established that the Government violated the Code.

VI. ANALYSIS

As a preliminary matter, I must sort out a characterization issue. The Court of Appeal seems to have understood the arbitrator as having held that the ability to meet the aerobic standard is necessary to the safe and efficient performance of the work of an Initial Attack Crew member. With respect, I cannot agree with this reading of the arbitrator's reasons.

The arbitrator held that the standard was one of the appropriate measurements available to the Government and that there is generally a reasonable relationship between aerobic fitness and the ability to perform the job of an Initial Attack Crew member. This falls short, however, of an affirmative finding that the ability to meet the aerobic standard chosen by the Government is necessary to the safe and efficient performance of the job. To the contrary, that inference is belied by the arbitrator's conclusion that, despite her failure to meet the aerobic standard, Ms. Meiorin did not pose a serious safety risk to herself, her colleagues, or the general public. I therefore proceed on the view that the arbitrator did not find that an applicant's ability to meet the aerobic standard is necessary to his or her ability to perform the tasks of an Initial Attack Crew member safely and efficiently. This leaves us to face squarely the issue of whether the aerobic standard is unjustifiably discriminatory within the meaning of the Code.

A. The Test

1. The Conventional Approach

The conventional approach to applying human rights legislation in the workplace requires the tribunal to decide at the outset into which of two categories the case falls: (1) "direct discrimination," where the standard is discriminatory on its face, or (2) "adverse effect discrimination," where the facially neutral standard discriminates in effect: [*O'Malley*, above, section 13:220] at p. 551, per McIntyre J. If a *prima facie* case of either form of discrimination is established, the burden shifts to the employer to justify it.

In the case of direct discrimination, the employer may establish that the standard is a BFOR by showing: (1) that the standard was imposed honestly and in good faith and was not designed to undermine the objectives of the human rights legislation (the subjective element); and (2) that the standard is reasonably necessary to the safe and efficient performance of the work and does not place an unreasonable burden on those to whom it applies (the objective element). [Citations omitted.] It is difficult for an employer to justify a standard as a BFOR where individual testing of the capabilities of the employee or applicant is a reasonable alternative: [citations omitted].

If these criteria are established, the standard is justified as a BFOR. If they are not, the standard itself is struck down: [citations omitted].

A different analysis applies to adverse effect discrimination. The BFOR defence does not apply. *Prima facie* discrimination established, the employer need only show: (1) that there is a rational connection between the job and the particular standard, and (2) that it cannot further accommodate the claimant without incurring undue hardship: [citations omitted]. If the employer cannot discharge this burden, then it has failed to establish a defence to the charge of discrimination. In such a case, the claimant succeeds, but the standard itself always remains intact.

. . . On the conventional analysis, I agree with the arbitrator that a case of prima facie adverse effect discrimination was made out and that, on the record before him and before this Court, the Government failed to discharge its burden of showing that it had accommodated Ms. Meiorin to the point of undue hardship.

However, the divergent approaches taken by the arbitrator and the Court of Appeal suggest a more profound difficulty with the conventional test itself. The parties to this appeal have accordingly invited this Court to adopt a new model of analysis that avoids the threshold distinction between direct discrimination and adverse effect discrimination and integrates the concept of accommodation within the BFOR defence.

2. Why is a New Approach Required?

The conventional analysis was helpful in the interpretation of the early human rights statutes, and indeed represented a significant step forward in that it recognized for the first time the harm of adverse effect discrimination. The distinction it drew between the available remedies may also have reflected the apparent differences between direct and adverse effect discrimination. However well this approach may have served us in the past, many commentators have suggested that it ill-serves the purpose of contemporary human rights legislation. I agree. In my view, the complexity and unnecessary artificiality of aspects of the conventional analysis attest to the desirability of now simplifying the guide-lines that structure the interpretation of human rights legislation in Canada.

[McLachlin C.J. then discussed several difficulties with the conventional analysis, including this one:]

Under the conventional analysis, if a standard is classified as being "neutral" at the threshold stage of the inquiry, its legitimacy is never questioned. The focus shifts to whether the individual claimant can be accommodated, and the formal standard itself always remains intact. The conventional analysis thus shifts attention away from the substantive norms underlying the standard, to how "different" individuals can fit into the "mainstream," represented by the standard.

Although the practical result of the conventional analysis may be that individual claimants are accommodated and the particular discriminatory effect they experience may be alleviated, the larger import of the analysis cannot be ignored. It bars courts and tribunals from assessing the legitimacy of the standard itself. . . .

3. Toward a Unified Approach

Whatever may have once been the benefit of the conventional analysis of discrimination claims brought under human rights legislation, the difficulties discussed show that there is much to be said for now adopting a unified approach that (1) avoids the problematic distinction between direct and adverse effect discrimination, (2) requires employers to accommodate as much as reasonably possible the characteristics of individual employees when setting the workplace standard, and (3) takes a strict approach to exemptions from the duty not to discriminate, while permitting exemptions where they are reasonably necessary to the achievement of legitimate work-related objectives.

. . .

Furthermore, some provinces have revised their human rights statutes so that courts are now required to adopt a unified approach: see s. 24(2) of the Ontario *Human Rights Code*. . . .

. . .

4. Elements of a Unified Approach

Having considered the various alternatives, I propose the following three-step test for determining whether a *prima facie* discriminatory standard is a BFOR. An employer may justify the impugned standard by establishing on the balance of probabilities:

(1) that the employer adopted the standard for a purpose rationally connected to the performance of the job;

(2) that the employer adopted the particular standard in an honest and good faith belief that it was necessary to the fulfilment of that legitimate work-related purpose; and

(3) that the standard is reasonably necessary to the accomplishment of that legitimate work-related purpose. To show that the standard is reasonably necessary, it must be demonstrated that it is impossible to accommodate individual employees sharing the characteristics of the claimant without imposing undue hardship upon the employer.

This approach is premised on the need to develop standards that accommodate the potential contributions of all employees in so far as this can be done without undue hardship to the employer. Standards may adversely affect members of a particular group, to be sure. But as Wilson J. noted in [*Central Alberta Dairy Pool v. Alberta (Human Rights Commission)*], "[i]f a reasonable alternative exists to burdening members of a group with a given rule, that rule will not be [a BFOR]." It follows that a rule or standard must accommodate individual differences to the point of undue hardship if it is to be found reasonably necessary. Unless no further accommodation is possible without imposing undue hardship, the standard is not a BFOR in its existing form and the *prima facie* case of discrimination stands.

Having set out the test, I offer certain elaborations on its application.

Step One

The first step in assessing whether the employer has successfully established a BFOR defence is to identify the general purpose of the impugned standard and determine whether it is rationally connected to the performance of the job. The initial task is to determine what the impugned standard is generally designed to achieve. The ability to work safely and efficiently is the purpose most often mentioned in the cases but there may well be other reasons for imposing particular standards in the workplace. In [*Brossard (Town) v. Quebec (Commission des droits de la personne)*] for example, the general purpose of the town's anti-nepotism policy was to curb actual and apparent conflicts of interest among public employees. In [*Caldwell v. Stuart*], the Roman Catholic high school sought to maintain the religious integrity of its teaching environment and curriculum. In other circumstances, the employer may seek to ensure that qualified employees are present at certain times. There are innumerable possible reasons that an employer might seek to impose a standard on its employees.

The employer must demonstrate that there is a rational connection between the general purpose for which the impugned standard was introduced and the objective requirements of the job. For example, turning again to *Brossard, supra,* Beetz J. held . . . that because of the special character of public employment, "[i]t is appropriate and indeed necessary to adopt rules of conduct for public servants to inhibit conflicts of interest." Where the general purpose of the standard is to ensure the safe and efficient performance of the job — essential elements of all occupations — it will likely not be necessary to spend much time at this stage. Where the purpose is narrower, it may well be an important part of the analysis.

The focus at the first step is not on the validity of the particular standard that is at issue, but rather on the validity of its more general purpose. This inquiry is necessarily more general than determining whether there is a rational connection between the performance of the job and the *particular standard* that has been selected, as may have been the case on the conventional approach. The distinction is important. If there is no rational relationship between the general purpose of the standard and the tasks properly required of the employee, then there is of course no need to continue to assess the legitimacy of the particular standard itself. Without a legitimate general purpose underlying it, the standard cannot be a BFOR. In my view, it is helpful to keep the two levels of inquiry distinct.

Step Two

Once the legitimacy of the employer's more general purpose is established, the employer must take the second step of demonstrating that it adopted the particular standard with an honest and good faith belief that it was necessary to the accomplishment of its purpose, with no intention of discriminating against the claimant. This addresses the subjective element of the test which, although not essential to a finding that the standard is not a BFOR, is one basis on which the standard may be struck down. . . . If the imposition of the standard was not thought to be reasonably necessary or was motivated by discriminatory animus, then it cannot be a BFOR.

It is important to note that the analysis shifts at this stage from the general purpose of the standard to the particular standard itself. It is not necessarily so that a particular standard will constitute a BFOR merely because its general purpose is rationally connected to the performance of the job. . . .

Step Three

The employer's third and final hurdle is to demonstrate that the impugned standard is reasonably necessary for the employer to accomplish its purpose, which by this point has been demonstrated to be rationally connected to the performance of the job. The employer must establish that it cannot accommodate the claimant and others adversely affected by the standard without experiencing undue hardship. When referring to the concept of "undue hardship," it is important to recall the words of Sopinka J. who observed in *Central Okanagan School District No. 23 v. Renaud* . . . , that "[t]he use of the term 'undue' infers that some hardship is acceptable; it is only 'undue' hardship that satisfies this test." It may be ideal from the employer's perspective to choose a standard that is uncompromisingly stringent. Yet the standard, if it is to be justified under the human rights legislation, must accommodate factors relating to the unique capabilities and inherent worth and dignity of every individual, up to the point of undue hardship.

. . .

Courts and tribunals should be sensitive to the various ways in which individual capabilities may be accommodated. Apart from individual testing to determine whether the person has the aptitude or qualification that is necessary to perform the work, the possibility that there may be different ways to perform the job while still accomplishing the employer's legitimate work-related purpose should be considered in appropriate cases. The skills, capabilities and potential contributions of the individual claimant and others like him or her must be respected as much as possible. Employers, courts and tribunals should be innovative yet practical when considering how this may best be done in particular circumstances.

Some of the important questions that may be asked in the course of the analysis include:

(a) Has the employer investigated alternative approaches that do not have a discriminatory effect, such as individual testing against a more individually sensitive standard?

(b) If alternative standards were investigated and found to be capable of fulfilling the employer's purpose, why were they not implemented?

(c) Is it necessary to have all employees meet the single standard for the employer to accomplish its legitimate purpose or could standards reflective of group or individual differences and capabilities be established?

(d) Is there a way to do the job that is less discriminatory while still accomplishing the employer's legitimate purpose?

(e) Is the standard properly designed to ensure that the desired qualification is met without placing an undue burden on those to whom the standard applies?

(f) Have other parties who are obliged to assist in the search for possible accommodation fulfilled their roles? As Sopinka J. noted in *Renaud, supra*, at pp. 992–96, the task of determining how to accommodate individual differences may also place burdens on the employee and, if there is a collective agreement, a union.

Notwithstanding the overlap between the two inquiries, it may often be useful as a practical matter to consider separately, first, the *procedure*, if any, which was adopted to assess the issue of accommodation and, second, the *substantive content* of either a more accommodating standard which was offered or alternatively the employer's reasons for not offering any such standard. . . .

If the *prima facie* discriminatory standard is not reasonably necessary for the employer to accomplish its legitimate purpose or, to put it another way, if individual differences may be accommodated without imposing undue hardship on the employer, then the standard is not a BFOR. . . . Conversely, if the general purpose of the standard is rationally connected to the performance of the particular job, the particular standard was imposed with an honest, good faith belief in its necessity, and its application in its existing form is reasonably necessary for the employer to accomplish its legitimate purpose without experiencing undue hardship, the standard is a BFOR. If all of these criteria are established, the employer has brought itself within an exception to the general prohibition of discrimination.

Employers designing workplace standards owe an obligation to be aware of both the differences between individuals, and differences that characterize groups of individuals. They must build conceptions of equality into workplace standards. . . . To the extent that a standard unnecessarily fails to reflect the differences among individuals, it runs afoul of the prohibitions contained in the various human rights statutes and must be replaced. The standard itself is required to provide for individual accommodation, if reasonably possible. . . .

B. Application of the Reformed Approach to the Case on Appeal

1. Introduction

Ms. Meiorin has discharged the burden of establishing that, *prima facie*, the aerobic standard discriminates against her as a woman. The arbitrator held that, because of their generally lower aerobic capacity, most women are adversely affected by the high aerobic standard. While the Government's expert witness testified that most women can achieve the aerobic standard with training, the arbitrator rejected this evidence as "anecdotal" and "not supported by scientific data." This Court has not been presented with any reason to revisit this characterization. . . .

Ms. Meiorin having established a *prima facie* case of discrimination, the burden shifts to the Government to demonstrate that the aerobic standard is a BFOR. For the reasons below, I conclude that the Government has failed to discharge this burden and therefore cannot rely on the defence provided by s. 13(4) of the Code.

2. Steps One and Two

The first two elements of the proposed BFOR analysis, that is (1) that the employer adopted the standard for a purpose rationally connected to the performance of the job; and (2) that the employer adopted the particular standard in an honest and good faith belief that it was necessary to the fulfilment of that legitimate work-related purpose, have been fulfilled. The Government's general purpose in imposing the aerobic standard is not disputed. It is to enable the Government to identify those employees or applicants who are able to perform the job of a forest firefighter safely and efficiently. It is also clear that there is a rational connection between this general characteristic and the performance of the particularly strenuous tasks expected of a forest firefighter. All indications are that the Government acted honestly and in a good faith belief that adopting the particular standard was necessary to the identification of those persons able to perform the job safely and efficiently. It did not intend to discriminate against Ms. Meiorin. To the contrary, one of the reasons the Government retained the researchers from the University of Victoria was that it sought to identify non-discriminatory standards.

3. Step Three

Under the third element of the unified approach, the employer must establish that the standard is reasonably necessary to the accomplishment of that legitimate work-related purpose. To show that the standard is reasonably necessary, it must be demonstrated that it is impossible to accommodate individual employees sharing the characteristics of the claimant without imposing undue hardship upon the employer. In the case on appeal, the contentious issue is whether the Government has demonstrated that this particular aerobic standard is reasonably necessary in order to identify those persons who are able to perform the tasks of a forest firefighter safely and efficiently. As noted, the burden is on the government to demonstrate that, in the course of accomplishing this purpose, it cannot accommodate individual or group differences without experiencing undue hardship.

The Government adopted the laudable course of retaining experts to devise a non-discriminatory test. However, because of significant problems with the way the researchers proceeded, passing the resulting aerobic standard has not been shown to be reasonably necessary to the safe and efficient performance of the work of a forest firefighter. The Government has not established that it would experience undue hardship if a different standard were used.

The procedures adopted by the researchers are problematic on two levels. First, their approach seems to have been primarily a descriptive one: test subjects were observed completing the tasks, the aerobic capacity of the test subjects was ascertained, and that capacity was established as the minimum standard required of every forest firefighter. However, merely describing the characteristics of a test subject does not necessarily allow one to identify the standard *minimally* necessary for the safe and efficient performance of the task. Second, these primarily descriptive studies failed to distinguish the female test subjects from the male test subjects, who constituted the vast majority of the sample groups. The record before this Court therefore does not permit us to say whether men and women require the same minimum level of aerobic capacity to perform safely and efficiently the tasks expected of a forest firefighter.

While the researchers' goal was admirable, their aerobic standard was developed through a process that failed to address the possibility that it may discriminate unnecessarily on one or more prohibited grounds, particularly sex. This phenomenon is not unique to the procedures taken towards identifying occupational qualifications in this case. . . .

The expert who testified before the arbitrator on behalf of the Government defended the original researchers' decision not to analyse separately the aerobic performance of the male and female, experienced and inexperienced, test subjects as an attempt to reflect the actual conditions of firefighting. This misses the point. The polymorphous group's average aerobic performance is irrelevant to the question of whether the aerobic standard constitutes a minimum threshold that cannot be altered without causing undue hardship to the employer. Rather, the goal should have been to measure whether members of all groups require the same minimum aerobic capacity to perform the job safely and efficiently and, if not, to reflect that disparity in the employment qualifications. There is no evidence before us that any action was taken to further this goal before the aerobic standard was adopted.

Neither is there any evidence that the Government embarked upon a study of the discriminatory effects of the aerobic standard when the issue was raised by Ms. Meiorin. In fact, the expert reports filed by the Government in these proceedings content themselves with asserting that the aerobic standard set in 1992 and 1994 is a minimum standard that women can meet with appropriate training. No studies were conducted to substantiate the latter assertion and the arbitrator rejected it as unsupported by the evidence.

Assuming that the Government had properly addressed the question in a procedural sense, its response — that it would experience undue hardship if it had to accommodate Ms. Meiorin — is deficient from a substantive perspective. The Government has presented no evidence as to the cost of accommodation. Its primary argument is that, because the aerobic standard is necessary for the safety of the individual firefighter, the other members of the crew, and the public at large, it would experience undue hardship if compelled to deviate from that standard in any way.

Referring to the Government's arguments on this point, the arbitrator noted that, "other than anecdotal or 'impressionistic' evidence concerning the magnitude of risk involved in accommodating the adverse-effect discrimination suffered by the grievor, the employer has presented no cogent evidence . . . to support its position that it cannot accommodate Ms. Meiorin because of safety risks." The arbitrator held that the evidence fell short of establishing that Ms. Meiorin posed a serious safety risk to herself, her colleagues, or the general public. Accordingly, he held that the Government had failed to accommodate her to the point of undue hardship. This Court has not been presented with any reason to interfere with his conclusion on this point, and I decline to do so. The Government did not discharge its burden of showing that the purpose for which it introduced the aerobic standard would be compromised to the point of undue hardship if a different standard were used.

This leaves the evidence of the Assistant Director of Protection Programs for the British Columbia Ministry of Forests, who testified that accommodating Ms. Meiorin would undermine the morale of the Initial Attack Crews. Again, this proposition is not supported by evidence. But even if it were, the attitudes of those who seek to maintain a discriminatory practice cannot be reconciled with the Code. These attitudes cannot therefore be determinative of whether the employer has accommodated the claimant to the point of undue hardship. . . . Although serious consideration must of course be taken of the "objection of employees based on well-grounded concerns that their rights will be affected," discrimination on the basis of a prohibited ground cannot be justified by arguing that abandoning such a practice would threaten the morale of the workforce. . . . If it were possible to perform the tasks of a forest firefighter safely and efficiently without meeting the prescribed aerobic standard (and the Government has not established the contrary), I can see no right of other firefighters that would be affected by allowing Ms. Meiorin to continue performing her job.

The Court of Appeal suggested that accommodating women by permitting them to meet a lower aerobic standard than men would constitute "reverse discrimination." I respectfully disagree. As this Court has repeatedly held, the essence of equality is to be treated according to one's own merit, capabilities and circumstances. True equality requires that differences be accommodated. . . . A different aerobic standard capable of identifying women who could perform the job safely and efficiently therefore does not necessarily imply discrimination against men. "Reverse" discrimination would only result if, for example, an aerobic standard representing a minimum threshold for *all* forest firefighters was held to be inapplicable to men simply because they were men.

The Court of Appeal also suggested that the fact that Ms. Meiorin was tested individually immunized the Government from a finding of discrimination. However, individual testing, without more, does not negate discrimination. The individual must be tested against a realistic standard that reflects his or her capacities and potential contributions. Having failed to establish that the aerobic standard constitutes the minimum qualification required to perform the job safely and efficiently, the Government cannot rely on the mere fact of individual testing to rebut Ms. Meiorin's *prima facie* case of discrimination.

. . .

[McLachlin C.J. concluded that the Government had not shown that the prima facie discriminatory aerobic standard was reasonably necessary to identify forest firefighters who could work safely and efficiently, so the Government was not able to rely on the BFOR defence. She therefore restored the order of the arbitrator reinstating Ms. Meiorin to her former position and compensating her for lost wages and benefits.]

✳ ✳ ✳

It has been argued that the standard in *Meiorin* focuses the analysis more on the system than on the individual, and that it recognizes the need to restructure organizations: Tamar Witelson, "From Here to Equality: Meiorin, TD Bank, and the Problems with Human Rights Law" (1999), 25 Queen's L.J. 347.

13:300 SOME MAJOR EMPLOYMENT-RELATED EQUALITY ISSUES

13:310 Sex Discrimination

The law's treatment of claims of sex discrimination illustrates how equality claims in the employment context have evolved, and how workplace discrimination issues reflect broader societal concerns.

Understanding the meaning of sex discrimination requires consideration of the societal impact of women's capacity to reproduce and the need to combine family care and work outside the home. In *Bliss v. Attorney General of Canada*, [1979] 1 S.C.R. 183, the Supreme Court of Canada held that discrimination on the basis of pregnancy was not discrimination on the basis of sex. In *Brooks v. Canada Safeway*, [1989] 1 S.C.R. 1219, the Court revisited that question. Canada Safeway's accident and sickness plan excluded pregnant women from benefits during the period prior to the birth and for seventeen weeks afterwards. Applying the test articulated under section 15 of the *Charter* in the *Andrews* case, mentioned above in section 13:220, Dickson C.J. noted that the plan treated pregnant women less favourably than non-pregnant employees, and was thus discriminatory on the basis of pregnancy. Pregnancy itself was not a prohibited ground of discrimination under the applicable human rights statute (the Manitoba *Human Rights Act*), but sex was. Dickson C.J. held that "[d]iscrimination on the basis of pregnancy is a form of sex discrimination because of the basic biological fact that only women have the capacity to become pregnant." He said:

> Over ten years have elapsed since the decision in *Bliss*. During that time there have been profound changes in women's labour force participation. With the benefit of a decade of hindsight and ten years of experience with claims of human rights discrimination and jurisprudence arising therefrom, I am prepared to say that *Bliss* was wrongly decided or, in any event, that *Bliss* would not be decided now as it was decided then. Combining paid work with motherhood and accommodating the childbearing needs of working women are ever-increasing imperatives. That those who bear children and benefit society as a whole thereby should not be economically or socially disadvantaged seems to bespeak the obvious. It is only women who bear children; no man can become pregnant. . . . [I]t is unfair to impose all of the costs of pregnancy upon one-half of the population.
>
> . . . The Safeway plan was no doubt developed . . . 'in an earlier era when women openly were presumed to play a minor and temporary role in the labor force'. . . .
>
> I am not persuaded by the argument that discrimination on the basis of pregnancy cannot amount to sex discrimination because not all women are pregnant at any one time. While pregnancy-based discrimination only affects parts of an identifiable group, it does not affect anyone who is not a member of the group. Many, if not most, claims of partial

discrimination fit this pattern. As numerous decisions and authors have made clear, this fact does not make the impugned distinction any less discriminating. . . .

Finally, on this point, the respondent referred to *Canada Safeway Ltd. v. Manitoba Food and Commercial Workers Union, Local 832,* . . . in which this Court restored an arbitration award which found Safeway's 'no beards' rule to be a 'reasonable' rule. Safeway argues that, by analogy, this Court has already found that discrimination because of pregnancy is not discrimination because of sex. Reference was also made to *Manitoba Human Rights Commission v. Canada Safeway Ltd.* . . . in which a panel of this Court dismissed the Human Rights Commission's application for leave to appeal the decision that Safeway's 'no beards' rule was not discrimination because of sex. The Manitoba Court of Appeal in a unanimous decision stated that the 'no beards' rule was 'definitely not a matter of sexual discrimination.' It is contended that there is an analogy between that case and the present situation; beards are peculiar to men as pregnancy is peculiar to women; however, not all men grow beards and not all women become pregnant. I do not find these cases helpful; I cannot find any useful analogy between a company rule denying men the right to wear beards and an accident and sickness insurance plan which discriminates against female employees who become pregnant. The attempt to draw an analogy at best trivializes the procreative and socially vital function of women and seeks to elevate the growing of facial hair to a constitutional right. . . .

* * *

Since the *Brooks* case was decided, human rights statutes have been amended to specify that discrimination on the basis of pregnancy is a form of sex discrimination.

From claims based on pregnancy itself have evolved claims based on experiences related to pregnancy. For example, *Carewest v. Health Sciences Association of Alberta* (2001), 93 L.A.C. (4th) 129, an employer's refusal to extend the maternity leave of a woman who wanted to breast feed her baby at home was held by an arbitrator to be sex discrimination. Similarly, sex discrimination claims (including those related to pregnancy) may have to be reconciled with claims based on other grounds. For example, in *Quintette Operating Corp. v. United Steelworkers of America, Local 9113,* [1997] B.C.D.L.A. 500.36.30.30, the union and employer had agreed that temporarily disabled employees would be given preference for light work that was available within their own department. A pregnant employee grieved unsuccessfully that it was discriminatory not to include her in that scheme. The arbitrator held that the scheme was not discriminatory — that the grievor was being treated not as a pregnant woman but as an employee who could do only office work when no such work was available in her department.

13:320 Sexual Harassment

13:321 Sexual Harassment as Sex Discrimination

Workplace harassment on the ground of sex, race, disability, or any other ground specified in human rights legislation is recognized in law as a form of discrimination in employment. Legal recognition that harassment is a form of discrimination was not immediate, particularly in the case of sexual harassment. Some courts and tribunals considered sexual harassment not to be a form of sex discrimination, because not every woman in a given workplace was subjected to it or because it was considered it to be an expression of personal attraction which with the law should not interfere. The Supreme Court of Canada considered the matter in the following case.

Janzen v. Platy Enterprises Ltd., [1989] 1 S.C.R. 1252

[The two complainants were waitresses at a restaurant. A male co-worker repeatedly kissed and touched them and made sexual advances toward them, despite their objections. When they complained to the manager, the sexual conduct ceased, but they were then subjected to verbal criticism and abuse from the co-worker and the manager. They quit their jobs and filed complaints of sex discrimination with the Manitoba Human Rights Commission. At the time, the Manitoba *Human Rights Act* prohibited sex discrimination but made no mention of sexual harassment.

The human rights adjudicator and the trial court upheld the complaint. The Manitoba Court of Appeal reversed, finding that the sexual harassment experienced by the complainants was not sex discrimination. They appealed to the Supreme Court of Canada.]

DICKSON C.J. (for the Court):

. . .

Without seeking to provide an exhaustive definition of the term, I am of the view that sexual harassment in the workplace may be broadly defined as unwelcome conduct of a sexual nature that detrimentally affects the work environment or leads to adverse job-related consequences for the victims of the harassment. . . . When sexual harassment occurs in the workplace, it is an abuse of both economic and sexual power. Sexual harassment is a demeaning practice, one that constitutes a profound affront to the dignity of the employees forced to endure it. By requiring an employee to contend with unwelcome sexual actions or explicit sexual demands, sexual harassment in the workplace attacks the dignity and self-respect of the victim both as an employee and as a human being.

. . .

There appear to be two principal reasons, closely related, for the decision of the Court of Appeal of Manitoba that the sexual harassment to which the appellants were subjected was not sex discrimination. First, the Court of Appeal drew a link between sexual harassment and sexual attraction. Sexual harassment, in the view of the Court, stemmed from personal characteristics of the victim, rather than from the victim's gender. Second, the appellate court was of the view that the prohibition of sex discrimination in s. 6(1) of the Human Rights Act was designed to eradicate only generic or categorical discrimination. On this reasoning, a claim of sex discrimination could not be made out unless all women were subjected to a form of treatment to which all men were not. If only some female employees were sexually harassed in the workplace, the harasser could not be said to be discriminating on the basis of sex. At most the harasser could only be said to be distinguishing on the basis of some other characteristic.

. . .

The fallacy in the position advanced by the Court of Appeal is the belief that sex discrimination only exists where gender is the sole ingredient in the discriminatory action and where, therefore, all members of the affected gender are mistreated identically. While the concept of discrimination is rooted in the notion of treating an individual as part of a group rather than on the basis of the individual's personal characteristics, discrimination does not require uniform treatment of all members of a particular group. It is sufficient that ascribing to an individual a group characteristic is one factor in the treatment of that individual. If a finding of discrimination required that every individual in the affected group be treated identically, legislative protection against discrimination would be of little or no value. . . .

The argument that discrimination requires identical treatment of all members of the affected group is firmly dismissed by this Court in *Brooks v. Canada Safeway Ltd.* In *Brooks* I stated that pregnancy-related discrimination is sex discrimination. The argument that pregnancy-related discrimination could not be sex discrimination because not all women become pregnant was dismissed for the reason that pregnancy cannot be separated from gender. All pregnant persons are women. Although, in *Brooks*, the impugned benefits plan of the employer, Safeway, did not mention women, it was held to discriminate on the basis of sex because the plan's discriminatory effects fell entirely upon women.

The reasoning in Brooks is applicable to the present appeal. Only a woman can become pregnant; only a woman could be subject to sexual harassment by a heterosexual male. . . . That some women do not become pregnant was no defence in *Brooks*, just as it is no defence in this appeal that not all female employees at the restaurant were subject to sexual harassment. The crucial fact is that it was only female employees who ran the risk of sexual harassment. No man would have been subjected to this treatment. . . .

. . . As the LEAF factum puts it, ". . . sexual harassment is a form of sex discrimination because it denies women equality of opportunity in employment because of their sex." It is one of the purposes of anti-discrimination legislation to remove such denials of equality of opportunity.

13:322 Defining Sexual Harassment

Around the time of *Janzen*, some legislatures amended their human rights or labour legislation to make specific reference to sexual harassment. Currently, four provinces (Manitoba, Newfoundland and Labrador, Ontario, and Quebec) and the federal jurisdiction have an explicit legislative prohibition against sexual harassment. The remaining jurisdictions continue to rely on the general prohibition against discrimination in employment. The federal government is the only jurisdiction to refer to sexual harassment in both human rights and labour legislation.

Shaw v. Levac Supply Ltd., (1991), 91 CLLC 17,007 (Ont. Bd. Inq.)

[Shaw worked for Levac Supply for fourteen years as a bookkeeper. During her employment, she was frequently teased by a male co-worker, Robertson, and her complaints to management went unanswered. The conduct included mimicking her speech, suggesting that she was incompetent, and making derogatory comments about her weight — for example, saying "waddle, waddle" when she walked around the office.]

HUBBARD, Chair: . . . It seems to me incontestable that to express or imply sexual unattractiveness is to make a comment of a sexual nature. Whether the harasser says, "you are attractive and I want to have sex with you," or says, "you are unattractive and no one is likely to want to have sex with you," the reference is sexual. It is verbal conduct of a sexual nature, and it is sexual harassment in the workplace if it is repetitive and has the effect of creating an offensive working environment; it is sexual harassment in the form of an inappropriate comment of a sexual nature. . . .

When a man chants "waddle, waddle" within her hearing every time an overweight woman walks about the office, or mimics the swishing sound made by her nylons rubbing together because of her weight, what purpose can he possibly have except to indicate that she is physically unattractive? Why draw attention to her bodily inelegance in such circumstances other than to indicate that she is sexually undesirable? What other way is the victim to take such comments? The respondent was not a disinterested observer simply making an objective comment upon someone's unfortunate condition. In my opinion, he knew, or ought to have known, that these gibes were . . . a "sexual put-down". . . .

I turn now to the alternative submission of the Commission that, even if it were found that Mr. Robertson's conduct did not amount to sexual harassment so as to bring it within the scope of [the provision of the Manitoba Human Rights Code which prohibited sex discrimination and sexual harassment], it was aimed at the complainant because she is a woman, and gender harassment in the workplace is an infringement of that provision. . . .

To begin with, the primary meaning of the word "sex" is the fact or character of being either male or female, "coitus" being a secondary meaning. Unless the context indicates otherwise, the word is to be given its primary meaning. . . . [E]arly decisions in the field of human rights found that sexual harassment was discrimination because of sex (i.e. "gender") in order to subject that conduct to provisions that prohibited discrimination but did not deal directly with sexual harassment. It would be odd to find that, now that harassment because of sex is dealt with in a separate provision, the word "sex" does not mean gender and that to harass a person non-sexually solely because of his or her gender does not come within the provision.

* * *

Similarly, for example, repeated sabotage by male employees of a female co-worker's safety equipment, due to resentment of the presence of a woman in the workplace, has been recognized as a form of sexual harassment. In such cases, the complainant must prove a link between the harassing conduct and her sex.

The difficult issues raised by same-sex harassment are discussed by Janine Benedet, "Same-Sex Sexual Harassment" (2000), 26 Queen's L.J. 101.

13:330 Discrimination on the Basis of Disability

Concern about discrimination on the ground of disability has become much more prominent over the last two decades. This reflects more understanding of different kinds of disabilities, and rising expectations on the part of people with disabilities. On the history of legal protection in this area, see Bernard Adell, "The Rights of Disabled Workers at Arbitration and under Human Rights Legislation," (1991) 1 Lab. Arb. Yrbk. 167. As Adell points out, collective bargaining can offer only a limited response to the problem of disability discrimination, because it focuses on people who are employed and, in the main, on full-time employees. People with disabilities, particularly severe disabilities, have a high rate of unemployment. Those who do have jobs tend to have held them for a relatively short time and to have a less stable connection with the workforce.

Traditionally, an employee with a physical or mental disability bore the entire burden of adapting to the requirements of the workplace, perhaps with the help of medical or vocational rehabilitation services. An employee who could not adapt was out of work. However, since the 1980s, with the rise of the duty to accommodate, adapting has become a two-way street. An employee with a disability must still be able to perform the core features of a job, but the employer must be prepared (to the threshold of undue hardship) to make changes to the workplace to accommodate the employee's particular needs.

Disability (both mental and physical) is now listed among the prohibited grounds of discrimination in human rights legislation across the country, but it has unique features that distinguish it from other prohibited grounds. Those features are discussed in the following excerpt.

Michael Lynk, "Disability and the Duty to Accommodate," [2001–2002] 1 Lab. Arb. Y.B. 51

First, persons with a disability are characterized by greater heterogeneity than virtually any other group covered by the legislation. Even within the same injury, disease or condition, the varieties of disabling experience are extremely wide. Moreover, the social environment has a substantial capacity either to compound or to alleviate a disability. As the late Justice John Sopinka stated in one of his last decisions [*Eaton v. Brant County Board of Education*]:

> It follows that disability, as a prohibited ground, differs from other enumerated grounds such as race or sex because there is no individual variation with respect to these grounds. However, with respect to disability, this ground means vastly different things depending upon the individual and the context.

Second, unlike the predominately fixed character of most other protected grounds, such as race or gender, the condition of disability is potentially quite mutable. A person with a disability may recover entirely, the particular condition may stabilize for an extended period of time, or the intervention of modern medicine and technology may permit the employee to work productively with few or no limitations. Conversely, a disability might deteriorate or fluctuate dramatically, both in the short and in the long term, thus rendering an employee's attempt to return to work unsuccessful. Furthermore, anyone —

regardless of her or his present state of health — can potentially acquire a permanent, total or long-lasting disability, and the chances of becoming disabled increase with age.

And third, the modes of accommodation, short of undue hardship, required to extend equality to persons with disabilities, because of the greater heterogeneity of disabling conditions, are invariably broader and more complex than those required by other protected grounds. In the case of most protected grounds, accommodations can be accomplished through a change in policies or programs, together with a campaign to reform social attitudes. The responses necessary to ameliorate the social disadvantages of disablement, however, will frequently be more diverse, more individually tailored, more reliant upon technology, and probably more costly. This will often require more creativity and co-operation, and will likely necessitate a greater number of long-lasting alterations and commitments. [Reprinted by permission of Lancaster House Publishing.]

* * *

Accommodating a disability in the workplace can be a very complex and painstaking process, as the following arbitration award shows.

Shuswap Lake General Hospital v. British Columbia Nurses' Union (Lockie Grievance), [2002] B.C.C.A.A.A. No. 21 (Gordon)

INTRODUCTION

¶ 1   Ms. Sharon Lockie, the grievor, has been employed as a registered nurse ("RN") at the Shuswap Lake General Hospital (the "hospital") since May 1994. In April 1997 she was diagnosed with bi-polar mood disorder ("bmd"). She has experienced several episodes of "mania," a manifestation of her disorder, since then. One such episode occurred in early April 2000. On that occasion, one of her co-workers noted behavior consistent with mania, and, following an intervention at the workplace, the grievor went off work. There is no dispute the grievor is not fit to practice as a nurse when she is unwell.

¶ 2   The grievor's psychiatrist, Dr. Keith Gibson, attended her for several weeks following the April 2000 episode. He subsequently confirmed she was fit to return to work effective June 1, 2000. Despite this medical opinion, the Employer was unwilling to allow the grievor to return to work in her position. The Employer encouraged the grievor to apply for long-term disability benefits. She applied for those benefits, but her application was denied due to her doctor's medical opinion, with which she agreed, that she was fit to return to work as a nurse.

¶ 3   When the grievor then sought to return to her nursing position at the hospital, the Employer refused to permit her to do so absent an assurance she would not relapse, or if she did, her relapse could be accurately predicted. As bmd is a disorder characterized by relapses that cannot be accurately predicted, such an assurance could not be given.

¶ 4   On July 31, 2000 the grievor filed a grievance against the Employer's refusal to allow her to return to her nursing position at the hospital despite Dr. Gibson's opinion that she was medically fit to do so. On August 20, 2000 she filed a complaint with the B.C. Human Rights Commission alleging the Employer's refusal to allow her to return to work constitutes discrimination due to her mental disability. The human rights complaint is being held in abeyance pending the outcome of this proceeding.

¶ 5   The Union's position is that by suspending the grievor from her nursing position due to the possibility of a relapse, the Employer is discriminating against her by reason of her mental disability contrary to Article 31 of the collective agreement, and has not discharged its duty to accommodate the grievor to the point of undue hardship. In Article 31, the parties agree to subscribe to the principles of the British Columbia Human Rights Code, R.S.B.C., c. 210 (the "Code").

¶ 6   The Employer advances a three-fold response to the grievance. It says it: 1) could not continue to accommodate the grievor in her position without incurring undue hardship; 2) canvassed and could not find any nursing position that would not similarly result in undue hardship; and, 3) offered to canvass the possibility of positions in the other two bargaining units in its facility, but the Union and the grievor were "not interested" in doing so pending the outcome of this proceeding.

. . .

BACKGROUND

¶ 9   The hospital is a small acute care facility with 49 acute care beds and 5 alternative care beds. There are 22 medical/surgical beds on the unit. On day shift, the unit is staffed with an RN team leader, 2 RNs, and 2 licensed practical nurses ("LPNs"). A "float" nurse is scheduled daily at the hospital. When nursing absences are experienced, either the float nurse or a replacement nurse is utilized to fill the absence. Staffing for the evening shift is 2 RNs and 2 LPNs. For the night shift, 2 RNs and 1 LPN are scheduled. Prior to April 2000, the grievor's shift schedule in a five or six-week rotation was typically five, 12-hour day shifts and the remainder 8-hour evening shifts.

. . .

¶ 12   The work on the unit is typically divided into two teams each consisting of an RN and an LPN. Each team is generally assigned 11 patients. RNs and LPNs meet at the outset of each shift to receive their patient assignments and to hear "report" about the patients from the nurses going off shift. This process takes approximately 30 minutes. The grievor testified that during their shifts, RNs have verbal and visual contact with each other in the hallways and at the medication carts. She said RNs communicate "frequently" about patient care information, and even though RNs may not actually work with LPNs, they have "a fair bit" of contact with each other at the nursing station throughout their shift.

. . .

Bi-Polar Mood Disorder

¶ 18   Bmd is an incurable relapsing condition. Individuals with this disorder experience changes in mood state from either normality to mania, or normality to "depression." These changes in mood state are commonly referred to as "decompensations."

¶ 19   Bmd can be treated and, for many individuals, well managed with appropriate medical and other interventions. Medications such as lithium, anti-convulsants and anti-depressants may be prescribed to stabilize mood. Physicians and psychiatrists also intervene by way of assessment, education and monitoring. Both the patient and his or her family members are educated about the nature of the illness, the ways to manage factors contributing to relapse, the detection of early symptoms of relapse, and support and early warning systems. In terms of monitoring, physicians are able to test blood levels for compliance to medications, side effects, and the need to change medications and/or dosages. Environmental and dietary factors may also be monitored and managed.

¶ 20   Dr. Gibson testified that approximately two-thirds of patients with bmd experience "very significant improvement" in their disorders through treatment, and approximately 50 percent of such patients are employed. He said the duration of episodes of mania can be greatly reduced with medication. Dr. Collins and Dr. Gibson agree that work is therapeutic for individuals with bmd as it provides structure to the day/week/month. In Dr. Gibson's experience, treated bmd patients in the following occupations have all continued to be employed: specialist physicians (including the Head of Psychiatry at a Calgary-based facility), engineers, lawyers, social workers, nurses, mill workers, taxi drivers, and restaurant workers. In the health care facility where Dr. Gibson works in Alberta, he is aware of two staff members with treated bmd who have direct patient care responsibilities. He said these individuals "function well" in their positions.

. . .

The History of the Grievor's Disability and the Events Giving Rise to this Dispute

¶ 35   . . . commencing in October 1999, the grievor experienced a number of extra-ordinary circumstances. From October to December 3, 1999 three close family members died. Another three family members died between December 1999 and October 2000. During the grievor's shift on October 23, 1999, she made several medication errors. The errors involved her failure to administer certain antibiotics. At meetings with management to discuss this situation, the grievor acknowledged the seriousness of the errors. She attributed the errors to fatigue as opposed to any medical or health issue. Consequently, management issued a written warning to her. The Employer does not rely on these errors as part of this case. It simply notes that management was aware of them when the events of December 1999 occurred. In her evidence, Ms. Thompson acknowledged that other nurses make medication errors, but said she has no prior experience with a nurse making as many mediation errors during one shift as the grievor made on October 23, 1999.

. . .

¶ 37   On December 14 the grievor made three medication errors. Ms. Simpson's shift that day overlapped with the grievor's shift by 4 hours that day. At approximately 6:30 pm, near the end of the grievor's shift, Ms. Simpson went into the nursing station and saw the grievor with a number of medication error forms on the desk. Ms. Simpson asked the grievor if she could help, and the grievor explained that she had missed a number of medications. Ms. Simpson inquired whether this was perhaps an indication that the grievor was not feeling well. According to Ms. Simpson, the grievor "became tearful and agreed that someone should be called." Ms. Simpson contacted the manager on call and then tried to support the grievor as best she could. Ms. Simpson estimated that as the replacement RN arrived on the floor that day between 7:30pm and 7:45pm, her (Ms. Simpson's) patients were left unattended from approximately 7:00pm until then. In cross-examination she conceded that although her patients were not attended by her for approximately one hour, she could not say they failed to receive proper care as a result of this situation.

¶ 38   Ms. Thompson's evidence about the December 1999 medication errors was that the grievor "caught" the errors at approximately 7:00pm, administered the missed medications, and noted the errors. Ms. Thompson does not dispute that the grievor took full responsibility for these errors. When Ms. Thompson attempted to give hearsay evidence about the effect of the medication errors on the affected patient, the Union objected. At the outset of the hearing the Union put the Employer on notice that strict proof of any patient safety issues due to these medication errors was required and that hearsay would be objected to. In any event, in her evidence Ms. Thompson could only speculate that the patient "may" have experienced more pain due to the missed medication.

. . .

¶ 41   The grievor went on sick leave following the mid-December episode. She began attending Dr. Gibson at that time. Dr. Gibson identified the indicators for the grievor's decompensation at that time as: irritability; sleep disturbance; spending money; rapid or pressured speech; and, repeated reference to a particular topic in her conversation. He also determined that the February to May period, when the grievor's husband is often absent due to the pressures of his own career, seems to be a "tough season" for the grievor in terms of her disorder. He decided to increase her dosage of lithium during this season. He prescribed anti-depressants and found that over time he and the grievor were able to determine that her sleep disturbance could be well regulated with the drug clopixol.

[The grievor returned to work in February 2000 in accordance with a return-to-work agreement between the employer and union].

¶ 50   The grievor successfully completed the supernumerary shifts provided for in the return-to-work agreements and subsequently returned to her regular rotation. There were no further episodes at the workplace until April 8, 2000.

. . .

¶ 53   As the [April 8] shift progressed, a palliative care patient came onto the ward from the emergency room. Ms. Sweeten observed at that time that the grievor became "quite involved" with the patient's admitting procedure and bed placement. According to Ms. Sweeten, the grievor "appeared stressed and upset that her patient was in pain and distress, and she [the grievor] appeared agitated." Ms. Sweeten encouraged the grievor to go for a break, but the grievor stayed on the unit. Ms. Sweeten observed the grievor repetitively paging an admitting doctor for an oral analgesic order for one of her patients. Ms. Sweeten advised the grievor that another patient needed analgesics. The other RN eventually settled that patient. Ms. Sweeten subsequently noted that the grievor "appeared to become more upset" and when she (Ms. Sweeten) suggested they take a break, the grievor "broke down at the desk crying and upset." The grievor also asked Ms. Sweeten to obtain a specific meal for her and, contrary to accepted practice, asked for a food tray for the new patient's husband.

. . .

¶ 58   Ms. Thompson concluded from the nurses' reports that the grievor did not have good insight into the seriousness of the April episode. She met with the grievor, her shop steward and Mr. Jackson. Ms. Thompson then sent a letter to Dr. Gibson on April 20, 2000 seeking his assurance that if the grievor returned to work, she would "meet her standards of practice on a consistent basis." Dr. Gibson's evidence was that, given the nature of bmd, he was puzzled by Ms. Thompson's use of the term "on a continuous basis." In his April 26th response to the request he wrote, in part, as follows:

> . . . The big problem I have is in terms of what you mean by on a "continuous basis." As I am sure you are aware, bi-polar mood disorder is a relapsing/remitting condition. Even with absolute compliance to medications and all other interventions, individuals afflicted with this disorder can have episodes of depression or mania evolve, sometimes quite quickly. It seems Sharon's struggles over the last four years have been particularly prominent in the spring time (months of April and May). In addition, I believe Sharon has been challenged with more than her usual share of stressors, which has likely contributed to her recent struggles. The best I can do is record once again what I believe I have made Sharon's employer aware of before, that being during periods of remission I would expect Sharon to be capable of competently completing her work in a manner consistent with the standards of nursing practice and professional behavior. On the other hand, it is impossible to predict when she might have another temporary relapse, beyond observing that April/May tends to be an especially challenging time for Sharon.

. . .

¶ 61   Mr. Jackson's evidence was that, after receiving Dr. Gibson's letter, he decided the Employer could not accommodate the grievor as an RN because "relapses are impossible to predict." He said all nursing positions in the facility were canvassed to determine if they involved direct patient care and, as they all did, no position was "available for accommodation."

. . .

¶ 66 Ms. Thompson agreed that after the April 2000 incident she did not consider the following accommodative measures: a return-to-work program similar to the February protocol; the grievor's provision of daily reports of her symptoms; a contract requiring the grievor's family members and doctors to communicate with her (Ms. Thompson) about the grievor's condition; a requirement that the grievor regularly report to either her or Lisa Wherry for assessment; more frequent blood lithium level reports from the grievor's doctor; or, a requirement that the grievor visit her doctor or her psychiatrist more frequently. She acknowledged that the Employer has not offered the grievor any other specific position as an accommodation. Moreover, she did not dispute that management told the grievor there were "too many problems with the other unions" to look for an accommodation in other bargaining units. Ms. Thompson's evidence in this regard was that "we needed her [the grievor's] ideas before we approached the other unions."

. . .

ANALYSIS AND DECISION

¶ 136 At issue in this dispute is whether the continued employment of the grievor as a nurse at the hospital would impose undue hardship on the Employer.

¶ 137 I accept the Employer's submission that this case does not involve general policy in health care; rather, it involves this grievor and this facility. I also accept the Employer's contention that it has accommodated the grievor's mental disability in the workplace in several ways since April 1997. The Employer has permitted various absences from work on sick leave ranging in duration from one week to approximately two months, and has replaced the grievor with casual RNs when she has had to go off work during a shift due to decompensation. The Employer designed and implemented a return-to-work plan including two weeks of supernumerary day shifts and certain reporting/monitoring mechanisms, some of which involved the grievor's co-workers. Following the April 2000 episode at work, the Employer sought further medical information to see if it could accommodate the grievor and canvassed all the nursing positions in its facility to see if the grievor could be accommodated in positions that did not entail direct patient care duties. Accordingly, this dispute involves an assessment of whether the Employer has reached the point of undue hardship in its efforts to accommodate the grievor as a nurse at its facility.

¶ 138 Applying the [*Meiorin*] principles to the evidence before me, I have no difficulty finding that a prima facie case of discrimination has been made out. The reason the Employer has refused to continue to employ the grievor as a nurse is her inability to assure management she will be able to accurately predict future relapses. As the inability to accurately predict relapse is a feature of bmd, I find the Employer's refusal to continue to employ the grievor is inextricably linked to her mental disability and is prima facie discriminatory.

¶ 139 The onus therefore shifts to the Employer to establish, on a balance of probabilities, that its standard constitutes a BFOR. The Employer's standard for the purposes of the BFOR analysis was succinctly summarized in Ms. Thompson's evidence. She said she would only permit a nurse with bmd to return to work in a position involving patient care duties if the nurse was "well controlled and no risk to patient safety and does not require other nurses to monitor [him or her] closely." In Ms. Thompson's and Mr. Jackson's opinion, the grievor did not meet this standard because she could not guarantee she would not relapse and could not assure them that relapse could be accurately predicted.

¶ 140 The Union only challenges the Employer's standard under the third part of the BFOR test. Thus, the question is whether the Employer has established that its standard is reasonably necessary by demonstrating it is impossible to accommodate the grievor in her nursing position without incurring undue hardship. . . . The facts of this case have been reviewed at some length because I share the view expressed by Arbitrator Munroe in *International Forest Products Ltd.*, . . . , that the answer to this inquiry involves an assessment of all of the particular facts of this case.

¶ 141 In terms of a risk to patient safety, I find the Employer's standard is effectively one of absolute safety or perfection, not one of reasonable safety. To use the words of the Supreme Court of Canada in PSERC, the Employer's test of "no" risk to patient safety set an "uncompromisingly stringent standard." The Employer's relapse prediction standard effectively negates a fundamental characteristic of the grievor's mental disability. I accept the Union's contention that the Employer focused too narrowly on whether relapse could be accurately predicted. Given the medical information relating to the nature of bmd, the Employer ought to have acknowledged the fact that relapse cannot be accurately predicted, and ought to have engaged in a search for reasonable accommodative measures that would reduce any risk to patient safety to an acceptable level and still allow the grievor to work as a nurse.

¶ 142 The Employer's contention in relation to safety is that the nature of the grievor's work, disability and insight, and the way in which her disability manifests itself at work, creates a "serious" risk to patient safety that is "too great" to permit her to work in patient care duties. The Employer says that as there is no reasonable way to test the grievor's safety on a day-to-day basis, obliging management to accommodate her in her nursing position would constitute undue hardship. The Employer must point to evidence establishing, on a balance of probabilities, that a serious or unacceptable risk to patient safety would arise from the grievor's continued employment as a nurse. . . . If the risk to patient safety is low, the Employer must establish that the loss or injury that may result would be serious. The evidence must clearly identify the risks and demonstrate that it is impossible to reduce those risks to an acceptable level through reasonable accommodative measures. . . .

¶ 143 On the evidence before me, I cannot find the Employer has established either a "serious" or "unacceptable" risk to patient safety, or the "impossibility" of reducing that risk to an acceptable level through reasonable accommodative measures. The identity of those who bear the risk to safety is the patients on the unit. This undoubtedly poses a legitimate concern for the Employer. Patients reasonably expect the Employer to protect their health and safety while they are in hospital. But the evidence fails to establish that the magnitude of the risk to patient safety is serious or unacceptable.

¶ 144 The evidence relating to medication errors establishes that institutionalized care at the hospital carries with it some risk to patient health arising from medication errors. Other nurses make medication errors and the Employer's records contain numerous examples of such errors. I find the risk to patient health from medication errors is slightly higher in relation to the grievor than in relation to other RNs. Ms. Thompson's uncontradicted evidence is that the grievor had made more medication errors on one shift than other RNs. Thus, given the nature of the grievor's work, a risk to patient health exists, and the magnitude of the risk is somewhat higher than it is in respect of other nurses.

¶ 145 However, there is no direct evidence of any specific loss or injury to any patient due to the grievor's medication errors, and no direct evidence relating to the seriousness of the loss or injury that may result. Medication errors were not a feature of the April 2000 episode. Ms. Thompson's hearsay evidence regarding the December 1999 medication errors does not support a finding of a serious or intolerable risk to patient safety. For these reasons, I find the Employer has failed to establish a serious or unacceptable risk to patient safety or, for that matter, to patient discomfort amounting to a safety risk due to medication errors.

¶ 146 In terms of the Employer's concern relating to patient disruption and/or nursing shortages leading to a direct risk to patient safety, I must again find the evidence falls short of establishing the Employer's factual contentions. There is no evidence that patient safety was ever jeopardized due to a shortage of nurses on the unit while nurses were assisting the grievor. Ms. Simpson expressed concern in this regard, but her evidence did not substantiate any direct risk to patient safety.

¶ 147 The evidence pertaining to the absence of nurses from the unit, or nursing shortages, when the grievor has been unwell at work is that Ms. Simpson assisted the grievor briefly at the outset of her shift in August 1999 and assigned an LPN to sit with the grievor for an unspecified amount of time until the social worker arrived. Ms. Simpson said that four years ago it was very difficult to find casual RN replacements, but there is no evidence that a replacement RN was not found on the day in question or on any other occasion when the grievor's illness manifested itself on the unit. Nor is there any evidence that any patient suffered discomfort or disruption due to either Ms. Simpson's or the LPN's absence from the unit. Further, in terms of unusual situations that may affect patient safety on the unit, the evidence as a whole does not persuade me that the unit is regularly short one RN. And, the evidence is that on day shift a "float" nurse, who could conceivably be temporarily utilized on the unit in the event that the staffing department experienced difficulty obtaining a replacement RN, is scheduled daily at the facility.

¶ 148 As to the December 1999 episode, Ms. Simpson's patients were unattended by her for a short time while she assisted the grievor. But Ms. Simpson could not say her patients failed to receive proper care during that time. Ms. Sweeten noted that due to the grievor's undue attention to one of her patients in April 2000, another RN had to attend to the needs of one of the grievor's patients. But again, there is no evidence that, as a result, the particular patient or any other patient suffered either discomfort or discomfort amounting to a risk to patient safety.

¶ 149 There was evidence that certain patients and family members who observed the grievor's behavior as she moved in and out of the palliative care room while awaiting Mr. Byer's arrival asked questions about the grievor's condition. I am prepared to infer that this situation created concern for these individuals in terms of both the grievor's well-being and patients' well-being. Nonetheless, there is no evidence the grievor approached these patients and attempted to provide patient care and no evidence establishing patient discomfort and/or disruption creating a risk to patient health or safety.

¶ 150 I find that any disruption experienced by patients and their families during the April 2000 incident is attributable to two factors: Ms. Sweeten's delayed reporting of the grievor's behavior to the nurse in charge; and the decision to keep the grievor on the unit. . . . I am satisfied that any risk of similar disruptions can be easily and substantially reduced or diminished by providing an educational workshop on bmd to the grievor's co-workers and supervisors as requested by staff in April 2000, and by instructing staff to ensure the grievor is removed from the unit if her behavior displays indicators of relapse.

¶ 151 Moreover, the evidence fails to demonstrate that it is impossible to reduce the identified risks to an acceptable level through reasonable accommodative measures. I find several material facts relating to the nature of the grievor's workplace, her disability and the way it manifests itself in the workplace must be considered.

¶ 152 First, the nature of the workplace provides certain implicit safeguards against any risk to patient health or safety escalating to a serious or unacceptable level. The grievor's duties are performed in a professional and team-based context. Unlike the solitary work of the fishing guide in *Oak Bay Marina Ltd.*, . . . , the grievor can be easily observed by her co-workers for approximately 30 minutes at the outset of each shift during report. The grievor is also in ongoing contact with her professional colleagues throughout a shift at the nursing station, medication carts and in the hallways. Further, by virtue of their professional obligations to observe and report co-worker impairments of all sorts, the grievor's co-workers will not be required to shoulder any significant additional accommodative responsibility or stress over and above that which exists in relation to all other co-workers. On the evidence before me, I accept that it would not be a reasonable accommodative measure to impose on the grievor's co-workers an obligation to closely scrutinize her behavior in a formal monitoring system. RNs and LPNs nonetheless have a professional responsibility to observe and report co-workers' impairments to their supervisors, and I am satisfied the concerns expressed by the grievor's co-workers in this regard can be satisfactorily addressed through the provision of an educational workshop on bmd and clear instructions from management.

¶ 153 Second, the grievor's particular indicators of relapse have, in the past, been readily observed by her co-workers and reported to supervisory or management staff. . . .

¶ 154 Third, supervisory and/or management staff are available for reporting purposes. On day shift, a team leader is on the unit and both Ms. Thompson and Ms. Wherry are scheduled to work. For evening and night shifts, managers are available on an on-call basis.

¶ 155 Fourth, although bmd is characterized by a loss of insight as an episode evolves, the evidence is that when fellow RNs have confronted the grievor with a possibility that she may be unwell, she has accepted their observations and has agreed she needs to be replaced. . . . The point here is that despite the predictable loss of insight as an episode evolves, the grievor is an individual who is receptive to her RN colleagues' observations of her condition at work and amenable to being relieved of her patient care duties.

¶ 156 I am also satisfied that it is possible to reduce the identified risk to an acceptable level by implementing reasonable accommodative measures that do not impose undue hardship on the Employer. . . . [A]ll of the evidence relating to the grievor's illness and possible accommodative measures must be considered and an assessment must be made as to the viability of various relapse-reduction mechanisms and strategies.

¶ 157 . . . Over time, and more specifically since the April 2000 episode, the grievor and Dr. Gibson have become more familiar with the specific features of her disorder. Together, they have developed some very effective approaches to her illness in terms of treatment, monitoring and prevention of episodes of mania. . . .

¶ 158 The grievor stabilizes quickly following an episode of mania, responds very well to treatment, and is entirely compliant to her medications. The medical evidence also establishes that the seasonal character of the grievor's illness is amendable to monitoring and medication. Moreover . . . , she has made significant strides since April 2000 in terms of self-education and self-identification of indicators for relapse. It is true, as the Employer submits, that the grievor's optimism in this regard has not yet been tested at its facility, but a significant fact remains. The grievor has experienced 14 months of relapse-free living during much of which she has been employed as an RN performing direct patient care duties for two different health care employers.

. . .

¶ 161 I find the Employer's willingness to engage in a meaningful search for reasonable accommodative measures enabling the grievor to return to her position as a nurse ceased when Dr. Gibson confirmed the impossibility of accurately predicting relapses. The Employer continued to focus on relapse prediction even after Dr. Gibson outlined various mechanisms that would assist in anticipating the grievor's decompensations. As I have said, the Employer's focus on relapse prediction was too narrow and its standard of "no" risk was too stringent. The evidence of both Dr. Collins and Dr. Gibson is that other nurses and doctors with bmd have returned to work and have performed their patient care duties safely with some workplace accommodations. . . .

. . .

¶ 167 For all of the foregoing reasons, I find the Employer has failed to satisfy the third test outlined in [*Meiorin*].

. . .

¶ 173 In all of the circumstances of this case, I find the grievor should be returned to work as a nurse on the following conditions. The grievor must:

1. continue to regularly attend her psychiatrist and physician and immediately report indicators for relapse to them;
2. continue to comply with her medical caregivers' testing, monitoring, treatment and medication recommendations;
3. continue to regularly use her familial support team to monitor her indicators for relapse;
4. authorize her psychiatrist, physician, and/or husband to contact her manager if any of them identifies indicators for decompensation or has a concern about the grievor's condition;
5. prepare a self-report of indicators of relapse and the need to increase medication and provide a copy of it to her manager, or designate, if and when requested to do so;
6. meet with supervisors or other administrative personnel to monitor her condition, if and when requested to do so;
7. not report for work if she has a suspicion she is not well;
8. agree to work predictable, routine shifts, and no night shifts;
9. agree not to work excessive overtime;
10. advise her co-workers and team leader about her disorder and the indicators for relapse;
11. comply with any reasonable accommodative measures the grievor, her Union representative and her manager negotiate for detecting early warning signs of decompensation in the workplace.

¶ 174 In terms of reasonable accommodative measures, the following will apply:

1. the grievor is to be scheduled for predictable, routine shifts with as few alterations as possible, and no night shifts;
2. the Employer is to provide the grievor's co-workers, supervisors, managers and other personnel such as the Occupational Health and Safety Officer, with an educational workshop on bmd and the detection of indicators for decompensation;
3. the Employer is to provide a facilitated discussion of co-worker concerns relating to the grievor's return to work;
4. in consultation with the grievor, her Union representative and Dr. Gibson, the Employer is to develop a procedure for staff to utilize if they detect signs of relapse at the workplace, and bring that procedure to the attention of the grievor's co-workers and supervisors;
5. the Employer is to permit the grievor to be absent from work if she identifies indicators of relapse;
6. the Employer may implement reasonable reporting mechanisms involving supervisors, other administrative personnel, or the local mental health unit to monitor the grievor's condition.

13:340 Who Is under a Duty to Accommodate?

The employer and the union share the duty to accommodate. According to the Supreme Court of Canada in *Central Okanagan School District No. 23 v. Renaud*, [1992] 2 S.C.R. 970 (excerpted below), the union not only may be liable for failure to accommodate if it has been involved in developing the relevant rule or practice, but also if it impedes the employer's efforts to accommodate. This view has been criticized because it is premised on an assumption that the employer and the union are equal partners in collective bargaining: see Beth Bilson, "Seniority and the Duty to Accommodate: A Clash of Values — A Neutral's Perspective," (1999–2000) 1 Lab. Arb. Yrbk. 73, 77–79.

Central Okanagan School District No. 23 v. Renaud, [1992] 2 S.C.R. 970

SOPINKA J.: The issue raised in this appeal is the scope and content of the duty of an employer to accommodate the religious beliefs of employees and whether and to what extent that duty is shared by a trade union. . . . Is a trade union liable for discrimination if it refuses to relax the provisions of a collective agreement and thereby blocks the employer's attempt to accommodate? Must the employer act unilaterally in these circumstances? These are issues that have serious implications for the unionized workplace.

THE FACTS

The appellant was employed by the Board of School Trustees, School District No. 23 (Central Okanagan) (the 'school board') and was a member of the Canadian Union of Public Employees, Local 523 (the 'union'). He had been employed by the school board since 1981 and in 1984 used his seniority to secure a Monday to Friday job at Spring Valley Elementary School ('SVE'). The gymnasium at SVE was rented out to a community group on Friday evenings and a custodian was required to be present for security and emergency purposes during this time. Pursuant to the employer's work schedule, which was included in the collective agreement, the job at SVE involved an afternoon shift from 3:00 p.m. until 11:00 p.m. during which only one custodian was on duty. As a Seventh-day Adventist, the appellant's religion forbade him from working on the church's Sabbath, which is from sundown Friday until sundown Saturday. The appellant met with a representative of the school board to try to accommodate his inability to work the full Friday shift. The school board representative was agreeable to the request but indicated that the school-board required the consent of the union if any accommodation involved an exception to the collective agreement. Many of the alternatives discussed by the representative and the appellant involved transfer to 'prime' positions which the appellant did not have enough seniority to secure. The appellant was reluctant to accept a further alternative, that he work a four-day week, as this would result in a substantial loss in pay. In spite of these possibilities and other alternatives that could perhaps have been implemented without the union's consent, the employer concluded that the only practical alternative was to create a Sunday to Thursday shift for the appellant which did require the consent of the union.

The union had a meeting to discuss making an exception for the appellant but instead passed the following motion:

> that the Kelowna sub-local of Local 523 demand that management of SD #23 rescind the proposal of placing any employee on a Sunday-Thursday shift. If, failing this agreement, a Policy Grievance be filed immediately to prevent the implementation of this proposal due to the severe violations of the Collective Agreement.

The appellant was informed of the rejection of the proposed accommodation and the ongoing requirement to work on Friday nights. He was also informed of the intention of the school board to continue to seek a viable accommodation. After further unsuccessful attempts to accommodate, the school board eventually terminated the appellant's employment as a result of his refusal to complete his regular Friday night shift.

The appellant filed a complaint pursuant to s. 8 of the British Columbia *Human Rights Act*, S.B.C. 1984, c. 22 (the Act), against the school board and pursuant to s. 9 against the Union. The proceedings were subsequently amended by the member designate (appointed by the British Columbia Council of Human Rights to investigate the complaints) to include a claim against the union under s. 8 as well.

[The member designate of the British Columbia Council of Human Rights upheld the complaints against both the respondent employer and the respondent union. The B.C. courts reversed that decision, and the complainant appealed to the Supreme Court of Canada.]

LEGISLATION

For convenience, the relevant legislation [the British Columbia *Human Rights Act*] is reproduced below:

8. (1) No person or anyone acting on his behalf shall
   (a) refuse to employ or refuse to continue to employ a person, or
   (b) discriminate against a person with respect to employment or any term or condition of employment,
   because of the . . . religion . . . of that person . . .

   (4) Subsections (1) and (2) do not apply with respect to a refusal, limitation, specification or preference based on a bona fide occupational requirement.

9. No trade union, employers' organization or occupational association shall
   (a) exclude any person from membership,
   (b) expel or suspend any member, or
   (c) discriminate against any person or member,
   because of the . . . religion . . . of that person or member. . . .

THE ISSUES

[The issue before the Supreme Court of Canada was expressed as follows by Sopinka J.:]

Whether an employer or a labour union representing him is under any duty to effect a reasonable accommodation where, for reasons of religious belief, the employee is unable to work a particular shift.

. . .

Nature and Extent of the Duty to Accommodate

The duty resting on an employer to accommodate the religious beliefs and practices of employees extends to require an employer to take reasonable measures short of undue hardship. In *O'Malley*, McIntyre J. explained that the words 'short of undue hardship' import a limitation on the employer's obligation so that measures that occasion undue interference with the employer's business or undue expense are not required.

The respondents submitted that we should adopt the definition of undue hardship articulated by the Supreme Court of the United States in *Trans World Airlines, Inc. v. Hardison*. . . . In that case, the court stated . . . :

> To require TWA to bear more than a *de minimis* cost in order to give Hardison Saturdays off is an undue hardship . . . to require TWA to bear additional costs when no such costs are incurred to give other employees the days off that they want would involve unequal treatment of employees on the basis of their religion. By suggesting that TWA should incur certain costs in order to give Hardison Saturdays off . . . would in effect require TWA to finance an additional Saturday off and then to choose the employee who will enjoy it on the basis of his religious beliefs. While incurring extra costs to secure a replacement for Hardison might remove the necessity of compelling another employee to work involuntarily in Hardison's place, it would not change the fact that the privilege of having Saturdays off would be allocated according to religious beliefs. . . .

This definition is in direct conflict with the explanation of undue hardship in *O'Malley*. This Court reviewed the American authorities in that case and referred specifically to *Hardison* but did not adopt the '*de minimis*' test which it propounded.

Furthermore, there is good reason not to adopt the '*de minimis*' test in Canada. *Hardison* was argued on the basis of the establishment clause of the First Amendment of the U.S. Constitution and its prohibition against the establishment of religion. This aspect of the *Hardison* decision was thus decided within an entirely different legal context. The case law of this Court has approached the issue of accommodation in a more purposive manner, attempting to provide equal access to the workforce to people who would otherwise encounter serious barriers to entry. . . .

The *Hardison de minimis* test virtually removes the duty to accommodate and seems particularly inappropriate in the Canadian context. More than mere negligible effort is required to satisfy the duty to accommodate. The use of the term 'undue' infers that some hardship is acceptable; it is only 'undue' hardship that satisfies this test. The extent to which the discriminator must go to accommodate is limited by the words 'reasonable' and 'short of undue hardship.' These are not independent criteria but are alternate ways of expressing the same concept. What constitutes reasonable measures is a question of fact and will vary with the circumstances of the case. Wilson J., in [*Central Alberta Dairy Pool v. Alberta (Human Rights Commission)*], listed factors that could be relevant to an appraisal of what amount of hardship was undue as . . . :

> . . . financial cost, disruption of a collective agreement, problems of morale of other employees, interchangeability of work force and facilities. The size of the employer's operation may influence the assessment of whether a given financial cost is undue or the ease with which the work force and facilities can be adapted to the circumstances.

Where safety is at issue both the magnitude of the risk and the identity of those who bear it are relevant considerations.

She went on to explain that . . . '[t]his list is not intended to be exhaustive and the results which will obtain from a balancing of these factors against the right of the employee to be free from discrimination will necessarily vary from case to case.'

The concern for the impact on other employees which prompted the court in *Hardison* to adopt the *de minimis* test is a factor to be considered in determining whether the interference with the operation of the employer's business would be undue. However, more than minor inconvenience must be shown before the complainant's right to accommodation can be defeated. The employer must establish that actual interference with the rights of other employees, which is not trivial but substantial, will result from the adoption of the accommodating measures. Minor interference or inconvenience is the price to be paid for religious freedom in a multicultural society.

. . .

The Threatened Grievance

The member designate refused to give effect to the submission that the economic impact of a grievance threatened by the respondent Union constituted undue hardship. She was of the view that the collective agreement was subject to the *Human Rights Act* and the only economic consequence to the employer would have been the costs of defending the grievance.

The proposition relied on by the member designate is fully supported by the authorities. In *Insurance Corporation of British Columbia v. Heerspink* . . . Lamer J. (as he then was) stated . . . :

Furthermore, as it [the *Human Rights Code*] is a public and fundamental law, no one, unless clearly authorized by law to do so, may contractually agree to suspend its operation and thereby put oneself beyond the reach of its protection.

In [*Ontario Human Rights Commission v. Etobicoke (Borough of)*], this principle was stated to apply to a collective agreement. . . . McIntyre J. stated:

While this submission is that the condition, being in a collective agreement, should be considered a *bona fide* occupational qualification and requirement, in my opinion to give it effect would be to permit the parties to contract out of the provisions of the *Ontario Human Rights Code*.

Although the Code contains no explicit restriction on such contracting out, it is nevertheless a public statute and it constitutes public policy in Ontario as appears from a reading of the statute itself and as declared in the preamble. It is clear from the authorities, both in Canada and in England, that parties are not competent to contract themselves out of the provisions of such enactments and that contracts having such effect are void, as contrary to public policy.

The respondent Board submits, however, that this principle does not apply in the case of adverse effect discrimination. The basis for this submission is that in the case of direct discrimination the offending provision is struck down but that in adverse effect discrimination it is upheld in its general application and the complainant is accommodated so that it does not affect him or her in a discriminatory fashion. I do not accept this submission. Adverse effect discrimination is prohibited by the *Human Rights Act* no less than direct discrimination. In both instances private arrangements, whether by contract or collective agreement, must give way to the requirements of the statute. . . .

While the provisions of a collective agreement cannot absolve the parties from the duty to accommodate, the effect of the agreement is relevant in assessing the degree of hardship occasioned by interference with the terms thereof. Substantial departure from the normal operation of the conditions and terms of employment in the collective agreement may constitute undue interference in the operation of the employer's business.

The member designate did not err in law in concluding that the collective agreement did not relieve the respondent employer of its duty to accommodate. She concluded that the sole impact of the threatened grievance which would have sought to enforce the collective agreement was the cost of defending it and that this did not constitute undue hardship. The only other alleged effect of the proposed accommodation was with respect to the effect on other employees and their reaction which the respondent Board feared would result from unilateral action on the part of the employer without Union approval. It is, therefore, necessary to consider whether the member designate erred in law in respect of this factor.

Effect on Other Employees

The respondent Board submits that the member designate erred in stating that the employer's fear that unilateral action on the part of the employer might bring forth reprisals from other employees was not a justification for refusing to accommodate the appellant. This submission is based on the following statement in the evidence of Harvey Peatman, the secretary-treasurer of the respondent Board:

> Q. What would have happened if the school district had moved unilaterally without union approval to accommodate him in some way in your view? What did you think would happen?

> A. Well, possible riot by the members of the union but — No, more seriously, very definitely being faced with a grievance which really would have been undefendable.

This statement would justify the conclusion that the alleged fear of employee reprisal was not the real reason for the employer's decision not to create the special shift for the appellant. The real reason was the concern relating to the threatened grievance which was based on a mistake of law. I have explained above that there was no error of law on the part of the member designate in this regard. If this concern played any part in the decision of the employer, it did not constitute justification for the refusal to accommodate the appellant.

The reaction of employees may be a factor in deciding whether accommodating measures would constitute undue interference in the operation of the employer's business. In Central Alberta Dairy Pool, Wilson J. referred to employee morale as one of the factors to be taken into account. It is a factor that must be applied with caution. The objection of employees based on well-grounded concerns that their rights will be affected must be considered. On the other hand, objections based on attitudes inconsistent with human rights are an irrelevant consideration. I would include in this category objections based on the view that the integrity of a collective agreement is to be preserved irrespective of its discriminatory effect on an individual employee on religious grounds. The contrary view would effectively enable an employer to contract out of human rights legislation provided the employees were ad idem with their employer. It was in this context that Wilson J. referred to employee morale as a factor in determining what constitutes undue hardship.

There is no evidence in the record before the Court that the rights of other employees would likely have been affected by an accommodation of the appellant. The fact that the appellant would be assigned to a special shift may have required the adjustment of the schedule of some other employee but this might have been done with the consent of the employee or employees affected. The respondents apparently did not canvass this possibility. The union objected to the proposed accommodation on the basis that the integrity of the collective agreement would be compromised and not that any individual employee objected on the basis of interference with his or her right. In my opinion, the member designate came to the right conclusion with respect to this issue.

Union's Duty to Accommodate

The duty to accommodate developed as a means of limiting the liability of an employer who was found to have discriminated by the *bona fide* adoption of a work rule without any intention to discriminate. It enabled the employer to justify adverse effect discrimination and thus avoid absolute liability for consequences that were not intended. Section 8 of the Act, like many other human rights codes, prohibits discrimination against a person with respect to employment or any term or condition of employment without differentiating between direct and adverse effect discrimination. Both are prohibited. Moreover, any person who discriminates is subject to the sanctions which the Act provides. By definition (s. 1) a union is a person. Accordingly, a union which causes or contributes to the discriminatory effect incurs liability. In order to avoid imposing absolute liability, a union must have the same right as an employer to justify the discrimination. In order to do so it must discharge its duty to accommodate.

The respondent union does not contest that it had a duty to accommodate but asserts that the limitations on that duty were not properly applied by the member designate. It submits that the focus must be on interference with the rights of employees rather than on interference with the union's business. It further submits, and is supported in this regard by the Canadian Labour Congress (CLC), that a union cannot be required to adopt measures which conflict with the collective agreement until the employer has exhausted reasonable accommodations that do not affect the collective rights of employees.

These submissions raise for determination the extent of a union's obligation to accommodate and how the discharge of that duty is to be reconciled and harmonized with the employer's duty. These are matters that have not been previously considered in this Court.

As I have previously observed, the duty to accommodate only arises if a union is party to discrimination. It may become a party in two ways.

First, it may cause or contribute to the discrimination in the first instance by participating in the formulation of the work rule that has the discriminatory effect on the complainant. This will generally be the case if the rule is a provision in the collective agreement. It has to be assumed that all provisions are formulated jointly by the parties and that they bear responsibility equally for their effect on employees. I do not find persuasive the submission that the negotiations be re-examined to determine which party pressed for a provision which turns out to be the cause of a discriminatory result. This is especially so when a party has insisted that the provision be enforced. . . .

Second, a union may be liable for failure to accommodate the religious beliefs of an employee notwithstanding that it did not participate in the formulation or application of a discriminatory rule or practice. This may occur if the union impedes the reasonable efforts of an employer to accommodate. In this situation it will be known that some condition of employment is operating in a manner that discriminates on religious grounds against an employee and the employer is seeking to remove or alleviate the discriminatory effect. If reasonable accommodation is only possible with the union's co-operation and the union blocks the employer's efforts to remove or alleviate the discriminatory effect, it becomes a party to the discrimination. In these circumstances, the union, while not initially a party to the discriminatory conduct and having no initial duty to accommodate, incurs a duty not to contribute to the continuation of discrimination. It cannot behave as if it were a bystander asserting that the employee's plight is strictly a matter for the employer to solve. . . .

The timing and manner in which the union's duty is to be discharged depends on whether its duty arises on the first or second basis as outlined above. I agree with the submissions of the respondent union and CLC that the focus of the duty differs from that of the employer in that the representative nature of a union must be considered. The primary concern with respect to the impact of accommodating measures is not, as in the case of the employer, the expense to or disruption of the business of the union but rather the effect on other employees. The duty to accommodate should not substitute discrimination against other employees for the discrimination suffered by the complainant. Any significant interference with the rights of others will ordinarily justify the union in refusing to consent to a measure which would have this effect. Although the test of undue hardship applies to a union, it will often be met by a showing of prejudice to other employees if proposed accommodating measures are adopted. As I stated previously, this test is grounded on the reasonableness of the measures to remove discrimination which are taken or proposed. Given the importance of promoting religious freedom in the workplace, a lower standard cannot be defended.

While the general definition of the duty to accommodate is the same irrespective of which of the two ways it arises, the application of the duty will vary. A union which is liable as a co-discriminator with the employer shares a joint responsibility with the employer to seek to accommodate the employee. If nothing is done both are equally liable. Nevertheless, account must be taken of the fact that ordinarily the employer, who has charge of the workplace, will be in the better position to formulate accommodations. The employer, therefore, can be expected to initiate the process. The employer must take steps that are reasonable. If the proposed measure is one that is least expensive or disruptive to the employer but disruptive of the collective agreement or otherwise affects the rights of other employees, then this will usually result in a finding that the employer failed to take reasonable measures to accommodate and the union did not act unreasonably in refusing to consent. This assumes, of course, that other reasonable accommodating measures were available which either did not involve the collective agreement or were less disruptive of it. In such circumstances, the union may not be absolved of its duty if it failed to put forward alternative measures that were available which are less onerous from its point of view. I would not be prepared to say that in every instance the employer must exhaust all the avenues which do not involve the collective agreement before involving the union. A proposed measure may be the most sensible one notwithstanding that it requires a change to the agreement and others do not. This does not mean that the union's duty to accommodate does not arise until it is called on by the employer. When it is a co-discriminator with the employer, it shares the obligation to take reasonable steps to remove or alleviate the source of the discriminatory effect.

In the second type of situation in which the union is not initially a contributing cause of the discrimination but by failing to co-operate impedes a reasonable accommodation, the employer must canvass other methods of accommodation before the union can be expected to assist in finding or implementing a solution. The union's duty arises only when its involvement is required to make accommodation possible and no other reasonable alternative resolution of the matter has been found or could reasonably have been found.

The member designate did not, therefore, err in applying the *O'Malley* definition of the duty to accommodate to the respondent union. Moreover, she found that the union was involved in the conduct which resulted in adverse effect discrimination and that its duty to accommodate arose by reason of this fact. The respondent union, therefore, owed a duty to accommodate jointly with the employer. The proposal for accommodation presented to the union was found to be reasonable. While it was submitted that the member designate failed to consider the trespass on the rights of other employees, I am satisfied that the only possible effect was the adjustment to the schedule of one employee to work the Friday afternoon shift in place of the appellant. The respondent union conceded in argument that there is no evidence that employees were canvassed to ascertain whether someone would volunteer to switch with the appellant. If this occurred, no employees' rights would have been adversely affected. The onus of proof with respect to this issue was on the respondent union. I agree with the member designate that it was not discharged.

Finally, in view of the fact that the duty to accommodate of the union was shared jointly with the employer, it was not incumbent on the member designate to determine whether all other reasonable accommodations had been explored by the employer before calling upon the union. Nevertheless, it appears to me that the member designate was of the view that the special shift proposal was not only reasonable but the most reasonable. This view is fully supported by the evidence. Accordingly, the decision of the member designate must be upheld unless the respondents are correct that there was an error in law on her part with respect to the complainant's duty to facilitate accommodation of his religious beliefs.

Duty of Complainant

The search for accommodation is a multi-party inquiry. Along with the employer and the union, there is also a duty on the complainant to assist in securing an appropriate accommodation. . . .

To facilitate the search for an accommodation, the complainant must do his or her part as well. Concomitant with a search for reasonable accommodation is a duty to facilitate the search for such an accommodation. Thus, in determining whether the duty of accommodation has been fulfilled, the conduct of the complainant must be considered.

This does not mean that, in addition to bringing to the attention of the employer the facts relating to discrimination, the complainant has a duty to originate a solution. While the complainant may be in a position to make suggestions, the employer is in the best position to determine how the complainant can be accommodated without undue interference in the operation of the employer's business. When an employer has initiated a proposal that is reasonable and would, if implemented, fulfil the duty to accommodate, the complainant has a duty to facilitate the implementation of the proposal. If failure to take reasonable steps on the part of the complainant causes the proposal to founder, the complaint will be dismissed. The other aspect of this duty is the obligation to accept reasonable accommodation. This is the aspect referred to by McIntyre J. in O'Malley. The complainant cannot expect a perfect solution. If a proposal that would be reasonable in all the circumstances is turned down, the employer's duty is discharged.

In my opinion the member designate did not err in this respect. The complainant did everything that was expected of him with respect to the proposal put forward by the employer. It failed because the Union refused consent and the employer refused to proceed unilaterally. The appellant had no obligation to suggest other measures. Moreover, it is not suggested that the appellant turned down any reasonable proposal which was offered to him.

. . .

* * *

Where the provisions of a collective agreement are found to discriminate against some members of the bargaining unit on a prohibited ground, the union may be held to be in breach of its duty to accommodate even though it had tried (and failed) to persuade the employer to accept non-discriminatory terms: *United Food and Commercial Workers, Local 401 v. Alberta Human Rights and Citizenship Commission*, 2003 ABCA 246 (Alta. C.A.).

13:350 The Interface between the Human Rights Forum and Grievance Arbitration in the Enforcement of Equality Rights

In *Cadillac Fairview Corp. v. Saskatchewan (Human Rights Code Board of Inquiry)* (1999), 173 D.L.R. (4th) 609 (Sask. CA) (leave to appeal to S.C.C. refused), employees of the unionized employer complained to the Saskatchewan Human Rights Commission of sexual harassment and discrimination, in breach of the Saskatchewan *Human Rights Code*. The Commission set up a board of inquiry to hear the matter. The employer sought to terminate the proceedings on judicial review. It claimed that because the applicable collective agreement prohibited sex discrimination, the principle of pre-eminence of the grievance arbitration forum affirmed by the Supreme Court of Canada in *Weber v. Ontario Hydro* (above, section 9:621 and 9:631) meant that the human rights forum had no authority to deal with the matter. Vancise J.A., for the Saskatchewan Court of Appeal, held as follows:

> [27] *Weber*, in my opinion, did not go so far as to state that any rights created by statute that affect employment rights must of necessity arise out of the collective agreement and can only be dealt with by arbitration. . . .

> [28] The right which was allegedly violated in this case is a fundamental human right which employees and the union need not bargain and cannot contract out of. . . .

> [29] The Supreme Court of Canada has stated that when human rights legislation comes into conflict with other, more specific legislation, the provisions of the Code prevail. Next to constitutional law, human rights provisions are more important than all other laws. They have been defined as basic quasi-constitutional rights and statutes. They are not treated as laws of general application but rather as fundamental laws. Unless the legislature has expressly provided otherwise, the Code takes precedence over all other laws when there is a conflict. . . .

> [35] The result in this case is clear. The Board of Inquiry appointed under the provisions of the Code has jurisdiction to hear and determine this matter. . . .

At other points in his judgment, Vancise J. seemed to suggest that the human rights forum not only had the jurisdiction to hear the complaint in question, but may even have had sole jurisdiction to do so, to the exclusion of the arbitral forum. That suggestion has been put to rest by the decision of the Supreme Court of Canada in *Parry Sound (District) Social Services Administration Board v. Ontario Public Service Employees Union, Local 324*, 2003 SCC 42, set out in section 9:610 above. In the *Parry Sound* case, the Supreme Court held (at para. 14) that "the substantive rights and obligations of the Human Rights Code are incorporated into a collective agreement over which [an arbitrator] has jurisdiction." Although *Parry Sound* came from Ontario, where the labour relations statute expressly gives arbitrators the authority to apply the human rights statute and other employment-related legislation, the Supreme Court's judgment seems to make clear that arbitrators can and must apply human rights legislation even where they are not given any specific statutory authority to that effect.

Is there a risk that, despite the fundamental nature of human rights legislation, grievance arbitration will be held to have sole jurisdiction to apply the provisions of that legislation in the unionized context, to the exclusion of the human rights forum? Like the *Cadillac Fairview* decision of the Saskatchewan Court of Appeal excerpted above, the decision of the Ontario Court of Appeal in *Ford Motor Company of Canada Ltd. et al. v. Ontario Human Rights Commission et al.* (2002), 209 D.L.R. (4th) 465, would appear to say no. In the Ford Motor case, the employer and union argued, among other things, that because an arbitration award had been issued on an employee's grievance alleging racial discrimination, a human rights board of inquiry had no jurisdiction to hear a complaint under the human rights statute on the same matter. In rejecting that argument, Abella J.A., for the court, said:

> [58] I am . . . of the view that *Weber* does not apply so as to oust the jurisdiction of the [board of inquiry] . . .
>
> [59] The [Ontario Human Rights Commission] now has authority under s. 34(1)(a) of the [*Ontario Human Rights Code*] to decide, in its discretion, not to deal with a complaint where it is of the view that the complaint "could or should be more appropriately dealt with" under another Act. Labour arbitrators now have statutory authority under the *Labour Relations Act, 1995* to apply the Code. Since the Commission has statutory authority under the Code to defer to another forum, the legislative intent has clearly shifted from according exclusive jurisdiction to the Commission for Code violations to offering concurrent jurisdiction to labour arbitrators when complaints arise from disputes under a collective agreement.
>
> [60] The underlying goal of these symmetrical amendments is to avoid the gratuitous bifurcation or proliferation of proceedings, especially when the arbitrable grievance and the human rights complaint emerge seamlessly from the same factual matrix. That goal was also, I think, at the heart of Weber. In my view, Weber stands for the proposition that when several related issues emanate from a workplace dispute, they should all be heard by one adjudicator to the extent jurisdictionally possible, so that inconsistent results and remedies . . . may be avoided.
>
> [61] On the other hand, there may be circumstances where an individual unionized employee finds the arbitral process foreclosed, since the decision whether to proceed with a grievance is the union's and not the employee's. Moreover, the alleged human rights violation may be against the union, as stipulated in the Code. . . .
>
> [62] In an arbitration under a collective agreement, only the employer and union have party status. The unionized employee's interests are advanced by and through the union, which necessarily decides how the allegations should be represented or defended. Applying Weber so as to assign exclusive jurisdiction to labour arbitrators could therefore render chimerical the rights of individual unionized employees. This does not mean, however, that the availability of jurisdictional concurrency should be seen as encouraging "forum" shopping. The jurisdictional outcome will depend upon the circumstances of each case, including the reasonableness of the union's conduct, the nature of the dispute, and the desirability of finality and consistency of result.

✳ ✳ ✳

For a more detailed analysis to the same effect, see Brian Etherington, "Promises, Promises: Notes on Diversity and Access to Justice" (2000), 26 Queen's L.J. 43.

Whatever risks might be posed by the growth of arbitral jurisdiction over equality issues in the workplace, it has brought those issues to the shop floor in a way that no other forum could. The following article considers both the complementarity and the tension between seniority rights and equality rights.

M. Kaye Joachim, "Seniority Rights and the Duty to Accommodate" (1998), 24 Queen's L.J. 131 at 151–63, 178–79, 187

II. SENIORITY

. . .

D. Similarities and Contrasts Between Seniority Systems and the Duty to Accommodate

It is important to recognize that both seniority systems and the duty to accommodate are designed to enhance the employment opportunities of workers. Seniority operates directly, by making length of service a factor in who receives work. Anti-discrimination legislation operates indirectly, by ensuring that certain factors do not determine who gets the work. Since both systems involve competition between workers, some will see their employment opportunities expanded and others will not.

While seniority rules insulate all employees from management discretion, senior workers will gain more than junior workers from the seniority system. Workers accept this as fair because they believe that they will, in time, share in the advantages of the senior worker. . . . Anti-discrimination laws similarly operate to protect all employees from discrimination on prohibited grounds, as all employees have a race or colour, gender, age, marital status and the like. Those individuals or groups who are most often discriminated against by employers will see their opportunities expanded, while those who are seldom discriminated against (young, white, able-bodied male workers), will not. The latter groups may never get their turn to benefit from anti-discrimination laws; they will become older and they may become disabled, but they will never become non-white or female. Similarly, many employees who might wish to have certain accommodations (such as transfer to a preferred shift or assignment) never seek them because they do not see the lack of those accommodations as discriminatory. Although employees commonly perceive as fair the uneven benefits offered by seniority systems, many of them do not see as fair the uneven benefits accords by anti-discrimination laws.

By contrasting management discretion to act arbitrarily, seniority systems can help prevent direct discrimination. Because seniority is "a neutral system that is colour-blind, gender-blind, and age-blind" it prohibits management from using those factors to the detriment of groups traditionally discriminated against.

A pure seniority system empowers workers to exercise their seniority for opportunities such as training, job shadowing, entering apprenticeship programs and job posting. With a clear seniority list, a worker knows she is eligible for an opportunity. Any intrusion of discriminatory factors into the selection of the worker is quickly revealed and can be handled through the grievance arbitration process.   By the same token, however, seniority systems will unavoidably come into conflict with the duty to accommodate. The essence of a seniority system is that the parties agree in advance on the factors to be taken into account (length of service, and to varying degrees, skill and ability). By implication, they agree that all other factors (such as net productivity of the employee, relationship with the employer, number of dependents and disability-related needs) may not be taken into account. Because relief from the adverse effects of discrimination requires an employer to consider a worker's disability-related needs, conflict is inevitable.

III. CONFLICTS BETWEEN THE ACCOMMODATION OF DISABLED WORKERS AND SENIORITY RIGHTS

Conflicts between seniority systems and the accommodation required by a disabled employee can arise in two ways. First, the seniority provisions of the collective agreement may discriminate (directly or indirectly) against a disabled worker, and the accommodation required by the employee may therefore involve modification to or exception from the collective agreement. The union shares the duty with the employer to find a suitable accommodation. While the employer is not obliged, under anti-discrimination legislation, to select the form of accommodation least disruptive to the collective agreement, the availability of less intrusive forms of accommodation is relevant to determining whether the parties acted reasonably in attempting to accommodate a worker.

Second, although the terms of the collective agreement may not have a discriminatory effect, a worker may need an accommodation that cannot be implemented without violating the seniority provisions. In this case, the employer must canvass other methods of accommodating the employee that do not require the participation of the union, before calling upon the union to grant an exception to or modification of the seniority provisions of the collective agreement. In the next section, I set out a series of scenarios illustrating different ways in which accommodating disabled workers can interfere with the seniority rules in a collective agreement. Some of these scenarios are hypothetical, and others are based on actual cases.

A. Accumulation of Seniority

(i) Competitive Seniority
(a) Date of Hire Seniority Systems
In the first scenario, the collective agreement provides that seniority accrues from the date of hire but ceases to accumulate after one year of absence. A disabled worker absent for a year and a half because of disability loses six months of seniority credits. When she applies for a promotion for which she is qualified, she loses out to an employee who moved ahead of her on the seniority list. She grieves, alleging that the loss of six months' competitive seniority is discriminatory. She requests that her lost seniority credits be restored, despite the provisions of the collective agreement.

(b) Hours Worked Seniority Systems
The same agreement provides that part-time workers accrue seniority based on hours worked, and that there are to be separate seniority lists for part-time and full-time workers. Because of a disability-related absence, an employee is unable to work her usual hours, and falls behind others on the part-time seniority list. She grieves that she should be credited for competitive seniority while absent due to disability.

(ii) Benefit Seniority

In each of the above scenarios, the disabled worker also claims that she should be credited with benefit seniority during the disability-related absence.

B. Application of Seniority

(i) Impact on Future Working Opportunities

(a) Hiring and Promotion Systems

An employer's workplace is divided into several seniority units, each with its own seniority list. Each seniority unit contains several job classifications, and progress from one classification to another is linear. The only access to the workplace is through entry-level positions at the bottom of each job ladder. Those positions have more arduous physical tasks and less desirable working hours. Progression or promotion to other positions higher on the job ladder is determined by seniority. Suppose an applicant with a hidden disability is offered a position with the employer, but it is subsequently discovered that she is unable to perform the physical tasks of the entry-level positions. Although she can perform the tasks of an upper-level position, the employer rescinds the offer, and the employee files a human rights complaint alleging that the employer's hiring practices discriminate against her because of disability. With respect to the career ladder, she seeks to be placed in one of the upper-level positions that she is physically capable of performing, contrary to the provisions of the collective agreement.

In a related example, a disabled employee wishes to advance in the workplace but is unable to perform the physical tasks of the next position up on the job ladder. She applies for a position even higher on the job ladder, the duties of which she is capable of performing, but is turned down because she has not progressed through the lower position. She also files a complaint alleging that the employer's system of promotion discriminates against her because of disability.

(b) Shift Selection

A worker develops a sleep disorder that prevents her from working during the night shift. In her unit, shift preferences are determined strictly by seniority, leaving her far down on the list of employees waiting in line for the day shift. The employer places her in the next available day-shift position, but the union files a grievance on behalf of the more senior employee who was passed over.

(c) Transfer to a Vacant Position within the Bargaining Unit

A worker becomes disabled (or a disabled worker becomes further disabled) and is unable to continue performing the functions of her position safely. Attempts to modify her position so that she can perform it safely and productively fail, and she faces the loss of employment or layoff unless an alternative position is provided. There are other positions within the bargaining unit that she could perform, but the agreement requires the employer to post all vacancies, and also provides that where applicants are relatively equal in ability, seniority is to prevail. The employer places the disabled worker in a position she can perform, without posting it, and the union grieves. Her seniority level is too low to allow her to compete successfully for any of the positions she is capable of performing.

(ii) Impact on Current Working Conditions: Bumping

A disabled worker cannot be accommodated in her own position, and there are no jobs vacant or likely to become vacant that she can perform. She could, however, perform the work of several employees who are junior to her, and the employer displaces one of them in order to accommodate her. In one situation, the junior worker is transferred to another position. In another example, the junior worker is laid off, with recall rights. In a third variation, no junior employees are doing work that is suitable for the disabled employee, but a senior employee is doing work that she can do. The employer therefore displaces the senior employee and transfers him against his wishes to the disabled employee's position, with o loss of compensation.

(iii) Impact on Ability to Maintain or Regain Employment Status

(a) Protection against Bumping

The employer reorganizes the workplace and eliminates some positions. A senior worker whose position is eliminated exercises his bumping rights to displace a junior disabled worker. The disabled worker is unable to perform the duties of the positions held by the more junior workers whom she is eligible to bump, and she is laid off. She grieves that her position should have been protected from bumping, since the senior worker could have bumped another junior worker.

(b) Recall Rights

Following a layoff, the next two workers in line for recall are a non-disabled worker and then a disabled worker. The employer recalls the disabled worker ahead of the more senior worker, because one of the few positions she is capable of performing becomes available. If she had not been recalled to this position, it is unlikely that a position she was capable of performing would become available for some time. The more senior worker is called to work two weeks later. He grieves the loss of two weeks' compensation, and seeks to be placed in the position given to the disabled worker.

(c) Transfer of Seniority Credits across Bargaining Units or Seniority Units

There are no suitable positions for the disabled worker within the bargaining unit. There is work which she could perform in another bargaining unit, but the two units are represented by different trade unions and are covered by different collective agreements that do not provide for inter-unit transfers. The employer transfers the disabled worker into a suitable vacant position in the other bargaining unit, contrary to the posting and seniority provisions. However, the employer declines to recognize her fifteen years of service, so she moves to the bottom of the seniority list in the new unit. The members of that unit grieve the failure to post the vacancy and fill it from within the unit. The disabled worker grieves the loss of her seniority.

IV. RESOLVING THE CONFLICT

A. The Duty to Accommodate and Its Limits

In each of the scenarios outlined above, the accommodation requested by the disabled worker interferes with the seniority provisions of the collective agreement, with varying impact on other employees. Some effect on other workers is inevitable as human rights legislation expands the work opportunities of groups that have been discriminated against. That legislation is used to rectify a refusal to hire or transfer an employee on a prohibited ground of discrimination, by placing the complainant in the position he or she would have obtained but for the discrimination. This remedy is considered appropriate, regardless of its impact on other workers aspiring to that position. Similarly, in cases of adverse-effect discrimination, the duty to accommodate increases the opportunities of some workers in order to rectify the effect of indirectly discriminatory rules on certain groups. This inevitably limits the work opportunities available to other workers, and in some cases it alters their current working conditions. Can those workers reasonably be expected to accept the consequences of interfering with seniority rules in order to accommodate disabled co-workers?

The right to equal treatment in employment is not absolute, as the Supreme Court of Canada indicated in *O'Malley* [*Ontario (Human Rights Commission) v. Simpsons Sears Ltd.*]:

> The Code must be construed and flexibly applied to protect the right of the employee who is subject to discrimination and also to protect the right of the employer to proceed with the lawful conduct of his business. The Code was not intended to accord rights to one to the exclusion of the rights of the other.
>
> In cases of direct discrimination, the limit of the right to equal treatment is reached where the differential treatment can be justified as a bona fide occupational requirement. In cases of adverse-effect discrimination, the limit on the right to equal treatment is reached where the accommodation required to correct the differential effect would cause undue hardship to the union or the employer. Similarly, there must be limits on the burden the state is willing to impose on co-workers. Where a proposed accommodation significantly or substantially interferes with the rights of other workers, the limit on the right to equal treatment has been reached. . . .

D. Conflicts Revisited

. . .

If the disabled worker were not accommodated in each of these examples, she would not be hired or would lose her employment altogether. In contrast, the burden on the co-workers in each example is that they would be denied the opportunity to use their seniority right to move to a preferred shift or position. In a workplace with regular turnover, that may mean a short delay in obtaining the desired opportunity. In other cases, the lost opportunity may never arise again. In a workplace where shift work is the norm, and jobs that involve straight days are the preferred positions, workers may wait years to accumulate sufficient seniority to entitle them to a day job. The variability between jobs in terms of salary, duties performed, working conditions, geographic location and opportunities for promotion may be enormous. Even minor differences between jobs may have large personal significance for individual workers. A promotion with a small increase in salary may have a significant effect on pension entitlement in later years. Is it justifiable to expect workers to make these sacrifices so that disabled workers can obtain or maintain access to the workplace?

In any situation where there are more candidates than work opportunities, requiring the employer to give an opportunity to one worker inevitably has an impact on other workers. Human rights legislation prohibits an employer from directly discriminating because of race in the assignment of work opportunities, and we do not consider the impact on other employees who might have benefitted from such discrimination in the particular case. Similarly, if an employer intended to modify a work station in order to enable a disabled applicant to do the work, we would not suggest that this accommodation should be discarded merely because another candidate had been hoping for the position and would have received it if the modifications had not been made.

In a non-unionized workplace, if an employer departs from its usual practice of filling middle level positions with internal candidates and hires a disabled external applicant into such a position, this will affect the career aspirations of inside workers. Similarly, if an employer transfers a disabled employee to a vacant shift or position as an accommodation to enable him or her to remain in the workplace, this will affect co-workers who may have aspired to that opening. We would not expect that these workers could block the accommodation by claiming that it would impact unreasonably on them.

In the unionized environment, the difference is that the employer and bargaining agent have agreed in advance that such openings will be posted and filled by bargaining unit members in accordance with seniority. Thus, it has been implicitly agreed that openings will not be used to accommodate disabled workers. This changes mere expectations into collectively bargained rights. Depending on the circumstances of the particular workplace, workers may develop concrete and defined expectations toward preferred positions or shifts. In other workplaces, different variables may not foster such defined expectations. If it is accepted that the existence of a collective agreement, in and of itself, should not bar the accommodation of disabled workers, then it is the actual impact on co-workers that should count. A worker who has taken courses to position himself for a foreseeable and long awaited promotion opportunity may be able to establish that its loss will have a significant impact on him. In other cases, such factors as the unpredictability of turnover, the existence of skill and ability requirements, or the uncertainties of the bumping system will preclude employees from developing concrete expectations with respect to vacancies. In those cases, the loss of the opportunity to bid on a preferred position may be a justifiable burden to impose in order to allow the accommodation of a disabled worker. . . .

CONCLUSION

The workplace poses many unintended barriers to persons whose disabilities impair their capacity to perform ordinary tasks in the same manner, at the same speed or on the same equipment as non-disabled workers. Requiring employers to adapt the workplace to accommodate disability-related needs allows disabled persons the opportunity to gain access to and remain in the workforce. Ideally, disabled workers could be accommodated to enable them to continue to perform the work they were performing before the onset or worsening of their disability. When this is not possible, employers may have to consider the availability of suitable alternative employment. This form of accommodation inevitably affects the working conditions and opportunities of other workers who may hold or aspire to the position sought by the disabled worker.

In a unionized environment, this conflict between workers is exacerbated by seniority provisions in collective agreements. The essence of these provisions is the agreement between employer and workers that specified work opportunities will be allocated on the basis of length of service, which is perceived as a fair and objective criterion. Conversely, those provisions constitute an agreement in advance that other factors (such as disability-related needs) will not be used to allocate work opportunities.

The credits accumulated under seniority provisions affect workers' economic security, and any interference with the operation of the seniority rules lessens the value of the credits.

The requirement to accommodate disability-related needs and the requirement to comply with seniority provisions both restrict the potential for arbitrary or discriminatory action by employers. When those requirements conflict, should the principle of non-discrimination be followed, or the principle of seniority?

Equality rights are not absolute. The limit of a disabled person's right to equal opportunity is reached when the accommodation required to achieve equality would cause substantial interference with the rights of other workers. However, the fact that a requested accommodation would interfere with the seniority provisions of the collective agreement should not in and of itself bar that accommodation, since it would be contrary to public policy to allow employees and employers to contract out of their obligation to accommodate disabled workers. What really matters is the actual impact of the accommodation on the working conditions and opportunities of other workers. Each departure from the seniority principle must be judged on its unique facts in order to determine whether that impact is substantial.

[Reprinted by permission.]

* * *

13:400 SYSTEMIC DISCRIMINATION

Systemic discrimination is the term used to refer to the operation of a web of factors which lead to the under-representation of particular groups in the workforce, or their over-representation in low-level jobs. As the following excerpt explains, dramatic shifts in the demographic profile of Canadian society have highlighted the degree of stratification in the workforce.

K. Kelly, "Visible Minorities: A Diverse Group" (1995), 37 Canadian Social Trends 2

Recent changes in immigration patterns have increased the size of Canada's visible minority population and have also changed its composition. In 1991, the 1.9 million adults in a visible minority in Canada represented 9% of the population aged 15 and over, doubling the 1981 proportion. More than three-quarters (78%) were immigrants, 15% were born in Canada and the remainder (7%) were non-permanent residents. As was the case during the 1980s, Chinese, Blacks and South Asians accounted for two-thirds of adults in a visible minority in 1991. During the past decade, however, there have been large increases in some of the smaller visible minority groups such as South East Asians and Latin Americans.

People in a visible minority in Canada have much in common. Most, for example, live and work in Canada's larger cities. Nonetheless, the visible minority population comprises groups which are, in many ways, very diverse. It includes not only recent immigrants, but also those who have lived in Canada for a long time or who were born here. Although some recent immigrants quickly adjust to their new life in this country, others may have a more difficult time accessing services or participating in the labour force because they lack the necessary language skills in English or French.

Visible minority groups also differ in their age structures, levels of educational attainment and the types of jobs they have. For example, South East Asians and Latin Americans, more than half of whom immigrated to Canada during the 1980s, are among the youngest of all visible minorities. They tend to have less formal education and have both the lowest rates of labour force participation and the highest rates of unemployment. In addition, over half of their populations are employed as clerical, service or manual workers. In contrast, those in the Japanese community, two-thirds of whom were born in Canada, are older than members of other visible minority groups. They are also among the most highly educated, have the lowest unemployment rate and are among those most likely to hold professional or managerial positions.

Despite education diversity among the various groups, visible minorities are generally more highly educated than are other adults. And yet, even among those aged 25 to 44 with a university degree, adults in a visible minority are less likely than others to be employed in professional or managerial occupations. Rather, many are concentrated in lower-paying clerical, service and manual labour jobs. . . .

UNDEREMPLOYMENT AMONG VISIBLE MINORITIES WITH POST-SECONDARY EDUCATION

Visible minorities aged 25 to 44 are as likely as other adults that age to have at least some education or training beyond high school. Among adults aged 25 to 44 who worked in the 18 months before the 1991 Census, visible minorities were more likely (25%) to have a university degree than were other adults (17%). They were, however, somewhat less likely to have some other post-secondary education (41% compared with 45%).

Nonetheless, visible minorities with a university education are not as likely as others with the same level of education to be employed in the higher-paying professional or managerial occupations. Among those aged 25 to 44 with a university degree who worked in the 18 months before the 1991 Census, just over one-half of visible minorities had either a professional (39%) or managerial (13%) job, compared with 70% of other adults (52% in professional and 18% in managerial positions). University-educated Japanese aged 25 to 44 were the most likely to be in professional or managerial occupations (65%), followed by Chinese adults in that age group (61%). In contrast, only 27% of university-educated Filipinos aged 25 to 44 were in these occupations, as were 42% of Latin Americans.

Similarly, among those aged 25 to 44 with other types of post-secondary education, 26% of visible minorities were in professional, semi-professional or managerial occupations, compared with 32% of other adults. The proportion in these occupations ranged from highs of 36% among Japanese and 33% among Koreans, to lows of 17% among Latin Americans and 20% among South East Asians and Filipinos.

A disproportionate share of Filipino adults with at least some education beyond high school worked in service jobs in the 18 months before the 1991 Census. Among adults aged 25 to 44 with a university degree, 17% of Filipinos were service workers, compared with 5% of visible minorities overall and 2% of other adults. Similarly, among those aged 25 to 44 with some other post-secondary education, 29% of Filipinos had service jobs, compared with 12% of visible minorities and 8% of other adults.

Manual labour jobs were relatively common among highly-educated South East Asians and Latin Americans who worked in the 18 months before the 1991 Census. Among those aged 25 to 44, about 25% of South East Asians and Latin Americans with some post-secondary education were in manual labour jobs, as were 11% of Latin Americans with a university degree. Overall, 12% of visible minorities aged 25 to 44 with a post-secondary education, and 4% of those with a university degree had such jobs. Among other adults that age, 8% of those with some post-secondary education and 2% of university graduates were manual labourers.

A LOOK TO THE FUTURE — THE VISIBLE MINORITY POPULATION IS EXPECTED TO INCREASE

As was the case during the 1980s, the visible minority population is expected to continue to increase faster than the total population. The number of visible minority adults is projected to triple between now and 2016 to just over six million. Canada's non-visible minority adult population, on the other hand, is projected to increase by about one-quarter. As a result of such different growth rates, adults in a visible minority could account for about 20% of all adults by 2016, more than double the proportion in 1991 (9%).

The number of adults in a visible minority is projected to increase during each of the five-year periods between 1991 and 2016. The growth rate, however, is expected to decline in each successive period, from a high of 42% between 1991 and 1996 to 17% between 2011 and 2016.

Individual visible minority groups are expected to increase at different rates. The West Asian and Arab adult community is expected to be the fastest growing, with the population in 2016 projected to be four times higher than in 1991. The Filipino and other Pacific Islander, Latin American, Chinese and most other Asian communities are expected to more than triple in size over the same period. Growth in the size of the adult populations of Blacks (2.9 times greater in 2016 than in 1991) and South Asians (2.5 times greater) will be somewhat slower. These differences in growth rates among individual groups could contribute to a further diversification of Canada's visible minority population.

[Reproduced by authority of the Ministry of Industry, 1997, Statistics Canada, *Canadian Social Trends*, Catalogue No. 11-008, Summer 1995, Number 37, pages 2–8.]

✳ ✳ ✳

The Supreme Court of Canada's approach to equality under section 15 of the *Charter* does not see the protected grounds as including economic grounds. In this regard, the Ontario Court of Appeal has held that section 15 does not require the provincial government to institute employment equity legislation: *Ferrell v. Ontario (Attorney General)* (1998), 42 O.R. (3d) 97 (C.A.) (leave to appeal to S.C.C. refused). Even if the *Charter* did require the government to take proactive measures to combat systemic discrimination in employment, that duty, in the Court of Appeal's view, had been met by the *Ontario Human Rights Code*, notwithstanding that statute's emphasis on individual rather than systemic complaints. The court added, in a dictum, that the *Charter* did not appear to impose a positive obligation on legislatures to enact measures to combat systemic discrimination.

However, section 15(2) of the *Charter* expressly allows laws and practices (in effect, affirmative action) that singles out particular groups in order to help them overcome historic inequities. In the following decision, the Supreme Court of Canada gave an affirmative action remedy for systemic discrimination in employment.

Canadian National Railway Co. v. Canada (Canadian Human Rights Commission), [1987] 1 S.C.R. 1114

[A human rights tribunal under the *Canadian Human Rights Act* found Canadian National [CN] guilty of discrimination on the basis of sex in its hiring practices for certain unskilled blue-collar jobs. Relying on the predecessor to section 53 of the Act (section 41(2)(a)), the tribunal ordered the company to cease certain discriminatory hiring and employment practices and to alter others, and also ordered that the company set a goal of 13 percent female participation in targeted jobs in its St. Lawrence region. The order established a requirement to hire at least one woman for every four job openings until the goal was reached. Finally, the company was required to file periodic reports with the commission. A majority of the Federal Court of Appeal set aside the measures dealing with hiring. The matter was appealed to the Supreme Court of Canada, which allowed the appeal.]

> DICKSON C.J.C.: By the end of 1981, there were only 57 women in 'blue-collar' posts in the St. Lawrence region of CN, being a mere 0.7 percent of the blue-collar labour force in the region. There were 276 women occupying unskilled jobs in all the regions where CN operated, again amounting to only 0.7 percent of the unskilled workforce. By contrast, women represented, in 1981, 40.7 percent of the total Canadian labour force. At the time, women constituted only 6.11 percent of the total workforce of CN. Among blue-collar workers in Canada, 13 percent were women during the period January to May 1982, yet female applicants for blue-collar jobs at CN constituted only 5 percent of the total applicant pool.
>
> The markedly low rate of female participation in so-called 'non-traditional' occupations at Canadian National, namely occupations in which women typically have been significantly under-represented considering their proportion in the workforce as a whole, was not for-

tuitous. The evidence before the Tribunal established clearly that the recruitment, hiring and promotion policies at Canadian National prevented and discouraged women from working on blue-collar jobs. The Tribunal held, a finding not challenged in this Court, that CN had not made any real effort to inform women in general of the possibility of filling non-traditional positions in the company. For example, the evidence indicated that Canadian National's recruitment program with respect to skilled crafts and trades workers was limited largely to sending representatives to technical schools where there were almost no women. When women presented themselves at the personnel office, the interviews had a decidedly 'chilling effect' on female involvement in non-traditional employment; women were expressly encouraged to apply only for secretarial jobs. According to some of the testimony, women applying for employment were never told clearly the qualifications which they needed to fill the blue-collar job openings. Another hurdle placed in the way of some applicants, including those seeking employment as coach cleaners, was to require experience in soldering. Moreover, the personnel office did not itself do any hiring for blue-collar jobs. Instead, it forwarded names to the area foreman, and Canadian National had no means of controlling the decision of the foreman to not to hire a woman. The evidence indicated that the foremen were typically unreceptive to female candidates. . . .

SYSTEMIC DISCRIMINATION AND THE SPECIAL TEMPORARY MEASURES ORDER

A thorough study of 'systemic discrimination' in Canada is to be found in the Abella Report on equality in employment. The terms of reference of the Royal Commission instructed it 'to inquire into the most efficient, effective and equitable means of promoting employment opportunities, eliminating systemic discrimination and assisting individuals to compete for employment opportunities on an equal basis'. . . . Although Judge Abella chose not to offer a precise definition of systemic discrimination, the essentials may be gleaned from the following comments . . . [from] the Abella Report:

> Discrimination . . . means practices or attitudes that have, whether by design or impact, the effect of limiting an individual's or a group's right to the opportunities generally available because of attributed rather than actual characteristics. . . .
>
> It is not a question of whether this discrimination is motivated by an intentional desire to obstruct someone's potential, or whether it is the accidental by-product of innocently motivated practices or systems. If the barrier is affecting certain groups in a disproportionately negative way, it is a signal that the practices that lead to this adverse impact may be discriminatory. This is why it is important to look at the results of a system. . . .

In other words, systemic discrimination in an employment context is discrimination that results from the simple operation of established procedures of recruitment, hiring and promotion, none of which is necessarily designed to promote discrimination. The discrimination is then reinforced by the very exclusion of the disadvantaged group because the exclusion fosters the belief, both within and outside the group, that the exclusion is the result of 'natural' forces, for example, that women 'just can't do the job' (see the Abella Report . . .). To combat systemic discrimination, it is essential to create a climate in which both negative practices and negative attitudes can be challenged and discouraged. The Tribunal sought to accomplish this objective through its 'Special Temporary Measures' Order. Did it have the authority to do so?

Section 41(2) of the *Canadian Human Rights Act* lists the orders that a Tribunal may make if it determines that a person has engaged in a discriminatory practice. Among the potential orders is an order for 'measures' to be taken under s. 41(2)(a) 'including adoption of a special program, plan or arrangement referred to in subsection 15(1), to prevent the same or a similar practice occurring in the future.' The 'program, plan or arrangement' referred to in s. 15(1) is any mechanism 'designed to prevent disadvantages that are likely to be suffered by, or to eliminate or reduce disadvantages that are suffered by, any group of individuals when those disadvantages would be or are based on or related to,' *inter alia*, sex.

Because of his stated emphasis upon the 'ordinary grammatical construction' of s. 41(2)(a), Hugessen J., for the majority in the Federal Court of Appeal, offered this reading of the paragraph . . . :

> Reduced to its essentials, this text permits the Tribunal to order the taking of measures aimed at preventing the future occurrence of a discriminatory practice on the part of a person found to have engaged in such a practice in the past.

He stressed that 'the sole permissible purpose for the order is prevention' and that the text 'does not allow restitution for past wrongs.' Therefore, the 'program, plan or arrangement' authorized by reference to s. 15(1) would necessarily be limited by the language of s. 41(2)(a) to a mechanism designed 'to prevent the same or a similar practice occurring in the future.' Hugessen J. recognized the special difficulties involved in dealing with systemic discrimination . . . :

> . . . I recognize that by its very nature systemic discrimination may require creative imaginative preventive measures. Such discrimination has its roots, not in any deliberate desire to exclude from favour, but in attitudes, prejudices, mindsets and habits which may have been acquired over generations. It may well be that hiring quotas are the proper way to achieve the desired result.

Hugessen J. simply did not believe, without some precise factual showing, that specific hiring goals could be related to prevention, and thereby fall within s. 41(2)(a). The 'Special Temporary Measures' ordered by the Tribunal were struck down because the employment objectives imposed in the order were expressed in terms which, in Justice Hugessen's view, indicated that the objective was remedial and not preventive.

To evaluate this argument it is important to remember exactly what was ordered by the Human Rights Tribunal. The impugned section of the Order was headed 'Special Temporary Measures' and the heart of the employment equity programme was contained in paragraph 2:

> . . . Canadian National is ordered to hire at least one woman for every four non-traditional positions in the future. . . . When it is in effect, daily adherence to the one-in-four ratio

will not be required in order to give the employer a better choice in the selection of candidates. However, it must be complied with over each quarterly period until the desired objective of having 13% of non-traditional positions filled by women is achieved.

It should be underscored once again that the objective of 13 percent female participation was not arbitrary, for it corresponded to the national average of women involved in the non-traditional occupations.

In his dissenting opinion in the Federal Court of Appeal, MacGuigan J. accepted, as I do, that s. 41(2)(a) was designed to allow human rights tribunals to prevent future discrimination against identifiable protected groups, but he held that 'prevention' is a broad term and that it is often necessary to refer to historical patterns of discrimination in order to design appropriate strategies for the future. He noted the deep roots of discrimination against women at CN. It is an uncontradicted fact that the hiring and promotion policies of CN and the enormous problems faced by the tiny minority of women in the blue-collar workforce amounted to a systematic denial of women's equal employment opportunities.

Justice MacGuigan's point is made abundantly clear when one considers the context in which the challenged order was issued. It bears repeating that the tribunal had found that at the end of 1981 only 0.7 percent of blue-collar jobs in the St. Lawrence Region of Canadian National were held by women. The Tribunal found, furthermore that the small number of women in non-traditional jobs tended to perpetuate exclusion and, in effect, to cause additional discrimination. Moreover, Canadian National knew that its policies and practices, although perhaps not discriminatory in intent, were discriminatory in effect, yet had done nothing substantial to rectify the situation. When confronted with such a case of 'systemic discrimination,' it may be that the type of order issued by the Tribunal is the only means by which the purpose of the Canadian Human Rights Act can be met. In any program of employment equity, there simply cannot be a radical dissociation of 'remedy' and 'prevention.' Indeed there is no prevention without some form of remedy. The point was explained clearly by Professors Greschner and Norman in their Case Comment on the majority judgment of the Federal Court of Appeal in this case. . . . They emphasize that an employment equity program:

> . . . tries to break the causal links between past inequalities suffered by a group and future perpetuation of the inequalities. It simultaneously looks to the past and to the future, with no gap between cure and prevention. Any such program will remedy past acts of discrimination against the group and prevent future acts at one and the same time. That is the very point of affirmative action.

This point demands repetition. . . . When a program is said to be aimed at remedying past acts of discrimination, such as by bringing women into blue-collar occupations, it necessarily is preventing future acts of discrimination because the presence of women will help break down generally the notion that such work is man's work and more specifically, will help change the practices within that workplace which resulted in the past discrimination against women. From the other perspective, when a program is said to be aimed at preventing future acts of discrimination (again by bringing women into blue-collar occupations), it necessarily is also remedying past acts of discrimination because women as a group suffered from the discrimination and are now benefiting from the program.

Unlike the remedies in s. 41(2)(b)–(d), the 'remedy' under s. 41(2)(a) is directed towards a group and is therefore not merely compensatory but is itself prospective. The benefit is always designed to improve the situation for the group in the future, so that a successful employment equity programme will render itself otiose.

To see more clearly why the Special Temporary Measures Order is prospective, it would be helpful to review briefly the theoretical underpinnings of employment equity programs. I have already stressed that systemic discrimination is often unintentional. It results from the application of established practices and policies that, in effect, have a negative impact upon the hiring and advancement prospects of a particular group. It is compounded by the attitudes of managers and co-workers who accept stereotyped visions of the skills and 'proper role' of the affected group, visions which lead to the firmly held conviction that members of that group are incapable of doing a particular job, even when that conclusion is objectively false. An employment equity program, such as the one ordered by the Tribunal in the present case, is designed to break a continuing cycle of systemic discrimination. The goal is not to compensate past victims or even to provide new opportunities for specific individuals who have been unfairly refused jobs or promotion in the past, although some such individuals may be beneficiaries of an employment equity scheme. Rather, an employment equity program is an attempt to ensure that future applicants and workers from the affected group will not face the same insidious barriers that blocked their forebears.

An employment equity program thus is designed to work in three ways. First, by countering the cumulative effects of systemic discrimination, such a program renders further discrimination pointless. To the extent that some intentional discrimination may be present, for example, in the case of a foreman who controls hiring and who simply does not want women in the unit, a mandatory employment equity scheme places women in the unit despite the discriminatory intent of the foreman. His battle is lost.

Secondly, by placing members of that group that had previously been excluded into the heart of the workplace and by allowing them to prove ability on the job, the employment equity scheme addresses the attitudinal problem of stereotyping. For example, if women are seen to be doing the job of 'brakeman' or heavy cleaner or signaler at Canadian National, it is no longer possible to see women as capable of fulfilling only certain traditional occupational roles. It will become more and more difficult to ascribe characteristics to an individual by reference to the stereotypical characteristics ascribed to all women.

Thirdly, an employment equity programme helps to create what has been termed a 'critical mass' of the previously excluded group in the work place. This 'critical mass' has important effects. The presence of a significant number of individuals from the targeted group eliminates the problems of 'tokenism'; it is no longer the case that one or two women, for example, will be seen to 'represent' all women. . . . Moreover, women will not be so easily placed on the periphery of management concern. The 'critical mass' also effectively remedies systemic inequities in the process of hiring:

There is evidence that when sufficient minorities/women are employed in a given estab-lishment, the informal processes of economic life, for example, the tendency to refer friends and relatives for employment, will help to produce a significant minority [or female] applicant flow.

(Alfred W. Blumrosen, 'Quotas, Common Sense and Law in Labour Relations: Three Dimensions of Equal Opportunity' in Walter S. Tarnopolsky, ed., *Some Civil Liberties Issues of the Seventies*. . . .) If increasing numbers of women apply for non-traditional jobs, the desire to work in blue collar occupations will be less stigmatized. Personnel offices will be forced to treat women's applications for non-traditional jobs more seriously. In other words, once a 'critical mass' of the previously excluded group has been created in the workforce, there is a significant chance for the continuing self-correction of the system.

When the theoretical roots of employment equity programs are exposed, it is readily apparent that, in attempting to combat systemic discrimination, it is essential to look to the past patterns of discrimination and to destroy those patterns in order to prevent the same type of discrimination in the future. It is for this reason that the language of the Tri-bunal's Order for Special Temporary Measures may appear 'remedial.' In any case, as was stressed by MacGuigan J. in his dissent, the important question is not whether the Tri-bunal's order tracked the precise wording of s. 41(2)(a), but whether the actual measures ordered could be construed fairly to fall within the scope of the section. One should look to the substance of the order and not merely to its wording.

For the sake of convenience, I will summarize my conclusions as to the validity of the employment equity program ordered by the Tribunal. To render future discrimination pointless, to destroy discriminatory stereotyping and to create the required 'critical mass' of target group participation in the workforce, it is essential to combat the effects of past systemic discrimination. In so doing, possibilities are created for the continuing amelio-ration of employment opportunities for the previously excluded group. The dominant purpose of employment equity programs is always to improve the situation of the target group in the future. MacGuigan J. stressed in his dissent that 'the prevention of systemic discrimination will reasonably be thought to require systemic remedies.' Systemic reme-dies must be built upon the experience of the past so as to prevent discrimination in the future. Specific hiring goals, as Hugessen J. recognized, are a rational attempt to impose a systemic remedy on a systemic problem. The Special Temporary Measures Order of the Tribunal thus meets the requirements of s. 41(2)(a) of the *Canadian Human Rights Act*. It is a 'special program, plan or arrangement' within the meaning of s. 15(1) and therefore can be ordered under s. 41(2)(a). The employment equity order is rationally designed to combat systemic discrimination in the Canadian National St. Lawrence Region by pre-venting 'the same or a similar practice occurring in the future.'

A secondary problem must now be addressed, the fact that the Order of the Tribunal was expressed in terms of an employment goal, rather than a hiring goal. This methodol-ogy might increase the belief that the Order was remedial and not, properly speaking, pre-ventive. The Tribunal held, however, that the systemic discrimination at CN occurred not only in hiring but once women were on the job as well. The evidence revealed that there was a high level of publicly expressed male antipathy towards women which contributed to a high turnover rate amongst women in blue-collar jobs. As well, many male workers and supervisors saw any female worker in a non-traditional job as an upsetting phenomenon and as a 'job thief.' To the extent that promotion was dependent upon the evaluations of male supervisors, women were at a significant disadvantage. Moreover, because women generally had a low level of seniority, they were more likely to be laid off. For the employment equity program to be effective in creating the 'critical mass' and in destroying stereotypes, the goals had to be expressed in terms of actual employment. Otherwise the reasonable objectives of the scheme would have been defeated. The dominant purpose remained to improve the employment situation for women at CN in the future. . . .

13:500 PAY EQUITY

REFERENCES

R. Robb, "Equal Pay for Work of Equal Value: Issues and Policies" (1987) 13 Can. Pub. Pol. 445; Paul Weiler, "The Wages of Sex: The Uses and Limits of Comparable Worth" (1986) 99 Harv. L. Rev. 1728; P. Hughes, "*P.S.A.C. v. Canada (Treasury Board)*: The Long and Winding Road to Equity" (2000), 8 C.L.E.L.J. 55

The existence of a gap between the wages of men and women is well known. Census statistics reveal that the wage gap, measured by taking the average earnings of full-time, year-round workers in each major occupation, declined from 35 percent in 1985 to 28 percent in 1998. See Statistics Canada, *Employment Income by Occupation* (Ottawa: Statistics Canada, 2001). Many factors, including education, age, race, training, labour market experience, length of service, health, marital status, and geographical region, influence the extent of the gap. Identifying the effects of these factors can lead to a better understanding of the causes of the gap and assist in the design of remedies. Of course, many of the gaps in these human capital factors are also influenced by sex discrimination in the labour market or in society at large.

Prior to the earliest pay equity legislation, it was not uncommon for employers to maintain two wage rates for the same position on the basis of sex, based partly on the reasoning that men needed more money because they were the family breadwinners. In the early 1950s, statutes began to address the relatively straightforward problem of unequal pay for equal work, by forbidding employers from paying women less when they did the same work as men.

That legislation did not address a far more significant component of the wage gap: the fact that women were overrepresented in lower-paying jobs. This problem of occupational segregation led to a campaign to go beyond equal pay for the same work and to require equal pay for work of equal *value* — what has come to be known as "pay equity." Advocates of pay equity legislation theorized that a gender-neutral job evaluation scheme would disclose that many lower-paying jobs done mostly by women required equivalent skills, effort, responsibility and working conditions to higher-paying jobs done mostly by men.

In Canada, such legislation has taken two forms. Originally, guarantees of equal pay for men and women doing the same work formed part of human rights and fair employment statutes. Those statutes require individual workers or groups of workers to file complaints of discrimination against their employer. Such complaints can be costly and time-consuming, and they tend to address the problem in a piecemeal fashion.

As a result, some provinces have enacted legislation that obliges some or all employers to take measures to attain pay equity between male and female job categories. In Quebec, this legislation applies to all employers. In most other provinces, it applies only in the public and quasi-public sector. The legislation requires employers to submit a pay equity plan in accordance with the specified calculation methods. Employees or unions may bring complaints of non-compliance to a specialized administrative tribunal, which will review the employer's actions.

The Conservative government elected in Ontario in 1995 repealed a portion of the *Pay Equity Act* that dealt with broader public sector workplaces, which were mostly female. Implementing pay equity in these workplaces was difficult, since there was no obvious male-dominated job category that could serve as a comparator. The repealed legislative provisions specified that in such cases, the "proxy comparison method" was to be used to calculate whether pay equity adjustments were called for, and almost all female-dominated workplaces in the public sector had been the subject of proxy comparison orders. (The proxy comparison method was never extended to the Ontario private sector.) The 1996 legislative amendment, Schedule J, capped existing proxy pay equity adjustments at 3 percent of the employer's 1993 payroll and prohibited any further use of the proxy comparison method. As a result, the women affected had only 22 percent of their pay differential corrected.

A union representing 5200 Ontario broader public-sector workers argued that Schedule J violated section 15(1) of the *Charter*. Their application for a declaration of invalidity was granted in the following decision.

Service Employees International Union, Local 204 v. Ontario (A.G.) (1997), 35 O.R. (3d) 508 (Gen. Div.)

O'LEARY J.: —

. . . The applicants attack Schedule J as violating ss. 15(1) and 28 of the *Charter*.

The Applicants' argument may be summarized as follows. The *Pay Equity Act*, in both its legislative intent and in its effects, is human rights legislation designed to provide a proactive, systemic remedy for systemic gender discrimination in women's compensation.

Women who work in predominantly female workplaces are particularly vulnerable to sex-based discrimination in compensation because they perform work which is most stereotypically identified as being "women's work" and which, accordingly, is most undervalued in comparison with work performed by men. That portion of the wage gap that is attributable to systemic sex discrimination is widest in predominantly female workplaces, and the women who work in these workplaces are among the most disadvantaged by sex-based discrimination in compensation, both as compared with men and as compared with other working women.

The *Pay Equity Act* contained as one of its original commitments the development of a pay equity remedy which could redress systemic discrimination in compensation for this most disadvantaged group of women. The proxy comparison method was enacted in 1993, after careful study and consideration, to carry out that commitment embodied in the original Act.

By contrast, the proxy comparison method was removed from the Act without any study as to the efficacy of the proxy remedy, or the impact of the amendment on the women affected.

. . .

Schedule J denies to a group who previously had a remedy under the *Pay Equity Act* the protection and benefit of the Act. Schedule J singles out one group for differential treatment. It is submitted that Schedule J clearly creates a discriminatory distinction which denies equal protection and equal benefit of the law to that group of women.

That group is the most disadvantaged by systemic discrimination in compensation on the basis of sex of any group of public sector employees in Ontario. In other words, they are among the most in need of pay equity remedies.

The women affected by Schedule J are identified by the fact that they are predominantly women who do "women's work" in predominantly female workplaces, distinguishing characteristics which are clearly "closely related" to the enumerated ground of sex.

It is submitted, on the basis of this group of characteristics, that Schedule J has a prejudicial effect on the enumerated ground of sex.

. . .

Section 15(2) Argument of Respondent

The applicants are clearly treated differently to their prejudice by the Pay Equity Act as it now exists as a result of the Schedule J amendment. The respondent argues that the Act is affirmative action legislation having as its objective the elimination of systemic gender pay inequity suffered by women and as such is protected against a s. 15(1) attack by s. 15(2) of the *Charter*. Section 15 of the *Charter* reads as follows:

> (2) Subsection (1) does not preclude any law, program or activity that has as its object the amelioration of conditions of disadvantaged individuals or groups including those that are disadvantaged because of race, national or ethnic origin, colour, religion, sex, age or mental or physical disability.

It is submitted that women cannot attack the Act under s. 15(1) of the *Charter* simply because the Act has helped them proportionately less than it has helped other women. It is said that women can attack the Act only if they have been excluded from the benefit of the Act because the Act discriminates against them on one of the prohibited grounds set out in s. 15(1) or on an analogous ground. If the applicants could say they have been discriminated against because they are women, then that would be a basis for invoking s. 15(1) of the *Charter*. Here, the complaint is not that the applicants have been excluded from the benefit of the Act because they are women. Rather, the complaint is that being women most in need of relief from pay inequity they have been removed from the protection that the Act once gave them. It is said that complaint is barred by s. 15(2).

A literal reading of s. 15(2) of the *Charter* appears to support that argument. However, constitutional law authors and the courts have pointed out that s. 15(2) was placed in the *Charter* to make clear that s. 15(1) does not preclude affirmative action programs in favour of disadvantaged individuals or groups even though such programs inevitably involve some element of reverse discrimination against those not belonging to the disadvantaged group. . . . Section 15(2) does not protect affirmative action legislation from attacks by members of the disadvantaged group it was designed to benefit. In *Lovelace v. Ontario* . . . , the Ontario Court of Appeal stated . . .:

> A s. 15(2) program that excludes from its reach disadvantaged individuals or groups that the program was designed to benefit likely infringes s. 15(1). The government would then have to justify the exclusion under s. 1.

There is no doubt that the applicants are members of the disadvantaged group the *Pay Equity Act* was designed to benefit and that they have been excluded from its reach by the Schedule J amendment. Accordingly, their claim of discrimination must succeed unless the government can justify the exclusion under s. 1 of the *Charter*.

WHAT RESPONDENT MUST JUSTIFY UNDER SECTION 1 OF THE *CHARTER*

It must be made clear just what the government of Ontario must justify under s. 1 of the *Charter*. The unfortunate state of women prior to the *Pay Equity Act, 1987* as the objects of systemic gender wage inequity was created by the marketplace and stereotypical attitudes, not by government. It was not because of any action by government that they were in the plight they were in. The *Charter* does not place a positive obligation on government to eliminate such inequity. Rather, the government must not create inequity. As was stated by L'Heureux-Dubé J. in *Thibaudeau v. R.* . . . :

> Although s. 15 of the *Charter* does not impose upon governments the obligation to take positive actions to remedy the symptoms of systemic inequality, it does require that the government not be the source of further inequality.

Leaving aside any responsibility of government to eliminate systemic gender wage inequality in its own employees, the government of Ontario was under no obligation to enact the *Pay Equity Act, 1987*. It could likewise have repealed the entire Pay Equity Act in 1996 without giving rise to any claims of discrimination.

Had the government simply repealed the *Pay Equity Act* in 1996, the applicants' position would be the same as that of the applicants in *Ferrel v. Ontario (Attorney General)*, heard by MacPherson J. . . . . There, the applicants brought a motion for an interlocutory injunction suspending the operation of Bill 8, also known as the *Job Quotas Repeal Act, 1995*, pending the resolution of an application questioning the validity of Bill 8 as being contrary to s. 15 of the *Charter*. At p. 2 of his reasons, MacPherson J. stated:

The problem with the applicants' position is that Bill 8 is a repealing statute. It repeals a statute, and several provisions in other statutes, enacted by a previous legislature. It does not enact any new substantive provisions that can be measured against the *Charter*, including s. 15. The purpose of the *Charter* is to ensure that governments comply with the *Charter* when they make laws. The *Charter* does not go further and require that governments enact laws to remedy societal problems, including problems of inequality and discrimination. One can hope that governments will regard this as part of their mission; however, the *Charter* does not impose this mission at the high level of constitutional obligation — section 32 of the *Charter* states that the *Charter* applies to governments. Governments speak through laws, regulations and practices. In Ontario, the current legislature has decided not to speak in the domain of employment equity. It has decided to leave this, at least for the time being, to the realm of private activity. Although many people, including the applicants, may regret and oppose this decision, the legislature is entitled to make it. . . .

Here, the government did not repeal the whole *Pay Equity Act*. Rather, it repealed just that part that provided for the proxy method of comparison. It is the removal of the proxy method that resulted in the applicants being treated differently to their prejudice by the *Pay Equity Act*.

Just as the government did not have to enact the *Pay Equity Act*, it likewise did not have to undertake to pay for the elimination of pay inequity amongst employees in the broader public sector. Leaving aside any rights employers in the broader public sector might have acquired against government because of its undertaking to pay the cost of pay equity wage adjustments (something that was not argued before me), the government in 1995 could have cancelled its contribution to the cost of pay equity. Certainly, it does not have to justify capping its contribution at $500 million per year.

What the government does have to justify is the Schedule J amendment. . . .

Denying proxy sector women 78 percent of the wage increase needed to remedy the systemic wage inequity fixed by their proxy pay equity plans was the method chosen by government to allow it to cap its pay equity costs at $500 million per year. The government then must justify its action in requiring in effect that 100 percent of the shortfall in funds created by the $500 million cap be borne by those women who had suffered the most from systemic wage discrimination because they perform traditional women's work in female-dominated sectors of the broader public sector, with no male comparators in their places of employment. It is to be noted that other women working in the broader public sector, many of whom suffered far less from systemic wage discrimination than those in the proxy sector, have had 100 percent of that inequity removed, but were not required to contribute in any way to the shortfall in pay equity funding.

. . .

[O'Leary J. went on to hold that the Ontario government had failed to provide an adequate section 1 justification for the repeal. Specifically, he rejected the government's expert evidence that the proxy method was not a valid method of quantifying gender-based systemic wage discrimination in the female-dominated broader public sector.

Therefore, the government did not have a pressing and substantial objective in enacting Schedule J. O'Leary J. continued:]

I point out there was no attempt by the respondent to establish that in order to live within the $500 million cap government placed on pay equity spending, the government had to remove the proxy method and throw the full weight of the funding reduction on those working in the proxy sector. It was not explained why the burden could not have been apportioned equitably amongst all workers in the broader public sector who benefited from the $380 million still paid annually by government towards the cost of wage adjustments in that sector.

It must also be noted that the Schedule J amendment cannot be justified as an incremental approach to pay equity. It is not a matter of putting off to another day, when the same can be afforded, the correction of the gender-based systemic wage inequity from which women in the proxy sector undoubtedly suffer. Schedule J and the government's position on this application tells proxy sector women they are not and cannot be covered under the *Pay Equity Act* even though other women in the broader public sector have had their systemic gender-based wage inequity 100 percent cured.

CONCLUSION

It is a matter of choice for government as to whether or not it legislates to remove inequity. When, however, government decides to legislate and identifies the disadvantaged group the legislation is intended to benefit, then it must, subject to s. 1 of the *Charter*, make the legislation apply fairly and equally to all within the group or government itself is guilty of discriminating. This is especially so where government itself picks up the cost of removing the inequality that is the focus of the legislation. Where legislation discriminates against a portion of the group the legislation is designed to help, the legislation contravenes s. 15(1) of the *Charter* and so is *ultra vires* unless the discrimination is demonstrably justified under s. 1 of the *Charter*.

The *Pay Equity Act*, because of the 1996 Schedule J amendment, discriminates against proxy sector women by denying them the opportunity of quantifying and correcting the systemic gender-based wage inequity from which they suffer, a benefit the *Act* grants to other women working in the broader public sector.

The discrimination has not been justified under s. 1 of the *Charter*, in that the stated objective of the Schedule J amendment does not warrant overriding the constitutional right of equal benefit of the law. Indeed, the stated objective — the restoring of the *Pay Equity Act* to true pay equity principles — I find to be mistaken. Proxy method was and is an appropriate pay equity tool in keeping with the intent of the *Pay Equity Act* to relieve women, including those working in female-segregated workplaces in the broader public sector, from systemic gender-based wage discrimination.

Since it was the 1996 Schedule J amendment that created the discrimination, I declare that Schedule J of the *Savings and Restructuring Act, 1996*, amending the *Pay Equity Act*, is unconstitutional and of no force and effect.

13:600 THE FUTURE OF EQUALITY

13:610 Economic Inequality

Canadian courts have repeatedly held that equality rights are concerned with the protection of human dignity. However, the courts have frequently excluded economic equality claims, either on the basis that the *Charter* is not a guarantor of economic rights or that such claims engage matters of social and economic policy rather than individual rights. Nor has occupational status or membership in a particular socioeconomic group, such as low income wage earners or welfare recipients, been found to be a ground "analogous" to those listed in section 15 and thus one which can support a *Charter* challenge. See, for example, *Reference re Workers' Compensation Act, 1983 (Nfld.)*, [1989] 1 S.C.R. 922. In general, unless a legislative or administrative action can be characterized as a denial of equal treatment on the basis of a listed or analogous ground, the fact that it creates, perpetuates or fails to ameliorate an economic disadvantage has so far been held insufficient to bring it within the definition of discrimination.

In *Delisle v. Canada (Deputy Attorney General)* [1999] 2 S.C.R. 989, discussed in Chapter 4 above, the Supreme Court of Canada reiterated its reluctance to consider occupational status as an analogous ground for the purposes of section 15 of the *Charter*. That case involved the statutory exclusion of Royal Canadian Mounted Police officers from eligibility for collective bargaining. In rejecting the argument of the appellant RCMP officers that the exclusion violated their equality rights under section 15, Bastarache J., for the majority of the Court, said (at paragraph 44):

> In this case the appellant has not established that the professional status or employment of RCMP members are analogous grounds. It is not a matter of functionally immutable characteristics in a context of labour market flexibility. A distinction based on employment does not identify, here, "a type of decision making that is suspect because it often leads to discrimination and denial of substantive equality" . . . , in view in particular of the status of police officers in society.

In the later case of *Dunmore v. Ontario (Attorney General)*, 2001 SCC 94, excerpted above in Chapter 4, it was agricultural workers who had been excluded from collective bargaining by statute, and they were a group that clearly had much lower social status than the RCMP officers in Delisle. However, the Supreme Court of Canada did not deal with the claim that their exclusion from collective bargaining violated their equality rights under section 15 of the *Charter*, because the Court held the exclusion to violate their right to freedom of association under section 2(d).

Earlier decisions also show a reluctance on the part of the Supreme Court of Canada to use section 15 of the *Charter* to interfere with the distributive decisions of legislatures, even where there is an arguable connection to a prohibited ground. For example, in *Symes v. Canada* [1993] 4 S.C.R. 695, a female lawyer incurred high childcare costs in order to have the time to practice her profession. The *Income Tax Act* did not allow her to deduct all of those costs as a professional expense, but allowed only the much small-

er childcare deduction. The Supreme Court rejected her section 15 claim that this effectively discriminated against women workers. In the view of the majority of the Court,
although it was clear that women disproportionately bore the burden of childcare, it was
not established that they disproportionately paid the costs of such care.

In general, claims of economic discrimination fare no better under human rights law
than under the *Charter*. Quebec is an exception. Its human rights statute lists "social
condition" as a prohibited ground. That term has been held to refer to a combination of
objective factors, such as income level or family background, and subjective factors
such as unfavourable perceptions held by others. No other jurisdiction includes social
condition or the equivalent as a prohibited ground of discrimination, although some
prohibit discrimination on the basis of "source of income" or "social origin." Section 7
of the Alberta *Human Rights, Citizenship and Multiculturalism Act* is an example.

The absence of protection from discrimination on the basis of social condition has
been a source of repeated criticism. The Canadian Labour Congress (CLC), in its submissions to the Canadian Human Rights Act Review Panel referred to above, argued
that various forms of economic discrimination "in fact impede access to equality of
opportunity probably almost as often as any other form of discrimination." It noted that
costs associated with obtaining or maintaining employment (such as paying for tests or
buying tools) may serve as barriers to employment for the poor. The CLC recommended that "social condition" be added to the federal Act, with a definition similar to that
developed in Quebec. It argued that such an amendment to the federal human rights
statute would have the added result of encouraging courts and tribunals to treat social
condition as an analogous ground when interpreting section 15 of the *Charter*.

Economic inequality, and the resulting problem of social exclusion, is increasing in
Canada and almost everywhere else. Wage rates have fallen in real terms in the last generation, and there is more dispersion, or inequality, of wages. Such changes are often
attributed to market forces, the effects of technology and greater communication, or
simply to globalization. However, the degree of economic inequality varies considerably
among industrialized countries, and there is evidence that it is affected by the extent of
collective bargaining and the relative strength of unions: see I. Bakker, "Globalization
and Human Development in the Rich Countries: Lessons from Labour Markets and Welfare States," Background Papers, United Nations Development Programme *Human
Development Report 1999*, vol. 2, 29). In turn, collective bargaining coverage and union
density are dependent upon the state of labour market rules and institutions.

Laws facilitating collective bargaining rules were originally introduced, in part, to
address economic equality. However, as is perhaps clear from Chapters 3 to 6 of this
book, it has become clear that under the *Wagner Act* model which prevails across Canada, collective bargaining is not equally available to all workers, or equally advantageous
when it is available. This has become all the more true with the proliferation of atypical
forms of work in the new economy. Those in "peripheral" rather than "core" labour markets and those engaged in non-standard forms of work typically face greater difficulties
achieving certification; where they succeed, they often face poor prospects of gains, if

not imminent decertification. Those same workers also benefit less from statutory protections and employment insurance schemes. As of yet, the *Charter* has not yet been successfully used to force legislatures to address the structural causes of workplace stratification, including those that may relate to labour market institutions. For example, it has been suggested that the fragmentation of bargaining units under Wagnerism creates an unconstitutional barrier to the attainment of workplace equality by women and ethnic or racial minorities, because it precludes them from having effective collective bargaining, or indeed any collective bargaining at all. This phenomenon is discussed in an excerpt by Judy Fudge in Chapter 6 (section 6:140) above. As mentioned in the *Ferrell* decision, section 13:400 above, even where governments have repealed existing legislation designed to ameliorate the position of disadvantaged groups in the workplace, the courts have generally refused to find a breach of s. 15. The only exception is provided by the decision of a trial court in *S.E.I.U. Local 204 v. Ontario*, above. In that case, certain provisions of the Ontario *Pay Equity Act* (the proxy comparison provisions) had made the benefits of that Act accessible to the most economically disadvantaged of the groups of female employees whom the Act was designed to benefit. The repeal of those provisions was held to be a breach of s. 15(1) because it "discriminate[d] against a portion of the group the legislation is designed to help. . . ."

13:620 Gender and Economic Discrimination

It is relatively uncontroversial to assert that labour markets are gendered in their structure and operation. It is one of the few truly universal gender traits that men and women everywhere do different types of work, although the particular roles that they play from society to society vary enormously. See Gillian Hadfield, "A Coordination Model of the Sexual Division of Labor," (1999) 40 Journal of Economic Behavior and Organization 125). It remains a fact that women perform most of the unpaid work, and that the allocation of unpaid work between men and women does not appear to shift appreciably when women enter the labour market. While the vast majority of women, including those with young children, now participate in the paid labour force, they also retain responsibility for domestic obligations and do disproportionate amounts of unpaid work. As described in the United Nations Development Programme, *Human Development Report 1999* (New York: Oxford, 1999), this produces a distinct set of burdens and costs for women.

Labour market regulations have traditionally been directed at regulating the conditions of paid work in core industrial sectors; in addition, their reach is, by definition, limited to the formal rather than the informal sector. The neglect of unpaid work is arguably discriminatory against women, as such work significantly constrains labour market participation. More to the point, however, is the discriminatory potential of workplace rules that do not accommodate or compensate for those non-market obligations, and that directly or indirectly relegate women to lower occupational status and income. The following excerpt deals with the relationship between paid and unpaid work, and with why it can be seen as a labour market issue.

Diane Elson, "Labor Markets as Gendered Institutions: Equality, Efficiency and Empowerment Issues" (1999), 27 World Development 611, at 612

. . . The most fundamental way in which labor markets are gendered institutions is in the way in which they operate at the intersection of ways in which people make a living and care for themselves, their children, their relatives and friends. Activities which make a living are recognized by economists as economic activities which should in principle be counted as part of national production. For brevity, we might call the sum of this largely market-oriented work the "productive economy." But, as feminist economists have pointed out, unpaid, unjacketed caring activities are also critical for the functioning of the "productive economy," since they reproduce, on a daily and intergenerational basis, the labor force which works in the productive economy. Moreover, feminist economists have argued that unpaid caring activities entail work, even though they are not market-oriented. For brevity, we might call the sum of unpaid, caring work, the "reproductive economy."

Labor markets form one of the points of intersection of these two economies. But they operate in ways that fail to acknowledge the contributions of the reproductive economy. Instead they operate in ways that disadvantage those who carry out most of the work in the reproductive economy: women. Labor market institutions are constructed in ways that represent only the costs to employers of the time that employees spend on unpaid caring for others. The benefits are not represented. Thus, for instance, employees' parenting duties are represented as liabilities and not assets to their employers. Labor market institutions are constructed in ways that reflect only the immediate costs of time off from paid work to have and rear children, and care for sick relatives and friends. They are not constructed to reflect the benefits of the reproduction and maintenance of a pool of labor from which employers can select their employees. Nor do they reflect the enhanced interpersonal skills which come from parenting and managing a household. In the language of economics, the reproductive economy produces benefits for the productive economy which are externalities, not reflected in market prices and wages. Or, as feminist economist Nancy Folbre puts it, labor market institutions fail to face up to the problem of "who pays for the kids?"

Of course, the operation of labor market institutions cannot escape the fact that someone has to pay for the kids. (Just as there is no such thing as a free lunch, there is also no such thing as a free replenishment of the pool of labor.) Most labor market institutions are constructed on the basis that the burdens of the reproductive economy will be, and should be, borne largely by women. For instance, arrangements for paternal leave are far less widespread than maternal leave, and where they do exist, there are many barriers to men taking up their entitlements, because promotion often depends upon showing "commitment" to the job, and taking paternal leave may be interpreted as a sign of weak commitment to the job. Domestic responsibilities penalize women in the labor market and are a key factor in women's weak position in terms of earnings and occupations.

LABOR MARKETS AS GENDERED INSTITUTIONS

It is sometimes claimed that labor markets adapt so as to allow women to combine paid work with unpaid work — for example, part-time work and home-based work. But, this kind of adaptation is generally one-sided — more designed to allow the productive economy access to workers whose entry into the labor market is constrained by domestic responsibilities than to give weight to the contribution that women's unpaid work makes to the productive economy. This is revealed in the way in which these more "informal" types of work typically do not have contracts which give employees any rights to paid time for meeting their responsibilities in the reproductive economy — rights such as maternity leave, and time-off for caring for sick relatives. Nor does such employment cover women's needs when they have retired from paid work, since pension rights are also not covered. Instead, the presumption appears to be that someone else (husband, children) will support such workers in their old age.

Thus labor market institutions are not only bearers of gender, they are also reinforcers of gender inequality. But different institutional configurations give different results: some labor markets are more equal than others. Moreover, improvements can be brought about by public action, i.e. by combined action by the state and by groups of active citizens. Public action can build upon the potential for change in labor market institutions themselves. For such institutions are not like fortresses of stone, rather they are combinations of overlapping and conflicting practices, norms and networks, whose seeming solidity at any moment masks subterranean pressures and fissures.

[Reprinted by permission.]

* * *

For further discussion, see Kerry Rittich, "Feminization and Contingency: Regulating the Stakes of Work for Women," in J.A.F. Conaghan *et al.*, *Labour Law in an Era of Globalization*, Oxford University, Press, 2002). To what extent do we already compensate unpaid labour through employment insurance and employment standards? To what extent are labour laws and other protective legislation implicated in the economic disadvantage of women in labour markets? How might existing equality jurisprudence serve as vehicles to ameliorate it? Consider, for example, the application to these issues of the *Vriend* and *Meoirin* cases, set out earlier in this chapter.

13:630 Equality and Human Rights in International Law

Conceptions of human rights at international law are significantly broader than those now reflected in most Canadian human rights legislation. Economic rights form an integral part of international human rights regimes and are incorporated into regional human rights treaties as well. Moreover, workers' rights and interests are central to efforts to promote social and economic rights. For example, article 55 of the *Charter* of the United Nations commits all nations to promote "higher standards of living, full employment, and conditions of economic and social progress and development." Among the rights recognized in the *Universal Declaration of Human Rights* (UDHR) are the right to work, to just and favourable working conditions, to rest and leisure, to reasonable hours of work and to paid holidays. Under the *UDHR*, every worker has the right to sufficient remuneration to support a family at a level worthy of human dignity.

Many of these rights are further elaborated in the *International Covenant on Economic, Social and Cultural Rights (ICESCR)*, to which Canada is a signatory. The *ICESCR* commits signatory states to the "progressive realization" of a broad range of economic rights through legislative measures. Protected rights include the right to fair wages and equal remuneration for work of equal value and the right to just and favourable conditions of work, including a decent living and safe and healthy working conditions. The *ICESCR* also recognizes the "right to work," which includes the right to technical and vocational guidance and training. In addition, the conventions of the International Labour Organization (ILO), many of which Canada has ratified, provide an extensive and detailed international code of workplace rights and standards. Some ILO conventions, such as those on the right to equal pay and the rights of migrant workers, attempt to ensure more equality for vulnerable groups at work. Rights set out in international treaties are not understood to be justiciable in the same way as domestic constitutional rights or human rights, but they nonetheless bind signatory countries. Failure to respect them places a state in breach of its international obligations.

In interpreting domestic legislation and the *Canadian Charter of Rights and Freedoms*, the Supreme Court of Canada is increasingly recognizing the value and importance of resort to customary international law, international human rights norms, and international treaty obligations. Sometimes these international norms are highly influential, even dispositive. For example, in *Baker v. Canada (Minister of Citizenship and Immigration)*, [1999] 2 S.C.R. 817, the Supreme Court considered whether the obligation that Canada had assumed to further the "best interests of the child" under the United Nations *Convention on the Rights of the Child* should be given primary importance in the interpretation and application of the humanitarian and compassionate provisions of the *Immigration Act*. The Court held that the values that should inform the interpretation of the Act could be derived from Canada's international obligations, and that a failure to give enough weight to the best interests of the child would render unreasonable an exercise of the statutory power. In *Slaight Communications Inc. v. Davidson* (1989), 59 D.L.R. (4th) 416 (S.C.C.), excerpted above in Chapter 12, a tribunal's remedial order had tightly restricted what an employer could say about an unjustly dismissed employee. Dickson C.J. referred to the ICESCR, and particularly to article 6 on the right to work, in support of the conclusion that the restriction, although it violated freedom of expression, was demonstrably justified within the meaning of section 1 of the *Charter*. In *Dunmore v. Ontario (Attorney General)*, 2001 SCC 94, excerpted above in Chapter 4, Bastarache J. noted (at paragraph 30) that "international labour jurisprudence . . . recognizes the inevitably collective nature of the freedom to organize." He used that fact in support of the conclusion (also at paragraph 30) that freedom of association under the *Charter* should be interpreted to include "not only the exercise in association of the constitutional rights and freedoms (such as freedom of assembly) and lawful rights of individuals, but the exercise of certain collective activities, such as making majority representations to one's employer." However, it is clear that international norms, like *Charter* rights, are susceptible to being interpreted in a way that limits the collective interests of workers in the name of individual rights. For example, in *R. v. Advance Cutting and Coring Ltd.*, discussed in Chapter 10 above, the majority of the Supreme Court of Canada held that the ICESCR's guarantee of the right to work supported the view that freedom of association included the right not to associate. The dissenting judges in that case held that it also supported their view that the latter right was infringed by a statute which required every Quebec construction worker, as a condition of employment in the industry, to designate one of a number of named unions as his or her bargaining representative.

The right to freedom of association and collective bargaining, and the right to freedom from discrimination in employment, are among the "core" rights emphasized in the ILO *Declaration on Fundamental Principles and Rights at Work* (86th Session, Geneva, June, 1998). The *International Covenant on Civil and Political Rights* obliges states to protect against discrimination "on any ground such as race, colour, sex, language, religion, political or other opinion, national or social origin, property, birth or other status." To what extent could such instruments be invoked in support of a claim that governments must, for example, amend existing statutes to give vulnerable groups more effective access to collective bargaining?

13:640 Procedural Reform

In the early decades after their enactment, human rights statutes generated high expectations. Those expectations were strikingly articulated in *Seneca College of Applied Arts and Technology v. Bhadauria*, [1981] 2 S.C.R. 181, excerpted above in Chapter 2 (section 2:300), where the Supreme Court of Canada held that the Ontario *Human Rights Code* constituted a "complete code" for the protection of the rights set out in it, and thus implicitly precluded recourse to common law court actions for redress against any of the statutorily prohibited forms of discrimination.

However, human rights statutes (or perhaps more precisely, their enforcement processes) are widely considered to have failed to live up to their expectations. The following excerpt, from a background paper to the Report of the Canadian Human Rights Act Review Panel, *Promoting Equality: A New Vision* (2000), describes some of the problems and discusses a range of possible responses. It addresses the federal legislation, but similar issues have arisen under provincial statutes.

Shelagh Day and Gwen Brodsky, "Screening and Carriage: Reconsidering the Commission's Function" (September, 1999)

Human rights commissions have been established in Canada to be stewards of the public interest in the effective enforcement of human rights. Stewardship over this public interest is essential. A human rights commission should be able to ensure that human rights claimants are assisted, and that human rights claims are dealt with in a manner that is appropriate to their importance in the society. It should also be able to nurture the jurisprudence, appearing before tribunals and courts to present arguments that promote the development of the law in ways that will help to eradicate persistent patterns of inequality. It should be able to develop concentrated expertise and to select and develop cases in light of their potentially broad impact on disadvantaged groups.

Commission stewardship over the public interest in human rights enforcement can be provided in different ways, as the options proposed here will illustrate. But changes which would move the human rights system closer to a private dispute resolution model will necessarily raise questions about whether, and how, the public interest can be protected.

In light of the public interest in achieving equality, it is not clear that in Canada we have created mechanisms for enforcing human rights that are adequate to the task and its importance.

At this time, there are major concerns about whether the federal human rights system is functioning adequately. Both human rights claimants and respondents are dissatisfied. Both groups are concerned about delays and inadequate processes. Claimants are also concerned about the small number of cases that are referred to the Canadian Human Rights Tribunal for hearing, and the underdeveloped role of the Commission in addressing systemic discrimination. The question arises: could changes to the statutorily-created relationship among the Commission, complainants and respondents bring improvement?

This paper is about the screening, investigation, and carriage functions of the Commission, that is, it concerns these elements:

1) the Commission's power, at a preliminary stage, to dismiss a complaint or decide not to deal with it because:
   a) it does not fall within the time limits set out in the Act,
   b) it is not within the jurisdiction of the Act,
   c) it is "trivial, frivolous, vexatious or made in bad faith" or
   d) in the Commission's view, the complainant should pursue another avenue of recourse;
2) the Commission's power to investigate a complaint and then decide whether to send it to conciliation, to refer it to the Canadian Human Rights Tribunal, or to dismiss it;
3) the Commission's power, if the complaint is sent to conciliation, to subsequently dismiss the complaint or to refer it to the Tribunal.

Taken together these are the core elements of the Commission's complaint-handling system.

Under the current statutory regime, there is no independent right of access to a Tribunal hearing. For the person who believes that their rights have been violated, the scheme places the Commission in the position of controlling access to the Tribunal.

CURRENT CONCERNS

The major concerns about the current functioning of the CHRC are these:

1 Delay

Between 1988 and 1997, the Canadian Human Rights Commission took from 23 to 27 months to reach decisions not to deal with a complaint, or to dismiss it or refer it for hearing. If a complaint was sent to conciliation this added additional months. If a complaint was referred to hearing, final resolution could take several more years. Delays in processing complaints now cause serious dissatisfaction among both claimants and respondents, and result in some complaints being dismissed by courts.

2   High Rejection Rate

Of the 6,550 complaints the CHRC received between 1988 and 1997, only 19% of complaints were settled with Commission participation and 6% were referred to the Canadian Human Rights Tribunal for hearing. The Commission decided not to proceed with or to dismiss about two thirds of all complaints. The high rejection rate and very low rate of referral for hearing raises serious questions among stakeholders about the credibility of the system as a mechanism for enforcing the right to equality. It also raises questions about whether the Commission's complaint-processing and decision-making is being driven by its lack of resources and fully-trained staff, and by the administrative need to reduce its backlog and workload, rather than by the central goals of human rights legislation.

3   Commission's Authority to Extinguish Rights

Concern regarding the high rejection rate is intensified by the fact that the only recourse available to a person whose complaint has been dismissed is to make an application in Federal Court for judicial review of the Commission's dismissal decision. Because of the 1981 decision of the Supreme Court of Canada in *Seneca College of Applied Arts and Technology v. Bhadauria* a person who believes that their human rights have been violated cannot go directly to court to seek a remedy.

The Federal Court can review the Commission's decisions to dismiss complaints for correctness on a question of law or jurisdiction, but principally these reviews consider only whether the Commission was procedurally fair in the manner in which it investigated and made its decision to dismiss. A successful outcome on judicial review, which is much less likely than an unsuccessful one, leads to the complaint being referred back to the Commission. Most complainants have their rights conclusively determined by the Commission without an oral hearing.

4   Participation

When a complaint is filed with the Commission, it is taken out of the hands of the complainant. Many complainants become witnesses and bystanders with respect to the framing, investigating, disposition and presentation to the Tribunal of their own complaints. The relationship with the Commission is experienced as disempowering. Further, organizations that have an interest in the outcome of human rights cases because they represent disadvantaged groups and stand to be affected directly or indirectly can only be involved by applying to intervene at the Tribunal stage. No funding is provided to support such interventions and there is no means for a third party to have input at the Commission decision-making stage. These groups are ready to play a larger role, and can make a significant contribution to the development of the law on equality, as they have demonstrated through their interventions in *Charter* cases.

5   Commission's Role in Addressing Systemic Discrimination Underdeveloped

Because the Commission has become bogged down in the process of screening and investigation, it has not fully developed its role as a strategic advocate, carrying forward cases that will have a broad impact on groups that are disadvantaged in Canadian society, and that will clarify and strengthen legal analysis of human rights protections. Given the current understanding that past discrimination has created serious disadvantages for major groups protected by human rights legislation, this is an essential role for a modern federal Commission.

OPTIONS

The combination of the Commission's power to extinguish rights and the high rate of rejection of complaints has created a serious sense of unfairness among human rights claimants. In our view, this perceived unfairness must be addressed in this review, as must the delays, the need to develop the Commission's focus on systemic discrimination, and the need for claimants and community organizations representing disadvantaged groups to participate more fully in the development of the law.

There are various possible changes that could be made in the federal human rights system to respond to current concerns. The following models represent a spectrum of possibilities for redesign. Elements of one model could be combined with those of another.

- Model A: Provide Fairer, Faster Screening
  1. clarify and narrow the Commission's discretion to decide not to deal with a complaint, and to decide that a Tribunal hearing is not warranted, and
  2. impose enforceable time limits on the Commission, and parties, to control delay.

- Model B: Guarantee Access to Tribunal
  1. establish an independent right of access to a Tribunal hearing for persons whose complaints the Commission decides not to deal with or not to refer, in addition to clarifying and narrowing the Commission's discretion, and imposing time limits on the Commission and parties (Model A), and
  2. give complainants who decide to exercise their right of independent access to the Tribunal full disclosure of the contents of the Commission's investigative file, and
  3. provide legal representation for complainants who decide to exercise their right of independent access to the Tribunal, and
  4. ensure that the Tribunal has the necessary resources to deal with an increased volume of complaints, and
  5. provide intervenor funding for equality-seeking groups.

- Model C: Enhance the Commission's Focus on Systemic Discrimination
  1. reduce the number of cases in which the Commission is responsible for investigation and carriage, by permitting the Commission to select the complaints that it will investigate and carry forward on the basis of their potential for broad impact on equality-seeking groups and/or their jurisprudential importance, and
  2. explicitly assign to the Commission a mandate to pursue strategic initiatives to address systemic discrimination, and
  3. create new standard-setting and audit powers for the Commission to enhance its ability to address systemic discrimination, and
  4. establish an independent right of access to a Tribunal hearing for persons whose cases are not selected by the Commission for carriage, and

5 impose enforceable time limits on the Commission's opportunity to select a case, and

6 provide legal representation for claimants who appear before the Tribunal without the assistance of the Commission, and

7 ensure that the Tribunal has the necessary powers, procedures, and resources, including disclosure procedures and wide subpoena and summons powers to provide an adequate substitute for Commission investigation, and

8 provide intervenor funding for equality-seeking groups.

- Model D: Permit Complainants to Bypass the Commission (Break *Bhadauria*)

1 remove all responsibility from the Commission for determining whether a complaint should be referred or dismissed, and

2 establish a right for any person who believes their human rights have been violated to take their case before the Tribunal, or

3 establish a right for any person who believes their human rights have been violated to take their case before a court.

Different models vary in their degree of emphasis on Commission responsibility for, and control over, individual complaints. Model A retains a high level of Commission responsibility for screening and carriage, and seeks to overcome unfairness and delay in Commission decision-making through narrowing the Commission's broad discretion and imposing time limits. Model B also retains a high level of Commission responsibility, seeks to overcome unfairness and delay in Commission decision-making, and also does away with the finality of the Commission's decision-making powers by opening up the alternative of independent Tribunal access for complainants whose claims have been rejected by the Commission. Model C combines the features of models A and B, and leaves open the possibility of the Commission advising and assisting people at the complaint-drafting stage, but shifts the purpose of Commission screening away from determining who gets access to the Tribunal to identifying cases for their test-case potential. Model C emphasizes the Commission focus on systemic discrimination and the means necessary to address it, a focus that has been underdeveloped largely due to the burden of screening and investigating a high volume of complaints. Participation for equality-seeking groups could be increased in Models A, B, or C through providing access for intervenors to participate in hearings and intervenor funding. Model D eliminates the screening and complaint carriage function of the Commission entirely, placing human rights complainants on the same footing as plaintiffs in ordinary civil litigation, and leaving open the question of the Commission's future role.

[Reprinted by permission.]

Chapter 14: Labour and Employment Law in the New Economy

14:100 THE CRISIS OF INDUSTRIAL RELATIONS AND LABOUR LAW

We have focused throughout this book on legal problems — employment contracts, bargaining units, strikes and picketing, labour standards, and the like. These are clearly important, but our preoccupation with them may have distracted us from some highly pertinent questions about the crisis that has affected our system of industrial relations and labour law for quite some time. A few examples from cases we have read will make the point.

- In *Cronk v. Canadian General Insurance*, above, section 2:420, at age fifty-five, after working there for twenty-nine years, a clerical employee "lost her job at a major Canadian insurance company when it made substantial organizational changes," although she "did nothing to cause the termination of her employment."
- In *Québec-Téléphone*, above, section 4:330, "increasing competition and rapid technological innovation" had led to a "progressive flattening of the hierarchical pyramid," pushing managerial responsibility down to employees at lower levels.
- In *Radio Shack*, above, section 7:421, officials of a multinational company waged a particularly vicious and protracted anti-union campaign — from their head office in Texas.
- In *Buhler Versatile Inc.*, also in section 7:421, U.S. competition law administrators required an American company to divest itself of a Canadian tractor factory that it had acquired in a takeover of another American company, and a Canadian entrepreneur began to run it without having much of an understanding of his collective bargaining obligations.
- In *White Spot Ltd.*, above, section 6:530, a restaurant chain franchised out one of its locations, and the labour board had to decide whether the employees of that restaurant would bargain as a separate unit or together with the other restaurants in the chain.
- In *Canadian National Railway Co.*, above, section 13:400, the CNR was shown to have practiced systemic discrimination against women who wanted to work in blue-collar jobs. The company was ordered to take significant remedial measures to ensure the hiring of women. This order was made at roughly the same time as the federal government was beginning to reduce its support for rail travel in favor of a user-pay policy, resulting in the abandonment of many rail services and drastic reductions in the CNR's workforce.

These cases and others we could easily identify amount to a catalogue of the causes of the present crisis: corporate restructuring and downsizing, technological change, globalization, privatization, and a changing workforce. That crisis — which is a complex, long-lasting, and worldwide phenomenon — manifests itself in ordinary cases that crop up every day in courts and labour boards and law offices. There is no hiding from it, no way of avoiding its consequences and implications in one's dealings with labour law clients, no possibility that it will leave unchanged most of what you have learned so far in reading this book. In this final chapter of the book, we will look at the impact of those factors and at some of the responses that are emerging to it. That is why this chapter may be the most important one of all.

Harry Arthurs, "Labour Law without the State?" (1996) 46 U.T.L.J. 1 at 4–7, 10–31, 43–45

The impact of the international economic and political system upon nation states has been discernible for half a millennium, although recent developments in information technology have certainly quickened the pace and magnified the consequences of globalization. Arguments over the state's responsibility for micro- and macro-economic policies have waxed and waned quite dramatically over the past two hundred years. Changes in technology, skills, knowledge, the organization of work, the structure of management and ownership, patterns of distribution and consumption, and the power of workers' collectivities have been recurring themes in discussions of industrial relations so long as there has been industry — and likely longer. So what is new about the new economy, the economy we are experiencing at the end of the twentieth century? As will be argued next, what is new is the convergence of these developments and their impact — admittedly, their variable impact — upon so many spheres and sectors of the economy and of social and political life. . . .

[W]e have become used to thinking of the nation state as three essentially congruent spaces: the political, the juridical and the economic. Consequently, we have operated on the assumption that a state which wishes to regulate its labour market is able to do so: the labour market lies within its economic space, and the relevant actors, institutions and processes inhabit its political and juridical space. This congruence of spaces, and the calculus of public policy-making which it supports, are being radically disturbed in the new economy.

Economic spaces are no longer co-terminous with the nation state (or are no longer perceived to be); now they extend across regional trade blocs such as NAFTA (North American Free Trade Agreement) and the EU (European Union), or are subsumed into global regimes, especially the GATT (General Agreement on Tariffs and Trade, now the World Trade Organization). Or more accurately, the economic spaces inhabited by some actors — especially multi-national corporations — extend beyond state boundaries. Other actors — trade unions, social movements, small businesses — generally continue to inhabit smaller spaces, associated with their traditional local constituencies.

Familiar political spaces — those conventionally defined by the boundaries of the nation state — are being dissolved by both centripetal and centrifugal forces. On the one hand, national sovereignties are shrinking and fracturing as their powers are devolved to smaller units, in response to efforts by ethno-cultural and other regional claimants to establish economic and cultural spaces in which their own interest and influence will dominate. On the other hand, supranational institutions — the EU is the leading, perhaps unique, example — are beginning to create political and juridical institutions which reach beyond the borders of individual states, and coincide with the larger economic space they are meant to govern.

Juridical spaces, by and large, remain formally aligned with political spaces, but there are important exceptions. Some supranational forums have been created, by treaty or by practise, in which norms are created or enforced at a higher level than the nation state. . . . And most importantly (however difficult it may be for lawyers to accept), in every site of social interaction, indigenous legal orders operate — often at arm's length from the legal order of the state. Thus juridical regimes governing the workplace in the new economy are not likely to remain forever those traditionally associated with the nation state. . . .

In the view of some observers, the present period is one in which we are experiencing a 'hollowing out of the state.' This arresting phrase is meant to call attention to the repeated and often successful attacks on the state's role in providing economic stimulus, regulation and a social safety net. At a minimum, the existing repertoire of such benign and purposeful state interventions is more likely to contract than to expand. . . .

What has all this to do with labour law?

The Canadian labour law system succeeded to the extent that it did during the post-war period — how well is a matter of debate — because it was lodged in a complex system of public policies, institutional arrangements and implicit and explicit understandings involving employers, unions and governments. We know this system by various names — fordism, corporatism, industrial pluralism — each of which emphasizes different causes and effects as distinguishing characteristics. However, as the system unravels, it becomes less important to debate or distinguish these than it is to point to the implications of their disappearance for the future of labour law as we have known it.

The most salient point is that however inclusive the consensus supporting the post-war system may have been, it has suffered important defections. Intellectuals and technocrats have become increasingly alienated from state-centred politics, after an attraction lasting three or four generations. Consequently, they are much less likely to argue for such important features of the labour law system as the efficacy of regulatory intervention, regional equalization, progressive taxation, public expenditure to offset the business cycle, or even the possibility that class differences can be mediated through state-sponsored collective bargaining.

The working class — a concept whose descriptive power always exceeded its emotive appeal — is divided within itself. Workers seem increasingly apathetic — even antipathetic — to labour organizations and labour parties; unions have failed to preserve old alliances with ethnic communities or to forge new ones with visible minority groups; and genders and generations seem to regard each other as opponents in a zero-sum competition for whatever is left of a depleting resource; regular employment. At the institutional level, unions are dismissive of the few vestigial traces of corporate noblesse oblige; corporations increasingly reject any conception of their own role which does not compute on next quarter's bottom line; and both mistrust government attempts to manage the economy, while seeking specific interventions favourable to their own interests or ideological beliefs.

As a result, long-established labour market institutions — unemployment insurance and workers compensation, for example — have come under devastating criticism and threat of fundamental revision. Labour law reforms, such as those initiated by Ontario's late NDP government, are perceived not as relatively minor technical adjustments to the existing system — which they were — but as a realignment of collective bargaining so fundamental that it could resuscitate a faltering trade union movement and/or bring capitalism to its knees. Systemic interventions, such as employment equity, were indeed introduced with relatively little resistance from major employers, but only because they were designed to have relatively little initial impact. And the symbolic significance of such innocuous measures as same-sex employment benefits has been allowed to eclipse their most important practical consequence: to adjust public policies so they no longer ignore well-established patterns of social behaviour.

In short, the Canadian version the new economy is characterized by fissiparous tendencies in politics and social life. These have created an environment hostile to the survival of the postwar labour law system and make its reform or renovation very difficult. Indeed, the fault lines in that system run right to its core: the nature and organization of paid work which labour law is meant to regulate. . . .

Most elements of our labour law system — collective bargaining, social security, workers' compensation, job training, employment equity, and even individual employment law — are based on a paradigm of industrial employment which prevailed in key economic sectors during the 1930s and 1940s, when essential elements of the system were first introduced. The paradigm envisages that an ideal-type worker with relatively long job tenure will perform standardized tasks under the direction of hierarchical management within an expanding economy of relatively large-scale production units. Obviously, this paradigm — and its ideal-type workers, employers, and jobs — never captured all of the varieties of employment to which postwar labour law applied. Indeed, this was the source of considerable tension within the system. For example, the pattern of short-term employment in construction and shipping effectively foreclosed access to lengthy procedures such as union certification, mediation, and grievance arbitration. Instead unions resorted to top-down organizing, whose consequences included violations of labour legislation, violence, and, in some cases, the demise of democratic unionism. Cyclical employment in seasonal industries, such as fishing, led to unexpected and unsustainable claims on the unemployment insurance fund. Traditions of collegial self-governance in universities cut across the labour-management dichotomy which is central to conventional collective bargaining structures. The presence of nationwide integrated operations in banks made them relatively impervious to unionization. Job training schemes for standardized tasks failed to meet the special needs of high tech employers. And plant- or company-based structures of employment relations proved unsuitable for dealing with industry- or economywide problems of labour market adjustment.

In the new economy, departures from the old ideal-types of production, management, and employment may be more than aberrations: they may become the norm. If so, they will constitute the crucial elements of a new paradigm of employment relations, which will require the development of a new system of labour law. This indeed is the argument of many students of the new economy. While their argument rests largely on an extrapolation of trends, rather than on current reality, it does seem that the old paradigm is rapidly losing its descriptive accuracy, and consequently its prescriptive power.

Indeed, it sometimes seems that almost everything is changing, at least in manufacturing. First and foremost, human labour is being replaced by machines, and increasingly by intelligent machines. From this, other changes follow.

Long production runs of standard products formerly compelled by the high cost of retooling are now being replaced by shorter runs of non-standard products utilizing more flexible technologies, which can be adjusted frequently and rapidly in response to consumer signals. Long production runs were what permitted employers to establish rigid job classifications, based on fixed functions and specific skill sets; job classifications were used in turn to define gradations of pay and entitlements to job progression and security. Now, job classifications — and the prerogatives built upon them — are being diluted or abandoned, as multi-skilled workers are regrouped into quality circles with shared responsibility for production and shared financial incentives. In the previous dispensation, control over technical specifications, quality standards, and production flows was most easily maintained by keeping the maximum number of operations within the firm. Now, computer-based information systems enable more and more firms to rely on networks of suppliers, contractors, and consultants to provide facilities, components, skills, and services as required. This in turn allows them to reduce their own cadre of employees to those required for core operations, and as a corollary, to some extent, to even out the peaks and valleys of demand and production by relying on dependable supplier networks. These networks may involve nearby feeder plants or, in some circumstances, production units in more distant regions and countries which offer the attraction of lower operating costs, especially lower labour costs.

These changes obviously affect workers individually and collectively. Old familiar job skills, and reward systems based on those skills, become obsolete. New forms of work knowledge, requiring different levels and types of education, are at a premium. In effect, one form of job property loses value and another gains it. But job property is not transferable from one company to another, much less from one person to another. The result is that there are winners and losers, and competition between them is waged on the basis of their relationship to old and new forms of job property. Thus different groups of workers compete with each other on the basis of geography (plant mandates), gender (men's — or women's — work), length of service (seniority rules), riparian rights (access to overtime), educational qualifications (computer skills), or other attributes. Unions are supposed to mediate amongst groups of workers with divergent interests and arguably have done so with some success. However, in the new economy, conflicts may become too frequent and too extreme for successful reconciliation. At some point, workers may opt instead to defend themselves by organizing along lines of skill or race or some other sharply defined identity. This would further weaken the union movement, which has been largely organized, at least since the 1930s, on the basis of common employment in a particular industry and firm.

The consequence of all of this is that employment in the manufacturing sector — the traditional mother-lode of good jobs and trade unionism — is being rapidly depleted. Nor do these changes affect only production workers. Clerical workers involved in recordkeeping and control functions have been replaced by computers. The ranks of shop-floor supervisors and middle managers have been thinned, and their responsibilities devolved, in order to 'empower' rank-and-file workers — or to force them to discipline themselves, depending on one's point of view. The result, possibly for the first time since the 1930s, is serious structural unemployment for all categories of workers in the relatively privileged — and paradigmatic — enclave of industrial employment.

By contrast, employment in the service sector has been growing apace, although here too information technology has prompted, or made possible, changes in the nature and organization of work. A growing and privileged cadre of 'knowledge workers' in the service sector, as in manufacturing, enjoys relatively attractive prospects, although often as consultants and contractors or in other non-standard forms of employment. But many service jobs have been lost to corporate 're-engineering' and restructuring, to the downsizing of government, to computerization and to other changes analogous to those which afflict the manufacturing sector. Consequently, the greatest area of growth in employment in the service sector appears to be the so-called mac-jobs — part-time, low-skilled, dead-end jobs.

Against this background, we can ask whether familiar labour law concepts are capable of capturing the emerging paradigm of employment in the new economy. Should workers in feeder plants be included in the same bargaining unit as those in core operations even though their employers are clearly not 'associated' or 'related' to the dominant firm they supply? Should the growing numbers of franchisees, contractors, and consultants in service industries be eligible for protection under employment standards or employment equity legislation?

To summarize, the new economy is characterized by a fairly dramatic decline in the stability and longevity of employment relations generally, and in the attachment of workers to particular trades, unions, employers, and industries — or even to the paid workforce.

This brings us to another change in the paradigm underlying employment. When one speaks of attachment to the workforce, as it was tacitly assumed to be fifty years ago, one was speaking of a workforce whose attitudes were shaped by experience of the depression and the war, a workforce with rising — but essentially modest — expectations, a relatively homogeneous workforce, and especially a male workforce. Of course, its composition has changed considerably in the intervening years. Homogeneity — if it ever really existed — is gone. Generational peristalsis has obviously complicated attempts to maintain something vaguely resembling full employment; now it will complicate attempts to continue to sustain the welfare state; and thus an aging population can be reckoned as a further crisis for the old labour law. Ethnic diversity is a challenge which was met (or evaded) relatively successfully in the postwar period; but diversity was not visible diversity then, and now it is. Race is definitely on the new agenda of labour law, at least in the larger metropolitan centres, and it forces us to confront equity issues at the very moment when we have a smaller margin of optimism, generosity, and social resources than we have had for some time. Moreover, reshaping labour policy with an eye to racial equity is all the more difficult because it cannot be done without at the same time reshaping virtually all social policies, including education, welfare, culture, and the justice system.

But of all of the changes in the workforce which undercut the old paradigm, none is more pervasive and powerful than changes in its gender composition. The war, as it turns out, was thought to have made the workplace safe only for men; women who were recruited into manufacturing and service work were rapidly displaced so that returning veterans could reclaim their jobs. But the feminist revolution which gathered momentum twenty years later has permanently changed the workplace: there will be no return to the early postwar years when women stayed at home and men went to work. This is not to say that the transformation of the labour force has proceeded smoothly: crude discrimination, pink ghettos, glass ceilings, and sexual harassment were all used as rearguard strategies to defend the old paradigm and those advantaged by it. Human rights legislation, pay equity, employment equity, rights for part-time — mostly women — workers, and other measures were mobilized in response, in part the cause, in part the effect, of attitudinal changes on the part of some employers and unions and the public in general. But while these measures modified the old paradigm, they did not wholly displace it.

Now the paradigm itself may be giving way. If, as seems almost certain, the workforce is going to contain a considerable contingent of women — and men — who want to reconcile the iron discipline of work with all that the rest of life offers and demands, the very notion of work is going to have to change. The direction, pervasiveness, and speed of change are subject to debate. To what extent the sociology of work can prevail over economics, and decades of law can prevail over centuries of culture, remains unclear. But what does seem likely is that as gender relations reshape employment relations, they will reshape labour law as well.

Finally, while the long-term trend in employment in advanced industrial countries is for the labour force to include an increasing proportion of knowledge-workers, it is not at all clear that our present labour law system is capable of accommodating this new and substantial presence. Egalitarian policies designed to ensure equitable access to jobs are more difficult to implement when recruitment is based on highly differentiated credentials, skills, and knowledge. Assumptions about an arm's-length relationship between workers and employers are less easily applied to what Galbraith calls the technostructure. The relatively clear line between workers and entrepreneurs blurs in the case of 'experts,' 'consultants,' or 'specialists' who survive from contract to contract, in effect practising serial monogamy in their working lives; their entitlement to bargain collectively or to be insured against unemployment or work-related injuries blurs likewise. . . .

Thus, if indeed there is something we can call the new economy, if the new economy does truly define the shape of a new paradigm of employment relations, we must be alert to all the nuances, variations, and contradictions which are likely to characterize any new system of labour law that may ensue. Indeed, precisely because of the contemporaneity, complexity and open-endedness of the processes of change, the new economy, the new paradigm of employment relations, the new labour law are all likely to be hybrids. They are likely to contain something of the past, present, and future, of supra-state, state, sub-state and non-state institutions, of law in all its pluralistic variants, of the public and private realm, of the global as well as the distinctively local. . . .

Free trade — first with the United States, then extending to Mexico . . . has brought many of these developments to the top of the Canadian public policy agenda. NAFTA is therefore a convenient point of entry into a discussion of the central issues.

. . . Although NAFTA does not purport to revise formal legal norms proclaimed and administered by competent Canadian legislative bodies — much less by private actors — it obviously does rearrange the complex web of social and economic, cultural, and political relations in which are embedded both state law and non-state normative systems. As those relations change profoundly, under the influence of NAFTA, so too does the 'living law' of both the state and the shop-floor.

. . . it has been argued that free trade is a 'conditioning device' deliberately adopted to habituate us to the acceptance of a particular set of values. As a conditioning device, it imposes coherence and discipline on our institutions and behaviours by restructuring the relationship between the state and civil society; it enhances the scope of the private market and the power of constituencies — such as transnational companies — which are perceived to benefit from liberalization of the economy; and it puts in question both the perceived feasibility and the legitimacy of alternative economic, social, and industrial policies. . . .

Various aspects of NAFTA produce this result. It removes tariff and non-tariff barriers behind which protected Canadian and Mexican industries have traditionally generated jobs and tax revenues; it allows already dominant US-owned industries to achieve further economies of scale; it reinforces US control over industrial and intellectual property upon which technology and technology-based industries depend; it facilitates capital flows and thus further exposes the relatively fragile Canadian and Mexican economies to punishing currency fluctuations; and it gives credibility to employer threats to move factories to wherever production costs are lowest, thus extracting wage concessions from workers and more favourable policies from governments.

The issue is not whether the positive consequences of free trade will, in the long term, outweigh the negative. Rather, it is whether free trade has helped to create a volatile environment in which, for some time to come, employers rather than workers or unions are likely to set the direction of labour law. . . .

Since Canada committed itself to a regime of free trade in October 1987, unions have suffered a series of significant setbacks at the hands of both governments and employers and, in the public sector, of governments-as-employers. Salary roll-backs, lost strikes, downsizing of public and private sector workforces, and other plagues and pestilences have fallen on labour's head throughout the period. But by and large, except in the public sector, these have not resulted from state labour law. Indeed, labour has even managed several legal victories — some perhaps pyrrhic, others ephemeral — which appear to refute the notion that free trade has destroyed the state's capacity to regulate the labour market, if it has the will to do so. . . .

Nor has free trade apparently influenced litigation outcomes, as might be expected.

. . . It is therefore tempting to conclude that the dog did not bark in the night, that the absence of tangible evidence of NAFTA's consequences demonstrates the absence of such consequences, that like Canadian legislatures, the Supreme Court and labour relations boards are not NAFTA-conditioned, and that the conditioning thesis is wrong, or at least overstated.

The temptation should, however, be resisted on two counts. First, conditioning does take time, and works its way back through the electoral and judicial process only after it has succeeded in changing public expectations and values. Indeed, it can be argued that the defeat of Ontario's NDP government, and the repeal of crucial elements of its labour legislation, is an early sign that conditioning is proceeding apace.

Second, to extrapolate somewhat from the original thesis, conditioning does not require that NAFTA should operate only by producing specific changes in the juridical character and content of labour law. Rather, it suggests that NAFTA should be perceived as part of a permanent institutional framework which helps to ensure that employers and workers, policy-makers and voters, will act routinely and reflexively in response to a set of 'givens' — baseline assumptions about what is possible and desirable — which express and facilitate neo-conservative values. . . .

These propositions, moreover, are regarded not as mere social constructs but as hard 'facts' which cannot be challenged. Indeed, there is an impressive body of experiential evidence to support each of them: restructured economies, sustained fiscal, exchange, and political crises; industries reconfigured, relocated or recumbent, persistent high levels of unemployment — and also just enough 'success stories' to provide positive reinforcement for individual, corporate, and governmental behaviour which conforms to the givens which NAFTA embodies and advances.

Thus, conditioning can work directly on the actors in the labour market without the necessity of enshrining the givens in legal rules. . . . Thus, the labour relations act need not be repealed or even amended: rather, as in the United States, it can be left to wilt and wither. . . .

Because of the special importance of workplace norms and processes in labour law, it is important to understand how free trade has affected management and labour, the primary actors whose episodic confrontations and daily interactions shape workplace relations.

. . . it is very pertinent to the future of Canadian society and the Canadian economy that many firms no longer have directors or a CEO with roots in Canada to make the case within the corporation for the preservation of Canadian jobs or the support of Canadian institutions. In terms of Canadian labour relations and labour law, it is also very pertinent that firms no longer have a resident industrial relations manager with authority to decide how to handle grievances, what to do when confronted with an organizing campaign or a strike, or whether to comply fully or minimally with human-rights legislation. Instead, corporate policies, made in and administered directly from the United States, and reflecting US experience and values, are projected directly into Canada through the agency of US-based directors and managers.

The consequence may well be that — even without a change in public policy or political power — Canadian employees, on the periphery of the corporate empire, will experience more determined employer resistance to unionism, less willingness to support the social safety net, and other changes in the law of the workplace as it emerges from labour-management encounters, company policies, operating manuals, and shop-floor behaviour by supervisors. . . .

There is a certain irony in this growing reincorporation of Canadian corporate structures, personnel, and strategies into those of American-based parent firms. It coincides with precisely the opposite phenomenon on the labour side of the equation. Whereas in 1980, about 50 per cent of Canadian workers were members of international unions, all with headquarters in the United States, by 1991 this had fallen to 30.5 per cent.

One might imagine that cross-border union alliances would be essential, if workers hoped to confront the power of multinational enterprises. . . . However, the spectacular secession of the Canadian Auto Workers from the United Auto Workers in 1985 might suggest that even the closest possible integration of manufacturing operations — under the umbrella of an intergovernmental sectoral agreement — is not regarded by unions as a sufficient reason to preserve their international affiliation. . . .

I have tried to suggest how the new economy is likely to transform the labour law system of the old fordist economy and why the new paradigm, the new labour law system, is likely to be characterized by serious and possibly irreconcilable conflict. To put the modest reach of my argument in perspective, several points must be restated. First, changes in labour law are not autonomous: they derive from changes in our political economy, although they also help to hasten or reinforce, and occasionally retard, those changes. Second, parts of the 'new' economy will continue to look pretty much like the old. There, fordist modes of production and management are likely to persist; familiar statutes may well remain on the books; there may be no dramatic rupture in patterns of social behaviour and legal regulation. And third, since some of the distinctive legal institutions of the new economy are being shaped by non-state agencies which tend to favour stability over disorder — even global corporations may so perceive their interests, in certain circumstances — continuities as well as discontinuities may characterize the new paradigm of labour law.

With these threshold reservations, what remains is for me to explore two particular institutional settings in which the labour law of the new economy might be shaped. . . .

It has been argued that, at some point, global 'spot market capitalism' will be displaced by a more orderly and regulated version of the free market. . . . In this view, some effort must be made to re-create something resembling state intervention at a level higher than that of the nation state, a level more nearly commensurate with the regional and global markets within which key corporate decisions are being made.

On present performance, the prospects for success are not brilliant. The ILO has been trying without much obvious success to promulgate and enforce trans-national norms of labour law since 1919. The NAFTA side accord on labour sets a very low standard of aspiration. Only the example of the European Union holds out some modest promise that transnational capitalism may try to create a social market, characterized by a floor of labour standards and rights sufficient to avoid the destabilizing effects of poverty and despair, and to forestall illicit low-wage competition from within the market and from external sources as well. However the European experiment is the product of special historical circumstances, is by no means an undiluted success, and may be very difficult to reproduce on a global scale.

Attempts to regulate labour conditions and practices on a transnational basis — however desirable — are problematic both conceptually and in practical terms. Transnational labour standards will obviously be attacked as intruding upon national sovereignty, as a form of disguised protectionism designed to preserve jobs in the advanced countries, as a device to prevent developing countries from industrializing, even as an attempt to force labour standards down to a lower transnational norm in those countries which exceed it. In practical terms, given the difficulty of setting and enforcing labour standards in a domestic context, it is hard to imagine that regulation could be accomplished transnationally. Nonetheless, we can probably look forward to a spirited debate over whether and how to establish transnational labour standards, and a good deal of experimentation with the production of law within transnational labour market institutions. . . .

The other important site in which law will be produced in the new economy is, ironically, the very site in which it has always been produced: the workplace itself.

. . . without understating the importance of power relations as a determinant of the indigenous law of the workplace, it is also true that other forces are highly influential. Among these are the specific architecture of authority and the organization of work within the firm; technology and associated requirements of skill and knowledge; established custom and usage in the workplace; and the power of pre-existing movements of solidarity in the surrounding society, including movements based on union organization, ethnicity, communal traditions, and culture. While some of the outcomes of these forces may well be explicit rules — operating manuals, collective agreements, local by-laws — much of the normative regime is almost certain to take the form of implicit understandings and tacit ways of doing things.

The indigenous and the implicit do not necessarily translate into the benign or the progressive. Employer power and state power are still strong conservative and coercive elements in the production of workplace norms. And other forces, indigenous to the workplace and the surrounding society, are not necessarily democratic or equitable: they may simply seek to reproduce hierarchy and hostility. Nonetheless, if we should not romanticize the corporation and workplace as institutions which produce labour law, neither should we underestimate their importance as a source of normativity and, therefore, as a focus of observation and analysis.

This, I suggest, would be an ironic conclusion after two centuries of state intervention and state labour law, and after perhaps two decades of globalization: the enfeeblement of the nation state and the failure to produce an effective substitute for the state at the transnational level may refocus attention on local struggles, on indigenous, implicit, and informal lawmaking, on movements which have not become juridified but which actually draw their strength and sustenance from grass-roots involvement.

14:110 What Is the "New Economy"?

What is the "new economy"? What does "globalization" mean? Many have been searching for answers to these questions. It is widely agreed that changing patterns and rules of trade and investment, technological innovation, and trajectories of national and international economic policies are leading us to a new context for, among other things, labour policy.

World Bank, *World Development Report 1995: Workers in an Integrating World* (New York: Oxford University Press, 1996) at 51–53

CHANNELS OF GLOBAL INTERACTIONS

International trade is the first avenue by which most countries feel the impact of economic integration. Volumes of goods and services traded across borders have grown tremendously in recent years, accounting for about 45 percent of world GDP in 1990, up from 25 percent in 1970. . . . In 1990, 17 percent of the labor force in developing and former centrally planned economies worked directly or indirectly in the export sector, with exports to the richer countries accounting for two-thirds of this employment effect. There was also a rapid shift to higher-value-added activities: the share of manufactures in developing countries' exports tripled between 1970 and 1990, from 20 percent to 60 percent. This rise marks a radical change in the international division of labor since the 1960s, when developing countries exported primary commodities almost exclusively. With the expansion of labor-intensive exports of manufactures, trade has come of age. . . .

Capital has also become increasingly mobile, ever in search of the best returns. Gross capital flows (inflows plus outflows), an admittedly imperfect measure of capital mobility, rose from 7 percent to 9 percent of GDP in developing and transitional economies during the past two decades. . . . Capital controls have been relaxed and are easily evaded anyway. Today capital moves more readily into successful countries and out of those countries where returns on investment are outweighed by the risks. . . .

International migration of people in search of work is the laggard in this story. Annual migratory flows from developing countries (total inflows and outflows) are no greater now, relative to population size, than in the early 1970s, at about one emigrant per thousand inhabitants. . . . The overall effect of international migration is much smaller than that of capital or trade: only about 2 percent of people born in low- and middle-income countries do not live in their country of origin. Migrants send home about $75 billion a year, about one-third the volume of net capital flows. Some 2 million to 3 million new migrants now leave developing countries each year (both legally and illegally), about half of whom go to industrial countries. For the latter, migration from developing countries translates into 1.5 new immigrants per thousand inhabitants per year, the same as in 1970. Migration between industrial countries has fallen since 1970 from 2.5 migrants per thousand inhabitants in 1970 to 1.5 per thousand in 1990. The foreign-born share of the population in industrial countries — currently about 5 percent — has been rising however, because of the slower growth of the native population.

United Nations Conference on Trade and Development, *World Investment Report 1994: Transnational Corporations, Employment and the Workplace* (New York: United Nations, 1995) at 117–20, 122–26, 146–49, 151–52, 156

The world economy can be described along two distinct, but interrelated, dimensions: *market* exchanges and *production* activities that link consumers, producers and suppliers within and across national economies. The extent to which these economic agents engage in cross-border relations varies with market size and location, technological and other domestic economic advantages, and the openness of the policy framework and the links established through markets or production activities can involve many elements, in particular, capital flows, goods, services, people, technology, information and ideas. International integration describes the spread and deepening of these linkages across national boundaries. . . .

International economic integration is often seen as the spread of market linkages through greater trade and factor flows, and government action to reduce obstacles to these flows is the main stimulus to increased integration. However, this type of *shallow integration* ignores participation in the international division of labour at the level of production. *International production* refers to a firm controlling productive assets in more than one country, whereby control is typically established through FDI [Foreign Direct Investment], but can also be exercised through various non-equity forms. As such, international production goes beyond arm's length market exchanges by internalising cross-border exchanges related to productive assets located in different countries under the common governance of TNCs [transnational corporations]. As soon as FDI becomes a chosen vehicle for establishing cross-border linkages, the character of international economic integration changes from shallow to *deep integration*. However, deep integration differs from shallow in ways other than the chosen channel of establishing cross-border activity. Because FDI, unlike market-based exchanges, does not end with the initial transaction, it establishes a more lasting linkage between economic agents located in different countries. Consequently, and this is a central contention of this chapter, the type of strategy adopted by TNCs matters very much to the nature of deep integration and, by implication, to the way in which deep integration and shallow integration interact to establish a wider globalization process. Corporate strategies related to international production initially involve the common governance by TNCs of a limited number of corporate functions, often in the framework of a vertical division of labour, and as more and more functions are included under the common governance — both along vertical and, increasingly, horizontal lines — international production takes on a more *integrated* character. . . .

A. GLOBALIZATION: A LONG-TERM PERSPECTIVE

The expansion of markets, the evolution of firms and the process of international integration

In a sense, all economic activity takes place within national boundaries. . . . More significantly, decisions with a bearing on economic growth and competitiveness — such as the decisions to invest and innovate — have traditionally been discussed as the product of national firms under the auspices of their national States. Accommodating the steady growth of cross-border economic activity has produced considerable disagreement among economists. On the one hand, international trade theorists have assumed a world of complete markets and perfect competition to explore the benefits of shallow integration in the absence of TNCs and FDI, where the choice between flows of factors and goods is essentially arbitrary. On the other hand, industrial organization theorists have assumed a world where firms must constantly choose between trade and FDI in their drive to expand activities across borders, and deeper integration reflects the strategic decision of firms to a world of cross-border market failures with significant transaction costs, in which the control over assets located in different countries certainly matters.

In recent years, these two perspectives have begun to converge on a view of the world economy with porous borders, in which TNCs are catalysts of fundamental change. In particular, the growth and complexity of cross-border economic linkages are embedding the national organization of economic activity within a global system of processes and transactions. . . .

For much of the nineteenth century, the interplay of these national and international forces created a turbulent world. The unchallenged industrial leadership of the United Kingdom translated into political control across large parts of the world economy. The birth of new nations and the consolidation of older powers was a difficult process, often reinforcing industrial and military ambitions. But as military conflicts subsided and economic challenges rose, a period of political stability and consolidation coincided with an unprecedented spread of cross-border linkages. The period 1870–1913 has, in particular, been seen as one in which a virtuous circle of rapid economic progress and international integration established a core global economy. Because the period is generally considered as representing a high point of integration, it provides a useful benchmark against which to measure contemporary changes in the world economy. . . .

B. REBUILDING INTERNATIONAL ECONOMIC INTEGRATION

Between the beginning of the First World War and the end of the Second World War, many of the linkages established across the world economy over the preceding forty years were severed. Wartime controls persisted after 1918 and, although economic growth accelerated in the 1920s, the international financial system was marked by increased instability, outflows of long-term capital from industrial countries slowed dramatically and world trade failed to recover to its pre-war level. The international economic order crumbled in 1929 with the world recession and the insularity of national recovery strategies.

Since the Second World War, during a period of unprecedented growth and macroeconomic stability, these linkages have been gradually rebuilt. Both domestically and internationally, post-war economic development has rested on the successful repair, expansion and regulation of market linkages. A new international economic order has slowly evolved, under which increased cross-border flows of goods, services and factors have reinforced the domestic consensus on economic growth. Two features of this order have been of particular importance to the renewal of the process of international integration: a facilitating international policy framework and technological progress. But, the wider impact of these features on international economic integration has been strongly conditioned by the strength of economic growth and a broad tendency for convergence (in terms of the structures of economic activity and productivity performance) across parts of the world economy over the past fifty years.

The new international policy framework

With the turmoil of the 1930s still very much in mind, a new international order to facilitate a more open trading arrangement and stable monetary conditions was an immediate concern of post-war policy makers:

- Initial efforts to create an International Trade Organization as part of the Havana Charter were stillborn. Instead, the promotion of trade was based upon a multilateral principle of reciprocity under the General Agreement on Tariffs and Trade (GATT). The successive rounds of GATT negotiations sought a more open trading environment through the steady diminution of border barriers and the removal of intentional discrimination against foreign goods, services and firms. Despite the undoubted increase in non-tariff barriers, notably in industries such as electronics and automobiles, the implementation of a wide range of bilateral and unilateral trade measures, in parallel with GATT rounds, further liberalized world trade. Measured in terms of tariff reductions, progress has been impressive (table III.1 [which shows that average tariff rates on manufactured products in developed countries dropped from the 20%–40% range in 1913 to around 10% in 1990]). With the conclusion of the Uruguay Round, the average tariff on industrial goods in developed countries will be below 4 per cent. Such measures have proceeded furthest within regional trading blocs (although it is arguable as to whether such developments divert, rather than create, trade). Overall — and especially in light of the conclusion of the Uruguay Round, the establishment of the single European market and the implementation of the North American Free Trade Agreement — it is clear that the current international trading environment is more open than at any time since 1945 and, arguably, than before the First World War.
- A primary objective of the 1944 Bretton Woods agreement was to create a more orderly and stable basis for dealing with balance-of-payments problems and for regulating longer-term financial transactions between countries on the basis of fixed exchange rates pegged to the United States dollar. The aim was to provide the necessary financial lubricant for a reconstructed world economy. In the late 1950s, the restoration of currency convertibility among the leading industrial nations began a long-term trend in the direction of financial liberalization and increased international capital mobility. The Code of Liberalisation of Capital Movements and the Code of Liberalisation of Invisible Operations, adopted by the Organisation for Economic Co-operation and Development (OECD) in 1961, went some way to institutionalize this consensus. A series of regional initiatives, such as the European Community's directives on capital movements, has pressed further in the direction of a complete liberalization of finan-

cial markets, particularly since the late 1980s. Although the breakdown of the Bretton Woods system in the early 1970s created a more volatile international financial environment, the general trend has remained one of increasing liberalization of financial markets. Indeed, since the late 1970s, unilateral measures to dismantle barriers to financial flows, coupled with the proliferation of new financial instruments, has transformed the international financial system.

. . .

- The international framework governing the flow of technology has, in part, been subsumed by other regulatory structures. Laws controlling mergers and acquisition, joint ventures, cooperation agreements and local-content legislation, in so far as they relate to technology transfer, have been liberalized in recent years. However, the flow of proprietary knowledge across borders has evolved separately from those governing other flows. Many of the international rules on intellectual property rights date back to the previous century. In the post-war period, the formation of the World Intellectual Property Organization (WIPO) in 1967 and various regional initiatives in Europe and Africa strengthened the framework on proprietary knowledge. The proliferation of domestic legislation and bilateral and multilateral agreements during the 1980s, culminating in the inclusion of intellectual property rights in the Uruguay Round negotiations, anticipates a common system of intellectual property protection consistent with higher standards of protection in more developed countries and covering a wider range of instruments. Parallel to this trend, much of the legislation — regional and national — introduced in developing countries in the 1960s and 1970s to screen and control the technology-transfer process has been relaxed or dismantled in areas such as royalty payments between parent firms and affiliates, authorization and duration of contracts, and registration procedures.

- The regulatory framework for *foreign direct investment* has evolved more unevenly than that for either trade or financial flows. A multilateral agreement on global investment principles was discussed in 1947 as part of the draft Havana Charter but failed to gain approval. In the following two decades, multilateral negotiations on the protection of foreign-owned assets were hindered by differences over a government's right to expropriate foreign property, and FDI legislation remained firmly grounded at the national level, with considerable variation in frameworks. Efforts to construct a more systematic FDI policy framework began in the mid-1960s, through bilateral investment treaties and expanding regional and multilateral negotiations. Bilateral investment treaties first emerged in the 1960s between European countries and their former colonies (predominantly in Africa). These have steadily grown in number — by January 1994 there were 570 such agreements — and have expanded in geographical scope over the past two decades. . . . In 1976, OECD conducted multilateral negotiations over a broad range of investment issues, the outcome of which was the Declaration on International Investment and Multinational Enterprises. Efforts in the United Nations and the World Bank have pushed further in that direction. So did the Uruguay Round in the area of services and trade-related investment measures. Given the nature of international service transactions, the General Agreement on Trade in Services, in particular, introduces a fledgeling FDI regime for the services sector, thus covering more than half of world-wide FDI flows. Regional efforts to construct a more open FDI regime have been organized in the European Union and North America (the United States-Canada Free Trade Agreement and, more recently, NAFTA). All these efforts have been complemented — and in many ways been overtaken — by a rapid liberalization of restrictive national laws since the mid-1980s. . . . As more countries liberalize, convergence to a common FDI framework is occurring in areas such as the right of establishment; national treatment; repatriation rules; and compensation payments.

- In contrast to capital markets, *labour markets* have remained largely closed at the national level. In general, tight controls on international flows of labour were introduced in the traditional migrant-receiving countries during the 1930s. The subsequent removal of these controls (with alternating periods of tightening and relaxing) over the period since the Second World War has been governed by economic conditions, as well as political and cultural legacies. More recently, however, regional initiatives, such as those within the European Union, the European Economic Area and NAFTA have eased restrictions on the mobility of labour, especially business and professional persons, and the Uruguay Round provides incipient rules for the negotiation of progressive liberalization of the temporary movement of persons supplying services.

Unlike the gold standard, this regulatory framework has been established through a purposeful process of institution building beginning at Bretton Woods, but gradually encompassing a growing body of international institutions. Over the past fifty years, this framework has created a more open — although uneven — environment for engaging in cross-border exchanges.

The enabling technologies

It is no accident that the major surges in international integration — during the period 1870–1913 and in the period since the Second World War — have been associated with new organizational and technological developments. . . .

. . . [A] key feature of the period since the Second World War has been the development and (since the late 1960s) the widespread diffusion of new technologies based upon the microelectronics revolution and, in particular, what has come to be seen as the major new generic technology: information technology. This defines a new techno-economic paradigm since the introduction of information technologies has 'such pervasive effects on the economy as a whole that they change the style of production and management throughout the system.' . . .

Growth and convergence

The underlying causes of the rapid growth after the Second World War are undoubtedly complex, and beyond the scope of this chapter. But of particular importance to the process of international economic integration, rapid economic growth, for much of the past fifty years, has been accompanied by a gradual convergence in economic performance. Its most visible manifestation has been a decline in the relative economic strength of the

United States and the emergence of Japan as a leading industrial centre. Albeit more circumscribed, there is some evidence that the convergence in economic structures and consumption patterns has not been confined to the core economies alone. The rise of the South East Asian 'miracle' economies has been the most visible indication of a wider convergence 'club.' But for much of the past fifty years, structural changes across the developing world have evolved in a similar direction; manufacturing is now a more spatially dispersed activity and manufacturing exports dominate the trade and investment profiles of many developing countries. Furthermore, structural changes have turned most countries into economies in which the services sector is the largest sector — in the case of all developed countries, accounting for over half of domestic output. This structural change has an increasingly important impact on the structure of the world economy and is becoming an increasingly prominent source of international transactions.

These factors have combined to re-establish the process of international economic integration that was lost during the period between the two world wars. To some extent, this process has been a continuation of trends established during the benchmark period 1870-1913; but it has also introduced important changes in the world economy, particularly in the sphere of international production. . . .

F. THE UNEVEN LANDSCAPE OF INTEGRATED INTERNATIONAL PRODUCTION

Despite the operation of powerful forces creating a higher degree of global integration of economic activities, it should not be assumed that there is a smooth, even or inevitable evolution towards a uniform system of integrated international production. Technological developments in transport and communications have not removed the influence of space — geography still matters. Furthermore, TNCs continue to operate on a rough surface of regulatory complexity and uneven factor availability, and do so in a variety of ways — governments still matter. In addition, TNCs originate in specific places and, through the influence of routine and inertia, carry with them some of the attributes acquired there. Consequently, a high level of diversity continues to exist.

Geography still matters

To begin with — and notwithstanding their geographical reach — TNCs are still substantially creatures of their domestic environments. Certainly, the argument that TNCs have, in effect, become de-nationalized is only a partial interpretation of the real world. As has been observed: 'However great the global reach of their operations, the national firm does, psychologically and sociologically, 'belong' to its home base. In the last resort, its directors will always heed the wishes and commands of the government which has issued their passports and those of their families.' In fact, the boards of directors of most TNCs continue to be predominantly of home-country origin; TNCs still continue to gain some clear advantages from their long-standing involvement with their 'domestic' economies; and 'mutual interest' between TNCs and their home-country governments continues to be strong.

Equally important, technological changes have not removed the relevance of location for many production activities; in fact, in some cases, rapid technological changes, including organizational innovations, such as lean production, in which trust and reliability are at a premium, appear to reinforce geographical differences. Furthermore, local and regional economies of agglomeration have not disappeared. High value-added functions continue to be attracted to locations with the right mix of complementary industries and skills. Thus, even as capital becomes more mobile, TNCs and their affiliates continue to derive their competitive advantages in part from interacting with the local economy. Consequently, 'differences in national economic structures, values, cultures, institutions, and histories contribute profoundly to competitive success. The role of the home nation seems to be as strong as or stronger than ever. While globalization of competition might appear to make the nation less important, instead it seems to make it more so.'

The influence of geography is apparent in FDI flows. . . . [C]ountries undertake a disproportionate share of their investment in the economies of their regional partners. Canada, for example, had 71 per cent of its FDI stock in the United States and Latin America in 1990. Italy had 74 percent of its investment stock in the European Union in 199. The intraregional share of investment is not quite as high in East Asia as in Europe and North America. . . .

Governments still matter

The reshaping of today's world economy, no less than in earlier periods, is an interactive process between firms, markets and states. The importance of the state in influencing the strategies, structures and behaviour of TNCs and, therefore, the nature and extent of integrated international production, lies in its dual role as regulator of specific activities and as container of specific assemblages of political, economic, social, cultural and institutional attributes. But it is this particular assemblage of both components that is likely to mold domestic businesses and affect their international nature: 'host governments wield the power to limit the extent of, or even to dismantle, the MNC integrated manufacturing and trade networks with more regulations and restrictions on foreign investments and market access.'

But governments can, and do, create, modify or even destroy comparative and competitive advantages. In imperfectly competitive markets, first-mover advantages, externalities and spillovers are still seen to require governments to intervene in favour of their domestic firms. In some countries, for example, in the United States, this has led to a growing demand for a more strategic policy stance. This shift is particularly evident with regard to high-technology industries that are seen to be at the centre of a country's competitiveness. Within the broad tendency towards greater deregulation, therefore, there are significant differences between individual states. And despite the undoubted changes that have occurred in its autonomy, the State remains a critical actor in the organization of the world economy and a major source of continued unevenness in the extent and form of integrated international production. . . .

G. GLOBALIZATION AND INTEGRATED INTERNATIONAL PRODUCTION

Globalization is often taken to connote fully integrated markets for final goods and services and for factors of production. This, which has been termed here shallow integration, implies the entry and exit of economic agents into markets, largely unhindered by political boundaries and regardless of their place of origin. Over the past fifty years, economic and political factors have combined to produce a level of shallow integration at least comparable to that reached before the First World War. The result is a considerably more complex pattern of international specialization and exchange than was present when the Bretton Woods institutions were established, a pattern, furthermore, that encompasses virtually all countries in the world. . . .

The domestic management of the integrated international production system

. . . [T]he system of integrated international production is particularly vulnerable to microeconomic and macroeconomic imbalances. Not only does integrated international production generate many more linkages, both vertical and horizontal (thus increasing complexity and, consequently, vulnerability to disruption), but also the high degree of specialization in an international division of labour implies that no firm or industry — or indeed national or regional economy — within this system can operate effectively without relying on many other firms and industries in the system. Furthermore, infrastructure and human-resource needs are particularly high under these circumstances; rates of investment may need to be higher than those prevailing under the simpler integration strategies of international production; and there appears to be a premium on maintaining such demanding — because of their intangible nature — institutional supports as trust and cooperation. Moreover, with such a high level of interdependence, shocks or disturbances in one part of the system are likely to be transmitted with considerable rapidity to other parts. . . .

Thus, whilst the desire of many countries to benefit simultaneously from their participation in world markets is perhaps unprecedented, it also gives rise to a *paradox in national policy making*. On the one hand, international linkages and interconnections have created a perception that effective national policies (and their implementation) for adapting to a more interdependent world economy have gained rather than declined in importance. On the other hand, these same pressures make the identification and targeting of purely national objectives increasingly complex and have narrowed the scope for independent action. . . .

The policy paradox becomes all the more challenging because many more policy issues that were previously the responsibility of national governments — including national technological systems, labour-market regulations and competition laws — become open to international concern, the stronger the linkages established through integrated international production. To date, the challenge posed by the internationalization of domestic policy issues has had its most dramatic effect in areas where economic and social assets are closely intertwined, reflecting furthermore the fact that social assets tend to be more rooted in their local or national environments. This is particularly true of labour markets. Although TNCs help to organize the international division of labour and exert considerable influence over national patterns of industrial activity and employment . . . , their impact on employment and workplace conditions is dependent upon macroeconomic, structural and technological factors that are mediated by domestic policies and organizations. The direct labour-market effects of FDI on employment are thus difficult to quantify. But international economic integration has widened the options available to TNCs in dealing with a dispersed labour force. Cross-border plant relocation is only the most visible — and drastic — option available to firms in their efforts to restructure under pressure from global competition; automation, diversification of product lines, product innovation and subcontracting have all been made easier by labour market deregulation and more decentralised negotiating and bargaining structures. The weakening of traditional institutional representation of labour may also make it easier for firms to respond to increased international competition through the option of rationalizing and reducing direct costs rather than seeking a longer-term — more expensive and riskier — commitment to invest in human capital and other created assets.

Given the nature of the integrated international production system, retraining and an effective welfare programme are as integral to it as to earlier systems. They are also as expensive, particularly at a time when a growing number of firms and industries need to adjust to new competitive pressures and a growing share of the labour force faces poor employment prospects. The widening mobility gap between capital and labour has, in part, contributed to the declining autonomy of national social and labour policies. For instance, taxes to ensure adequate social programmes may encourage the exit of the more mobile factors, further increasing the burden on the least mobile. The destructive potential of this logic lies behind European Union efforts to devise a transnational social policy. More generally, because the systemic interdependence of economic relations occurs across an increasing number of national borders to reach the global level, the governance pressures of integrated international production are likely to be particularly pronounced. But in important respects, existing policy frameworks — because they are still defined by national parameters — are inadequate for dealing with such pressures many of which are now international in character.

[The United Nations is the author of the original material. Reprinted by permission.]

✳ ✳ ✳

A crucial and very difficult question is: what should federal and provincial governments do as a matter of domestic labour policy (or human capital policy), in response to the "new environment"? In the new economy, human capital policy is more important than ever. Most other factors of production (capital, services, ideas, information, raw materials and so on) are mobile, but labour remains largely immobile, for reasons of both fact and law. Thus, labour may provide a margin of competitive advantage on which state policy can be of use. On the other hand, in the new economy individual states find it increasingly difficult to establish adequate labour policies. And, as always, labour policy is highly contestable.

What has happened in the Canadian labour market in the recent past within the areas we have been looking at? What has been the domestic impact of globalization?

Report of the Advisory Group on Working Time and the Distribution of Work (Ottawa: Supply and Services Canada, 1994) (Chair: Arthur Donner) at 6–8, 27–35

CHANGING PRESSURES ON FAMILIES AND INDIVIDUALS

Families of today face three major, and often competing, pressures: the need to care for children, especially pre-schoolers; the need to care for aging parents; and the need to maintain family incomes, which now often require that two people have paid work.

In one of every three dual-earner families, the wife's earnings account for more than 40 percent of the family's total income. Clearly, few people have jobs that, by themselves, enable their families to live according to a standard they deem to be comfortable. For the past 20 years, with stagnant real wages, the standard has been maintained because people are working longer hours and because more women have entered the work force. Consequently, there has been an unbroken rise in the labour force participation of married women. The number of families headed by single parents is also on the rise. These trends have created a difficult situation for those, especially women, who combine work with household responsibilities. The statistics confirm that women's work on the job and at home has increased in the new environment.

A generation ago the 'typical' Canadian family had a male breadwinner with a female homemaker running the household. Almost three-quarters (70 percent) of families were configured in this way in 1961. By 1991, less than one in five households looked like this. Even among families with children under age six, less than a third fit this stereotypical image. Indeed, by 1991 the stereotype had flipped on its head: over 60 percent of 'nuclear' families in Canada (two parents and children) were dual-earner families. More than 55 percent of lone parents were also working by 1991.

Canadians working outside the home for pay, especially women, still have important and time-consuming family responsibilities. For example, while the full impact of a greying population is still more than two decades away, 51 percent of employees currently provide some care to an elderly person.

The real social revolution of this generation has to do with increasing female labour force participation rates, particularly among those who are raising young children. In 1981, 48 percent of women with young children were in the labour market. By 1993, the figure was 63 percent. Consequently, there is a growing need and demand for parental or family-related leaves and more flexible hours.

At the same time, more people are working long hours. Unusually long hours of work result not only from employers' demands but also from the need of families for more income. As well, long hours of work are the consequence of down-sizing; those who remain are expected to do more and often feel less secure. The effects of rapidly changing job prospects are personal as well as society-wide. While people worried about the 'empty-nest' syndrome in the 1970s and 1980s, the 1990s are marked by an increasing number of young adults who remain or have returned home because they are unemployed or underemployed.

There is a 'time crunch' counterpart to the income and jobs polarization described. Family incomes are being squeezed in the 1990s. To the extent that they are being maintained it has been at a cost — the lost time with partners, children, friends and in the community.

If one factor unites the unemployed, the precariously employed, the fully employed, and those who usually work long hours ('the over-employed'), it is stress.

. . .

Research shows that most people are happy in their work, but satisfaction levels have declined as job security has diminished in a time of high unemployment and a jobless recovery.

According to a 1992 Statistics Canada survey (reported in *Profiling Canada's Families*, The Vanier Institute of the Family, and the Canadian Committee for the International Year of the Family, 1994), one-third of Canadians say they are constantly under stress, trying to do more than they can handle.

CHANGING PRESSURES IN THE WORKPLACE

In today's economy the buoyant optimism of the 1950s and 1960s is missing. The result is a sense of insecurity that is especially harsh in the modern workplace — whether it is experienced in the corporate boardroom, in the managerial office, or on the plant floor. For it is in the context of work that some of the most complex, most subtle transformations to modern society are taking place.

The nature of work, the hours, the place, the responsibilities, the people, the future — the likelihood of employment itself — have changed and will continue to do so. Not only has work changed, the way work is done has altered significantly. . . .

The real costs of technological change are imposed most painfully on those who cannot adapt, such as older workers or businesses that cannot keep up with or acquire the new technologies. Moreover, while technology creates some jobs, it displaces others. Employers must find skilled workers. Employees must learn new skills, which may quickly be overtaken by the next round of new technology.

The pressures of ever-increasing competition and changes in the organization of work have intruded into even the more sheltered sectors of the economy. They ultimately reflect demands by customers for longer business hours, higher quality products, and better and friendlier service. The broader public sector is also under pressure to maintain and improve services, while responding to fiscal restraint. . . .

NON-STANDARD WORK

The Industrial Revolution in the 19th century moved most work from the home and the field to the factory and the office. In the 20th century the growth of the service economy has generated new jobs in stores, restaurants and hotels, as well as in hospitals, schools, and government offices. In the past, people produced goods or services according to a known schedule. Today, by contrast, more and more of us work irregular hours, uncertain schedules, for ourselves, for more than one employer, at several locations, or from home.

But fewer and fewer of us work full-time, for the full year, for a single employer. Profound changes to the way working time is structured have important implications for society. These must be addressed by employers and workers, by unions, and by political, social, and economic policy makers.

A 'standard' job is usually defined as a full-year, full-time job with a single employer. Most employees still hold such jobs but, according to the landmark 1990 report of the Economic Council of Canada, *Good Jobs, Bad Jobs*, fully one-half of all of new jobs created between 1980 and 1988 were 'non-standard.'

The most common form of non-standard employment is part-time work, defined by Statistics Canada as a job of fewer than 30 hours a week. Short-term, temporary or contract jobs, which may be full-time or part-time, are also considered non-standard. Individual workers may find that these jobs meet their own needs, or they may try to combine part-time and temporary work to obtain the hours of work and income they want. The final major type of non-standard employment is known as 'own-account self-employment,' that is, people selling goods or services who do not employ people themselves.

After more than a decade of major changes in the job market, non-standard employment has grown to the point where the standard job is still the norm, but only just. In 1992, six of every 10 Canadian earners worked full-time hours for the entire year. (In the vast majority of cases, they would have worked for the same employer, though some changed jobs during the year.) Only one woman in two held a full-time, full-year job, compared with two of three men.

Part-time and temporary jobs have grown faster than full-time permanent jobs partly because of such temporary factors as the recessions of the early 1980s and early 1990s. But it is also clear that a major structural change is well under way in Canada, as in other advanced economies. It is thus quite possible, and even likely, that the non-standard job of today will become the 'standard' job of tomorrow. . . .

It is important to underline the fact that non-standard jobs are not necessarily 'bad' jobs. Some part-time jobs provide good pay and benefits, as well as stable employment and prospects for advancement. They are preferred by many working people, particularly women with young children. . . . Some temporary workers gain valuable experience that leads to a permanent job. Among non-standard workers are highly paid consultants and contractors, whether professionals or tradespeople, who have left regular jobs to make more money, find more independence, or gain more satisfaction from their work.

However, many non-standard jobs do not provide individuals with predictable hours or a predictable income. Both are important . . . , especially for lower-paid workers.

As a society, we should be concerned less with the growth of non-standard jobs as such and much more with the growth of precarious, contingent, 'just-in-time,' dead-end jobs that do not give employees adequate access to the rights, standards, and opportunities most of us usually take for granted. It is a particular cause for concern that the line that tends to divide standard from non-standard jobs also often separates men from women and divides visible minorities from the rest of the community.

. . .

A permanent job provides greater assurance of stability of income than a contract job, even in today's uncertain world. Full-time permanent jobs are much more likely to provide access to such non-wage or salary benefits as pensions and health, dental, and other benefits. They are also much more likely to be unionized and to be protected by the terms and conditions of a collective agreement regarding promotions, layoffs, and dismissals. Finally, prospects for advancement in a given firm and in the labour market in general are probably much brighter for permanent than for non-standard employees.

As discussed later in more detail, employees in non-standard jobs may also have difficulty gaining access to some of the rights and benefits we often assume come with any job, including protection under employment standards legislation regarding hours of work and wages or access to Unemployment Insurance and Canada/Quebec Pension Plan benefits.

The Advisory Group on Working Time and the Distribution of Work believes that basic fairness requires that ways be found to improve the conditions of workers in non-standard jobs. An equitable redistribution of work time means that disparities between standard and non-standard workers should be addressed and that conditions for those at the bottom should be improved. Such changes are relevant to the job creation potential of work-time redistribution. Changes to conditions of part-time work will be necessary if there is to be an easier transition between full-time and part-time jobs.

FORCES BEHIND THE GROWTH OF NON-STANDARD JOBS

The growth in non-standard work is the result of several interrelated changes — some driven by the shift to a post-industrial society, some by technological and organizational change, and some by intensifying competition in national and international markets.

The Service Economy

In the early post-war years, a large proportion of the paid labour force were men employed as blue collar, hourly paid workers (or as salaried managers) in the goods-producing sector: resources, manufacturing, the transportation industries that moved the goods, and construction. Many aspects of these traditional industries have changed profoundly but, in the main, they still employ men working full-time and still generate much of our national output. However, the proportion of the national work force directly employed in these sectors has fallen precipitously because of weak demand, substantial increases in productivity (output per employee) and, to some degree, because of the loss of labour-intensive manufacturing industries to other countries.

From the 1960s to well into the 1980s, while those industries declined, another important long-term social and economic change was taking place. Retail, hospitality, tourism, entertainment, and personal services industries grew in terms of their share of the total labour force. Because many of these jobs in offices, stores, hotels, and restaurants have always been part-time, part-time employment now accounts for a larger proportion of all jobs.

. . .

. . . One significant result of the increased participation of women in the paid labour force has been greater need for services that replace some of the unpaid work these women did in the home. Another consequence has been a growing demand for services outside 'normal' working hours. These changes have fuelled further growth in the non-standard work force in stores, fast-food outlets, and such personal service industries as house cleaning, and child care.

A 'Just-in-Time' World

Another major factor behind changes in the work force has been the need or demand by employers for 'just-in-time workers' to accommodate the demands of 'just-in-time production.'

In the 1980s, North American manufacturers (led by the auto industry) began to emulate the just-in-time production techniques of Japanese industry, based on the recognition that low inventory of both production inputs and final product translates into significant bottom-line savings. Such new computerized technologies as programmable machine tools have also made possible a major shift from mass production of standardized goods to more customized products made in smaller batches.

In the 1920s, Henry Ford said that you could have a Model T Ford in any colour you wanted, as long as it was black. By contrast, an assembly line in a modern auto plant today can produce several varieties of the same basic models with a wide range of options. . . .

Today, some clothing retailers directly and immediately transmit sales information to suppliers, so that production responds almost instantaneously to changes in the market. A run on red denim shirts one day will result in immediate orders to the manufacturer for more red shirts, to be delivered within days.

The result is more variety for consumers and lower inventory costs for retailers and producers. But the price of variety and speed in delivering services and products is variability and uncertainty in the labour market. A company must be prepared to produce and deliver small orders rapidly, on demand.

Inevitably, demand fluctuates from one week to the next, even in a growing market, making the supplier want to hire people who will also work variable hours, on demand. This flexibility is often gained by reducing the number of core, permanent, full-time workers to a minimum, making the regular hours of work more variable, or increasing reliance on people whose hours of work can be easily changed: temporary workers, part-time workers without fixed hours, or so-called self-employed contractors such as homeworkers.
. . .

The phenomenon of just-in-time production and delivery has spread rapidly to the service sector. From law offices and accounting firms to advertising agencies to restaurants, people are expected to provide service as and when it is needed, at the same time that consumers are demanding unlimited availability of service. Seven-day-a-week retail and consumer service operations are now the norm, and 24-hour-a-day coffee shops have been joined by all-night copy shops and round-the-clock international financial operations. Increasingly, employers and employees are living in a just-in-time world.
. . .

There is a constant ratcheting effect as enterprises and individuals operating on non-standard hours demand goods and services from those who have not yet made the shift. Every company working on a just-in-time basis has a ripple effect, causing uncertainty in its own work force and for the companies and employees it touches.

Heightened Competition and the Lean Workplace

Another major factor behind the growth of non-standard employment has been the intensification of business competition, both nationally and internationally. Increased international trade and the increased mobility of investment capital have led to strong pressures on employers to lower labour costs.

Costs are certainly not the only factor in competition, and wages are not the only — or necessarily the most important — cost factor for employers. Businesses can succeed in highly competitive markets and still provide decent wages and benefits through high productivity and by offering high-quality goods and sophisticated services. But the reality remains that many enterprises have felt forced to deal with the changing competitive environment, or with demanding shareholders, by lowering their wage costs.

Costs can be reduced by increased reliance on temporary and contract workers who, by definition, do not participate in the private pension and benefit plans that are common among large employers and can easily add 25 to 30 percent to the bill for wages. Use of self-employed contract workers also often means that the company does not have to pay social security premiums to governments on behalf of those persons.

In recent years, many larger companies and governments have contracted out services that used to be performed in-house. There are many reasons businesses have focused on their 'core' operations. Among them is cost reduction. A contract worker providing a service may receive lower wages and benefits than an in-house employee and regular full-time employees are much more likely to be covered by the terms of a union collective agreement than are temporary, contract, or part-time workers.

Business analysts have applauded the emergence of 'leaner' organizational structures in both the private and public sector. There is a strong tendency to reduce the regular, full-time, permanent ('standard') work force to the minimum possible. Several employers frankly told the Advisory Group that, after several years of down-sizing and restructuring, any decision to hire a new, permanent employee is treated as a major, even a 'million-dollar' decision. . . .

Part-time Work

Today, more than two million Canadians, or about one in every six employees (17 percent of workers as of July, 1994), work part-time. Their presence in the labour force has approximately doubled over the past two decades because of the slow growth of full-time jobs. Indeed, only half of all new jobs created between 1979 and 1993 were full-time, the result of two recessions that wiped out much of the full-time work created in periods of recovery.

Almost one in four jobs (23%) in 1993 were part-time jobs. The proportion of such jobs is higher than the proportion of part-time workers since some people — 6 percent of the labour force — combine two part-time jobs so as to become 'full-time workers.'

. . .

Many part-timers are excluded from the benefit plans that regular full-time workers take for granted. Only one in 10 part-time workers belongs to a private pension plan, compared with about one-half of all full-time workers. A Labour Canada survey (mainly of large employers in federally regulated industries) found that, in 1985, 60 percent of part-timers were not covered by extended health and dental plans, 70 percent were not covered in the case of long-term disability, and 80 percent did not belong to a pension plan. By contrast, virtually all full-timers (95 percent) were eligible to receive these benefits. Coverage is much lower for non-regular part-timers working for smaller organizations.

Those working less than 15 hours per week do not qualify for Unemployment Insurance, even if they combine part-time jobs.

Eleven years have passed since the federal government appointed a Royal Commission on Part-Time Work (the Wallace Commission), which recommended that regular part-timers receive the same benefits coverage, on a prorated basis, as those working full-time. As the commission and others have argued, equal coverage is important not only to secure better treatment for people in part-time jobs, but to facilitate easier movement between part-time and full-time work. A full-time clerical worker or nurse, for example, will think twice — if at all — about reducing hours if this means giving up pension benefits, even if she or he is prepared to trade some income for more free time.

Increasingly, responsible employers, including the federal government itself, have recognized the need to extend pension and other benefits to part-timers, and pension legislation in most jurisdictions has been amended to allow part-timers to be included in pension plans. The government of Saskatchewan recently introduced prorated benefits coverage for most part-timers, prompting considerable discussion in the business community. This coverage has also been recommended by the recent Thompson Report on Employment Standards in British Columbia.

The Economic Council's report *Good Jobs, Bad Jobs* confirmed the Wallace Commission's finding that, on average, part-time jobs pay about 25 percent less than comparable full-time jobs, as defined by occupation and industry. However, little or no systematic information is available on pay gaps between full-time and part-time workers occupying similar positions with the same employer, although many collective agreements specify pay rates that apply to both groups.

Some of the pay differences may be due to differences in experience and skill requirements. Others may be the result of the fact that, for complex and varied historical reasons, part-time workers are much less likely to be unionized than those who are employed full-time. Even in a unionized environment, the part-timers may not be covered by the collective agreement that applies to the organization's full-time workers.

Many employers and unions have seen the need to close the pay gap and have taken action to do so. There has also been some reconsideration of the provisions of labour legislation that allow for full-time and part-time workers to be divided into different bargaining units.

Not much information exists on the opportunities for advancement available to part-time workers. The Advisory Group learned that some large private-sector employers have consciously implemented human resource policies that allow, and even encourage, movement from full-time to part-time and back to full-time over the course of a career. This, as we note in the next chapter, is certainly a leading-edge practice.

The Advisory Group also learned that in some unionized organizations, the City of Winnipeg for example, part-timers not only receive the same pay and benefits as full-time workers, they also accumulate seniority on the same basis — from the date they are hired. This effectively means that, over time, someone initially hired as a part-timer can, if he or she wishes, move into a suitable full-time job as it becomes available.

The Province of Saskatchewan recently passed legislation that requires employers of more than 50 people to offer suitably qualified part-time workers first access to additional hours of work as those become available, thus effectively allowing part-timers to move to full-time status over time.

Temporary and Contract Work

Many Canadians have always worked in full-time jobs that are temporary because of purely seasonal factors — agriculture, logging and fishing, for example. Jobs in construction tend to be short-term because they are seasonal, but also because workers must move from project to project and often from contractor to contractor. Artists and performers usually go from one full-time temporary job to another. Generally speaking, people in these sectors do not expect to work full-time for the same employer throughout the year, and a variety of policies have been developed to respond to their economic needs (e.g., Unemployment Insurance, multi-employer pension plans, and sectoral rather than individual employer-based bargaining in construction).

More recently, economic restructuring and the recession have negatively affected workers in a wide range of jobs, from manufacturing to transportation, from the plant floor to the boardroom. In the recession from 1990 to 1993, nearly one in three working Canadians suffered at least one period of unemployment. . . .

Far from doing much to help those for whom part-time work is not a matter of choice, or is meant to act as a stepping stone, governments appear to have taken the lead in creating the temporary labour force that is having a particularly serious impact on young people trying to gain access to full-time, continuing employment.

The Self-employed and the Return of Homeworking

The instability that has rocked Canada's industrial and commercial world has moved many thousands of people into a new kind of business — their own — and into a new workplace — home. Ironically, the organizational and technological revolutions of the late 20th century are unwinding the world of paid office and factory employment brought about by the Industrial Revolution and are creating new cottage industries.

Excluding farmers and fishermen, fewer than one-tenth of working Canadians are self-employed, and that category includes such traditional types as lawyers, small retailers, and independent tradespeople as well as such new groups as computer consultants and workers, formerly employed in factories, who now produce goods in their own homes.

Among the sectors with significant levels of self-employment are construction (one in five workers); transportation (one in 10 workers, including taxi drivers and independent truckers); trade (one in 10); insurance and real estate agencies (also one in 10); and business services (one in five).

Over the past decade, self-employment has grown about twice as fast as regular employment, as many companies and public-sector bodies have contracted out services that used to be provided in-house by regular employees. Self-employment seems to have grown particularly rapidly among older workers: approximately four in 10 are 45 years of age or older.

A Statistics Canada study found that, in the past decade, self-employed workers in most sectors have suffered declines in their inflation-adjusted income, probably in part because of intense competition. However, it is likely that incomes vary substantially within a sector.

The Advisory Group found particular grounds for concern in the situation of a subgroup of the self-employed, those often referred to as 'dependent contractors.'

The term self-employed often implies that the individual concerned controls his or her own hours and other aspects of work, but the term may mean simply that the terms of the employment relationship have been altered by an employer who wants to be free of obligations. This is most clearly the case when someone who used to be an employee — such as a garment worker in a factory — becomes a homeworker with a sewing machine, selling all of her production to her former employer. The former factory worker turned homeworker may well lose standard benefits of employment (a minimum wage for time worked, vacation pay, UI and CPP/QPP coverage) even though the real nature of the employment relationship has not changed.

A 1993 survey of Chinese-speaking homeworkers in Metro Toronto conducted by the International Ladies Garment Workers Union found that 58 percent were working very long hours (61 to 75 hours per week), that 62 percent had hourly earnings below the minimum wage, and 87 percent were not receiving vacation pay as mandated by minimum employment standards. Some homeworkers work in the same kind of conditions that spawned popular outrage and legislative action in the late 19th century.

We do not really know how widespread abuses are, precisely because homework is hidden. Homeworkers are individuals isolated in the home. That is why at least one province, Ontario, now requires contractors using homeworkers to hold a permit.

Today, some of the world's largest corporations are contracting out production to smaller companies that, in turn, subcontract to even smaller firms and ultimately to homeworkers. Sophisticated computer systems link sales to a new — and very old — point of production, the worker's home.

Homeworking exists in a number of sectors. Electronics manufacturers employ homeworkers doing routine assembly tasks in their own homes. Because of modern technologies, homework has surfaced as well in such unexpected areas as fast food delivery or customer service. Using a phone installed by the company, a person sitting in her own home and being paid on a per-call basis takes calls and passes on information via computer. Many large organizations, including the federal government, are encouraging some office workers to work at home, linked to the office through fax and modem. Conditions of work undoubtedly vary a great deal, and some individuals welcome the opportunity to work at home. What is common to all these situations, though, is the potential for isolation of the individual and exclusion from the benefits of a 'normal' employment relationship.

Theoretically (most often legally), people who are nominally 'self-employed' but, in practice, work continuously for a single client should be considered employees and have access to the same rights, benefits, and protection as standard employees. Legally and morally, a woman working for a business in her home should receive at least the vacation pay that she would get if employed on the employer's premises. The same is true of sick pay, coverage for Unemployment Insurance and Canada Pension Plan benefits, and other services. In practice, however, it appears that even basic observance of employment standards by some employers of 'dependent contractors' is not being enforced.

One basic problem is lack of information regarding the nominally self-employed who are really dependent contractors working for others on a regular and continuing basis.

A second problem is more general and has to do with enforcement of labour standards. There are grounds for concern regarding a system that generally requires an employee, who may well feel vulnerable to dismissal, to formally file a complaint before an investigation will be undertaken. There have been suggestions that the authorities should take a more active stance, for example by carrying out periodic audits of compliance with labour standards.

A third problem is the uncertain and ambiguous line dividing the truly self-employed from dependent contractors. Is a taxi driver self-employed because he or she is paid by the fare, or is she or he an employee of the taxi company that dispatches those fares in return for a fee? Generally, taxi drivers qualify for Unemployment Insurance benefits and, in some provinces, have been able to join unions that collectively bargain with taxi companies. However, groups of comparable dependent contractors in other jurisdictions are still considered to be self-employed and do not have access to the protection of employment standards and labour legislation.

A fourth problem relates to the pay of dependent contractors. A home-based worker is often paid by the piece or by the customer served rather than according to the time spent on the job. Even highly experienced workers may earn below — well below — the statutory minimum wage for time actually worked.

In today's economy and society there is a growing group of own-account and precariously employed workers — many of them immigrant and visible minority women — who are working under conditions that the great majority of Canadians, including most employers, would deem to be unacceptable. There is a clear need both for more analysis of the changes under way and for a rethinking of the way employment standards are defined and enforced.

[The *Report* is a publication of Human Resources Development Canada. Reproduced with the permission of the Minister of Public Works and Government Services Canada, 1997.]

✳ ✳ ✳

Seeking a Balance: Canada Labour Code Part I Review (Ottawa: Supply and Services Canada, 1996) (Chair: A. Sims; Members: P. Knopf & R. Blouin) at 21–29

THE NEW LABOUR RELATIONS ENVIRONMENT

The Changing Workplace

In the past ten years, we have witnessed rapid change in the structure of work and workplaces regulated by the *Canada Labour Code*. However, while new types of work are emerging, much traditional work continues, particularly in the federal jurisdiction. In this section we discuss some of the more profound changes and their consequences for labour relations.

Deregulation and Enhanced Competition

Ten years ago, the workplace governed by the *Canada Labour Code* was, in many areas, highly regulated without much real competition. There was also a great deal of government ownership. Over the past decade, regulation and government ownership have diminished rapidly and competition has increased.

Examples of deregulation include the 'Open Skies' policy and the revisions to trucking regulations. The federal government has withdrawn from ownership of major employers such as Canadian National and Air Canada and has adopted a more arm's length relationship with the Canada Post Corporation. More recently, the federal government arranged to sell its air traffic control system and announced its intention to do the same with marine transportation and the St. Lawrence Seaway.

The elimination of the subsidies known as 'the Crow rate,' payable under the *Western Grain Transportation Act*, has introduced new competition into the grain trade. Whereas in the past there was an economic incentive to move all grain through Canadian ports by rail, there is now the possibility of exploring alternate routes, either in the event of a work stoppage, or on a long term basis.

Free trade has added a further competitive element. In several industries, the removal of tariff and other barriers to doing business with or through the United States has exposed Canadian businesses and their employees to the need to remain competitive with their American counterparts.

The competition created by deregulation and free trade is breaking up some of the more traditional bargaining patterns. When a small number of bargaining relationships (one or two unions with one or two employers) negotiated for major industries, they tended to negotiate together, or at least to negotiate pattern agreements where wage rates and working conditions were very similar. The new competitiveness has put wage rates and, as a result, comparative operating costs, back onto the bargaining table.

This increased competition is having a profound impact on collective bargaining in the federal sector. In the past, a strike or lockout might carry little or no risk of loss of market share; the same event today can result in a major loss of business. Unions and management have had to adjust their strategies appropriately. This new reality may have served to reduce the number of stoppages and their severity.

Privatization and Government Cutbacks

To reduce costs and the level of services provided, government continues to transfer jobs to the private sector, or to eliminate them completely, including many of its own support services such as printing and security. This change puts public sector unions in a defensive mode, as this type of work tends to go to smaller employers where unionization rates are lower and organizing tends to be more difficult. In many cases, when the federal government contracts out work that it previously performed itself, the work not only ceases to be covered by the *Public Service Staff Relations Act*, but ceases to be in the federal jurisdiction at all. Employment functions, such as caretaking or printing, when removed from a federal department or agency or a federally regulated private enterprise, generally fall under provincial legislative competence.

This trend has also had an impact on the overall labour movement, of which the public sector unions are a major part. Government cutbacks make it that much more difficult for government and organized labour to communicate freely concerning government's role as legislator. The government is seen frequently to be wearing two hats in its dealings with organized labour: legislator and policy maker on the one hand; and the country's largest employer (and in a cutback mode) on the other.

Changes in Technology

. . .

Changing technology has had a number of important impacts on the workplace. The most obvious impact has been the automation of many jobs, resulting in large scale layoffs and seemingly intractable unemployment problems.

A second and more subtle impact has been the increase in the ability of management to monitor and control the way work is performed. The computer can now keep much closer track of the costs, performance, time-frames and profitability of various forms of work. This information has made it safer for employers to have much secondary work done outside of the traditional enterprise, heightening concern at the bargaining table over job security for employees of the core enterprise. Another feature of this facility to contract out work is the trend away from stockpiling products and supplies in favour of 'just in time' delivery systems, where producers and suppliers carry the responsibility for maintaining a steady supply of goods and raw materials to major manufacturers.

Technology also affects styles of management and forms of workplace communication, subjects which we address later in this report.

The Compaction of Work

The catch-phrase 'doing more with less' applies to each worker as much as the entire workplace. Increasingly, fewer and fewer employees are doing more and more work. At the same time, unemployment figures remain alarmingly high. This is an important area for policy consideration by governments and others, although one largely beyond the scope of this report.

Part-time, short term and casual work is increasing in importance, and in the 1980s accounted for 44% of total employment growth. These types of jobs typically involve lower wages, fewer benefits, and less security than more traditional employment. This in turn is leading to a polarization of our workforce; full-time secure workers making comparatively more income, while workers with less security making comparatively less.

This results in several social issues. At a time when government is trying to reduce its liability for social service benefits like old age security, an increasing segment of the population is losing access to the type of private pension and benefit plan arrangements that could make them self-sufficient in their retirement.

The emergence of an underemployed and poorly paid class of workers impacts unduly on those who already find their job opportunities restricted, exacerbating the problems of gender, race, age and disability discrimination.

This also creates the occasional backlash against those who are organized, who are seen, by some, as the fortunate beneficiaries of this polarization of jobs. An unsettling resentment of the organized can develop among those who face bleak opportunities for employment.

Training, Innovation and Adjustment Strategies

More than ever, employees will have to retrain at least once in their careers, and training is no longer just something employees acquire outside of the workplace. Increasingly, training is an important part of work itself. Training is not just learning to do something, but learning to adapt and innovate, to do the work better. Workplace training and workplace innovation are merging areas.

Training is as important for growing industries as to those that are in decline. In the latter case, retraining is a vital part of employee adjustment programs, necessary for the development of new skills to meet new challenges.

Training, innovation and workplace adjustment are areas where government can play a key role as facilitator. So too can joint committees of labour and management. Government already promotes sectoral councils and other tri-partite institutions. Labour and management clearly have a common interest in responding to the needs and opportunities created by change.

The New Involvement of the Parties

There is a belief by some commentators that collective bargaining has become a system opposed to change, a brake on much needed industrial restructuring. Unions are accused of being the new conservatives, resisting change and seeking to preserve the status quo. This viewpoint may be due to institutionalized unemployment which has made the labour market a buyers' market, and to the economic restructuring which has led to a reduction in the overall number of jobs in many workplaces.

Unions reflect and represent the concerns of their members. The loss of benefits and potentially, the loss of work, frequently put unions into a defensive posture. What is probably more significant is that employers are now using collective bargaining to achieve industrial change. The demands of employers rather than the demands of unions are now increasingly the focus of negotiations.

Styles of Management

There has been a steady evolution from a rather hierarchical style of management to a new form of 'flattened' management. Beneath all the buzz words is the fact that restructuring has led to a reduction in the numbers of managers in many Canadian businesses. These fewer people now have increased responsibilities, and there is a need for new, and often more collegial ways of getting work done. Increasingly, this means having employees in a bargaining unit make or at least participate in some of the decisions previously reserved exclusively to management. . . .

A side effect of this reduction in the number of managers is the employer's increased vulnerability to strike action. . . . A reduced management complement means less flexibility in this area and explains some of the new importance attached to the question of replacement employees.

Management itself is changing rapidly. Managing no longer means simply maintaining order and predictability according to a set of established rules, but rather keeping pace with changing priorities and finding innovative and effective ways to meet new challenges. This requires new types of leadership skills, emphasizing cooperation, teamwork and flexibility. This can lead to impatience with old style confrontational collective bargaining and contract administration approaches. At the same time, it does open up new opportunities for improved labour-management relationships.

Union Structures and Approaches

As workplaces change, so do unions. The past decade has seen the merger or amalgamation of many major trade unions, including several that play an important role in federal collective bargaining. This is partly a response to the actions of the Canada Labour Relations Board which consolidated bargaining units with several large national employers in order to reduce fragmentation. It is also partly a natural process, as unions consolidate into larger structures for greater efficiency and strength.

In many cases, as unions have amalgamated, they have broadened the base of services offered and their range of activities. Major unions now have legal departments and highly developed training and research facilities. These help educate union members in the bargaining, arbitration and dispute resolution processes, and labour economics. Most unions have also developed a very sophisticated understanding of the industries in which they operate, contributing new depth to the overall bargaining process.

Styles of Negotiation

One must be wary of the allure of new styles of negotiation which come into fashion every few years. However, one must be sensitive to the voices of those who have been through years of traditional adversarial forms of bargaining and who are saying that there must be a better way to do things.

One of the most promising trends we observed across the country was a growing awareness of the advantages of more principled styles of negotiation, compared to the more traditional position-based approach. Change is clearly taking place, but it comes hard in some industries where old behaviour patterns run deep, and old rivalries and animosities are difficult to replace.

. . .

Our traditional style of bargaining, at its worst involved labour and management each putting forward elaborate and often exaggerated lists of demands, meeting together to 'horse trade' over those demands, while at the same time bluffing, threatening and posturing in support of their positions. This could go on for months, or even years, until intense negotiations occurred only at the eleventh hour, when compromise was sought to avert a work stoppage. Many settlements were achieved by this process. However, the focus tended to be on the demands and the arguments in favour of those demands, rather than on the underlying interests of the parties in the dispute. This form of negotiation tended to achieve a collective agreement, but often did not concern itself with long-term problem solving.

This style of negotiation has been changing, not only in labour relations. Much has been written on new negotiation practices, and parties are trying out these techniques both at the bargaining table and in their day to day work. Encouraging the process is the growing recognition that effective labour-management relations requires an ongoing relationship built on mutual respect and continuous problem solving. The growing availability of training in workplace problem solving also helps this process.

Two impediments, however, continue to hinder the growth of this new attitude to labour-management relations. First, some unions remain wary that employers engage in this sort of dialogue only when they need labour's cooperation because of problems ahead, such as difficult downsizing. All the elaborate mechanisms do not disguise the bad news, and this generates understandable cynicism in some circles. The second barrier is the very out-dated public stereotype of labour-management relations. Bargaining always seems to be described in its worst form. Labour and management dialogue is considered ineffective unless it is confrontational and involves colourful posturing full of ten second media clips. The resulting public misconception often makes it difficult for union leaders to convince their membership that a better informed participatory form of negotiation is more effective.

No labour code could or should prescribe bargaining styles for the parties. Each set of negotiations will take on its own dynamic that reflects the history and culture of the relationship of the parties and the direction they will take during the term of the agreement that is being negotiated. All a labour statute can do is to foster a culture of responsible problem solving and give the parties the affordable supports that are necessary to bring that about.

The International Environment and Obligations

Canada is a trading nation. Canadian businesses and unions cannot operate in isolation. They work and thrive in the international context and must gain the respect of the global community as well as pay heed to global competition. Consequently, any considerations about the future of collective bargaining and the *Canada Labour Code* must be made in light of Canada's international situation and obligations.

Impacts of Global Competition

The labour component of exports is becoming increasingly important. It is easy to say that our labour relations environment must help us be competitive; both labour and management recognize that without markets there are no jobs. But we must decide the types of jobs we wish to develop and sustain, and the social and economic values that will support our overall competitiveness.

Each of our competitors has different labour policies, just as they have different resources and different strengths within their workforces. When we compare ourselves to other nations, we must be cautious not to compare ourselves with only one element of each society. Canada, like every country, faces an integrated set of possibilities: a low wage economy comes with low domestic consumption; high levels of education increase the ability to compete in areas of high technology; an innovative and flexible workforce can adapt quickly to new competitive situations.

Our choices, taken together, determine our ability to compete. A country cannot simply adopt one aspect of another nation's strategy without recognizing the impact that this will have on other domestic policies. We may be tempted, for example, to modify our labour laws and other aspects of our social policy to attract investment. Where laws can be improved within Canada's overall labour and social context, such ideas should be adopted. But we must be cautious of an unthinking downward spiral, where we strip our laws of their balance and protection in the name of economic flexibility, without regard to the social consequences. To make these choices sensibly, we must be conscious of the way our system of labour relations actually works and, we must be confident that, despite occasional conflict, it will help to keep Canadian labour productive and competitive.

This is particularly true in our dealings with the United States, because of its importance not only as a trading partner, but also as a principal investor in our economy. American laws are in some respects similar to Canadian laws, but there are subtle differences. For example, American employers spend much more on third party insurance programs to cover health care. Americans also customarily spend more of their own funds on higher education. We make no comment on which social policy is right, but simply point out that one cannot extract particular aspects of a country's labour policy for comparison without looking at the undertaking compromises and consequences.

[The report is a publication of Human Resources Development Canada. Reproduced with the permission of the Minister of Public Works and Government Services Canada, 1997.]

14:200 NEW RESPONSES

The state's authority largely stops at its borders, even though business activities and labour disputes can cross borders. Thus, one of the most difficult challenges presented by the new paradigm is that of somehow creating industrial relations systems — and legal-regulatory institutions — that are congruent with the global or transnational dimensions of large multinational corporations.

14:210 The International Labour Organization and the World Trade Organization

The International Labour Organization (ILO) was founded in 1919, in the aftermath of the First World War. The quotation below from Albert Thomas of France, one of the ILO's founders, reflects a noble view of the organization's transnational role. The subsequent excerpt suggests that the historical project of building a transnational regime of labour regulation may call for new tools. Some of those tools are already within the ILO's institutional arsenal, but others will require greater interaction with the international trade system and with private actors in the economy and in civil society.

Albert Thomas, "The ILO: Its Origins, Development and Future," reprinted in (1996) 135 Int'l Labour Review 261 at 276

> Even if the ILO should only be a scientific information service at the disposal of all employers, workers and students, who are seeking the social justice which is the guarantee of international peace, even if the Office only registers the progress made in various countries, even then the ILO would be an invaluable cog in the machinery of social evolution. Even then it would still be worthy to hold the attention and to utilise the activity of men who would still keep in their hearts a more daring ideal, but who, in the present confusion, see no other effective means of ameliorating poverty immediately or of hastening the advent of a juster world.

Werner Sengenberger, "Restructuring at the Global Level: The Role of International Labour Standards" in W. Sengenberger & D. Campbell, eds., *Creating Economic Opportunities: The Role of Labour Standards in Industrial Restructuring* (Geneva: International Institute for Labour Studies, 1994) 394 at 403ff

INTERNATIONAL LABOUR STANDARDS AND THE ILO

> Labour standards are set at various organizational levels, such as the establishment, enterprise, industry, region, nation and international economy. The need for providing standards at the international level was increasingly felt as the opportunity of competing through wages and working conditions expanded with increasing cross-border competition in Europe in the late nineteenth and early twentieth centuries. In the international debate which culminated in the foundation of the International Labour Organization (ILO) under Article 19 of the Treaty of Versailles in 1919, labour standards at the international level were opposed by some countries on the grounds that they would handicap them on the international market by increasing their costs relative to other countries not covered by the common rule. For example, the ratification of the Hours of Work Convention, which was the first Convention adopted by the ILO in 1919, was slowed down by this consideration. Others, on the contrary, argued that international agreements to set standards would ensure that competition was not at the workers' expense and would in fact amount to a code of fair competition between employers and between countries. This argument was in fact embodied in the Preamble of the Constitution of the ILO which

states that 'the failure of any nation to adopt humane conditions of labour is an obstacle in the way of other nations which desire to improve the conditions in their own countries.'

It was perhaps not by accident that the ILO was created as an autonomous body at the end of the First World War, when nations had just passed through a period of political and social disaster. At this time there existed — as was the case later after the Second World War — the 'community of suffering' which can give rise to sufficient consensus capable of generating international order. There was agreement in the industrialized countries in 1919 to seek to create an organization apt to set international labour standards in order to relieve the social effects of international economic competition, and, more generally, advance justice in relation to the social conditions aggravated by the ravages of industrialization and the appalling working environment caused by it. The principles that 'universal and lasting peace can be established only if it is based on social justice' and 'labour is not a commodity' form cornerstones of ILO philosophy.

The following more specific objectives of the ILO are stated in its Constitution:

(a) regulation of working hours, including the establishment of a maximum working day and week;
(b) regulation of the labour supply;
(c) prevention of unemployment;
(d) provision of an adequate living wage;
(e) protection of the worker against sickness, disease and injury arising out of employment;
(f) protection of children, young persons, and women;
(g) provision for old age and injury;
(h) protection of the interests of those working in countries other than their own;
(i) equal remuneration for work of equal value;
(j) recognition of the freedom of association;
(k) organization of vocational and technical education.

From the beginning, the ILO was heavily involved in normative work and the setting of international labour standards has been its core activity. The ILO, which at present has 156 member States, has a unique tripartite structure which enables national governments and workers' and employers' organizations to share power in its decision-making bodies, of which the Governing Body is the executive organ, and the International Labour Conference elaborates and adopts international labour standards. Once standards are adopted by the Conference, member States must submit them within a year to their parliaments or other legislative authorities for the enactment of national legislation or action. These authorities remain free to decide whether or not they put them into effect, but they are in any case obliged to inform the Director-General of the ILO of the action taken.

Today's International Labour Code consists of 174 Conventions and 181 Recommendations, the two forms that ILO standards can take. Conventions have a legal status similar to international treaties. Once ratified by the competent national authority, they involve binding international commitments. Appropriate documentation has to be supplied by the country's government about how the Convention will function. The ILO Constitution also requires non-ratifying member countries to report periodically on the extent to which their laws and practices implement the provisions of unratified Conventions. They must indicate what is preventing or delaying the ratification. Recommendations do not create any international obligation but are designed to provide guidance to governments in formulating their social policies. They have been found most suitable or appropriate whenever a subject is not yet ripe for the adoption of a Convention, or to supplement a Convention, or where it seems desirable to leave a wide latitude to states as to which action should be taken.

The application of ratified Conventions is closely monitored through ILO's reporting and review machinery, involving the International Labour Office as the secretariat of the ILO, as well as tripartite committees of the Conference, and independent experts. Reports are scrutinized with a view to helping governments to overcome difficulties which they may have in making standards effective. As concerns compliance, any member has the right to file a formal complaint with the International Labour Office if it is not satisfied that any other member is securing the effective observance of a Convention which both have ratified. The matter is then made subject to inquiry, and eventually recommendations are made as to the necessary steps to be taken to meet the complaint. The governments in question then have to either accept the recommendations or refer the complaint to the International Court of Justice, whose decision is final.

About 6,000 ratifications of Conventions have been made so far by member States, which averages more than 30 per member. Among the Conventions most commonly ratified are the Convention of 1930 on Forced Labour (No. 29), the Convention of 1957 on the Abolition of Forced Labour (No. 105), the Convention of 1948 on Freedom of Association and Protection of the Right to Organize (No. 87), the Convention of 1949 on the Right to Organize and Collective Bargaining (No. 98), the Convention of 1951 on Equal Remuneration (No. 100), the Convention of 1958 on Discrimination in Employment and Occupation (No. 111), and the Convention of 1964 on Employment Policy (No. 122). These key Conventions, each of which has been ratified by more than 100 member States, are seen as fundamental human rights, which are of particular concern to the ILO.

It is recognized as a problem that the record of ratification varies vastly across countries. With some notable exceptions, most ratifications are made by the industrialized or near-industrialized countries, while the developing countries have ratified far fewer Conventions. It has been debated at great length, both inside and outside the ILO, whether the developing countries can even afford to apply the minimum standards laid down in the International Labour Code. The ILO itself has responded to this question by providing some flexibility in introducing standards to take account of the widely varying economic and social conditions and legal and political systems. In view of such variety, two extremes are to be avoided. One is to set standards which can be accepted at once by the greatest possible number of countries, with the risk that the common denominator is apt to result in a standard too low to produce any significant progress. The other would be to aim at too high a standard which would not be immediately practicable in most countries. Many standards are formulated in fairly general language, thus giving governments latitude either in the scope of setting the standard or in the methods of application.

It is generally held that the standards promulgating fundamental human rights mentioned above should apply independently of the state of a country's development. For example, no matter how rich or poor a country is, it cannot be accepted that trade union leaders be harassed, jailed, disappear, or be murdered. Substantive standards, on the other hand, usually contain flexible formulas of one kind or another. For example, with regard to minimum wages, Convention No. 131 (1970) specifies that a country should have a system of minimum wages in one form or another, but it does not stipulate the minimum wage required. It would be unrealistic to set a substantive rule, given the enormous wage differentials across member States. (In the United States, for example, the average wage per hour is about the same as that for a full working day in adjacent Mexico. In Finland, a carpenter's wage on one day is nowadays equivalent to a worker's wage for one month in neighbouring Russia.) Even so, it is the ambition of the ILO to adhere to the principle of universality in setting and enforcing standards, and not admit regional standards for groupings of countries of different degrees of development. Regional standards would accentuate rather than reduce differences in development, and would mean that in certain regions there would be 'substandards' for 'sub-human people.' . . .

The other way in which the ILO, together with other specialized United Nations agencies, has attempted to deal with the wide differential in national labour conditions, has been through *technical cooperation*. This includes education, consultation and technical assistance, and is given primarily to the countries of the South to assist them in their development process, e.g. through public works projects, setting up vocational training and rehabilitation centres, promoting full employment, forming rural cooperatives, building safety and health systems, and establishing systems of social security. The setting and application of labour standards and technical cooperation are seen to complement and strengthen each other. Technical cooperation is to be designed with the aim of achieving progress towards the ratification of and compliance with international labour standards. [Reprinted by permission.]

* * *

The World Trade Organization (WTO), founded in 1995, administers and enforces agreements negotiated by its member states for the purpose of liberalizing international trade. The question of the impact of differing levels of labour standards on international trade has repeatedly come before the WTO. In response, it has repeatedly asserted that labour standards should be addressed through the ILO, rather than through trade protectionism or trade sanctions.

Organisation for Economic Co-operation and Development, *Trade, Employment and Labour Standards* (Paris: OECD, 1996) at 169–76

LABOUR STANDARDS AND WTO DISCIPLINES

Introduction

The debate about linkages between trade disciplines and labour standards is not new. Indeed, Article 7 of the Havana Charter [1948], which was meant to establish an International Trade Organization (ITO), referred to the importance of satisfactory social conditions for the smooth operation of the trading system and invited Members to work for the establishment of such conditions within their territory. However, this article was among the provisions of the Charter that never entered into force.

Suggestions have been made recently to establish closer links between trade and core labour standards, in particular as regards the operation of the GATT/WTO system of multilateral rules and disciplines for international trade. For instance, in 1983, the European Parliament called for the negotiation of a GATT provision on labour standards engaging all GATT Members to respect ILO Conventions on freedom of association, collective bargaining, forced labour and non-discrimination. In 1986 and in 1994, the United States suggested, without success, to add worker's rights to the Uruguay Round and to the WTO agenda. In 1994, the European Parliament further suggested that GATT Article XX(e) on prison labour be amended to include forced and child labour, as well as violations of the principle of freedom of association and collective bargaining. Some have suggested making use of the WTO Trade Policy Review Mechanism (TPRM). There have been other proposals (e.g. by TUAC [the Trade Union Advisory Committee to the OECD]) for the introduction of a "social clause" into the WTO, with the aim in particular of strengthening the enforcement of "basic" labour standards.

Discussions have also taken place within the ILO. The objective was to ensure that the gradual liberalisation of markets be accompanied by improvements in conditions of work, or at least by the elimination of the most flagrant abuses and forms of exploitation. The ILO Secretariat discussed the applicability of using anti-dumping and countervailing duties provisions, general exceptions provisions, or nullification and impairment provisions for that purpose.

Subsequent debate on these ideas within the ILO Working Party on the Social Dimension of the Liberalisation of World Trade underlined their controversial nature. Many participants, in particular among the employers and the developing countries, were opposed to the implementation of a "social clause" in the WTO. In fact, the consensus that emerged at an important session of the ILO Working Party was that it "should not pursue the question of trade sanctions and that any discussion of the link between international trade and social standards, through a sanction-based social clause, should be suspended". . . . Instead, the Working Party will look at ways to promote core labour standards through encouragement, support and assistance and at the means to strengthen ILO's effectiveness in achieving this task.

Whether to introduce additional objectives, to negotiate new provisions and mechanisms or to interpret existing WTO provisions would imply the existence of sufficient political will among WTO Members, and would be a matter for their consideration and decision. Accordingly, the comments below simply draw attention to certain key elements that would need to be addressed satisfactorily in relation to specific proposals to establish links between WTO disciplines and core standards. Certain OECD governments, while proposing that the trade and labour standards issues be discussed among WTO Members, have not presented precise suggestions so far on how the existing WTO system of rules and disciplines might be adapted. The debate on the possible "introduction of a social clause in the WTO" thus remains speculative, in the absence of agreement to consider the issue in the WTO and of detailed proposals regarding its scope and implementation mechanisms. As such, it is not discussed here.

Elements of proposals concerning the use of WTO provisions

"Social dumping"

Low levels of labour standards applied by exporting firms are considered by some as a form of "social dumping" which unfairly affects firms in countries adopting more advanced standards. It has been proposed that there be application of anti-dumping duties against so-called "social dumping."

As currently formulated in the WTO Agreement on Implementation of Article VI of GATT 1994, a product is considered as being dumped when it is introduced into the commerce of another country at less than its normal value. This occurs if the export price is less than the comparable price in the ordinary course of trade for the like product when destined for consumption in the exporting country .When there are no sales, or when, because of insufficient sales volume or a particular market situation, such sales do not permit a proper comparison, the margin of dumping is to be determined on the basis of either a comparable price of the like product exported to a third country or on the basis of constructed value. Investigating authorities must, therefore, base their determination either on actual price discrimination or on an actual comparison of production costs to export price as set forth in the Agreement. It is to be noted also that anti-dumping duties can be levied in respect of an imported product determined to have been dumped, only if that product is causing or threatening to cause material injury to the domestic producers of the like product in the importing country; and also, that the anti-dumping duty shall not exceed the margin of dumping.

All of these, and other requirements, must be met if a WTO Member is to act in a manner consistent with its WTO obligations. Thus, to the extent that application by an investigating authority of anti-dumping duties rested on any other separate or distinct criterion in its own right, such as "violation of core labour standards" per se, this would not be compatible with the existing provisions of the Agreement. These provisions do not allow for the determination of a margin of dumping on the basis of non-enforcement of core standards. Moreover, if determination of a dumping margin involves an assessment of costs of production, these must be actual, and not notional or hypothetical costs.

"Social subsidies"

The concern has been expressed that governments may, in effect, assist production and/or exports by enforcing either low labour standards, or labour standards that deviate from those that are generally applicable at the national level, for example by instituting "union-free" export-processing zones within a country that otherwise permits the establishment of independent unions. This action is characterised by some as a subsidy, or as an indirect export subsidy. In this context it has been proposed that countervailing duties be applied against exports from such countries. Although the analysis in Part II indicates that the suppression of core standards is not an effective "social subsidy" and that there is little evidence that core standards influence trade patterns in practice, the discussion below deals with the problems in applying remedial actions in any case.

First, it would depend on whether "abnormally" low labour conditions represent a form of subsidy within the meaning of GATT Article XVI and the definition of the WTO Agreement on Subsidies and Countervailing Measures. The definition of a subsidy in the WTO Agreement includes a number of situations in which a benefit is conferred either by a financial contribution granted by the government or public bodies, or by "any income or price support in the sense of Article XVI of the GATT 1994." Violation of core standards does not involve any financial contribution by the government, as defined under the existing WTO Agreement. There remains a question of whether it could be deemed to meet the latter criteria relating to income or price support. It is unclear how any measure to *reduce* core labour standards could constitute income "support." It is also difficult to envisage how the criterion of "price support" could be satisfied, given that non-enforcement of core standards is not a governmental measure that supplies assistance to firms or producers through regulation of prices.

Even if a measure is deemed to satisfy the criteria for definition as a "subsidy" within the terms of the Agreement, action against it can only be taken if it is also "specific" within the meaning of the Agreement. There are a number of tests which apply; *inter alia*, the "granting authority" must limit access to a subsidy to "certain enterprises." A subsidy which is "limited to certain enterprises located within a designated geographical region" shall be determined to be specific.

This would seem to suggest, for instance, that a country-wide, objective implementation of labour standards, albeit at a low level, would be unlikely to meet the specificity test in any case, as it would appear to be generally applicable by definition.

The more limited case of lower core standards in export-processing zones would, to the extent that these satisfied the criteria for determination of the existence of a subsidy, need to be evaluated precisely against the criteria related to specificity, as well as the other relevant provisions of the Agreement.

Furthermore, the primary means for taking "remedial" action against any subsidy that satisfies the specificity test are countervailing actions (often called "Track one") or recourse to the procedures for dispute resolution in relation to nullification and impairment or serious prejudice (often called "Track two").

Recourse to either of these tracks gives rise to a further set of requirements. In the case of any measures that satisfied the criteria for countervailability, it would be necessary, *inter alia*, to satisfy all the requirements for a determination of injury to the domestic producers of the subsidised product. It should be noted that in the absence of such injury or threat of injury, it is not permissible to apply countervailing measures. It would also be necessary to be consistent with the requirements for the calculation of the amount of a subsidy, in particular the requirement that the countervailing duty should not exceed the level of subsidisation. This would be vital if it was in principle possible to quantify any specific benefit arising from non-observation/non-enforcement of core labour standards.

General exceptions provisions

GATT 1994 provides for certain general exceptions, such as Article XX(a) on public morals, Article XX(b) on human life or health and Article XX(e) on products of prison labour. As exceptions to other provisions of the Agreement, any party seeking to invoke these provisions would bear the burden of demonstrating that it satisfied the relevant criteria, including those specified in the "chapeau" to Article XX, viz. that "measures are not applied in a manner which would constitute a means of arbitrary or unjustifiable discrimination between countries where the same conditions prevail; or a disguised restriction on international trade." Article XXI provides also for certain security exceptions.

Subject to the above-mentioned "chapeau" requirements, a WTO Member may, under Article XX(e), restrict imports of goods made with prison labour. Other provisions under the General Exceptions Article include Article XX(d) and Article XX(h). The idea of using Article XX(d) (on measures necessary to secure compliance with laws or regulations not inconsistent with the GATT) in relation to labour standards was envisaged and abandoned during the negotiations on the Havana Charter. The Sub-committee which considered the general exceptions to Chapter IV noted that

> in discussing an amendment to [Article XX(d)], designed to exempt measures against so-called 'social dumping' from the provisions of Chapter IV, the Sub-committee expressed the view that this objective was covered for short-term purposes by paragraph I of Article 40 [Article XIX] and for long-term purposes by Article 7 [on worker rights] in combination with Articles 93,94 and 95 [on dispute settlement].

The text of Article 7 was not, of course, included in the GATT.

Article XX(h) allows GATT Members to adopt measures "undertaken in pursuance of obligations under any inter-governmental commodity agreement which conforms to criteria submitted to the Contracting Parties and not disapproved by them or which is itself so submitted and not so disapproved." Within the framework of the Integrated Programme for Commodities of the UNCTAD, a number of international commodity agreements contain provisions on "fair labour standards." These provisions, however, seem to be more declarations of intent than precise contractual undertakings; they are limited to a general reference to fair working conditions without quoting any concrete provisions referring to existing international agreements. Special sanctions or control mechanisms are not provided for, and their effects in practice depend largely on the leverage which concerned countries can exert in securing compliance with such clauses. None of the commodity agreements, nor criteria with respect to commodity agreements, have ever been formally submitted to the GATT Members.

Nullification and impairment provisions

It has been suggested by some that the dispute-settlement provision of the WTO might offer a means to address enforcement of core labour standards in certain circumstances. Under Article XXIII, l(b) or (c), and Article 26 of the Understanding on Rules and Procedures Governing the Settlement of Disputes, a Member may bring an action if it believes that any benefit accruing to it under the Agreement is being nullified or impaired, or that the attainment of any objective of the Agreement is being impeded, as a result of inter alia "the application by another of any measure, whether or not it conflicts with the provisions of the Agreement" or the "existence of any other situation." Paragraph 2 of that Article also refers to the scope for Contracting Parties to consult with other inter-governmental organisations. Under the terms of Article 26, the complainant shall present a detailed justification of any complaint relating to Article XXIII, l(b). There is no obligation to withdraw the measure if a panel or Appellate Body rules that it did nullify or impair benefits. The panel or Appellate Body shall recommend that the Member concerned make "a mutually satisfactory adjustment." There is no case law on complaints of the type described in Article XXIII, l(c) of GATT 1994.

The original Article 7 of the Havana Charter would have involved incorporating workers' rights provisions in the Agreement as a potential basis for any invocation of nullification and impairment provisions. With respect to all such matters referred to dispute-settlement procedures, co-operation was to be instituted between the ITO and the ILO. In 1953, when a US proposal to re-insert the provision in the GATT was rejected, the United States declared that, taking into account the distortions likely to be created by unfair labour conditions, it considered the possibility of invoking nullification or impairment in terms of Article XXIII as existing already under the current provisions. No action was ever taken in this direction, although the United States indicates that it still considers it has reserved its right to do so.

"Opt-out" provisions

It has been argued that GATT Article XXXV presented an opportunity for contracting parties to exercise a de facto labour rights exception to GATT rules. This was the so-called "opt-out" clause, under which a contracting party had the right upon the accession of a new Contracting Party (or upon its own accession to GATT) to declare that it will not apply GATT in its trade relations with a specific Contracting Party. There were no limitations placed on a country's decision to exercise this option, apart from the requirements that it be invoked only at the time of accession, and that it could not be invoked if tariff negotiations had taken place between the two parties in the course of GATT-accession negotiations. This provision of the GATT first emerged in response to India's concerns over the accession of South Africa in 1948. To the extent that one considers the specific opposition to apartheid to have been, *inter alia*, a labour rights issue, those countries that invoked Article XXXV against South Africa employed this provision as a labour-related political exception. Of the 12 invocations of the Article that were still in effect as of 1990, four related to South Africa. The issue has since been rendered moot by the abolition of apartheid and the establishment of the WTO, although it remains an option for any WTO Member to take recourse to the provision of Article XIII regarding future new WTO Members for whatever reason. There are, however, good reasons to consider such an approach as rather inflexible and probably disproportionate in regard to most of the labour standards issues presently under consideration.

Labour standards in the Trade Policy Review Mechanism (TPRM)

It has also been suggested that policies that deliberately attempt to reduce core labour standards in certain export sectors or export-processing zones be included and discussed in the country reviews undertaken in the framework for the Trade Policy Review Mechanism on the grounds that the publicity and peer pressure involved in this exercise might eventually improve the situation of core labour standards in some countries. It has been proposed that the ILO might play an active part in such a procedure, first by defining the set of core labour standards and then by participating in the elaboration of that part of the WTO Secretariat report dealing with labour policies. This TPRM option would provide a peer review process that would not be substantially different from the existing procedures in the ILO.

The TPRM focuses on trade and trade policies. Export-processing zones per se can be the subject of TPRM discussions. Any proposals to deal with core labour standards issues would need to be consistent with, inter alia, Articles A(i) and (ii) of the TPRM annex, whereby the subject matter of review is to be a background for better understanding and assessment of the country's trade policies and practices, and cannot in any case be used as a basis either for dispute-settlement procedures or for imposing new policy commitments on Members. It should be noted that all proposals to include labour policies in trade policy reviews undertaken in the past have encountered strong opposition from developing countries.

Concluding remarks

Applying the proposals reviewed in this section would pose, in the first place, a number of questions concerning the appropriateness and the effectiveness of various WTO mechanisms which, in their present forms, are directed towards the enforcement of trade policies and practices. A second observation is that the use of various WTO articles or procedures would, in all appearance, require amendments, reinterpretations or common understandings. These remain, ultimately, a matter for WTO members themselves to determine. It is, however, apparent that there is presently a lack of consensus within WTO to move in such a direction. . . .

[Extracted from *Trade Employment and Labour Standards: A Study of Core Workers' Rights and International Trade*. Copyright © OECD, 1996. Reprinted by permission.]

＊ ＊ ＊

World Trade Organization, *Singapore Ministerial Declaration*, adopted 13 December 1996

. . .

PURPOSE

2. For nearly 50 years Members have sought to fulfill, first in the GATT and now in the WTO, the objectives reflected in the preamble to the WTO Agreement of conducting our trade relations with a view to raising standards of living worldwide. The rise in global trade facilitated by trade liberalization within the rules-based system has created more and better-paid jobs in many countries. The achievements of the WTO during its first two years bear witness to our desire to work together to make the most of the possibilities that the multilateral system provides to promote sustainable growth and development while contributing to a more stable and secure climate in international relations.

TRADE AND ECONOMIC GROWTH

3. We believe that the scope and pace of change in the international economy, including the growth in trade in services and direct investment, and the increasing integration of

economies offer unprecedented opportunities for improved growth, job creation, and development. These developments require adjustment by economies and societies. They also pose challenges to the trading system. We commit ourselves to address these challenges.

INTEGRATION OF ECONOMIES; OPPORTUNITIES AND CHALLENGES

4. We renew our commitment to the observance of internationally recognized core labour standards. The International Labour Organization (ILO) is the competent body to set and deal with these standards, and we affirm our support for its work in promoting them. We believe that economic growth and development fostered by increased trade and further trade liberalization contribute to the promotion of these standards. We reject the use of labour standards for protectionist purposes, and agree that the comparative advantage of countries, particularly low-wage developing countries, must in no way be put into question. In this regard, we note that the WTO and ILO Secretariats will continue their existing collaboration.

CORE LABOUR STANDARDS

5. We commit ourselves to address the problem of marginalization for least-developed countries, and the risk of it for certain developing countries. We will also continue to work for greater coherence in international economic policy-making and for improved coordination between the WTO and other agencies in providing technical assistance.

* * *

World Trade Organization, *Qatar Ministerial Declaration*, Ministerial Conference, Fourth Session, Doha, Qatar, 14 November 2001

. . .

8. We reaffirm our declaration made at the Singapore Ministerial Conference regarding internationally recognized core labour standards. We take note of work underway in the International Labour Organization (ILO) on the social dimension of globalization. [Reprinted by permission.]

* * *

The ILO sought to focus its activities and strengthen its normative structure through the adoption, in 1998, of the Declaration on Fundamental Principles and Rights at Work, which gives higher priority to a few "core labour standards" and sets out new follow-up procedures to try to increase the level of observance of those core standards. The thrust of the Declaration has been summarized as follows by an officer of the ILO.

Hilary Kellerson, "The ILO Declaration of 1998 on Fundamental Principles and Rights: A Challenge for the Future" (1998) 137 Int'l. Lab. Rev. 223

After several years of discussion and intense negotiations, on 18 June 1998 the International Labour Conference adopted a Declaration on fundamental principles and rights at work and its follow-up to promote the implementation of these principles and rights.

The principles thus given expression are those concerning the fundamental rights of (a) freedom of association and the effective recognition of the right to collective bargaining; (b) the elimination of all forms of forced or compulsory labour; (c) the effective abolition of child labour; and (d) the elimination of discrimination in respect of employment and occupation (Article 2). This Declaration is the culmination of a process which, within the ILO, has its origins in proposals for establishing a procedure similar to that of the Committee on Freedom of Association for the other rights recognized as fundamental. The freedom of association procedure, like the Declaration, is based on the principles laid down in the ILO Constitution but, unlike the Declaration's follow-up, is a complaints-based procedure and thus will continue to operate in parallel with the Declaration.

Concurrent with the debate within the ILO, discussions on the economic and social implications of the globalization of the world economy in other fora were reaching consensus on the identification of fundamental workers' rights. At the World Summit for Social Development, held in Copenhagen in March 1995, the Heads of State and Government committed themselves to "Pursue the goal of ensuring quality jobs, and safeguard the basic rights and interests of workers and to this end, freely promote respect for relevant International Labour Organization Conventions, including those on the prohibition of forced and child labour, the freedom of association, the right to organize and bargain collectively, and the principle of non-discrimination." The following year, the World Trade Organization's (WTO) Ministerial Conference at Singapore, in its Final Declaration, stated, "We renew our commitment to the observance of internationally recognized core labour standards. The International Labour Organization (ILO) is the competent body to set and deal with these standards, and we affirm our support for its work in promoting them. We believe that economic growth and development fostered by increased trade and further trade liberalization contribute to the promotion of these standards."

It was in this context that, in his Report to the 85th Session (1997) of the International Labour Conference on the ILO, standard setting and globalization (ILO, 1997), the Director-General put forward proposals for the adoption by the Conference of a solemn Declaration of fundamental rights. The discussions at the Conference that year led the Governing Body to add to the agenda of the 1998 Session of the Conference the question of the adoption of such a Declaration.

THE CONTENT OF THE DECLARATION

The first element in the Declaration is the reaffirmation of the obligation of Members of the Organization to respect the principles concerning fundamental rights. As was repeatedly emphasized during the discussions, the Declaration does not seek to impose any new obligations on member States. It is based on the fact that, in voluntarily joining the ILO, each Member has endorsed the principles and rights set out in its Constitution and in the Declaration of Philadelphia which expressly, or implicitly in the case of the abolition of forced labour, recognize the rights enshrined in the 1998 Declaration (Article 1). Thus, while these principles and rights have been expressed and developed in the fundamental ILO Conventions, member States, even if they have not ratified these Conventions, have an obligation, as Members, to respect, to promote and to realise the principles concerning these fundamental rights (Article 2). Their recognition moreover confirms the status of the Conventions embodying them as core labour standards.

The reason why these principles and rights are regarded as fundamental is spelled out in the Preamble, which affirms that "in seeking to maintain the link between social progress and economic growth, the guarantee of fundamental principles and rights at work is of particular significance in that it enables the persons concerned to claim freely and on the basis of equality of opportunity their fair share of the wealth which they have helped to generate, and to achieve fully their human potential." They are thus an essential cornerstone in a world of growing economic interdependence, in which economic growth is essential but not sufficient to ensure equity, social progress and the eradication of poverty.

An issue addressed in the Declaration in this context is the relationship between social progress and trade liberalization. It was repeatedly emphasized during the discussions that the Declaration should not be seen as creating a link between labour standards and international trade or as providing a pretext for protectionist measures. On this issue the Declaration, echoing the Singapore Ministerial Declaration of the WTO, "stresses that labour standards should not be used for protectionist trade purposes, and that nothing in this Declaration and its follow-up shall be invoked or otherwise used for such purposes; in addition, the comparative advantage of any country should in no way be called into question by this Declaration or its follow-up" (Article 5).

The second major element of the Declaration is its promotional character. This finds expression in the recognition of the obligation of the ILO to assist its Members to attain the objectives of the Declaration, by offering technical cooperation and advisory services to promote ratification and implementation of the fundamental Conventions, by assisting Members' efforts to realize the principles concerning the fundamental rights which are the subject of the fundamental Conventions, and by helping Members create a climate for economic and social development. It obliges the ILO to make full use of its constitutional, operational and budgetary resources for this purpose and encourages other organizations to support these efforts (Article 3). The broad context of this promotional effort is expressed in the Preamble "confirming the need for the ILO to promote strong social policies, justice and democratic institutions."

The Declaration thus envisages a new emphasis in the use of ILO resources — constitutional, operational and budgetary as well as external — on promoting respect for the principles and rights reaffirmed in the Declaration.

THE FOLLOW-UP

There was agreement from the outset that the Declaration should be accompanied by a meaningful and effective follow-up, which would be strictly promotional in nature and not involve any punitive aspect, duplication of existing procedures or new obligations. Its aim is to encourage member States to promote the fundamental principles and rights reaffirmed in the Declaration, and for this purpose to allow the identification of areas in which the ILO's technical cooperation may be useful in supporting the efforts of member States.

Certain details of its implementation are still to be determined by the Governing Body at its 273rd Session in November 1998, but the essentials are clearly laid down in the "Follow-up to the Declaration" annexed to the Declaration and adopted integrally with it.

The follow-up will consist of two complementary elements. The first element is an annual follow-up in which States will be asked to provide reports every year on each of the fundamental Conventions which they have not ratified. The purpose of these reports is to provide an opportunity to review, every year, the efforts made in the four areas of fundamental rights and principles specified in the Declaration by States which have not ratified the relevant Conventions. This process concerning non-ratified fundamental Conventions is based on article 19, paragraph 5 (e), of the Constitution under which member States are required to report, when requested by the Governing Body, on the position of their law and practice in regard to the matters dealt with in a Convention which they have not ratified.

. . .

The second element is a global report which will cover, each year, one of the four categories of fundamental principles and rights in turn, and review developments during the preceding four-year period. Its purpose will be, firstly, to provide a general overview of the situation in all member States (since ratification does not necessarily imply full implementation, and non-ratifying States do not necessarily fail to respect the fundamental principles) and establish the major trends and developments. Secondly, it will serve to assess the effectiveness of assistance provided by the ILO for the furtherance of the implementation of this Declaration in the period covered and determine priorities for technical cooperation in the following period. . . .

THE SIGNIFICANCE OF THE DECLARATION

There is intrinsic value in this solemn Declaration in that it represents a reaffirmation, by governments and both social partners, of the universality of fundamental principles and rights at a time of widespread uncertainty and questioning of those rights. That is not a small achievement.

There is also great potential value in the Declaration which depends on a dynamic implementation of its follow-up. The promotional effort called for in this Declaration implies a reorientation of the ILO's constitutional, operational and budgetary resources in support of the priorities determined in the global reports, themselves based on annual reports and other official information available to the ILO.

A remarkable aspect of this approach is that it represents a collective decision to pursue social justice by the high road — drawing on people's aspiration for equity, social progress and the eradication of poverty — rather than by sanctions which can be abused for protectionist purposes in international trade.

While affirming the importance of linking social progress to economic growth, in adopting the Declaration the International Labour Conference places the whole question of the promotion of fundamental labour standards and their underlying principles squarely in the framework of the constitutional principles and procedures of the ILO. The full value of the Declaration, which depends on the active implementation of the follow-up by many in and outside the ILO, will only emerge in the course of time. The challenge facing the ILO in the next millennium will be to ensure that the Declaration achieves the significance and the impact it offers.

[Reprinted by permission.]

* * *

The following is a somewhat more critical assessment of the significance of the Declaration on Fundamental Principles and Rights at Work.

Brian Langille, "The ILO and the New Economy: Recent Developments"(1999) 15 Int'l. J. Comparative Lab. Law and Ind. Rel. at 230–56

The adoption of this Declaration was regarded by many within and outside the ILO as an absolute priority — it was necessary for the ILO to do something in order to reassert itself and its mandate in what may be referred to as the 'new global economy.' . . . In fact, the ILO regarded itself as having to respond to a de facto invitation issued by other international institutions, especially the WTO at its December 1996 Ministerial Meeting in Singapore, to reassert its institutional priority in connection with its traditional set of concerns.

. . .

. . . For the sceptics, the Declaration does not mark a new beginning, but a kind of collective evasion, or worse — a consensus in favour of (continued) irrelevance and marginalization for the ILO. From this perspective the ILO has been historically powerless. It has no real world 'bite,' no sanctions or real incentives with which to affect behaviour in the world. It is a debating society which has been pushed to the sidelines by the overpowering nature of private global market forces and by the other public international institutions constructing the rules for the international marketplace — the WTO, the IMF, the World Bank, the OECD, etc. On the sceptical view, these are the only institutions with real clout, i.e. real incentives (access to WTO membership, IMF packages, World Bank loans) and sanctions, capable of guiding behaviour in the real world, even if only at the margins. . . .

Nevertheless, a realistic appraisal of recent events must treat this package of views as too simplistic as well. . . .

Following the WTO Ministerial Meeting in Singapore in December 1996 the ILO was placed in a very perplexing position. The official text of the WTO Singapore Declaration included a ringing reaffirmation of the importance of core labour rights and of the centrality of the ILO in advancing the core labour rights agenda. Nevertheless, the subtext was large and transparently clear for all to see — the rejection of labour standards, core or otherwise, as a fit subject matter of WTO debate, and the dismissal of the ILO as marginal and irrelevant at best, to the efforts of the WTO to set the ground rules for production and trade in the global economy. These ground rules now within the WTO mandate range across a number of issues going well beyond the traditional trade agenda, i.e. trade in goods, and are now legitimately considered to include, at least potentially, competition policy, intellectual property, the environment, and investment — but not labour. So, the referral of these issues back to the ILO could be seen at the same time as a large and positive reaffirmation of the ILO mandate, and as a broadside undermining it.

The options facing the ILO after Singapore were not altogether attractive. An obvious option was to accept the official WTO text at face value and carry on, as before, but also deeply aware of the risk of compromise this involved — that of continuity, but of continued marginalization and the relegation to a role of keeping labour issues on a very distant back burner.

The option actually taken, and appropriately so in my view, was to attempt to use the official text, and the overwhelming reaffirmation of faith in the ILO, as a vehicle to animate change within the ILO. . . .

However, the concrete manifestation of this strategy — to make the most out of a difficult situation — was revealed by the Director General's 1997 report to the June Conference entitled *The ILO, Standard Setting and Globalization.* Of the proposals for institutional renewal suggested by the Director-General in his 1997 Report two are of interest here: (1) the idea of a 'Declaration' on fundamental rights; and (2) the idea of 'social labelling.' While these ideas share much in common, only the declaration proposal made it out of the starting blocks. The social labelling idea was 'shot down' immediately. . . .

. . . No one believed that there had been a mass conversion at Singapore. On the other hand, the risk in the strategy pursued by the ILO was that in taking up the public words of Singapore as an invitation and as a spur to renewal, it might simply fail. This would result in the worst of all possible worlds — a very public demonstration of inability, internally, to deliver on announced reform agendas, and therefore of irrelevancy. . . .

. . .

The idea of a Declaration is both evocative and evasive in the ILO context. The ILO Constitution does not mention 'Declarations' — nor for that matter, does the constitution of any other international organization. Yet Declarations are a familiar part of the institutional vocabulary or grammar of many international organizations — the Universal Declaration of Human Rights being the most obvious example. . . .

On the other hand, the ILO is clearly empowered to act, and has acted in a more direct manner, through the creation and adoption of Conventions which are, when ratified, binding international treaties with attached monitoring and complaint processes (although no 'hard' sanctions at the end of the day). The ILO is also expressly empowered to adopt non-binding recommendations aimed at guiding policies within member states. What then is the point of a 'Declaration' of general principle concerning core labour rights? Is there not a risk of detracting from the seven concrete Conventions dealing with the four core rights? This was an obvious concern to worker representatives at the ILO — that a Declaration of principle would be a vehicle for diluting concrete and detailed obligations contained in the relevant Conventions. On the other hand, from the perspective of governments and employers, Conventions concerning the core rights often remained unratified because of concrete problems in reconciling the details of domestic legislation with the specific demands of the conventions.

. . . There was another historical precedent within the ILO which cast a long shadow over the proposal for a Declaration — the precedent of the 'freedom of association machinery.' In 1951 the ILO established the Committee on Freedom of Association (CFA), technically a tripartite committee of the Governing Body of the ILO. The basic constitutional idea sustaining the CFA is of profound importance — that all member states of the ILO, simply by virtue of membership, are constitutionally committed to the promotion, recognition, and respect of the principle of freedom of association. . . .

The CFA and its processes were originally conceived of as a 'promotional' mechanism. Indeed, that is, as we see, its formal constitutional basis. The CFA was not to duplicate the monitoring or 'enforcement' mechanisms established for the relevant Conventions on freedom of association (Nos. 87 and 98). The Committee is a Tripartite 'political' committee of the Governing Body; it is not a panel of legal experts like the 'Committee of experts' which monitors compliance with ratified Conventions. Nonetheless, it is commonly observed that the 1951 special procedure on freedom of association has increasingly moved away from a 'promotional' mandate to a more legalistic, complaint driven, heavily used mechanism which has resulted in a complex and detailed jurisprudence. This jurisprudence, although not technically based upon the details of the relevant Conventions, is large and is now distributed in an ILO monograph running to approximately 200 pages.

Thus, on the one hand, the CFA precedent offers the appealing prospect for workers of a 'hard process' applying to all states regardless of whether the relevant Conventions have been ratified. On the other hand, it demonstrates to others the difficulty of preventing mechanisms designed for the 'promotion' of fundamental values from becoming another layer of detailed institutional complication aimed at 'enforcement.'

In this complex and sometimes contradictory interplay of interests — between the advantages and disadvantages of principle versus detailed commitment, of constitutional versus normal 'legislative' grounding of obligations, and of 'promotion' versus 'enforcement' lies, of course, the promise, or at least the possibility of political compromise, coalition building, and the finding of common ground, and this indeed proved to be the path forward. . . .

. . .

The four core labour rights are basic and sound in affirming a deep and profound respect for human beings as ends in themselves (and not commodities, to use the ILO language) with an equal right to concern for their well being, and respect for their ability and need to exercise personal autonomy in leading fully developed lives. The core rights agenda is aimed at helping to provide the necessary circumstances for, and to remove obvious obstacles to, the achievement of this end. It is, of course, not a complete recipe for eternal peace, but it is a necessary part of that human project. As we have seen, part of its normative, as well as its rhetorical power, is that the core rights agenda transcends the traditional divide between the language of human rights and the language of economics.

Yet it seems clear that, in spite of their universal character and cross-disciplinary appeal, the core rights agenda is at once controversial and contested when any effort is made to establish a link between those core standards and access to the global marketplace — whether in terms of trade in goods or in terms of investment, and whether couched in market friendly terms such as labelling. Any effort to move the ILO, and its international labour code, beyond its current 'sanctionless' modes of monitoring and review is, it seems, politically impossible even if such proposals are limited to providing market incentives to respect core standards. In fact, it seems that efforts to gain universal acceptance of the core rights, even in a sanctionless environment, has led to a Declaration in which members of the ILO could only agree on language which fails to take the core rights as seriously as they should be taken. . . .

. . . [O]ne of the basic features of the debates and discussions about the ILO and international labour standards is the seemingly unrelenting focus upon one aspect of the ILO — the standard setting and monitoring process. The focus is upon the legislative and enforcement process, that is, the 'legal machinery' of the ILO. This focus is centred upon Geneva and upon the Conventions. Perhaps this is an entirely natural focus of attention at this stage of our debates about globalization and its discontents. However, the fact is that the legislative and monitoring functions of the ILO — that is, the official legal function — is only one face of the organization and, in spite of its high profile, this legal aspect of the ILO in fact represents substantially less than 50 percent of ILO functions, as calculated in budgetary terms.

The ILO is much more than a Convention producing and monitoring machine. The ILO has in fact three dimensions, only one of which is the legal function. The other two may be described as being the world's centre of excellence for research and understanding of labour related issues, and second, a programme delivery organization actually delivering results through global, regional, and member state based programme initiatives, such as the *International Program on the Elimination of Child Labour* (IPEC).

A grasp of these fundamental points provokes the following thought. We have noticed that ILO member states were deeply resistant to, and suspicious of, any obligations or restrictions which the new Declaration would impose upon them, so much so that they included the extraordinary paragraph 5 . . . in the text of the Declaration. However, a reading of the Declaration reveals that it is not only a Declaration about the obligations of member states, it is also a Declaration concerning the obligations of the organization itself. . . .

. . .

Viewed against the backdrop of the sprawling ILO mandate and range of activities, the Declaration's legacy may indeed lie in its potential as a disciplining and focussing device for the activities of the organization itself. In so doing, the focus would not be upon imposing obligations upon the members, or upon the market-based incentives inherent in the labelling idea, but upon the use of direct aid and assistance in the form of institutional expertise, resources, 'technical cooperation' etc. to 'promote' the core values. Having rejected any notion of a 'social clause,' or trade sanctions, or other disciplining devices, no matter how market friendly, the essence of the Declaration's achievement is to focus the organization in its programme delivery, at least within one of its fundamental substantive provisions — promoting basic rights. . . . It is too early to say how effective this strategy will be. . . . The new Director-General, Juan Somavia, has in his Report to the 1999 Conference, entitled Decent Work, and in his proposals for the ILO program and budget (adopted unanimously at the 1999 Conference) outlined a streamlined and focused management by (four core) objectives approach — the first objective of which is promotion of the fundamental rights of the Declaration. The whole drift of the Report is internal restructuring and rededication of ILO program work to the promotion of the core objectives. The idea of 'linkage' is explicitly rejected. The letters WTO do not appear in the Report.

✻ ✻ ✻

As is noted in the above excerpt, the front-line administration of the ILO's Conventions on freedom of association (especially Conventions 87 and 98) is in the hands of the Committee on Freedom of Association. Like the ILO itself, that Committee is tripartite in nature, consisting of representatives of employers, employees, and governments. In the half-century since it was established, it has heard over 2000 complaints. By way of example, the following excerpt from its March 2003 report deals with a complaint about a 2000 amendment to the Ontario *Labour Relations Act, 1995*. Because the provinces have no standing at the ILO, complaints against provincial legislation are nominally brought against the federal government.

Case No. 2182: Report of Committee on Complaint against the Government of Canada concerning the Province of Ontario, in International Labour Office, *330th Report of the Committee on Freedom of Association*, March 2003, GB.286/11 (part 1), 286th Session of Governing Body

<http://www.ilo.org/public/english/standards/relm/gb/docs/gb286/pdf/gb-11-p1.pdf>

> Allegations: The complainants allege that some provisions of the Ontario Labour Relations Act encourage the decertification of workers' organizations by requiring employers to post and distribute in the workplace documents setting out the process to terminate trade union bargaining rights.

> 306. The complaint in the present case is contained in a communication from the Ontario Federation of Labour and the Canadian Labour Congress, dated 9 March 2002.

> 307. In a communication of 10 October 2002, the Federal Government transmitted the reply of the Government of the Province of Ontario.

> 308. Canada has ratified the Freedom of Association and Protection of the Right to Organise Convention, 1948 (No. 87). It has not ratified the Right to Organise and Collective Bargaining Convention, 1949 (No. 98), the Labour Relations (Public Service) Convention, 1978 (No. 151), nor the Collective Bargaining Convention, 1981, (No. 154).

> A. THE COMPLAINANTS' ALLEGATIONS

> 309. The Ontario Federation of Labour (OFL), affiliated to the Canadian Labour Congress, is made up of 650,000 workers in more than 1,500 affiliated local unions. This complaint concerns some provisions of the Labour Relations Amendment Act, 2000 (Bill No. 139) which, according to the OFL, infringe guarantees of freedom of association and, in particular, ILO Conventions Nos. 87, 98 and 151. These provisions encourage the decertification of workers' organizations by requiring employers to post and distribute in the workplace documents prepared by the Minister of Labour, setting out the process to terminate trade union bargaining rights.

> 310. Bill No. 139 passed third reading and received royal assent in December 2000. These provisions are now contained in section 63.1 of the Labour Relations Act (the LRA), which provides:

63.1(1) Within one year after the day the Labour Relations Amendment Act, 2000, receives royal assent, the Minister shall cause to be prepared and published a document describing the process for making an application for a declaration that the trade union no longer represents the employees in a bargaining unit. . . .

63.1(3) The document shall explain who may make an application, when an application may be made and the procedure, as set out in this Act and in any rules made by the chair of the Board . . . that the Board follows in dealing with an application.

63.1(4) An employer with respect to whom a trade union has been certified as a bargaining agent . . . shall use reasonable efforts:

(a) to post and keep posted a copy of a document published under this section in a conspicuous place in every workplace of the employer at which employees represented by the trade union perform work;

(b) to post and keep posted with that copy a notice that any employee represented by the trade union may request a copy of the document from the employer;

(c) once in each calendar year, to provide a copy of the document to all employees of the employer who are represented by the trade union; and

(d) upon the request of an employee . . . to provide a copy of the document to him or her, even though the employer has previously provided or will subsequently provide the employee with a copy of the document.

63.1(5) An employer shall not be found to be in violation of this Act as a result of doing anything set out in subsection (4).

311. In accordance with these provisions, the Minister of Labour prepared and published a document describing the process for decertification in December 2001. A copy of the poster and brochure were mailed that same month to all employers who had registered a collective bargaining relationship with the Ministry of Labour.

312. The complainants allege that section 63.1 of the LRA contravenes Convention No. 87, ratified by Canada, and is entirely inconsistent with the Government's obligations under international law to encourage, promote and protect the right of employees to bargain collectively. This provision constitutes a powerful message by the State of its opposition to the unionization of employees and a clear interference with that right. By virtue of freedom of association principles [in Convention No. 87], all workers have the right to establish and join organizations of their own choosing; governments must take measures to encourage and promote the full development and utilization of machinery for voluntary negotiation between unions and employers, and must allow trade unions to operate in full freedom.

313. The complainants submit that this provision constitutes a significant interference with the rights of employees to join and participate in the activities of trade unions. . . . Rather than encouraging the exercise of the right to collective bargaining the Government has chosen in a discriminatory and one-sided manner to promote the decertification of existing trade unions by conducting a campaign which can only be seen as designed to encourage interference with the exercise of trade union freedoms.

314. Labour relations boards and academics have consistently noted that communications by employers to employees interfering with decisions relating to certification and decertification constitute unfair labour practices. Given the responsive nature of the employment relationship, messages sent by an employer may overly influence employees in the exercise of their right to join a union. Where that message from an employer is coupled with the imprimatur of the State, it cannot but interfere with the rights of employees to join workers' organizations and to participate in their activities. The fact that the distribution of such documents by an employer would otherwise be viewed as an unfair labour practice and unlawful interference with employees' rights under the LRA is made plain by subsection 63.1(5) which absolves an employer from liability under the Act for complying with the requirements to post and distribute.

315. The legislation in question is noteworthy in that it advises employees only of their rights to decertify under the Labour Relations Act. It does not mention any of the rights that are intended to protect freedom of association including the right to engage in certification and in lawful activities of trade unions and to be free from discrimination or anti-union reprisal, all matters which are covered by the LRA. . . .

316. In addition, the Government has not chosen to require that similar posters or brochures be distributed in non-union workplaces advising employees of their rights to unionize. . . .

B. THE GOVERNMENT'S REPLY

318. In its communication of 3 October 2002, the Government of Ontario submits that the obligation made to employers in unionized workplaces to post a decertification information poster under Bill No.139 does not violate ILO Conventions Nos. 87, 98, 151 and 154. . . .

320. The document sets out neutral factual information about union decertification. It explains who may make an application, when an application may be made and the procedure as set out in the Act and in the rules of the Ontario Labour Relations Board (OLRB). . . .

323. The Government of Ontario submits that these provisions support workplace democracy and the individual right of workers freely to decide whether they wish to be represented by a union and continue with union representation. Certification information is made available to employees by unions during an organization drive but, until now, there had been little information available to employees about decertification. Unions did not provide it and employers were generally prohibited from doing so. The purpose of the decertification poster is simply to inform employees of their rights under the LRA, which they may otherwise not be aware of, by providing neutral, factual information.

324. . . . The document clearly states that the employer must not be involved in the decertification process under section 63 of the LRA. Employees are protected from employer interference with their right to freedom of association pursuant to section 63(16) of the

LRA, which states as follows: "Despite subsections (5) and (14), the Board may dismiss the application [for decertification] if the Board is satisfied that the employer or a person acting on behalf of the employer initiated the application or engaged in threats, coercion or intimidation in connection with the application."

325. Several sections of the LRA provide further protections for employees of their right to unionize. . . .

C. THE COMMITTEE'S CONCLUSIONS

. . .

329. The Committee recalls that measures should be taken to guarantee freedom of association, which includes the effective recognition of collective bargaining. This necessarily implies the taking of positive steps, conducive to achieving freedom of association and the collective regulation of employment terms and conditions.

330. The Committee considers that the provisions challenged in the present case cannot promote and encourage freedom of association. Quite the contrary, the poster and accompanying notice . . . may be considered, at best, as a message by the Government that a decertification application would be entertained favourably and, at worst, as an incitement to apply for decertification, thus contravening Convention No. 87 ratified by Canada.

331. The Government's argument that the objective of this provision is to provide neutral and factual information might have been more convincing had the amending legislation introduced parallel provisions, with the official endorsement of the Labour Ministry, to inform workers in all non-unionized workplaces (not only in "remote logging or mining camps") of their right to organize and the procedures to do so, and of the various existing legal guarantees to ensure the free exercise of that right. . . .

332. . . . The Committee can only conclude that section 63.1(5) constitutes a preemptive provision to avoid possible unfair labour practice proceedings from being filed by trade unions; this also removes much weight to the Government's argument as to the wide redress powers of the OLRB, in respect of acts done by employers in accordance with section 63.1.

333. The Committee considers that section 63.1 of the LRA does not encourage the promotion of freedom of association, is not conducive to harmonious labour relations and may rather ultimately prove counterproductive by creating a recurring climate of confrontation over certification issues. . . .

THE COMMITTEE'S RECOMMENDATION

334. In light of the foregoing conclusions, the Committee invites the Governing Body to approve the following recommendation:

> The Committee requests the Government of Ontario to repeal section 63.1 of the Labour Relations Act and to keep it informed of developments in this respect.

✻ ✻ ✻

The March 2003 report of the ILO Committee on Freedom of Association also dealt with a series of other complaints brought by Canadian unions with respect to British Columbia statutes on labour relations in health care and education enacted in 2001. In addition, the report contained follow-up material on other Canadian complaints that were first dealt with in earlier years. Those earlier complaints related to certain statutory provisions in Ontario and New Brunswick, including two items referred to in Chapter 4 above: the *Prevention of Unionization Act (Ontario Works), 1998*, with respect to workfare recipients (referred to in section 4:220), and the provisions of the Ontario *Labour Relations Act, 1995* excluding agricultural workers from the scope of that Act (referred to in section 4:300).

The Committee's report also dealt with complaints brought against Argentina, Belarus, Brazil, Bulgaria, Colombia, and China. However, of the the 334 paragraphs that made up the entire report, 220 were devoted to complaints against labour laws in one country — Canada. Why do you think our law attracted so much of the Committee's attention?

14:220 A Regional Endeavour: The North American Agreement on Labour Co-operation

The North American Free Trade Agreement (NAFTA), between Canada, the United States, and Mexico, which has been in force since 1994, makes no mention of labour issues. However, one of its supplementary documents, the North American Agreement on Labour Cooperation (NAALC) — widely known as the labour side agreement — addresses failures by any of the three governments to enforce its own labour laws.

The full text of NAALC can be found at <http://www.naalc.org/english/agreement.shtml>.The following are some of its main substantive provisions.

North American Agreement on Labor Co-operation Between the Government of the United States of America, the Government of Canada and the Government of the United Mexican States, 13 September 1993

. . .

PART ONE: OBJECTIVES

Article 1: Objectives

The objectives of this Agreement are to:
a. improve working conditions and living standards in each Party's territory;
b. promote, to the maximum extent possible, the labor principles set out in Annex 1;
c. encourage cooperation to promote innovation and rising levels of productivity and quality;
d. encourage publication and exchange of information, data development and coordination, and joint studies to enhance mutually beneficial understanding of the laws and institutions governing labor in each Party's territory;
e. pursue cooperative labor-related activities on the basis of mutual benefit;
f. promote compliance with, and effective enforcement by each Party of, its labor law; and
g. foster transparency in the administration of labor law.

PART TWO: OBLIGATIONS

Article 2: Levels of Protection

Affirming full respect for each Party's constitution, and recognizing the right of each Party to establish its own domestic labor standards, and to adopt or modify accordingly its labor laws and regulations, each Party shall ensure that its labor laws and regulations provide for high labor standards, consistent with high quality and productivity workplaces, and shall continue to strive to improve those standards in that light.

Article 3: Government Enforcement Action

1. Each Party shall promote compliance with and effectively enforce its labor law through appropriate government action, subject to Article 42, such as:
a. appointing and training inspectors;
b. monitoring compliance and investigating suspected violations, including through on-site inspections;
c. seeking assurances of voluntary compliance;
d. requiring record keeping and reporting;
e. encouraging the establishment of worker-management committees to address labor regulation of the workplace;
f. providing or encouraging mediation, conciliation and arbitration services; or
g. initiating, in a timely manner, proceedings to seek appropriate sanctions or remedies for violations of its labor law.

2. Each Party shall ensure that its competent authorities give due consideration in accordance with its law to any request by an employer, employee or their representatives, or other interested person, for an investigation of an alleged violation of the Party's labor law.

Article 4: Private Action

1. Each Party shall ensure that persons with a legally recognized interest under its law in a particular matter have appropriate access to administrative, quasi-judicial, judicial or labor tribunals for the enforcement of the Party's labor law.

2. Each Party's law shall ensure that such persons may have recourse to, as appropriate, procedures by which rights arising under:
a. its labor law, including in respect of occupational safety and health, employment standards, industrial relations and migrant workers, and
b. collective agreements,
can be enforced.

Article 5: Procedural Guarantees

1. Each Party shall ensure that its administrative, quasi-judicial, judicial and labor tribunal proceedings for the enforcement of its labor law are fair, equitable and transparent and, to this end, each Party shall provide that:
a. such proceedings comply with due process of law;

b. any hearings in such proceedings are open to the public, except where the adminis-
    tration of justice otherwise requires;

c. the parties to such proceedings are entitled to support or defend their respective posi-
    tions and to present information or evidence; and

d. such proceedings are not unnecessarily complicated and do not entail unreasonable
    charges or time limits or unwarranted delays.

. . .

Article 49: Definitions

1. For purposes of this Agreement:

A Party has not failed to "effectively enforce its occupational safety and health, child labor
or minimum wage technical labor standards" or comply with Article 3(1) in a particular
case where the action or inaction by agencies or officials of that Party:

a. reflects a reasonable exercise of the agency's or the official's discretion with respect to
    investigatory, prosecutorial, regulatory or compliance matters; or

b. results from bona fide decisions to allocate resources to enforcement in respect of
    other labor matters determined to have higher priorities;

"labor law" means laws and regulations, or provisions thereof, that are directly related to:

a. freedom of association and protection of the right to organize;

b. the right to bargain collectively;

c. the right to strike;

d. prohibition of forced labor;

e. labor protections for children and young persons;

f. minimum employment standards, such as minimum wages and overtime pay, cover-
    ing wage earners, including those not covered by collective agreements;

g. elimination of employment discrimination on the basis of grounds such as race, reli-
    gion, age, sex, or other grounds as determined by each Party's domestic laws;

h. equal pay for men and women;

i. prevention of occupational injuries and illnesses;

j. compensation in cases of occupational injuries and illnesses;

k. protection of migrant workers;

"mutually recognized labor laws" means laws of both a requesting Party and the Party whose
laws were the subject of ministerial consultations under Article 22 that address the same general subject matter in a manner that provides enforceable rights, protections or standards;

"pattern of practice" means a course of action or inaction beginning after the date of entry
into force of the Agreement, and does not include a single instance or case;

"persistent pattern" means a sustained or recurring pattern of practice;

"province" means a province of Canada, and includes the Yukon Territory and the Northwest Territories and their successors;

"publicly available information" means information to which the public has a legal right under the statutory laws of the Party;

"technical labor standards" means laws and regulations, or specific provisions thereof, that are directly related to subparagraphs (d) through (k) of the definition of labor law. For greater certainty and consistent with the provisions of this Agreement, the setting of all standards and levels in respect of minimum wages and labor protections for children and young persons by each Party shall not be subject to obligations under this Agreement. Each Party's obligations under this Agreement pertain to enforcing the level of the general minimum wage and child labor age limits established by that Party; . . .

[Published by the Secretariat of the Commission for Labour Co-operation. Reprinted by permission.]

* * *

Parts 4 and 5 of NAALC (articles 20 to 41) embody an elaborate process for the handling of complaints. That process is outlined in the following excerpt.

Organisation for Economic Co-operation and Development, *Trade, Employment and Labour Standards* (Paris: OECD, 1996) at 178–83

THE NORTH AMERICAN AGREEMENT ON LABOUR COOPERATION

The North American Agreement on Labour Cooperation (NAALC) — more commonly known as the labour supplemental agreement to the NAFTA — links each of the North American countries' labour laws to the regional trade agreement. Both agreements entered into force on January 1st, 1994. The NAALC promotes mutually recognised labour principles including core labour standards and other standards such as the occupational health and safety of workers and the protection of migrant workers. . . .

The main objective of the NAALC is to improve working conditions and living standards in the United States, Mexico and Canada. The emphasis of the agreement is to encourage transparent and effective enforcement of the existing labour laws in each country through cooperation and the exchange of information. The agreement also provides for consultations between the National Administrative Offices (NAO) or at the Ministerial level, as well as comparative assessments among the three countries. Should these steps fail to solve a matter in dispute, a dispute resolution process can be invoked. This process may ultimately result in fines (monetary enforcement assessments) backed by trade sanctions in the event Mexico or the United States does not observe and enforce its own labour laws, but it must be noted that trade sanctions are not available against Canada [NAALC, Part 4 and Part 5]. Complaints or petitions can be submitted by any person with a legally recognized interest under the law of any party to the NAALC. However, the dispute settlement procedure can be quite lengthy: over two years may elapse before measures such as the imposition of action plans, or fines or trade sanctions can be enforced. In addition, trade sanctions are only possible in the areas of child labour, minimum wages and occupational safety and health, but not in cases relating to freedom of association, right to bargain collectively, and forced labour (see the table below on the NAALC dispute settlement process and time-frame). Furthermore, it must be noted that the NAALC does not refer to internationally-agreed minimum labour standards as the European GSP system (see below), but to standards defined under the national legislation of the parties. In particular, complaints must be both trade-related and covered by mutually recognized labour laws, and there must have been a persistent pattern of non-enforcement of the relevant labour legislation. . . .

NAALC Dispute Settlement Process

	Action	Timing
Step 1	Submission filed with NAO (full coverage of NAALC dispositions)	NAO must accept or reject submission for review within 60 days
Step 2	Review process: information gathering through consultation with other NAOs, and/or public hearing (in the U.S.), final report published (in Mexico and the U.S.)	Final report must be published within 120 days from acceptance of submission, with possible 60 days extension
If unresolved:		
Step 3	Ministerial consultations (full coverage). *If unresolved,* and object of dispute is (i) trade related; (ii) concerns mutually recognized labour laws in the areas of health and safety, child labour, and technical labour standards; any consulting party may request:	No set time limit
Step 4	Establish an Evaluation Committee of Experts, prepare draft evaluation report that may be reviewed by the parties, and then present final evaluation report	Draft report shall be presented to the parties within 120 days after establishment, and final report presented to the Council no later than 60 days later. Written responses by the Parties must be provided within 90 days, and submitted to the Council along with the final report at the next regular Council session
If unresolved **AND related to health and safety, child labor, or minimum wages:**		
Step 5	Ministerial Council Consultations. *If unresolved,* within 60 days party may request a Special Session of the Council to convene within 20 days and have 60 days to reach a resolution, and if unresolved, then at the request of any consulting Party and by a two-third vote, the Council shall:	60 days
Step 6	Convene an Arbitral Panel	Initial Report presented to the Parties within 180 days after selection of the panelists. Final report due within 60 days after submission of initial report
If unresolved		
	(a) no action (b) parties cannot agree on whether implemented	Under (a), request to reconvene between 60–120 days, under (b) no earlier than 180 days

Action	Timing
Step 7 Panel may be reconvened and may impose a monetary enforcement assessment	Under (a) Panel has 90 days to take action, under (b) 60 days

If a Party fails to pay a monetary enforcement assessment within 180 days after it is imposed by panel:

Step 8 Complaining Party or Parties may suspend application of NAFTA benefits in an amount no greater than that sufficient to collect the monetary enforcement assessment (only for Mexico and the U.S.)

Sources: NAALC, Final Draft, 1993; NAALC: A Guide, U.S. NAO, U.S. Dept of Labor, Washington, D.C., 1995, Appendix 1, Appendix 2.

[© OECD, 1996, *Trade, Employment and Labour Standards: A Study of Core Workers' Rights and International Trade.* Reproduced with permission of the OECD.]

✵ ✵ ✵

The above process has not been followed through to its final stages in any of the approximately thirty complaints that have been brought so far with respect to alleged failures by one or other of the three signatory countries to give effect to the provisions of its labour legislation. This factor, among others, has led some observers to conclude that NAALC is ineffectual. However, the following excerpt provides an example of its use to spotlight a regulatory problem and to induce government to consult with workers and employers in an effort to remedy the problem.

NAALC Secretariat, Communications submitted to the United States National Administrative Office (NAO): Summary of U.S. NAO 9803

On December 18, 1998, the U.S. NAO accepted for review a public communication alleging a failure by Quebec, Canada, to provide an effective remedy for plant closings with anti-union motivations, and unwarranted delays in union certification procedures. The communication also alleged that, by limiting union certifications to single employer bargaining units, Quebec labor law made it unduly difficult for workers in nonstandard employment (part-time, casual, contractual work) to organize unions. The allegations related to attempts to organize the employees at a McDonald's restaurant in St. Hubert, Quebec, Canada. The communication was submitted on October 21, 1998, by the International Brotherhood of Teamsters, Teamsters Canada, the Quebec Federation of Labor, Teamsters Local 973 (Montreal) and the International Labor Rights Fund.

On January 20, 1999 the U.S. NAO requested information from the Canadian NAO regarding plant closures with anti-union motivations in the province of Quebec. The Canadian NAO's response of January 29, 1999 extended an invitation from the Quebec labor department to officials of the U.S. NAO to meet regarding the issue. After a meeting between the U.S. NAO, Quebec labor officials and union representatives, it was agreed that a Quebec government council would commence a study of sudden anti-union plant closures.

This submission was short lived. Once submitted, the Québec government quickly met with labour and came to an agreement to address the question legislatively. The unions withdrew the submission. The NAALC decided to study the issue of sudden plant closings, producing a thorough discussion paper on the topic that canvassed practices across North America.

[Reprinted by permission.]

Lance Compa, "NAFTA's Labour Side Agreement and International Labour Solidarity," Antipode: A Radical Journal of Geography, vol. 33, no. 3, July 2001, pp. 451–67

. . .

EXPERIENCE UNDER THE NAALC

For labour rights advocates with patience and willingness to put it to the test, the NAALC has emerged as a viable new arena for creative transnational action. With its unusual "cross-border" complaint mechanism, the Agreement provides an opportunity for workers, trade unions and their allies in the United States, Mexico and Canada to work together concretely to defend workers' rights against abuses by corporations and governments.

This is not meant to exaggerate the NAALC's effects. It is not a full-fledged international enforcement mechanism. Critics fault it, for example, for not resulting in reinstatement orders for workers unjustly dismissed for union organizing efforts, or orders to recognize and bargain with independent unions instead of company or government-sponsored unions. But advocates need to be practical about how far governments are prepared to go to hand over traditional sovereignty on labour issues to new international tribunals. Even the European Union, with extensive labour rights provisions that can be enforced by the European Court of Justice, leaves issues of salaries, union organizing and collective bargaining, and the right to strike untouched by EU directives. Single member countries hold veto power over EU policy on social security and social protection, redundancies and other key matters.

In the six years since it took effect, NAFTA's labour side agreement has given rise to a varied, rich experience of international labour rights advocacy. More than twenty complaints and cases on behalf of workers in all three countries have arisen under the NAALC. They embrace workers' organizing and bargaining efforts, occupational safety and health, migrant worker protection, minimum employment standards, discrimination against women, compensation for workplace injuries, and other issues.

A rapid summary of just a few cases — and later a more detailed look at one — suggests how advocates get results. Gains are not made through direct enforcement by an international tribunal, but through indirection, by exploiting the spaces created by this new labour rights instrument to strengthen cross-border ties among labour rights advocates and to generate unexpected pressures on governments and on transnational enterprises. To be effective, labor rights advocates using the Agreement must seek help from their counterparts across the border.

- In 1996 the provincial government of Alberta, Canada announced plans to privatize workplace health and safety enforcement. Labour inspectors would be sacked and become independent contractors. The public employees' union declared it would file a NAALC complaint charging Alberta with not just failure, but with a complete abdication, of its responsibility to effectively enforce health and safety laws. The government dropped the plan.

- In 1996 Mexican labour authorities dissolved a small, democratic trade union in the Fisheries ministry when that agency was merged into the larger environmental ministry, where a bigger pro-government held bargaining rights. Together with U.S. human rights groups, the dissident union filed a NAALC complaint in the United States charging failure to enforce Mexican constitutional guarantees of freedom of association. At a public hearing in Washington, D.C., Mexican government officials and leaders of both Mexican unions, labour law experts from both countries, and U.S. labour and human rights advocates testified, generating wide publicity in both countries and a sharply critical report by the U.S. NAO. The smaller, dissident union regained its registration and has continued its activity in the democratic union movement.

- Mexican and U.S. telephone workers unions filed a 1997 complaint with the U.S. NAO when workers at the Maxi-Switch electronics factory in Sonora, Mexico tried to form an independent union but were denied registration. Two days before a scheduled public hearing in Tucson, Arizona (near the Sonora plant) the Mexican government and the Mexican telephone workers union agreed to settle the complaint and cancel the hearing. Registration was granted to the independent union.

- A 1997 complaint by a coalition of U.S. and Mexican labour, human rights and women's rights groups challenged the widespread practice of pregnancy testing in the maquiladora factories. A public hearing in Texas near the border area exposed the involvement of well-known U.S. companies like General Motors and Zenith and led to a U.S. NAO report confirming the abuses. Several U.S. multinational firms announced they would halt the practice, and advocacy groups in Mexico launched new efforts for reform legislation to halt pregnancy testing in employment.

- U.S. and Mexican labour, human rights, and local community advocacy groups filed a NAALC complaint with the U.S. NAO in 1997 against interference with an independent union organizing effort and health and safety violations at a Hyundai Motors supplier called Han Young. A 1998 public hearing in San Diego, California and follow up governmental consultations and public forums made the case an international incident. The Mexican labour department applied the first substantial fines against any company for health and safety violations. The independent union gained bargaining rights and has maintained an active, high-profile campaign with international support for securing a collective agreement.

- More than twenty trade union and allied organizations filed NAALC complaints in 1998 both with the U.S. NAO and with the Canadian NAO on violations of workers' organizing rights and health and safety laws at a U.S. company-owned auto parts factory in Mexico City called ITAPSA. The coalition mounted broad-based activity in connection with public hearings in both countries, as well as protests at corporate shareholder meetings. International support has allowed the union to maintain its struggle for recognition.

- A 1999 complaint to the U.S. NAO by flight attendants' unions in the United States and Mexico charged Mexico with failing to enforce freedom of association by denying flight attendants represented by a "wall-to-wall" pro-government union at the TAESA airline the right to form an independent union. A March 2000 public hearing in Washington, D.C. buttressed workers' claims and demonstrated international support for Mexican flight attendants, who undertook protest actions in major airports. Later in 2000, in a parallel situation at another airline, the Mexican government reversed its stance and allowed flight attendants to vote separately on union representation to avoid a new round of international scrutiny.

- Canadian and U.S. unions filed a NAALC complaint with the U.S. NAO in 1998 after McDonald's closed a Montreal restaurant where workers had formed a union. The complaint targeted flaws in Quebec's labour law that allowed companies to close work sites for anti-union motivation. When the U.S. NAO accepted the complaint and scheduled public hearings, Quebec trade unions, employer federations, and labour department officials agreed to take up the matter in a labour code reform bill rather than have Quebec's "dirty laundry" aired in a U.S. public hearing. The unions withdrew the complaint, and the hearing was cancelled.

- Twenty-five unions, health and safety advocacy groups, human rights organizations and allied community support networks filed a major new complaint with the U.S. NAO in 2000 for workers suffering egregious health and safety violations at two Auto-Trim manufacturing plants in the maquiladora region. The 100-page complaint reflects long and careful collaboration among the filing organizations, a high level of technical competency and legal argument, and a powerful indictment of the government's failure to enforce health and safety laws. A public hearing was set for early 2001.

In each of these cases new alliances were built among groups that had hardly ever communicated until the NAALC complaint gave them a concrete venue for working together. For leaders and activists of independent Mexican trade unions in particular, access to international allies and to a mechanism for scrutiny of repressive tactics long hidden from international public view provided strength and protection to build their movement.

This accounting is not meant to overstate the Agreement's impact. Each of the cases noted here is more complicated than these capsule summaries can convey, and the advantages gained are uneven. Using the NAALC does not mean going from triumph to triumph. But the nature of trade union work, both in the national context and in the context of globalization, is anything but a triumphant march forward. It is more of a hard slog through rocks and mud, usually with more backsliding and side-slipping than progress.

Any request of workers to turn to the NAALC to air their grievances must be joined by honest cautions that it cannot directly result in regained jobs, union recognition, or back pay for violations. Unions and allied groups have to weigh the value of using the Agreement in light of staff time, energy and resources that might be allocated elsewhere, when a specific payoff in new members or new collective agreements cannot be promised. Gains come obliquely, over time, by pressing companies and governments to change their behavior, by sensitizing public opinion, by building ties of solidarity, and taking other steps to change the climate for workers' rights advances in North America. Perhaps, in time, even direct gains can be achieved as the NAALC system elaborates a kind of labour law jurisprudence for North America that informs decisions by national bodies. That goal is still to be met.

The Problem of Sovereignty

It could hardly be otherwise at this stage of regional integration among such diverse countries. Take one of the early NAALC cases, for example, involving Sprint Corp., the U.S. telecommunications giant. In 1994, Sprint closed a San Francisco facility shortly before more than 200 workers there were to vote for union representation. In national legal proceedings, the highest U.S. federal court authorities ruled in the company's favor, saying the evidence showed the closing was a lawful one motivated by business considerations, not anti-unionism.

On a separate track, a NAALC complaint led to widely noted public hearings in San Francisco that gave an international platform to affected workers and union leaders from the United States, Mexico and Europe who exposed Sprint's antiunion actions and challenged the company's joint ventures in Mexico and other countries. The NAALC's permanent secretariat published a 250-page study comparing each country's legal regime for antiunion plant closures that highlighted widespread abuses in the U.S. system. Trade unionists involved in the Sprint case denounced the NAALC as worthless because it did not overturn the federal court's decision and order the company to reopen the plant, rehire the workers with back pay, and recognize the union. Tactically, such denunciations are fair enough as a way to attack Sprint. But to expect the agreement to create an international labour tribunal empowered to independently take evidence and overrule national courts is completely unrealistic.

The Agreement was negotiated by countries with highly developed and highly divergent labour law and labour relations systems. Each is a product of unique time, space, and language-bound social histories. The result was inevitably a compromised hybrid. The states opened themselves to a cross-border oversight mechanism, with limited enforcement powers, while guarding sovereignty over key elements of their national systems. It is not the agreement trade unionists and workers' rights advocates would have written were it left to them, but it was not left to them.

The challenge is to exploit what was written, and to change it over time to strengthen workers' rights. In some cases unwittingly, NAALC negotiators created new space for advocates to communicate, collaborate, strategize and act together, seizing opportunities that had never existed.

A TRANSNATIONAL ADVOCACY PERSPECTIVE

NAALC "Platforms"

Metaphorically, the NAALC can be seen creating a series of sliding platforms crossing the space of one, two or three countries where trade unionists and their allies can stand to direct fire at their own and the others' governments, their own and the others' national and multinational corporations, even their own and the others' corrupted trade unions.

The platforms can cross borders in equal proportion, or be anchored mostly in one country. They rest first on the Agreement's unique, accessible cross-border complaint mechanism. Workers who suffer abuses, and their defenders, have to file a complaint with the government of another country, not the country where violations occurred. Under the agreement, "any person" can file such complaints. There are no citizenship requirements or requirements that a complainant be an injured party or have a material stake in a case.

The result is that social actors that use the NAALC seek partners in the country or countries where they intend to file complaints. Indeed, most of the more than twenty cases filed so far have involved transnational coalitions of unions and allied human rights and community groups who find in the Agreement's institutional mechanisms new opportunities to develop relationships and joint action.

Before the NAALC was created, cross-border trade union relationships mostly consisted of thin contacts at two levels. One was between high-level union leaders who attended conferences and conventions and agreed on resolutions of support without much followup. The other consisted of sporadic local-union-to-local-union contacts and occasional worker-to-worker delegations that usually were aimed at helping the poor Mexicans. These links paled in comparison with the business-to-business contacts and boss-to-boss delegations that occur every day in North American commerce.

The new NAALC platforms allow transnational social actors to demand investigations, public hearings and government consultations on workers' rights violations. Advocates now have the opportunity to strategize and plan together in a sustained fashion, gathering evidence for drafting a complaint, crafting its elements, setting priorities, defining demands, launching media campaigns, meeting with government officials to set the agenda for a hearing and to press them for thorough reviews and followup, preparing to testify in public hearings, engaging technical experts to buttress a case with scientific elements (a health and safety case, for example), influencing the composition of independent experts' panels and the terms of reference of their investigation, and other concrete tasks that go far beyond adopting resolutions or arranging serial worker-to-worker meetings.

Why Bother?

The criticism can be fairly made that this is staff work, not rank-and-file mobilization. It occupies lawyers, researchers, publicists and other union and NGO professionals without engaging workers. Worse, it can create false illusions of relief through bureaucratic legal mechanisms instead of workers' own power. It looks for help from the same governments that are chiefly interested in protecting capital, not labour. For labour radicals, why bother?

Bother for the same reasons workers have to bother with national legal systems: because those are the mechanisms workers have gained after long political organizing and bargaining struggles in a system that is stacked against them.

Legal work, media advocacy, lobbying and other "inside game" moves are deeply compromised, flawed and frustrating. They are poor, pale, anemic substitutes for rich, red, robust worker mobilization and struggle against corporate power. But the balance of

power in a capitalist society — or rather the imbalance of power, accentuated now by globalization of production and investment flows — constricts the space for worker action and
makes all the more precious the spaces that become available.

Of course workers must take up the struggle through organizing, strikes, demonstrations, protests and other forms of direct action. But they cannot do it all the time, every
day, in every dispute. There are inherent limits to time, space, energy, resources and other
factors affecting capacity for workers' struggle. More fundamentally, the balance of power
is unfavorable. Workers are not now in a position to vanquish the capitalist class or the
capitalist state. Their agenda is necessarily a "Plan B" involving selective struggle, incremental gains through politics and legislation, and creative exploitation of national legal
institutions as well as new international mechanisms like the NAALC to advance their
interests.

Transnational advocacy networks have to work around the lack of "hard law" features
which create accountability through trials of evidence, findings of guilt, and enforcement
by state power — putting lawbreakers in jail, or seizing their assets to satisfy a financial
judgment. Instead, they must exploit the potential for "soft law" mechanisms typical of
the NAALC and other international instruments and mechanisms. Soft law is marked by
investigations, reviews, research, reports, information exchanges, public hearings (as distinct from trials of evidence), consultations, evaluations, recommendations, declarations,
publicity, exposés; the "mobilization of shame," as it is sometimes put, to enforce judgments in the court of public opinion.

These measures should not be scorned or boycotted by social actors, and least by
transnational actors looking for openings, spaces, platforms or other bases for creative
intervention and exploitation. The challenge is to integrate involvement in institutional
settings with action in extra-institutional settings.

This is not meant as a wide-eyed endorsement of using the NAALC at every opportunity. Choices about resource allocation and measurement of potential gains have to be
made. Actors face unavoidable compromises using instruments and procedures created
by governments more attuned to corporate concerns than to workers' interests. It is just
a short step to cooptation if advocates become so enamored of international labour rights
instruments like the NAALC that they devalue struggle against the neoliberal agenda, like
that in the streets of Seattle.

Given the structurally defensive position of workers in a corporate-dominated system,
sole reliance on denunciation, confrontation and rejection, while scorning involvement in
efforts to link workers' rights to trade or to use the inevitably flawed agreements that follow, is a self-limiting strategy. Putting all the energy of the international movement
against corporate power into protesting WTO and international bankers' conclaves, or
launching ad hoc media campaigns against Wal-Mart's latest sale of products made by
child labour, is only one side of a strategic whole. Both sides are needed, and both sides
need each other. One is a sharp "no" to the corporate agenda and related mobilization that
denounces, exposes, protests and even shuts down — if only for a few hours — the gears
of global trade and investment. The other is a savvy, strategic exploitation of pressure
points found in international human rights and labour rights instruments, however

flawed they may be compared with what labour rights advocates would create on their own without governments or transnational enterprises to contend with.

Contrary to the scornful dismissal of the NAALC by skeptics and critics on the left, fear and loathing mark the views of government and corporate officials at the opposite pole. Former Mexican government officials who made light of the Agreement when it was negotiated in 1993 later condemned it for the scrutiny and condemnation it brought to Mexican labour practices under the spotlight of complaints, public hearings, public reports, government-to-government consultations. One denounced "indiscriminate acceptance" of complaints and warned that the NAALC served "the tactical interests of U.S. unions and so-called 'independent trade unions' in Mexico."

U.S. corporate executives and attorneys think the Agreement has been hijacked by trade union radicals to attack company conduct throughout North America, and demand an end to contentious complaint procedures where unions and their allies brand companies as workers' rights violators. An executive of the Washington State apple industry said "unions on both sides of the border are abusing the NAFTA process in an effort to expand their power . . . NAFTA's labour side agreement is an open invitation for specific labour disputes to be raised into an international question . . . and could open the door to a host of costly and frivolous complaints against U.S. employers."

THE WASHINGTON APPLE CASE

The Washington state apple case is a rich example "platform-building" by strategic use of the NAALC and how it can foster new ties of solidarity and sustained work among labour rights advocates in the United States and Mexico. More than 50,000 Mexican workers labour in the orchards and processing plants of the largest apple-growing region in the United States. Employers crushed their efforts throughout the 1990s to form trade unions, to bargain collectively, to have job health and safety protection, to end discrimination, and to make other workplace gains.

In 1997 the Teamsters union and the United Farm Workers agreed to develop a NAALC case on these issues. They reached out for support to Mexican unions, farmworker advocacy groups, and human rights organizations. A complaint was drafted, translated and redrafted to the satisfaction of the newly-formed network. In May 1998 the question was then posed: who should sign the complaint, which would be filed with the Mexican labour department? Put another way, who would be publicly identified as the parties that triggered international scrutiny of labour abuses in Washington State that might result in sanctions against apple exports to Mexico? Mexico is the largest single export market for Washington apples, and since the complaint addressed health and safety violations among many others, it was susceptible to sanctions.

The two U.S. unions were each trying to organize apple workers, one in the orchards and one in the processing plants. They wanted to avoid employers' countercharges that they were out to destroy apple workers' jobs. On the Mexican side, the independent union allies in the *Unión Nacional de Trabajadores* (UNT), the *Frente Auténtico del Trabajo* (FAT), the *Frente Democrático de Campesinos* (FDC) and other groups working with their U.S.

counterparts were sensitive to government and official union accusations that they were "puppets" of protectionist U.S. unions. At the same time, from an inside-Mexico competitive standpoint, they wanted to be seen as frontline defenders of migrant workers in the United States, ahead of the official unions and ahead of the PRI government.

After careful consultations through personal visits, telephone conference calls, e-mail exchanges and other communications among key leaders and staffers of all these organizations, the complaint was officially signed by just the Mexican organizations, not by any U.S. groups. An American NGO, the International Labour Rights Fund, became the public face of a media campaign in the United States, issuing press releases and sending an investigator to the apple growing region to meet with workers about the cases and to interview potential witnesses for a hearing to be held in Mexico, with behind-the-scenes help from the unions. An experienced organizer from the FAT came to Washington to help the unions in their organizing efforts. The AFL-CIO's Solidarity Center pledged financial support to send Washington apple workers to Mexico for the hearings. Less than one month after the Washington State apple complaint was filed in Mexico, the CTM — the official, pro-government union federation in Mexico — filed its own first-ever NAALC complaint over treatment of migrant Mexican workers at an opposite corner of the United States, in the Easternmost state of Maine.

In December 1998 a hearing in the case was held in Mexico City. Advocates faced another strategic decision: should worker witnesses be Mexican migrants alone, which would obviate the need for translation and allow more workers to testify, or should non-Mexican, English-speaking workers also participate (many Anglo workers are employed in the processing plants, not in the orchards, which are entirely Mexican migrants) at the cost of a bumpier hearing process. U.S. advocates first suggested an all-Mexican, Spanish-only project. But Mexicans thought the effort would be strengthened by presenting united interests of both Mexican and American workers. Long-time Anglo workers joined the delegation and the unions provided interpretation for them during press conferences, during meetings with Mexican workers and trade unionists, and at the hearing at the Mexican labour department. Their shoulder-to-shoulder stance with Mexican coworkers lent a powerful image of solidarity to the public face of the campaign.

The hearing in Mexico City itself was a dramatic example of the reach of the NAALC "platform" and the leaping of spatial, language and cultural boundaries in the North American context. Half a dozen officials from an agency of the Mexican government heard, in their own language, accounts of labour rights abuses by a delegation of Mexican workers employed in the United States thousands of miles to the North in an industry for which Mexico is a major consumer market. The hearing was prompted by a complaint initiated by U.S. trade unionists in Washington State, Washington D.C. and California (site of the United Farm Workers union headquarters; the Teamsters union headquarters are in Washington, D.C.), then filed by allies in Mexican labour and human rights organizations in Mexico City after lengthy cross-border planning.

At the hearing, the Mexican workers were joined by Spanish-speaking U.S. trade union representatives and human rights attorneys, by Mexican independent union and farmworker advocates, and by English-speaking co-workers who delivered their own duly interpreted testimony in English.

The Mexican labour department later issued a report demanding consultations between the labour secretaries of the two countries. They agreed on a program, due to be implemented in early 2001, of public outreach and public hearings chaired by U.S. and Mexican officials from the two federal governments and from the state government. The forums would take place in the apple-growing region of Washington, where large numbers of workers are prepared to testify about conditions in both Spanish and English.

In succession, the NAALC provided concrete means of pressing the apple growing industry to improve conditions or risk losing the Mexican market, pressing the government of Mexico to conduct a thorough review of the complaint, hold public hearings for workers from the United States, and issue a strong report seeking ministerial consultations; pressing the *officialista* Mexican labour unions to take their own action on behalf of Mexican migrants in the United States by filing the NAALC complaint on Maine, pressing the U.S. government to agree to public events in Washington State and to devote its own energies to seeking improved conditions, and pressing the state government to take steps in matters of state competence to improve conditions, especially with regard to safety and health. While cycling from national to transnational arenas, every step was accompanied by a media campaign that kept the dispute in the public eye and shaped a new, rights-based discourse linked to North American economic integration.

CONCLUSION

The apple case shows how expanding coalitions of trade union, human rights, migrant workers, women's rights and other progressive communities involved in using the NAALC are adding new chapters to stories already known of transnational advocacy networks using new international instruments and institutions to promote their goals. Admittedly, the new networks until now have mostly engaged trade union and NGO leaders, organizers, lawyers, researchers, publicists and other cadres, not masses of workers in a genuine transnational social movement. But constructing and strengthening ties among these cadres is a precondition to a new global solidarity unionism that is the longer-term goal.

The instruments and institutions are flawed. But they create spaces, terrains, platforms and other metaphorical foundations where advocates can unite across frontiers and plant their feet to promote new norms, mobilize actors, call to account governments and corporations, disseminate research findings, launch media campaigns, educate each other and the public, challenge traditional notions of sovereignty, give legitimacy to their cause by invoking human rights and labour rights principles — in sum, to redefine debates and discourse by breaking up old frameworks and shaping new ones.
[Preprinted by permission of Blackwell Publishing.]

* * *

Negotiations have been underway since 1994 for a Free Trade Area of the Americas. Those negotiations include every country in North, South, and Central America, except Cuba. A meeting of trade ministers in November 2003 affirmed that the target date for an agreement is January 2005. Working groups have been meeting in many trade-related areas, but labour is not one of them. However, the Third Draft FTAA Agreement, dated November 21, 2003 (http://www.ftaa-alca.org/FTAADraft03/Index_e.asp), includes the following provisions.

Third Draft of the Free Trade Area of the Americas Agreement

CHAPTER VII: LABOR PROVISIONS AND NON-IMPLEMENTATION PROCEDURES FOR ENVIRONMENT AND LABOR PROVISIONS

Article 1. Statement of Shared Commitment

1.1. The Parties reaffirm their obligations as members of the International Labor Organization (ILO) and their commitments under the *1998 ILO Declaration on Fundamental Principles and Rights at Work*. Each Party shall strive to ensure that such labor principles and the internationally recognized labor rights set forth in Article 7.1. (Definitions) of this Chapter, are recognized and protected by domestic labor laws.

1.2. Recognizing the right of each Party to establish its own labor standards, and to adopt or modify its labor laws accordingly, each Party shall strive to ensure that its laws provide for labor standards consistent with the internationally recognized labor rights set forth in Article 7.1. (Definitions) of this Chapter, and shall strive to improve those standards.

Article 2. Application and Enforcement of Labor Laws

2.1. A Party shall not fail to effectively enforce its labor laws, through a sustained or recurring course of action or inaction, in a manner affecting trade between the Parties, after the date of entry into force of this Agreement.

2.2. The Parties recognize that each Party retains the right to exercise discretion with respect to investigatory, prosecutorial, regulatory, and compliance matters and to make decisions regarding the allocation of resources to enforcement with respect to other labor matters determined to have higher priorities. . . .

2.3. The Parties recognize that it is inappropriate to encourage trade or investment by weakening or reducing the protections afforded in domestic labor laws. Accordingly, each Party shall strive to ensure that it does not waive or otherwise derogate from, or offer to waive or otherwise derogate from, such laws in a manner that weakens or reduces adherence to the internationally recognized labor rights referred to in Article 7.1. (Definitions) of this Chapter, as an encouragement for trade with another Party, or as an encouragement for the establishment, acquisition, expansion, or retention of an investment in its territory.
. . .

Article 4. Labor Cooperation

. . .

4.2. Cooperative activities and capacity building in support of the objectives of this Chapter may include, but need not be limited to the following subjects:

a) Fundamental labor rights and their effective application;

b) Elimination of the worst forms of child labor;

c) Labor administration;

d) Labor inspectorates and inspection systems;

e) Labor justice;

f) Labor-management relations; and

g) Working conditions: hours of work, minimum wages, and occupational safety and health.

. . .

[Article 5 provides that a consultative procedure, or the agreement's dispute settlement provisions, may be invoked if a member state alleges that another has failed to enforce its own labour laws. Article 6 provides that every member state must have fair and accessible administrative or judicial processes for enforcing its labour laws without undue cost or delay.]

Article 7. Definitions

7.1. For purposes of this Chapter, *labor laws* means a Party's statutes or regulations, or provisions thereof, that are directly related to the following internationally recognized labor rights:

a) the right of association;

b) the right to organize and bargain collectively;

c) a prohibition on the use of any form of forced or compulsory labor;

d) labor protections for children, including a minimum age for the employment of children and the prohibition and elimination of the worst forms of child labor; and

e) acceptable conditions of work with respect to minimum wages, hours of work, and occupational safety and health.

14:230 Self-regulatory Initiatives

Even if there is a sense that transnational institutions are needed to regulate the labour market, and especially the behaviour of multinational companies, we are a long way from having such institutions. That is true even in Europe, where one might expect to find the most progress. However, a considerable range of organizations that operate transnationally do have some capacity to regulate corporate behaviour, local labour standards, or workers' rights. Space permits only a brief overview.

Unions have made some efforts to establish transnational alliances and strategies, with a view to presenting a united front to employers who do business in several countries or in such industries as shipping and air transport, where an employer may have a presence in many countries. Such alliances are rare, however. The most powerful one — the United Auto Workers — which once represented employees of the major automobile, aircraft, and farm implement manufacturers in the U.S. and Canada, split some time ago into two national unions that now have relatively little contact. As Compa points out in the above excerpt, a few links have developed between Canadian and American unions and those in Mexico since NAALC came into force, but there is little collaboration between workers in the advanced economies and their counterparts in the less developed world. Even in the European Union, trade unions have not yet been able to create effective structures for continent-wide collective bargaining, although some stimulus in that direction may be provided by the current requirement of EU law that a large company which does business in a number of EU countries must have a European Works Council with employee representatives from each of those countries. On the whole, the workers of the world, whom Marx invited to unite 150 years ago, have yet to take up the invitation. Indeed, in their loyalties they have proven to be more parochial than their employers.

International nongovernmental organizations (NGOs) have proliferated during the last ten or twenty years. These organizations defend the rights of women, aboriginal peoples, workers, and others in a variety of ways. They lobby their host governments and also take their campaigns to the home countries of offending corporations and to the markets in which those corporations want to sell goods or raise capital. They provide funds, training, and other assistance to local unions and citizens' groups, and they work for the adoption of international conventions to protect workers. They sponsor investigations into abuses of workers' interests, their goal being to enhance public awareness and provide a basis for the imposition of sanctions.

Corporations themselves sometimes establish codes of conduct, by which they commit themselves to act responsibly and ethically when doing business abroad. These codes may cover such matters as occupational health, child labour, discrimination against women, environmental protection, and the avoidance of corrupt practices, but they seldom address collective bargaining rights. They tend to be most significant in industries that sell to retail markets in developed nations, where they can be used as a marketing tool to assuage the social concerns of consumers. For example, fire hazards and low wages in shoe factories have garnered media coverage, and public campaigns have led some reputation-sensitive corporations (such as Nike) to adopt codes for the treatment of workers by the corporations themselves and by suppliers.

A 1998 ILO study of all known corporate codes of conduct (215 at that time) found that they were not very consistent or credible. Their content varied greatly, and they lacked transparency, external monitoring, and enforcement mechanisms. They often failed to mention existing international labour standards, and they tended to address only "hot" issues such as child labour, while ignoring important but lower-profile matters such as collective bargaining rights and hours of work. Often, codes that were highly publicized in consumer countries were unavailable or untranslated in the countries where the work was being done.

Social labels managed by international institutions or NGOs have been proposed as one way of overcoming the consistency and credibility problems of private corporate codes of conduct. In 1997, the ILO proposed an international labelling system as a response to the refusal to include a social clause in the WTO agreements. More recently, Belgium introduced a labelling scheme that it hopes will spread to other countries through multilateral treaties. Still, the only successful social labelling programmes have been industry-sponsored initiatives developed by marketing or import associations in response to negative publicity. Examples are Rugmark and other labels certifying hand-woven Indian carpets as free of child labour, and ProChild and other domestic social labelling programmes in Brazil.

The International Standards Organization (ISO) has been very successful in setting up a system of universal quality control standards (ISO9000) and environmental management standards (ISO14000). There are over half a million ISO9000 certifications in 161 countries, and over 35,000 ISO14000 certifications in 112 countries. An attempt to follow the ISO model in the area of standards for the treatment of employees has been made by a New York-based organization called Social Accountability International (SAI), through its SA8000 standards package. The following excerpt, from the SAI website, outlines the SA8000 initiative. A sobering factor to keep in mind is that, according to data on the website, only 310 companies worldwide (employing less than 200,000 workers in total) had received SA8000 certification as of October 2003. About three-quarters of those companies were in six countries (Italy, China, Brazil, India, Vietnam, and Pakistan).

Social Accountability International <http://www.sa-intl.org> (Accessed 18 January 2004)

Social Accountability International (SAI) works to improve workplaces and combat sweat-shops through the expansion and further development of the currently operative international workplace standard, SA8000, and its associated verification system.

SAI is a U.S.-based, nonprofit organization dedicated to the development, implementation and oversight of voluntary verifiable social accountability standards. SAI is committed to ensuring that standards and the systems for verifying compliance with such standards are highly reputable and publicly accessible. To accomplish this, SAI:

- Convenes key stakeholders to develop consensus-based voluntary standards
- Accredits qualified organizations to verify compliance
- Promotes understanding and encourages implementation of such standards worldwide

SAI's social accountability system approach is based on transparency, credibility and verification.

SAI ADVISORY BOARD

In 1996, SAI convened an international multi-stakeholder Advisory Board to develop Social Accountability 8000 (SA8000), a voluntary standard for workplaces based on ILO (International Labour Organization) and other human rights conventions. Its independent verification method draws many key elements from the widely accepted quality management system certification in the ISO programs.

The SAI advisory board includes experts from trade unions, businesses and NGOs. Among the Advisory Board members there is a broad range of expertise: human rights, child labor, and labor rights, and socially responsible investment firms, as well as auditing techniques and the management of large supply chains. Reaching consensus among this diverse group is a continuing challenge, but the strength of SA8000, notably its rigorous requirements and in its clear, auditable language, is the product of such diversity.

CODES OF CONDUCT BACKGROUND

. . .

The diverse codes of conduct published by individual companies have become somewhat problematic, both for consumers who want clear information and for companies seeking to enforce these codes. Studies carried out by a number of institutions, including the OECD, the ILO, and MHC International, have found that corporate internal codes of conduct tend to be highly inconsistent, expensive, and inefficient to monitor. This is due to unclear definitions and a lack of trained auditors. Such codes and their monitoring systems also tend to be weak on audibility and sensitivity to local laws and customs.

In response to the inconsistencies among workplace codes of conduct, SAI developed a standard for workplace conditions and a system for independently verifying factories' compliance. The standard, Social Accountability 8000 (SA8000), and its verification system draw from the United Nations and ILO conventions and declarations, and the ISO9000 quality management system. The SA8000 standard was created with input from the SAI advisory board, and is designed to assure decent working conditions at companies around the globe.

In order to ensure maximum effectiveness of this system, SAI seeks to continually improve techniques for verifying factories'' compliance with the standard. These techniques can also help employers develop more effective management systems that have the potential to reduce the risk of accidents and improve productivity. To this end, SAI consults with a broad range of stakeholders — workers, employers, and other interested parties such as NGOs and unions — thus continually working to make the SA 8000 system responsive to regional and cultural differences.

. . .

SA8000 STANDARD ELEMENTS

SA8000 is based on international workplace norms in the ILO conventions and the UN''s Universal Declaration of Human Rights and the Convention on Rights of the Child. The official standard is at www.sa-intl.org, but a summary follows:

1. Child Labor:
   - no workers under the age of 15;
   - minimum lowered to 14 for countries operating under the ILO Convention 138 developing-country exception;
   - remediation of any child found to be working

2. Forced Labor:
   - No forced labor, including prison or debt bondage labor;
   - no lodging of deposits or identity papers by employers or outside recruiters

3. Health and Safety:
   - Provide a safe and healthy work environment; take steps to prevent injuries;
   - regular health and safety worker training;
   - system to detect threats to health and safety;
   - access to bathrooms and potable water

4. Freedom of Association and Right to Collective Bargaining:
   - respect the right to form and join trade unions and bargain collectively;
   - where law prohibits these freedoms, facilitate parallel means of association and bargaining

5. Discrimination:
   - no discrimination based on race, caste, origin, religion, disability, gender, sexual orientation, union or political affiliation, or age;
   - no sexual harassment

6. Discipline:
   - no corporal punishment, mental or physical coercion, or verbal abuse

7. Working Hours:
   - comply with the applicable law but, in any event, no more than 48 hours per week with at least one day off for every seven-day period;
   - voluntary overtime paid at a premium rate and not to exceed 12 hours per week on a regular basis;
   - overtime may be mandatory if part of a collective bargaining agreement

8. Compensation:
   - wages paid for a standard work week must meet the legal and industry standards and be sufficient to meet the basic need of workers and their families;
   - no disciplinary deductions

9. Management Systems:
   - facilities seeking to gain and maintain certification must go beyond simple compliance to integrate the standard into their management systems and practices.

HOW COMPANIES CAN IMPLEMENT SA8000

There are two options, certification to SA8000 and involvement in the Corporate Involvement Program (CIP).

1. Certification to SA8000: Companies that operate production facilities can seek to have individual facilities certified to SA8000 through audits by one of the accredited certification bodies. Since the SA8000 system became fully operational in 1998, there are certified facilities in 30 countries on five continents and across 22 industries.
2. SA8000 Corporate Involvement Program: Companies that focus on selling goods or that combine production and selling can join the SA8000 Corporate Involvement Pro-

gram. The CIP is a two-level program that helps companies evaluate SA8000, implement the standard, and report publicly on implementation progress.

- SA8000 Explorer (CIP Level One): Evaluate SA8000 as an ethical sourcing tool via pilot audits.
- SA8000 Signatory (CIP Level Two):
  — Implement SA8000 over time in some or all of the supply chain through certification.
  — Communicate implementation progress to stakeholders via SAI-verified public reporting.

The CIP was launched in late 1999 and has attracted entities representing more than $100 billion in annual revenue including Amana SA, Avon, Cutter & Buck, Dole, Eileen Fisher, Otto Versand, Tex Line, Toys-R-Us, UNOPS, and Vöögele Mode. Program benefits include training courses for managers, suppliers and workers, technical assistance in implementing SA8000, access to a shared database of suppliers, and the right to use the SAI and SA8000 logos to communicate with stakeholders.

CERTIFICATION

. . .

Achieving SA8000 certification of a facility is not easy. However, there is a well-defined process for getting there. . . .

1. Learn What SA8000 Requires and Seek SA8000 Applicant Status . . .

- For training on SA8000, you may wish to take an accredited SA8000 four-day Auditor Training Course or an SA8000 two-day Supplier Training Course.
- Contact an accredited SA8000 certification auditing firm to get an application and initiate the process. Toys R Us can provide help in selecting an accredited auditing firm and negotiating fees.

You should apply for SA8000 Applicant status by requesting an application form from an accredited certification auditing body. Submit the application with supporting documentation showing that your facility complies with relevant national and local regulations, assessing your facility against the SA8000 standard and making the commitment to apply for a certification audit within one year. . . . Buyers that have committed to implementing SA8000 through the SA8000 Corporate Involvement Program (CIP) must give preference to suppliers who are SA8000 applicants. . . .

2. Initial Assessment

- Once you have completed your internal assessment of compliance to SA8000 and made any changes to conditions, policies and management systems required by the standard, you can arrange for an assessment audit (also known as a "pre-audit" by one of the accredited auditing firms).

- Do not be discouraged by any non-compliances with SA8000 (referred to as corrective action requests) that the assessment audit identifies. We do not know any facility that has not had at least one corrective action request after an assessment audit.
- You may want to seek assistance in addressing these corrective actions from buyers who have requested that you seek SA8000 certification. . . . You may contact SAI for referrals to certified facilities, trade unions, NGOs, multi-lateral organizations, and consultants.

. . .

3. Certification Audit and Surveillance Audits

. . .

- A specially trained local audit team will be assigned to your business. The team should know applicable local laws, local NGOs will brief them and trade unions and speak the local language(s) of your managers and workers.
- You will be asked to provide the audit team with access to relevant records as well as the freedom to interview your employees. If any aspect of your operations does not meet what is required by the standard, the audit team will issue a major or minor corrective action request. . . . The audit team will review your responses to any corrective action requests and then make a recommendation on whether or not to issue a certificate to their management who will then make a final decision and communicate it to you.
- An SA8000 certification is good for 3 years. There will be surveillance audits every 6 months or once a year if the certification auditor deems that the facility is performing very well in complying with the standard. Every three years, the facility must undergo a full certification audit to maintain its certification. . . .

✻ ✻ ✻

The following are the SAI's reports on the disposition of two of the small number of complaints that have so far been dealt with against workplaces with SA8000 certification.

Complaint #002: Certification Improper <http://www.sa-intl.org/Accreditation/CertificationComplaints/Complaint002.htm>

Details of Facility

Chung Hoo Shoes Factory, Manufacturer of Athletic Footwear, Zhongshan, Guangdong Province
Certified 12/08/99 ...

Details of Complaint

- High heat and poor ventilation system
- Poor meals and poor dormitory conditions
- Long working hours
- Insufficient wages
- Illegal penalties and deductions

. . .

Actions Taken

September 7, 2000: complaint lodged with SAI and forwarded to the certification body.

Later in September 2000: the certifier attempted to investigate via an unannounced audit, but found the factory closed for a holiday. The certification of the factory was suspended until such time as an audit could take place.

November 7–8: audit took place and the factory was found to be far out of compliance, evidence was found supporting the specific violations in the complaint.

November 2000: certificate cancelled by certification body.

Factory has not since reapplied for certification.

SA8000 Complaint System Leads to Positive Change for Kenyan Fruit Workers
<http://www.sa-intl.org/AboutSAI/March2003.htm>

In 2000, global fruit company Del Monte faced a boycott in Italy, one of the key export markets for its subsidiary, Del Monte Kenya Ltd. Italian unions, NGOs and representatives of the Catholic Church organized the boycott in protest over labor issues on the company's plantations near Thika, Kenya. Now, thanks in large part to the good offices and excellent complaints handling of Coop Italia, just three years later, the company has instituted procedures for assessing all employees' performance, converted 1,500 "casual" plantation workers to seasonal staff, donated policing booths to police in Thika, revised its medical policy to fully cover all seasonal workers, compensated plantation workers who had previously been underpaid, and built housing with windows, potable water, electricity, and pesticide protection for 5,000 workers.

These changes were brought about through the efforts of Coop Italia, Centro Nuovo Modello di Sviluppo (CNMS — an Italian NGO), the Kenya Human Rights Commission (a non-profit NGO based in Nairobi), and Del Monte Kenya Ltd., using the SA8000 complaint system. CNMS, in conjunction with the Kenya Human Rights Commission, initially brought a complaint to Coop Italia. Since Coop Italia's private label is SA8000-certified, it asked Del Monte to respond under the SA8000 "control of supplier" requirement. Del Monte's response included inviting the Kenya Human Rights Commission to conduct seminars for management on worker rights, and allowing shop stewards to form the Workers Rights Watch, an association with a dual role of promoting and protecting the rights of the workers at Del Monte. With the help of a NGO and a local trade union, Del Monte's pineapple plantation recently achieved SA8000 certification.

[All SAI material reprinted with permission.]

✽ ✽ ✽

For assessments of other self-regulatory initiatives, see B. Hepple, "A Race to the Top? International Investment Guidelines and Corporate Codes of Conduct," (1999) 20 Comp. Lab. Law & Pol'y J. 347; J. Diller, "A Social Conscience in the Global Marketplace? Labour Dimensions of Codes of Conduct, Social Labelling, and Investor Initiatives," (1999) 138 Int'l Lab. Rev. 99. A unique approach to private standards is described in

Charles Sabel et. al., "Ratcheting Labor Standards: Regulation for Continuous Improvement in the Global Workplace," The World Bank, Social Protection Discussion Paper No.11 (Washington D.C., 2000).

Harry W. Arthurs, "Private Ordering and Workers Rights in the Global Economy: Corporate Codes of Conduct as a Regime of Labour Market Regulation," in Joanne Conaghan, Michael Fischl, & Karl Klare, eds., *Labour Law in an Era of Globalization: Transformative Practices and Possibilities* (Oxford: OUP, 2001), c. 24, pp. 475–85, 487

. . .

WHY "VOLUNTARY" EMPLOYMENT CODES?

There is nothing new under the sun, certainly not codes governing employment in transnational enterprises. From the 17th to the 19th century, the Crowley steel works — near Sunderland, in the north of England — were governed by a "book of laws" (sometimes called the "ancient constitution") which laid down the rights and obligations of workers in this huge paternalistic proto-global enterprise. The great global trading companies — the Hudson's Bay Company, the East India Company — became quasi-governments and promulgated legal codes which comprehensively regulated the behaviour of their employees (and other people) all over the world. Early Victorian manufacturers and mine owners — a formidable presence in Imperial and international trade — had statutory power to establish their own codes or "special rules" dealing with safety and work practices. Codes — work rules and employment manuals, adopted unilaterally, and collective agreements, adopted bilaterally — have been a fixture of modern industrial employment. And even thoroughly globalized, post-modern, post-industrial "empowered" employees have continued to be ruled by employment codes.

All of these codes share two main characteristics. They operate internally, within the enterprise, to define terms of employment such as wages, working conditions, discipline, and quality standards; to educate workers to adhere to them; and to ensure orderly and consistent enforcement of those terms by supervisors and managers. And they operate externally, by mimicking the rhetoric, forms and processes of law to convince conscientious investors, consumers, NGOs and governments of the legitimacy of what are characteristically unequal, and sometimes exploitative, employment relations. Indeed the ultimate legitimation strategy is to coopt potential critics by enlisting them as sponsors of a code regime. Finally, some codes are adopted on a sectoral or industry-wide basis. Such codes give each signatory a stake in policing the others, diminish the risk that "free riders" will benefit from goodwill accruing to the sector as a whole, and make it more difficult for non-complying firms to compete on the basis of their lower labour costs and standards. All of this contributes to the operational efficacy of the code, which in turn makes it a more convincing legitimating device.

The internal functions of codes — their tutelary and disciplinary functions — have been dealt with elsewhere, by authors from E.P. Thompson to Stuart Henry; the appearance of rival, even subversive, normative systems "in the shadow" of these corporate codes has been documented by Burowoy; the reflexive, rule-generating tendency of large corporations has been addressed by Teubner and others; and I have attempted to situate all of these approaches to workplace codes within a general theory of legal and industrial pluralism. Their external functions — their legitimating and market regulating functions — are the focus of this essay.

Of course, there is no clear division between internal and external audiences. For workers and consumers, managers and government officials to be persuaded to accept voluntary codes as the equivalent of legal protections, all must acquiesce in roughly similar values and assumptions. Hence the importance of the dominant neo-liberal discourse which disparages state regulation and stresses the inevitability of globalization, the positive contributions of TNCs and the invincible logic of their structures and policies. Moreover, codes must be perceived to achieve results roughly comparable to those achieved through alternate means such as statutory regulation or collective bargaining. If there is excessive dissonance between the reality of workplace life and the rhetoric of an employment code, workers will be disillusioned, the public will be disenchanted, TNCs [transnational corporations] will be publicly embarrassed and self-regulation will cease to be regarded as legitimate. Hence the need to create "legal" procedures which can both bring about and testify to the positive consequences of self-regulation. What is puzzling about the recent proliferation of voluntary employment codes, however, is that their underlying values remain somewhat obscure, their procedures deeply flawed and their outcomes unverified.

Values first. Traditional hierarchy and reciprocal obligation may have seemed the natural order of things to several generations of Crowleys, their workers and their latter-day counterparts in developing countries; the inexorable logic of market forces acting upon "free" contracting parties (backed by occasional state coercion) may have been all that was needed to justify employment practices in the dark satanic mills of nineteenth century England; and the Wagner Act's promise that workers were to be given democratic voice and vote in their relations with their employer may have been for a time persuasive to enlightened employers, militant employees and an American public concerned about escalating industrial warfare. But none of these seems to have much salience today. Procedures next. Only a minority of codes summarized in the OECD study — and in other studies — actually include any procedural arrangements at all, only a handful involve anything approaching independent monitoring, and virtually none involve third party enforcement. And finally outcomes. To put it plainly, there is little or no evidence about how codes actually affect the behaviour of TNCs. Thus, it is something of a mystery as to why voluntary codes should have become so numerous in recent years.

Several alternative hypotheses may be advanced. First, transnational corporations are often said to depend upon their "human capital" for success in a knowledge-based global economy. If they are to attract and retain the workers they need, enlightened self-interest dictates that they should both preach high employment standards — by adopting voluntary codes — and practice them. This hypothesis may indeed hold true for a privileged cadre of peripatetic executives, technical experts and professionals. However, it does not seem to have much to do with millions of rank-and-file production workers, who — if treated as "human capital" at all — seem to be regarded as low-yield and essentially disposable assets. . . .

A second hypothesis is that globalization has not only benefited investors and other privileged elites, but that it has also strengthened the world-wide acceptance of human rights and worker entitlements. Voluntary codes, on this view, are no less important a source of such rights and entitlements than international treaties and agreements or national legislation: indeed, they are proof that the appropriate norms have percolated into and become operational in actual workplaces, where they count most. Again, there is modest evidence to support this hypothesis; but there is also considerable experience to the contrary. In the *maquiladoras*, the enterprise zones of the People's Republic of China, the carpet factories of Pakistan or, for that matter, the manufacturing plants of southern Ontario or South Wales, expanded investment, employment opportunities and markets are premised on government policies designed to establish a "business friendly" environment. These policies generally involve derogation from established worker rights and entitlements, and in extreme cases, forceable suppression of worker and community organizations. Nonetheless, it is relatively rare for businesses — the intended beneficiaries of these policies — to protest against repressive labour legislation or strategies, or to insist that they would prefer to apply the high standards set out in their voluntary codes, such as protection of the right to organize and bargain collectively. One must ask, therefore, whether a deep attachment to the notion of labour rights and entitlements is in fact what animates the adoption of voluntary codes by transnational business.

The third hypothesis is, to me, the most persuasive. The interconnectedness of the global economy, some note, has made it vulnerable to disruption. . . . Stoppages by production workers, refusals to handle by transport workers, consumer boycotts and political pressures in any one of a score of countries may have ramifying consequences. This is not to suggest that workers, their unions or transnational advocacy groups can mobilize support easily, that the legal systems of most countries tolerate such mobilization, or that transnationals lack ample power to defend themselves in most conflictual situations. Nonetheless, it is in the interests of transnational corporations to cosmeticise conflict, if they can, to pacify workers, neutralize unions, and reassure NGOs, governments and consumers — all objectives which can be facilitated by adopting voluntary codes. This is the most obvious explanation of the recent popularity of "voluntary codes" which are, in this perspective, not quite so voluntary as all that.

THE SUCCESSFUL REPRODUCTION OF LEGALITY?

Voluntary codes may cover safe and healthy working conditions, grievance procedures, collective bargaining, measures forbidding discrimination, child labour or substandard wages. They may establish procedures for inspection, processing complaints and resolving disputes. Thus, at a superficial glance, voluntary codes of employment may seem capable of reproducing — approximately, if not precisely — many of the substantive and procedural characteristics of state labour legislation.

At a middle distance, however, the differences between state law and voluntary regimes become more apparent. Legislation applies to the generality of enterprises; codes only to those which have chosen to promulgate a code or make themselves subject to one. Unlike the relatively precise and directory language of regulatory statutes, the language of most codes is vague, hortatory and not well suited to compelling compliance in circumstances which are unclear or controversial. Virtually all statutes are enforced ultimately by the coercive agencies of the state; with rare exceptions, no coercive power is available to enforce voluntary codes. And, in principle those charged with violating state labour standards are judged by a court or independent regulatory tribunal; those charged with violating codes are generally judged by themselves or their nominees. Codes, then, are at best only a rough approximation of liberal legality, not a strict replication of it.

But on close examination, the picture is not quite so clear. In effect, we have been comparing an ideal model of legislation and state regulation with the current, flawed reality of self-regulation. If we revisit each of the points just made, we will see that voluntary codes bear a closer resemblance to state regimes than we might care to admit.

Because of constitutional limitations, political influence and materiality thresholds, the coverage of state regulatory regimes in practice is less than universal, and sometimes no more comprehensive than that of voluntary regimes administering codes adopted by sectoral or stakeholder organizations. Statutory language — especially in labour statutes — may appear clear, but even longstanding interpretations can be frustrated by lengthy challenges or overturned by unsympathetic courts; in both state and self-regulating systems, corporations tend to have the last word. While in principle, the state's coercive power can be mobilized to secure compliance with labour laws, this seldom takes place in practice. Recently, many states have abandoned aggressive and costly inspection and enforcement programs in favour of self-reporting and self-discipline by employers, and formal adjudication and punitive action in favour of alternative dispute resolution. State enforcement systems, in practice, have often become no more rigorous than those established under voluntary codes. Even independent adjudication — which supposedly guarantees the integrity of state regulatory practice, and which has no counterpart under voluntary schemes — does not operate as cleanly and decisively as it is supposed to. Even in their golden age, state regulators were susceptible to "regulatory capture," the outcome of symbiotic association with their "clientele," of lobbying and patronage, of inadequate resources. Judges, by contrast, remained independent and were never "captured"; but they did not need to be: they seldom demonstrated much sympathy for workers' interests, or much understanding of their organizations and strategies.

Ironically, then, given that state regulation of the workplace is in disrepair and disrepute, voluntary corporate regimes may not produce such very different outcomes. And now a further irony: intentionally or unintentionally, voluntary regimes sometimes become entangled with state policy-making and state legality instead of merely providing an alternative to the one and a facsimile of the other.

VOLUNTARY CODES AND THE STATE

If, as hypothesized, voluntary code regimes are evidence of the immunity of TNCs from state regulation, it must also be said that states themselves actively or passively promote the adoption of such codes and even become directly involved in drafting and administering them.

Governments formulating labour market policies have always conducted an ongoing process of implicit — even explicit — negotiation with advisory bodies, industry representatives, major corporations, unions, NGOs and other stakeholder groups. In recent times, however, the focus of negotiations has shifted as a result of the desire of neo-liberal governments to win the approval of investors and maintain the confidence of financial markets especially for their macro-economic policies. In the result, public policies affecting the labour market have arguably become even more negotiable than they were during the heyday of corporatism. However, negotiations now virtually exclude the labour movement, although macro-economic policies shape the labour market and in turn appear to play "a major role in shaping the trajectory of employer strategies and employment relations."

How does this new dynamic of policy negotiation lead to the adoption of voluntary codes? Employers in general have been emboldened by their dominant position in the policy process and the labour market and by widespread acknowledgement of their need to resort to domestic or offshore labour practices which will enable them to respond to global competition. Consequently, some of them may choose — or, from their perspective, be driven — to engage in egregious, irresponsible and exploitative practices: the use of child labour, brutal repression of a strike, a fatal failure to adhere to safety standards. The consequences of such practices are then publicized by a union or social advocacy group, widely reported by the media, and used as the rallying cry for a boycott of the company's goods or a campaign for legislation designed to suppress the practice and exclude the offending goods from market. Governments, confronted with public demands that they "do something," often respond by asking the employer in question to promise to behave in the future, a promise which is likely to be expressed in the form of a voluntary code.

Voluntary codes for employers are obviously attractive for employers: no legal controls or sanctions, lower compliance costs (or none) and good publicity eclipsing bad. And codes are attractive for governments: they permit them to be seen to be concerned and responsive without provoking negative reactions from investors, breaking current ideological taboos against regulation, or incurring the transaction costs associated with inspection, prosecution and other traditional forms of intervention. Moreover, voluntary codes may actually resolve problems, or at least alleviate them to the point where they cease to be a political issue. And of course, if they do not — if codes fail to produce the desired practical or political outcomes, if in the end conventional regulation is unavoidable — governments will at least be able to say to employers, investors and ideological critics that it was the last resort, not the first. Parenthetically, in some federal states, codes have the additional attraction of offering a way around potential jurisdictional conflicts over who can regulate what.

When legislation is ultimately enacted — with or without the acquiescence of important constituencies — negotiation does not cease. It continues on a daily basis in the context of administration and enforcement. This crucially important element of "negotiation" results from the fact that the state's resources — its juridical powers, personnel and political credibility — are seldom sufficient to support inspection of every workplace, prosecution of every offending employer or proscription of every new hazardous process or practice. Consequently, from the earliest Victorian labour legislation to the present governments have sought to enhance compliance and lighten the burdens of administration by persuading or compelling employers to take "ownership" of labour legislation, to internalize its values so that they are routinely translated into workplace norms, without the need for government inspection, admonition or prosecution. Codes appear to be a promising strategy for enhancing compliance: they are written by employers, administered by employers, and hopefully internalized in the operating procedures of employers.

Nowhere is the challenge of securing compliance more difficult than in the case of the offshore operations of domestic employers, investors or traders. Here the inspector's writ does not legally run; here practices are likely to be most egregious; here workers see confirmation of their worst fears of a "race to the bottom." Codes once again may provide the answer. Firms which adopt and adhere to codes in their foreign operations effectively relieve their own governments of the legal, practical and political challenges of extraterritorial inspection and enforcement. Various privileges — participation in trade missions, export loan guarantees, access to government purchasing programs — can be extended to firms which are code-compliant, and denied to those which are not. And finally, if these privileges do not suffice to shield compliant employers from competition by non-compliant firms with lower labour costs, codes can be used as the template for legislation or regulations designed to bar "rogue" firms from domestic markets. For all of these reasons, states have pursued an active policy of promoting code regimes for locally-based corporations trading abroad through technical initiatives, mediation amongst stakeholders and public endorsement of specific high profile code initiatives, as well as through direct or symbolic commitment as code signatories.

Finally, voluntary codes of labour standards may, paradoxically, give rise to explicit consequences in domestic and international law. There is little litigation so far involving codes, especially in the labour area, and what follows is largely conjectural. However, in principle it seems possible that codes might, in given circumstances, materially affect the outcome of litigation. For example, codes which originate in agreements within sectoral organizations or amongst stakeholder groups may constitute legally binding contracts. Governments may make compliance with employment codes a formal condition of tendering and performance in procurement contracts or in order to gain access to markets. And codes may be used by judges to pour substantive content into vague normative standards — "implied" terms on which to ground an unlawful dismissal suit, a standard of "reasonableness" to define the duty of care owed to injured workers, evidence of what constitutes "due diligence" by corporate directors who are sued for failing to prevent workplace harassment.

Thus, state regulation and voluntary code regimes are not mutually exclusive alternatives, nor do voluntary code regimes simply reproduce systems of state regulation. To some extent the two systems exist in a state of symbiosis, and are more similar in their strategies and outcomes, more ideologically aligned, more mutually dependent and operationally integrated than is generally believed. . . .

So we return to the issue of legitimacy. Voluntary codes are emerging as the most significant feature of a fragile, inchoate regime of transnational labour market regulation. Employers are supposed to be the object of that regulation, but they are also its primary authors and administrators; they can conjure it up or make it disappear pretty much whenever and for whatever reason they wish. But workers — supposedly the subjects, the beneficiaries, of this regulation — lack the power to create it, to significantly influence its terms, or even to insist that they receive its promised benefits; they can only denounce it and try to rob it of its legitimacy. We must somehow square this circle.

[By permission of Oxford University Press.]

* * *

14:300 A NEW PARADIGM

Globalization and the other forces that have helped to shape the new paradigm have had destabilizing effects on political, social, and economic arrangements, even in advanced industrialized countries such as Canada. In part, these effects flow from the exercise of real power by multinationals, who have acquired the ability to face down governments and unions by threatening to disinvest, reduce their workforces or take other harmful actions. In part, however, the effects arise not so much from the actual exercise of power by multinationals, but from the fear or anticipation of its exercise. This situation creates a dynamic that even ardent proponents of globalization see as presenting a serious risk of social unrest.

Klaus Schwab & Claude Smadja, "Globalization Backlash Is Serious: Another Perspective" *The Globe and Mail* (16 February 1996) B10

Economic globalization has entered a critical phase. A mounting backlash against its effects, especially in the industrial democracies, is threatening to disrupt economic activity and social stability in many countries.

. . .

Popular skepticism about the win-win effect of the global economy is compounded by two phenomena.

First, it is becoming harder in the industrial democracies to ask the public to go through the pains and uncertainties of structural adjustment for the sake of future benefits. The social impact of these pressures is being felt at the very moment when economic activity has slowed markedly in most industrial democracies.

The second phenomenon is that globalization tends to de-link the fate of the corporation from the fate of its employees. In the past, higher profits meant more job security and better wages. The way corporations have to operate to compete in the global economy means that it is now routine to have companies announce new profit increases along with a new wave of layoffs.

Some estimates put at three million the number of layoffs since the end of the 1980s in the United States, and more are expected. It is no consolation for a laid-off employee to hear analysis explain how the re-engineering of which he is a victim will help his former employer prosper.

For those who keep their jobs, the new sense of insecurity means the demise of corporate loyalty bonds. It is not yet clear that corporations have fully realized the consequences that this will have on their future performance.

All this confronts political and economic leaders with the challenge of demonstrating how the new global capitalism can function to the benefit of the majority and not only for corporate managers and investors.

But if the key issue today is to make apparent the social returns of global capitalism, we have to be equipped to reap these returns. This is where the critical question of setting national priorities comes to the fore.

The effort of focusing on training and education, on the constant overhauling of telecommunication and transportation infrastructures, on entrepreneur-incentive fiscal policies, on recalibrating social policies has to be a central part of a national competitiveness policy going beyond the traditional concept of economic policy.

Meanwhile, the globalized economy must not become synonymous with 'free-market on the rampage,' a brakeless train wreaking havoc. The social responsibilities of corporations (and governments) remain as important as ever. What is on the agenda is the need to redefine and recalibrate them.

Moral considerations aside, there can be no sustainable growth without the public at large seeing itself as the major stakeholder in the successful functioning of the economy.

. . .

Public opinion in the industrial democracies will no longer be satisfied with articles of faith about the virtues and future benefits of the global economy. It is pressing for action.

[Reprinted by permission.]

E. Kapstein, "Workers and the World Economy" (1996) 75:3 Foreign Affairs 16 at 16–17

BREAKING THE POSTWAR BARGAIN

The global economy is leaving millions of disaffected workers in its train. Inequality, unemployment, and endemic poverty have become its handmaidens. Rapid technological change and heightening international competition are fraying the job markets of the major industrialized countries. At the same time systemic pressures are curtailing every government's ability to respond with new spending. Just when working people most need the nation-state as a buffer from the world economy, it is abandoning them.

This is not how things were supposed to work. The failure of today's advanced global capitalism to keep spreading the wealth poses a challenge not just to policymakers but to modern economic 'science' as well. For generations, students were taught that increasing trade and investment, coupled with technological change, would drive national productivity and create wealth. Yet over the past decade, despite a continuing boom in international trade and finance, productivity has faltered, and inequality in the United States and unemployment in Europe have worsened.

President Bill Clinton may have been right to proclaim that 'the era of big government is over,' and perhaps the American people will ultimately decide that those who need assistance should look elsewhere for help. But if the post-World War II social contract with workers — of full employment and comprehensive social welfare — is to be broken, political support for the burgeoning global economy could easily collapse. For international economic integration is not some uncontrollable fact of life, but has deepened because of a series of policy decisions taken by the major industrial powers over the last 45 years. It is time to recognize that those decisions, while benefiting the world economy as a whole, have begun to have widespread negative consequences. The forces acting on today's workers inhere in the structure of today's global economy, with its open and increasingly fierce competition on the one hand and fiscally conservative units — states — on the other. Countermeasures, therefore, must also be deep, sustained, and widespread. Easing pressures on the 'losers' of the new open economy must now be the focus of economic policy if the process of globalization is to be sustained.

It is hardly sensationalist to claim that in the absence of broad-based policies and programs designed to help working people, the political debate in the United States and many other countries will soon turn sour. Populists and demagogues of various stripes will find 'solutions' to contemporary economic problems in protectionism and xenophobia. Indeed, in every industrialized nation, such figures are on the campaign trail. Growing income inequality, job insecurity, and unemployment are widely seen as the flip side of globalization. That perception must be changed if Western leaders wish to maintain the international system their predecessors created. After all, the fate of the global economy ultimately rests on domestic politics in its constituent states.

The spread of the dogma of restrictive fiscal policy is undermining the bargain struck with workers in every industrial country. States are basically telling their workers that they can no longer afford the postwar deal and must minimize their obligations. The current obsession with balanced budgets in the United States and the Maastricht criteria in Europe must be replaced by an equally vigilant focus on growth and equity. National responses to this global problem are likely to fail, as any state that deviates from 'responsible' economic policies will be punished by currency markets and bondholders. States must now reorient their economic policies toward growth, but it should be done as part of a coordinated international effort. Calling for such economic policy coordination might seem utopian in the current political environment, but it has been done before.

The world may be moving inexorably toward one of those tragic moments that will lead future historians to ask, why was nothing done in time? Were the economic and policy elites unaware of the profound disruption that economic and technological change were causing working men and women? What prevented them from taking the steps necessary to prevent a global social crisis?

[Reprinted by permission of *Foreign Affairs*. Copyright 1996 by the Council on Foreign Relations, Inc.]

Harry Arthurs, "Reinventing Labour Law for the Global Economy: The Benjamin Aaron Lecture"(2001) 22 Berkeley J. Emp'ment and Lab. Law 271 at 285–91

All in all, then, this has been a pretty melancholy account of where labor law stands today, and where it seems to be going in an age of globalization. On the basis of what I have said so far, one might conclude that labor's prospects at the beginning of the 21st century are no better than they were 100 years earlier, that John R. Commons launched us on a project doomed to failure, and that the workers of the world ought to be uniting to thank management for their chains, not trying to shed them. Perhaps, indeed some of you actually have reached those conclusions. But I have not. I do not believe we have arrived at the end of history; I do not believe we will see the gradual withering away of state intervention or the ultimate demise of labor law and industrial relations as we have known them; and I do not believe that workers or citizens will continue indefinitely to accept whatever cards they are dealt by the invisible hand of the market. To the contrary, I believe that there will be a new dawn for labor law and industrial relations, and that workers, states, enlightened employers and sympathetic citizens are already beginning to build a just and effective law of labor for the new, global economy....

This brings me to my final point: how, despite the inability of many lawyers to detect it, a new labor law is actually emerging in the global economy. This new labor law has not yet begun to affect U.S. domestic labor law, but it is gradually beginning to shape relations between transnational employers and their workers, and to influence the industrial relations and labor law systems of many of America's trading partners and competitors. In the long run, therefore, it may leach back into the United States, just as it did under the New Deal and during the postwar period. This emerging global labor law has at least five components.

The first is international treaties and conventions. Obviously, these have a direct juridical effect only on the countries that sign them — which, in most cases, the United States has not. However, the United States has been arguing for some time that those countries that do not adhere to "core labor standards" should be denied membership in the WTO, in which the United States is very much a dominant player. Ironically, since "core labor standards" are, in fact, taken directly from the ILO'S large catalogue of Conventions — many of which the United States has not ratified — if the United States succeeds in making compliance a condition of WTO membership, it will have extended the reach of the ILO not only to cover other countries, but possibly itself as well. Indeed, at least one scholarly study has argued that these standards have already become part of customary international law, adherence to which is already required by the WTO statute.

Moreover, the United States obviously is a member of NAFTA and has signed the so-called "labor side accord," the NAALC. This agreement commits each NAFTA partner to adhere to its own labor laws, establishes a dispute resolution process to ensure compliance, and allows this process to be accessed not only by the other governments, but by their aggrieved citizens. As a result, over the past five or six years, American workers, unions, and social movements have filed twenty or thirty complaints with the NAALC National Administrative Office in Washington against the failure of the Mexican government to extend protection to its own workers, especially in cases involving foreign subsidiaries doing business in the *maquiladoras*. A number of these complaints have given rise to hearings, and the resulting findings and publicity have embarrassed the employers involved, the official Mexican trade unions, and the Mexican government. As a result, some improvements have taken place in the administration of Mexican labor law. More to the point, the complaints process has helped to launch a new independent trade union movement in

Mexico, has been the catalyst for much greater cooperation amongst Mexican, Canadian and American unions, and has also legitimated and reinforced the activities of churches, women's groups and other social activists on behalf of Mexican workers. Complaints against the United States in Mexico and Canada have been relatively infrequent, but on at least one occasion they have resulted in a change in administrative practice by the U.S. Department of Labor. Here, then, we see a beginning — albeit a very modest one — of a new treaty-based regime of labor law that reaches across national boundaries. This new regime has the capacity to alter the way in which national labor law is administered and may significantly change the industrial relations dynamic of the countries bound by it.

Another example is the Treaty of Rome, which established the European Union (EU), by far the world's most elaborate and effective transnational regime. So far, the EU has not developed a significant body of collective labor law, in part because of objections from the United Kingdom. However, it does have legislation governing workplace discrimination, plant closings and layoffs, employer insolvency, and Works Councils. Whether a more comprehensive regime of EU labor law will grow up alongside EU competition, transport, consumer, and agricultural law remains to be seen. Some observers favor it, some claim to see it in the offing and some doubt that it will ever emerge. I mention the EU specifically, however, to point out that it is possible for national labor law to be explicitly reconfigured as a result of globalization and regional economic integration. I doubt very much that the United States would accede to anything like the Treaty of Rome; if it did, I can imagine that attempts to use treaty obligations to trump domestic labor law would be frustrated by both legal and political strategies. But this does not diminish the fact that treaties are in fact legally binding, and that they are a potential source of transnational or global labor law.

The dissemination of "best practices" is the second major component of developing global labor law. This is essentially the optimistic obverse of a process I mentioned earlier, in which the law of the shop is degraded by globalization. The optimistic version begins with the proposition that best practices are indispensable for success in technology-based economies, where human capital is a strategic asset. The United States has become such an economy and, over many decades, has contributed to a virtuous circle in which ideas about law, management and work originated in the United States, were exported and re-engineered abroad, and ultimately returned to challenge — even change — thinking in their country of origin. Seniority, quality circles and flexible production are all cases in point. It is pretty likely, the optimists argue, that such a virtuous circle will increasingly shape labor practices in the global economy in the future, as America and its trading partners compete with each other, learn from each other, imitate each other's successes, and avoid each other's mistakes. If this is true, the dissemination of "best practices" will proceed both by way of borrowings amongst national legal systems and by way of non-legislated changes in company philosophy and shop-floor practice. Specifically, as someone once suggested to me, lawyers are likely to function as "bees and wasps." They gather best practices from one set of clients, incorporate them into legal forms, and then cross-pollinate them into the practices and forms of a second set of clients.

Third, management is constructing a kind of global labor law in the form of corporate voluntary codes of conduct. These codes, which have been appearing at a great rate over the past decade, have been adopted by individual corporations and sectoral organizations voluntarily, under pressure from labor unions, consumer organizations and human rights groups and in response to the urgings of national governments, the OECD, the ILO, and other international organizations. These codes are "voluntary" in the sense that they are not imposed by law and do not appear to give rise to enforceable third party claims. However, in another sense they are not voluntary. Many were adopted under pressure by reluctant corporations in order to ward off adverse publicity, strikes, boycotts, embargoes, or political and legal sanctions. This pressure may become more intense. Scholars have proposed that codes of conduct should be made transparent and their enforcement "ratcheted" ever-upward through structured, systematic exposure to market sanctions. And some form of legal enforceability may not be far off. For example, a U.S. court recently mandated adoption, independent monitoring, and third-party enforcement of an employment code as part of the settlement of a massive claim under anti-peonage, indentured servitude, anti-racketeering, false advertising, and Fair Labor Standards laws; and legislators in both Australia and the U.S. have recently been asked to consider legislation that would in effect force corporations seeking various government benefits to adopt and implement codes of conduct.

Of course, apart from the issue of legal consequences, the provenance and the procedural, structural, substantive, and remedial features of codes vary considerably. Most are purely internal and can be activated, if at all, only by the corporation's own compliance officer. Only a few carry the imprimatur of third parties, provide for independent monitoring or are enforceable through neutral complaint bodies. They also differ in their content and coverage. Some offer specific guarantees of "core labor rights," and even of a so-called "living wage;" others amount to no more than a vague promise of good intentions. Some extend to all domestic and foreign suppliers and subsidiaries of the corporation; others only to its core operations. Many are no more than words on paper; others have produced at least modest changes in employment conditions. In other words, one can hardly point to voluntary, unenforceable, and unenforced corporate codes as a substitute for effective labor legislation. But then, the same can be said of some Acts of Congress.

Fourth, corporations are not the only actors shaping global labor law. Unions are making a modest contribution too, whether through national unions and labor congresses, international labor bodies such as the so-called "trade secretariats," or *ad hoc* union alliances built around specific disputes and for limited purposes. Needless to say, union efforts to build solidarity across national boundaries have not been hugely successful, for reasons mentioned earlier. But in a few celebrated cases, unions have been able to win at least battles, if not actual wars. Employers have been forced to abandon plant closings or compensate dismissed workers, improve wages and working conditions, recognize unions, and respect local health and safety standards. In other words, unions have been able to do on a small scale globally what they aspire to do on a large scale nationally.

Fifth, the new actors in the formation of global economy are social movements — women, consumers, university students, religious communities, environmentalists, aboriginal peoples, anti-poverty and anti-child labor activists, and human rights groups. These social movements, often working with unions in both the advanced and developing economies, have been able to arouse public indignation against abusive labor practices which, in turn, has forced retailers, investors, and ultimately governments to bring pressure to bear on offending employers.

It is difficult to imagine that governments, unions, corporations, and social movements might create and administer a system of global labor law by pasting together a collage of treaties and conventions, best practices, corporate codes, *ad hoc* settlements, and vestigial remnants of national legislation. But this, after all, is pretty much how we originally constructed our "old" system of labor law. Lest we forget, there was collective bargaining before the Wagner Act, employer- and union-sponsored welfare funds before Social Security, and grievance arbitration before the War Labor Board. Thus, I want to conclude by arguing that it is just possible that in these scattered, episodic episodes of rule-making and dispute resolution, we may spy the shape of the future.

Table of Cases

This table of cases contains only those cases discussed or mentioned in the Group's commentary, or those cases from which excerpts have been included. Excerpts are marked in bold.